XML and Web Services

Ron Schmelzer et al.

SAMS

XML and Web Services Unleashed

International Standard Book Number: 0-672-323419

Library of Congress Catalog Card Number: 2001097282

Printed in the United States of America

First Printing: February 2002

05 04 03 02 4 3 2 1

Trademarks

Warning and Disclaimer

Executive Editor
Rochelle J. Kronzek

Development Editor
Songlin Qiu

Managing Editor
Matt Purcell

Project Editor
George E. Nedeff

Copy Editor
Bart Reed

Indexer
Kelly Castell

Proofreader
Karen Whitehouse

Technical Editor
Mike Farley

Interior Designer
Anne Jones

Cover Designer
Aren Howell

Page Layout
D&G Limited, LLC

Contents at a Glance

Contents

15 Web Services Building Blocks: SOAP 629

16 Web Services Building Blocks: WSDL and UDDI 677

PART IV The Semantic Web 995

23 RDF for Information Owners 997

24 The Semantic Web for Information Owners 1039

PART V Appendix 1069

A Extensible Markup Language (XML) 1.0 (Second Edition) Specification 1071

About the Lead Author

Ron Schmelzer, founder and senior analyst of ZapThink, an XML-focused industry analyst group, is a well-known expert in the field of XML and XML-based standards and initiatives. Ron has been featured in and written for periodicals, and he has spoken at numerous industry conferences, including XML One, Comdex, and Internet World, on the topic of XML.

Prior to ZapThink, Ron Schmelzer was a founder and "ePostle of Partners" for ChannelWave, where he was responsible for identifying the needs of channel partners and making sure all partners received the full benefit of partner relationship management systems. Prior to co-founding ChannelWave, Ron worked on advanced Internet applications for U.S. Robotics and was a founding partner of Dynamic Data Services, a data-networking services company.

Ron was named "Geek of the Week" in *Internet Magazine* and was listed among *Boston Magazine's* Internet Top 40. Ron received a B.S. degree in Computer Science and Electrical Engineering from the Massachusetts Institute of Technology (MIT).

About the Contributing Authors

Travis Vandersypen is a senior software developer working for EPS Software Corporation, located in Houston, Texas. He concentrates on building distributed applications using COM+, XML, Visual Studio .NET, SQL Server, and other supporting technologies. He is an internationally published author and speaker, a three-time Microsoft Visual FoxPro Excellence Award nominee, and co-author of several development utilities and libraries. He can be reached via e-mail at `tvandersypen@msn.com` or at `travis@eps-software.com`.

Jason Bloomberg is an e-business technology manager and industry analyst with a diverse background in the business and technology of e-business. He is currently the Director of E-Services at Ashton Services, a Massachusetts-based boutique Web firm. He has been a senior analyst in IDC's e-business advisory group as well as serving in e-business management positions at USWeb/CKS (later marchFIRST) and WaveBend Solutions (now Experio Solutions). Bloomberg is a widely published business and technical writer, whose articles have appeared in *Electronic Commerce World*, *Intranet Journal*, *Datamation*, *The Rational Edge*, *DM Review Interactive*, and *ZDNet: Developer*. He also co-authored the book *Web Page Scripting Techniques* (Hayden Books, 1996). He can be reached at `wizard@rhodes.com`.

Madhu Siddalingaiah is a consultant and technical trainer. Since 1995, Madhu has focused on Web technologies. He has authored several books and articles on Java, embedded systems, and XML. Madhu works with organizations to architect and develop Web-based systems to achieve their business goals. Madhu relates much of his experience through lectures at technology conferences all over the world. He is also a rated helicopter pilot and enjoys flying when the weather and his schedule permits.

Michael D. Qualls is a Webmaster and developer currently working with Marketing Information Network, a leading data provider for the direct marketing industry. Michael has worked extensively with the creation of Web applications since 1996, utilizing Visual Basic, Active Server Pages, Microsoft SQL Server, and XML. More recently, Michael has specialized in creating custom online order applications for e-commerce companies. He lives in Oklahoma City, Oklahoma with his wife, Holly, and two daughters, Alexandra and Michaela. In his spare time, Michael enjoys practicing a wide variety of martial arts, including Brazilian Jiujitsu, Muay Thai kickboxing, Western boxing, and Buguazhang.

Sam Hunting is the CEO of eTopicality, Inc., a consultancy that provides analytical services for the Semantic Web and content providers, including schema development, topic maps, and all phases of DTD development. He specializes in complex content where rapid and flexible development of quality solutions is paramount. His expertise includes legal content, medical content, interactive electronic technical manuals for aircraft, textbooks, encyclopedias, electronic commerce, and workflow. His specifications work includes co-editorship of XML Topic Maps (XTM) and co-authorship of the XTM 1.0 DTD. When he is not analyzing content, he is dabbling in programming languages with clean syntax, such as Python and Eiffel, listening to music, or improving his rudimentary French.

Chád Darby has experience developing *n*-tier Web applications for Fortune 500 companies and the Department of Defense. Chád is a contributing author for the books *Professional Java E-commerce* and *Java Networking*. He has also published articles in *Java Report*, *Java Developer's Journal*, and *Web Techniques*. He has been an invited speaker at conferences, including SD West 99, XML DevCon 2000, and JavaCon 2000. Chád recently gave a presentation on JSP custom tags in Mumbai, India. He holds a B.S. in Computer Science from Carnegie Mellon University.

David Houlding is a software architect at The Technical Resource Connection. With 10 years of experience in software design and development, he is responsible for leading the creation of secure enterprise wireless, voice, and Web-enabled distributed object systems that leverage the power of XML, XSL, WML, VoiceXML, and other powerful XML technologies to deliver real business value. He has extolled the virtues of distributed and mobile computing with presentations at numerous major industry conferences, article publications in major trade journals, contributions to book publications, and interviews for newspaper and other articles. David's interests include visualizing software architectures, and he led the creation of, and currently manages, the Architecture Zone Web-based ASP service dedicated to the SVG-based interactive visualization of complex systems. He may be contacted at `david@houlding.net`.

Dianne Kennedy has a long history in publishing, beginning with her experience as a editor/writer for the textbook division of Doubleday. Dianne began working with information technologies in 1986, when she was one of the pioneers in SGML. In 1997, Dianne founded XMLXperts and began work as an independent XML consultant. She is CEO and principal consultant for XMLXperts.

Dianne also serves as Chief Technical Consultant for IDEAlliance, is an editor of the XML Files, participates as an invited expert on the ICE authoring group, and was chairperson for the XML1998–2000 Conferences. She is also the chairperson for the Knowledge Technologies Conference (2001–2002), the Open Publish 2002 Conference, and the XML in Publishing Day at the Seybold Seminars, both in San Francisco and New York.

Dedication

Dedicated to my family, Jennifer Fairman, Milo, and Rudy—people and cats of distinction.

—Ronald Schmelzer

Dedicated to Karen, Joshua, Simon, and Melanie for their inspiration and support.

—David Houlding

Dedicated to my mother, Constance Hunting.

—Sam Hunting

Dedicated to my family Janine, Chade, and Ty. Thanks for giving me a purpose in life.

—Chád Darby

Acknowledgments

Ronald Schmelzer. It would be difficult to say that authoring a book, even in part, is an effortless and challenge-free process. Many people and lots of resources have gone into making this a successful endeavor. It goes without saying that the Sams publication staff deserves much of the kudos and thanks for helping to shepherd this process in a compressed timeframe with the excellent results contained within. In particular, I would like to acknowledge Shelley Kronzek, the Executive Editor for this project, Songlin Qiu, the development editor, Mike Farley, the technical editor, and Bart Reed, copy editor. Without their help, many of our authors would be ships without rudders in the sea. Of course, none of this would be possible without the tremendous and superlative effort of the other co-authors on this project: Jason Bloomberg, Chád Darby, Sam Hunting, David Houlding, Dianne Kennedy, Mike Qualls, Madhu Siddalingaiah, and Travis Vandersypen. I commend each of them for their dedication in helping to make this a book to be proud of. On a personal note, I would like to acknowledge Jennifer E. Fairman of Fairman Studios for her understanding, time, and constant inspiration. She planted the seed in my mind that writing a book was more than just a hope, but a soon-to-be realized goal.

Jason Bloomberg. I would like to thank Steve Stassen and the rest of the Ashton Services development team for assistance with the source code for the chapters on Web Services.

Sam Hunting. My thanks to the editors of Sams Publishing for their hard work.

Tell Us What You Think!

As the reader of this book, *you* are our most important critic and commentator. We value your opinion and want to know what we're doing right, what we could do better, what areas you'd like to see us publish in, and any other words of wisdom you're willing to pass our way.

As an Executive Editor for Sams Publishing, I welcome your comments. You can fax, e-mail, or write me directly to let me know what you did or didn't like about this book—as well as what we can do to make our books stronger.

Please note that I cannot help you with technical problems related to the topic of this book, and that due to the high volume of mail I receive, I might not be able to reply to every message.

When you write, please be sure to include this book's title and author as well as your name and phone or fax number. I will carefully review your comments and share them with the author and editors who worked on the book.

Fax: 317-581-4770

E-mail: `feedback@samspublishing.com`

Mail: Shelley Kronzek
Executive Editor
Sams Publishing
201 West 103rd Street
Indianapolis, IN 46290 USA

Introduction

Congratulations! Whether you are a recent newcomer to the Extensible Markup Language (XML) or are already a power user, you have just chosen a book that will give you a leg-up on understanding and using the power and flexibility of the XML language. No doubt, you have seen a considerable amount about XML and have heard what it can do. Some of it is grounded in technical reality, and some of it is just hype. In general, though, the technology has piqued your interest enough that you are willing to dive headfirst into learning how XML can benefit you.

It is well known that XML as a technology is a moving target. What may be new and cutting edge one month is already old news the next. However, this book has been written in an in-depth manner by experts in the space. You will find this book to be useful long after it first hits the shelves because the concepts introduced in this book will help guide you in crafting XML strategies and implementations that leverage today's standards while making room for tomorrow's innovations.

Rather than just skimming the surface of what XML has to offer, this book provides an overarching view of how XML impacts different vertical industries, implementations, and technological needs.

Who This Book's Intended Audience Is

This book is focused on those intermediate-to-advanced users who already know something about XML but still are unsure of its various intricacies, technical complexities, and implementations that allow one to make the most of XML and its related technologies. Although the book starts with a level-setting definition of what XML is and how it has evolved, most of the chapters are focused on detailed, relevant, and timely explanations of XML implementation in areas as diverse as databases, content management, e-business, and the Semantic Web.

What You Need to Know Prior to Reading This Book

This book is aimed at the developer who is itching to implement XML technologies, but at the same time it offers full coverage of XML topics. Therefore, the only things you need to know prior to reading this book are the fundamentals of the Internet and the basic concepts of XML. You'll also want to be in possession of at least a basic set of tools for experimenting with the concepts explained within.

What You Will Learn from Reading This Book

This book covers a wide range of implementation and development tools, techniques, and technologies for use with XML. You will learn everything from the basic foundation and history of XML to how to read, transform, process, and make programmatic use of XML. In particular, you will gain a fundamental knowledge of processing technologies such as SAX and the Document Object Model, XML document structure, including XML Schema, XPath, XLink, and XPointer, in-depth and cutting-edge knowledge of Web Services and Microsoft's .NET Framework, and specific XML implementations in areas such as content management, e-business, voice and wireless, vertical industries, and the Semantic Web. In general, this book will give you the knowledge you need to unleash your XML capabilities!

What Software You Will Need to Complete the Examples Provided with This Book

Various chapters in this book contain different requirements for tools and processing technologies. In some cases, the choice of tools will be left up to you, with a listing of the available toolsets included in the chapter. In other cases, most notably the .NET chapters, the use of Microsoft- or Java-specific tools will be mandated. In any case, the open nature of XML and the availability of cheap, and often free, tools will make it easy to obtain the technology necessary to follow along and implement the XML and related code as specified in this book.

How This Book Is Organized

Although it is understood that many readers don't read a book in sequential order, this book is set up so that general and fundamental topics of XML are covered first, and more specific implementation and technologies are covered later.

This book is divided into the following parts:

- **Part I: Essentials of XML**

  This part gives you a foundation upon which all technologies and strategies around XML are based. The first chapter covers XML history and basics, whereas the rest of the chapters cover the essential elements of XML, XML validation technologies, including Document Type Definitions (DTDs), XML Schema and other schema types, and supporting XML technologies, including XLink, XPath, and XPointer.

- **Part II: Building XML-Based Applications**

  Once you have a good understanding of XML and its components, you can start building robust applications. Part II of this book covers all the technologies and techniques needed to read, process, and make use of XML, including using the Document Object Model (DOM), using the Simple API for XML (SAX), transforming XML, integrating XML with databases, formatting XML for presentation, using the Simple Vector Graphics (SVG) specification, working with XML-based content management, understanding and using Web Services, and making use of Microsoft's .NET Framework.

- **Part III: Applied XML**

  Given a thorough understanding of XML fundamentals and the tools and techniques needed to make use of XML in a robust manner, you are guided through several chapters in Part III that illustrate how XML can be used in specific scenarios. First, you are introduced to the world of XML-based standards and specifications by means of the "standards stack." Next, you gain an understanding of how XML is used in e-business systems, in voice and wireless applications, and in various vertical industries, such as healthcare, manufacturing, and finance.

- **Part IV: The Semantic Web**

  Finally, after learning the new directions that XML is taking us, you are introduced to the complex and sophisticated world of the Semantic Web. Given how XML is transforming the use of data and its exchange between organizations and systems, the Semantic Web will soon be a major technology that will change the way we deal with systems. The two chapters contained here give you an understanding of the framework behind many Semantic Web efforts and the Resource Description Framework (RDF) as well as provide a more general treatment of the Semantic Web and what it has to offer.

- **Appendix A**

  This appendix is a copy of the World Wide Web Consortium (W3C) specification for the XML 1.0 Recommendation. It is included as a reference and a source for various technologies and concepts mentioned in this book. Other resources are referenced within specific chapters because their contents may change over time.

What's on the Sams Web Site for This Book

The chapter-by-chapter code files described in this book are available on the Sams Web site at `http://www.samspublishing.com/`. Enter this book's ISBN (without the hyphens) in the Search box and click Search. When the book's title is displayed, click the title to go to a page where you can download all the code in a chapter-by-chapter zip file format.

Conventions Used in This Book

The following conventions are used in this book:

- Code lines, commands, statements, variables, and any text you type or see onscreen appears in a `monospace` typeface. **`Bold monospace`** typeface is used to represent text you need to input.
- Placeholders in syntax descriptions appear in an *`italic monospace`* typeface. Replace the placeholder with the actual filename, parameter, or whatever element it represents.
- *Italics* highlight technical terms when they're being defined.
- The ➥ icon is used before a line of code that is really a continuation of the preceding line. Sometimes a line of code is too long to fit as a single line on the page. If you see ➥ before a line of code, remember that it's part of the line immediately above it.
- The book also contains notes, tips, and cautions to help you spot important or useful information more quickly. Some of these are helpful shortcuts to help you work more efficiently.
- In addition, you will see the use of sidebars to highlight additional resources and information, case studies, and guides to help you make the most of what you are reading.

Essentials of XML

Part I

In This Part

XML in Context

In This Chapter

We are truly living in wonderful and privileged times. We can schedule airfare and book hotels from the convenience of our homes. Finding restaurants and mapping directions to a 3 P.M. meeting is as simple as opening a Web browser. Gone are the long waits in service lines and the 30-minute hold times with the inevitably rude customer service personnel. We can order phone service, view real estate and apartments, shop and bid on flea market items, lodge customer-service complaints, and even file our tax returns without ever having to leave our homes or pick up the phone. We don't even have to interact with a single human being. In fact, we can now live our entire lives without ever having to leave our homes. All these wondrous things would have seemed impossible a mere decade ago, and some of them are only now beginning to be realized.

Of course, none of this would be possible without data—the lifeblood of information flow. Everywhere we look, data is present. It's in the phone bill we receive in the mail, the bar code on our soft drink beverage, the e-mail we exchange, the tax forms we prepare, and the millions of financial and banking transactions that occur on a daily basis without our knowledge. In the context of our discussion, data is any and all information that can be represented in a computer. Data is so intertwined with computing that to say one can exist without the other is akin to saying that humans can exist without organs.

What's more, the Extensible Markup Language (XML) is powering this data revolution. This book, *XML Unleashed!*, is designed to get you well on your way toward developing XML applications and systems that enable your most important business processes as well as your simplest visions for data representation and exchange. Written for those already familiar with many of the concepts of XML but still not sure how to make best use of the technologies, this book aims to help you become a more advanced user of XML. Although this chapter covers the way that XML came to be, the "meat" of this book starts very soon in Chapter 2, "The Fundamentals of XML."

Written for intermediate-to-advanced XML developers, this book covers all the necessary topics, from the basics of Document Type Definitions (DTDs) to the more advanced topics in XML database integration and the semantic Web. The foundations of XML as well as specific development methodologies and applications are contained within. By reading this book, you can *unleash* the XML developer within.

In this chapter you will learn:

- What XML is
- Why XML is important
- Why the timing of XML is right
- What other technologies, such as EDI, SGML, and HTML, have brought to the table

- Why those technologies are insufficient to solve our problems
- Where XML is heading

XML: A Brief Glimpse

Although Chapter 2, "The Fundamentals of XML," lays the foundation work for XML, in order to have a good discussion about what XML can do for you and how it differs from past efforts, it does make sense to give you a brief glimpse of what XML is. XML stands for *Extensible Markup Language*, a series of three words that mean a whole lot. The basic idea is that with XML, you can encode information in a text document that not only has data in it but also has information that describes what the information means—and in a structured manner that humans can read. This may sound abstract or extremely simple, depending on your viewpoint, but it is the truly basic core of the language. XML is simply a text document that allows users to store data in a structured manner that also encodes information, or "metadata," as to what that data means.

For a more detailed introduction to XML, you should read Chapter 2. The remainder of this book details extensions to this basic concept to power robust applications and make XML work in a real-world context.

With this explanation in mind, we can now address the bigger questions: Why does XML matter? Why will it solve our data-representation problems? Why is it different from other formats that have attempted to solve the same problems? Why will it make a difference in the way we run our businesses, day-to-day tasks, and lives?

The Time Is Right

Before we talk about what XML is and how it began, it makes sense to talk about why the revolution in structured data is happening now. As you'll learn later in this section, although XML has many compelling features, as a technology, it offers little that others have not attempted with differing degrees of success. So, the question that begs to be asked is, "how is XML different?"

As a partial answer to this question, timing is everything. There are many reasons why XML may not have worked as a technology or movement even a decade ago. Some of these reasons are technology based, whereas others deal more with the sociological ramifications of how technology is used and adopted.

The simplest of reasons why XML is becoming popular is that our machines are only now capable of the processing requirements of this data format. It simply would have been extremely difficult, if not impossible, to support the processing, data storage, and bandwidth requirements for the exchange of XML documents 20 years ago. We started approaching the ability to process this information in an effective manner only a decade ago. Simply put, processing power, data storage, and bandwidth is becoming incredibly cheap these days. Processing XML now is not as big a challenge as it would have been in 1980.

The driving force for the use of a technology like XML is the desire to exchange information in an open, nonproprietary manner. The terms *open systems* and *open software* imply that a particular application or data format can be created by Corporation A's tools and processed by Corporation B, C, or D's tools or by open-source applications and tools. Open systems can be created and processed in any combination of different tools and applications by different or competing tool vendors. For vendors of software applications who open their data formats and programming layers, this means their software can be replaced more easily. Obviously, this primarily represents an advantage to the consumers, who have increased choices in how they choose to have their problems addressed. But this is also an advantage for the software vendors in that they can develop open interfaces that keep their software applications always current and open for modification. In the past few years, the movement to open-source systems and platforms has been tremendous. In part, this has been a reaction to the dominance of the industry by particular software corporations, and in part this is due to the general demand for systems that can interoperate with each other. Ten years ago, this cry for openness was hardly a whisper. It simply would have been impossible to demand open, nonproprietary systems in 1990 when most desktop computers ran DOS and back-office servers ran either Novell or Unix. However, the environment today is ripe for the use of open, nonproprietary data formats.

Of course, the development of the Internet itself is a reason why XML could not have existed in any widespread manner a decade or more ago. Although the Internet was developed in the late 1960s, widespread commercial use of the vast worldwide network was not possible until the early 1990s. Without the Internet, it would be costly, inefficient, and difficult to exchange data in a format such as XML. In fact, the Electronic Data Interchange (EDI) format thrived mainly because it provided both a means for representing data as well as a method for transporting it from place to place. With the widespread use of the Internet, however, technologies such XML could be used in a more extensive manner than formats requiring the use of a closed, proprietary network.

Furthermore, we have had experience now with many technologies that have worked to varying degrees of success. Our experience with EDI has given us an understanding of what it takes to perform electronic transactions. Usage of the Standard Generalized Markup Language (SGML) and the widely popular Hypertext Markup Language

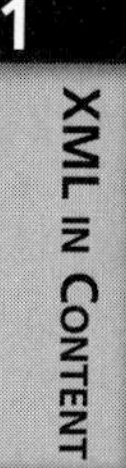

(HTML) has given us experience in what it takes to create, manage, and maintain structured data stores. The development and use of various object-oriented and distributed application technologies such as Microsoft's Component Object Model (COM) and the Common Object Request Broker Architecture (CORBA) have given us the required know-how of when and how to apply distributed processing techniques and methodologies. All that XML has given us is another means for expressing this experience. Without that experience, there is no doubt that XML would simply be another step in the path towards a more perfect data-representation technology. Although XML may not be that final step, it surely is a product of all the experience, mistakes, and wisdom learned from our previous attempts to exchange information in an open manner.

The advent of HTML has brought a new kind of developer to the forefront. These "developers" are not programmers, EDI data wranglers, or publishing industry workers but rather the hordes of individuals who create and manage content on a daily basis. The Web has taught them that they, too, can be part of the information revolution—and now they will be part of the XML revolution. These are the very same developers who would be capable of implementing XML in all its different forms. After all, how can the revolution be fought without any soldiers?

So, not only does XML solve some of the key problems facing data interchange, but its technology comes at a time when we can deal with its existence. In technology, timing is everything.

How We Got Here

The development of XML was not an epiphany that came to a lone inventor working in isolation, nor was it conceived of as part of a corporation's product-development efforts. Rather, XML is an evolution of data formats that existed previously but solved problems of different sorts. In understanding XML, one needs to understand these formats and how their limitations prevented their widespread adoption.

Standard Generalized Markup Language (SGML)

With its roots originating all the way back in 1969 and its standardization by the ISO in 1986, SGML is really the forefather of all markup languages. It introduced the notion that data processing and document processing could be one and the same thing—but we're getting ahead of ourselves here.

Note

SGML is formally standardized as ISO specification 8879:1986. You can obtain more information from the World Wide Web Consortium (W3C) Web site at `http://www.w3.org/MarkUp/SGML/`.

Computers have long been used for document and text processing. In the early days, computers were used to assist in document preparation and typesetting. They allowed copy creators and editors to quickly prototype how a specific document would look prior to its printing on a traditional printing press. As computing progressed, so did its application in the document-preparation industry. The advent of word processors necessitated the invention of a means to indicate how the content was to be modified for printing. Because software applications at the time were text based with no graphical capabilities to speak of, the text contained in the documents were "marked up" using textual commands that were later processed by the final printing destination. These so-called *markups* surrounded the text and explained how it was to be handled for printing. This included notations for boldface, underline, font sizing, placement, and other such commands. Word processors didn't invent markup as a concept—markup is common in document creation and editing. Editors have used markup for decades, if not centuries, to indicate their revisions and changes to text. Word processors merely implemented a way by which markup could be encoded in a computer-based system.

The number and type of such markups proliferated with the number of word processing formats. Markup languages such as troff, rich-text format (RTF), and LaTeX were created to meet these needs. An example of LaTeX can be found in Listing 1.1 (This code is from a Web site on LaTeX at `http://www.oxy.edu/~jquinn/home/Math400/LaTeX/thesis-example-latexcode.html`). Finally, the development of graphical WYSIWYG (What You See Is What You Get) systems eliminated the need for textual markup of documents to indicate their final presentation format. However, the legacy of markup lives on.

LISTING 1.1 LaTeX Example

```
\documentclass[11pt]{article}
\setlength{\textwidth}{6in}
\setlength{\textheight}{9in}
\setlength{\oddsidemargin}{0.2in}
\setlength{\evensidemargin}{0.2in}
\setlength{\topmargin}{-.6in}
\begin{document}
\newtheorem{lemma}{Lemma}[section]
```

LISTING 1.1 continued

```
\newtheorem{theorem}[lemma]{Theorem}
\newtheorem{corollary}[lemma]{Corollary}
\newtheorem{conjecture}[lemma]{Conjecture}
\newtheorem{proposition}[lemma]{Proposition}
\newtheorem{definition}[lemma]{Definition}
\def\square{{\Box}}
\title{Title For a Sample Comprehensive Paper}
\author{ Your Name Here \\Department of Mathematics \\Occidental College \\ \\
{\it Submitted in partial fulfillment of the requirements for the degree}\\
{\sc Bachelor of Arts}}
\maketitle
\begin{abstract}
Every paper needs to begin with an abstract. This is a brief overview of the
entire paper. It should be independent of the body of the paper (i.e. no
referencing things to come). If you feel a definition is needed to make the
ideas here clear, then by all means include it. A lazy reader should be able
to get the entire gist of your work by reading the abstract to be able to
determine if it is worth reading more of the paper.
\end{abstract}
\section{Introduction}
The introduction serves to acquaint the reader with your topic and place it in
 a greater perspective. Notation and definitions which are used throughout the
 work should be presented here. You may find yourself repeating the ideas in
the abstract --- that's okay. They should be more fleshed out in the
introduction.
\section{Main Body}
```

SGML built upon this markup history by providing a common format for defining and exchanging markups between systems that may not share the same markup language inherently. In 1969, IBM sought to simplify the tasks of creating, archiving, searching, and managing legal documents. Charles Goldfarb headed up this task of creating the system and defining a format to meet these needs. In the process of doing so, Goldfarb, along with his coworkers Ed Mosher and Ray Lorie, realized that IBM's multiple systems stored their information in different formats. Producing an application and data format that would cross these systems and produce a unified result would mean that a standard format would have to be created. The solution to this set of problems took the form of the Generalized Markup Language (GML), the initials of which are also the creators' initials. GML was designed to provide a standard means for marking up content that could then be archived, managed, and searched. See Listing 1.2 for an example of an SGML document.

LISTING 1.2 SGML Example

```
<!DOCTYPE book [
<!ELEMENT book O O ((title & subject & author & ISBN?), body)>
<!ELEMENT body - O (bodylines+)>
<!ELEMENT bodylines O O (#PCDATA)>
<!ELEMENT (title, subject, author, ISBN) - O (#PCDATA)>
]>
<title>Little Miss Muffet</title>
<subject>Children's fairy tale</subject>
<author>Mother Goose</author>
<body>
       <bodylines>Little Miss Muffet</bodylines>
       <bodylines>Sat on her tuffet</bodylines>
</body>
```

SGML also introduced the notion of a generalized document format. Rather than having proprietary, custom markup languages that could not be exchanged between systems, a common means for markup definition was defined. Systems that complied with the SGML specification could communicate with each other, even if competing vendors created them. SGML also brought forth the idea that documents can have custom types that indicate the nature and purpose of the information contained within. Rather than specifying a single, monolithic specification that was to be used across all industries, SGML conceived that individual industries would be concerned specifically with the way they represent information. Each of these industries would be able to maintain a Document Type Definition (DTD) for itself and thus be able to exchange documents in an even more specific, standardized manner.

All these features in SGML have transformed the simple document into a representation of text content and its associated data. SGML proved, at a very early age, that document processing and data processing could be one and the same. This idea would be carried forward in the development of its subsequent successor formats: XML and HTML.

However, as SGML development progressed, it became increasingly more overweight and complicated. Both the creation and parsing of SGML documents were difficult and complex, and the various "optional" features of SGML started to bog down its ability to become widely adopted. By necessity, the SGML specification was pulled and influenced by many conflicting industry groups, each of which wanted to make sure the language was able to meet their needs. As a result, the creation of a simple, generic parser for the language was a difficult proposition, at best.

However, the legacy of SGML continued to live on, not only in the number of documents created in the language, but in subsequent formats that borrowed heavily from its creative direction while attempting to side-step some of its complexities.

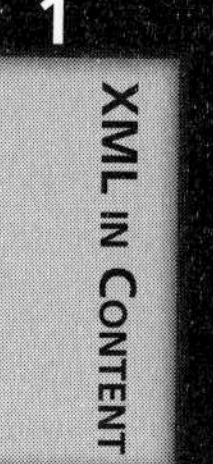

Hypertext Markup Language (HTML)

SGML could have continued its steady growth as the only generalized markup language in use if it weren't for the sudden emergence of the Web and its own format for data exchange—the Hypertext Markup Language (HTML).

Although the Internet has been around since the late 1960s, it was the development of the Web that truly brought the Internet into its current prominence and widespread usage. The Web finally put a visual, interactive, and easy-to-use front end on a network system that had formerly been dominated by applications such as Telnet, FTP, and Gopher. The Web provided users a means to easily create repositories of knowledge that could be linked with one another as well as contain graphical images and well-formatted layouts. What's more, the Web was based, in part, on SGML.

In 1989, a physics researcher at the CERN European Nuclear Research Facility named Tim Berners-Lee proposed that information collected and produced by the facility could be shared in a more interactive and visual manner. Berners-Lee took a peek at what SGML had to offer on this subject, and upon further exploration, he realized that he could create a simple DTD based on SGML that would allow users to create simple hypertext-linked documents. He named this DTD and subsequent development the Hypertext Markup Language (HTML), a sample of which can be seen at Listing 1.3.

LISTING 1.3 HTML Example

```
<HTML>
  <HEAD>
    <TITLE>This an HTML Hello World!</TITLE>
  </HEAD>
  <BODY>
    <H1>Hello World!</H1>
    <FONT SIZE="2">Using a Font Tag, with <B>Boldface</B>
     and <I>Italics</I></FONT>
  </BODY>
</HTML>
```

However, HTML is nothing like SGML when it comes to the strictness and complexity of the language. HTML was developed relatively quickly and was meant to solve a fairly simple job. It was created with simple developers in mind; therefore, "sloppiness" was allowed to thrive. In fact, this sloppiness may be the very reason why the Web exists in the first place. Because it was so easy to create HTML documents and browsers, the format flourished in the vacuum of the Internet. Users simply were craving a document format that could express their ideas in a visual, linked manner. HTML met this need.

Because it borrows much of its functionality from SGML, HTML provides many similar features: the use of angle-bracketed elements and attributes as well as a structure defined by a DTD that was independent of display mechanisms. Of course, this latter part became increasingly fuzzy as the various Internet browser vendors started to battle over control of the market. In particular, Microsoft and Netscape sought to add their own proprietary elements to the HTML language that would be understandable only by their respective browser platforms. Of course, this violated the basic tenets of SGML in that the markup language should be standardized and generalized.

In addition, HTML solved only one part of the SGML realm of problems—namely the presentational and layout aspects. HTML was aimed squarely at representing information for display on a browser or other display devices such as cell phones and handheld devices. The language was never intended as a means for storing data and *metadata* (information that describes data) or for providing a framework for users to exchange data in a structured manner. HTML had separated the notions of data processing from document processing.

It soon became clear that once again a need for a language such as SGML was needed on the Internet. HTML was not adequate for the extensible, data-oriented nature of information exchange, and SGML was too complex and not native to the Internet environment.

Electronic Data Interchange

Of course, HTML and SGML were not the only data formats in existence prior to the emergence of XML. In the electronic commerce and business communities, another acronym held even more sway than SGML.

The Transportation Data Coordinating Committee (TDCC) developed the Electronic Data Interchange (EDI) format in the early 1970s as a means for transportation industry vendors to specify transaction sets that enabled electronic processing of purchase orders and bills. At the time, computing power was concentrated in isolated mainframes that had low storage capacity and even lower bandwidth capabilities for exchanging information.

Because freight transactions were dominated by high-volume, low-dollar transactions, transportation suppliers were early adopters of EDI standards. Many large carriers and shippers achieved significant productivity gains by switching their internal, paper-oriented systems to electronic transactions enabled by EDI.

Because the presence of an established message-transport infrastructure, standardized business process rules, and file formats did not exist in the early years of EDI's formation, the EDI format carried with it specifications for how the messages were to be exchanged and processed. Before the Internet came into widespread use, EDI messages were sent across private value-added networks (VANs) that ensured that transactional messages reached their destination with security, integrity, and messaging validity, along with receipts that guaranteed the messages were received. The EDI transaction sets also contained strict business rules on how the messages were to be handled.

The EDI file format used a fairly arcane syntax that was unintelligible to most humans. Just looking at Listing 1.4 is enough to give many of us headaches. The structure was aimed at efficiency and compactness over flexibility and human readability. As such, EDI parsers and processors were used to create, read, and manage these files. In general, two parties that wished to conduct an EDI transaction would need to enter into a trading agreement, choose a VAN for message delivery, build or buy software to conduct mapping between data formats and EDI messages, and build translators to interpret the sender's message into the company's native data format. Each of these operations would have to be accomplished for every new trading partner added to the network. In addition, VANs charge monthly and per-transaction fees for the handling of these messages. It is no wonder that implementation cost and complexity is so high with EDI systems. It is also no wonder that only the large manufacturers were able to afford to participate!

LISTING 1.4 EDI Example

```
ISA*00* *00* *01*003897733 *12*PARTNER ID*980923*1804*U*00200*000000002*0*T*@
GS*PO*MFUS*PARTNER ID*19980924*0937*3*X*004010
ST*850*0001
BEG*00*SA*4560006385**19980923
CUR*BY*USD
TAX*1-00-123456-6
FOB*DF***02*DDP
ITD*01*ZZ*****45*****NET 45 - Payment due 45 days from Document Date
TD5*Z****Ship via Airborne
N9*L1**NOTE FOLLOWING TEXT
MSG*PLEASE CONFIRM PRICE IF NOT CORRECT.
N9*L1**NOTE FOLLOWING TEXT
MSG*CONTACT JACK WITH QUESTIONS 212-555-1212
N1*BT**92*USA1
N1*BY*ACME HARDWARE CORPORATION*92*MFUS
PER*BD*JOHN DOE
N1*SE*PARTNER COMPANY NAME*92*0010001000
N1*ST*Acme Hardware Corporation*92*0000002924
N3*123 Random Hill Rd
N4*Megalopolis*NY*01429*US
PO1*00010*3600*EA*1.233*CT*BP*123456-123*EC*AM*VP*123456*123
PID*F****STROMBOLI, 4000,XCR-P5
SCH*3300*EA***002*19981101
CTT*1
SE*23*0001
GE*1*2
IEA*1*000000002
```

Each of the EDI transaction sets defines which fields of data are contained in a specific transactional message. The format defines the fields themselves, their order of appearance, and the length of the information contained within. A number of "implementation guidelines" are also applied to the transaction sets to assist in the development of valid EDI messages.

The EDI transaction sets were developed by two separate bodies: the American National Standards Institute's (ANSI) Accredited Standards Committee (ASC) X12 and the United Nations Standards Messages Directory for Electronic Data Interchange for Administration, Commerce, and Transport (EDIFACT). Whereas ANSI X12 met the needs of North American commerce users, EDIFACT was focused on meeting more international needs. Later, the ANSI ASC X12 effort was moved to the Data Interchange Standards Association (DISA) for ongoing management. As such, the specifications deviated somewhat and the "standard" nature of EDI was rapidly degraded.

EDI has been used as the basis for a number of industry-specific standards efforts. In particular, the healthcare industry has used EDI to define its Health Level Seven (HL7) standard, which is in use by most of the world's hospitals and insurance companies for exchanging healthcare and health insurance information. In addition, other groups including automotive, insurance, government, retail, and grocery industries have looked to EDI as a format on which to base their business-to-business interactions.

However, many of the supposed gains that EDI was to deliver were never realized due to the inability of the electronic applications to eliminate the paper processes necessary to support the business processes. EDI exhibits the "80/20 rule," which states that the last 20 percent of a company's trading partners to be implemented in EDI will represent 80 percent of its savings. The reason for this is simple: The trading partners that still conduct business in paper formats and processes still need to be supported. That means dual and somewhat-redundant processes—one electronic and one paper—need to be supported. This is very inefficient in the long run. In addition, EDI was never really able to help the small and medium-sized trading partners to participate in the electronic commerce game. This is primarily due to EDI's cost and the complexity of implementation. It was simply too expensive to get all the small-business suppliers to switch from their paper processes to EDI. This meant that the returns for everyone were greatly diminished.

Another of EDI's problems is its reliance on fixed transaction sets. The rigidity of these transaction sets makes EDI somewhat impervious to the natural changes that occur in business processes and methodologies. This rigidity is reflected in the somewhat-strict manner in which EDI messages must be processed and the standardization process by which these transaction sets are defined. Transaction sets have a well-defined field

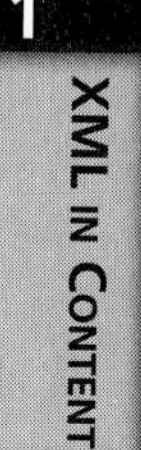

format and structure. Companies are not free to add their own data elements or redefine data structures. This has required many users to implement EDI in a nonstandard manner in order for it to serve their business needs.

However, the EDI industry sought to fix many of these shortcomings by embracing the Internet as a means for transportation, and by relaxing many of the strict processing requirements. EDI has actually made some significant strides in the past five or so years in trying to adapt to the rapidly changing business frontier. In this regard, it is unlikely that EDI is going to disappear entirely. Rather, we may find that within EDI's already large community base, its use will solidify. However, as a means for transporting data in general or as a solution for e-business for the community at large, EDI has had its day in the sun, and now XML is due to bask in some of the sunlight.

The investment that many companies have made in EDI is not going to simply be thrown away, however. Many companies are looking to leverage their EDI expertise into crafting XML solutions that take advantage of the EDI infrastructure, business processes, and architecture. In fact, a number of XML proposals seek to "XML-enable" EDI by simply replacing the arcane EDI format with XML tags. Others seek to mirror the transaction sets using a similar XML-based element structure. In any case, many companies are seeking to soften the transition from EDI to XML-based systems by utilizing the decades of experience in EDI systems and using this experience to create robust XML-based systems.

The Beginnings of XML

As the Internet emerged and rapidly became a viable place to conduct business, communicate, and entertain, it became apparent that the need to exchange data in an open manner was still unmet. SGML provided a solution for exchanging data in a structured, standardized manner, but it was inappropriate for direct application on the Internet. HTML was a pure-Internet approach for displaying and presenting information in a platform-independent manner, but it was wholly inadequate for representing data structures. EDI had proven its merit in conducting electronic business transactions but was ill-suited to being exchanged on the Internet and lacked the sophisticated features of either HTML or SGML. It was obvious something more was needed.

In this environment, an initiative led Jon Bosak and supported by a group of SGML and industry notables, including Tim Bray, C. M. Sperberg-McQueen, Jean Paoli, and James Clark, sought to take some of the best features of SGML and "put them on the Web." Their goal was to take the standard, generalized manner for marking up data and extend it with metadata while stripping out all the complexities and optional features that made

SGML too difficult to implement. On top of that, the new language would be designed inherently for the Internet and have the support of the Internet's top standards-setting body, the World Wide Web Consortium (W3C). Originally called *Web SGML*, this new language was later named the Extensible Markup Language (XML) .

Note

A great history of XML in Jon Bosak's own words can be found at `http://java.sun.com/xml/birth_of_xml.html`.

The Promise of XML

What can XML offer that these other various formats have been unable to deliver at this point? How will XML make our lives better, make our systems more efficient, lower our costs, and increase our revenues? How will XML make the task of representing, storing, and exchanging data an easier process than using SGML, HTML, or EDI?

Benefits of XML

The very nature of XML is that it is a structured document format that represents not only the information to be exchanged but also the metadata encapsulating its meaning. Most information has structure of some type. For example, information about a book contains information about the title, author, chapters, body text, and index. In turn, body text contains paragraphs, line text, and footnotes. This information is structured because a document that describes a book would need to describe that information in a way that a person or machine can understand it. Author information should not be contained within the index section, and vice versa. Although SGML has provided this functionality to XML by virtue of being a "parent language," XML has simplified the process of defining and using this metadata.

Although XML is fairly simple in nature, in that it only needs to follow basic syntax rules to be considered "well-formed," one of the biggest features of the language is its ability to provide a means for guaranteeing the validity of a document. This means that not only can you send a document to a receiving party but you can also send criteria, in the form of Document Type Definitions (DTDs) or other schema formats, with which the document must comply. For example, criteria may specify that an XML document should contain only the listed set of elements and attributes in a specific order and in given quantities. XML documents, on the other hand, come built in with error and validity checking. The DTD or schema that is referred to by an XML document can guarantee,

at the time of document creation, that all the elements are correctly specified and in the correct order. Furthermore, the usage of a more advanced validity-guaranteeing mechanism such as XML Schema can help guarantee that the values of the element content itself are valid and fall within acceptable ranges. Documents can be validated at their time of creation or at their time of receipt, and they can be rejected or accepted on an automated basis without human intervention. At design time, these errors can be fixed before transmission, and upon receipt, they can be sent back to the sender for further human processing with an exact pinpointing as to where these errors have occurred.

Validity-checking software is also very low cost, if not free. Most parsers on the market are available in open-source form and come with validation capabilities built in. Although many of these are currently only DTD compliant, the move to XML Schema–based validity checking is well under way. Batches of documents can be checked for compliance against a single DTD or schema, or they can be checked against different schema based on their destination or origination. Although the use of a DTD and schema does not guarantee 100-percent validity, it goes a long way toward ensuring that the vast majority of documents exchanged and received fit an acceptable policy.

One benefit of using XML with DTDs or schemas is that XML editors provide structured editing "for free." As a developer, how many times have you run a processor on some formatted file only to get a complaint about a syntax error at line 37? Editing software that only allows you to enter valid XML will catch many of these errors as you type them. From another perspective, editors can automatically create a form-style interface from a DTD or schema. Therefore, XML can provide a simpler user interface and eliminate some of the complexity of creating XML documents.

XML takes advantage of existing Internet protocols, and as such, designers choosing to use XML in their solutions don't have to create new protocols as a means for transporting their documents. Designing a new protocol today may not make sense when existing and well-understood protocols such as HTTP exist. Using these protocols makes the document more portable across multiple platforms, more easily debugged, and easier to understand how to qualify and route. In addition, HTTP as a protocol is well understood, and IT engineers know how to manage the HTTP traffic. Using a new protocol would require inventing a protocol to go over the wires, which would necessitate identifying new data streams for firewalls, management of the traffic, and a whole ball of wax that is simply not necessary for a structured data format.

Because XML is a structured document that shares many of the same processing and parsing requirements as SGML and HTML, plenty of generally available parsers have been built. Many of these parsers are now built in to general browsers and server-side agents. Chapter 2 talks about these various client-side and server-side parsers and processors and explains which tools are available for use today.

In addition, the Document Object Model (DOM) has been created by the W3C as a general model for how parsers and processors should interact and process XML documents for representation as a data-bound tree. As a result, the DOM has produced a generic, universal method for processing XML documents. Applications that require XML processing can access this wealth of tools and specifications and thus add parsing in a relatively pain-free way. Developers do not have to write new parsers, unless they really want to. Many parsers exist in a wide variety of languages, and many of these are free.

Another oft-cited benefit of XML is its ability to be read and written by humans, rather than created by applications in a machine-only readable format. Although many say that XML will be primarily used for machine-to-machine communication and can be created using visual tools that don't necessitate the actually editing of the code, experience with HTML has shown that there are numerous occasions when a developer has to "dip in" to the actual document and make adjustments. It is for this reason that XML is plain text and uses elements that represent actual words or phrases that contain some semantic meaning.

XML represents information and the metadata about that information; therefore, it does not specify any particular manner for how the data should be processed or provide any constraints for mechanisms with which to handle the information. This is in contrast to other formats, such as EDI, certain types of text files, and databases, that explicitly require accessing the documents in a specific manner. Furthermore, the files themselves define how the information is to be processed and what requirements systems must have in order to make sense of the documents. In contrast, XML documents simply encode information and their metadata without specifying how the information is to be processed or displayed.

Often, the capability of XML to separate its process and data content is known as being *future-proof* or *loosely coupled*, depending on which end of the marketing spectrum you stand. *Future-proof* in this instance means that no future changes in the data-exchange layer should affect the programming layer, and vice versa. Loosely coupled systems allow for "arms-length" exchange of information, where one party does not need to know details of how the other party plans to process the information. These systems are then "loosely coupled" from the existing systems they need to integrate with or whatever system is to be in place in future. This allows for changes in the presentation, process, and data layers without affecting the other layers.

Due to XML's popularity, ease of use, and increasing proliferation of tools, the number of individuals and organizations skilled in XML use is increasing exponentially. It is becoming considerably easier to find skilled employees and contractors who are familiar with XML, the standards, and best practices for implementing XML in multiple environments. Perhaps one of the best arguments for the use of XML is that the more people there are who make use of the language, the more it will be supported and capable of meeting your needs. Sometimes the best technologies are the ones that are the most in use, regardless of their technological advantages.

Advantages of XML over SGML

Although XML borrows much of its functionality from SGML, it provides a number of distinct advantages. Although SGML may still be suitable for content and data representation, the tide of public opinion is definitely shifting in XML's favor. As such, it makes sense to at least consider XML in place of existing or proposed SGML implementations.

XML permits well-formed documents to be parsed without the need for a DTD, whereas many SGML implementations require some DTD for processing. XML is much simpler and more permissive in its syntax than SGML. The XML specification is very small, includes a bare-bones set of features (rather than a bunch of optional features that can make implementation costs difficult to judge), and avoids some of the stigma associated with the SGML name.

XML was created because a direct implementation of SGML on the Internet was difficult. SGML simply did too much. One of SGML's benefits is that it provides significant flexibility for a diverse community of users by providing a wide array of choices, which resulted in a wide range of syntactical variations for documents. This produced a specification that was very difficult for developers to implement. XML 1.0 simplified the specification by eliminating unnecessary flexibility. This resulted in a specification that was both powerful and easy to implement. The goal was to aim at meeting the majority of users' needs, without aiming to meet all the users' needs.

Advantages of XML over HTML

HTML was created to meet a very different need than XML. It is clear that XML will not now, or perhaps ever, completely replace HTML. Except of course with regard to the XML-enabled version of HTML, known as *XHTML*. HTML was designed as a language to present hyperlinked, formatted information in a Web browser. It has no capability to represent metadata, provide validation, support extensibility by users, or support even the basic needs of e-business. Fundamentally, the difference is that HTML is intended for consumption by humans, whereas XML is meant for both machine and human consumption.

Advantages of XML over EDI

EDI adoption has been fairly widespread, even though mainly among larger-sized businesses. The cost of EDI implementation and ongoing maintenance can be measured in the billions in aggregate. Millions of dollars in transactions occur on a daily basis using EDI-mediated messages. It would be very difficult, if not impossible, to uproot all this activity and replace it with exclusively XML-based transactions. These businesses have so much money and time invested in ANSI X12/EDI that they will be fairly slow to adopt a new standard, which would necessitate new processing technology, mapping software, and back-end integration. For them, it would seem that they would need to discard their existing, working technology in favor of an unproven and still immature technology.

However, XML offers a number of clear advantages over EDI, which has long had its time in the sun. XML is a good replacement for EDI because it uses the Internet for the data exchange. There have been efforts to provide mechanisms for EDI to also be transported over the Internet, but many of these have not met with much success. Recent efforts have attempted to make use of Internet protocols such as SMTP, FTP, and HTTP to transport EDI, but it is clear that the format was not originally designed or intended for such use.

Compared to EDI and other electronic commerce and data-interchange standards, XML offers serious cost savings and efficiency enhancements that make implementation of XML good for the bottom line. There are many components to document exchange and electronic commerce systems: document creation tools, processing components, validity checking, data mapping, back-end integration, access to a communications backbone, security, and other pieces of the commerce puzzle. XML greatly simplifies, if not eliminates, many of these steps.

XML's built-in validity checking, low-cost parsers and processing tools, Extensible Stylesheet Language (XSL) based mapping, and use of the Internet keep down much of the e-commerce chain cost. In many cases, general XML tools can be found that are not only applicable to the problem to be solved, but are flexible and very inexpensive. Whereas EDI is a specific domain of knowledge and expertise that comes with a comparable price tag, XML makes use of technology that has been in use for years, if not decades. Systems that take advantage of this wealth of available processing power and know-how will greatly reduce not only their costs but also their time to implementation.

The use of the Internet itself greatly lowers the barrier for small and medium-sized companies that have found EDI too costly to implement. Simple functionality and low-cost tools will go a long way in helping these companies afford to exchange high-quality, structured documents that are capable of supporting commercial exchange and back-end integration.

As one XML user states, "XML is hip, happening, now." EDI is perceived as crusty and old. Text files are blasé, and databases have increasingly become a staple of data storage locked in a proprietary format. The idea that XML represents a new, fresh approach to solving many lingering problems in a flexible manner appeals to many in senior management. In many instances, buying into a new technology requires the approval of the senior levels of IT, if not the corporate and management levels. With XML's continuing positive exposure, getting management approval on an XML project is become an increasingly simpler endeavor.

Another of the drawbacks to EDI and some text file and database formats is that they don't easily support the needs for internationalization and localization. Specifically, in those languages it is difficult to represent information contained in a non-Latin alphabet. XML, as part of its initial specification, supports these needs inherently.

XML syntax allows for international characters that follow the Unicode standard to be included as content in any XML element. These can then be marked up and included in any XML-based exchange. The use of internationalization features helps to surpass one of the early problems of other formats that cause unnecessary schism and conflict between different geographies. For example, it is not fair that an English technical manual can be marked up in a file format if a Japanese manual can't be likewise formatted. XML sought to solve this problem from the get-go.

Advantages of XML over Databases and Flat Files

XML is a structured document format that includes not only the data but also metadata that describes that data's content and context. Most text files simply cannot offer this clear advantage. They either represent simply the information to be exchanged without metadata or include metadata in a flat, one-level manner. Common file exchange formats such as comma-delimited and tab-delimited text files merely contain data in predefined locations or delimitations in the files. Complex file formats such as Microsoft Excel contain more structured information but are machine-readable only and still do not contain the level of structuring present in XML.

Relational and object-oriented databases and formats can represent data as well as metadata, but for the most part, their formats are not text based. Most databases use a proprietary binary format to represent their information. There are other text-based formats that include metadata regarding information and are structured in a hierarchical representation, but they have not caught on in popularity nearly to the extent that XML or even SGML has.

Although text files can also be transmitted via e-mail and over the Web, structured formats such as relational and object-oriented databases are not easily accessible over the Internet. Their binary-based formats and proprietary connection mechanisms preclude their ability to be easily accessible via the Internet. Many times, gateway software and other mechanisms are needed to access these formats, and when they are made accessible it usually is through one particular transport protocol, such as HTTP. Other means for accessing the data, such as through e-mail and FTP, are simply not available.

One of the primary issues faced by alternate file format and database languages is that processing tools are custom, proprietary, or expensive. When tools are widespread, they are usually specific to the particular file format in question. One of XML's greatest strengths is that processing tools have become relatively widespread and inexpensive, if not free.

Drawbacks to XML

One of the most notable and significant "knocks" against XML is that it's huge. XML takes up lots of space to represent data that could be similarly modeled using a binary format or a simpler text file format. The reason for this is simple: It's the price we pay for human-readable, platform-neutral, process-separated, metadata-enhanced, structured, validated code.

And this space difference is not insignificant. XML documents can be 3 to 20 times as large as a comparable binary or alternate text file representation. The effects of this space should not be underestimated. It's possible that 1GB of database information can result in over 20GB of XML-encoded information. This information then needs to get stored and transmitted over the network—facts that should make computer, storage, and network hardware manufacturers very happy indeed!

Let's not also forget that computers need to process this information. Large XML documents may need to be loaded into memory before processing, and some XML documents can be gigabytes in size! This can result in sluggish processing, unnecessary reparsing of documents, and otherwise heavy system loads. In addition, much of the "stack" of protocols requires fairly heavy processing to make it work as intended. For example, the Simple Object Access Protocol (SOAP), which is a cross-platform messaging and communication platform for use in remote procedure calls (RPCs) between and within server systems, is a very heavy protocol to manipulate on-the-fly. The marshalling that occurs in the process of working with the protocol can cause system performance to be quite poor because XML is, after all, a text-based protocol that is being used to make RPCs between systems. Using XML in this transactional, real-time manner may impose more requirements on the system as far as parsing and processing than the system can handle.

In addition, a problem of many current XML parsers is that they read an entire XML document into memory before processing. This practice can be disastrous for XML documents of very large sizes. XML is not only a data language but a complicated one at that (from a parsing perspective). It oftentimes increases code complexity, because XML can be more difficult to parse than a simpler data format such as comma- or tab-delimited fields.

Despite all the added value in representing data and metadata in a structured manner, some projects simply don't require the complexity that XML introduces. In these cases, simple text files do the job more efficiently. For example, a configuration file that includes a short list of a few commands and their values doesn't require a multilevel, metadata-enhanced file format for its communication. Therefore, one shouldn't take the stance that simply because XML contains structure and metadata it should be used for *all* file formatting and document-exchange needs.

Although XML does offer validation technology, it is not currently as sophisticated as many of the EDI syntax checkers. XML editors often lack the detail and helpfulness found in common EDI editors. Many EDI syntax editors can report error details throughout a document and can complete the parsing of the entire document. Many XML editors are unable to proceed beyond the first syntax.

In addition, XML inherits the notorious security issues associated with the Internet, but it also inherits the possible solutions to those problems as well. As long as a system is designed with security in mind, exchanging XML over the Internet should be fairly problem free.

XML-Based Standards

We have already discussed the advantages of the "ML" in XML, but the "X" presents advantages of its own. *Extensibility*, as applied to XML, is the ability for the language to be used to define specific vocabularies and metadata. Rather than being fixed in describing a particular set of data, XML, in conjunction with its DTDs and schema, is able to define any number of documents that together form a language of their own.

Indeed, hundreds, if not thousands, of specific document vocabularies have been created based on XML to meet the different needs of healthcare, manufacturing, user interface design, petroleum refining, and even chess games. Text files and relational database schemas are rigid in that they are meant to represent the information contained within and nothing more. It would be a difficult proposition at best to add a new set of information to a text file or relational database management system (RDBMS). XML files, especially those created using an "open content model," can easily be extended by adding additional elements and attributes. Whole classes of documents can be defined simply by sending a document with a new DTD or schema. Sharing a DTD and schema within a user community results in a joint specification—if not a de facto or explicit standard.

Where Is XML Heading?

Someone once said that XML is better than sliced bread—it doesn't mold. With all this XML hubbub, people tend to forget that XML isn't an application. It's not a programming language. It's not the answer to world peace and starvation. It's not even a breakfast cereal. XML is simply a document format that has characteristics that make it very well suited to sending structured information containing metadata that is easily validated.

However, with a standard language that has all the capabilities of XML, tremendous advancements can be made in areas dealing with the representation, storage, and exchange of information. In particular, XML is making it easier to conduct e-business and e-commerce, manage online content, work with distributed applications, communicate, and otherwise provide value.

E-Business and E-Commerce

In the past few years, the Internet and the Web have revolutionized the way we communicate. As part of this revolution, the way in which we do business has likewise been radically altered. We can finally be liberated from paper-based processes and be empowered to conduct business and improve our customer support. We have moved from "traditional" business to "e-business," and XML is helping every step of the way.

E-commerce is not a concept that was invented with the Web. Rather, it has been around as long as there have been electronic means for exchanging commercial transactions. EDI has been around since the late 1960s and has been in use to exchange supply, shipping, and purchase information. However, the technology is rather arcane, relatively expensive, and cumbersome to implement. The promise of being able to exchange vital business information using open protocols such as XML and the Internet have tickled more than one idle mind.

It is widely understood that *e-business*, as a term, refers to a collection of business concepts and processes that are enabled by a variety of electronic or online solutions. In general, e-business often refers to the practice of using electronically-enabled processes to manage and run portions of a company's business practices, or managing its overall business approach using an electronic or online mentality. Particular e-business practices include delivering information to customers via the Internet, implementing customer relationship management systems, and connecting branches together utilizing electronically distributed methods.

Although overlapping somewhat with the definition of e-business, *e-commerce* generally refers to the ability to perform a particular transaction with a customer in an electronic or online format. E-commerce is usually much smaller in scope and focused than overall e-business and usually implies a direct transaction between two parties. To make the distinction with e-business clear, buying a book online is considered an e-commerce transaction, whereas enabling the fulfillment and delivery of that book using electronic methods is considered e-business.

One of the main uses of XML in e-business is the representation of the various business transactions that occur on a daily basis between partners in a trading process. This includes purchase orders, invoices, shipping, bills of lading, and warehousing information. Because these transactions represent billions, if not trillions, of dollars on a daily basis, it's no wonder that the first target of many XML standards-setting bodies is to specify these very transactions.

In addition to the actual transactions themselves, XML is helping to standardize the process by which these messages are exchanged among trading partners. One of the biggest values that EDI brought to implementing companies was that in addition to getting a file format, you also got a message-transport mechanism. In order for XML to truly be enabled for e-business, it also needs a means for guaranteeing that messages reach their final destination in the order and quantity necessary. As such, business-oriented standards groups have been creating the means for transporting, routing, and packaging XML messages for consumption in business processes.

One of the major steps in any e-business process is payment for services rendered or goods sold. Even in this area, XML is making a major impact. XML has been used to send payment information of all types, including credit cards, cash, vouchers, barter exchanges, and electronic funds transfers. Of course, security remains one of the biggest concerns when it comes to sending payment information, and in this area too, XML is making waves. XML has been used for security specifications of all sorts, ranging from encryption and authorization to privacy.

Content Management

The proliferation of computing power and the means to connect these machines has resulted in an explosion of data. All of a sudden, any application or document can instantly be shared with others. This has led to the concept that all information or data can be considered "content" that can be accessible and integrated with other systems. XML is being used to enable all forms of content management and application integration.

In particular, content that formerly was locked into proprietary file formats has been encoded with a variety of XML-based formats. XML is now enabling this content to be searched, located, and integrated with applications. "Legacy" systems, such as Customer Relationship Management (CRM), Enterprise Resource Planning (ERP), accounting, finance, Human Resources (HR), and other systems, are now communicating with each other using XML as the "lingua franca" of exchange. In addition, documents that have been sitting in various file repositories are being marked up and made available to users, both internal and external, through the Web.

XML is not only being used to mark up and integrate with existing content but also to assist in its creation and management. A variety of new technologies based on XML are being used to help in authoring, versioning, posting, and maintenance of content of all sorts. These new XML formats allow many types of users to work with content in an open, nonproprietary manner. As well as giving users the ability to control how their content is viewed, XML is enabling developers to "syndicate" content by distributing it to subscribers of all types. This means that a single source of data can be placed on multiple Web servers and destinations, without having to key in the data multiple times. Truly, XML has liberated data to serve its function of conveying information.

Web Services and Distributed Computing

XML even aims to solve some of the long-standing challenges in getting computer systems to interact with each other on a programmatic level. *Distributed computing* (the ability to distribute processing responsibilities and functions among machines on a local or wide area network) has long faced challenges in the way that programming functionality encapsulated within "objects" is exchanged. Over the past few decades, many different approaches have been attempted at getting systems of even the same operating system type to be able to efficiently exchange programming functionality. This ability to call remote computing functionality, known as *remote procedure calls* (RPCs) or *distributed computing*, has been attempted through technologies such as the Component Object Model (COM) and CORBA. However, each of these technologies has its supporters from different, proprietary implementation camps. COM is supported mainly by the Microsoft camp, whereas CORBA is supported by competing vendors. XML aims to put this divisiveness to rest by specifying a platform-neutral approach by which objects and programmatic functionality can be operated on a global, distributed basis.

This ability to access computing functionality through XML and Web technologies is becoming known as *Web Services* and will no doubt play a major role in the next few years. Backed by such industry notables as IBM, Microsoft, Sun, and Oracle, Web Services are poised to change the way computing is accomplished on a distributed, open basis. XML is being used to define and transport application functionality as well as allow users a means to register and locate these Web Services for their own internal use. For example, a Web site developer who wants to create complex shipping and delivery options can locate a Web Service offered by the United Parcel Service (UPS) and instantly "plug it in" to his company's Web site in a seamless fashion without having to make any modifications to the internal systems.

Peer-to-Peer Networking and Instant Messaging

In the past few years, another major revolution in communication and data exchange has swept the Internet. With the increasing number of machines and individuals now able to access the Internet, file sharing has moved from centralized servers to the desktop. Individuals can quickly exchange messages, files, and other information with each other on an on-demand basis. Known as *peer-to-peer networks* (P2P), this "instant file sharing" technology was popularized by the Napster movement, which aimed to facilitate the sharing of music, albeit often copyrighted. Despite the negative publicity attached to Napster, P2P technology has shown that it can be useful in many other arenas, both within and external to the walls of an organization.

In a similar vein, the ability to quickly send messages to colleagues, friends, acquaintances, and business partners has been greatly enhanced by the ubiquity of Internet connectivity. Originally popularized by AOL and ICQ, instant messaging of all sorts has become very popular. Instant messaging has spread to many different devices, ranging from desktop computers to cell phones, and has included such features as desktop application sharing, video conferencing, and voice communications.

XML is quickly making its presence felt in both of these rapidly growing technology areas. Various XML specifications and protocols are being used to allow individuals and organizations to send instant messages, locate other users, and locate, exchange, and store files on peer-to-peer networks in an open and nonproprietary manner.

Getting More Meaning out of the Web: The Semantic Web

The very nature of XML allows users to create their own tags that represent the context and meaning of data. However, there is nothing that prevents two or more organizations from calling the same data element different things or using the same name for different data elements. Furthermore, how will computers be able to understand the various ways of representing the same information? To a human, "PO," "Purchase Order," and "PurchOrd" all mean the same thing, but to a computer, they are all as different as "cow," "swim," and "Volkswagen." Crossing language boundaries makes things even more difficult. Not only do element names change dramatically, but their context and possible meanings do as well.

The Semantic Web aims to change all this by giving data elements additional ways of specifying their meaning in a semantically relevant manner. A variety of XML-enabled initiatives are on the front burner of the W3C and other major standards-setting organizations. We will soon be introduced to the terms *ontology* and *topic maps* and learn how these new ways of looking at information and its meaning can help computers and humans make better decisions about how to use data.

In the words of the World Wide Web Consortium (W3C), "The Semantic Web is an extension of the current Web in which information is given well-defined meaning, better enabling computers and people to work in cooperation."

Note

You can find more information about the Semantic Web by visiting the W3C home page at `http://www.w3.org/2001/sw/`.

The most practical of these implementations will help enable users to make better, more relevant searches. How many times have you used a search engine and found that 90 percent of the returned results are completely irrelevant? With a context-aware search engine, it is possible to turn that ratio on its head. Now, rather than wading through a zillion dead-end search engine entries, a user can zero in on the specific item of interest and make use of the information in the best means possible. The implications of the Semantic Web, made possible only through the use of XML, are tremendous.

Summary

The amazing information revolution of the past few years has resulted in tremendous changes in the way we represent, store, and exchange data. These changes have brought us to where we are today. However, in the process of trying to deal with the onslaught of information, we have created an overwhelming number of different file formats, standards, and mechanisms for exchanging information. This proliferation of data formats has increasingly complicated our lives as we attempt to interconnect systems that were not originally created to speak to each other. Furthermore, our use of proprietary systems and applications has unpleasantly pigeonholed many of us into trying to shoehorn new uses for our old "legacy" systems.

XML hopes to change all this. Stemming from a heritage of structured data formats, starting with SGML and ending most recently with HTML, XML combines the sophistication of structured, metadata-enriched, self-describing data with the ubiquity and simplicity of the Internet. It also presents major advantages over other file format and exchange mechanisms such as EDI, text files, and relational database formats.

Furthermore, the timing is right for XML to take root and grow. The market craves open and nonproprietary systems. The user base of trained developers familiar with HTML, SGML, EDI, and other technologies is growing tremendously. The prevalence and widespread use of the Internet provides a perfect platform for the exchange of information and integration of systems. What's more, XML has firmly jumped on the positive publicity bandwagon. XML may not have been the first technology of its kind, but it is at the right place at the right time.

Although XML may not be the answer to all the world's ills, it represents the latest iteration of steadily improving ways for us to communicate and interact.

This book will help you find the best ways to use XML in a manner that is not only detailed and comprehensive for the intermediate user but also in a way that borrows from experience and practical use of XML in the real world. The authors of this book reflect a wide range of experiences with XML in practical implementation and include industry notables and professionals in the field who have been using XML, in some instances, almost since its very day of inception.

CHAPTER 2

The Fundamentals of XML

In This Chapter

In the previous chapter, you were introduced to the ocean of possibilities that XML provides. Now, it is time to get your feet wet. You have seen how XML has emerged from a rich history of structured data representation formats to meet the current needs of developers and content generators. However, the question remains, "Now what?" How can you make use of XML to meet your specific application and development needs? What are the basics of XML so that you can get started and create XML applications today?

In this chapter, you will learn the basic elements and fundamentals of the structure and meaning of XML. You will learn what tools and technologies are needed to read, write, and process XML documents. In addition, this chapter identifies the various portions of the XML document, how they interrelate, and the specifications in working with those various document components. Finally, you will be introduced to the tools you need to create, read, and process XML documents. These tools allow you to unlock the wealth that XML promises.

We'll explore the details in a sample XML document, and in the process you'll learn all about

- Markup languages
- The XML document structure
- Elements
- Attributes
- Entities
- Document types
- The well-formed and valid XML document
- Unicode and internationalization
- Reading and processing XML

Introduction to XML Syntax

Every language and document representation format needs to have a goal. The "goal" of a document's format gives it meaning and a long-term direction. After all, it is not possible for a single data-representation format to be used for all possible data needs. The goal of the Microsoft Word format is to represent a word-processing document; the goal of the Microsoft Excel format is to represent a spreadsheet of numerical information. Although it is possible to use Excel to represent a word-processing document and Word to encode numerical data, these are not the "intended uses" of these document formats. Continuing development of the formats will not make Word a better spreadsheet or Excel a better word processor. It's like fitting a square peg in a round hole.

So, what is the goal of XML and its intended use? We have spent a chapter talking about how XML can be used to encode any structured information, but the one-size-fits-all document format simply doesn't exist. XML is good at representing information that has an *extensible*, *hierarchical* format and requires encoding of *metadata*. These three concepts form the basis of the XML language's structure and data model.

NOTE

If you're interested in hearing about XML syntax straight from the horse's mouth, you can find the complete W3C XML 1.0 Recommendation in Appendix A of this book.

Markup Languages and Self-Describing Data

One of the early design goals of XML was that it should be fairly easy to create XML documents using standard text editors and widely available editing tools. This is actually a legacy of the SGML and HTML languages, which are also text based. These languages use "markup" in order to encode metadata in a text format. The main concept behind markup languages is that they use special text strings to surround data or text with information that indicates the context, meaning, or interpretation of the data encapsulated in the markup. In effect, markup languages in general and XML in particular really contain only two kinds of information: markup elements and actual data that are given meaning by these markup elements. Together, these are known as *XML text*.

Caution

It is a mistake to call just the text that is being marked up in an XML document "XML text," because this term refers to the combination of markup elements and character data, and not just character data alone.

Markup text has a couple rules. First, it needs to be differentiated from the rest of the document text by a unique set of characters that delineates where the markup information starts and ends. These special characters are known as *delimiters*. The XML language has four special delimiters, as outlined in Table 2.1.

TABLE 2.1 XML Delimiter Characters

Character	*Meaning*
<	The start of an XML markup tag
>	The end of an)> less than angle brackets> XML markup tag
&	The start of an XML entity
;	The end of an XML entity

In XML, angle brackets (less-than and greater-than signs) are used to delimit an XML "tag," and the ampersand and semicolon characters delimit "entity" information. Tags are a unit of information that we will refer to later when we start talking about XML elements, and entities provide another way of encoding specific information within an XML document.

Of course, the data contained within the delimiting characters is where all the information lies. Because XML is a plain-text language, markup tags can actually indicate what information is being described. This is actually a major feature of XML and similar languages—namely, the ability for the XML document to self-describe what it is talking about. The following example in Listing 2.1 shows a simple XML document that demonstrates the self-describing property of XML.

LISTING 2.1 XML As a Self-Describing Language

```
<?xml version="1.0"?>
<the_following_text_is_my_first_name>Ron</the_following_text_is_my_first_name>
```

It is clear from this example that the markup tag is talking about someone's first name, and the encapsulated text is the actual first name. The power of a self-describing language is tremendous. It simplifies document creation, maintenance, and debugging. This also makes it easier to communicate with others who may not have prior knowledge of a document's contents. Of course, the big drawback of such languages is that they take up a lot of space. But nowadays, disk space and memory are plentiful and cheap.

A Simple XML Document

Throughout this chapter, we will refer to a simple XML document to demonstrate the various portions of an XML document and how it is structured. In this case, we'll talk about a shirt. There's actually a lot we can talk about with regard to a shirt: size, color, fabric, price, brand, and condition, among other properties. Listing 2.2 shows one possible XML rendition of a document describing a shirt. Of course, there are many other possible ways to describe a shirt, but this example provides a foundation for our further discussions.

LISTING 2.2 A Simple XML document

```
<?xml version="1.0"?>

<shirt>
    <model>Zippy Tee</model>
    <brand>Tommy Hilbunger</brand>
    <price currency="USD">14.99</price>
    <on_sale/>
    <fabric content="60%">cotton</fabric>
    <fabric content="40%">polyester</fabric>
    <options>
    <colorOptions>
            <color>red</color>
            <color>white</color>
        </colorOptions>
        <sizeOptions>
        <size>Medium</size>
            <size>Large</size>
    </sizeOptions>
</options>
    <description>
This is a <b>funky</b> Tee shirt similar to the
Floppy Tee shirt
</description>
</shirt>
```


XML Document Structure

As you can tell from the example in Listing 2.2, an XML document consists of a number of discrete components or sections. Although not all the sections of an XML document may be necessary, their use and inclusion helps to make for a well-structured XML document that can easily be transported between systems and devices.

The major portions of an XML document include the following:

- The XML declaration
- The Document Type Declaration
- The element data
- The attribute data
- The character data or XML content

Each of these major components will be explored in great detail in this section of the chapter. By the end of this section, you should have a thorough understanding of what comprises an XML document.

XML Declaration

The first part of an XML document is the declaration. A declaration is exactly as it sounds: It is a definite way of stating exactly what the document contains. Just like the *Declaration of Independence* states that the United States planned to separate itself from Great Britain, the XML declaration states that the following document contains XML content.

The XML declaration is a processing instruction of the form `<?xml ...?>`. Although it is not required, the presence of the declaration explicitly identifies the document as an XML document and indicates the version of XML to which it was authored. In addition, the XML declaration indicates the presence of external markup declarations and character encoding. Because a number of document formats use markup similar to XML, the declaration is useful in establishing the document as being compliant with a specific version of XML without any doubt or ambiguity. In general, every XML document should use an XML declaration. As documents increase in size and complexity, this importance likewise grows.

The XML declaration consists of a number of components. Table 2.2 lists these various components and their specifications.

TABLE 2.2 Components of the XML Declaration

Component	*Description*
`<?xml`	Starts the beginning of the processing instruction (in this case, for the XML declaration).
`Version="xxx"`	Describes the specific version of XML being used in the document (in this case, version 1.0 of the W3C specification). Future iterations could be 2.0, 1.1, and so on.
`standalone="xxx"`	This standalone option defines whether documents are allowed to contain external markup declarations. This option can be set to `"yes"` or `"no"`.
`encoding="xxx"`	Indicates the character encoding that the document uses. The default is `"US-ASCII"` but can be set to any value that XML processors recognize and can support. The most common alternate setting is `"UTF-8"`.

The standalone document declaration defines whether an external DTD will be processed as part of the XML document. When `standalone` is set to `"yes"`, only internal DTDs will be allowed. When it is set to `"no"`, an external DTD is required and an internal DTD becomes an optional feature. Listing 2.3 illustrates a few valid XML declarations.

LISTING 2.3 Valid XML Declarations

```
<?xml version="1.0" standalone="yes"?>
<?xml version="1.0" standalone="no"?>
<?xml version="1.0" encoding="UTF-8" standalone="no"?>
```


The first declaration defines a well-formed XML document, whereas the second defines a well-formed and valid XML document. The third declaration shows a more complete definition that states a typical use-case for XML. Namely, the declaration states that the XML document complies with version 1.0 of the specification and requires external markup declarations that are encoded in UTF-8.

Document Type Declaration

Once we are aware that we are talking about a specific version of an XML document, the next step is to be more specific about the content contained within. The Document Type Declaration (`DOCTYPE`) gives a name to the XML content and provides a means to guarantee the document's validity, either by including or specifying a link to a Document Type Definition (DTD). Although SGML requires a Document Type Declaration, XML has no restrictions of the sort, although one should be included to avoid an ambiguous understanding of document content.

Caution

Don't confuse the Document Type Declaration with the Document Type Definition (DTD). When abbreviated using a "normal" abbreviation method, both terms would seem the same, but the reality is quite different. A Document Type Declaration (`DOCTYPE`) and a DTD serve very different, although related purposes. The former is used to identify and name the XML content, whereas the latter is used to validate the metadata contained within.

Although well-formed XML documents don't require the inclusion of the `DOCTYPE`, valid XML documents do. This discussion of "well formed" and "valid" will be covered later in this document, but the basic gist is that XML documents can be fairly freeform or comply to a strict guideline of what content can be contained within. Valid XML documents must declare the document type to which they comply, whereas well-formed XML documents can include the DOCTYPE to simplify the task of the various tools that will be manipulating the XML document.

A Document Type Declaration names the document type and identifies the internal content by specifying the *root element*, in essence the first XML tag that the XML-processing tools will encounter in the document. A DOCTYPE can identify the constraints on the validity of the document by making a reference to an external DTD subset and/or include the DTD internally within the document by means of an internal DTD subset. The general forms of Document Type Declarations follow the forms identified in Listing 2.4.

LISTING 2.4 General Forms of the Document Type Declarations

```
<!DOCTYPE NAME SYSTEM "file">
<!DOCTYPE NAME [ ]>
<!DOCTYPE NAME SYSTEM "file" [ ]>
```

In the first form listed, the DOCTYPE is referring to a document that only allows use of an externally defined DTD subset. The second declaration only allows an internally defined subset within the document. The final listing provides a place for inclusion of an internally defined DTD subset between the square brackets while also making use of an external subset. In the preceding listing, the keyword NAME should be replaced with the actual root element contained in the document, and the "file" keyword should be replaced with a path to a valid DTD. In the case of our shirt example, the DOCTYPE is

```
<!DOCTYPE shirt SYSTEM "shirt.dtd">
```

because the first tag in the document will be the <shirt> element and our DTD is saved to a file named shirt.dtd, which saved in the same path as the XML document.

The only real difference between internally and externally defined DTD subsets is that the DTD content itself is contained within the square brackets, in the case of internal subsets, whereas external subsets save this content to a file for reference, usually with a .dtd extension. The actual components of the Document Type Declaration are listed in Table 2.3.

TABLE 2.3 Components of the Document Type Declaration

Component	*Description*
<	The start of the XML tag (in this case, the beginning of the Document Type Declaration).

TABLE 2.3 continued

Component	*Description*
`!DOCTYPE`	The beginning of the Document Type Declaration.
`NAME`	Specifies the name of the document type being defined. This must comply with XML naming rules.
`SYSTEM`	Specifies that the following system identifier will be read and processed.
`"file"`	Specifies the name of the file to be processed by the system.
`[`	Starts an internal DTD subset.
`]`	Ends the internal DTD subset.
`>`	The end of the XML tag (in this case, the end of the Document Type Declaration) .

Markup and Content

In addition to the XML declaration and the Document Type Declaration, XML documents are composed of markup and content. In general, six kinds of markup can occur in an XML document: elements, entity references, comments, processing instructions, marked sections, and Document Type Declarations. The following sections explore these markup types and illustrate how they are used. Of course, needless to say, that which is not markup is content, and this content must comply with rules of its own.

Elements

Within an XML document, elements are the most common form of markup. XML elements are either a matched pair of XML tags or single XML tags that are "self-closing." Matching XML tags consist of markup tags that contain the same content, except that the ending tag is prefixed with a forward slash. For example, our shirt element begins with `<shirt>` and ends with `</shirt>`. Everything between these tags is additional XML text that has either been defined by a DTD or can exist by virtue of the document merely being well formed. When elements do not come in pairs, the element name is suffixed by the forward slash. For example, if we were merely making a statement that a shirt existed, we may use `<on_sale/>`. In this case, there would be no other matching element of the same name used in a different manner. These "unmatched" elements are known as *empty elements*. The trailing "`/>`" in the modified syntax indicates to a program processing the XML document that the element is empty and no matching end tag should be sought. Because XML documents do not require a Document Type Declaration, without this clue it could be impossible for an XML parser to determine which tags were intentionally empty and which had been left empty by mistake.

A question arises about the difference between empty elements and matched element tags that simply contain no content. In reality, there is basically no distinction between the two. It is valid in XML to use the empty-element tag syntax in either case. Therefore, it is legal to use a matched start and end tag pair for elements that are declared as empty. However, for concerns of interoperability and parser compliance, it is best to use the empty-element syntax for elements declared as empty and to make sure that other elements have some content contained within.

Elements can be arbitrarily nested within other elements ad infinitum. In essence, XML is a hierarchical tree. This means that XML elements exist within other elements and can branch off with various children nodes. Although these elements may be restricted by DTDs or schema, the nature of XML is to allow for the growth of these elements in a manner that's as "wide" or "deep" as possible. This means that a single XML element can contain any number of child elements, and the depth of the XML tree can consist of any number of nodes.

You can pretty much name XML elements anything you want, but specific rules need to be followed so that the elements aren't confused with other markup content. XML elements can contain letters, numbers, and other characters, but names cannot start with a number or any punctuation character. XML names cannot contain spaces because whitespace is used within an element to separate the various attribute sections. Also, XML elements cannot contain the greater-than or less-than characters for obvious reasons. For less-obvious reasons, XML elements cannot start with the letters "xml" because they are reserved for future use. Also, XML elements cannot contain the colon character because it is reserved for use in XML namespaces (covered later in this chapter).

In particular, no XML element names are reserved because namespaces can be used to avoid inadvertent conflicts. Although punctuation marks (other than the colon) can be used within an XML element name, you should avoid the hyphen (`-`) and period (`.`) characters in element names because some software applications might confuse them for arithmetic or object operations. Element names should be descriptive and not confusing. After all, one of the main values of XML is that it can be read by humans! For example, what does `<jxf12>` mean to anyone but a computer—if anything at all? Document creators should use descriptive terms that accurately and as specifically as possible describe the content contained within.

Element names can be as long as you like, with almost no real size limitation. This means that the element `<wow_this_really_is_one_heck_of_a_long_element_name>` is actually valid, but what programmer would want to type that element repeatedly or encode a software application to key on that particular element name. Also, some devices with constrained memory capabilities may not work well with overly long XML tag names. In any case, long names are an annoyance to developers, systems, and users alike, despite XML's support for this feature. It's best to leave long content strings to the XML content and keep them out of element and attribute names. XML also allows for the use of non-English letters, such as á, é, and ò, in a document. In fact, XML allows all Unicode 2.3 characters to be used, although there is an effort to upgrade the specification to further use Unicode 3.0 characters in attribute and element names. However, there is no such restriction on XML content, which allows any valid Unicode character to be used.

Attributes

Within elements, additional information can be communicated to XML processors that modifies the nature of the encapsulated content. For example, we may have specified a `<price>` element, but how do we know what currency this applies to? Although it's possible to create a `<currency>` subtag, another more viable approach is to use an attribute. Attributes are name/value pairs contained within the start element that can specify text strings that modify the context of the element. Listing 2.5 shows an example of possible attributes in our shirt example.

LISTING 2.5 Attribute Examples

```
<price currency="USD">…</price>
<on_sale start_date="10-15-2001"/>
```

One of the significant features of attributes is that the content described by them can follow strict rules as to their value. Attributes can be required, optional, or contain a fixed value. Required or optional attributes can either contain freeform text or contain one of a set list of enumerated values. Fixed attributes, if present, must contain a specific value. Attributes can specify a default value that is applied if the attribute is optional but not present. With these properties, attributes can add a considerable amount of value to element content. For example, we may wish to restrict the possible currency values submitted to a list of acceptable three-character ISO currency codes. Or, we may only allow the value `"USD"` to be submitted. Likewise, we can specify that if no currency value is submitted, the system will assume `"USD"` as the default value.

Attributes vs. Elements: What's the Right Approach?

As you have seen, we can represent information in either elements or attributes. So, when is the right time to communicate information in an element versus using an attribute to communicate the same information. For instance, in our shirt example, when should we use `<shirt><color>red</color></shirt>` versus `<shirt color="red">`? This issue of elements versus attributes is a constantly recurring question that can be traced back to the SGML days. Of course, the answer is, it depends! After all, both formats are valid.

The main way to determine whether an element approach is more favorable to an attribute approach, or vice versa, is to identify how the information is to be used. Because most XML users agree that the decision is dependent on the implementation, many would argue that XML is not really an ideal language for data modeling, which requires a more strict sense for how data should be represented. Some of the common arguments are as follows.

Some visual XML browsers display element information but ignore attribute values for purposes of display. Of course, many technologies display both element and attribute values. For those that don't, the use of elements may prevail over attributes.

When DTDs are used, attributes allow default or enumerated values as well as provide a means to restrict the possible data entered. Of course, various XML-based schema technologies are allowing these very same features in elements. However, for those using exclusively DTDs, these features may be a deciding point for the choice of attributes.

Because attributes are nonstructural (that is, they are merely name/value pairs), if you need further internal structure, the use of elements will be the logical choice.

If you are producing an application that is keyed on the name of elements, you should choose elements as the source of information. However, if that information is mainly in empty elements, using attributes can be equally useful and more simple.

Attributes can simplify the level of XML element nesting but can complicate document processing.

Various technologies are keyed on the element name rather than the attribute name or value. For this reason, using either elements or attributes may be the right approach.

If an item needs to occur multiple times, only elements can be used because attributes are restricted to appearing once within an element.

In general, elements are logical, structural units of information that represent objects of information. These objects can either contain textual information or subelements. However, attributes represent the characteristics of this information and therefore can only contain textual information. So, elements represent objects, whereas attributes represent the properties of those objects. Therefore, elements should be used for information chunks that are considered to be informational objects that can be related in a parent/child relationship, whereas attributes should be used to represent any information that describes the objects in context.

In any case, neither approach is right or wrong. The use of elements or attributes is a choice that a designer needs to make upon implementation, taking into consideration all the benefits and advantages of each approach.

Entity References

There are times when we want to introduce special characters or make use of content that is constantly repeated without having to enter it multiple times. This is the role of the XML entity. Entities provide a means to indicate to XML-processing applications that a special text string is to follow that will be replaced with a different literal value. Entities can solve some otherwise intractable problems. For example, how do we insert a greater-than or less-than sign in our text? XML processors would interpret those characters as parts of an XML tag, which may not be our desired result. As such, the entity gives us a way to provide a character sequence that will be replaced with these otherwise invalid characters.

Each entity has a unique name that is defined as part of an entity declaration in a DTD or XML Schema. Entities are used by simply referring to them by name. Entity references are delimited by an ampersand at the beginning and a semicolon at the ending. The content contained between the delimiters is the entity that will be replaced. For example, the `<` entity inserts the less-than sign (<) into a document. Elements can be encoded so they aren't processed or replaced by their entity equivalents in order to be used for display or encoding within other element values. For example, the string `<element>` can be encoded in an XML document as `<element>`, and it therefore will not be processed. Listing 2.6 shows a number of sample entity references.

LISTING 2.6 Sample Entity References

```
<description>The following says that 8 is greater than 5</description>
<equation>4 &gt; 5</equation>
<prescription>The Rx prescription symbol is &#8478;
       which is the same as &#x211E;</prescription>
```

Entities can also be used to refer to often repeated or varying text as well as to include the content of external files. For example, an entity `&legal;` can be replaced with an organization's legal disclaimer, consisting of any XML text that is included in the DTD or read from a file.

There are internal and external entities, and they both can be general or parameter entities. Internal entities are defined and used within the context of a document, whereas external entities are defined in a source that is accessible via a URI. Internal entities are largely simple string replacements, whereas external entities can consist of entire XML documents or non-XML text, such as binary files. When using an external entity, you must define the type of the file. External entities that refer to these files must declare that the data they contain is not XML by using a notation. Parameter entities are entities that are declared and used within the context of a DTD or schema. They allow users to create replacement text that can be used multiple times to modularize the creation of valid documents. Parameter entities can be either internal or external, but they cannot refer to non-XML data because you can't have a parameter entity with a notation.

Another special form of entity is the character reference, which is used to insert arbitrary Unicode characters into an XML document. This allows international characters to be entered even if they can't be typed directly on a keyboard. Character entities use decimal or hexadecimal references to describe their Unicode data values. For example, `℞` and `℞` both encode the "Rx" character, also known as character number `U+211E` in Unicode.

Comments

One of the key benefits of XML is that humans can read it. A side effect of this feature is that there is a necessity to provide documentation around XML content that describes the intent or context of a given XML markup. Comments are quite simple to include in a document. The character sequence `<!--` begins a comment and `-->` ends the comment. Between these two delimiters, any text at all can be written, including valid XML markup. The only restriction is that the comment delimiters cannot be used; neither can the literal string `--`. Comments can be placed anywhere in a document and are not considered to be part of the textual content of an XML document. As a result, XML processors are not required to pass comments along to an application. An example of a comment is shown in Listing 2.7.

LISTING 2.7 A Sample Comment

```
<!-- The below element talks about an Elephant I once owned... -->
<animal>Elephant</animal>
```

Processing Instructions

Processing instructions (PIs) perform a similar function as comments in that they are not a textual part of an XML document but provide information to applications as to how the content should be processed. Unlike comments, XML processors are required to pass along PIs. Processing instructions have the following form:

```
<?instruction options?>
```

The instruction name, called the *PI target*, is a special identifier that the processing application is intended to understand. Any following information can be optionally specified so that the application is able to understand the context or further requirements of the PI. PI names can be formally declared as notations (a structure for sending such information). The only restriction is that PI names may not start with `xml`, which is reserved for the core XML standards. Listing 2.8 shows a sample processing instruction.

LISTING 2.8 Example of a Processing Instruction

```
<?send-message "process complete"?>
```

Marked CDATA Sections

Some documents will contain a large number of characters and text that an XML processor should ignore and pass to an application. These are known as character data (or `CDATA`) sections. Within an XML document, a `CDATA` section instructs the parser to ignore all markup characters except the end of the `CDATA` markup instruction. This allows for a section of XML code to be "escaped" so that it doesn't inadvertently disrupt XML processing.

`CDATA` sections follow this general form:

```
<![CDATA[content]]>
```

In the content section, any characters can be included, with the necessary exception of the character string `]]>`. All content contained in the `CDATA` section is passed directly to the application without interpretation. This means that elements, entity references, comments, and processing instructions are all ignored and passed as string literals to processing applications. `CDATA` instructions must exist in the context of XML elements and not as standalone entities. Listing 2.9 shows sample `CDATA` information.

LISTING 2.9 A Sample `CDATA` Section

```
<object_code>
    <![CDATA[
    function master(poltice integer) {
```

LISTING 2.9 continued

```
      if poltice<=3 then {
        intMaster=poltice+IntToString(FindElement("<chicken>"));
      }
    }
    ]]>
</object_code>
```

Document Type Definitions

Document Type Definitions (DTDs) provide a means for defining what XML markup can occur in an XML document. Basically, the DTD provides a mechanism to guarantee that a given XML document complies with a well-defined set of rules for document structure and content. These rules provide a framework for guaranteeing the "validity" of a document. DTDs and the more recent XML Schema are the means for defining the validity constraints on XML documents. Each of these are covered in great detail in later chapters of this book, but for now it is important to recognize that DTDs represent a specific form of XML text that is allowable in an XML document.

Caution

Don't confuse the Document Type Definition (DTD) with the Document Type Declaration (DOCTYPE). See the earlier caution in the "Document Type Declaration" section for a more precise clarification of these two terms.

XML Content

Of course, the value of XML is greatly enhanced by the presence of content within the elements. The content between XML elements is where most of the value lies in an XML document. In fact, that is almost exclusively where all the variable content lies. XML elements are usually well defined and strict in their application. When a DTD or XML Schema is used, users can't change these portions of the document. Therefore, the informational content that the metadata describes is precisely where the variable data resides. Of course, it then behooves XML to be as widely lenient about XML content as possible.

In fact, XML content can consist of any data at all, including binary data, as long as it doesn't violate rules that would confuse the content with valid XML metadata instructions. This means that XML metadata delimiters must be escaped if they are not to be processed, and entities should be referenced if they are needed. XML content can contain any characters, including any valid Unicode and international characters. The content can be as long as necessary and contain hundreds of megabytes of textual information, if required. Of course, the size of the content is an implementation decision.

XML Content Models

Because elements, attributes, and content are the most important parts of the XML document, figuring out the restrictions on how those elements and attributes can be created, modified, or removed from a document is of extreme importance. Should an XML document creator allow additional, unforeseen elements to be added to the document in an arbitrary fashion, or should the creator restrict elements to only those that are allowed by the DTD or XML Schema? These questions are the main concepts behind the use of XML content models. A content model provides a framework around which the extensibility features of XML can be taken advantage of, if at all. At the very least, the model provides an indication of the intent of the document creator as to the explicit extensibility of the document, because users can extend a document using an internal DTD subset if they are so inclined. However, by doing so, the users are "overriding" the content model as intended by the document creator.

An "open" content model enables a user to add additional elements and attributes to a document without them having to be explicitly declared in a DTD or schema. In an open content model, users can take full advantage of the extensibility of XML without having to make changes to a DTD. As expected, the use of a DTD precludes an open content model. In fact, you cannot have an open content model when using a DTD, except if a user chooses to override the DTD by using an internal DTD subset. However, new schema formats, such as XML Schema, provide this mechanism. Also, the use of an open content model isn't completely freeform. For example, you cannot add or remove content that will result in the existing content model being broken. In an open content model, all required elements must be present, but it is not invalid for additional elements to also be present. This means that content must follow the rules of the schema before extensibility features can be taken advantage of. If these rules are not followed, XML validation will fail. In addition, you can add undeclared XML elements in an open content model as long as they are defined in a different namespace. By definition, well-formed XML documents that have no validity constraints are open content models.

On the other hand, a "closed" content model restricts elements and attributes to only those that are specified in the DTD or schema. By definition, a DTD is a closed content model because it describes what may exclusively appear in the content of the element. In a closed model, the XML document creator maintains strict control of specifically which elements and attributes as well as the order that markup may appear in a given compliant document. Closed models are helpful when you're enforcing strict document exchange and provide a means to guarantee that incoming data complies with data requirements.

A more focused content model is a "mixed" content model, which enables individual elements to allow an arbitrary mixture of text and additional elements. These mixed elements are useful when freeform fields, with possible XML or other markup data are to be included. This allows the majority of the document to remain closed while portions of the document are noted as extensible. Mixed models represent a good compromise that can allow for strictness while providing a limited means for extensibility.

Handling Whitespace in XML

Whitespace is the term used for character spaces, tabs, linefeeds, and carriage returns in documents. Issues around the handling of these seemingly "invisible" characters are important for many reasons. It is hard to tell whether whitespace should be ignored or passed "as is" to documents. Listing 2.10 illustrates our shirt example with various whitespace issues.

LISTING 2.10 Shirt Example with Whitespace

```
<?xml version="1.0"?>
<!DOCTYPE shirt SYSTEM "shirt.dtd">
<shirt>

    <model>Zippy Tee</model>
    <brand>Tommy

Hilbunger</brand>
    <price currency="USD">14.99</price>
    <on_sale/>
    <fabric content="60%">cotton</fabric>
    <fabric content="40%">polyester</fabric>
    <options>

    <colorOptions>
            <color>red</color>
            <color>white</color>
        </colorOptions>

        <sizeOptions>
        <size>Medium</size>
            <size>Large</size>
    </sizeOptions>
</options>
    <description>
This is a <b>funky</b> Tee shirt similar
```

LISTING 2.10 continued

```
to the
Floppy Tee shirt
</description>
</shirt>
```

Are these various whitespace issues significant? The whitespace between the initial `<shirt>` element and the `<model>` element may not be significant, but the whitespace within the `<description>` tag might be. How are we to know?

It turns out that the only way XML processors can determine whether whitespace is significant is by knowing the content model of the XML document. Basically, in a mixed content model, whitespace is significant because the application is not sure as to whether or not the whitespace will be used in processing, but in an open or closed model, it is not. However, the rule for XML processors is that they must pass all characters that are not markup intact to the application. Validating processors also inform applications about the significance of the various whitespace characters. In addition, a special attribute called `xml:space` with the value `preserve` or `default` can be used to explicitly indicate that the whitespace contained within the element is significant. For example, `xml:space='preserve'` indicates that all whitespace contained in the element is significant. Of course, the `xml:space` attribute must be defined in the DTD as an enumerated type with only those two values.

Also, XML processors simplify cross-platform portability issues by normalizing all end-of-line characters to the single linefeed character "`&#A;`".

Rules of XML Structure

We have explored the structure of XML documents, but there are various rules that XML documents must comply with in order for them to be appropriately processed and parsed. Some of these rules enforce the hierarchical, structured nature of XML, whereas others impose restrictions to simplify the task of XML processing for applications.

All XML Elements Must Have a Closing Tag

Even though other markup languages such as HTML allow their markup tags to remain "open" or contain only a beginning element tag, XML requires all tags to be closed. They can be closed by matching a beginning element tag with a closing tag, or they can be closed by the use of empty elements. In either case, no tag may be left unclosed. Listing 2.11 shows this incorrect use of XML.

LISTING 2.11 Incorrect XML Due to Unclosed Tags

```
<markup>This is not valid XML
<markup>Since there is no closing tag
```

XML Tags Are Case Sensitive

In XML, the use of capitalization is incredibly important. XML elements and attributes are case sensitive. This means that differences in capitalization will be interpreted as different elements or attributes. This differs from HTML, where tags are not case sensitive and arbitrary capitalization is allowed. In XML, the elements `<shirt>` and `<Shirt>` are as different as `<egg>` and `<house>`. Listing 2.12 shows an example of the incorrect matching of element capitalization.

LISTING 2.12 Incorrect XML Due to Capitalization Mismatch

```
<Markup>These two tags are very different</markup>
```

All XML Elements Must Have Proper Nesting

Unlike languages such as HTML, XML requires that elements be nested in proper hierarchical order. Tags must be closed in the reverse order in which they are opened. A proper analogy is to think of XML tags as envelopes. There must never be a case where one envelope is closed when an envelope contained within it is still open. Listing 2.13 shows an incorrect nesting order of XML elements.

LISTING 2.13 Incorrect XML Due to Improper Element Nesting

```
<oxygen><nitrogen>These tags are improperly nested</oxygen></nitrogen>
```

All XML Documents Must Contain a Single Root Element

XML documents must contain a single root element—no less, and certainly no more. All other elements in the XML document are then nested within this root element. Once the root element is defined, any number of child elements can branch off it as long as they follow the other rules mentioned in this section. The root element is the most important one in the document because it contains all the other elements and reflects the document type as declared in the Document Type Declaration. Root elements can be listed only once and not repeated, nor can there be multiple, different root elements. Listing 2.14 illustrates the improper use of root elements.

LISTING 2.14 Incorrect XML Due to Multiple Root Elements

```
<?xml version="1.0"?>
<Father>
    <Son>
        <Daughter>
        </Daughter>
    </Son>
</Father>
<Mother>
    <Son>
        <Daughter>
        </Daughter>
    </Son>
</Mother>
```


Attribute Values Must Be Quoted

When attributes are used within XML elements, their values must be surrounded by quotes. Although most systems accept single or double quotes for attribute values, it is generally accepted to use double quotes around attribute values. If you need to use the quote literal within an attribute value, you can use the quote entity `"` or `'` to insert the required quote character. Listing 2.15 illustrates the improper use of non-quoted attributes.

LISTING 2.15 Incorrect XML Due to Improper Quoting of Attributes

```
<?xml version=1.0?>
<shirt>
  <price currency=USD>14.99</price>
</shirt>
```

Attributes May Only Appear Once in the Same Start Tag

Even though attributes may be optional, when they are present, they can only appear once. This simple restriction prevents ambiguity when multiple, conflicting attribute name/value pairs are present. By only allowing a single attribute name/value pair to be present, the system avoids any conflicts or other errors. Listing 2.16 shows the improper use of multiple attributes within a single element.

LISTING 2.16 Incorrect XML Due to Multiple Attribute Names in Start Tag

```
<shirt size="large" size="small">Zippy Tee</shirt>
```

Attribute Values Cannot Contain References to External Entities

Although external entities may be allowed for general markup text, attribute values cannot contain references to external entities. However, attribute values can make use of internally defined entities and generally available entities, such as < and ".

All Entities Except amp, lt, gt, apos, and quot Must Be Declared Before They Are Used

Although this goes without saying, entities cannot be used before they are properly declared. Referring to an undeclared entity would obviously result in an XML document that is not well formed and proper. However, there are a number of entities that can be assumed to be defined by XML processors. So far, these are limited to the entities &, <, >, ', and ".

Other Rules of XML Structure

Other rules exist for well-formed XML. For example, binary entities cannot be referenced in the general content of an XML document. Rather, these entities can only be used in an attribute declared as ENTITY or ENTITIES. Also, text and parameter entities are not allowed to be directly or indirectly recursive, and the replacement text for all parameter entities referenced inside a markup declaration must be complete markup declarations.

Well-Formed and Valid Documents

Not all XML documents are the same. In particular, two specific descriptions can be applied to XML documents to describe the content contained within them. XML documents can be well formed, and they can also be valid. Validity implies "well-formedness," but not vice versa. That's because a valid XML document is a more strict form of a well-formed XML document. It's like saying that a square is a rectangle, but not vice versa.

Well-Formed Documents

An XML document is well formed if it follows all the preceding syntax rules of XML. On the other hand, if it includes inappropriate markup or characters that cannot be processed by XML parsers, the document cannot be considered well formed. It goes without saying that an XML document can't be partially well formed. And, by definition, if a document is not well formed, it is not XML. This means that there is no such thing as an XML document that is not well formed, and XML processors are not required to process these documents.

Valid Documents

Although the property of "well-formedness" is a matter of making sure the XML document complies to syntactical rules, the property of validity is a different ballgame. A well-formed XML document is considered valid only if it contains a proper Document Type Declaration and if the document obeys the constraints of that declaration. In most cases, the constraints of the declaration will be expressed as a DTD or an XML Schema. Well-formed XML documents are designed for use without any constraints, whereas valid XML documents explicitly require these constraint mechanisms. In addition to constraining the possible elements and the ordering of those elements in a document, valid XML documents can take advantage of certain advanced features of XML that are not available to merely well-formed documents due to their lack of a DTD or XML Schema. Some of these advanced features include linking mechanisms, value and range bounding, and data typing.

Although the creation of well-formed XML is a simple process, the use of valid XML documents can greatly improve the quality of document processes. Valid XML documents allow users to take advantage of content management, business-to-business transactions, enterprise integration, and other processes that require the exchange of constrained XML documents. After all, any document can be well formed, but only specific documents are valid when applied against a constraining DTD or schema.

Linking XML Documents Together

The clear benefit and *raison d'étre* of HTML is that documents can be linked together to form an aggregate system of information and value. XML has a similar value proposition when taking into account the XLink and XPointer specifications. These specifications allow users to link related XML documents together in a structured manner.

XLink provides XML document links that express a relationship between XML documents and resources. A resource is any location within an XML document, such as an element, document tree, or any portion of content that can be addressed in a link. The nature of the link relationship between resources is determined by applications that process the link within its context.

XPointers provide a means to locate these resources, without explicitly requiring that the resource be identified with an ID attribute. Links are not identified by name because

XML does not have a fixed set of elements. XML processors instead use a specific attribute to identify links. Additional attributes provide further information to the XML processor as well as provide a facility to avoid link name collisions and a means to control linking behavior.

Namespaces in XML

As XML documents become more predominate, the increasing interdependence of XML documents will require the use of technologies to separate XML documents with multiple, possibly conflicting tag sets. For example, our shirt XML DTD may include part of a more general "apparel" DTD. In this case, a mechanism is provided to associate these various XML data sources. In order for a processing application to properly understand and associate the correct elements, it must know which tag set the elements come from.

XML solves this problem with namespaces. Namespaces use a colon-delimited prefix to associate external semantics with elements that can be identified via a Universal Resource Identifier (URI). The use of the namespace-identified element then acts as if the element was defined in a local manner. Listing 2.17 shows an example of namespace usage.

LISTING 2.17 Namespace Example

```
<?xml version="1.0"?>
<shirt:shirt xmlns:shirt="http://xmlshirts.org/schema"
 xmlns:apparel="http://xmlapparel.org/schema">
    <shirt:model>Zippy Tee</shirt:model>
      <apparel:mfgID>KFL233562</apparel:mfgID>
    <shirt:description>This is a <b>funky</b> Tee shirt
        similar to the Floppy Tee shirt
</shirt:description>
</shirt:shirt>
```

Because XML is an open standard in which XML authors are free to create whatever elements and attributes they wish, it's inevitable that multiple XML developers will choose the same element and attribute names for their standards. However, they could mean, depending on the document, entirely different things. For instance, let's examine the following sample XML document:

```
<Customer>
   <Name>John Smith</Name>
</Customer>
```

This sample document contains the root element <Customer>, which contains a child element called <Name>. We can clearly determine that the <Name> element contains the name of the customer referred to by the <Customer> element.

Now, let's look at another sample XML document. This time, however, the XML document contains details regarding a product, as shown here:

```
<Product>
   <Name>Hot Dog Buns</Name>
</Product>
```

You can see that this document contains a <Product> element as the root element and a <Name> element, which contains the name of the product. Now, let's look at another typical scenario. Let's imagine that the customer places an order for a product (a very typical scenario for a Web store). The following XML document could be constructed to indicate that a customer has placed an order for a particular product:

```
<Customer>
   <Name>John Smith</Name>
   <Order>
      <Product>
         <Name>Hot Dog Buns</Name>
      </Product>
   </Order>
</Customer>
```

We can easily distinguish the differences between the two <Name> elements. The first <Name> element, which appears as a child of the <Customer> element, contains the customer's name. The second <Name> element, on the other hand, contains the product's name. However, how can the parser tell the difference? It can't, not unless we explicitly tell it what the difference is. This is where XML namespaces come in. By using namespaces, XML parsers can easily tell the difference between the two <Name> elements.

Therefore, modifying the preceding XML document to specify the appropriate namespaces turns it into this:

```
<Customer>
   <cust:Name xmlns:cust="customer-namespace-URI">John Smith</cust:Name>
   <Order>
      <Product>
         <prod:Name xmlns:prod="product-namespace-URI">Hot Dog Buns</prod:Name>
      </Product>
   </Order>
</Customer>
```

Now, the XML parsers can easily tell the difference between any validation rules between the customer's <Name> element and the product's <Name> element.

Declaring Namespaces

Within an XML document, namespaces can be declared using one of two methods: a default declaration or an explicit declaration. Which method to use is completely open and left up to you; either way will suffice.

A default namespace declaration specifies a namespace to use for all child elements of the current element that do not have a namespace prefix associated with them. For instance, in the following XML document, a default declaration for the `<Customer>` element is defined by using the `xmlns` attribute on the parent element without specifying or attaching a prefix to the namespace:

```
<Customer xmlns="http://www.eps-software.com/po">
   <Name>Travis Vandersypen</Name>
   <Order>
      <Product>
         <Name>Hot Dog Buns</Name>
      </Product>
   </Order>
</Customer>
```

For this XML document, all child elements of the `<Customer>` element are specified as belonging to the `http://www.eps-software.com/po` namespace.

Sometimes, however, it may be necessary and more readable to explicitly declare an element's namespace. This is accomplished much the same way in which a default namespace is declared, except a prefix is associated with the `xmlns` attribute. If you examine the following XML document, you can see that a prefix of `po` is with the elements within the document:

```
<po:Customer xmlns:po="http://www.eps-software.com/po">
   <po:Name>Travis Vandersypen</po:Name>
   <po:Order>
      <po:Product>
         <po:Name>Hot Dog Buns</po:Name>
      </po:Product>
   </po:Order>
</po:Customer>
```

One thing worth pointing out here is that the prefix associated with the elements is a shorthand notation to be used in place of the full namespace. Although the preceding XML document provides a rather simple scenario for explicitly identifying namespaces, the true power behind explicitly declaring namespaces becomes clear when you utilize elements from different namespaces, as is the case in the following XML document:

```
<cust:Customer xmlns:cust="http://www.eps-software.com/customer"
➥xmlns:ord="http://www.eps-software.com/order">
```

```
    <cust:Name>Travis Vandersypen</cust:Name>
    <ord:Order>
       <ord:Product>
          <ord:Name xmlns:prod="product-namespace-URI">Hot Dog Buns</ord:Name>
       </ord:Product>
    </ord:Order>
</cust:Customer>
```

From looking at this example, you can see that two different namespaces are referenced: one for customers and one for orders. This allows a different set of rules to be applied for customer names versus product names.

Identifying the Scope of Namespaces

By default, all child elements within a parent element, unless indicated otherwise by referencing another namespace, appear within the parent's namespace. This allows all child elements to "inherit" their parent element's namespace. However, this "inherited" namespace can be overwritten by specifying a new namespace on a particular child element. Let's examine the following XML document:

```
<Customer xmlns="http://www.eps-software.com/customer">
  <Name>Travis Vandersypen</Name>
    <Order xmlns="http://www.eps-software.com/order">
      <Product>
         <Name>Hot Dog Buns</Name>
      </Product>
   </Order>
</Customer>
```

In the preceding XML document, the <Customer> element declares a default namespace located at `http://www.eps-software.com/customer`. All elements contained within the <Customer> element that do not explicitly qualify a namespace "inherit", the namespace declared by the <Customer> element. However, the <Order> element also declares a default namespace. Starting at the <Order> element, all unqualified elements within the <Order> element will inherit the namespace declared by the <Order> element.

Applying Style to XML

Because XML largely represents information, it is separated from how that information is to be displayed and represented to the end user. HTML is a language that strongly connects its metadata with presentation. For example, the <hr> element always displays a horizontal rule. However, there is no such limitation for the <horizontal_rule> element in XML, which can be displayed as a horizontal, vertical, or diagonal line, a string of asterisks, an image of the prime minister, or anything at all! Therefore, styling and presentation-level specificity needs to be applied to XML.

In HTML, the concept of applying style sheets to further abstract the presentation layer was introduced in the form of Cascading Style Sheets (CSS). The intent was to provide a mechanism to allow for the flexible display of HTML across multiple devices, browsers, and display formats. Of course, because XML doesn't have any presentation capability at all, it makes sense to use a similar approach. XML borrows from this concept; the result is the XML Stylesheet Language (XSL). In XML, no element includes a notion of how it is to be displayed, but XSL provides a mechanism to convert the XML element to a visual or other rendition for output. XSL can convert an XML document into HTML, SGML, RTF, another XML format, or any other file format possible. In this method, XML truly separates its content from presentation by providing an abstraction as to how the information specified is to be displayed.

Basics of Reading and Processing XML

Now that you have learned the basics of how to write well-formed XML documents (learning how to write valid XML documents is covered in the chapters on DTDs and the XML Schema), it is now important that you learn how to process and handle these XML documents. After all, the value of XML is not in its creation but in its use.

Along these lines, processing XML follows a few major lines: parsing the XML document, processing and making use of the parsed elements, and integrating with other systems and programming languages. Because XML is just a text document format and not a programming language, it provides no mechanism to instruct machines how to process the content contained within it. That's actually a good thing. Because there are no specific processing requirements, XML documents can be processed by all types of devices, operating systems, clients, servers, and other information consumers, all which only need to understand how to read XML. XML not only has separated the presentation from data, it has separated the strict processing requirements from data. In essence, XML is as pure a data format as possible.

The following sections explore the various steps of processing XML and the tools available to accomplish these tasks.

Parsers

The first step for any system that plans to make use of XML documents is to actually read the documents into memory. Although this may seem like a simple task, the structured nature of XML imposes several requirements on parsers. In addition, the behavior of parsing applications needs to be consistent so that XML documents can be reliably exchanged between disparate systems. As a result, XML parsers must adhere to a certain accepted level of compliance.

Because an XML document is just a text file, any user can write his or her own program to read in the XML text file and take it apart for use in a programming application. However, the amount of time and complexity it would take to write such an XML document reader (which, by the way, would have to be written over and over again for the different programs that need access to the information in XML documents) would make the adoption of XML an onerous task. The WC3 (the XML standardization body) came to the realization that a standard mechanism was needed to parse these XML documents and promoted the use of compliant XML parsers. As a result, a number of widely available XML parsers exist that allow the application developer to focus on application-specific code rather than on XML document reading or processing.

In actuality, there are really two types of XML parsers: validating parsers and nonvalidating parsers. Nonvalidating parsers merely read XML documents and verify that the documents are well formed. Validating parsers read well-formed documents in addition to checking their compliance against a DTD, XML Schema, or other validation set. Obviously, nonvalidating parsers are much easier to program and can be made extremely efficient and space conserving. The first iteration of XML parsers were nonvalidating because the DTD and XML Schema proposals were far from stable. As the specifications became more stable, the number of validating parsers likewise increased. As a result, many of the parsers currently on the market (commercial or open source) are validating parsers that have progressively become more robust and efficient.

Because of the added complexity of ensuring validity and compliance with a DTD or schema, validating parsers tend to be much larger in memory and processing footprint than nonvalidating parsers. If most of the XML in a particular system is well formed and doesn't need to be checked for validity, the use of a nonvalidating parser may be a better idea.

Examples of nonvalidating parsers include James Clark's expat, XP, and Lark. Examples of validating parsers include IBM's XML for Java, the DataChannel XML Parser (DXP), Daniel Veillard's libXML, and Apache's Xerces. Microsoft's MSXML includes both validating and nonvalidating parsers that support a variety of platforms. These parsers run the gamut from open source efforts to commercial products, from extremely tiny implementations to large, robust efforts. Information about these tools and links to find out more information are included in the chapters that cover them in more detail.

The Document Object Model (DOM)

Parsing XML is essential to working with XML documents, but applications that plan to actually use and manipulate XML content require a more robust model for programmatic interaction with XML data. To this effect, the Document Object Model (DOM) was created as a means to allow developers to refer to, retrieve, and change the content and structure of XML documents. The Document Object Model offers two levels of interface implementation: the DOM Core, which supports basic XML document integration, and DOM HTML, which extends the model to HTML documents.

DOM converts XML documents into a programmatic object model that can then be used and processed by standard applications. Once the XML document has been parsed, an object model representation exists in the memory of the processing client. This object model allows users to manipulate the XML document without having to write and reread the XML document multiple times. In effect, DOM allows a user to manipulate an XML file in memory using an object-oriented approach. The document object that is created consists of a tree of nodes that represents the structure of the XML document and the data contained within. This in-memory tree is accessed via DOM.

As the DOM parser creates an object model based on the XML document, it also expands all entities used in the file and compares the structure of the information in the XML document to a DTD or XML Schema, if one is used. Then, a reference object is created of some class type that can call methods on the document objects. The W3C also provides a set of Java interfaces known as the DOM API that provide a core set of methods for interacting with XML document objects. However, because the DOM API is just a specification, the actual implementation of the XML objects is up to individual XML parser applications.

The SAX API

Both DOM and the Simple API for XML (SAX) provide a programmatic layer that allows a user to directly access the information contained within an XML document. However, each of these mechanisms provides a different approach to accessing this information. Whereas DOM creates an object that represents a hierarchical tree of nodes that reflects the structure of an XML document, SAX processes an XML document by giving applications a stream of parsing events around that document. Rather than interacting with an in-memory XML tree, a user is interacting with a stream of data that can be acted upon. DOM is great for in-memory tree manipulation, whereas SAX is great for linear processing of large XML documents.

Event-based parsers such as SAX provide a view of XML documents that is data centric and event driven. When a user reads an XML document using SAX, elements that are encountered by the parser are read, processed, and then forgotten. The event-based parser reads the elements from the document and returns them to the application with a list of attributes and content. By taking this approach, a user obtains a more efficient means of processing XML documents because the search time is greatly optimized, requiring less code and memory. The primary reason for this is that an in-memory tree representation of the XML document is not required. Event-based APIs merely report parsing events such as the start and end of XML markup, which are processed by application event handlers through callbacks. This mechanism is widely used in many "process-and-forget" systems and is especially appropriate for XML-based messaging and transaction systems, where keeping the XML tree in memory is simply not appropriate.

International Language Support in XML

Because XML is by and large just a text document format with features for validation checking and representing structured, hierarchical metadata, there is nothing that restricts it from being applicable in only certain geographies. As a result, the W3C and other standards organizations have gone through great pains to make sure XML can support various international and localization needs that have plagued the adoption of other document formats. In particular, XML is capable of supporting a number of languages, data formats, character sets, and peculiarities of localization that allow the format to not only cross geographic boundaries but logical boundaries as well.

Unicode

Developed prior to the emergence of XML, the Unicode standard is a universal character set whose goal is to provide an unambiguous encoding of the content of plain text that can be written in any and all languages of the world. The latest version of Unicode, version 3.0, covers almost all the languages and dialects used in the world, including languages that are no longer actively spoken. Unicode 3.0 contains all the characters needed by these languages as well as additional characters used for interoperability with older character encodings and for control functions.

Because XML is a text-based language, it is dependent on characters and the representation of those characters. As such, it has relied on a version of Unicode to encode its elements, attributes, and data content. Therefore, XML can support as part of its native specification any of a number of major language and character sets, thus enabling the encoding of almost any text document. However, it should be noted that some inconsistencies in Unicode adoption are present. For example, a wider use of Unicode characters is permitted in general XML content than is allowable for element and attribute names. A movement is underway to correct this shortfall and allow for an equally wide use of arbitrary and complete characters as are possible in Unicode 3.0 and future versions.

Summary

Writing XML documents is a fairly simple endeavor that only requires a user to understand the basics of creating well-formed, structural markup. In essence, all one needs to do is open a text editor of choice and start writing XML. By understanding how the various elements of XML syntax are composed, a user can almost immediately start making XML work for him or her. It is to XML's credit that creating useful XML applications is so easy—and often extremely low cost.

The various portions of an XML document, ranging from the XML declaration to the actual construction of XML elements and attributes, interact in a manner that allows for the creation of a document that truly separates data content from its presentation and processing requirements. The use of nonvalidating and validating parsers gives the user the ability to turn such text-based documents into a programming model that provides all the power and capability of any data-based access mechanism. And if simple parsing of XML documents is not enough, the DOM and SAX APIs provide a robust means for translating XML documents directly into programmatic APIs for inclusion in the most sophisticated of applications. In addition, the international features of XML give it scope beyond any single geography, operating system, or display device platform.

In essence, XML is a simple markup language with simple rules that nevertheless provide robust support for even the most complex of data interchange and representation requirements. All that is needed is to follow the simple rules of XML document creation to find the appropriate tools that match one's needs. For this reason, XML is being used in an ever-increasing scale.

Validating XML with the Document Type Definition (DTD)

In This Chapter

XML is a meta-markup language that is fully extensible. As long as it is well formed, XML authors can create any XML structure they desire in order to describe their data. However, an XML author cannot be sure that the structure he poured so much time and effort into creating won't be changed by another XML author or for that matter an application. There needs to be a way to ensure that the XML structure cannot be changed at random. This type of assurance for XML document structure is vital for e-commerce applications and business-to-business processing, among other things. This is where the Document Type Definition (DTD) steps in. A DTD provides a roadmap for describing and documenting the structure that makes up an XML document. A DTD can be used to determine the validity of an XML document.

In this chapter we will start with several examples and a brief overview of the DTD and what it does. Then we will break down the different items that make up the structure of the DTD. The coverage of the DTD structure will begin with a discussion of the Document Type Declaration. Then we will move on to the functional items that make up the DTD. The DTD includes element definitions, entity definitions, and parameters. Finally, before closing the chapter, we will explore some of the drawbacks of DTDS and emerging alternatives for validation. Now, let's start by defining the Document Type Definition.

Document Type Definitions

DTD stands for *Document Type Definition*. A Document Type Definition allows the XML author to define a set of rules for an XML document to make it valid. An XML document is considered "well formed" if that document is syntactically correct according to the syntax rules of XML 1.0. However, that does not mean the document is necessarily valid. In order to be considered valid, an XML document must be validated, or verified, against a DTD. The DTD will define the elements required by an XML document, the elements that are optional, the number of times an element should (could) occur, and the order in which elements should be nested. DTD markup also defines the type of data that will occur in an XML element and the attributes that may be associated with those elements. A document, even if well formed, is not considered valid if it does not follow the rules defined in the DTD.

Note

DTDs are part of the W3C's XML 1.0 recommendation. This recommendation may be found at `http://www.w3.org/TR/REC-xml`.

When an XML document is validated against a DTD by a validating XML parser, the XML document will be checked to ensure that all required elements are present and that no undeclared elements have been added. The hierarchical structure of elements defined in the DTD must be maintained. The values of all attributes will be checked to ensure that they fall within defined guidelines. No undeclared attributes will be allowed and no required attributes may be omitted. In short, every last detail of the XML document from top to bottom will be defined and validated by the DTD.

Although validation is optional, if an XML author is publishing an XML document for which maintaining the structure is vital, the author can reference a DTD from the XML document and use a validating XML parser during processing. Requiring that an XML document be validated against a DTD ensures the integrity of the data structure. XML documents may be parsed and validated before they are ever loaded by an application. That way, XML data that is not valid can be flagged as "invalid" before it ever gets processed by the application (thus saving a lot of the headaches that corrupt or incomplete data can cause).

Imagine a scenario where data is being exchanged in an XML format between multiple organizations. The integrity of business-to-business data is vital for the smooth functioning of commerce. There needs to be a way to ensure that the structure of the XML data does not change from organization to organization (thus rendering the data corrupt and useless). A DTD can ensure this.

An extra advantage of using DTDs in this situation is that a single DTD could be referenced by all the organization's applications. The defined structure of the data would be in a centralized resource, which means that any changes to the data structure definition would only need to be implemented in one place. All the applications that referenced the DTD would automatically use the new, updated structure.

A DTD can be internal, residing within the body of a single XML document. It can also be external, referenced by the XML document. A single XML document could even have both a portion (or subset) of its DTD that is internal and a portion that is external. As mentioned in the previous paragraph, a single external DTD can be referenced by many XML documents. Because an external DTD may be referenced by many documents, it is a good repository for global types of definitions (definitions that apply to all documents). An internal DTD is good to use for rules that only apply to that specific document. If a document has both internal and external DTD subsets, the internal rules override the external rules in cases where the same item is defined in both subsets.

Given this brief overview, you can quickly see why a DTD would be important to applications that exchange data in an XML format. Before diving into the actual coverage of the structure of DTDs, take a look at a couple of quick examples. This will give you a better impression of what we are talking about as we go forward.

Some Simple DTD Examples

Let's take a quick look at two DTDs—one internal and one external. Listing 3.1 shows an internal DTD.

LISTING 3.1 An Internal DTD

```
<?xml version="1.0"?>
<!DOCTYPE message [
<!ELEMENT message (#PCDATA)>
]>
<message>
Let the good times roll!
</message>
```

In Listing 3.1, the internal DTD is contained within the Document Type Declaration, which begins with `<!DOCTYPE` and ends with `]>`. The Document Type Declaration will appear between the XML declaration and the start of the document itself (the document or root element) and identify that section of the XML document as containing a Document Type Definition. Following the Document Type Declaration (`DOCTYPE`), the root element of the XML document is defined (in this case, `message`). The DTD tells us that this document will have a single element, `message`, that will contain parsed character data (`#PCDATA`).

> **Note**
>
> The Document Type Declaration should not be confused with the Document Type Definition. These are two exclusive items. Also confusing is the acronym DTD, which is only ever used in reference to the Document Type Definition. The Document Type Declaration is the area of the XML document after the XML declaration that begins with `<!DOCTYPE` and ends with `]>`. It actually encompasses the Document Type Definition. The Document Type Definition will be contained within an opening bracket (`[`) and a closing bracket (`]`).

Now, let's take a look at Listing 3.2 and see how this same DTD and XML document would be joined if the DTD were external.

LISTING 3.2 An External DTD

```
<?xml version="1.0"?>
<!DOCTYPE message SYSTEM "message.dtd">
<message>
Let the good times roll!
</message>
```

In Listing 3.2 the DTD is contained in a separate file, `message.dtd`. The contents of `message.dtd` are assumed to be the same as the contents of the DTD in Listing 3.1. The keyword `SYSTEM` in the Document Type Declaration lets us know that the DTD is going to be found in a separate file. A URL could have been used to define the location of the DTD. For example, rather than `message.dtd`, the Document Type Declaration could have specified something like `../DTD/message.dtd`.

Note

The keyword `SYSTEM` used in a Document Type Declaration will always be indicative of the Document Type Definition being contained in an external file.

Both of these examples show us a well-formed XML document. Additionally, because both XML documents contain a single element, `message`, which contains only parsed character data, both adhere to the DTD. Therefore, they are both also valid XML documents.

A document that looks like what's shown in Listing 3.3 would not be valid according to the DTD in these examples.

LISTING 3.3 Document Not Valid According to Defined DTD

```
<?xml version="1.0"?>
<!DOCTYPE message SYSTEM "message.dtd">
<message>
<text>
Let the good times roll!
</text>
</message>
```

Even though this is a well-formed XML document, it is not valid. When this document is validated against `message.dtd`, a flag will be raised because `message.dtd` does not define an element named `text`.

Don't worry if you do not completely understand what is going on at this point. As long as you get the gist, everything will become very clear in the sections that follow.

Structure of a Document Type Definition

The structure of a DTD consists of a Document Type Declaration, elements, attributes, entities, and several other minor keywords. We will take a look at each of these topics, in that order. As we progress from topic to topic, we will follow a mini case study about the use of XML to store employee records by the Human Resources department of a fictitious company.

Our coverage of the DTD structure shall begin with the Document Type Declaration.

The Document Type Declaration

In order to reference a DTD from an XML document, a Document Type Declaration must be included in the XML document. Listings 3.1, 3.2, and 3.3 gave some examples and brief explanations of using a Document Type Declaration to reference a DTD. There may be one Document Type Declaration per XML document. The syntax is as follows:

```
<!DOCTYPE rootelement SYSTEM | PUBLIC DTDlocation [ internalDTDelements ] >
```

- The exclamation mark (`!`) is used to signify the beginning of the declaration.
- `DOCTYPE` is the keyword used to denote this as a Document Type Definition.
- `rootelement` is the name of the root element or document element of the XML document.
- `SYSTEM` and `PUBLIC` are keywords used to designate that the DTD is contained in an external document. Although the use of these keywords is optional, to reference an external DTD you would have to use one or the other. The `SYSTEM` keyword is used in tandem with a URL to locate the DTD. The `PUBLIC` keyword specifies some public location that will usually be some application-specific resource reference.
- `internalDTDelements` are internal DTD declarations. These declarations will always be placed within opening (`[`) and closing (`]`) brackets.

Note

This book typically uses the more common `SYSTEM` keyword when referencing external DTDs.

It is possible for a Document Type Declaration to contain both an external DTD subset and an internal DTD subset. In this situation, the internal declarations take precedence over the external ones. In other words, if both the external and internal DTDs define a rule for the same element, the rule of the internal element will be the one used. Consider the Document Type Declaration fragment shown in Listing 3.4.

LISTING 3.4 Internal and External DTDs

```
<!DOCTYPE rootelement SYSTEM "http://www.myserver.com/mydtd.dtd"
[
<!ELEMENT element1 (element2,element3)>
<!ELEMENT element2 (#PCDATA)>
<!ELEMENT element3 (#PCDATA)>
]>
```

Here in Listing 3.4, we see that the Document Type Declaration references an external DTD. There is also an internal subset of the DTD contained in the Document Type Declaration. Any rules in the external DTD that apply to elements defined in the internal DTD will be overridden by the rules of the internal DTD.

> **Note**
>
> You will also notice in Listing 3.4 that the Document Type Declaration is spread out over several lines. Whitespace is unimportant in Document Type Declarations as long as there is no whitespace on either side of the `!` symbol. Multiple lines are used for clarity.

Now that you have seen how to reference a DTD from an XML document, we will begin our coverage of the items that make up the declarations in DTDs.

DTD Elements

All elements in a valid XML document are defined with an element declaration in the DTD. An element declaration defines the name and all allowed contents of an element. Element names must start with a letter or an underscore and may contain any combination of letters, numbers, underscores, dashes, and periods. Element names must never start with the string "xml". Colons should not be used in element names because they are normally used to reference namespaces.

Each element in the DTD should be defined with the following syntax:

```
<!ELEMENT elementname rule >
```

- `ELEMENT` is the tag name that specifies that this is an element definition.
- `elementname` is the name of the element.
- `rule` is the definition to which the element's data content must conform.

In a DTD, the elements are processed from the top down. A validating XML parser will expect the order of the appearance of elements in the XML document to match the order of elements defined in the DTD. Therefore, elements in a DTD should appear in the order you want them to appear in an XML document. If the elements in an XML document do not match the order of the DTD, the XML document will not be considered valid by a validating parser.

Listing 3.5 demonstrates a DTD, `contactlist.dtd`, that defines the ordering of elements for referencing XML documents.

LISTING 3.5 `contactlist.dtd`

```
<!ELEMENT contactlist (fullname, address, phone, email) >
<!ELEMENT fullname (#PCDATA)>
<!ELEMENT address (addressline1, addressline2)>
<!ELEMENT addressline1 (#PCDATA)>
<!ELEMENT addressline2 (#PCDATA)>
<!ELEMENT phone (#PCDATA)>
<!ELEMENT email (#PCDATA)>
```

The first element in the DTD, `contactlist`, is the document element. The rule for this element is that it contains (is the parent element of) the `fullname`, `address`, `phone`, and `email` elements. The rule for the `fullname` element, the `phone` element, and the `email` element is that each contains parsed character data (`#PCDATA`). This means that the elements will contain marked-up character data that the XML parser will interpret. The `address` element has two child elements: `addressline1` and `addressline2`. These two children elements contain `#PCDATA`. This DTD defines an XML structure that is nested two levels deep. The root element, `contactlist`, has four child elements. The `address` element is, in turn, parent to two more elements. In order for an XML document that references this DTD to be valid, it must be laid out in the same order, and it must have the same depth of nesting.

The XML document in Listing 3.6 is a valid document because it follows the rules laid out in Listing 3.5 for `contactlist.dtd`.

LISTING 3.6 contactlist.xml

```
<?xml version="1.0"?>
<!DOCTYPE contactlist SYSTEM "contactlist.dtd">
<contactlist>
<fullname>Bobby Soninlaw</fullname>
<address>
<addressline1>101 South Street</addressline1>
<addressline2>Apartment #2</addressline2>
</address>
<phone>(405) 555-1234</phone>
<email>bs@mail.com</email>
</contactlist>
```

The second line of this XML document is the Document Type Declaration that references `contactlist.dtd`. This is a valid XML document because it is well formed and complies with the structural definition laid out in the DTD.

> **Note**
>
> In Listing 3.6, the element name listed in the Document Type Declaration matches the name of the root element of the XML document. If the element name listed in the Document Type Declaration did not match the root element of the XML document, the XML document would immediately be deemed invalid and the XML parser would halt.

The element rules govern the types of data that may appear in an element.

DTD Element Rules

All data contained in an element must follow a set rule. As stated previously, the rule is the definition to which the element's data content must conform. There are two basic types of rules that elements must fall into. The first type of rule deals with content. The second type of rule deals with structure. First, we will look at element rules that deal with content.

Content Rules

The content rules for .elements deal with the actual data that defined elements may contain. These rules include the `ANY` rule, the `EMPTY` rule, and the `#PCDATA` rule.

The ANY Rule

An element may be defined. using the ANY rule. This rule is just what it sounds like: The element may contain other elements and/or normal character data (just about anything as long as it is well formed). An element using the ANY rule would appear as follows:

```
<!ELEMENT elementname ANY>
```

The drawback to this rule is that it is so wide open that it defeats the purpose of validation. A DTD that defines all its elements using the ANY rule will always be valid as long as the XML is well formed. This really precludes any effective validation. The XML fragments as shown in Listing 3.7 are all valid given the definition of elementname.

LISTING 3.7 XML Fragments Using the ANY Rule

```
<elementname>
This is valid content
</elementname>

<elementname>
<anotherelement>
This is more valid content
</anotherelement>
This is still valid content
</elementname>

<elementname>
<emptyelement />
<yetanotherelement>
This is still valid content!
</yetanotherelement>
Here is more valid content
</elementname>
```

You should see from this listing why it is not always a great idea to use the ANY rule. All three fragments containing the element elementname are valid. There is, in effect, no validation for this element. Use of the ANY rule should probably be limited to instances where the XML data will be freeform text or other types of data that will be highly variable and have difficulty conforming to a set structure.

The EMPTY Rule

This rule is the exact opposite of the ANY rule. An element that is defined with this rule will contain no data. However, an element with the EMPTY rule could still contain attributes (more on attributes in a bit). The following element is an example of the EMPTY rule:

```
<!ELEMENT elementname EMPTY>
```

This concept is seen a lot in HTML. There are many tags such as the break tag (`<br />`) and the paragraph tag (`<p />`) that follow this rule. Neither one of these tags contains any data, but both are very important in HTML documents. The best example of an empty tag used in HTML is the image tag (`<img>`). Even though the image tag does not contain any data, it does have attributes that describe the location and display of an image for a Web browser.

In XML, the `EMPTY` rule might be used to define empty elements that contain diagnostic information for the processing of data. Empty elements could also be created to hold metadata describing the contents of the XML document for indexing purposes. Empty elements could even be used to provide clues for applications that will render the data for viewing (such as an empty "gender" tag, which designates an XML record as "male" or "female"—male records could be rendered in blue, and female records could be rendered in pink) .

The `#PCDATA` *Rule*

The `#PCDATA` rule indicates that parsed character data will be contained in the element. Parsed character data is data that may contain normal markup and will be interpreted and parsed by any XML parser accessing the document. The following element demonstrates the `#PCDATA` rule:

```
<!ELEMENT elementname (#PCDATA)>
```

An element in an XML document that adheres to the `#PCDATA` rule might appear as follows:

```
<data>
This is some parsed character data
</data>
```

It is possible in an element using the `#PCDATA` rule to use the `CDATA` keyword to prevent the character data from being parsed. You can see an example of this in Listing 3.8.

LISTING 3.8 CDATA

```
<sample>
<data>
<![CDATA[<tag>This will not be parsed</tag>]]>
</data>
</sample>
```

All the data between `<![CDATA[` and `]]>` will be ignored by the parser and treated as normal characters (markup ignored).

Structure Rules

Whereas the content rules. deal with the actual content of the data contained in defined elements, structure rules deal with how that data may be organized. There are two types of structure rules we will look at here. The first is the "element only" rule. The second rule is the "mixed" rule.

The "Element Only" Rule

The "element only" rule .specifies that only elements may appear as children of the current element. The child element sequences should be separated by commas and listed in the order they should appear. If there are to be options for which elements will appear, the listed elements should be separated by the pipe symbol (|). The following element definition demonstrates the "element only" rule:

```
<!ELEMENT elementname (element1, element2, element3)>
```

You can see here that a list of elements are expected to appear as child elements of `elementname` when the referencing XML document is parsed. All these child elements must be present and in the specified order. Here is how an element that is listing a series of options will appear:

```
<!ELEMENT elementname (element1 | element2)>
```

The element defined here will have a single child element: either `element1` or `element2`.

The "Mixed" Rule

The "mixed" rule is used to help define elements that may have both character data (`#PCDATA`) and child elements in the data they contain. A list of options or a sequential list will be enclosed by parentheses. Options will be separated by the pipe symbol (|), whereas sequential lists will be separated by commas. The following element is an example of the "mixed" rule:

```
<!ELEMENT elementname (#PCDATA | childelement1 | childelement2)*>
```

In this example, the element may contain a mixture of character data and child elements. The pipe symbol is used here to indicate that there is a choice between `#PCDATA` and each of the child elements. However, the asterisk symbol (`*`) is added here to indicate that each of the items within the parentheses may appear zero or more times (we will cover the use of element symbols in the next section). This can be useful for describing data sets that have optional values. Consider the following element definition:

Note

The asterisk symbol used in these examples indicates that an item may occur zero or more times. Element symbols are covered in detail in Table 3.1.

```
<!ELEMENT Son (#PCDATA | Name | Age)*>
```

This definition defines an element, `Son`, for which there may be character data, elements, or both. A man might have a son, but he might not. If there is no son, then normal character data (such as "N/A") could be used to describe this condition. Alternatively, the man might have an adopted son and would like to indicate this. Consider the XML fragments shown in Listing 3.9 in relation to the definition for the element `Son`.

LISTING 3.9 The "Mixed" Rule

```
<Son>
N/A
</Son>

<Son>
Adopted Son
<Name>Bobby</Name>
<Age>12</Age>
</Son>
```

The first fragment contains only character data. The second fragment contains a mixture of character data and the two defined child elements. Both fragments conform to the definition and are valid.

Element Symbols

In addition to the normal rules that apply to element definitions, element symbols can be used to control the occurrence of data. Table 3.1 shows the symbols that are available for use in DTDs.

TABLE 3.1 Element Symbols

Symbol	*Definition*
Asterisk (*)	The data will appear zero or more times (0, 1, 2, …). Here's an example: `<!ELEMENT children (name*)>` In this example, the element children could have zero or more occurrences of the child element name. This type of

TABLE 3.1 continued

Symbol	*Definition*
	rule would be useful on a form asking a person about his or her children. It is possible that the person could have no children or many children.
Comma (,)	Provides separation of elements in a sequence. Here's an example: `<!ELEMENT address (street, city, state, zip)>` In this example, the element address will have four child elements: street, city, state, and zip. Each of the child elements must appear in the defined order in the XML document.
Parentheses [( )]	The parentheses are used to contain the rule for an element. Parentheses may also be used to group a sequence, subsequence, or a set of alternatives in a rule. Here's an example: `<!ELEMENT address (street, city, (state | province), zip)>` In this example, the parentheses enclose a sequence. Additionally, a subsequence is nested within the sequence by a second set of parentheses. The subsequence indicates that there will be either a state or a province element in that spot in the main sequence.
Pipe (|)	Separates choices in a set of options. Here's an example: `<!ELEMENT dessert (cake | pie)>` The element dessert will have one child element: either cake or pie.
Plus sign (+)	Signifies that the data must appear one or more times (1, 2, 3, …). Here's an example: `<!ELEMENT appliances (refrigerator+)>` The appliances element will have one or more refrigerator child elements. This assumes that every household has at least one refrigerator.
Question mark (?)	Data will appear either zero times or one time in the element. Here's an example: `<!ELEMENT employment (company?)>` The element employment will have either zero occurrences or one occurrence of the child element company.

TABLE 3.1 continued

Symbol	Definition
No symbol	When no symbol is used (other than parentheses), this signifies that the data must appear once in the XML file. Here's an example: `<!ELEMENT contact (name)>` The element `contact` will have one child element: `name`.

Element symbols can be added to element definitions for another level of control over the XML documents that are being validated against it. Consider the DTD in Listing 3.10, which makes very limited use of XML symbols.

LISTING 3.10 Limited Use of Symbols

```
<!ELEMENT contactlist (contact) >
<!ELEMENT contact (name, age, sex, address, city, state, zip, children) >
<!ELEMENT name (#PCDATA) >
<!ELEMENT age (#PCDATA) >
<!ELEMENT sex (#PCDATA) >
<!ELEMENT address (#PCDATA) >
<!ELEMENT city (#PCDATA) >
<!ELEMENT state (#PCDATA) >
<!ELEMENT zip (#PCDATA) >
<!ELEMENT children (child) >
<!ELEMENT child (childname, childage, childsex) >
<!ELEMENT childname (#PCDATA) >
<!ELEMENT childage (#PCDATA) >
<!ELEMENT childsex (#PCDATA) >
```


You can see in Listing 3.10 that a contact record for a contactlist file is being laid out. It is very straight forward and includes the basic address information you would expect to see in this type of file. Information on the contact's children is also included. This looks like a well-laid-out, easy-to-use file format. However, there are several problems. What if you are not sure about a contact's address? What if the contact does not have children? What if the user is a lady and you are afraid to ask her age? The way that this DTD is laid out, it will be very difficult for a referencing XML document to be deemed valid if any of this information is unknown.

Using element symbols, you can create a more flexible DTD that will take into account the possibility that you might not always know all of a contact's personal information. Take a look at a similar DTD laid out in Listing 3.11.

LISTING 3.11 Broader Use of Symbols

```
<!ELEMENT contactlist (contact+) >
<!ELEMENT contact (name, age?, sex, address?, city?, state?, zip?, children?) >
<!ELEMENT name (#PCDATA) >
<!ELEMENT age (#PCDATA) >
<!ELEMENT sex (#PCDATA) >
<!ELEMENT address (#PCDATA) >
<!ELEMENT city (#PCDATA) >
<!ELEMENT state (#PCDATA) >
<!ELEMENT zip (#PCDATA) >
<!ELEMENT children (child*) >
<!ELEMENT child (childname, childage?, childsex) >
<!ELEMENT childname (#PCDATA) >
<!ELEMENT childage (#PCDATA) >
<!ELEMENT childsex (#PCDATA) >
```

Listing 3.11 is much more flexible than Listing 3.10. There is still a single root element, `contactlist`, which will contain one or more instances (+) of the element `contact`. Under each `contact` element is a list of child elements that make up the description of the contact record. It is assumed here that the name and sex of the contact will be known. However, the definition indicates that there will be zero or one occurrence (?) of the `age`, `address`, `city`, `state`, `zip`, and `children` elements. These elements are set for zero or one occurrence because the definition is taking into account that this information might not be known. Looking further down the listing, you see that the `children` element is marked to have zero or more instances (*) of the `child` element. This is because a person might have no children or many children (or we might not know how many children the person has). Under the `child` element, it is assumed that `childname` and `childsex` information will be known (if there is at least one `child` element). However, the `childage` element is marked as zero or one (?), just in case it is unknown how old the child is.

You can easily see how Listing 3.11 is more flexible than Listing 3.10. Listing 3.11 takes into account that much of the contact data could be missing or unknown. An XML document being validated against the DTD in Listing 3.10 could still be validated and accepted by a validating parser even though it might not have all the contact's personal data. However, an XML document being validated against the DTD in Listing 3.10 would be rejected as invalid if it did not include the `children` element.

Now that you have seen how DTDs define element declarations, let's take a look at how attributes are used in a mini case study.

Zippy Human Resources: XML for Employee Records, Part I

Now that you have seen how elements are defined in a DTD, you have enough tools to follow along with a mini case study that shows how a company could use XML in its Human Resources department.

The Human Resources department for a small but growing company, Zippy Delivery Service, has decided that in order to make their employee data flexible across all the applications used by the company, the employee data should be stored in XML. The Zippy Human Resources department's first task is to decide on the fields to be included in the XML structure:

- Employee Name
- Position
- Age
- Sex
- Race
- Marital Status
- Address Line 1
- Address Line 2
- City
- State
- Zip Code
- Phone Number
- E-Mail Address

After determining which elements are needed, they decide to put together a DTD in order to ensure that the structure of the employee records in the XML data file never changes. Additionally, the decision is made that multiple employee records should be stored in a single file. Because this is the case, they need to declare a document (root) element to hold employee records and a parent element for the elements making up each individual employee record. The Human Resources department also realizes that some of the data might not be applicable to all employees. Therefore, they need to use element symbols to account for varying occurrences of data. They've come up with the following DTD structure as the first draft:

```
Employees1.dtd
<!ELEMENT employees (employee+) >
<!ELEMENT employee (name, position, age, sex, race, m_status, address1,
address2?, city, state, zip, phone?, email?) >
```

```
<!ELEMENT name (#PCDATA) >
<!ELEMENT position (#PCDATA) >
<!ELEMENT age (#PCDATA) >
<!ELEMENT sex (#PCDATA) >
<!ELEMENT race (#PCDATA) >
<!ELEMENT m_status (#PCDATA) >
<!ELEMENT address1 (#PCDATA) >
<!ELEMENT address2 (#PCDATA) >
<!ELEMENT city (#PCDATA) >
<!ELEMENT state (#PCDATA) >
<!ELEMENT zip (#PCDATA) >
<!ELEMENT phone (#PCDATA) >
<!ELEMENT email (#PCDATA) >
```

The Human Resources department has decided that the document element `employees` is required to have one or more (+) child elements (`employee`). The `employee` element would be the container element for each individual employee's data. Out of the elements comprising the employee data, the Human Resources department knows that not all employees have a second line to their street address. Also, some employees do not have home telephone numbers or e-mail addresses. Therefore, the elements `address2`, `phone`, and `email` are marked to appear zero or one time in each record (?). The new DTD structure is saved in a file named `employees1.dtd` (which, by the way, you can download from the Sams Web site).

The first several employee records are then entered into an XML document, called `Employees1.xml`:

```
<?xml version="1.0"?>
<!DOCTYPE employees SYSTEM "employees1.dtd">
<employees>
<employee>
<name>Bob Jones</name>
<position>Dispatcher</position>
<age>37</age>
<sex>Male</sex>
<race>African American</race>
<m_status>Married</m_status>
<address1>202 Carolina St.</address1>
<city>Oklahoma City</city>
<state>OK</state>
<zip>73114</zip>
<phone>4055554321</phone>
<email>bobjones@mail.com</email>
</employee>
<employee>
<name>Mary Parks</name>
<position>Delivery Person</position>
```

```
<age>19</age>
<sex>Female</sex>
<race>Caucasian</race>
<m_status>Single</m_status>
<address1>1015 Empire Blvd.</address1>
<address2>Apt. D3</address2>
<city>Oklahoma City</city>
<state>OK</state>
<zip>73107</zip>
<phone>4055559876</phone>
<email>maryparks@mail.com</email>
</employee>
<employee>
<name>Jimmy Griffin</name>
<position>Delivery Person</position>
<age>23</age>
<sex>Male</sex>
<race>African American</race>
<m_status>Single</m_status>
<address1>1720 Maple St.</address1>
<city>Oklahoma City</city>
<state>OK</state>
<zip>73107</zip>
<phone>4055556633</phone>
</employee>
</employees>
```

The XML document `Employees1.xml` (also available for download from the Sams Web site) initially has three employee records entered into it. The Document Type Declaration is entered after the XML declaration and before the document element, `employees`, and it uses the `SYSTEM` keyword to denote that it is referencing the DTD, `employees1.dtd`, externally.

The Human Resources department at Zippy Delivery Service feels that they are off to a good start. They have defined a DTD, `employees1.dtd`, for their XML data structure and have created an XML document, `Employees1.xml` (containing three employee records), that is valid according to the DTD. However, you'll find out during the course of this chapter that the Human Resources department's DTD can be improved.

DTD Attributes

So far you have seen that it is possible to use intricate combinations of elements and symbols to create complex element definitions. Now let's take a look at how XML attribute definitions can be added into this mix.

XML attributes are name/value pairs that are used as metadata to describe XML elements. XML attributes are very similar to HTML attributes. In HTML, `src` is an attribute of the `img` tag, as shown in the following example:

```
<img src="images/imagename.gif" width="10" height="20">
```

In this example, `width` and `height` are also attributes of the `img` tag. This is very similar to the markup in Listing 3.12, which demonstrates how an image element might be structured in XML.

LISTING 3.12 Attribute Use in XML

```
<image src="images/" width="10" height="20">
imagename.gif
</image>
```

In Listing 3.12, `src`, `width`, and `height` are presented as attributes of the XML element `image`. This is very similar to the way that these attributes are used in HTML. The only difference is that the `src` attribute merely contains the relative path of the image's directory and not the actual name of the image file.

In Listing 3.12, the attributes `width`, `height`, and `src` are used as metadata to describe certain aspects of the content of the `image` element. This is consistent with the normal use of attributes. Attributes can also be used to provide additional information to further identify or index an element or even give formatting information.

Attributes are also defined in DTDs. Attribute definitions are declared using the `ATTLIST` declaration. An `ATTLIST` declaration will define one or more attributes for the element that it is referencing.

> **Note**
>
> Attribute definitions do not follow the same "top-down" rule that element definitions do. However, it is still a good coding practice to list the attributes in the order you would like them to appear in the XML document. Usually this means listing the attributes directly after the element to which they refer.

Attribute list declarations in a DTD will have the following syntax:

```
<!ATTLIST elementname attributename type defaultbehavior defaultvalue>
```

- `ATTLIST` is the tag name that specifies that this definition will be for an attribute list.
- `elementname` is the name of the element that the attribute will be attached to.

- `attributename` is the actual name of the attribute.
- `type` indicates which of the 10 valid kinds of attributes this attribute definition will be.
- `defaultbehavior` dictates whether the attribute will be required, optional, or fixed in value. This setting determines how a validating parser should relate to this attribute.
- `defaultvalue` is the value of the attribute if no value is explicitly set.

Take a look at Listing 3.13 for an example of how this declaration may be used.

LISTING 3.13 ATTLIST Declaration

```
<!ATTLIST name
sex CDATA #REQUIRED
age CDATA #IMPLIED
race CDATA #IMPLIED >
```

In Listing 3.13, an attribute list is declared. The `name` element is being referenced by the declaration. Three attributes are defined; `sex`, `age`, and `race`. The three attributes are character data (`CDATA`). Only one of the attributes, `sex`, is required (`#REQUIRED`). The other two attributes, `age` and `race`, are optional (`#IMPLIED`). An XML element using the attribute list declared here would appear as follows:

```
<name sex="male" age="30" race="Caucasian">Michael Qualls</name>
```

The `name` element contains the value "Michael Qualls". It also has three attributes of Michael Qualls: sex, age, and race. The attributes in Listing 3.13 are all character data (`CDATA`). However, attributes actually have 10 possible data types.

Attribute Types

Before going over a more detailed example of using attributes in your DTDs, let's first review Table 3.2, which presents the 10 valid types of attributes that may be used in a DTD. Then we will look at Table 3.3, which shows the default values for attributes.

TABLE 3.2 Attribute Types

Type	*Definition*
CDATA	Characterdata only. The attribute will contain no markup. Here's an example: `<ATTLIST box height CDATA "0">`

TABLE 3.2 continued

Type	*Definition*
	In this example, an attribute, height, has been defined for the element box. This attribute will contain character data and have a default value of "0".
`ENTITY`	The name of an unparsed general entity that is declared in the DTD but refers to some external data (such as an image file). Here's an example: `<!ATTLIST img src ENTITY #REQUIRED>` The src attribute is an `ENTITY` type that refers to some external image file.
`ENTITIES`	This is the same as the `ENTITY` type but represents multiple values listed in sequential order, separated by whitespace. Here's an example: `<!ATTLIST imgs srcs ENTITIES #REQUIRED>` The value of the `imgs` element using the `srcs` attribute would be something like `img1.gif img2.gif img3.gif`. This is simply a list of image files separated by whitespace.
`ID`	An attribute that uniquely identifies the element. The value for this type of attribute must be unique within the XML document. Each element may only have a single `ID` attribute, and the value of the `ID` attribute must be a valid XML name, meaning that it may not start with a numeric digit (which precludes the use of a simple numbering system for IDs). Here's an example: `<!ATTLIST cog serial ID #REQUIRED>` Each cog element in the XML document will have a required attribute, `serial`, that uniquely identifies it.
`IDREF`	This is the value of an ID attribute of another element in the document. It's used to establish a relationship with other tags when there is not necessarily a parent/child relationship. Here's an example: `<!ATTLIST person cousin IDREF #IMPLIED>` Each person element could have a cousin attribute that references the value of the `ID` attribute of another element.
`IDREFS`	This is the same as `IDREF`; however, it represents multiple values listed in sequential order, separated by whitespace.

TABLE 3.2 continued

Type	*Definition*
	Here's an example: `<!ATTLIST person cousins IDREFS #IMPLIED>` Each `person` element could have a `cousins` attribute that contains references to the values of multiple `ID` attributes of other elements.
`NMTOKEN`	Restricts the value of the attribute to a valid XML name. Here's an example: `<!ATTLIST address country NMTOKEN "usa">` Each address element will have a country attribute with a default value of "`usa`".
`NMTOKENS`	This is the same as `NMTOKENS`; however, it represents multiple values listed in sequential order, separated by whitespace. Here's an example: `<!ATTLIST region states NMTOKENS "KS OK" >` Each region element will have a states attribute with a default value of "`KS OK`".
`NOTATION`	This type refers to the name of a notation declared in the DTD (more on notations later). It is used to identify the format of non-XML data. An example would be using the `NOTATION` type to refer to an external application that will interact with the document. Here's an example: `<!ATTLIST music play NOTATION "mplayer2.exe ">` In this example, the element music has an attribute, `play`, that will hold the name of a notation that determines the type of music player to use. The default value (notation) is "`mplayer2.exe `".
Enumerated	This type is not an actual keyword the way the other types are. It is actually a listing of possible values for the attribute separated by pipe symbols (`|`). Here's an example: `<!ATTLIST college grad (1|0) "1">` The element `college` has an attribute, `grad`, that will have a value of either "`1`" or "`0`" (with the default value being "`1`").

You saw during the coverage of the 10 valid attribute types that we used two preset default behavior settings: `#REQUIRED` and `#IMPLIED`. There are four different default types that may be used in an attribute definition, as detailed in Table 3.3.

TABLE 3.3 Default Value Types

Type	*Definition*
`#REQUIRED`	Indicates that the value of the attribute must be specified. Here's an example `<!ATTLIST season year CDATA #REQUIRED >` In this example, the element `season` has a character data attribute, `year`, that is required.
`#IMPLIED`	Indicates that the value of the attribute is optional. Here's an example: `<!ATTLIST field size CDATA #IMPLIED >` In this case, each `field` element may have a `size` attribute, but it is not required.
`#FIXED`	Indicates that the attribute is optional, but if it is present, it must have a specified set value that cannot be changed. Here's an example: `<!ATTLIST bcc hidden #FIXED "true" >` Each bcc element has an attribute, `hidden`, that has a fixed value of "`true`".
Default	This is not an actual default behavior type. The value of the default is supplied in the DTD. Here's an example: `<!ATTLIST children number CDATA "0">` This represents that the `children` element has a `number` attribute with a default value of "`0`".

So far you have element (`ELEMENT`) declarations and attribute (`ATTLIST`) declarations under your belt. You have seen that you can create some very complex hierarchical structures using elements and attributes. Next, we will take a look at a way to save some time when building DTDs. DTD entities offer a way to store repetitive or large chunks of data for quick reference. First, however, we are going to revisit our mini case study.

Zippy Human Resources: XML for Employee Records, Part II

This is the second part of our mini case study on the use of XML in the Human Resources department at Zippy Delivery Service. You saw in Part I that the Human Resources department was able to put together a DTD (`Employees1.dtd`) and an XML document with some employee records (`Employees1.xml`). The DTD was referenced from the XML file for purposes of validation.

Upon review of their DTD, the members of the Human Resources department have decided that they are not quite satisfied. They feel that they have two types of information about each employee: personal information and contact information. They've decided that the personal information would be better stored as attributes of the employee `name` element rather than as individual elements. Additionally, they've decided that they need an ID type of attribute for each `employee` element in order to be able to quickly search the XML document. The DTD, therefore, has been amended as follows (you can download the DTD `Employees2.dtd` from the Sams Web site):

```
<!ELEMENT employees (employee+) >
<!ELEMENT employee (name, position, address1, address2?, city, state,
zip, phone?, email?) >
<!ATTLIST employee serial ID #REQUIRED >
<!ELEMENT name (#PCDATA) >
<!ATTLIST name
age CDATA #REQUIRED
sex CDATA #REQUIRED
race CDATA #IMPLIED
m_status CDATA #REQUIRED >
<!ELEMENT position (#PCDATA) >
<!ELEMENT address1 (#PCDATA) >
<!ELEMENT address2 (#PCDATA) >
<!ELEMENT city (#PCDATA) >
<!ELEMENT state (#PCDATA) >
<!ELEMENT zip (#PCDATA) >
<!ELEMENT phone (#PCDATA) >
<!ELEMENT email (#PCDATA) >
```

You can see that a new ID attribute, `serial`, has been added for the `employee` element. The `serial` attribute is marked as required (`#REQUIRED`). The `age`, `sex`, `race`, and `m_status` elements have been removed and changed to attributes of the `name` element. Each of these attributes is character data (`CDATA`). Also, the `race` attribute has been deemed optional (`#IMPLIED`).

The XML document has also been updated to reflect the new requirements of the changed DTD (you can download XML document `Employees2.xml` from the Sams Web site):

```
<?xml version="1.0"?>
<!DOCTYPE employees SYSTEM "employees2.dtd">
<employees>
<employee serial="emp1">
<name age="37" sex="Male" race="African American" m_status="Married">
Bob Jones
</name>
<position>Dispatcher</position>
<address1>202 Carolina St.</address1>
```

```
<city>Oklahoma City</city>
<state>OK</state>
<zip>73114</zip>
<phone>4055554321</phone>
<email>bobjones@mail.com</email>
</employee>
<employee serial="emp2">
<name age="19" sex="Female" race="Caucasian" m_status="Single">
Mary Parks
</name>
<position>Delivery Person</position>
<address1>1015 Empire Blvd.</address1>
<address2>Apt. D3</address2>
<city>Oklahoma City</city>
<state>OK</state>
<zip>73107</zip>
<phone>4055559876</phone>
<email>maryparks@mail.com</email>
</employee>
<employee serial="emp3">
<name age="23" sex="Male" race="African American" m_status="Single">
Jimmy Griffin
</name>
<position>Delivery Person</position>
<address1>1720 Maple St.</address1>
<city>Oklahoma City</city>
<state>OK</state>
<zip>73107</zip>
<phone>4055556633</phone>
</employee>
</employees>
```

In order for the XML document to remain valid according to the DTD, a `serial` attribute has been added for each `employee` element. Each `serial` attribute is set to a unique value. The `age`, `sex`, `race`, and `m_status` elements have been removed and added as attributes of the `name` element.

The Zippy Human Resources department now feels that they are getting pretty close to having the DTD and XML structure they need in order to have an effective solution for storing their employee records. However, as you'll see in Part III, there is still a bit more tweaking that can be done with the addition of entities.

DTD Entities

Entities in DTDs are storage units. They can also be considered placeholders. Entities are special markups that contain content for insertion into the XML document. Usually this will be some type of information that is bulky or repetitive. Entities make this type of information more easily handled because the DTD author can use them to indicate where the information should be inserted in the XML document. This is much better than having to retype the same information over and over.

An entity's content could be well-formed XML, normal text, binary data, a database record, and so on. The main purpose of an entity is to hold content, and there is virtually no limit on the type of content an entity can hold.

The general syntax of an entity is as follows:

```
<!ENTITY entityname [SYSTEM | PUBLIC] entitycontent>
```

- `ENTITY` is the tag name that specifies that this definition will be for an entity.
- `entityname` is the name by which the entity will be referred in the XML document.
- `entitycontent` is the actual contents of the entity—the data for which the entity is serving as a placeholder.
- `SYSTEM` and `PUBLIC` are optional keywords. Either one can be added to the definition of an entity to indicate that the entity refers to external content.

Note

The keyword `SYSTEM` or `PUBLIC` used in an entity declaration will always be indicative of the contents of the entity being contained in an external file. Think of this as something like a pointer in C and C++. The entity is used as a reference to an external source of data.

Note

Entity declarations do not follow the same "top-down" rule that element definitions do. They may be listed anywhere in the body of the DTD. However, it is good practice to list them first in the DTD as they may be referenced later in the document.

Entities may either point to internal data or external data. Internal entities represent data that is contained completely within the DTD. External entities point to content in another location via a URL. External data could be anything from normal parsed text in another file, to a graphics or audio file, to an Excel spreadsheet. The type of data to which an external entity can refer is virtually unlimited.

An entity is referenced in an XML document by inserting the name of the entity prefixed by `&` and suffixed by `;`. When referenced in this manner, the content of the entity will be placed into the XML document when the document is parsed and validated. Let's take a look at an example of how this works (see Listing 3.14).

Listing 3.14 Using Internal Entities

```
<?xml version="1.0"?>
<!DOCTYPE library [
<!ENTITY cpy "Copyright 2000">
<!ELEMENT library (book+)>
<!ELEMENT book (title,author,copyright)>
<!ELEMENT title (#PCDATA)>
<!ELEMENT author (#PCDATA)>
<!ELEMENT copyright (#PCDATA)>
]>
<library>
<book>
<title>How to Win Friends</title>
<author>Joe Charisma</author>
<copyright>&cpy;</copyright>
</book>
<book>
<title>Make Money Fast</title>
<author>Jimmy QuickBuck</author>
<copyright>&cpy;</copyright>
</book>
</library>
```

Listing 3.14 uses an internal DTD. In the DTD, an entity called `cpy` is declared that contains the content "Copyright 2000". In the `copyright` element of the XML document, this entity is referenced by using `&cpy;`. When this document is parsed, `&cpy;` will be replaced with "Copyright 2000" in each instance in which it is used. Using the entity `&cpy;` saves the XML document author from having to type in "Copyright 2000" over and over. This is a fairly simple example, but imagine if the entity contained a string of data that was several hundred characters long. It is much more convenient (and easier on the fingers) to be able to reference a three- or four-character entity in an XML document than to type in all that content.

Predefined Entities

There are five predefined entities, as shown in Table 3.4. These entities do not have to be declared in the DTD. When an XML parser encounters these entities (unless they are contained in a CDATA section), they will automatically be replaced with the content they represent.

TABLE 3.4 Predefined Entities

Entity	*Content*
&	&
<	<
>	>
"	"
'	'

The XML fragment in Listing 3.15 demonstrates the use of a predefined entity.

LISTING 3.15 Using Predefined Entities

```
<icecream>
<flavor>Cherry Garcia</flavor>
<vendor>Ben &amp; Jerry's</vendor>
</icecream>
```

In this listing, the ampersand in “Ben & Jerry’s” is replaced with the predefined entity for an ampersand (&) .

External Entities

External entities are used to reference external content. As stated previously, external entities get their content by referencing it via a URL placed in the entitycontent portion of the entity declaration. Either the SYSTEM keyword or the PUBLIC keyword is used here to let the XML parser know that the content is external.

XML is incredibly flexible. External entities can contain references to almost any type of data—even other XML documents. One well-formed XML document can contain another well-formed XML document through the use of an external entity reference. Taking this a step further, it can be easily extrapolated that a single XML document can be made up of references to many small XML documents. When the document is parsed, the XML parser will gather all the small XML documents, merging them into a whole.

The end-user application will only see one document and never know the difference. One useful way to apply the principle of combining XML documents through the use of external entities would be in an employee-tracking application, like the one shown in Listing 3.16.

LISTING 3.16 Using External Entities

```
<?xml version="1.0"?>
<!DOCTYPE employees [
<!ENTITY bob SYSTEM "http://srvr/emps/bob.xml">
<!ENTITY nancy SYSTEM "http://srvr/emps/nancy.xml">
<!ELEMENT employees (clerk)>
<!ELEMENT clerk (#PCDATA)>
]>
<employees>
<clerk>&bob;</clerk>
<clerk>&nancy;</clerk>
</employees>
```

In this listing, two external entity references are used to refer to XML documents outside the current document that contain the employee data on "bob" (`bob.xml`) and "nancy" (`nancy.xml`). The `SYSTEM` keyword is used here to let the XML parser know that this is external content. In order to insert the external content into the XML document, the entities `&bob;` and `&nancy;` are used. It is useful to be able to contain the employee information in a separate file and "import" it using an entity reference. This is because this same information could be easily referenced by other XML documents, such as an employee directory and a payroll application. Defining logical units of data and separating them into multiple documents, as in this example, makes the data more extensible and reduces the need to reproduce redundant data from document to document.

Caution

Use prejudice when splitting up your XML data into multiple documents. Splitting up employee records into 100 different XML documents so that they will have increased extensibility across multiple applications might be a good idea. Taking the orders table from your order tracking database and splitting it into 100,000 documents would be a horrible idea. External entities are parsed at runtime. Could you imagine parsing thousands of entities that point to XML documents at runtime? Applications would suddenly be forced to search through 100,000 separate documents to find what they need instead of a single indexed table. Performance would be destroyed. So, keep in mind that although the approach mentioned here does have very applicable uses, it should not represent an overall data storage solution.

Non-Text External Entities and Notations

Some external entities will contain non-text data, such as an image file. We do not want the XML parser to attempt to parse these types of files. In order to stop the XML parser, we use the NDATA keyword. Take a look at the following declaration:

```
<!ENTITY myimage SYSTEM "myimage.gif" NDATA gif>
```

The NDATA keyword is used to alert the parser that the entity content should be sent unparsed to the output document.

The final part of the declaration, gif, is a reference to a notation. A *notation* is a special declaration that identifies the format of non-text external data so that the XML application will know how handle the data. Any time an external reference to non-text data is used, a notation identifying the data must be included and referenced. Notations are declared in the body of the DTD and have the following syntax:

```
<!NOTATION notationname [SYSTEM | PUBLIC ] dataformat>
```

- ENTITY is the tag name that specifies that this definition will be for an entity.
- notationname is the name by which the notation will be referred in the XML document.
- SYSTEM is a keyword that is added to the definition of the notation to indicate that the format of external data is being defined. You could also use the keyword PUBLIC here instead of SYSTEM. However, using PUBLIC requires you to provide a URL to the data format definition.
- dataformat is a reference to a MIME type, ISO standard, or some other location that can provide a definition of the data being referenced.

Note

Notation declarations do not follow the same "top-down" rule that element definitions do. They may be listed anywhere in the body of the DTD. However, it is good practice to list them after the entity that references them in order to increase clarity.

Listing 3.17 is an example of using notation declarations for non-text external entities.

LISTING 3.17 Using External Non-Text Entities

```
<!NOTATION gif SYSTEM "image/gif" >
<!ENTITY employeephoto SYSTEM "images/employees/MichaelQ.gif" NDATA gif >
<!ELEMENT employee (name, sex, title, years) >
<!ATTLIST employee pic ENTITY #IMPLIED >
…
<employee pic="employeephoto">
…
</employee>
```

In this example, an `ENTITY` type of attribute, `pic`, is defined for the element `employee`. In the XML document, the `pic` attribute is given the value `employeephoto`, which is an external entity that serves as a placeholder for the GIF file `MichaelQ.gif`. In order to aid the application process and display the GIF file, the external entity (using the `NDATA` keyword) references the notation `gif`, which points to the MIME type for GIF files.

Parameter Entities

The final type of entity we will look at is the parameter entity, which is very similar to the internal entity. The main difference between an internal entity and a parameter entity is that a parameter entity may only be referenced inside the DTD. Parameter entities are in effect entities specifically for DTDs.

Parameter entities can be useful when you have to use a lot of repetitive or lengthy text in a DTD. Use the following syntax for parameter entities:

```
<!ENTITY % entityname entitycontent>
```

The syntax for a parameter entity is almost identical to the syntax for a normal, internal entity. However, notice that in the syntax, after the declaration, there is a space, a percent sign, and another space before `entityname`. This alerts the XML parser that this is a parameter entity and will be used only in the DTD. These types of entities, when referenced, should begin with `%` and end with `;`. Listing 3.18 shows an example of this.

LISTING 3.18 Using Parameter Entities

```
<!ENTITY % pc "(#PCDATA)">
<!ELEMENT name %pc;>
<!ELEMENT age %pc;>
<!ELEMENT weight %pc;>
```

In this listing, `pc` is used as a parameter entity to reference `(#PCDATA)`. All entities in the DTD that hold parsed character data use the entity reference `%pc;`. This saves the DTD author from having to type #PCDATA over and over. This particular example is somewhat trivial, but you can see where this can be extrapolated out to a situation where you have a long character string that you do not want to have to retype.

We are almost finished. Having covered the use of element, attribute, and entity declarations in DTDs, we have just a few more loose ends to tie up. In the next section, we will look at the use of the IGNORE and INCLUDE directives. Then we will discuss the use of comments in DTDs. In the final part of the chapter, we will look at the future of DTDs, some possible shortcomings of DTDs, and a possible alternative for DTD validation. Before moving on though, let's pay one more quick visit to the Zippy Human Resources department in our mini case study.

Zippy Human Resources: XML for Employee Records, Part III

This is the final part of the mini case study on the use of XML in the Human Resources department at Zippy Delivery Service. In Part II, the Human Resources department decided to change the structure of their DTD by moving the employees' personal data into attributes. This created a separation between personal data and contact data (which remained stored in elements).

At this point, the Human Resources department felt pretty satisfied with their work. Now, however, there are just a couple more minor areas where they feel the DTD (Employees2.dtd) could be improved. They've decided that they need to add several entities in order to speed the entry process for new records and to cut down on having to retype redundant information. First, they've added an entity for "Delivery Person". This makes sense to them because all but a few of the employees of Zippy Delivery Service are delivery people, and this will save them from having to type it over and over. The second entity they've decided to add is a parameter entity to give them a shortcut for entering #PCDATA type elements.

Here's the updated DTD (you can download Employees3.dtd from the Sams Web site):

```
<!ENTITY dp "Delivery Person">
<!ENTITY % pc "#PCDATA">
<!ELEMENT employees (employee+) >
<!ELEMENT employee (name, position, address1, address2?, city, state,
zip, phone?, email?) >
<!ATTLIST employee serial ID #REQUIRED >
<!ELEMENT name (%pc;) >
<!ATTLIST name
age CDATA #REQUIRED
sex CDATA #REQUIRED
```

```
race CDATA #IMPLIED
m_status CDATA #REQUIRED >
<!ELEMENT position (%pc;) >
<!ELEMENT address1 (%pc;) >
<!ELEMENT address2 (%pc;) >
<!ELEMENT city (%pc;) >
<!ELEMENT state (%pc;) >
<!ELEMENT zip (%pc;) >
<!ELEMENT phone (%pc;) >
<!ELEMENT email (%pc;) >
```

In the new DTD, the entity `dp` is declared first. This entity is used to insert the value "Delivery Person" into the XML document when it is referenced. Next, the entity `pc` is declared. This is a parameter entity that holds the value "#PCDATA" for insertion into the DTD when referenced.

The XML document `Employees2.xml` has been updated to reflect the addition of the `dp` entity (the whole XML document is not listed because only a few lines actually changed; data not shown here should be assumed to be the same as in Parts I and II of this case study). Here's the code for `Employees3.xml` (which you can download from the Sams Web site):

```
<?xml version="1.0"?>
<!DOCTYPE employees SYSTEM "employees3.dtd">
<employees>
<employee serial="emp1">
<name age="37" sex="Male" race="African American" m_status="Married">
Bob Jones
</name>
<position>Dispatcher</position>
...
</employee>
<employee serial="emp2">
<name age="19" sex="Female" race="Caucasian" m_status="Single">
Mary Parks
</name>
<position>&dp;</position>
...
</employee>
<employee serial="emp3">
<name age="23" sex="Male" race="African American" m_status="Single">
Jimmy Griffin
</name>
<position>&dp;</position>
...
</employee>
</employees>
```

For the first employee, Bob Jones, the `dp` entity was not used for his `position` value because he is the company's dispatcher. However, for Mary Parks and Jimmy Griffin, the entity reference `&dp;` was inserted as the value for their `position` elements because they are both delivery people. This entity reference would also be used for any new employees added to the XML document that are delivery people.

The DTD for Zippy Deliver Service's Human Resources department is now complete. The DTD contains all the information required. It takes account for information that might not be applicable. The employees' personal and contact information has been logically separated between attributes and elements. Also, entities have been added to serve as timesaving devices for future additions to the XML document. The Zippy Human Resource department has built a DTD that will serve to validate their XML employee records effectively and efficiently.

More DTD Directives

Just a few more DTD keywords are left to cover. These are keywords that do not neatly fit into any particular topic, so they're lumped together here. These keywords are `INCLUDE` and `IGNORE`, and they do just what their names suggest—they indicate pieces of markup that should either be included in the validation process or ignored.

The IGNORE Keyword

When developing or updating a DTD, you may need to comment out parts of the DTD that are not yet reflected in the XML documents that use the DTD. You could use a normal comment directive (which will be covered in the next section), or you can use an `IGNORE` directive. The syntax for `IGNORE` is shown in Listing 3.19.

LISTING 3.19 Using `IGNORE` Directives

```
<![ IGNORE
This is the part of the DTD ignored
]]>
```

You can choose to ignore elements, entities, or attributes. However, you must ignore entire declarations. You may not attempt to ignore a part of a declaration. For example, the following would be invalid:

```
<!ELEMENT Employee <![ IGNORE (#PCDATA) ]]> (Name, Address, Phone) >
```

In this example, the DTD author has attempted to ignore the rule #PCDATA in the middle of an element declaration. This is invalid and would trigger an error.

The INCLUDE Keyword

The INCLUDE directive marks declarations to be included in the document. It might seem interesting that this keyword exists at all because not using an INCLUDE directive is the same as using it! In the absence of the INCLUDE directive, all declarations (unless they are commented out or enclosed in an IGNORE directive) will be included anyway. The syntax for INCLUDE, as shown in Listing 3.20, is very similar to the syntax for the IGNORE directive.

LISTING 3.20 Using INCLUDE Directives

```
<![ INCLUDE
This is the part of the DTD included
]]>
```

The INCLUDE directive follows the same basic rules as the IGNORE directive. It may enclose entire declarations but not pieces of declarations. The INCLUDE directive can be useful when you're in the process of developing a new DTD or adding to an existing DTD. Sections of the DTD can be toggled between the INCLUDE directive and the IGNORE directive in order to make it clear which sections are currently being used and which are not. This can make the process of developing a new DTD easier, because you are able to quickly "turn on" or "turn off" different sections of the DTD.

> **Note**
>
> If an INCLUDE directive is enclosed by an IGNORE directive, the INCLUDE directive and its declarations will be ignored.

Comments Within a DTD

Comments can also be added to DTDs. Comments within a DTD are just like comments in HTML and take the following syntax:

```
<!-- Everything between the opening tag and closing tag is a comment -->
```

As in HTML, comments in a DTD may not be nested. Comments may, however, span multiple lines. Generally comments in a DTD are used to demarcate different sections of the DTD or to help human readers understand different abbreviations used in the declarations. Comments will be ignored by the XML parser during processing. Listing 3.21 shows how to insert comments into a DTD.

LISTING 3.21 Using Comments

```
<!-- This is a comment -->
<!ELEMENT rootelement (element1, element2)>
<!ELEMENT element1 (#PCDATA)>
<!-- This is another comment -->
<!ELEMENT element2 (#PCDATA)>
<!-- This is a comment
that spans multiple lines -->
```

Comments provide a useful way to explain the meaning of different elements, attribute lists, and entities within the DTD. They can also be used to demarcate the beginning and end of different sections in the DTD.

The DTD is a powerful tool for defining rules for XML documents to follow. DTDs have had and will continue to have an important place in the XML world for some time to come. However, DTDs are not perfect. As XML has expanded beyond a simple document markup language, these limitations have become more apparent. XML is quickly becoming the language of choice for describing more abstract types of data. DTDs are hard-pressed to keep up. We will now take a look at some of the drawbacks to DTDs and what future alternatives will be available.

DTD Drawbacks and Alternatives

Throughout this book, we will continue to document new growths, changes, and permutations to XML as a technology to enhance data exchange, data structuring, e-commerce, the Internet, and so on. As newer uses for XML come into being, the needs for validation expand. XML is being used to describe the data structure of video files, audio files, and Braille devices, among other things—not to mention the ever-growing plethora of alternative data devices such as cellular phones, handheld computers, televisions, and even appliances. There are several drawbacks that limit the ability of DTDs to meet these growing and changing validation needs.

First and foremost, DTDs are composed of non-XML syntax. Given that one of the central tenets of XML is that it be totally extensible, it may not seem to make a lot of sense that this is the case for DTDs. However, you must consider that XML is a child of SGML, and in SGML, DTDs are the method used to validate documents. Therefore, XML inherited DTDs from its parent. Although DTDs are effective at defining the structure for document markup, as XML evolves, the fact that DTDS are not formed of XML syntax and are nonextensible becomes constraining.

Additionally, there can only be a single DTD per document. It is true that there can be internal and external subsets of DTDs, but there can only be a single DTD referenced. In the modern programming world, we are used to being able to draw the programming constructs we use from different modules or classes. If we applied this idea to DTDs, we might expect to be able to use a DTD for customers, a separate DTD for inventory, and a separate DTD for orders. However, this is not the case. All aspects of an XML document must be within a single DTD. This limitation is similar to what programmers faced back in the days of monolithic applications before object-oriented programming became a normal standard for application development. This leads into the next limitation.

DTDS are not object oriented. There is no inheritance in DTDs. As programmers, we have gotten used to describing new objects based on the characteristics of existing objects. One classic example is having Porsche, Ford, and Chevrolet classes that inherent some characteristics from a base car class. DTDs have no capability to do this.

DTDs do not support namespaces very well. For a namespace to be used, the entire namespace must be defined within the DTD. If there are more than one namespace, each of them must be defined within the DTD. This totally defeats the purpose of namespaces—being able to define multiple namespaces from many different external sources.

Additionally, DTDs have weak data typing and no support for the XML DOM. DTDs basically have one data type: the text string. There are a few restraints, such as the element rules and attribute types covered in this chapter, but these are pretty weak considering the types of applications for which XML is now being used (especially in e-commerce). The Document Object Model has become a powerful tool to manipulate XML data; however, the DTD is totally cut off from the reach of the DOM.

Finally, and possibly most important from a security standpoint, is the ability of the internal DTD subset to override the external DTD subset. An company could spend a great deal of time and effort crafting a DTD to validate the XML data in its e-commerce transactions only to have the settings in the DTD overridden by the internally defined elements of a DTD. The implications on this from a transaction security standpoint should be fairly clear.

So, what is to be done about the DTD? The DTD is still an effective mechanism for validating XML documents and will be so for a long time to come. It just does not "scale" to meet the needs of the expanding XML world. At the time of this writing, the W3C organization has just recently finished the final touches on the recommendation for the XML

Schema, which is a new validation mechanism for XML that corrects all the shortcomings of DTDs. XML Schema is a powerful and important technology for the future of XML. The next chapter of this book will be devoted to covering the XML Schema.

Note

The W3C organization's Web resources page for the XML Schema may be viewed at `http://www.w3.org/XML/Schema`.

Summary

In this chapter, we have covered the Document Type Definition (DTD) and how it is used to validate XML documents. Well-formed XML documents are documents that are syntactically correct according to the syntax rules of XML. However, in order to be a valid XML document, it must be validated against a DTD using a validating XML parser. A DTD serves as a roadmap for defining what structure a valid XML document should have.

We covered the following items in relation to using DTDs:

- A DTD may be internal to the XML document or external and referenced by the XML document.
- A DTD is attached to an XML document through a Document Type Declaration. A Document Type Declaration appears after the XML declaration and before the root element of the XML document. The Document Type Declaration may include a reference to an external DTD, encompass an internal DTD, or both.
- XML elements are declared and defined within the DTD. Elements are parsed from the top down, and elements in the XML document should appear in the same order they appear in the DTD. Element declarations have a specific set of rules and symbols that may be used in their definitions.
- XML attributes are declared and defined within the DTD. Attributes are not processed in a top-down fashion, but it is good programming practice to insert them after the element they reference. Attribute declarations have a specific set of types that may be used in their definitions.
- Entities are used in DTD as storage spaces or placeholders for data. Normally entities are used to store repetitive or bulky data for easy reference. There are four types of entities: internal, predefined, external, and parameter. Notations are used as references to help define the format of the external data.

- The `IGNORE` directive is used to indicate blocks of declarations that should not be included when the document is processed.
- The `INCLUDE` directive is used to indicate blocks of declarations that should be included when the document is processed. This directive is totally unnecessary to the successful processing of a DTD.
- Comments may be included in DTDs. Comments in DTDs are used in exactly the same way they are used in HTML.
- The DTD has several drawbacks that limit its scalability with respect to new and future XML applications. The XML Schema is the new recommendation from the W3C organization for XML validation. The XML Schema will be covered in detail in the next chapter.

Throughout the chapter, we followed a mini case study in which the Human Resources department for Zippy Delivery Service used XML to store employee records. The Human Resources department required a DTD to ensure that all XML records were of a uniform structure. To start, they built a simple DTD that was functional and worked. However, they were able to expand upon and improve their DTD to coincide with the introduction of new DTD topics in this chapter. Ultimately, they produced a DTD that effectively defined all the needs of the Human Resources department and enabled them to build a good roadmap for a valid XML document containing employee records.

CHAPTER 4

Creating XML Schemas

In This Chapter

Document Type Definitions have generated quite a few complaints since they were introduced. As a result, the W3C set about creating a new standard for defining a document's structure. What the W3C created is something even more complex and flexible than DTDs: the XML Schema Definition Language.

The XML Schema Definition Language solves a number of problems posed with Document Type Definitions. For instance, because the language for specifying DTDs is inherently different from the XML document it is describing, DTDs can be difficult to read and understand. Another limitation of DTDs is the method in which data is handled. Unfortunately, DTDs only support character data types: DTDs are unable to make a distinction between the various data types, such as numerics, dates, and so on. They are all considered character data types. Probably the most important and notable drawback of using DTDs is their inability to provide support for mixing elements from different documents stored in separate namespaces.

Schemas, while more complex than DTDs, also give an individual much more power and control over how XML documents are validated. For instance, with the new W3C standard, a document definition can specify the data type of an element's contents, the range of values for elements, what the minimum as well as maximum number of times an element may occur, annotations to schemas, and much more.

In this chapter, we'll cover the following topics:

- The various XML data types
- How to define and declare an attribute
- How to define and declare simple as well as complex elements
- How to create an enumerated set of values
- How to specify various constraints
- The different facets for the various data types
- How to create groups of related elements and attributes
- How to "inherit" elements and attributes from other schemas
- How to define a schema for a sample purchase order XML document
- How to associate and link an XML schema with an XML document

Introduction to the W3C XML Schema Recommendation

In May of 2001, the W3C finalized its recommendation for the XML Schema Definition Language. This standard allows an author to define simple and complex elements and the rules governing how those elements and their attributes may show up within an instance document. The author has a large amount of control over how the structure of a conforming XML document must be created. The author can apply various restrictions to the elements and attributes within the document, from specifying the length to specifying an enumerated set of acceptable values for the element or attribute. With the XML Schema Definition Language, an XML schema author possesses an incredible amount of control over the conformance of an associated XML document to the specified schema. You can find more information on the W3C at `www.w3c.org`. Additionally, the W3C XML Schema recommendation is separated into three main documents:

- The XML Schema Primer (Part 0), which can be found at `http://www.w3c.org/TR/xmlschema-0/`.
- The XML Schema Structures (Part 1), which can be found at `http://www.w3c.org/TR/xmlschema-1/`.
- The XML Schema Data Types (Part 2), which can be found at `http://www.w3c.org/TR/xmlschema-2/`.

You can find additional information on the XML Schema Definition Language at `http://www.w3c.org/XML/Schema`.

Sample XML Document

The rest of this chapter is devoted to creating and understanding the XML schema for the XML document shown in Listing 4.1, which details a purchase order for various items that can commonly be found in a grocery store. This document allows one individual to receive the shipment of the goods and an entirely different individual to pay for the purchase. This document also contains specific information about the products ordered, such as how much each product is, how many were ordered, and so on.

LISTING 4.1 `PurchaseOrder.xml` Contains a Sample Purchase Order for Common Items Found in a Grocery Store

```
<PurchaseOrder Tax="5.76" Total="75.77">

  <ShippingInformation>
    <Name>Dillon Larsen</Name>
    <Address>
      <Street>123 Jones Rd.</Street>
      <City>Houston</City>
      <State>TX</State>
      <Zip>77381</Zip>
    </Address>
    <Method>USPS</Method>
```

LISTING 4.1 continued

```
    <DeliveryDate>2001-08-12</DeliveryDate>
  </ShippingInformation>

  <BillingInformation>
    <Name>Madi Larsen</Name>
    <Address>
      <Street>123 Jones Rd.</Street>
      <City>Houston</City>
      <State>TX</State>
      <Zip>77381</Zip>
    </Address>
    <PaymentMethod>Credit Card</PaymentMethod>
    <BillingDate>2001-08-09</BillingDate>
  </BillingInformation>

  <Order SubTotal="70.01" ItemsSold="17">
    <Product Name="Baby Swiss" Id="702890" Price="2.89"
➥Quantity="1"/>
    <Product Name="Hard Salami" Id="302340" Price="2.34"
➥Quantity="1"/>
    <Product Name="Turkey" Id="905800" Price="5.80"
➥Quantity="1"/>
    <Product Name="Caesar Salad" Id="991687" Price="2.38"
➥Quantity="2"/>
    <Product Name="Chicken Strips" Id="133382" Price="2.50"
➥Quantity="1"/>
    <Product Name="Bread" Id="298678" Price="1.08"
➥Quantity="1"/>
    <Product Name="Rolls" Id="002399" Price="2.24"
➥Quantity="1"/>
    <Product Name="Cereal" Id="066510" Price="2.18"
➥Quantity="1"/>
    <Product Name="Jalapenos" Id="101005" Price="1.97"
➥Quantity="1"/>
    <Product Name="Tuna" Id="000118" Price="0.92"
➥Quantity="3"/>
    <Product Name="Mayonnaise" Id="126860" Price="1.98"
➥Quantity="1"/>
    <Product Name="Top Sirloin" Id="290502" Price="9.97"
➥Quantity="2"/>
    <Product Name="Soup" Id="001254" Price="1.33"
➥Quantity="1"/>
    <Product Name="Granola Bar" Id="026460" Price="2.14"
➥Quantity="2"/>
    <Product Name="Chocolate Milk" Id="024620" Price="1.58"
➥Quantity="2"/>
    <Product Name="Spaghetti" Id="000265" Price="1.98"
➥Quantity="1"/>
```

LISTING 4.1 continued

```
    <Product Name="Laundry Detergent" Id="148202" Price="8.82"
➥Quantity="1"/>
  </Order>

</PurchaseOrder>
```

As you can see, Listing 4.1 represents a fairly small and simple order that could be placed online. It contains the necessary information regarding how payment is to be made, how the order is to be shipped, and on what day the order is to be delivered. The preceding listing should by no means be construed as an all-inclusive document for an online grocery store order; it has been constructed for use as an example within this book only.

Until the XML Schema Definition Language recommendation was finalized, most authors, in the face of ever-changing standards, decided to stick with a finalized standard of DTDs. For the preceding listing, an author might construct the DTD shown in Listing 4.2.

LISTING 4.2 `PurchaseOrder.dtd` Contains a Sample DTD for *`PurchaseOrder.xml`*

```
<?xml version="1.0" encoding="UTF-8"?>
<!ELEMENT PurchaseOrder (ShippingInformation, BillingInformation, Order)>
<!ATTLIST PurchaseOrder
  Tax CDATA #IMPLIED
  Total CDATA #IMPLIED
>
<!ELEMENT ShippingInformation (Name, Address, (((BillingDate,
➥PaymentMethod)) | ((DeliveryDate, Method))))>
<!ELEMENT BillingInformation (Name, Address, (((BillingDate,
➥PaymentMethod)) | ((DeliveryDate, Method))))>
<!ELEMENT Order (Product+)>
<!ATTLIST Order
  SubTotal CDATA #IMPLIED
  ItemsSold CDATA #IMPLIED
>
<!ELEMENT Name (#PCDATA)>
<!ELEMENT Address (Street, City, State, Zip)>
<!ELEMENT BillingDate (#PCDATA)>
<!ELEMENT PaymentMethod (#PCDATA)>
<!ELEMENT DeliveryDate (#PCDATA)>
<!ELEMENT Method (#PCDATA)>
<!ELEMENT Product EMPTY>
<!ATTLIST Product
  Name CDATA #IMPLIED
  Id CDATA #IMPLIED
```

LISTING 4.2 continued

```
  Price CDATA #IMPLIED
  Quantity CDATA #IMPLIED
>
<!ELEMENT Street (#PCDATA)>
<!ELEMENT City (#PCDATA)>
<!ELEMENT State (#PCDATA)>
<!ELEMENT Zip (#PCDATA)>
```

Schema for XML Document

So, now that you've seen the DTD for the XML document in Listing 4.1, what would the comparative XML schema for it look like? Although the DTD in Listing 4.2 manages to describe the XML document in Listing 4.1 in a total of 30 lines, creating an XML schema is not quite so easy. Given the document in Listing 4.1, the XML schema for it is shown in Listing 4.3.

LISTING 4.3 `PurchaseOrder.xsd` Contains the Schema Definition for `PurchaseOrder.xml`

```
<xsd:schema xmlns:xsd="http://www.w3.org/2001/XMLSchema">

  <xsd:annotation>
    <xsd:documentation>
      Purchase Order schema for an online grocery store.
    </xsd:documentation>
  </xsd:annotation>

  <xsd:element name="PurchaseOrder" type="PurchaseOrderType"/>

  <xsd:complexType name="PurchaseOrderType">
    <xsd:all>
      <xsd:element name="ShippingInformation" type="InfoType"
➥minOccurs="1" maxOccurs="1"/>
      <xsd:element name="BillingInformation" type="InfoType"
➥minOccurs="1" maxOccurs="1"/>
      <xsd:element name="Order" type="OrderType"
➥minOccurs="1" maxOccurs="1"/>
    </xsd:all>
    <xsd:attribute name="Tax">
      <xsd:simpleType>
        <xsd:restriction base="xsd:decimal">
          <xsd:fractionDigits value="2"/>
        </xsd:restriction>
      </xsd:simpleType>
    </xsd:attribute>
    <xsd:attribute name="Total">
```

LISTING 4.3 continued

```
      <xsd:simpleType>
        <xsd:restriction base="xsd:decimal">
          <xsd:fractionDigits value="2"/>
        </xsd:restriction>
      </xsd:simpleType>
    </xsd:attribute>
  </xsd:complexType>

  <xsd:group name="ShippingInfoGroup">
    <xsd:all>
      <xsd:element name="DeliveryDate" type="DateType"/>
      <xsd:element name="Method" type="DeliveryMethodType"/>
    </xsd:all>
  </xsd:group>

  <xsd:group name="BillingInfoGroup">
    <xsd:all>
      <xsd:element name="BillingDate" type="DateType"/>
      <xsd:element name="PaymentMethod" type="PaymentMethodType"/>
    </xsd:all>
  </xsd:group>

  <xsd:complexType name="InfoType">
    <xsd:sequence>
      <xsd:element name="Name" minOccurs="1" maxOccurs="1">
        <xsd:simpleType>
          <xsd:restriction base="xsd:string"/>
        </xsd:simpleType>
      </xsd:element>
      <xsd:element name="Address" type="AddressType" minOccurs="1"
➥maxOccurs="1"/>
      <xsd:choice minOccurs="1" maxOccurs="1">
        <xsd:group ref="BillingInfoGroup"/>
        <xsd:group ref="ShippingInfoGroup"/>
      </xsd:choice>
    </xsd:sequence>
  </xsd:complexType>

  <xsd:simpleType name="DateType">
    <xsd:restriction base="xsd:date"/>
  </xsd:simpleType>

  <xsd:simpleType name="DeliveryMethodType">
    <xsd:restriction base="xsd:string">
      <xsd:enumeration value="USPS"/>
      <xsd:enumeration value="UPS"/>
      <xsd:enumeration value="FedEx"/>
      <xsd:enumeration value="DHL"/>
      <xsd:enumeration value="Other"/>
```

LISTING 4.3 continued

```
    </xsd:restriction>
  </xsd:simpleType>

  <xsd:simpleType name="PaymentMethodType">
    <xsd:restriction base="xsd:string">
      <xsd:enumeration value="Check"/>
      <xsd:enumeration value="Cash"/>
      <xsd:enumeration value="Credit Card"/>
      <xsd:enumeration value="Debit Card"/>
      <xsd:enumeration value="Other"/>
    </xsd:restriction>
  </xsd:simpleType>

  <xsd:complexType name="AddressType">
    <xsd:all>
      <xsd:element name="Street" minOccurs="1">
        <xsd:simpleType>
          <xsd:restriction base="xsd:string"/>
        </xsd:simpleType>
      </xsd:element>
      <xsd:element name="City" minOccurs="1" maxOccurs="1">
        <xsd:simpleType>
          <xsd:restriction base="xsd:string"/>
        </xsd:simpleType>
      </xsd:element>
      <xsd:element name="State" type="StateType" minOccurs="1"
➥maxOccurs="1"/>
      <xsd:element name="Zip" type="ZipType" minOccurs="1"
➥maxOccurs="1"/>
    </xsd:all>
  </xsd:complexType>

  <xsd:simpleType name="ZipType">
    <xsd:restriction base="xsd:string">
      <xsd:minLength value="5"/>
      <xsd:maxLength value="10"/>
      <xsd:pattern value="[0-9]{5}(-[0-9]{4})?"/>
    </xsd:restriction>
  </xsd:simpleType>

  <xsd:simpleType name="StateType">
    <xsd:restriction base="xsd:string">
      <xsd:length value="2"/>
      <xsd:enumeration value="AR"/>
      <xsd:enumeration value="LA"/>
      <xsd:enumeration value="MS"/>
      <xsd:enumeration value="OK"/>
      <xsd:enumeration value="TX"/>
```

LISTING 4.3 continued

```
    </xsd:restriction>
  </xsd:simpleType>

  <xsd:complexType name="OrderType">
    <xsd:sequence>
      <xsd:element name="Product" type="ProductType"
➥minOccurs="1" maxOccurs="unbounded"/>
    </xsd:sequence>
    <xsd:attribute name="SubTotal">
      <xsd:simpleType>
        <xsd:restriction base="xsd:decimal">
          <xsd:fractionDigits value="2"/>
        </xsd:restriction>
      </xsd:simpleType>
    </xsd:attribute>
    <xsd:attribute name="ItemsSold" type="xsd:positiveInteger"/>
  </xsd:complexType>

  <xsd:complexType name="ProductType">
    <xsd:attribute name="Name" type="xsd:string"/>
    <xsd:attribute name="Id" type="xsd:positiveInteger"/>
    <xsd:attribute name="Price">
      <xsd:simpleType>
        <xsd:restriction base="xsd:decimal">
          <xsd:fractionDigits value="2"/>
        </xsd:restriction>
      </xsd:simpleType>
    </xsd:attribute>
    <xsd:attribute name="Quantity" type="xsd:positiveInteger"/>
  </xsd:complexType>

</xsd:schema>
```


Examining the preceding XML schema, you can see that defining a schema for a document can become fairly complicated. However, for all the extra complexity involved, the schema gives the author virtually limitless control over how an XML document can be validated against it. For instance, you may notice the use of the `<xsd:choice>` element. You'll learn later in the "Model Groups" section of this chapter that this element can be used to indicate when one of a group of elements or attributes may show up, but not all, as is the case with the `DeliveryDate` and `BillingDate` attributes.

Also, notice the use of the `xsd` namespace. This namespace can be anything, but for convention in this chapter, we'll use `xsd` to indicate an XML Schema Definition Language element.

Creating XML Schemas

One of the first things that comes to mind for most people when authoring an XML schema is the level of complexity that accompanies it. However, the example in Listing 4.3 demonstrates only a small portion of the power and flexibility within the XML Schema Definition Language. Table 4.1 shows a complete list of every element the XML Schema Definition Language supports.

TABLE 4.1 XML Schema Elements Supported by the W3C Standard

Element Name	*Description*
`All`	Indicates that the contained elements may appear in any order within a parent element.
`Any`	Indicates that any element within the specified namespace may appear within the parent element's definition. If a type is not specifically declared, this is the default.
`anyAttribute`	Indicates that any attribute within the specified namespace may appear within the parent element's definition.
`annotation`	Indicates an annotation to the schema.
`Appinfo`	Indicates information that can be used by an application.
`Attribute`	Declares an occurrence of an attribute.
`attributeGroup`	Defines a group of attributes that can be included within a parent element.
`Choice`	Indicates that only one contained element or attribute may appear within a parent element.
`complexContent`	Defines restrictions and/or extensions to a `complexType`.
`complexType`	Defines a complex element's construction.
`documentation`	Indicates information to be read by an individual.
`Element`	Declares an occurrence of an element.
`Extension`	Extends the contents of an element
`Field`	Indicates a constraint for an element using `XPath`.

TABLE 4.1 continued

Element Name	*Description*
`Group`	Logically groups a set of elements to be included together within another element definition.
`import`	Identifies a namespace whose schema elements and attributes can be referenced within the current schema.
`include`	Indicates that the specified schema should be included in the target namespace.
`Key`	Indicates that an attribute or element value is a key within the specified scope.
`keyref`	Indicates that an attribute or element value should correspond with those of the specified key or unique element.
`List`	Defines a `simpleType` element as a list of values of a specified data type.
`notation`	Contains a notation definition.
`redefine`	Indicates that simple and complex types, as well as groups and attribute groups from an external schema, can be redefined.
`restriction`	Defines a constraint for the specified element.
`schema`	Contains the schema definition.
`selector`	Specifies an `XPath` expression that selects a set of elements for an identity constraint.
`sequence`	Indicates that the elements within the specified group must appear in the exact order they appear within the schema.
`simpleContent`	Defines restrictions and/or extensions of a `simpleType` element.
`simpleType`	Defines a simple element type.
`Union`	Defines a `simpleType` element as a collection of values from specified simple data types.
`unique`	Indicates that an attribute or element value must be unique within the specified scope.

Each of the elements in Table 4.1 has its own series of attributes and elements, including a series of constraints that can be placed on each element.

Authoring an XML schema consists of declaring elements and attributes as well as the "properties" of those elements and attributes. We will begin our look at authoring XML schemas by working our way from the least-complex example to the most-complex example. Because attributes may not contain other attributes or elements, we will start there.

Declaring Attributes

Attributes in an XML document are contained by elements. To indicate that a complex element has an attribute, use the <attribute> element of the XML Schema Definition Language. For instance, if you look at the following section from the PurchaseOrder schema, you can see the basics for declaring an attribute:

```
<xsd:complexType name="ProductType">
  <xsd:attribute name="Name" type="xsd:string"/>
  <xsd:attribute name="Id" type="xsd:positiveInteger"/>
  <xsd:attribute name="Price">
    <xsd:simpleType>
      <xsd:restriction base="xsd:decimal">
        <xsd:fractionDigits value="2"/>
      </xsd:restriction>
    </xsd:simpleType>
  </xsd:attribute>
  <xsd:attribute name="Quantity" type="xsd:positiveInteger"/>
</xsd:complexType>
```

From this, you can see that when declaring an attribute, you must specify a type. This type must be one of the simple types defined in Table 4.2.

TABLE 4.2 The Simple XML Data Types

Data Type	*Description*
anyURI	Represents a Uniform Resource Identifier (URI).
base64Binary	Represents Base-64-encoded binary data.
boolean	Represents Boolean values (True and False).
byte	Represents an integer ranging from -128 to 127. This type is derived from short.
date	Represents a date.

TABLE 4.2 continued

Data Type	*Description*
`dateTime`	Represents a specific time on a specific date.
`decimal`	Represents a variable-precision number.
`double`	Represents a double-precision, 64-bit, floating-point number.
`duration`	Represents a duration of time.
`ENTITIES`	Represents a set of values of the `ENTITY` type.
`ENTITY`	Represents the `ENTITY` attribute type in XML 1.0. This type is derived from `NCName`.
`float`	Represents a single-precision, 32-bit, floating-point number.
`gDay`	Represents a recurring Gregorian day of the month.
`gMonth`	Represents a Gregorian month.
`gMonthDay`	Represents a recurring Gregorian date.
`gYear`	Represents a Gregorian year.
`gYearMonth`	Represents a specific Gregorian month in a specific Gregorian year.
`hexBinary`	Represents hex-encoded binary data.
`ID`	Represents the `ID` attribute type defined in XML 1.0. This type is derived from `NCName`.
`IDREF`	Represents a reference to an element with the specified `ID` attribute value. This type is derived from `NCName`.
`IDREFS`	Represents a set of values of `IDREF` attribute types.
`int`	Represents an integer with a range of -2,147,483,648 to 2,147,483,647. This type is derived from `long`.
`integer`	Represents a sequence of decimal digits with an optional leading sign (+ or -). This type is derived from `decimal`.

TABLE 4.2 continued

Data Type	Description
`language`	Represents natural language identifiers. This type is derived from `token`.
`long`	Represents an integer with a range of -9,223,372,036,854,775,808 to 9,223,372,036,854,775,807. This type is derived from `integer`.
`Name`	Represents a token that begins with a letter, underscore, or colon and continues with letters, digits, and other characters. This type is derived from `token`.
`NCName`	Represents "noncolonized" names. This type is derived from `Name`.
`negativeInteger`	Represents an integer that is less than zero. This type is derived from `nonPositiveInteger`.
`NMTOKEN`	Represents a set of letters, digits, and other characters in any combination with no restriction on the starting character. This type is derived from `token`.
`NMTOKENS`	Represents a set of values of `NMTOKEN` types.
`nonNegativeInteger`	Represents an integer that is greater than or equal to zero. This type is derived from `integer`.
`nonPositiveInteger`	Represents an integer that is less than or equal to zero. This type is derived from `integer`.
`normalizedString`	Represents whitespace-normalized strings. This type is derived from `string`.
`NOTATION`	Represents a set of `QNames`.
`positiveInteger`	Represents an integer that is greater than zero. This type is derived from `nonNegativeInteger`.

TABLE 4.2 continued

Data Type	*Description*
`QName`	Represents a qualified name.
`short`	Represents an integer with a value range of -32,768 to 32,767. This type is derived from `int`.
`string`	Represents a character string.
`time`	Represents a recurring instance of time.
`token`	Represents tokenized strings. This type is derived from `normalizedString`.
`unsignedBtye`	Represents an integer with a value range of 0 to 255. This type is derived from `unsignedShort`.
`unsignedInt`	Represents an integer with a value in the range of 0 to 4,294,967,295. This type is derived from `unsignedLong`.
`unsignedLong`	Represents an integer with a value in the range of 0 to 18,446,744,073,709,551,615. This type is derived from `nonNegativeInteger`.
`unsignedShort`	Represents an integer with a value in the range of 0 to 65,535. This type is derived from `unsignedInt`.

The types in Table 4.2 can each be further categorized as either a "primitive" data type or a "derived" data type. Here's a list of the primitive data types:

- `anyURI`
- `base64Binary`
- `Boolean`
- `date`
- `dateTime`
- `decimal`
- `double`
- `duration`

- `float`
- `gDay`
- `gMonth`
- `gMonthDay`
- `gYear`
- `gYearMonth`
- `hexBinary`
- `NOTATION`
- `QName`
- `string`
- `time`

The derived data types are "primitive" or other "derived" data types with restrictions placed on them, such as `integer`, `positiveInteger`, and `byte`. Here's a list of the derived data types:

- `byte`
- `ENTITIES`
- `ENTITY`
- `ID`
- `IDREF`
- `IDREFS`
- `int`
- `integer`
- `language`
- `long`
- `Name`
- `NCName`
- `negativeInteger`
- `NMTOKEN`
- `NMTOKENS`
- `nonNegativeInteger`
- `nonPositiveInteger`
- `short`

- `token`
- `unsignedByte`
- `unsignedInt`
- `unsignedLong`
- `unsignedShort`

Note

From the simple types specified in Table 4.2, you may notice what appears to be a group of duplicate or unnecessary types, such as `nonNegativeInteger` and `positiveInteger`. Aren't those two types the same? No, they're not. If you look closely, you'll see that `nonNegativeInteger` is an integer whose value is greater than or equal to zero, whereas the `positiveInteger` type is an integer whose value is greater than zero, which means a `positiveInteger` type cannot be zero. Keep this in mind when deciding on the base data type for your elements and attributes, because these small details can greatly influence their acceptable value ranges.

Aside from defining the type of an attribute, the `<attribute>` element within the XML Schema Definition Language contains attributes to assist in defining when an attribute is optional, whether its values are fixed, what its default value is, and so on. Here's the basic syntax for the `<attribute>` element:

```
<attribute name="" type="" [use=""] [fixed=""] [default=""] [ref=""]/>
```

The `use` attribute can contain one of the following possible values:

- `optional`
- `prohibited`
- `required`

If the `use` attribute is set to `required`, the parent element must have the attribute; otherwise, the document will be considered invalid. A value of `optional` indicates the attribute may or may not occur in the document and the attribute may contain any value. By assigning a value of `prohibited` to the `use` attribute, you can indicate that the attribute may not appear at all within the parent element.

Specifying a value for the `default` attribute indicates that if the attribute does not appear within the specified element of the XML document, it is assumed to have the value. A value within the `fixed` attribute indicates the attribute has a constant value.

Caution

If you specify a value for the `fixed` attribute of the `<attribute>` element, the resulting attribute must have the value specified for the attribute to be valid. If you mean to indicate that the attribute should have a default value of some sort, use the default attribute instead. It should be noted that the `default` and `fixed` attributes are mutually exclusive of each other.

The `ref` attribute for the `<attribute>` element indicates that the attribute declaration exists somewhere else within the schema. This allows complex attribute declarations to be defined once and referenced when necessary. For instance, let's say you've "inherited" elements and attributes from another schema and would like to simply reuse one of the attribute declarations within the current schema; this would provide the perfect opportunity to take advantage of the `ref` attribute.

Just as attributes can be defined based on the simple data types included in the XML Schema Definition Language, they can also be defined based on `<simpleType>` elements. This can easily be accomplished by declaring an attribute that contains a `<simpleType>` element, as the following example demonstrates:

```
<xsd:attribute name="exampleattribute">
   <xsd:simpleType base="string">
      <xsd:length value="2"/>
   </xsd:simpleType>
</xsd:attribute>

<xsd:complexType name="exampleelement">
   <xsd:attribute ref="exampleattribute"/>
</xsd:complexType>
```

From this example, you can see that the XML Schema Definition Language gives the schema author a great deal of control over how attributes are validated. One of the wonderful side effects of the XML Schema Definition Language is its similarity to object-oriented programming. Consider each attribute definition and element definition to be a class definition. These class definitions describe complex structures and behaviors among various different classes, so each individual class definition, whether it's a simple class or complex class, encapsulates everything necessary to perform its job. The same holds true for the declaration of attributes and elements within an XML document. Each item completely describes itself.

Declaring Elements

Elements within an XML schema can be declared using the <element> element from the XML Schema Definition Language. If you look at the following example from Listing 4.3, you can see a simple element declaration using the XML Schema Definition Language:

```
<xsd:element name='PurchaseOrder' type='PurchaseOrderType'/>

<xsd:complexType name="PurchaseOrderType">
  <xsd:all>
    <xsd:element name="ShippingInformation" type="InfoType"
➥minOccurs="1" maxOccurs="1"/>
    <xsd:element name="BillingInformation" type="InfoType"
➥minOccurs="1" maxOccurs="1"/>
    <xsd:element name="Order" type="OrderType"
➥minOccurs="1" maxOccurs="1"/>
  </xsd:all>
  <xsd:attribute name="Tax">
    <xsd:simpleType>
      <xsd:restriction base="xsd:decimal">
        <xsd:fractionDigits value="2"/>
      </xsd:restriction>
    </xsd:simpleType>
  </xsd:attribute>
  <xsd:attribute name="Total">
    <xsd:simpleType>
      <xsd:restriction base="xsd:decimal">
        <xsd:fractionDigits value="2"/>
      </xsd:restriction>
    </xsd:simpleType>
  </xsd:attribute>
</xsd:complexType>
```

From this example, you can see that an element's type may be defined elsewhere within the schema. The location at which an element is defined determines certain characteristics about its availability within the schema. For instance, an element defined as a child of the <schema> element can be referenced anywhere within the schema document, whereas an element that is defined when it is declared can only have that definition used once. An element's type can be defined with either a <complexType> element, a <simpleType> element, a <complexContent> element, or a <simpleContent> element. The validation requirements for the document will influence the choice for an element's type. For instance, going back our object-oriented analogy, let's say you define a high-level abstract class and then need to refine its definition for certain situations. In that case, you would create a new class based on the existing one and change its definition as needed. The <complexContent> and <simpleContent> elements work much the same way: They provide a way to extend or restrict the existing simple or complex type definition as needed by the specific instance of the element declaration.

The basic construction of an element declaration using the `<element>` element within the XML Schema Definition Language is as follows:

```
<element name="" [type=""] [abstract=""] [block=""]
➥ [default=""] [final=""] [fixed=""] [minOccurs=""]
➥ [maxOccurs=""] [nillable=""] [ref=""]
➥ [substitutionGroup=""]/>
```

From this, you can see that element declarations offer a myriad of possibilities to the author. For instance, the `abstract` attribute indicates whether the element being declared may show up directly within the XML document. If this attribute is `true`, the declared element may not show up directly. Instead, this element must be referenced by another element using the `substitutionGroup` attribute. This substitution works only if the element utilizing the `substitutionGroup` attribute occurs directly beneath the `<schema>` element. In other words, for one element declaration to be substituted for another, the element using the `substitutionGroup` attribute must be a top-level element. Why would anyone in his right mind declare an element as abstract? The answer is really quite simple. Let's say you need to have multiple elements that have the same basic values specified for the attributes on the `<element>` element. A `<complexType>` element definition does not allow for those attributes. So, rather than define and set those attribute values for each element, you could make an "abstract" element declaration, set the values once, and substitute the abstract element definition as needed.

Note

You may omit the `type` attribute from the `<element>` element, but you should have either the `ref` attribute or the `substitutionGroup` attribute specified.

The `type` attribute indicates that the element should be based on a `complexType`, `simpleType`, `complexContent`, or `simpleContent` element definition. By defining an element's structure using one of these other elements, the author can gain an incredible amount of control over the element's definition. We will cover these various element definitions in the "Declaring Complex Elements" section and the "Declaring Simple Types" section later in this chapter.

The `block` attribute prevents any element with the specified derivation type from being used in place of the element. The `block` attribute may contain any of the following values:

- #all
- extension
- restriction
- substitution

If the value #all is specified within the block attribute, no elements derived from this element declaration may appear in place of this element. A value of extension prevents any element whose definition has been derived by extension from appearing in place on this element. If a value of restriction is assigned, an element derived by restriction from this element declaration is prevented from appearing in place of this element. Finally, a value of substitution indicates that an element derived through substitution cannot be used in place of this element.

The default attribute may only be specified for an element based on a simpleType or whose content is text only. This attribute assigns a default value to an element.

Caution

You cannot specify a value for both a default attribute and a fixed attribute; they are mutually exclusive. Also, if the element definition is based on a simpleType, the value must be a valid type of the data type.

The minOccurs and maxOccurs attributes specify the minimum and maximum number of times this element may appear within a valid XML document. Although you may explicitly set these attributes, they are not required. To indicate that an element's appearance within the parent element is optional, set the minOccurs attribute to 0. To indicate that the element may occur an unlimited number of times within the parent element, set the maxOccurs attribute to the string "unbounded".

Caution

You may not specify the minOccurs attribute for an element whose parent element is the <schema> element.

The nillable attribute indicates whether an explicit null value can be assigned to the element. If this particular attribute is omitted, it is assumed to be false. If this attribute has a value of true, the nil attribute for the element will be true. So what exactly does this do for you, this nillable attribute? Well, let's say you are writing an application that uses a database that supports NULL values for fields and you are representing your data as XML. Now let's say you request the data from your database and convert it into some XML grammar. How do you tell the difference between those elements that are empty and those elements that are NULL? That's where the `nillable` attribute comes into play. By appending an attribute of `nil` to the element, you can tell whether it is empty or is actually NULL.

> **Note**
>
> The `nillable` attribute applies only to an element's contents and not the attributes of the element.

The `fixed` attribute specifies that the element has a constant, predetermined value. This attribute only applies to those elements whose type definitions are based on `simpleType` or whose content is text only.

Declaring Complex Elements

Many times within an XML document, an element may contain child elements and/or attributes. To indicate this within the XML Schema Definition Language, you'll use the `<complexType>` element. If you examine the following sample section from Listing 4.3, you'll see the basics used to define a complex element within an XML schema:

```
<xsd:complexType name="PurchaseOrderType">
  <xsd:all>
    <xsd:element name="ShippingInformation" type="InfoType"
➥minOccurs="1" maxOccurs="1"/>
    <xsd:element name="BillingInformation" type="InfoType"
➥minOccurs="1" maxOccurs="1"/>
    <xsd:element name="Order" type="OrderType"
➥minOccurs="1" maxOccurs="1"/>
  </xsd:all>
  <xsd:attribute name="Tax">
    <xsd:simpleType>
      <xsd:restriction base="xsd:decimal">
        <xsd:fractionDigits value="2"/>
      </xsd:restriction>
    </xsd:simpleType>
  </xsd:attribute>
  <xsd:attribute name="Total">
    <xsd:simpleType>
      <xsd:restriction base="xsd:decimal">
        <xsd:fractionDigits value="2"/>
      </xsd:restriction>
```

```
    </xsd:simpleType>
  </xsd:attribute>
</xsd:complexType>
```

The preceding sample section specifies the definition of `PurchaseOrderType`. This particular element contains three child elements—`ShippingInformation`, `BillingInformation`, and `Order`—as well as two attributes: `Tax` and `Total`. You should also notice the use of the `maxOccurs` and `minOccurs` attributes on the element declarations. With a value of 1 indicated for both attributes, the element declarations specify that they must occur one time within the `PurchaseOrderType` element.

The basic syntax for the `<complexType>` element is as follows:

```
<xsd:complexType name='' [abstract=''] [base=''] [block='']
➥[final=''] [mixed='']/>
```

The `abstract` attribute indicates whether an element may define its content directly from this type definition or it must define its content from a type derived from this type definition. If this attribute is `true`, an element must define its content from a derived type definition. If this attribute is omitted or its value is `false`, an element may define its content directly based on this type definition.

The `base` attribute specifies the data type for the element. This attribute may hold any value from the included simple XML data types listed in Table 4.2.

The `block` attribute indicates what types of derivation are prevented for this element definition. This attribute can contain any of the following values:

- `#all`
- `extension`
- `restriction`

A value of `#all` prevents all complex types derived from this type definition from being used in place of this type definition. A value of `extension` prevents complex type definitions derived through extension from being used in place of this type definition. Assigning a value of `restriction` prevents a complex type definition derived through restriction from being used in place of this type definition. If this attribute is omitted, any type definition derived from this type definition may be used in place of this type definition.

The `mixed` attribute indicates whether character data is permitted to appear between the child elements of this type definition. If this attribute is `false` or is omitted, no character may appear. If the type definition contains a `simpleContent` type element, this value must be `false`. If the `complexContent` element appears as a child element, the `mixed` attribute on the `complexContent` element can override the value specified in the current type definition.

A `<complexType>` element in the XML Schema Definition Language may contain only one of the following elements:

- `all`
- `choice`
- `complexContent`
- `group`
- `sequence`
- `simpleContent`

For a short description of these elements, refer back to Table 4.1.

Declaring Simple Types

Sometimes, it's not necessary to declare a complex element type within an XML schema. In these cases, you can use the `<simpleType>` element of the XML Schema Definition Language. These element type definitions support an element based on the simple XML data types listed in Table 4.2 or any `simpleType` declaration within the current schema. For example, let's take the following section from the `PurchaseOrder` schema in Listing 4.3:

```
<xsd:simpleType name="PaymentMethodType">
  <xsd:restriction base="xsd:string">
    <xsd:enumeration value="Check"/>
    <xsd:enumeration value="Cash"/>
    <xsd:enumeration value="Credit Card"/>
    <xsd:enumeration value="Debit Card"/>
    <xsd:enumeration value="Other"/>
  </xsd:restriction>
</xsd:simpleType>
```

This type definition defines the `PaymentMethodType` element definition, which is based on the `string` data type included in the XML Schema Definition Language. You may notice the use of the `<enumeration>` element. This particular element is referred to as a *facet*, which we'll cover in the next section in this chapter.

The basic syntax for defining a `simpleType` element definition is as follows:

```
<xsd:simpleType name=''>
   <xsd:restriction base=''/>
</xsd:simpleType>
```

The base attribute type may contain any simple XML data type listed in Table 4.2 or any simpleType declared within the schema. Specifying the value of this attribute determines the type of data it may contain. A simpleType may only contain a value; not other elements or attributes.

You may also notice the inclusion of the <restriction> element. This is probably the most common method in which to declare types, and it helps to set more stringent boundaries on the values an element or attribute based on this type definition may hold. So, to indicate that a type definition's value may hold only string values, you would declare a type definition like the following:

```
<xsd:simpleType name='mySimpleType'>
   <xsd:restriction base='xsd:string'/>
</xsd:simpleType>
```

Two other methods are available to an XML schema author to "refine" a simple type definition: <list> and <union>. The <list> element allows an element or attribute based on the type definition to contain a list of values of a specified simple data type. The <union> element allows you to combine two or more simple type definitions to create a collection of values.

Refining Simple Types Using Facets

To give greater control over the definition of elements and attributes, the W3C added *facets* to the XML Schema Definition Language. A facet can only be specified for a <simpleType> element, and it helps determine the set of values for a <simpleType> element. For example, a facet may help determine the length or size that an element based on the <simpleType> element may have, an enumeration of acceptable values, and so on. Here's a list of the facets included within the XML Schema Definition Language:

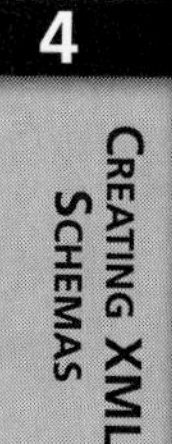

- enumeration
- fractionDigits
- length
- maxExclusive
- maxInclusive
- maxLength
- minExclusive
- minInclusive
- minLength
- pattern

- `totalDigits`
- `whiteSpace`

The `<enumeration>` facet constrains the data type to the specified values. For each valid value for a data type, another `<enumeration>` element must be defined. The following sample section from Listing 4.3 demonstrates the use of the `<enumeration>` facet:

```
<xsd:simpleType name="PaymentMethodType">
  <xsd:restriction base="xsd:string">
    <xsd:enumeration value="Check"/>
    <xsd:enumeration value="Cash"/>
    <xsd:enumeration value="Credit Card"/>
    <xsd:enumeration value="Debit Card"/>
    <xsd:enumeration value="Other"/>
  </xsd:restriction>
</xsd:simpleType>
```

This example indicates that the only valid values for an element based on `PaymentMethodType` are the following:

- Check
- Cash
- Credit Card
- Debit Card
- Other

The `<fractionDigits>` facet specifies the maximum number of decimal digits in the fractional part. The value for this facet must be a `nonNegativeInteger`. This may sound a bit confusing, but `<fractionDigits>` determines the number of decimal places allowed to appear within the value for the data type. For example, look at the following attribute declaration from Listing 4.3:

```
<xsd:attribute name="SubTotal">
  <xsd:simpleType>
    <xsd:restriction base="xsd:decimal">
      <xsd:fractionDigits value="2"/>
    </xsd:restriction>
  </xsd:simpleType>
</xsd:attribute>
```

The `<length>` facet determines the number of units of length for the specified data type. For instance, let's examine the following sample section from the `PurchaseOrder` schema in Listing 4.3:

```
<xsd:simpleType name="StateType">
   <xsd:restriction base="xsd:string">
```

```
      <xsd:length value="2"/>
      <xsd:enumeration value="AR"/>
      <xsd:enumeration value="LA"/>
      <xsd:enumeration value="MS"/>
      <xsd:enumeration value="OK"/>
      <xsd:enumeration value="TX"/>
   </xsd:restriction>
</xsd:simpleType>
```

The preceding sample section indicates that elements derived from the `StateType` type definition have a `string` value of `"2"` (that is, two spaces in length). Furthermore, the only acceptable values for elements derived from the `StateType` type definition are TX, LA, MS, OK, and AR, as indicated by the `<enumeration>` elements.

The `<maxExclusive>` facet specifies the upper bound for the values that can be assigned to the element or attribute. This facet ensures that all values are less than the value specified in this facet. The `<maxInclusive>` facet specifies the maximum value that can be assigned to the element or attribute.

Note

When specifying value-bounding facets, be sure the values assigned to those facets are valid values for the type definition's data type.

The `<maxLength>` and `<minLength>` facets specify the maximum and minimum lengths for values in the type definition. Keep in mind that the values specified in these facets are units of length that depend on the data type of the type definition's value. Also, remember these facets must have a `nonNegativeInteger` value assigned to them.

The `<minExclusive>` facet specifies the lower bound for the values that can be assigned to the element or attribute. This facet ensures that all values are greater than the value specified in this facet. The `<minInclusive>` facet specifies the minimum value that can be assigned to the element or attribute.

The `<pattern>` facet applies a specific pattern that the type definition's value must match. This facet constrains the type definition's data type to literals, which must match the pattern specified. Furthermore, the value specified for a `<pattern>` facet must be a regular expression. So what exactly qualifies as a regular expression? Put simply, a regular expression is composed of one or more "atoms" and optional quantifiers combined together with the pipe character (`|`). For instance, let's examine the following sample section from Listing 4.3:

```
<xsd:simpleType name="ZipType">
  <xsd:restriction base="xsd:string">
    <xsd:minLength value="5"/>
    <xsd:maxLength value="10"/>
    <xsd:pattern value="[0-9]{5}(-[0-9]{4})?"/>
  </xsd:restriction>
</xsd:simpleType>
```

The preceding type definition is for a zip code. In this particular definition, we declare that a valid zip code may only contain numbers 0 through 9; nothing else is allowed. Furthermore, the value for the type definition may contain five numbers listed together; then, if the additional four digits are included, the whole value is separated by a hyphen (-) between the fifth and sixth digits.

Tip

The regular expressions for use with the <pattern> facet are, in essence, Perl regular expressions. More specifics on Perl regular expressions can be found at `http://www.cpan.org/doc/manual/html/pod/perlre.html`.

The `<totalDigits>` facet specifies the maximum number of digits for a type definition's value. This value must be a `positiveInteger` value.

The `<whiteSpace>` facet specifies how whitespace is treated for the type definition's value. This particular facet can hold one of three values:

- `collapse`
- `preserve`
- `replace`

Specifying `collapse` indicates that all whitespace consisting of more than a single space will be converted to a single space and that all leading and trailing blanks will be removed. A value of `preserve` leaves the value as is. Assigning a value of `replace` causes all tabs, line feeds, and carriage returns to be replaced with a single space.

Not all type definitions, however, support every facet. The type definition's data type determines which facets are available. Table 4.3 shows which data types will support which facets.

TABLE 4.3 The Simple XML Data Types and Applicable Facets

Type	*Applicable Facets*
anyURI	enumeration, length, maxLength, minLength, pattern, whiteSpace
base64Binary	enumeration, length, maxLength, minLength, pattern, whiteSpace
boolean	pattern, whiteSpace
byte	enumeration, fractionDigits, maxExclusive, maxInclusive, minExclusive, minInclusive, pattern, totalDigits, whiteSpace
date	enumeration, maxExclusive, maxInclusive, minExclusive, minInclusive, pattern, whiteSpace
dateTime	enumeration, maxExclusive, maxInclusive, minExclusive, minInclusive, pattern, whiteSpace
decimal	enumeration, fractionDigits, maxExclusive, maxInclusive, minExclusive, minInclusive, pattern, totalDigits, whiteSpace
double	enumeration, maxExclusive, maxInclusive, minExclusive, minInclusive, pattern, whiteSpace
duration	enumeration, maxExclusive, maxInclusive, minExclusive, minInclusive, pattern, whiteSpace
ENTITIES	enumeration, length, maxLength, minLength, whiteSpace
ENTITY	enumeration, length, maxLength, minLength, pattern, whiteSpace
float	enumeration, maxExclusive, maxInclusive, minExclusive, minInclusive, pattern, whiteSpace
gDay	enumeration, maxExclusive, maxInclusive, minExclusive, minInclusive, pattern, whiteSpace

TABLE 4.3 continued

Type	*Applicable Facets*
gMonth	enumeration, maxExclusive, maxInclusive, minExclusive, minInclusive, pattern, whiteSpace
gMonthDay	enumeration, maxExclusive, maxInclusive, minExclusive, minInclusive, pattern, whiteSpace
gYear	enumeration, maxExclusive, maxInclusive, minExclusive, minInclusive, pattern, whiteSpace
gYearMonth	enumeration, maxExclusive, maxInclusive, minExclusive, minInclusive, pattern, whiteSpace
hexBinary	enumeration, length, maxLength, minLength, pattern, whiteSpace
ID	enumeration, length, maxLength, minLength, pattern, whiteSpace
IDREF	enumeration, length, maxLength, minLength, pattern, whiteSpace
IDREFS	enumeration, length, maxLength, minLength, whiteSpace
int	enumeration, fractionDigits, maxExclusive, maxInclusive, minExclusive, minInclusive, pattern, totalDigits, whiteSpace
integer	enumeration, fractionDigits, maxExclusive, maxInclusive, minExclusive, minInclusive, pattern, totalDigits, whiteSpace
language	enumeration, length, maxLength, minLength, pattern, whiteSpace
long	enumeration, fractionDigits, maxExclusive, maxInclusive, minExclusive, minInclusive, pattern, totalDigits, whiteSpace
Name	enumeration, length, maxLength, minLength, pattern, whiteSpace

TABLE 4.3 continued

Type	*Applicable Facets*
`NCName`	`enumeration`, `length`, `maxLength`, `minLength`, `pattern`, `whiteSpace`
`negativeInteger`	`enumeration`, `fractionDigits`, `maxExclusive`, `maxInclusive`, `minExclusive`, `minInclusive`, `pattern`, `totalDigits`, `whiteSpace`
`NMTOKEN`	`enumeration`, `length`, `maxLength`, `minLength`, `pattern`, `whiteSpace`
`NMTOKENS`	`enumeration`, `length`, `maxLength`, `minLength`, `whiteSpace`
`nonNegativeInteger`	`enumeration`, `fractionDigits`, `maxExclusive`, `maxInclusive`, `minExclusive`, `minInclusive`, `pattern`, `totalDigits`, `whiteSpace`
`nonPositiveInteger`	`enumeration`, `fractionDigits`, `maxExclusive`, `maxInclusive`, `minExclusive`, `minInclusive`, `pattern`, `totalDigits`, `whiteSpace`
`normalizedString`	`enumeration`, `length`, `maxLength`, `minLength`, `pattern`, `whiteSpace`
`NOTATION`	`enumeration`, `length`, `maxLength`, `minLength`, `pattern`, `whiteSpace`
`positiveInteger`	`enumeration`, `fractionDigits`, `maxExclusive`, `maxInclusive`, `minExclusive`, `minInclusive`, `pattern`, `totalDigits`, `whiteSpace`
`QName`	`enumeration`, `length`, `maxLength`, `minLength`, `pattern`, `whiteSpace`
`short`	`enumeration`, `fractionDigits`, `maxExclusive`, `maxInclusive`, `minExclusive`, `minInclusive`, `pattern`, `totalDigits`, `whiteSpace`
`string`	`enumeration`, `length`, `maxLength`, `minLength`, `pattern`, `whiteSpace`

TABLE 4.3 continued

Type	*Applicable Facets*
`time`	`enumeration`, `maxExclusive`, `maxInclusive`, `minExclusive`, `minInclusive`, `pattern`, `whiteSpace`
`token`	`enumeration`, `length`, `maxLength`, `minLength`, `pattern`, `whiteSpace`
`unsignedBtye`	`enumeration`, `fractionDigits`, `maxExclusive`, `maxInclusive`, `minExclusive`, `minInclusive`, `pattern`, `totalDigits`, `whiteSpace`
`unsignedInt`	`enumeration`, `fractionDigits`, `maxExclusive`, `maxInclusive`, `minExclusive`, `minInclusive`, `pattern`, `totalDigits`, `whiteSpace`
`unsignedLong`	`enumeration`, `fractionDigits`, `maxExclusive`, `maxInclusive`, `minExclusive`, `minInclusive`, `pattern`, `totalDigits`, `whiteSpace`
`unsignedShort`	`enumeration`, `fractionDigits`, `maxExclusive`, `maxInclusive`, `minExclusive`, `minInclusive`, `pattern`, `totalDigits`, `whiteSpace`

Anonymous Type Declarations

Sometimes within an XML schema it may not be necessary to create a separate type definition for an element or attribute. In such cases, you may use "anonymous" type declarations. Let's pull another sample section from the `PurchaseOrder` schema in Listing 4.3 and examine it:

```
<xsd:complexType name="InfoType">
  <xsd:sequence>
    <xsd:element name="Name" minOccurs="1" maxOccurs="1">
      <xsd:simpleType>
        <xsd:restriction base="xsd:string"/>
      </xsd:simpleType>
    </xsd:element>
    <xsd:element name="Address" type="AddressType" minOccurs="1"
➥maxOccurs="1"/>
```

```
    <xsd:choice minOccurs="1" maxOccurs="1">
      <xsd:group ref="BillingInfoGroup"/>
      <xsd:group ref="ShippingInfoGroup"/>
    </xsd:choice>
  </xsd:sequence>
</xsd:complexType>
```

This section defines the type definition for `InfoType`. If you look closely, you'll see the declaration of a `<Name>` element that does not have a `type` attribute specified. Instead, the `<element>` element, itself, contains a `<simpleType>` element without a `name` attribute specified. This is known as an "anonymous" type definition. If you're only using this type definition once, there is no need to go through the trouble of declaring and naming it. However, anonymous type declarations are not limited to `<simpleType>` elements; you can also create an anonymous type definition for a `<complexType>` element. For instance, let's look at the following example from Listing 4.3:

```
<xsd:complexType name="OrderType">
  <xsd:sequence>
    <xsd:element name="Product" type="ProductType"
➥minOccurs="1" maxOccurs="unbounded"/>
  </xsd:sequence>
  <xsd:attribute name="SubTotal">
    <xsd:simpleType>
      <xsd:restriction base="xsd:decimal">
        <xsd:fractionDigits value="2"/>
      </xsd:restriction>
    </xsd:simpleType>
  </xsd:attribute>
  <xsd:attribute name="ItemsSold" type="xsd:positiveInteger"/>
</xsd:complexType>

<xsd:complexType name="ProductType">
  <xsd:attribute name="Name" type="xsd:string"/>
  <xsd:attribute name="Id" type="xsd:positiveInteger"/>
  <xsd:attribute name="Price">
    <xsd:simpleType>
      <xsd:restriction base="xsd:decimal">
        <xsd:fractionDigits value="2"/>
      </xsd:restriction>
    </xsd:simpleType>
  </xsd:attribute>
  <xsd:attribute name="Quantity" type="xsd:positiveInteger"/>
</xsd:complexType>
```


This example shows the type definition for elements based on `OrderType`. This type definition contains an element named `Product`, which is based on the `ProductType` type definition. Because we only reference the `ProductType` type definition once, this would be a good candidate for which to use an anonymous type definition. Using an anonymous type definition, the preceding example changes to the following:

```
<xsd:complexType name="OrderType">
  <xsd:sequence>
    <xsd:element name="Product" minOccurs="1" maxOccurs="unbounded">
      <xsd:complexType>
        <xsd:attribute name="Name" type="xsd:string"/>
        <xsd:attribute name="Id" type="xsd:positiveInteger"/>
        <xsd:attribute name="Price">
          <xsd:simpleType>
            <xsd:restriction base="xsd:decimal">
              <xsd:fractionDigits value="2"/>
            </xsd:restriction>
          </xsd:simpleType>
        </xsd:attribute>
        <xsd:attribute name="Quantity" type="xsd:positiveInteger"/>
      </xsd:complexType>
    </xsd:element>
  </xsd:sequence>
  <xsd:attribute name="SubTotal">
    <xsd:simpleType>
      <xsd:restriction base="xsd:decimal">
        <xsd:fractionDigits value="2"/>
      </xsd:restriction>
    </xsd:simpleType>
  </xsd:attribute>
  <xsd:attribute name="ItemsSold" type="xsd:positiveInteger"/>
</xsd:complexType>
```

You can see from this example that the only real change necessary was to move the `<complexType>` element for the `ProductType` type definition to be contained by the `<element>` declaration for `Product`.

Specifying Mixed Content for Elements

So far we have declared a variety of different elements in Listing 4.3. Some of the elements have text only, some contain elements only, and some contain elements and attributes. However, we have not specified, yet, how to mix the content of elements—that is, mix text with child elements. One of the most overlooked attributes of the `<complexType>` element is the `mixed` attribute. If this attribute is set to `true`, elements based on this type definition can mix their contents with both text and child elements. For instance, let's examine the following sample XML document:

```
<Letter>
   <Greeting>Dear Mr.<Name>John Smith</Name>.</Greeting>
Your order of <Quantity>1</Quantity> <Product>Big Screen TV
➥</Product> has been shipped.
</Letter>
```

Notice the appearance of text among the child elements of <Letter>. The schema for this XML document would appear as follows:

```
<xsd:element name="Letter">
   <xsd:complexType mixed="true">
      <xsd:element name="Greeting">
         <xsd:complexType mixed="true">
            <xsd:element name="Name" type="xsd:string"/>
         </xsd:complexType>
      </xsd:element>
      <xsd:element name="Quantity" type="xsd:postiveInteger"/>
      <xsd:element name="Product" type="xsd:string"/>
   </xsd:complexType>
</xsd:element>
```

So what's the point of having mixed content? Well, if you needed to uniquely identify something within a paragraph or sentence, specifying an element as having mixed content might be useful. For one, you could easily format that one unique element differently from its parent element. You could also perform some special processing of that element within an application. However, unless it is absolutely necessary to use mixed content within an element, it is highly recommended that each element contain either text or other elements (not both, because some undesirable side effects may arise). For instance, in the preceding sample XML document, if you check the value of the `text` property for the <Greeting> element using the XMLDOM provided by Microsoft, it would contain this:

```
Dear Mr.John Smith,
```

Annotating Schemas

In a perfect world, everyone would be able to look at our XML schemas and automatically know what everything is and why it shows up in particular places. Although a good self-describing document can accomplish this to some extent with sensible element and attribute names, the truth of the matter is that most people I've met—well, all of them actually—are not mind readers. What may seem obvious to you may not be obvious to others. For that very reason, it helps to document your schemas. Within the XML Schema Definition Language, this can be accomplished using annotations. The XML Schema Definition Language defines three new elements to add annotations to an XML schema:

- <annotation>
- <appInfo>
- <documentation>

The <annotation> element contains the <appInfo> and <documentation> elements. In other words, you cannot use the <appInfo> and <documentation> elements by themselves—they must be contained within an <annotation> element. To see how this works, let's examine the following sample section from Listing 4.3:

```
<xsd:annotation>
   <xsd:documentation>
      Purchase order schema for an online grocery store.
   </xsd:documentation>
</xsd:annotation>
```

In the preceding example, the <annotation> and <documentation> elements help to identify the purpose of this particular XML schema. In Listing 4.3, the <annotation> element appears as a child element of the <schema> element. However, the <annotation> element can appear as a child of any elements listed in Table 4.2, with the exception of the <documentation> and <appInfo> elements. Really, the only difference between the two elements is the target audience. For the <documentation> element, the information it contains is meant to be read by users, whereas the information contained within an <appInfo> element is meant to be read and utilized by applications.

Model Groups

A *model group*, at least in terms of a schema definition, is a logically grouped set of elements. A model group within the XML Schema Definition Language consists of a "compositor" and a list of "particles" (or element declarations). A model group can be constructed using one of the following XML Schema Definition elements:

- <all>
- <choice>
- <sequence>

You can declare a group of elements that should be logically associated together by using the <group> element from the XML Schema Definition Language. Here's the basic syntax for the <group> element:

```
<group name="" [maxOccurs=""] [minOccurs=""] [ref=""]>
   .
   .
   .
</group>
```

By default, the maxOccurs and minOccurs attributes are set to 1. The ref attribute is used after you have defined the <group> element and you wish to reference it, as the following example shows:

```
<xsd:group name="exampleGroup">
   <xsd:all>
      <xsd:element name="Element1" type="xsd:string"/>
      <xsd:element name="Element2" type="xsd:string"/>
      <xsd:element name="Element3" type="xsd:string"/>
   </xsd:all>
</xsd:group>

<xsd:element name="ParentElement">
   <xsd:complexType>
      <xsd:group ref="exampleGroup"/>
   </xsd:complexType>
</xsd:element>
```

All Groups

When the order in which child elements appear within their parent element is not important, you may use an `<all>` element from the XML Schema Definition Language. The `<all>` element indicates that the elements declared within it may appear in any order within the parent element. For instance, let's examine the `InfoType` type definition from Listing 4.3:

```
<xsd:group name="ShippingInfoGroup">
  <xsd:all>
    <xsd:element name="DeliveryDate" type="DateType"/>
    <xsd:element name="Method" type="DeliveryMethodType"/>
  </xsd:all>
</xsd:group>

<xsd:group name="BillingInfoGroup">
  <xsd:all>
    <xsd:element name="BillingDate" type="DateType"/>
    <xsd:element name="PaymentMethod" type="PaymentMethodType"/>
  </xsd:all>
</xsd:group>

<xsd:complexType name="InfoType">
  <xsd:sequence>
    <xsd:element name="Name" minOccurs="1" maxOccurs="1">
      <xsd:simpleType>
        <xsd:restriction base="xsd:string"/>
      </xsd:simpleType>
    </xsd:element>
    <xsd:element name="Address" type="AddressType"
➥minOccurs="1" maxOccurs="1"/>
    <xsd:choice minOccurs="1" maxOccurs="1">
      <xsd:group ref="BillingInfoGroup"/>
      <xsd:group ref="ShippingInfoGroup"/>
```

```
    </xsd:choice>
  </xsd:sequence>
</xsd:complexType>

<xsd:simpleType name="DateType">
  <xsd:restriction base="xsd:date"/>
</xsd:simpleType>

<xsd:simpleType name="DeliveryMethodType">
  <xsd:restriction base="xsd:string">
    <xsd:enumeration value="USPS"/>
    <xsd:enumeration value="UPS"/>
    <xsd:enumeration value="FedEx"/>
    <xsd:enumeration value="DHL"/>
    <xsd:enumeration value="Other"/>
  </xsd:restriction>
</xsd:simpleType>

<xsd:simpleType name="PaymentMethodType">
  <xsd:restriction base="xsd:string">
    <xsd:enumeration value="Check"/>
    <xsd:enumeration value="Cash"/>
    <xsd:enumeration value="Credit Card"/>
    <xsd:enumeration value="Debit Card"/>
    <xsd:enumeration value="Other"/>
  </xsd:restriction>
</xsd:simpleType>
```

Notice the occurrence of the <all> elements. In this particular case, either the <DeliveryDate> and <Method> elements may appear in any order or the <BillingDate> and <PaymentMethod> elements may appear in any order.

Choices

Sometimes you might want to declare that any one of a possible group of elements may appear within an element, but not all of them. This is accomplished by using the <choice> element of the XML Schema Definition Language. Let's examine the following sample section from Listing 4.3:

```
<xsd:complexType name="PurchaseOrderType">
  <xsd:all>
    <xsd:element name="ShippingInformation" type="InfoType"
➥minOccurs="1" maxOccurs="1"/>
    <xsd:element name="BillingInformation" type="InfoType"
➥minOccurs="1" maxOccurs="1"/>
    <xsd:element name="Order" type="OrderType" minOccurs="1"
➥maxOccurs="1"/>
  </xsd:all>
  <xsd:attribute name="Tax">
    <xsd:simpleType>
```

```
        <xsd:restriction base="xsd:decimal">
          <xsd:fractionDigits value="2"/>
        </xsd:restriction>
      </xsd:simpleType>
    </xsd:attribute>
    <xsd:attribute name="Total">
      <xsd:simpleType>
        <xsd:restriction base="xsd:decimal">
          <xsd:fractionDigits value="2"/>
        </xsd:restriction>
      </xsd:simpleType>
    </xsd:attribute>
  </xsd:complexType>

  <xsd:group name="ShippingInfoGroup">
    <xsd:all>
      <xsd:element name="DeliveryDate" type="DateType"/>
      <xsd:element name="Method" type="DeliveryMethodType"/>
    </xsd:all>
  </xsd:group>

  <xsd:group name="BillingInfoGroup">
    <xsd:all>
      <xsd:element name="BillingDate" type="DateType"/>
      <xsd:element name="PaymentMethod" type="PaymentMethodType"/>
    </xsd:all>
  </xsd:group>

  <xsd:complexType name="InfoType">
    <xsd:sequence>
      <xsd:element name="Name" minOccurs="1" maxOccurs="1">
        <xsd:simpleType>
          <xsd:restriction base="xsd:string"/>
        </xsd:simpleType>
      </xsd:element>
      <xsd:element name="Address" type="AddressType"
➥minOccurs="1" maxOccurs="1"/>
      <xsd:choice minOccurs="1" maxOccurs="1">
        <xsd:group ref="BillingInfoGroup"/>
        <xsd:group ref="ShippingInfoGroup"/>
      </xsd:choice>
    </xsd:sequence>
  </xsd:complexType>

  <xsd:simpleType name="DateType">
    <xsd:restriction base="xsd:date"/>
  </xsd:simpleType>

  <xsd:simpleType name="DeliveryMethodType">
    <xsd:restriction base="xsd:string">
      <xsd:enumeration value="USPS"/>
```

```
    <xsd:enumeration value="UPS"/>
    <xsd:enumeration value="FedEx"/>
    <xsd:enumeration value="DHL"/>
    <xsd:enumeration value="Other"/>
  </xsd:restriction>
</xsd:simpleType>

<xsd:simpleType name="PaymentMethodType">
  <xsd:restriction base="xsd:string">
    <xsd:enumeration value="Check"/>
    <xsd:enumeration value="Cash"/>
    <xsd:enumeration value="Credit Card"/>
    <xsd:enumeration value="Debit Card"/>
    <xsd:enumeration value="Other"/>
  </xsd:restriction>
</xsd:simpleType>
```

In this case, because the information between the `<ShippingInformation>` and `<BillingInformation>` elements is so similar, we only want to define that type definition once. However, because the two date elements—`<DeliveryDate>` and `<BillingDate>`—could not appear in both places, we've decided to create a choice: either the `<DeliveryDate>` element can appear within the element or the `<BillingDate>` element can appear, but not both. Furthermore, you can specify the minimum and maximum number of times the selected item may appear within the parent element by using the `minOccurs` and `maxOccurs` attributes of the `<choice>` element.

> **Note**
>
> Within a `<group>` or `<complexType>` element, the `<choice>` element may only appear once. For any other valid XML Schema Definition Language element that can contain the `<choice>` element, the `<choice>` element may appear an unlimited number of times.

Sequences

The `<sequence>` element in the XML Schema Definition Language requires the elements contained within it to appear in the same order in the parent element. For instance, let's examine the following sample section from Listing 4.3:

```
<xsd:complexType name="PurchaseOrderType">
  <xsd:all>
    <xsd:element name="ShippingInformation" type="InfoType"
➥minOccurs="1" maxOccurs="1"/>
    <xsd:element name="BillingInformation" type="InfoType"
➥minOccurs="1" maxOccurs="1"/>
```

```
    <xsd:element name="Order" type="OrderType" minOccurs="1"
➥maxOccurs="1"/>
  </xsd:all>
  <xsd:attribute name="Tax">
    <xsd:simpleType>
      <xsd:restriction base="xsd:decimal">
        <xsd:fractionDigits value="2"/>
      </xsd:restriction>
    </xsd:simpleType>
  </xsd:attribute>
  <xsd:attribute name="Total">
    <xsd:simpleType>
      <xsd:restriction base="xsd:decimal">
        <xsd:fractionDigits value="2"/>
      </xsd:restriction>
    </xsd:simpleType>
  </xsd:attribute>
</xsd:complexType>
```

According to this type definition, the `<ShippingInformation>`, `<BillingInformation>`, and `<Order>` elements may appear within the `<PurchaseOrder>` element in any order. If we want to indicate that the `<ShippingInformation>` element must appear first, then the `<BillingInformation>` element, and then the `<Order>` element, we could do the following:

```
<xsd:complexType name="PurchaseOrderType">
  <xsd:sequence>
    <xsd:element name="ShippingInformation" type="InfoType"
➥minOccurs="1" maxOccurs="1"/>
    <xsd:element name="BillingInformation" type="InfoType"
➥minOccurs="1" maxOccurs="1"/>
    <xsd:element name="Order" type="OrderType" minOccurs="1"
➥maxOccurs="1"/>
  </xsd:sequence>
  <xsd:attribute name="Tax">
    <xsd:simpleType>
      <xsd:restriction base="xsd:decimal">
        <xsd:fractionDigits value="2"/>
      </xsd:restriction>
    </xsd:simpleType>
  </xsd:attribute>
  <xsd:attribute name="Total">
    <xsd:simpleType>
      <xsd:restriction base="xsd:decimal">
        <xsd:fractionDigits value="2"/>
      </xsd:restriction>
    </xsd:simpleType>
  </xsd:attribute>
</xsd:complexType>
```

Caution

Keep in mind that when you declare a <sequence> element, the elements you place in it must appear in that exact order within the XML document being validated.

Attribute Groups

Just as you can logically group a set of elements together using the <group> element within the XML Schema Definition Language, you can create a logical group of attributes to do the same thing. In this case, though, you will need to use the <attributeGroup> element. Here's the basic syntax for the <attributeGroup> element:

```
<attributeGroup [name=""] [ref=""]>
   <attribute …/>
   <attribute …/>
   .
   .
   .
</attributeGroup>
```

Following the preceding syntax, we could define a group of attributes that can be associated with one another, as the following example shows:

```
<xsd:attributeGroup name="exampleGroup">
   <xsd:attribute name="Attr1" type="xsd:string"/>
   <xsd:attribute name="Attr2" type="xsd:positiveInteger"/>
   <xsd:attribute name="Attr3" type="xsd:date"/>
</xsd:attributeGroup>

<xsd:element name="exampleElement">
   <xsd:complexType>
      <xsd:attributeGroup ref="exampleGroup"/>
   </xsd:complexType>
</xsd:element>
```

The preceding example creates a group of attributes named `exampleGroup`. This group consists of three attributes: `Attr1`, `Attr2`, and `Attr3`. Also, we've defined a complex element named <exampleElement>, which then references the group of attributes. It is the equivalent of the following:

```
<xsd:element name="exampleElement">
   <xsd:complexType>
      <xsd:attribute name="Attr1" type="xsd:string"/>
      <xsd:attribute name="Attr2" type="xsd:positiveInteger"/>
```

```
      <xsd:attribute name="Attr3" type="xsd:date"/>
   </xsd:complexType>
</xsd:element>
```

Targeting Namespaces

You can view an XML schema as a collection of type definitions and element declarations targeted for a specific namespace. Namespaces allow us to distinguish element declarations and type definitions of one schema from another. We can assign an intended namespace for an XML schema by using the `targetNamespace` attribute on the `<schema>` element. By assigning a target namespace for the schema, we indicate that an XML document whose elements are declared as belonging to the schema's namespace should be validated against the XML schema. We will discuss namespaces in Chapter 5, "The X-Files: XPath, XPointer, and XLink." For instance, we could indicate a target namespace for our `PurchaseOrder` schema as indicated in Listing 4.4.

LISTING 4.4 `PurchaseOrder1.xsd` Contains the Schema Definition for `PurchaseOrder.xml` with a Target Namespace

```
<xsd:schema targetNamespace="http://www.eps-software.com/poschema"
➥xmlns:xsd="http://www.w3.org/2001/XMLSchema"
➥xmlns="http://www.eps-software.com/poschema"
➥elementFormDefault="unqualified"
➥attributeFormDefault="unqualified">

  <xsd:annotation>
    <xsd:documentation>
      Purchase Order schema for an online grocery store.
    </xsd:documentation>
  </xsd:annotation>

  <xsd:element name="PurchaseOrder" type="PurchaseOrderType"/>

  <xsd:complexType name="PurchaseOrderType">
    <xsd:all>
      <xsd:element name="ShippingInformation" type="InfoType"
➥minOccurs="1" maxOccurs="1"/>
      <xsd:element name="BillingInformation" type="InfoType"
➥minOccurs="1" maxOccurs="1"/>
      <xsd:element name="Order" type="OrderType"
➥minOccurs="1" maxOccurs="1"/>
    </xsd:all>
    <xsd:attribute name="Tax">
      <xsd:simpleType>
        <xsd:restriction base="xsd:decimal">
          <xsd:fractionDigits value="2"/>
        </xsd:restriction>
```

LISTING 4.4 continued

```
      </xsd:simpleType>
    </xsd:attribute>
    <xsd:attribute name="Total">
      <xsd:simpleType>
        <xsd:restriction base="xsd:decimal">
          <xsd:fractionDigits value="2"/>
        </xsd:restriction>
      </xsd:simpleType>
    </xsd:attribute>
  </xsd:complexType>

  <xsd:group name="ShippingInfoGroup">
    <xsd:all>
      <xsd:element name="DeliveryDate" type="DateType"/>
      <xsd:element name="Method" type="DeliveryMethodType"/>
    </xsd:all>
  </xsd:group>

  <xsd:group name="BillingInfoGroup">
    <xsd:all>
      <xsd:element name="BillingDate" type="DateType"/>
      <xsd:element name="PaymentMethod" type="PaymentMethodType"/>
    </xsd:all>
  </xsd:group>

  <xsd:complexType name="InfoType">
    <xsd:sequence>
      <xsd:element name="Name" minOccurs="1" maxOccurs="1">
        <xsd:simpleType>
          <xsd:restriction base="xsd:string"/>
        </xsd:simpleType>
      </xsd:element>
      <xsd:element name="Address" type="AddressType" minOccurs="1"
➥maxOccurs="1"/>
      <xsd:choice minOccurs="1" maxOccurs="1">
        <xsd:group ref="BillingInfoGroup"/>
        <xsd:group ref="ShippingInfoGroup"/>
      </xsd:choice>
    </xsd:sequence>
  </xsd:complexType>

  <xsd:simpleType name="DateType">
    <xsd:restriction base="xsd:date"/>
  </xsd:simpleType>

  <xsd:simpleType name="DeliveryMethodType">
    <xsd:restriction base="xsd:string">
      <xsd:enumeration value="USPS"/>
      <xsd:enumeration value="UPS"/>
```

LISTING 4.4 continued

```
      <xsd:enumeration value="FedEx"/>
      <xsd:enumeration value="DHL"/>
      <xsd:enumeration value="Other"/>
    </xsd:restriction>
  </xsd:simpleType>

  <xsd:simpleType name="PaymentMethodType">
    <xsd:restriction base="xsd:string">
      <xsd:enumeration value="Check"/>
      <xsd:enumeration value="Cash"/>
      <xsd:enumeration value="Credit Card"/>
      <xsd:enumeration value="Debit Card"/>
      <xsd:enumeration value="Other"/>
    </xsd:restriction>
  </xsd:simpleType>

  <xsd:complexType name="AddressType">
    <xsd:all>
      <xsd:element name="Street" minOccurs="1">
        <xsd:simpleType>
          <xsd:restriction base="xsd:string"/>
        </xsd:simpleType>
      </xsd:element>
      <xsd:element name="City" minOccurs="1" maxOccurs="1">
        <xsd:simpleType>
          <xsd:restriction base="xsd:string"/>
        </xsd:simpleType>
      </xsd:element>
      <xsd:element name="State" type="StateType" minOccurs="1"
➥maxOccurs="1"/>
      <xsd:element name="Zip" type="ZipType" minOccurs="1"
➥maxOccurs="1"/>
    </xsd:all>
  </xsd:complexType>

  <xsd:simpleType name="ZipType">
    <xsd:restriction base="xsd:string">
      <xsd:minLength value="5"/>
      <xsd:maxLength value="10"/>
      <xsd:pattern value="[0-9]{5}(-[0-9]{4})?"/>
    </xsd:restriction>
  </xsd:simpleType>

  <xsd:simpleType name="StateType">
    <xsd:restriction base="xsd:string">
      <xsd:length value="2"/>
      <xsd:enumeration value="AR"/>
      <xsd:enumeration value="LA"/>
      <xsd:enumeration value="MS"/>
```

LISTING 4.4 continued

```
      <xsd:enumeration value="OK"/>
      <xsd:enumeration value="TX"/>
    </xsd:restriction>
  </xsd:simpleType>

  <xsd:complexType name="OrderType">
    <xsd:sequence>
      <xsd:element name="Product" type="ProductType"
➥minOccurs="1" maxOccurs="unbounded"/>
    </xsd:sequence>
    <xsd:attribute name="SubTotal">
      <xsd:simpleType>
        <xsd:restriction base="xsd:decimal">
          <xsd:fractionDigits value="2"/>
        </xsd:restriction>
      </xsd:simpleType>
    </xsd:attribute>
    <xsd:attribute name="ItemsSold" type="xsd:positiveInteger"/>
  </xsd:complexType>

  <xsd:complexType name="ProductType">
    <xsd:attribute name="Name" type="xsd:string"/>
    <xsd:attribute name="Id" type="xsd:positiveInteger"/>
    <xsd:attribute name="Price">
      <xsd:simpleType>
        <xsd:restriction base="xsd:decimal">
          <xsd:fractionDigits value="2"/>
        </xsd:restriction>
      </xsd:simpleType>
    </xsd:attribute>
    <xsd:attribute name="Quantity" type="xsd:positiveInteger"/>
  </xsd:complexType>

</xsd:schema>
```

Now that we've modified our schema file to specify a target namespace, how do we associate the schema with the XML document? This can be accomplished using the `http://www.w3.org/2001/XMLSchema-instance` namespace and specifying the schema file's location using the `<schemaLocation>` element defined within the namespace. Typically, this namespace is given the prefix of `xsi`. We could then change our `PurchaseOrder` XML document as indicated in Listing 4.5.

LISTING 4.5 `PurchaseOrder1.xml` Contains a Sample Purchase Order Based on the `PurchaseOrder1` Schema Definition in `PurchaseOrder1.xsd`

```
<po:PurchaseOrder xmlns:po="http://www.eps-software.com/poschema"
➥xmlns:xsi="http://www.w3.org/2001/XMLSchema-instance"
➥xsi:schemaLocation="PurchaseOrder1.xsd"
➥Tax="5.76" Total="75.77">

<ShippingInformation>
    <Method>USPS</Method>
    <DeliveryDate>08/12/2001</DeliveryDate>
    <Name>Dillon Larsen</Name>
    <Address>
      <Street>123 Jones Rd.</Street>
      <City>Houston</City>
      <State>TX</State>
      <Zip>77381</Zip>
    </Address>
  </ShippingInformation>

  <BillingInformation>
    <PaymentMethod>Credit Card</PaymentMethod>
    <BillingDate>08/09/2001</BillingDate>
    <Name>Madi Larsen</Name>
    <Address>
      <Street>123 Jones Rd.</Street>
      <City>Houston</City>
      <State>TX</State>
      <Zip>77381</Zip>
    </Address>
  </BillingInformation>

  <Order SubTotal="70.01" ItemsSold="17">
    <Product Name="Baby Swiss" Id="702890" Price="2.89"
➥Quantity="1"/>
    <Product Name="Hard Salami" Id="302340" Price="2.34"
➥Quantity="1"/>
    <Product Name="Turkey" Id="905800" Price="5.80"
➥Quantity="1"/>
    <Product Name="Caesar Salad" Id="991687" Price="2.38"
➥Quantity="2"/>
    <Product Name="Chicken Strips" Id="133382" Price="2.50"
➥Quantity="1"/>
    <Product Name="Bread" Id="298678" Price="1.08"
➥Quantity="1"/>
    <Product Name="Rolls" Id="002399" Price="2.24"
➥Quantity="1"/>
    <Product Name="Cereal" Id="066510" Price="2.18"
➥Quantity="1"/>
    <Product Name="Jalapenos" Id="101005" Price="1.97"
➥Quantity="1"/>
```

LISTING 4.5 continued

```
    <Product Name="Tuna" Id="000118" Price="0.92"
➥Quantity="3"/>
    <Product Name="Mayonnaise" Id="126860" Price="1.98"
➥Quantity="1"/>
    <Product Name="Top Sirloin" Id="290502" Price="9.97"
➥Quantity="2"/>
    <Product Name="Soup" Id="001254" Price="1.33"
➥Quantity="1"/>
    <Product Name="Granola Bar" Id="026460" Price="2.14"
➥Quantity="2"/>
    <Product Name="Chocolate Milk" Id="024620" Price="1.58"
➥Quantity="2"/>
    <Product Name="Spaghetti" Id="000265" Price="1.98"
➥Quantity="1"/>
    <Product Name="Laundry Detergent" Id="148202" Price="8.82"
➥Quantity="1"/>
  </Order>

</po:PurchaseOrder>
```

By assigning a namespace to the `<PurchaseOrder>` element, we associate that element with the global `<PurchaseOrder>` element declaration within our XML schema. Notice, however, that the `<PurchaseOrder>` element is the only qualified element. If you look back at our `<schema>` element from Listing 4.4, you'll see two attributes: `elementFormDefault` and `attributeFormDefault`. These attributes can possess one of two values:

- `qualified`
- `unqualified`

If a value of `unqualified` is specified or the `elementFormDefault` and `attributeFormDefault` attributes are omitted, the elements or attributes that are not globally declared within the schema (those that are not children of the `<schema>` element) do not require a prefix within the XML instance document. However, if a value of `qualified` is specified, all elements and attributes must have a prefix associated with them. For instance, we could make a change to our `PurchaseOrder` schema and specify that the `elementFormDefault` and `attributeFormDefault` attributes have a value of `qualified`, as shown in Listing 4.6.

LISTING 4.6 `PurchaseOrder2.xsd` Contains the Schema Definition for `PurchaseOrder.xml` with a Target Namespace and Qualified Elements and Attributes

```
<xsd:schema targetNamespace="http://www.eps-software.com/poschema"
➥xmlns:xsd="http://www.w3.org/2001/XMLSchema"
➥xmlns="http://www.eps-software.com/poschema"
```

LISTING 4.6 continued

```
➥elementFormDefault="qualified"
➥attributeFormDefault="qualified">

  <xsd:annotation>
    <xsd:documentation>
      Purchase Order schema for an online grocery store.
    </xsd:documentation>
  </xsd:annotation>

  <xsd:element name="PurchaseOrder" type="PurchaseOrderType"/>

  <xsd:complexType name="PurchaseOrderType">
    <xsd:all>
      <xsd:element name="ShippingInformation" type="InfoType"
➥minOccurs="1" maxOccurs="1"/>
      <xsd:element name="BillingInformation" type="InfoType"
➥minOccurs="1" maxOccurs="1"/>
      <xsd:element name="Order" type="OrderType"
➥minOccurs="1" maxOccurs="1"/>
    </xsd:all>
    <xsd:attribute name="Tax">
      <xsd:simpleType>
        <xsd:restriction base="xsd:decimal">
          <xsd:fractionDigits value="2"/>
        </xsd:restriction>
      </xsd:simpleType>
    </xsd:attribute>
    <xsd:attribute name="Total">
      <xsd:simpleType>
        <xsd:restriction base="xsd:decimal">
          <xsd:fractionDigits value="2"/>
        </xsd:restriction>
      </xsd:simpleType>
    </xsd:attribute>
  </xsd:complexType>

  <xsd:group name="ShippingInfoGroup">
    <xsd:all>
      <xsd:element name="DeliveryDate" type="DateType"/>
      <xsd:element name="Method" type="DeliveryMethodType"/>
    </xsd:all>
  </xsd:group>

  <xsd:group name="BillingInfoGroup">
    <xsd:all>
      <xsd:element name="BillingDate" type="DateType"/>
      <xsd:element name="PaymentMethod" type="PaymentMethodType"/>
    </xsd:all>
  </xsd:group>
```

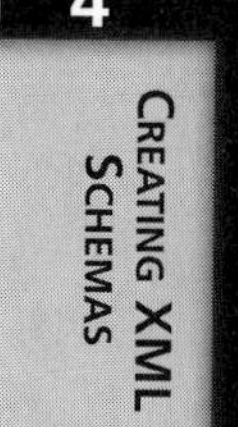

LISTING 4.6 continued

```
  <xsd:complexType name="InfoType">
    <xsd:sequence>
      <xsd:element name="Name" minOccurs="1" maxOccurs="1">
        <xsd:simpleType>
          <xsd:restriction base="xsd:string"/>
        </xsd:simpleType>
      </xsd:element>
      <xsd:element name="Address" type="AddressType" minOccurs="1"
➥maxOccurs="1"/>
      <xsd:choice minOccurs="1" maxOccurs="1">
        <xsd:group ref="BillingInfoGroup"/>
        <xsd:group ref="ShippingInfoGroup"/>
      </xsd:choice>
    </xsd:sequence>
  </xsd:complexType>

  <xsd:simpleType name="DateType">
    <xsd:restriction base="xsd:date"/>
  </xsd:simpleType>

  <xsd:simpleType name="DeliveryMethodType">
    <xsd:restriction base="xsd:string">
      <xsd:enumeration value="USPS"/>
      <xsd:enumeration value="UPS"/>
      <xsd:enumeration value="FedEx"/>
      <xsd:enumeration value="DHL"/>
      <xsd:enumeration value="Other"/>
    </xsd:restriction>
  </xsd:simpleType>

  <xsd:simpleType name="PaymentMethodType">
    <xsd:restriction base="xsd:string">
      <xsd:enumeration value="Check"/>
      <xsd:enumeration value="Cash"/>
      <xsd:enumeration value="Credit Card"/>
      <xsd:enumeration value="Debit Card"/>
      <xsd:enumeration value="Other"/>
    </xsd:restriction>
  </xsd:simpleType>

  <xsd:complexType name="AddressType">
    <xsd:all>
      <xsd:element name="Street" minOccurs="1">
        <xsd:simpleType>
          <xsd:restriction base="xsd:string"/>
        </xsd:simpleType>
      </xsd:element>
      <xsd:element name="City" minOccurs="1" maxOccurs="1">
        <xsd:simpleType>
```

LISTING 4.6 continued

```
          <xsd:restriction base="xsd:string"/>
        </xsd:simpleType>
      </xsd:element>
      <xsd:element name="State" type="StateType" minOccurs="1"
➥maxOccurs="1"/>
      <xsd:element name="Zip" type="ZipType" minOccurs="1"
➥maxOccurs="1"/>
    </xsd:all>
  </xsd:complexType>

  <xsd:simpleType name="ZipType">
    <xsd:restriction base="xsd:string">
      <xsd:minLength value="5"/>
      <xsd:maxLength value="10"/>
      <xsd:pattern value="[0-9]{5}(-[0-9]{4})?"/>
    </xsd:restriction>
  </xsd:simpleType>

  <xsd:simpleType name="StateType">
    <xsd:restriction base="xsd:string">
      <xsd:length value="2"/>
      <xsd:enumeration value="AR"/>
      <xsd:enumeration value="LA"/>
      <xsd:enumeration value="MS"/>
      <xsd:enumeration value="OK"/>
      <xsd:enumeration value="TX"/>
    </xsd:restriction>
  </xsd:simpleType>

  <xsd:complexType name="OrderType">
    <xsd:sequence>
      <xsd:element name="Product" type="ProductType"
➥minOccurs="1" maxOccurs="unbounded"/>
    </xsd:sequence>
    <xsd:attribute name="SubTotal">
      <xsd:simpleType>
        <xsd:restriction base="xsd:decimal">
          <xsd:fractionDigits value="2"/>
        </xsd:restriction>
      </xsd:simpleType>
    </xsd:attribute>
    <xsd:attribute name="ItemsSold" type="xsd:positiveInteger"/>
  </xsd:complexType>

  <xsd:complexType name="ProductType">
    <xsd:attribute name="Name" type="xsd:string"/>
    <xsd:attribute name="Id" type="xsd:positiveInteger"/>
    <xsd:attribute name="Price">
      <xsd:simpleType>
```

LISTING 4.6 continued

```
        <xsd:restriction base="xsd:decimal">
          <xsd:fractionDigits value="2"/>
        </xsd:restriction>
      </xsd:simpleType>
    </xsd:attribute>
    <xsd:attribute name="Quantity" type="xsd:positiveInteger"/>
  </xsd:complexType>

</xsd:schema>
```

Based on the `PurchaseOrder` schema in Listing 4.6, the new version of the `PurchaseOrder` XML would appear as shown in Listing 4.7.

LISTING 4.7 `PurchaseOrder2.xml` Contains a Sample Purchase Order Based on the `PurchaseOrder2` Schema Definition in `PurchaseOrder2.xsd`

```
<po:PurchaseOrder xmlns:po="http://www.eps-software.com/poschema"
  xmlns:xsi="http://www.w3.org/2001/XMLSchema-instance"
  xsi:schemaLocation="purchaseorder2.xsd"
  Tax="5.76" Total="75.77">

   <po:ShippingInformation>
      <po:Method>USPS</po:Method>
      <po:DeliveryDate>08/12/2001</po:DeliveryDate>
      <po:Name>Dillon Larsen</po:Name>
      <po:Address>
         <po:Street>123 Jones Rd.</po:Street>
         <po:City>Houston</po:City>
         <po:State>TX</po:State>
         <po:Zip>77381</po:Zip>
      </po:Address>
   </po:ShippingInformation>

   <po:BillingInformation>
      <po:PaymentMethod>Credit Card</po:PaymentMethod>
      <po:BillingDate>08/09/2001</po:BillingDate>
      <po:Name>Madi Larsen</po:Name>
      <po:Address>
         <po:Street>123 Jones Rd.</po:Street>
         <po:City>Houston</po:City>
         <po:State>TX</po:State>
         <po:Zip>77381</po:Zip>
      </po:Address>
   </po:BillingInformation>

   <po:Order SubTotal="70.01" ItemsSold="17">
      <po:Product Name="Baby Swiss" Id="702890" Price="2.89" Quantity="1"/>
```

LISTING 4.7 continued

```
      <po:Product Name="Hard Salami" Id="302340" Price="2.34" Quantity="1"/>
      <po:Product Name="Turkey" Id="905800" Price="5.80" Quantity="1"/>
      <po:Product Name="Caesar Salad" Id="991687" Price="2.38" Quantity="2"/>
      <po:Product Name="Chicken Strips" Id="133382" Price="2.50" Quantity="1"/>
      <po:Product Name="Bread" Id="298678" Price="1.08" Quantity="1"/>
      <po:Product Name="Rolls" Id="002399" Price="2.24" Quantity="1"/>
      <po:Product Name="Cereal" Id="066510" Price="2.18" Quantity="1"/>
      <po:Product Name="Jalapenos" Id="101005" Price="1.97" Quantity="1"/>
      <po:Product Name="Tuna" Id="000118" Price="0.92" Quantity="3"/>
      <po:Product Name="Mayonnaise" Id="126860" Price="1.98" Quantity="1"/>
      <po:Product Name="Top Sirloin" Id="290502" Price="9.97" Quantity="2"/>
      <po:Product Name="Soup" Id="001254" Price="1.33" Quantity="1"/>
      <po:Product Name="Granola Bar" Id="026460" Price="2.14" Quantity="2"/>
      <po:Product Name="Chocolate Milk" Id="024620" Price="1.58" Quantity="2"/>
      <po:Product Name="Spaghetti" Id="000265" Price="1.98" Quantity="1"/>
      <po:Product Name="Laundry Detergent" Id="148202" Price="8.82"
➥Quantity="1"/>
   </po:Order>

</po:PurchaseOrder>
```

Note

Just because you may specify a value of `qualified` for `elementFormDefault` or `attributeFormDefault` doesn't mean the other attribute must be the same. You could specify that elements within the schema must be "qualified," but attributes may be "unqualified," and vice versa.

"Inheriting" from Other Schemas

As you can see from the XML schema in Listing 4.6, things can get rather complex and long. Plus, you may wish, at times, to define a common piece for multiple XML schemas and maintain and extend it separately from the individual schemas that need it. For this reason, the W3C included the `<include>` and `<import>` elements in the XML Schema Definition Language. Through the use of these elements, you can effectively "inherit" elements and attributes from the referenced schema. For instance, if you look at Listing 4.3, you can see the declaration of an `<Address>` element. We may want to use this same element over and over again in multiple schemas. However, we wouldn't want to redefine this element in each schema. Instead, it would be nice to have that element declaration and type definition within a separate document.

As long as the targetNamespace attribute on the <schema> element of both schemas match, or the targetNamespace attribute for the <schema> element in the referenced XML schema is empty, you can "inherit" any and all elements and attributes within the XML schema using the <include> element. The <import> element doesn't care what the target namespace is in the referenced schema.

Going back Listing 4.3, we can separate out the <Address> element declaration (and the various type definitions that go along with it) into its own schema, as shown in Listing 4.8.

LISTING 4.8 Address.xsd Contains a Sample Address Schema Definition

```
<xsd:schema xmlns:xsd="http://www.w3.org/2001/XMLSchema">

  <xsd:annotation>
    <xsd:documentation>
      Address schema for a typical US address
    </xsd:documentation>
  </xsd:annotation>

  <xsd:element name="Address" type="AddressType"/>

  <xsd:complexType name="AddressType">
    <xsd:all>
      <xsd:element name="Street" minOccurs="1">
        <xsd:simpleType>
          <xsd:restriction base="xsd:string"/>
        </xsd:simpleType>
      </xsd:element>
      <xsd:element name="City" minOccurs="1" maxOccurs="1">
        <xsd:simpleType>
          <xsd:restriction base="xsd:string"/>
        </xsd:simpleType>
      </xsd:element>
      <xsd:element name="State" type="StateType" minOccurs="1" maxOccurs="1"/>
      <xsd:element name="Zip" type="ZipType" minOccurs="1" maxOccurs="1"/>
    </xsd:all>
  </xsd:complexType>

  <xsd:simpleType name="ZipType">
    <xsd:restriction base="xsd:string">
      <xsd:minLength value="5"/>
      <xsd:maxLength value="10"/>
      <xsd:pattern value="[0-9]{5}(-[0-9]{4})?"/>
    </xsd:restriction>
  </xsd:simpleType>
```

LISTING 4.8 continued

```
  <xsd:simpleType name="StateType">
    <xsd:restriction base="xsd:string">
      <xsd:length value="2"/>
      <xsd:enumeration value="AR"/>
      <xsd:enumeration value="LA"/>
      <xsd:enumeration value="MS"/>
      <xsd:enumeration value="OK"/>
      <xsd:enumeration value="TX"/>
    </xsd:restriction>
  </xsd:simpleType>

</xsd:schema>
```

Notice in the new `Address` schema that we did not specify a value for the `targetNamespace` attribute. This will allow us to include the schema in a modified version of the `PurchaseOrder` schema by using the `<include>` element as shown in Listing 4.9.

LISTING 4.9 `PurchaseOrder3.xsd` Includes the Contents of *`Address.xsd`*

```
<xsd:schema xmlns:xsd="http://www.w3.org/2001/XMLSchema">

  <xsd:include schemaLocation="Address.xsd"/>

  <xsd:annotation>
    <xsd:documentation>
      Purchase Order schema for an online grocery store.
    </xsd:documentation>
  </xsd:annotation>

  <xsd:element name="PurchaseOrder" type="PurchaseOrderType"/>

  <xsd:complexType name="PurchaseOrderType">
    <xsd:all>
      <xsd:element name="ShippingInformation" type="InfoType"
➥minOccurs="1" maxOccurs="1"/>
      <xsd:element name="BillingInformation" type="InfoType"
➥minOccurs="1" maxOccurs="1"/>
      <xsd:element name="Order" type="OrderType" minOccurs="1" maxOccurs="1"/>
    </xsd:all>
    <xsd:attribute name="Tax">
      <xsd:simpleType>
        <xsd:restriction base="xsd:decimal">
          <xsd:fractionDigits value="2"/>
        </xsd:restriction>
      </xsd:simpleType>
    </xsd:attribute>
```

LISTING 4.9 continued

```
    <xsd:attribute name="Total">
      <xsd:simpleType>
        <xsd:restriction base="xsd:decimal">
          <xsd:fractionDigits value="2"/>
        </xsd:restriction>
      </xsd:simpleType>
    </xsd:attribute>
  </xsd:complexType>

  <xsd:group name="ShippingInfoGroup">
    <xsd:all>
      <xsd:element name="DeliveryDate" type="DateType"/>
      <xsd:element name="Method" type="DeliveryMethodType"/>
    </xsd:all>
  </xsd:group>

  <xsd:group name="BillingInfoGroup">
    <xsd:all>
      <xsd:element name="BillingDate" type="DateType"/>
      <xsd:element name="PaymentMethod" type="PaymentMethodType"/>
    </xsd:all>
  </xsd:group>

  <xsd:complexType name="InfoType">
    <xsd:sequence>
      <xsd:element name="Name" minOccurs="1" maxOccurs="1">
        <xsd:simpleType>
          <xsd:restriction base="xsd:string"/>
        </xsd:simpleType>
      </xsd:element>
      <xsd:element ref="Address" minOccurs="1" maxOccurs="1"/>
      <xsd:choice>
        <xsd:group ref="BillingInfoGroup"/>
        <xsd:group ref="ShippingInfoGroup"/>
      </xsd:choice>
    </xsd:sequence>
  </xsd:complexType>

  <xsd:simpleType name="DateType">
    <xsd:restriction base="xsd:date"/>
  </xsd:simpleType>

  <xsd:simpleType name="DeliveryMethodType">
    <xsd:restriction base="xsd:string">
      <xsd:enumeration value="USPS"/>
      <xsd:enumeration value="UPS"/>
      <xsd:enumeration value="FedEx"/>
      <xsd:enumeration value="DHL"/>
      <xsd:enumeration value="Other"/>
```

LISTING 4.9 continued

```
    </xsd:restriction>
  </xsd:simpleType>

  <xsd:simpleType name="PaymentMethodType">
    <xsd:restriction base="xsd:string">
      <xsd:enumeration value="Check"/>
      <xsd:enumeration value="Cash"/>
      <xsd:enumeration value="Credit Card"/>
      <xsd:enumeration value="Debit Card"/>
      <xsd:enumeration value="Other"/>
    </xsd:restriction>
  </xsd:simpleType>

  <xsd:complexType name="OrderType">
    <xsd:sequence>
      <xsd:element name="Product" type="ProductType"
➥minOccurs="1" maxOccurs="unbounded"/>
    </xsd:sequence>
    <xsd:attribute name="SubTotal">
      <xsd:simpleType>
        <xsd:restriction base="xsd:decimal">
          <xsd:fractionDigits value="2"/>
        </xsd:restriction>
      </xsd:simpleType>
    </xsd:attribute>
    <xsd:attribute name="ItemsSold" type="xsd:positiveInteger"/>
  </xsd:complexType>

  <xsd:complexType name="ProductType">
    <xsd:attribute name="Name" type="xsd:string"/>
    <xsd:attribute name="Id" type="xsd:positiveInteger"/>
    <xsd:attribute name="Price">
      <xsd:simpleType>
        <xsd:restriction base="xsd:decimal">
          <xsd:fractionDigits value="2"/>
        </xsd:restriction>
      </xsd:simpleType>
    </xsd:attribute>
    <xsd:attribute name="Quantity" type="xsd:positiveInteger"/>
  </xsd:complexType>

</xsd:schema>
```


Because we did not explicitly declare a target namespace for the `Address` schema, we can include it within the new `PurchaseOrder` schema. Because there is no reference to a namespace, however, we can simply refer to the declared `<Address>` element in the `Address` schema without having to qualify it. However, to prevent schemas from getting confused with other <Address> elements from other schemas, we may want to specify a value for the targetNamespace attribute for our Address schema as shown in Listing 4.10.

LISTING 4.10 Address1.xsd Modified to Specify a Target Namespace

```
<xsd:schema targetNamespace=http://www.eps-software.com/addressschema
➥xmlns:xsd="http://www.w3.org/2001/XMLSchema"
➥xmlns="http://www.eps-software.com/addressschema">

  <xsd:annotation>
    <xsd:documentation>
      Address schema for a typical US address
    </xsd:documentation>
  </xsd:annotation>

  <xsd:element name="Address" type="AddressType"/>

  <xsd:complexType name="AddressType">
    <xsd:all>
      <xsd:element name="Street" minOccurs="1">
        <xsd:simpleType>
          <xsd:restriction base="xsd:string"/>
        </xsd:simpleType>
      </xsd:element>
      <xsd:element name="City" minOccurs="1" maxOccurs="1">
        <xsd:simpleType>
          <xsd:restriction base="xsd:string"/>
        </xsd:simpleType>
      </xsd:element>
      <xsd:element name="State" type="StateType" minOccurs="1" maxOccurs="1"/>
      <xsd:element name="Zip" type="ZipType" minOccurs="1" maxOccurs="1"/>
    </xsd:all>
  </xsd:complexType>

  <xsd:simpleType name="ZipType">
    <xsd:restriction base="xsd:string">
      <xsd:minLength value="5"/>
      <xsd:maxLength value="10"/>
      <xsd:pattern value="[0-9]{5}(-[0-9]{4})?"/>
    </xsd:restriction>
  </xsd:simpleType>

  <xsd:simpleType name="StateType">
    <xsd:restriction base="xsd:string">
      <xsd:length value="2"/>
      <xsd:enumeration value="AR"/>
      <xsd:enumeration value="LA"/>
      <xsd:enumeration value="MS"/>
```

LISTING 4.10 continued

```
      <xsd:enumeration value="OK"/>
      <xsd:enumeration value="TX"/>
    </xsd:restriction>
  </xsd:simpleType>

</xsd:schema>
```

Because we have just specified a target namespace for the `Address` schema, unless the target namespace for the `PurchaseOrder` schema is the same, we can no longer use the `<include>` element to “inherit” the element declarations from the `Address` schema. However, we can use the `<import>` element to include the newly modified `Address` schema as shown in Listing 4.11.

LISTING 4.11 `PurchaseOrder4.xsd` "Imports" the Contents of `Address1.xsd`

```
<xsd:schema xmlns:adr="http://www.eps-software.com/addressschema"
➥xmlns:xsd="http://www.w3.org/2001/XMLSchema">

  <xsd:import namespace=http://www.eps-software.com/addressschema
➥schemaLocation="Address1.xsd"/>

  <xsd:annotation>
    <xsd:documentation>
      Purchase Order schema for an online grocery store.
    </xsd:documentation>
  </xsd:annotation>

  <xsd:element name="PurchaseOrder" type="PurchaseOrderType"/>

  <xsd:complexType name="PurchaseOrderType">
    <xsd:all>
      <xsd:element name="ShippingInformation" type="InfoType"/>
      <xsd:element name="BillingInformation" type="InfoType"/>
      <xsd:element name="Order" type="OrderType"/>
    </xsd:all>
    <xsd:attribute name="Tax">
      <xsd:simpleType>
        <xsd:restriction base="xsd:decimal">
          <xsd:fractionDigits value="2"/>
        </xsd:restriction>
      </xsd:simpleType>
    </xsd:attribute>
    <xsd:attribute name="Total">
      <xsd:simpleType>
        <xsd:restriction base="xsd:decimal">
          <xsd:fractionDigits value="2"/>
        </xsd:restriction>
```

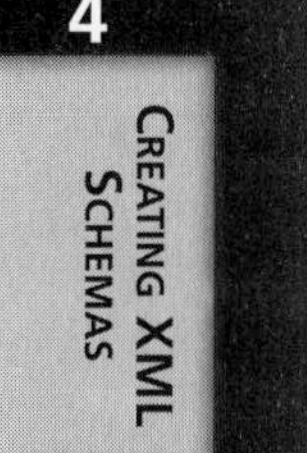

LISTING 4.11 continued

```
      </xsd:simpleType>
    </xsd:attribute>
  </xsd:complexType>

  <xsd:group name="ShippingInfoGroup">
    <xsd:all>
      <xsd:element name="DeliveryDate" type="DateType"/>
      <xsd:element name="Method" type="DeliveryMethodType"/>
    </xsd:all>
  </xsd:group>

  <xsd:group name="BillingInfoGroup">
    <xsd:all>
      <xsd:element name="BillingDate" type="DateType"/>
      <xsd:element name="PaymentMethod" type="PaymentMethodType"/>
    </xsd:all>
  </xsd:group>

  <xsd:complexType name="InfoType">
    <xsd:sequence>
      <xsd:element name="Name">
        <xsd:simpleType>
          <xsd:restriction base="xsd:string"/>
        </xsd:simpleType>
      </xsd:element>
      <xsd:element ref="adr:Address"/>
      <xsd:choice>
        <xsd:group ref="BillingInfoGroup"/>
        <xsd:group ref="ShippingInfoGroup"/>
      </xsd:choice>
    </xsd:sequence>
  </xsd:complexType>

  <xsd:simpleType name="DateType">
    <xsd:restriction base="xsd:date"/>
  </xsd:simpleType>

  <xsd:simpleType name="DeliveryMethodType">
    <xsd:restriction base="xsd:string">
      <xsd:enumeration value="USPS"/>
      <xsd:enumeration value="UPS"/>
      <xsd:enumeration value="FedEx"/>
      <xsd:enumeration value="DHL"/>
      <xsd:enumeration value="Other"/>
    </xsd:restriction>
  </xsd:simpleType>

  <xsd:simpleType name="PaymentMethodType">
    <xsd:restriction base="xsd:string">
```

LISTING 4.11 continued

```
      <xsd:enumeration value="Check"/>
      <xsd:enumeration value="Cash"/>
      <xsd:enumeration value="Credit Card"/>
      <xsd:enumeration value="Debit Card"/>
      <xsd:enumeration value="Other"/>
    </xsd:restriction>
  </xsd:simpleType>

  <xsd:complexType name="OrderType">
    <xsd:sequence>
      <xsd:element name="Product" type="ProductType"
➥maxOccurs="unbounded"/>
    </xsd:sequence>
    <xsd:attribute name="SubTotal">
      <xsd:simpleType>
        <xsd:restriction base="xsd:decimal">
          <xsd:fractionDigits value="2"/>
        </xsd:restriction>
      </xsd:simpleType>
    </xsd:attribute>
    <xsd:attribute name="ItemsSold" type="xsd:positiveInteger"/>
  </xsd:complexType>

  <xsd:complexType name="ProductType">
    <xsd:attribute name="Name" type="xsd:string"/>
    <xsd:attribute name="Id" type="xsd:positiveInteger"/>
    <xsd:attribute name="Price">
      <xsd:simpleType>
        <xsd:restriction base="xsd:decimal">
          <xsd:fractionDigits value="2"/>
        </xsd:restriction>
      </xsd:simpleType>
    </xsd:attribute>
    <xsd:attribute name="Quantity" type="xsd:positiveInteger"/>
  </xsd:complexType>

</xsd:schema>
```

You can see that the <import> element supports two attributes: namespace and schemaLocation. You'll also notice the declaration of the adr namespace within the <schema> element. This namespace declaration is necessary for the <import> element to work correctly. The namespace attribute on the <import> element refers to a namespace that has been previously declared within the <schema> element.

Note

The major difference between the `<include>` and `<import>` elements within the XML Schema Definition Language is that the `<import>` element allows you to include schema components from schemas with different target namespaces, which will allow you to use schema components from any schema.

Summary

An XML schema consists of components, primarily elements, attributes, and type definitions. These components are assembled within an XML schema to indicate whether an XML document conforms to the schema specified. In May 2001, the W3C finalized its recommendation for the XML Schema Definition Language, which provides the individual language elements needed to create an XML schema.

The XML Schema Definition Language provides a very powerful and flexible way in which to validate XML documents. It includes everything from declaring elements and attributes to "inheriting" elements from other schemas, from defining complex element definitions to defining restrictions for even the simplest of data types. This gives the XML schema author such control over specifying a valid construction for an XML document that there is almost nothing that cannot be defined with an XML schema.

DTDs and XML schemas are two very different means to the same end: providing a "roadmap" with which to validate XML documents. However, so much more detail can be specified with an XML schema than with a DTD. Schemas support varying data types and namespaces, and they allow the author to define the structure of an XML document using XML syntax. DTDs are limited to character data types, provide no support for namespaces, and define the structure of an XML document using a very archaic and cumbersome standard. Because an XML schema is nothing more than an XML document in itself, it can be loaded into an XML parser just like any other XML document that allows applications to provide added functionality with a very common interface through the XMLDOM.

CHAPTER 5

The X-Files: XPath, XPointer, and XLink

In This Chapter

Now that you have a decent understanding of what XML is, the next obvious question is how can we find the pieces of information we desire. The answer is the XML Path Language, or *XPath*. The XML Path Language provides a standard syntax for querying an XML document for specific pieces of information. This syntax provides an independent mechanism for "querying" or locating the desired elements or attributes within the XML document.

XPath, itself, is a very powerful mechanism for finding the elements or attributes you want to work with. Imagine if you had to traverse the hierarchy one element and one attribute at a time and perform a conditional test to see whether the current element or attribute matched the search criteria you specified. For small XML documents, you probably wouldn't notice much. However, for larger XML documents, the speed issue immediately appears. This is one of the reasons XPath was created—to reduce the amount of time to find the elements and attributes desired by an author or developer.

XLink allows an XML document to specify a link from the current document to another document in another location. This facilitates the dispersion and compartmentalization of data much the same way a normalized database would. You could think of each document as a table within a database and the XLink specification of each document as a relation between the tables. This means instead of having to duplicate information among the documents, you could specify information once and be able to access it via XLink.

XPointer expands on the functionality of XLink by building on the XPath specification and identifying a node or node set to link to in the target document. This provides much the same functionality as a foreign key within a table of a database. Because the information within a normalized database exists in one location only, it becomes necessary to relate to that information to prevent duplication of information. XPointers provide the same functionality within a group of XML documents.

In this chapter, you will learn

- What namespaces are and how they can be useful within an XML document
- The relationship among XPath, XLink, and XPointer
- What XPath is and how it can be used to find the desired node(s) within an XML document
- The syntax of an XPath expression
- How XPointer can be used to locate specific nodes within a related XML document
- How XLink can be used to link various XML documents together

XPath

The XML Path Language (XPath) is a standard for creating expressions that can be used to find specific pieces of information within an XML document. XPath expressions are used by both XSLT (for which XPath provides the core functionality) and XPointer to locate a set of nodes. To understand how XPath works, it helps to imagine an XML document as a tree of nodes consisting of both elements and attributes. An XPath expression can then be considered a sort of roadmap that indicates the branches of the tree to follow and what limbs hold the information desired. The complete documentation for the XPath recommendation can be found at `http://www.w3c.org/TR/xpath`.

XPath expressions have the ability to locate nodes based on the nodes' type, name, or value or by the relationship of the nodes to other nodes within the XML document. In addition to being able to find nodes based on these criteria, an XPath expression can also return any of the following:

- A node set
- A Boolean value
- A string value
- A numeric value

XML documents are, in essence, a hierarchical tree of nodes. Curiously, there is a similarity between URLs and XPath expressions. Why? Quite simply, URLs represent a navigation path of a hierarchical file system, and XPath expressions represent a navigation path for a hierarchical tree of nodes.

Operators and Special Characters

XPath expressions are composed using a set of operators and special characters, each with its own meaning. Table 5.1 lists the various operators and special characters used within the XML Path Language.

TABLE 5.1 Operators and Special Characters for the XML Path Language

Operators and Special Characters	*Description*
/	Selects the children from the node set on the left side of this character
//	Specifies that the matching node set should be located at any level within the XML document

TABLE 5.1 continued

Operators and Special Characters	*Description*
`.`	Specifies the current context should be used
`*`	A wildcard character that selects all elements or attributes regardless of name
`@`	Selects an attribute
`:`	Namespace separator
`()`	Indicates a grouping within an XPath expression
`[`*`expression`*`]`	Indicates a filter expression
`[`*`n`*`]`	Indicates that the node with the specified index should be selected
`+`	Addition operator
`-`	Subtraction operator
`div`	Division operator
`*`	Multiplication operator
`mod`	Returns the remainder of a division operation

Table 5.1 only provides a list of operators and special characters that can be used within an XPath expression. However, the table does not indicate what the order of precedence is. The priority for evaluating XPath expressions is as follows:

1. Grouping
2. Filters
3. Path operations

Note

Keep the precedence order in mind when constructing your XPath queries because the results can be dramatically different when a grouping or filter is applied within an expression.

XPath Syntax

The XML Path Language provides a declarative notation, termed a *pattern*, used to select the desired set of nodes from XML documents. Each pattern describes a set of matching nodes to select from a hierarchical XML document. Each pattern describes a "navigation" path to the desired set of nodes similar to the Uniform Resource Identifier (URI) syntax. However, instead of navigating a file system, the XML Path Language navigates a hierarchical tree of nodes within an XML document.

Each "query" of an XML document occurs from a particular starting node that defines the context for the query. The context for the query has a very large impact on the results. For instance, the pattern that locates a node from the root of an XML document will most likely be a very different pattern when looking for the same node from somewhere else in the hierarchy.

As mentioned earlier in this chapter, one possible result from performing an XPath query is a node set, or a collection of nodes matching a specified search criteria. To receive these results, a "location path" is needed to locate the result nodes. These location paths select the resulting node set relative to the current context. A location path is, itself, made up of one or more location steps. Each step is further comprised of three pieces:

- An axis
- A node test
- A predicate

Therefore, the basic syntax for an XPath expression would be something like this:

```
axis::node test[predicate]
```

Using this basic syntax and the XML document in Listing 5.1, we could locate all the <c> nodes by using the following XPath expression:

```
/a/b/child::*
```

Alternatively, we could issue the following abbreviated version of the preceding expression:

```
/a/b/c
```

All XPath expressions are dependant on the current context. The context is the current location within the tree of nodes. Therefore, if we're currently on the second <b> element within the XML document in Listing 5.1, we can select all the <c> elements contained within that <b> element by using the following XPath expression:

```
./c
```

This is what's known as a "relative" XPath expression.

Axes

The axis portion of the location step identifies the hierarchical relationship for the desired nodes from the current context. An axis for a location step could be any of the items listed within Table 5.2.

TABLE 5.2 XPath Axes for a Location Step

Axis	*Description*
`ancestor`	Specifies that the query should locate the ancestors of the current context node, which includes the parent node, the parent's parent node, and ultimately the root node.
`ancestor-or-self`	Indicates that in addition to the ancestors of the current context node, the context node should also be included in the resulting node set.
`attribute`	Specifies that the attributes of the current context node are desired.
`child`	Specifies that the immediate children of the current context node are desired.
`descendant`	Specifies that in addition to the immediate children of the current context node, the children's children are also desired.
`descendant-or-self`	Indicates that in addition to the descendants of the current context node, the current context node is also desired.
`following`	Specifies that nodes in the same document as the current context node that appear after the current context node should be selected.
`following-sibling`	Specifies that all the following siblings of the current context node should be selected.
`namespace`	Specifies that all the nodes within the same namespace as the current context node should be selected.
`parent`	Selects the parent of the current context node.
`preceding`	Selects the nodes within the document that appear before the current context node.
`preceding-sibling`	Selects the siblings of the current context node that appear before the current context node.
`self`	Selects the current context node.

All the axes in Table 5.2 depend on the context of the current node. This raises the question, How do you know what the current context node is? The easiest way to explain this is through example, so let's use the XML document shown in Listing 5.1 as the basis for the explanation of how the current context node is defined.

LISTING 5.1 `Sample1.xml` Contains a Simple XML Document

```
<a>
  <b>
    <c d="Attrib 1">Text 1</c>
    <c d="Attrib 2">Text 2</c>
    <c d="Attrib 3">Text 3</c>
  </b>
  <b>
    <c d="Attrib 4">Text 4</c>
    <c d="Attrib 5">Text 5</c>
  </b>
  <b>
    <c d="Attrib 6">Text 6</c>
    <c d="Attrib 7">Text 7</c>
    <c d="Attrib 8">Text 8</c>
    <c d="Attrib 9">Text 9</c>
  </b>
  <b>
    <c d="Attrib 10">Text 10</c>
    <c d="Attrib 11">Text 11</c>
    <c d="Attrib 12">Text 12</c>
  </b>
</a>
```

Using this sample XML document as a reference, and the following XPath query, we can examine how the current context node is determined:

```
/a/b[1]/child::*]
```

The preceding XPath query consists of three location steps, the first of which is `a`. The second location step in the XPath query is `b[1]`, which selects the first `<b>` element within the `<a>` element. The final location step is `child::*`, which selects all (signified by `*`) child elements of the first `<b>` element contained within the `<a>` element. It is important to understand that each location step has a different context node. For the first location step, the current context node is the root of the XML document. It should be noted that the node `<a>` is not the root of the XML document; it's the first element within the hierarchy, but the root of an XML document is denoted by "`/`" as the first character within an XPath query. The context for the second location step is the node `<a>`. The third location step has the first `<b>` node as its context.

Now that you have a better understanding of how the context for an XPath query axis is defined, we can look at the resulting node sets for the axes described in Table 5.2. Using the XML document in Listing 5.1, Table 5.3 lists some XPath queries with the various axes and the resulting node sets.

TABLE 5.3 XPath Queries and the Resulting Node Sets

XPath Query	*Resulting Node Set*
`a/b[1]/c[1]/ancestor::*`	<a> <b> <c d="Attrib 1">Text 1</c> <c d="Attrib 2">Text 2</c> <c d="Attrib 3">Text 3</c> </b> <b> <c d="Attrib 5">Text 5</c> </b> <b> <c d="Attrib 6">Text 6</c> <c d="Attrib 7">Text 7</c> <c d="Attrib 8">Text 8</c> <c d="Attrib 9">Text 9</c> </b> <b> <c d="Attrib 10">Text 10</c> <c d="Attrib 11">Text 11</c> <c d="Attrib 12">Text 12</c> </b> </a> <b> <c d="Attrib 1">Text 1</c> <c d="Attrib 2">Text 2</c> <c d="Attrib 3">Text 3</c> </b>
`a/b[1]/c[1]/ancestor-or-self::*`	<a> <b> <c d="Attrib 1">Text 1</c> <c d="Attrib 2">Text 2</c> <c d="Attrib 3">Text 3</c> </b> <b> <c d="Attrib 4">Text 4</c>

TABLE 5.3 continued

XPath Query	*Resulting Node Set*
	<c d="Attrib 5">Text 5</c> </b> <b> <c d="Attrib 6">Text 6</c> <c d="Attrib 7">Text 7</c> <c d="Attrib 8">Text 8</c> <c d="Attrib 9">Text 9</c> </b> <b> <c d="Attrib 10">Text 10</c> <c d="Attrib 11">Text 11</c> <c d="Attrib 12">Text 12</c> </b> </a> <b> <c d="Attrib 1">Text 1</c> <c d="Attrib 2">Text 2</c> <c d="Attrib 3">Text 3</c> </b> <c d="Attrib 1">Text 1</c>
`a/b[1]/c[1]/attribute::*`	d="Attrib 1"
`a/b[1]/child::*`	<c d="Attrib 1">Text 1</c> <c d="Attrib 2">Text 2</c> <c d="Attrib 3">Text 3</c>
`a/descendant::*`	<b> <c d="Attrib 1">Text 1</c> <c d="Attrib 2">Text 2</c> <c d="Attrib 3">Text 3</c> </b> <c d="Attrib 1">Text 1</c> <c d="Attrib 2">Text 2</c> <c d="Attrib 3">Text 3</c> <b> <c d="Attrib 4">Text 4</c> <c d="Attrib 5">Text 5</c> </b> <c d="Attrib 4">Text 4</c> <c d="Attrib 5">Text 5</c>

TABLE 5.3 continued

XPath Query	*Resulting Node Set*
	<b> <c d="Attrib 6">Text 6</c> <c d="Attrib 7">Text 7</c> <c d="Attrib 8">Text 8</c> <c d="Attrib 9">Text 9</c> </b> <c d="Attrib 6">Text 6</c> <c d="Attrib 7">Text 7</c> <c d="Attrib 8">Text 8</c> <c d="Attrib 9">Text 9</c> <b> <c d="Attrib 10">Text 10</c> <c d="Attrib 11">Text 11</c> <c d="Attrib 12">Text 12</c> </b> <c d="Attrib 10">Text 10</c> <c d="Attrib 11">Text 11</c> <c d="Attrib 12">Text 12</c>
`a/descendant-or-self::*`	<a> <b> <c d="Attrib 1">Text 1</c> <c d="Attrib 2">Text 2</c> <c d="Attrib 3">Text 3</c> </b> <b> <c d="Attrib 4">Text 4</c> <c d="Attrib 5">Text 5</c> </b> <b> <c d="Attrib 6">Text 6</c> <c d="Attrib 7">Text 7</c> <c d="Attrib 8">Text 8</c> <c d="Attrib 9">Text 9</c> </b> <b> <c d="Attrib 10">Text 10</c> <c d="Attrib 11">Text 11</c> <c d="Attrib 12">Text 12</c> </b>

TABLE 5.3 continued

XPath Query	*Resulting Node Set*
	</a> <b> <c d="Attrib 1">Text 1</c> <c d="Attrib 2">Text 2</c> <c d="Attrib 3">Text 3</c> </b> <c d="Attrib 1">Text 1</c> <c d="Attrib 2">Text 2</c> <c d="Attrib 3">Text 3</c> <b> <c d="Attrib 4">Text 4</c> <c d="Attrib 5">Text 5</c> </b> <c d="Attrib 4">Text 4</c> <c d="Attrib 5">Text 5</c> <b> <c d="Attrib 6">Text 6</c> <c d="Attrib 7">Text 7</c> <c d="Attrib 8">Text 8</c> <c d="Attrib 9">Text 9</c> </b> <c d="Attrib 6">Text 6</c> <c d="Attrib 7">Text 7</c> <c d="Attrib 8">Text 8</c> <c d="Attrib 9">Text 9</c> <b> <c d="Attrib 10">Text 10</c> <c d="Attrib 11">Text 11</c> <c d="Attrib 12">Text 12</c> </b> <c d="Attrib 10">Text 10</c> <c d="Attrib 11">Text 11</c> <c d="Attrib 12">Text 12</c>
`a/b[1]/c[1]/following::*`	<c d="Attrib 2">Text 2</c> <c d="Attrib 3">Text 3</c> <b> <c d="Attrib 4">Text 4</c> <c d="Attrib 5">Text 5</c> </b>

TABLE 5.3 continued

XPath Query	*Resulting Node Set*

	`<c d="Attrib 4">Text 4</c>`
	`<c d="Attrib 5">Text 5</c>`
	`<b>`
	`  <c d="Attrib 6">Text 6</c>`
	`  <c d="Attrib 7">Text 7</c>`
	`  <c d="Attrib 8">Text 8</c>`
	`  <c d="Attrib 9">Text 9</c>`
	`</b>`
	`<c d="Attrib 6">Text 6</c>`
	`<c d="Attrib 7">Text 7</c>`
	`<c d="Attrib 8">Text 8</c>`
	`<c d="Attrib 9">Text 9</c>`
	`<b>`
	`  <c d="Attrib 10">Text 10</c>`
	`  <c d="Attrib 11">Text 11</c>`
	`  <c d="Attrib 12">Text 12</c>`
	`</b>`
	`<c d="Attrib 10">Text 10</c>`
	`<c d="Attrib 11">Text 11</c>`
	`<c d="Attrib 12">Text 12</c>`

`a/b[1]/c[1]/following-sibling::*`	`<c d="Attrib 2">Text 2</c>` `<c d="Attrib 3">Text 3</c>`

`a/b[1]/c[1]/parent::*`	`<b>`
	`  <c d="Attrib 1">Text 1</c>`
	`  <c d="Attrib 2">Text 2</c>`
	`  <c d="Attrib 3">Text 3</c>`
	`</b>`

`a/b[1]/c[2]/preceding::*`	`<c d="Attrib 1">Text 1</c>`
`a/b[1]/c[3]/preceding-sibling::*`	`<c d="Attrib 1">Text 1</c>` `<c d="Attrib 2">Text 2</c>`
`a/b[1]/c[1]/self::*`	`<c d="Attrib 1">Text 1</c>`

Note

For all the XPath expressions contained within this chapter, the corresponding results are listed as they are returned by the Microsoft XML DOM version 3. Some other DOM implementations may produce different results; it depends on the interpretation of the XPath specifications and how that interpretation is implemented as to what the resulting node set would be. However, you are not limited to working with only one version of a DOM provided by one company. You can test the XPath expressions by using the following URL:

`http://www.fivesight.com/downloads/xpathtester.asp`

From the contents of Table 5.3, you can see what may be some strange results. However, it's important to remember that a resulting node set contains the entire hierarchy for the nodes contained within the set. Keeping that in mind, the results for the XPath queries in Table 5.3 begin to make more sense.

Node Tests

The node test portion of a location step indicates the type of node desired for the results. Every axis has a principal node type: If an axis is an element, the principal node type is `element`; otherwise, it is the type of node the axis can contain. For instance, if the axis is `attribute`, the principal node type is `attribute`.

A node test may also contain a node name, or `QName`. In this case, a node with the specified name is sought, and if found, it's returned in the node set. However, the nodes selected in this manner must be the principal node type sought and have an expanded name equal to the `QName` specified. This means that if the node belongs to a namespace, the namespace must also be included in the node test for the node to be selected. For instance, `ancestor::div` and `ancestor::test:div` will produce two entirely different node sets. In this first case, only nodes that have no namespace specified and have a name of `div` will be selected. In the second case, only those `div` nodes belonging to the `test` namespace will be selected.

In addition to specifying an actual node name, other node tests are available to select the desired nodes. Here's a list of these node tests:

- `comment()`
- `node()`
- `processing-instruction()`
- `text()`

As you can see, a small number of node tests are available for use within a location step. The `comment()` node test selects comment nodes from an XML document. The `node()` node test selects a node of any type, whereas the `text()` node test selects those nodes that are text nodes. Special consideration should be given to the `processing-instruction()` node test, because this node test will accept a literal string parameter to specify the name of a desired processing instruction.

Note

Most people believe that a document such as the one in Listing 5.1 contains 17 nodes. Although it's true that the document does contain 17 nodes, those aren't the only nodes the document contains. Most people simply count the number of elements within a document. However, each node that contains text also has a text node associated with it. So, when a node test for `text()` is conducted, a node set is returned with all the text nodes, but those nodes will not have a name—they simply contain text. The node test for `node()` will return the desired nodes, and if there are any elements that contain text, those text nodes will also be returned in the node set.

Predicates

The predicate portion of a location step filters a node set on the specified axis to create a new node set. Each node in the preliminary node set is evaluated against the predicate to see whether it matches the filter criteria. If it does, the node ends up in the filtered node set. Otherwise, it doesn't.

A predicate may consist of a filter condition that is applied to an axis that either directs the condition in a forward or reverse direction. A forward axis predicate contains the current context node and nodes that follow the context node. A reverse axis predicate contains the current context node and nodes that precede the context node.

A predicate within a location step may contain an expression that, when evaluated, results in a Boolean (or *logical*) value that can be either True or False. For instance, if the result of the expression is a number, such as in the expression `/a/b[position()=2]`, then the predicate `[position()=2]` is evaluated for each node in the axis to see whether it is the second node, and if so, it returns `True` for the predicate. In fact, the expressions for a predicate can get rather complex because you are not limited to one test condition within a predicate—you may use the Boolean operators `and` and `or`. Using these two operators, you can create very powerful filter conditions to find the desired node set. Predicates may also consist of a variety of functions.

XPath predicates may, and most probably will, contain a Boolean comparison, as listed in Table 5.4.

TABLE 5.4 Boolean Operators and Their Respective Descriptions

Boolean Operator	*Description*
>	Greater than
>=	Greater than or equal to
<	Less than
<=	Less than or equal to
=	Equal to
!=	Not equal to

Caution

Remember that these Boolean operators may contain special characters that are invalid within an XML document, such as an XSLT style sheet. In those cases, to perform these Boolean operations, you would need to use an escape sequence, such as `<` for < or `>` for >.

Note

Predicates within a location step can also contain other location steps. For instance, using Listing 5.1, a predicate could be specified as `//*[attribute::d]`, which will return all the `d` attributes.

XPath Functions

XPath functions are used to evaluate XPath expressions and can be divided into one of four main groups:

- Boolean
- Node set
- Number
- String

Each of these main groups contains a set of functions that deal with specific operations needed with respect to the items covered. Table 5.5 lists each XPath function available as well as the arguments accepted, the return type, and a brief description.

TABLE 5.5 XPath Functions as Recommended by the W3C

Type	*Syntax*	*Return Type*	*Description*
Boolean	`boolean(object)`	Boolean	Converts the argument into a Boolean value
	`false()`	Boolean	Returns `False`
	`lang(string)`	Boolean	Returns `True` if the `xml:lang` attribute of the context node is the same as the sublanguage specified by the argument
	`not(expression)`	Boolean	Returns `True` if the expression argument is `False`
	`true()`	Boolean	Returns `True`
Node set	`count(node-set)`	Number	Returns the number of nodes in the node set argument
	`Document (variant, [node-set])`	Node set	Creates an XML document from the variant argument
	`id(object)`	Node set	Returns a node set based on the node's unique ID
	`key(name, value)`	Node set	Returns a node set with the specified key name and value
	`last()`	Number	Returns the context size for the expression evaluation context
	`local-name ([node-set])`	String	Returns the local part of the expanded name of the first node in the node set
	`name([node-set])`	String	Returns the expanded name of the first node in the node set

TABLE 5.5 continued

Type	*Syntax*	*Return Type*	*Description*
	`namespace-uri ([node-set])`	String	Returns the namespace URI for the namespace of the first node in the node set
	`position()`	Number	Returns the index number of the node within the parent
Number	`ceiling(number)`	Number	Returns the smallest integer that is not less than the argument
	`floor(number)`	Number	Returns the largest integer that is not greater than the argument
	`number(variant)`	Number	Converts the argument to a number
	`round(number)`	Number	Returns the integer closest in value to the argument
	`sum(node-set)`	Number	Sums the value of all the nodes within the node set after being converted to a number
String	`concat(string, string, [string*])`	String	Returns the concatenation of the `string` arguments
	`contains(string, string)`	Boolean	Returns `True` if the first string contains the second
	`normalize-space()`	String	Returns the string with the whitespace removed
	`starts-with (string, string)`	Boolean	Returns `True` if the first string begins with the second string
	`string(variant)`	String	Converts the argument into a string

TABLE 5.5 continued

Type	*Syntax*	*Return Type*	*Description*
	`string-length (string)`	Number	Returns the length of the string
	`substring (string, start, length)`	String	Returns a substring of the specified string starting at the start position indicated by `startpos` of the length specified by `length`
	`substring-after (string, string)`	String	Returns the substring of the first string that follows the first occurrence of the second string
	`substring-before chars, replace)`	String	Returns the substring of the first string that precedes the first occurrence of the second string
	`translate (string, chars, replace)`	String	Replaces the string specified in `chars` within the specified string with the string specified in `replace`.

As you can see in Table 5.5, a large number of functions are available that perform a myriad of operations. These functions can be used within a location-step predicate to help filter out undesired nodes. They also help in providing functionality that without which would make the XPath language quite limiting.

XPath Examples

You have seen the basic construction of each piece of an XPath query, but in truth, it helps to see the XPath expressions and the results for them. Therefore, to help with this and to provide as many examples as possible, we will use the code in Listing 5.2, which provides a good baseline sample XML document we can use for the XPath examples.

LISTING 5.2 `Sample2.xml` Provides the XML Document Against Which the Sample XPath Expressions Will Be Evaluated

```
<PurchaseOrder Tax="5.76" Total="75.77">

  <ShippingInformation>
    <Method>USPS</Method>
    <DeliveryDate>08/12/2001</DeliveryDate>
    <Name>Dillon Larsen</Name>
    <Address>
      <Street>123 Jones Rd.</Street>
      <City>Houston</City>
      <State>TX</State>
      <Zip>77381</Zip>
    </Address>
  </ShippingInformation>

  <BillingInformation>
    <PaymentMethod>Credit Card</PaymentMethod>
    <BillingDate>08/09/2001</BillingDate>
    <Name>Madi Larsen</Name>
    <Address>
      <Street>123 Jones Rd.</Street>
      <City>Houston</City>
      <State>TX</State>
      <Zip>77381</Zip>
    </Address>
  </BillingInformation>

  <Order SubTotal="70.01" ItemsSold="17">
    <Product Name="Baby Swiss" Id="702890" Price="2.89"
➥Quantity="1"/>
    <Product Name="Hard Salami" Id="302340" Price="2.34"
➥Quantity="1"/>
    <Product Name="Turkey" Id="905800" Price="5.80"
➥Quantity="1"/>
    <Product Name="Caesar Salad" Id="991687" Price="2.38"
➥Quantity="2"/>
    <Product Name="Chicken Strips" Id="133382" Price="2.50"
➥Quantity="1"/>
    <Product Name="Bread" Id="298678" Price="1.08"
➥Quantity="1"/>
    <Product Name="Rolls" Id="002399" Price="2.24"
➥Quantity="1"/>
    <Product Name="Cereal" Id="066510" Price="2.18"
➥Quantity="1"/>
```

LISTING 5.2 continued

```
    <Product Name="Jalapenos" Id="101005" Price="1.97"
➥Quantity="1"/>
    <Product Name="Tuna" Id="000118" Price="0.92"
➥Quantity="3"/>
    <Product Name="Mayonnaise" Id="126860" Price="1.98"
➥Quantity="1"/>
    <Product Name="Top Sirloin" Id="290502" Price="9.97"
➥Quantity="2"/>
    <Product Name="Soup" Id="001254" Price="1.33"
➥Quantity="1"/>
    <Product Name="Granola Bar" Id="026460" Price="2.14"
➥Quantity="2"/>
    <Product Name="Chocolate Milk" Id="024620" Price="1.58"
➥Quantity="2"/>
    <Product Name="Spaghetti" Id="000265" Price="1.98"
➥Quantity="1"/>
    <Product Name="Laundry Detergent" Id="148202" Price="8.82"
➥Quantity="1"/>
  </Order>

</PurchaseOrder>
```

As you can see, Listing 5.2 looks very similar to Listing 4.1. This is basically the same sample XML document we used in Chapter 4, "Creating XML Schemas," but it has been slightly modified to perform as a better example for XPath queries. Using this sample XML document, Table 5.6 contains sample XPath expressions and their respective results.

TABLE 5.6 Sample XPath Queries and Their Results

Expression	*Results*

`/PurchaseOrder/child::Order`	`<Order SubTotal="70.01" ItemsSold="17">`
	`<Product Name="Baby Swiss" Id="702890"`
	`➥Price="2.89" Quantity="1"/>`
	`<Product Name="Hard Salami" Id="302340"`
	`➥Price="2.34" Quantity="1"/>`
	`<Product Name="Turkey" Id="905800" Price="5.80"`
	`➥Quantity="1"/>`
	`<Product Name="Caesar Salad" Id="991687"`
	`➥Price="2.38" Quantity="2"/>`

TABLE 5.6 continued

Expression	*Results*
	<Product Name="Chicken Strips" Id="133382" ➥Price="2.50" Quantity="1"/> <Product Name="Bread" Id="298678" Price="1.08" ➥Quantity="1"/> <Product Name="Rolls" Id="002399" Price="2.24" ➥Quantity="1"/> <Product Name="Cereal" Id="066510" Price="2.18" ➥Quantity="1"/> <Product Name="Jalapenos" Id="101005" ➥Price="1.97" Quantity="1"/> <Product Name="Tuna" Id="000118" Price="0.92" ➥Quantity="3"/> <Product Name="Mayonnaise" Id="126860" ➥Price="1.98" Quantity="1"/> <Product Name="Top Sirloin" Id="290502" ➥Price="9.97" Quantity="2"/> <Product Name="Soup" Id="001254" Price="1.33" ➥Quantity="1"/> <Product Name="Granola Bar" Id="026460" ➥Price="2.14" Quantity="2"/> <Product Name="Chocolate Milk" Id="024620" ➥Price="1.58" Quantity="2"/> <Product Name="Spaghetti" Id="000265" ➥Price="1.98" Quantity="1"/> <Product Name="Laundry Detergent" Id="148202" ➥Price="8.82" Quantity="1"/> </Order>
/PurchaseOrder/child::*	<ShippingInformation> <Method>USPS</Method> <DeliveryDate>08/12/2001</DeliveryDate> <Name>Dillon Larsen</Name> <Address>

TABLE 5.6 continued

Expression	*Results*

```
    <Street>123 Jones Rd.</Street>
    <City>Houston</City>
    <State>TX</State>
    <Zip>77381</Zip>
  </Address>
</ShippingInformation>

<BillingInformation>
  <PaymentMethod>Credit Card</PaymentMethod>
  <BillingDate>08/09/2001</BillingDate>
  <Name>Madi Larsen</Name>
  <Address>
    <Street>123 Jones Rd.</Street>
    <City>Houston</City>
    <State>TX</State>
    <Zip>77381</Zip>
  </Address>\
</BillingInformation>

<Order SubTotal="70.01" ItemsSold="17">
  <Product Name="Baby Swiss" Id="702890"
➥Price="2.89" Quantity="1"/>
  <Product Name="Hard Salami" Id="302340"
➥Price="2.34" Quantity="1"/>
  <Product Name="Turkey" Id="905800" Price="5.80"
➥Quantity="1"/>
  <Product Name="Caesar Salad" Id="991687"
➥Price="2.38" Quantity="2"/>
  <Product Name="Chicken Strips" Id="133382"
➥Price="2.50" Quantity="1"/>
  <Product Name="Bread" Id="298678" Price="1.08"
➥Quantity="1"/>
  <Product Name="Rolls" Id="002399" Price="2.24"
➥Quantity="1"/>
```

TABLE 5.6 continued

Expression	*Results*
	<Product Name="Cereal" Id="066510" Price="2.18" ➥Quantity="1"/> <Product Name="Jalapenos" Id="101005" ➥Price="1.97" Quantity="1"/> <Product Name="Tuna" Id="000118" Price="0.92" ➥Quantity="3"/> <Product Name="Mayonnaise" Id="126860" ➥Price="1.98" Quantity="1"/> <Product Name="Top Sirloin" Id="290502" ➥Price="9.97" Quantity="2"/> <Product Name="Soup" Id="001254" Price="1.33" ➥Quantity="1"/> <Product Name="Granola Bar" Id="026460" ➥Price="2.14" Quantity="2"/> <Product Name="Chocolate Milk" Id="024620" ➥Price="1.58" Quantity="2"/> <Product Name="Spaghetti" Id="000265" ➥Price="1.98" Quantity="1"/> <Product Name="Laundry Detergent" Id="148202" ➥Price="8.82" Quantity="1"/> </Order>
/PurchaseOrder/descendant ➥::text()	USPS08/12/2001Dillon Larsen123 Jones ➥Rd.HoustonTX77381 Credit Card08/09/2001Madi ➥Larsen123 Jones Rd. HoustonTX77381
/PurchaseOrder/Order/ ➥child::node()	<Product Name="Baby Swiss" Id="702890" Price="2.89" ➥Quantity="1"/> <Product Name="Hard Salami" Id="302340" ➥Price="2.34" Quantity="1"/>

TABLE 5.6 continued

Expression	*Results*
	<Product Name="Turkey" Id="905800" Price="5.80" ➥Quantity="1"/> <Product Name="Caesar Salad" Id="991687" ➥Price="2.38" Quantity="2"/> <Product Name="Chicken Strips" Id="133382" ➥Price="2.50" Quantity="1"/> <Product Name="Bread" Id="298678" Price="1.08" ➥Quantity="1"/> <Product Name="Rolls" Id="002399" Price="2.24" ➥Quantity="1"/> <Product Name="Cereal" Id="066510" Price="2.18" ➥Quantity="1"/> <Product Name="Jalapenos" Id="101005" Price="1.97" ➥Quantity="1"/> <Product Name="Tuna" Id="000118" Price="0.92" ➥Quantity="3"/> <Product Name="Mayonnaise" Id="126860" Price="1.98" ➥Quantity="1"/> <Product Name="Top Sirloin" Id="290502" ➥Price="9.97" Quantity="2"/> <Product Name="Soup" Id="001254" Price="1.33" ➥Quantity="1"/> <Product Name="Granola Bar" Id="026460" ➥Price="2.14" Quantity="2"/> <Product Name="Chocolate Milk" Id="024620" ➥Price="1.58" Quantity="2"/> <Product Name="Spaghetti" Id="000265" Price="1.98" ➥Quantity="1"/> <Product Name="Laundry Detergent" Id="148202" ➥Price="8.82" Quantity="1"/>
/PurchaseOrder/Order/Product/ ➥attribute::Name	Name="Baby Swiss"Name="Hard Salami"Name="Turkey" ➥Name="Caesar Salad"Name="Chicken Strips" ➥Name="Bread"Name="Rolls"Name="Cereal"

TABLE 5.6 continued

Expression	*Results*
	➥Name="Jalapenos"Name="Tuna"Name="Mayonnaise" ➥Name="Top Sirloin"Name="Soup"Name="Granola Bar" ➥Name="Chocolate Milk"Name="Spaghetti" ➥Name="Laundry Detergent"
/PurchaseOrder/Order/Product/ ➥attribute::*	Name="Baby Swiss"Id="702890"Price="2.89" ➥Quantity="1" ➥Name="Hard Salami"Id="302340"Price="2.34" ➥Quantity="1"Name="Turkey"Id="905800"Price="5.80" ➥Quantity="1"Name="Caesar Salad"Id="991687" ➥Price="2.38"Quantity="2"Name="Chicken Strips" ➥Id="133382"Price="2.50"Quantity="1"Name="Bread" ➥Id="298678"Price="1.08"Quantity="1"Name="Rolls" ➥Id="002399"Price="2.24"Quantity="1"Name="Cereal" ➥Id="066510"Price="2.18"Quantity="1" ➥Name="Jalapenos"Id="101005"Price="1.97" ➥Quantity="1"Name="Tuna"Id="000118"Price="0.92" ➥Quantity="3"Name="Mayonnaise"Id="126860" ➥Price="1.98"Quantity="1"Name="Top Sirloin" ➥Id="290502"Price="9.97"Quantity="2"Name="Soup" ➥Id="001254"Price="1.33"Quantity="1" ➥Name="Granola Bar"Id="026460"Price="2.14" ➥Quantity="2"Name="Chocolate Milk"Id="024620" ➥Price="1.58"Quantity="2"Name="Spaghetti" ➥Id="000265"Price="1.98"Quantity="1" ➥Name="Laundry Detergent"Id="148202"Price="8.82" ➥Quantity="1"/>
/PurchaseOrder/descendant ➥::Name	<Name>Dillon Larsen</Name> <Name>Madi Larsen</Name>
//Product/ancestor::*	<PurchaseOrder Tax="5.76" Total="75.77"> <ShippingInformation> <Method>USPS</Method> <DeliveryDate>08/12/2001</DeliveryDate> <Name>Dillon Larsen</Name> <Address> <Street>123 Jones Rd.</Street> <City>Houston</City> <State>TX</State>

Table 5.6 continued

Expression	Results
	(see code below)

```
    <Zip>77381</Zip>
  </Address>
</ShippingInformation>

<BillingInformation>
  <PaymentMethod>Credit Card</PaymentMethod>
  <BillingDate>08/09/2001</BillingDate>
  <Name>Madi Larsen</Name>
  <Address>
    <Street>123 Jones Rd.</Street>
    <City>Houston</City>
    <State>TX</State>
    <Zip>77381</Zip>
  </Address>
</BillingInformation>

<Order SubTotal="70.01" ItemsSold="17">
  <Product Name="Baby Swiss" Id="702890"
➥Price="2.89" Quantity="1"/>
  <Product Name="Hard Salami" Id="302340"
➥Price="2.34" Quantity="1"/>
  <Product Name="Turkey" Id="905800"
➥Price="5.80" Quantity="1"/>
  <Product Name="Caesar Salad" Id="991687"
➥Price="2.38" Quantity="2"/>
  <Product Name="Chicken Strips" Id="133382"
➥Price="2.50" Quantity="1"/>
  <Product Name="Bread" Id="298678" Price="1.08"
➥Quantity="1"/>
  <Product Name="Rolls" Id="002399" Price="2.24"
➥Quantity="1"/>
  <Product Name="Cereal" Id="066510"
➥Price="2.18" Quantity="1"/>
```

TABLE 5.6 continued

Expression	*Results*

	`<Product Name="Jalapenos" Id="101005" ➥Price="1.97" Quantity="1"/>`
	`<Product Name="Tuna" Id="000118" Price="0.92" ➥Quantity="3"/>`
	`<Product Name="Mayonnaise" Id="126860" ➥Price="1.98" Quantity="1"/>`
	`<Product Name="Top Sirloin" Id="290502" ➥Price="9.97" Quantity="2"/>`
	`<Product Name="Soup" Id="001254" Price="1.33" ➥Quantity="1"/>`
	`<Product Name="Granola Bar" Id="026460" ➥Price="2.14" Quantity="2"/>`
	`<Product Name="Chocolate Milk" Id="024620" ➥Price="1.58" Quantity="2"/>`
	`<Product Name="Spaghetti" Id="000265" ➥Price="1.98" Quantity="1"/>`
	`<Product Name="Laundry Detergent" Id="148202" ➥Price="8.82" Quantity="1"/>`
	`</Order>`
	
	`</PurchaseOrder>`
	`<Order SubTotal="70.01" ItemsSold="17">`
	`<Product Name="Baby Swiss" Id="702890" ➥Price="2.89" Quantity="1"/>`
	`<Product Name="Hard Salami" Id="302340" ➥Price="2.34" Quantity="1"/>`
	`<Product Name="Turkey" Id="905800" Price="5.80" ➥Quantity="1"/>`
	`<Product Name="Caesar Salad" Id="991687" ➥Price="2.38" Quantity="2"/>`

TABLE 5.6 continued

Expression	*Results*
	<Product Name="Chicken Strips" Id="133382" ➥Price="2.50" Quantity="1"/> <Product Name="Bread" Id="298678" Price="1.08" ➥Quantity="1"/> <Product Name="Rolls" Id="002399" Price="2.24" ➥Quantity="1"/> <Product Name="Cereal" Id="066510" Price="2.18" ➥Quantity="1"/> <Product Name="Jalapenos" Id="101005" ➥Price="1.97" Quantity="1"/> <Product Name="Tuna" Id="000118" Price="0.92" ➥Quantity="3"/> <Product Name="Mayonnaise" Id="126860" ➥Price="1.98" Quantity="1"/> <Product Name="Top Sirloin" Id="290502" ➥Price="9.97" Quantity="2"/> <Product Name="Soup" Id="001254" Price="1.33" ➥Quantity="1"/> <Product Name="Granola Bar" Id="026460" ➥Price="2.14" Quantity="2"/> <Product Name="Chocolate Milk" Id="024620" ➥Price="1.58" Quantity="2"/> <Product Name="Spaghetti" Id="000265" ➥Price="1.98" Quantity="1"/> <Product Name="Laundry Detergent" Id="148202" ➥Price="8.82" Quantity="1"/> </Order>
//Name/ancestor:: ➥BillingInformation	<BillingInformation> <PaymentMethod>Credit Card</PaymentMethod> <BillingDate>08/09/2001</BillingDate>

TABLE 5.6 continued

Expression	*Results*

	`<Name>Madi Larsen</Name>`
	`<Address>`
	`<Street>123 Jones Rd.</Street>`
	`<City>Houston</City>`
	`<State>TX</State>`
	`<Zip>77381</Zip>`
	`</Address>`
	`</BillingInformation>`

`//*/ancestor-or-self::Order`	`<Order SubTotal="70.01" ItemsSold="17">`
	`<Product Name="Baby Swiss" Id="702890"`
	`➥Price="2.89" Quantity="1"/>`
	`<Product Name="Hard Salami" Id="302340"`
	`➥Price="2.34" Quantity="1"/>`
	`<Product Name="Turkey" Id="905800" Price="5.80"`
	`➥Quantity="1"/>`
	`<Product Name="Caesar Salad" Id="991687"`
	`➥Price="2.38" Quantity="2"/>`
	`<Product Name="Chicken Strips" Id="133382"`
	`➥Price="2.50" Quantity="1"/>`
	`<Product Name="Bread" Id="298678" Price="1.08"`
	`➥Quantity="1"/>`
	`<Product Name="Rolls" Id="002399" Price="2.24"`
	`➥Quantity="1"/>`
	`<Product Name="Cereal" Id="066510" Price="2.18"`
	`➥Quantity="1"/>`
	`<Product Name="Jalapenos" Id="101005"`
	`➥Price="1.97" Quantity="1"/>`
	`<Product Name="Tuna" Id="000118" Price="0.92"`
	`➥Quantity="3"/>`
	`<Product Name="Mayonnaise" Id="126860"`
	`➥Price="1.98" Quantity="1"/>`
	`<Product Name="Top Sirloin" Id="290502"`

TABLE 5.6 continued

Expression	*Results*
	➥Price="9.97" Quantity="2"/> <Product Name="Soup" Id="001254" Price="1.33" ➥Quantity="1"/> <Product Name="Granola Bar" Id="026460" ➥Price="2.14" Quantity="2"/> <Product Name="Chocolate Milk" Id="024620" ➥Price="1.58" Quantity="2"/> <Product Name="Spaghetti" Id="000265" ➥Price="1.98" Quantity="1"/> <Product Name="Laundry Detergent" Id="148202" ➥Price="8.82" Quantity="1"/> </Order>
//*/descendant-or-self::Name	<Name>Dillon Larsen</Name> <Name>Madi Larsen</Name>
//*/self::Product	<Product Name="Baby Swiss" Id="702890" Price="2.89" ➥Quantity="1"/> <Product Name="Hard Salami" Id="302340" ➥Price="2.34" Quantity="1"/> <Product Name="Turkey" Id="905800" Price="5.80" ➥Quantity="1"/> <Product Name="Caesar Salad" Id="991687" ➥Price="2.38" Quantity="2"/> <Product Name="Chicken Strips" Id="133382" ➥Price="2.50" Quantity="1"/> <Product Name="Bread" Id="298678" Price="1.08" ➥Quantity="1"/> <Product Name="Rolls" Id="002399" Price="2.24" ➥Quantity="1"/> <Product Name="Cereal" Id="066510" Price="2.18" ➥Quantity="1"/>

TABLE 5.6 continued

Expression	*Results*
	<Product Name="Jalapenos" Id="101005" Price="1.97" ➥Quantity="1"/> <Product Name="Tuna" Id="000118" Price="0.92" ➥Quantity="3"/> <Product Name="Mayonnaise" Id="126860" Price="1.98" ➥Quantity="1"/> <Product Name="Top Sirloin" Id="290502" ➥Price="9.97" Quantity="2"/> <Product Name="Soup" Id="001254" Price="1.33" ➥Quantity="1"/> <Product Name="Granola Bar" Id="026460" ➥Price="2.14" Quantity="2"/> <Product Name="Chocolate Milk" Id="024620" ➥Price="1.58" Quantity="2"/> <Product Name="Spaghetti" Id="000265" Price="1.98" ➥Quantity="1"/> <Product Name="Laundry Detergent" Id="148202" ➥Price="8.82" Quantity="1"/>
/PurchaseOrder/child:: ➥ShippingInformation/ ➥descendant::Zip	<Zip>77381</Zip>
/PurchaseOrder/*/child::Name	<Name>Dillon Larsen</Name> <Name>Madi Larsen</Name>
/	<PurchaseOrder Tax="5.76" Total="75.77"> <ShippingInformation> <Method>USPS</Method> <DeliveryDate>08/12/2001</DeliveryDate> <Name>Dillon Larsen</Name> <Address> <Street>123 Jones Rd.</Street> <City>Houston</City> <State>TX</State> <Zip>77381</Zip>

TABLE 5.6 continued

Expression	*Results*

```
  </Address>
</ShippingInformation>

<BillingInformation>
  <PaymentMethod>Credit Card</PaymentMethod>
  <BillingDate>08/09/2001</BillingDate>
  <Name>Madi Larsen</Name>
  <Address>
    <Street>123 Jones Rd.</Street>
    <City>Houston</City>
    <State>TX</State>
    <Zip>77381</Zip>
  </Address>
</BillingInformation>

<Order SubTotal="70.01" ItemsSold="17">
  <Product Name="Baby Swiss" Id="702890"
➥Price="2.89" Quantity="1"/>
  <Product Name="Hard Salami" Id="302340"
➥Price="2.34" Quantity="1"/>
  <Product Name="Turkey" Id="905800"
➥Price="5.80" Quantity="1"/>
  <Product Name="Caesar Salad" Id="991687"
➥Price="2.38" Quantity="2"/>
  <Product Name="Chicken Strips" Id="133382"
➥Price="2.50" Quantity="1"/>
  <Product Name="Bread" Id="298678" Price="1.08"
➥Quantity="1"/>
  <Product Name="Rolls" Id="002399" Price="2.24"
➥Quantity="1"/>
  <Product Name="Cereal" Id="066510"
➥Price="2.18" Quantity="1"/>
```

TABLE 5.6 continued

Expression	*Results*
	<Product Name="Jalapenos" Id="101005" ➥Price="1.97" Quantity="1"/> <Product Name="Tuna" Id="000118" Price="0.92" ➥Quantity="3"/> <Product Name="Mayonnaise" Id="126860" ➥Price="1.98" Quantity="1"/> <Product Name="Top Sirloin" Id="290502" ➥Price="9.97" Quantity="2"/> <Product Name="Soup" Id="001254" Price="1.33" ➥Quantity="1"/> <Product Name="Granola Bar" Id="026460" ➥Price="2.14" Quantity="2"/> <Product Name="Chocolate Milk" Id="024620" ➥Price="1.58" Quantity="2"/> <Product Name="Spaghetti" Id="000265" ➥Price="1.98" Quantity="1"/> <Product Name="Laundry Detergent" Id="148202" ➥Price="8.82" Quantity="1"/> </Order> </PurchaseOrder>
/descendant::Product	<Product Name="Baby Swiss" Id="702890" Price="2.89" ➥Quantity="1"/> <Product Name="Hard Salami" Id="302340" ➥Price="2.34" Quantity="1"/> <Product Name="Turkey" Id="905800" Price="5.80" ➥Quantity="1"/> <Product Name="Caesar Salad" Id="991687" ➥Price="2.38" Quantity="2"/>

TABLE 5.6 continued

Expression	*Results*
	<Product Name="Chicken Strips" Id="133382" ➥Price="2.50" Quantity="1"/> <Product Name="Bread" Id="298678" Price="1.08" ➥Quantity="1"/> <Product Name="Rolls" Id="002399" Price="2.24" ➥Quantity="1"/> <Product Name="Cereal" Id="066510" Price="2.18" ➥Quantity="1"/> <Product Name="Jalapenos" Id="101005" Price="1.97" ➥Quantity="1"/> <Product Name="Tuna" Id="000118" Price="0.92" ➥Quantity="3"/> <Product Name="Mayonnaise" Id="126860" Price="1.98" ➥Quantity="1"/> <Product Name="Top Sirloin" Id="290502" ➥Price="9.97" Quantity="2"/> <Product Name="Soup" Id="001254" Price="1.33" ➥Quantity="1"/> <Product Name="Granola Bar" Id="026460" ➥Price="2.14" Quantity="2"/> <Product Name="Chocolate Milk" Id="024620" ➥Price="1.58" Quantity="2"/> <Product Name="Spaghetti" Id="000265" Price="1.98" ➥Quantity="1"/> <Product Name="Laundry Detergent" Id="148202" ➥Price="8.82" Quantity="1"/>
/descendant::Address/ ➥child::Zip	<Zip>77381</Zip> <Zip>77381</Zip>
/PurchaseOrder/Order/child:: ➥Product[position()=3]	Product Name="Turkey" Id="905800" Price="5.80" ➥Quantity="1"/> <
/PurchaseOrder/Order/child:: ➥Product[last()]	<Product Name="Laundry Detergent" Id="148202" ➥Price="8.82" Quantity="1"/>

TABLE 5.6 continued

Expression	*Results*
/PurchaseOrder/Order/child:: ➥Product[last()-1]	<Product Name="Spaghetti" Id="000265" Price="1.98" ➥Quantity="1"/>
/PurchaseOrder/Order/child:: ➥Product[position()>3]	<Product Name="Caesar Salad" Id="991687" ➥Price="2.38" Quantity="2"/> <Product Name="Chicken Strips" Id="133382" ➥Price="2.50" Quantity="1"/> <Product Name="Bread" Id="298678" Price="1.08" ➥Quantity="1"/> <Product Name="Rolls" Id="002399" Price="2.24" ➥Quantity="1"/> <Product Name="Cereal" Id="066510" Price="2.18" ➥Quantity="1"/> <Product Name="Jalapenos" Id="101005" Price="1.97" ➥Quantity="1"/> <Product Name="Tuna" Id="000118" Price="0.92" ➥Quantity="3"/> <Product Name="Mayonnaise" Id="126860" Price="1.98" ➥Quantity="1"/> <Product Name="Top Sirloin" Id="290502" ➥Price="9.97" Quantity="2"/> <Product Name="Soup" Id="001254" Price="1.33" ➥Quantity="1"/> <Product Name="Granola Bar" Id="026460" ➥Price="2.14" Quantity="2"/> <Product Name="Chocolate Milk" Id="024620" ➥Price="1.58" Quantity="2"/> <Product Name="Spaghetti" Id="000265" Price="1.98" ➥Quantity="1"/> <Product Name="Laundry Detergent" Id="148202" ➥Price="8.82" Quantity="1"/>

TABLE 5.6 continued

Expression	*Results*
/PurchaseOrder/Order/Product/ ➥following-sibling:: ➥Product[position()>3]	<Product Name="Chicken Strips" Id="133382" ➥Price="2.50" Quantity="1"/> <Product Name="Bread" Id="298678" Price="1.08" ➥Quantity="1"/> <Product Name="Rolls" Id="002399" Price="2.24" ➥Quantity="1"/> <Product Name="Cereal" Id="066510" Price="2.18" ➥Quantity="1"/> <Product Name="Jalapenos" Id="101005" Price="1.97" ➥Quantity="1"/> <Product Name="Tuna" Id="000118" Price="0.92" ➥Quantity="3"/> <Product Name="Mayonnaise" Id="126860" Price="1.98" ➥Quantity="1"/> <Product Name="Top Sirloin" Id="290502" Price="9.97 ➥Quantity="2"/> <Product Name="Soup" Id="001254" Price="1.33" ➥Quantity="1"/> <Product Name="Granola Bar" Id="026460" ➥Price="2.14" Quantity="2"/> <Product Name="Chocolate Milk" Id="024620" ➥Price="1.58" Quantity="2"/> <Product Name="Spaghetti" Id="000265" Price="1.98" ➥Quantity="1"/> <Product Name="Laundry Detergent" Id="148202" ➥Price="8.82" Quantity="1"/>
/PurchaseOrder/Order/Product ➥[position()=4]/ ➥preceding-sibling:: ➥Product	<Product Name="Baby Swiss" Id="702890" Price="2.89" ➥Quantity="1"/> <Product Name="Hard Salami" Id="302340" ➥Price="2.34" Quantity="1"/> <Product Name="Turkey" Id="905800" Price="5.80" ➥Quantity="1"/>

TABLE 5.6 continued

Expression	*Results*
/descendant::Product [position()=3]	<Product Name="Turkey" Id="905800" ➥Price="5.80" Quantity="1"/>
/descendant::Product ➥[attribute:: ➥Name="Turkey"]	<Product Name="Turkey" Id="905800" Price="5.80" ➥Quantity="1"/>
/descendant::Product ➥[attribute:: ➥Price>"2.00"] ➥[position()=7]	<Product Name="Cereal" Id="066510" Price="2.18" ➥Quantity="1"/>
/PurchaseOrder/child::* ➥[self:: ➥ShippingInformation or ➥self:: ➥BillingInformation]	<ShippingInformation> <Method>USPS</Method> <DeliveryDate>08/12/2001</DeliveryDate> <Name>Dillon Larsen</Name> <Address> <Street>123 Jones Rd.</Street> <City>Houston</City> <State>TX</State> <Zip>77381</Zip> </Address> </ShippingInformation> <BillingInformation> <PaymentMethod>Credit Card</PaymentMethod> <BillingDate>08/09/2001</BillingDate> <Name>Madi Larsen</Name> <Address> <Street>123 Jones Rd.</Street> <City>Houston</City> <State>TX</State> <Zip>77381</Zip> </Address> </BillingInformation>

As you can see from the examples in Table 5.6, XPath expressions can get rather long and complex. For this reason, an abbreviated syntax has also been introduced. Table 5.7 lists the XPath expressions and their respective abbreviations.

TABLE 5.7 XPath Expressions and Their Abbreviations

Expression	*Abbreviation*
`self::node()`	`.`
`parent::node()`	`..`
`child::nodename`	`nodename`
`attribute::nodename`	`@nodename`
`descendant-or-self::node()`	`//`

Using the abbreviations in Table 5.7, the XPath expressions in Table 5.6 can be rewritten as shown in Table 5.8.

TABLE 5.8 Abbreviated XPath Expressions from Table 5.6

Full Expression	*Abbreviated Expression*
`/PurchaseOrder/child::Order`	`/PurchaseOrder/Order`
`/PurchaseOrder/child::*`	`/PurchaseOrder/*`
`/PurchaseOrder/descendant::text()`	`/PurchaseOrder//text()`
`/PurchaseOrder/Order/child::node()`	`/PurchaseOrder/Order/node()`
`/PurchaseOrder/Order/Product/` ➥`attribute::Name`	`/PurchaseOrder/Order/Product/@Name`
`/PurchaseOrder/Order/Product/` ➥`attribute::*`	`/PurchaseOrder/Order/Product/@*`
`/PurchaseOrder/descendant::Name`	`/PurchaseOrder//Name`
`//Product/ancestor::*`	`//*[.//Product]`
`//Name/ancestor::BillingInformation`	`//BillingInformation[.//Name]`
`//*/ancestor-or-self::Order`	N/A
`//*/descendant-or-self::Name`	`//Name`
`//*/self::Product`	`//Product`
`/PurchaseOrder/child::` ➥`ShippingInformation/` ➥`descendant::Zip`	`/PurchaseOrder/ShippingInformation//Zip`
`/PurchaseOrder/*/child::Name`	`PurchaseOrder/*/Name`
`/`	`/`
`/descendant::Product`	`//Product`
`/descendant::Address/child::Zip`	`//Address/Zip`

TABLE 5.8 continued

Full Expression	*Abbreviated Expression*
`/PurchaseOrder/Order/child::` `➥Product[position()=3]`	`PurchaseOrder/Order/Product[3]`
`/PurchaseOrder/Order/child::` `➥Product[last()]`	`PurchaseOrder/Order/Product[last()]`
`/PurchaseOrder/Order/child::` `➥Product[last()-1]`	`PurchaseOrder/Order/Product[last()-1]`
`/PurchaseOrder/Order/child::` `➥Product[position()>3]`	`PurchaseOrder/Order/Product[position()>3]`

`/PurchaseOrder/Order/Product/`
`➥following-sibling::`
`➥Product[position()>3]`
	N/A

`/PurchaseOrder/Order/Product`
`➥[position()=4]/`
`➥preceding-sibling::`
`➥Product`
	N/A

`/descendant::Product[position()=3]`	`//Product[3]`
`/descendant::Product` `➥[attribute::Name="Turkey"]`	`//Product[@Name="Turkey"]`

`/descendant::Product`
`➥[attribute::Price>"2.00"]`
`➥[position()=7]`
	`//Product[@Price>"2.00"][7]`

`/PurchaseOrder/child::*`
`➥[self::ShippingInformation`
`➥or self::BillingInformation]`
	`/PurchaseOrder/ShippingInformation|`
	`➥BillingInformation`

You can see from the examples in Table 5.8 that not every expression has an abbreviated equivalent. For instance, the XPath expression `/PurchaseOrder/Order/Product/following-sibling::Product[position()>3]` has no abbreviated equivalent.

XPointer

The XML Pointer Language (XPointer), currently in the candidate recommendation stage of the W3C approval process, builds on the XPath specification. An XPointer uses location steps the same as XPath but with two major differences: Because an XPointer describes a location within an external document, an XPointer can target a point within that XML document or a range within the target XML document. You can find the complete specification at `http://www.w3.org/TR/xptr`.

Because XPointer builds on the XPath specification, the location steps within an XPointer are comprised of the same elements that make up XPath location steps. The axes for XPointer are the same as the axes for XPath, as indicated in Table 5.2.

The node tests for an XPointer are, for the most part, the same as for an XPath node test. However, in addition to the node tests already listed for XPath expressions, XPointer provides two more important node tests:

- `point()`
- `range()`

These two additional node tests correspond to the new functionality added by XPointer. For this new functionality to work correctly, the XPointer specification added the concept of a location within an XML document. Within XPointer, a location can be an XPath node, a point, or a range. A point can represent the location immediately before or after a specified character or the location just before or just after a specified node. A range consists of a start point and an endpoint and contains all XML information between those two points. In fact, the XPointer specification extends the node types to include points and ranges.

XPointer expressions also allow predicates to be specified as part of a location step in much the same fashion XPath expressions allow for them. As with XPath expressions, XPointer expressions have specific functions to deal with each specific predicate type. However, the XPointer specification also adds an additional function named `unique()`. This new function indicates whether an XPointer expression selects a single location rather than multiple locations or no locations at all.

For an XPath expression, the result from a location step is known as a *node set*; for an XPointer expression, the result is known as a *location set*. To reduce the confusion, the XPointer specification uses a different term for the results of an expression: Because an XPointer expression can yield a result consisting of points or ranges, the idea of the *node set* had to be extended to include these types. Therefore, to prevent confusion, the results of an XPointer expression are referred to *location sets*. Four of the functions that return location sets, `id()`, `root()`, `here()`, and `origin()`, have the differences noted in Table 5.9.

TABLE 5.9 Some XPointer Functions That Return Location Sets

Function	*Description*
`id()`	Selects all nodes with the specified ID
`root()`	Selects the root element as the only location in a location set
`here()`	Selects the current element location in a location set
`origin()`	Selects the current element location for a node using an out-of-line link

The `id()` function works exactly the same as the `id()` function for an XPath expression. The `root()` function works just like the `/` character—it indicates the root element of an XML document.

The next two functions, `here()` and `origin()`, are interesting functions in their own right. The `here()` function, as indicated, refers to the current element. Because an XPointer expression can be located in a text node or in an attribute value, this function could be used to refer to the current element rather than simply the current node. The `origin()` function works much the same as the `here()` function, except that it refers to the originating element. The key idea here is that the originating element does not need to be located within the same document as the resulting location set.

Not every target for an XPointer must be a node. Targeting nodes works great when you're designing or utilizing an application that handles XML documents as node trees, such as the XML DOM, but it doesn't lend itself well to other application types. What happens when the user desires a location at a particular point or a range within an XML document that may cover various nodes and child nodes? This is where much of the power behind XPointers surfaces.

Points

Many times a link from one XML document into another must locate a specific point within the target document. XPointer points solve this problem for XML developers by allowing a context node to be specified and an index position indicating how far from the context node the desired point is. However, how do you know whether you're referring to the number of characters from the context node to locate the point or the number of nodes from the context node? In truth, it all depends on which XPointer point type you decide to use. Two different types of points can be represented using XPointer points:

- Node points
- Character points

Node points are location points in an XML document that are nodes that contain child nodes. For these node points, the index position indicates after which child node to navigate to. If 0 is specified for the index, the point is considered to be immediately before any child nodes. A node point could be considered to be the gap between the child nodes of a container node.

> **Note**
>
> When you're specifying an index position for a node point, the index position cannot be greater than the total number of child nodes contained by the origin node.

When the origin node is a text node, the index position indicates the number of characters. These location points are referred to as *character points*. Because you are indicating the number of characters from the origin, the index specified must be an integer greater than or equal to 0 and less than or equal to the total length of the text within the text node. By specifying 0 for the index position in a character point, the point is considered to be immediately before the first character in the text string. For a character point, the point, conceptually, represents the space between the characters of a text string.

> **Note**
>
> The index position for XPointer points indicates the number of units to move from the origin. For instance, in a character point, an index of 3 means the point is located immediately after the third character in the text string.

Now that you have a better understanding of the different types of points supported within the XPointer Language, how do you indicate that you want a point within an XPointer expression? By using a point identifier called `start-point()`.

To understand better how XPointer points work, we will use the sample XML document shown in Listing 5.3. This is a simple XML document containing a list of names and addresses.

LISTING 5.3 `Sample3.xml` Contains a Small List of Names and Addresses

```
<People>

  <Person>
    <Name>Dillon Larsen</Name>
```

LISTING 5.3 continued

```
    <Address>
      <Street>123 Jones Rd.</Street>
      <City>Houston</City>
      <State>TX</State>
      <Zip>77380</Zip>
    </Address>
  </Person>

  <Person>
    <Name>Madi Larsen</Name>
    <Address>
      <Street>456 Hickory Ln.</Street>
      <City>Houston</City>
      <State>TX</State>
      <Zip>77069</Zip>
    </Address>
  </Person>

  <Person>
    <Name>John Doe</Name>
    <Address>
      <Street>214 Papes Way</Street>
      <City>Houston</City>
      <State>TX</State>
      <Zip>77301</Zip>
    </Address>
  </Person>

  <Person>
    <Name>John Smith</Name>
    <Address>
      <Street>522 Springwood Dr.</Street>
      <City>Houston</City>
      <State>TX</State>
      <Zip>77069</Zip>
    </Address>
  </Person>

  <Person>
    <Name>Jane Smith</Name>
    <Address>
      <Street>522 Springwood Dr.</Street>
      <City>Houston</City>
      <State>TX</State>
      <Zip>77069</Zip>
    </Address>
  </Person>
```

LISTING 5.3 continued

```
  <Person>
    <Name>Mark Boudreaux</Name>
    <Address>
      <Street>623 Fell St.</Street>
      <City>Houston</City>
      <State>TX</State>
      <Zip>77380</Zip>
    </Address>
  </Person>

</People>
```

Using the sample XML document in Listing 5.3, you can more clearly understand the ideas behind XPointer points and how they work, as shown in Table 5.10.

TABLE 5.10 Examples of XPointer Points and the Resulting Locations

XPointer Expression	*Location*
`/People/Person[1]/Name/text()/point()[position()=4]`	Just after the *l* and just before the `start-`*o* in Dillon
`/People/Person[1]/Name/text()/start-point()[position()=0]`	Just before the *D* in Dillon
`/People/Person[2]/Address/start-point()[position()=2]`	Just before the `<State>` element in the `<Person>` element for Madi Larsen
`/People/Person[2]/Address/start-point()[position()=0]`	Just before the `<Street>` element in the `<Person>` element for Madi Larsen

From the examples in Table 5.10, you can see how the types of points behave and their resulting locations.

Note

The XPointer Language specification does not distinguish between the endpoint of one node and the start point of another. The conceptual space between each node represents one point so that as one node ends, another begins, but both share the same conceptual point.

Ranges

An XPointer range defines just that—a range consisting of a start point and an endpoint. A range will contain the XML between the start point and endpoint but does not necessarily have to consist of neat subtrees of an XML document. A range can extend over multiple branches of an XML document. The only criterion is that the start point and endpoint must be valid.

Note

A range can only be specified to contain an XML structure within the same document. This means both the start point and endpoint must be within the XML document. Furthermore, the start point cannot fall after the endpoint within an XML document. However, the start point and endpoint can be the same point, in which case the range is considered collapsed. If the container node for the start point is a node type other than element, text, or root, the container node of the endpoint must be the same node type. For instance, you can specify a start point for a range using a processing instruction node as the container node to the end of an element, but you cannot specify that the range covers text from inside the processing instruction node to text outside that node.

Within the XPointer Language, a range can be specified by using the keyword `to` within the XPointer expression in conjunction with the `start-point()` and `end-point()` functions. For instance, the following expression specifies a range beginning at the first character in the `<Name>` element for Dillon Larsen and ending after the ninth character in the `<Name>` element for Dillon Larsen:

```
/People/Person[1]/Name/text()start-point()[position()=0] to
➥/People/Person[1]/Name/text()start-point()[position()=9]
```

In this example, two node points are used as the starting and ending points for the range. The result is the string `Dillon La`. Table 5.11 lists the various range functions available.

TABLE 5.11 XPointer Range Functions

Function	*Description*
`end-point()`	Selects a location set consisting of the endpoints of the desired location steps
`range-inside()`	Selects the range(s) covering each location in the `location-set` argument

TABLE 5.11 continued

Function	*Description*
`range-to()`	Selects a range that completely covers the locations within the `location-set` argument
`start-point()`	Selects a location set consisting of the start points of the desired location steps

The XML Pointer Language also has the ability to perform basic string matching by using a function named `string-range()`. This function returns a location set with one range for every nonoverlapping match to the search string by performing a case-sensitive search. The general syntax for `string-range()` is as follows:

```
string-range(location-set, string, [index, [length]])
```

The `location-set` argument for the `string-range()` function is any XPointer expression that would create a location set as its result—for instance, `/`, `/People/Person`, `/People/Person[1]`, and so on. The `string` argument contains the string searched for. It does not matter, when you're using the `string-range()` function, where this string occurs; only that is does occur. By specifying the `index` and `length` arguments, you can indicate the range you wish returned. For instance, to return the letters *Ma* from the Madi Larsen `<Name>` element, you could pass an `index` value of 1 and a `length` value of 2.

Abbreviating XPointer Notation

When you're creating XPointer expressions, generally elements will be referenced by ID or by location. For just this reason, the XML Pointer Language added a few abbreviated forms of reference. In addition to all the standard XPath abbreviations, XPointer goes one step beyond that: XPointer allows you to remove the `[` and `]` characters from the index position. Therefore, the expression

```
/People/Person[1]/Name[1]
```

becomes this:

```
1/1/1
```

Overall, it's a much shorter expression. However, speaking from experience, this does not tend to lend itself well to actual implementation. The reasoning behind this goes back to what XML was designed for in the first place: to give meaning and structure to data. By specifying the XPointer expression as `1/1/1`, we lose all documentation regarding what it is we're looking for—we have to know, off the tops of our heads, that we're going to be selecting the first <Name> element of the first <Person> element of the <People> element.

Although it's perfectly acceptable to use the new abbreviated notation, consider this possible scenario: Your company asks you to link two documents together using XLinks and XPointers. Two years later, you no longer work at that company and the company did not have the foresight to document any of your work. The individual who inherits your work must now perform some research on her own to figure out what exactly you were selecting using your abbreviated syntax. However, if you had used the abbreviated XPath version, it makes that individual's job a little easier—she knows, by virtue of the XPath expression itself, that the first <Name> element of the first <Person> element beneath the <People> element should be selected.

XLink

The anchor element, <a>, within HTML indicates a link to another resource on an HTML page. This could be a location within the same document or a document located elsewhere. In HTML terms, the anchor element creates a hyperlink to another location. The hyperlink can either appear as straight text, a clickable image, or a combination of both. Although HTML anchor elements contain a lot of functionality, they are still limiting—they require the use of the anchor element (<a>) itself, and they basically sit there waiting for someone to click them before navigating to the specified location.

The XML Linking Language, XLink, addresses and overcomes these limitations by allowing a link to another document to be specified on any element within an XML document. What's more, those links to other documents can be much more complex than the simple links supported by the HTML specification. You can find the complete specification at `http://www.w3.org/TR/xlink`.

The XML Linking Language creates a link to another resource through the use of attributes specified on elements, not through the actual elements themselves. The XML Linking Language specification supports the attributes listed in Table 5.12.

TABLE 5.12 XLink Attributes

Attribute	*Description*
`xlink:type`	This attribute must be specified and indicates what type of XLink is represented or defined.
`xlink:href`	This attribute contains the information necessary to locate the desired resource.

TABLE 5.12 continued

Attribute	*Description*
`xlink:role`	This attribute describes the function of the link between the current resource and another.
`xlink:arcrole`	This attributes describes the function of the link between the current resource and another.
`xlink:title`	This attribute describes the meaning of the link between the resources.
`xlink:show`	This attribute indicates how the resource linked to should be displayed.
`xlink:actuate`	This attribute specifies when to load the linked resource.
`xlink:label`	This attribute is used to identify a name for a target resource.
`xlink:from`	This attribute identifies the starting resource.
`xlink:to`	This attribute identifies the ending resource.

The `xlink:type` attribute must contain one of the following values:

- `simple`
- `extended`
- `locator`
- `arc`
- `resource`
- `title`
- `none`

A value of `simple` creates a simple link between resources. Indicating a value of `extended` creates an extended link, which is discussed in the "Extended Links" section later in this chapter. A value of `locator` creates a link that points to another resource. A value of `arc` creates an arc with multiple resources and various traversal paths. A `resource` value creates a link to indicate a specific resource. A value of `title` creates a title link. By specifying a value of `none` for the `xlink:type` attribute, the parent element has no XLink meaning, and no other XLink-related content or attributes have any relationship to the element. For all intents and purposes, a value of `none` removes the ability to link to another resource from an element.

As indicated in Table 5.12, the `xlink:href` attribute supplies the location of the resource to link to. This attribute is a URI reference that can be used to find the desired resource. In a case where you wish to link to a specific area of the target resource, you may optionally include an XPointer expression to specify a point or range within that document with which to link.

The `xlink:role` attribute specifies the function of the link. However, you cannot use this attribute with just any type of XLink. This attribute may only be used for the following XLink types:

- `extended`
- `simple`
- `locator`
- `resource`

Similarly, the `xlink:arcrole` attribute may only be used with two types of XLinks:

- `arc`
- `simple`

The `xlink:title` attribute is completely optional and is provided for us to make some sense of and document, in a way, what a particular link is. If the `xlink:title` attribute is specified, it should contain a string describing the resource.

Note

The `xlink:role`, `xlink:arcrole`, and `xlink:title` attributes are classified collectively as semantic attributes according to the XLink recommendation.

The `xlink:show` attribute is an optionally specified attribute for a link for the `simple` and `arc` XLink types and will accept the following values:

- `new`
- `replace`
- `embed`

- `other`
- `none`

If a value of `new` is specified, the resource will be loaded into a new window. A value of `replace` indicates that the resource should be loaded into the current window. Indicating a value of `embed` will load the resource into the specified location and wrap the originating resource around it, as appropriate. This effect is similar to specifying an `src` attribute on a `<img>` tag in HTML. A value of `other` allows each application using XLinks to look for other indications within the XML document to determine what needs to be done. Specifying a value of `none` has essentially the same effect as specifying a value of `other`, with the exception that the application is not expected to look for other indications as to what to do to display the link.

The `xlink:actuate` attribute is used to indicate when the linked resource should be loaded. This attribute will accept the following values:

- `onLoad`
- `onRequest`
- `other`
- `none`

A value of `onLoad` indicates that when the current resource is loading, the linked resource should be loaded as well. Specifying a value of `onRequest` means the linked document should only be loaded when some post-loading event triggers a message for traversal. A value of `other` indicates, again, that the application should look for other indications as to what the desired behavior is. Indicating a value of `none` specifies that the application is free to handle the loading of the linked resource in whatever manner seems appropriate.

Note

The `xlink:show` and `xlink:actuate` attributes are known as *behavior attributes* within the XLink recommendation.

The `xlink:label` attribute is used to name `resource` and `locator` XLink types. This value will end up being used as values within the `xlink:from` and `xlink:to` attributes to indicate the starting and ending resources for an `arc` XLink type.

Note

The `xlink:label`, `xlink:from`, and `xlink:to` attributes are known as *traversal attributes* according to the XLink recommendation.

The XML Linking Language offers two major types of links: simple and extended. Within XLink, a simple link is a convenient, shorthand notation by which to associate two resources. These resources—one local and one remote—are connected by an arc, always making a simple link an outbound link. An extended link associates any number of resources together. Furthermore, those resources may be both local and remote.

Simple Links

A simple link combines the functionality provided by the different pieces available through an extended link together into a shorthand notation. A simple link consists of an `xlink:type` attribute with a value of `simple` and, optionally, an `xlink:href` attribute with a specified value. A simple link may have any content, and even no content; it is up to the application to provide some means to generate a traversal request for the link. If no target resource is specified with the `xlink:href` attribute, the link is simply considered "dead" and will not be traversable.

Simple links play multiple roles in linking documents. For instance, the simple link, itself, acts as a `resource` XLink type for the local document. It is the combination of this functionality that shortens the XLink definition for a simple link.

However, as stated earlier, simple links are just that—simple. They link exactly two resources together: one local and one remote. Therefore, if something more complex must be handled, an extended link is necessary.

Extended Links

Within the XML Linking Language, extended links give you the ability to specify relationships between an unlimited number of resources, both local and remote. In addition, these links can involve multiple paths between the linked resources. Local resources are part of the actual extended link, whereas remote resources identify external resources to the link. An out-of-line link is created when there are no local resources at all for a link. It is up to individual applications to decide how to handle extended links; there's no magic formula for this one.

Understanding extended links can be rather frustrating. Therefore, let's look at a sample XML document that incorporates XLinks, as shown in Listing 5.4, to see how this all works.

LISTING 5.4 `Sample4.xml` Contains a Modified Version of the Names List in `Sample3.xml`

```
<People xmlns:xlink="http://www.w3.org/1999/xlink"
➥xlink:type="extended" xlink:title="Phone book">

  <Person>
    <Name>Dillon Larsen</Name>
    <Address>
      <Street>123 Jones Rd.</Street>
      <City>Houston</City>
      <State>TX</State>
      <Zip>77380</Zip>
    </Address>
  </Person>

  <Person>
    <Name>Madi Larsen</Name>
    <Address>
      <Street>456 Hickory Ln.</Street>
      <City>Houston</City>
      <State>TX</State>
      <Zip>77069</Zip>
    </Address>
  </Person>

  <Person>
    <Name>John Doe</Name>
    <Address>
      <Street>214 Papes Way</Street>
      <City>Houston</City>
      <State>TX</State>
      <Zip>77301</Zip>
    </Address>
  </Person>

  <Person xlink:type="resource" xlink:label="John">
    <Name>John Smith</Name>
    <Spouse xlink:type="resource" xlink:label="JohnSpouse">Jane Smith</Spouse>
    <Address>
      <Street>522 Springwood Dr.</Street>
      <City>Houston</City>
      <State>TX</State>
      <Zip>77069</Zip>
```

LISTING 5.4 continued

```
    </Address>
  </Person>

  <Person xlink:type="resource" xlink:label="Jane">
    <Name>Jane Smith</Name>
    <Spouse xlink:type="resource" xlink:label="JaneSpouse">John Smith</Spouse>
    <Address>
      <Street>522 Springwood Dr.</Street>
      <City>Houston</City>
      <State>TX</State>
      <Zip>77069</Zip>
    </Address>
  </Person>

  <Marriage xlink:type="arc" xlink:from="JohnSpouse"
➥xlink:to="Jane" xlink:actuate="onRequest" xlink:show="new"/>
  <Marriage xlink:type="arc" xlink:from="JaneSpouse"
➥xlink:to="John" xlink:actuate="onRequest" xlink:show="new"/>

</People>
```

From Listing 5.4, you can see that we've slightly modified the XML document from Listing 5.3. The difference here is that we're specifying XLinks within this document. Notice the addition of two new elements in Listing 5.4: `<Spouse>` and `<Marriage>`.

The basic idea here is that clicking the `<Spouse>` element will open up a new window with the spousal information on it. So how would this occur? The actual mechanics are up to the individual applications, but ideally, the `<Marriage>` element serves as an arc, or navigation path, from the local resource, which could be `Jane Smith` or `John Smith`, depending on which element you're looking at, to another resource. The `<Marriage>` element with the appropriate `xlink:from` attribute would be selected, and the application would find where the destination resource is by looking in the `xlink:to` attribute. Then, locating the element with that value in its `xlink:label` attribute, the application would navigate there and open up that information in a new window.

Summary

In this chapter, we've covered how to find desired pieces of information within an XML document using the XML Path Language and how to link XML documents together using the XML Linking Language and the XML Pointer Language. XPath, XLink, and XPointer, together, make up a set of protocols by which you can perform most any function pertaining to XML documents. We can consider XPath to be a sort of query language, whereas XLink and XPointer can be considered advanced forms of hyperlinks.

But what does it all mean? How can all this complicated mess be of some use to us? If you look at the heart of all three of these specifications, they all involve some method of locating information—whether it's a standard method to find information within the current XML document, or how to link various pieces of information within one XML document to another, or even to find a location within an XML document. These specifications empower us to find information. That's the power behind them, and let's face it, that's why most of us write applications to begin with—to manage information. And you can't manage information if you can't find it to begin with.

CHAPTER

Defining XML Using Alternate Schema Representations

IN THIS CHAPTER

Within the XML world, the XML Schema Definition Language is emerging as a supported standard for creating XML Schemas since its final recommendation given by the W3C in May of 2001. However, it is not the only supported standard defining XML schemas. Over time, while the W3C was busy refining its formal schema definition language, the rest of the world created its own. For every markup language, there is probably one schema definition language. Depending on the technologies you're used to incorporating within your applications, you may be more familiar with some of these alternate schema definition languages than others.

These alternate schema definition languages cover everything from being subsets of other schema definition languages to serving a specialized purpose, as is the case with the Schema for Object-Oriented XML (SOX) schema definition language, which is geared for, you guessed it, object-oriented XML documents. We'll take the rest of the chapter to discuss these other formats, briefly, which include the following:

- XML Data Reduced (XDR) schemas
- Document Structure Definition (DSD) schemas
- Document Content Description (DCD) schemas
- Schema for Object-Oriented XML (SOX)
- RELAX NG
- Schematron

A chapter could be devoted to each of these alternate schema formats. However, this chapter is meant to give you a brief overview of some of the other schema formats available. For each format, a URL is listed where you can find more information if needed.

A Brief Review of XML Schemas

To get an idea of how these various other schema definition languages might appear for an XML document, let's go back to our online grocery store sample XML document from Chapter 4, "Creating XML Schemas," which is shown in Listing 6.1.

LISTING 6.1 `PurchaseOrder.xml` Provides a Sample XML Document for an Online Grocery Store Order

```
<PurchaseOrder Tax="5.76" Total="75.77">

  <ShippingInformation>
    <Name>Dillon Larsen</Name>
    <Address>
      <Street>123 Jones Rd.</Street>
```

LISTING 6.1 continued

```
      <City>Houston</City>
      <State>TX</State>
      <Zip>77381</Zip>
    </Address>
    <Method>USPS</Method>
    <DeliveryDate>2001-08-12</DeliveryDate>
  </ShippingInformation>

  <BillingInformation>
    <Name>Madi Larsen</Name>
    <Address>
      <Street>123 Jones Rd.</Street>
      <City>Houston</City>
      <State>TX</State>
      <Zip>77381</Zip>
    </Address>
    <PaymentMethod>Credit Card</PaymentMethod>
    <BillingDate>2001-08-09</BillingDate>
  </BillingInformation>

  <Order SubTotal="70.01" ItemsSold="17">
    <Product Name="Baby Swiss" Id="702890" Price="2.89"
➥Quantity="1"/>
    <Product Name="Hard Salami" Id="302340" Price="2.34"
➥Quantity="1"/>
    <Product Name="Turkey" Id="905800" Price="5.80"
➥Quantity="1"/>
    <Product Name="Caesar Salad" Id="991687" Price="2.38"
➥Quantity="2"/>
    <Product Name="Chicken Strips" Id="133382" Price="2.50"
➥Quantity="1"/>
    <Product Name="Bread" Id="298678" Price="1.08"
➥Quantity="1"/>
    <Product Name="Rolls" Id="002399" Price="2.24"
➥Quantity="1"/>
    <Product Name="Cereal" Id="066510" Price="2.18"
➥Quantity="1"/>
    <Product Name="Jalapenos" Id="101005" Price="1.97"
➥Quantity="1"/>
    <Product Name="Tuna" Id="000118" Price="0.92"
➥Quantity="3"/>
    <Product Name="Mayonnaise" Id="126860" Price="1.98"
➥Quantity="1"/>
    <Product Name="Top Sirloin" Id="290502" Price="9.97"
➥Quantity="2"/>
    <Product Name="Soup" Id="001254" Price="1.33"
➥Quantity="1"/>
    <Product Name="Granola Bar" Id="026460" Price="2.14"
➥Quantity="2"/>
```

LISTING 6.1 continued

```
    <Product Name="Chocolate Milk" Id="024620" Price="1.58"
➥Quantity="2"/>
    <Product Name="Spaghetti" Id="000265" Price="1.98"
➥Quantity="1"/>
    <Product Name="Laundry Detergent" Id="148202" Price="8.82"
➥Quantity="1"/>
  </Order>

</PurchaseOrder>
```

As you can see, Listing 6.1 represents a fairly small and simple order that could be placed online. It contains the information necessary regarding how payment is to be made, how the order is to be shipped, and what day delivery should be. For comparison purposes with the other schema formats discussed in the rest of this chapter, we'll also include the W3C schema for our sample XML document, as shown in Listing 6.2.

LISTING 6.2 `PurchaseOrder.xsd` Contains a W3C Schema for `PurchaseOrder.xml`

```
<xsd:schema xmlns:xsd="http://www.w3.org/2001/XMLSchema">

  <xsd:annotation>
    <xsd:documentation>
      Purchase Order schema for an online grocery store.
    </xsd:documentation>
  </xsd:annotation>

  <xsd:element name="PurchaseOrder" type="PurchaseOrderType"/>

  <xsd:complexType name="PurchaseOrderType">
    <xsd:all>
      <xsd:element name="ShippingInformation" type="InfoType"
➥minOccurs="1" maxOccurs="1"/>
      <xsd:element name="BillingInformation" type="InfoType"
➥minOccurs="1" maxOccurs="1"/>
      <xsd:element name="Order" type="OrderType"
➥minOccurs="1" maxOccurs="1"/>
    </xsd:all>
    <xsd:attribute name="Tax">
      <xsd:simpleType>
        <xsd:restriction base="xsd:decimal">
          <xsd:fractionDigits value="2"/>
        </xsd:restriction>
      </xsd:simpleType>
    </xsd:attribute>
    <xsd:attribute name="Total">
      <xsd:simpleType>
        <xsd:restriction base="xsd:decimal">
```

LISTING 6.2 continued

```
        <xsd:fractionDigits value="2"/>
      </xsd:restriction>
    </xsd:simpleType>
  </xsd:attribute>
</xsd:complexType>

<xsd:group name="ShippingInfoGroup">
  <xsd:all>
    <xsd:element name="DeliveryDate" type="DateType"/>
    <xsd:element name="Method" type="DeliveryMethodType"/>
  </xsd:all>
</xsd:group>

<xsd:group name="BillingInfoGroup">
  <xsd:all>
    <xsd:element name="BillingDate" type="DateType"/>
    <xsd:element name="PaymentMethod" type="PaymentMethodType"/>
  </xsd:all>
</xsd:group>

<xsd:complexType name="InfoType">
  <xsd:sequence>
    <xsd:element name="Name" minOccurs="1" maxOccurs="1">
      <xsd:simpleType>
        <xsd:restriction base="xsd:string"/>
      </xsd:simpleType>
    </xsd:element>
    <xsd:element name="Address" type="AddressType" minOccurs="1"
➥maxOccurs="1"/>
    <xsd:choice minOccurs="1" maxOccurs="1">
      <xsd:group ref="BillingInfoGroup"/>
      <xsd:group ref="ShippingInfoGroup"/>
    </xsd:choice>
  </xsd:sequence>
</xsd:complexType>

<xsd:simpleType name="DateType">
  <xsd:restriction base="xsd:date"/>
</xsd:simpleType>

<xsd:simpleType name="DeliveryMethodType">
  <xsd:restriction base="xsd:string">
    <xsd:enumeration value="USPS"/>
    <xsd:enumeration value="UPS"/>
    <xsd:enumeration value="FedEx"/>
    <xsd:enumeration value="DHL"/>
    <xsd:enumeration value="Other"/>
  </xsd:restriction>
</xsd:simpleType>
```

LISTING 6.2 continued

```
  <xsd:simpleType name="PaymentMethodType">
    <xsd:restriction base="xsd:string">
      <xsd:enumeration value="Check"/>
      <xsd:enumeration value="Cash"/>
      <xsd:enumeration value="Credit Card"/>
      <xsd:enumeration value="Debit Card"/>
      <xsd:enumeration value="Other"/>
    </xsd:restriction>
  </xsd:simpleType>

  <xsd:complexType name="AddressType">
    <xsd:all>
      <xsd:element name="Street" minOccurs="1">
        <xsd:simpleType>
          <xsd:restriction base="xsd:string"/>
        </xsd:simpleType>
      </xsd:element>
      <xsd:element name="City" minOccurs="1" maxOccurs="1">
        <xsd:simpleType>
          <xsd:restriction base="xsd:string"/>
        </xsd:simpleType>
      </xsd:element>
      <xsd:element name="State" type="StateType" minOccurs="1"
➥maxOccurs="1"/>
      <xsd:element name="Zip" type="ZipType" minOccurs="1"
➥maxOccurs="1"/>
    </xsd:all>
  </xsd:complexType>

  <xsd:simpleType name="ZipType">
    <xsd:restriction base="xsd:string">
      <xsd:minLength value="5"/>
      <xsd:maxLength value="10"/>
      <xsd:pattern value="[0-9]{5}(-[0-9]{4})?"/>
    </xsd:restriction>
  </xsd:simpleType>

  <xsd:simpleType name="StateType">
    <xsd:restriction base="xsd:string">
      <xsd:length value="2"/>
      <xsd:enumeration value="AR"/>
      <xsd:enumeration value="LA"/>
      <xsd:enumeration value="MS"/>
      <xsd:enumeration value="OK"/>
      <xsd:enumeration value="TX"/>
    </xsd:restriction>
  </xsd:simpleType>
```

LISTING 6.2 continued

```
  <xsd:complexType name="OrderType">
    <xsd:all>
      <xsd:element name="Product" type="ProductType"
➥minOccurs="1" maxOccurs="unbounded"/>
    </xsd:all>
    <xsd:attribute name="SubTotal">
      <xsd:simpleType>
        <xsd:restriction base="xsd:decimal">
          <xsd:fractionDigits value="2"/>
        </xsd:restriction>
      </xsd:simpleType>
    </xsd:attribute>
    <xsd:attribute name="ItemsSold" type="xsd:positiveInteger"/>
  </xsd:complexType>

  <xsd:complexType name="ProductType">
    <xsd:attribute name="Name" type="xsd:string"/>
    <xsd:attribute name="Id" type="xsd:positiveInteger"/>
    <xsd:attribute name="Price">
      <xsd:simpleType>
        <xsd:restriction base="xsd:decimal">
          <xsd:fractionDigits value="2"/>
        </xsd:restriction>
      </xsd:simpleType>
    </xsd:attribute>
    <xsd:attribute name="Quantity" type="xsd:positiveInteger"/>
  </xsd:complexType>

</xsd:schema>
```

For a more detailed explanation regarding the schema in the preceding listing, refer to Chapter 4. As you can see from this listing, the XML Schema Definition Language can get rather complex and very detailed. But what about some of the other schema formats that have been proposed over time? We'll take the rest of the chapter to discuss these alternative schema formats and compare them against the XML Schema from the preceding listing.

Dead Formats: XDR, DSD, and DCD

Along the way to the final XML Schema recommendation given by the W3C, many other schema formats were proposed. Some of these proposals gave the W3C ideas on what needed to be included in an "all-inclusive" and robust schema definition language.

For example, some of these proposals build or solve problems in other schema proposals. There has been a long-recognized need to have way in which to define a schema for an XML document using XML syntax. As a result, many proposals were created and submitted to the W3C, and you'll see aspects from some of these proposals in the formal recommendation by the W3C for the XML Schema Definition Language.

Still, some companies created their own versions because they needed an immediate schema definition language and couldn't wait for the W3C to complete its formal recommendation on the XML Schema Definition Language. However, these formats, although still supported by many systems, will most likely be phased out in favor of the new W3C XML Schema Definition Language, and they are now considered inactive, on hold, or outright "dead." The major formats that we will concentrate on are the XML Data Reduced, Document Structure Definition, and Document Content Description languages, all of which helped to contribute to the formal XML Schema recommendation.

XML Data Reduced (XDR) Schema

In 1998, a proposal was created based on the XML-Data submission to the W3C called XML Data Reduced (XDR). This proposal refined the ideas and concepts found in the XML-Data submission down to a more manageable size in the hopes that faster progress toward adopting a formal schema definition language would be made. The main purpose of this proposal was to create a schema definition language by which elements and attributes of an XML document could be defined using XML syntax rather than using DTDs, which were recognized as being inadequate. The proposal for XDR can be found at `http://www.ltg.ed.ac.uk/~ht/XMLData-Reduced.htm`.

Going back to our online grocery store order example in Listing 6.1, the XDR schema for that sample document could appear as shown in Listing 6.3. Note the use of the word *could*. As there are many different ways to reach the same definition, this is one example of how this schema might be defined; the details regarding how this schema is constructed could vary from author to author. For instance, the `<AttributeType>` elements could be declared globally rather than locally. This doesn't change the overall results of this schema, however.

LISTING 6.3 `PurchaseOrder.xdr` Contains an XDR Schema for `PurchaseOrder.xml`

```
<Schema name="Untitled-schema"
➥xmlns="urn:schemas-microsoft-com:xml-data"
➥xmlns:dt="urn:schemas-microsoft-com:datatypes">

  <ElementType name="Address" model="closed" content="eltOnly"
➥order="seq">
    <element type="Street" minOccurs="1" maxOccurs="1"/>
```

LISTING 6.3 continued

```
    <element type="City" minOccurs="1" maxOccurs="1"/>
    <element type="State" minOccurs="1" maxOccurs="1"/>
    <element type="Zip" minOccurs="1" maxOccurs="1"/>
  </ElementType>

  <ElementType name="BillingDate" model="closed"
➥content="textOnly" dt:type="date"/>

  <ElementType name="BillingInformation" model="closed"
➥content="eltOnly" order="seq">
    <element type="Name" minOccurs="1" maxOccurs="1"/>
    <element type="Address" minOccurs="1" maxOccurs="1"/>
    <element type="PaymentMethod" minOccurs="1" maxOccurs="1"/>
    <element type="BillingDate" minOccurs="1" maxOccurs="1"/>
  </ElementType>

  <ElementType name="City" model="closed" content="textOnly"
➥dt:type="string"/>

  <ElementType name="DeliveryDate" model="closed"
➥content="textOnly" dt:type="date"/>

  <ElementType name="Method" model="closed" content="textOnly"
➥dt:type="string"/>

  <ElementType name="Name" model="closed" content="textOnly"
➥dt:type="string"/>

  <ElementType name="Order" model="closed" content="eltOnly"
➥order="seq">
    <AttributeType name="SubTotal" dt:type="fixed.14.4"
➥required="yes"/>
    <AttributeType name="ItemsSold" dt:type="i1"
➥required="yes"/>

    <attribute type="SubTotal"/>
    <attribute type="ItemsSold"/>
    <element type="Product" minOccurs="1" maxOccurs="*"/>
  </ElementType>

  <ElementType name="PaymentMethod" model="closed"
➥content="textOnly" dt:type="string"/>

  <ElementType name="Product" model="closed" content="empty">
    <AttributeType name="Name" dt:type="string" required="yes"/>
    <AttributeType name="Id" dt:type="string" required="yes"/>
    <AttributeType name="Price" dt:type="fixed.14.4"
➥required="yes"/>
```

LISTING 6.3 continued

```
    <AttributeType name="Quantity" dt:type="i1" required="yes"/>

    <attribute type="Name"/>
    <attribute type="Id"/>
    <attribute type="Price"/>
    <attribute type="Quantity"/>
  </ElementType>

  <ElementType name="PurchaseOrder" model="closed"
➥content="eltOnly" order="seq">
    <AttributeType name="Tax" dt:type="fixed.14.4"
➥required="yes"/>
    <AttributeType name="Total" dt:type="fixed.14.4"
➥required="yes"/>
    <AttributeType name="xmlns" dt:type="string"/>

    <attribute type="Tax"/>
    <attribute type="Total"/>
    <attribute type="xmlns"/>

    <element type="ShippingInformation" minOccurs="1"
➥maxOccurs="1"/>
    <element type="BillingInformation" minOccurs="1"
➥maxOccurs="1"/>
    <element type="Order" minOccurs="1" maxOccurs="1"/>
  </ElementType>

  <ElementType name="ShippingInformation" model="closed"
➥content="eltOnly" order="seq">
    <element type="Name" minOccurs="1" maxOccurs="1"/>
    <element type="Address" minOccurs="1" maxOccurs="1"/>
    <element type="Method" minOccurs="1" maxOccurs="1"/>
    <element type="DeliveryDate" minOccurs="1" maxOccurs="1"/>
  </ElementType>

  <ElementType name="State" model="closed" content="textOnly"
➥dt:type="string"/>

  <ElementType name="Street" model="closed" content="textOnly"
➥dt:type="string"/>

  <ElementType name="Zip" model="closed" content="textOnly"
➥dt:type="i4"/>

</Schema>
```

So, what can you tell from Listing 6.3? Well, for one, you see many similarities between an XDR schema and the W3C schema shown in Listing 6.2. Attributes are defined separately and then declared within the element or elements in which they are needed. Also, elements are defined separately and then placed inside the parent elements' definitions, as needed. Also, you can see that XDR supports an intrinsic set of data types similar to the ones supported by the W3C schema. As such, it makes sense then that some of the standards developed for XML Data Reduced schemas made it into the final recommendation by the W3C for the XML Schema Definition Language.

However, upon closer examination of Listings 6.2 and 6.3, we can quickly identify some major differences. For one, there is one way in which to define all element definitions within an XDR schema: the `<ElementType>` element. Whereas in the XSD schema, you can choose between `<complexType>` and `<simpleType>`, depending on the content you expect the element to hold. Also, you'll notice that to include a declaration of some data type in the XDR schema, you must use the `type` attribute from the `urn:schemas-microsoft-com:datatypes` namespace. You'll also notice that there's no support for an anonymous type declaration within an XDR schema: You must still create an `<ElementType>` element to define the element's contents, although you can declare it within the parent element, in which case it is referred to as a *local type definition*. Lastly, although you cannot tell simply from comparing the two schemas, an XDR schema does not support inheriting elements and attributes from another schema.

Document Structure Description (DSD) Schema

In 1999, AT&T Labs in New Jersey and BRICS at the University of Aarhus, Denmark collaborated to create the proposal for the Document Structure Description (DSD) language. The DSD language came about from a need to describe XML documents to Web programmers with a very limited background in computer science. The DSD language was designed to further the W3C-sponsored XML technologies, such as XSL Transformations (XSLT) and Cascading Style Sheets (CSS).

The benefit, at the time, was that DSD did not require specialized knowledge of XML or SGML because the technology was based on general and familiar concepts that allowed for stronger XML document descriptions than were possible with a DTD or the XML Schema proposal as it existed at the time; remember, the XML Schema Definition Language was not made into a formal recommendation until 2001. More complete information on this schema format can be found at `http://www.brics.dk/DSD/`.

Looking back to our online grocery store order example in Listing 6.1, the DSD schema for that sample document could appear as shown in Listing 6.4. (Note the use of the word *could*.) Again, different authors may define the same structure for an XML document slightly differently.

LISTING 6.4 PurchaseOrder.dsd Contains a DSD Schema for PurchaseOrder.xml

```
<DSD IDRef="PurchaseOrder" DSDVersion="1.0">

  <Title>DSD for PurchaseOrder.xml</Title>
  <Version>1.0</Version>
  <Author>Travis Vandersypen</Author>

  <ElementDef ID="PurchaseOrder">
    <AttributeDecl Name="Tax">
      <OneOrMore>
        <CharRange Start="0" End="9"/>
      </OneOrMore>
    </AttributeDecl>

    <AttributeDecl Name="Total">
      <OneOrMore>
        <CharRange Start="0" End="9"/>
      </OneOrMore>
    </AttributeDecl>

    <OneOrMore>
      <Sequence>
        <Element IDRef="ShippingInformationType"/>
        <Element IDRef="BillingInformationType"/>
        <Element IDRef="OrderType"/>
      </Sequence>
    </OneOrMore>
  </ElementDef>

  <ElementDef ID="CityType" Name="City">
    <Content>
      <StringType/>
    </Content>
  </ElementDef>

  <ElementDef ID="StateType" Name="State">
    <Content>
      <StringType/>
    </Content>
  </ElementDef>

  <ElementDef ID="StreetType" Name="Street">
    <Content>
      <StringType/>
    </Content>
  </ElementDef>

  <ElementDef ID="ZipType" Name="Zip">
    <Content>
      <StringType/>
```

LISTING 6.4 continued

```
    </Content>
  </ElementDef>

  <ElementDef ID="AddressType" Name="Address">
    <Sequence>
      <Element IDRef="StreetType"/>
      <Element IDRef="CityType"/>
      <Element IDRef="StateType"/>
      <Element IDRef="ZipType"/>
    </Sequence>
  </ElementDef>

  <ElementDef ID="BillingDateType" Name="BillingDate">
    <Content>
      <StringType/>
    </Content>
  </ElementDef>

  <ElementDef ID="PaymentMethodType" Name="PaymentMethod">
    <Content>
      <StringType/>
    </Content>
  </ElementDef>

  <ElementDef ID="BillingInformationType"
➥Name="BillingInformation">
    <Sequence>
      <Element IDRef="NameType"/>
      <Element IDRef="AddressType"/>
      <Element IDRef="PaymentMethodType"/>
      <Element IDRef="BillingDateType"/>
    </Sequence>
  </ElementDef>

  <ElementDef ID="DeliveryDateType" Name="DeliveryDate">
    <Content>
      <StringType/>
    </Content>
  </ElementDef>

  <ElementDef ID="DeliveryMethodType" Name="Method">
    <Content>
      <StringType/>
    </Content>
  </ElementDef>

  <ElementDef ID="NameType" Name="Name">
    <Content>
      <StringType/>
```

LISTING 6.4 continued

```
    </Content>
  </ElementDef>

  <ElementDef ID="ShippingInformationType"
➥Name="ShippingInformation">
    <Sequence>
      <Element IDRef="NameType"/>
      <Element IDRef="AddressType"/>
      <Element IDRef="DeliveryMethodType"/>
      <Element IDRef="DeliveryDateType"/>
    </Sequence>
  </ElementDef>

  <ElementDef ID="OrderType" Name="Order">
    <AttributeDecl Name="SubTotal">
      <OneOrMore>
        <CharRange Start="0" End="9"/>
      </OneOrMore>
    </AttributeDecl>

    <AttributeDecl Name="ItemsSold">
      <OneOrMore>
        <CharRange Start="0" End="9"/>
      </OneOrMore>
    </AttributeDecl>

    <OneOrMore>
      <Element IDRef="ProductType"/>
    </OneOrMore>
  </ElementDef>

  <ElementDef ID="ProductType" Name="Product">
    <AttributeDecl IDRef="Name"/>

    <AttributeDecl Name="Id">
      <OneOrMore>
        <AnyChar/>
      </OneOrMore>
    </AttributeDecl>

    <AttributeDecl Name="Price">
      <OneOrMore>
        <CharRange Start="0" End="9"/>
      </OneOrMore>
    </AttributeDecl>

    <AttributeDecl Name="Quantity">
      <OneOrMore>
        <CharRange Start="0" End="9"/>
```

LISTING 6.4 continued

```
      </OneOrMore>
    </AttributeDecl>

  </ElementDef>

</DSD>
```

You can see that the major difference in Listing 6.4 from the sample W3C schema in Listing 6.2 is that cardinality can be expressed via special elements such as `<OneOrMore>` and `<ZeroOrMore>`. Furthermore, strings have special element type definitions using the `<StringType>` element, by which an author can specify that an element contains string content. Again, however, you see the same basic trend with the W3C schema repeated here: Elements have their definitions declared separately from where they are actually used and placed within a parent element. Also, the DSD schema definition language uses a grammar-based approach to indicate how conforming XML documents should be structured.

Upon close inspection, though, you can see some major limitations with the DSD language. For one, it makes the assumption that everything is a string data type. Although that may be true in a sense, it's rather limiting when you wish to represent data that possesses a different data type other than string. For instance, does it make sense to define an element or attribute that should contain a monetary value as some string representation of that? Not really. And the DSD also does not provide support for inheriting elements and attributes from other schemas.

Document Content Description (DCD) Schema

In 1998, IBM, Microsoft, and Textuality collaborated and created a proposal which was then submitted to the W3C to create a new standard by which rules governing the structure and content of XML documents could be represented in an XML syntax. This submission was titled the *Document Content Description* (DCD). The DCD standard incorporates a subset of the XML-Data Submission and expresses it in a way consistent with the W3C Resource Description Framework (RDF). The DCD standard was intended to be a viable option to a DTD. However, with the formal recommendation of the XML Schema Definition Language, this proposal, like so many others, has become obsolete. The submission made to the W3C can be found at `http://www.w3.org/TR/NOTE-dcd`.

As an example of a Document Content Description schema, we'll again use the online grocery store example in Listing 6.1 as the sample document we'll attempt to describe. The resulting DCD schema is shown in Listing 6.5.

LISTING 6.5 `PurchaseOrder.dcd` Contains a DCD Schema for `PurchaseOrder.xml`

```
<DCD xmlns:RDF="http://www.w3.org/1999/02/22-rdf-syntax-ns#">

  <ElementDef Type="Address" Root="True" Content="Closed"
➥Model="Elements">
    <Group RDF:Order="Seq">
      <Element>Street</Element>
      <Element>City</Element>
      <Element>State</Element>
      <Element>Zip</Element>
    </Group>
  </ElementDef>

  <ElementDef Type="BillingDate" Root="True" Content="Closed"
➥Model Model="Data" Datatype="date"/>

  <ElementDef Type="BillingInformation" Root="True"
➥Model Content="Closed" Model="Elements">
    <Group RDF:Order="Seq">
      <Element>Name</Element>
      <Element>Address</Element>
      <Element>PaymentMethod</Element>
      <Element>BillingDate</Element>
    </Group>
  </ElementDef>

  <ElementDef Type="City" Root="True" Content="Closed"
➥Model Model="Data" Datatype="string"/>

  <ElementDef Type="DeliveryDate" Root="True" Content="Closed"
➥Model Model="Data" Datatype="date"/>

  <ElementDef Type="Method" Root="True" Content="Closed"
➥Model Model="Data" Datatype="string"/>

  <ElementDef Type="Name" Root="True" Content="Closed"
➥Model Model="Data" Datatype="string"/>

  <ElementDef Type="Order" Root="True" Content="Closed"
➥Model Model="Elements">
    <AttributeDef Name="SubTotal" Datatype="fixed.14.4"
➥Model Occurs="Required"/>
    <AttributeDef Name="ItemsSold" Datatype="i1"
➥Model Occurs="Required"/>

    <Group RDF:Order="Seq" Occurs="OneOrMore">
      <Element>Product</Element>
    </Group>
  </ElementDef>
```

LISTING 6.5 continued

```
  <ElementDef Type="PaymentMethod" Root="True" Content="Closed"
➥Model Model="Data" Datatype="string"/>

  <ElementDef Type="Product" Root="True" Content="Closed"
➥Model Model="Empty">
    <AttributeDef Name="Name" Datatype="string"
➥Model Occurs="Required"/>
    <AttributeDef Name="Id" Datatype="string"
➥Model Occurs="Required"/>
    <AttributeDef Name="Price" Datatype="fixed.14.4"
➥Model Occurs="Required"/>
    <AttributeDef Name="Quantity" Datatype="i1"
➥Model Occurs="Required"/>
  </ElementDef>

  <ElementDef Type="PurchaseOrder" Root="True" Content="Closed"
➥Model Model="Elements">
    <AttributeDef Name="Tax" Datatype="fixed.14.4"
➥Model Occurs="Required"/>
    <AttributeDef Name="Total" Datatype="fixed.14.4"
➥Model Occurs="Required"/>

    <Group RDF:Order="Seq">
      <Element>ShippingInformation</Element>
      <Element>BillingInformation</Element>
      <Element>Order</Element>
    </Group>
  </ElementDef>

  <ElementDef Type="ShippingInformation" Root="True"
➥Model Content="Closed" Model="Elements">
    <Group RDF:Order="Seq">
      <Element>Name</Element>
      <Element>Address</Element>
      <Element>Method</Element>
      <Element>DeliveryDate</Element>
    </Group>
  </ElementDef>

  <ElementDef Type="State" Root="True" Content="Closed"
➥Model Model="Data" Datatype="string"/>

  <ElementDef Type="Street" Root="True" Content="Closed"
➥Model Model="Data" Datatype="string"/>

  <ElementDef Type="Zip" Root="True" Content="Closed"
➥Model Model="Data" Datatype="i4"/>
</DCD>
```

From the schema definition in Listing 6.5, you can see that many similarities exist among a DCD schema, an XDR schema, and a W3C XML Schema. All three have demonstrated that element contents are defined separately and then referenced elsewhere, where they are needed; the same goes for attributes. Plus, all three take the basic approach of building from the smallest piece outward; that is to say that the simplest pieces are defined and then compounded together as needed to create more complex structures that can then be included in even more complex structures, and so on. All in all, it's very similar to the method in which a house would be built: The wood is acquired and cut to the lengths needed, then the frame is built, and so on.

Again, though, if you take a closer look, you'll see many important differences between the W3C schema and the DCD schema. For instance, as with the XDR schema, every element must have a separate type definition somewhere in the document. That means every time you wish to use an element, you must separately define its type definition and then declare that element where it will actually be used.

Schema for Object-Oriented XML (SOX)

In 1997, Veo Systems Inc., submitted a note to the W3C concerning a new schema definition language referred to as the *Schema for Object-Oriented XML* (SOX). SOX was developed primarily to assist in the development of large-scale, distributed electronic commerce applications. SOX provides a better alternative to DTDs for the creation of efficient software-development processes in distributed applications. SOX provides basic data types that can be extended, inheritance for attributes and content models, a powerful namespace mechanism, and documentation that can be embedded. Compared with DTDs, the Schema for Object-Oriented XML decreases the complexity of supporting interoperation among distributed applications by allowing various SOX processors to crunch the schema file to produce varying outputs in an automated fashion.

The SOX schema definition language is a grammar-based language very similar to that of the XML Schema Definition Language. Elements have "type" definitions and then are placed within parent elements through a declaration statement. In the case of the SOX schema definition language, the type definition comes in the form of the `<elementtype>` element. This element contains the basic type definition for an element. By using the `<model>` element within the `<elementtype>` element, a schema author can define the elements' definitions using element declarations, choices, attribute declarations, and so on. A sample SOX schema for Listing 6.1 is shown in Listing 6.6.

LISTING 6.6 `PurchaseOrder.sox` Contains a Sample SOX Schema for `PurchaseOrder.xml`

```
<schema name="PurchaseOrder">

  <elementtype name="PurchaseOrder">
    <model>
      <attdef name="Tax" datatype=""/>
      <attdef name="Total" datatype=""/>

      <sequence>
        <element name="ShippingInformation"/>
        <element name="BillingInformation"/>
        <element name="Order"/>
      </sequence>
    </model>
  </elementtype>

  <elementtype name="ShippingInformation">
    <model>
      <sequence>
        <element name="Name"/>
        <element name="Address"/>
        <element name="Method"/>
        <element name="DeliveryDate"/>
      </sequence>
    </model>
  </elementtype>

  <elementtype name="BillingInformation">
    <model>
      <sequence>
        <element name="Name"/>
        <element name="Address"/>
        <element name="PaymentMethod"/>
        <element name="BillingDate"/>
      </sequence>
    </model>
  </elementtype>

  <elementtype name="Name">
    <model>
      <string/>
    </model>
  </elementtype>

  <elementtype name="Method">
    <model>
      <string/>
    </model>
  </elementtype>
```

LISTING 6.6 continued

```
<elementtype name="DeliveryDate">
  <model>
    <string datatype="date"/>
  </model>
</elementtype>

<elementtype name="PaymentMethod">
  <model>
    <string/>
  </model>
</elementtype>

<elementtype name="DeliveryDate">
  <model>
    <string datatype="date"/>
  </model>
</elementtype>

<elementtype name="Address">
  <model>
    <sequence>
      <element name="Street"/>
      <element name="City"/>
      <element name="State"/>
      <element name="Zip"/>
    </sequence>
  </model>
</elementtype>

<elementtype name="Street">
  <model>
    <string/>
  </model>
</elementtype>

<elementtype name="City">
  <model>
    <string/>
  </model>
</elementtype>

<elementtype name="State">
  <model>
    <string/>
  </model>
</elementtype>

<elementtype name="Zip">
  <model>
```

LISTING 6.6 continued

```
      <string/>
    </model>
  </elementtype>

  <elementtype name="Order">
    <model>
      <attdef name="SubTotal" datatype="number"/>
      <attdef name="ItemsSold" datatype="int"/>
      <sequence>
        <element name="Product" occurs="+"/>
      </sequence>
    </model>
  </elementtype>

  <elementtype name="Product">
    <model>
      <empty/>
      <attdef name="Name" datatype="string"/>
      <attdef name="Id" datatype="string"/>
      <attdef name="Price" datatype = "number"/>
      <attdef name="Quantity" datatype="number"/>
    </model>
  </elementtype>

</schema>
```

From Listing 6.6, you can tell that the SOX schema definition language contains many similarities to the XML Schema Definition Language, XDR schemas, DCD schemas, and DSD schemas. The `<elementtype>` element contains the type definition for an element, which is then declared or referenced in other element type definitions.

The major difference between the W3C schema and the SOX schema is that in a SOX schema, if you redefine an element's type definition, any other element that makes a reference to the parent element type definition can also use the redefined or "subclassed" type definition in its place.

RELAX NG Schema

RELAX NG is the combination of two schema definition languages: RELAX and TREX. This schema definition language was proposed, in its current form at least, in August of 2001. On December 3rd of 2001, the specification committee proposed a formal version 1.0 for RELAX NG. You can find the current specification for RELAX NG at `http://www.oasis-open.org/committees/relax-ng/spec-20011203.html`.

One of the major advantages of the RELAX NG schema definition language over its predecessors is the ability to specify data types and simultaneously use a simple definition syntax to build a schema. However, before we explore the details for the RELAX NG schema definition language, it's important that you understand the sources for it: RELAX and TREX.

RELAX

In March of 2000, because of how complex the XML Schema Definition Language was getting, a new schema proposal was generated called *Regular Language Description for XML* (RELAX). This new schema definition language promised to define RELAX grammars using XML syntax, including the data types contained as part of the XML Schema Definition Language, and to be aware of namespaces. According to the RELAX specification, the RELAX schema definition language combines many features of DTDs with the data types supported by the XML Schema Definition Language. The main idea, as the XML Schema Definition Language was not a formal recommendation at the time RELAX was proposed, was that RELAX schemas could be created using XML syntax and then, when the formal recommendation came around for the XML Schema Definition Language, the schemas created using RELAX could be easily migrated over to the new XML schema standard recommended by the W3C.

The RELAX schema definition language, itself, consists of two parts: RELAX Core and RELAX Namespace. RELAX Core allows schema authors to create XML schemas that define elements and attributes for a single namespace, whereas RELAX Namespace allows authors to develop schemas utilizing multiple namespaces. A sample RELAX schema for the XML document in Listing 6.1 is shown in Listing 6.7.

LISTING 6.7 `PurchaseOrder.rlx` Contains a Sample RELAX Schema for `PurchaseOrder.xml`

```
<module moduleVersion="1.0" relaxCoreVersion="1.0"
➥targetNamespace=""
➥xmlns="http://www.xml.gr.jp/xmlns/relaxCore">

  <interface>
    <export label="PurchaseOrder"/>
  </interface>

  <elementRule role="PurchaseOrder">
    <sequence>
      <ref label="ShippingInformation" occurs="1"/>
      <ref label="BillingInformation" occurs="1"/>
      <ref label="Order" occurs="1"/>
    </sequence>
  </elementRule>
```

LISTING 6.7 continued

```
<elementRule role="ShippingInformation">
  <sequence>
    <ref label="Name" occurs="1"/>
    <ref label="Address" occurs="1"/>
    <ref label="Method" occurs="1"/>
    <ref label="DeliveryDate" occurs="1"/>
  </sequence>
</elementRule>

<elementRule role="BillingInformation">
  <sequence>
    <ref label="Name" occurs="1"/>
    <ref label="Address" occurs="1"/>
    <ref label="PaymentMethod" occurs="1"/>
    <ref label="BillingDate" occurs="1"/>
  </sequence>
</elementRule>

<elementRule role="Order">
  <sequence>
    <ref label="Product" occurs="*"/>
  </sequence>
</elementRule>

<elementRule role="Address">
  <sequence>
    <ref label="Street" occurs="1"/>
    <ref label="City" occurs="1"/>
    <ref label="State" occurs="1"/>
    <ref label="Zip" occurs="1"/>
  </sequence>
</elementRule>

<elementRule role="Street" type="string"/>

<elementRule role="City" type="string"/>

<elementRule role="State" type="string"/>

<elementRule role="Zip" type="string"/>

<elementRule role="Name" type="string"/>

<elementRule role="Product">
  <empty/>
</elementRule>

<elementRule role="Method" type="string"/>

<elementRule role="DeliveryDate" type="date"/>
```

LISTING 6.7 continued

```
  <elementRule role="PaymentMethod" type="string"/>

  <elementRule role="BillingDate" type="date"/>

  <tag name="ShippingInformation"/>

  <tag name="BillingInformation"/>

  <tag name="Order">
    <attribute name="SubTotal" type="decimal"/>
    <attribute name="ItemsSold" type="positiveInteger"/>
  </tag>

  <tag name="Product">
    <attribute name="Name" type="string"/>
    <attribute name="Id" type="string"/>
    <attribute name="Price" type="decimal"/>
    <attribute name="Quantity" type="positiveInteger"/>
  </tag>

  <tag name="Name"/>

  <tag name="Street"/>

  <tag name="City"/>

  <tag name="State"/>

  <tag name="Zip"/>

  <tag name="Address"/>

  <tag name="Method"/>

  <tag name="PaymentMethod"/>

  <tag name="DeliveryDate"/>

  <tag name="BillingDate"/>

  <tag name="PurchaseOrder">
    <attribute Name="Tax" type="decimal"/>
    <attribute Name="Total" type="decimal"/>
  </tag>

</module>
```

The schema shown in Listing 6.7 may seem a bit strange, but once you understand the grammar behind it, it becomes a very easily understandable schema. The basis for a

RELAX schema is that elements are defined using the `<elementRule>` element. This element can then reference, using the `<ref>` element, other elements that have been defined using the `<elementRule>` element. However, a separate element, `<tag>` with the same `name` attribute value as the `role` attribute on the `<elementRule>` element contains the attribute declarations for that element. Regardless of whether an element has attributes, it must have a corresponding `<tag>` element. The jury is still out as to whether this separation of element declarations from attribute declarations causes more complication than a regular DTD or XML Schema.

TREX

In the early part of 2001, another schema definition language proposal emerged, called *Tree Regular Expressions for XML* (TREX). This schema definition language took the approach of creating "patterns" by which to compare XML instance documents against in order to decide conformity. These patterns represented an unordered collection of attributes and an ordered sequence of elements. A sample TREX schema for the XML document in Listing 6.1 is shown in Listing 6.8.

LISTING 6.8 `PurchaseOrder.trex` Contains a Sample TREX Schema for `PurchaseOrder.xml`

```
<grammar>

  <start>
    <element name="PurchaseOrder">
      <attribute Name="Tax">
        <string/>
      </attribute>

      <attribute Name="Total">
        <string/>
      </attribute>

      <element name="ShippingInformation">
        <element name="Name">
          <anyString/>
        </element>

        <ref name="Address"/>

        <element name="Method">
          <anyString/>
        </element>

        <element name="DeliveryDate">
          <anyString/>
```

LISTING 6.8 continued

```
        </element>
      </element>

      <element name="BillingInformation">
        <element name="Name">
          <anyString/>
        </element>

        <ref name="Address"/>

        <element name="PaymentMethod">
          <anyString/>
        </element>

        <element name="BillingDate">
          <anyString/>
        </element>
      </element>

      <element name="Order">
        <attribute name="SubTotal">
          <anyString/>
        </attribute>

        <attribute name="ItemsSold">
          <anyString/>
        </attribute>

        <oneOrMore>
          <element name="Product">
            <attribute name="Name">
              <anyString/>
            </attribute>

            <attribute name="Id">
              <anyString/>
            </attribute>

            <attribute name="Price">
              <anyString/>
            </attribute>

            <attribute name="Quantity">
              <anyString/>
            </attribute>
          </element>
        </oneOrMore>
      </element>
    </element>
```

LISTING 6.8 continued

```
      <define name="Address">
        <element name="Street">
          <anyString/>
        </element>

        <element name="City">
          <anyString/>
        </element>

        <element name="State">
          <anyString/>
        </element>

        <element name="Zip">
          <anyString/>
        </element>
      </define>

    </start>

  </grammar>
```

The schema in Listing 6.8 is a little easier to understand than the RELAX schema listed in Listing 6.7. Truly the TREX schema appears self-explanatory by defining an element's contents in the traditional hierarchical XML fashion so that it becomes very easy to locate and understand what each element contains. However, the TREX schema definition language has a huge lack of support for any data types other than strings. This can be a major limitation when you're building an application.

Combining RELAX and TREX

The two different schemas we have just discussed, RELAX and TREX, each have their advantages and disadvantages. RELAX supports the XML Schema data types, but TREX does not; TREX treats content within elements and attributes as strings, the same as a DTD. However, the syntax for TREX is much simpler to understand and implement. As a result, the two schemas were merged into one: RELAX NG. This new schema proposal combines the best of both worlds: support for the XML Schema data types and a simplified schema definition language. You can see the outcome of this combination of schema definition languages in Listing 6.9.

LISTING 6.9 `PurchaseOrder.rlxng` Contains a Sample RELAX NG Schema for `PurchaseOrder.xml`

```
<grammar>

  <start>
    <element name="PurchaseOrder">
      <attribute Name="Tax">
        <data type="decimal" datatypeLibrary=
➥"http://www.w3.org/2001/XMLSchema-datatypes"/>
      </attribute>

      <attribute Name="Total">
        <data type="decimal" datatypeLibrary=
➥"http://www.w3.org/2001/XMLSchema-datatypes"/>
      </attribute>

      <element name="ShippingInformation">
        <element name="Name">
          <data type="string" datatypeLibrary=
➥"http://www.w3.org/2001/XMLSchema-datatypes"/>
        </element>

        <ref name="Address"/>

        <element name="Method">
          <data type="string" datatypeLibrary=
➥"http://www.w3.org/2001/XMLSchema-datatypes"/>
          <choice>
            <value>USPS</value>
            <value>UPS</value>
            <value>FedEx</value>
            <value>DHL</value>
            <value>Other</value>
          </choice>
        </element>

        <element name="DeliveryDate">
          <data type="date" datatypeLibrary=
➥"http://www.w3.org/2001/XMLSchema-datatypes"/>
        </element>
      </element>

      <element name="BillingInformation">
        <element name="Name">
          <data type="string" datatypeLibrary=
➥"http://www.w3.org/2001/XMLSchema-datatypes"/>
        </element>

        <ref name="Address"/>
```

LISTING 6.9 continued

```
        <element name="PaymentMethod">
          <data type="string" datatypeLibrary=
➥"http://www.w3.org/2001/XMLSchema-datatypes"/>
          <choice>
            <value>Check</value>
            <value>Cash</value>
            <value>Credit Card</value>
            <value>Debit Card</value>
            <value>Other</value>
          </choice>
        </element>

        <element name="BillingDate">
          <data type="date" datatypeLibrary=
➥"http://www.w3.org/2001/XMLSchema-datatypes"/>
        </element>
      </element>

      <element name="Order">
        <attribute name="SubTotal">
          <data type="decimal" datatypeLibrary=
➥"http://www.w3.org/2001/XMLSchema-datatypes"/>
        </attribute>

        <attribute name="ItemsSold">
          <data type="positiveInteger" datatypeLibrary=
➥"http://www.w3.org/2001/XMLSchema-datatypes"/>
        </attribute>

        <oneOrMore>
          <element name="Product">
            <attribute name="Name">
              <data type="string" datatypeLibrary=
➥"http://www.w3.org/2001/XMLSchema-datatypes"/>
            </attribute>

            <attribute name="Id">
              <data type="string" datatypeLibrary=
➥"http://www.w3.org/2001/XMLSchema-datatypes"/>
            </attribute>

            <attribute name="Price">
              <data type="decimal" datatypeLibrary=
➥"http://www.w3.org/2001/XMLSchema-datatypes"/>
            </attribute>

            <attribute name="Quantity">
              <data type="positiveInteger" datatypeLibrary=
➥"http://www.w3.org/2001/XMLSchema-datatypes"/>
```

LISTING 6.9 continued

```
            </attribute>
          </element>
        </oneOrMore>
      </element>
    </element>

    <define name="Address">
      <element name="Street">
        <data type="string" datatypeLibrary=
➥"http://www.w3.org/2001/XMLSchema-datatypes"/>
      </element>

      <element name="City">
        <data type="string" datatypeLibrary=
➥"http://www.w3.org/2001/XMLSchema-datatypes"/>
      </element>

      <element name="State">
        <data type="string" datatypeLibrary=
➥"http://www.w3.org/2001/XMLSchema-datatypes"/>
      </element>

      <element name="Zip">
        <data type="string" datatypeLibrary=
➥"http://www.w3.org/2001/XMLSchema-datatypes"/>
      </element>
    </define>

  </start>

</grammar>
```

You can see many similarities between the schema in Listing 6.9 and the TREX schema in Listing 6.8. Most of the element definitions and grammar remain the same between TREX and RELAX NG, but with one important addition: the `<data>` element. This is probably the single biggest reason for the creation of RELAX NG. Previously in TREX, a schema author was very limited in data type representation. Now, with the new `<data>` element, the RELAX NG schemas can support data types other than strings. In addition, due to the inclusion of the `datatypelibrary` attribute on the `<data>` element, the data types do not necessarily have to belong to the XML Schema Definition Language; they can come from anywhere.

By adopting the TREX-style schema definition, RELAX NG removes the cumbersome language associated with the RELAX schema definition language. Now, rather than having to specify both `<elementRule>` and `<tag>` elements to define an element's contents, you can accomplish everything within the `<element>` element.

So, what is it about Listing 6.9 that, without one necessarily knowing anything about the RELAX NG language itself, makes it intuitive to understand? For one, now that cardinality is expressed using element definitions, it becomes very clear as to how many of a particular element may appear within another. Remember that in the W3C schema recommendation, cardinality is expressed using the `minOccurs` and `maxOccurs` attributes. However, at the same time, you can no longer specify, say, that an element must occur between two to five times within another element, which is a major limiting factor in the RELAX NG schema recommendation.

Schematron

Most of the schema definition languages we have explored to this point have been based on grammatical structures. Now it's time for a drastic change in direction and concept. A new schema definition language titled Schematron has been introduced that has changed the way of thinking about schemas entirely: Rather than basing them on some grammatical structure, Schematron uses patterns to define schemas. By using patterns, Schematron allows schema authors to represent various structures that would otherwise be difficult to accomplish in a more traditional grammar-based schema definition language. By basing its definition language on XPath and XSLT, Schematron's learning curve drops sharply compared to other schema definition languages. For more information on Schematron, visit `http://www.ascc.net/xml/resource/schematron/`.

The general idea behind Schematron is to find a node set, typically elements, using XPath expressions and check the node set against some other XPath expressions to see whether they are true. A nice feature of the Schematron schema definition language is that you can actually embed Schematron schemas inside the XML Schema Definition Language's `<appinfo>` element.

Currently in version 1.5, Schematron schemas may be created using what are termed *assertions*, *rules*, *patterns*, and *phases*. Assertions within a Schematron schema are simple declarative statements contained within an `<assert>` or `<report>` element. The statement within an `<assert>` element is one that is expected to be true for an XML document conforming to the schema being defined. A statement within the `<report>` element, however, is one that is expected to be false for an XML document conforming to the schema. So, to create an assertion statement you wish to show up when an element does not have, say, a particular child element, you'd use an `<assert>` element, saying something like "Element A must have an Element B." Alternatively, you could use a `<report>` element with a statement saying something like "Element B is missing from Element A."

Each of the elements used for assertions within a Schematron schema make use of an attribute called `test`. This attribute contains an XSLT pattern, which may combine one or more XPath expressions using the `or` operator (`|`) to specify a condition that the assertion must meet. In addition, each element may also contain the following three elements:

- `<name>`
- `<emph>`
- `<span>`

The `<name>` element, when appearing in the statement for an assertion, is used to indicate that the name of the context node should be inserted at the location where the `<name>` element is. This removes the need to know the exact name of an element or elements for which an assertion will fail or hold true. Also, you may optionally specify a `path` attribute that contains an XPath expression to locate a specific node within the document, allowing a different element or attribute to be used instead of the context node. The `<emph>` element has been provided to allow for better formatting control so that elements within the assertion statement can have the same formatting as those within the `<name>` element. The `<span>` element performs exactly the same function as the `<span>` element within HTML.

Within a Schematron schema, a rule can be specified by using a `<rule>` element, which can contain both `<assert>` and `<report>` elements. The `<rule>` element itself has a `context` attribute that contains an XPath expression used to identify when the assertions contained within the rule should be tested. The combination of the `<rule>`, `<assert>` and `<report>` elements is the core behind the Schematron schema definition language.

Rules are grouped together using patterns, indicated by the `<pattern>` element. This `<pattern>` element is the nearest equivalent to a type. Patterns may contain one or more `<rule>` elements and may also contain a variety of attributes, including the following:

- `name`
- `id`
- `fpi`
- `see`

The `name` attribute allows you to specify text that can be easily read by humans, whereas the `id` attribute assigns a unique ID to the `<pattern>` element. The `fpi` element, which stands for *Formal Public Identifier*, allows an SGML Formal Public Identifier to be attached to the `<pattern>` element. The `see` attribute allows you to specify a URL that would give more documentation regarding the tests.

> **Note**
>
> One important note to keep in mind is that a context node can only be used as the context node for a rule one time. This means that the first rule that uses the context node as its context node will be evaluated normally, but every other rule that specifies the same context node will be skipped.

Now that you have a general understanding of the elements that comprise a Schematron schema, let's look at an example. Listing 6.10 shows a sample Schematron schema for the sample XML document in Listing 6.1.

LISTING 6.10 `PurchaseOrder.xst` Contains a Sample Schematron Schema for `PurchaseOrder.xml`

```
<schema>
  <pattern name="Sample">
    <rule context="PurchaseOrder">
      <assert test="@Tax">The <name/> element must have a
➥<emph>Tax</emph> attribute.</assert>

      <assert test="@Total">The <name/> element must have a
➥<emph>Total</emph> attribute.</assert>
    </rule>

    <rule context="ShippingInformation">
      <assert test="Name">The <name/> element must have a
➥<emph>Name</emph> element.</assert>

      <assert test="Address">The <name/> element must have an
➥<emph>Address</emph> element.</assert>

      <assert test="Method">The <name/> element must have a
➥<emph>Method</emph> element.</assert>

      <assert test="DeliveryDate">The <name/> element must have a
➥<emph>DeliveryDate</emph> element.</assert>
    </rule>

    <rule context="BillingInformation">
      <assert test="Name">The <name/> element must have a
➥<emph>Name</emph> element.</assert>

      <assert test="Address">The <name/> element must have an
➥<emph>Address</emph> element.</assert>
```

LISTING 6.10 continued

```
      <assert test="PaymentMethod">The <name/> element must have a
➥<emph>PaymentMethod</emph> element.</assert>

      <assert test="BillingDate">The <name/> element must have a
➥<emph>BillingDate</emph> element.</assert>
    </rule>

    <rule context="Address">
      <assert test="Street">The <name/> element must have a
➥<emph>Street</emph> element.</assert>

      <assert test="City">The <name/> element must have a
➥<emph>City</emph> element.</assert>

      <assert test="State">The <name/> element must have a
➥<emph>State</emph> element.</assert>

      <assert test="Zip">The <name/> element must have a
➥<emph>Zip</emph> element.</assert>
    </rule>

    <rule context="Order">
      <assert test="@SubTotal">The <name/> element must have a
➥<emph>SubTotal</emph> attribute.</assert>

      <assert test="@ItemsSold">The <name/> element must have a
➥<emph>ItemsSold</emph> attribute.</assert>

      <assert test="Product">The <name/> element must have a
➥<emph>Product</emph> element.</assert>
    </rule>

    <rule context="Product">
      <assert test="@Name">The <name/> element must have a
➥<emph>Name</emph> attribute.</assert>

      <assert test="@Id">The <name/> element must have a
➥<emph>Id</emph> attribute.</assert>

      <assert test="@Price">The <name/> element must have a
➥<emph>Price</emph> attribute.</assert>

      <assert test="@Quantity">The <name/> element must have a
➥<emph>Quantity</emph> attribute.</assert>
    </rule>

  </pattern>

</schema>
```

As you can tell from the code in Listing 6.10, there is a dramatic difference in complexity between it and the schema listed in Listing 6.2. Using the Schematron definition language, we have been able to efficiently describe the rules by which an XML document can be verified against conformance in a fraction of the complexity of the formal XML Schema Definition Language. Plus, now that we can actually see the schema created using the Schematron definition language, we can easily see how effective the idea of basing the schema on patterns can be compared with the very rigid and structured grammar-based method.

Alternatively, the schema in Listing 6.10 could be written as shown in Listing 6.11 to create messages that would indicate when an element or attribute is in compliance.

LISTING 6.11 `PurchaseOrder2.xst` **Contains a Sample Schematron Schema for** `PurchaseOrder.xml`

```
<schema>
  <pattern name="Sample">
    <rule context="PurchaseOrder">
      <report test="@Tax">The <name/> element has a
➥<emph>Tax</emph> attribute.</report>

      <report test="@Total">The <name/> element has a
➥<emph>Total</emph> attribute.</report>
    </rule>

    <rule context="ShippingInformation">
      <report test="Name">The <name/> element has a
➥<emph>Name</emph> element.</report>

      <report test="Address">The <name/> element has an
➥<emph>Address</emph> element.</report>

      <report test="Method">The <name/> element has a
➥<emph>Method</emph> element.</report>

      <report test="DeliveryDate">The <name/> element has a
➥<emph>DeliveryDate</emph> element.</report>
    </rule>

    <rule context="BillingInformation">
      <report test="Name">The <name/> element has a
➥<emph>Name</emph> element.</report>

      <report test="Address">The <name/> element has an
➥<emph>Address</emph> element.</report>

      <report test="PaymentMethod">The <name/> element has a
➥<emph>PaymentMethod</emph> element.</report>
```

LISTING 6.11 continued

```
      <report test="BillingDate">The <name/> element has a
➥<emph>BillingDate</emph> element.</report>
    </rule>

    <rule context="Address">
      <report test="Street">The <name/> element has a
➥<emph>Street</emph> element.</report>

      <report test="City">The <name/> element has a
➥<emph>City</emph> element.</report>

      <report test="State">The <name/> element has a
➥<emph>State</emph> element.</report>

      <report test="Zip">The <name/> element has a
➥<emph>Zip</emph> element.</report>
    </rule>

    <rule context="Order">
      <report test="@SubTotal">The <name/> element has a
➥<emph>SubTotal</emph> attribute.</report>

      <report test="@ItemsSold">The <name/> element has a
➥<emph>ItemsSold</emph> attribute.</report>

      <report test="Product">The <name/> element has a
➥<emph>Product</emph> element.</report>
    </rule>

    <rule context="Product">
      <report test="@Name">The <name/> element has a
➥<emph>Name</emph> attribute.</report>

      <report test="@Id">The <name/> element has a
➥<emph>Id</emph> attribute.</report>

      <report test="@Price">The <name/> element has a
➥<emph>Price</emph> attribute.</report>

      <report test="@Quantity">The <name/> element has a
➥<emph>Quantity</emph> attribute.</report>
    </rule>

  </pattern>

</schema>
```

The main difference between the schema in Listing 6.10 and the one in Listing 6.11 is that the messages in the schema for Listing 6.10 will only show up in the output when the test condition for the `<assert>` element fails. The messages in the schema in Listing 6.11 show up in the output when the test for the `<report>` element succeeds. The examples shown in Listing 6.10 and Listing 6.11 could be further combined into one schema so that output would be produced in either case, failure or success, as shown in Listing 6.12.

LISTING 6.12 `PurchaseOrder3.xst` Contains a Schematron Schema for `PurchaseOrder.xml`

```
<schema>
  <pattern name="Sample">
    <rule context="PurchaseOrder">
      <assert test="@Tax">The <name/> element must have a
➥<emph>Tax</emph> attribute.</assert>

      <assert test="@Total">The <name/> element must have a
➥<emph>Total</emph> attribute.</assert>

      <report test="@Tax">The <name/> element has a
➥<emph>Tax</emph> attribute.</report>

      <report test="@Total">The <name/> element has a
➥<emph>Total</emph> attribute.</report>
    </rule>

    <rule context="ShippingInformation">
      <assert test="Name">The <name/> element must have a
➥<emph>Name</emph> element.</assert>

      <assert test="Address">The <name/> element must have an
➥<emph>Address</emph> element.</assert>

      <assert test="Method">The <name/> element must have a
➥<emph>Method</emph> element.</assert>

      <assert test="DeliveryDate">The <name/> element must have a
➥<emph>DeliveryDate</emph> element.</assert>

      <report test="Name">The <name/> element has a
➥<emph>Name</emph> element.</report>

      <report test="Address">The <name/> element has an
➥<emph>Address</emph> element.</report>

      <report test="Method">The <name/> element has a
➥<emph>Method</emph> element.</report>
```

LISTING 6.12 continued

```
      <report test="DeliveryDate">The <name/> element has a
➥<emph>DeliveryDate</emph> element.</report>
    </rule>

    <rule context="BillingInformation">
      <assert test="Name">The <name/> element must have a
➥<emph>Name</emph> element.</assert>

      <assert test="Address">The <name/> element must have an
➥<emph>Address</emph> element.</assert>

      <assert test="PaymentMethod">The <name/> element must have a
➥<emph>PaymentMethod</emph> element.</assert>

      <assert test="BillingDate">The <name/> element must have a
➥<emph>BillingDate</emph> element.</assert>

      <report test="Name">The <name/> element has a
➥<emph>Name</emph> element.</report>

      <report test="Address">The <name/> element has an
➥<emph>Address</emph> element.</report>

      <report test="PaymentMethod">The <name/> element has a
➥<emph>PaymentMethod</emph> element.</report>

      <report test="BillingDate">The <name/> element has a
➥<emph>BillingDate</emph> element.</report>
    </rule>

    <rule context="Address">
      <assert test="Street">The <name/> element must have a
➥<emph>Street</emph> element.</assert>

      <assert test="City">The <name/> element must have a
➥<emph>City</emph> element.</assert>

      <assert test="State">The <name/> element must have a
➥<emph>State</emph> element.</assert>

      <assert test="Zip">The <name/> element must have a
➥<emph>Zip</emph> element.</assert>

      <report test="Street">The <name/> element has a
➥<emph>Street</emph> element.</report>

      <report test="City">The <name/> element has a
➥<emph>City</emph> element.</report>
```

LISTING 6.12 continued

```
      <report test="State">The <name/> element has a
➥<emph>State</emph> element.</report>

      <report test="Zip">The <name/> element has a
➥<emph>Zip</emph> element.</report>
    </rule>

    <rule context="Order">
      <assert test="@SubTotal">The <name/> element must have a
➥<emph>SubTotal</emph> attribute.</assert>

      <assert test="@ItemsSold">The <name/> element must have a
➥<emph>ItemsSold</emph> attribute.</assert>

      <assert test="Product">The <name/> element must have a
➥<emph>Product</emph> element.</assert>

      <report test="@SubTotal">The <name/> element has a
➥<emph>SubTotal</emph> attribute.</report>

      <report test="@ItemsSold">The <name/> element has a
➥<emph>ItemsSold</emph> attribute.</report>

      <report test="Product">The <name/> element has a
➥<emph>Product</emph> element.</report>
    </rule>

    <rule context="Product">
      <assert test="@Name">The <name/> element must have a
➥<emph>Name</emph> attribute.</assert>

      <assert test="@Id">The <name/> element must have a
➥<emph>Id</emph> attribute.</assert>

      <assert test="@Price">The <name/> element must have a
➥<emph>Price</emph> attribute.</assert>

      <assert test="@Quantity">The <name/> element must have a
➥<emph>Quantity</emph> attribute.</assert>

      <report test="@Name">The <name/> element has a
➥<emph>Name</emph> attribute.</report>

      <report test="@Id">The <name/> element has a
➥<emph>Id</emph> attribute.</report>

      <report test="@Price">The <name/> element has a
➥<emph>Price</emph> attribute.</report>
```

LISTING 6.12 continued

```
      <report test="@Quantity">The <name/> element has a
➥<emph>Quantity</emph> attribute.</report>
    </rule>

  </pattern>

</schema>
```

In the schema shown in Listing 6.12, an XML instance document would be evaluated and a very detailed report of the level of its conformity could be generated by virtue of having both `<assert>` and `<report>` elements within it. This allows applications to test for either condition depending on what sort of process is being attempted. But why would you ever want to use a pattern-based schema versus a grammar-based one? Well, imagine our sample Purchase Order XML document in Listing 6.1. Using Schematron, we could create a pattern that says the sum of all the prices times the quantities of the `<Product>` elements within the `<Order>` element must equal the value of the `SubTotal` attribute on the `<Order>` element.

Summary

In this chapter, we have explored a myriad of other schema definition languages, including XDR, DSD, DCD, SOX, RELAX NG, and Schematron. For the most part, you can see a striking similarity between these schema definition languages and the XML Schema Definition Language. Elements are first defined and then declared; the same goes for attributes. However, one schema language, Schematron, is drastically different.

You have seen that the formats that are now considered "dead" (XDR, DSD and DCD) have contributed to the formal XML Schema Definition Language recommendation by the W3C. You can see elements in each that show up within the formal recommendation, such as the concepts of element and attribute type definitions as well as element and attribute declarations.

The SOX schema definition language provides a more object-oriented approach to defining schemas, whereas RELAX NG provides a simpler approach to schema definitions than what is capable within the W3C schema recommendation. The Schematron schema definition language provides a completely different concept for defining schemas for XML documents in that it uses patterns rather than grammar to validate XML instance documents against the schema. This particular schema format raises some interesting possibilities, especially because a schema defined using the XML Schema Definition

Language can contain a Schematron schema inside an `<appinfo>` element. This would enable a schema author to define a schema using both a grammar-based and pattern-based approach—the best of both worlds.

You should keep your eye on the RELAX NG and Schematron languages as more and more companies become aware of them and begin to provide more and more support for them. SOX will begin to take a more important role for those companies that wish to enable the substitution of subclassed elements for a referenced superclass element.

Building XML-Based Applications

Part II

In This Part

CHAPTER 7

Parsing XML Using Document Object Model

In This Chapter

Up to now, we have been talking about the basics of XML. You know what an XML document looks like as well as the difference between well-formed and validated documents. Also, we have looked at several schema representations. There are tools that you can use to create XML documents and ways to exchange these documents with commercial software, such as databases and word processors. But what if you want to work with XML documents programmatically? How do you go about writing your own software that creates and reads an XML document?

As you know, XML is made up of human-readable text, so you can write your own code to manipulate XML. As you can probably guess, lots of people want to do this, so there are standard ways of working with XML. You don't have to write a lot of the code yourself. Two of the most common tools for working with XML are the Document Object Model (DOM) and the Simple API for XML (SAX).

In this chapter, we will explore DOM and look at several examples. We will look at JDOM, a Java-centric API that is similar to DOM. We will explore JAXB (or Java API for XML) binding. This is an effective way to map Java objects to XML directly using automatically generated classes. Finally, we will consider a real-world application of DOM by building an XML data server.

Note

Code examples in Java are used throughout this chapter. The source code is available on the Sams Web site. In order to compile and execute the sample code, you will need a Java 2 development environment and possibly a `make` utility. You can use just about any Java 2 development environment, such as the Software Development Kit (SDK), which is freely available from Sun Microsystems (`http://java.sun.com/j2se`), or an integrated environment like Borland JBuilder. Additional information, such as configuration hints, how to compile and execute examples, and links to resources is included with the source code. This information is contained in a file called `faq.html` in the source code directory.

In addition, you will need supplemental class libraries for DOM, JDOM, and so on. These libraries are all freely available for download at several sites on the Internet. The download sites are listed in the text for each code example and also listed in `faq.html`. Once a library is downloaded, simply follow the installation instructions available at the download site. Typically, installation simply involves unpacking a zip file and adding the class library to your `CLASSPATH`. If you still have difficulty, consult the documentation supplied with the class libraries or Frequently Asked Questions (FAQs).

What Is DOM, Anyway?

The Document Object Model (DOM) provides a way of representing an XML document in memory so that it can be manipulated by your software. DOM is a standard application programming interface (API) that makes it easy for programmers to access elements and delete, add, or edit content and attributes. DOM was proposed by the World Wide Web Consortium (W3C) in August of 1997 in the User Interface Domain. The Activity was eventually moved to the Architecture Domain in November of 2000. Here's a good place to start looking for DOM-related information:

```
http://www.w3.org/DOM
```


DOM by itself is just a specification for a set of interfaces defined by W3C. In fact, the DOM interfaces are defined independent of any particular programming language. You can write DOM code in just about any programming language, such as Java, ECMAScript (a standardized version of JavaScript/JScript), or C++. There are DOM APIs for each of these languages. W3C uses the Object Management Group's (OMG) Interface Definition Language (IDL) to define DOM in a language-neutral way. Language-specific *bindings*, or DOM interfaces, exist for these languages. The DOM specification itself includes bindings for Java and ECMAScript, but third parties have defined bindings for many other languages.

Any number of organizations provide implementations in accordance with the DOM specification. An *implementation* is a complete set of APIs for a given programming language that supports the DOM specification. You might suspect that commercial software vendors would sell DOM implementations, but it turns out that there are several open-source and freely available implementations. These implementations are well documented and of high quality. They are commonly used in production software with very good results. This is a result of a well-written specification by W3C. Due to the availability of high-quality free implementations, few if any implementations are sold for profit. We will look at some of these implementations along with sample code throughout this chapter.

What DOM Is Not

From the preceding discussion, it might be clear to you what the DOM is, but it is also important to highlight what the DOM is not. Here is a brief summary:

- DOM is not a mechanism for persisting, or *storing*, objects as XML documents. Think of it the other way: DOM is an object model for representing XML documents in your code.

- DOM is not a set of data structures; rather it is an object model describing XML documents.
- DOM does not specify what information in a document is relevant or how information should be structured.
- DOM has nothing to do with COM, CORBA, or other technologies that include the words *object model*.

Why Do I Need DOM?

The main reason for using DOM is to create or modify an XML document programmatically. You can use DOM just to read an XML document, but as you will see in the next chapter, SAX is often a better candidate for the read-only case. If you want to create a document, you start by creating a root element and then add attributes, content, sub-elements, and so on. Once you are finished, you can write the document out to disk or send it over a network. The output looks just like an XML document prepared in a text editor or XML tool.

If you want to modify an existing XML document, you can read it in from a file or other I/O source. The entire document is read into memory all at once, so you can change any part of it at any time. The representation in memory is a tree structure that starts with a root element that contains attributes, content, and sub-elements. You can traverse this tree, search for a specific node, and change its attributes or data. You can also add attributes or elements anywhere in the tree, as long as you don't violate the rules of a well-formed document. Again, you can write the modified document back out to disk or to the network.

It is possible to process XML documents using other, simpler techniques, such XSLT. The problem is that XSLT is not always expressive enough to solve complex problems. For example, let's say you want to search for elements described by another element, in the case of a master/detail relationship. This is difficult if not impossible to accomplish with XSLT.

Learning to use DOM saves you considerable time by leveraging existing parsers. Additionally, a standard interface makes it easy to change parsers in the event that an improved implementation becomes available.

Disadvantages of Using DOM

Although DOM is a W3C specification with support for a variety of programming languages, it's not necessarily the best solution for all problems. One of the big issues is that DOM can be memory intensive. As mentioned earlier, when an XML document is loaded, the entire document is read in at once. A large document will require a large amount of memory to represent it. Other parsing methods, such as SAX, don't read in the entire document, so they are better in terms of memory efficiency for some applications.

Some have argued that the DOM API is too complex. Although this is somewhat subjective, it is true that DOM is not practical for small devices such as PDAs and cellular phones. With the rapid proliferation of these devices and demand for greater functionality, XML will very likely play a role in this market. In these cases, DOM as specified by the W3C might not be the best way to go. Fortunately, there are smaller, simpler APIs for XML manipulation that follow the spirit, if not the letter, of DOM. Some of these alternative APIs are discussed later in this chapter.

Of course, everything is relative. If you want to write a quick-and-dirty program without the need for a lot of functionality, you might not require a sophisticated API at all. If all you want to do is generate a relatively simple XML document, you can always write out XML directly and avoid DOM entirely. However, as any veteran programmer knows, that quick-and-dirty code you wrote the midnight before the demo somehow always finds its way into production and becomes a maintenance nightmare!

DOM Levels

The DOM working group works on phases (or *levels*) of the specification. At the time of this writing, three levels are in the works. The DOM Level 1 and Level 2 specifications are W3C recommendations. This means that the specifications are final and can be implemented without fear of things changing. Level 1 allows traversal of an XML document as well as the manipulation of the content in that document. Level 2 extends Level 1 with additional features such as namespace support, events, ranges, and so on. Level 3 is currently a working draft. This means that it is under active development and subject to change. Details of the developments can be found at the DOM working group Web site (`www.w3.org/DOM`).

DOM Core

The DOM core is available in DOM Level 1 and beyond. It permits you to create and manipulate XML documents in memory. As mentioned earlier, DOM is a tree structure that represents elements, attributes, and content. As an example, let's consider a simple XML document, as shown in Listing 7.1.

LISTING 7.1 Simple XML Document

```
<purchase-order>
    <customer>James Bond</customer>
    <merchant>Spies R Us</merchant>
    <items>
        <item>Night vision camera</item>
        <item>Vibrating massager</item>
    </items>
</purchase-order>
```

Figure 7.1 shows a diagram of the tree structure representing the XML document from Listing 7.1.

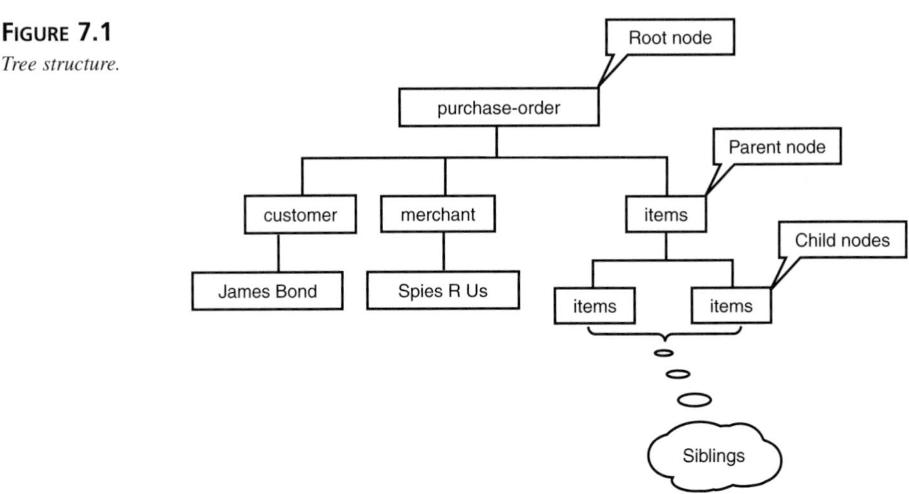

FIGURE 7.1
Tree structure.

As you can see, elements and text in the XML document are represented by nodes in the tree structure. A *node* is an abstract concept that can take the form of an element, attribute, text, or some other information.

Parents, Children, and Siblings

In formal computer science literature, lots of different terms are used to describe the parts of a tree structure. You may have run into words such as *root*, *branches*, and *leaves*. This is a bit abstract and doesn't describe relationships very well, so the DOM specification uses the words *parents*, *children*, and *siblings* to represent nodes and their relationships to one another.

Parent nodes may have zero or more child nodes. Parent nodes themselves may be the child nodes of another parent node. The ultimate parent of all nodes is, of course, the *root* node. Siblings represent the child nodes of the same parent. These abstract descriptions of nodes are mapped to elements, attributes, text, and other information in an XML document.

DOM interfaces contain methods for obtaining the parent, children, and siblings of any node. The root node has no parent, and there will be nodes that have no children or siblings. After all, the tree has to start and end somewhere!

DOM Interfaces

As mentioned earlier, the DOM interfaces are defined in IDL so that they are language neutral. The DOM specification goes into excruciating detail with respect to the interfaces. Of course, it must—what good is a spec if it is incomplete? A few fundamental interfaces are the most important. If you understand how these interfaces work, you can solve most problems without learning the entire spec inside and out.

The fundamental interfaces are listed in Table 7.1, along with a brief description of each.

TABLE 7.1 Fundamental Interfaces

Interface	*Description*
`Node`	The primary interface for the DOM. It can be an element, attribute, text, and so on, and contains methods for traversing a DOM tree.
`NodeList`	An ordered collection of `Node`s.
`NamedNodeMap`	An unordered collection of `Node`s that can be accessed by name and used with attributes.
`Document`	An `Node` representing an entire document. It contains the root `Node`.
`DocumentFragment`	A `Node` representing a piece of a document. It's useful for extracting or inserting a fragment into a document.
`Element`	A `Node` representing an XML element.
`Attr`	A `Node` representing an XML attribute.
`CharacterData`	A `Node` representing character data.
`Text`	A `CharacterData` node representing text.
`Comment`	A `CharacterData` node representing a comment.
`DOMException`	An exception raised upon failure of an operation.
`DOMImplementation`	Methods for creating documents and determining whether an implementation has certain features.

The diagram in Figure 7.2 shows the relationships among the interfaces described in Table 7.1.

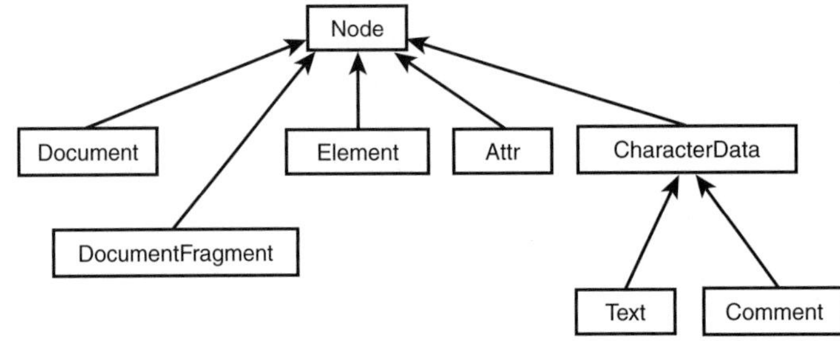

FIGURE 7.2
Interface relationships.

A number of extended interfaces are not mandatory but may be available in some implementations. These interfaces are beyond DOM Level 1 and are discussed later in this chapter. You can determine whether these interfaces are supported by calling the `hasFeature()` method of the `DOMImplementation` interface. You can use the arguments "XML" and "2.0" for the feature and version parameters of the `hasFeature()` method. For a detailed explanation, refer to the DOM specification on the W3C Web site.

The extended interfaces are listed in Table 7.2, along with a brief description of each.

TABLE 7.2 Extended Interfaces

Interface	*Description*
`CDATASection`	Text representing `CDATA`
`DocumentType`	A node representing document type
`Notation`	A node with public and system IDs of a notation
`Entity`	A node representing an entity that's either parsed or unparsed
`EntityReference`	A node representing an entity reference
`ProcessingInstruction`	A node representing an XML processing instruction

Java Bindings

The DOM working group supplies Java language bindings as part of the DOM specification. The specification and Java language bindings are available at the W3C Web site. These bindings are sets of Java source files containing Java interfaces, and they map exactly to the DOM interfaces described earlier. The package `org.w3c.dom` contains the

Java interfaces but does not include a usable implementation. In order to make the interfaces do something useful, you will need an implementation, or a *parser*.

A number of DOM implementations are available for Java. Two of the most popular are Java APIs for XML Processing (JAXP), developed by Sun Microsystems, and Xerces, developed as part of the Apache XML project. Both JAXP and Xerces are freely available in source and binary (`.class`) form. JAXP is available on the Sun Web site at `http://java.sun.com/xml/xml_jaxp.html`, and Xerces is available on the XML Apache Web site at `http://xml.apache.org/xerces2-j/index.html`.

Walking Through an XML Document

Let's look at an example in which we load an XML document from disk and print out some of its contents. This example will help you understand how the API works and how to traverse nodes in a number of ways. In the first example, we will print out just the element names using `getNodeName()` from the `Node` interface. We will start from the root and recursively print all child node names, indenting for clarity. The source code for `SimpleWalker.java` is shown in Listing 7.2.

> **Note**
>
> Note that source code for all examples in this chapter are available on the Sams Web site.

LISTING 7.2 `SimpleWalker.java`

```
package com.madhu.xml;

import java.io.*;

import org.w3c.dom.*;
import javax.xml.parsers.*;

public class SimpleWalker {
    protected DocumentBuilder docBuilder;
    protected Element root;

    public SimpleWalker() throws Exception {
        DocumentBuilderFactory dbf = DocumentBuilderFactory.newInstance();
        docBuilder = dbf.newDocumentBuilder();
        DOMImplementation domImp = docBuilder.getDOMImplementation();
        if (domImp.hasFeature("XML", "2.0")) {
```

LISTING 7.2 continued

```
            System.out.println("Parser supports extended interfaces");
        }
    }

    public void parse(String fileName) throws Exception {
        Document doc = docBuilder.parse(new FileInputStream(fileName));
        root = doc.getDocumentElement();
        System.out.println("Root element is " + root.getNodeName());
    }

    public void printAllElements() throws Exception {
        printElement("", root);
    }

    public void printElement(String indent, Node aNode) {
        System.out.println(indent + "<" + aNode.getNodeName() + ">");
        Node child = aNode.getFirstChild();
        while (child != null) {
            printElement(indent + "\t", child);
            child = child.getNextSibling();
        }
        System.out.println(indent + "</" + aNode.getNodeName() + ">");
    }

    public static void main(String args[]) throws Exception {
        SimpleWalker sw = new SimpleWalker();
        sw.parse(args[0]);
        sw.printAllElements();
    }
}
```

Looking at the code, the first thing we need to do is import the necessary packages. We need the DOM package, which is in `org.w3c.dom`, and we also need the `javax.xml.parsers` package. The DOM package we know about, but the `javax.xml.parsers` package is different. It's not part of the W3C DOM specification at all. It contains two critical classes for DOM: `DocumentBuilder` and `DocumentBuilderFactory`. These classes are needed because the DOM interfaces do not provide a way to load or create documents; this is up to the implementation. The `javax.xml.parsers` package is part of Java API for XML Processing (JAXP) and is defined through the Java Community Process (JCP JSR-005). Details on JSR-005 can be found at `http://jcp.org/jsr/detail/005.jsp`. Apache Xerces includes this package as part of the distribution. The classes in the `javax.xml.parsers` package are implementation independent, so it is possible to write application code that is completely separate from a particular DOM implementation. If you find a better implementation tomorrow, you can plug it in without changing your application code.

Execution begins at the main method, which will create an instance of our `SimpleWalker` class and call a couple of its methods to do the work. There are several methods in the `DocumentBuilder` class (`javax.xml.parsers` package) for loading and parsing an XML file. You can supply a `java.io.File`, an `InputStream`, or other source. We will use `FileInputStream` to load our file, but first we need to get an instance of `DocumentBuilder`, which is an abstract class, so we can't create an instance directly. That's the job of `DocumentBuilderFactory`, which is also abstract, but it has a static factory method, `newInstance()`, that we can use to create a `DocumentBuilder`. From there we can use one of the `parse()` methods to give us a `Document` object. Now we are totally in the DOM world. We can also obtain a `DOMImplementation` to find out what features our parser has. In this case, we are trying to find out whether extended interfaces are supported.

Once we have a `Document` object, we can get the root element by calling the `getDocumentElement()` method. It turns out that the `Document` object itself is a node, but it's not the root node. We must call `getDocumentElement()` to get the root.

The method `printElement()` in `SimpleWalker` does all the heavy lifting. It prints out the node name and then iterates through the child nodes recursively. Indenting is added for clarity. A sample XML file, `library.xml`, is used for testing and is shown in Listing 7.3.

LISTING 7.3 `library.xml`—Sample XML File

```
<?xml version="1.0" encoding="UTF-8"?>
<library>
    <fiction>
        <book>Moby Dick</book>
        <book>The Last Trail</book>
    </fiction>
    <biography>
        <book>The Last Lion, Winston Spencer Churchill</book>
    </biography>
</library>
```

The example can be executed using the following command:

```
java SimpleWalker library.xml
```

The output is shown in Listing 7.4.

LISTING 7.4 Output from `SimpleWalker`

```
Parser supports extended interfaces
Root element is library
<library>
```

LISTING 7.4 continued

```
        <#text>
        </#text>
        <fiction>
                <#text>
                </#text>
                <book>
                        <#text>
                        </#text>
                </book>
                <#text>
                </#text>
                <book>
                        <#text>
                        </#text>
                </book>
                <#text>
                </#text>
        </fiction>
        <#text>
        </#text>
        <biography>
                <#text>
                </#text>
                <book>
                        <#text>
                        </#text>
                </book>
                <#text>
                </#text>
        </biography>
        <#text>
        </#text>
</library>
```

The output is mostly what we expect—all the element names are indented nicely to show contained elements. However, what are all those `<#text>` elements? As mentioned earlier, any text in an XML document becomes a child node in DOM. If we call `getNodeName()` on a text node, we get `#text`, not the text itself. If we want to get the text, we must determine whether we have a text node and then call `getNodeValue()`. We need only make a minor modification to the `printElement()` method, as shown in Listing 7.5.

LISTING 7.5 Modified `printElement()` Method

```
    public void printElement(String indent, Node aNode) {
        if (aNode.getNodeType() == Node.TEXT_NODE) {
            System.out.println(indent + aNode.getNodeValue());
```

LISTING 7.5 continued

```
        } else {
            System.out.println(indent + "<" + aNode.getNodeName() + ">");
            Node child = aNode.getFirstChild();
            while (child != null) {
                printElement(indent + "\t", child);
                child = child.getNextSibling();
            }
            System.out.println(indent + "</" + aNode.getNodeName() + ">");
        }
    }
```


As you can see, the modified method checks the node type and formats the output as needed. The output after the modification is shown in Listing 7.6.

LISTING 7.6 Output After `printElement()` Modification

```
Parser supports extended interfaces
Root element is library
<library>


        <fiction>


                <book>
                        Moby Dick
                </book>


                <book>
                        The Last Trail
                </book>


        </fiction>


        <biography>


                <book>
                        The Last Lion, Winston Spencer Churchill
                </book>


        </biography>


</library>
```

Notice the extra blank lines before and after each element. That's because the DOM parser treats any whitespace between elements as text.

Depending on the type of node, we might need to use `getNodeName()`, `getNodeValue()`, or maybe `getAttributes()`. Table 7.3 summarizes what each of the methods gives you, depending on the interface type.

TABLE 7.3 Node Method Result Summary

Interface	`getNodeName()`	`getNodeValue()`	`getAttributes()`
`Attr`	Name of the attribute	Value of the attribute	`null`
`CDATASection`	`#cdata-section`	Content of the CDATA section	`null`
`Comment`	`#comment`	Content of the comment	`null`
`Document`	`#document`	`null`	`null`
`DocumentFragment`	`#document-fragment`	`null`	`null`
`DocumentType`	Document type name	`null`	`null`
`Element`	Tag name	`null`	`NamedNodeMap`
`Entity`	Entity name	`null`	
`EntityReference`	Name of the entity referenced	`null`	`null`
`Notation`	Notation name	`null`	`null`
`ProcessingInstruction`	Target	Entire content excluding the target	`null`
`Text`	`#text`	Content of the text node	`null`

It's important to note that attributes are not child nodes of elements. You must explicitly call `getAttributes()` to obtain a `NamedNodeMap` containing the attributes. `NamedNodeMap` is convenient for attributes because you can easily get a specific attribute by name or by index (starting from 0).

Something else to keep in mind is that many of the methods can throw a `DOMException` or some other exception. `DOMException` is a checked exception, meaning it must be caught or thrown. In our simple example, we just throw all exceptions to the caller. If an exception gets to main, the Java Virtual Machine (JVM) will catch the exception, print out a stack trace, and terminate the program. That's okay for this simple case, but in production you might want to handle exceptions yourself.

Creating an XML Document

In this example, we will create an XML document in memory, from scratch, and then write it out to disk. You might do something like this if you have data from a non-XML source, such as a database, and you want to create an XML document based on the data. You could do this by just printing out raw tags and avoid DOM altogether. This will work fine in many cases, but there are potential maintenance problems. First, you might not generate well-formed XML due to coding errors. Second, it's a lot more work!

For the data source, we will use the directory of the local disk. The XML document produced will be a directory listing in XML. The source code for `DocBuilder.java` is shown in Listing 7.7.

Note

Remember that source code for all examples in this chapter are available on the Sams Web site.

LISTING 7.7 DocBuilder.java

```
package com.madhu.xml;

import java.io.*;

import org.w3c.dom.*;
import javax.xml.parsers.*;

public class DocBuilder {
    protected DocumentBuilder docBuilder;
    protected Element root;
    protected Document doc;
    protected PrintWriter writer;

    public DocBuilder() throws Exception {
        DocumentBuilderFactory dbf = DocumentBuilderFactory.newInstance();
        docBuilder = dbf.newDocumentBuilder();
    }

    public void buildDOM(String startDir) throws Exception {
        doc = docBuilder.newDocument();
        root = doc.createElement("directory-listing");
```

LISTING 7.7 continued

```
        appendFile(root, new File(startDir));
        doc.appendChild(root);
    }

    public void appendFile(Node parent, File aFile) throws Exception {
        if (aFile.isDirectory()) {
            Element dirElement = doc.createElement("directory");
            dirElement.setAttribute("name", aFile.getName());
            File[] files = aFile.listFiles();
            int n = files.length;
            for (int i=0; i<n; i+=1) {
                appendFile(dirElement, files[i]);
            }
            parent.appendChild(dirElement);
        } else {
            Element fileElement = doc.createElement("file");
            Text fileName = doc.createTextNode(aFile.getName());
            fileElement.appendChild(fileName);
            parent.appendChild(fileElement);
        }
    }

    public void writeDOM(PrintWriter bw) throws Exception {
        writer = bw;
        writer.println("<?xml version=\"1.0\" encoding=\"UTF-8\"?>");
        writeNode("", root);
    }

    public void writeNode(String indent, Node aNode) {
        switch (aNode.getNodeType()) {
            case Node.TEXT_NODE:
                writer.println(indent + aNode.getNodeValue());
                break;

            case Node.ELEMENT_NODE:
                writer.print(indent + "<" + aNode.getNodeName());
                NamedNodeMap attrs = aNode.getAttributes();
                int n = attrs.getLength();
                for (int i=0; i<n; i+=1) {
                    Node attr = attrs.item(i);
                    writer.print(" " + attr.getNodeName() + "=\"");
                    writer.print(attr.getNodeValue() + "\"");
                }
                writer.println(">");
                Node child = aNode.getFirstChild();
                while (child != null) {
                    writeNode(indent + "\t", child);
                    child = child.getNextSibling();
                }
```

LISTING 7.7 continued

```
                writer.println(indent + "</" + aNode.getNodeName() + ">");
                break;
        }
    }

    public static void main(String args[]) throws Exception {
        DocBuilder db = new DocBuilder();
        db.buildDOM(args[0]);
        PrintWriter bw = new PrintWriter(
            new FileWriter(args[1]));
        db.writeDOM(bw);
        bw.close();
    }
}
```


To create an XML document, we use the `DocumentBuilderFactory` and the `DocumentBuilder` interfaces as before. However, instead of calling `parse()` in `DocumentBuilder` to create a `Document` object, we will call the `newDocument()` method. This creates an empty `Document` object. Then we create elements and attributes as needed and attach them appropriately.

The bulk of the work can be found in the methods `buildDOM()` and `appendFile()`. Directories and files are treated as elements. The name of a directory becomes an attribute for a directory element, whereas the name of a file is added as a text child node for a file element. A portion of the output from the program is shown in Listing 7.8.

LISTING 7.8 Partial Output from DocBuilder

```
<?xml version="1.0" encoding="UTF-8"?>
<directory-listing>
    <directory name="..">
        <directory name="com">
            <directory name="madhu">
                <directory name="xml">
                    <file>
                        DocBuilder.class
                    </file>
                    <file>
                        SimpleWalker.class
                    </file>
                </directory>
            </directory>
        </directory>
        <directory name="test">
            <file>
                Makefile
```

LISTING 7.8 continued

```
</file>
<file>
    personal-schema.xml
</file>
<file>
    personal.dtd
</file>
<file>
    personal.xml
</file>
...
```

The `Document` interface contains the methods needed for creating any type of node. Element nodes contain a method called `setAttribute()` that conveniently creates and adds an attribute in one step. If an attribute with the same name already exists, its value is replaced.

You'll also notice that the code in the `writeNode()` method is improved over similar code in `SimpleWalker`. It handles elements, text nodes, and attributes as well.

DOM Traversal and Range

Traversal and range are features added in DOM Level 2. They are supported by Apache Xerces. You can determine whether traversal is supported by calling the `hasFeature()` method of the `DOMImplementation` interface. For traversal, you can use the arguments "Traversal" and "2.0" for the feature and version parameters of the `hasFeature()` method.

Traversal

Traversal is a convenient way to walk through a DOM tree and select specific nodes. This is useful when you want to find certain elements and perform operations on them.

Traversal Interfaces

The traversal interfaces are listed in Table 7.4, along with a brief description of each.

TABLE 7.4 Summary of Traversal Interfaces

Interface	*Description*
`NodeIterator`	Used to walk through nodes linearly. Represents a subtree as a linear list.

TABLE 7.4 continued

Interface	*Description*
`TreeWalker`	Represents a subtree as a tree view.
`NodeFilter`	Can be used in conjunction with `NodeIterator` and `TreeWalker` to select specific nodes.
`DocumentTraversal`	Contains methods to create `NodeIterator` and `TreeWalker` instances.

Traversal Example

Let's look at an example in which traversal is used. Let's say we want to print out just the names of books in our library. One way to do this is to write code to iterate through every node recursively and look for book elements. This will work, but we don't need to do all that work ourselves. Instead, we can use `NodeIterator` to iterate through all the nodes and define a `NodeFilter` to select only the nodes with the name "book." When we find a book node, we can get the value of the text content and print it out.

There are two classes we need to define. The first one, `IteratorApp.java`, contains the application code. The second one, `NameNodeFilter.java`, selects nodes with a given name. The source code for `IteratorApp.java` is shown in Listing 7.9, and the source code for `NameNodeFilter.java` is shown in Listing 7.10. Both source files must import `org.w3c.dom.traversal` in order to reference the traversal interfaces.

LISTING 7.9 `IteratorApp.java`

```
package com.madhu.xml;

import java.io.*;

import org.w3c.dom.*;
import org.w3c.dom.traversal.*;
import javax.xml.parsers.*;

public class IteratorApp {
    protected DocumentBuilder docBuilder;
    protected Document document;
    protected Element root;

    public IteratorApp() throws Exception {
        DocumentBuilderFactory dbf = DocumentBuilderFactory.newInstance();
        docBuilder = dbf.newDocumentBuilder();
        DOMImplementation domImp = docBuilder.getDOMImplementation();
        if (domImp.hasFeature("Traversal", "2.0")) {
```

LISTING 7.9 continued

```
            System.out.println("Parser supports Traversal");
        }
    }

    public void parse(String fileName) throws Exception {
        document = docBuilder.parse(new FileInputStream(fileName));
        root = document.getDocumentElement();
        System.out.println("Root element is " + root.getNodeName());
    }

    public void iterate() {
        NodeIterator iter =
        ((DocumentTraversal)document).createNodeIterator(
            root, NodeFilter.SHOW_ELEMENT,
            new NameNodeFilter("book"), true);

        Node n = iter.nextNode();
        while (n != null) {
            System.out.println(n.getFirstChild().getNodeValue());
            n = iter.nextNode();
        }
    }

    public static void main(String args[]) throws Exception {
        IteratorApp ia = new IteratorApp();
        ia.parse(args[0]);
        ia.iterate();
    }
}
```

LISTING 7.10 NameNodeFilter.java

```
package com.madhu.xml;

import org.w3c.dom.*;
import org.w3c.dom.traversal.*;

public class NameNodeFilter implements NodeFilter {
    protected String name;

    public NameNodeFilter(String inName) {
        name = inName;
    }

    public short acceptNode(Node n) {
        if (n.getNodeName().equals(name)) {
            return FILTER_ACCEPT;
```

LISTING 7.10 continued

```
        } else {
            return FILTER_REJECT;
        }
    }
}
```

Looking at `IteratorApp.java`, you'll see that the traversal code is found in the `iterate()` method. We can create an instance of `NodeIterator` from the `DocumentTraversal` interface. But how do we get an instance of a `DocumentTraversal` interface? It turns out that if traversal is supported, the `Document` instance will also implement `DocumentTraversal`. If you look carefully at the `iterate()` method, you will see that the document is downcast into `DocumentTraversal`. The cast succeeds because traversal is supported by our implementation (Xerces). If it wasn't supported, a `ClassCastException` would be raised at runtime.

The method for creating a `NodeIterator` is `createNodeIterator(...)`, which accepts four parameters: the root node, a flag determining which nodes to show, a possible `NodeFilter`, and a flag determining whether entity references are to be expanded. In our example, we start at the document root, because we want to search the entire document. Constants in the `NodeFilter` interface define which nodes will be visible. You can choose options such as elements, attributes, text, and so on. The `NodeFilter` is optional. If you don't want to use a `NodeFilter`, just supply "null" and no filter will be applied.

In our example, we define a node filter that looks for nodes with a given name. To define a node filter, we need to implement `NodeFilter` and fill in one method: `acceptNode()`. As we iterate through nodes, the traversal API will call our `acceptNode()` method, which can return either `FILTER_ACCEPT`, `FILTER_REJECT`, or `FILTER_SKIP`. For node iterators, `FILTER_REJECT` and `FILTER_SKIP` do the same thing. The behavior is slightly different for `TreeWalker` interfaces (refer to the documentation for the details). In our `acceptNode()` method, we just compare the name of the node and return `FILTER_ACCEPT` if the node name matches the name supplied when `NameNodeFilter` was created. We created an instance of `NameNodeFilter` with the name "book," so we should find only book elements.

Going back to the `iterate()` method in the `IteratorApp` class, we can use a `while` loop to go through the nodes. The method `nextNode()` will return null when we get to the end of the list. Only element nodes with name "book" are returned. Once we find a book element, we can obtain the text content node by calling `getFirstChild()` and then calling `getNodeValue()` on that node. The input XML file is shown in Listing 7.11.

LISTING 7.11 library.xml—Input XML Document

```
<?xml version="1.0" encoding="UTF-8"?>
<library>
    <fiction>
        <book>Moby Dick</book>
        <book>The Last Trail</book>
    </fiction>
    <biography>
        <book>The Last Lion, Winston Spencer Churchill</book>
    </biography>
</library>
```

Here's the output from `IteratorApp`:

```
Parser supports MutationEvents
Root element is library
Moby Dick
The Last Trail
The Last Lion, Winston Spencer Churchill
```

The `TreeWalker` interface provides many of the same benefits as `NodeIterator`. The main difference is that `TreeWalker` presents a tree-oriented view of the nodes instead of a list-oriented view. An iterator allows you to move forward and backward, but a `TreeWalker` interface allows you to also move to the parent of a node, to one of its children, or to a sibling. The DOM specification explains this in greater detail.

Range

Range interfaces provide a convenient way to select, delete, extract, and insert content. You can determine whether range is supported by calling the `hasFeature(...)` method of the `DOMImplementation` interface. You can use the arguments "Range" and "2.0" for feature and version. There are a number of applications for which the range interfaces are useful.

A range consists of two boundary points corresponding to the start and the end of the range. A boundary point's position in a `Document` or `DocumentFragment` tree can be characterized by a node and an offset. The node is the container of the boundary point and its position. The container and its ancestors are the ancestor containers of the boundary point and its position. The offset within the node is the offset of the boundary point and its position. If the container is an `Attr`, `Document`, `DocumentFragment`, `Element`, or `EntityReference` node, the offset is between its child nodes. If the container is a `CharacterData`, `Comment`, or `ProcessingInstruction` node, the offset is between the 16-bit units of the UTF-16 encoded string contained by it.

The boundary points of a range must have a common ancestor container that is either a `Document`, `DocumentFragment`, or `Attr` node. That is, the content of a range must be entirely within the subtree rooted by a single `Document`, `DocumentFragment`, or `Attr` node. This common ancestor container is known as the *root container* of the range. The tree rooted by the root container is known as the range's *context tree*.

The container of a boundary point of a range must be an `Element`, `Comment`, `ProcessingInstruction`, `EntityReference`, `CDATASection`, `Document`, `DocumentFragment`, `Attr`, or `Text` node. None of the ancestor containers of the boundary point of a range can be a `DocumentType`, `Entity`, or `Notation` node.

Range Interfaces

The range interfaces are listed in Table 7.5, along with a brief description of each.

TABLE 7.5 Summary of Range Interfaces

Interface	*Description*
`Range`	This interface describes a range and contains methods to define, delete, insert content.
`DocumentRange`	This interface creates a range.

Range Example

Let's look at an example in which range is used. Let's say we want to delete the first child node under the root. One way to do this is to write code to iterate through every node under the first child and remove it. However, we can accomplish the same operation with less code using ranges.

The source code for `RangeApp.java` is shown in Listing 7.12. We must import `org.w3c.dom.range` in order to refer to the range interfaces.

LISTING 7.12 `RangeApp.java`

```
package com.madhu.xml;

import java.io.*;

import org.w3c.dom.*;
import org.w3c.dom.ranges.*;
import javax.xml.parsers.*;
```

LISTING 7.12 continued

```
public class RangeApp {
    protected DocumentBuilder docBuilder;
    protected Document document;
    protected Element root;

    public RangeApp() throws Exception {
        DocumentBuilderFactory dbf = DocumentBuilderFactory.newInstance();
        docBuilder = dbf.newDocumentBuilder();
        DOMImplementation domImp = docBuilder.getDOMImplementation();
        if (domImp.hasFeature("Range", "2.0")) {
            System.out.println("Parser supports Range");
        }
    }

    public void parse(String fileName) throws Exception {
        document = docBuilder.parse(new FileInputStream(fileName));
        root = document.getDocumentElement();
        System.out.println("Root element is " + root.getNodeName());
    }

    public void deleteRange() {
        Range r = ((DocumentRange)document).createRange();
        r.selectNodeContents(root.getFirstChild());
        r.deleteContents();
    }

    public static void main(String args[]) throws Exception {
        RangeApp ra = new RangeApp();
        ra.parse(args[0]);
        ra.deleteRange();
    }
}
```

Looking at `RangeApp.java`, you'll see that the traversal code is found in the `deleteRange()` method. We can create an instance of a range from the `DocumentRange` interface. We obtain a `DocumentRange` instance similar to the traversal example. If range is supported, the `Document` instance will also implement `DocumentRange`. In the `deleteRange()` method, you will see that the document is downcast into `DocumentRange`. The cast succeeds because range is supported by our implementation (Xerces). If it wasn't supported, a `ClassCastException` would be raised at runtime.

The method for creating a range is `createRange()`, with no arguments. A number of methods in the `Range` interface set the range. In the example, we used `selectNodeContents()` to select all the content under the first child node under he root. We can delete this content using `deleteContents()`.

Other DOM Implementations

For a variety of reasons, some have argued that DOM as specified by the W3C is not the best way to go. One reason is that it's too complex. In this case, JDOM has appeared as an alternative. Another reason is that DOM takes too much memory and is not practical for resource-constrained devices such as PDAs and cellular phones. For these applications, a number of DOM-like APIs have appeared. In this section, we'll look at some of these alternative implementations.

JDOM

JDOM is not an acronym. It was originally developed as an open-source API for XML but has been accepted by the Java Community Process (JCP JSR-102). The home of JDOM is `www.jdom.org`.

JDOM was designed specifically for Java. In contrast, DOM is purely an interface specification independent of any language. For example, a Java parser can leverage standard Java types and collections, such as the `String` class and the Collections API. The goal of W3C DOM is to be language independent, which works but can add a lot of unnecessary complications. Here are some of the guiding principles of JDOM:

- JDOM should be straightforward for Java programmers.
- JDOM should support easy and efficient document modification.
- JDOM should hide the complexities of XML wherever possible, while remaining true to the XML specification.
- JDOM should integrate with DOM and SAX.
- JDOM should be lightweight and fast.
- JDOM should solve 80 percent (or more) of Java/XML problems with 20 percent (or less) of the effort when compare with DOM.

JDOM is a class-based API, whereas DOM is an interface-based API. There are classes that encapsulate documents, elements, attributes, text, and so on. This simplifies usage by minimizing downcasts. DOM is a strict hierarchy based on a node, which leads to lots of downcasts. Downcasts add complexity to source code and also reduce performance.

JDOM does not parse XML by itself; rather, it can build JDOM objects from a DOM tree or a SAX parser. In general, it is more efficient to use JDOM's `SAXBuilder` class if all you want to do is read XML from a file or stream.

JDOM Example

Let's create an XML document using JDOM. The source code for `JDOMCreate.java` appears in Listing 7.13.

LISTING 7.13 `JDOMCreate.java`

```
package com.madhu.xml;

import org.jdom.*;
import org.jdom.output.*;

public class JDOMCreate {
    public static void main(String args[]) throws Exception {
        Element root = new Element("library");
        Document doc = new Document(root);
        Element fiction = new Element("fiction");
        Element book = new Element("book");
        book.setAttribute("author", "Herman Melville");
        book.addContent("Moby Dick");
        fiction.addContent(book);
        root.addContent(fiction);
        XMLOutputter outputter = new XMLOutputter("\t", true);
        outputter.output(doc, System.out);
    }
}
```

Most of the JDOM classes are in the `org.jdom` package. We only need the `org.jdom.output` package in order to write the output using `XMLOutputter`. As advertised, JDOM code is very simple. To create a document, all we need to do is create elements, using any of the `Element` class constructors. Once that is done, we can set attributes and add content. The `addContent()` method is overridden, so you can add text or elements using the same method. Notice that you must create the `Document object` given a root element. This is done to make sure the document is always well formed.

Once the object graph representing our document is created, we can write it out to a stream using the `XMLOutputter` class. In the example, we write the document to `System.out`. We could write it to a file using `FileOutputStream` as well. The output appears in Listing 7.14.

LISTING 7.14 `JDOMCreate` Output

```
<?xml version="1.0" encoding="UTF-8"?>
<library>
        <fiction>
```

LISTING 7.14 continued

```
            <book author="Herman Melville">Moby Dick</book>
        </fiction>
</library>
```

Notice the nice formatting of the output. Indenting and new lines make the document look as if it was hand-edited. Formatting can be controlled through constructor parameters of the `XMLOutputter` class. In the example, we specified a Tab character (`\t`) for indenting and set new lines to `true`. This can be particularly handy if the XML documents you create are available for human consumption (which they often are).

Reading and parsing an XML document is even easier. As mentioned earlier, JDOM is not meant to be a parser replacement. JDOM uses existing parsers to avoid reinventing the wheel. If you have an existing DOM or SAX parser, you can use it with JDOM. The JDOM distribution includes Apache Xerces, so you can be up and running right away.

The following example parses an XML document and then prints it out using `XMLOutputter`. The source code for `JDOMParse.java` appears in Listing 7.15.

LISTING 7.15 `JDOMParse.java`

```
package com.madhu.xml;

import java.io.*;

import org.jdom.*;
import org.jdom.input.*;
import org.jdom.output.*;

public class JDOMParse {
    public static void main(String args[]) throws Exception {
        SAXBuilder builder = new SAXBuilder();
        Document doc = builder.build(new File(args[0]));
        XMLOutputter outputter = new XMLOutputter("\t", true);
        outputter.output(doc, System.out);
    }
}
```

You can use either a DOM or SAX parser in order to parse a document and produce a JDOM `Document` object. In practice, SAX parsers tend to be more efficient in terms of memory because the entire document is not read in at once, as is the case with DOM. The `SAXBuilder` class can build a document given a `File` object, `InputStream`, or a number of other sources.

Small DOM-like Implementations

PDAs and cellular phones are rapidly becoming the terminals of choice for people on the run. They are a lot easier to carry compared to a laptop. (Remember the "luggables" of the mid-1980s? We've come a long way since then!)

With the availability of Java 2 Micro Edition (J2ME) and the wireless Web, XML is becoming more important on these small devices. If you're going to work with XML on a PDA, something like DOM is a great help. Of course, a full-blown DOM implementation is too much for a PDA, but there are smaller, simpler alternatives, and you have several solutions from which to choose.

NanoXML

NanoXML is a nonvalidating parser available at `http://nanoxml.sourceforge.net`. It looks a lot like DOM, but it's much smaller. Version 2.0 is about 33KB, but a light version is available that's less than 6KB! The API contains a class called `XMLElement`, which is very similar to the `Node` interface found in DOM.

TinyXML

TinyXML is a nonvalidating parser available at `http://www.gibaradunn.srac.org/tiny/index.shtml`. It's primarily for reading in an XML document, because it does not provide facilities to create a document. It's extremely simple, based primarily on one class, `TinyParser`, and one interface, `ParsedXML`. All you need to do is call a static method in `TinyParser` to parse a stream, file, or URL. This gives you an instance of a `ParsedXML` interface that has only seven methods. The uncompressed class files are about 16KB.

kXML

kXML is a DOM-like parser in the spirit of JDOM. The primary difference is that it is designed specifically for J2ME resource-constrained devices. kXML can be found at `http://www.kxml.org`. kXML is probably the most sophisticated of the three small parsers mentioned.

Java Architecture for XML Binding (JAXB)

JAXB provides a means of automatically binding XML with Java objects. JAXB is being developed through the Java Community Process (JCP) under JSR-31. The home of JAXB is `http://java.sun.com/xml/jaxb/index.html`.

JAXB can be considered a *serialization* mechanism from Java objects to XML. Serialization is the process of converting an object in memory into a stream of data, and vice versa. Serialization is a convenient way of storing objects on disk or sending them over a network. Object serialization based on serializable and externalizable interfaces performs a similar function but requires the developer to simply implement one of these interfaces. In the case of JAXB, a set of binding classes is generated using a schema compiler. The classes manage *marshalling*, meaning translating Java objects to XML and back again. Here is a brief summary of some of benefits of JAXB:

- Valid data is guaranteed. Marshalling is based on a schema, which constrains the structure of the XML.
- JAXB is faster and requires less memory when compared with DOM. DOM includes a lot of functionality for manipulating arbitrary documents. JAXB applications are specific to a given schema, so they can be more efficient.
- JAXB is relatively easy to use. All you need to do is supply a schema and generate binding classes using a schema compiler. From there, reading, writing, and modifying XML is simply a matter of a few method calls.
- JAXB applications are extensible. The generated classes can be used as is, or they can be subclassed for reusability and added functionality.

Data Binding

If you think about it, a class and a schema perform similar functions. Classes describe Java objects, whereas schemas describe XML documents. An object is an instance of a class, and a document follows a schema. The diagram in Figure 7.3 illustrates the relationships between schemas, classes, documents, and objects.

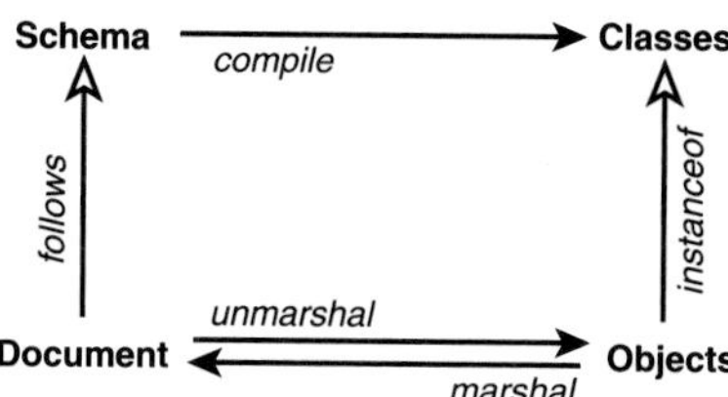

FIGURE 7.3
Binding relationships.

If we have a schema, perhaps in the form of a DTD, we can automatically generate classes that translate between objects and documents. Of course, in the real world, we might want to customize some of the details of the generated classes. Fortunately, JAXB provides facilities for customization through an optional binding schema.

One way to define a binding is to generate one Java class for every element in a schema. If you don't provide any extra information, this is basically what JAXB does. Attributes within an element are mapped to `String` fields. Content within an element is a little more complicated. Table 7.6 summarizes how the content is mapped within a Java class.

TABLE 7.6 Default Content Binding

Content Type	*Field Type*
PCDATA	`String`
Fixed number of elements	References to sub-element types
Varying number of elements	`java.util.List`
Any	Can be defined using additional information described in a binding schema

JAXB Example

Let's look at an example using JAXB. A sample DTD is shown in Listing 7.16. We will use this DTD as our schema for generating binding classes. As of this writing, the JAXB schema compiler only accepts DTDs. In the future, other schema formats may be accepted.

LISTING 7.16 `library.dtd`

```
<?xml version="1.0" encoding="US-ASCII"?>
<!ELEMENT library (fiction|biography|science)*>
<!ELEMENT fiction (book)+>
<!ELEMENT biography (book)+>
<!ELEMENT science (book)+>
<!ELEMENT book (#PCDATA)>
<!ATTLIST book author CDATA #REQUIRED>
```

This DTD describes a simple library with three categories of books: fiction, biography, and science. Each of these categories can contain one or more book elements. Each book element contains an author attribute, and the title will be defined in the content of the book element. This isn't necessarily a practical example, but it will give you a good idea how JAXB works. It can be easily expanded as needed.

In order to generate binding classes, we need to run the schema compiler shipped with JAXB. The schema compiler is itself written in Java and can be invoked like this:

```
java com.sun.tools.xjc.Main -d outdir -roots library library.dtd
```

Of course, the schema compiler JAR file must be in your classpath (dropping the JAR into your `JDK/jre/lib/ext` directory is the simplest way). The `-d` option specifies an output directory for the generated classes. If it's not included, the current directory is used. The `-roots` option specifies a comma-separated list of root elements. This is needed because DTDs don't provide a way to define root elements. The last argument is the filename of our DTD.

The schema compiler can also accept an optional binding schema. The binding schema is an XML file with the extension `.xjs`. It can include information such as the root elements, names of classes and methods, which elements to bind to classes, types for attributes, and data conversions. If you specify a binding schema, you can avoid the `-roots` option. If you don't use a binding schema, you must supply the `-roots` option. There's quite a bit you can do with binding schemas, so it's best to refer to the JAXB specification to get it all. We will stick with the default bindings provided automatically with the schema compiler. In many cases, this is good enough.

Once the schema compiler is run on our sample DTD, five Java source files are generated containing the classes that describe each of the elements in `library.dtd`. The code for the root element, `Library.java`, is shown in Listing 7.17.

LISTING 7.17 `Library.java`

```
// imports not shown

public class Library
    extends MarshallableRootElement
    implements RootElement
{

    private List _Content = PredicatedLists.createInvalidating(this,
       new ContentPredicate(), new ArrayList());
    private PredicatedLists.Predicate pred_Content = new ContentPredicate();

    public List getContent() {
        return _Content;
    }

    public void deleteContent() {
        _Content = null;
        invalidate();
    }

    public void emptyContent() {
        _Content = PredicatedLists.createInvalidating(this,
               pred_Content, new ArrayList());
    }
```

LISTING 7.17 continued

```
    public void validateThis()
        throws LocalValidationException
    {
    }

    public void validate(Validator v)
        throws StructureValidationException
    {
        for (Iterator i = _Content.iterator(); i.hasNext(); ) {
            v.validate(((ValidatableObject) i.next()));
        }
    }

    public void marshal(Marshaller m)
        throws IOException
    {
        XMLWriter w = m.writer();
        w.start("library");
        if (_Content.size()> 0) {
            for (Iterator i = _Content.iterator(); i.hasNext(); ) {
                m.marshal(((MarshallableObject) i.next()));
            }
        }
        w.end("library");
    }

    public void unmarshal(Unmarshaller u)
        throws UnmarshalException
    {
        XMLScanner xs = u.scanner();
        Validator v = u.validator();
        xs.takeStart("library");
        while (xs.atAttribute()) {
            String an = xs.takeAttributeName();
            throw new InvalidAttributeException(an);
        }
        {
            List l = PredicatedLists.create(this, pred_Content,
                new ArrayList());
            while ((xs.atStart("fiction")||xs.atStart("biography"))||
                   xs.atStart("science")) {
                l.add(((MarshallableObject) u.unmarshal()));
            }
            _Content = PredicatedLists.createInvalidating(this,
                pred_Content, l);
        }
        xs.takeEnd("library");
    }
```

LISTING 7.17 continued

```
    public static Library unmarshal(InputStream in)
        throws UnmarshalException
    {
        return unmarshal(XMLScanner.open(in));
    }

    public static Library unmarshal(XMLScanner xs)
        throws UnmarshalException
    {
        return unmarshal(xs, newDispatcher());
    }

    public static Library unmarshal(XMLScanner xs, Dispatcher d)
        throws UnmarshalException
    {
        return ((Library) d.unmarshal(xs, (Library.class)));
    }

    public boolean equals(Object ob) {
        if (this == ob) {
            return true;
        }
        if (!(ob instanceof Library)) {
            return false;
        }
        Library tob = ((Library) ob);
        if (_Content!= null) {
            if (tob._Content == null) {
                return false;
            }
            if (!_Content.equals(tob._Content)) {
                return false;
            }
        } else {
            if (tob._Content!= null) {
                return false;
            }
        }
        return true;
    }

    public int hashCode() {
        int h = 0;
        h = ((127 *h)+((_Content!= null)?_Content.hashCode(): 0));
        return h;
    }

    public String toString() {
        StringBuffer sb = new StringBuffer("<<library");
```

LISTING 7.17 continued

```
        if (_Content!= null) {
            sb.append(" content=");
            sb.append(_Content.toString());
        }
        sb.append(">>");
        return sb.toString();
    }

    public static Dispatcher newDispatcher() {
        return Biography.newDispatcher();
    }

    private static class ContentPredicate
        implements PredicatedLists.Predicate
    {
        public void check(Object ob) {
            if (!(ob instanceof MarshallableObject)) {
                throw new InvalidContentObjectException(ob,
                        (MarshallableObject.class));
            }
        }
    }
}
```

There is a field named `_Content` of type `java.util.List`. This object can contain any number of elements—specifically, the categories of books in our library. A `List` object is used for the content because we didn't specify a particular type in a binding schema. In this case, the schema compiler chose a `List` object because our library element can contain a variable number of sub-elements. There are a few validation methods that can validate this class and all content. The `marshal()` and `unmarshal()` methods read and write XML to and from streams.

A simple application that exercises the generated classes is shown in Listing 7.18. This application reads an XML file, adds another book element, validates the XML, and writes all the content to a second XML file. This is typical of the kinds of applications that can be developed with JAXB.

LISTING 7.18 `LibraryApp.java`

```
import java.io.*;
import java.util.*;
import javax.xml.bind.*;
import javax.xml.marshal.*;
```

LISTING 7.18 continued

```
public class LibraryApp {
    protected Library myLibrary;

    public LibraryApp() {
        myLibrary = new Library();
    }

    public static void main(String[] args) throws Exception {
        LibraryApp la = new LibraryApp();

        la.readXML("library.xml");
        la.addBook();
        la.validate();
        la.writeXML("new_library.xml");
    }

    public void readXML(String fileName) throws Exception {
        System.out.println("Reading " + fileName);
        FileInputStream fIn = new FileInputStream(fileName);
        try {
            myLibrary = myLibrary.unmarshal(fIn);
        } finally {
            fIn.close();
        }
        System.out.println(myLibrary);
    }

    public void addBook() {
        List entryList = myLibrary.getContent();
        for (ListIterator i = entryList.listIterator(); i.hasNext();) {
            Object element = i.next();
            if (element instanceof Science) {
                Book qmBook = new Book();
                qmBook.setAuthor("Eisberg, Resnick");
                qmBook.setContent("Quantum Mechanics");
                Science sb = (Science) element;
                List sl = sb.getBook();
                sl.add(qmBook);
                break;
            }
        }
    }

    public void validate() throws Exception {
        myLibrary.validate();
    }

    public void writeXML(String fileName) throws Exception {
        System.out.println("Writing " + fileName);
```

LISTING 7.18 continued

```
        FileOutputStream fOut = new FileOutputStream(fileName);
        try {
            myLibrary.marshal(fOut);
        } finally {
            fOut.close();
        }
    }
}
```

The two imported packages of interest are `javax.xml.bind` and `javax.xml.marshal`. The first one, `javax.xml.bind`, contains most of the classes for JAXB. The second package, `javax.xml.marshal`, contains a few classes needed for marshalling. These classes were split into two packages because marshalling is not specific to XML. There could be marshalling classes for all kinds of data bindings.

The `readXML()` method reads an XML file into a `Library` object using the `unmarshal()` method. This could throw an `UnmarshalException` caused by invalid XML.

The `addBook()` method obtains a reference to the content of the `Library` object as a `List` object. It then searches for a category of type science, creates a book object, and adds it to the science category. Notice the `setAuthor()` method defined in the `Book` class. This was also generated by the schema compiler.

The `validate()` method validates the `Library` object before it is written using the `writeXML()` method. Validation is required if any of the objects describing our document were modified. If validation is not done, an exception would be thrown by the `marshal()` method.

As you can see, JAXB is fairly easy to use. A lot of functionality can be added automatically by specifying a binding schema. As mentioned earlier, you might want to explore binding schemas in detail to get the most out of JAXB.

Case Study: Building an XML Data Server

Let's take a look at a case study so you can see how DOM works in the real world. We will build a Java servlet that accepts a SQL statement to query a database and returns the results in the form of XML. This might seem like overkill. Why not just connect to the database through ODBC or JDBC and obtain a result set? Of course, you could do that, but there are firewall constraints and possibly the need for a persistent connection to the client. HTTP is a simple protocol that any firewall will pass without complaining. HTTP is easy to implement and easy to debug. Most importantly, it's an open protocol with wide industry support.

What we will end up with is something like an XML data server. Of course, commercial-quality data servers do a lot more, such as manage scalability through caching and load balancing. Even still, we can build an effective data server for illustration purposes, and scalability can be addressed later.

A servlet accepts a request from a client and returns results in XML. The servlet acts as the "glue" between the Internet and the database. Figure 7.4 illustrates the operation of the servlet and database.

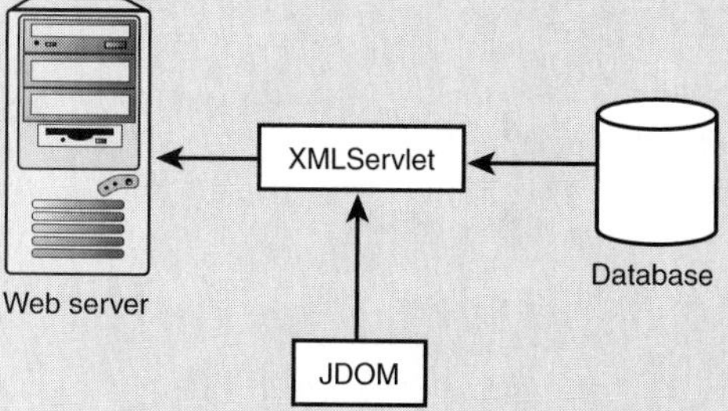

FIGURE 7.4
Servlet operation.

It would be nice to automate as much of the XML generation as possible. What we can do is use the column names of the database result set as the element names of our XML output. We can use `ResultSetMetaData` from JDBC to give us this information. The source code for our XML servlet is shown in Listing 7.19.

The complete source code is available on the Sams Web site. Our sample database contains information from the *2000 CIA World Fact Book*. In order to experiment with XMLServlet, you will need a servlet engine such as Apache Tomcat. Tomcat is freely available for download from `http://Jakarta.apache.org/tomcat`. The download includes detailed installation instructions along with a number of examples. You can use almost any database for testing. Any one of the sample databases supplied with Microsoft Access will work well.

Sample output is shown in Listing 7.20.

LISTING 7.19 `XMLServlet.java`

```
package com.madhu.xml;

import java.io.*;
import java.util.*;
import java.sql.*;
```

LISTING 7.19 continued

```
import javax.servlet.*;
import javax.servlet.http.*;

import org.jdom.*;
import org.jdom.output.*;

public class XMLServlet extends HttpServlet {
    protected Connection connection;

    public void init() {
        try {
            Class.forName("sun.jdbc.odbc.JdbcOdbcDriver");
            connection = DriverManager.getConnection(
                    "jdbc:odbc:worldfactbook");
        } catch (Exception e) {
            e.printStackTrace();
        }
    }

    public void doGet(HttpServletRequest request,
                  HttpServletResponse response) throws IOException {

        ServletConfig config = getServletConfig();
        PrintWriter out = response.getWriter();
        response.setContentType("text/xml");
        try {
            String sql = request.getParameter("sql");
            Statement stat = connection.createStatement();
            ResultSet rs = stat.executeQuery(sql);
            ResultSetMetaData rsMeta = rs.getMetaData();
            int rowNumber = 1;
            Element root = new Element("resultset");
            root.setAttribute("query", sql);
            while (rs.next()) {
                Element row = new Element("row");
                row.setAttribute("index", Integer.toString(rowNumber));
                int nCols = rsMeta.getColumnCount();
                for (int i=1; i<=nCols; i+=1) {
                    String colName = rsMeta.getColumnName(i);
                    Element column = new Element(colName);
                    column.addContent(rs.getString(i));
                    row.addContent(column);
                }
                root.addContent(row);
                rowNumber += 1;
            }
```

LISTING 7.19 continued

```
                rs.close();
                stat.close();

                Document doc = new Document(root);

                XMLOutputter outputter = new XMLOutputter("\t", true);
                outputter.output(doc, out);
            } catch (Exception e) {
                e.printStackTrace(out);
            }
        }
}
```

LISTING 7.20 `XMLServlet` Sample Output

```
<?xml version="1.0" encoding="UTF-8"?>
<resultset query="select * from people where country like 'united%'">
    <row index="1">
        <ID>220</ID>
        <Country>United Arab Emirates</Country>
        <Population>2369153.0</Population>
        <GrowthRate>1.61</GrowthRate>
        <BirthsPer1000>18.0</BirthsPer1000>
        <DeathsPer1000>3.68</DeathsPer1000>
        <NetMigrationPercent>1.82</NetMigrationPercent>
        <NetMigration>43118.5846</NetMigration>
        <InfantMortalityPer1000>17.17</InfantMortalityPer1000>
        <TotalLifeExpectency>74.06</TotalLifeExpectency>
        <MaleLifeExpectency>71.64</MaleLifeExpectency>
        <FemaleLifeExpectency>76.61</FemaleLifeExpectency>
        <TotalLiteracy>79.2</TotalLiteracy>
        <MaleLiteracy>78.9</MaleLiteracy>
        <FemalLiteracy>79.8</FemalLiteracy>
    </row>
    <row index="2">
        <ID>221</ID>
        <Country>United Kingdom</Country>
        <Population>59511464.0</Population>
        <GrowthRate>0.25</GrowthRate>
        <BirthsPer1000>11.76</BirthsPer1000>
        <DeathsPer1000>10.38</DeathsPer1000>
        <NetMigrationPercent>1.07</NetMigrationPercent>
        <NetMigration>636772.6648</NetMigration>
        <InfantMortalityPer1000>5.63</InfantMortalityPer1000>
```

LISTING 7.20 continued

```
        <TotalLifeExpectency>77.66</TotalLifeExpectency>
        <MaleLifeExpectency>74.97</MaleLifeExpectency>
        <FemaleLifeExpectency>80.49</FemaleLifeExpectency>
        <TotalLiteracy>99.0</TotalLiteracy>
        <MaleLiteracy>0.0</MaleLiteracy>
        <FemalLiteracy>0.0</FemalLiteracy>
    </row>
    <row index="3">
        <ID>222</ID>
        <Country>United States</Country>
        <Population>275562673.0</Population>
        <GrowthRate>0.91</GrowthRate>
        <BirthsPer1000>14.2</BirthsPer1000>
        <DeathsPer1000>8.7</DeathsPer1000>
        <NetMigrationPercent>3.5</NetMigrationPercent>
        <NetMigration>9644693.555</NetMigration>
        <InfantMortalityPer1000>6.82</InfantMortalityPer1000>
        <TotalLifeExpectency>77.12</TotalLifeExpectency>
        <MaleLifeExpectency>74.24</MaleLifeExpectency>
        <FemaleLifeExpectency>79.9</FemaleLifeExpectency>
        <TotalLiteracy>97.0</TotalLiteracy>
        <MaleLiteracy>97.0</MaleLiteracy>
        <FemalLiteracy>97.0</FemalLiteracy>
    </row>
    </resultset>
```

As in any servlet, the bulk of the work is performed in the `goGet()` method. The `doGet()` method will only be called in response to a `GET` request. If responses to both `GET` and `POST` requests are necessary, you can override the `service()` method instead.

The SQL query is supplied as part of the query string. We can obtain this string using the `getParameter()` method while supplying the name of the parameter. In our example, the parameter name is simply `sql`. Once we have the SQL, we can issue standard JDBC calls to obtain a result set.

Now the interesting part begins. We will use JDOM to create the DOM tree. As you saw earlier, JDOM can be easier to use when creating a document. The result set is translated into a DOM tree by using the `ResultSet` column names as element names. The column names are obtained through `ResultSetMetaData`. The resulting DOM tree is written to the response output stream using `XMLOutputter`.

Summary

Document Object Model (DOM) is a set of language-independent interfaces defined by the W3C DOM working group. DOM parsers can be used to read, create, and modify XML documents. At the time of this writing, DOM Level 1 and Level 2 are recommended specifications, meaning they are available for use in production software. DOM Level 3 is a working draft, meaning the specification is not yet ready for implementation. The DOM specification includes Java language bindings described as Java interfaces. All the specifications may be found at the DOM Web site (`www.w3.org/DOM`).

There are several freely available implementations of DOM Level 1 and Level 2. The most common are JAXP from Sun Microsystems and Xerces from the Apache XML group. JDOM is another popular variant that can be easier to use in some cases. Several small DOM-like implementations are available for use in resource-constrained applications such as cell phones and PDAs.

JAXB provides yet another way to create and parse XML using an object model. JAXB is defined by the Java Community Process and can be used to bind an XML schema into Java classes. This can be more efficient when compared to DOM in many cases.

CHAPTER

Parsing XML Using SAX

IN THIS CHAPTER

In the last chapter, you saw how XML data could be parsed using the Document Object Model (DOM). In this chapter, we will explore another tool for parsing XML—the Simple API for XML (SAX). DOM can also be used for creating documents. Unlike DOM, SAX can only be used for parsing existing documents. We will look at some of the reasons why SAX is preferred for certain applications. We will explore several examples that demonstrate how the SAX API works, and finally we will look at a practical example as a case study using SAX.

SAX has an interesting development history. Many of the APIs commonly used today (even outside the XML community) have been developed through some kind of formal process. A standards body, such as the W3C, is often involved. SAX, on the other hand, was the result of collaboration by the members of the XML-DEV mailing list, principally Dave Megginson. The home of SAX is Dave Megginson's site: `http://www.megginson.com/SAX`. The history of SAX can be found at `http://www.megginson.com/SAX/SAX1/history.html`, and the XML-DEV mailing list is located at `http://www.xml.org/xml/xmldev.shtml`.

Despite the lack of a formal standards body guiding the development of SAX, it has rapidly become one of the most popular APIs for parsing XML. This is due, in part, to the fact that it is available in the public domain, free of charge, in both source and binary form. The copyright is probably the least restrictive of any available today. Unlike the GNU Public License (GPL) and others, the SAX copyright is just one short paragraph:

> *SAX2 is Free!*
>
> *I hereby abandon any property rights to SAX 2.0 (the Simple API for XML), and release all of the SAX 2.0 source code, compiled code, and documentation contained in this distribution into the Public Domain. SAX comes with NO WARRANTY or guarantee of fitness for any purpose.*
>
> *David Megginson, david@megginson.com*

Basically, you can do whatever you want with SAX—there are no strings attached. Then again, there is no formal support. Documentation is limited to the API and source code. One might argue that you get what you pay for, but SAX has been around for several years and the quality is quite high. As with any open-source software, if you run into a problem, you can dive in and fix it yourself. In many cases, this is more effective than high-priced technical support from a large corporation.

What Is SAX, Anyway?

SAX is an API that can be used to parse XML documents. A *parser* is a program that reads data a character at a time and returns manageable pieces of data. For example, a parser for the English language might break up a document into paragraphs, words, and punctuation. In the case of XML, the important pieces of data include elements, attributes, text, and so on. This is what SAX does.

SAX provides a framework for defining event listeners, or *handlers*. These handlers are written by developers interested in parsing documents with a known structure. The handlers are registered with the SAX framework in order to receive events. Events can include start of document, start of element, end of element, and so on. The handlers contain a number of methods that will be called in response to these events. Once the handlers are defined and registered, an input source can be specified and parsing can begin.

What SAX Is Not

SAX by itself is just an API, and a number of implementations are available from many of the familiar sources. The most commonly used parsers are Xerces from the Apache XML project and Java API for XML Processing (JAXP) from Sun Microsystems. A good list of parsers can be found at `http://www.xmlsoftware.com`.

SAX was originally developed in Java, but similar implementations are available in other languages as well. There are implementations for Perl, Python, and C++, for example. You can find more information at `http://www.megginson.com/SAX/applications.html`.

Why Do I Need SAX?

If you have an XML document, at some point you will need to read it programmatically. Let's say you want to pull out the text from a document or maybe look for attributes of specific tags. You might be able to do some of the work using a tool or maybe XSLT, but these solutions have their limitations. When you need to do something more complex, you'll have to write a program. That's where SAX comes in.

If you are writing a tool or a standalone program to process XML, SAX is a good way to do it. Many applications today can be customized using an XML file. These files have replaced the traditional "properties" files for reasons of uniformity and richness of expression. Instead of spending a lot of your time writing a parser to read XML files, you might as well use SAX. As mentioned earlier, SAX is completely free, so it can be embedded in a larger application without royalty fees or even copyright notices.

Some SAX parsers can validate a document against a Document Type Definition (DTD). Validating parsers can also tell you specifically where validation has failed. You will see an example demonstrating how to do that in this chapter.

SAX vs. DOM

As you know, DOM is an in-memory tree structure of an XML document or document fragment. DOM is a natural object model of an XML document, but it's not always practical. Large documents can take up a lot of memory. This is overkill if all you want to do is find a small piece of data in a very large document.

SAX is, in many ways, much simpler than DOM. There is no need to model every possible type of object that can be found in an XML document. This makes the API easy to understand and easier to use. DOM contains many interfaces, each containing many methods. SAX is comprised of a handful of classes and interfaces. SAX is a much lower-level API when compared with DOM. For these reasons, SAX parsers tend to be smaller than DOM implementations. In fact, many DOM implementations use SAX parsers under the hood to read in XML documents.

SAX is an *event-based* API. Instead of loading an entire document into memory all at once, SAX parsers read documents and notify a client program when elements, text, comments, and other data of interest are found. SAX parsers send you events continuously, telling you what was found next.

The DOM parses XML *in space*, whereas SAX parses XML *in time*. In essence, the DOM parser hands you an entire document and allows you to traverse it any way you like. This can take a lot of memory, so SAX can be significantly more efficient for large documents. In fact, you can process documents larger than available system memory, but this is not possible with DOM. SAX can also be faster, because you don't have to wait for the entire document to be loaded. This is especially valuable when reading data over a network.

In some cases, you might want to build your own object model of an XML document because DOM might not describe your specific document efficiently or in the way you would like. You could solve the problem by loading a document using DOM and translating the DOM object model into your own object model. However, this can be very inefficient, so SAX is often a better solution.

Disadvantages

SAX is not a perfect solution for all problems. For instance, it can be a bit harder to visualize compared to DOM because it is an event-driven model. SAX parsing is "single pass," so you can't back up to an earlier part of the document any more than you can back up from a serial data stream. Moreover, you have no random access at all. Handling parent/child relationships can be more challenging as well.

Another disadvantage is that the current SAX implementations are read-only parsers. They do not provide the ability to manipulate a document or its structure (this feature may be added in the future). DOM is the way to go if you want to manipulate a document in memory.

There is no formal specification for SAX. The interfaces and behavior are defined through existing code bases. This means there is no way to validate a SAX parser or to determine whether it works correctly. In the words of Dave Megginson, "It's more like English Common Law rather than the heavily codified Civil Code of ISO or W3C specifications."

Even considering these limitations, SAX does its job well. It's lightweight, simple, and easy to use. If all you want to do is read XML, SAX will probably do what you need.

SAX Versions

The first version, SAX 1.0, was released in May 1998. It provided the basic functionality needed to read elements, attributes, text, and to manage errors. There was also some DTD support. The details of SAX 1.0 can be found at `http://www.megginson.com/SAX/SAX1/index.html`.

The current version, SAX 2.0, was released two years later in May 2000. Many of the SAX 2.0 interfaces are departures from SAX 1.0. Older interfaces are included, but deprecated, for backward compatibility. Adapters are included for using SAX 1.0 parsers with SAX 2.0, and vice versa. SAX 2.0 also includes support for namespaces and extensibility through features and properties. Documentation is improved as well.

Note

Code examples in Java are used throughout this chapter. The source code is available on the Sams Web site. In order to compile and execute the sample code, you will need a Java 2 development environment and possibly a `make` utility. You can use just about any Java 2 development environment, such as the Software Development Kit (SDK) freely available from Sun Microsystems (`http://java.sun.com/j2se`) or an integrated environment such as Borland JBuilder.

In addition, you will need supplemental class libraries for SAX. Most of the examples use SAX 2.0 libraries available from Dave Megginson's site. Alternatively, Apache Xerces includes a SAX 2.0 parser. Xerces is available at `http://xml.apache.org`. Once you've downloaded it, simply follow the installation instructions by unpacking a zip file and adding the class libraries to your classpath. If you still have difficulty, consult the documentation supplied with the class libraries or Frequently Asked Questions (FAQs) .

SAX Basics

To illustrate how SAX works, let's say you have a simple document, like this one:

```
<?xml version="1.0" encoding="UTF-8"?>
<fiction>
    <book author="Herman Melville">Moby Dick</book>
</fiction>
```

If you want to parse this document using SAX, you would build a *content handler* by creating a Java class that implements the `ContentHandler` interface in the `org.xml.sax` package. Convenience adapters are available that simplify some of this.

Once you have a content handler, you simply register it with a SAX `XMLReader`, set up the input source, and start the parser. Next, the methods in your content handler will be called when the parser encounters elements, text, and other data. Specifically, the events generated by the preceding example will look something like this:

```
start document
start element: fiction
start element: book (including attributes)
characters: Moby Dick
end element: book
end element: fiction
end document
```

As you can see, the events reported follow the content of the document in a linear sequence. There are a number of other events that might be generated in response to processing instructions, errors, and comments. We will look at these in the examples that follow.

SAX Packages

The SAX 2.0 API is comprised of two standard packages and one extension package. The standard packages are `org.xml.sax` and `org.xml.helpers`. The `org.xml.sax` package contains the basic classes, interfaces, and exceptions needed for parsing documents. There, you will find most of the interfaces needed to create handlers for various types of events. We will use many of these classes and interfaces in the sample code later in this chapter. A summary of the `org.xml.sax` package is shown in Table 8.1.

TABLE 8.1 The `org.xml.sax` Package

Name	*Description*
Interfaces	
`AttributeList`	Deprecated. This interface has been replaced by the SAX2 `Attributes` interface, which includes namespace support.

TABLE 8.1 continued

Name	*Description*
`Attributes`	Interface for a list of XML attributes.
`ContentHandler`	Receives notification of the logical content of a document.
`DocumentHandler`	Deprecated. This interface has been replaced by the SAX2 `ContentHandler` interface, which includes namespace support.
`DTDHandler`	Receives notification of basic DTD-related events.
`EntityResolver`	Basic interface for resolving entities.
`ErrorHandler`	Basic interface for SAX error handlers.
`Locator`	Interface for associating a SAX event with a document location.
`Parser`	Deprecated. This interface has been replaced by the SAX2 `XMLReader` interface, which includes namespace support.
`XMLFilter`	Interface for an XML filter.
`XMLReader`	Interface for reading an XML document using callbacks.
Classes	
`HandlerBase`	Deprecated. This class works with the deprecated `DocumentHandler` interface.
`InputSource`	A single input source for an XML entity.
Exceptions	
`SAXException`	Encapsulates a general SAX error or warning.
`SAXNotRecognizedException`	Exception class for an unrecognized identifier.
`SAXNotSupportedException`	Exception class for an unsupported operation.
`SAXParseException`	Encapsulates an XML parse error or warning.

The `org.xml.sax.helpers` package contains additional classes that can simplify some of your coding and make it more portable. You will find a number of adapters that implement many of the handler interfaces, so you don't need to fill in all the methods defined in the interfaces. Factory classes provide a mechanism for obtaining a parser independent of the implementation. We will use many of these classes and interfaces in the sample code later in this chapter. A summary of the `org.xml.sax.helpers` package is shown in Table 8.2.

TABLE 8.2 The `org.xml.sax.helpers` Package

Class	*Description*
`AttributeListImpl`	Deprecated. This class implements a deprecated interface, `AttributeList` that has been replaced by `Attributes`, which is implemented in the `AttributesImpl` helper class.
`AttributesImpl`	Default implementation of the `Attributes` interface.
`DefaultHandler`	Default base class for SAX2 event handlers.
`LocatorImpl`	Provides an optional convenience implementation of `Locator`.
`NamespaceSupport`	Encapsulate namespace logic for use by SAX drivers.
`ParserAdapter`	Adapts a SAX1 `Parser` as a SAX2 `XMLReader`.
`ParserFactory`	Deprecated. This class works with the deprecated `Parser` interface.
`XMLFilterImpl`	Base class for deriving an XML filter.
`XMLReaderAdapter`	Adapts a SAX2 `XMLReader` as a SAX1 `Parser`.
`XMLReaderFactory`	Factory for creating an XML reader.

The `org.xml.sax.ext` package is an extension that is not shipped with all implementations. It contains two handler interfaces for capturing declaration and lexical events. We will use some of these classes and interfaces in the sample code later in this chapter. A summary of the `org.xml.sax.ext` package is shown in Table 8.3.

TABLE 8.3 The `org.xml.sax.ext` Package

Interface	*Description*
`DeclHandler`	SAX2 extension handler for DTD declaration events
`LexicalHandler`	SAX2 extension handler for lexical events

SAX Implementations

As mentioned earlier, a number of SAX implementations exist. SAX implementations include all the underlying classes needed to parse documents. The SAX API by itself does not include these underlying classes, so you will need to obtain an implementation. You can find a list of implementations at `http://www.megginson.com/SAX/applications.html`. When looking for an implementation, you might want to consider several factors, such as version support, validating/nonvalidating, DTD/XML Schema support, and so on.

As in the case of DOM, several high-quality free implementations exist, so cost is not an issue. If you want to validate documents while parsing XML, you will need a validating SAX implementation. Most validating implementations support DTDs, and some even support XML Schema.

In terms of performance, there is not much hard data. You might have to do some benchmarking yourself to determine whether it's fast enough for you. For the examples in this chapter, we will use Xerces, developed by the Apache XML group. Xerces is a validating parser with full support for SAX 2.0. Xerces is very popular and widely regarded as a high-quality parser. It is freely available at `http://xml.apache.org`.

Working with SAX

In this section, we will explore a series of examples. The examples will exercise different parts of the SAX API to illustrate how they are used and demonstrate how they work.

Note

Like the other examples in this book, the source code for these examples is available on the Sams Web site. Details on compiling and executing the examples is contained in a file called `faq.html` supplied with the download.

Walking Through an XML Document

Let's look at a simple example in which we read an XML document from disk and print out some of the contents. This example will help you understand how the SAX API works. In this example, we will print out just the element names and the text between the elements. The source code for `SAXDemo.java` is shown in Listing 8.1.

LISTING 8.1 `SAXDemo.java`

```
package com.madhu.xml;

import java.io.*;
import org.xml.sax.*;
import org.xml.sax.helpers.*;
import javax.xml.parsers.*;

public class SAXDemo extends DefaultHandler {
    public void startDocument() {
        System.out.println("***Start of Document***");
```

LISTING 8.1 continued

```
    }

    public void endDocument() {
        System.out.println("***End of Document***");
    }

    public void startElement(String uri, String localName,
        String qName, Attributes attributes) {

        System.out.print("<" + qName);
        int n = attributes.getLength();
        for (int i=0; i<n; i+=1) {
            System.out.print(" " + attributes.getQName(i) +
                "='" + attributes.getValue(i) + "'");
        }
        System.out.println(">");
    }

    public void characters(char[] ch, int start, int length) {
        System.out.println(new String(ch, start, length).trim());
    }

    public void endElement(String namespaceURI, String localName,
        String qName) throws SAXException {

        System.out.println("</" + qName + ">");
    }

    public static void main(String args[]) throws Exception {
        if (args.length != 1) {
            System.err.println("Usage: java SAXDemo <xml-file>");
            System.exit(1);
        }

        SAXDemo handler = new SAXDemo();

        SAXParserFactory factory = SAXParserFactory.newInstance();

        SAXParser parser = factory.newSAXParser();
        parser.parse(new File(args[0]), handler);
    }
}
```

The first thing we need to do is import the necessary packages. For this example, we will need the `org.xml.sax` package and the `org.xml.helpers` package. In addition, we have imported the `javax.xml.parsers` package. This package is part of JAXP, defined by the Java Community Process (JCP). Although this package is outside the scope of SAX proper, it is helpful in locating and creating a default SAX parser. It is not absolutely required, as you will see in later examples, but it shows one of the recommended ways of creating a SAX parser. This package is shipped with Xerces as well as JAXP from Sun Microsystems.

Our class extends `DefaultHandler` in order to capture events. `DefaultHandler` is a convenience adapter class defined in `org.xml.sax.helpers`. It implements four interfaces: `EntityResolver`, `DTDHandler`, `ContentHandler`, and `ErrorHandler`. We could have implemented `ContentHandler` alone, but then we would be required to fill in all the methods of `ContentHandler`, even if we were not interested in all the events. `DefaultHandler` defines empty stub methods for all these events. That way, we are free to fill in only the methods we are interested in. All other events are discarded.

In order to register our handler, we can create a `SAXParser` instance and call its `parse()` method with a file and handler instance. The code to do this is located in the `main()` method of the example. This uses a factory class defined in JAXP. In later examples, we will see other ways of creating a parser and registering handlers.

In the example, we have defined five methods: `startDocument()`, `endDocument()`, `startElement()`, `characters()`, and `endElement()`. These methods will be called in response to related events, and they are defined in the `ContentHandler` interface, along with a number of others. Once the `parse()` method is called, our methods will be called in response to events until the end of input is reached or an error occurs. Descriptions of all the methods defined in `ContentHandler` are provided in Table 8.4.

TABLE 8.4 The `ContentHandler` Methods

Method	*Description*
`characters()`	Receives notification of character data
`endDocument()`	Receives notification of the end of a document
`endElement()`	Receives notification of the end of an element
`endPrefixMapping()`	Ends the scope of a prefix-URI mapping
`ignorableWhitespace()`	Receives notification of ignorable whitespace in element content
`processingInstruction()`	Receives notification of a processing instruction
`setDocumentLocator()`	Receives an object for locating the origin of SAX document events
`skippedEntity()`	Receives notification of a skipped entity
`startDocument()`	Receives notification of the beginning of a document
`startElement()`	Receives notification of the beginning of an element
`startPrefixMapping()`	Begins the scope of a prefix-URI namespace mapping

The `startElement()` and `endElement()` methods accept several arguments: namespace URI, local name, qualified name, and attributes. The first three are defined depending on whether namespaces are used. The `characters()` method provides an array of characters and locations where valid characters are found in the array. This is done for performance reasons. Typically, a `String` can be easily created, as shown earlier.

A sample XML document, `library.xml`, is used for testing and is shown in Listing 8.2.

LISTING 8.2 `library.xml`—Sample XML Document

```
<?xml version="1.0" encoding="UTF-8"?>
<!DOCTYPE library SYSTEM "library.dtd">
<library>
    <fiction>
        <book author="Herman Melville">Moby Dick</book>
        <book author="Zane Grey">The Last Trail</book>
    </fiction>
    <biography>
        <book author="William Manchester">
            The Last Lion, Winston Spencer Churchill
        </book>
    </biography>
    <science>
        <book author="Hecht, Zajac">Optics</book>
    </science>
</library>
```

To execute `SAXDemo`, you can enter the following command:

```
java com.madhu.xml.SAXDemo library.xml
```

This command specifies that the input file, `library.xml`, is located in the current directory. The output of `SAXDemo` is shown in Listing 8.3. It shows beginning and end of document events, elements, and text. Note that formatting such as tabs and spaces is lost. This happens because text is trimmed of whitespace by calling the `trim()` method of the `String` class.

LISTING 8.3 Output from `SAXDemo`

```
***Start of Document***
<library>
<fiction>
<book author='Herman Melville'>
Moby Dick
</book>
<book author='Zane Grey'>
The Last Trail
```

LISTING 8.3 continued

```
</book>
</fiction>
<biography>
<book author='William Manchester'>
The Last Lion, Winston Spencer Churchill
</book>
</biography>
<science>
<book author='Hecht, Zajac'>
Optics
</book>
</science>
</library>
***End of Document***
```

Validation

SAX parsers come in two varieties: validating and nonvalidating. Validating parsers can determine whether an XML document is valid based on a Document Type Definition (DTD) or Schema.

The SAX parser shipped with Apache Xerces is a validating parser. In order to use validation, you must turn it on by setting the validation feature to `true`. If you attempt to turn on validation with a nonvalidating parser, a `SAXNotSupportedException` will be thrown. If the parser does not recognize the feature, a `SAXNotRecognizedException` will be thrown. This helps in determining whether you mistyped the feature name.

In the following example, we will write a simple program to validate an XML document. The document is expected to include a reference to its DTD, and the DTD is expected to be accessible. In this example, the DTD will be located on the local hard drive in the same directory as the document itself. SAX parsers are smart enough to understand URLs, so if an HTTP URL is specified, the parser will go out to the network to get the DTD. Later, you will see how this automatic resolution of DTDs can be controlled in our code. The source code for `SAXValidator.java` is shown in Listing 8.4.

LISTING 8.4 `SAXValidator.java`

```
package com.madhu.xml;

import java.io.*;
import org.xml.sax.*;
import org.xml.sax.helpers.*;

public class SAXValidator extends DefaultHandler {
```

Listing 8.4 continued

```
    private boolean valid;
    private boolean wellFormed;

    public SAXValidator() {
        valid = true;
        wellFormed = true;
    }

    public void startDocument() {
        System.out.println("***Start of Document***");
    }

    public void endDocument() {
        System.out.println("***End of Document***");
    }

    public void error(SAXParseException e) {
        valid = false;
    }

    public void fatalError(SAXParseException e) {
        wellFormed = false;
    }

    public void warning(SAXParseException e) {
        valid = false;
    }

    public boolean isValid() {
        return valid;
    }

    public boolean isWellFormed() {
        return wellFormed;
    }

    public static void main(String args[]) throws Exception {
        if (args.length != 1) {
            System.err.println("Usage: java SAXValidate <xml-file>");
            System.exit(1);
        }

        XMLReader parser = XMLReaderFactory.createXMLReader(
            "org.apache.xerces.parsers.SAXParser");

        parser.setFeature("http://xml.org/sax/features/validation", true);

        SAXValidator handler = new SAXValidator();
        parser.setContentHandler(handler);
```

LISTING 8.4 continued

```
        parser.setErrorHandler(handler);

        parser.parse(new InputSource(new FileReader(args[0])));
        if (!handler.isWellFormed()) {
            System.out.println("Document is NOT well formed.");
        }
        if (!handler.isValid()) {
            System.out.println("Document is NOT valid.");
        }
        if (handler.isWellFormed() && handler.isValid()) {
            System.out.println("Document is well formed and valid.");
        }
    }
}
```

In this example, we will avoid the use of JAXP classes in order to create a parser. Instead, we will use `XMLReaderFactory`. This is needed to set features and properties. In order to validate the document, we will enable validation by setting the feature `http://xml.org/sax/features/validation` to `true`. We will register an error handler in addition to a `ContentHandler`. Remember that `DefaultHandler` implements `ErrorHandler`.

`ErrorHandler` contains three methods that can be used to determine whether a document is well formed and valid. A summary of the `ErrorHandler` methods is provided in Table 8.5.

TABLE 8.5 The `ErrorHandler` Methods

Method	*Description*
`error()`	Receives notification of a recoverable error
`fatalError()`	Receives notification of a nonrecoverable error
`warning()`	Receives notification of a warning

Either `error()` or `warning()` will be called if the document is well formed but not valid (that is, it violates the rules of the DTD), and `fatalError()` will be called if the document is not well formed. In this example, we will set flags for different types of errors and report the results when parsing is finished.

We will use an invalid XML document, `invalid-library.xml`, for testing. The document and referenced DTD, `library.dtd`, is shown in Listings 8.5 and 8.6, respectively. If you look closely, you will notice what is wrong with the document. If you can't find the problem, it will become clear in the next example.

LISTING 8.5 `invalid-library.xml`—Invalid XML Document

```
<?xml version="1.0" encoding="UTF-8"?>
<!DOCTYPE library SYSTEM "library.dtd">
<library>
    <fictions>
        <book author="Herman Melville">Moby Dick</book>
        <book author="Zane Grey">The Last Trail</book>
    </fictions>
    <biography>
        <book author="William Manchester">
            The Last Lion, Winston Spencer Churchill
        </book>
    </biography>
    <science>
        <book author="Hecht, Zajac">Optics</book>
    </science>
</library>
```

LISTING 8.6 `library.dtd`—DTD File

```
<?xml version="1.0" encoding="US-ASCII"?>
<!ELEMENT library (fiction|biography|science)*>
<!ELEMENT fiction (book)+>
<!ELEMENT biography (book)+>
<!ELEMENT science (book)+>
<!ELEMENT book (#PCDATA)>
<!ATTLIST book author CDATA #REQUIRED>
```

The output is shown in Listing 8.7.

LISTING 8.7 Output from `SAXValidator`

```
***Start of Document***
***End of Document***
Document is NOT valid.
```

A number of features are defined in SAX. A detailed list can be found at `http://www.megginson.com/SAX/Java/features.html`. Features are enabled by calling the `setFeature()` method with the feature name and the value `true`. Features are disabled with the value `false`. Here is a brief summary of SAX 2.0 features:

- `http://xml.org/sax/features/namespaces`

  `true`: Performs namespace processing.

- `http://xml.org/sax/features/namespace-prefixes`

  `true`: Reports the original prefixed names and attributes used for namespace declarations.

- `http://xml.org/sax/features/string-interning`

  `true`: All element names, prefixes, attribute names, namespace URIs, and local names are internalized using `java.lang.String.intern`.

- `http://xml.org/sax/features/validation`

  `true`: Reports all validation errors (implies external-general-entities and external-parameter-entities).

- `http://xml.org/sax/features/external-general-entities`

  `true`: Includes all external general (text) entities.

- `http://xml.org/sax/features/external-parameter-entities`

  `true`: Includes all external parameter entities, including the external DTD subset.

Handling Errors

Did you figure out what was wrong with the XML document in the last example? Don't worry if you didn't. We'll write a program to tell us what's wrong. The previous example told us the document was not valid, but it didn't tell us where or what was not valid. The `Locator` interface can give us the parse position within a `ContentHandler` method. The position information includes line number and column number. It is important to note that the `Locator` object should *not* be used in any other methods, including `ErrorHandler` methods. Fortunately, `ErrorHandler` methods supply a `SAXParseException` object that can also give us position information.

The source code for `SAXErrors.java` is shown in Listing 8.8.

LISTING 8.8 `SAXErrors.java`

```
package com.madhu.xml;

import java.io.*;
import org.xml.sax.*;
import org.xml.sax.helpers.*;

public class SAXErrors extends DefaultHandler {
    private Locator locator;

    public void startDocument() {
        System.out.println("***Start of Document***");
```

LISTING 8.8 continued

```
    }

    public void endDocument() {
        System.out.println("***End of Document***");
    }

    public void setDocumentLocator(Locator inLocator) {
        System.out.println("***Got Locator***");
        locator = inLocator;
        int line = locator.getLineNumber();
        int column = locator.getColumnNumber();
        String publicID = locator.getPublicId();
        String systemID = locator.getSystemId();

        System.out.println("Line " + line + ", column " + column);
        if (publicID != null) {
            System.out.println("Public ID " + publicID);
        }
        if (systemID != null) {
            System.out.println("System ID " + systemID);
        }
    }

    public void printLocation(SAXParseException e) {
        int line = e.getLineNumber();
        int column = e.getColumnNumber();
        String publicID = e.getPublicId();
        String systemID = e.getSystemId();

        System.out.println("Line " + line + ", column " + column);
        if (publicID != null) {
            System.out.println("Public ID " + publicID);
        }
        if (systemID != null) {
            System.out.println("System ID " + systemID);
        }
    }

    public void error(SAXParseException e) {
        printLocation(e);
        System.out.println("Recoverable error: " + e.getMessage());
        Exception ex = e.getException();
        if (ex != null) {
            System.out.println("Embedded exception: " + ex.getMessage());
        }
    }

    public void fatalError(SAXParseException e) {
        printLocation(e);
```

LISTING 8.8 continued

```
            System.out.println("Non-recoverable error: " + e.getMessage());
            Exception ex = e.getException();
            if (ex != null) {
                System.out.println("Embedded exception: " + ex.getMessage());
            }
        }

    public void warning(SAXParseException e) {
        printLocation(e);
        System.out.println("Warning: " + e.getMessage());
        Exception ex = e.getException();
        if (ex != null) {
            System.out.println("Embedded exception: " + ex.getMessage());
        }
    }

    public static void main(String args[]) throws Exception {
        if (args.length != 1) {
            System.err.println("Usage: java SAXErrors <xml-file>");
            System.exit(1);
        }

        XMLReader parser = XMLReaderFactory.createXMLReader(
            "org.apache.xerces.parsers.SAXParser");

        parser.setFeature("http://xml.org/sax/features/validation", true);

        SAXErrors handler = new SAXErrors();
        parser.setContentHandler(handler);
        parser.setErrorHandler(handler);

        parser.parse(new InputSource(new FileReader(args[0])));
    }
}
```


This example is very similar to the previous example, but the `ContentHandler` method `setDocumentLocator()` is added to obtain a `Locator` instance. Detailed information is printed in the error methods.

We will use the same invalid document and DTD from the previous example for testing. The output is shown in Listing 8.9.

LISTING 8.9 Output from `SAXErrors`

```
***Got Locator***
Line 1, column 1
***Start of Document***
```

LISTING 8.9 continued

```
Line 4, column 12
Recoverable error: Element type "fictions" must be declared.
Line 16, column 11
Recoverable error: The content of element type "library" must match
[ic:ccc]"(fiction|biography|science)*".
***End of Document***
```

As expected, a validation error occurs at line 4. The `fictions` tag should be `fiction`. Another error is encountered at the ending `library` tag. This is caused by the same error.

Entity References

SAX parsers will resolve entity references automatically. However, there are cases when you might want to resolve an entity reference yourself. In the following example, we will define an entity for hardcover books. It will be referenced as `&hc;` and defined in our DTD. If we use an HTTP URL to define the entity, the SAX parser will go out to the network to resolve it. What we want to do here is resolve the entity using a local file. We can accomplish this using an `EntityResolver`. The source code for `SAXEntity.java` is shown in Listing 8.10.

LISTING 8.10 `SAXEntity.java`

```
package com.madhu.xml;

import java.io.*;
import org.xml.sax.*;
import org.xml.sax.helpers.*;

public class SAXEntity extends DefaultHandler {
    public SAXEntity() {
    }

    public void startDocument() {
        System.out.println("***Start of Document***");
    }

    public void endDocument() {
        System.out.println("***End of Document***");
    }

    public void startElement(String uri, String localName,
        String qName, Attributes attributes) {

        System.out.print("<" + qName);
```

LISTING 8.10 continued

```
        int n = attributes.getLength();
        for (int i=0; i<n; i+=1) {
            System.out.print(" " + attributes.getQName(i) +
                "='" + attributes.getValue(i) + "'");
        }
        System.out.println(">");
    }

    public void characters(char[] ch, int start, int length) {
        System.out.println(new String(ch, start, length).trim());
    }

    public void endElement(String namespaceURI, String localName,
        String qName) throws SAXException {

        System.out.println("</" + qName + ">");
    }

    public InputSource resolveEntity(String publicId, String systemId) {
        try {
            if (systemId.equals("http://www.madhu.com/xml/hardcover.txt")) {
                return new InputSource(
                    new FileReader("hardcover.txt"));
            }
        } catch (IOException e) {
        }
        return null; // for default behavior
    }

    public static void main(String args[]) throws Exception {
        if (args.length != 1) {
            System.err.println("Usage: java SAXEntity <xml-file>");
            System.exit(1);
        }

        XMLReader parser = XMLReaderFactory.createXMLReader(
            "org.apache.xerces.parsers.SAXParser");

        parser.setFeature("http://xml.org/sax/features/validation", true);

        SAXEntity handler = new SAXEntity();
        parser.setContentHandler(handler);
        parser.setEntityResolver(handler);

        parser.parse(new InputSource(new FileReader(args[0])));
    }
}
```

EntityResolver is also implemented by DefaultHandler. EntityResolver contains only one method, resolveEntity(), which will be called with the system ID and public ID, depending on how the entity is defined. Once we determine what the entity is, we must return an InputSource pointing to where the entity resides.

InputSource is a class defined in package org.xml.sax. InputSource can be created given an InputStream or Reader. If an entity with our ID is referenced, we will return an InputSource pointing to a local file named hardcover.txt. In all other cases, null is returned, meaning use the default behavior and resolve all other entities automatically.

We will use an XML document that uses the hardcover entity, entity-ref.xml, for testing. The document and referenced DTD, library.dtd, is shown in Listings 8.11 and 8.12, respectively.

LISTING 8.11 entity-ref.xml—XML Document with Entity Reference

```
<?xml version="1.0" encoding="UTF-8"?>
<!DOCTYPE library SYSTEM "library.dtd">
<library>
    <fiction>
        <book author="Herman Melville">Moby Dick</book>
        <book author="Zane Grey">The Last Trail</book>
    </fiction>
    <biography>
        <book author="William Manchester">
            The Last Lion, Winston Spencer Churchill &hc;
        </book>
    </biography>
    <science>
        <book author="Hecht, Zajac">Optics &hc;</book>
    </science>
</library>
```

LISTING 8.12 library.dtd—DTD with Entity Reference Definition

```
<?xml version="1.0" encoding="US-ASCII"?>
<!ELEMENT library (fiction|biography|science)*>
<!ELEMENT fiction (book)+>
<!ELEMENT biography (book)+>
<!ELEMENT science (book)+>
<!ELEMENT book (#PCDATA)>
<!ATTLIST book author CDATA #REQUIRED>
<!ENTITY hc SYSTEM "http://www.madhu.com/xml/hardcover.txt">
```

The output is shown in Listing 8.13.

LISTING 8.13 Output from `SAXEntity`

```
***Start of Document***
<library>
<fiction>
<book author='Herman Melville'>
Moby Dick
</book>
<book author='Zane Grey'>
The Last Trail
</book>
</fiction>
<biography>
<book author='William Manchester'>
The Last Lion, Winston Spencer Churchill
(hardcover)

</book>
</biography>
<science>
<book author='Hecht, Zajac'>
Optics
(hardcover)
</book>
</science>
</library>
***End of Document***
```


Parsers can skip entities if they are nonvalidating or if entity features are set to `false`. In either case, the `skippedEntity()` method defined in `ContentHandler` will be called with the name of the entity.

Lexical Events

You saw earlier how to capture basic events, such as elements and characters, but what about comments, `CDATA`, and DTD references? We can receive these events as well using an extension interface called `LexicalHandler`. `LexicalHandler` is part of the `org.xml.sax.ext` package, which is not necessarily supported by all SAX implementations. Xerces, of course, provides support for the extension package.

The source code for `SAXLexical.java` is shown in Listing 8.14.

LISTING 8.14 `SAXLexical.java`

```
package com.madhu.xml;

import java.io.*;
import org.xml.sax.*;
```

LISTING 8.14 continued

```
import org.xml.sax.ext.*;
import org.xml.sax.helpers.*;

public class SAXLexical extends DefaultHandler implements LexicalHandler {
    public SAXLexical() {
    }

    public void startDocument() {
        System.out.println("***Start of Document***");
    }

    public void endDocument() {
        System.out.println("***End of Document***");
    }

    public void startElement(String uri, String localName,
        String qName, Attributes attributes) {

        System.out.print("<" + qName);
        int n = attributes.getLength();
        for (int i=0; i<n; i+=1) {
            System.out.print(" " + attributes.getQName(i) +
                "='" + attributes.getValue(i) + "'");
        }
        System.out.println(">");
    }

    public void characters(char[] ch, int start, int length) {
        System.out.println(new String(ch, start, length).trim());
    }

    public void endElement(String namespaceURI, String localName,
        String qName) throws SAXException {

        System.out.println("</" + qName + ">");
    }

    public void startDTD(String name, String publicId,
        String systemId) throws SAXException {

        System.out.print("*** Start DTD, name " + name);
        if (publicId != null) {
            System.out.print(" PUBLIC " + publicId);
        }
        if (systemId != null) {
            System.out.print(" SYSTEM " + systemId);
        }
        System.out.println(" ***");
    }
```

LISTING 8.14 continued

```
    public void endDTD() throws SAXException {
        System.out.println("*** End DTD ***");
    }

    public void startEntity(String name) throws SAXException {
        System.out.println("*** Start Entity " + name + " ***");
    }

    public void endEntity(String name) throws SAXException {
        System.out.println("*** End Entity " + name + " ***");
    }

    public void startCDATA() throws SAXException {
        System.out.println("*** Start CDATA ***");
    }

    public void endCDATA() throws SAXException {
        System.out.println("*** End CDATA ***");
    }

    public void comment(char[] ch, int start, int length)
        throws SAXException {

        System.out.println("<!— " +
            new String(ch, start, length) + " —>");
    }

    public static void main(String args[]) throws Exception {
        if (args.length != 1) {
            System.err.println("Usage: java SAXLexical <xml-file>");
            System.exit(1);
        }

        XMLReader parser = XMLReaderFactory.createXMLReader(
            "org.apache.xerces.parsers.SAXParser");

        parser.setFeature("http://xml.org/sax/features/validation", true);

        SAXLexical handler = new SAXLexical();
        parser.setContentHandler(handler);
        parser.setProperty("http://xml.org/sax/properties/lexical-handler",
            handler);

        parser.parse(new InputSource(new FileReader(args[0])));
    }
}
```

Notice that we are explicitly implementing `LexicalHandler`. This is necessary because `DefaultHandler` does not implement `LexicalHandler`. We must fill in all methods of `LexicalHandler` whether we are interested in them or not. That's just the way interfaces work. The methods for `LexicalHandler` are listed in Table 8.6.

TABLE 8.6 The `LexicalHandler` Methods

Method	*Description*
`comment()`	Reports an XML comment anywhere in the document
`endCDATA()`	Reports the end of a `CDATA` section
`endDTD()`	Reports the end of DTD declarations
`endEntity()`	Reports the end of an entity
`startCDATA()`	Reports the start of a `CDATA` section
`startDTD()`	Reports the start of DTD declarations, if any
`startEntity()`	Reports the beginning of some internal and external XML entities

In the `main()` method, notice that in order to register a lexical handler, we must call `setProperty()`. This is different from the standard handlers because `LexicalHandler` is an extension. If a method in the standard API includes a reference to `LexicalHandler`, it will not compile unless the extension package is included. The `setProperty()` method accepts a `String` property name and an `Object` property. This avoids the direct reference to `LexicalHandler` in the API. The property, in this case, is the handler itself.

A sample XML document, `comment.xml`, is used for testing and is shown in Listing 8.15.

LISTING 8.15 `comment.xml`—Sample XML Document

```
<?xml version="1.0" encoding="UTF-8"?>
<!DOCTYPE library SYSTEM "library.dtd">

<!— A short list of books in a library —>

<library>
    <fiction>
        <book author="Herman Melville">Moby Dick</book>
        <book author="Zane Grey">The Last Trail</book>
    </fiction>
    <biography>
        <book author="William Manchester">
            The Last Lion, Winston Spencer Churchill
        </book>
    </biography>
    <science>
```

LISTING 8.15 continued

```
        <book author="Hecht, Zajac">Optics</book>
    </science>
</library>
```

The output is shown in Listing 8.16.

LISTING 8.16 Output from SAXLexical

```
***Start of Document***
*** Start DTD, name library SYSTEM library.dtd ***
*** Start Entity [dtd] ***
*** End Entity [dtd] ***
*** End DTD ***
<!—  A short list of books in a library  —>
<library>
<fiction>
<book author='Herman Melville'>
Moby Dick
</book>
<book author='Zane Grey'>
The Last Trail
</book>
</fiction>
<biography>
<book author='William Manchester'>
The Last Lion, Winston Spencer Churchill
</book>
</biography>
<science>
<book author='Hecht, Zajac'>
Optics
</book>
</science>
</library>
***End of Document***
```

Notice the DTD and entity references in the beginning and the comment immediately following the DTD events.

Case Study: Parsing Web Pages

Thus far, you have seen lots of examples of how to use SAX. Now let's look at a practical example where we can put it to use. The U.S. Census Bureau conducts a survey of all residents and businesses in the U.S. every 10 years. The product of this survey is a vast quantity of information on everything from population and salaries to retail sales and education. The information is primarily used by the government for zoning and redistricting, but it has many uses in the private sector as well.

Historically, the census was recorded on paper. In the late 1800s, it was projected that the population of the U.S. had grown to such a point that more than 10 years would have been required to process and tabulate all the data! As soon as the census data was tabulated, it would have become obsolete and a new census would be required. The problem was solved by inventor Herman Hollerith, who devised a scheme of punching holes in paper that could be tabulated quickly using a machine. This was the first punch-card machine. Hollerith founded the Tabulating Machine Company in 1896, which, after mergers and acquisitions, grew into International Business Machines (IBM).

Because the census is conducted by the federal government and paid for by public funds, the information is available to the public free of charge. In fact, it is available on the U.S. Census Web site (probably stored in an IBM database!). The problem is that the data is prepared for human consumption in HTML, which is not easily digested by databases.

The census has a site dedicated to state and county quick facts. It can be found at `http://quickfacts.census.gov/qfd/index.html`. This site contains just a small portion of the data compiled by the Census Bureau, but it's still a lot of data! It would be useful to grab this data and reformat it so that it can be bulk-loaded into a database. Once the data is in a database, we can perform interesting queries on people, businesses, and geography.

This is where SAX fits in. What we need to do is write a program that parses these Web pages and pulls out the important information. There are, in fact, hundreds of pages of information, because there is data on every state and every county in every state. For our case study, we will just collect the data for each state. The program can easily be extended to collect data for each county as well.

As you are probably aware, common HTML is usually not well formed. So it is not possible to use standard SAX parsers such as Xerces. Fortunately, Anders Kristensen has developed HTML Enabled XML Parser (HEX) for just this purpose. HEX is a SAX 1.0 parser that accepts HTML and tolerates all its problems. HEX can be found at `http://www-uk.hpl.hp.com/people/sth/java/hex.html`.

The Census Quick Facts Web pages are organized in a hierarchy. The home page contains links to state pages, and each state page contains links to county pages. What we need to do is first parse the home page, grab the links for the state pages, and then parse each state page. The home page and the state pages are formatted differently, so there are different content handlers for each. The source code for the main class, `Spider.java`, is shown in Listing 8. 17.

LISTING 8.17 `Spider.java`

```
package com.madhu.spider;

import java.io.*;
import java.util.*;
import java.net.*;

import org.xml.sax.*;
import hplb.xml.Tokenizer;

public class Spider {
    private int numberOfStates;
    private PrintWriter out;

    public void process(String nStates, String outFile)
        throws Exception {

        numberOfStates = Integer.parseInt(nStates);
        out = new PrintWriter(new FileWriter(outFile));
        processUSA();
        out.close();
    }

    public void processUSA() throws Exception {
        USAHandler usa = new USAHandler();
        Tokenizer t = new Tokenizer();
        t.setDocumentHandler(usa);
        t.setErrorHandler(usa);
        URL u = new URL("http://quickfacts.census.gov/qfd/index.html");
        InputStream is = u.openStream();
        t.parse(is);
        is.close();

        int nStates = numberOfStates;
        Iterator it = usa.getStateNames();
        while (it.hasNext() && nStates— > 0) {
            String state = (String) it.next();
            String url = "http://quickfacts.census.gov" +
                    usa.getStateURI(state);
            processState(state, url);
        }
```

LISTING 8.17 continued

```
    }

    public void processState(String state, String url)
        throws Exception {

        StateHandler st = new StateHandler();
        Tokenizer t = new Tokenizer();
        t.setDocumentHandler(st);
        t.setErrorHandler(st);
        URL u = new URL(url);
        InputStream is = u.openStream();
        t.parse(is);
        is.close();

        System.out.println(state);
        out.print("\"" + state + "\"");
        ArrayList dataList = st.getDataList();
        int n = dataList.size();
        for (int i=0; i<n; i+=1) {
            String[] data = (String[]) dataList.get(i);
            out.print(", \"" + data[1] + "\"");
        }
        out.println();
    }

    public static void main(String args[]) throws Exception {
        if (args.length != 2) {
            System.err.println(
                    "Usage: java Spider <# of states> <out-file>");
            System.exit(1);
        }
        Spider m = new Spider();
        m.process(args[0], args[1]);
    }
}
```

When compiling this code, make sure there are no other SAX class libraries in your classpath. HEX includes classes in the same package as other SAX parsers, so a name conflict might arise. Make certain that you have not placed Xerces or other SAX APIs in your `java/jre/lib/ext` directory, because these classes are automatically added to your classpath.

The API for HEX is slightly different from SAX, but the principles are the same. `Spider` creates a `Tokenizer` (similar to `XMLReader`) and registers a handler, `USAHandler`, for the home page. This handler grabs the names of each state and the links to each state page.

Once this is done, a `StateHandler` is registered and input is accepted from the state Web pages. This is done for each state Web page. The output is stored in a text file named as a command-line parameter.

The source code for `USAHandler.java` is shown in Listing 8.18.

LISTING 8.18 USAHandler.java

```
package com.madhu.spider;

import java.io.*;
import java.util.*;

import org.xml.sax.*;
import hplb.xml.Tokenizer;

public class USAHandler extends HandlerBase {
    private HashMap linkMap;
    private String actionURL;
    private String stateParamName;
    private boolean grabText;
    private String statePage;
    private String optionText;
    private String url;

    public USAHandler() {
        linkMap = new HashMap(75);
        grabText = false;
    }

    public void startElement(String name, AttributeMap atts) {
        if (name.equalsIgnoreCase("form")) {
            actionURL = atts.getValue("ACTION");
            return;
        }
        if (name.equalsIgnoreCase("SELECT")) {
            stateParamName = atts.getValue("NAME");
            url = actionURL + "?" + stateParamName + "=";
            return;
        }
        if (name.equalsIgnoreCase("OPTION")) {
            statePage = atts.getValue("value");
            if (statePage == null) {
                statePage = atts.getValue("VALUE");
            }
            grabText = true;
            return;
        }
```

LISTING 8.18 continued

```
    }

    public void characters(char ch[], int start, int length)
        throws Exception {

        if (grabText) {
            String text = new String(ch, start, length);
            text = text.replace('\n', ' ');
            text = text.replace('\r', ' ');
            optionText = text.trim();
            linkMap.put(optionText, statePage);
        }
    }

    public void endElement(String name) {
        grabText = false;
    }

    public void warning(String message, String systemID,
        int line, int column) throws Exception {
            // ignore errors
    }

    public Iterator getStateNames() {
        return linkMap.keySet().iterator();
    }

    public String getStateURI(String state) {
        String htmlPage = (String) linkMap.get(state);
        if (htmlPage == null) {
            return null;
        }
        return url + htmlPage;
    }
}
```

The home page contains an HTML form with a drop-down list in a form for each state. `USAHandler` grabs the `ACTION` attribute from the form, which is needed to get the state pages. It also grabs the state names and values from the drop-down list.

`StateHandler` does the real work of collecting the raw data. Each state Web page contains three tables with information on people, businesses, and geography. `StateHandler` grabs the data in each of these tables and puts it all in an array list. `Spider` takes this list and pulls out the state data, formats it, and writes it out to a file. The source code for `StateHandler.java` is shown in listing 8.19.

LISTING 8.19 StateHandler.java

```
package com.madhu.spider;

import java.io.*;
import java.util.*;

import org.xml.sax.*;
import hplb.xml.Tokenizer;

public class StateHandler extends HandlerBase {
    public static final int MAX_COLUMNS = 3;

    private HashMap linkMap;
    private ArrayList dataList;

    private String actionURL;
    private String countyParamName;
    private String countyPage;
    private String optionText;
    private String url;

    private boolean grabOptionText;
    private boolean grabTable;
    private String[] row;
    private int columnIndex;

    public StateHandler() {
        linkMap = new HashMap(75);
        dataList = new ArrayList(100);
        grabOptionText = false;
        row = new String[MAX_COLUMNS];
        columnIndex = -1;
        grabTable = false;
    }

    public void startElement(String name, AttributeMap atts) {
        if (name.equalsIgnoreCase("form")) {
            actionURL = atts.getValue("ACTION");
            return;
        }
        if (name.equalsIgnoreCase("SELECT")) {
            countyParamName = atts.getValue("NAME");
            url = actionURL + "?" + countyParamName + "=";
            return;
        }
        if (name.equalsIgnoreCase("OPTION")) {
            countyPage = atts.getValue("value");
            if (countyPage == null) {
```

LISTING 8.19 continued

```
                countyPage = atts.getValue("VALUE");
            }
            grabOptionText = true;
            return;
        }
        if (grabTable && name.equalsIgnoreCase("TR")) {
            columnIndex = 0;
        }
    }

    public void characters(char ch[], int start, int length)
        throws Exception {

        String text = new String(ch, start, length);
        text = text.replace('\n', ' ');
        text = text.replace('\r', ' ');
        text = text.trim();
        if (text.length() == 0) {
            return;
        }
        if (grabOptionText) {
            grabOptionText = false;
            optionText = text;
            linkMap.put(optionText, countyPage);
        }
        if (text.equals("People QuickFacts") ||
            text.equals("Business QuickFacts") ||
            text.equals("Geography QuickFacts")) {

            grabTable = true;
        }
        if (columnIndex >= 0 && columnIndex < MAX_COLUMNS) {
            row[columnIndex++] = text;
        }
        if (columnIndex == MAX_COLUMNS) {
            columnIndex = -1;
            dataList.add(row);
            row = new String[MAX_COLUMNS];
        }
    }

    public void endElement(String name) {
        grabOptionText = false;
        if (name.equalsIgnoreCase("table")) {
            grabTable = false;
        }
```

LISTING 8.19 continued

```
    }

    public void warning(String message, String systemID,
        int line, int column) throws Exception {
            // ignore errors
    }

    public Iterator getCountyNames() {
        return linkMap.keySet().iterator();
    }

    public String getCountyURI(String state) {
        String htmlPage = (String) linkMap.get(state);
        if (htmlPage == null) {
            return null;
        }
        return url + htmlPage;
    }

    public ArrayList getDataList() {
        return dataList;
    }
}
```

The program will take some time to run completely, depending on your Internet connection. What comes out is a file with one row for each state containing data on that state. The data is all quoted, so it can be easily bulk-loaded into most databases.

As mentioned earlier, the program can be extended to collect information on each county in every state. This is quite a bit of data, but it will contain a lot of interesting information on specific regions of the U.S. To collect county information, another handler, similar to `StateHandler`, can be created that parses data from the county Web pages. Fortunately, `StateHandler` also grabs the links for the counties, so a lot of the work is already done.

The output is shown in Listing 8.20. Note that the output is comma separated, which is acceptable by any database. Many databases now accept XML as an input format for bulk loading. XML format is also attractive for further processing or reformatting using XSLT. The program can be easily modified to produce valid XML by changing the `print` statements. Making other adjustments, such as removing percent symbols and commas in large numbers, might be a good idea also. These modifications are left as an exercise for you, the reader.

LISTING 8.20 Output from `Spider`

```
"Utah", "2,233,169", "29.6%", "9.4%", "32.2%", "8.5%", "89.2%", "0.8%",
"Maryland", "5,296,486", "10.8%", "6.7%", "25.6%", "11.3%", "64.0%",
"New Mexico", "1,819,046", "20.1%", "7.2%", "28.0%", "11.7%", "66.8%",
"North Carolina", "8,049,313", "21.4%", "6.7%", "24.4%", "12.0%",
"Washington", "5,894,121", "21.1%", "6.7%", "25.7%", "11.2%", "81.8%",
. . .
```

Summary

SAX is an easy-to-use API for parsing XML data. It's available in source and binary form free of charge. SAX has become one of the most popular tools for parsing XML due to its ease of use and widespread availability.

Unlike DOM, SAX is an event-based parser. SAX reads XML serially and generates events when elements, text, comments and other data are found. To use SAX, you simply extend or implement the relevant handler (`DefaultHandler` will work in most cases) and register it. Once this is done, the parser is pointed to an XML source and parsing can begin.

The event-based parsing scheme used by SAX does not solve all problems. It is not possible to traverse a document at random or modify a document's structure. Even still, SAX solves a large class of XML parsing problems easily and efficiently.

CHAPTER 9

Transforming XML with XSL

IN THIS CHAPTER

XML is quickly becoming an integral component of enterprise applications. XML provides a vendor-independent, data-exchange mechanism used among applications or companies. Within the same industry, standard XML vocabularies have been developed to describe common business processes, such as purchase orders and parts requisition. However, there are times when we'd like to convert XML data to a different format. For example, if a supplier provides a list of parts as an XML document, we might like to convert the XML document to use a different set of elements that are supported by our internal applications. The XML Stylesheet Language (XSL) solves this problem of document conversion.

This chapter contains complete examples that utilize the XSL technology for document publishing and B2B communication.

XSL Technologies

XSL has two independent languages:

- The XSL Transformation Language (XSLT)
- The XSL Formatting Object Language (XSL-FO)

XSLT is used to convert an XML document to another format. XSL-FO provides a way of describing the presentation of an XML document. Both technologies use a supporting XML technology, XPath. XPath defines a standard mechanism for accessing elements within a document. See Chapter 5, "The X-Files: XLink, XPath, and XPointer," for more information on XPath.

We'll start with XSLT and cover the details of XSL-FO later in the chapter.

This chapter illustrates the practical features of XSLT that are commonly used on development projects. If you would like to view the XLST specification, visit `http://www.w3.org/TR/xslt`.

In this chapter, you will learn how to

- Create XSL style sheets
- Perform client-side XSLT processing with XSL-enabled browsers
- Perform server-side XSLT processing with Active Server Pages and JavaServer Pages
- Retrieve data from XML documents using XSLT and XPath
- Convert XML documents to HTML
- Convert XML documents to other XML formats

- Generate PDF documents with XSL-FO
- Integrate XSLT and XSL-FO with Java servlets

XSLT for Document Publishing

XSL technology has an important role in the field of document publishing. Imagine, for example, that we have an XML document for a list of books. We would like to publish this document in various formats. Using XSL, we can convert the book list to an HTML file, PDF document, or other format. The key to this example is the XML document, which serves as a single data source. By applying an XSL style sheet, we render a new view of the data. The development of multiple style sheets allows us to have multiple views of the same data. This approach provides a clean separation of the data (the XML document) and the view (the XSL style sheet). We'll implement the book list example in this chapter.

We can also extend this example to support wireless Internet clients. A growing number of mobile phones and PDAs support the Wireless Application Protocol (WAP). These WAP-enabled devices contain a minibrowser for rendering Wireless Markup Language (WML) documents. To support the wireless Internet clients, all we have to do is design an appropriate XSL style sheet to convert the XML document to WML. No modifications are required to the original XML document. This process is illustrated in Figure 9.1.

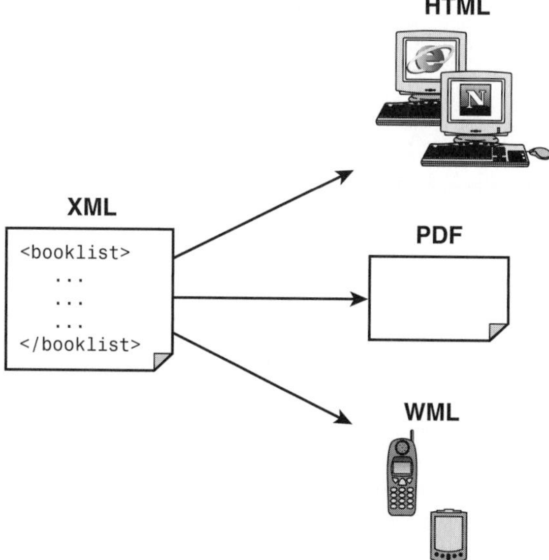

FIGURE 9.1
Publishing documents with XSLT.

XSLT provides the mechanism for converting an XML document to another format. This is accomplished by applying an XSLT style sheet to the XML document. The style sheet contains conversion rules for accessing and transforming the input XML document to a different output format. An XSLT processor is responsible for applying the rules defined in the style sheet to the input XML document. The process is illustrated in Figure 9.2.

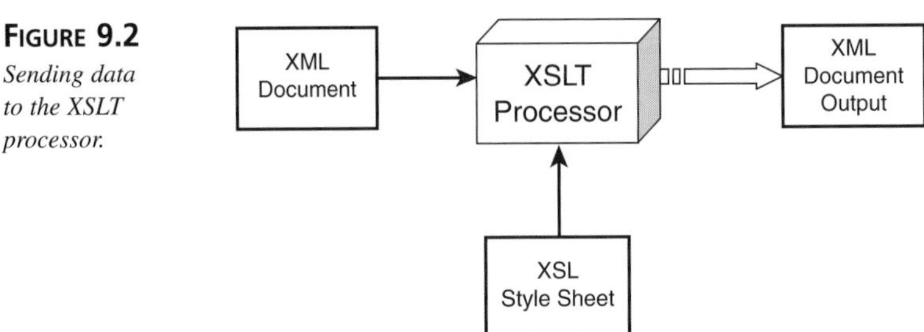

FIGURE 9.2
Sending data to the XSLT processor.

Later in the chapter, implementation details are provided on how to construct the XSL style sheet and apply the conversion rules with an XSLT processor.

Note

All of the source code in this chapter is available at the Sams Web site. You can download the code and extract it to a directory on your file system. The remainder of this chapter will use `<install_dir>` as the root location where you installed the code. Here's a description of the source code directories:

Directory	*Description*
`ch9_xsl\browser_demo`	Sample code for client-side XSLT processing
`ch9_xsl\public_html`	Sample code for server-side XSLT processing (ASP and JSP)
`ch9_xsl\public_html\WEB-INF`	Support files for JSP
`ch9_xsl\b2b`	Sample code for B2B (covered later in the chapter)
`ch9_xsl\xsl_fo`	Sample code for XSL-FO (covered later in the chapter)

Getting Started with XSLT

In the next example we'll convert an XML document to an HTML document. The XML document contains a list of books, as shown is Listing 9.1.

LISTING 9.1 `<install_dir>\ch9_xsl\browser_demo\book.xml`

```
<?xml version="1.0"?>
<?xml-stylesheet type="text/xsl" href="book_view.xsl"?>

<book>
    <author>Michael Daconta et al</author>
    <title>XML Development with Java 2</title>
    <category>Java</category>
    <price currency="USD">44.99</price>
    <summary>
        XML Development with Java 2 provides the information
        and techniques a Java developer will need to integrate
        XML into Java-based applications.
    </summary>
</book>
```

The desired output of the HTML table is shown in Figure 9.3.

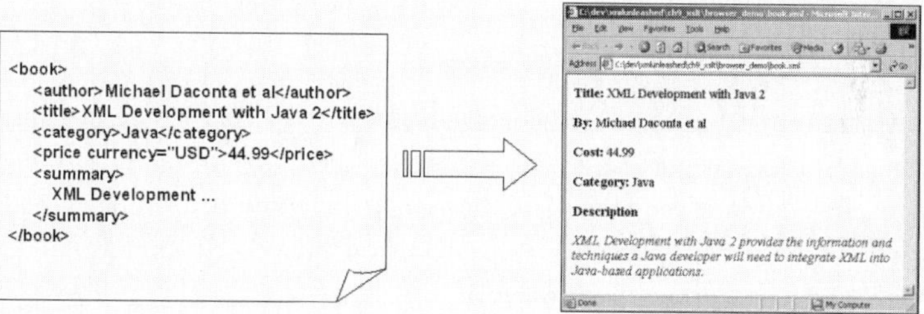

FIGURE 9.3
Converting `book.xml` *to an HTML table.*

Creating the XML Document

The XML document, `book.xml`, contains elements for the author, title, price, summary, and category. Listing 9.2 has the complete code for `book.xml`.

LISTING 9.2 `<install_dir>\ch9_xsl\browser_demo\book.xml`

```
<?xml version="1.0"?>

<book>
    <author>Michael Daconta et al</author>
    <title>XML Development with Java 2</title>
```

LISTING 9.2 continued

```
    <category>Java</category>
    <price currency="USD">44.99</price>
    <summary>
        XML Development with Java 2 provides the information
        and techniques a Java developer will need to integrate
        XML into Java-based applications.
    </summary>
</book>
```

In this example, we will apply the style sheet in a client-side Web browser. The XML document makes a reference to a style sheet using the following code:

```
<?xml-stylesheet type="text/xsl" href="book_view.xsl"?>
```

Creating the XSL Style Sheet

The next step is to create the XSL style sheet. XSL style sheets are XML documents; as a result, they must be well formed. An XSL style sheet has the following general structure:

```
<?xml version="1.0"?>
<xsl:stylesheet xmlns:xsl="URI" version="1.0">

<!--XSL-T CONVERSION RULES-->

</xsl:stylesheet>
```

The `<xsl:stylesheet>` element defines how the XSLT processor should process the current XSL document. The `xmlns` attribute is the namespace definition. The XSL Transformation engine reads the `xmlns` attribute and determines whether it supports the given namespace. The `xmlns` attribute specifies the XSL prefix. All XSL elements and types in the document use the prefix.

The `xmlns` attribute value contains a Uniform Resource Identifier (URI), which serves as a generic method for identifying entities on the World Wide Web. It is important to note that the XSLT processor will not connect to the URI; it simply compares the URI against a collection of URIs that it supports.

The XSLT 1.0 specification defines the following URI for the XSL namespace:

```
http://www.w3.org/1999/XSL/Transform
```

The "1999" in the URI indicates the year the URI was allocated by the World Wide Web Consortium (W3C). It does not relate to the version of XSLT that is being used. The XSLT version reference is specified using the `version` attribute of the `<xsl:stylesheet>` element. The `version` attribute is required.

The XSL style sheet contains HTML text and XSL elements. The HTML text forms the basis of the desired output page. The XSL elements are template rules for the XSLT processor. A template is associated with a given element in the XML document. In our example, a template is defined to match on the `<book>` element using the following code:

```
<xsl:template match="/book">

   <!--static text and xsl rules -->

</xsl:template>
```

XSLT defines the `<xsl:value-of>` element for retrieving data from a XML document. The `<xsl:value-of>` element contains a `select` attribute. This attribute value is the name of the actual XML element you want to retrieve. For example, the following code will retrieve the title of the book:

```
<xsl:value-of select="title" />
```

Now let's create the file `book_view.xsl`. This style sheet will create an HTML page that contains information about the book, which is stored in the file `book.xml`. The style sheet contains the basic format of an HTML page and uses XSL elements to retrieve the data. Currently, the XSL elements are merely placeholders in the document. Once an XSL processor accesses the XSL style sheet, the processor executes the XSL elements and replaces them with the appropriate data from the XML document. Listing 9.3 contains the complete code for `book_view.xsl`.

LISTING 9.3 `<install_dir>\ch9_xsl\browser_demo\book_view.xsl`

```
<?xml version="1.0"?>
<xsl:stylesheet xmlns:xsl="http://www.w3.org/1999/XSL/Transform" version="1.0">

<xsl:template match="/book">
    <html><body>

    <b>Title: </b>  <xsl:value-of select="title" />
    <p/>
    <b>By: </b> <xsl:value-of select="author" />
    <p/>
    <b>Cost: </b> <xsl:value-of select="price" />
    <p/>
    <b>Category: </b> <xsl:value-of select="category" />
    <p/>
    <b>Description</b>
    <p/>
    <i><xsl:value-of select="summary" /></i>
```

LISTING 9.3 continued

```
    </body></html>
</xsl:template>
</xsl:stylesheet>
```

The Missing Piece: The XSLT Processor

So far, we've developed the XML document and the XSL style sheet. Now we need an XSLT processor to generate the output document, as shown in Figure 9.2.

XSLT processors are widely available. When you select an XSLT processor, you must ensure that it is fully compliant with the XSLT 1.0 specification. Table 9.1 contains a list of the most popular XSLT 1.0–compliant processors.

TABLE 9.1 XSLT 1.0 Processors

Company	*Product*	*Web Site*
Apache	Xalan-J 1.2.2	`xml.apache.org`
Microsoft	MS XML Parser 3.0	`msdn.microsoft.com`
Sun Microsystems	JAXP 1.1	`java.sun.com/xml`
James Clark	XT	`www.jclark.com/xml/`

Many other XSLT processors are available at `www.xslt.com`. The main difference between the various processors is the programming language supported. For example, the parsers from Apache, Sun Microsystems, and James Clark provide a Java API. The Microsoft parser provides an API for Visual Basic and Visual C++. The Apache parser also provides a C++ API; however, development on the C++ version of Xalan has been suspended.

Two techniques are available for performing the XSLT processing: client-side processing and server-side processing.

Client-side XSLT processing commonly occurs in a Web browser. The Web browser includes an XSLT processor and retrieves the XML document and XSL style sheet, as shown in Figure 9.4.

The client-side technique offloads the XSLT processing to the client machine. This minimizes the workload on the Web server. However, the disadvantage is that the Web browser must provide XSLT support. At the time of this writing, Netscape Communicator 6 and Microsoft Internet Explorer 6 support the XSLT 1.0 specification.

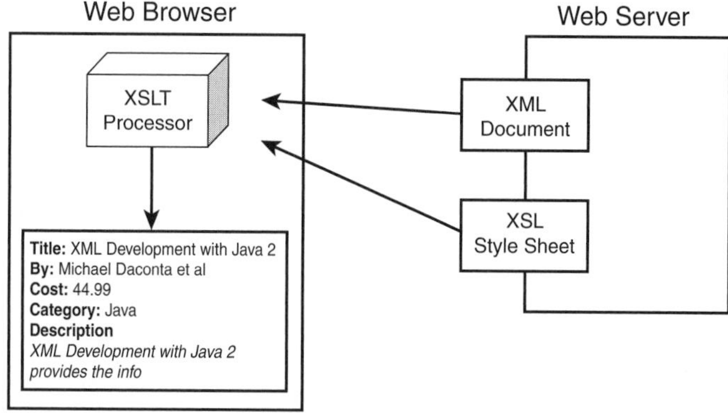

FIGURE 9.4
Processing XSLT in a Web browser.

Microsoft Internet Explorer 5.*x* has very limited support for XSLT 1.0. The previous version of the Netscape browser, 4.*x*, provides no support for XSLT.

Note

Microsoft Internet Explorer 5.*x* provides very limited support for XSLT 1.0. A number of XSLT elements are not supported, such as `<xsl:sort>`, `<xsl:if>`, and `<xsl:number>`, among others. Also, the browsers use `http://www.w3.org/TR/WD-xsl` for the XSL namespace. This is not compatible with the XSLT 1.0 specification.

Microsoft provides a service pack for IE 5.*x* that includes Microsoft XML Parser 3.0, which supports the XSLT 1.0 specification. This service pack is available at `http://msdn.microsoft.com`.

However, it's recommended that you upgrade to IE 6.0 because it is fully XSLT 1.0 compliant.

The exercises in this chapter assume that you have a browser that adheres to the XSLT 1.0 specification.

The client-side technique is applicable when you're deploying an application in a controlled environment. For example, in a corporate environment, the system administrators can install the latest version of the Web browser that conforms to the XSLT 1.0 specification. Implementation details for client-side XSLT processing are provided later in this chapter.

If you are deploying the application on an extranet or the Internet, you will probably have little control over the type/version of browser installed on the client machines. If this is the case, you should implement the server-side technique.

Server-side XSLT processing occurs on the Web server or application server. A server-side process such as an Active Server Page (ASP), JavaServer Page (JSP), or Java servlet will retrieve the XML document and XSL style sheet and pass them to an XSLT processor. The output of the XSLT processor is sent to the client Web browser for presentation. The output is generally a markup language, such as HTML, that is understood by the client browser. The application interaction is illustrated in Figure 9.5.

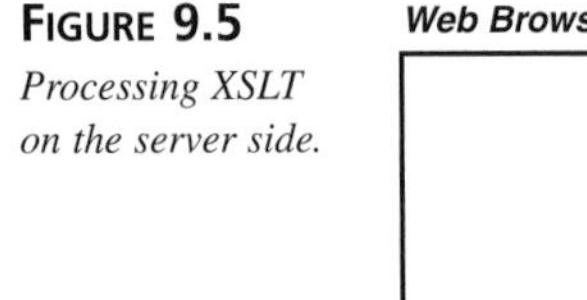

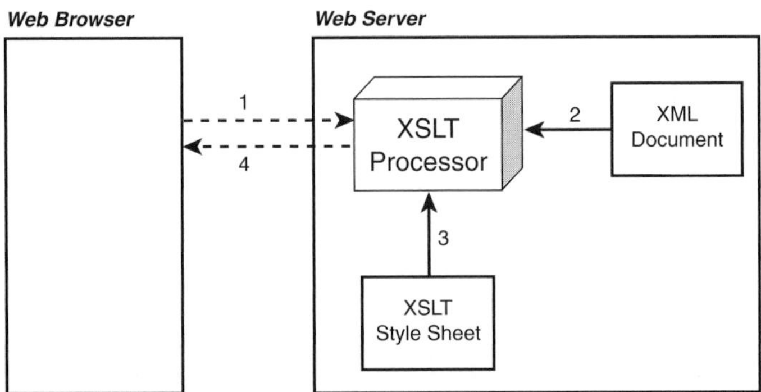

FIGURE 9.5
Processing XSLT on the server side.

An advantage of the server-side technique is browser independence. As shown in the preceding figure, the output document is simply an HTML file. This technique supports the older browser versions and makes the application more robust and versatile. Implementation details are provided later in this chapter.

Also, by utilizing the server-side technique, the application can support a diverse collection of clients. The application can detect the user-agent, such as a WAP-enabled mobile phone, and send back a document containing a Wireless Markup Language (WML) tag. The WAP-enabled phone can render the content using the built-in WML mini-browser.

Implementing Client-Side XSLT Processing

In this section, we'll implement client-side XSLT processing. As mentioned before, you will need a browser that supports XSLT 1.0, such as Netscape Communicator 6 or Microsoft Internet Explorer 6.

For client-side processing, the XML document requires a special processing instruction to reference the XSL style sheet. The processing instruction is `<?xml-stylesheet>`, and it has two attributes: `type` and `href`. The `type` attribute specifies the content type of the document to be retrieved (in this case, `text/xsl`). The `href` attribute is a URL reference to the style sheet. The `href` attribute supports absolute and relative URL references.

The following code example uses a relative URL reference for the style sheet `book_view.xsl`:

```
<?xml-stylesheet type="text/xsl" href="book_view.xsl"?>
```

Listing 9.4 shows the updated version of the `book.xml` document. This version contains the special processing instruction to reference an XSL style sheet.

LISTING 9.4 <install_dir>\ch9_xsl\browser_demo\book.xml

```
<?xml version="1.0"?>
<?xml-stylesheet type="text/xsl" href="book_view.xsl"?>

<book>
    <author>Michael Daconta et al</author>
    <title>XML Development with Java 2</title>
    <category>Java</category>
    <price currency="USD">44.99</price>
    <summary>
        XML Development with Java 2 provides the information
        and techniques a Java developer will need to integrate
        XML into Java-based applications.
    </summary>
</book>
```

No changes are required to the XSL style sheet. You only have to make sure the XSL style sheet is accessible by the reference in the XML document. In this example, the style sheet is located in the same directory as the XML document. Listing 9.5 contains the style sheet.

LISTING 9.5 <install_dir>\ch9_xsl\browser_demo\book_view.xsl

```
<?xml version="1.0"?>
<xsl:stylesheet xmlns:xsl="http://www.w3.org/1999/XSL/Transform" version="1.0">

<xsl:template match="/book">
    <html><body>

    <b>Title: </b>  <xsl:value-of select="title" />
    <p/>
    <b>By: </b> <xsl:value-of select="author" />
    <p/>
    <b>Cost: </b> <xsl:value-of select="price" />
    <p/>
    <b>Category: </b> <xsl:value-of select="category" />
    <p/>
    <b>Description</b>
    <p/>
```

LISTING 9.5 continued

```
    <i><xsl:value-of select="summary" /></i>

    </body></html>
</xsl:template>
</xsl:stylesheet>
```

This example requires a browser that supports XSLT 1.0, such as Netscape Communicator 6 or Microsoft Internet Explorer 6.

Start the Web browser and open the file `<install_dir>\ch9_xsl\browser_demo\book.xml`. The XML document, `book.xml`, references the style sheet, `book_view.xsl`. When the `book.xml` file is loaded in the browser, the style sheet is applied and the output is rendered in the browser, as shown in Figure 9.6.

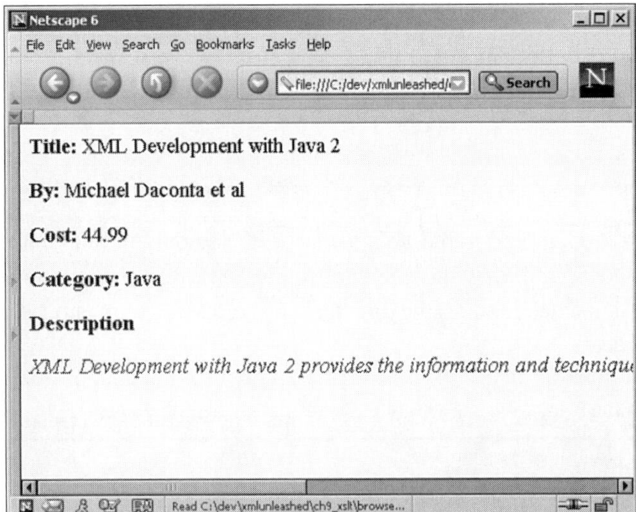

FIGURE 9.6
XSLT rendered in a Web browser.

Implementing Server-Side XSLT Processing

In this section, we'll implement the server-side processing technique. A number of server-side technologies are available, including Common Gateway Interface (CGI), ColdFusion, Hypertext Processor (PHP), and so on. This chapter focuses on server-side processing with Microsoft's Active Server Pages (ASP) and Sun Microsystems' JavaServer Pages (JSP).

ASP: Server-Side XSLT Processing

In order to develop using ASP, you will need the IIS Web server and the latest version of the Microsoft XML parser. The required components are listed below.:

- *Microsoft IIS Web Server 5.0.* This version of IIS is included with Microsoft Windows 2000 Professional. You can also use IIS 4.0 or Personal Web Server (PWS); however, you will have to install the Windows NT Option Pack 4. Refer to Microsoft's Web site for details on adding ASP support to IIS 4.0 and PWS.
- *Microsoft XML Parser 3.0.* If you have IE 6 installed on your server machine, then MS XML Parser 3.0 is included. The MS XML Parser 3.0 is also available as a separate download from `http://msdn.microsoft.com`.

The setup instructions at the beginning of the chapter showed you how to download and extract the source code. You have two options for publishing the source code on the IIS server:

- Copy the files in `<install_dir>\ch9_xsl\public_html` to `c:\Inetpub\wwwroot`.
- Set up a virtual directory that points to `<install_dir>\ch9_xsl\public_html`

An ASP file accesses the Microsoft XML parser as a server object. The following ASP code creates an input source for the XML document and XSL style sheet. Once the documents are loaded, the XML document is transformed based on the rules in the style sheet. The output of the document is returned to the Web browser using the `Response` server object. Listing 9.6 contains the file `book_test.asp`.

LISTING 9.6 `<install_dir>\ch9_xsl\public_html\book_test.asp`

```
<%@ Language=VBScript %>
<%
set xml = Server.CreateObject("Microsoft.XMLDOM")
xml.load(Server.MapPath("book.xml"))

set xsl = Server.CreateObject("Microsoft.XMLDOM")
xsl.load(Server.MapPath("book_view.xsl"))

Response.Write(xml.transformNode(xsl))
%>
```

You can test this example by starting the IIS server and then accessing the file `book_test.asp` in a Web browser. For this example you can use any Web browser. Remember that server-side processing is browser independent, so there is no requirement for XSL in the browser. Figure 9.7 illustrates this concept by accessing the ASP file using an older version of the Netscape Communicator browser, version 4.7.

FIGURE 9.7
A Web browser rendering HTML.

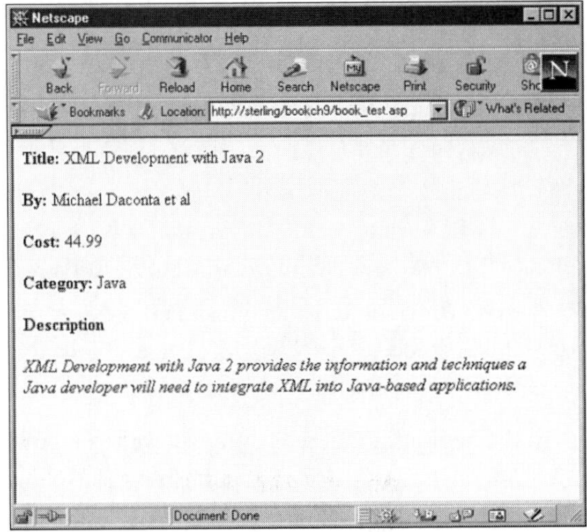

JSP: Server-Side XSLT Processing

Sun Microsystems provides a server-side technology that is very similar to ASP. Of course, the server-side scripting is accomplished in Java. In order to perform the server-side processing with JSP, you will need to install the Java Software Development Kit (SDK) along with a compliant JSP server container. Here's a list of required components:

- Sun Microsystems' Software Development Kit (SDK) 1.3 (or higher). The SDK is available at Sun's Web site, `http://java.sun.com/j2se`. Follow the installation instructions provided with the SDK.
- *Apache Tomcat Server 4*. Apache Tomcat 4 is the official reference implementation for JSP 1.2 and Java Servlets 2.3. If your application server already supports JSP 1.1 or higher, there is no requirement to install Tomcat. Apache Tomcat 4 is available from the Apache Web site, `http://jakarta.apache.org/tomcat`. Follow the installation instructions provided with the Tomcat server.

Once Tomcat 4 is installed, you need to add a new Web application that points to the source code directory. This is accomplished by editing the file `<tomcat_install_dir>\conf\server.xml`. Move to the section where the `<Context>` elements are listed and then add the following entry:

```
<Context path="/bookch9"
         docBase="<install_dir>/ch9_xsl/public_html"
         debug="0"
         reloadable="true" />
```

Be sure to update <install_dir> with the installation directory for the book's source code. This configuration allows you to access the Web application named bookch9. This Web application's document base is located at <install_dir>\ch9_xsl\public_html.

Restart the Tomcat server to pick up the new configuration. By default, the Tomcat server is listening on port 8080. You can access files for the bookch9 Web application using the URL http://localhost:8080/bookch9/book_test.jsp.

This example makes use of a JSP custom tag for the XSLT processing. A JSP custom tag is a special tag that is created by a developer. When the JSP server encounters the custom tag, it executes the handler code associated with the tag. JSP custom tags are conceptually similar to ASP server objects. However, the custom action is represented in the JSP page as a custom tag instead of scripting code.

The Apache <jakarta:apply> tag provides the XSLT processing. The JSP code example shown in Listing 9.7 utilizes the <jakarta:apply> tag. This listing contains the file book_test.jsp.

LISTING 9.7 <install_dir>\ch9_xsl\public_html\book_test.jsp

```
<%@ taglib uri="http://jakarta.apache.org/taglibs/xsl-1.0" prefix="jakarta" %>

<jakarta:apply xml="book.xml" xsl="book_view.xsl" />
```

The first line in this example informs the JSP server to use the tag library that is identified by the URI http://jakarta.apache.org/taglibs/xsl-1.0. This URI is defined in the Web application's deployment description. The URI is actually mapped to the file jakarta-xsl.tld, located in the directory <install_dir>\ch9_xsl\public_html\WEB-INF. The file jakarta-xsl.tld is the Tag Library Descriptor (TLD). The TLD file provides a description of the custom tags available in the class library. It also provides a mapping between the custom tag name and the tag handler class. The tag handler class is located in the directory <install_dir>\ch9_xsl\public_html\WEB-INF\lib.

The next line of code is the actual <jakarta:apply> tag. This tag has two attributes—one defines the XML input source and the other defines the XSL style sheet. The results of the XSLT process are returned to the Web browser.

To test this example, make sure the Tomcat server is running. In a Web browser, access the JSP with the URL http://localhost:8080/bookch9/book_test.jsp. The output should resemble Figure 9.7.

Advanced Features of XSLT

The previous section covered the basics of XSLT processing. Now that you have the required components for XSLT processing installed and configured, we'll explore some advanced XSLT concepts. In this section, you'll learn how to loop over a collection of XML elements, sort the elements, and perform conditional filtering on the data.

Looping

The XSLT element `<xsl:for-each>` is used for looping through a list of elements. This is very useful when you have a collection of related items and you'd like to process them in a sequential fashion. The `<xsl:for-each>` element is commonly used in the Web development world to convert an XML document to an HTML table.

Here's the syntax for `<xsl:for-each>`:

```
<xsl:for-each select=node-set-expression>
    <!-- content -->
</xsl:for-each>
```

The `<xsl:for-each>` element has a required attribute: `select`. The value of the `select` attribute is an expression. The expression contains an XPath expression for selecting the appropriate elements from the list.

Let's take the previous `book.xml` example one step further. Instead of describing a single book, let's create an XML document that contains a list of books. This could describe the books available at an e-commerce site or a list of books available in your company's technical library. Listing 9.8 contains the file `booklist.xml`.

LISTING 9.8 `<install_dir>\ch9_xsl\public_html\loop\booklist.xml`

```
<?xml version="1.0"?>
<booklist>
    <book>
        <author>Michael Daconta et al</author>
        <title>XML Development with Java 2</title>
        <category>Java</category>
        <price currency="USD">37.99</price>
    </book>
    <book>
        <author>Mark Grand</author>
        <title>Patterns in Java</title>
        <category>Java</category>
        <price currency="USD">44.99</price>
    </book>
    <book>
        <author>Richard Monson-Haefel</author>
```

LISTING 9.8 continued

```
        <title>Enterprise JavaBeans</title>
        <category>Java</category>
        <price currency="USD">34.95</price>
    </book>
    <book>
        <author>Chad Darby et al</author>
        <title>Professional Java E-Commerce</title>
        <category>Java</category>
        <price currency="USD">59.95</price>
    </book>
    <book>
        <author>E. Lynn Harris</author>
        <title>Any Way The Wind Blows</title>
        <category>Fiction-Romance</category>
        <price currency="USD">19.95</price>
    </book>
    <book>
        <author>E. Lynn Harris</author>
        <title>Invisible Life</title>
        <category>Fiction-Romance</category>
        <price currency="USD">16.95</price>
    </book>
    <book>
        <author>E. Lynn Harris</author>
        <title>And This Too Shall Pass</title>
        <category>Fiction-Romance</category>
        <price currency="USD">18.95</price>
    </book>
    <book>
        <author>Tom Clancy</author>
        <title>Executive Orders</title>
        <category>Fiction-Thriller</category>
        <price currency="USD">7.99</price>
    </book>
    <book>
        <author>Tom Clancy</author>
        <title>Hunt for Red October</title>
        <category>Fiction-Thriller</category>
        <price currency="USD">27.95</price>
    </book>
    <book>
        <author>Tom Clancy</author>
        <title>The Sum of All Fears</title>
        <category>Fiction-Thriller</category>
        <price currency="USD">7.99</price>
    </book>
</booklist>
```

Now, let's design an XSL style sheet to convert the XML document to an HTML table. The <xsl:for-each> element loops over a list of items. This example performs a loop for each <book> element in the <booklist> element. This process is described in the select attribute with the expression booklist/book. See the following code snippet:

```
<xsl:for-each select="booklist/book" >
        <!-- insert table rows and table data -->
</xsl:for-each>
```

Inside of the <xsl:for-each> element, the appropriate HTML elements are used for the table rows and table data. To retrieve the data from the XML document, each table cell uses the <xsl:value-of> element. Listing 9.9 contains the complete style sheet, booklist_loop.xsl.

LISTING 9.9 <install_dir>\ch9_xsl\public_html\loop\booklist_loop.xsl

```
<?xml version="1.0"?>
<xsl:stylesheet xmlns:xsl="http://www.w3.org/1999/XSL/Transform" version="1.0">

<xsl:template match="/">
<html><body>
<h3>Looping Example</h3>
<hr></hr>
<table border="1" cellpadding="5">
    <tr>
        <th>Author</th>
        <th>Title</th>
        <th>Category</th>
        <th>Price</th>
    </tr>

    <!-- Perform loop for each book in the book list -->
    <xsl:for-each select="booklist/book" >
        <tr>
            <td>  <xsl:value-of select="author" /> </td>
            <td>  <xsl:value-of select="title" />      </td>
            <td>  <xsl:value-of select="category" />    </td>
            <td>  <xsl:value-of select="price" />    </td>
        </tr>
    </xsl:for-each>
</table>

</body></html>
</xsl:template>
</xsl:stylesheet>
```

You can test the server-side scripts using the techniques presented earlier in this chapter. The test files are named `booklist_test.jsp` and `booklist_test.asp`. They are located in the directory `<install_dir>\ch9_xsl\public_html\loop`.

The server-side scripts refer to the appropriate XML document and XSL style sheet. Listing 9.10 contains the code for `booklist_test.jsp`.

LISTING 9.10 `<install_dir>\ch9_xsl\public_html\loop\book_test.jsp`

```
<%@ taglib uri="http://jakarta.apache.org/taglibs/xsl-1.0" prefix="jakarta" %>

<jakarta:apply xml="/loop/booklist.xml" xsl="/loop/booklist_loop.xsl" />
```

To view the test file, start the Tomcat server. In the Web browser, open `http://localhost:8080/bookch9/loop/booklist_test.jsp`. Figure 9.8 shows the result.

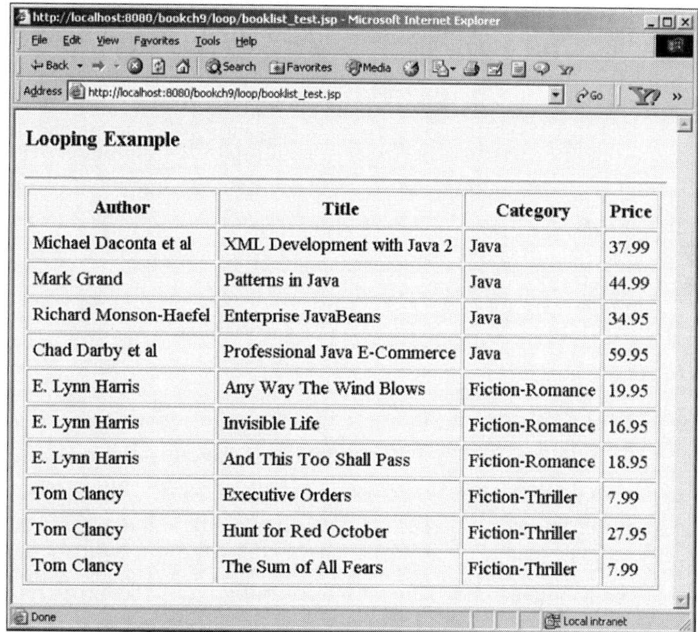

Author	Title	Category	Price
Michael Daconta et al	XML Development with Java 2	Java	37.99
Mark Grand	Patterns in Java	Java	44.99
Richard Monson-Haefel	Enterprise JavaBeans	Java	34.95
Chad Darby et al	Professional Java E-Commerce	Java	59.95
E. Lynn Harris	Any Way The Wind Blows	Fiction-Romance	19.95
E. Lynn Harris	Invisible Life	Fiction-Romance	16.95
E. Lynn Harris	And This Too Shall Pass	Fiction-Romance	18.95
Tom Clancy	Executive Orders	Fiction-Thriller	7.99
Tom Clancy	Hunt for Red October	Fiction-Thriller	27.95
Tom Clancy	The Sum of All Fears	Fiction-Thriller	7.99

FIGURE 9.8
The result of applying the style sheet to the XML document.

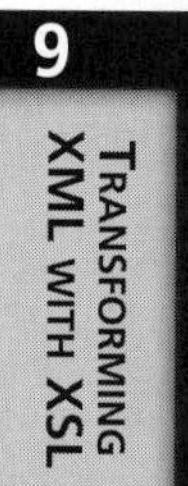

You can also test this example using the client-side techniques described earlier in the chapter by adding a reference to the XSL in the XML document.

Sorting

In XSLT, the <xsl:sort> element is used for sorting the XML data. It is possible to sort based on a single key or multiple keys. The syntax for the <xsl:sort> element is shown here:

```
<xsl:sort
    select = string-expression
    order = { "ascending" | "descending" }
    data-type = { "text" | "number" }
    case-order = {"upper-first" | "lower-first" }
    lang = { nmtoken } />
```

The <xsl:sort> element is used in conjunction with the <xsl:for-each> element. For example, the following code snippet sorts the book titles in alphabetical order:

```
<!-- Sort by the book title -->
<xsl:for-each select="booklist/book" >
    <xsl:sort select="title" />
         <!-- insert table rows and table data -->
</xsl:for-each>
```

Sort Order: Ascending or Descending?

By default, the information is sorted in ascending order. Set the `order` attribute to `descending` for a descending sort. The following code snippet sorts the titles in descending order:

```
    <!-- Sort by the book title, descending -->
    <xsl:for-each select="booklist/book">
        <xsl:sort select="title" order="descending"/>
<!-- insert table rows and table data -->
    </xsl:for-each>
```

It is important to note that the <xsl:sort> element assumes that the sort key is a text element. If you need to sort numerical data, you have to set the `data-type` attribute to `number`. If you don't set the `data-type` attribute, the XSLT processor will use the default value, `text`. When sorting numerical data, the default value of `text` will not generate the desired output. To demonstrate this point, let's attempt to sort the books in `booklist.xml` by price. The following code snippet purposefully omits the `data-type` attribute:

```
<xsl:for-each select="booklist/book">
    <xsl:sort select="price" />
    <tr>
        <td>  <xsl:value-of select="author" /> </td>
        <td>  <xsl:value-of select="title" />      </td>
        <td>  <xsl:value-of select="category" />    </td>
        <td>  <xsl:value-of select="price" />    </td>
    </tr>
</xsl:for-each>
```

When applied to `booklist.xml`, this style sheet fragment generates the output in Figure 9.9.

FIGURE 9.9
Incorrect sorting of XML data by price.

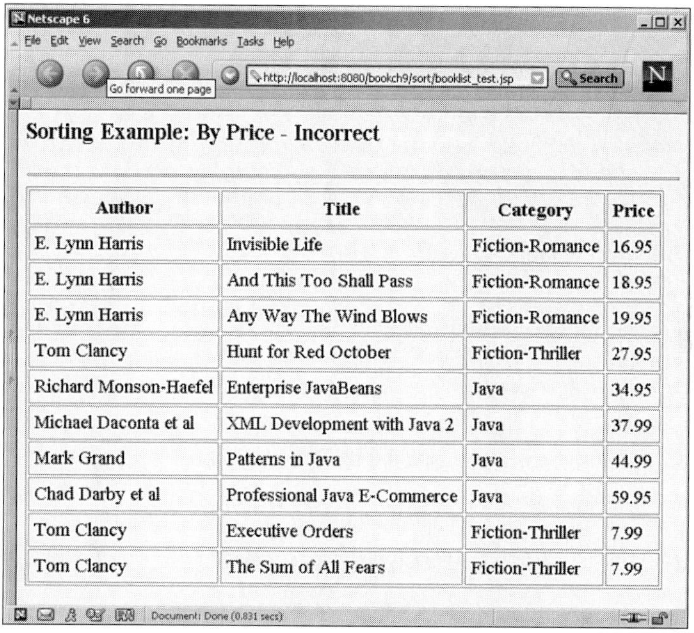

Netscape 6
File Edit View Search Go Bookmarks Tasks Help
http://localhost:8080/bookch9/sort/booklist_test.jsp
Go forward one page

Sorting Example: By Price - Incorrect

Author	Title	Category	Price
E. Lynn Harris	Invisible Life	Fiction-Romance	16.95
E. Lynn Harris	And This Too Shall Pass	Fiction-Romance	18.95
E. Lynn Harris	Any Way The Wind Blows	Fiction-Romance	19.95
Tom Clancy	Hunt for Red October	Fiction-Thriller	27.95
Richard Monson-Haefel	Enterprise JavaBeans	Java	34.95
Michael Daconta et al	XML Development with Java 2	Java	37.99
Mark Grand	Patterns in Java	Java	44.99
Chad Darby et al	Professional Java E-Commerce	Java	59.95
Tom Clancy	Executive Orders	Fiction-Thriller	7.99
Tom Clancy	The Sum of All Fears	Fiction-Thriller	7.99

Document: Done (0.831 secs)

Notice that the prices are *not* sorted in an ascending order.

To achieve numerical sorting, you have to specify `<xsl:sort select="price" data-type="number" />`. Listing 9.11 provides the correct usage of the `<xsl:sort>` element for numerical sorting.

LISTING 9.11 `<install_dir>\ch9_xsl\public_html\sort\booklist_sort.xsl`

```
<?xml version="1.0"?>
<xsl:stylesheet xmlns:xsl="http://www.w3.org/1999/XSL/Transform" version="1.0">

<xsl:template match="/">
<html><body>
<h3>Sorting Example: By Price</h3>
<hr></hr>
<table border="1" cellpadding="5">
    <tr>
        <th>Author</th>
        <th>Title</th>
        <th>Category</th>
        <th>Price</th>
```

LISTING 9.11 continued

```
    </tr>

    <!-- Perform loop for each book in the book list -->
    <xsl:for-each select="booklist/book" >
        <xsl:sort select="price" order="ascending" data-type="number" />
        <tr>
            <td>  <xsl:value-of select="author" /> </td>
            <td>  <xsl:value-of select="title" />     </td>
            <td>  <xsl:value-of select="category" />    </td>
            <td>  <xsl:value-of select="price" />    </td>
        </tr>
    </xsl:for-each>
</table>

</body></html>
</xsl:template>
</xsl:stylesheet>
```

When applied to `booklist.xml`, the revised style sheet generates the correct output, as shown in Figure 9.10.

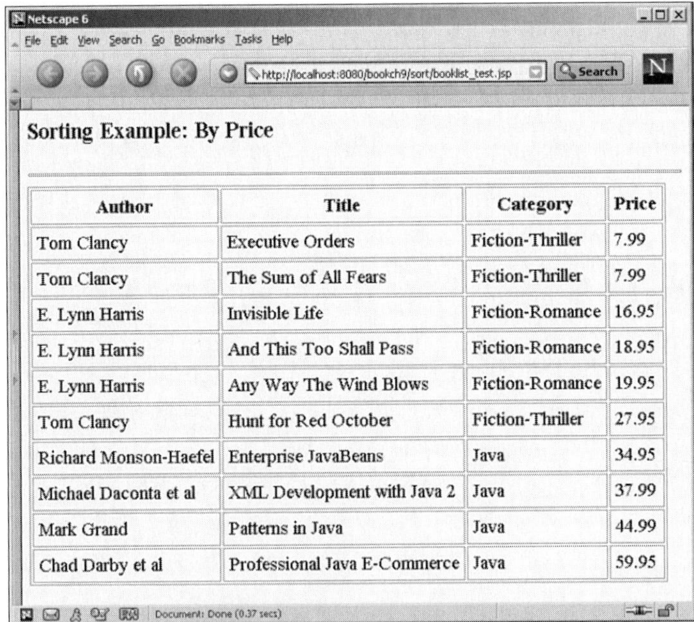

FIGURE 9.10
XML data correctly sorted by price.

Note

I've discovered a bug with the client-side XSLT implementation in Netscape 6.1. Netscape 6.1 does not support numerical sorting with the `<xsl:sort>` element. Even when explicitly set in the style sheet (using `<xsl:sort select="price" data-type="number" />`), the Netscape browser does not sort the prices in numerical order.

This bug is only encountered when using the client-side XSLT support in the Netscape 6.1 browser. The server-side technique applies the transformation on the server side, so this bug is never encountered. As a best practice, you should apply the server-side technique whenever possible.

Sorting by Case

The `case-order` attribute is used to specify whether uppercase or lowercase has precedence during the sort. For example, if the `case-order` attribute is set to `upper-case`, then

```
a b A B
```

is sorted as follows:

```
A a B b
```

If the `lower-case` attribute value is applied, then

```
a b A B
```

is sorted like this:

```
a A b B
```

The `case-order` attribute should only be used when the `data-type` attribute is set to `text`.

Sorting with Multiple Keys

In certain situations, you might want to sort using multiple keys. For example, you could sort the books by category and then by price. This is accomplished by inserting multiple `<xsl:sort>` elements within an `<xsl:for-each>` element. Listing 9.12 sorts by category and then by price.

LISTING 9.12 `<install_dir>\ch9_xsl\public_html\sort\booklist_sort_categoryprice.xsl`

```
<?xml version="1.0"?>
<xsl:stylesheet xmlns:xsl="http://www.w3.org/1999/XSL/Transform" version="1.0">
```

LISTING 9.12 continued

```
<xsl:template match="/">
<html><body>
<h3>Sorting Example: By Price</h3>
<hr></hr>
<table border="1" cellpadding="5">
    <tr>
        <th>Author</th>
        <th>Title</th>
        <th>Category</th>
        <th>Price</th>
    </tr>

    <!-- Perform loop for each book in the book list -->
    <xsl:for-each select="booklist/book" >
        <xsl:sort select="category" />
        <xsl:sort select="price" data-type="number" />
        <tr>
            <td> <xsl:value-of select="author" /> </td>
            <td> <xsl:value-of select="title" />     </td>
            <td> <xsl:value-of select="category" />   </td>
            <td> <xsl:value-of select="price" />   </td>
        </tr>
    </xsl:for-each>
</table>

</body></html>
</xsl:template>
</xsl:stylesheet>
```

When applied to `booklist.xml`, this style sheet generates the output shown in Figure 9.11. The implementation details are left as an exercise for you, the reader.

The server-side test scripts are available in the directory `<install_dir>\ch9_xsl\public_html\sort`.

Conditionals

During an XSLT transformation, the style sheet can perform conditional tests on the data. XSLT contains a very simple `if-then` conditional. The syntax for the `<xsl:if>` element is shown here:

```
<xsl:if test=Boolean-expression>
    <!-- content -->
</xsl:if>
```

The `test` attribute refers to a Boolean expression. If the Boolean expression evaluates to `true`, the content within the `<xsl:if>` element is included in the output.

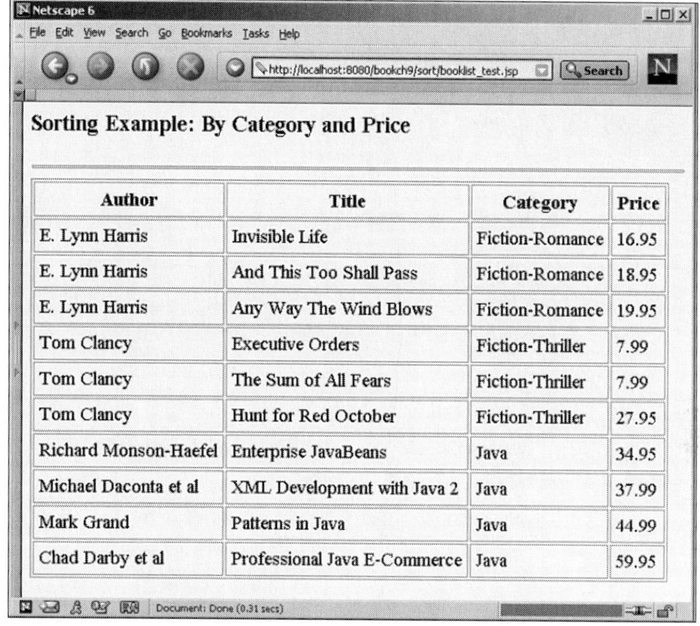

Sorting Example: By Category and Price

Author	Title	Category	Price
E. Lynn Harris	Invisible Life	Fiction-Romance	16.95
E. Lynn Harris	And This Too Shall Pass	Fiction-Romance	18.95
E. Lynn Harris	Any Way The Wind Blows	Fiction-Romance	19.95
Tom Clancy	Executive Orders	Fiction-Thriller	7.99
Tom Clancy	The Sum of All Fears	Fiction-Thriller	7.99
Tom Clancy	Hunt for Red October	Fiction-Thriller	27.95
Richard Monson-Haefel	Enterprise JavaBeans	Java	34.95
Michael Daconta et al	XML Development with Java 2	Java	37.99
Mark Grand	Patterns in Java	Java	44.99
Chad Darby et al	Professional Java E-Commerce	Java	59.95

FIGURE 9.11
Sorting XML data with multiple sort keys.

The following code snippet performs a test for Fiction-Thriller books:

```
<xsl:for-each select="booklist/book" >
    <tr>
        <xsl:if test="category='Fiction-Thriller'">
            <xsl:attribute name="bgcolor">red</xsl:attribute>
        </xsl:if>
        <td>  <xsl:value-of select="author" /> </td>
        <td>  <xsl:value-of select="title" />      </td>
        <td>  <xsl:value-of select="category" />    </td>
        <td>  <xsl:value-of select="price" />    </td>
    </tr>
</xsl:for-each>
```

If a Fiction-Thriller book is found, the background color of the row is set to red. In this example, we've introduced a new XSLT element, `<xsl:attribute>`. The `<xsl:attribute>` element creates a new attribute for the parent element. In this example, the parent is the `<tr>` element. If the conditional is `true`, the `<tr>` element will have the attribute `bgcolor` and its value set to `red`. The end result is `<tr bgcolor="red">`.

When applied to `booklist.xml`, the XSLT processor generates the output shown in Figure 9.12. The server-side test scripts are available in the directory `<install_dir>\ch9_xsl\public_html\if`.

> **Note**
>
> Of course, the figure in the book is in black and white. However, the desired output will be displayed on your color monitor.

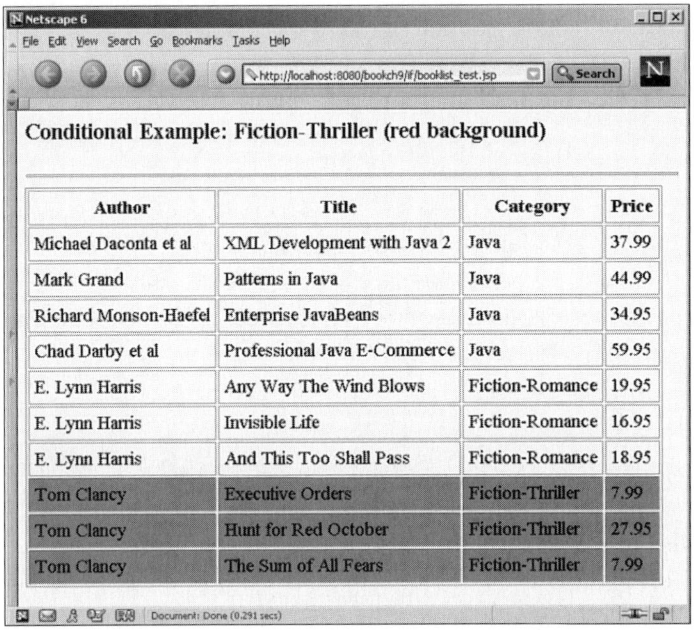
Netscape 6
File Edit View Search Go Bookmarks Tasks Help
http://localhost:8080/bookch9/if/booklist_test.jsp
Search
Conditional Example: Fiction-Thriller (red background)
Author | Title | Category | Price
Michael Daconta et al | XML Development with Java 2 | Java | 37.99
Mark Grand | Patterns in Java | Java | 44.99
Richard Monson-Haefel | Enterprise JavaBeans | Java | 34.95
Chad Darby et al | Professional Java E-Commerce | Java | 59.95
E. Lynn Harris | Any Way The Wind Blows | Fiction-Romance | 19.95
E. Lynn Harris | Invisible Life | Fiction-Romance | 16.95
E. Lynn Harris | And This Too Shall Pass | Fiction-Romance | 18.95
Tom Clancy | Executive Orders | Fiction-Thriller | 7.99
Tom Clancy | Hunt for Red October | Fiction-Thriller | 27.95
Tom Clancy | The Sum of All Fears | Fiction-Thriller | 7.99
Document: Done (0.291 secs)

FIGURE 9.12
Using conditionals in XSLT.

Filters

In relation to conditional tests, XSLT can also filter the data based on a given expression. When data is selected using the <xsl:for-each> element, the expression can contain a filter. For example, you can filter the data to contain only Java books. The following code snippet performs the desired operation:

```
<xsl:for-each select="booklist/book[category='Java']" >
    <tr>
        <td>  <xsl:value-of select="author" /> </td>
        <td>  <xsl:value-of select="title" />     </td>
        <td>  <xsl:value-of select="category" />    </td>
        <td>  <xsl:value-of select="price" />    </td>
    </tr>
</xsl:for-each>
```

XSL for Business-to-Business (B2B) Communication

The previous section leveraged XSLT for document publishing. However, XSLT can also be used in for B2B communication—the process of exchanging data between two different companies. Developers can leverage XML to describe the data in a vendor-independent fashion. In the ideal case, both companies will agree upon a standard vocabulary for describing the data using a DTD or schema. The vocabulary is composed of the XML element names used in the XML document. However, in certain cases one of the companies might like to use a different vocabulary. This is where XSL enters the picture.

The example in this section describes a B2B scenario between a training company, Hot Shot Training, and a software development company, AcmeSoft. The computer training company maintains a database for the students that have attended its courses. The training company has developed an XML application that produces the list of students for a given class.

The management team at AcmeSoft would like to retrieve this list from the training company's XML application. However, once the data is retrieved, AcmeSoft would like to store the data in a different XML format using its own XML element names. The application interaction is illustrated in Figure 9.13.

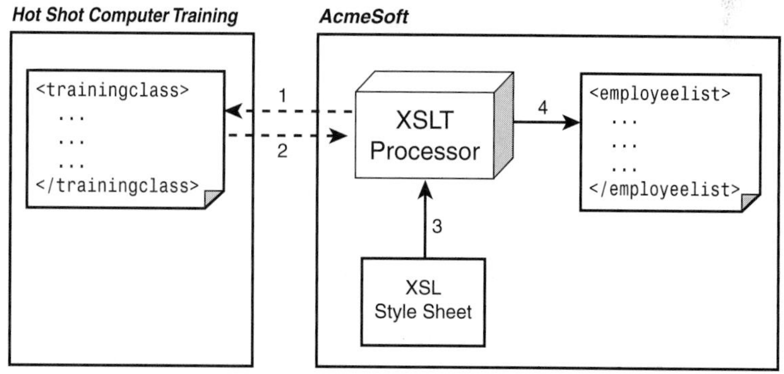

FIGURE 9.13
Converting XML data in B2B communication.

The XML application at the training company is accessible using the HTTP protocol. The first step is to request the XML document from the training company. In step 2, the XML document is retrieved. In step 3, the document is transformed using the supplied XSLT style sheet. Finally, the desired output document is produced in step 4.

A sample output of the XML document is shown here:

```
<?xml version="1.0"?>
<trainingclass>
    <title>J2EE Essentials</title>
    <start_date>24 Sep 2001</start_date>
    <end_date>28 Sep 2001</end_date>
    <location>Philadelphia, PA</location>

    <student>
        <first_name>Riley</first_name>
        <last_name>Scott</last_name>
        <email>riley@acmesoft.web</email>
    </student>

    <student>
        <first_name>Torrance</first_name>
        <last_name>Lee</last_name>
        <email>torrance.lee@acmesoft.web</email>
    </student>
</trainingclass>
```

The development team at AcmeSoft has a different collection of element names to describe a training class. The desired output of the converted XML document for AcmeSoft is shown here:

```
<?xml version="1.0"?>
<employeelist>
    <course_title>J2EE Essentials</course_title>
    <course_date start="24 Sep 2001" end="28 Sep 2001" />
    <location>Philadelphia, PA</location>

    <employee>
        <name>
            <first>Riley</first>
            <last>Scott</last>
        </name>
        <email>riley.scott@acmesoft.web</email>
    </employee>

    <employee>
        <name>
            <first>Torrance</first>
            <last>Lee</last>
        </name>
        <email>torrance.lee@acmesoft.web</email>
    </employee>
</employeelist>
```

Notice in both instances that the data is the same; it's simply in a different format. The format is different because of the element names used by AcmeSoft. In the context of

AcmeSoft, there are no students on the payroll; instead, AcmeSoft has employees. Also, the AcmeSoft team has a different approach for storing the class date. Finally, notice that AcmeSoft uses a different structure for the employee name.

Therefore, a mechanism is needed to convert an XML document to another XML format. XSLT offers a solution to this problem. An XSL style sheet can be developed to convert the `<trainingclass>` document to the `<employeelist>` document. This approach will not require any changes by the training company. The training company can continue to publish XML documents for its training classes. The development team at AcmeSoft can develop an XSL style sheet that contains the transformation rules. Once the style sheet is developed, the XML document and style sheet can be passed to the XSLT processor, which will generate the desired XML document for `<employeelist>`.

Creating the XSL Style Sheet

The XSL style sheet will contain the template for the `<employeelist>` document, and the XSL elements will be leveraged to retrieve the data from the `<trainingclass>` document. The transformation is fairly straightforward, except for one area. The training company describes the date for the class using the elements `<start_date>` and `<end_date>`, as shown here:

```
<start_date>24 Sep 2001</start_date>
<end_date>28 Sep 2001</end_date>
```

AcmeSoft stores the date as a single element with two attributes for the start and end:

```
<course_date start="24 Sep 2001" end="28 Sep 2001" />
```

In this case, `<xsl:attribute>` can be used to create attributes for `<course_date>`:

```
<course_date>
<xsl:attribute name="start"><xsl:value-of select="start_date"/>
➥</xsl:attribute>
<xsl:attribute name="end"><xsl:value-of select="end_date"/></xsl:attribute>
</course_date>
```

The `<xsl:attribute>` element creates attributes for the parent element. In this example, the parent element is `course_date`. This transformation will result in the following code:

```
<course_date start="24 Sep 2001" end="28 Sep 2001" />
```

The complete code for the style sheet is shown in Listing 9.13.

LISTING 9.13 `<install_dir>\ch9_xsl\public_html\b2b\train2employee.xsl`

```
<?xml version="1.0"?>
<xsl:stylesheet xmlns:xsl="http://www.w3.org/1999/XSL/Transform" version="1.0">
```

LISTING 9.13 continued

```
<xsl:template match="/trainingclass">
    <employeelist>

        <course_title><xsl:value-of select="title" /></course_title>

        <!-- create attributes for the start and end course dates -->
        <course_date>
            <xsl:attribute name="start">
                              <xsl:value-of select="start_date"/>
                            </xsl:attribute>
            <xsl:attribute name="end">
                              <xsl:value-of select="end_date"/>
                            </xsl:attribute>
        </course_date>

        <location><xsl:value-of select="location" /></location>

        <!-- Perform a loop for each student in the training class -->
        <xsl:for-each select="student"
            <employee>
                <name>
                    <first><xsl:value-of select="first_name"/></first>
                    <last><xsl:value-of select="last_name"/></last>
                </name>
                <email><xsl:value-of select="email"/></email>
            </employee>
        </xsl:for-each>

    </employeelist>
</xsl:template>
</xsl:stylesheet>
```

Using the XSLT Processor

So far in this chapter, we've used client-side and server-side techniques for XSLT processing. The client-side technique utilized a Web browser that has support for XSLT. The server-side technique leveraged server scripts developed in JSP and ASP. The JSP examples used a JSP custom tag for the XSLT processing, whereas the ASP examples leveraged the Microsoft XML server object.

For most B2B applications, the source XML document is retrieved by another application. This may be a standalone application or a component of a larger B2B application. In the case of a standalone application, the necessary code to perform the XSLT processing needs to be developed. For example, a Visual Basic or Visual C++ application can use the XSLT processor available with the Microsoft XML API. In a similar fashion, a

Java application can use the XSLT processor available with the Apache Xalan API. The Apache Xalan API is available at `http://xml.apache.org`.

Here's the code for a standalone Java application that uses the Apache Xalan API (note that the application accepts three command-line arguments—one each for the input XML document, the XSL style sheet, and the name of the output file):

```
java XslTester <input XML> <input XSL> <output file>
```

The input XML document and the input XSL style sheet can be referenced using filenames or URLs. Listing 9.14 contains the complete code for `XslTester.java`.

LISTING 9.14 `<install_dir>\ch9_xsl\b2b\XslTester.java`

```
import org.apache.xalan.xslt.*;

/**
 *  Usage:  java XslTester <input XML> <input XSL> <output file>
 */
public class XslTester{

    public static void main(String[] args) {

        try {
            // Verify the correct arguments are passed in
            if (args.length != 3) {

System.out.println("Usage:  java XslTester <input XML> <input XSL>
➥<output file>");
                System.exit(1);
            }

            System.out.println("Processing: " + args[0] + " and " + args[1]);

            // Step 1:  Get a reference to the XSLT Processor
            XSLTProcessor myEngine = XSLTProcessorFactory.getProcessor();

            // Step 2:  Get the XML input document
            XSLTInputSource xmlSource = new XSLTInputSource(args[0]);

            // Step 3:  Get the XSL style sheet
            XSLTInputSource xslStylesheet = new XSLTInputSource(args[1]);

            // Step 4:  Setup the output target
            XSLTResultTarget xmlOutput = new XSLTResultTarget(args[2]);

            // Step 5:  Now process it!
            myEngine.process(xmlSource, xslStylesheet, xmlOutput);
```

LISTING 9.14 continued

```
            System.out.println("Created => " + args[2]);
            System.out.println("Done!");
        }
        catch (Exception exc) {
            exc.printStackTrace();
        }
    }
}
```

The first task of the main method is verifying the correct number of parameters. Next, the application retrieves a reference to the XSLT processing engine using the factory method `XSLTProcessorFactory.getProcessor()`. The application then retrieves the input XML document and XSL style sheet based on the first two command-line arguments. The result target for the XSLT translation is configured to use the filename supplied as the third command-line argument. Finally, the XSLT processing engine is invoked using the objects `xmlSource`, `xslStylesheet`, and `xmlOutput`.

Running the Example

This example requires the Java Development Kit version 1.3 or higher. Follow these steps to test it:

1. Open an MS-DOS window.
2. Move to the directory `<install_dir>\ch9_xsl\b2b\`.
3. Set up the Java classpath by typing **`setpaths`**.
4. Execute the application by typing the following:

   `java XslTester trainingclass.xml train2employee.xsl testoutput.xml`
5. View the `testoutput.xml` file in a text editor. Verify that your document resembles this:

```
<?xml version="1.0" encoding="UTF-8"?>
<employeelist>
    <course_title>J2EE Essentials</course_title>
    <course_date start="24 Sep 2001" end="28 Sep 2001"/>
    <location>Philadelphia, PA</location>
    <employee>
        <name>
            <first>Riley</first>
            <last>Scott</last>
        </name>
        <email>riley@acmesoft.web</email>
    </employee>
    <employee>
```

```
            <name>
                <first>Torrance</first>
                <last>Lee</last>
            </name>
            <email>torrance.lee@acmesoft.web</email>
        </employee>
    </employeelist>
```

The `trainingclass.xml` document is also available on the Web server at `http://localhost:8080/bookch9/hotshot/trainingclass.xml`. The `XslTester` application also supports a URL for the XML document and XSL style sheet. You can access the `trainingclass.xml` document via the Web server by simply supplying the following URL:

```
java XslTester http://localhost:8080/bookch9/hotshot/trainingclass.xml

train2employee.xsl testoutput.xml
```

This example demonstrates the technique used to retrieve an XML document and perform the XSLT conversion. Once the XML data is converted to the desired XML output, the application can process it accordingly. For example, the application can use the SAX and DOM APIs to parse the XML document and store the results in a database. By leveraging the SAX and DOM APIs, the application is very flexible in how it processes/stores the converted XML document.

XSL Formatting Objects

The XSL technology is also composed of XSL Formatting Objects (XSL-FO). XSL-FO was designed to assist with the printing and displaying of XML data. The main emphasis is on the document layout and structure. This includes the dimensions of the output document, including page headers, footers, and margins. XSL-FO also allows the developer to define the formatting rules for the content, such as font, style, color, and positioning. XSL-FO is a sophisticated version of Cascading Style Sheets (CSS). In fact, XSL-FO borrows a lot of the terminology and elements from CSS.

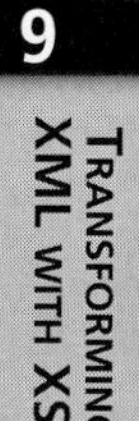

XSL-FO documents are well-formed XML documents. An XSL-FO formatting engine processes XSL-FO documents. You can use two techniques for creating XSL-FO documents. The first is to simply develop the XSL-FO file with the included data. The second technique is to dynamically create the XSL-FO file using an XSLT translation.

XSL-FO Formatting Engines

The current W3C Candidate Recommendation for XSL-FO is 15 October 2001 and is available at `http://www.w3.org/TR/2001/REC-xsl-20011015`. Many of the XSL-FO formatting engines implement a subset of the XSL-FO specification. Also, the browser support for XSL-FO is nonexistent.

However, don't be discouraged. Engines are available that allow you to experiment with the basic features of XSL-FO. In fact, we'll use the Apache XSL-FOP to generate PDF documents from XML. Table 9.2 contains a list of XSL-FO formatting engines.

The source code distribution for this chapter includes the Apache XSL-FO formatting engine. You have everything you need to run the examples. You can download additional engines if you'd like to experiment with them.

TABLE 9.2 XSL-FO Formatting Engines

XSL-FO Engine	*Web Site*
Apache XSL-FOP	`xml.apache.org`
XEP	`www.renderx.com`
iText	`www.lowagie.com/iText/`
Unicorn	`www.unicorn-enterprises.com`

The examples in this chapter are based Apache XSL-FOP version 0.20.1.

Note

Directions for downloading the source code were given at the beginning of the chapter. The initial download also includes the XSL-FO sample code. Here are descriptions of the directories specific to the XSL-FO examples:

Directory	*Description*
`ch9_xsl\xsl_fo`	Sample code for XSL-FO
`ch9_xsl\xsl_fo\lib`	Supporting JAR files
`ch9_xsl\xsl_fo\dynamic`	Sample code to create XSL-FO from XSLT
`ch9_xsl\xsl_fo\ezfop.war`	Web app archive for servlet demo

In this section, we will create a simple XSL-FO document. Once the document is created, we will use the Apache XSL-FOP formatter to convert the document to a PDF file. The application interaction is illustrated in Figure 9.14.

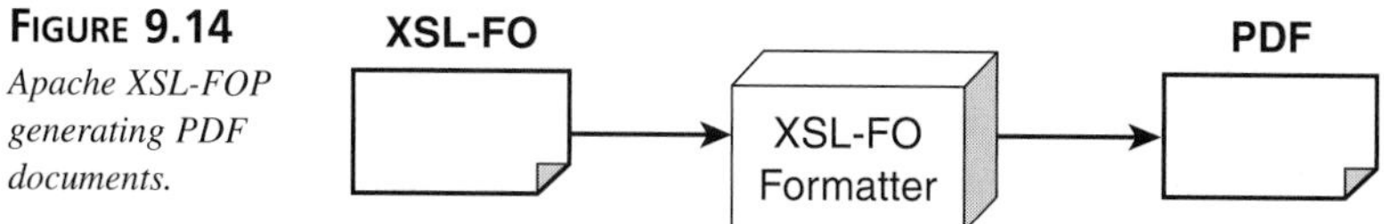

FIGURE 9.14
Apache XSL-FOP generating PDF documents.

Basic Document Structure

An XML-FO document follows the syntax rules of XML; as a result, it is well formed. XSL-FO elements use the following namespace:

```
http://www.w3.org/1999/XSL/Format
```

The following code snippet shows the basic document setup for XSL-FO:

```
<?xml version="1.0" encoding="utf-8"?>

<fo:root xmlns:fo="http://www.w3.org/1999/XSL/Format">
  <!-- layout master set -->
    <!-- page masters: size and layout -->

  <!-- page sequences and content -->
</fo:root>
```

The element `<fo:root>` is the root element for the XSL-FO document. An XSL-FO document can contain the following components:

- Page master
- Page master set
- Page sequences

Page Master: `<fo:page-master>`

The page master describes the page size and layout. For example, we could use an 8.5×11-inch page or an A4 letter. The page master contains the dimensions for a page, including width, height, and margins. The page master is similar to a slide master in Microsoft PowerPoint. The components of the page master are shown in Figure 9.15.

The `<fo:simple-page-master>` element defines the layout of a page. The following code snippet describes a U.S. letter:

```
<fo:simple-page-master master-name="simple"
              page-height="11in"
              page-width="8.5in"
              margin-top="1in"
              margin-bottom="1in"
              margin-left="1.25in"
              margin-right="1.25in">
</fo:simple-page-master>
```

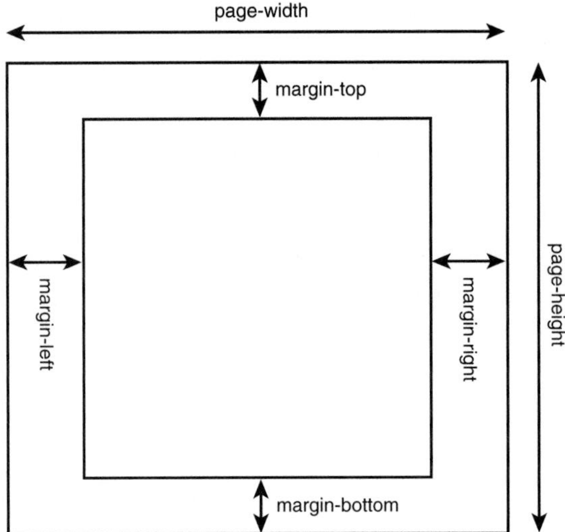

FIGURE 9.15
Components of the page master.

Notice the attributes for `<fo:simple-page-master>`. The attributes define the height and width of the page, along with the size of the margins. The dimensions in this example are listed in inches (in). Table 9.3 lists the dimensions supported in XSL-FO.

TABLE 9.3 XSL-FO Dimensions

Unit Suffix	*Description*
in	Inches (1 inch equals 2.54 centimeters)
mm	Millimeters
cm	Centimeters
pt	Points (1 point equals 1/72 inch)
pc	Picas (1 pica equals 12 points)
em	Font size of the relevant font
ex	X-height of the relevant font
px	Pixels

To set the page height to 210 millimeters, use the following syntax:

```
page-height="210mm"
```

The `<fo:simple-page-master>` element can also be used to describe an A4 letter (height 210 mm and width 297 mm):

```
<fo:simple-page-master master-name="A4-example"
             page-height="210mm"
             page-width="297mm"
             margin-top="0.5in"
             margin-bottom="0.5in"
             margin-left="0.5in"
             margin-right="0.5in">
</fo:simple-page-master>
```

Each page is divided into five *regions*. Regions serve as containers for the document content. The regions are depicted below in Figure 9.16.

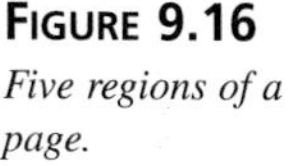

FIGURE 9.16
Five regions of a page.

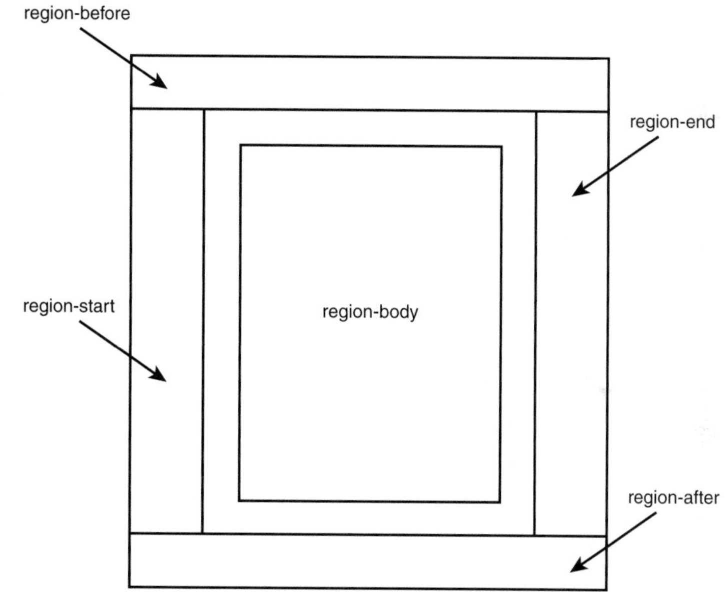

The `region-before` and `region-after` areas are commonly used for page headers and footers. The `region-body` area is the center of the page and contains the main content. The `region-start` and `region-end` sections are commonly used for left and right sidebars, respectively. During the definition of a page master, you specify the size of the regions using the following elements:

- `<fo:region-before>`
- `<fo:region-after>`
- `<fo:region-body>`
- `<fo:region-start>`
- `<fo:region-end>`

The following example defines the dimensions for <fo:region-body>, <fo:region-before>, and <fo:region-after>:

```
<fo:simple-page-master master-name="simple"
              page-height="11in"
              page-width="8.5in">
  <fo:region-body margin-top="0.5in"/>
  <fo:region-before extent="0.5in"/>
  <fo:region-after extent="0.5in"/>
</fo:simple-page-master>
```

The extent attribute has a different meaning, depending on the region. For <fo:region-end> and <fo:region-start>, the extent attribute specifies the width. For <fo:region-before> and <fo:region-after>, it specifies the height.

Page Master Set: <fo:page-master-set>

A document can be composed of multiple pages, each with its own dimensions. The page master set refers to the collection of page masters.

In the following code example, a page master set is defined that contains one page set:

```
<fo:layout-master-set>
  <fo:simple-page-master master-name="simple"
              page-height="11in"
              page-width="8.5in"
              margin-top="1in"
              margin-bottom="1in"
              margin-left="1.25in"
              margin-right="1.25in">
    <fo:region-body margin-top="0.5in"/>
    <fo:region-before extent="3cm"/>
    <fo:region-after extent="1.5cm"/>
  </fo:simple-page-master>
</fo:layout-master-set>
```

Let's integrate the new elements into the basic document structure. Recall from earlier in this section that an XSL-FO document has the following structure:

```
<?xml version="1.0" encoding="utf-8"?>
<fo:root xmlns:fo="http://www.w3.org/1999/XSL/Format">
  <!-- layout master set -->
    <!-- page masters: size and layout -->

  <!-- page sequences and content -->
</fo:root>
```

With the information provided thus far, we can fill in the blanks for the page master set. The following code example contains a page master set with a simple page master:

```
<?xml version="1.0" encoding="utf-8"?>
<fo:root xmlns:fo="http://www.w3.org/1999/XSL/Format">
  <!-- layout master set -->
  <fo:layout-master-set>

    <!-- page masters: size and layout -->
    <fo:simple-page-master master-name="simple"
                  page-height="11in"
                  page-width="8.5in"
                  margin-top="1in"
                  margin-bottom="1in"
                  margin-left="1.25in"
                  margin-right="1.25in">
      <fo:region-body margin-top="0.5in"/>
      <fo:region-before extent="3cm"/>
      <fo:region-after extent="1.5cm"/>
    </fo:simple-page-master>

  </fo:layout-master-set>

  <!-- page sequences and content -->
</fo:root>
```

Now that we have the page layout defined, we can start adding content with page sequences.

Page Sequences: <fo:page-sequence>

A page sequence defines a series of printed pages. Each page sequence refers to a page master for its dimensions. The page sequence contains the actual content for the document.

The `<fo:page-sequence>` element contains `<fo:static-content>` and `<fo:flow>` elements.

The `<fo:static-content>` element is used for page headers and footers. For example, we can define a header for the company name and page number, and this information will appear on every page.

The `<fo:flow>` element contains a collection of text blocks. The `<fo:flow>` element is similar to a collection of paragraphs. A body of text is defined using the `<fo:block>` element. The `<fo:block>` element is a child element of `<fo:flow>`. The `<fo:block>` element contains free-flowing text that will wrap to the next line in a document if it overflows.

In this example, we'll use the `<fo:flow>` and `<fo:block>` elements to create a document for a fictional company, Ez Books Online. The desired output for the document as a PDF is shown in Figure 9.17.

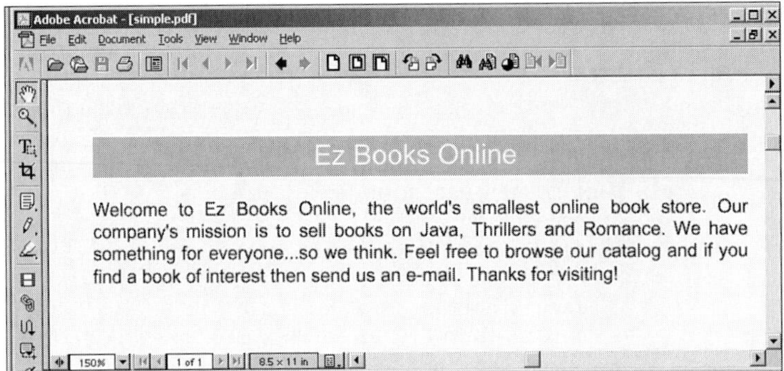

FIGURE 9.17
PDF document for Ez Books Online.

The following code fragment defines a page sequence. This sequence uses the simple page master we defined earlier in this section. Also, the `<fo:flow>` element contains two `<fo:block>` elements. Here's the code:

```
<fo:page-sequence master-name="simple">

  <fo:flow flow-name="xsl-region-body">

    <!-- this defines a level 1 heading with orange background -->
    <fo:block font-size="18pt"
          font-family="sans-serif"
          line-height="24pt"
          space-after.optimum="15pt"
          background-color="orange"
          color="white"
          text-align="center"
          padding-top="3pt">
          Ez Books Online
    </fo:block>

    <!-- Paragraph that contains info about the company -->
    <fo:block font-size="12pt"
              font-family="sans-serif"
              line-height="15pt"
              space-after.optimum="14pt"
              text-align="justify">
Welcome to Ez Books Online, the world's smallest online book store.
Our company's mission is to sell books on Java, Thrillers and Romance.
We have something for everyone...so we think.  Feel free to browse our
catalog and if you find a book of interest then send us an e-mail.
Thanks for visiting!
    </fo:block>

    </fo:flow>
  </fo:page-sequence>
```

The <fo:flow> element has to specify a region for its content. In this example, the content is placed in the main body region.

The first <fo:block> element defines a heading with an orange background. Notice how the content of each <fo:block> can be customized using font and line attributes.

The second <fo:block> element contains information about the company. The text for <fo:block> is free flowing. The text will automatically wrap. Ample space is provided at the end of the paragraph using the `space-after.optimum` attribute.

Now let's integrate the new elements into the basic document structure. Recall from earlier that an XSL-FO document has the following structure:

```
<?xml version="1.0" encoding="utf-8"?>
<fo:root xmlns:fo="http://www.w3.org/1999/XSL/Format">
  <!-- layout master set -->
    <!-- page masters: size and layout -->

  <!-- page sequences and content -->
</fo:root>
```

Listing 9.15 contains the additional code for the page sequence.

LISTING 9.15 <install_dir>\ch9_xsl\xsl_fo\simple.fo

```
<?xml version="1.0" encoding="utf-8"?>
<fo:root xmlns:fo="http://www.w3.org/1999/XSL/Format">
  <!-- layout master set -->
  <fo:layout-master-set>

    <!-- page masters: size and layout -->
    <fo:simple-page-master master-name="simple"
                  page-height="11in"
                  page-width="8.5in"
                  margin-top="1in"
                  margin-bottom="1in"
                  margin-left="1.25in"
                  margin-right="1.25in">
      <fo:region-body margin-top="0.5in"/>
      <fo:region-before extent="3cm"/>
      <fo:region-after extent="1.5cm"/>
    </fo:simple-page-master>

  </fo:layout-master-set>

  <!-- page sequences and content -->
  <fo:page-sequence master-name="simple">

    <fo:flow flow-name="xsl-region-body">
```

LISTING 9.15 continued

```
      <!-- this defines a level 1 heading with orange background -->
      <fo:block font-size="18pt"
            font-family="sans-serif"
            line-height="24pt"
            space-after.optimum="15pt"
            background-color="orange"
            color="white"
            text-align="center"
            padding-top="3pt">
            Ez Books Online
      </fo:block>

      <!-- Paragraph that contains info about the company -->
      <fo:block font-size="12pt"
                font-family="sans-serif"
                line-height="15pt"
                space-after.optimum="14pt"
                text-align="justify">
Welcome to Ez Books Online, the world's smallest online book store.
Our company's mission is to sell books on Java, Thrillers and Romance.
We have something for everyone...so we think.  Feel free to browse our
catalog and if you find a book of interest then send us an e-mail.
Thanks for visiting!
    </fo:block>

    </fo:flow>
  </fo:page-sequence>
</fo:root>
```

Generating a PDF Document

Now that we have the XSL-FO document `simple.fo`, let's convert it to a PDF file. In this chapter, we are using the open-source Apache-FOP formatting engine. It is included in the source code download for this chapter. Apache-FOP requires the Java Development Kit from Sun Microsystems. The Adobe Acrobat Reader is required to view the PDF documents. The Acrobat Reader is freely available at `http://www.adobe.com`.

Follow these steps to generate a PDF document from `simple.fo`:

1. Open an MS-DOS window.
2. Move to the directory `<install_dir>\ch9_xsl\xsl_fo\`.
3. Set up the Java classpath by typing **`setpaths`**.
4. Execute Apache-FOP by typing **`fop simple.fo simple.pdf`**.

The Apache-FOP formatter now reads the input file `simple.fo` and generates the output file `simple.pdf`.

5. View the `simple.pdf` file in Adobe Acrobat Reader. Your screen should resemble what's shown in Figure 9.17.

Page Headers and Footers

The `<fo:static-content>` element defines content that should appear on every page. The `<fo:static-content>` element is commonly used to set up page headers and footers. The `<fo:static-content>` element is a component of `<fo:page-sequence>`.

In this example, we'll define a page header that contains the company name and current page number. We'll also define a footer that lists the company's Web site. This example is also composed of multiple pages to illustrate the fact that the header and footer are repeated on each page.

The header is defined using the following code fragment:

```
<!-- header -->
<fo:static-content flow-name="xsl-region-before">
  <fo:block text-align="end"
        font-size="10pt"
        font-family="serif"
        line-height="14pt" >
    Ez Books Catalog - page <fo:page-number/>
  </fo:block>
</fo:static-content>
```

The content for the header is placed in `xsl-region-before`, which is the top of the page in this example. The `<fo:block>` element uses the `text-align` attribute to place the text at the end of the region. This example uses the English language, so the text is right justified. The current page number is determined using the `<fo:page-number>` element.

The footer is defined using the following code fragment:

```
<!-- footer -->
<fo:static-content flow-name="xsl-region-after">
  <fo:block text-align="center"
        font-size="10pt"
        font-family="serif"
        line-height="14pt" >
    Visit our website http://www.ezbooks.web
  </fo:block>
</fo:static-content>
```

The footer content is placed at the bottom of the page in `xsl-region-after`. A message containing the company's Web site is listed in the footer.

New pages are generated using `<fo:block break-before="page">`. The following code fragment generates a page break before the content is rendered. The static content, header, and footer will also appear on the new page. Here's the code:

```
<!-- insert page break for second page -->
<fo:block break-before="page">
A page break is inserted before this block.
Notice we have the headers and footers
in place.  This was accomplished with the
fo-static-content elements.  We can continue
on...business as usual.
</fo:block>
```

Now that we've discussed the smaller pieces of this example, let's pull it all together. Listing 9.16 contains the complete code for `header_footer.fo`.

LISTING 9.16 `<install_dir>\ch9_xsl\xsl_fo\header_footer.fo`

```
<?xml version="1.0" encoding="utf-8"?>

<fo:root xmlns:fo="http://www.w3.org/1999/XSL/Format">

  <fo:layout-master-set>
    <!-- layout information -->
    <fo:simple-page-master master-name="simple"
                  page-height="11in"
                  page-width="8.5in"
                  margin-top="1in"
                  margin-bottom="1in"
                  margin-left="1.25in"
                  margin-right="1.25in">
      <fo:region-body margin-top="0.5in"/>
      <fo:region-before extent="0.5in"/>
      <fo:region-after extent="0.5in"/>
    </fo:simple-page-master>
  </fo:layout-master-set>

  <fo:page-sequence master-name="simple">
    <!-- header -->
    <fo:static-content flow-name="xsl-region-before">
      <fo:block text-align="end"
            font-size="10pt"
            font-family="serif"
            line-height="14pt" >
        Ez Books Catalog - page <fo:page-number/>
      </fo:block>
    </fo:static-content>

    <!-- footer -->
    <fo:static-content flow-name="xsl-region-after">
```

LISTING 9.16 continued

```
      <fo:block text-align="center"
            font-size="10pt"
            font-family="serif"
            line-height="14pt" >
        Visit our website http://www.ezbooks.web
      </fo:block>
    </fo:static-content>

     <!-- body -->
     <fo:flow flow-name="xsl-region-body">

      <!-- this defines a level 1 heading with orange background -->
      <fo:block font-size="18pt"
            font-family="sans-serif"
            line-height="24pt"
            space-after.optimum="15pt"
            background-color="orange"
            color="white"
            text-align="center"
            padding-top="3pt">
            Ez Books Online
      </fo:block>

      <!-- Paragraph that contains info about the company -->
      <fo:block font-size="12pt"
                font-family="sans-serif"
                line-height="15pt"
                space-after.optimum="14pt"
                text-align="justify">
Welcome to Ez Books Online, the world's smallest online book store.
Our company's mission is to sell books on Java, Thrillers and Romance.
We have something for everyone...so we think.  Feel free to browse our
catalog and if you find a book of interest then send us an e-mail.
Thanks for visiting!
</fo:block>

    <!-- insert page break for second page -->
    <fo:block break-before="page">
A page break is inserted before this block.
Notice we have the headers and footers in place.
This was accomplished with the fo-static-content elements.
We can continue on...business as usual.
    </fo:block>

    <!-- insert page break for third page -->
    <fo:block break-before="page">
Information on our third page.  Again...notice the page number is
incrementing for us...automagically.  Wouldn't it be great to generate
this XSL-FO page dynamically?  Hold
```

LISTING 9.16 continued

```
tight, dynamic demos are coming up!
    </fo:block>

    </fo:flow>

  </fo:page-sequence>
</fo:root>
```

Notice that `<fo:static-content>` is a component of `<fo:page-sequence>`. Also, `<fo:static-content>` has to be listed *before* any `<fo:flow>` elements. If not, the formatting engine will generate a parsing error.

You can generate the PDF document from `header_footer.fo` using the steps from the previous section. Once you've set up the Java classpath, perform the conversion by typing the following:

```
fop header_footer.fo header_footer.pdf
```

The PDF document should resemble what's shown in Figure 9.18. Navigate to the different pages in the document to verify the existence of the header and footer.

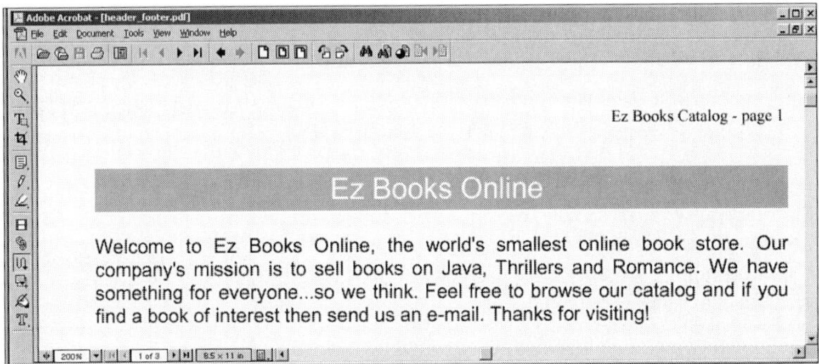

FIGURE 9.18
PDF document with header and footer.

Graphics

XSL-FO also allows for the insertion of external graphic images. The graphic formats supported are dependent on the XSL-FO formatting engine. The Apache-FOP formatting engine supports the popular graphics formats: GIF, JPEG, and BMP.

The following code fragment inserts the image `smiley.jpg`:

```
<fo:block text-align="center">
    <fo:external-graphic src="smiley.jpg" width="200px" height="200px"/>
</fo:block>
```

We can incorporate this image in a letter from the company president. Converting the file `<install_dir>\ch9_xsl\xsl_fo\graphic.fo` to a PDF generates what's shown in Figure 9.19.

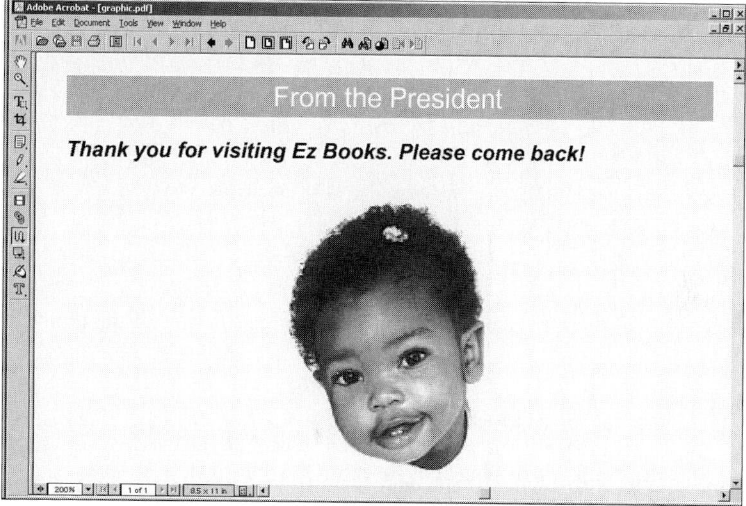

FIGURE 9.19
Inserting a graphic image in a PDF document.

Tables

XSL-FO has rich support for structuring tabular data. In fact, there are many similarities between HTML tables and XSL-FO tables. Table 9.4 lists the HTML table elements with their corresponding XSL-FO table elements.

TABLE 9.4 Comparing HTML Table Elements and XSL-FO Table Elements

HTML Element	*XSL-FO Element*
`TABLE`	`fo:table-and-caption`
Not applicable	`fo:table`
`CAPTION`	`fo:table-caption`
`COL`	`fo:table-column`
`COLGROUP`	Not applicable
`TH`	`fo:table-header`
`TBODY`	`fo:table-body`
`TFOOT`	`fo:table-footer`
`TD`	`fo:table-cell`
`TR`	`fo:table-row`

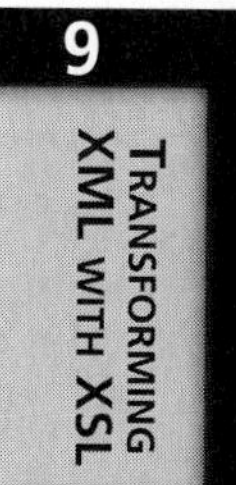

In this example, we'll create a table for our books. The desired output for the table is shown in Figure 9.20.

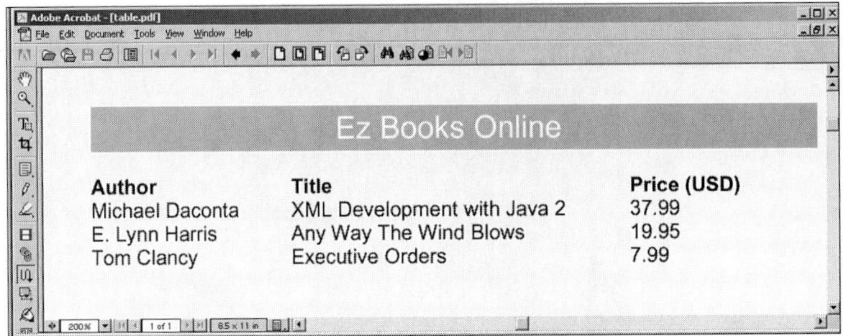

FIGURE 9.20
Creating a table in a PDF document.

The following code fragment defines the basic structure of the table:

```
<fo:table>
      <!-- define column widths -->
      <fo:table-column column-width="120pt"/>
      <fo:table-column column-width="200pt"/>
      <fo:table-column column-width="80pt"/>

    <fo:table-header>
        <fo:table-row>

                   <fo:table-cell>
                      <fo:block font-weight="bold">Author</fo:block>
                   </fo:table-cell>

                   <fo:table-cell>
                       <fo:block font-weight="bold">Title</fo:block>
                    </fo:table-cell>

                    <fo:table-cell>
                        <fo:block font-weight="bold">Price (USD)</fo:block>
                    </fo:table-cell>
        </fo:table-row>
    </fo:table-header>

    <!-- insert table body and rows here -->

</fo:table>
```

The column widths are specified using the `<fo:table-column>` element. Next, the table headers are defined. In HTML, the table headers are automatically formatted using a bold font. However, this is not the case in XSL-FO. If a bold font is desired for the table heading, it must be set explicitly using the `font-weight` attribute.

The following code fragment inserts the table body and rows:

```
<fo:table-body>
    <fo:table-row>
        <fo:table-cell>
                            <fo:block>Michael Daconta</fo:block>
                        </fo:table-cell>
        <fo:table-cell>
                            <fo:block>XML Development with Java 2</fo:block>
                        </fo:table-cell>
        <fo:table-cell>
                            <fo:block>37.99</fo:block>
                        </fo:table-cell>
    </fo:table-row>
    <fo:table-row>
        <fo:table-cell>
                            <fo:block>E. Lynn Harris</fo:block>
                        </fo:table-cell>
        <fo:table-cell>
                            <fo:block>Any Way The Wind Blows</fo:block>
                        </fo:table-cell>
        <fo:table-cell>
                            <fo:block>19.95</fo:block>
                        </fo:table-cell>
    </fo:table-row>
    <fo:table-row>
        <fo:table-cell>
                            <fo:block>Tom Clancy</fo:block>
                        </fo:table-cell>
        <fo:table-cell>
                            <fo:block>Executive Orders</fo:block>
                        </fo:table-cell>
        <fo:table-cell>
                            <fo:block>7.99</fo:block>
                        </fo:table-cell>
    </fo:table-row>
</fo:table-body>
```

As you can see, the table body is very similar to HTML. Simply replace the HTML table elements with the appropriate XSL-FO elements. However, note that the table cell data must be wrapped in an `<fo:block>` element.

Let's pull it all together. Listing 9.17 contains the complete code for `table.fo`.

LISTING 9.17 `<install_dir>\ch9_xsl\xsl_fo\table.fo`

```
<?xml version="1.0" encoding="utf-8"?>
<fo:root xmlns:fo="http://www.w3.org/1999/XSL/Format">

  <fo:layout-master-set>
    <!-- layout information -->
```

LISTING 9.17 continued

```
    <fo:simple-page-master master-name="simple"
                  page-height="11in"
                  page-width="8.5in"
                  margin-top="1in"
                  margin-bottom="1in"
                  margin-left="1.25in"
                  margin-right="1.25in">
      <fo:region-body margin-top="0.5in"/>
      <fo:region-before extent="3cm"/>
      <fo:region-after extent="1.5cm"/>
    </fo:simple-page-master>
  </fo:layout-master-set>

  <fo:page-sequence master-name="simple">

    <fo:flow flow-name="xsl-region-body">

      <!-- this defines a level 1 heading with orange background -->
      <fo:block font-size="18pt"
            font-family="sans-serif"
            line-height="24pt"
            space-after.optimum="15pt"
            background-color="orange"
            color="white"
            text-align="center"
            padding-top="3pt">
            Ez Books Online
      </fo:block>

    <!-- table start -->
    <fo:table>
        <!-- define column widths -->
      <fo:table-column column-width="120pt"/>
      <fo:table-column column-width="200pt"/>
      <fo:table-column column-width="80pt"/>

    <fo:table-header>
        <fo:table-row>
            <fo:table-cell>
                            <fo:block font-weight="bold">Author</fo:block>
                        </fo:table-cell>
            <fo:table-cell>
                             <fo:block font-weight="bold">Title</fo:block>
                        </fo:table-cell>
            <fo:table-cell>
                              <fo:block font-weight="bold">Price
(USD)</fo:block>
                        </fo:table-cell>
```

LISTING 9.17 continued

```
        </fo:table-row>
    </fo:table-header>

    <fo:table-body>
        <fo:table-row>
            <fo:table-cell>
                                  <fo:block>Michael Daconta</fo:block>
                               </fo:table-cell>
            <fo:table-cell>
                                  <fo:block>XML Development with Java 2</fo:block>
                               </fo:table-cell>
            <fo:table-cell>
                                  <fo:block>37.99</fo:block>
                               </fo:table-cell>
        </fo:table-row>
        <fo:table-row>
            <fo:table-cell>
                                  <fo:block>E. Lynn Harris</fo:block>
                               </fo:table-cell>
            <fo:table-cell>
                                  <fo:block>Any Way The Wind Blows</fo:block>
                               </fo:table-cell>
            <fo:table-cell>
                                  <fo:block>19.95</fo:block>
                               </fo:table-cell>
        </fo:table-row>
        <fo:table-row>
            <fo:table-cell>
                                 <fo:block>Tom Clancy</fo:block>
                               </fo:table-cell>
            <fo:table-cell>
                                  <fo:block>Executive Orders</fo:block>
                               </fo:table-cell>
            <fo:table-cell>
                                  <fo:block>7.99</fo:block>
                               </fo:table-cell>
        </fo:table-row>
    </fo:table-body>    </fo:table>
    <!-- table end -->

    </fo:flow>
  </fo:page-sequence>
</fo:root>
```

Converting the file `<install_dir>\ch9_xsl\xsl_fo\table.fo` to a PDF generates what's shown in Figure 9.20.

Generating XSL-FO Tables Using XSLT

The previous example only listed three books. Imagine the size of the document if we wanted to list 500 books. The document would be extremely large and verbose. In this section, we'll use XSLT to automatically generate the XSL-FO document.

The file, `booklist.xml`, contains a list of the books. We can develop an XSL style sheet that will automatically construct the XSL-FO document. This process is illustrated in Figure 9.21.

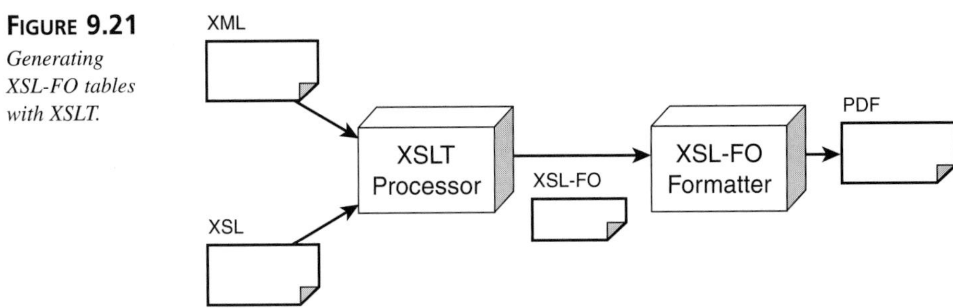

FIGURE 9.21
Generating XSL-FO tables with XSLT.

After reviewing the XSL-FO document for the book table, you can see that the dynamic portion is the construction of each table row. We can use the element `<xsl:for-each>` to loop over each book and build the table row. This is accomplished with the following code:

```
<!-- Perform loop for each book in the book list -->
<xsl:for-each select="booklist/book" >

    <fo:table-row>
        <fo:table-cell>[sr]
                  <fo:block><xsl:value-of select="author" /></fo:block>
                </fo:table-cell>
        <fo:table-cell>
                  <fo:block><xsl:value-of select="title" /></fo:block>
                </fo:table-cell>
        <fo:table-cell>
                  <fo:block><xsl:value-of select="price" /></fo:block>
                </fo:table-cell>
    </fo:table-row>

</xsl:for-each>
```

As you can see, this example is very similar to constructing an HTML table with XSLT. Instead of using the HTML table elements, we're using the appropriate XSL-FO table elements. Also, this example uses table borders via the values specified for the border-style and border-width attributes. By leveraging XSLT and XSL-FO, we can dynamically generate a PDF file based on an XML document.

Listing 9.18 contains the complete code for this example.

LISTING 9.18 <install_dir>\ch9_xsl\xsl_fo\dynamic\table\booklist_table.xsl

```
<?xml version="1.0"?>
<xsl:stylesheet xmlns:xsl="http://www.w3.org/1999/XSL/Transform"
                xmlns:fo="http://www.w3.org/1999/XSL/Format"
                version="1.0">

<xsl:template match="/">


<fo:root xmlns:fo="http://www.w3.org/1999/XSL/Format">

  <fo:layout-master-set>
    <!-- layout information -->
    <fo:simple-page-master master-name="simple"
                  page-height="11in"
                  page-width="8.5in"
                  margin-top="1in"
                  margin-bottom="2in"
                  margin-left="1.25in"
                  margin-right="1.25in">
      <fo:region-body margin-top="0.5in"/>
      <fo:region-before extent="3cm"/>
      <fo:region-after extent="1.5cm"/>
    </fo:simple-page-master>
  </fo:layout-master-set>
  <!-- end: defines page layout -->


  <fo:page-sequence master-name="simple">

    <fo:flow flow-name="xsl-region-body">

      <!-- this defines a level 1 heading with orange background -->
      <fo:block font-size="18pt"
            font-family="sans-serif"
            line-height="24pt"
            space-after.optimum="15pt"
            background-color="orange"
            color="white"
            text-align="center"
            padding-top="3pt">
            Ez Books Online
      </fo:block>
```

LISTING 9.18 continued

```
    <!-- table start -->
    <fo:table border-style="solid" border-width=".1mm" >
        <!-- define column widths -->
      <fo:table-column column-width="120pt"/>
      <fo:table-column column-width="200pt"/>
      <fo:table-column column-width="80pt"/>

    <fo:table-header>
        <fo:table-row >
            <fo:table-cell border-style="solid" border-width=".1mm">
                <fo:block font-weight="bold">Author</fo:block>
            </fo:table-cell>
            <fo:table-cell border-style="solid" border-width=".1mm">
                <fo:block font-weight="bold">Title</fo:block>
            </fo:table-cell>
            <fo:table-cell border-style="solid" border-width=".1mm">
                <fo:block font-weight="bold">Price (USD)</fo:block>
            </fo:table-cell>
        </fo:table-row>
    </fo:table-header>

    <fo:table-body>
        <!-- Perform loop for each book in the book list -->
        <xsl:for-each select="booklist/book" >

            <fo:table-row>
                <fo:table-cell border-style="solid" border-width=".1mm">
                    <fo:block><xsl:value-of select="author" /></fo:block>
                </fo:table-cell>
                <fo:table-cell border-style="solid" border-width=".1mm">
                    <fo:block><xsl:value-of select="title" /></fo:block>
                </fo:table-cell>
                <fo:table-cell border-style="solid" border-width=".1mm">
                    <fo:block><xsl:value-of select="price" /></fo:block>
                </fo:table-cell>
            </fo:table-row>

        </xsl:for-each>
    </fo:table-body>

    </fo:table>
    <!-- table end -->

    </fo:flow>
  </fo:page-sequence>
</fo:root>

</xsl:template>
</xsl:stylesheet>
```

Generating a PDF Document

This example involves a two-step process. The first step involves XSLT processing the `booklist.xml` document with `booklist_table.xsl`. The second step involves converting the output of the XSLT conversion to a PDF file using XSL-FO.

The Apache-FOP product can perform both of these steps internally. All we have to do is provide the XML document and XSL style sheet.

Follow these steps to generate the PDF document:

1. Open an MS-DOS window.
2. Move to the directory `<install_dir>\ch9_xsl\xsl_fo\dynamic\table`.
3. Set up the Java classpath by typing **`setpaths`**.
4. Execute Apache-FOP by typing the following:

   `fop -xml booklist.xml -xsl booklist_table.xsl dyntable.pdf`

5. View the `dyntable.pdf` file in Adobe Acrobat Reader. Figure 9.22 shows what your screen should look like.

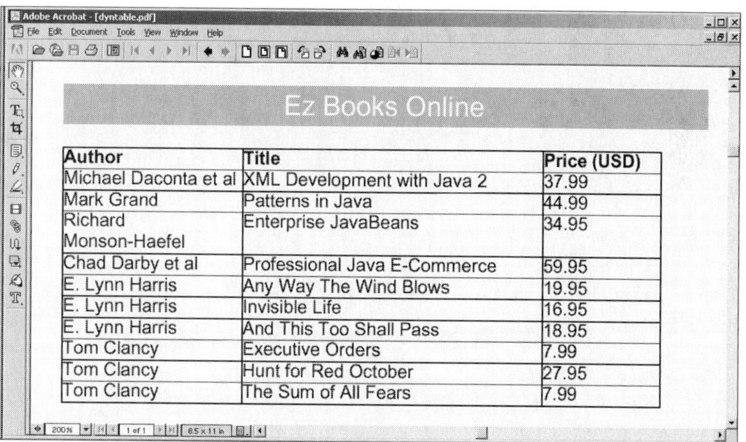

Ez Books Online

Author	Title	Price (USD)
Michael Daconta et al	XML Development with Java 2	37.99
Mark Grand	Patterns in Java	44.99
Richard Monson-Haefel	Enterprise JavaBeans	34.95
Chad Darby et al	Professional Java E-Commerce	59.95
E. Lynn Harris	Any Way The Wind Blows	19.95
E. Lynn Harris	Invisible Life	16.95
E. Lynn Harris	And This Too Shall Pass	18.95
Tom Clancy	Executive Orders	7.99
Tom Clancy	Hunt for Red October	27.95
Tom Clancy	The Sum of All Fears	7.99

FIGURE 9.22
Output of `dyntable.pdf`.

Web Application Integration: Java Servlets, XSLT, and XSL-FO

In this section, we will pull all the parts together and develop a Web application that integrates Java servlets, XSLT, and XSL-FO. We will develop a Java servlet to pass an XML document and XSL style sheet to the Apache-FOP formatting engine. The XML document is `booklist.xml`. The XSL style sheet, `booklist_table.xsl`, contains the XSL-FO template code to generate a table. The servlet will respond with the PDF document generated by the Apache-FOP formatting engine. The application interaction is shown in Figure 9.23.

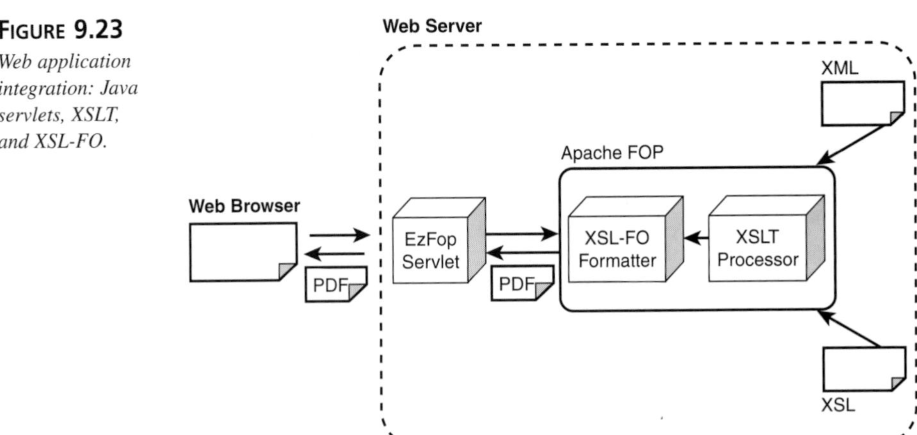

FIGURE 9.23
Web application integration: Java servlets, XSLT, and XSL-FO.

Developing the Java Servlet

The Java servlet handles an HTTP `GET` request. The servlet sets up a reference to the files `booklist.xml` and `booklist_table.xsl`. The Apache-FOP API provides access to the Apache-FOP formatting engine via the class `org.apache.fop.apps.Driver`. The following code creates an instance of the driver and sets the renderer to PDF:

```
// setup the driver for PDF
Driver driver = new Driver();
driver.setRenderer(Driver.RENDER_PDF);
```

Next, the servlet creates a file reference for the XML document and XSL style sheet. Because the servlet is running in the context of a servlet engine, we need to retrieve the real path to the Web application's root (`c:\foo\ch9_xsl\xsl_fo\public_html`). The `XSLTInputHandler` class transforms the XML document using the XSL style sheet, and the resulting document is input for the Apache-FOP processing engine. This is accomplished in the following code fragment:

```
 String appRoot  = getServletContext().getRealPath("/");

String xmlFileName = "booklist.xml";
String xslFileName = "booklist_table.xsl";
File xmlFile = new File(appRoot + xmlFileName);
File xslFile = new File(appRoot + xslFileName);
```

```
// create an input handler for the XSLT transformation
XSLTInputHandler inputHandler = new XSLTInputHandler(xmlFile, xslFile);
XMLReader parser = inputHandler.getParser();
```

Now, we need to set up an output for the XSL-FO formatter process. We'll use a `ByteArrayOutputStream` object to serve as a temporary buffer. The XSL-FO processor generates the PDF document using the following code:

```
// setup the output for XSL-FO formatter process
// temporarily place in a ByteArrayOutputStream
ByteArrayOutputStream out = new ByteArrayOutputStream();
driver.setOutputStream(out);

// Run the formatter based on the XSL-FO document
driver.render(parser, inputHandler.getInputSource());
```

Finally, we need to send the PDF document back to the Web browser. Recall from the previous step that the document was placed in a temporary buffer. All we have to do is access the content of the temporary buffer and send the content using the response. This is accomplished in the following code:

```
// The out object has the result of the XSL-FO formatter process
//  Retrieve the content from ByteArray
byte[] content = out.toByteArray();

// Setup the response for the web browser
response.setContentType("application/pdf");
response.setContentLength(content.length);

// Finally, send the result to the browser!
OutputStream outputToBrowser = response.getOutputStream();
outputToBrowser.write(content);
outputToBrowser.flush();
```

Listing 9.19 contains the complete code for the `EzFopServlet`.

LISTING 9.19 `<install_dir>\ch9_xsl\xsl_fo\servlet_source\EzFopServlet.java`

```
import java.io.File;
import java.io.OutputStream;
import java.io.ByteArrayOutputStream;
import java.io.IOException;

import javax.servlet.ServletException;
import javax.servlet.http.HttpServlet;
import javax.servlet.http.HttpServletRequest;
import javax.servlet.http.HttpServletResponse;

import org.xml.sax.XMLReader;
```

LISTING 9.19 continued

```
import org.apache.fop.apps.Driver;
import org.apache.fop.apps.XSLTInputHandler;

/**
 * Example servlet to generate a PDF from an XSL-FO document
 */
public class EzFopServlet extends HttpServlet {

    public void doGet(HttpServletRequest request, HttpServletResponse response)
        throws ServletException, IOException {

        try {
            // get the application root for this web app
            String appRoot  = getServletContext().getRealPath("/");

            String xmlFileName = "booklist.xml";
            String xslFileName = "booklist_table.xsl";
            File xmlFile = new File(appRoot + xmlFileName);
            File xslFile = new File(appRoot + xslFileName);

            // diagnostic messages
            System.out.println("EzFopServlet:  XSL-FO formatting:");
            System.out.println("xml = " + xmlFile);
            System.out.println("xsl = " + xslFile + "\n\n");

            // setup the driver for PDF
            Driver driver = new Driver();
            driver.setRenderer(Driver.RENDER_PDF);

            // create an input handler for the XSLT transformation
            XSLTInputHandler inputHandler =
                                new XSLTInputHandler(xmlFile, xslFile);
            XMLReader parser = inputHandler.getParser();

            // setup the output for XSL-FO formatter process
            // temporarily place in a ByteArrayOutputStream
            ByteArrayOutputStream out = new ByteArrayOutputStream();
            driver.setOutputStream(out);

            // Run the formatter based on the XSL-FO document
            driver.render(parser, inputHandler.getInputSource());

            // The out object has the result of the XSL-FO formatter process
            //  Retrieve the content from ByteArray
            byte[] content = out.toByteArray();

            // Setup the response for the web browser
            response.setContentType("application/pdf");
            response.setContentLength(content.length);
```

LISTING 9.19 continued

```
            // Finally, send the result to the browser!
            OutputStream outputToBrowser = response.getOutputStream();
            outputToBrowser.write(content);
            outputToBrowser.flush();
        }
        catch (Exception exc) {
            log(exc.toString());
            throw new ServletException(exc);
        }
    }
}
```

Testing the Example

This example is stored in a separate Web application archive (WAR) file, called `ezfop.war`. The WAR file contains the compiled class for `EzFopServlet`. The WAR file can be deployed on any JSP or servlet engine that supports the Servlet 2.3 API or JSP 1.2.

Follow these steps to deploy it on a Tomcat 4 server:

1. Copy the file `<install_dir>\ch9_xsl\xsl_fo\ezfop.war` to `<tomcat_install_dir>\webapps`.
2. Restart the Tomcat server.
3. Access the `ezfop` Web application using `http://localhost:8080/ezfop`. Figure 9.23 shows what your screen should look like.

Summary

This chapter covered a lot of ground. We started out by discussing the role of XSL in application development. In the realm of document publishing, XSL can be used to create multiple views of the same XML document. This is accomplished by creating an XSL style sheet that contains the template code for the view and the XSLT constructs for retrieving the data. XSL also has a key role in the area of B2B communications. We can easily convert XML documents to other XML formats using the XSL technology.

Next, we covered the implementation details for constructing XSL style sheets. We discussed the XSL elements used to retrieve XML data, loop over sequential data, and perform conditional tests and sorting of the XML data.

We also discussed the various techniques for performing the XSLT translation. If the browser supports XSLT, you can leverage the client-side technique. This approach offloads the XSLT processing to the client machine. However, if you are in an environment where the XSLT browser support is unknown, you can apply the server-side strategy. The server-side strategy is implemented with a server scripting language such as Active Server Pages or JavaServer Pages. The server-side technique performs the XSLT processing on the server, and the result is normally an HTML document that is widely supported in Web browsers.

The XSL-FO language was explored for document publishing. In particular, we utilized the Apache-FOP formatting engine to generate PDF documents from XSL-FO documents. By applying the XSLT technology, we were able to dynamically populate the XSL-FO document with a list of books that were stored in a separate XML document.

The grand finale of the chapter was the integration of XSLT, XSL-FO, and Java servlets. The resulting Web application consisted of a Java servlet that retrieved an XML document and XSL style sheet. These documents were fed into the Apache-FOP formatting engine to generate a PDF document directly back to the Web browser.

Using the techniques presented, you can create Web applications that transform XML on the server side. This chapter covered the essential elements to jumpstart your XSLT and XSL-FO projects. Good luck!

CHAPTER 10

Integrating XML with Databases

IN THIS CHAPTER

Data is king! This statement is often made by IT professionals because a large percentage of their applications are data driven. With the emergence of XML as a technique for describing data, the frequently asked question is, "How can we integrate XML with our existing relational database?" In particular, developers need a solution to dynamically generate XML documents using information stored in databases.

XML and database integration is important because XML provides a standard technique to describe data. By leveraging XML, a company can convert its existing corporate data into a format that is consumable by its trading partners. XML allows the development team to define a set of custom tags specific to its industry. A trading partner can import the XML data into its system using the given format. The trading partner also has the option of converting the data to a different XML format using XSLT. XSLT is covered in Chapter 9, "Transforming XML with XSL."

In this chapter, you will learn how to

- Use XML as a database integration format
- Model databases in XML
- Leverage XML data binding with Java Architecture for XML Binding (JAXB)
- Create a data access object
- Generate XML documents with Java servlets

Note

All the source code in this chapter is available at the Sams Web site. You can download the code and extract it to a directory on your file system. For the remainder of this chapter, I'll use `<install_dir>` as the root location where you've installed the code. The installation contains a number of directories. Here's a description of the source code directories (partial list):

Directory	*Description*
`ch10_xmldb\source_code`	Source code files
`ch10_xmldb\public_html`	Web application root directory
`ch10_xmldb \public_html\WEB-INF`	Web application support files
`ch10_xmldb\lib`	JAXB JAR files
`ch10_xmldb\data`	MS Access database used in the chapter

XML Database Solutions

A large number of XML database solutions are available, and they generally come in two flavors: database mapping and native XML support.

XML Database Mapping

The first type of XML database solution provides a mapping between the XML document and the database fields. The system dynamically converts SQL result sets to XML documents. Depending on the sophistication of the product, it may provide a graphical tool to map the database fields to the desired XML elements. Other tools support a configuration file that defines the mapping. These tools continue to store the information in relational database management system (RDBMS) format. They simply provide an XML conversion process that is normally implemented as a server-side Web application. This solution is depicted in Figure 10.1.

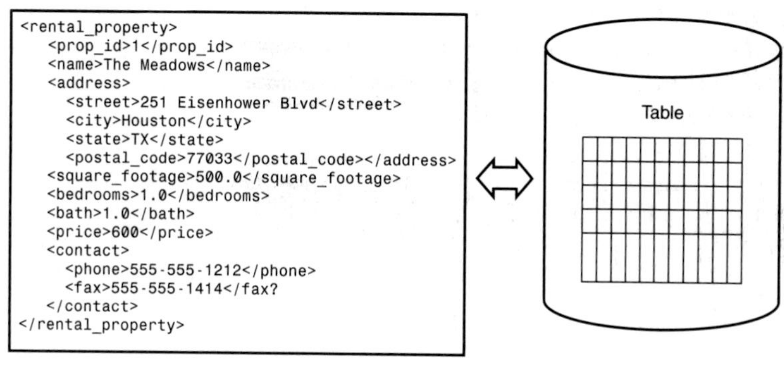

FIGURE 10.1
Mapping XML documents to database fields.

Table 10.1 contains a list of products that provide XML database mappings. Note that this list is not exhaustive. Additional product offerings are available at `www.xml.com`.

TABLE 10.1 XML Database Mapping Products

Product	*Company*	*Web Site*
DB2 Extender	IBM	`www.ibm.com`
SQL Server 2000	Microsoft	`www.microsoft.com`
Oracle 8i & 9i	Oracle	`www.oracle.com`
DataMirror DB/XML	DataMirror	`www.datamirror.com`

TABLE 10.1 continued

Product	*Company*	*Web Site*
webMethods	webMethods	`www.webmethods.com`
Excelon	Excelon	`www.exceloncorp.com`

Native XML Support

The second type of XML database solution actually stores the XML data in the document in its native format. Each product uses its own proprietary serialization technique to store the data. However, when the data is retrieved, it represents an XML document. This solution is depicted in Figure 10.2.

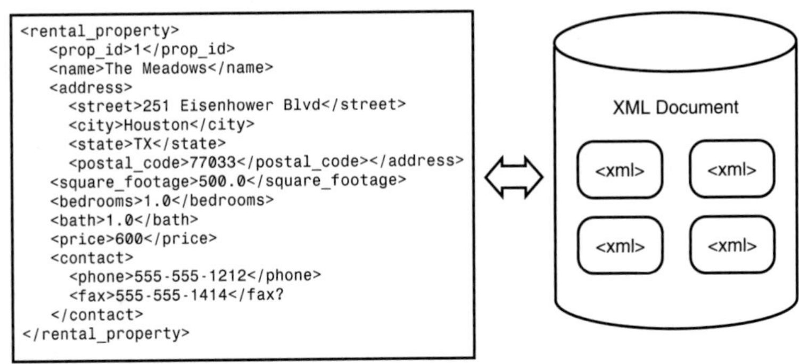

FIGURE 10.2
Native XML databases.

Table 10.2 lists some of the products that provide native XML document support. See `www.xml.com` for additional products.

TABLE 10.2 Native XML Database Products

Product	*Company*	*Web Site*
TEXTML	IXIA Soft	`www.ixiasoft.com`
Oracle 8i and 9i	Oracle	`www.oracle.com`
Excelon	Excelon	`www.exceloncorp.com`
dbXML	dbXML Group	`www.dbxml.org`
Tamino	Software AG	`www.softwareag.com`

Noted XML author Ronald Bourret maintains a list of XML database products that you can visit at `www.rpbourret.com/xml`.

Modeling Databases in XML

In this section, you'll learn how to model a database in XML using Java. When we model a database, we provide an external representation of the database contents. For our sample program, we'll utilize a database that contains information on rental properties. We'll model the rental property database as an XML document. Figure 10.3 shows the desired output.

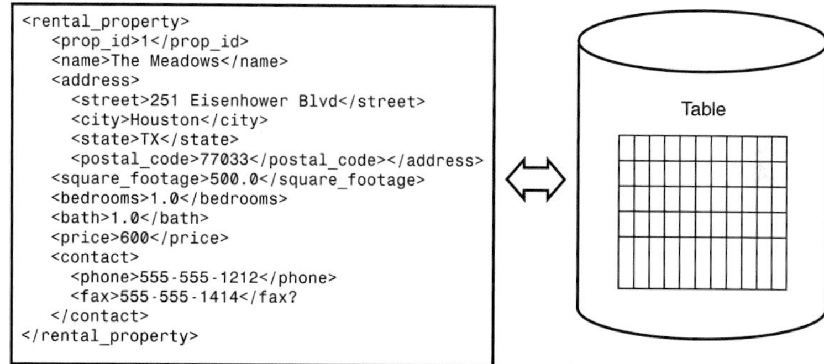

FIGURE 10.3
Desired output for rental properties.

One possible solution is to use Java servlets and JDBC. Java servlets are server-side components that reside in a Web server or application server. Java servlets are commonly used to handle requests from Web browsers using the HTTP protocol.

A key advantage to using servlets is the thin-client interface. The servlets handle the request on the server side and respond by generating an HTML page dynamically. This lowers the requirement on the client browser. The browser only has to provide support of HTML. As a result, there is zero client-side administration.

In contrast, Java applets require the browser to support the correct version of the Java Virtual Machine (JVM). This has been a thorny issue with the Java community since the early days of applet development. If the browser doesn't support Java, the applet will not execute. Of course, there are a number of workarounds, such as the Java Plug-In and Java Web Start. However, these technologies still require an initial installation on the client machine—which can prove to be time consuming and error prone.

We can develop a servlet that uses JDBC. The servlet will make the appropriate query to the database and use Java Database Connectivity (JDBC) API result set metadata to create the elements. In fact, a servlet that performs this operation is presented in Chapter 7, "Parsing XML Using Document Object Model." This is a simple and elegant solution because it leverages the result set metadata.

In this section, we'll leverage the XML data binding features of Java Architecture for XML Binding (JAXB). JAXB provides a framework for representing XML documents as Java objects. Using the JAXB framework, we can guarantee that the documents processed by our system are well formed. Also, we have the option of validating the XML data against a schema.

In the JAXB framework, we can parse XML documents into a suitable Java object. This technique is referred to as *unmarshaling*. The JAXB framework also provides the capability to generate XML documents from Java objects, which is referred to as *marshaling*. The process is illustrated in the Figure 10.4.

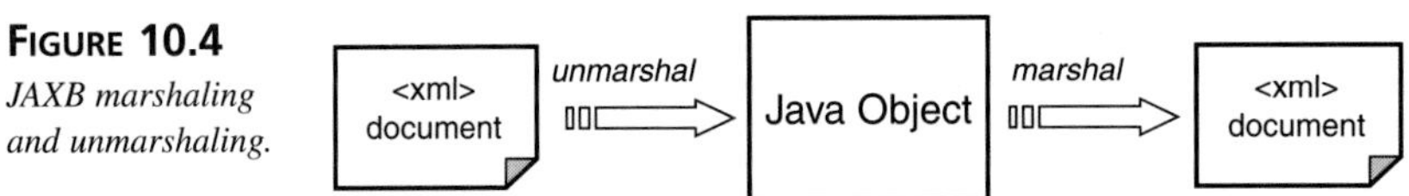

FIGURE 10.4
JAXB marshaling and unmarshaling.

JAXB is easier to use and a more efficient technique for processing XML documents than the SAX or DOM API. Using the SAX API, you have to create a custom content handler for each XML document structure. Also, during the development of the content, you have to create and manage your own state machine to keep track of your place in the document. For very complex XML documents, the development process is very cumbersome. Using JAXB, an application can parse an XML document by simply unmarshaling the data from an input stream.

JAXB is similar to DOM in that we can create XML documents programmatically and perform validation. However, the hindrance with DOM is the complex API. If we have an XML tree, using the DOM API, we have to traverse through the tree to retrieve elements. However, with JAXB, we retrieve the data from the XML document by simply calling a method on an object. JAXB allows us to define Java objects that map to XML documents, so we can easily retrieve data. The JAXB framework also ensures the type safety of the data.

See Chapter 7 for an introduction to JAXB. Also, detailed information on JAXB is available in the JAXB specification at `java.sun.com/xml`. This chapter assumes you understand the basics of JAXB. We'll apply JAXB in an enterprise application later in this chapter.

JAXB Solution

In the JAXB solution, we will model the rental property database as an XML document. First we need to review the database schema. After reviewing the schema, we will develop our desired XML document based on an XML schema. After we have the XML schema developed, we can create the JAXB binding schema. The JAXB binding schema contains instructions on how to bind the XML schema to a Java class. We'll take the JAXB binding schema and generate the appropriate Java classes.

To summarize, we'll follow these steps:

1. Review the database schema.
2. Construct the desired XML document.
3. Define a schema for the XML document.
4. Create the JAXB binding schema.
5. Generate the JAXB classes based on the schema.
6. Develop a Data Access Object (DAO).
7. Develop a servlet for HTTP access.

Figure 10.5 illustrates the application architecture. `RentalXMLServlet` communicates with `RentalDAO` to retrieve information from the database. Once the information is retrieved by `RentalDAO`, `RentalXMLServlet` generates an XML document.

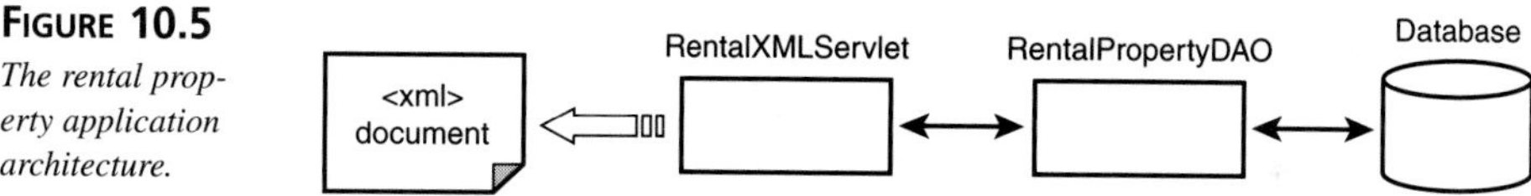

FIGURE 10.5
The rental property application architecture.

Reviewing the Database Schema

We have an existing database for the rental properties. Table 10.3 contains the database schema.

TABLE 10.3 Rental Property Database Schema

Field	*Type*
prop_num	NUMBER
name	VARCHAR2
street_address	VARCHAR2
city	VARCHAR2
state	VARCHAR2
zip_code	VARCHAR2
size_sq	NUMBER
bed_count	NUMBER

TABLE 10.3 continued

Field	*Type*
bath_count	NUMBER
monthly_rent	NUMBER
voice_phone	VARCHAR2
fax_phone	VARCHAR2

The source code for this chapter includes a sample MS Access database. The file is located at `<install_dir>\ch10_xmldb\data\rental_property.mdb`.

Constructing the Desired XML Document

The desired output XML document describes the rental property. However, the XML document does not use the exact field names listed in the database schema. Instead, the XML document provides a custom mapping of the database fields to XML element names. Table 10.4 contains the mapping.

TABLE 10.4 XML Database Mapping

Database Field	*XML Element Name*
prop_num	`<prop_id>`
name	`<name>`
street_address	`<street>`
city	`<city>`
state	`<state>`
zip_code	`<postal_code>`
size_sq	`<square_footage>`
bed_count	`<bedrooms>`
bath_count	`<bath>`
monthly_rent	`<price>`
voice_phone	`<phone>`
fax_phone	`<fax>`

A rental property is described with a root element of `<rental_property>`, as shown in the following code:

```
<rental_property>
    <prop_id>1</prop_id>
    <name>The Meadows</name>
    <address>
        <street>251 Eisenhower Blvd</street>
        <city>Houston</city>
        <state>TX</state>
        <postal_code>77033</postal_code>
    </address>
    <square_footage>500.0</square_footage>
    <bedrooms>1.0</bedrooms>
    <bath>1.0</bath>
    <price>600</price>
    <contact>
        <phone>555-555-1212</phone>
        <fax>555-555-1414</fax>
    </contact>
</rental_property>
```

Notice how the `<address>` element contains the subelements `<street>`, `<city>`, `<state>`, and `<postal_code>`. A similar approach is taken for the contact information. The `<contact>` element contains the `<phone>` and `<fax>` elements for the voice number and fax number, respectively.

In our system, we'll normally work with a collection of rental properties. This collection is modeled using a `<rental_property_list>` element, as shown here:

```
<rental_property_list>
  <rental_property> … </rental_property>
  <rental_property> … </rental_property>
  … …
</rental_property_list>
```

Defining a Schema for the XML Document

Based on the desired document format, we can create a schema definition. In this section, we will define the Document Type Definition (DTD). The DTD schema format was chosen because JAXB 1.0 (early access) only supports DTDs. In the future, JAXB is supposed to support the formal XML Schema definition.

Listing 10.1 contains the DTD for our rental property list.

LISTING 10.1 `<install_dir>\ch10_xmldb\rental_property.dtd`

```
<!ELEMENT rental_property_list (rental_property)*>
<!ELEMENT rental_property (prop_id, name, address, square_footage,
➥bedrooms, bath, price, contact)>
```

LISTING 10.1 continued

```
<!ELEMENT prop_id (#PCDATA)>
<!ELEMENT name (#PCDATA)>

<!ELEMENT address (street, city, state, postal_code)>
<!ELEMENT street (#PCDATA)>
<!ELEMENT city (#PCDATA)>
<!ELEMENT state (#PCDATA)>
<!ELEMENT postal_code (#PCDATA)>

<!ELEMENT square_footage (#PCDATA)>
<!ELEMENT bedrooms (#PCDATA)>
<!ELEMENT bath (#PCDATA)>
<!ELEMENT price (#PCDATA)>

<!ELEMENT contact (phone, fax)>
<!ELEMENT phone (#PCDATA)>
<!ELEMENT fax (#PCDATA)>
```

Creating the JAXB Binding Schema

Now that the DTD is defined for our document, we need to define the JAXB binding schema. The JAXB binding schema is an XML document that contains instructions on how to bind a DTD to a Java class.

Using the JAXB binding schema, we can define the names of the generated Java classes, map element names to specific properties in the Java class, and provide the mapping rules for attributes. The following code example informs the JAXB system that the element `<rental_property_list>` should be mapped to a Java class and that it is the root element for the XML document:

```
<element name="rental_property_list" type="class" root="true"/>
```

There's no requirement to define a mapping for every element in the XML document. JAXB uses a default binding schema that will create properties in the Java class based on the XML element name.

The binding schema also allows us to define a conversion rule for elements. For example, the numerical data for the rental property, such as price, square footage, and number of rooms, is always represented in the DTD as text data (`#PCDATA`). This is one of the limitations of the DTD format. However, by using JAXB, we can specify that a given element should be converted to a Java primitive type or class. In the following code example, we inform JAXB to convert the values of `<square_footage>`, `<bedrooms>`, and `<bath>` to the `double` type; also, `<price>` is converted to an instance of the `java.math.BigDecimal` class:

```
<element name="square_footage" type="value" convert="double"/>
<element name="bedrooms" type="value" convert="double"/>
<element name="bath" type="value" convert="double"/>
<element name="price" type="value" convert="BigDecimal"/>
<conversion name="BigDecimal" type="java.math.BigDecimal"/>
```

We can also use the binding schema to define enumerated types, constructors, and interfaces. However, in the JAXB 1.0 early access version, constructors are not yet implemented.

The binding schema includes a section for controlling the output of the generated Java source code. For example, we can inform the system to use a given package name. The following code defines the package name as `xmlunleashed.ch10.jaxb`:

```
<options package="xmlunleashed.ch10.jaxb"/>
```

See the JAXB specification for details on the binding schema file format.

Now, let's look at the JAXB binding schema file for our rental property example. The schema files normally use the filename extension `.xjs` (for XML Java schema). Listing 10.2 contains the complete code for our JAXB binding schema, `rental_property.xjs`.

LISTING 10.2 `<install_dir>\ch10_xmldb\rental_property.xjs`

```
<?xml version="1.0" encoding="ISO-8859-1" ?>
<!DOCTYPE xml-java-binding-schema SYSTEM
➥"http://java.sun.com/dtd/jaxb/1.0-ea/xjs.dtd">

<xml-java-binding-schema version="1.0-ea">
    <options package="xmlunleashed.ch10.jaxb"/>
      <element name="rental_property_list" type="class" root="true">
          <content property="list"/>
      </element>
    <element name="square_footage" type="value" convert="double"/>
    <element name="bedrooms" type="value" convert="double"/>
    <element name="bath" type="value" convert="double"/>
    <element name="price" type="value" convert="BigDecimal"/>

    <conversion name="BigDecimal" type="java.math.BigDecimal"/>
</xml-java-binding-schema>
```

Generating the JAXB Classes Based on Schemas

Now we are ready to generate the Java source files based on our schemas. JAXB provides a schema compiler for generating the Java source files. The schema compiler takes as input the DTD and the JAXB binding schema. Figure 10.6 illustrates the process.

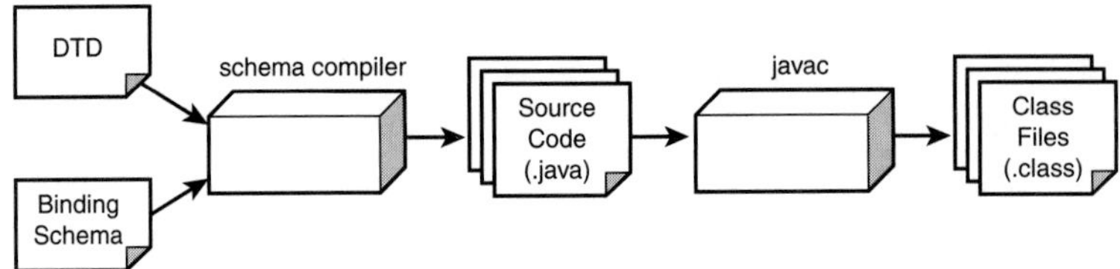

FIGURE 10.6
Generating Java classes with the JAXB compiler.

We pass our DTD (`rental_property.dtd`) and binding schema (`rental_property.xjs`) to the JAXB schema compiler with the `xjc` command. The command should be entered in the directory `<install_dir>\ch10_xmldb\`. Type everything on one line:

```
java com.sun.tools.xjc.Main rental_property.dtd
➥rental_property.xjs -d source_code
```

This command generates source code in the `source_code` directory. The following files are generated:

- `RentalPropertyList.java`. This file models the `<rental_property_list>` element.
- `RentalProperty.java`. This file models the `<rental_property>` element.
- `Address.java`. This file models the `<address>` subelement.
- `Contact.java`. This file models the `<contact>` subelement.

Figure 10.7 contains the Unified Modeling Language (UML) diagram for the generated Java classes.

Using the default schema-binding definition, the JAXB schema compiler generates a property in the Java class for each XML element. In the event the XML element contains subelements, the schema compiler will create a new class.

Listing 10.3 contains the partial source code for `RentalProperty.java`. Some of the code and methods are not listed to preserve space.

FIGURE 10.7
Rental property UML diagram.

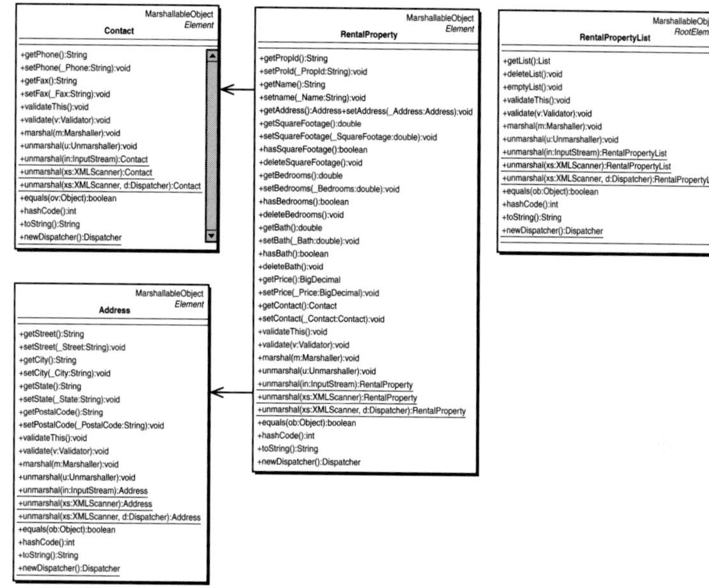

LISTING 10.3 `<install_dir>\ch10_xmldb\source_code\xmlunleashed\ch10\jaxb\RentalProperty.java`

```
package xmlunleashed.ch10.jaxb;

import java.io.IOException;
import java.io.InputStream;
import java.math.BigDecimal;
import javax.xml.bind.ConversionException;
import javax.xml.bind.Dispatcher;
import javax.xml.bind.Element;
import javax.xml.bind.InvalidAttributeException;
import javax.xml.bind.LocalValidationException;
import javax.xml.bind.MarshallableObject;
import javax.xml.bind.Marshaller;
import javax.xml.bind.MissingContentException;
import javax.xml.bind.NoValueException;
import javax.xml.bind.StructureValidationException;
import javax.xml.bind.UnmarshalException;
import javax.xml.bind.Unmarshaller;
import javax.xml.bind.Validator;
import javax.xml.marshal.XMLScanner;
import javax.xml.marshal.XMLWriter;
import xmlunleashed.ch10.jaxb.Address;
import xmlunleashed.ch10.jaxb.Contact;
```

LISTING 10.3 continued

```
public class RentalProperty
    extends MarshallableObject
    implements Element
{

    private String _PropId;
    private String _Name;
    private Address _Address;
    private double _SquareFootage;
    private boolean has_SquareFootage = false;
    private double _Bedrooms;
    private boolean has_Bedrooms = false;
    private double _Bath;
    private boolean has_Bath = false;
    private BigDecimal _Price;
    private Contact _Contact;

    public String getPropId() {
        return _PropId;
    }

    public void setPropId(String _PropId) {
        this._PropId = _PropId;
        if (_PropId == null) {
            invalidate();
        }
    }

    public String getName() {
        return _Name;
    }

    public void setName(String _Name) {
        this._Name = _Name;
        if (_Name == null) {
            invalidate();
        }
    }

    public Address getAddress() {
        return _Address;
    }

    public void setAddress(Address _Address) {
        this._Address = _Address;
        if (_Address == null) {
            invalidate();
        }
    }
```

LISTING 10.3 continued

```
   public void validateThis()
        throws LocalValidationException
    {
        ... ...
    }

    public void marshal(Marshaller m)
        throws IOException
    {
       // code to output the XML document
    }

    public void unmarshal(Unmarshaller u)
        throws UnmarshalException
    {
       // code to read in the XML document
    }
    ... ...
}
```

The source code for RentalProperty.java contains private data members for the elements defined in <rental_property>. The public get/set methods provide access to the properties. For example, to retrieve the name of the rental property from the Java object, we call the getName() method. In the case of a nested element, such as address, we call the getContact() method, which returns a Contact object. The Contact class is defined in a similar manner with get/set methods for the properties.

Also, we can validate the object by calling the validateThis() method. Recall that this source code was generated based on the DTD, so we can verify that the contents of the object adheres to the grammar rules of the DTD. The validate() method is very useful if the contents of the RentalProperty object are modified using the setter methods. It is also useful if we construct a RentalProperty object from scratch.

Finally, the RentalProperty class contains methods to marshal and unmarshal the content.

The source code for the remaining files is available in the source code download in the directory <install_dir>\ch10_xmldb\source_code\xmlunleashed\ch10\jaxb. Feel free to investigate these files' contents.

Developing a Data Access Object (DAO)

A Data Access Object (DAO) provides access to the backend database. The goal of the DAO design pattern is to provide a higher level of abstraction for database access. The

DAO encapsulates the complex JDBC and SQL calls. The DAO provides access to the backend database via public methods. The DAO converts a result set to a collection of objects. The objects model the data stored in the database. The application interaction with a DAO is shown in Figure 10.8.

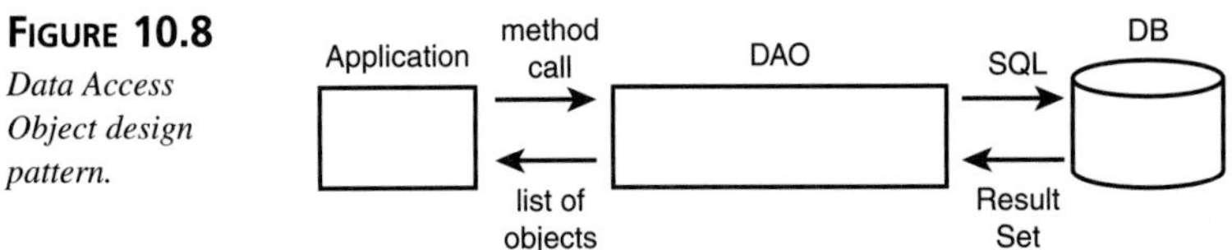

FIGURE 10.8
Data Access Object design pattern.

By using a DAO, the implementation details of the database are hidden from the application clients. The implementation details include the database schema and database vendor. This follows closely with the design principle of encapsulation. A benefit of using the DAO is improved application maintenance. If the database schema changes, such as a column name being modified, we only have to update the DAO. No modifications are required to the client programs. Also, if we decide to change the database implementation from Sybase to Oracle, modifications are only required to the DAO. The clients can continue to use the DAO without any modification. The DAO design pattern is widely used in the industry and is documented in Sun's J2EE Patterns Catalog, found at `java.sun.com/j2ee`.

In our solution, we'll create a DAO called `RentalPropertyDAO`. This version of the DAO will only provide the method `getRentalProperties()`. Later in the chapter, we'll provide additional methods. The `getRentalProperties()` method submits a SQL query to the database and converts the result set to a collection of JAXB `RentalProperty` objects. This process is illustrated in Figure 10.9.

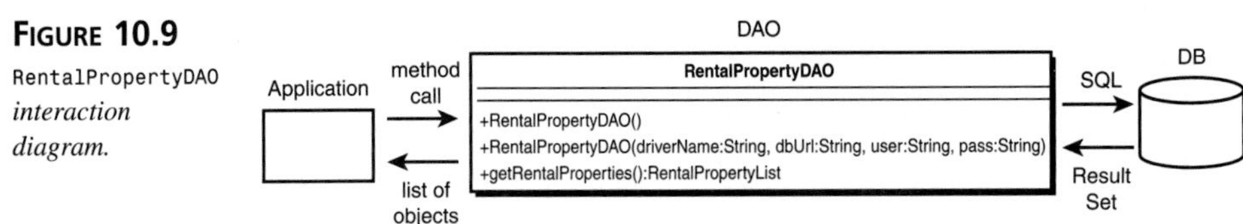

FIGURE 10.9
`RentalPropertyDAO` *interaction diagram.*

Let's examine the components of the `RentalPropertyDAO` source code. The class definition and constructor for `RentalPropertyDAO` are shown here:

```
public class RentalPropertyDAO {

    /**
     *  The database connection
```

```
     */
    protected Connection myConn;

    /**
     *  Constructor for DAO.  Setup the database connection.
➥*  Use the default properties.
     */
    public RentalPropertyDAO()
        throws DAOException {
            this("sun.jdbc.odbc.JdbOdbcDriver",
➥"jdbc:odbc:RentalPropertyDSN",
➥"test", "test");
    }

    /**
     *  Constructor for DAO.  Setup the database connection.
     */
    public RentalPropertyDAO(String driverName, String dbUrl,
➥String user, String pass)
        throws DAOException {

        try {
            // Load the driver
            log("Loading driver: "  + driverName);
            Class.forName(driverName);

            // Get a connection
            log("Connecting to the database: "  + dbUrl);
            log("User id: "  + user);
            myConn = DriverManager.getConnection (dbUrl, user, pass);

            log("DB connection successful at " + new java.util.Date());
        }
        catch (Exception exc) {
            throw new DAOException(exc);
        }
    }
…
}
```

The class `RentalPropertyDAO` defines a data member for a `java.sql.Connection` object. This will serve as our connection to the database. For the sake of simplicity, we're using a single connection. We could also utilize a database connection pool to increase the scalability of the application.

`RentalPropertyDAO` can be constructed by using the default constructor. In this case, the DAO will use default properties for the JDBC driver name, the JDBC database URL, and the user ID and password. This constructor shields the client code for knowing the details of the database implementation. The typical JDBC steps are followed to load a database driver and to obtain a connection to the database.

`RentalPropertyDAO` also provides a constructor, where the client program supplies the appropriate JDBC parameters. This constructor provides flexibility and would be typically used in a distributed computing environment such as Remote Method Invocation (RMI) or Enterprise JavaBeans (EJB). A remote server object would instantiate the DAO using server-side parameters. The DAO would then be available remotely via a server-side proxy interface. In this scenario, the client application would simply look up the remote object and invoke its methods. The client object is not involved with the construction of the DAO and therefore is shielded from the implementation details of JDBC driver name, URL, and so on.

Once the `RentalPropertyDAO` Data Access Object is constructed, clients can retrieve data from the database by calling the `getRentalProperties()`method. The code for `getRentalProperties()` is shown here:

```
/**
 *  Get a list of rental properties from the database
 *
 *  @return a list of RentalProperty objects
 *  @exception SQLException thrown for SQL errors
 */
public RentalPropertyList getRentalProperties() throws DAOException {

    RentalPropertyList theRentalPropertyList = new RentalPropertyList();
    List theList = theRentalPropertyList.getList();

    try {
        Statement myStmt = myConn.createStatement();

        String rentalSql = "SELECT prop_num, name, street_address, "
➥+ "city, state, zip_code, "
➥+ "size, sq, bed_count, bath_count, "
➥+ "monthly_rent, voice_phone, "
                                + "fax_phone FROM rental_properties";

        ResultSet myRs = myStmt.executeQuery(rentalSql);

        RentalProperty tempProperty = null;

        // build a collection of JAXB RentalProperty objects
        while (myRs.next()) {
            tempProperty = createRentalProperty(myRs);
            theList.add(tempProperty);
        }

        // be sure to validate the new list
```

```
            theRentalPropertyList.validate();

            myRs.close();
            myStmt.close();
        }
        catch (Exception exc) {
            throw new DAOException(exc);
        }

        return theRentalPropertyList;
    }
```

This method queries the database and returns a collection of `RentalProperty` objects.

After the SQL is executed, the method processes the result set to build a collection of `RentalProperty` objects. Because the early access version of JAXB does not support the code generation of constructors, we've created a simple constructor method in `RentalPropertyDAO`. The code for the `createRentalProperty()`method is shown here:

```
    /**
     *  Create a JAXB RentalProperty object based on the result set.
     *  This method provides the mapping between database schema and object
     */
    protected RentalProperty createRentalProperty(
➥ResultSet theRs) throws DAOException {

        RentalProperty theProperty = new RentalProperty();
        Address theAddress = new Address();
        Contact theContact = new Contact();

        try {
            // set the rental property number and name
            theProperty.setPropId(theRs.getString("prop_num"));
            theProperty.setName(theRs.getString("name"));

            // set the address
            theAddress.setStreet(theRs.getString("street_address"));
            theAddress.setCity(theRs.getString("city"));
            theAddress.setState(theRs.getString("state"));
            theAddress.setPostalCode(theRs.getString("zip_code"));
            theProperty.setAddress(theAddress);

            // set the square footage, bedrooms, bath count and rent
            theProperty.setSquareFootage(theRs.getDouble("size_sq"));
            theProperty.setBedrooms(theRs.getDouble("bed_count"));
            theProperty.setBath(theRs.getDouble("bath_count"));
            theProperty.setPrice(new BigDecimal(
➥theRs.getDouble("monthly_rent")));
```

```
            // set the contact information
            theContact.setPhone(theRs.getString("voice_phone"));
            theContact.setFax(theRs.getString("fax_phone"));
            theProperty.setContact(theContact);
        }
        catch (SQLException exc) {
            throw new DAOException(exc);
        }

        return theProperty;
    }
```

The `createRentalProperty()`method creates an instance of a `RentalProperty` object using the default constructor. It then populates the object based on information from the result set. This method actually handles the mapping between the database fields and the XML elements.

Listing 10.4 contains the complete code for `RentalPropertyDAO.java`.

LISTING 10.4 `<install_dir>\ch10_xmldb\source_code\xmlunleashed\ch10\RentalPropertyDAO.java`

```
package xmlunleashed.ch10;

import java.sql.DriverManager;
import java.sql.Connection;
import java.sql.Statement;
import java.sql.ResultSet;
import java.sql.SQLException;

import java.math.BigDecimal;

import xmlunleashed.ch10.jaxb.RentalProperty;
import xmlunleashed.ch10.jaxb.RentalPropertyList;
import xmlunleashed.ch10.jaxb.Contact;
import xmlunleashed.ch10.jaxb.Address;


/**
 *  Data Access Object (DAO) for the rental_property database. <br>
 *
 */
public class RentalPropertyDAO {

    /**
     *  The database connection
     */
    protected Connection myConn;
```

LISTING 10.4 continued

```
    /**
     *  Constructor for DAO.  Setup the database connection.
     */
    public RentalPropertyDAO(String driverName, String dbUrl,
➥String user, String pass)
        throws DAOException {

        try {
            // Load the driver
            log("Loading driver: "  + driverName);
            Class.forName(driverName);

            // Get a connection
            log("Connecting to the database: "  + dbUrl);
            log("User id: "  + user);
            myConn = DriverManager.getConnection (dbUrl, user, pass);

            log("DB connection successful at " + new java.util.Date());
        }
        catch (Exception exc) {
            throw new DAOException(exc);
        }
    }

    /**
     *  Get a list of rental properties from the database
     *
     *  @return a list of RentalProperty objects
     *  @exception SQLException thrown for SQL errors
     */
    public RentalPropertyList getRentalProperties() throws DAOException {

        RentalPropertyList theRentalPropertyList = new RentalPropertyList();
        java.util.List theList = theRentalPropertyList.getList();

        try {
            Statement myStmt = myConn.createStatement();

            String rentalSql = "SELECT prop_num, name, street_address, "
➥+ "city, state, zip_code, "
➥+ "size, sq, bed_count, bath_count, "
➥+ "monthly_rent, voice_phone, "
➥+ "fax_phone FROM rental_properties";

            ResultSet myRs = myStmt.executeQuery(rentalSql);

            RentalProperty tempProperty = null;
```

LISTING 10.4 continued

```
            // build a collection of JAXB RentalProperty objects
            while (myRs.next()) {
                tempProperty = createRentalProperty(myRs);
                theList.add(tempProperty);
            }

            // be sure to validate the new list
            theRentalPropertyList.validate();

            myRs.close();
            myStmt.close();
        }
        catch (Exception exc) {
            throw new DAOException(exc);
        }

        return theRentalPropertyList;
    }

    /**
     *  Create a JAXB RentalProperty object based on the result set.
     *  This method provides the mapping between database schema and object
     */
    protected RentalProperty createRentalProperty(
➥ResultSet theRs) throws DAOException {

        RentalProperty theProperty = new RentalProperty();
        Address theAddress = new Address();
        Contact theContact = new Contact();

        try {
            // set the rental property number and name
            theProperty.setPropId(theRs.getString("prop_num"));
            theProperty.setName(theRs.getString("name"));

            // set the address
            theAddress.setStreet(theRs.getString("street_address"));
            theAddress.setCity(theRs.getString("city"));
            theAddress.setState(theRs.getString("state"));
            theAddress.setPostalCode(theRs.getString("zip_code"));
            theProperty.setAddress(theAddress);

            // set the square footage, bedrooms, bath count and rent
            theProperty.setSquareFootage(theRs.getDouble("size_sq"));
            theProperty.setBedrooms(theRs.getDouble("bed_count"));
            theProperty.setBath(theRs.getDouble("bath_count"));
            theProperty.setPrice(new BigDecimal(
➥theRs.getDouble("monthly_rent")));
```

LISTING 10.4 continued

```
            // set the contact information
            theContact.setPhone(theRs.getString("voice_phone"));
            theContact.setFax(theRs.getString("fax_phone"));
            theProperty.setContact(theContact);
        }
        catch (SQLException exc) {
            throw new DAOException(exc);
        }

        return theProperty;
    }

    /**
     *  Utility method for logging
     */
    protected void log(Object message) {
        System.out.println("RentalPropertyDAO: " + message);
    }
}
```

Now that we have the DAO in place, a client program can easily retrieve information from the database. The `RentalPropertyList` collection contains JAXB `RentalProperty` objects. These objects are capable of producing an XML representation of their data thanks to the JAXB support. The XML data is available by calling the `marshal()` method.

Creating a Test Harness for `RentalPropertyDAO`

Before we move to the next section, let's create a test harness for `RentalPropertyDAO`. A *test harness* is a small program that tests the basic functionality of the application. If designed properly, The test harness provides a way of producing predictable results from an application.

The `TestApp` program will construct the `RentalPropertyDAO` Data Access Object and then retrieve a list of `RentalProperty` objects by calling the method `getRentalPropertyList()`. The XML data is displayed by calling the `marshal()` method on `RentalPropertyList`.

Listing 10.5 contains the code for `TestApp.java`.

LISTING 10.5 `<install_dir>\ch10_xmldb\source_code\TestApp.java`

```
import xmlunleashed.ch10.RentalPropertyDAO;
import xmlunleashed.ch10.DAOException;
```

LISTING 10.5 continued

```
import xmlunleashed.ch10.jaxb.RentalPropertyList;

import java.io. IOException;

/**
 * Test harness for the RentalPropertyDAO.
➥* Retrieves a rental property list and displays the
 * results to standard out.
 */
public class TestApp {

    /**
     * DAO data member
     */
    protected RentalPropertyDAO myRentalDAO;

    /**
     * Constructs the RentalPropertyDAO
     */
    public TestApp() throws DAOException {
        myRentalDAO = new RentalPropertyDAO();
    }

    /**
     * Retrieves a rental property list and displays the results to standard out
     */
    public void process() throws DAOException, IOException {
        // Get the list of rental properties
        RentalPropertyList theList = myRentalDAO.getRentalProperties();

        // Send the XML data to standard out.
        theList.marshal(System.out);
    }

    /**
     *  Main routine.  Constructs the test app and runs the process.
     */
    public static void main(String[] args) {
        try {
            TestApp myApp = new TestApp();

            myApp.process();
        }
        catch (Exception exc) {
            exc.printStackTrace();
        }
    }
}
```

When we run the test harness, it retrieves a collection of rental properties from the DAO. The test harness then displays an XML document similar to this one:

```
<?xml version="1.0" encoding="UTF-8"?>

<rental_property_list>
    <rental_property>
    <prop_id>1</prop_id>
    <name>The Meadows</name>
    <address>
        <street>251 Eisenhower Blvd</street>
        <city>Houston</city>
        <state>TX</state>
        <postal_code>77033</postal_code>
    </address>
    <square_footage>500.0</square_footage>
    <bedrooms>1.0</bedrooms>
    <bath>1.0</bath>
    <price>600</price>
    <contact>
        <phone>555-555-1212</phone>
        <fax>555-555-1414</fax>
    </contact>
    </rental_property>

    <rental_property>
        ...
    </rental_property>
</rental_property_list>
```

Developing a Servlet for HTTP Access

At this point, we have constructed the `RentalPropertyDAO` Data Access Object. This DAO is capable of retrieving information from a database and providing a collection of objects. Thanks to the JAXB framework, these objects can be marshaled into XML.

Now we need to provide an HTTP interface for `RentalPropertyDAO` so that a Web browser can interact with our system. Java servlets provides support for the HTTP protocol. If you are interested in Web-based interaction, you should also read about the Web Services technology, which is covered later in this book.

In our solution, we'll use a servlet to handle the requests to the DAO. In the servlet, we'll call the appropriate method and return the result as an XML document. Figure 10.10 depicts the application interaction.

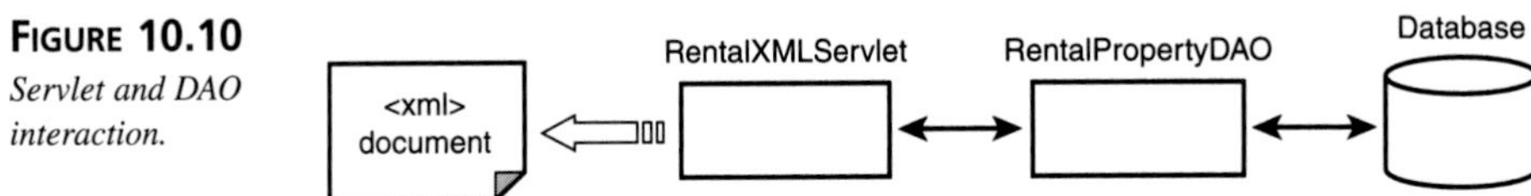

FIGURE 10.10
Servlet and DAO interaction.

The servlet is responsible for creating an instance of `RentalPropertyDAO`. The servlet reads JDBC parameters from the `web.xml` configuration file and constructs `RentalPropertyDAO` accordingly. An excerpt from the `web.xml` file is shown here (make note of the definitions for the parameters `driverName`, `dbUrl`, `user`, and `pass`) :

```
<servlet>
    <servlet-name>RentalXMLServlet</servlet-name>
    <servlet-class>xmlunleashed.ch10.RentalXMLServlet</servlet-class>
    <init-param>
        <param-name>driverName</param-name>
        <param-value>sun.jdbc.odbc.JdbcOdbcDriver</param-value>
    </init-param>
    <init-param>
        <param-name>dbUrl</param-name>
        <param-value>jdbc:odbc:RentalPropertyDSN</param-value>
    </init-param>
    <init-param>
        <param-name>user</param-name>
        <param-value>test</param-value>
    </init-param>
    <init-param>
        <param-name>pass</param-name>
        <param-value>test</param-value>
    </init-param>
    <load-on-startup/>
</servlet>
```

The servlet reads the parameters and constructs the `RentalPropertyDAO` Data Access Object in the `init()` method. The code for the `init()` method is shown here:

```
/**
 *  Create an instance of the RentalPropertyDAO
 */
public void init() throws ServletException {

    // retrieve database connection parameters
    String dbUrl = getInitParameter("dbUrl");
    String driverName = getInitParameter("driverName");
    String user = getInitParameter("user");
    String pass = getInitParameter("pass");

    // create an instance of the RentalPropertyDAO
    try {
```

```
            myRentalDAO = new RentalPropertyDAO(driverName, dbUrl, user, pass);
        }
        catch (Exception exc) {
            log(exc.toString());
            throw new ServletException(exc);
        }
    }
```

The servlet handles HTTP `GET` requests, so we have to override the `doGet()` method. In this method, we set the content type of the response to `text/xml`. This informs the client that we are returning XML-formatted text data. Next, we set up `ServletOutputStream`. Then we retrieve a list of rental properties from `RentalPropertyDAO`. The list is then marshaled to the `ServletOutputStream` object, `out`. Finally, the output stream is closed. The code for the `doGet()` method is shown here:

```
    /**
     *  Perform the following steps for GET requests.
     *
     *  <ol>
     *  <li>Retrieve a list of rental properties from RentalPropertyDAO<li>
     *  <li>Marshal the list as an XML document<li>
     *  </ol>
     */
    public void doGet(HttpServletRequest request, HttpServletResponse response)
        throws ServletException, IOException {

        ServletOutputStream out = null;
        RentalPropertyList theList = null;

        try {
            // Set the content type to text/xml
            response.setContentType("text/xml");

            // Retrieve the servlet output stream
            out = response.getOutputStream();

            // Retrieve a list of rental properties
            theList = myRentalDAO.getRentalProperties();

            // Marshal the list as an XML document
            theList.marshal(out);
        }
        catch (DAOException exc) {
            exc.getRootCause().printStackTrace();
            throw new ServletException(exc.getRootCause());
        }
        catch (Exception exc) {
            log(exc.toString());
            exc.printStackTrace();
            throw new ServletException(exc);
```

```
        }
        finally {
            out.close();
        }
    }
```

Testing the Application

In order to test the application, you need to download and install the following important components.

Here's what's required to test the application:

- *Sun Microsystems' Software Development Kit (SDK) 1.3 (or higher)*. The SDK is available at Sun's Web site, `http://java.sun.com/j2se`. Follow the installation instructions provided with the SDK.
- *Apache Tomcat Server 4*. Apache Tomcat 4 is the official reference implementation for JSP 1.2 and Java Servlets 2.3. If your application server already supports JSP 1.1 or higher, there's no requirement to install Tomcat. Apache Tomcat 4 is available from the Apache Web site, `http://jakarta.apache.org/tomcat`. Follow the installation instructions provided with the Tomcat server.
- *Microsoft Internet* Explorer *6 or Netscape 6*. In this section, you will need a browser that has client-side XML support. This is useful for viewing the raw XML output of our servlet.

Note

The Java SDK provides the compilation and runtime tools for the Java platform. The Tomcat server is the servlet container. The servlet container provides an execution environment for the Java servlets. Finally, the Web browser is for viewing the output of the servlets.

Once Tomcat 4 is installed, we need to add a new Web application that points to the source code directory. This is accomplished by editing the file `<tomcat_install_dir>\conf\server.xml`. Move to the section where the `<Context>` elements are listed and then add the following entry:

```
<Context path="/bookch10"
         docBase="<install_dir>/ch10_xmldb/public_html"
         debug="0"
         reloadable="true" />
```

Be sure to update `<install_dir>` with the installation directory for the book's source code. This configuration allows us to access the Web application named `bookch10`. This Web application's document base is located at `<install_dir>\ch10_xmldb\public_html`.

Now, restart the Tomcat server to pick up the new configuration. By default, the Tomcat server is listening on port 8080. You can access files for the `bookch10` Web application using the following URL:

```
http://localhost:8080/bookch10/test.jsp
```

The file `test.jsp` should display a welcome message and the current date.

Next, follow these steps to compile the source code:

1. Open a Microsoft command prompt window.
2. Move to the source code directory by typing this:
   ```
   cd <install_dir>\ch10_xmldb
   ```
   This directory includes the batch file `setpaths.bat`. This file will place the following JAR files in the classpath: `lib\servlet.jar`, `lib\jaxb-rt-1.0-ea.jar`, and `lib\jaxb-xjc-1.0-ea.jar`.
3. Set up the classpath by typing the following:
   ```
   setpaths.bat
   ```
4. Move to the source code directory by typing this:
   ```
   cd source_code
   ```
5. Compile the code by typing this:
   ```
   javac -d ..\public_html\WEB-INF\classes *.java
   ```
   If you are accustomed to using ANT, note that this directory also contains a `build.xml` file.

Now we need to set up an ODBC Data Source Name (DSN) for `RentalPropertyDSN`. This DSN should point to the file `<install_dir>\ch10_xmldb\data\rental_property.mdb`.

Now we need to test `RentalXMLServlet`. In a Web browser, open `http://localhost:8080/bookch10/RentalXMLServlet`.

If you are using Microsoft Internet Explorer 6, you will see the XML content shown in Figure 10.11.

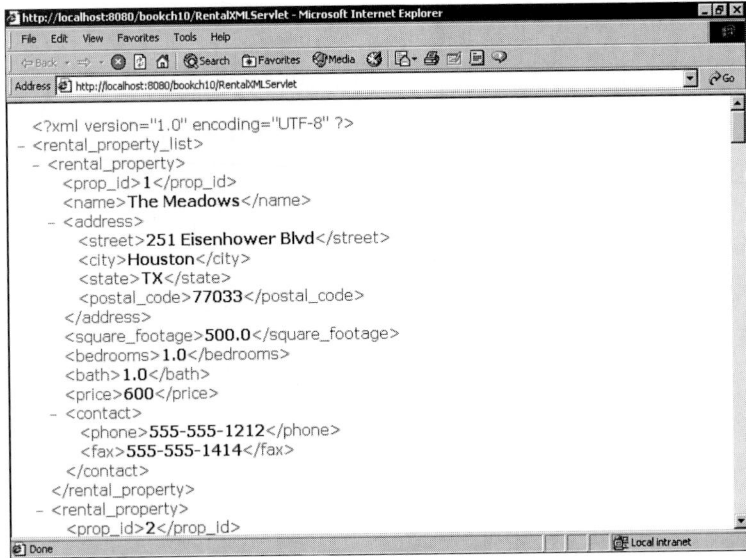


```
  <?xml version="1.0" encoding="UTF-8" ?>
- <rental_property_list>
  - <rental_property>
      <prop_id>1</prop_id>
      <name>The Meadows</name>
    - <address>
        <street>251 Eisenhower Blvd</street>
        <city>Houston</city>
        <state>TX</state>
        <postal_code>77033</postal_code>
      </address>
      <square_footage>500.0</square_footage>
      <bedrooms>1.0</bedrooms>
      <bath>1.0</bath>
      <price>600</price>
    - <contact>
        <phone>555-555-1212</phone>
        <fax>555-555-1414</fax>
      </contact>
    </rental_property>
  - <rental_property>
      <prop_id>2</prop_id>
```


FIGURE 10.11
`RentalXMLServlet` *output in Microsoft Internet Explorer 6.*

If you are using Netscape 6, select the menu option View, Page Source. This will display the raw XML output as shown in Figure 10.12.

Source for: http://localhost:8080/bookch10/RentalXMLServlet - Netscape
File Edit View Help

```
<?xml version="1.0" encoding="UTF-8"?>

<rental_property_list>
  <rental_property>
    <prop_id>1</prop_id>
    <name>The Meadows</name>
    <address>
      <street>251 Eisenhower Blvd</street>
      <city>Houston</city>
      <state>TX</state>
      <postal_code>77033</postal_code></address>
    <square_footage>500.0</square_footage>
    <bedrooms>1.0</bedrooms>
    <bath>1.0</bath>
    <price>600</price>
    <contact>
      <phone>555-555-1212</phone>
      <fax>555-555-1414</fax></contact></rental_property>
  <rental_property>
    <prop_id>2</prop_id>
    <name>The Meadows</name>
    <address>
      <street>251 Eisenhower Blvd</street>
      <city>Houston</city>
      <state>TX</state>
      <postal_code>77033</postal_code></address>
    <square_footage>700.0</square_footage>
    <bedrooms>2.0</bedrooms>
    <bath>1.5</bath>
```

FIGURE 10.12
`RentalXMLServlet` *output in Netscape Navigator 6.*

Great! We've developed `RentalXMLServlet` to provide an HTTP interface to `RentalPropertyDAO`. The end product is an XML model of the data stored in the database.

Now we can take this one step further by applying a style sheet to the data.

Converting the XML Data to HTML with XSLT

We can leverage the functionality of XSLT to convert the XML data to HTML. In particular, we will convert the rental property list to an HTML table, as shown in Figure 10.13.

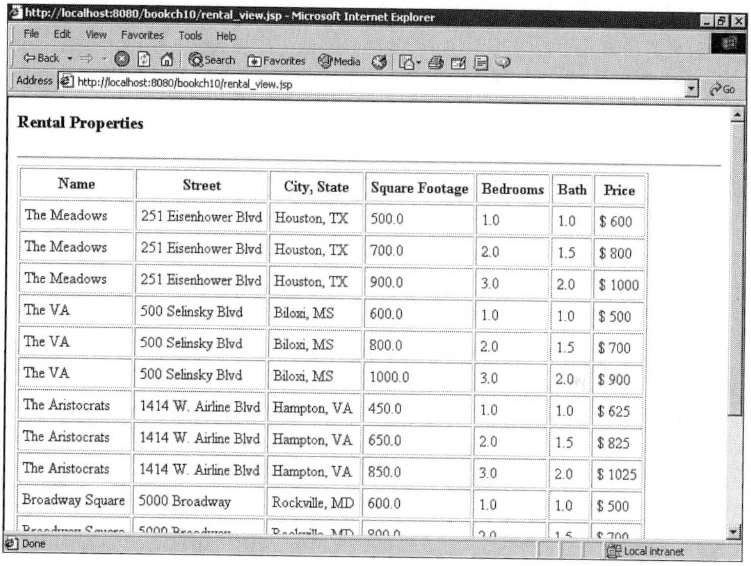
http://localhost:8080/bookch10/rental_view.jsp - Microsoft Internet Explorer
File Edit View Favorites Tools Help
Address http://localhost:8080/bookch10/rental_view.jsp
Rental Properties
Done
Local intranet

Name	Street	City, State	Square Footage	Bedrooms	Bath	Price
The Meadows	251 Eisenhower Blvd	Houston, TX	500.0	1.0	1.0	$ 600
The Meadows	251 Eisenhower Blvd	Houston, TX	700.0	2.0	1.5	$ 800
The Meadows	251 Eisenhower Blvd	Houston, TX	900.0	3.0	2.0	$ 1000
The VA	500 Selinsky Blvd	Biloxi, MS	600.0	1.0	1.0	$ 500
The VA	500 Selinsky Blvd	Biloxi, MS	800.0	2.0	1.5	$ 700
The VA	500 Selinsky Blvd	Biloxi, MS	1000.0	3.0	2.0	$ 900
The Aristocrats	1414 W. Airline Blvd	Hampton, VA	450.0	1.0	1.0	$ 625
The Aristocrats	1414 W. Airline Blvd	Hampton, VA	650.0	2.0	1.5	$ 825
The Aristocrats	1414 W. Airline Blvd	Hampton, VA	850.0	3.0	2.0	$ 1025
Broadway Square	5000 Broadway	Rockville, MD	600.0	1.0	1.0	$ 500

FIGURE 10.13
HTML table for rental properties.

This section assumes you are familiar with XSLT. If not, then read Chapter 9.

The XSLT style sheet contains the HTML template along with the XSLT constructs to retrieve the data. Our style sheet defines an HTML table with instructions to create a table row for each rental property in the list. Listing 10.6 contains the code for `rental_view.xsl`.

LISTING 10.6 <install_dir>\ch10_xmldb\public_html\rental_view.xsl

```
<?xml version="1.0"?>
<xsl:stylesheet xmlns:xsl=
➥"http://www.w3.org/1999/XSL/Transform" version="1.0">
```

LISTING 10.6 continued

```
<xsl:template match="/rental_property_list">
<html><body>
<h3>Rental Properties</h3>
<hr></hr>
<table border="1" cellpadding="5">
    <tr>
        <th>Name</th>
        <th>Street</th>
        <th>City, State</th>
        <th>Square Footage</th>
        <th>Bedrooms</th>
        <th>Bath</th>
        <th>Price</th>
    </tr>

    <!— Perform loop for each rental property in the list —>
    <xsl:for-each select="rental_property" >
        <tr>
            <td>  <xsl:value-of select="name" /> </td>
            <td>  <xsl:value-of select="address/street" />      </td>
            <td>  <xsl:value-of select="address/city" />,
➥<xsl:value-of select="address/state" /> </td>
            <td>  <xsl:value-of select="square_footage" /> </td>
            <td>  <xsl:value-of select="bedrooms" /> </td>
            <td>  <xsl:value-of select="bath" /> </td>
            <td>  $ <xsl:value-of select="price" />    </td>
        </tr>
    </xsl:for-each>
</table>

</body></html>
</xsl:template>
</xsl:stylesheet>
```

We'll use the Apache-Jakarta custom tag, `<jakarta:apply>`, for XLST processing. Instead of specifying an XML document by filename, we need to refer to `RentalXMLServlet`. The `<jakarta:apply>` element supports the subelement `<jakarta:include>`, which refers to an XML resource to include. This includes the output of `RentalXMLServlet`. Listing 10.7 shows the code for `rental_test.jsp`.

LISTING 10.7 `<install_dir>\ch10_xmldb\public_html\rental_view.jsp`

```
<%@taglib uri="http://jakarta.apache.org/taglibs/xsl-1.0" prefix="jakarta" %>

<jakarta:apply xsl="rental_view.xsl">
  <jakarta:include page="/RentalXMLServlet"/>
</jakarta:apply>
```

Testing the JSP Page

To test this example, make sure the Tomcat server is running. In a Web browser, access the JSP page with the URL `http://localhost:8080/bookch10/rental_view.jsp`.

Your browser should resemble what's shown in Figure 10.13 shown previously.

Summary

We started this chapter by reviewing commercial solutions for XML database integration. These products provide a mapping between the database fields and XML documents. Also, you learned that certain products bypass the relational database and store XML documents in their native format.

The bulk of the chapter was dedicated to XML data binding with JAXB. In the rental property example, we modeled a database as an XML document. This included the development of a DTD and JAXB binding schema. We utilized the DTD and binding schema to generate Java classes. The classes allowed us to quickly and easily map XML documents to Java objects. This eliminated the need to use the SAX and DOM APIs, which prove to be cumbersome for complex XML documents.

We also applied J2EE design patterns by developing a Data Access Object (DAO) for the database interface. The DAO encapsulated the low-level SQL and JDBC code and provided a public method to retrieve information from the database. The DAO leveraged the JAXB framework by returning a collection of JAXB-aware objects. These objects modeled our XML document structure.

A Java servlet was developed to provide HTTP access to our system. The servlet used the DAO to retrieve a list of rental properties. The servlet then used the JAXB framework to marshal the objects as an XML document. Finally, a JSP page converted the XML data to an HTML table using an XSLT style sheet.

This technique can be easily extended for the development of B2B or B2C applications. There is a large amount of synergy between JAXB and XML database integration. This chapter has opened a treasure chest of knowledge. I challenge you to cash in on the riches!

CHAPTER 11

Formatting XML for the Web

In This Chapter

XML is a data structuring language. XML provides meaning for your data. However, something that XML does not do is provide formatting for your data. There is no indication in an XML document or in the XML specification for how XML data should be displayed for human consumption. This is an important consideration. Although XML is designed to be multiplatform compatible and easily consumable by machines across the entire spectrum of operating systems, there is no indication of how XML should be consumed by humans.

XML does, however, allow tags to be defined in a self-describing manner (this is indeed recommended). When viewing the XML tag `Dog`, you can be fairly certain what the tag is referring to. However, if the XML file gets large or the structure gets overly complicated (such as a mathematical formula or a chemical element definition), the XML file might not be easily legible to the human eye. Therefore, an easy way to format XML data is needed so that humans can easily consume it.

In HTML, the structure and formatting for data are combined. Although HTML is very effective at formatting data for appearing on the Web, HTML is, for all intents and purposes, limited to the Web. XML has separated itself from formatting. This serves to make XML far more flexible in terms of how it may be used and displayed. XML may have formatting applied so that it appears in a desktop PC application, a handheld PC application, a mainframe terminal, a Web browser, and so on.

This chapter focuses on several of the technologies used for formatting, delivering, and gathering XML data on the Web. First, we'll cover some of the history of data formatting, starting with a brief look at the Document Style Semantics and Specification Language (DSSSL) and Cascading Style Sheets (CSS). You will see how CSS can be used to provide some formatting for XML data. Then we will look at XHTML—a reformulation of HTML into an XML application. Finally, we will briefly look into the future by covering XForms, another XML application, which is the intended replacement for HTML forms.

Before covering some of the newer technologies used for displaying XML on the Web, we will take a look at some older data-formatting technologies: DSSSL and CSS. This should give you a good overview of where we have come from so that you might better understand where we are going.

A Brief History of DSSSL

Standard Generalized Markup Language (SGML) is a platform-independent (neutral), application-independent, ISO-standardized metalanguage for structuring data. More important, SGML is the mother of HTML and XML. HTML and XML are derivations or special applications of SGML. However, before the advent of HTML and XML, SGML was the most prominent metalanguage describing the structure of data.

Note

This section is not intended to provide detailed coverage of SGML and DSSSL. If you would like to do more in-depth research of SGML and DSSSL, an excellent online resource is `http://ourworld.compuserve.com/homepages/hoenicka_markus/sgmlintro.html`.

SGML was published as an international standard (ISO 8879) in 1986. SGML allows for the creation of structured documents that describe data. The markup of data in SGML is highly descriptive and defined using a Document Type Definition (DTD). It is completely data independent, which means that data coded in SGML is not dependent on any specific display mechanism, platform, or software. Does this sound familiar? These are some of the same features that XML has. Of course, because XML is a child (descendent) of SGML, this should make perfect sense.

Although SGML does a good job describing and structuring data, it does nothing for the formatting of data. In 1996, ISO approved the final draft of the Document Style Semantics and Specification Language (DSSSL) for SGML documents. DSSSL's specific purpose is to provide processing instructions for SGML documents. The two main types of instructions that DSSSL provides have to do with transformations (transforming a SGML document from one structure to another) and formatting or styles (applying style sheets to SGML documents). We are going to be covering the DSSSL style language here.

As is true for any style language, DSSSL defines syntax for how different elements in a SGML document will be mapped to formatting objects for display. For example, a SGML document might contain an element, `X`. A DSSSL style sheet could be applied to the SGML document that maps the contents of the element `X` to a specific font size, font weight, color, and so on. Listing 11.1 gives a very simple example of an SGML document.

LISTING 11.1 Very Simple SGML Document

```
<!DOCTYPE Note [
<!ELEMENT Note - - (From, To, Subject, Body) >
<!ELEMENT From - - (#PCDATA) >
<!ELEMENT To - - (#PCDATA)>
<!ELEMENT Subject - - (#PCDATA)>
```

LISTING 11.1 continued

```
<!ELEMENT Body - - (#PCDATA)>
]>
<Note>
<From>Bob</From>
<To>Jenny</To>
<Subject>Hello Friend!</Subject>
<Body>Just thought I would drop you a line.</Body>
</Note>
```

You can see that, indeed, Listing 11.1 is an example of what a simple message structure might look like in SGML. There is a document element, `Note`, which has four children: `From`, `To`, `Subject`, and `Body`. There is a Document Type Declaration containing an internal DTD. It is interesting to note that in SGML, a DTD is always required. In the DTD element declarations, there are two dashes (`-`) after each element name. The dashes signify whether opening and closing tags are required. A dash indicates a required tag, whereas the letter `o` stands for `optional` (because XML always requires a closing tag, this feature of the element definition was dropped from the XML DTD).

Although Listing 11.1 is complete and does accurately depict a "note" according to the DTD, there is nothing that explains how the note should be displayed. In SGML, DSSSL is the standard for defining the formatting. If a DSSSL style sheet were created for this SGML document, it would appear something like what's shown in Listing 11.2.

LISTING 11.2 DSSSL Style Sheet

```
<!DOCTYPE style-sheet public "-//James Clark//DTD DSSSL Style Sheet//EN" >
(element Note (make simple-page-sequence))
(element To
(make paragraph
font-family: arial
font-size: 15pt
font-weight: bold ))
(element From
(make paragraph
font-family: arial
font-size: 15pt
font-weight: bold ))
(element Subject
(make paragraph
font-family: arial
font-size: 13pt
font-weight: bold ))
(element body
(make paragraph
font-family: arial
font-size: 12pt ))
```

The first thing you'll notice in Listing 11.2 is that there is a Document Type Declaration. In DSSSL, style sheets are very complicated; therefore, it is normal practice to reference a larger, public style sheet from a style sheet you are creating. The public style sheet defines the layout schemes. In this case, the publicly defined style sheet for rendering HTML is being referenced. You can see that the remainder of the style sheet defines the font, size, and weight of each of the elements in the SGML document. The settings in the DSSSL style sheet override the settings in the referenced style sheet if both define styles for the same elements.

Note

James Clark is the creator of the HTML DSSSL style sheet used as the public DTD reference for the Document Type Declaration in Listing 11.2. It is considered to be the standard for DSSSL-defined HTML. Clark is responsible for writing the majority of the DSSSL standard and has worked extensively to help create and expand the standards by which SGML and XML are used and applied. More information about Clark's work can be found at `www.jclark.com`.

The markup used in SGML and DSSSL should look fairly familiar to you. It is not that different from the markup we see today in XML, XML DTDs, and CSS. In fact, SGML and DSSSL work well and are still used today. A Web-enabled version of DSSSL, called DSSSL-Online, has been produced. However, SGML and DSSSL are very complicated technologies. Newer innovations in data metalanguages have introduced an easier-to-follow syntax, tighter definitions, and superior implementations.

Next, we are going to review a more recent formatting option, Cascading Style Sheets.

A Brief History of CSS

In 1996, about the time the DSSSL standard was being finalized by the ISO, the W3C organization was finalizing its own style language. On December 17, 1996, Cascading Style Sheets Level 1 (CSS1) became an official W3C recommendation. CSS1 was introduced with the intention of separating, as much as possible, the formatting (visual rendering) from HTML-structured documents.

Note

This section is not intended to provide detailed coverage of CSS. To learn more about CSS, visit the W3C organization's CSS resource page at `http://www.w3c.org/Style/CSS/`.

HTML, an SGML application, was originally introduced to simplify the visual rendering of structured data for Web-enabled audiences. However, as vendors (especially Netscape and Microsoft) introduced new versions of their Web browsers, more custom extensions to HTML for rendering were introduced. Some features of HTML were adopted by the Web browsers, whereas others were ignored or changed. The original intent of HTML became increasingly splintered as the HTML implementations of competing Web browsers became more and more incompatible. For this reason, CSS1 was an attempt to separate much of the rendering (font sizes, colors, spacing, and so on) from HTML—that is, to help remove the disparities between the Web browsers.

In addition to separating rendering from HTML, CSS1 is much simpler to implement than DSSSL-Online, the Web version of DSSSL. CSS1 has a simpler, easier-to-understand syntax. It allows for a much more granular control of layout and formatting. CSS1 was developed to be very flexible and maintainable through the use of separate style sheets that can be referenced by many HTML pages simultaneously.

Note

This overview of CSS will mainly deal with CSS Level 1. Although CSS Level 2 is the most recent Cascading Style Sheet recommendation, at the time of writing, only the newest versions of the most popular Web browsers support much of CSS Level 2. Therefore, in order to reach the widest audience possible, CSS Level 1 will be covered in much more detail.

Listing 11.3 shows a very simple example of what a message might look like in a HTML page (building upon the SGML message example in Listing 11.1). The code from this listing, `simplemessage.HTML`, can be downloaded from the Sams Web site.

LISTING 11.3 Very Simple HTML Page

```
<html>
<head>
<title>Simple Message</title>
```

LISTING 11.3 continued

```
</head>
<body>
<h1>Note</h1>
<h2>From: Bob</h2>
<h2>To: Jenny</h2>
<h3>Subject: Hello Friend!</h3>
<h4>Just thought I would drop you a line.</h4>
</body>
</html>
```

Listing 11.3 has no special formatting applied to it. It is a simple HTML page that gives no indication about the type of font, font size, colors, and so on that should be applied to it when rendered in a Web browser. In this case, the formatting applied will be the default settings associated with the HTML tags for a Web browser that loads the page. Figure 11.1 shows how this page would be rendered using the default settings in Internet Explorer 5.5.

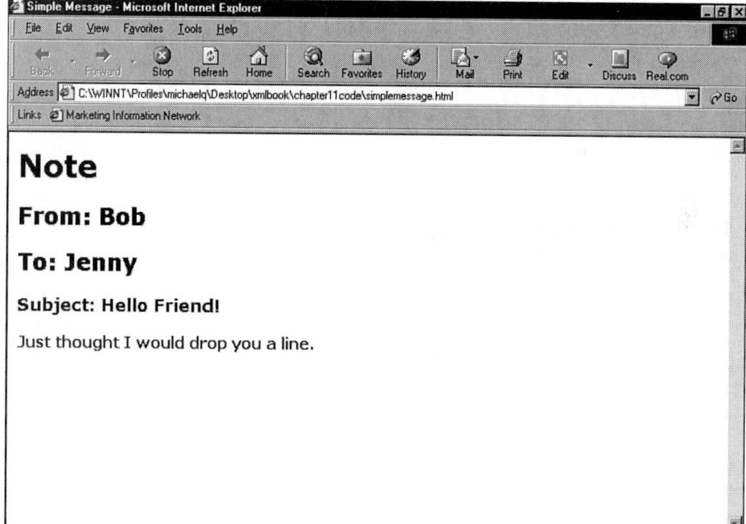

FIGURE 11.1
Default Web browser formatting is applied to Listing 11.3.

You can see there is nothing fancy about the formatting for this page. However, it is possible to apply a CSS1 style sheet to this page to affect the rendering. Applying a style sheet to the page will override the default formatting of the Web browser. Listing 11.4 shows a CSS1 style sheet that could be used to apply styles to the HTML page in Listing 11.3. The code for this listing, `simplecss.css`, can be downloaded from the Sams Web site.

LISTING 11.4 Simple CSS1 Style Sheet

```
h1
{
font-family:verdana;
font-size:20px;
font-weight:bold;
color:#0000ff
}
h2
{
font-family:arial;
font-size:15px;
font-weight:bold;
color:#00ff00
}
h3
{
font-family:sans serif;
font-size:13px;
font-weight:bold;
color:#ff0000
}
h4
{
font-family:courier;
font-size:12px;
color:#000000
}
```

On the surface, a CSS1 style sheet is very similar to a DSSSL style sheet. However, beyond some subtle syntax differences (CSS is a bit more straightforward), the big difference is that the CSS style sheet does not have a Document Type Declaration. This is because the rules for applying and parsing CSS style sheets are built in to the Web browser's parsing engine. There is no need for a DTD in a CSS1 style sheet. This removes a lot of the overhead inherent in DSSSL.

Only a single line of code must be added to the HTML page (from Listing 11.3) in order to reference the style sheet in Listing 11.4. Listing 11.5 shows the updated HTML page. The code for this listing, `simplemessage_css.HTML`, can be downloaded from the Sams Web site.

LISTING 11.5 Very Simple HTML Page

```
<html>
<head>
<title>Simple Message</title>
```

LISTING 11.5 continued

```
<!-- references the style sheet from Listing 11.4 -->
<link rel="STYLESHEET" type="text/css" href="simplecss.css" />
</head>
<body>
<h1>Note</h1>
<h2>From: Bob</h2>
<h2>To: Jenny</h2>
<h3>Subject: Hello Friend!</h3>
<h4>Just thought I would drop you a line.</h4>
</body>
</html>
```

The only change from Listing 11.3 to Listing 11.5 is that the `link` element has been added to the page right after the `title` element inside the `head` element. The `link` element is an empty element with three attributes. The `rel` attribute establishes that the link is for a style sheet. The `type` attribute establishes the MIME type for a CSS style sheet. Finally, the `href` attribute is, of course, the URL for the style sheet. Now, when visited by a Web browser, the page will be rendered using the settings found in the style sheet that is referenced by the `href` attribute of the `link` element. Figure 11.2 shows how the page in Listing 11.5 would appear in Internet Explorer 5.5.

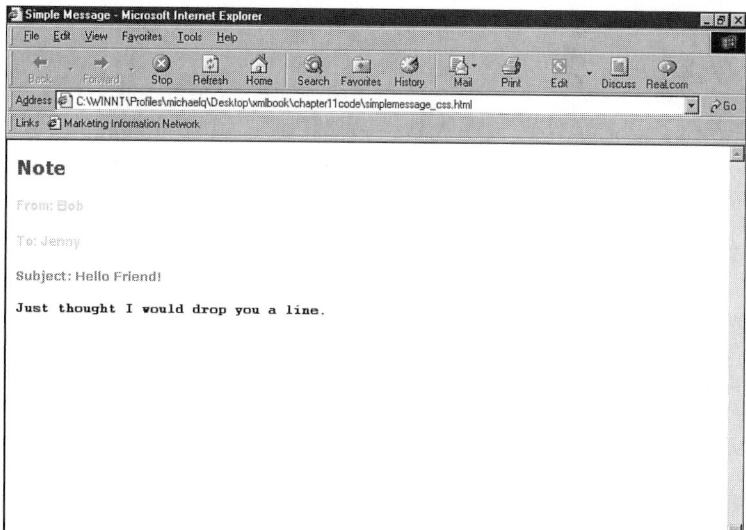

FIGURE 11.2
Formatting is applied to Listing 11.3 using the Cascading Style Sheet from Listing 11.4.

Compare Figure 11.2 to Figure 11.1. It is easy to see that applying the CSS1 style sheet from Listing 11.4 has radically affected the rendering of the HTML. Each of the elements—<h1>, <h2>, <h3>, and <h4>—are rendered differently according to the `font-family`, `font-size`, `font-weight`, and `color` settings from the style sheet.

Of course, this all becomes academic if Web browsers do not adopt W3C recommendations such as CSS1. In the last few years, the major Web browser vendors have finally finished adding (almost) complete support for CSS1. The only problem with this is that CSS2 is the newest recommendation for Cascading Style Sheets. CSS2 was ratified as a W3C recommendation in May 1998. Since CSS2 was ratified in 1998, at the time of this writing, only Opera 5 and Netscape 6 have broad support for CSS2. It is this lag in adopting new CSS technology by the Web browser vendors that has been instrumental in Web developers continuing to use older HTML formatting tags such as <font>, <u>, and <i>.

CSS is not only used to apply formatting to HTML. In the next section, we will cover how CSS may be used to apply formatting to XML documents for display in Web browsers.

XML Presentation Using CSS

Interestingly enough, CSS actually works better with XML than it does with HTML. This is because XML has none of the problems that CSS was designed to correct—namely the mingling of data structure and data formatting in HTML. Because XML has no data formatting included in its specification, CSS works perfectly with XML. Structure and formatting are totally separated. Listing 11.6 shows a style sheet that could be used with an XML document to format XML data for display in a Web browser. The code for this listing, `notestyle.css`, can be downloaded from the Sams Web site.

LISTING 11.6 CSS for an XML Document

```
<!-- This style sheet will be referenced as notestyle.css -->
Note
{
display: block
}
From, To
{
display:block;
font-family:verdana;
font-size:15px;
margin-bottom:5px
}
Subject
{
display:block;
```

LISTING 11.6 continued

```
font-family:verdana;
font-size:13px;
font-weight:bold;
margin-bottom:10px
}
Body
{
display:block;
font-family:verdana;
font-size:12px
}
```

In this listing are five style selectors: `Note`, `From`, `To`, `Subject`, and `Body`. Each selector listed represents the name of an XML element. The styles associated with each selector will be applied to XML elements that have matching names (that is, styles associated with the `Note` selector would be applied to an XML element with the name `Note`). Notice that two of the selectors, `From` and `To`, are grouped by being listed in a sequence separated by a comma. Selectors may be grouped this way to indicate that they will have the same style settings.

A CSS style sheet may be attached to an XML document through the use of the special XML processing instruction `<?xml-stylesheet?>`. There are two attributes to the `xml-stylesheet` processing instruction: `type` and `href`. The `type` attribute sets the MIME type for the CSS style sheet. Its value should always be `text/css`. The `href` attribute gives the URL for the location of the CSS style sheet. Listing 11.7 demonstrates linking the CSS style sheet from Listing 11.6 to an XML document. The code for this listing, `notestyle.XML`, can be downloaded from the Sams Web site.

LISTING 11.7 Applying CSS to an XML Document

```
<?xml version="1.0"?>
<!--
This is referencing the style sheet from Listing 11.6 -
we are calling it notestyle.css here
-->
<?xml-stylesheet type="text/css" href="notestyle.css"?>
<Note>
<From>From: Bob</From>
<To>To: Jenny</To>
<Subject>Subject: Hello Friend!</Subject>
<Body>Just thought I would drop you a line.</Body>
</Note>
```

In Listing 11.7, the `href` attribute of the `xml-stylesheet` processing instruction assumes that the CSS style sheet is located in the same directory. The `href` attribute value could also be a relative URL or an absolute URL. You can see that Listing 11.7 is very similar to Listing 11.5, except that in this case the document is structured with XML rather than HTML. Figure 11.3 shows how Listing 11.7 looks in Internet Explorer 5.5.

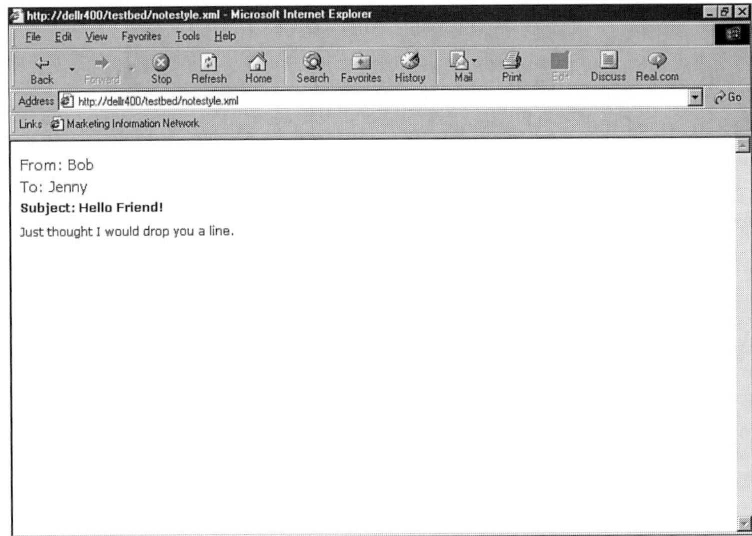

FIGURE 11.3
Listing 11.7 is formatted using the Cascading Style Sheet from Listing 11.6.

The XML elements have been nicely formatted for display according to the rules of the style sheet. This is a handy, easy way to make XML data viewable over the Web. However, I am not advocating XML formatted with CSS to replace HTML. Only the newest browsers have this capability; therefore, you should only use this approach when you know that your target audience will be using a compatible Web browser. As you will see in the next section, HTML has been reformulated into an XML application. This has been done with the intention of making the use of XML for broader applications on the Web an easier transition. Before we go on to our coverage of XHTML, however, let's take a look at one more way that CSS can be used with XML.

Note

If you are going to be using XML formatted with CSS for Web browser display, you must make sure your audience is using at least Internet Explorer 4+, Netscape Navigator 6+, or Opera 5+. At the time of writing, these are the only browsers that support this capability well.

CSS also supports the use of "classes." So far, we have seen CSS applied to specific elements. It is also possible to create a CSS class that can be applied to specific elements and not others. This might be handy if you have a group of elements, each with the same name that you wish to display, but you want the formatting to vary from element to element (such as alternating background colors). Because the elements have the same name, you will need a different way to alternate formatting. Listing 11.8 demonstrates how you can accomplish this. The code for this listing, `alternate.css`, can be downloaded from the Sams Web site.

LISTING 11.8 Alternating Styles with Classes

```
<!--This style sheet shall be referenced as alternate.css -->
Catalog
{
display:block
}
Item
{
display:block;
margin-bottom:5px
}
Item.Odd
{
background:#dcdcdc
}
Name
{
display:block;
font-family:verdana;
font-size:14px;
font-weight:bold
}
Description, Price
{
display:block;
font-family:arial;
font-size:12px
}
```

The CSS style sheet in this listing is similar to the CSS style sheet in Listing 11.6. The difference (other than the different element names) is that there has been a class added. You will notice that there is an `Item` selector and that a class called `Odd` has been added for the `Item` selector. `Item` elements that specifically reference the `Odd` class will have the style setting `background:#dcdcdc` applied to them. This class will give the effect of being able to alternate the background color of the XML document referencing this style sheet. Listing 11.9 is an XML document that references the style sheet in Listing 11.8. The code for this listing, `alternate.XML`, can be downloaded from the Sams Web site.

LISTING 11.9 Referencing the Alternating Styles CSS Class

```
<?xml version="1.0"?>
<!--
This is a reference to the style sheet in Listing 11.8
- It is referred to as alternate.css here
-->
<?xml-stylesheet type="text/css" href="alternate.css"?>
<!DOCTYPE Catalog [
<!ELEMENT Catalog (Item+) >
<!ELEMENT Item (Name,Description,Price) >
<!ATTLIST Item Class CDATA #IMPLIED >
<!ELEMENT Name (#PCDATA) >
<!ELEMENT Description (#PCDATA) >
<!ELEMENT Price (#PCDATA) >
]>
<Catalog>
<Item Class="Odd">
<Name>Gloves</Name>
<Description>10 oz. sparring gloves</Description>
<Price>$29.99</Price>
</Item>
<Item>
<Name>Head Gear</Name>
<Description>Padded foam head protection for sparring</Description>
<Price>$49.99</Price>
</Item>
<Item Class="Odd">
<Name>Speed Bag</Name>
<Description>5 lb. punching bag</Description>
<Price>$50.00</Price>
</Item>
<Item>
<Name>Heavy Bag</Name>
<Description>100 lb. punching bag</Description>
<Price>$109.95</Price>
</Item>
<Item Class="Odd">
<Name>Judo Dogi</Name>
<Description>Single weave Judo uniform</Description>
<Price>$59.95</Price>
</Item>
<Item>
<Name>Karate Dogi</Name>
<Description>Light weight karate uniform</Description>
<Price>$19.95</Price>
</Item>
</Catalog>
```

This listing is a bit more complex than some of the listings we have looked at so far, but if you break it down into pieces, you will see that it is very easy to follow. The second line of the document is the processing instruction, `xml-stylesheet`, that references the `alternate.css` style sheet. There is a DTD included in this listing that defines the structure of the XML document. This is included for the purpose of demonstrating how the CSS class `Odd` (from Listing 11.8) will be referenced. In the DTD, the element `Item` has an optional attribute defined, `Class`. When this attribute is included for the element `Item` in the XML document and set to the value `Odd`, the style associated with the `Odd` class in the style sheet will be applied to the element. Figure 11.4 shows how this XML document will be rendered in Internet Explorer 5.5.

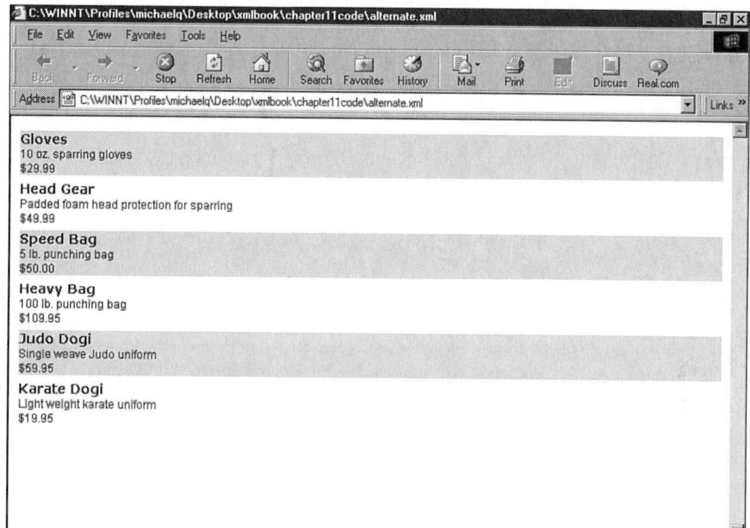

FIGURE 11.4
Formatting Listing 11.9 using the Cascading Style Sheet from Listing 11.8.

In the XML document (from Listing 11.9), all the odd-numbered `Item` elements have the optional attribute `Class` set to `Odd`. When rendered, this has the effect of making ever other `Item` element have a silver background. This definitely makes it much easier to quickly view the items in this catalog.

We have now seen a couple ways that CSS can be applied to XML. However, as I mentioned previously, don't be too quick to jump on the XML bandwagon for displaying your data on the Web! The Web browser vendors (and users) are still working on catching up. Unless you have a captive audience, such as in an intranet setting, using XML as demonstrated here is probably not a good idea yet. In order to help ease along the transition to XML, the W3C organization has created XHTML—and that is what we will look at next.

An Overview of XHTML

Someday the Web will be standardized. All Web pages will be completely cross-platform compatible and will load faster. Also, work will get done more quickly (especially for us Web developers). However, the standardization of the Web is still over the horizon, and movement toward that goal is painfully slow. In order to help prepare for the future, the W3C organization introduced XHTML 1.0 as an official recommendation on January 26, 2000. XHTML is a step toward the goal of standardizing markup for the Web. It is also a step toward making the Web "XML compatible." XHTML is an XML application. XHTML is a reformulation of HTML into an XML application. Therefore, HTML is made XML compatible and open to interaction with future XML technologies.

XHTML 1.0: The Transition

XHMTL 1.0 was introduced in order to serve as a bridge (or transition) from older technologies (such as the splintered and incompatible variations of HTML) to newer technologies (such as XML). XHTML 1.0 creates a markup that is compatible with older Web browsers but also will be compatible as support is picked up for emerging technologies. XHTML 1.0 is very similar to HTML 4. Basically, it has simply taken HTML 4 and reformulated it as an XML application.

Note

The official XHTML 1.0 recommendation can be found at `http://www.w3.org/TR/xhtml1/`.

Making HTML XML Compliant

The main goals of XHTML are to make documents XML compliant and to address the incompatibilities of HTML in the major Web browsers. Once this compliance is achieved, support will be ensured for XML technologies such as XSL, and pages will be able to be parsed and edited with standard XML tools. Also, because XHTML 1.0 is so close to HTML 4, existing Web pages can be updated to XHTML 1.0 compliance with mostly only minor changes. Developers and Webmasters of sites consisting of hundreds or thousands of pages should not break into a cold sweat at the thought of upgrading to XHTML 1.0. It is really quite easy. Before going into the three variations (DTDs) of XHTML 1.0, let's take a look at Listings 11.10 and 11.11. These listings give you a quick before-and-after picture of how a document would be upgraded from HTML to XHTML 1.0 compliance. The code for this listing, `beforexhtml.HTML`, can be downloaded from the Sams Web site.

LISTING 11.10 Document Before XHTML 1.0 Compliance

```
<HTML>
<HEAD>
<TITLE>Sample HTML Page: Pre-XHTML 1.0 Conversion</TITLE>
</HEAD>
<BODY>
<H1>My Favorite Musical Groups</H1>
<P>
<UL>
<LI>Dave Mathews Band
<LI>Beck
<LI>Offspring
</UL>
<P>
<H4>Pretty eclectic tastes, ay?
</BODY>
</HTML>
```

Listing 11.10 is a pretty typical HTML document. You can see that the tags are capitalized and the `<P>`, `<LI>`, and `<H4>` tags are not closed with ending tags. However, despite not being well formed, a Web browser will render this page with no problems. Listing 11.10, although okay for HTML, is wrong in XHTML 1.0. Listing 11.11 shows how this page would be changed to be XHTML 1.0 compliant. The code for this listing, `afterxhtml.HTML`, can be downloaded from the Sams Web site.

LISTING 11.11 Document After XHTML 1.0 Compliance

```
<!DOCTYPE html PUBLIC
"-//W3C//DTD XHTML 1.0 Transitional//EN"
"http://www.w3.org/TR/xhtml1/DTD/xhtml1-transitional.dtd">
<html>
<head>
<title>Sample HTML Page: Post-XHTML 1.0 Conversion</title>
</head>
<body>
<h1>My Favorite Musical Groups</h1>
<p />
<ul>
<li>Dave Mathews Band</li>
<li>Beck</li>
<li>Offspring</li>
</ul>
```

LISTING 11.11 continued

```
<p />
<h4>Pretty eclectic tastes, ay?</h4>
</body>
</html>
```

The first thing you will notice in this listing is that a Document Type Declaration has been added. The Document Type Declaration contains a public reference to the Transitional DTD for XHTML 1.0 (this will be covered in detail in the next section). Additionally, all the HTML tags have been set to lowercase according to XHTML rules. HTML is notably lax about capitalization and will accept both lowercase and uppercase tags (or even mixtures of both). XML (XHTML) is strict about requiring lowercase tag names. Also, all the opening tags have been closed. The `<p>` tags are empty tags and have had closing "`/`" symbols added. A closing tag could have been added (`<p></p>`); however, it is easier to simply treat them like empty tags. This is the same rule for empty tags in XML. The difference being that in XHTML, in order for these tags to display properly in a Web browser, a space is inserted before the "`/`" symbol.

Listing 11.11 could potentially be displayed using any HTML extension, an XHTML extension, or an XML extension (when viewed with Internet Explorer 5.5). However, with the XML extension, the file may be verified for well-formedness and validated against a DTD. This provides a clear picture of the use of XHTML as a bridge from HTML to XML. Although Listing 11.10 and Listing 11.11 will be rendered by the browser equally well with an HTML extension, only Listing 11.11 will be rendered with an XML extension. This is because only Listing 11.11 is valid XML. XHTML is used to make the HTML into valid XML.

There is no difference between how Listing 11.10 and 11.11 will be displayed in today's Web browsers. Figure 11.5 demonstrates how both Listing 11.10 and Listing 11.11 would be rendered in Internet Explorer 5.5.

The two renderings are exactly the same! The big difference is that Listing 11.11 is now a well formed XHTML document. Listing 11.11 is compatible with XML technology and may be fully integrated with future XML technology applications. What's more, this was all relatively painless to do! Certainly there will be varying degrees of work that needs to be done on existing pages to make them compatible, but you can see that you won't ever have to scrap your whole Web site to achieve compatibility. More than likely you will only have to make minor changes.

Specific syntax rules apply to XHTML in order to make a document well formed. We will cover those rules in a moment, but first let's take a look at the three variants, or DTDs, that have been created for XHTML 1.0.

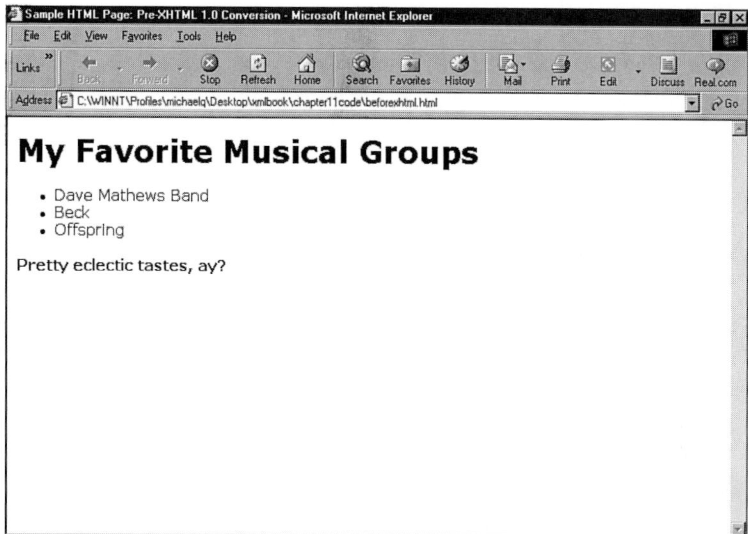

FIGURE 11.5
Rendering of Listings 11.10 and 11.11 in Internet Explorer 5.5.

Variants of XHTML

In order to conform to XHTML, a document must be validated against one of three DTDs that have been defined for XHTML. These DTDs are reformulations of the DTDs defined for HTML 4: Strict, Transitional, and Frameset.

> **Note**
>
> If you are just beginning with your migration to XHTML for your existing Web site, using the Transitional DTD would probably be the best choice because it has the loosest restrictions. If you are building from scratch, it might not be a bad idea to go ahead and use the Strict DTD. That way, you are ensured of the highest level of compliance.

Strict DTD

A strictly conforming XHTML document that references the Strict DTD will have the following Document Type Declaration:

```
<!DOCTYPE html
PUBLIC "-//W3C//DTD XHTML 1.0 Strict//EN"
"http://www.w3.org/TR/xhtml1/DTD/xhtml1-strict.dtd">
```

Adherence to the Strict DTD means that the XHTML document will have the following characteristics:

- There will be a strict separation of presentation from structure. Style sheets are used for formatting, and the XHTML markup is very clean and uncluttered. There are no optional vendor-specific HTML extensions.
- The Document Type Definition must be present and placed before the `<html>` element in the document.
- The root element of the document will be `<html>`.
- The `<html>` element will have the `xmlns` attribute in order to designate the XHTML namespace.
- The document, of course, is valid according to the rules defined in the Strict DTD.

Note

The namespace for XHMTL 1.0 that should be referenced by the `xmlns` attribute of the root element `<html>` is `http://www.w3.org/1999/xhtml`.

Listing 11.12 gives a very simple example of an XHTML page that conforms to the Strict DTD. The code for this listing, `strictdtd.HTML`, can be downloaded from the Sams Web site.

LISTING 11.12 Strict DTD Reference

```
<!DOCTYPE html
PUBLIC "-//W3C//DTD XHTML 1.0 Strict//EN"
"http://www.w3.org/TR/xhtml1/DTD/xhtml1-strict.dtd">
<html xmlns="http://www.w3.org/1999/xhtml">
<head>
<title>Strict XHTML DTD Reference</title>
</head>
<body>
<h1>Strict XHTML DTD Reference</h1>
<table>
<tr>
<td>
This is a plain, vanilla page.
</td>
</tr>
<tr>
<td>
```

LISTING 11.12 continued

```
There are no special formatting elements included.
</td>
</tr>
<tr>
<td>
If any formatting is needed a CSS style sheet could be referenced.
</td>
</tr>
</table>
</body>
</html>
```

In this listing, no special formatting HTML elements are included. Additionally, this is, according to XML rules, a well-formed document. Therefore, this page would be valid according the Strict DTD. Any special formatting needed could be added by referencing a CSS style sheet.

Note

The XHTML Strict DTD can be found at `http://www.w3.org/TR/xhtml1/DTD/xhtml1-strict.dtd`.

The most important requirement for the Strict DTD is the separation of presentation and structure. How many of your existing Web pages meet this requirement? How difficult would it be to get your Web pages to meet this requirement? In most of your existing Web pages, you will have an almost terminal mixture of presentation and structure in your HTML. In order to comply with the Strict DTD, you would probably have to make fairly extensive changes to your existing Web pages. In order to address this potential problem, the Transitional DTD was created to be much more lenient in its rules. It is much simpler to make an HTML page "Transitional compliant" than it is to make a page "Strict compliant." The Transitional DTD is covered next.

Transitional DTD

The Transitional DTD for XHTML has more loosely defined requirements than the Strict DTD. As such, it is much easier to use with current Web browsers than the Strict DTD. To be more specific, you have to make far fewer changes to your existing Web pages. As long as the Transitional DTD is referenced from the Document Type Definition, the HTML is well formed, and it follows the basic XHTML syntax rules (more on the syntax rules in a moment), there should not be any problems.

Note

The XHTML Transitional DTD can be found at `http://www.w3.org/TR/xhtml1/DTD/xhtml1-transitional.dtd`.

A Document Type Declaration containing a reference to the Transitional DTD will appear as follows:

```
<!DOCTYPE html
PUBLIC "-//W3C//DTD XHTML 1.0 Transitional//EN"
"http://www.w3.org/TR/xhtml1/DTD/xhtml1-transitional.dtd">
```

This DTD is also useful if you are using or have Web site visitors that use Web browsers that do not support CSS style sheets. If you must support a lot of the formatting HTML elements, such as `<font>`, `<b>`, `<u>`, and so on, due to the necessity of supporting Web browsers that do not support CSS, then the Transitional DTD is your best bet to becoming XHTML compliant. Listing 11.13 shows an XHTML page that uses a lot of formatting elements but is still valid because it references the Transitional DTD. The code for this listing, `transdtd.HTML`, can be downloaded from the Sams Web site.

LISTING 11.13 Transitional DTD Reference

```
<!DOCTYPE html
PUBLIC "-//W3C//DTD XHTML 1.0 Transitional//EN"
"http://www.w3.org/TR/xhtml1/DTD/xhtml1-transitional.dtd">
<html xmlns="http://www.w3.org/1999/xhtml">
<head>
<title>Transitional XHTML DTD Reference</title>
</head>
<body>
<h1><font face="arial" color="#ff0000">
<b>Transitional</b> XHTML DTD Reference</font></h1>
<table>
<tr>
<td>
<font size="13px" face="arial">This page has
<em>quite a bit</em> of <u>formatting</u> added!</font></td>
</tr>
<tr>
<td>
<font size="13px" face="arial"><em>Many</em>
formatting elements are <strong>included</strong>.</font>
</td>
</tr>
<tr>
<td>
```

LISTING 11.13 continued

```
<font size="13px" face="sans serif">
This type of formatting works for
<big>older browsers</big> that do not <small>support CSS</small>!
</font>
</td>
</tr>
</table>
</body>
</html>
```

Listing 11.13 includes many formatting elements. This is okay because these elements are supported by the Transitional DTD for the purposes of backward compatibility. This document is well formed, all elements are in lowercase, and attribute values are quoted. This document is XHTML compliant, according to the Transitional DTD, and it will still work with older Web browsers.

The third type of DTD that we will take a look at is the Frameset DTD.

Frameset DTD

The XHTML Frameset DTD is designed specifically to work with HTML frame pages. Frame pages are pages in which the browser has been broken up into several semi-independent navigable windows. Each frame, or window, will have its own content that is maintained in a file separate from the content in the other windows. Normally, one frame will contain navigation links and the other frame serves as the target for the link, loading whatever content the link points to when clicked. A frame page might be useful if you want to be able to load content from another Web site in one frame while keeping your navigation links available in another window. In addition to the files that make up the content for each of the frames, one main frame page "binds" the other frames together. From this main page, you will reference the Frameset DTD. The Frameset DTD contains rules that apply specifically to the special setup of a frame page. In order to reference the XHTML Frameset DTD, use the following Document Type Declaration:

```
<!DOCTYPE html
PUBLIC "-//W3C//DTD XHTML 1.0 Frameset//EN"
"http://www.w3.org/TR/xhtml1/DTD/xhtml1-frameset.dtd">
```

Note

The XHTML Frameset DTD can be found at `http://www.w3.org/TR/xhtml1/DTD/xhtml1-frameset.dtd`.

Any time you are splitting the Web browser page into two or more frames, you should reference this DTD in order to be XHTML compliant.

Now that you have seen the DTDs that are used with XHTML 1.0, you probably have a dozen or so questions dancing around in your head about the exact differences between XHTML and HTML 4.

Syntax and Definitions

This section explains the syntax requirements for an XHTML document and the differences between XHTML and HTML 4.

XHTML Must Be Well Formed

As mentioned previously, according to XML syntax rules, all elements that are opened in an XHTML document must be closed. This is a departure from HTML, where many elements, such as `<p>` or `<li>`, are not closed.

For example, the following would be okay for HTML but not XHTML:

```
<p>The paragraph element is not closed
```

In order to be okay for XHTML, the preceding example would have to look like this:

```
<p>The paragraph element is now closed</p>
```

For the opening paragraph element, `<p>`, a closing paragraph element, `</p>`, has been added.

There are also many empty elements in HTML—the most notable being the `<img>` element. You will also see a lot of `<br>` and `<hr>` elements in HTML. In XHTML, empty elements are handled just as they are in XML. A slash character (/) is added before the closing ">" symbol. The only difference in XHTML is that, in order to be compliant with today's Web browsers, a space must be added before the "/" symbol in the element. If this is not done, the element will not be rendered properly. Therefore, the HTML elements `<img>`, `<br>`, and `<hr>` become `<img />`, `<br />`, `<hr />` in XHTML. This rule should be applied to any empty elements, not just the ones listed here.

Elements must be properly nested. In HTML, elements *should* be properly nested, but Web browsers are pretty forgiving if they are not. Oftentimes, when looking at an HTML page, you will see something like this:

```
<p>There elements are not <b>properly nested!</p></b>
```

Even though the <p> elements and the <b> elements are overlapping and not properly nested, most Web browsers will still properly render the page. In XHTML, this overlapping must be corrected as follows

```
<p>There elements are <b>properly nested!</b></p>
```

Here, you can see that the nesting has been corrected. The <b> elements are properly contained within the <p> elements.

All Elements and Attributes Must Be Lowercase

This is another departure from HTML. In HTML, elements can be uppercase, lowercase, or even a mixture of cases. Therefore, the elements <br>, <BR>, and <Br> would be rendered identically in HTML. However, in XHTML, only <br> would be correct.

The same rule goes for attribute names. In HTML, there are no case rules for attribute names. In XHTML, attribute names must be lowercase.

Attribute Values Must Always Appear in Quotes

All attribute values must appear in quotes. Both string values and numeric values must appear in quotes as well. In HTML, however, this is optional.

For example, HTML would allow the following:

```
<td colspan=4>
```

In XHTML, however, this must be rewritten as follows:

```
<td colspan="4">
```

> **Note**
>
> Values can appear in single quotes (`colspan='4'`) or double quotes (`colspan="4"`). Either way is equally acceptable.

If there is a quote sign or double quote sign in your attribute value, you must use the other quote sign to quote your attribute value. For example, if you have an attribute called `lastname`, with the value `O'Malley`, then the attribute would be written `lastname="O'Malley"`. In this case, double quotes are used to delimit the value because a single quote is contained in the value.

Attributes May Not Be Minimized

It is common to have attributes in HTML such as `checked` or `nowrap` that are minimized. In XHTML, minimization of attributes is not allowed. Attribute/value pairs must be written out in full.

In HTML, an attribute could be minimized as follows:

```
<td nowrap>
```

In XHTML, in order to be compliant with the Transitional DTD, this would be rewritten like so:

```
<td nowrap="nowrap">
```

> **Note**
>
> It is important to note that some of the implied HTML attributes are supported in the Strict DTD and some are not. For example, `checked` is supported and `nowrap` is not. The Transitional DTD supports both.

You simply take the minimized value in HTML and turn it into an attribute name/value pair in XHTML.

Script and Style Elements Must Be Enclosed in CDATA Sections

In order to avoid the values of script and style elements being parsed by the XML parser, you should enclose the values in `CDATA` sections. Listing 11.14 gives an example of this.

LISTING 11.14 Style Element in XHTML

```
<style>
<![CDATA[
Insert all of the pages style settings here
]]>
</style>
```

`CDATA` sections will be ignored by the XML parser and sent directly to the Web browser for interpretation and rendering.

Note

If you prefer not to use CDATA sections in your XHTML pages, you can use external script and style documents. Either method works and is really a choice of personal preference.

Element Identifier References Are to the id Attribute

In HTML, the name attribute and the id attribute are both used to identify specific elements. The id attribute in XHTML is an XML id type of attribute and therefore uniquely identifies the element throughout the document. In XML, references to the identifier for an element will be to the id attribute.

Caution

Some current Web browsers do not yet support the id attribute. In order to ensure forward and backward compatibility, always use both the id and name attributes.

HTML 4 defines the name attribute for the elements a, applet, form, frame, iframe, img, and map. In XHTML, the name attribute has been deprecated, or marked as outdated by newer constructs, and will be completely removed in future releases. Until support is actually dropped for the name attribute and all Web browsers begin using the id attribute instead, both should be used. Listing 11.15 demonstrates this.

LISTING 11.15 Using the id and name Attributes

```
<frame id="frame1" name="frame1">
Frame content goes here
</frame>
```

Here, the id attribute and the name attribute both have the same value: frame1. The id attribute is included to provide an XHTML-valid identifier for this frame element. The name attribute is also included to ensure that existing Web browsers uniquely recognize the element.

You should be fairly comfortable with XHTML 1.0 by now. This would be a good time to start our mini case study and see how a small Internet retailer would use XHTML 1.0 on their Web site.

Coca Cabana Technology Shop Case Study: Building a Web Site for the Future, Part I

XHTML 1.0 is a tremendous tool for helping Web site developers get their Web sites quickly transitioned to XML compatibility. In this mini case study, we will take a quick visit to the Coca Cabana Technology Shop to see how they made their Web site XHTML 1.0 Transitional compliant.

The owners of Coca Cabana Technology Shop have always prided themselves on being up to date on the latest technology for the computers they sell. However, recently it was pointed out to them by one of their clients that although their computers are great, their Web site is beginning to fall behind the times. The owners decided that in order to keep up the appearance of being on top of their industry, they would need to upgrade their Web site.

After a bit of research, they found out that XHTML, an XML application, would better serve their e-commerce needs and move them to the cutting edge of technology on the Web.

Because most of Coca Cabana Technology Shop's business is over the Internet, they decided that they better upgrade their Web site to XHTML 1.0 immediately. In order to achieve compatibility as quickly as possible, they went with the XHTML 1.0 Transitional DTD.

The first step was to review the HTML code currently used to make up their Web site (for expediency purposes, we are simply going to look at the home page of Coca Cabana Technology Shop). Here's the code for `Prexhtml_Home.html` (which you can download from the Sams Web site):

```
<HTML>
<HEAD>
<TITLE>Welcome to Coca Cabana</TITLE>
<META name="description" content="Welcome to Coca Cabana, The best
technology
shop on the Web!">
<META name="keywords" content="technology, web, internet, computers,
palm-tops, lap-tops, modems, hard drives">
</HEAD>
<BODY  BGCOLOR="BEIGE">
<BASEFONT FACE="VERDANA" SIZE="2">
<H1>Welcome to Coca Cabana Technology Shop!</H1>
<H3>The <FONT COLOR="RED">best</FONT> darn shop on the internet!</H3>
<P>
Here at Coca Cabana we pride ourselves on having the most up to date
technology at the best prices you will find anywhere.
<HR>
<TABLE BGCOLOR="BLACK" CELLPADDING="0" CELLSPACING="1"
BORDER="0" WIDTH="100%">
```

```
<TR>
<TD WIDTH=15% VALIGN=TOP BGCOLOR=TAN>
<FONT SIZE="2">
<!--
These links do not actually go anywhere - they are included for
demonstration purposes
-->
<H4>Site Links:</H4>
<UL>
<LI><A HREF=home.html>Home</A>
<LI><A HREF=news.html>Latest News</A>
<LI><A HREF=catalog.html>Catalog</A>
<LI><A HREF=support.html>Support</A>
<LI><A HREF=aboutus.html>About us</A>
</TD>
<TD VALIGN="TOP">
<TABLE BGCOLOR="BLACK" CELLPADDING="4" CELLSPACING="0" WIDTH="100%">
<TR>
<TD BGCOLOR="TEAL">
<H2>Check out our laptop blowout!</H2>
<FONT SIZE="4">Special selections from our award winning laptop line!
<UL>
<FONT SIZE="3" COLOR=MAROON>
<LI>COCA PENTIUM III Laptop - <b>$999.00</B>
<LI>COCA PENTIUM II Laptop - <b>$799.00</B>
<LI>COCA PENTIUM Laptop - <b>$599.00</FONT></B>
</TD>
</TR>
<TR>
<TD BGCOLOR=KHAKI>
<H4>We have some other great specials that you should see!</H4>
<FONT SIZE="3">The following low prices are always
available at Coca Cabana!
<UL>
<FONT SIZE="3" COLOR="MAROON">
<LI>COCA PENTIUM III DESKTOP - <b>$1299.00</B>
<LI>COCA PALM-TOP - <b>$299.00</B>
<LI>COCA 10 GIGABYTE HARDDRIVES - <b>$109.00</B>
</TD>
</TR>
</TABLE>
</TD>
</TR>
</TABLE>
<HR>
<CENTER><FONT SIZE=2>Thanks for shopping at the Coca Cabana Technology
shop!<BR><B>Please come again soon!
</BODY>
</HTML>
```

What the owners of Coca Cabana Technology Shop discovered was that although their Web site displayed on the Internet well, the HTML code making up the page was not XHTML compliant and, in some cases, was down right sloppy. Here's a list of the major problems they found:

- The XHTML 1.0 specification dictates that element names and attribute names should not be capitalized. This needs to be changed on the Coca Cabana Technology Shop site.
- All attribute values must appear in quotes. Only some of the attribute values were quoted on the Coca Cabana Technology Shop site.
- All elements must have both opening and closing tags. Also, empty elements must have the slash character (/) before the closing ">". This is also a problem on the site.
- Finally, they found several instances of elements not properly nested.

In addition to these needed changes, they also have to make sure they add the proper Document Type Declaration with a reference to the XHTML 1.0 Transitional DTD. The document that they came up with after making all the necessary changes is shown in the following file, `Postxhtml_Home.html` (which you can download from the Sams Web site):

```
<!DOCTYPE html PUBLIC
"-//W3C//DTD XHTML 1.0 Transitional//EN"
"http://www.w3.org/TR/xhtml1/DTD/xhtml1-transitional.dtd">
<html>
<head>
<title>Welcome to Coca Cabana</title>
<meta name="description" content="Welcome to Coca Cabana, The best
technology shop on the Web!" />
<meta name="keywords" content="technology, web, internet, computers,
palm-tops, lap-tops, modems, hard drives" />
</head>
<body  bgcolor="BEIGE">
<basefont face="VERDANA" size="2" />
<h1>Welcome to Coca Cabana Technology Shop!</h1>
<h3>The <font color="RED">best</font> darn shop on the internet!</h3>
<p>
Here at Coca Cabana we pride ourselves on having the most up to date
technology at the best prices you will find anywhere.
</p>
<hr />
<table bgcolor="BLACK" cellpadding="0" cellspacing="1"
border="0" width="100%">
<tr>
```

```
<td width="15%" valign="top" bgcolor="TAN">
<h4>Site Links:</h4>
<!--
These links do not actually go anywhere - they are included for
demonstration purposes
-->
<ul>
<li><font size="2"><a href="home.html">Home</a></font></li>
<li><font size="2"><a href="news.html">Latest News</a></font></li>
<li><font size="2"><a href="catalog.html">Catalog</a></font></li>
<li><font size="2"><a href="support.html">Support</a></font></li>
<li><font size="2"><a href="aboutus.html">About us</a></font></li>
</ul>
</td>
<td valign="top">
<table bgcolor="BLACK" cellpadding="4" cellspacing="0" width="100%">
<tr>
<td bgcolor="TEAL">
<h2>Check out our lap top blowout!</h2>
<font size="4">Special selections from our award winning
laptop line!</font>
<ul>
<li><font size="3" color="MAROON">COCA PENTIUM III Laptop -
<b>$999.00</b></font></li>
<li><font size="3" color="MAROON">COCA PENTIUM II Laptop -
<b>$799.00</b></font></li>
<li><font size="3" color="MAROON">COCA PENTIUM Laptop -
<b>$599.00</b></font></li>
</ul>
</td>
</tr>
<tr>
<td bgcolor="KHAKI">
<h4>We have some other great specials that you should see!</h4>
<p>
<font size="3">The following low prices are always available at
Coca Cabana!</font>
</p>
<ul>
<li><font size="3" color="MAROON">COCA PENTIUM III DESKTOP -
<b>$1299.00</b></font></li>
<li><font size="3" color="MAROON">COCA PALM-TOP -
<b>$299.00</b></font></li>
<li><font size="3" color="MAROON">COCA 10 GIGABYTE HARDDRIVES -
<b>$109.00</b></font></li>
</ul>
</td>
</tr>
```

```
</table>
</td>
</tr>
</table>
<hr />
<center><font size="2">Thanks for shopping at the Coca Cabana Technology
shop!<br /><b>Please come again soon!</b></font></center>
</body>
</html>
```

After making all the necessary changes to ensure their Web site is XHTML 1.0 Transitional compliant, the owners of Coca Cabana Technology Shop decided to add one more little touch to their home page. Just before the closing </body> tag, they added the following five lines of code:

```
<p>
<a href="http://validator.w3.org/check/referer"><img
src="http://www.w3.org/Icons/valid-xhtml10"
alt="Valid XHTML 1.0!" height="31" width="88" /></a>
</p>
```

These lines of code add an image to the home page that, when clicked, redirects visitors to a validator on the W3C organization's Web site. This validator checks to ensure that the referring Web page is made up of valid XHTML. Even though the validator is not required for the page to actually be valid, They thought this would be a neat touch to let visitors know that they are up with the latest Web technology as well as the latest computer technology. Anyone clicking the image would instantly know that his Web site is XHTML 1.0 valid.

XHTML 1.1: Modularization

If the analogy of a bridge is used for XHTML 1.0, then possibly the analogy of an elevator could be used for XHTML 1.1. XHTML 1.0 creates a bridge to easily span the gap between HTML 4 and XML 1.0 compliance. XHTML 1.1 creates an elevator for raising the level of conformance of XHTML 1.0. Once a series of Web pages have become XHTML 1.0 compliant, they are on the ground floor. There is nowhere to go but up!

On April 10, 2001 the Modularization of XHTML became an official W3C organization recommendation.

Note

This section is not intended to provide complete coverage of the Modularization of XHTML. It is recommended that you also take a look at the official Modularization of XHTML recommendation found at `http://www.w3.org/TR/2001/REC-xhtml-modularization-20010410/`.

XHTML modularization is a dissection of XHTML 1.0 into a collection of abstract modules, with each module representing a specific type of XHTML functionality (such as an abstract module for defining XHTML tables or an abstract module for defining XHTML text formatting). Modules are implemented through the use of XML DTDs. XHTML modularization allows different modules to be "mixed and matched" together within XML DTDs in order to create XHTML subsets and extensions.

Note

The Modularization of XHTML could be thought of in terms of breaking XHTML 1.0 (and, by extension, HTML 4) into class objects, similar to what is found in an object-oriented programming (OOP) language. Think of each module as a class object that can be referenced to add functionality to the DTDs you create. Each module (class object) exposes a specific set of functionality that may be added to your DTD (project). Of course, you don't have to reference a module the same way you reference a class object in OOP, but the analogy still should give you an idea of how to think about XHTML modularization.

After making the Modularization of XHTML an official recommendation, the W3C moved quickly and on May 31, 2001, XHTML 1.1 (module-based XHTML) also became an official recommendation.

Note

The official XHTML 1.1 module-based XHTML recommendation can be found at `http://www.w3.org/TR/2001/REC-xhtml11-20010531/`.

XHTML 1.1 is basically the reformulation of the XHTML 1.0 Strict DTD into a module-based document type. This new module-based document type is designed to be portable and easily applicable across a broad collection of clients and platforms. With the advent of XHTML 1.1, end-user device vendors will be able to create DTDs that specify specifically which XHTML modules their devices support. Each of the modules will be consistent and conform with the Modularization of XHTML recommendation. This ensures that although a vendor might only be using a subset of XHTML, the subset will completely conform with XHTML 1.1. Compatibility will always be ensured.

In this section, we will take a quick rundown of the changes that have been made from XHTML 1.0. We will then go into a more detailed look at modularization in XHTML and its main areas of divergence from XHTML 1.0. Finally, in the subsection on syntax and definitions, we will run down the modules that make up the Modularization of XHTML and XHTML 1.1 document type.

Caution

Before you get too excited about XHTML 1.1 and all the implications of Modularized XHTML, be aware that application and browser support for XHTML 1.1 is pretty much nonexistent at this point. XHTML 1.1 is covered here mainly to show you where XHTML is going—not necessarily where it is currently. You could probably write an XHTML page that references the XHTML 1.1 DTD and get it to load in one of the newest Web browsers. However, unless you are writing your own custom applications that will use XHTML 1.1, that is about all you will get. Hopefully vendors will be fast to jump on the bandwagon and we will see tons of cool implementations of Modularized XHTML very soon.

Changes from XHTML 1.0

As previously stated, XHTML 1.1 is basically a reformulation of the XHTML 1.0 Strict DTD into a module-based document type. Many of the facilities available in other XHTML 1.0 document types (Transitional and Frameset) are not available in XHTML 1.1. The same general rules for strict adherence from XHTML 1.0 apply in XHTML 1.1.

The main differences between an XHTML 1.0 Strict DTD and XHTML 1.1 (apart from being defined in modules) are summarized here:

- All features that were deprecated have been completely removed in XHTML 1.1. Most of the removed features dealt with layout and formatting. The goal here is as much separation as possible between data structure and visual formatting. The strategy is to rely on style sheets for presentation.
- For all elements, the `lang` attribute as been removed and replaced with the `xml:lang` attribute.

- For the a and map elements, the name attribute has been removed and replaced with the id attribute.
- The Ruby collection of elements has been added to the document type.

Note

The Ruby collection is derived from Ruby Annotation, which is another W3C recommendation. It may be viewed at http://www.w3.org/TR/2001/REC-ruby-20010531/. Ruby Annotation defines an XHTML module that specifies the markup to be used for Ruby, which is a term used for a run of text that is associated with another run of text (base text). Ruby text provides a short annotation for the base text. Ruby is used frequently along with Japanese and Chinese ideographs in order to provide alternate readings that have the same meanings. The Ruby Annotation recommendation will make Ruby readily available on the Web through XHTML markup.

Listing 11.14 demonstrates a simple example of a document that conforms to XHTML 1.1. The code for this listing, simplexhtml11.HTML, can be downloaded from the Sams Web site.

LISTING 11.16 Simple XHTML 1.1 Document

```
<?xml version="1.0" encoding="UTF-8"?>
<!DOCTYPE html PUBLIC "-//W3C//DTD XHTML 1.1//EN"
"http://www.w3.org/TR/xhtml11/DTD/xhtml11.dtd">
<html xmlns="http://www.w3.org/1999/xhtml" xml:lang="en" >
<head>
<title>A Simple XHTML 1.1 Document</title>
</head>
<body>
<p>This document valid according to the XHTML 1.1 DTD.</p>
</body>
</html>
```

This listing is very similar to the ones you saw earlier in the section on XHTML 1.0. The main difference is that the Document Type Declaration references the XHTML 1.1 DTD. Of course, the XHTML 1.1 DTD defines a stricter set of validation standards. Notice also that the XML declaration is included. This is not strictly required but is always highly recommended.

Now, let's delve a bit further into XHTML modularization.

Modularization of XHTML

The Web is becoming more and more pervasive. It is creeping into almost every aspect of our lives. The Web is on our cellular phones, handheld devices, automobiles, and televisions. Soon it will be on our appliances. HTML has become the content language that is most used by vendors developing new Web-enabled devices. However, the splintering of HTML into different supported features across different vendors, combined with the introduction of new extensions and the mingling of data structure and presentation, has rendered HTML less than optimal for this purpose.

XHTML 1.0 was introduced in order to reformulate HTML 4 into an XML application. This reformulation allows vendors to tap in to the ever-expanding myriad of XML technologies. However, XHTML 1.0 still defines a pretty broad markup. It encompasses basically all of HTML 4. Simpler devices have little use for (or are totally incapable of using) much of what is available in XHTML 1.0. XHTML 1.0 is not necessarily cross-platform compatible in its Transitional and Frameset DTDs. XHTML 1.0 is an XML application, but it is not extensible.

The Modularization of XHTML makes XHTML extensible. XHTML has been broken down into abstract modules. Each module represents a building block that can be combined with other building blocks to create unique subsets of XHTML. This means that content developers and vendors can define new document types comprised only of the modules they require for their application or device. These new document types are still fully conforming subsets of XHTML because they are derived directly from combinations of XHTML modules.

To take this a step further, developers and vendors can actually create hybrid document types that define their own element structure and still reference XHTML modules. Developers and vendors can, in effect, create their own markup languages by combining elements that they define with modules from XHTML.

Note

An excellent reference/example for creating hybrid document types has been put together by the W3C organization and can be found at `http://www.w3.org/MarkUp/Guide/xhtml-m12n-tutorial/`.

XHTML Is Separated into Modules

XHTML 1.1 separates XHTML 1.0 into 20 different abstract modules. Table 11.1 shows the modules that XHTML has been broken into.

TABLE 11.1 XHTML 1.1 Modules

Module	*Contained Elements*
Structure Module	`body`, `head`, `html`, `title`
Text Module	`abbr`, `acronym`, `address`, `blockquote`, `br`, `cite`, `code`, `dfn`, `div`, `em`, `h1`, `h2`, `h3`, `h4`, `h5`, `h6`, `kbd`, `p`, `pre`, `q`, `samp`, `span`, `strong`, `var`
Hypertext Module	`A`
List Module	`dl`, `dt`, `dd`, `ol`, `ul`, `li`
Object Module	`object`, `param`
Presentation Module	`b`, `big`, `hr`, `I`, `small`, `sub`, `sup`, `tt`
Edit Module	`del`, `ins`
Bidirectional Text Module	`Bdo`
Forms Module	`button`, `fieldset`, `form`, `input`, `label`, `legend`, `select`, `optgroup`, `option`, `textarea`
Table Module	`caption`, `col`, `colgroup`, `table`, `tbody`, `td`, `tfoot`, `th`, `thead`, `tr`
Image Module	`Img`
Client-side Image Map Module	`area`, `map`
Server-side Image Map Module	Attribute `ismap` on `img`
Intrinsic Events Module	`Events` attributes
Meta-information Module	`Meta`
Scripting Module	`noscript`, `script`
Stylesheet Module	`style` element
Style Attribute Module *	`style` attribute
Link Module	`Link`
Base Module	`Base`
Ruby Module	`ruby`, `rbc`, `rb`, `rt`, `rp`

* *Marked as deprecated*

There is one additional module that has been added to the recommendation. The XHTML 1.1 DTD also uses the Ruby Annotation module. The Ruby Module and its contents have been added to the end of Table 11.1

Any XHTML 1.1 document that is validated against the XHTML 1.1 DTD will not be considered valid if it contains any element(s) not contained in one the modules listed in

Table 11.1 or in the Ruby Annotation Module. In the next section, we will expand on this by covering strict conformance with XHTML 1.1.

Strict Conformance Is Required

Strict conformance of a document with XHTML 1.1 requires absolute adherence to the following criteria:

- The document must conform to the definitions expressed in the XHTML 1.1 DTD. The XHTML 1.1 DTD may be referenced using the following Document Type Declaration:

```
<!DOCTYPE html PUBLIC "-//W3C//DTD XHTML 1.1//EN"
"http://www.w3.org/TR/xhtml11/DTD/xhtml11.dtd">
```

- The root element of the document must be `<html>`.
- The `<html>` element must designate the XHTML namespace using the `xmlns` attribute. The value of the attribute should always be `http://www.w3.org/1999/xhtml`.
- The Document Type Declaration must be made prior to the root element.

Now that we have covered the specifics of strict conformance, let's see exactly which of XHTML 1.0's features have been removed from XHTML 1.1.

Deprecated Features Have Been Removed

In XHTML 1.0, the `name` attribute of the `a`, `applet`, `form`, `frame`, `iframe`, `img`, and `map` elements was deprecated. In XHTML 1.1, this attribute has been completely removed.

In addition to removing the deprecated features from XHTML 1.0, XHTML 1.1 removes all the deprecated elements from HTML 4. The elements that were deprecated in HTML 4 are `applet`, `basefont`, `center`, `dir`, `font`, `isindex`, `menu`, `s`, `strike`, and `u`.

XHTML 1.1 attempts to make a clean break with much of the outdated features of HTML and moves to separate structure from presentation. This is getting us closer to the original intent of HTML. XHTML 1.1 will rely on style sheets for any special presentation formatting.

So far, we have covered XHTML 1.0, which reformulates HTML into an XML application, and we have seen the Modularization of XHTML in our coverage of XHTML 1.1. However, because XHTML 1.1 is virtually unsupported at this point, you might be wondering how alternative devices such as cellular phones and handheld devices are being supported currently. In the next section, you'll see how XHTML Basic was created in order to provide an easy, stripped-down, modularized version of XHTML 1.0 for alternative devices.

XHTML Basic

Based on the proposed recommendation (at the time) of the Modularization of XHTML, XHTML Basic became a W3C recommendation on December 19, 2000. XHTML Basic was based on a minimal set of XHTML modules in order to provide a subset of XHTML for the purpose of delivering XML-conforming content to alternative devices such as pagers, cellular phones, handheld devices, televisions, and so on. Most alternative devices are characterized by their limited processing power, bandwidth, and screen sizes. Therefore, a very streamlined markup is required in order to be able to provide content. There's just no room for any type of complex interpretation of detailed code, and XHTML Basic was designed specifically to fit this need.

Note

The official XHTML Basic recommendation can be found at `http://www.w3.org/TR/xhtml-basic/`.

First, we are going to cover the recent history behind creating XHTML-based markup for alternative devices. Then we will look at the supported HTML features found in XHTML Basic. Finally, we will go over the modules that make up the XHTML Basic document type.

XHTML for Alternative Devices

The two previously existing HTML subsets that are designed for alternative devices are Compact HTML (CHTML) and Wireless Markup Language (WML). Both of these markup languages have strengths and some weaknesses. CHTML is not a recognized standard and is not XML compliant. However, it does have expanded support of colors, animations, and other rich display features. WML is a standard that is recognized as part of the Wireless Application Protocol, as implemented by the WAP Forum.

Note

The WAP Forum is comprised of most of the world's big mobile-computing companies, including Nokia, Ericsson, Motorola, and Phone.com. The official WAP Forum Web site can be found at `http://www.wapforum.org/`.

WML is also an XML 1.0 application. This, of course, means that WML is well formed, may be validated, and is open to XML technology applications. However, WML is not extensible. Although WML is an XML 1.0 application, it is defined with a fixed set of tags and may not be expanded upon.

Even though WML and CHTML are competing languages, they do have several features in common. They both support basic text features, hyperlinks and links to documents, basic forms, basic tables, images, and meta-information. It was from these common features that XHTML Basic was started. Both representatives of CHTML and WML took part in the formulation of the XHTML Basic standard. Shortly after XHTML Basic was approved as a recommendation, the WAP Forum announced that it would be adopting XHTML Basic in its WAP 2.0 release. On July 31, 2001 the WAP Forum made its 2.0 specification public with WML reformulated as a modularized subset of XHTML. This means that WML is now fully XHTML (and XHTML Basic) compatible. The idea of XHTML for alternative devices is taking hold.

So, what XHTML features are actually supported in XHTML Basic? The next section covers this topic.

Supported XHTML Features

The first thing that should be noted here is that XHTML Basic is extensible. This is an important supported feature from the Modularization of XHTML. Even though very limited features are supported, it is possible for the XHTML Basic DTD to be expanded on by referencing other XHTML modules. For example, the Scripting Module could be referenced to extend XHTML Basic to support scripting for alternative devices that are powerful enough to allow script processing.

> **Note**
>
> The exact XHTML modules and all the supported elements that make up XHTML Basic will be listed in Table 11.2 in the next section, "The XHTML Basic Document."

Before going into the specifics of what is supported, let's take a quick look at what is not supported by XHTML Basic. The `style` element is not supported. This is because external style sheets are the only supported style method (because many devices may not support style sheets at all). The `script` and `noscript` elements are not supported. Many alternative devices have very limited processing power and attempting script processing is simply not practical or possible. Additionally, because many of these simple devices only display monospaced text, things like bidirectional text, boldfaced font, and other text extension elements are not supported.

There are quite a few things that are not supported! So, what is supported? Let's take a look at the supported items now.

Text Support

Basic text formatting features are supported in XHTML Basic. These include simple text-formatting markup such as paragraphs, breaks, lists, and headers. Listing 11.17 gives an example of a simple XHTML Basic document using text formatting. The code for this listing, `xhtmlbasic.HTML`, can be downloaded from the Sams Web site.

LISTING 11.17 Simple Text Formatting in XHTML Basic

```
<?xml version="1.0" encoding="UTF-8"?>
<!DOCTYPE html PUBLIC "-//W3C//DTD XHTML Basic 1.0//EN"
"http://www.w3.org/TR/xhtml-basic/xhtml-basic10.dtd">
<html xmlns="http://www.w3.org/1999/xhtml" xml:lang="en" >
<head>
<title>XHTML Basic text features</title>
</head>
<body>
<h3>Some supported text features</h3>
<p>The following list represents several of the
supported XHTML Basic text formatting.</p>
<ul>
<li>Lists</li>
<li>Paragraphs</li>
<li>Headings</li>
</ul>
</body>
</html>
```

Listing 11.17 is a very simple listing that demonstrates a valid XHTML Basic document. The first line contains the XML declaration. Then the Document Type Declaration is included and contains a public reference to the XHTML Basic DTD. The markup within the document is limited to the `html` root element, `head`, `title`, `body`, `h3`, `p`, `ul`, and `li`. You will find that this is very typical of an XHTML Basic document. They are simple and streamlined, as their intended clients, alternative devices, require.

Hyperlinks and Linking to Documents

Both normal hyperlinks and the `link` element are supported in XHTML Basic. The hyperlink is the most basic and central feature of linking content on the Web. Therefore, it must be included.

The inclusion of the `link` element allows for the linking of external documents to the Web page. This is also an important feature because it allows style sheets to be linked to the document. In XHTML Basic external style sheets are the main media for providing formatting to documents. Listing 11.18 provides a simple example of using a `link` element and a hyperlink in an XHTML Basic document. The code for this listing, `basiclink.HTML` and `mystylesheet.css`, can be downloaded from the Sams Web site.

LISTING 11.18 Using Hyperlinks and the *link* Element in XHTML Basic

```
<?xml version="1.0" encoding="UTF-8"?>
<!DOCTYPE html PUBLIC "-//W3C//DTD XHTML Basic 1.0//EN"
"http://www.w3.org/TR/xhtml-basic/xhtml-basic10.dtd">
<html xmlns="http://www.w3.org/1999/xhtml" xml:lang="en" >
<head>
<title>XHTML Basic hyperlinks and link elements</title>
<link rel="stylesheet" type="text/css" href="mystylesheet.css" />
</head>
<body>
<h3>XML Tutorial Web Sites</h3>
<p>Here are some good XML Web sites</p>
<ul>
<li><a href="http://www.xml101.com">XML101.com</a></li>
<li><a href="http://www.w3schools.com">W3Schools.com</a></li>
<li><a href="http://www.xhtmlguru.com">XHTMLguru.com</a></li>
</ul>
</body>
</html>
```

In this listing, we use the same type of text formatting features used in Listing 11.18. However, now we have added a `link` element in order to link to an external style sheet, and we have added hyperlinks to three really good XML tutorial sites. Notice in the `link` element, because this is an empty element, that we have added "/" before the closing ">". This is consistent with the requirements of the XML 1.0 specification.

Table Support

Very basic tables are supported. Keep in mind that tables can be very difficult to display on small devices. Therefore, you should use tables sparingly. Limit their use to displaying information that requires a tabular presentation. Avoid using tables for the entire page layout. Listing 11.19 shows how a table might be used in XHTML Basic. The code for this listing, `basictables.HTML`, can be downloaded from the Sams Web site.

LISTING 11.19 Using Tables in XHTML Basic

```
<?xml version="1.0" encoding="UTF-8"?>
<!DOCTYPE html PUBLIC "-//W3C//DTD XHTML Basic 1.0//EN"
```

LISTING 11.19 continued

```
"http://www.w3.org/TR/xhtml-basic/xhtml-basic10.dtd">
<html xmlns="http://www.w3.org/1999/xhtml" xml:lang="en" >
<head>
<title>XHTML Basic tables</title>
<link rel="stylesheet" type="text/css" href="mystylesheet.css" />
</head>
<body>
<h3>Today's Weather Forecast</h3>
<table>
<tr><td>Current Temp</td><td>77 F</td></tr>
<tr><td>High Temp</td><td>85 F</td></tr>
<tr><td>Low Temp</td><td>72 F</td></tr>
</table>
</body>
</html>
```

This listing uses a very simple table structure to provide a layout for a weather forecast. Only the `table`, `tr`, and `td` elements are used. You really should try to keep it this simple due to the processing limitations and display limitations of the devices that will be loading your XHTML Basic pages.

> **Caution**
>
> XHTML Basic (the Basic Tables Module) does not support the nesting of tables. If you attempt to nest tables in your XHTML Basic pages, they will not be conforming (valid) documents.

Forms Support

Basic XHTML forms are supported. Similar to using tables in XHTML Basic, your use of forms should be very limited. File and image input types are not supported. Listing 11.20 shows a simple form in XHTML Basic. The code for this listing, `basicforms.HTML`, can be downloaded from the Sams Web site.

LISTING 11.20 Using Simple Forms in XHTML Basic

```
<?xml version="1.0" encoding="UTF-8"?>
<!DOCTYPE html PUBLIC "-//W3C//DTD XHTML Basic 1.0//EN"
"http://www.w3.org/TR/xhtml-basic/xhtml-basic10.dtd">
<html xmlns="http://www.w3.org/1999/xhtml" xml:lang="en" >
<head>
<title>XHTML Basic Forms</title>
</head>
```

LISTING 11.20 continued

```
<body>
<h3>Please enter your name and email address</h3>
<form method="post" action="anotherpage.asp">
Name: <input type="text" id="txtName" name="txtName" />
<br />
E-Mail Address: <input type="text" id="txtEMail" name="txtEMail" />
<br />
<input type="submit" value="Submit" />
</form>
</body>
</html>
```

In this example, you can see that the form is kept very simple. Only two types of `input` elements are used: `text` and `submit`. No special formatting is applied here either. In many cases, in a normal HTML page, a form will be laid out with a table. In XHTML Basic, as mentioned in the previous subsection, this would not be a good idea because it takes undue processing to render the table. Finally, notice that the empty elements are closed with the "/" symbol. At the end of this chapter, we will take a quick look at XForms. XForms will represent a more robust means for supporting user input on alternate devices in the future.

Style Sheet Support

The `style` element is not supported in XHTML Basic. The XHTML Basic recommendation supports linking to include external style sheets. This is preferred because an external style sheet can be linked to and used by clients that support style sheets and ignored by clients that do not support style sheets. In XHTML Basic, the `div` and `span` elements may be used along with the `class` attribute to hook style information to the structure of the document. Listing 11.18 showed you how to use a `link` element to include an external style sheet. Listing 11.21 demonstrates using the `div` element to apply a style from an external style sheet using a `class` attribute. The code for this listing, `basicdiv.HTML`, can be downloaded from the Sams Web site.

LISTING 11.21 Using `div` to Apply Styles in XHTML Basic

```
<?xml version="1.0" encoding="UTF-8"?>
<!DOCTYPE html PUBLIC "-//W3C//DTD XHTML Basic 1.0//EN"
"http://www.w3.org/TR/xhtml-basic/xhtml-basic10.dtd">
<html xmlns="http://www.w3.org/1999/xhtml" xml:lang="en" >
<head>
<title>XHTML Basic Style</title>
<link rel="stylesheet" type="text/css" href="mystylesheet.css" />
</head>
<body>
```

LISTING 11.21 continued

```
<div class="SectionTitle">Applying Style</div>
<div class="SectionContent">This is a demonstration of adding
style to XHTML Basic</div>
</body>
</html>
```

In this listing is a link to an external style sheet: `mystylesheet.css`. In the body of the document, two `div` elements are used to format the text. Each `div` element has a `class` attribute that is used to reference a class in the style sheet (for the purposes of this example, we are assuming that the style sheet contains the classes `SectionTitle` and `SectionContent`). The appropriate formatting for each class will be applied to the text contained within each `div` element. This is assuming that the device viewing this page supports style sheets; otherwise, default formatting for that device will be applied.

Images Support

Yes, images are supported in XHTML Basic, but before you get too excited, think about how slowly those huge, image-laden pages load on your desktop browser. Now think about how that page would load on your handheld! Personally, I would recommend not even using images in your XHTML Basic page. If you do decide to use images, use them very sparingly and make them very small. In its WAP 2.0 specification, the WAP Forum supports the use of *pictograms*, which are tiny images (such as the smiley faces you often see on bulletin boards on the Internet) that can be used to convey some additional meaning. According to the WAP forum, pictograms are supported in order to enhance communication across language boundaries.

Now that we have gone over the main features supported in XHTML Basic, let's take a look at the exact modules supported in XHTML Basic and the criteria used for XHTML Basic document conformance.

XHTML Basic Document

The XHTML Basic document type is composed of a set of XHTML modules. The included modules are listed in Table 11.2.

> **Note**
>
> These XHTML modules are defined in the Modularization of XHTML, which can be found at `http://www.w3.org/TR/2001/REC-xhtml-modularization-20010410/`.

TABLE 11.2 XHTML Basic Modules

Module	*Contained Elements*
Structure Module	`body`, `head`, `html`, `title`
Text Module	`abbr`, `acronym`, `address`, `blockquote`, `br`, `cite`, `code`, `dfn`, `div`, `em`, `h1`, `h2`, `h3`, `h4`, `h5`, `h6`, `kbd`, `p`, `pre`, `q`, `samp`, `span`, `strong`, `var`
Hypertext Module	`A`
List Module	`dl`, `dt`, `dd`, `ol`, `ul`, `li`
Basic Forms Module	`form`, `input`, `label`, `select`, `option`, `textarea`
Basic Tables Module	`caption`, `table`, `td`, `th`, `tr`
Image Module	`img`
Object Module	`object`, `param`
Metainformation Module	`meta`
Link Module	`link`
Base Module	`base`

A document that meets the requirements of XHTML Basic is a strictly conforming document. In order to be considered a strictly conforming document, the following criteria must be met:

- The document must validate against the XHTML Basic DTD, which is comprised of the modules listed in Table 11.2.
- The root element of the document must be `<html>`.
- The root element must have the `xmlns` attribute with a value of `http://www.w3.org/1999/xhtml`.
- There must be a Document Type Declaration that references the XHTML Basic DTD. The XHTML Basic DTD can be found in the following location:

```
<!DOCTYPE html PUBLIC "-//W3C//DTD XHTML Basic 1.0//EN"
"http://www.w3.org/TR/xhtml-basic/xhtml-basic10.dtd">
```

- The DTD subset must not be used to override any parameter entities in the DTD.

As long as these requirements are met, a document will be considered a conforming document.

So far in this chapter we have looked at some background on electronic data by covering DSSSL. Then we moved on to CSS and how they can be used to format HTML on the Web. We then looked at how CSS can be used to display XML on the Web. Next, we spent quite a bit of time covering what is going to be one of the centerpieces of data delivery and formatting on the Web in the future: XHTML. Before we wrap up this chapter, we are going to look at one more emerging XML technology: XForms. XForms is an XHTML-compatible application that is intended to replace HTML forms in the future.

Before going on to our coverage of XForms, however, let's revisit Coca Cabana Technology Shop and see how they applied XHTML Basic to their Web site.

Coca Cabana Technology Shop: Building a Web Site for the Future, Part II

During the course of their research on XHTML 1.0, the owners of Coca Cabana Technology Shop realized that XHTML Basic was becoming an important markup language for delivering content to alternative devices. In line with the idea that they should be on the cutting edge with their Web site, they decided that they needed to make a version of their site that would be easily accessible to alternative devices.

Because XHTML Basic is such a simplified language and considering the limited bandwidth and processing power that alternative devices possess, the Coca Cabana Technology Shop owners decided that they would simply put together an XHTML Basic page that advertises their specials. First, they reviewed the portion of their home page that lists their specials. This is shown in the file `Postxhtml_Home.html`, which you can download from the Sams Web site:

```
<!DOCTYPE html PUBLIC
"-//W3C//DTD XHTML 1.0 Transitional//EN"
"http://www.w3.org/TR/xhtml1/DTD/xhtml1-transitional.dtd">
<html>
<!-- Please note that this is only a partial listing of
Postxhtml_Home.html that was originally listed in part
one of this mini-case study
-->
...
<table bgcolor="BLACK" cellpadding="4" cellspacing="0" width="100%">
<tr>
<td bgcolor="TEAL">
<h2>Check out our lap top blowout!</h2>
<font size="4">Special selections from out award
winning laptop line!</font>
<ul>
<li><font size="3" color="MAROON">COCA PENTIUM III Laptop -
<b>$999.00</b></font></li>
<li><font size="3" color="MAROON">COCA PENTIUM II Laptop -
<b>$799.00</b></font></li>
<li><font size="3" color="MAROON">COCA PENTIUM Laptop -
<b>$599.00</b></font></li>
```

```
</ul>
</td>
</tr>
<tr>
<td bgcolor="KHAKI">
<h4>We have some other great specials that you should see!</h4>
<p>
<font size="3">The following low prices are always available at
Coca Cabana!</font>
</p>
<ul>
<li><font size="3" color="MAROON">COCA PENTIUM III DESKTOP -
<b>$1299.00</b></font></li>
<li><font size="3" color="MAROON">COCA PALM-TOP -
<b>$299.00</b></font></li>
<li><font size="3" color="MAROON">COCA 10 GIGABYTE HARDDRIVES -
<b>$109.00</b></font></li>
</ul>
</td>
</tr>
</table>
</td>
</tr>
</table>
…
</html>
```

One of the main things they realized after reviewing the specials listed on their home page was that some of the markup was no longer supported by XHTML Basic (such as the `<font>` elements). These would need to be removed. Another thing they noticed was that they used a nested table on their home page. Table nesting is not supported in XHTML Basic. Also, the Document Type Declaration would need to be updated to point to the XHTML Basic DTD. Taking these items into consideration, they came up with the following XHTML Basic document, `Xhtmlbasic_home.html` (which you can download from the Sams Web site):

```
<?xml version="1.0" encoding="UTF-8"?>
<!DOCTYPE html PUBLIC "-//W3C//DTD XHTML Basic 1.0//EN"
"http://www.w3.org/TR/xhtml-basic/xhtml-basic10.dtd">
<html xmlns="http://www.w3.org/1999/xhtml" xml:lang="en" >
<head>
<title>Welcome to Coca Cabana Technology Shop</title>
</head>
<body>
<h1>Welcome to Coca Cabana Technology Shop!</h1>
<h3>The best darn shop on the internet!</h3>
<h2>Check out our lap top blowout!</h2>
<ul>
```

```
<li>COCA PENTIUM III Laptop - <b>$999.00</b></li>
<li>COCA PENTIUM II Laptop - <b>$799.00</b></li>
<li>COCA PENTIUM Laptop - <b>$599.00</b></li>
</ul>
<h4>We have some other great specials that you should see!</h4>
<ul>
<li>COCA PENTIUM III DESKTOP - <b>$1299.00</b></li>
<li>COCA PALM-TOP - <b>$299.00</b></li>
<li>COCA 10 GIGABYTE HARDDRIVES - <b>$109.00</b></li>
</ul>
<h5>Thank you!</h5>
</body>
</html>
```

You can see from the XHTML Basic version of the Coca Cabana Technology Shop home page that it has been simplified a great deal. All unsupported elements and attributes have been removed. Also, all table structures have been removed. Removing the table structures makes the page easier to render for alternative devices(although, consider that this would probably still be too much to display on a cell phone—it is probably better suited for a handheld PC display). The owners of Coca Cabana Technology Shop can now proudly say that their Web site is accessible by alternative devices on the Internet.

An Overview of XForms

One of the primary uses of the Web by businesses is to gather data from the visitors to their Web sites. Forms provide a powerful mechanism for users to interact with Web sites. HTML forms, and more recently XHTML forms, have been used for this purpose. Currently, the W3C organization is working on the next generation of Web forms: XForms. On August 28, 2001 the XForms 1.0 working draft was released.

Note

The official XForms 1.0 working draft can be found at `http://www.w3.org/TR/xforms/`.

Even though XForms is only a working draft at this point, it is important to at least get a good general understanding of XForms. XForms is going to be one of the vital technologies that drives the Web in the future.

Introduction to XForms

Forms were first introduced to the Web in 1993. Since then, forms have grown to be a vital part of the user interaction with Web sites. More recently, HTML forms developers have been able to start restructuring their forms to be XHTML compliant. This makes forms XML 1.0 compatible; however, this does not really change any of the shortcomings of old HTML forms. HTML forms fail to provide any separation of presentation from data and logic. There are very limited facilities in HTML forms (short of doing a bunch of script programming, which is not even supported in all browsers) for tracking user input during form filling. XForms is being designed to solve these problems.

Next Generation of Web Forms

XForms provides the next logical step in the evolvement of forms on the Web. The XML standard dictates that structure be separated from presentation. XForms as an XML application accomplishes this.

Successor to HTML Forms

As stated, XForms is being designed to be the successor to HTML forms. Let's take a quick look at Listing 11.22, which shows a typical HTML form.

LISTING 11.22 Typical HTML Form

```
<html>
<head>
<title>Typical HTML Form</title>
</head>
<body>
<form action="processexample.asp" method="post">
<p>Please enter your personal information:</p>
<table>
<tr>
<td>Name:</td>
<td><input type="text" id="txtName" name="txtName"></td>
</tr>
<tr>
<td>Age:</td>
<td>
<select id="cboAge" name="cboAge">
<option>Less than 18</option>
<option>18 - 35</option>
<option>Over 35</option>
</select>
</td>
</tr>
```

LISTING 11.22 continued

```
<tr>
<td>Gender:</td>
<td>
<select id="cboGender" name="cboGender">
<option>Male</option>
<option>Female</option>
</select>
</td>
</tr>
<tr>
<td colspan="2"><input type="submit" value="Submit"></td>
</tr>
</table>
</form>
</body>
</html>
```

You can see that this is a regular HTML form typical of what you will find on most Web sites. Presentation of the form is combined with the purpose of the form. Additionally, there is no control over the data entered by the user prior to form submission. Figure 11.6 demonstrates how this form would be rendered in Internet Explorer 5.5.

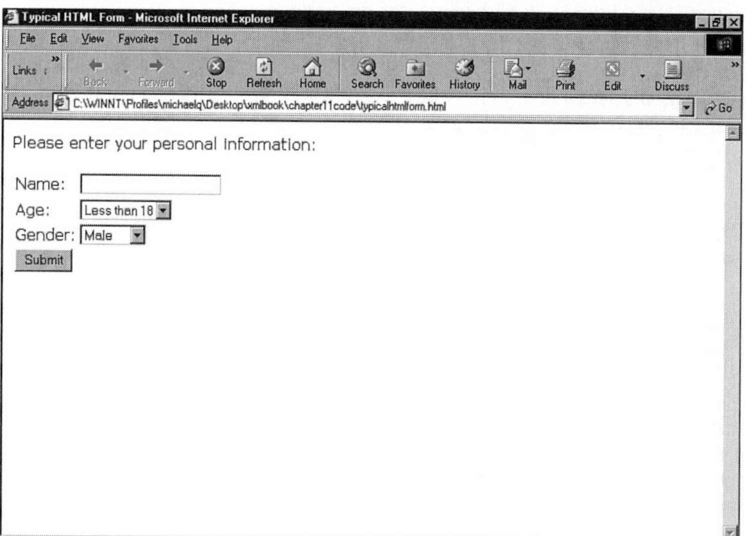

FIGURE 11.6 *Listing 11.22 rendered in Internet Explorer 5.5.*

In XForms, there are separate sections used to describe the purpose of the form and the presentation of the form. This provides a great advantage over HTML because XForms makes no requirement of how the form should be presented. This makes XForms very rich and flexible. XForms may just as easily be displayed using XHTML form controls as WML form controls. This is because XForms does not predetermine the type of control that must be used to collect the data. XForms merely dictates the type of data that should be collected. Listing 11.23 shows how the form in Listing 11.22 would be rewritten using XForms.

LISTING 11.23 XForms Web Form

```
<xform:input ref="txtName">
<xform:caption>Name</xform:caption>
</xform:input>
<xform:selectOne ref="cboAge">
<xform:caption>Age</xform:caption>
<xform:choices>
<xform:item value="Less than 18"><xform:caption>Less than 18
</xform:caption></xform:item>
<xform:item value="18 - 35"><xform:caption>18 - 35</xform:caption></xform:item>
<xform:item value="Over 35"><xform:caption>Over 35</xform:caption></xform:item>
</xform:choices>
</xform:selectOne>
<xform:selectOne ref="cboGender">
<xform:caption>Gender</xform:caption>
<xform:choices>
<xform:item value="Male"><xform:caption>Male</xform:caption></xform:item>
<xform:item value="Female"><xform:caption>Female</xform:caption></xform:item>
</xform:choices>
</xform:selectOne>
<xform:submit>
<xform:caption>Submit<xform:caption>
</xform:submit>
```

You can immediately see in this listing that the user interface is not hard-coded to use select boxes and text boxes, as is the case in the HTML form in Listing 11.22. The listing merely specifies that the data that should be gathered. Different clients can render the interface as appropriate. The `id` and `name` attributes have been replaced by the `ref` attribute, which is an XML ID type of attribute that uniquely identifies the XForms control.

Several other things should be noted about Listing 11.23. There is no `form` element. This is not required in XForms. Also, when the form is submitted, the data will be submitted as XML data. Data entered in this XForms form by a user might look like what appears in Listing 11.24.

LISTING 11.24 Submitted XForms Data

```
<Envelope>
<Body>
<txtName>Michael Qualls</txtName>
<cboAge>18 - 34</cboAge>
<cboGender>Male</cboGender>
</Body>
</Envelope>
```

XForms submits well-formed XML data. Once this data is received by the server, it may be validated against a DTD by an XML parser.

Comparing Listing 11.23 with Listing 11.22 shows the very clear divergence of XForms with HTML forms. Before we go on to look at the specific parts of XForms, let's take a quick look at the other ways that XForms differs from HTML forms.

Based on XML

XForms is, of course, an XML technology. This opens up XForms to using all the different permutations of XML on the Web, such as XHTML, WML, and XSL. It appears that XSL is going to be very important in relation to XForms. As stated, the XForms working draft makes no requirements for how forms should be presented. XSL will be able to be used to transform XForms documents to meet the presentation requirements of any clients using the form.

Platform Neutral

XForms is platform neutral. As an XML technology, no specific requirements are made in order to use XForms. XForms may be formatted for display as easily for handheld devices, as for cellular phones, and as for desktop computers (within reason, of course; the display limitations of some devices would have to be taken into account).

Works with XHTML

XForms may be displayed using XHTML. As a matter of fact, the W3C is working on a DTD that combines XHTML 1.1 with XForms. Once integrated, XForms will not only provide complete separation of purpose and presentation but will be completely modularized. At the time of this writing, the DTD has not been completed.

XForms: Three Layers

XForms forms technology is split into three layers. These layers are purpose, presentation, and data. We will now look at each of these layers and see how they relate to the overall design goals of XForms.

Purpose Layer

As has been stated several times previously, the purpose of the form and the presentation of the form are separated in XForms. But what does this actually mean? As you saw in Listing 11.22, the purpose and the presentation were combined in the HTML form. In that listing, HTML form elements were hard-coded into the page. The presentation was predetermined for any clients loading the page. When viewing Listing 11.23, you quickly see that there is no defined presentation. The actual main form elements, referenced from the XForms namespace, are `input` and `selectOne`. Both of these elements make their purpose very clear. The `input` element expects some input from the user, and `selectOne` allows the user to choose one of several defined options (the `choices` child element contains the options available). However, although the purpose of the form is clear, there is no indication of how the form should be displayed. It is left totally to the client to configure the presentation.

Presentation Layer

The presentation layer of XForms is actually dependent on the client loading the XForms document. An XForms document could be rendered in HTML, XHTML, or WML. XForms could even be configured for delivery to an audio device or a Braille device. This is one area where the presentation capabilities truly transcend the abilities of HTML forms. The handicapped accessibility to XForms documents is greatly enhanced over the abilities of more traditional forms of electronic data gathering.

Data Layer

It might seem odd to say that there is a data layer. The data is entered into the form fields that are rendered by the client device. It would seem that data should be part of the presentation layer, or it might seem appropriate to make data part of the purpose layer because the purpose layer defines the type of data being gathered. However, there is indeed a data layer to XForms. You see, although data might be entered into the form fields, there is another part of the XForms document that is actually tracking this data as it is being entered: the data layer. There is actually an XForms construct placed within the `head` element of the XForms document. Listing 11.25 shows what the data layer might look like for the XForms form from Listing 11.23.

LISTING 11.25 XForms Data Layer

```
<xform:xform>
<xform:submitinfo action="processexample.asp" method="post" />
<xform:instance>
<personalinfo >
<txtName />
```

LISTING 11.25 continued

```
<cboAge />
<cboGender />
</personalinfo>
</xform:instance>
</xform:xform>
```

Three elements in this listing have names that match the values of the `ref` attributes of the form elements defined in Listing 11.23. These elements serve as placeholders for the values entered into the form elements. These elements are wrapped inside of the wrapper element `personalinfo`. The wrapper element may be of the author's choosing. It is these placeholders that give us the ability to perform instance tracking of the values users input while filling out the form. This is the next factor that makes XForms superior to HTML forms. We will now take a look at instance data tracking.

Instance Data Tracking

Instance data tracking gives the XForms author greater control over user input. As stated previously, data submitted by an end user via an XForms document could be validated against a DTD on the server. Using instance data tracking, it's even possible to validate user input during form entry—prior to form submission. Sure, this type of validation is available in HTML if you want to write a bunch of JavaScript to track user entries, but then you have to rewrite the JavaScript to achieve compatibility for each of the Web browsers used to visit your Web site. No extra code is needed to write with XForms. This will be a feature included with the XForms parser.

Tracks Partially Filled Forms

Listing 11.25 demonstrated the data layer in XForms. In order to use the data layer to track form filling for partially filled forms, a namespace is created for the placeholder elements in the data layer. Listing 11.26 demonstrates how a namespace could be referenced for a XForms data layer in a document that is using a combination of XHTML and XForms to create the form.

Caution

Please be aware that the next several examples of XForms instance data are not technically valid. The Document Type Declaration references the XHTML 1.1 DTD, which does not yet include XForms elements. At time of writing the W3C XForms Working Group is still in the process of developing the DTD for combining XHTML and XForms.

LISTING 11.26 XForms Data Instance Tracking—Namespace

```
<?xml version="1.0" encoding="UTF-8"?>
<!DOCTYPE html PUBLIC "-//W3C//DTD XHTML 1.1//EN">
<html xmlns="http://www.w3.org/1999/xhtml"
xmlns:xform="http://www.w3.org/2001/08/xforms"
xmlns:info="http://mydomain.example.com/personalinformation"xml:lang="en">
<head>
<title>Referencing a namespace for instance data tracking</title>
<xform:xform>
<xform:submitinfo action="processexample.asp" method="post" />
<xform:instance>
<info:personalinfo >
<info:txtName />
<info:cboAge />
<info:cboGender />
</info:personalinfo>
</xform:instance>
</xform:xform>
</head>
…
</html>
```

Listing 11.26 is not a complete document. It only includes the declaration statements, the `head` element and its contents, and the root element, `html`. In the `html` element, three namespace are referenced. The first two are for the XHTML and XForms namespaces. The third is the namespace for placeholder elements. The namespace is referenced by attaching the prefix "`info:`" to the wrapper element, `personalinfo`, and to the placeholder elements, `txtName`, `cboAge`, and `cboGender`.

Now we are ready to start tracking partial form filling. We just need to connect the actual form elements to the placeholder elements.

Connects with Form Elements

In order to connect our form elements with the placeholder elements in the XForms data layer, we must reference the placeholder elements from the `ref` attribute of each of the form elements. Listing 11.27 shows how the placeholder elements are referenced.

LISTING 11.27 Connecting with Form Elements

```
<xform:input ref="info:personalinfo/info:txtName">
<xform:caption>Name</xform:caption>
</xform:input>
<xform:selectOne ref="info:personalinfo/info:cboAge">
<xform:caption>Age</xform:caption>
<xform:choices>
```

LISTING 11.27 continued

```
<xform:item value="Less than 18"><xform:caption>Less than 18
</xform:caption></xform:item>
<xform:item value="18 - 35"><xform:caption>18 - 35</xform:caption></xform:item>
<xform:item value="Over 35"><xform:caption>Over 35</xform:caption></xform:item>
</xform:choices>
</xform:selectOne>
<xform:selectOne ref="info:personalinfo/info:cboGender">
<xform:caption>Gender</xform:caption>
<xform:choices>
<xform:item value="Male"><xform:caption>Male</xform:caption></xform:item>
<xform:item value="Female"><xform:caption>Female</xform:caption></xform:item>
</xform:choices>
</xform:selectOne>
<xform:submit>
<xform:caption>Submit<xform:caption>
</xform:submit>
```

Listing 11.27 is very similar to Listing 11.23. However, there is one major difference: The value of the `ref` attribute for each form element has been updated to point to a placeholder element.

Now the form elements are connected with the placeholder elements. During the form-filling process, prior to form submission, the XForms parser will have access to the values that the end user is entering into the form elements.

Is XPath Based

In Listing 11.27, XPath statements were used as the values of the `ref` attributes to connect the form elements with the placeholder elements. This is another example of how using XForms, an XML application, will enable us to incorporate more XML technologies to complete our tasks.

Rich Data Type and Form Validation

XForms adopts the XML Schema data typing system. This enables the author to specify the type of data that is expected to be entered into the form fields. From this, the XForms parser can be used to enforce the proper data typing. A very simple example of how validation and data typing can be used is demonstrated in Listing 11.28.

LISTING 11.28 Data Typing and Form Validation

```
<xform:xform>
…
<xform:bind ref="info:personalinfo/info:txtName"
required="true"
```

LISTING 11.28 continued

```
type="xsd:string"
/>
<xform:bind ref="info:personalinfo/info:cboAge"
required="true"
type="xsd:string"
/>
<xform:bind ref="info:personalinfo/info:cgoGender"
required="true"
type="xsd:string"
/>
...
</xform:xform>
```

The XForms `bind` element is used to indicate that each of the form elements is required and that the data type will be a character string. The `ref` attribute, once again, has its value set to an XPath expression that points to the placeholder elements in the data layer. Now the XForms parser can make sure that the required elements are present and that the proper data types are entered.

Multiple Form Documents

Finally, it should be noted that XForms places no limitations on the number of forms per document. When multiple forms share the same document, multiple `xform` elements will be required. Each of the `xform` elements following the first `xform` element must have a unique ID type of attribute so that it can be referenced uniquely from other parts of the document. Additionally, when multiple `xform` elements are used, each of the form elements on the document will need an `IDREF` type of attribute, `xform`, along side its `ref` attribute so that it can be associated with the proper `xform` element. Listing 11.29 shows how an `xform` element would be referenced from a form element in a multiple-form document.

LISTING 11.29 `xform` Element Reference from a Form Element

```
<xform:input ref="txtEMailAddress" xform="contactinfo">
<xform:caption>Email Address</xform:caption>
</xform:input>
<xform:submit xform="contactinfo">
<xform:caption>Submit</xform:caption>
</xform:submit>
```

In this listing, a new attribute, `xform`, has been added to the XForms `input` element and `submit` element. The `xform` attribute is an `IDREF` that references the `ID` attribute for an `xform` element defined elsewhere in the document. This establishes a clear relationship between the form elements and the `xform` element in a multiple-form document.

Summary

In this chapter, we covered quite a bit of ground related to formatting and delivering XML on the Web. We covered items ranging from the history of data formatting, to cutting-edge XML formatting, to future cutting-edge XML formatting in the following topics:

- DSSSL was developed in 1996 to provide transformations and layout rendering for SGML, the wellspring of XML.
- Around the same time, the W3C organization released its recommendation for CSS in order to provide layout guidelines for HTML. This was done in an attempt to separate structure from presentation on the Web.
- CSS actually works better with XML to provide presentation. This is because XML closely resembles the original intent of HTML—it's a simple, straightforward delivery mechanism for content on the Internet that includes no special embedded formatting instructions.
- XHTML 1.0 is the next generation of HTML on the Web. XHTML 1.0 is actually HTML 4 reformulated as an XML application.
- In order to make XHTML truly extensible, the W3C organization modularized XHTML. This recommendation splits XHTML into separate abstract modules, each of which represents some specific functionality in XHTML.
- In order to provide XHTML-compliant content for alternative devices such as handheld computers, cellular phones, and pagers, XHTML Basic was created. XHTML Basic is a very simplified, modularized version of XHTML intended to be easily processed by the limited resources of these alternative devices.
- XForms is the next generation of forms on the Web. Fully XML 1.0 compatible, XForms will provide a separation of purpose and presentation. Also, XForms offers instance data tracking, rich data typing, and validation. Although only a working draft now, XForms when completed will offer a great improvement over current forms technology.

We also reviewed a mini case study in this chapter that demonstrated how XHTML 1.0 and XHTML Basic could be applied. Coca Cabana Technology Shop, a small technology company, applied XHTML 1.0 to their Web site so that they would be XML compliant and able to take advantage of future e-commerce advances. Also, they created an XHTML Basic version of their Web site so that customers using alternative devices would have easy access to the specials Coca Cabana Technology Shop advertises on the Internet.

CHAPTER 12

Interactive Graphical Visualizations with SVG

IN THIS CHAPTER

In the information age, we are growing to depend on being able to quickly and accurately identify relevant information and make good decisions based on it. Nowhere is this more true than on the Internet, where there is a veritable sea of information we are only beginning to harness the power of. An often quoted rule of thumb is that making a good decision involves 90 percent presentation and only 10 percent interpretation. One of the most effective ways of presenting information in a form that can be rapidly assimilated is graphically—thus the saying, "A picture is worth a thousand words." We are all familiar with the bitmap GIF and JPEG images, which are already pervasive across the Internet. Although bitmap graphics are powerful and appropriate for certain types of applications (in particular, photographs), they are not appropriate for many of the uses for which they are currently employed, due in part to primitive support for graphics in the early stages of the growth of the Web. Vector graphics, on the other hand, is a powerful, well-established type of graphical representation that is complementary to bitmap graphics. This chapter introduces, discusses, and demonstrates how a new vector graphics language called Scalable Vector Graphics (SVG) may be used to deliver powerful new interactive business applications. This chapter shows how SVG, an XML vector graphics standard, may be used to visualize and make sense of any type of XML content (for example, over the Web). Beyond simply showing the ability to apply SVG as an alternative graphics presentation language, this chapter shows how the power of SVG may be rapidly and easily applied to visualize and make sense of a sea of XML data in a variety of XML formats.

In this chapter you will learn

- The differences between bitmap and vector graphics and how they complement each other
- The SVG implementation of vector graphics, including the standard, structure, and elements
- How to develop interactive graphical applications that visualize XML data using SVG
- About future SVG developments

Vector Graphics to Complement Bitmap Graphics

This section presents bitmap and vector graphics and discusses how they complement each other to deliver comprehensive graphics capabilities across a variety of applications.

Bitmap Graphics

Bitmaps are made up of a rectangular matrix of pixels. These pixels are assigned integer values that determine their state. The state of a pixel determines its shade of gray or color in a grayscale or color bitmap image, respectively. For example, Figure 12.1 shows a simple bitmap with a diagonal line composed of a set of dark pixels.

FIGURE 12.1
Bitmap graphics example.

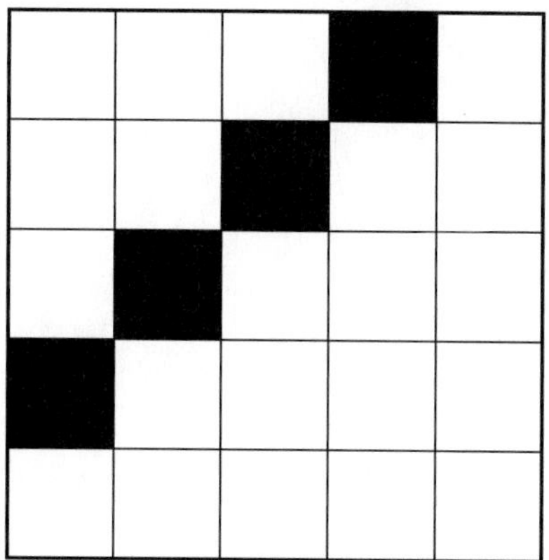

Color bitmap images may be composed of multiple component bitmap images for each of the primary colors—red, green and blue. Bitmap images are typically represented in binary format and are not readily editable with text editors. There is typically a high correlation between adjacent pixels in a bitmap image because nearby pixels typically have similar intensities or colors. Consequently, a large amount of redundancy exists in bitmap images, which typically makes bitmap images in their raw form inefficient graphical representations. Therefore, uncompressed bitmap images can be relatively large in terms of file sizes. Without degradation, "lossless" compression can typically achieve a compression factor of approximately two times. On the other hand, with degradation that is insignificant to a human viewer at a normal viewing distance, "lossy" compression typically achieves a compression factor of up to 10 times. Bitmap graphics on the Web include GIF and JPEG images for which there is broad support among Web browsers. GIF bitmap images support "lossless" compression, whereas JPEG bitmap images support both "lossless" and "lossy" compression. Photos lend themselves well to representation in the bitmap graphical format.

Vector Graphics

Aside from photographs, many other applications lend themselves better to an alternative graphical representation, called *vector graphics*. In this representation, graphics are composed of graphical primitives, including lines and text. For example, Figure 12.2 shows a simple vector graphics diagram with a diagonal line defined by its start and endpoints `(sx,sy)` and `(ex,ey)`, respectively. This is the vector diagram equivalent of the bitmap diagram shown previously in Figure 12.1.

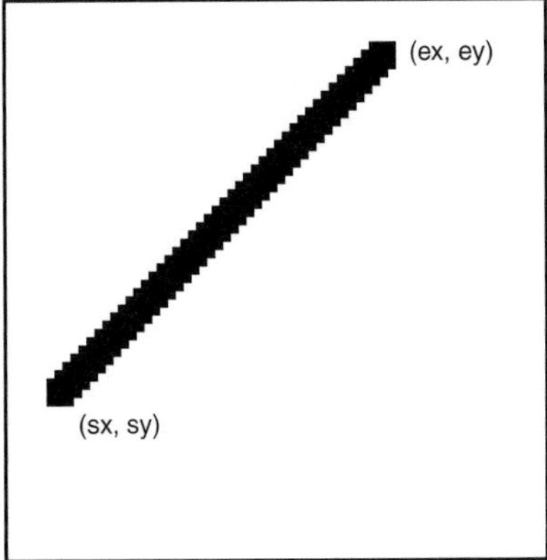

FIGURE 12.2
Vector graphics example.

Vector graphics information is kept symbolic rather than in a flat pixel format. Vector graphics files are typically represented in a text format, such as XML, and are therefore easily editable using a simple text editor. Because information is kept symbolic in vector graphics, these types of graphics may be easily manipulated. This makes them well suited to interactive applications. Examples of manipulations that are easily achievable with vector graphics include scaling, rotating, and panning. Furthermore, scaling does not result in pixelation (or "blockiness"), as is the case with bitmap images, when one zooms in too far. Instead of representing graphics in a flat, exhaustive format like bitmap graphics, which without compression has the same size regardless of content, vector graphics more efficiently represent graphics from graphical elements. Consequently, vector graphics may be very efficiently represented and are therefore easily stored and downloaded. In a Web application, this leads to faster client response time, less network and server load, and less storage requirement on the server side.

It is notoriously difficult to extract meaning from bitmap graphics. Vector graphics, on the other hand, contain primitive elements, including text from which meaning may easily be extracted in an automated fashion. This is particularly true of XML-based vector graphics formats, which not only leverage the power of vector graphics but also the standard well-formed structure of XML that enables them to be processed efficiently, robustly, and in an automated fashion. Bitmap graphics are difficult to reduce. In extracting subsections of bitmap graphics, users are typically forced to use simple rectangular cropping. On the other hand, you can easily reduce the vector graphic by identifying and extracting the primitives that constitute the desired subsection of the graphic.

Raster displays, such as those used for televisions and computer monitors, are made up of a matrix of pixels. Therefore, bitmap images may be readily displayed on them, in some cases with subsampling or supersampling to change their size. Vector graphics, on the other hand, don't define the pixels to be displayed directly but rather how to compute them from a set of primitive graphics elements, including lines and text, for example.

Complementary Bitmap and Vector Graphics

Photos are best represented in bitmap format, typically with either lossless or lossy compression. Most other types of graphics are best represented as vector graphics. However, due to the early Web browser support for bitmap formats (in particular, GIF and JPEG formats), most Web content does not make use of vector graphics, even in applications traditionally dominated by vector graphics (for example, mapping). A good example of this are the map Web sites, such as MapBlast (`www.mapblast.com`) and MapQuest (`www.mapquest.com`), that enable users to retrieve and view maps in bitmap format over the Internet. Due to the use of bitmap graphics, a simple manipulation such as zooming in on the map results in a new request to the server and a whole new image being downloaded. In contrast, the use of vector graphics in such applications would enable such transformations to be achieved on the client side without further server requests. One of the main reasons for the use of bitmap graphics in these types of applications is the lack of vector graphics formats widely supported on the client side, such as by the major Web browsers. SVG promises to address this issue by delivering the power of vector graphics in a widely supported standard XML-based format that may be easily applied to power a variety of interactive graphical applications on the Internet. Although the previous clear distinction drawn between bitmap and vector graphics is convenient from a conceptual standpoint, in practice they are not mutually exclusive. For example, vector graphics may be composed of graphical primitives, including embedded bitmap image subcomponents. On the Web and across all practical graphical applications, bitmap and vector graphics will be used together as well as in combination with each other in various hybrid forms.

SVG: An XML Standard for Vector Graphics

SVG is an XML-based vector graphics language for describing two-dimensional graphics. It builds on well-established vector graphics concepts that are also implemented in other popular vector formats, including Encapsulated Postscript (EPS) and Windows

Meta File (WMF). However, SVG differs from other vector graphics formats in that it is solidly based in XML standards. Aside from enabling the use of XML tools and technologies with SVG, this gives SVG the unique advantage of being particularly well suited for visualizing XML data. There are three basic types of graphic objects in the SVG language: vector graphic shapes (including lines, curves and shapes), images, and text. These objects may be grouped, styled, and transformed. SVG graphics can be dynamic, such as incorporating animation and interactivity, thus enabling them to change in response to user input. Being an XML-based language, an SVG vector graphics diagram is generally represented for visualization as a Document Object Model (DOM), although it may be processed using other methods, such as Simple API for XML (SAX). This DOM may be manipulated with scripting to change its presentation and make it interactive. Conversely, SVG elements may trap user input events, including `onmouseover` and `onclick` events, and then make scripting callbacks in response to the se events. SVG graphics may be embedded in Web pages to create dynamic, interactive vector graphic visualizations for Web applications, and they may also be printed in documents formatted with XSL-formatted objects.

The SVG Standard

The SVG standard is overseen by the W3C (`www.w3.org`). The first draft of the specification was released in February 1999. The latest W3C recommendation for the SVG 1.0 specification was released September 2001. The MIME content type for SVG is image/svg+xml. SVG has wide industry support, both in terms of its development and the provision of tools, APIs, and content. It is based on well-established, proven vector graphics techniques but differs from its predecessors in that it is both well formed and valid XML. The XML DTD may be found at the W3C. A key area in which SVG is being applied is in Web pages, where it is rendered in a Web browser using a plug-in, the most popular of which is currently the Adobe SVG Viewer (`www.adobe.com`).

XML Technologies Related to SVG

Aside from simply providing another vector graphics format, SVG brings significant power to vector graphics in that it is an XML-based language. This enables users to leverage other XML standards in delivering and enhancing SVG vector graphics. This section briefly outlines various key XML technologies and how SVG relates to them:

- *Document Type Definition (DTD)*. SVG is valid XML and therefore has its own DTD that may be used to validate SVG documents. XML documents may be transformed into SVG for vector graphics visualizations. These XML documents may be validated with their own DTDs to ensure their validity prior to transformation into SVG.

- *eXtensible Markup Language (XML)*. XML documents may contain content and data that may be transformed into SVG vector graphics visualizations.
- *eXtensible Stylesheet Language Transformations (XSLT)*. XSL documents may be used to transform XML documents containing data into SVG documents that contain vector graphics visualizations of the XML data. This usage pattern is similar to the use of XSL in adding presentation information to XML for the generation of XHTML Web pages, except in the case of SVG, where the output of the transformation is an SVG document rather than an XHTML document.
- *eXtensible Hypertext Markup Language (XHTML)*. SVG documents may be embedded in XHTML to deliver Web pages with dynamic and interactive vector graphics.
- *Cascading Style Sheets (CSS)*. SVG vector graphics may incorporate styles, such as colors and fonts. It is often necessary to have consistent SVG styles across multiple SVG vector graphics—for example, on a business Web site with a well-defined look and feel for marketing its brand. To do this in a manageable way, it is desirable to consolidate style information in a central place referenced by all the SVG diagrams. CSS may be used to consolidate style information that may then be referenced from and incorporated into SVG vector graphics diagrams.
- *ECMAScript and JavaScript*. SVG vector graphics may be dynamic and interactive. To define dynamic and interactive behavior of SVG diagrams, it is necessary to provide executable logic. This is conveniently done in the form of scripts (ECMAScript and JavaScript) that are associated with the SVG vector graphics diagrams.
- *XSL Formatting Objects (XSL-FO)*. In addition to XSLT, the other component of XSL is XSL-FO, which adds precise formatting information to XML documents (for example, for printing). These diagrams may incorporate embedded SVG vector graphics diagrams.
- *Synchronized Multimedia Integration Language (SMIL)*. Pronounced *smile*, this XML language enables simple authoring of interactive audiovisual presentations that may incorporate SVG vector graphics diagrams.

Creating an Interactive Graphical Visualization

This section shows you how SVG goes beyond being just another vector graphics language in that it provides a powerful tool to automatically visualize any XML data. This tool provides a powerful new "window" that may be used to reveal the meaning of the data. Given the structure and meaning of an XML data source, this section shows how XML tools may be used to automatically generate SVG visualizations that are dynamic, interactive, and may be embedded in Web pages or formatted as documents for printing. To illustrate the concepts presented here, we use a loan calculation example. The meaning of this example is most concisely presented in the formula

```
m = p * ( i / ( 1 - ( 1 + i )^( -t )))
```

where

- `m` is the monthly payment dollar amount on the loan.
- `p` is the principal dollar amount of the loan.
- `i` is the monthly interest rate on the loan, which is the same as the annual interest rate divided by 12.
- `t` is the term of the loan in months, which is the same as the term of the loan in years multiplied by 12.

Given `p`, `i` and `t`, we can calculate `m` and the monthly payments over the term of the loan. For each monthly payment over the term of the loan, we can compute first the interest and then the principal components of the payment using the formulas

```
mi = b * i
mp = m - mi
```

where

- `mi` is the interest component of the current monthly payment on the loan.
- `b` is the previous month's principal outstanding balance of the loan.
- `i` is the monthly interest rate, as defined previously.
- `mp` is the principal component of the current monthly payment on the loan.

Given an XML data set that defines a loan, our task in this example will be to create an SVG visualization that enables users to easily see the principal balance of the loan at any point over the loan's duration. Later in this chapter, you'll see how interactive behavior may be added to the SVG visualization that enables the user to determine for any monthly payment the outstanding principal as well as the interest and principal components of the monthly payment. You'll also see how the SVG visualization may be further enhanced to give the user the power to experiment with different "what-if" scenarios to compare loan performances for different loan interest rates.

This example was chosen because it is meaningful and minimal, yet sufficient to illustrate the presented concepts. The same principles may be easily applied to generate either alternative SVG visualizations of the same data or visualizations of completely different data. Note also that the presentation capabilities of SVG in terms of visual effects go way beyond what is feasible to cover in this chapter. Near the end of this chapter, some excellent URL references are given that you are encouraged to use as starting points to further investigate some of the more advanced capabilities of SVG.

After a brief definition of the XML loan data structure, an XML document is presented for a sample loan. We then prototype an SVG visualization of this data manually and present the resulting SVG. The style information in this visualization is then abstracted out into a separate document using CSS. The source XML data and corresponding simplified SVG visualization are then used to define the source and target, respectively, in order to develop an XSL transformation that may be used subsequently to automatically visualize any XML loan. You'll see how to embed the SVG visualization in Web pages and enhance it with interactive behavior. Finally, you'll learn how to embed a visualization in a XSL-FO document (for example, for printing) .

Defining the Content DTD

The DTD that defines the valid structure of any XML loan document is shown in Listing 12.1. The root of the document is a `loan` element that has attributes to define the principal, the term in months, interest rate, and optionally the monthly payment (because this can be derived from the former three attributes) of the loan. This root element contains a `payment` child element for each monthly payment on the loan. Each `payment` element contains attributes that define the index of the monthly payment over the lifetime of the loan, the principal and interest components of the payment, as well as the outstanding principal on the loan at the point of that payment.

LISTING 12.1 Loan.dtd—Sample Loan DTD

```
<?xml version='1.0' encoding='UTF-8' ?>

<!ELEMENT loan (payment+)>
<!ATTLIST loan  principal      CDATA  #REQUIRED
                termInMonths   CDATA  #REQUIRED
                interestRate   CDATA  #REQUIRED
                monthlyPayment CDATA  #IMPLIED >

<!ELEMENT payment EMPTY>
<!ATTLIST payment  monthIndex           CDATA  #REQUIRED
                   principalPayment     CDATA  #REQUIRED
                   interestPayment      CDATA  #REQUIRED
                   principalOutstanding CDATA  #REQUIRED >
```

Creating the XML Content

Listing 12.2 shows a sample XML loan document that is valid according to the DTD in Listing 12.1. Because we created this sample XML loan document manually, we intentionally simplified our task by making the term of the loan short—three months. Given the principal, the term in months, and interest rate key loan criteria, we used the formulas presented previously to compute the derived values in the document, including the monthly payment amount and payment data points over the lifetime of the loan.

Listing 12.2 `3MonthLoan.xml`--Sample Loan XML (Three Month)

```
<?xml version="1.0" encoding="UTF-8"?>
<!DOCTYPE loan SYSTEM "Loan.dtd">

<loan principal="10000.00" termInMonths="3" interestRate="30"
➥monthlyPayment="3501.37">
  <payment monthIndex="0" principalOutstanding="10000.00"
➥principalPayment="0.00" interestPayment="0.00"/>
  <payment monthIndex="1" principalOutstanding="6748.63"
➥principalPayment="3251.37" interestPayment="250.00"/>
  <payment monthIndex="2" principalOutstanding="3415.97"
➥principalPayment="3332.66" interestPayment="168.72"/>
  <payment monthIndex="3" principalOutstanding="0.00"
➥principalPayment="3415.97" interestPayment="85.40"/>
</loan>
```

Creating an SVG Content Presentation Prototype

Given the sample XML loan document in Listing 12.2, the next step is to create a sample SVG visualization of this loan. Although given a thorough knowledge of SVG it is possible to create such a visualization manually, in practice the fastest and easiest way to create such a visualization is to use a WYSIWYG (What You See Is What You Get) SVG editor, such as JASC WebDraw (`www.jasc.com`). The XML document created using such a tool may then be fine-tuned by hand to get the exact desired result. The coordinate system used by SVG is shown in Figure 12.3. Note, in particular, the orientation of the y axis so that a y coordinate of zero is at the "top" of the coordinate system and increases downwards. The default units of this coordinate system, when no units are specified, are pixels (px). SVG does, however, enable coordinates to be explicitly specified in a variety of other units, including inches (in), millimeters (mm), and centimeters (cm). The unit of a given measurement or coordinate can be specified explicitly by appending the associated two-letter suffix to the number.

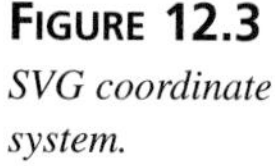

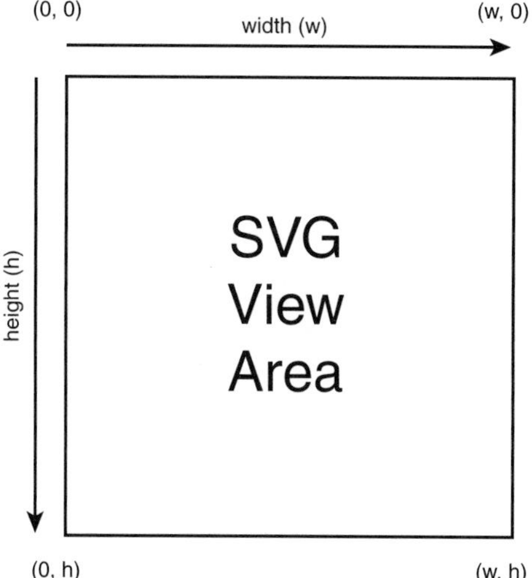

FIGURE 12.3
SVG coordinate system.

Listing 12.3 shows the prototype SVG document created for the XML loan document shown in Listing 12.2 using JASC WebDraw editor (`www.jasc.com`). You are encouraged to download and install WebDraw and then load the SVG in Listing 12.3 to get a hands-on feeling for editing SVG.

LISTING 12.3 *3MonthLoan.svg*—Sample Loan SVG

```
<?xml version="1.0" standalone="no"?>
<!DOCTYPE svg PUBLIC "-//W3C//DTD SVG 1.0//EN"
➥"http://www.w3.org/TR/2001/REC-SVG-20010904/DTD/svg10.dtd">
<svg width="485" height="290">
  <rect x="0" y="0" width="485" height="290" stroke="rgb(0,0,0)"
➥stroke-width="1" fill="none"/>

  <rect x="68.5" y="11.7" width="384" height="224" stroke="rgb(0,0,0)"
➥stroke-width="3" fill="none"/>

  <line x1="67" y1="58.8" x2="451" y2="58.8" fill="none" stroke="rgb(0,0,0)"
➥stroke-width="1" stroke-opacity="0.25"/>
  <line x1="67" y1="103.6" x2="451" y2="103.6" fill="none" stroke="rgb(0,0,0)"
➥stroke-width="1" stroke-opacity="0.25"/>
  <line x1="67" y1="148.4" x2="451" y2="148.4" fill="none" stroke="rgb(0,0,0)"
➥stroke-width="1" stroke-opacity="0.25"/>
  <line x1="67" y1="193.2" x2="451" y2="193.2" fill="none" stroke="rgb(0,0,0)"
➥stroke-width="1" stroke-opacity="0.25"/>
  <line x1="143.8" y1="14" x2="143.8" y2="238" fill="none" stroke="rgb(0,0,0)"
➥stroke-width="1" stroke-opacity="0.25"/>
```

LISTING 12.3 continued

```
  <line x1="220.6" y1="14" x2="220.6" y2="238" fill="none" stroke="rgb(0,0,0)"
➥stroke-width="1" stroke-opacity="0.25"/>
  <line x1="297.4" y1="14" x2="297.4" y2="238" fill="none" stroke="rgb(0,0,0)"
➥stroke-width="1" stroke-opacity="0.25"/>
  <line x1="374.2" y1="14" x2="374.2" y2="238" fill="none" stroke="rgb(0,0,0)"
➥stroke-width="1" stroke-opacity="0.25"/>

  <text x="10px" y="155px" transform="rotate(-90) translate(-220,-115)"
➥fill="rgb(0,0,0)" font-family="Arial" font-size="24">Principal Dollars</text>
  <text x="227.08px" y="283.289px" fill="rgb(0,0,0)" font-size="24"
➥font-family="Arial">Month</text>
  <text x="67px" y="258.072px" fill="rgb(0,0,0)" font-family="Arial"
➥font-size="12">0</text>
  <text x="55px" y="238px" fill="rgb(0,0,0)" text-anchor="end"
➥font-family="Arial" font-size="12">0.00</text>
  <text x="451px" y="258.072px" fill="rgb(0,0,0)" font-family="Arial"
➥font-size="12">3</text>
  <text x="55px" y="14px" fill="rgb(0,0,0)" text-anchor="end"
➥font-family="Arial" font-size="12">10000.00</text>

  <polyline fill="none" stroke="rgb(255,0,0)" stroke-width="2"
➥points="68.5,11.7 196.5,85.87 324.5,160.53 452.5,235.7"/>

  <circle cx="68.5" cy="11.7" r="4" fill="rgb(255,0,0)" stroke="rgb(0,0,0)"
➥stroke-width="1"/>
  <circle cx="196.5" cy="85.87" r="4" fill="rgb(255,0,0)" stroke="rgb(0,0,0)"
➥stroke-width="1"/>
  <circle cx="324.5" cy="160.53" r="4" fill="rgb(255,0,0)" stroke="rgb(0,0,0)"
➥stroke-width="1"/>
  <circle cx="452.5" cy="235.7" r="4" fill="rgb(255,0,0)" stroke="rgb(0,0,0)"
➥stroke-width="1"/>
</svg>
```

Figure 12.4 shows a screenshot of the SVG loan prototype diagram that appears in Listing 12.3. Key aspects of this SVG prototype are discussed subsequently.

The `svg` root element shown below contains the entire vector graphics diagram and defines its width and height in pixels.

```
<svg width="485" height="290">
```

The first child `rect` element shown below defines the bounding box or border of the SVG diagram. This box is defined by its top-left corner `x` and `y` coordinates and its `width` and `height`, all in pixels. The `stroke` of the rectangle indicates the color of the rectangle outline, which in this case is black (red=0, blue=0, green=0), whereas `stroke-width` indicates its line width, again in pixels. Because this is an outline of the diagram, `fill` is set to `none`, making the rectangle transparent.

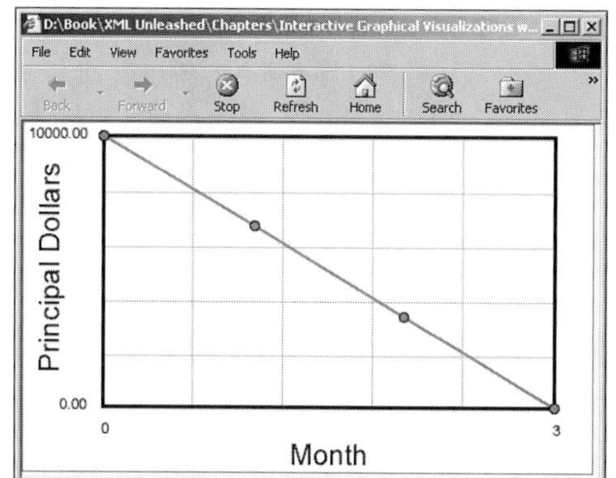

FIGURE 12.4
Sample loan SVG view.


```
<rect x="0" y="0" width="485" height="290" stroke="rgb(0,0,0)"
➥stroke-width="1" fill="none"/>
```

The second child `rect` element listed below defines a similar transparent rectangle with a black border that's 3 pixels in width, only this time the rectangle is serving as the bounding box of the plot *within* the SVG view area, rather than the border for the SVG view area, as before.

```
<rect x="68.5" y="11.7" width="384" height="224" stroke="rgb(0,0,0)"
➥stroke-width="3" fill="none"/>
```

The plot has a gray grid of lines as a background. The following `line` child element defines one of those lines. The other lines of the matrix are defined similarly. Note that the line is defined by its start coordinates, `x1` and `y1`, together with its end coordinates, `x2` and `y2`. The `fill`, `stroke`, and `stroke-width` attributes define the style of the line in the same way as for the rectangles defined previously. The `stroke-opacity` attribute defines the opacity of the line, which is a number between `0.0` for invisible and `1.0` for opaque (the default). Because we want the lines to be faded in the background of the plot in this case, we set the `stroke-opacity` to `0.25`.

```
<line x1="67" y1="58.8" x2="451" y2="58.8" fill="none" stroke="rgb(0,0,0)"
➥stroke-width="1" stroke-opacity="0.25"/>
```

The text labels for the axes' titles and values are specified with the `text` child elements, the first of which is shown next. Others are defined similarly. Each `text` element has a set of attributes that determines the positioning and style of the label, whereas its `text` child element specifies the actual text for the label. Note that the text positioning is specified using the bottom-left x and y coordinates of the label. The `transform` element is optionally specified to change the appearance of the text in some way. In this case, the `transform` element serves to rotate the text label 90 degrees counterclockwise so that it reads upwards for the vertical axis of the plot and then translate the rotated text to move it into position near the vertical axis of the plot.

```
<text x="10px" y="155px" transform="rotate(-90) translate(-220,-115)"
➥fill="rgb(0,0,0)" font-family="Arial" font-size="24">Principal Dollars</text>
```

The polyline child element shown below specifies a multisegment line in the vector diagram. The endpoints of the line segments making up this polyline child element are specified using the points attribute of this element. These points are x, y coordinates in sequence, moving along the polyline segment from start to end. Note that this polyline child element could also be represented as a set of line elements; however, this would be much more verbose and slower to render for complex datasets.

```
<polyline fill="none" stroke="rgb(255,0,0)" stroke-width="2"
➥points="68.5,11.7 196.5,85.87 324.5,160.53 452.5,235.7"/>
```

The data points of the plot that appear along the polyline are represented using circle child elements. Each circle is specified by its center coordinates, cx and cy, together with its radius, r. The fill, stroke, and stroke-width attributes define the style of the circle in the same manner as for the rectangles discussed previously. Note that the circles in this case are opaque and red in color. The first data point circle child element is shown here (others are defined similarly) :

```
<circle cx="68.5" cy="11.7" r="4" fill="rgb(255,0,0)" stroke="rgb(0,0,0)"
➥stroke-width="1"/>
```

SVG with Style Using CSS

From Listing 12.3, you can see that different vector graphics elements within the SVG document share the same style attributes. This includes, for example, line elements for the plot grid, text elements to label the plot axes, and circle elements for the plot data points. Although it is valid to produce an SVG document as in Listing 12.3, in practice it can lead to increased costs and errors due to the fact that if someone needs to make a change to a style, multiple elements need to be edited. For example, if someone wanted to change the style of the circle elements used for the data points in the plot, he would have to edit each circle element in the SVG document. This problem is compounded by the fact that content repositories, such as Web sites, often have a consistent style applied across them. This means that if someone wanted to make a change to the style of SVG diagrams embedded in the content, he would not only have to visit multiple elements within each document, as outlined earlier, but also multiple documents across the repository. Fortunately, CSS provides a way to centralize this style information so that it can be shared both across elements within an SVG document as well as across different SVG documents. Using CSS, it is possible to make global style changes across documents in a repository by simply editing one attribute value in a central CSS document. This central CSS document is referenced by each SVG document and is used by the SVG viewer at runtime to render the SVG document with the styles in the CSS document. Listing 12.4 shows the sample SVG loan document from Listing 12.3, only this time with CSS applied.

LISTING 12.4 `3MonthLoan_WithCss.svg`—Sample Loan SVG with CSS

```
<?xml version="1.0" standalone="no"?>
<!DOCTYPE svg PUBLIC "-//W3C//DTD SVG 1.0//EN"
➥"http://www.w3.org/TR/2001/REC-SVG-20010904/DTD/svg10.dtd">
<?xml-stylesheet href="Loan.css" type="text/css"?>
<svg width="485" height="290">
  <rect x="0" y="0" width="485" height="290" class="border"/>

  <rect x="68.5" y="11.7" width="384" height="224" class="plotbox"/>

  <line x1="67" y1="58.8" x2="451" y2="58.8" class="axisvalue"/>
  <line x1="67" y1="103.6" x2="451" y2="103.6" class="axisvalue"/>
  <line x1="67" y1="148.4" x2="451" y2="148.4" class="axisvalue"/>
  <line x1="67" y1="193.2" x2="451" y2="193.2" class="axisvalue"/>
  <line x1="143.8" y1="14" x2="143.8" y2="238" class="axisvalue"/>
  <line x1="220.6" y1="14" x2="220.6" y2="238" class="axisvalue"/>
  <line x1="297.4" y1="14" x2="297.4" y2="238" class="axisvalue"/>
  <line x1="374.2" y1="14" x2="374.2" y2="238" class="axisvalue"/>

  <text x="10px" y="155px" transform="rotate(-90) translate(-220,-115)"
➥class="axis">Principal Dollars</text>
  <text x="227.08px" y="283.289px" class="axis">Month</text>
  <text x="67px" y="258.072px" class="axisvalue">0</text>
  <text x="55px" y="238px" class="axisvalue" text-anchor="end">0.00</text>
  <text x="451px" y="258.072px" class="axisvalue">3</text>
  <text x="55px" y="14px" class="axisvalue" text-anchor="end">10000.00</text>

  <polyline class="data" points="68.5,11.7 196.5,85.87 324.5,160.53
➥452.5,235.7"/>

  <circle cx="68.5" cy="11.7" r="4" class="datapoint"/>
  <circle cx="196.5" cy="85.87" r="4" class="datapoint"/>
  <circle cx="324.5" cy="160.53" r="4" class="datapoint"/>
  <circle cx="452.5" cy="235.7" r="4" class="datapoint"/>
</svg>
```

The following line in the SVG document in Listing 12.4 references the CSS style sheet on which it depends:

```
<?xml-stylesheet href="Loan.css" type="text/css"?>
```

Listing 12.5 shows the CSS document to which the SVG document in Listing 12.4 refers. This CSS document contains style information used to render the SVG document in Listing 12.4. At the top of the SVG document in Listing 12.4, the following line appears:

```
<?xml-stylesheet href="Loan.css" type="text/css"?>
```

This line references the CSS document in Listing 12.5 and is used by the SVG viewer at runtime to locate the CSS document with the required style information.

Various elements throughout the SVG document in Listing 12.4 make use of the style information in the CSS style sheet in Listing 12.5 using the `class` attribute, for example, as shown for the first SVG `rect` element:

```
<rect x="0" y="0" width="485" height="290" class="border"/>
```

LISTING 12.5 `Loan.css`—Sample Loan CSS

```
rect.border
   {
   stroke:rgb(0,0,0);
   stroke-width:1;
   fill:none;
   }

rect.plotbox
   {
   stroke:rgb(0,0,0);
   stroke-width:3;
   fill:none;
   }

line.axisvalue
   {
   fill:none;
   stroke:rgb(0,0,0);
   stroke-width:1;
   stroke-opacity:0.25;
   }

text.axis
   {
   font-size:24;
   font-family:Arial;
   fill:rgb(0,0,0);
   }

text.axisvalue
   {
```

LISTING 12.5 continued

```
    font-size:12;
    font-family:Arial;
    fill:rgb(0,0,0);
    }

circle.datapoint
    {
    fill:rgb(255,0,0);
    stroke:rgb(0,0,0);
    stroke-width:1;
    }

circle.analysisDatapoint
    {
    fill:rgb(255,255,0);
    stroke:rgb(0,0,0);
    stroke-width:1;
    }

polyline.data
    {
    fill:none;
    stroke:rgb(255,0,0);
    stroke-width:2;
    }

polyline.analysisData
    {
    fill:none;
    stroke:rgb(255,255,0);
    stroke-width:2;
    }
```

Elements in the SVG document in Listing 12.4 refer to style information in Listing 12.5. For example, `circle` elements for plot data points in Listing 12.4 have `class` attributes with values that are used to determine the specific style of information to use from the CSS document in Listing 12.5. In the case of the `circle` elements, the `class` attribute has the value `datapoint`. This value is used together with the type of the element (in this case, `circle`) to create the key `circle.datapoint`, which is then used to locate the required style information in the CSS document in Listing 12.5, as shown here:

```
circle.datapoint
    {
    fill:rgb(255,0,0);
    stroke:rgb(0,0,0);
    stroke-width:1;
    }
```

Notice the similarity of this information to the style information embedded in each of the `circle` elements in the SVG document in Listing 12.3, as shown for the following `circle` elements in bold:

```
<circle cx="68.5" cy="11.7" r="4" fill="rgb(255,0,0)" stroke="rgb(0,0,0)"
➥stroke-width="1"/>
```

For more information on CSS in general, see Chapter 11 "Formatting XML for the Web."

Defining the XSL to Transform XML Content to SVG Presentation

One of the advantages SVG has over other vector graphics formats is that it is both a well-formed and valid XML format. This enables developers to leverage many other powerful XML technologies to automatically create SVG visualizations. XSL is one such technology that enables the creation of style sheets that, together with an XSLT engine, automatically transform XML data into SVG presentations. Listing 12.6 shows an XSL style sheet that transforms any XML loan document into an SVG loan visualization in the format shown in Listing 12.4. Furthermore, the SVG result of this transformation also uses the CSS document shown in Listing 12.5, so not only are we able to generate SVG visualizations automatically for all loans, but we can do so with consistent and easily maintainable styles. Following Listing 12.6, some of the XSL aspects specifically related to SVG are discussed. For more information on XSL, see Chapter 9, "Transforming XML."

Tip

Before attempting to define XSL style sheets to transform XML data into SVG presentations, it is a good idea that you first create some sample XML data and a corresponding SVG presentation. Together, these serve as a source and target for which the mapping may easily be defined. This is the reason the prototype XML loan document in Listing 12.2 and the corresponding SVG visualization in Listing 12.4 were created before attempting to define the XSL style sheet in Listing 12.6. Although given the XML loan data structure, it is theoretically possible to define an XSL style sheet without first defining the prototype target SVG visualization; however, in practice, this approach generally proves too difficult and error prone.

LISTING 12.6 Loan.xsl—Sample Loan XSL

```
<?xml version="1.0"?>
<xsl:stylesheet version="1.0" xmlns:xsl="http://www.w3.org/1999/XSL/Transform"
➥xmlns:xlink="http://www.w3.org/1999/xlink">

  <xsl:output method="xml" version="1.0" encoding="iso-8859-1" indent="yes"
➥doctype-public="-//W3C//DTD SVG 1.0//EN" doctype-system=
➥"http://www.w3.org/TR/2001/REC-SVG-20010904/DTD/svg10.dtd"/>

  <xsl:param name="plotTopLeftX">68.5</xsl:param>
  <xsl:param name="plotTopLeftY">11.7</xsl:param>
  <xsl:param name="plotWidth">384</xsl:param>
  <xsl:param name="plotHeight">224</xsl:param>

  <xsl:template match="/loan">

    <xsl:processing-instruction name="xml-stylesheet">href="Loan.css"
➥type="text/css"</xsl:processing-instruction>

    <svg width="485" height="290">
      <rect x="0" y="0" width="485" height="290" class="border"/>

      <rect x="68.5" y="11.7" width="384" height="224" class="plotbox"/>

      <line x1="67" y1="58.8" x2="451" y2="58.8" class="axisvalue"/>
      <line x1="67" y1="103.6" x2="451" y2="103.6" class="axisvalue"/>
      <line x1="67" y1="148.4" x2="451" y2="148.4" class="axisvalue"/>
      <line x1="67" y1="193.2" x2="451" y2="193.2" class="axisvalue"/>
      <line x1="143.8" y1="14" x2="143.8" y2="238" class="axisvalue"/>
      <line x1="220.6" y1="14" x2="220.6" y2="238" class="axisvalue"/>
      <line x1="297.4" y1="14" x2="297.4" y2="238" class="axisvalue"/>
      <line x1="374.2" y1="14" x2="374.2" y2="238" class="axisvalue"/>

      <text x="10px" y="155px" transform="rotate(-90) translate(-220,-115)"
➥class="axis">Principal Dollars</text>
      <text x="227.08px" y="283.289px" class="axis">Month</text>
      <text x="67px" y="258.072px" class="axisvalue">0</text>
      <text x="55px" y="238px" text-anchor="end" class="axisvalue">0.00</text>
      <text x="451px" y="258.072px" class="axisvalue"><xsl:value-of
➥select="@termInMonths"/></text>
      <text x="55px" y="14px" text-anchor="end" class="axisvalue"><xsl:value-of
➥select="@principal"/></text>

      <polyline class="data">
        <xsl:attribute name="points">
          <xsl:for-each select="payment">
            <xsl:variable name="paymentX"><xsl:value-of select="( @monthIndex *
➥$plotWidth div ../@termInMonths ) + $plotTopLeftX"/></xsl:variable>
```

LISTING 12.6 continued

```
        <xsl:variable name="paymentY"><xsl:value-of select="$plotHeight * (1 -
➥( @principalOutstanding div ../@principal )) + $plotTopLeftY"/>
➥</xsl:variable>

          <xsl:value-of select="$paymentX"/>,<xsl:value-of
➥select="$paymentY"/><xsl:text> </xsl:text>
        </xsl:for-each>
      </xsl:attribute>
    </polyline>

    <xsl:for-each select="payment">
      <xsl:variable name="paymentX"><xsl:value-of select="( @monthIndex *
➥$plotWidth div ../@termInMonths ) + $plotTopLeftX"/></xsl:variable>
      <xsl:variable name="paymentY"><xsl:value-of select="$plotHeight * (1 -
➥( @principalOutstanding div ../@principal )) + $plotTopLeftY"/>
➥</xsl:variable>

      <circle r="4" class="datapoint">
        <xsl:attribute name="cx"><xsl:value-of select="$paymentX"/>
➥</xsl:attribute>
        <xsl:attribute name="cy"><xsl:value-of select="$paymentY"/>
➥</xsl:attribute>
      </circle>
    </xsl:for-each>
  </svg>
 </xsl:template>
</xsl:stylesheet>
```

To simplify the maintenance of the XSL, it is a good idea to put any constants at the top of the document in the form of `xsl:param` variables, as shown here:

```
<xsl:param name="plotTopLeftX">68.5</xsl:param>
```

These constants are referred to from `xsl:value-of` elements elsewhere in the XSL. For example, the following code shows how the value of the parameter named `plotTopLeftX` is used in a formula to compute the value of a new XSL variable named `paymentX`:

```
<xsl:variable name="paymentX"><xsl:value-of select="( @monthIndex *
➥$plotWidth div ../@termInMonths ) + $plotTopLeftX"/></xsl:variable>
```

The CSS document in Listing 12.5 is referenced from the SVG result of the transformation using the following `xsl:processing-instruction`:

```
<xsl:processing-instruction name="xml-stylesheet">href="Loan.css"
➥type="text/css"</xsl:processing-instruction>
```

For each payment in the XML loan document being transformed with the XSL in Listing 12.6, the following code adds a point to the `polyline` element used to visualize the loan plot:

```
<polyline class="data">
  <xsl:attribute name="points">
    <xsl:for-each select="payment">
      <xsl:variable name="paymentX"><xsl:value-of select="( @monthIndex *
➥$plotWidth div ../@termInMonths ) + $plotTopLeftX"/></xsl:variable>
     <xsl:variable name="paymentY"><xsl:value-of select="$plotHeight * (1 -
➥( @principalOutstanding div ../@principal )) + $plotTopLeftY"/>
➥</xsl:variable>

      <xsl:value-of select="$paymentX"/>,<xsl:value-of
➥select="$paymentY"/><xsl:text> </xsl:text>
    </xsl:for-each>
  </xsl:attribute>
</polyline>
```

The formulas in this XSL use the location and dimensions of the loan plot, as defined in the `xsl:param` elements earlier in the XSL document, together with a knowledge of the SVG coordinate system shown in Figure 12.3 to determine the x and y coordinates of each payment point and to store them in the variables `paymentX` and `paymentY`. The values of these variables are then output to the value of the `points` attribute of the SVG `polyline` element.

Similarly, the following XSL code creates the SVG `circle` elements that represent each of the payment data points in the loan plot:

```
<xsl:for-each select="payment">
  <xsl:variable name="paymentX"><xsl:value-of select="( @monthIndex *
➥$plotWidth div ../@termInMonths ) + $plotTopLeftX"/></xsl:variable>
  <xsl:variable name="paymentY"><xsl:value-of select="$plotHeight * (1 -
➥( @principalOutstanding div ../@principal )) + $plotTopLeftY"/>
➥</xsl:variable>

  <circle r="4" class="datapoint">
    <xsl:attribute name="cx"><xsl:value-of select="$paymentX"/>
➥</xsl:attribute>
    <xsl:attribute name="cy"><xsl:value-of select="$paymentY"/>
➥</xsl:attribute>
  </circle>
</xsl:for-each>
```

Powering Web Pages with SVG

This section discusses how to embed SVG graphics in Web pages and then how to make these graphics interactive in order to deliver interactive graphical visualizations over the Web.

Embedding SVG Graphics in Web Pages

Listing 12.7 shows an XHTML Web page with an embedded SVG diagram. To view SVG diagrams, including the one in this example, in your Web browser you must first install a plug-in capable of rendering SVG—for example, the SVG Viewer from Adobe at www.adobe.com/svg/viewer/install.

LISTING 12.7 3MonthLoan.htm—Sample Loan XHTML

```
<html>
  <head>
    <title>Loan Visualization</title>
  </head>
  <body>
    <embed src="3MonthLoan_WithCss.svg" width="485" height="290"
➥type="image/svg-xml" border="1"
➥pluginspage="http://www.adobe.com/svg/viewer/install/main.html" />
  </body>
</html>
```

The key element in this Web page is the `embed` element, shown here:

```
    <embed src="3MonthLoan_WithCss.svg" width="485" height="290"
➥type="image/svg-xml" border="1"
➥pluginspage="http://www.adobe.com/svg/viewer/install/main.html" />
```

The value of the `src` attribute of the `embed` element provides the URL for the SVG document to embed in the Web page. In this case, the SVG document is in the same directory on the Web content tree as the Web page in which it is embedded. The `width` and `height` attributes, on the other hand, define the dimensions of the SVG embedded diagram. The `type` attribute gives the MIME content type of the embedded SVG diagram (in this case, `image/svg-xml`). The SVG diagram has a border of 1 pixel, as defined by the `border` element. In the event that the Web browser viewing the Web page does not have the capability to view documents of type `image/svg-xml`, the `pluginspage` attribute defines the Web page on the Internet to which the Web browser user may go to get an appropriate plug-in to view the embedded SVG document. In this case, the user is directed to the Adobe Web site (`www.adobe.com`) to get the Adobe SVG Viewer Web browser plug-in.

Adding Interactive Behavior

Another key advantage of SVG over other vector graphics formats is the ability to add interactive behavior to SVG diagrams. This section looks at a small cross section of types of behavior that may be added to an SVG diagram to make it interactive, including those listed here:

- Scaling
- Panning
- Highlighting
- Descriptions
- Analysis

For each type of behavior, code snippets are given in this discussion. These snippets are additions to the various documents already presented in this section in order to give them the desired interactive behavior. The complete resulting documents created by adding all the interactive behavior discussed here may be downloaded from the Web site resource center for this book. Refer to these files to see how the code snippets in this section fit into the overall loan application. You may also load the file named `120MonthLoan_Advanced.htm` in your Web browser to try out the interactive behavior. The complete documents with all the interactive behavior discussed in this section include the following:

- `120MonthLoan.xml`. An XML loan document for a 120-month loan
- `Loan_Advanced.xsl`. An XSL style sheet used to transform an XML loan document to get an SVG visualization
- `120MonthLoan_Advanced.svg`. An SVG visualization of a 120-month loan
- `120MonthLoan_Advanced.htm`. An XHTML document with embedded SVG visualization of a 120-month loan suitable for delivery over the Web
- `120MonthLoan_Advanced.xsl`. An XSL-FO document with an embedded SVG visualization of a 120-month loan suitable for printing

Note

The advanced version of the XHTML contains elements that depend on the source XML. Therefore, it would be created dynamically from an XSL transformation, in the same manner as the creation of the SVG. In other words, viewing this XHTML Web page would result in two XSL transformations—the first for the XHTML document and the second for the SVG embedded within it. The XSL used to transform the source XML into the XHTML is a straightforward application of the same concepts applied in the transformation to get the SVG, as discussed in this chapter.

Scaling

Scaling changes the zoom factor of the diagram. This enables the user to either zoom in for a magnified look at a subset of the diagram or to zoom out for an overview of the entire diagram. It is useful to enable the user to progressively change the zoom factor by a fixed delta. To implement this, we first add a form with the following input fields to the XHTML document in Listing 12.7:

```
<input type="button" value=" - " onclick="scale( scaleFactor -
➥scaleFactorDelta )" />

<input type="button" value=" + " onclick="scale( scaleFactor +
➥scaleFactorDelta )" />
```

It is also useful to enable the user to change the zoom factor directly to an explicitly specified value, as shown here:

```
<input name="scaleFactorTextField" type="text" value="1.0" size="3" />
<input type="button" value="Ok" onclick="scale(
➥this.form.scaleFactorTextField.value )" />
```

These input fields catch the `onclick` event and make a JavaScript callback to the `scale` function in response. The value passed to the `scale` function is the new zoom factor, which is computed from two JavaScript variables also added to the same document and shown here:

```
var scaleFactor = 1.0;
var scaleFactorDelta = 0.1;
```

The `scaleFactor` variable holds the value of the current scale factor, whereas the `scaleFactorDelta` variable is the progressive change in the scale factor when the user is zooming in or out.

The `scale` function implements the interactive scaling behavior, as shown here:

```
function scale( newScaleFactor ) {
  scaleFactor = newScaleFactor;
  scaleFactorTextField.value = newScaleFactor;
  updateSvgLoanPlot();
}
```

This function updates the current scale factor and reflects that value in the text field in the XHTML GUI. It then updates the SVG diagram with a call to the following function:

```
function updateSvgLoanPlot() {
  svgLoanPlot.setAttribute( "transform", "scale(" + scaleFactor + ")
➥translate(" + plotX + "," + plotY + ")" );
}
```

This function sets an attribute named `transform` on an element in the SVG DOM to a value that contains a `scale` transformation with the new scale factor. This element corresponds to the single child "group" element, named `g`, in the SVG DOM, as shown here:

```
<svg height="290" width="485" xmlns:xlink="http://www.w3.org/1999/xlink">
  <g transform="scale(1.0) translate(0,0)" id="LoanPlot">
    ...
  </g>
</svg>
```

The `g` element groups all the vector graphics elements of the SVG loan plot. Therefore, applying a scale transformation to this element causes the scale factor to be applied to every element in the SVG diagram. The JavaScript variable `svgLoanPlot`, which corresponds to the SVG `g` element discussed previously, is initialized when the Web page is loaded, as shown here:

```
svgDoc = document.embeds[ 0 ].getSVGDocument();
svgLoanPlot = svgDoc.getElementById( "LoanPlot" );
```

Note that the ID of the `g` element is `LoanPlot`. Also, note how this is used to locate the element in the SVG DOM. This technique may be used to locate other elements in the DOM with different IDs as well. Figure 12.5 shows a screenshot of the SVG diagram with a scale factor of `0.25` applied, causing a reduction in the size of the diagram to one quarter its default size. It is also possible to scale subsections of the SVG diagram through other vector graphic element groupings. Note that the default scale factor is `1.0`, corresponding to no scaling. This type of interactive behavior is particularly important in SVG applications in the field of mapping. In these types of applications, the amount of detail visible in the diagram is changed according to the level of magnification of the diagram. For example, at the highest zoom factor, street names may not be shown because they would be too small to be legible anyway and would obscure other higher-level detail. For details of how to toggle the visibility of elements, see the upcoming subsection titled "Highlighting." Note that other transformations are possible, including rotations and translations, as discussed in the following subsection. For a complete list of possible transformations, see the SVG specification at `www.w3.org`.

Panning

Panning involves the movement of all or part of the SVG diagram up, down, left, or right (or some combination thereof). This type of interactive behavior is particularly useful in combination with scaling, discussed previously. For example, on an SVG diagram where the user has zoomed in for a detailed look at part of the diagram, panning may be used to "move around" in order to look in detail at different parts of the SVG diagram. The following button controls may be added to the XHTML shown in Listing 12.7 in order to enable the user to perform the panning:

```
<input type="button" value=" Up " onclick="pan( plotX, plotY - panDelta )" />
<input type="button" value=" Left " onclick="pan( plotX - panDelta, plotY )" />
<input type="button" value=" Zero " onclick="pan( 0, 0 )" />
<input type="button" value="Right" onclick="pan( plotX + panDelta, plotY )" />
<input type="button" value="Down" onclick="pan( plotX, plotY + panDelta )" />
```

FIGURE 12.5
Scaled loan visualization.

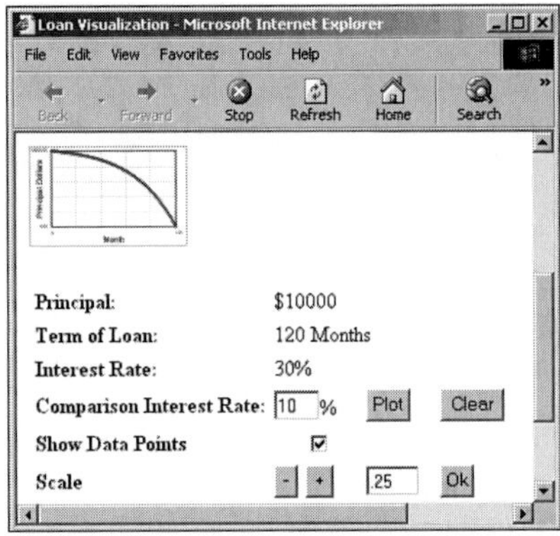

When the user clicks one of these buttons, the `onclick` event is caught and new x and y coordinates for the translation are computed from the three JavaScript variables shown here:

```
var plotX = 0;
var plotY = 0;
var panDelta = 25;
```

In this case, `plotX` and `plotY` values of `0` indicate no translation, and the SVG diagram is in its original position, where it first renders. The variable `panDelta` is the change in pixels applied to either the `plotX` or the `plotY` coordinate for each step that the user pans. Once the new values have been computed, a call is made to the JavaScript `pan` function, shown here, to update the SVG diagram:

```
function pan( newPlotX, newPlotY ) {
  plotX = newPlotX;
  plotY = newPlotY;
  updateSvgLoanPlot();
}
```

Once the `plotX` and `plotY` coordinates have been updated, a call is made to the `updateSvgLoanPlot` function, shown previously in the discussion on scaling behavior. This changes the transformation applied to the SVG diagram to include the desired panning. Figure 12.6 shows the SVG loan visualization with a scale factor of `1.75` applied, together with some panning, to show the first few data points of the plot.

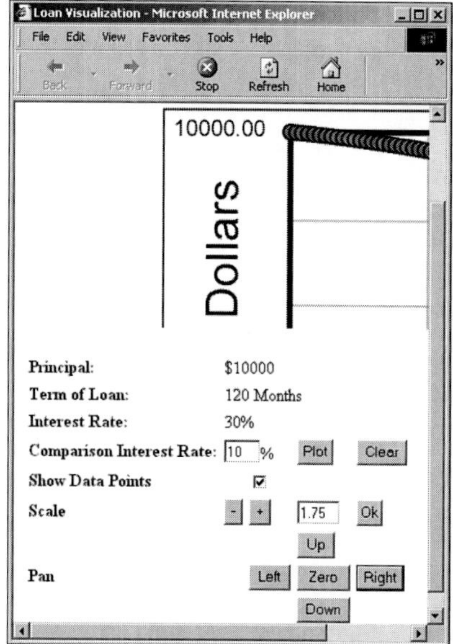

FIGURE 12.6
Scaled and panned loan visualization.

Highlighting

In this discussion, *highlighting behavior* means toggling the visibility of SVG vector graphics elements. In this example, we show how the circles representing the data points in the plot may be toggled on or off so that they are either visible or invisible. A checkbox may be added to the XHTML in Listing 12.7, as shown here, to enable users to toggle data points on or off:

```
<input type="checkbox" name="showDataPoints" value="on" checked="true"
➥onclick="setDataPointVisibility( this.form.showDataPoints.checked )" />
```

When the user either checks or unchecks this box, the `onclick` event is caught and the JavaScript function `setDataPointVisibility` is invoked:

```
function setDataPointVisibility( showDataPoints ) {
  var visibility = "hidden";
  if( showDataPoints ) {
    visibility = "visible";
  }

  for( var i = 0; i <= loanTermInMonths; ++i ) {
    svgPaymentDataPoint = svgDoc.getElementById( "Month" + i );
    svgPaymentDataPoint.setAttribute( "visibility", visibility );
  }
}
```

Just as the g (group) element was used in the previous discussions on scaling and panning, it can also be used for highlighting. Each of the data points represented by `circle` elements in the SVG may be contained by a g element, as shown here:

```
<g onmousedown="showPayment(0, 0.00, 0.00, 263.62, 10000.00 )">
  <circle class="datapoint" visibility="visible" r="4" id="Month0" cx="68.5"
➥cy="11.7"/>
</g>
```

The `setDataPointVisibility` function, shown previously, first determines whether the data points are being turned on or off and stores the result in the `visibility` variable. It then loops over each data point over the duration of the loan stored in the `loanTermInMonths` variable, which is initialized when the Web page is loaded (in this case, to the value `120`). For each data point `X`, it looks up the g element with the ID `MonthX`, as shown in the SVG for `Month0`. The function then sets the attribute named `visibility` on this g element to either `visible` or `hidden`, depending on whether the data points are being turned on or off, respectively. Figure 12.7 shows the SVG loan diagram with all the data points turned off. This is another good example of how the SVG DOM may be manipulated by JavaScript functions to provide interactive behavior. This type of interactive behavior is particularly useful in SVG diagrams that include the concept of layering (for example, maps where the user may want to either view or hide a certain set of features in a layer, depending on how she is using the SVG diagram) .

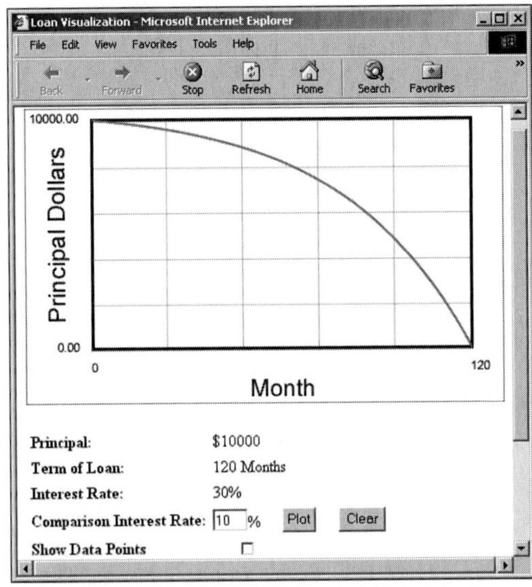

FIGURE 12.7
Loan visualization with data points off.

Descriptions

This type of interactive behavior involves the user selecting an element of the SVG diagram to view more detailed information. To illustrate this concept with our loan example, we will enable the user to select any loan payment data point on the plot to view details for that payment, including the index of the month, the principal and interest components of the payment, the total payment, and the balance of the outstanding principal at the point of the payment. In this case, the event of the user clicking a component of the SVG diagram is caught by the payment data point of the SVG diagram, as shown here:

```
<g onmousedown="showPayment(1, 13.62, 250.00, 263.62, 9986.38 )">
  <circle class="datapoint" visibility="visible" r="4" id="Month1" cx="71.7"
➥cy="12.0"/>
</g>
```

The g element enclosing the `circle` element used to represent the data point has an attribute, `onmousedown`, that traps a user click on the data point and calls the JavaScript `showPayment` function, shown here, in response:

```
function showPayment( month, principalPayment, interestPayment, totalPayment,
➥principalOutstanding ) {
  alert( "Month: " + month + "\n" + "Principal Payment: $" + principalPayment
➥+ "\n" + "Interest Payment: $" + interestPayment + "\n"
➥+ "Total Payment: $" + totalPayment + "\n"
➥+ "Principal Outstanding: $" + principalOutstanding );
}
```

This function is in the XHTML document shown in Listing 12.7, in which the SVG diagram is embedded. The arguments to this function are the values of the detailed information for the data point. This function simply creates a JavaScript alert to show the detailed information for the data point in a pop-up window, as shown in Figure 12.8.

This type of interactive behavior is very important in a broad range of visualizations for which there may be a vast amount of associated information, but displaying it all at once would lead to too much information for the user to assimilate. Enabling the user to interactively request the specific information he is interested in helps the SVG visualization stay clean and effective.

Analysis

In many interactive applications, the user is presented with information that she wishes to analyze (for example, by testing a few "what-if" scenarios and immediately seeing the effect). In our loan example, we illustrate this by enabling the user to specify an alternative interest rate for her loan and have the visualization plot a curve showing the performance of the loan with the new interest rate, together with the original plot for comparison. The first step in this interaction is to acquire the new interest rate from the user—for example, by adding the form input fields shown here to the XHTML document shown in Listing 12.7:

```
<input name="comparisonInterestRateTextField" type="text" value="10"
➥size="2" />%
<input type="button" value="Plot"
➥onclick="plot( comparisonInterestRateTextField.value )" />
<input type="button" value="Clear" onclick="clearPlot()" />
```

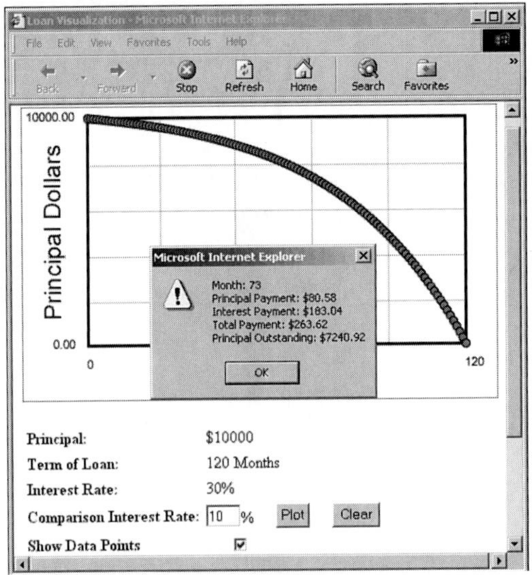

FIGURE 12.8
Loan visualization with an informational pop-up window.

The first input field, named `comparisonInterestRateTextField`, is the text field in which the user types the new interest rate she wishes to try. The next input field is a button labeled `Plot` that the user clicks to initiate the plotting of the loan performance for the new interest rate. Note that when the user selects this button, the form is not being submitted to a server. Rather, the `onclick` event for the button is caught and the JavaScript function named `plot`, which is embedded in the XHTML document containing the SVG diagram, is invoked with the value of the new test interest rate. The last input in the form is another button, labeled Clear, that enables the user to clear a "what-if" test case plot. Similarly, this button causes the JavaScript `clearPlot` function to be invoked. The `plot` function is shown here:

```
function plot( interestRate ) {
  var monthlyInterestRate = ( interestRate / 100.0 ) / 12.0;
  var monthlyPayment = round( principal * ( monthlyInterestRate / ( 1.0 -
➥Math.pow( 1.0 + monthlyInterestRate, -loanTermInMonths ) ) ) );
```

```
  var outstandingPrincipal = principal;
  var dataPoints = "";
  for( var i = 0; i <= loanTermInMonths; ++i ) {
    var interestPayment = 0.00;
    var principalPayment = 0.00;
    if( i > 0 ) {
      interestPayment = round( outstandingPrincipal * monthlyInterestRate );
      principalPayment = round( monthlyPayment - interestPayment );
    }
    outstandingPrincipal = outstandingPrincipal - principalPayment;

    testDataPointGroups[ i ].setAttribute(
      "onmousedown",
      "alert( '" +
      "Month: " + i + "\\n" +
      "Principal Payment: $" + principalPayment + "\\n" +
      "Interest Payment: $" + interestPayment + "\\n" +
      "Total Payment: $" + monthlyPayment + "\\n" +
      "Principal Outstanding: $" + round( outstandingPrincipal ) +
      "' )" );

    var cx = plotTopLeftX + ( i * ( plotWidth / loanTermInMonths ) );
    testDataPoints[ i ].setAttribute( "cx", cx );

    var cy = plotTopLeftY + ( plotHeight - ( plotHeight / principal ) *
➥outstandingPrincipal );
    testDataPoints[ i ].setAttribute( "cy", cy );

    testDataPoints[ i ].setAttribute( "visibility", "visible" );

    dataPoints += " " + cx + "," + cy;
  }
  testDataLine.setAttribute( "points", dataPoints );
  testDataLine.setAttribute( "visibility", "visible" );
}
```

The first step in this function is to compute the monthly interest rate and loan payment from the given annual interest rate using the formulas presented earlier in this chapter. For each month in the term of the loan, this function computes the principal, interest, and total monthly payments, rounded to the nearest cent, using the simple `round` function shown here:

```
function round( x ) {
  return Math.round( x * 100.0 ) / 100.0;
}
```

The detailed information for each loan payment is then set in the SVG DOM in order to show the loan performance for the new interest rate. In this case, the elements of the DOM that are affected are stored in the `testDataPointGroups` array, which is initialized when the Web page is first loaded, as shown here:

```
testDataLine = svgDoc.createElement( "polyline" );
testDataLine.setAttribute( "class", "analysisData" );
testDataLine.setAttribute( "visibility", "hidden" );
svgLoanPlot.appendChild( testDataLine );

for( var i = 0; i <= loanTermInMonths; ++i ) {
  var testDataPoint = svgDoc.createElement( "circle" );
  testDataPoint.setAttribute( "id", "TestMonth" + i );
  testDataPoint.setAttribute( "visibility", "hidden" );
  testDataPoint.setAttribute( "r", "4" );
  testDataPoint.setAttribute( "cx", "10" );
  testDataPoint.setAttribute( "cy", "10" );
  testDataPoint.setAttribute( "class", "analysisDatapoint" );

  var testDataPointGroup = svgDoc.createElement( "g" );
  testDataPointGroup.appendChild( testDataPoint );

  svgLoanPlot.appendChild( testDataPointGroup );

  testDataPoints[ i ] = testDataPoint;
  testDataPointGroups[ i ] = testDataPointGroup;
}
```

This initialization creates a new `polyline` element as well as a `g` element that encloses a `circle` element for each loan payment data point. The attributes that are set on these elements are similar to those for the current loan interest rate already discussed, with the important exception of the `visibility` attribute, which is set to a value of `hidden` to ensure that the elements of the test plot are not visible until the user tries a "what-if" scenario by specifying a new interest rate. Lastly, the new `polyline` and `g` elements are appended as children of the `svg` root element node in the DOM that is represented by the `svgLoanPlot` variable.

Note

Before elements of the SVG DOM may be modified to reflect changes in the SVG visualization required for interactive behavior, they first have to be located. This is achieved by obtaining a reference to the elements in the SVG DOM, such as by using the `getElementById` function discussed previously. Obtaining such references can be done either once during initialization of the Web page or each time the user does something interactive. Clearly the former is going to lead to an interactive visualization that is faster and more responsive because the logic does not have to hunt for the elements in the SVG DOM each time the user does something that requires a change. Storing references to key elements of the SVG DOM in JavaScript variables during initialization of the Web page—

including the svgLoanPlot variable for the root svg element and the testDataPointGroups and testDataLine variables for the elements representing the test loan plot—and thereafter modifying these elements through their JavaScript variable references leads to a significant performance enhancement over hunting for each of these in the SVG DOM each time a modification is required.

Given the initialization of our testDataLine and testDataPointGroups variables, as discussed earlier, the plot function listed previously modifies the attributes of these elements in order to show loan performance for any specified interest rate. In particular, the cx and cy attributes of the circle elements, representing the coordinates of the center of the circles, are modified to move the data points into the correct positions in the plot to reflect the new interest rate. The visibility attribute of each circle is also set to a value of visible to make its data point visible. Recall that the plot is composed not only of data points but also a multisegment line represented as a polyline element in the SVG DOM. Similarly, this element is created during initialization and is set during a call to the plot function to reflect loan performance for a new interest rate. In this case, it is the points and visibility attributes of the polyline element represented by the testDataLine variable that are set to show the new multisegment line in the correct location on the plot and make it visible, respectively.

To clear a test plot for a new interest rate, the user clicks the form button labeled Clear (presented previously). This results in a callback to the clearPlot JavaScript function listed here:

```
function clearPlot() {
  testDataLine.setAttribute( "visibility", "hidden" );
  for( var i = 0; i <= loanTermInMonths; ++i ) {
    testDataPoints[ i ].setAttribute( "visibility", "hidden" );
  }
}
```

This function simply sets the values of the visibility attributes of each of the test data point circles and the underlying multisegment lines to a value of hidden in order to make them invisible. Figure 12.9 shows an SVG loan visualization with a plot of our default 30-percent interest rate, together with a plot for a test interest rate of 10 percent. In this case, the user has clicked the test plot to get a pop-up window with detailed information on one of the data points, as discussed previously.

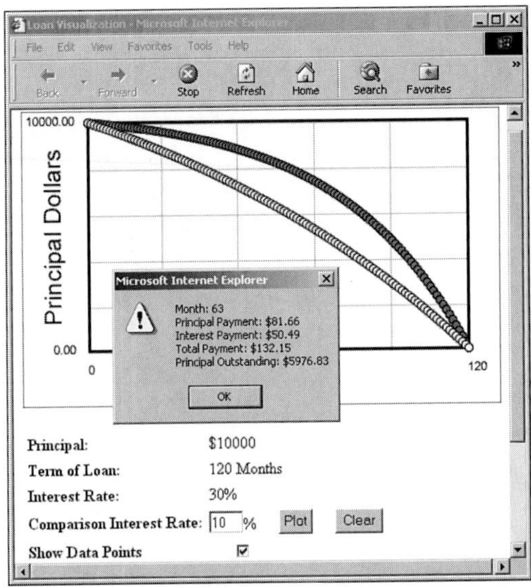

FIGURE 12.9
Loan visualization with a test data set plotted.

This important example shows that interactive SVG visualizations may be realized not only by modifying attributes on existing elements in the SVG DOM, as shown previously, but also by adding new elements to the SVG DOM, as shown here. In fact, it is also possible to delete elements of the SVG DOM, although doing this would have the same visible effect as making the element invisible, as discussed previously. This example also shows how the user may change the SVG visualization interactively in an arbitrary way in response to input to realize any kind of interactive behavior. This flexible yet simple-to-use capability paves the way for powerful, new interactive visualizations using SVG. The next few subsections outline some of the key advantages of using SVG to add visualizations to content.

The Benefits of Web Pages Powered by SVG

SVG enables powerful and compelling visualizations to be created. This enables Web pages to be more interactive and engaging for the user. Although in many cases it is possible to understand concepts through static information only, for many situations we learn more rapidly by manipulating items and viewing responses to our actions. Such situations indicate good potential target applications for interactive SVG visualizations.

Faster Client Response Time

Many Web applications today are made pseudo-interactive through the use of client/server interaction. In this case, when the user performs some action on a Web page, the Web browser sends a request to the Web server to get another Web page that reflects the changes associated with the user action. In practice, this approach results in unpredictable and frustrating application behavior, especially when the client/server interaction is occurring over a network without any guarantee of quality of service—a prime example of which is the Internet. In such cases, any user action is followed by a frustrating wait while the updated Web page is loaded. In the case of SVG, however, it is possible to realize true interactive behavior completely on the client side without any network requests to the server after the initial loading of the Web page containing the visualization. In practice, this leads to significantly faster client response time and more user-friendly interactive content.

Reduced Server Load

Because content that is interactive completely on the client side (without server interaction beyond initial loading) does not require subsequent server requests to deliver interactive behavior, there is less demand on the server. This enables both improved performance for existing clients and improved ability to scale to service more clients.

Improved User Privacy

Many useful interactive applications involve the user entering and manipulating sensitive information (for example, financial information associated with a loan).

Where applications are pseudo-interactive, as defined earlier, this information needs to be exchanged with the server. Where the network connection between the client Web browser and target Web server is secured with HTTPS, some assurance is given to users that their sensitive information will not be compromised while in transit over the public, untrusted Internet. However, in many of these applications, this assurance may not be enough to engage users because they may not even want their sensitive information to propagate to the target Web server, where they fear it will be compromised or used against them (for marketing purposes, for example).

SVG, however, enables completely client-side interactive behavior that allows users to enter and interact with their sensitive information totally on the client side with no need to share this information with the server. This enables users to gain a better understanding of their options and make decisions before opting to share their sensitive information, such as in the case of a loan application.

SVG-To-Go with XSL-FO

HTML has excelled in delivering content reliably to a variety of Web browsers with different capabilities. It has achieved this to a large extent by carefully restricting the syntax of the HTML language from specifying exactly how content should be displayed. However, in some applications, such as printing apps, it is desirable to be able to specify exactly how content should be formatted. XSL-FO complements XSLT, as discussed earlier in this chapter, in enabling the specification of the exact layout of content. An XSL-FO document may be used, for example, both to transform content into other formats, such as PDF, and to print content. Figure 12.10 shows a simple flow diagram of how XSL-FO documents are created and used.

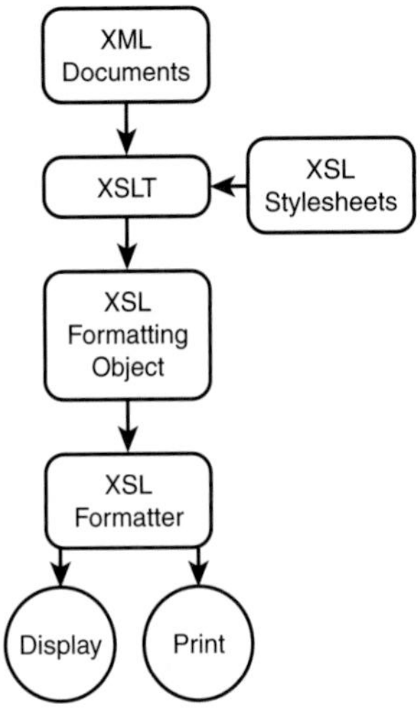

FIGURE 12.10
XSL-FO flow diagram.

SVG diagrams may be embedded in XSL-FO diagrams. For example, Listing 12.8 shows an XSL-FO document with an embedded loan visualization.

LISTING 12.8 `120MonthLoan_Advanced.xsl` – Loan Visualization Document with XSL-FO

```
<?xml version="1.0" encoding="UTF-8"?>

<xsl:stylesheet version="1.0" xmlns:xsl="http://www.w3.org/1999/XSL/Transform">
  <xsl:template match="/">

    <fo:root xmlns:fo="http://www.w3.org/1999/XSL/Format">
      <fo:layout-master-set>
        <fo:simple-page-master master-name="Loan" page-width="8.5in"
➥page-height="11.0in" margin="1.6in">
          <fo:region-body/>
        </fo:simple-page-master>
      </fo:layout-master-set>
```

LISTING 12.8 continued

```
      <fo:page-sequence master-name="Loan">
        <fo:flow flow-name="xsl-region-body">

          <fo:block font-size="24pt" space-after="0.25in">
            Loan
          </fo:block>

          <fo:block space-after="0.25in">
            This loan is for $<xsl:value-of select="loan/@principal"/> over a
➥period of <xsl:value-of select="loan/@termInMonths"/> months. The
➥interest rate is <xsl:value-of select="loan/@interestRate"/>% and the
➥monthly payment is $<xsl:value-of select="loan/@monthlyPayment"/>.
          </fo:block>

          <fo:block>
            <fo:external-graphic content-width="485px" content-height="290px"
➥src="120MonthLoan_Advanced.svg"/>
          </fo:block>

        </fo:flow>
      </fo:page-sequence>
    </fo:root>
  </xsl:template>
</xsl:stylesheet>
```

This XSL-FO example document, itself, contains information about the loan and, as in the case of an SVG loan visualization, may also be generated using an XSLT transformation, where the source is the XML loan document. The key code from this document that involves embedding the SVG visualization is the `fo:external-graphic` element, which specifies the width and height of the SVG diagram in pixels, as well as the source file, where the SVG document for the diagram may be found in the `content-width`, `content-height`, and `src` attributes. For more information on XSL-FO, see Chapter 9. Figure 12.11 shows the XSL-FO document in Listing 12.8 displayed using the Antenna House XSL Formatter (`www.antennahouse.com`). Once this tool is started, you may load both the XML document named `120MonthLoan.xml` and the XML style sheet named `120MonthLoan_Advanced.xsl` and then invoke the Run Formatter option of the tool to view the results shown in Figure 12.11. Using this tool, the XSL-FO document may be printed. Alternatively, this XSL-FO document may be converted into PDF format using the Apache FOP engine (`xml.apache.org/fop`) .

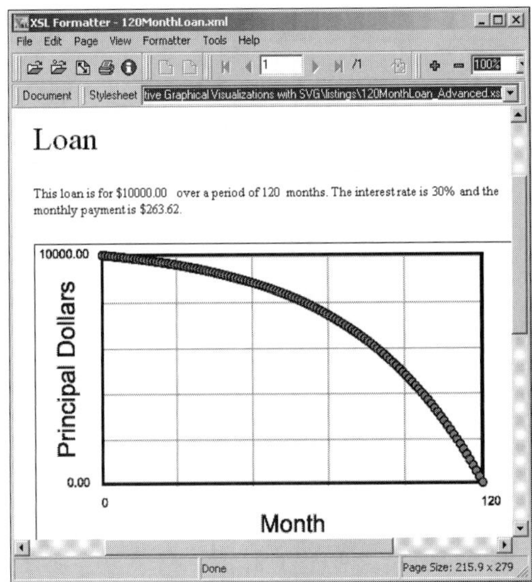

FIGURE 12.11
Loan visualization with XSL-FO.

SVG Structure and Elements

A previous discussion has shown how to use SVG together with other XML technologies to deliver an interactive graphical visualization and has illustrated these concepts with the loan example. Although this discussion has already touched on the key SVG elements and has shown the SVG structure implicitly, it is useful now to explicitly review the overall structure and elements of the SVG language.

Structure

Figure 12.12 shows the high-level structure of an SVG document with the key elements that are valid in such a document.

Elements

Table 12.1 lists the key elements of an SVG document, each with a brief description. For more detailed coverage, see the SVG specification available from the W3C (`www.w3.org`). For some elements references are made to the SMIL specification that may be found at W3C (`www.w3.org`) .

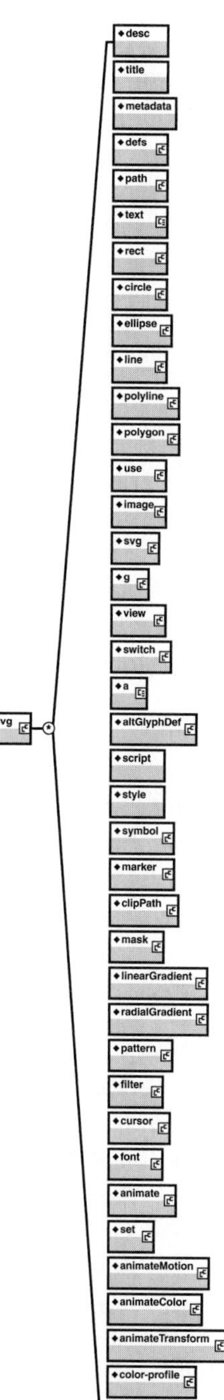

FIGURE 12.12
SVG document high-level element structure.

TABLE 12.1 SVG Key Elements

Element	*Description*
`a`	Analogous to HTML's `a` element, this element is used to indicate a hyperlink associated with the SVG elements that are children of this element. When a child element is clicked in the SVG visualization, the associated hyperlink is loaded.
`altGlyphDef`	Defines a candidate set of possible glyph substitutions. Note that fonts consist of a set of glyphs and associated information, such as font tables. This element provides controls over the glyphs used to render particular character data.
`animate`	Used to animate a single property or attribute over time in order to make SVG visualizations "live." See also the `animate` element in the SMIL specification.
`animateColor`	Specifies a color transformation over time. See also the `animateColor` element in the SMIL specification.
`animateMotion`	Causes a referenced element to move along a specified motion path. See also the `animateMotion` element in the SMIL specification.
`animateTransform`	Animates a transformation attribute on a target element. This enables animation of an element consisting of translation (panning), scaling, rotation, and skewing, or any combination thereof.
`circle`	Defines a circle based on a center point and radius.
`clipPath`	Defines a clipping path that may be used/referenced using a clip-path property. A clipping path restricts the region to which paint can be applied. Any parts of the diagram that lie outside the region bounded by the currently active clipping path are not drawn. You can think of this as a one-bit mask.
`color-profile`	Enables a color profile to be defined. A color profile may be used to build a transformation that corrects visual data for viewing on a particular device.
`cursor`	May be used to define a platform-independent custom cursor. For example, you could create a PNG image with the custom icon for a cursor and then reference this icon image from a `cursor` element in an SVG document. A `cursor` property may then be associated with an SVG element to cause the cursor to change to the custom cursor when the pointer moves over that element.

TABLE 12.1 continued

Element	*Description*
`defs`	Elements in SVG may reference other elements—for example, enabling a `circle` element to be filled with a linear gradient fill defined in a `linearGradient` element. In this case, the `circle` element would reference the `linearGradient` element. The `defs` element is used to group elements that are referenced by other elements, including, in this example, the `linearGradient` element.
`desc`	Used to add accessibility to SVG elements by providing text equivalents for graphics. Where descriptions are concise, the `title` element is used. Otherwise, the `desc` element is used. The text specified in a `desc` element is not generally visible but may, for example, be delivered to a user in aural form.
`ellipse`	Used to define an ellipse with a center point and two radii. The axes of the ellipse are aligned with the current coordinate system. However, this element may be rotated using a rotation transformation.
`filter`	Can define a region on the canvas in which a given filter effect applies.
`font`	Defines an SVG font.
`font-face`	Can be used to describe the characteristics of any font, SVG or otherwise. See also the `font` element.
`g`	Used to group and name collections of SVG elements. These child elements may share attributes defined by the parent `g` element. The `g` element may have an `id` attribute that can be used, for example, to locate the element in the SVG DOM.
`image`	Specifies that the contents of a file are to be rendered inside a rectangle on the SVG canvas. It may be used to embed a bitmap image in an SVG diagram, including PNG, GIF, or JPG images. This element may also be used to embed an SVG subdiagram inside another.
`line`	Defines a line segment that starts at one point and ends at another.
`linearGradient`	Defines a linear gradient, for example, in a fill.

TABLE 12.1 continued

Element	*Description*
`marker`	Defines the graphics that are to be used to draw arrowheads or polymarkers, for example, on a `path`, `line`, `polyline`, or `polygon` element.
`mask`	Used to define a mask that may be referenced from another element using a `mask` property to change some aspect of that element's appearance.
`metadata`	Used to identify the document-level metadata that may, in turn, be used, for example, to locate the document.
`path`	Defines a path that may be used to represent the outline of a shape that can be filled, stroked, used as a clipping path, or any combination thereof.
`pattern`	Used to fill or stroke an object using a predefined graphic object that may be replicated or tiled at fixed intervals in `x` and `y` to cover an area being painted.
`polygon`	Defines a closed shape consisting of a set of connected straight-line segments.
`polyline`	Defines a set of connected straight-line segments. Polylines typically define open shapes. See the `polygon` element for how to define a closed shape.
`radialGradient`	Defines a radial gradient, for example, in a fill.
`rect`	Defines a rectangle that is "axis aligned" with the current coordinate system. Rectangles with rounded corners may also be specified with this element.
`script`	Equivalent to the `script` element in HTML, this element is used to embed ECMAScript scripts in SVG documents. Functions defined in a `script` element are visible within the scope of the entire SVG document.
`set`	Enables the value of an attribute to be set to a specified value for a finite time interval. See also the `set` element in the SMIL specification.
`style`	Enables style sheets to be embedded directly in SVG content. This element has the same meaning as the `style` element in HTML.
`svg`	Root element of any SVG diagram. It may specify the width, height, and origin of the coordinate system for the SVG content.

TABLE 12.1 continued

Element	*Description*
`switch`	May be used to evaluate characteristics of the user agent being used. For example, to view the SVG content and then to select appropriate SVG child content based on those capabilities for rendering.
`symbol`	Used to define a graphical template object that may be instantiated with a `use` element.
`text`	Used to define a graphics element consisting of text.
`title`	Used to add accessibility to SVG elements by providing text equivalents for graphics. Where descriptions are concise, this element is used. Otherwise, the `desc` element is used. The text specified in this element is not generally visible but may be shown, for example, in a pop-up "tool-tip" form above a graphic element with which it is associated.
`use`	Indicates that an instance of a referenced graphical object (for example, defined with a `symbol` element) is to be created at a specified location on the SVG canvas.
`view`	Used to specify a predefined view on an SVG visualization.

Development Primer

This section discusses some resources that may be used to get started with SVG.

For a detailed list of resources for working with SVG, see the "Implementations" section at the W3C site (`w3.org/Graphics/SVG`). Some of the key resources available for working with SVG are also listed next. The following tutorials provide great starting points for learning SVG:

- *Adobe*. `www.adobe.com/svg/tutorial/intro.html`
- *KevLinDev*. `www.kevlindev.com`

To create your own SVG, you will need an editor. The following are examples of WYSIWYG SVG editors:

- *JASC WebDraw*. `www.jasc.com`
- *Amaya*. `www.w3.org/Amaya/Amaya.html`

Once you have created your SVG, you will need a viewer to render it for testing and deployment. The following two tools are examples of SVG viewers:

- *Adobe SVG Viewer.* www.adobe.com/svg/viewer/install
- *Batik.* xml.apache.org/batik

For inspiration and examples to help you create your own vector graphics, see the SVG used at the following Web sites:

- *Adobe.* www.adobe.com
- *Corda.* www.corda.com
- *ArchitectureZone.* www.architecturezone.trcinc.com

The Future of SVG

This section presents a few probable directions the future of SVG could take. When you're designing SVG systems with an intended lifespan of more than a few years, it is prudent to review these future directions to ensure the system design is flexible enough to accommodate probable changes.

Direct Web Browser Support for SVG

Currently, major Web browsers are enabled for SVG via plug-ins, most notably the Adobe SVG Viewer. Gradually, SVG support will be added to the core capabilities of the major Web browsers, and it will no longer be necessary to install plug-ins separately. When this is achieved, vector graphics support will exist alongside bitmap graphics support currently available in Web browsers.

New SVG Applications

New SVG applications will appear across a variety of application domains, including data visualization, games, and animation. The breadth of SVG applications will expand.

Expanding the Scope of SVG

Graphical applications that are currently realized using bitmap graphics will start using vector graphics in the form of SVG. The scope of SVG use will expand and it will displace the use of bitmap graphics in many areas, prime examples of which include mapping and GIS applications.

Summary

SVG is a vector graphics language that is both well formed and valid XML. Whereas bitmap graphics, such as GIF and JPG images, are appropriate for photos, SVG is appropriate for many other types of graphics. Many applications for which vector graphics are much better suited are currently using bitmap graphics due mostly to previously lacking Web browser support for vector graphics. SVG is much more than just another vector graphics format because it is built on the XML standard. This enables the use of other powerful XML tools and technologies with SVG. SVG may be used to create compelling interactive visualizations that may be embedded in Web pages and can incorporate scaling, panning, highlighting, descriptions, and analyze types of interactive behavior. Furthermore, this interactive behavior can occur completely on the client side, thus leading to more interactive content, faster client response time, less server load, and improved user privacy. SVG visualizations may also be embedded in XSL-FO documents for conversion to other formats, such as PDF, or for printing. There is currently wide industry support for the SVG standard, and a variety of mature tools are currently available for creating, viewing, printing, and manipulating SVG visualizations. New applications are appearing daily that demonstrate the power of SVG and stretch the limits of what can be achieved with this versatile and easy-to-use vector graphics language.

CHAPTER 13

XML and Content Management

In This Chapter

In the beginning, when all we had was HTML, the Internet was basically a publishing channel. By the mid 1990s, the Internet had become a viable alternative to print media for authors and publishers. In the late 1990s, as the sophistication of the Internet grew and XML was deployed, a growing number of companies that were not publishers began to use their Web sites to distribute/publish new forms of content. Everything from price lists to contact/telephone lists, home pages, and fax numbers became Internet content. Today, as the volume of content on the Internet continues to grow in size and types of content, it has become clear that online publishing requires a solid Web content-management solution and dynamic content distribution.

Web content management is generally defined as a combination of clearly defined roles, formal processes, and a supporting system architecture used to produce, collaborate on, maintain, publish, and distribute content on the Web. But what role should XML play in a Web content-management solution? Are other standards critical as well? And how do you select a Web content-management solution? In order to answer these questions, you must understand the core technologies and processes of Web content management. That's the goal of this chapter.

In this chapter, you'll learn:

- The definition of content management and the processes within the content-management workflow
- The XML-based components of a Web content-management system
- How to design the XML content environment
- WebDAV single-source, Web-based document creation
- The role of metadata (RDF and PRISM) for Web content management
- Content syndication with RSS and ICE
- Selecting a content-management system

What Is Web Content Management?

Web content management, when reduced to the lowest common denominator, comes down to the basics of working with content. By Web content, we mean any information or data on the Web. We must identify the types of content we need to manage and how content assets relate to one another. We must define the roles that need to be supported as we work with content. We must identify formal processes required to enable managed workflow based on these roles. Although we can probably enable Web content management with manual processes for small volumes of content, we will need a supporting systems architecture and Web content-management tools to handle content efficiently as the volume and variability of content grows.

Web content management does not have an out-of-the-box definition or solution. In fact, the definition of content management must be based on the characteristics of the content and the business model. For some organizations, content management is a straightforward publishing process—from a database to the Web. Other organizations rely on sophisticated content assembly that supports the automated, dynamic generation of a Web site. In some organizations, content management is limited to managing text files. In other organizations, content management requires structuring of large volumes of multimedia collections based on metadata attached to each rich media asset. Some organizations are only concerned with the management of newly created content. Others must consider management of legacy data as well. As you can see, Web content management requires human understanding of the business process, content analysis, and system design. Investment in information modeling and design are critical to the success of a Web content-management solution.

What Are the Components of a Content-Management Workflow?

The components of a content-management workflow, or event sequence, for the Web are much like the components of traditional content-management workflow. Typically components of Web content-management workflow include a content-input phase, a content-repository phase, and a content-delivery phase shown in Figure 13.1. Because the definition of content management differs based on the profile of the organization, its business goals, and the content it must manage, the components within each phase of any particular content-management workflow can vary as well.

Each component of content-management workflow has unique functionality and requires specialized tools. Content is entered into the workflow in the content-input phase, stored and maintained in the content-repository phase, and distributed in the content-delivery phase. The following subsections describe each component/phase of content-management workflow in greater detail.

Content-Input Phase

The content-input phase is the phase within the content-management workflow where content is introduced into the content-management system. Content input may come from one or more sources, as detailed in the following subsections.

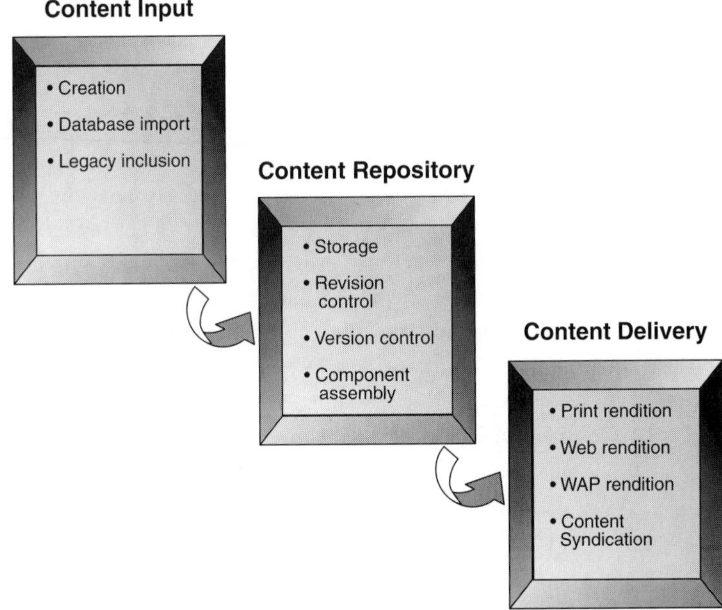

FIGURE 13.1
Components of a Web content - management system.

Original Creation

Original content creation occurs when content is authored by the organization and imported into the content-management system. Such content can be created in a variety of formats. For example, original content could be authored in a word processing system, in a desktop publishing system, with an HTML authoring tool, or even with an SGML or XML authoring tool. Original content may also be entered into a Web content-management system through the use of database forms.

It is not critical that all original content created for the Web be created in a data standard format, such as all content being required to conform to a particular XML tag set. However, this does make delivery easier. If the intent is to dynamically assemble content for Web delivery, it is critical that content be created in a delivery-neutral format. Often, organizations prepare content for a particular product or delivery media, thus rendering it relatively unusable in a dynamic content-assembly environment.

Note

A delivery-neutral format requires that content be created in such a manner that it can be effectively assembled in a variety of ways for a variety of media types. Delivery-neutral content is authored (words/phrases) in a way that it can stand as a logical unit and hence be assembled in a number of different ways. Delivery-neutral content is also encoded in a standard, open data format so that it can easily be presented in a number of media types.

Database Import

Although original content may be created directly in the content-management database system, often content comes from external databases within the same organization or from partner organizations. For example, content within an Enterprise Resource Planning (ERP) system may be valuable to import into a Web content-management system. Here, an import mechanism is a critical component of the Web content-management system.

Legacy Inclusion

Many times existing content is a critical ingredient for the Web. In this case, the content-management solution must account for the inclusion of the existing, or legacy, content. For example, a Web site for researching scientific journal articles requires the integration of past (legacy) journal articles with each new journal article that is published. A major issue is the data format of the legacy content and determining how that content can be integrated with "new" data on an ongoing basis. If the legacy data format cannot be easily included and managed, data conversion into a more viable format must be considered.

Content-Repository Phase

The second component of Web content management is the content-repository phase. In this phase, content that has been input is stored and managed.

At the heart of every Web content-management system is some sort of database or mechanism for maintaining persistent Web content over time. End users require not only the ability to store Web content but to track how and why it has been changed and to be assured that they can access the most up-to-date version of the content. So, a content-management database often has other features that you will find detailed in the following subsections.

Storage

The basic function of any content repository is to store data. Different storage options are available. For example, the database may be an inverted index, relational, or object oriented. The data may be stored directly in the database, or the database may simply be responsible for storing pointers to the data within some sort of file-storage system.

Revision Control

Revision control is important when a body of content is divided into small, logical units that may be worked on by a pool of authors, perhaps on different projects altogether. Revision control, often known as *check-out/check-in*, provides the capability to track when the content was last updated, who updated it, and why. Revision-control systems often "lock" the content from being updated by a second author while the first author is making updates.

Version Control

Version control enables end users to access a complete body of content that is valid at either a point in time or by a defined version number. This differs from revision control because it freezes all logical units in a body of content into a single unit that is valid when considered as an entity.

Component Assembly

A final functionality of a content repository is the ability to automate the assembly content components from the content repository for final delivery. In some cases, this is as simple as exporting the latest version of an entire document for delivery. In other cases, this is far more sophisticated. For example, component assembly may involve analysis of metadata associated with content assets to use as the basis for assembling content into a highly customized view of the content for Web delivery.

Content-Delivery Phase

Once the content has been assembled for delivery into a document or product, it must then be *delivered*. Content often comes to the final delivery in a variety of formats. Content that is stored in a Web content repository is fragmented into content objects that do not have a presentation interface for final delivery. Content may be stored as XML that is not intended to be viewed directly. Alternatively, content may be stored as records and fields of a database—again, not intended for direct viewing. Yet, in order to be presented, a common interface between the content and the end user must be set in place. Typically, this involves employing transformation/rendering/presentation software.

If content is in a delivery-neutral format such as XML, presentation delivery should be relatively straightforward. In addition, the ability to manage and control the delivery of dynamic content to the Web is a growing component of the content-delivery phase. This implies the application of automated Web publishing processes.

Print Rendition

Even though we are concentrating on content management for the Web, many times print delivery is also a consideration. This requirement is validated by the print support found in the W3C XSL Recommendation (October 16, 2001). According to the W3C, "XSL stylesheets are used to express how source content should be styled, laid out, and paginated onto a presentation medium such as a browser window, a pamphlet or a book." XSL 1.0 provides for the formatting of paged media that can drive professional printing capabilities and functions from XML source documents. XSL 1.0 assumes that we want to be able to specify how to format and render XML content in order to produce versions for both Web and print media using a single style sheet language.

Web Rendition

Again, we need some sort of style sheet to produce output for the Web. Today, the most common Web delivery mechanisms transform content into HTML so it can be delivered to the broadest number of browsers. An alternative to HTML delivery, favored by those that want/need page image rendition, is PDF, or Adobe's Portable Document Format, delivery for the Web.

WAP/Mobile Rendition

Accessibility of content anywhere, at any time, on any device is a trend in content delivery. The importance of new lightweight delivery devices was a clear focus of W3C standards development activity during 2000–2001. XHTML (a well-formed, modular, XML version of HTML), along with the Wireless Markup Language (WML) has emerged as delivery choices for Wireless Application Protocol (WAP) and mobile devices. Cascading Style Sheets (CSS) now comes with a new *Mobile Profile* that specifically tailors style sheet properties and values for mobile devices such as wireless phones.

In the page-rendition environment, tagged PDF technology now makes the automated resizing and reflowing of PDF page images for WAP/mobile devices a reality.

Content Syndication

The classic definition of *syndication* is the delivery of a single body of content to multiple end users, or *subscribers*. It began in the earliest days of the newspaper business when news services distributed news stories to multiple local newspapers. Today, Web-based content aggregation and content syndication make a compelling value proposition for content consumers and for content suppliers alike. XML-enabled syndication mechanisms address the need to automate reliable redistribution for both commercial and non-commercial content.

The Role of XML in Web Content Management

Because each organization's definition of Web content management is so personalized, it is rare that a complete content-management solution can be purchased "out of the box." Usually, Web content-management solutions vendors spend a good deal of time customizing their tools to meet customer requirements and integrating tools from a number of vendors. Other content-management tools vendors simply provide low-level APIs and let you do the rest!

Whether you are purchasing a content-management system or integrating your own, it is important to realize the critical role XML can play in your Web content-management solution. First, XML can enable the components of the content-management solution to communicate and pass data from one to another. Second, application components within the content-management system can themselves be XML based. These roles of XML in Web content management are discussed in the following subsections.

XML to Integrate System Components

Perhaps the most important role XML can play in the success of a Web content-management solution is when it is the "glue" used to integrate the applications that make up the content-management solution. As you know, XML is a standard, neutral, data-encoding format. Each component of a Web content-management system you purchase or a solution that you integrate yourself will be easier to plug and play if it is XML compliant. This means that each application component uses XML as a nonproprietary data format when it talks to other applications and that it uses XML when it passes data to another application component.

XML-Based Application Components

XML can also serve as the basis for certain application components within the content-management solution. The following content-management applications rely on XML functionality:

- The creation of XML-encoded structured content
- The validation of XML content
- The automated transformation/rendition/presentation of content across a variety of media

- The attachment of metadata to facilitate the management, discovery, and assembly of content
- Automated, reliable, secure content distribution over the Web

WebDAV Document Creation

WebDAV, the Web-based Distributed Authoring and Versioning protocol, was designed to add interoperability and collaborative capabilities to the Internet. WebDAV is a set of extensions to the HTTP protocol that allows users to collaboratively edit and manage files on a remote Web server, as you can see in Figure 13.2. It is a specification of the Internet Engineering Task Force (IETF). You can find the WebDAV specification at `http://www.ietf.org/html.charters/webdav-charter.html`.

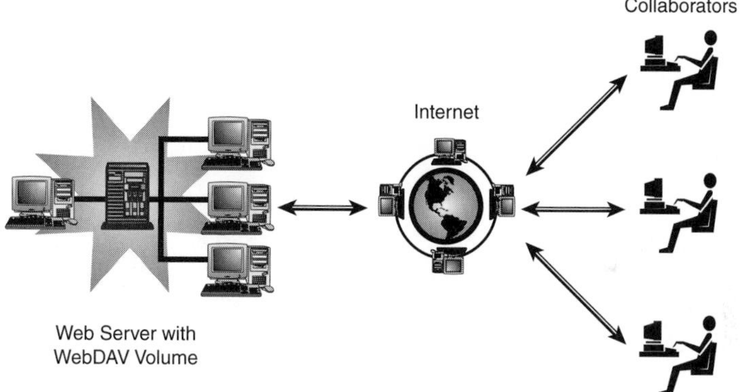

FIGURE 13.2
WebDAV enables collaborative authoring using the Internet.

WebDAV is a broad industry effort. Participants from Microsoft, Netscape, Novell, IBM, and Xerox are among those who helped develop the base WebDAV protocol. You can find out more about those who developed this specification at `http://www.webdav.org`.

The Role of WebDAV

Many believe that WebDAV will enable the original vision for the Web as a writeable, collaborative medium. Others see WebDAV meeting goals that extend beyond collaboration in Web page authoring. WebDAV may evolve into a network file system suitable for the Internet, one that works on entire files at a time, with good performance in high-latency environments. Others believe that WebDAV will become a protocol for manipulating the contents of a document-management system via the Web. Perhaps the best assessment is that WebDAV will support virtual enterprises, becoming the primary protocol supporting a wide range of collaborative applications. So, WebDAV could even be used to support remote software-development teams if you consider software development an extension of authoring. In fact, because WebDAV is based on HTTP it provides authoring support for Web resources of *any* media type—HTML, GIF, JPEG, and even software.

WebDAV-Enabled Authoring Environments

Simply put, WebDAV allows teams creating any sort of content to use a remote Web server as easily as if it were a local file server. This means that individuals separated by great geographic distances can trade information, develop ideas, and create and edit content as if they were sharing a single office network. This all works by mounting a WebDAV volume on a shared Web server. Everyone can then access files as they would any other networked volume.

WebDAV provides the following editorial features:

- *Locking*. WebDAV enables concurrency control by providing exclusive and shared write-locks to prevent file overwriting when two or more collaborators write to the same resource. The duration of WebDAV locks is independent of any individual network connection so that network connections may be disconnected arbitrarily.
- *Metadata properties*. The XML metadata properties of WebDAV provide storage for arbitrary metadata, such as a list of authors for Web resources. These properties can be set, deleted, and retrieved using the WebDAV protocol. DAV Searching and Locating (DASL) provides searches based on these XML metadata property values to locate Web resources.
- *Namespace support*. Web resources may need to be copied or moved as a Web site evolves. WebDAV supports copy and move operations using namespaces. Collections, similar to file system directories, may be created and listed.

The WebDAV community continues to extend WebDAV functionality in order to enable a richer authoring environment. Proposed extensions to WebDAV include the following:

- *Versioning and configuration management***.** Versioning support within WebDAV, similar to that provided by Revision Control System (RCS) or Source Code Control System (SCCS) will be the entry level of WebDAV functionality. The versioning level will support operations such as check-out, check-in, and retrieval of the history list.
- *Access control***.** WebDAV will provide the ability to set and clear access-control lists. This will enable the management of collaborators remotely by adding or deleting users from the list of collaborators on a single resource.

Note

WebDAV is an underlying protocol. It is like an enhanced remote file system. Although a content-management system can be built on top of the WebDAV protocol, it is important to recognize that WebDAV, by itself, is not a content-management system. Likewise, WebDAV is not a workflow-management system, but it could be used as the foundation for one.

Currently WebDAV is implemented in both open-source and commercial software. For example, Kiwi is an open-source file system built on WebDAV that was developed at Stanford University. Another open-source implementation of WebDAV is the Jigsaw Java-based WebDAV server at `http://www.w3.org/Jigsaw/`. Among the commercial products that include WebDAV implementations are Adobe Acrobat 5.0, Dreamweaver, and Microsoft Internet Explorer 5.0. You can learn more about WebDAV-based products at `http://www.webdav.org/projects`.

WebDAV and XML

WebDAV is an XML vocabulary. The WebDAV XML tag set defines a number of WebDAV methods for examining and maintaining Web content. In WebDAV, users and groups are represented as principals. The ability to perform a given method on a resource is controlled by one or more privileges assigned to a principal. For example, privileges might give a principal the ability to update a collection of Web content. WebDAV sets up an Access Control List (ACL) made up of Access Control Entries (ACEs), which define what principals are to get what privileges for a specific resource.

In Listing 13.1, the principal identified by the URL `http://www.foo.com/users/dkennedy` (that is, the user "dkennedy") is granted read and write privileges.

LISTING 13.1 Example of WebDAV Syntax

```
<?xml version="1.0" encoding="utf-8" ?>
<D:acl xmlns:D="DAV:">
<D:ace>
<D:principal>
<D:href>http://www.foo.com/users/dkennedy</D:href>
</D:principal>
<D:grant>
<D:privilege><D:read/></D:privilege>
<D:privilege><D:write/></D:privilege>
</D:grant>
</D:ace>
```

How to Design the XML Content Environment

If you are building a Web content-management solution, you may consider coding the textual content in XML. That certainly is not a requirement. However, one of the advantages of coding content in XML is the promise that content can be recombined and repurposed to create customized content deliverables.

Reusable Document Objects

If reuse is a major goal of coding content in XML, then the XML design should facilitate reuse. Here, the design should focus on the creation of small documents that contain concise topics. Because each piece of content can stand alone, it becomes a relatively easy task to combine pieces of content in new ways.

It is important to understand how you intend to reuse content and then to design the XML encoding and eventually the content storage to support that goal. Let's suppose, for example, that our content is scientific journals. What is the element of content reuse in this scenario? At first, glance it is the articles. It makes little sense to reuse anything but a complete article. Our XML encoding for the journal should enable each article to be a small, reusable document.

But if we take a close look, we can imagine that two other elements within the article might be reused as well. The first is the art. Photos and illustrations might have a reuse value of their own. Likewise, tables that summarize findings in the article might have use as an independent content object. What can we do in our XML design to support the specific reuse of these subelements.

Again, we must go back to the idea that each piece of reusable content is a small document. This means that each figure and table in the journal article is its own little document, is stored independently, and is called into this article or any other content-based product when the product is assembled for delivery.

XML Document Design Principles

Many times users of XML-based content-management systems come from an SGML background. Certainly conversion of data from SGML to XML is quite straightforward. However, the straightforward conversion of SGML documents into XML documents may not be the best design solution for data to be managed in a content-management system. If your original DTD was designed for a monolithic document to drive a print product, it most likely will not provide the functionality you want when you make an investment in a content-management solution.

Your content-management system will only be as flexible and versatile as the structures you impose on it. If you simply convert your monolithic SGML into monolithic XML (such as a large aircraft maintenance manual coded in compliance with ATA Spec 2100), you will end up managing the content as a large document that has very little potential for reuse in the future. Such large documents also have a huge impact on system performance.

An alternate approach to designing a monolithic XML tag set is to create small document definitions. Often times these small document definitions are based on an object model for reuse. Let's consider a scientific journal once more. In the days of SGML, we would define a DTD for the whole journal. This would imply the journal issue, containing all articles are managed and used as a unit. A slightly better approach would be to define a schema for the article. Then, we could call the article schema (and content stored on an article basis) as appropriate to construct the journal. We would store and use articles as independent information objects.

An even better approach would be to fragment the article into other useful objects or small documents that themselves might be reused. Here, we could envision having a schema for the journal that includes the schema for articles. The article schema might include other small XML documents such as the abstract, the citation header information for the article, the summary tables, and all graphics. Each of these content objects could then be managed independently, providing the functionality expected when we decided to use a content-management system.

Note

You can learn more about the principles of XML document design in the book, *Information Architecture for the WWW* (ISBN 1-56592-282-4).

The Role of Metadata (RDF and PRISM) in Web Content Management

A problem that everyone experiences, whether on the job or in one's personal life, is information overload. Let's just consider your daily mail. If you are like me, each day that you go to the mailbox, you cannot believe the amount of mail you receive. Usually I pick up the mail after a hard day at work. I don't have time to deal with each item that I have received right at that time. So what do I do? I carefully place the mail on top of my dining room table. By the weekend, I am suffering from information overload. There are bills to pay, important items such as insurance policies to file, magazines that I should read, and lots of junk mail to throw away. Fortunately, with just a few file folders, I can divide my mail into these four categories and quickly be able to find what I want.

Now imagine the problems facing those whose job it is to create content. It might be a magazine publisher or it might be a bank, an insurance company, or an electronics manufacturer. Very quickly these organizations discover the problems that information overload can bring. So don't they do what I do with my mail? Simply divide the content into neat categories and store it?

Well, the answer is, of course, that most content is far more complex than my mail. There may be several different schemes that people could use to find the content they need. Each piece of content has characteristics that are critical to its use and reuse. If I am storing images, for example, I need to know not only the subject matter but also the format and whether I have rights to use the images.

To effectively manage content, I need more than just a filing system. I need a way to specify critical information about each item of content as well. What I need is metadata!

What Is Metadata?

One of the formal definitions of metadata is *data about data*. In this context, we can consider metadata to be *data about content*. Consider an image. Data about the image is what will enable me to discover and use the image. This data—the subject matter, the photographer, the format, and the rights—is an example of metadata. Metadata gives us a mechanism to associate lookup information (images about the Internet) with the content we want to discover.

Note

Metadata can be used to store other kinds of information than just look-up information. For example, in a content-management system, metadata might be used to track how many times an image has been used and where. In fact, most content-management systems have their own internal metadata that enables the system functionality!

Another place where metadata will be most useful is the Web. The Web is much like a giant library. Instead of being made up of books, it is made up of resources such as e-mail messages, images, and Web pages. Today, if you know the URL of what you want to find, you can find it. However, if we had metadata about Web resources (much like the metadata in a card catalog in a library) we could navigate the Web a lot more easily.

About the Resource Description Framework

The effective use of metadata among applications on the Web requires common conventions about the semantics, syntax, and structure of metadata. In other words, it requires a metadata specification standard. Such a standard must also allow for individual communities of use, to define their own semantics, or *meaning*, of metadata to address their particular needs.

It's only natural that such a metadata specification was developed under the auspices of the World Wide Web Consortium. This specification is known as the *Resource Description Framework* (RDF), which is the result of a number of metadata communities bringing together their needs to provide a robust and flexible architecture for supporting metadata on the Web. RDF is very much a collaborative work. It became a W3C Recommendation in February 1999. An RDF Schema Model became a W3C Recommendation in March of 2000. RDF relies on XML syntax as well as the W3C syntax for URI.

The Resource Description Framework, as its name implies, is a framework for describing and interchanging metadata. In particular, RDF focuses on Web resources. It should come as no surprise that the world's librarians had a great deal of input into the development of RDF.

RDF Basics

RDF was designed based on the following basic concepts:

- *Resource*. All the world's Web content is a resource, and a resource must have a URI. Therefore, all the world's Web pages, as well as individual elements within these Web pages, are resources. A resource is the W3C home page, `http://www.w3.org/`, for example.
- *Property type*. Resources have names and can be used as properties (for example, subject or author). Typically, all we really care about is the name of the property type, but a property type needs to be a resource so that it can have its own properties.
- *Property*. A property is the resource along with its property type and a value for that property. For the resource `http://www.idealliance.org/xmlfiles/issue32/book.htm`, the property type is *subject*, and the value of the property type is *XML Book Review*.

- *Description.* A collection of properties that describe the same resource as a description. Taken together, the properties make up a metadata set that describes the resource.

RDF provides a model for attaching metadata to Web resources. It also provides a syntax so that it can be exchanged and used. That's really all RDF provides and all RDF is. It is simply a framework for defining metadata.

An RDF property can be represented as a directed labeled graph. Let's refer to the property "The subject of `http://www.idealliance.org/xmlfiles/issue32/book.htm` is XML Book Review." In Figure 13.3, you can see how resources are identified as nodes, property types are defined as directed label arcs, and string values are quoted.

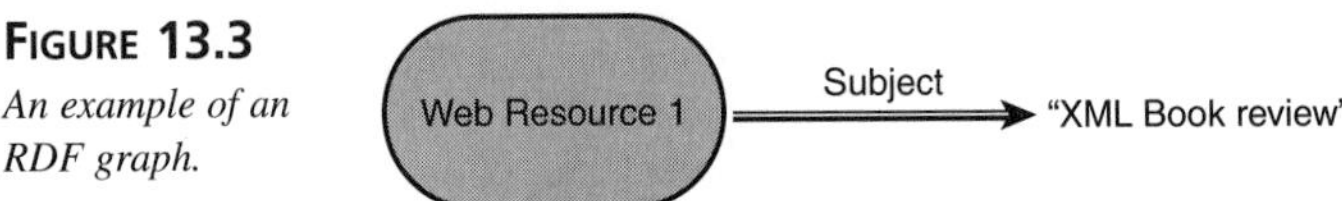

FIGURE 13.3
An example of an RDF graph.

RDF does not come with any predefined property types or value sets of its own. The metadata properties, property types, and values are left to the user to define according to the function metadata is to serve. These sets of RDF metadata are called *RDF vocabularies*. An example of an RDF vocabulary is Dublin Core. This is an initiative of the library community to develop a simple resource description for discovery.

Note

Dublin Core is not named for Dublin, Ireland. Nor is it an acronym. Actually, Dublin Core is named for Dublin, Ohio, home of the Online Computer Library Center (OCLC), where the original metadata specification for library resources was developed.

RDF is expressed in XML. Listing 13.2 represents "The subject of `http://www.idealliance.org/xmlfiles/issue32/book.htm` is XML Book Review. The editor of `http://www.idealliance.org/xmlfiles/issue32/book.htm` is Dianne Kennedy." In this example, we use XML namespaces to indicate the RDF namespace. We use the IDEAlliance namespace to identify the XML Files tags unambiguously. You can see the graph for this listing in Figure 13.4.

LISTING 13.2 Example of RDF Syntax

```
<?xml:namespace ns = "http://www.w3.org/RDF/RDF/" prefix ="RDF" ?>
<?xml:namespace ns = "http://idealliance.org/XMLFiles/" prefix = "XMLFiles" ?>
<RDF:RDF>
  <RDF:Description RDF:HREF = "http://uri-of-Document-1">
    <XMLFiles:subject>XML Book Review</XMLFiles:subject>
    <XMLFiles:publisher>IDEAlliance</ XMLFiles:publisher >
    <XMLFiles:editor>Dianne Kennedy</XMLFiles:editor>
  </RDF:Description>
</RDF:RDF>
```

FIGURE 13.4
An RDF graph for a resource description.

Why RDF and Not XML for Metadata?

XML can be used to model almost anything. It seems that we could just invent XML tags to code metadata. So why isn't XML the W3C recommended vehicle for metadata?

It turns out that the issue with using XML to represent metadata has to do with scalability. Two problems exist when we try to represent metadata directly with XML according to RDF specialists:

- Element order in an XML document is meaningful. In a metadata environment, where all metadata properties are equal, this doesn't make much sense. Who cares whether the subject or the editor of an XML Files article is listed first or second. And why take on the overhead of maintaining the correct order (XML modeling) when it is not meaningful. This can be expensive in overhead and difficult to implement.
- XML enables us to embed elements and entities within a description field (mixed content). When you represent these mixed-content structures in computer memory, you get data structures that mix hierarchical XML trees, graphs, and character strings. These become difficult to handle when billions of metadata fields are applied to Web resources.

Interestingly enough, even though XML by itself does not provide metadata functionality that we require for the next generation of the Web, XML remains a necessary ingredient for RDF interchange.

About XMP

XMP, Adobe's *eXtensible Metadata Platform*, is a framework for adding metadata to application files, databases, and content-management systems. Adobe announced XMP as a "standard" in September of 2001. XMP is built on W3C standards but is not, itself, a W3C standard. It is, however, an Adobe standard. As such, XMP will be implemented across the Adobe family of products and will be intimately integrated into the PDF output of Adobe publishing tools.

According to Adobe, the lack of standardized metadata has been a problem for the evolution of the Web. A standardized metadata framework is required for machines to be able to read and understand metadata associated with content. Only when this happens can we move toward automated content handling on the Web.

XMP is Adobe's attempt to remedy the lack of a standardized metadata framework. XMP relies on RDF to express metadata in XML. Within XMP, Adobe had defined its own starter set of metadata tags called the *XMP Schemas*. This XMP set of metadata tags is not a standard set of metadata tags; it is an Adobe set of metadata tags. Adobe is quick to point out that the value of XMP is not in this XMP Schema but the fact that XMP sets up a framework for applying metadata to content. According to Adobe, XMP can carry any metadata vocabulary. For example, XMP can serve as a platform for PRISM metadata in the publishing world. You can learn more about XMP at `http://www.adobe.com/products/xmp/main.html`.

About PRISM

PRISM is the *Publishing Requirements for Industry Standard Metadata*. It is an extensible XML metadata vocabulary designed to facilitate the multipurposing, aggregating, and syndicating, personalizing, and postprocessing of any kind of content. PRISM is a standardized metadata vocabulary developed by publishers to describe all kinds of published content. Examples of PRISM content types include advertisements, articles, books, catalogs, e-books, home pages, journals, magazines, news, interviews, and even cartoons.

Who Developed PRISM?

PRISM is hosted by IDEAlliance and sponsored by a group of companies such as Adobe Systems, Vignette, Time Inc., McGraw-Hill, CMP, Artesia Technologies, Getty Images, Interwoven, Kinecta, Netscape, and Quark. These companies all have a shared business interest in creating and using a common metadata standard as a basic part of their content infrastructures. The group consists of software developers as well as content suppliers and consumers who are involved in content creation, consumption, management, aggregation, and distribution, whether commercially or within intranet and extranet frameworks.

PRISM and Other Standards

When PRISM was developed, one of the goals was to build on existing metadata frameworks and vocabularies. It is natural that PRISM recommends the use of both XML and RDF as well as the Dublin Core metadata specification. It also makes extensive use of XML namespaces as a mechanism to include these related metadata standards. You can learn more about PRISM at `http://www.prismstandard.org/`.

PRISM metadata is expressed as an XML document, which begins with the standard XML declaration:

```
<?xml version="1.0"?>
```

A character encoding may be given if necessary. Because PRISM is an RDF vocabulary, the next element in a PRISM document is just like the first statement of an RDF document. The XML namespaces that you are using must be indicated as an attribute of RDF. This is done by adding attributes beginning with `xmlns:`. Note that we define both the RDF namespace and the namespace for Dublin Core because PRISM uses elements from each. This is shown in Listing 13.3.

LISTING 13.3 PRISM Uses XML, RDF, XML Namespaces and Dublin Core as a Basis

```
<?xml version="1.0" encoding="UTF-8"?>
<rdf:RDF xmlns:rdf="http://www.w3.org/1999/02/22-rdf-syntax-ns#"
xmlns:dc="http://purl.org/dc/elements/1.1/">
```

Tip

Namespaces are the primary extension mechanism for PRISM metadata. If you want to add metadata fields from other metadata specifications, or even from your own, just specify a namespace in the namespace declaration and add metadata tags from that namespace. You can learn more about XML namespaces and how to use them at `http://www.w3.org/TR/1999/REC-xml-names-19990114/`.

PRISM Elements

The goal of PRISM is to provide a framework for the interchange and preservation of content and metadata. It therefore is made up of a collection of elements to describe content and a set of controlled vocabularies listing values for the elements. The working group has focused on defining metadata for the following purposes:

- To provide general-purpose descriptions of the content resource
- To specify the relationship of one resource to another
- To indicate rights and permissions
- To enable inline metadata within the resource itself

PRISM elements can be categorized by functional group. As you know, some PRISM elements have been specifically defined within the PRISM specifications. Others have been borrowed from Dublin Core metadata, see `http://dublincore.org/`. PRISM elements can be categorized as follows:

- *General purpose*. These elements, for the most part, have been borrowed from Dublin Core. They include `dc:identifier`, `dc:author`, `dc:contributor`, `dc:title`, `dc:description`, and `dc:format`.
- *Provenance*. These elements include `dc:publisher`, `prism:distributor`, and `dc:source`.
- *Timestamps*. A number of timestamps have been developed as PRISM elements. These include `prism:creationtime`, `prism:pubicationtime`, and `prism:expiretime`.
- *Subject descriptions*. These elements describe the subject of a resource. These include `dc:subject`, `dc:description`, `prism:person`, and `prism:organization`.
- *Resource relationships*. PRISM has added numerous metadata fields that enable us to express relationships between content resources. These include `prism:isPartOf`, `prism:isBasedOn`, and `prism:isReferencedBy`.
- *Rights information*. PRISM uses Dublin Core rights and has developed its own set of rights metadata. This includes `prism:copyright`, `prism:rightsAgent`, and `prism:expirationTime`.

In addition to the PRISM namespace metadata elements, PRISM has defined some specialized elements that are in specialized namespaces. These include the following:

- `prl:`. The `prl:` namespace stands for *PRISM Rights Language*. This set of metadata elements is specific to a portion of the PRISM specification known as the *rights language*. Some examples of these tags are `prl:industry` and `prl:usage`.
- `pim:`. The `pim:` namespace stands for *PRISM Inline Markup*. These elements were specifically designed to enable inline markup of organizations, locations, product names, and personal names. Examples of these elements are `pim:organization`, `pim:location`, and `pim:person`.
- `pcv:`. The `pcv:` namespace stands for *PRISM Controlled Vocabulary*. This namespace provides a mechanism for describing and conveying all or a portion of a

controlled vocabulary or authority file. This may be used to define entire new taxonomies. Examples of these metadata elements include `pcv:broaderTerm`, `pcv:narrowerTerm`, and `pcv:relatedTerm`.

Using PRISM

PRISM descriptions are compliant with RDF, and they begin with the `rdf:RDF` element. PRISM requires that resources have unique identifiers. In Listing 13.4, a photograph is identified by a URI in the `rdf:about` attribute of the `rdf:Description` element. The `dc:identifier` element can be used for other identifiers, such as International Standard Book Numbers (ISBNs) or system-specific identifiers. In this example, the `dc:identifier` element contains an asset ID for *Cameramaster's* asset management system. In this simple example of PRISM, only the basic Dublin Core elements `dc:description`, `dc:title`, `dc:creator`, `dc:contributor`, and `dc:format` are used.

LISTING 13.4 Simple PRISM Description

```
<?xml version="1.0" encoding="UTF-8"?>
<rdf:RDF xmlns:rdf="http://www.w3.org/1999/02/22-rdf-syntax-ns#"
xmlns:dc="http://purl.org/dc/elements/1.1/">
<rdf:Description rdf:about="http://cameramasters.com/2001/08/IndianaDunes.jpg">
<dc:identifier rdf:resource="http://cameramasters.com/content/042249X"/>
<dc:description>Photograph taken at 2:00 PM on
➥the beach at Indiana Dunes State Park
</dc:description>
<dc:title>Indiana Beach in Summer</dc:title>
<dc:creator>Darold Vredberg</dc:creator>
<dc:contributor>Michelle Leigh, lighting</dc:contributor>
<dc:format>image/tiff</dc:format>
</rdf:Description>
</rdf:RDF>
```

A PRISM description can either be simple or quite complex. Like determining the level of XML tagging in content, one must ultimately consider the business application of PRISM to decide how much metadata should be attached to any information asset. If, for example, you have rights to all the content you want to track and manage, then including complex rights metadata in your PRISM description would be inappropriate. If, however, you routinely make use of content that has varying rights and permissions, specifying this data in your PRISM description is critical.

Listing 13.5 shows a more complex use of PRISM metadata. Here, we have expanded beyond the Dublin Core metadata set and are using PRISM metadata elements to indicate that the photo is part of an article as well as to indicate the rights ownership and management.

LISTING 13.5 Simple PRISM Description

```
<?xml version="1.0" encoding="UTF-8"?>
<rdf:RDF xmlns:rdf="http://www.w3.org/1999/02/22-rdf-syntax-ns#"
xmlns:dc="http://purl.org/dc/elements/1.1/">
<rdf:Description rdf:about="http://cameramasters.com/2001/08/IndianaDunes.jpg"
➥xmlns:pcv="http://prismstandard.org/namespaces/pcv/1.0/">
<dc:identifier rdf:resource="http://cameramasters.com/content/042249X"/>
<dc:description>Photograph taken at 2:00 PM
➥on the beach at Indiana Dunes State Park
</dc:description>
<prism:isPartOf rdf:resource=
➥"http://IndianaHome.com/2000/08/IndianaArticle.xml"/>
<dc:title>Indiana Beach in Summer</dc:title>
<dc:creator>Darold Vredberg</dc:creator>
<dc:contributor>Michelle Leigh, lighting</dc:contributor>
<dc:format>image/tiff</dc:format>
<prism:copyright>Copyright 2001, Indiana Home Publications. All
rights reserved.</prism:copyright>
<prism:rightsAgent>PhotoRights, Munster, IN</prism:rightsAgent>
</rdf:Description>
</rdf:RDF>
```

Web Content Syndication with RSS and ICE

Not only does metadata play a critical role in the content-repository phase of content management, but it plays an important role in the content-delivery phase as well. Content delivery on the Web is often referred to as *syndication*.

In its simplest sense, syndication is the delivery of content from a content provider, or *syndicator*, to a content consumer, or *subscriber*. Syndication may be a one-to-one relationship, but typically is a one-to-many relationship.

In the early days, syndicated content was distributed by wire services. Today, the Web makes a perfect channel for almost instantaneous syndication for all kinds of Web content.

Note

Many early Web syndication models were built on custom software platforms. But content syndicators soon found that ad-hoc syndication mechanisms were not only expensive to develop but were more expensive to maintain and extend over time. Syndicators were limited by ad-hoc syndication systems because custom development was required for each subscriber added. Their syndication network could not grow and be profitable following the ad-hoc model.

Lack of a standard Web-based syndication mechanism was troublesome for those who wanted to aggregate content on Web sites or portals as well. Aggregators found that they might need to have to implement a different content-handling mechanism for each relationship with a content syndicator that they wanted to establish. Again, this was costly and did not enable aggregators to add or vary the content on their portals in an inexpensive or flexibly fashion.

Two standard content-syndication mechanisms have emerged since the late 1990s to enable automated syndication on the Web. The first, RSS, emerged from the open-source community as a simple mechanism to enable the syndication of headlines. This lightweight syndication protocol is simple to use and inexpensive to implement. A second, more robust syndication protocol, Information and Content Exchange (ICE), was developed by industry content-providers and software vendors. ICE was developed to automate the negotiation of subscription characteristics and to address the need to automate the scheduled, reliable, secure redistribution of any content for publishers and for non-commercial content providers.

RSS Content Syndication

RSS is a number of things to a number of different communities. RSS is an XML vocabulary for describing a Web site that happens to be ideal for lightweight content syndication. Today, RSS is one of the most widely used Web site XML applications. Its popularity and wide use has uncovered utility in many more scenarios than originally was anticipated by its creators. Therefore, RSS can also be thought of as a portal content language, as a metadata syndication framework, and even as a content syndication system.

You can see the model for RSS in Figure 13.5. Content providers embed RSS into their HTML pages. These pointers are aggregated and then made available to a larger audience through the aggregator portal.

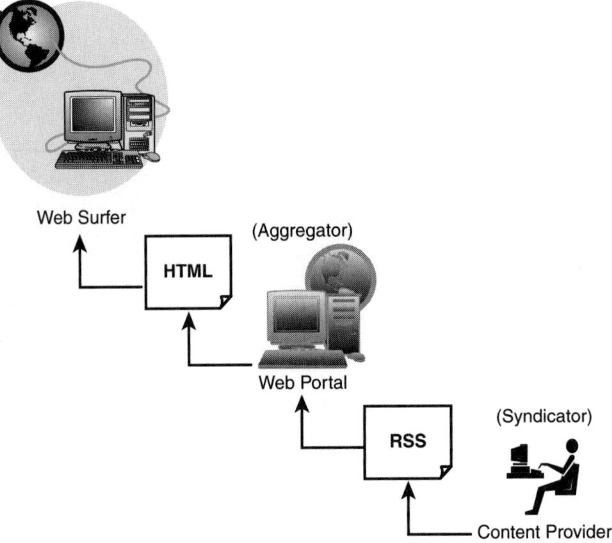

FIGURE 13.5
The RSS content syndication model.

History of RSS

RSS was originally introduced in 1999 by Netscape as a channel description framework for its My Netscape Network (MNN) portal (`http://dmoz.org/Netscape/My_Netscape_Network/`). RSS is simply an XML application that provides a novel content-gathering mechanism that's beneficial to Netscape, those providing content, and those using the content on the Web. RSS enables content gathering by providing a simple "snapshot in a document" for Web sites. This document enables Web sites to acquire an audience through the presence of their content on the My Netscape portal. Also, RSS gives users a centralized location into which content from their favorite Web sites flow to enable a one-stop reading experience.

Note

If you noticed that no acronym was given for RSS, that was not an oversight. It is intentional. According to UserLand, one of the open-source developers of RSS 0.91, "There is no consensus on what RSS stands for, so it's not an acronym, it's a name."

However, because we work in a world of acronyms, numerous ones have been attached to RSS. The acronyms most commonly associated with RSS include the following:

- R(DF) Site Summary
- Rich Site Summary
- Really Simple Syndication

Rich Site Summary is the acronym favored by the RSS-DEV community.

As a result of My Netscape Network, users soon found that RSS could be used as an XML-based lightweight syndication format for headlines. Using RSS, headlines could be taken outside the My Netscape Network site and used in other RSS-based portals. Examples such as xmlTree (`http://www.xmltree.com`) began to cater to general subject markets and to specialized vertical markets as well. RSS gained grassroots acceptance and quickly became a viable option to ad-hoc syndication systems being developed by commercial interests. RSS adoption has flourished because it provides for simple syndication without unnecessary complexity or bulk. Today, RSS feeds carry various content types to thousands of Web sites, including CNET, CNN, Disney, Forbes, Motley Fool, Wired, Red Herring, Salon, Slashdot, and ZDNet.

RSS Registries

In order for RSS to work, a mechanism for finding RSS feeds was needed. One solution is the RSS registry. The first step toward establishing an RSS registry was Internet Alchemy's OCS format. This format provides a way of listing RSS channels that have been made available on a Web site. As the number of RSS feeds grew, the next step was the establishment of registries. XmlTree (`http://www.xmltree.com`) is a registry that provides a facility for RSS content to be registered and classified for end use. UserLand (`http://my.userland.com`) provides a registry facility as well.

RSS Shift Toward Syndication

If My Netscape Network was the first RSS portal, UserLand was the first *RSS aggregator*. The main difference between My Netscape Network and UserLand is archiving. My Netscape Network displays only the latest version of RSS channel feeds. UserLand archives snapshots of content on a hourly basis. The revolutionary advance that aggregators brought was the ability to decouple items from the parent channels. This means that RSS can be presented as the intersection of simultaneous feeds from disparate sources to focus on timeliness, not on the channel. Meerkat (`http://www.oreillynet.com/meerkat`), an open wire service, presents items in reverse chronological order, but also allows for filtering, grouping, sharing, and searching.

The real shift of RSS toward syndication began when RSS 0.91 was released. In this version, RSS dropped RDF and became a simple XML vocabulary. RSS 0.91 added new item-level `<description>` tags that enabled RSS to clearly move into content syndication. The description field had a 500-character constraint. This enabled RSS to carry more than a headline but still limited its ability to carry heavyweight content.

RSS V1.0

As use of RSS increased, the user audience began to voice a need for enhancements. The item-level title and description elements were being overloaded with metadata and HTML, as some tried to use RSS for more than what it was intended. Some people began to insert unofficial ad-hoc elements to augment the metadata facilities within RSS 0.91. Therefore, we see the use of elements such as `<category>`, `<date>`, and `<author>`. The evolution of RSS seemed to be inevitable. RSS needed a richer metadata framework and a way to become extensible. But it also needed to be backward compatible so that the entrenched user base could continue to work with RSS. The issue was how to make this happen in a unified fashion.

It turns out that a new group, RSS-DEV, began to work on a new version of RSS that met its requirements. This version of RSS moved ahead to include namespaces and bring RSS back to RDF for metadata specification. RSS-DEV released RSS 1.0 in December of 2000.

The original version of RSS (RSS 0.9+) is currently being maintained and advanced by the open-source community working with UserLand. One of the goals of the RSS 0.9+ group is to advance RSS capabilities while maintaining its simplicity. According to Dave Winer of UserLand, "Today, RSS *is* simple, largely because it only builds on XML 1.0 and does not use namespaces or schemas, and it isn't a dialect of RDF. There's a logical route forward for RSS that says it should adapt to include all these concepts, but in doing so it would become vastly more complex, and, at the content provider level, would buy us almost nothing for the added complexity."

This leaves us with a lack of clarity about what RSS is and which version of RSS we should use. The reality is that some sites have a preference for one RSS version over the other. Other sites support both versions of RSS. This is not too much different from the browser wars between Netscape and Microsoft—and the implications for those trying to use the "standard" are much the same! There has been talk of giving new names for each different flavor of RSS, retaining RSS for 0.9+ and earlier, and giving RSS 1.0 a new name. To date, there has not even been consensus among the communities on the name, so for the moment, everyone continues to use "RSS" for both flavors of RSS.

Tip

If you want to access free software tools for RSS, you might consider joining the RSS-DEV group at Yahoogroups. You can link to sample content for this group at `http://www.yahoogroups.com/groups/rss-dev/message/15`.

Using RSS

Three easy steps are required to use RSS on your Web site:

1. Create and maintain RSS files for your Web site.
2. Register your RSS files with an RSS aggregator.
3. Publish relevant RSS content from others on your site.

You'll learn more about using RSS in this section.

Introduction to RSS Elements

Because RSS is an XML vocabulary, it follows the XML well-formedness rule that all RSS elements must nest inside one root element. For RSS, that element is `<rss>`. RSS has a single, required child element, `<channel>`. See Listing 13.6 for the XML element declaration for RSS.

LISTING 13.6 Root Element Declaration in RSS .91 DTD

```
<!ELEMENT rss (channel)>
<!ATTLIST rss
          version  CDATA #REQUIRED><!--version must be filled in here!> -->
```

Caution

Because there are two very different versions of RSS (RSS 0.9+ and RSS 1.0), it is most important to specify the RSS version number as an attribute of `<RSS>`.

RSS is made up a rather simple set of elements and subelements. The basic layout of the RSS file is as follows:

- XML declaration
- RSS root element

- Channel metadata
- Image listings (optional, you can list several)
- Item listings (one or more)

The channel element is made up of a number of channel metadata fields. In RSS .91, these fields are predefined, and hence not extensible. Some fields within `<channel>` are optional and others are required. Here's a list of these fields:

- `title`. The title of the RSS channel. The title is how people identify your service. The title of your channel should be the same as the title of your HTML Web site. The maximum length is 100 characters. This field is required.
- `link`. A URL pointing to the Web site named in the `<title>` element. The maximum length is 500 characters. This field is required.
- `description`. A phrase that describes your channel—your channel's positioning statement. The maximum length is 500 characters. This field is required.
- `language`. Indicates the content language of the channel. This is intended to allow aggregators to group all Spanish language sites, for example, on a single page. This field is required (enumerated value selection in RSS specification).
- `copyright`. The copyright notice for content. The maximum length is 100. This field is optional.
- `managingEditor`. The e-mail address of the managing editor of the channel. The maximum length is 100. This field is optional.
- `webmaster`. The e-mail address of the Webmaster of the channel. The maximum length is 100. This field is optional.
- `rating`. The PICS rating for the channel. The maximum length is 500. This field is optional.
- `pubDate`. The publication date of the channel. It must conform to the date/time standard (RFC 822). This field is optional.
- `lastBuildDate`. The last time the content of the channel was updated (RFC 822). This field is optional.
- `docs`. The URL for the documentation for the coding of the RSS site. This field is optional.
- `textInput`. Contains the required subelements `<title>`, `<link>`, `<description>`, and `<language>` for each text input field. This field is optional.
- `skipDays`. Contains any number of `<day>` subelements, such as `<day>Friday</day>`, that indicate days on which aggregrators may not read this channel.

- `skipHours`. Contains any number of `<hour>` subelements, such as `<hour>14 </hour>`, that indicate hours in GMT on which aggregrators may not read this channel.

Note

PICS stands for *Platform for Internet Content Selection*. This is a W3C Specification that enables labels (metadata) to be associated with Internet content. You can learn more about PICS at `http://www.w3.org/PICS/`.

In addition to the elements that give aggregrators information about the channel, the channel element contains one or more `<item>` elements. Each `<item>` element is an item of content, such as a news story. The `<item>` element is made up of three required subelements designed to assist aggregrators.

- `title`. The title of the item. The title is how people identify the content within the channel. The maximum length is 100 characters.
- `link`. A URL pointing to the Web page named in the item `<title>`. The maximum length is 500 characters.
- `description`. A phrase that describes the item. The maximum length is 500 characters.

Finally, a channel may contain one or more images. The images contain the following subelements, which enable aggregrators to locate and use images within the channel:

- `title`. The title of the image. The title is how people identify image. The maximum length is 100 characters. *Required.*
- `url`. A URL pointing to the image named in the `<title>` element. The maximum length is 500 characters. *Required.*
- `link`. A URL pointing to the site where the image named in the `<title>` element can be found. In practice, this should be the same as the URL of the channel. The maximum length is 500 characters. *Required.*
- `description`. A phrase that describes the image. The maximum length is 500 characters. *Optional.*
- `height`. Indicates the height of the image in pixels. The maximum value is 400; the default value is 31. *Optional.*
- `width`. Indicates the width of the image in pixels. The maximum value is 144; the default value is 88. *Optional.*

Creating Your Own RSS File

One of the easiest ways to create an RSS file for your Web content is to look at an example and modify it to fit your needs. Therefore, let's look at Listing 13.7.

LISTING 13.7 A Simple RSS File

```
<?xml version="1.0" encoding="ISO-8859-1" ?>
<rss version="0.91">
  <channel>
    <title>IDEAlliance</title>
    <link>http://idealliance.org</link>
    <description>XML Resources, XML Conferences,
➥XML Tutorials, User-Driven XML Standards,
➥XML Files Newsletter, XML Users Association
➥</description>
    <language>us-en</language>
    <copyright>Copyright 2001, idealliance.org.</copyright>
    <managingEditor>melledge@idealliance.org</managingEditor>
    <webMaster>webmaster@idealliance.org</webMaster>
    <image>
      <title>IDEAlliance Logo</title>
      <url>http://idealliance.org/images/idealogo.gif</url>
      <link>http://idealliance.org</link>
      <width>88</width>
      <height>31</height>
      <description>Logo for IDEAlliance</description>
    </image>
    <item>
      <title>XML Files: Monthly Newsletter</title>
      <link>http://www.idealliance.org/whats_xml/whats_xml_xmlfiles.htm/</link>
      <description>Monthly XML Newsletter.  Highlights
➥W3C standards development for the month,
 ➥XML-related events, XML Book Review
➥</description>
    </item>
    <item>
      <title>XML Roadmap</title>
      <link>http://www.idealliance.org/whats_xml/xmlroadmap/TOC/toc.htm</link>
      <description>A roadmap to all XML related
➥standards and vocabularies, completely
➥indexed and hyperlinked.
➥</description>
    </item>
  </channel>
</rss>
```

This RSS file is an example of RSS 0.91. It describes some content on the IDEAlliance.org Web site. One image and two items have been included in the

IDEAlliance RSS channel. The first item makes the XML Files monthly newsletter available for syndication. The second item makes the XML Roadmap available for syndication. Of course, you may add as many items and images as you want when you modify this RSS file for your own uses.

Note

IDEAlliance, or *International Digital Enterprise Alliance*, is a member organization that promotes the development and use of user-driven standards for the publishing industry. IDEAlliance (`http://www.idealliance.org`) is the host organization for numerous XML-based e-business standards for publishing. In addition, IDEAlliance serves as the host organization for both the ICE and PRISM specifications.

Publishing Your RSS File

When you have created your own RSS file, put it somewhere on your Web server. Remember that the value of your RSS file is only as good at the information in the file itself. This means that you should update your RSS file every time you change the content on your Web site or when your Web site layout changes. If the RSS file is outdated, it is of little value. Once you have created a baseline RSS file for your Web site, you may want to consider writing scripts that will "read" your Web site and automatically update fields within your RSS file.

Registering Your RSS File with RSS Aggregators

You have now created an RSS file and placed it on your site. How can you let others know that you are making content available to them? Well, of course, you can notify others using e-mail and listservs. However, the best approach is to register with one of the services that posts RSS directories.

Each RSS directory has a slightly different method for registering. Some are automated, and others are not. The major RSS directories include (in alphabetical order) `http://www.MoreOver.com`, `http://dmoz.org/Netscape/My_`*`Netscape`*`_Network`, `http://My.UserLand.com`, and `http://www.xmlTree.com`.

Registering with MoreOver.com

MoreOver.com offers a wide array of possibilities for content syndication. You can add news channels to your own sites by stepping through a wizard on the MoreOver Web site. You just have to select channels, specify their visual appearance, and the code will be mailed to you for inclusion on your Web site.

Getting your content listed with MoreOver is time consuming because it does not have an automated process. To register content, just send an e-mail to `newssource@moreover.com` that includes a pointer to your RSS file. MoreOver evaluates each listing personally. Your addition to MoreOver may take as long as three months, so be patient.

Registering with My Netscape

My Netscape publishes a huge collection of channels from organizations and individuals. Examples of channels offered through My Netscape include the Weather Channel and Nasdaq. My Netscape offers no support for publishing its channels anywhere else than `my.netscape.com`.

In order to get your channel included in the listings at `my.netscape.com`, you must first register with Netscape's Netcenter at `http://www.netscape.com`. Only registered members can submit a channel. Also, each registered member can submit only one RSS file of 8KB or less in size. You must have a valid e-mail address associated with your membership in order to register your RSS channel.

You can then register at `http://my.netscape.com`. To register, you must read and agree to the terms of use, enter the full URL of your RSS 0.91 file, and select an update frequency for your channel (the interval at which you would like Netscape to retrieve your RSS file). When My Netscape retrieves your RSS file, it will send you an e-mail to let you know that you are now listed. It will also provide you with an "add this site" button for your site that enables others to add your content to their site.

Registering with UserLand

UserLand also enables users to submit their RSS channels. UserLand divides between frontend and backend: the Web interface for reading news is the frontend, whereas the backend offers the same content in various formats, over different protocols. For example, content may be XML offered over SOAP.

UserLand uses an aggregator tool to update its RSS listings. To list your channel, you must first go to `http://aggregator.userland.com` and register. The UserLand aggregator reads all the registered XML files every hour and picks up all new items. It flows the items out to the affiliate sites using XML-RPC.

Publishing RSS Content from Others on Your Site

Now that you have made your content available to others using RSS, you may want to add content from the outside to your own Web site.

My Netscape will be of limited use here. The channels on My Netscape are designed for use on your own personalized interface at `http://my.netscape.com`. There, you can build and customize your own page. But that is really the extent of this use of RSS.

Options for including content from UserLand are much more viable. Here, you will want to go to `http://backend.userland.com`. Backend is an open technology that enables you to build your own applications based on its content flow. Most content is archived in XML form and is publicly accessible through HTTP.

MoreOver.com currently has over 250 publicly available free news categories. The headlines of these free categories can be read at `http://www.MoreOver.com`. MoreOver harvests news headline links from 1,500 online news sources and uses both human- and computer-editing to produce the newsfeeds in various formats, such as JavaScript and XML.

Content Syndication Using ICE

RSS is a simple mechanism for enabling the syndication of lightweight content. RSS was designed to be simple to use and inexpensive to implement. Although RSS has proven quite useful for the syndication of free content, RSS remains limited in its ability to enforce business rules in the content syndication environment. To fill this role, a second, more robust syndication protocol, Information and Content Exchange (ICE), was developed by industry content providers and software vendors. ICE was developed to automate the negotiation of subscription characteristics and to address the need to automate scheduled, reliable, secure redistribution of any content for publishers and for non-commercial content providers.

The History of ICE

On October 27, 1998, a press summit held in San Francisco announced the completion of a new XML-based Web protocol called ICE. On October 28, W3C acknowledged the submission of a Note on ICE. Today, the ICE protocol stands at version 1.1, and work on a Web services version of ICE—ICE 2.0—has begun. ICE was initially designed to meet the syndication requirements of Web content providers of all kinds. Today, ICE is important to anyone who wants to distribute information on the Web according to controlled business rules. ICE has been incorporated into many products, including Vignette, Kinecta, Oracle, Interwoven, 3Path, HP Bluestone, and Active Data Exchange.

ICE provides support for the syndication process. The theory behind ICE is that all online businesses have a syndication problem. Here, syndication is defined in a much broader sense than just the distribution of published content. Certainly publishers want a standard way to establish a reliable syndication business process. However, the truth is that all business partners need a reliable and accountable mechanism to exchange information on a routine basis. What publishers as well as those involved in e-business must do is establish online, networked information-based partnerships. Today, this process is often ad hoc, fragile, error prone, and expensive. This cannot prevail as the predominant Web model for syndication.

ICE provides us with a standard model that can be automated to support syndication for all. The importance of adopting a standard interchange mechanism is that it will lower costs of entry by eliminating the requirement to write customized scripts for each business partner that is added to the value chain. This, in turn, will increase opportunity by enabling a quick, inexpensive, and standard way to add new trading partners. The existence of a standard format for interoperating between business partners is critical.

ICE is not a file format but rather a bidirectional protocol designed specifically to support content dissemination on the Web. New opportunities created by ICE include the following:

- The ability for publishers to generate new revenue streams from existing content
- The ability to lower cost of content exchange among networked trading partners
- The ability to expand distribution of information (increased market share and increased revenue)
- The ability to create Internet Value Networks, not islands of information

ICE Authoring Group

The initial members of the ICE Authoring Group were Web pioneers who recognized that they needed a standard protocol for interoperating. These pioneers included Con O'Connell, Neil Webber, and Brad Husick from Vignette, Laird Popkin from News America Digital Publishing, Rick Levine from Sun Microsystems, Doug Bayer from Microsoft Corporation, Jay Brodsky from Chicago Tribune Media Services, Bruce Hunt of Adobe Systems, Andy Werth from CNET, John Petrone from Preview Travel, Gord Larose from ChannelWare, and Phil Gibson from National Semi-Conductor. The companies that developed ICE were evenly split between software vendors and users of technology, ensuring that it was a standard that met real user requirements. ICE is therefore known as a *user-driven technology standard*. The ICE Authoring Group and all ICE activities are hosted by IDEAlliance, the International Digital Enterprise Alliance. IDEAlliance provides administrative support for the group and plays a major role in helping to promote the adoption of the standard at conferences and summits.

You can learn more about ICE at its Web site, `http://www.icestandard.org`.

Caution

The ICE protocol manages and automates syndication relationships and the managed, scheduled transfer of content. *ICE should not be confused with PRISM.* They are not the same. PRISM provides an industry-standard metadata vocabulary to describe content assets. This vocabulary can work with ICE to automate content reuse and syndication processes, but it is not a syndication protocol. PRISM is a discovery mechanism and enables us to select content that will be syndicated using ICE. There is a natural synergy between ICE and PRISM. ICE provides the protocol for syndication processes, and PRISM provides a description of the resource being syndicated.

The ICE Syndication Model

The ICE syndication model differs from the RSS syndication model because RSS enables content providers to make their content free for use across the Web by anyone. However, ICE is specifically designed to enable the managed, reliable, scheduled delivery of content in a business environment. RSS assumes that those using the content may be unknown to the content provider. ICE, on the other hand, assumes that a business relationship has been established before ICE transactions begin. The business agreement can involve personal discussions, legal review, and contracts, just as any business agreement does. ICE transactions begin only after the business agreement has been established.

ICE Terminology

Before we begin to consider a step-by-step example to illustrate the ICE syndication model, it will be helpful to review a few definitions:

- *Syndicator*. A content provider or aggregator. A content distributor.
- *Subscriber*. A content consumer or receiver.
- *Subscription*. An agreement between a subscriber and a syndicator for the delivery of content according to the delivery policy and other parameters in the agreement.
- *Catalog*. A listing of ICE offerings. This is the listing of all content being offered for subscriptions and the delivery terms for the content.
- *ICE offer*. A particular subscription offering found within the ICE catalog.
- *Delivery policy*. The terms of delivery for ICE content. The delivery policy can include start date, stop date, mode (push or pull), delivery days, delivery times, update mode, and delivery URL.
- *Collection*. The current content of a subscription.

- *ICE package.* A delivery instance of commands to update a collection such as the addition of content items.
- *ICE payload.* The XML document used by ICE to carry protocol information. Examples include requests for packages, catalogs of subscription offers, usage logs, and other management information.

ICE Usage Example

ICE is an XML protocol that defines the business rules and processes needed for reliable content syndication among Web servers. Currently ICE uses HTTP as a transport layer. ICE messages, coded in XML, always come in request/response pairs.

Two parties (Web servers) are involved in ICE transactions. The first is the *syndicator*. The syndicator is the party that provides content—either its own or content it has aggregated from other sources. The second party in ICE transactions is the *subscriber*. The subscriber is the one who wants data from the syndicator. In ICE, certain messages are reserved for the syndicator. Other messages are reserved for the subscriber—and some messages can be used by either party.

Let's look at a typical ICE scenario so you can follow the steps in the ICE syndication process. In this scenario, a business relationship is established between the syndicator and the subscriber. This process is done in person or by telephone. The subscriber provides the syndicator with an identifier that will be used as the basis for automated ICE transactions.

The next step is for the subscriber to select subscription content. The subscriber sends a message to request a catalog that lists all content offers using the `ice-get-catalog` request. Listing 13.8 shows the `ice-get-catalog` request message in XML.

LISTING 13.8 An `ice-get-catalog` Request

```
<?xml version="1.0"?>
<!DOCTYPE ice-payload SYSTEM "http://www.icestandard.org/dtds/ICE1_1.dtd">
<ice-payload payload-id="PL-2000-08-24T22:10:33.901-DKennedy-423"
     timestamp="22:10:33,741" ice.version="1.1">
   <ice-header>
      <ice-sender sender-id="4af37b30-2c35-11d2-be4a-204c4f4f5020"
                  name="D Kennedy " role="subscriber"/>
      <ice-user-agent>
         IceBlock Systems ICE Processor, V7.0
      </ice-user-agent>
   </ice-header>
   <ice-request request-id="2000-08-24T22:10:33_RQ_DKennedyl_1888">
      <ice-get-catalog/>
   </ice-request>
</ice-payload>
```

At this point, the syndicator responds by delivering a catalog to the subscriber. Listing 13.9 shows the ice-response message in XML.

LISTING 13.9 ICE Catalog Response

```
<?xml version="1.0" ?>
<!DOCTYPE ice-payload SYSTEM "http://www.icestandard.org/dtds/ICE1_1.dtd">
<ice-payload payload-id="PL-2000-08-24T22:10:45-XMLFiles-2761"
     timestamp="22:10:45,321"
     location="xmlfiles.idealliance.org"
     ice.version="1.1">
   <ice-header >
     <ice-sender sender-id="4a2180c9-9435-d00f-9317-204d974e3410"
                 name="IDEAlliance" role="syndicator"/>
     <ice-user-agent>
       Northstar Protocols ICE Processor, V17
     </ice-user-agent>
   </ice-header>
   <ice-response response-id="RSP-2000-07-21T02:03:45-XMLFiles-9876">
     <ice-code numeric="200"
               phrase="OK"
               message-id="REQ-2000-07-21T02:02:23-DKennedy-345"/>
   </ice-response>
   <ice-catalog name="XML Files 2001 Newsletters"
               url="http://xmlfiles.idealliance.org/offers/xmlfiles.html">
     <ice-contact name="XML Files">
        For information please contact
        Catalog Offers:    Dianne Kennedy, 650-555-1212
        Technical Support: David Steinhardt,     650-555-1313
     </ice-contact>
     <ice-offer product-name="XMLFiles 2001 Newsletter"
                offer-id="XMLFiles-2001-V1-R1"
                subscription-id="ICE-NEW-SUBSCRIPTION"
                expiration-date="2001-12-30"
                quantity="12">
       <ice-delivery-policy stopdate="2002-01-01">
         <ice-delivery-rule mode="pull"
                max-num-updates="24"
                min-num-updates="12"
                max-update-interval="P2678400S"
                min-update-interval="P43200S"/>
         <!-- max-num-updates is two per month,
              min-num-updates is 12 per year,
              max-update-interval is 31 days,
              min-update-interval is 12 hours -->
       </ice-delivery-policy>
     </ice-offer>
   </ice-catalog>
</ice-payload>
```

ICE has functions that will enable the automated negotiations of any ICE offer. Suppose, for example, an offer in the catalog is the content that the subscriber wants, but the delivery policy is not acceptable. The subscriber could use ICE messages to negotiate acceptable delivery parameters.

When the subscriber is satisfied with the offer, acceptance for the offer is sent to the syndicator. The syndicator will then verify that it accepts the subscription and provides the subscriber with a subscription ID.

The next step is for the subscriber to request initial subscription content. The subscriber uses `ice-get-package` with the `current-state="ICE-INITIAL"` message (see Listing 13.10). The syndicator will provide the initial content for the subscription according to the delivery policy for the subscription in response to this request.

LISTING 13.10 Example of an `ice-get-package` Message

```
<?xml version="1.0"?>
<!DOCTYPE ice-payload SYSTEM "http://www.icestandard.org/dtds/ICE1_1.dtd">
<ice-payload payload-id="PL-2000-08-24T22:10:33.901-DKennedy-423"
     timestamp="22:10:33,741" ice.version="1.1">
   <ice-header>
      <ice-sender sender-id="4af37b30-2c35-11d2-be4a-204c4f4f5020"
                  name="D Kennedy " role="subscriber"/>
      <ice-user-agent>
         IceBlock Systems ICE Processor, V7.0
      </ice-user-agent>
   </ice-header>
   <ice-request request-id="2000-08-24T22:10:33_RQ_DKennedyl_1888">
      <ice-get-package current-state="ICE-INITIAL" subscription-id="1"/>
   </ice-request>
</ice-payload>
```

Following the initial delivery of subscription content, new content will be delivered from the syndicator to the subscriber according to the delivery policy of the subscription. The content is contained within the `ice-payload` as an `ice-package` made up of one or more `ice-items`. The ICE message may include any kind of content directly in the message (that is, HTML, database records, XML, graphics, PDF, and so on). Typically, though, the ICE item just sends a URL where the content is made available. The ICE message itself can be thought of as an envelope for content and data about the content delivery. When the ice message delivers content, it is always as an `ice-response`. You can see this message flow in Figure 13.6.

FIGURE 13.6
ICE enables messaging between the syndicator and subscriber.

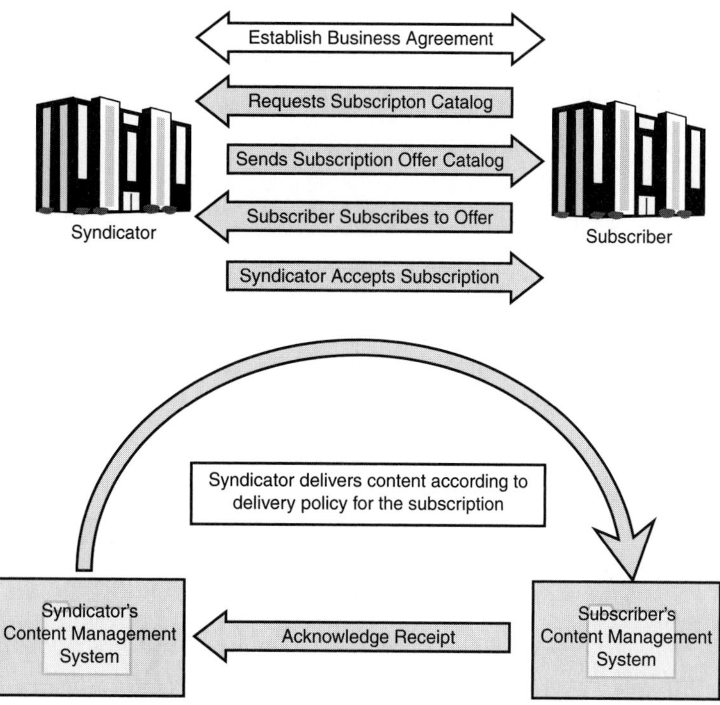

ICE Error Messages

One of the features of ICE that provides a great business advantage is the reliability of content delivery. The ICE protocol is designed so that every request must have a matching response. It is these request/response message pairs that enable us to verify and log the receipt of content. The ICE specification has built in a number of ICE error message codes that specifically support automation of syndication. These codes are used within the `ice-code` element. Listing 13.11 shows how `ice-code` is used to indicate an error.

LISTING 13.11 Example of `ice-code` with Error Indication

```
<ice-response response-id="REQ-2000-07-21T02:03:00-DKennedy-1873">
      <ice-code numeric="331"
                phrase="Failure fetching external data"
                message-id="REQ-2000-07-21T02:02:23-XMLFiles-2397">
        Unable to obtain content from URL:
        http://xmlfiles.idealliance.org/xmlfiles/xmlfiles2001.htm
      </ice-code>
</ice-response>
```

The following list shows some examples of ICE messages. The protocol has been developed based on use-case scenarios. Error messages are designed from these scenarios. Here's the list:

- *200 – OK*. The operation successfully completed.
- *201 – Confirmed*. The subscriber has successfully processed the package.
- *331 – Failure Fetching External Data.*
- *401 – Incomplete/Cannot Parse*. You couldn't even get the parser started!
- *402 – Not Well Formed XML*. Your XML tags didn't balance.
- *404 – Broken Link*. Content is not available at the specified link.
- *405 – Unrecognized Sender*. Who are you?
- *406 – Unrecognized Subscription*. You have to have a valid subscription ID.
- *407 – Unrecognized Operation*. An operation in the package was not one that you recognized.
- *408 – Unrecognized Operation Arguments*. The attributes on the element were unknown.
- *430 – Not Confirmed*. A generic error indicating that the subscriber didn't complete processing.
- *501 – Temporary Responder Error*. An "I'm too busy right now to do it" message.
- *603 – No More Confirmations To Send*. When you've confirmed everything, respond with this.

Note

The ICE codes fall into seven categories. The 200 series codes are success codes, such as OK. The 300 series codes are payload-level status codes. The 400 series codes are request-level status codes. The 500 series codes are operational failure codes, and the 600 series codes are pending state codes, where the subscriber is expected to send something to the syndicator, or vice versa. The 700 series codes are local use codes. These codes are reserved for use by the local ICE implementation and *must not* ever be sent to another ICE processor over the transport medium. Finally, the 900 series codes are experimental codes that enable ICE implementers to experiment new facilities without fear of collision with future versions of ICE codes.

ICE clearly contains many more features and imposes many disciplines on the process of content syndication. Therefore, one may make the false assumption that using ICE is a complex and expensive undertaking. It turns out that there are different levels of ICE implementation and ICE conformance. However, actually setting up minimal ICE implementation is easy for anyone.

Simple ICE Syndication

Very simple ICE implementations can provide a basic ability to syndicate content, just as RSS can. You would make syndicated material available in this way by following these steps:

1. Create content that you wish to syndicate. Place it on your Web site so that it will be available. Suppose you put the new issue of XML Files at the following URL:

   `http://www.idealliance.org/xmlfiles/issue30/default.htm`

2. Construct the following ICE message that describes the location of the content to be syndicated:

```
<?xml version="1.0"?>
<!DOCTYPE ice-package SYSTEM "http://www.icestandard.org/dtds/ICE1_1.dtd">
<ice-package>
<ice-item-ref url="http://www.idealliance.org/xmlfiles/issue30/default.htm"
item-id="xmlfilesissue30"/>
</ice-package>
```

3. Now place the ICE package on your Web site, such as `http://www.idealliance.org/ice/xmlfiles.ice`.

That's all that is required of the syndicator. If you are the subscriber to content that is posted using this simple ICE mechanism, you have two steps you must follow:

1. Obtain the URL for the ICE package on the Web site. You might receive this via e-mail. Alternatively, it might be posted on the home page of the site.
2. Parse the `ice-item-ref` URLs out of the ICE package and either download the content or reference it using the URL.

Note

Note that in this simple scenario we are only using `xmlfiles.ice` to point to content that is available for syndication. We are not establishing a business relationship, negotiating delivery policy, or enabling any sort of content control. When used in this way, ICE and RSS are very comparable. Just as the RSS syndicator must notify potential subscribers that content is available, the ICE syndicator, in this simple scenario, will need to publicize the ICE location on the Web site to enable subscribers to find the content for syndication.

Full ICE Compliance

If you intend to take advantage of the power of ICE to manage content according to business rules, you will most likely need the full power of ICE and the full range of ICE messaging at your disposal. This means that you will need to purchase a tool that provides ICE capabilities. Because ICE is a server-to-server messaging protocol, you can't really "see" ICE. However, you can look for it as a standard protocol supported by Web content-management systems.

The `ice-payload` is the XML document used by ICE to carry protocol information, or *ice messages*. The `ice-payload` is homogenous. This means that an `ice-payload` can only carry one kind of message. The DTD for ICE, shown in Listing 13.12, shows that the payload may carry one or more responses, one or more requests, but may never mix requests with responses.

LISTING 13.12 The DTD for an `ice-payload`

```
<!ELEMENT ice-payload ( ice-header, ( ice-request+ | ice-response+ |
          ice-unsolicited-now | ice-unsolicited-request+ |
          ice-unsolicited-response+) )
>
<!ATTLIST ice-payload
          payload-id      CDATA #REQUIRED
          timestamp       CDATA #REQUIRED
          ice.version     CDATA #REQUIRED  >
```

There are many different kinds of ICE requests and ICE responses. The syndicator sometimes makes requests and sometimes gives responses. Likewise, the subscriber sometimes makes requests and other times makes responses. Do not just assume that the subscriber is the requestor. That is not at all the case!

Here's a list of the standard ICE requests that are supported within full ICE compliance (as you can see, an automated tool to handle all messaging and track states of syndicated content is a must for full ICE syndication support):

- `ice-cancel`. Cancels the subscription.
- `ice-change-subscription`. Changes the subscription.
- `ice-code`. Passes an ICE message code.
- `ice-get-catalog`. Requests for the syndicator to request an ICE catalog.
- `ice-get-events`. Returns an ICE events log.
- `ice-get-package`. Requests for the syndicator to return an ICE package.
- `ice-get-sequence`. Returns the current ICE subscription state.

- ice-get-status. Returns the status of the subscription.
- ice-nop. Sends a no operation message. Used for debugging.
- ice-notify. Mechanism for sending a text message.
- ice-offer. The ICE subscription offer sent by Syndicator
- ice-package. The ICE package sent from syndicator to subscriber.
- ice-send-confirmations. Returns confirmation from the subscriber that a package has been received.
- ice-repair-item. Repairs a subscription collection by replacing missing items.

Enabling Content Management with ICE

ICE is designed to give both syndicators and subscribers the ability to manage their content. In the following simple example, the ice-access element specifies the span of time that the URL will be available. This means the subscriber knows how long the link will last. Also, the syndicator has made a commitment to provide it for a specific length of time. Therefore, the duration of the content is now made explicit, meaning each party can avoid the "404" broken link problem.

In Listing 13.13, you can see how we used ice-access-control to limit who may access the content via login and password. A security notice is printed to indicate that even though we are granting access for syndication, the copyright remains with IDEAlliance.

LISTING 13.13 Using ice-access to Manage Content

```
<?xml version="1.0"?>
<!DOCTYPE ice-package SYSTEM "http://www.icestandard.org/dtds/ICE1_1.dtd">
<ice-package>
<ice-item-ref url="http://www.idealliance.org/xmlfiles/issue30/default.htm"
item-id="xmlfilesissue30" />
<ice-access>
<ice-access-window starttime="2001-10-01T08:00:00"
➥stoptime="2001-10-31T017:00:00"/>
➥<ice-access-control control-type="password"
➥user="XMLFiles Subscriber" password="xmlgo">
          2001 IDEAlliance, Inc. All Rights Reserved.
          Use of the content in this item reference
          implies acceptance of the use license at
          http://www.idealliance.com/licenses/subscriber.html
          including honoring all copyrights and trademarks.
          You agree not to provide others with the
          access control password above.</ice-access-control>
</ice-access>
</ice-package>
```

Selecting a Content-Management Solution

Because Web content management does not have an out-of-the-box definition, what one looks for in selecting a content-management solution is difficult to specify. Clearly each definition of content management must be based on the characteristics of the content and the goals of the business model. Certain features of the content-management system may be critical to your business model, whereas others are not. About 100 different companies sell content-management solutions or components. Some are XML based, and some are not. Content-management solutions range from inexpensive desktop solutions to million-dollar solutions.

So where do you start? What do you look for?

First, you should begin with business requirements. Today, justifying the investment in a content-management solution must have clear benefits. Will the system save money for the company? Will the system position your company to be more competitive? Will the system position your company to develop new product offerings based on content reuse or new kinds of content-based products?

When you have clear business requirements for the system, you will want to make a decision about whether to purchase an integrated system or whether to integrate the system yourself. You can try to determine whether any off-the-shelf system comes close to meeting your business requirements. If it does, you should study the areas where the integrated system does not meet your requirements. Can you live with these deficiencies? Is it possible to customize the system to meet your requirements? What impact on your business goals will these deficiencies have?

If you cannot select an off-the-shelf solution, you must then look at the options for integrating your own custom system. You must also consider the capabilities of the information technologies staff within your company. Are they capable of integrating a complex system? Will you have to hire consultants to do the integration for you? You must understand the components that could be integrated, weigh those against your business requirements, and determine which components/functionalities are must-haves. Then you must narrow the field. If you choose to integrate a system, always be aware of the cost. At some point the cost may exceed the benefits that you seek!

Investigate the following features of any content-management solution (these features can be critical):

- Standards based
- System performance

- Scalability
- Cost of implementation
- The ability to provide ongoing support and services

Is the Solution Standards Based?

As you select a content-management solution, you should look for systems/components that use XML and other Web standards for messaging, content coding, and metadata coding. These are likely to be most flexible and easier to integrate than proprietary solutions. Always make this a priority.

System Performance

When selecting a content-management solution, you must always consider the performance of the system. System performance can make a real difference in how positively users view the new system. In addition, performance impacts real dollars and cents in your business. How long do backups take? How quickly can content be assembled for online delivery? How much downtime can be expected? When does the number of users begin to affect the speed of the system? Ask vendors for benchmarks. Conduct them yourself as part of your selection process.

Can the System Scale?

Before you select a content-management system, you should have some projections for the growth you expect. Do you expect to add a significant number of new users? Do you expect to increase the volume of the content on the system significantly? Do you expect to add new kinds or configurations of content output from the system? And most importantly, can the system meet your future goals? Will it cost more money? How much?

Cost of Implementation

In selecting a content-management system, you must have a clear understanding of what comes with the system and what must be added in order to implement the system as you have specified. During the sales cycle, all things are possible. During the implementation of the system, you might find hidden costs for which you had not budgeted. Must you add new components to get the functionality you need? How much will this cost? Try to understand all implementation costs up front.

Ongoing Support

Of course, once a system is installed, you will need to have ongoing support. A good Web content-management system will not be implemented in a day or even a month. The solutions provider will be your partner. Therefore, be sure you select a good one. Content-management systems are mission critical, so you need the assurance of having a good support and service team behind you. How many people are in the customer and technical support teams for the system you have purchased? Is the company stable? Is there an office nearby? Can the vendor support your investment over time?

Summary

As mention at the beginning of this chapter, Web content management can have many different meanings and solutions, depending on the types of content you have and your business goals. Despite the differences from solution to solution, Web content management is typified by standard workflow steps. Components of Web content-management workflow include a content-input phase, a content-repository phase, and a content-delivery phase.

In this chapter, we have discussed the processes within the content-management workflow in detail. You have also learned that XML provides the best way to integrate the components of the system. Basing a Web content-management solution on XML means that it will be far easier to integrate software components and will help to ensure the flexibility of your new content-management solution.

CHAPTER 14

Architecting Web Services

In This Chapter

No topic in this book is getting more attention and pure hype than the area of Web Services. Dozens of vendors, led by Microsoft and IBM, are pouring enormous resources into developing Web Services frameworks as well as the tools to support them. Part of the hype is unquestionably due to technology vendors' need to sell new products (as well as new versions of old products). However, the potential for Web Services goes far beyond a straightforward economic need to innovate.

In fact, Web Services signal a paradigm shift in distributed computing. Web Services have the potential to change the way distributed systems interact, which will fundamentally affect the operation of the Internet. As a result, Web Services might form the backbone of a new global e-business infrastructure.

However, many economic and political battles remain to be fought before Web Services can realize their enormous potential. Today, Web Services are on the bleeding edge, in the hands of the technologists and a few early adopters. As with other paradigm shifts, most of the work going on in the Web Services area involve new ways of solving *old* problems. People still follow the old ways of thinking about distributed computing and e-business frameworks. In order to break out of the old way of thinking and apply Web Services to *new* problems, you must understand how the core technologies of Web Services enable a new way of thinking about distributed computing. That's the goal of this chapter.

In this chapter, you'll learn the following:

- The definition of Web Services and the Web Services model
- The business and technical motivations for the development of Web Services
- The definition and structure of the service-oriented architecture, which is analogous to the now-familiar object-oriented architectures
- How to define and implement the service-oriented architecture's four key functional components: service implementation, publication, discovery, and invocation
- About current work in the areas of security and quality of service as well as the composition of Web Services and conversations among Web Services
- How to approach the service-oriented architecture from different viewpoints
- How the Just-In-Time capabilities of the Web Services model can create a new paradigm for distributed computing

What Are Web Services?

Simply put, Web Services are loosely coupled, contracted components that communicate via XML-based interfaces. Let's take a closer look at this definition:

- *Loosely coupled* means that Web Services and the programs that invoke them can be changed independently of each other. Loose coupling also implies that Web Services are platform independent.
- *Contracted* means that a Web Service's behavior, its input and output parameters, and how to bind to it are publicly available.
- A *component* is encapsulated code, which means that the implementation of each component is hidden from outside the component. Each component's functionality is only known by the interface it exposes.
- Because all Web Services' interfaces are built with XML, they all share the advantages of XML: They have a human readable, text-based format that is firewall friendly and self-describing. All Web Services are described using a standard XML notation called its *service description*.

Put another way, Web Services are self-contained applications that can be described, published, located, and invoked over the Internet (or any network, for that matter).

We will also talk extensively about the Web Services model of distributed computing, which is the overall approach to distributed technology enabled by Web Services. Web Services can be thought of merely as enabling a new remote procedure call (RPC) architecture, but the power of the technology goes far beyond what existing RPC architectures can provide. These new capabilities are part of the Web Services model.

Business Motivations for Web Services

The vision of global e-business largely remains unrealized. Executives dream about seamless interactions both with other companies as well as e-marketplaces, but the technology lags behind the vision. Today's information technology is still extraordinarily complex and expensive. Even with standards such as Electronic Data Interchange (EDI), Java 2 Enterprise Edition (J2EE), Common Object Request Broker Architecture (CORBA), and Windows Distributed interNet Application (Windows DNA), communicating between different corporate systems is still filled with hair-pulling detail work.

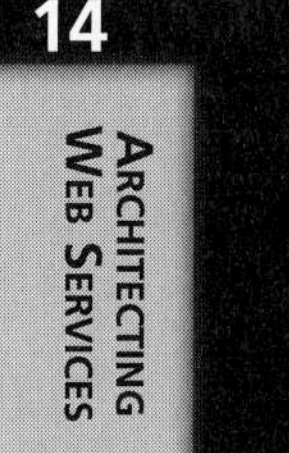

The business world needs more powerful techniques to scale business solutions without increasing complexity to unmanageable levels. In addition, there is a clear need for open, flexible, and dynamic solutions for enabling global e-business interactions among systems. The Web Services model promises to deliver these solutions by addressing complexity and costs, providing a common language for B2B e-commerce, and enabling the vision of a global e-marketplace.

Managing Complexity and IT Costs

In the early days of business computing, mainframes were large, complex, and expensive, and so were the programs that ran on them. As these systems aged, it was often prohibitively expensive to replace them, so programmers added functionality by adding code, thus building layer upon layer of complexity.

Object-oriented programming arose in this environment as an answer to the problems resulting from the ever-increasing complexity of the legacy systems. Modularity and reusability were touted as the solutions to the problems of legacy programming. Unfortunately, the promised gains generally did not materialize because of the complexities inherent in distributed systems.

Remote procedure call (RPC) architectures arose to address the problems that developed when components on different systems needed to communicate with each other. The two most successful RPC architectures, DCOM and CORBA, have gained widespread acceptance, but they are still too complex to provide convenient interoperability among different systems.

The conventional view of complex systems is that complexity and power are directly correlated: Powerful systems are necessarily complex, and simple systems are necessarily of limited use. However, current research on complex systems contradicts this conventional wisdom. It is possible to build powerful systems with simple components (such as Web Services) that are smart enough to organize themselves into large, powerful systems. Such systems would retain the simplicity of their components as well as reduce the costs inherent in large, complex systems. (A good place to learn about complex systems is at `http://www.brint.com/Systems.htm`.)

Lingua Franca of B2B E-Commerce

Business to Business (B2B) e-commerce has been around for more than a decade in the form of the Electronic Data Interchange (EDI). EDI is quite powerful and has gained widespread acceptance but is limited by its semantic ambiguity. For example, a "quantity" field in a given form may stand for number of boxes for one company but the number of pallets for another. People have to resolve each ambiguity manually, making EDI useful primarily in a hub-and-spoke arrangement, where one large company can dictate the meaning of each field to its suppliers.

When the Internet opened up the prospect of many-to-many e-commerce, it soon became clear that there needed to be a way to agree upon a single business vocabulary for all participants in each trading group. XML provided the basis for building such vocabularies because of its inherent extensibility. However, XML's greatest strength also proved to be a weakness, because its extensibility led to hundreds of different business vocabularies, often with overlapping applicability.

The Web Services model addresses this Tower of Babel problem by providing for dynamic service descriptions. Individual Web Services can describe their interfaces at runtime, allowing for dynamic interpretation of the semantics of the XML that underlies the messages Web Services send and receive.

Global E-Marketplace Vision

The overarching vision behind e-business is a world with global, seamless, automated e-commerce. Each company's systems should be able to locate and transact with other companies' systems automatically. Unfortunately, this vision is still far from becoming a reality.

Today, integrating commerce systems from two companies requires preexisting business and technical relationships between the companies. Only then can the technology teams of the two companies get together and decide how they will communicate and handle business transactions.

Business requires a way for companies to locate, identify, contact, and transact with other companies around the world on a "just in time" basis—that is, without having to establish a technical relationship beforehand.

Technical Motivations for Web Services

The technical motivations for Web Services are far more complex than the business motivations. Fundamentally, technologists are looking for the simplicity and flexibility promised, but never delivered, by RPC architectures and object-oriented technologies.

Limitations of CORBA and DCOM

Programming has been performed on a computer-by-computer basis for much of the history of computing. Programs were discrete chunks of computer code that ran on individual computers. Even object-oriented programming originated in a single-computer environment. This isolated computer mindset has been around so long that it pervades all thinking about software.

Then along came networks, and technologists looked for ways to break up program functionality onto multiple computers. Early communication protocols, such as the Network

File System for Unix and Microsoft's Distributed Computing Environment, focused on the network layer. These protocols, in turn, led to the development of wire protocols for distributed computing—in particular, the Object Remote Procedure Call (ORPC) protocol for Microsoft's DCOM and the Object Management Group's Internet Inter-ORB Protocol (IIOP) that underlies CORBA.

RPC architectures such as DCOM and CORBA enabled programs to be broken into different pieces running on different computers. Object-oriented techniques were particularly suited to this distributed environment for a few reasons. First, objects maintained their own discrete identities. Second, the code that handles the communication between objects could be encapsulated into its own set of classes so that programmers working in a distributed environment needn't worry about how this communication worked.

However, programmers still had that isolated computer mindset, which colored both DCOM's and CORBA's approach: Write your programs so that the remote computer appears to be a part of your own computer. RPC architectures all involved marshalling a piece of a program on one computer and shipping it to another system.

Note

Marshalling means taking an object or other form of structured data and breaking it up so that it can be transmitted as a stream of bytes over a network in such a way that the original object or data structure can be reassembled on the other end. Another word for marshalling is *serializing*, and objects that can be marshalled are described as *serializable*.

Unfortunately, both DCOM and CORBA share many of the same problems. DCOM is expressly a Microsoft-only architecture, and although CORBA is intended to provide cross-platform interoperability, in reality it is too complex and semantically ambiguous to provide any level of interoperability without a large amount of manual integration work. In addition, the specter of marshalling executable code and shipping it over the Internet opens up a Pandora's box of security concerns, such as viruses and worms.

Furthermore, each of these technologies handles key functionality in its own, proprietary way. CORBA's payload parameter value format is the Common Data Representation (CDR) format, whereas DCOM uses the incompatible Network Data Representation (NDR) format (Web Services use XML). Likewise, CORBA uses Interoperable Object References (IORs) for endpoint naming, whereas DCOM uses OBJREFs (Web Services use URIs, which are generalized URLs).

In addition, both CORBA and DCOM use binary wire protocols: the IIOP and ORPC, respectively. Because these protocols are binary, they are not humanly readable, and more significantly, they often have difficulties moving through firewalls. As a result, these architectures are usually relegated to use within the enterprise rather than between companies. (Web Services solve these problems with SOAP, to be covered in Chapter 15, "Web Services Building Blocks: SOAP".)

Problems with Business Modeling

Business modeling takes distributed computing with objects to its logical extreme, where objects are rolled into business components that correspond to coarse-grained business concepts or processes. A business component consists of all the software artifacts necessary to implement a business concept (such as "customer" or "order") as an autonomous, reusable element of a distributed information system.

In essence, business modeling is a way to apply object-oriented principles to large, enterprise systems in a recursive manner, where component systems are made up of business components, which in turn consist of individual distributed software components, which in turn contain object classes. As companies' use of technology matures, they move from using structured programming to object-oriented architectures, as shown in Figure 14.1.

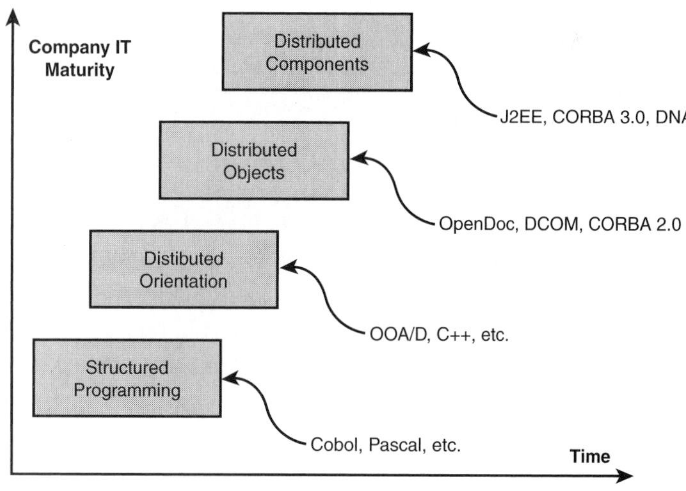

FIGURE 14.1
The evolution of business components.

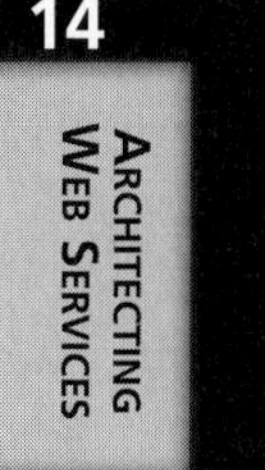

By representing business concepts with systems of business components, business modelers seek to achieve the following objectives:

- Limit complexity and costs by developing coarse-grained software units.
- Support high levels of reuse of business components.

- Speed up the development cycle by combining preexisting business components and continuous integration.
- Deliver systems that can easily evolve.
- Allow different vendors to provide competing business components that serve the same purpose, leading to a market in business components.

Unfortunately, large-scale business modeling has not widely achieved any of these objectives, for several reasons, including the following:

- Business components in reality typically have complex, nonstandard interfaces, which makes reuse and substitutability difficult to achieve.
- As systems of business components evolve into increasingly complex, comprehensive systems, it becomes very difficult to maintain the encapsulation of the components. Ideally, each component is a black box that can be plugged into the underlying framework; in reality, developers must spend time tweaking the internal operations of the components.
- The business drivers behind the development of the business components lead to custom development, which makes each component unique and custom in its own right. Every company handles its business models differently, so every business component is different.

The Web Services model can be thought of as the next step in the evolution of business components. Whereas business components are large, recursively defined collections of objects, Web Services should be relatively small, self-organizing components with well-defined, dynamic interfaces.

Problems with Vendor Dependence

Early leaders in every nascent industry find that they must integrate their companies vertically. For example, Standard Oil drilled the wells, transported the petroleum, refined it, distributed it, and then ran the gas stations that sold it. It had to follow this business model, because there were no other companies that could provide each of these services at a low-enough cost or with adequate quality.

The same is true of the software industry. ERP systems were essential to companies' operations, because the only cost-effective way to get all the operational components that make up ERP systems to work together was to get them from the same company. If you tried to cobble together accounting and manufacturing software back in 1995, you would have found large variations in quality and extremely high integration costs.

Simply put, the single main advantage to single-vendor distributed software solutions is that they work. When the cost of integration is high, going with a single vendor will save money. However, there are also several disadvantages to obtaining software from a single vendor. The disadvantages are as follows:

- As the market matures, other vendors will offer individual packages that are of a higher quality than the single vendor, making a "best-of-breed" approach more attractive.
- The purchasing company's business grows to depend on the business strategy of the vendor. Shifts in strategic direction or business problems at the vendor can filter down to the vendor's customers (the "all-the-eggs-in-one-basket" problem).
- It is very difficult to integrate a "one-stop shop" vendor's product with other vendors' products at other companies. As a result, a single vendor approach limits the potential of e-business.

Taking a vendor-independent software strategy solves the problems of vendor dependence but is only cost effective when certain conditions are met:

- A "best-of-breed" approach makes sense because the market is mature enough to offer competing packages of sufficient quality.
- There is a broadly accepted integration framework that allows for inexpensive integration of different packages, both within companies and between companies.

The Web Services model has the potential to meet both of these conditions. In particular, Web Services' loose coupling is the key to flexible, inexpensive integration capabilities.

Reuse and Integration Goals

Software reuse has been a primary goal of object-oriented architectures but, like the Holy Grail, has always been just out of reach. Creating objects and components to be reusable takes more development time and design skill, and therefore more money up front. However, conventional wisdom says that coding for reusability saves money in the long run, so why isn't coding for reusability more prevalent?

The problem is that the goal of software reuse presupposes a world with stable business requirements, and such a world just doesn't exist. Building a component so that it can handle future situations different from the current ones tends to be wasted work, because the future always brings surprises. Instead, it usually makes more sense to take an agile approach to components and include only the functionality you need right now. Such an approach keeps costs down and is more likely to meet the business requirements, but the resulting component is rarely reusable.

Simple integration of software applications is likewise just out of reach. This problem is especially onerous in the area of legacy integration. Today's approach to integrating legacy systems into component architectures is to create a "wrapper" for the legacy system so that it will expose a standard interface that all the other components know how to work with. What ends up happening is that getting that wrapper to work becomes the major expense and takes the most time. Maybe 90 percent of your software is easy to integrate, but the remaining 10 percent takes up most of your budget.c

The Service-Oriented Architecture (SOA)

Web Services can be thought of as components that can be described, published, located, and invoked over the Internet (or in general, any network). The true power of Web Services, however, comes from the fact that all these activities can take place at runtime. In essence, Web Services can figure out how to work with each other, without having been designed to do so specifically.

In order for Web Services to be able to work well together, they must participate in a set of shared organizing principles we call a *service-oriented architecture* (SOA). The term *service-oriented* means that the architecture is described and organized to support Web Services' dynamic, automated description, publication, discovery, and use.

The SOA organizes Web Services into three basic roles: the service provider, the service requester, and the service registry. The relationships among these three roles are shown in Figure 14.2.

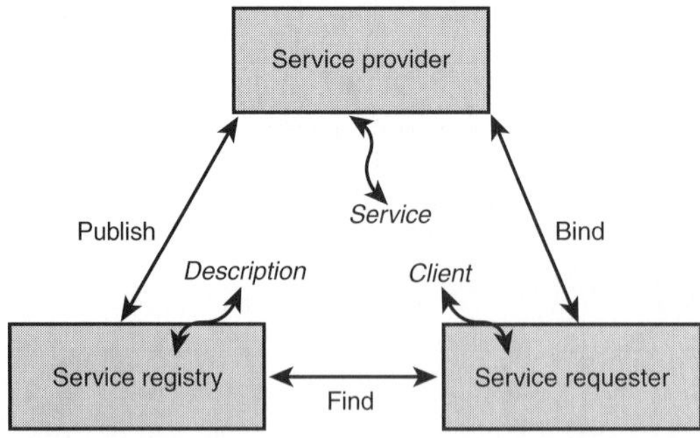

FIGURE 14.2
Web Service roles and relationships.

Service providers publish (and unpublish) their services to a service registry. Then, service requesters can find the desired Web Services by searching for their descriptions at the service registry. Once the requester locates the desired service, its client binds with the service at the service provider and then invokes the service.

The SOA is responsible for describing and organizing the mechanisms and practices for each of these actions. In addition, the SOA is responsible for describing how Web Services can be combined into larger services.

Flexibility of E-Business Services

The ability of Web Services to discover, bind to, and invoke other services automatically at runtime—what we call *Just In Time* (JIT) integration—is actually a tall order for any component in a distributed system to fill. JIT integration presupposes that the SOA has reached critical mass across the globe, where there is a sufficient number of Web Services exposing their interfaces available for discovery and invocation. Furthermore, how are we ever going to get to that global SOA if we don't already have a mature set of Web Services protocols that everyone agrees upon?

The fact of the matter is, there needs to be a way to bootstrap the SOA so that we can build it piece by piece, even though the underlying protocols are still maturing. Fortunately, this flexibility is built into the SOA, because although it would be really nice for Web Services to support discovery, binding, and invocation at runtime, these features are actually not required in order to use Web Services.

In fact, the SOA provides for a hierarchy of integration options, as shown in Figure 14.3.

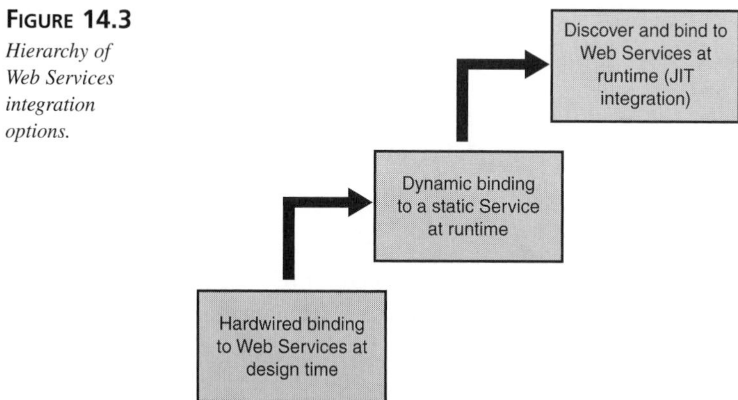

FIGURE 14.3
Hierarchy of Web Services integration options.

At the lowest level, Web Services are "hardwired" at design time. This option essentially mimics a tightly coupled distributed architecture such as a client/server or *n*-tier architecture. The developer handles the discovery manually and codes the interface to the desired service into the service requester.

At the next level, the desired Web Service is also identified beforehand, but the service requester is smart enough to bind to it dynamically at runtime. In this way, the service requester can vary its request to the service provider, depending on the particular situation. In addition, the service provider can change its interface from time to time (say, as part of a functionality upgrade), and service requesters will be able to adjust to the change on-the-fly.

The third level indicates JIT integration to the service provider: The service requester can search a registry dynamically for a provider and then bind to the one it selects. This is the only level that requires the participation of a service registry.

Tip

The hierarchy of Web Services integration options serves two important roles. When the SOA is fully formed, this hierarchy will describe the different ways that Web Services can interact, from the simplest to the most complex. In the meantime, this hierarchy also describes what Web Services will be useful for, as the SOA is in the process of being fleshed out. If you try to build Web Services that support JIT integration today, you'll likely be disappointed, because the technologies that go into the service registries are still being defined (and there aren't that many services registered in today's registries, anyway). However, it is possible today to create Web Services that interact at the first two levels. The first level can be thought of as a "training" level, because it doesn't provide much functionality beyond what more mature distributed architectures provide. Creating Web Services at the second level, however, can provide a new level of functionality beyond the existing architectures.

Lessons Learned from Object Orientation

There are several features an architecture must have to be considered *object oriented* (OO). An OO architecture's most important features are encapsulation, message sending, and hierarchical inheritance. Of these, the organizing power of class hierarchies has turned out to be the most useful feature of all, because class hierarchies allow the software-development process itself to scale.

Architectures that share encapsulation and message sending, but not inheritance, are referred to as *object based*. Object-based architectures are not nearly as powerful as object-oriented ones, for several reasons. First, encapsulation tends to make an application brittle, because an object's internal functionality can be difficult to update without breaking the system. Second, sending messages by exposing methods for remote objects to call is inefficient: If a remote object has a number of requests for an object, it must make a number of method calls, as opposed to one call that marshals all the requests.

Tip

One of the greatest performance advantages Web Services have over traditional RPC architectures is that a service requester can marshal multiple parameters into a single request, using the dynamic, hierarchical structure of XML. For complex requests that contain a large number of parameters, this advantage can be substantial, especially if the two systems are remote.

However, it is up to the architect and the Web Service developer to take advantage of this capability. A Web Service could easily be designed to make requests with single parameters, thus losing this performance advantage.

The important lesson that the SOA can learn from object-oriented architectures is that the organizing power of the SOA is the key to its success: The way that Web Services are published, located, invoked, and organized over the Internet is much more important than the internal structure of the Web Services themselves, or the specifics of the message protocols that enable the communication among services.

Architectures that focus on the details of how Web Services communicate, rather than what they say to each other, are called *service-based architectures* (corresponding to the distinction between object-oriented and object-based architectures). Now, service-based architectures are still useful, but not nearly as powerful as the SOA in a global e-business environment. Instead, service-based architectures are most useful within a single enterprise, where a single architecture team can define and manage the semantics behind the services.

Note

A typical example of a service-based architecture would be one that included Web-based data feeds—for example, a news headline service. Such a service sits at a particular URL and receives parameters in an ordinary HTTP GET request. Depending on the value of those parameters, it sends back the desired data.

A similar example that uses a service-oriented architecture would be a system that negotiates contracts with various news services on-the-fly for individual content feeds and then connects to the selected feeds dynamically at runtime.

The service-based architecture will continue to be quite useful but lacks the power and flexibility of the Web Services model's self-organization provided in the service-oriented architecture example.

Key Functional Components

The SOA has four key functional components: service implementation, publication, discovery, and invocation. This section introduces the architectural issues involved in each of these functional components. In essence, we'll provide a conceptual framework for the various protocols and technologies detailed in Chapters 15, "Web Services Building Blocks: SOAP," and 16, "Web Services Building Blocks: WSDL and UDDI."

Service Implementation

There are two basic approaches to building a Web Service: Build one from scratch, or provide a wrapper to an existing application or service so that it exposes a Web Service interface. As Web Services become more prevalent, developers will also have another set of options: Creating a new service interface for an existing Web Service, or taking advantage of an existing service interface to act as a skeleton for building or modifying a Web Service. Combining the choice of service interface with the two basic approaches to building a Web Service gives developers four methods for building Web Services:

- *Develop a new Web Service and a new service interface.* This "green field" method gives the developer the most leeway and is the most straightforward of the different methods. The best approach is simply to develop the Web Service as specified by the business requirements, define its interface, and then publish the interface and deploy the Web Service. This approach may be the most practical today, given the lack of existing Web Services. However, it will be the most expensive option.
- *Develop a new Web Service when there is an existing service interface.* The best method to use in this situation is a "top-down" approach. First, locate the existing service interface by searching a registry of Web Services. Next, generate a service implementation template, or *skeleton*, that contains all the methods and parameters that the Web Service must support to be in compliance with the interface. Then, develop the Web Service as before. This approach will become increasingly practical as useful Web Services become more prevalent in existing registries.
- *Develop a new service interface for an existing application.* You must develop a Web Service wrapper for your existing application in this "bottom-up" method. The wrapper then exposes the service interface. This approach will likely be the least expensive but also the least flexible.
- *Create a Web Service that wraps an existing application when you have an existing service interface.* This method is the most complex of the four, because you must first find the service interface and then use it to generate the service implementation template (skeleton). You must then use this template to develop the wrapper for the existing application.

Once your Web Service is complete and has a well-defined service interface, the next step is to publish your Web Service.

Publication

There are three steps to publishing a Web Service:

1. Author the Web Service description document. Written in the Web Services Description Language (WSDL), this document describes what the Web Service will do, where it can be found, and how to invoke it. (See Chapter 16 for a complete discussion of WSDL.)
2. Publish the Web Service description document on a Web server so that it is accessible to your desired audience (typically the Internet or one company's intranet, but it might also be published to a private e-marketplace). It is also possible to "direct-publish" the Web Service description to the service requester via e-mail, FTP, or even sneakernet. Direct publication is only possible when the access to the Web Service will be hardwired.
3. Publish the existence of your document in a Web Services registry using the Universal Description, Discovery, and Integration (UDDI) specification, which describes how Web Service registries are organized and how to work with them. A key aspect to UDDI is the UDDI registry, which acts as a repository for information about published Web Services (more about UDDI in Chapter 16). UDDI registries can be global, public registries, or they can be restricted to an individual enterprise (for a single application or department or for an enterprise portal) or to a closed group of companies (say, an e-marketplace or a partner catalog). WSDL and UDDI will be covered in Chapter 16.

Discovery

Once your Web Service appears in a registry, any application can discover your service and therefore locate the Web Service description document you published. UDDI registries support pattern queries for automated lookups and return the location of the WSDL file for the desired service. Once you have obtained the location of this file in the form of a Uniform Resource Indicator (URI), which is a generalization of the familiar Uniform Resource Locator (URL), you are able to download the WSDL file itself.

Invocation

There are two steps to invoking a Web Service:

1. Author a client using the Simple Object Access Protocol (SOAP). The WSDL file you downloaded contains the information you need to create a client using SOAP.

Because you are authoring clients on-the-fly based on information you found in the Web Service description document, you are able to invoke the Web Service dynamically at runtime. For more information on SOAP, see Chapter 15.

2. Make a SOAP call. Your client then creates a SOAP message describing what it wants the remote Web Service to do and then sends it to the URI specified in the WSDL document. Typically, the Web Service returns a SOAP message in the format detailed in the Web Service description document.

Note

The SOAP request/response exchange can be either synchronous or asynchronous. Some SOAP requests do not require a response, and some SOAP notifications generated by Web Services do not require a request. These messages (as well as others, such as error messages) are covered in Chapter 15: "Web Services Building Blocks: SOAP."

Just In Time Integration

Just as early object-oriented programming attempts looked a lot like the structural programming that preceded it, much of the early work with Web Services and the SOA can be expected to look like objects in OO architectures. However, just as programmers learned the true power of OO architectures and went beyond the capabilities of structured programming, so too will programmers learn the power of the SOA and go beyond what was practical with the techniques that came before.

The JIT integration capabilities of the SOA provide new organizing principles for the world of IT. Imagine an Internet full of Web Services: some globally available, and others available on intranets or other closed networks. This global set of Web Services grows and changes organically; the owner of each one determines what functionality the service will have and what interface it exposes, as well as which registries to submit the service to. In this global picture there is no master architect or executive committee who is responsible for maintaining the system. Instead, there's a set of simple, widely accepted open protocols that everybody is welcome to share.

So, if you were wondering why Web Services are named as they are, here is the answer. Sure, they run on HTTP, which means they drive on the same roads as the World Wide Web. However, that's not why they are "Web" Services. No, it's the global self-organizing power of technology based on simple, open protocols that puts the "Web" into Web Services.

Semantic Issues and Taxonomies

Semantics refers to the meaning, in human and business terms, of a Web Service's actions and parameters. Semantics have always been a sticking point for any distributed system. For example, EDI's rigid approach to its document formats led to semantic ambiguities. Business partners who use EDI must have an ad hoc agreement on the semantics of the fields in each document.

Object-oriented (OO) systems address the problem of semantics when the systems are small, but ambiguity creeps in when OO systems are scaled up. In a small OO implementation, the naming conventions of the methods as well as their signatures (the parameters the methods take in different situations) often connote to the developer the meaning of the methods and arguments. In a large-scale system, however, the semantics of a given class cannot typically be deduced by its interface alone. The problem only gets worse when many companies (possibly in different countries) attempt to participate in a distributed e-business system.

The advent of XML did little to cut through the morass of semantic issues because of XML's inherent extensibility. Due to the fact that the meaning of given XML tags were specified in an XML document's DTD or schema, developers were welcome to create their own sets of definitions, leading to a Tower of Babel situation.

Note

Different groups are attempting to solve the problems of semantic ambiguity. Industry groups and standards organizations are attempting to formulate XML schemata that provide the meaning of terms either within a particular vertical industry (as RosettaNet is attempting to do with the electronics industry) or across all of e-commerce (which is what the United Nations' ebXML standard is aiming to accomplish). RosettaNet can be found at `http://www.rosettanet.org`, and you can find ebXML at `http://www.ebxml.org`. Both ebXML and RosettaNet are covered in Chapter 20, "Implementing XML in E-Business."

Other groups, loosely affiliated under the Semantic Web Community banner, are trying to address the limitations of XML schemata by incorporating the human context missing in XML-based approaches through the development of *ontologies*. An ontology specifies a conceptualization of the objects, concepts, and other entities that exist in some area of interest, as well as the relationships among them. In other words, ontologies establish a joint terminology among members of a particular community of interest. You can learn more about the Semantic Web Community at `http://www.semanticweb.org`. You can also learn more about the Semantic Web in Chapter 24, "Semantic Web."

While the work on semantic issues is ongoing, some of the developments have been incorporated into the Web Services arena in the form of *taxonomies*. A taxonomy is a hierarchical representation of a set of concepts: Think of an area of interest (say, a vertical market) organized like a Yahoo! directory. UDDI registries take advantage of taxonomies, which can either be based on standard classifications of businesses or custom built to serve special purposes. The simplest taxonomy used in UDDI registries is geographical: country followed by political division—for example, United States, Massachusetts or United Kingdom, Wales.

Because XML is self-describing, a Web Services description can refer to any available schema as the basis for the services it describes. If the description takes advantage of the taxonomies that are available in the service registries that the service provider wishes to use, however, then service requesters will be able to discover such services by looking up terms that have meaning to the requester. Today, however, the use of taxonomies in UDDI registries is still quite rudimentary.

Security and Quality of Service Issues

Up to this point, we have covered building, publishing, finding, and invoking Web Services. Much of the nuts and bolts of the SOA is now in place. However, in order to conduct e-business in the real world, a few features are missing. Most notably, there must be a security infrastructure available for Web Services. Equally important is the need for some way to guarantee different levels of quality of service for messages sent to and from Web Services.

Security

Because Web Services typically run over HTTP and TCP/IP, many of the security requirements for Web Services can be satisfied with the well-established Secure Sockets Layer (SSL) protocol as well as the newer Internet Protocol Security (IPSec) protocol. SSL applies specifically to point-to-point messages sent over HTTP, whereas IPSec allows for the encryption of messages on the network layer. Are these two standards sufficient for securing Web Services, or is there a need for a more sophisticated or complete Web Services security layer?

There are four basic requirements that a Web Services security layer must provide:

- *Confidentiality*. The contents of the messages must not be available to unauthorized parties.
- *Authentication*. The sender of a message must be authorized to send a message, and the recipient of the message must be able to confirm the identity of the sender of the message.

- *Data integrity*. The recipient of a message must be able to guarantee that the message hasn't been tampered with in transit.
- *Nonrepudiation*. The recipient of a message must be able to guarantee the circumstances surrounding the sending of the message (for example, the time the message was sent and the fact that the sender sent only one copy of the message).

SSL and IPSec guarantee data integrity and confidentiality for messages that go from the sender directly to the recipient, but they aren't able to provide authentication or nonrepudiation. They are also unable to guarantee either data integrity or confidentiality if there is a third-party intermediary in between the sender and the recipient. Because SOAP messages are typically processed by intermediaries, SSL and IPSec are most useful if there is a preexisting trust relationship among sender, recipient, and intermediary. In the world of Web Services, however, this is unlikely to happen very often.

It is also possible to secure the messages to and from Web Services at the application layer or via a secure network. These two approaches may work inside single enterprises but will not work when multiple companies exchange Web Services messages. Instead, it makes more sense to include security information as meta-information in the SOAP header. The SOAP specification allows for such information but doesn't actually specify it. (More about SOAP headers in Chapter 15.) The security information to be sent in the SOAP headers is some kind of asymmetric key message digest, as provided for by authentication systems such as Kerberos and the Public Key Infrastructure (PKI).

Note

Several standards bodies are currently working on different asymmetric key systems for securing Web Services (and XML messages in general), including the W3C (which is working on XML Digital Signatures, XML Encryption, and XML Key Management Services) and OASIS, which is currently developing the Security Assertion Markup Language (SAML) and the Extensible Access Control Markup Language (XACML). The W3C can be found at `http://www.w3c.org`, and OASIS is located at `http://www.oasis-open.org`. You can also learn about Kerberos at `http://web.mit.edu/kerberos/www/`. There is no single source for information about PKI, but a good starting point is at `http://www.opengroup.org/public/tech/security/pki/`.

The problem with all asymmetric key systems is that they require the services of a trusted third party. This third party must provide the ultimate authority to generate the keys as well as provide a list of revoked key-generation authorities. All parties involved in secure interactions among Web Services must agree upon this trusted third party beforehand.

An adequate Web Services security layer, therefore, should contain both IPSec or SSL (in particular, HTTP over SSL, which is abbreviated HTTPS) for network security as well as some kind of asymmetric key technology for XML message security. Until such time as the asymmetric key technology issues have been resolved, SSL may be the best security available, even though it does not provide authentication or nonrepudiation and only works "point to point."

Caution

Web Services security is still a bleeding-edge topic. Work goes on in many groups, trying to develop the best approaches to handling security. Today, however, SSL affords the best security, in spite of its limitations.

The fact that asymmetric key solutions require a third party that is trusted by all participants in an exchange of information provides a serious limitation on this category of solution that no one has resolved at this time.

In addition to the security concerns that apply to the XML messages that go between Web Services, there is also the question of how service registries should secure their systems. Depending on the situation, there are three access control models that Web Service registries might follow:

- A *promiscuous registry* doesn't authenticate the publishers or the requesters. Such registries don't make any claims about the correctness of the data in the registry or the integrity of the participants. Although a promiscuous registry is the simplest form of registry to set up, its usefulness is limited by its lack of access control.
- An *authenticated registry* authenticates both service requesters and service publishers. Because it knows the identities of the parties involved in the registry, it can set up coarse-grained access control for specific categories of data within the registry. Typically, such a registry would require communication via SSL and might also include support for XML Digital Signatures so that it can validate the XML messages it receives.
- A *fully authorized registry* goes beyond the security offered by authenticated registries by implementing a fine-grained authorization paradigm, allowing it to secure individual data entries by storing access information for each one. Such a registry would have to support a more complex management and administration infrastructure in order to enforce such complex security. A fully authorized registry

might also act as a public key authority, providing the individual authority (often called *certificates*) to both Web Services publishers and requesters necessary to generate the asymmetric keys.

Quality of Service and Reliable Messaging

Quality of service (QoS) means different things at different layers. At the network layer, QoS refers to the ability of the network to transmit information with the desired accuracy and promptness. On the messaging layer, however, QoS refers to the reliability of the messaging—that is, the ability of the infrastructure to deliver a message exactly once to its intended recipient or to deliver a particular error message (typically to the sender) if the message cannot be sent.

The sending of messages to and from Web Services will fall into three basic modes:

- *Best effort.* The service requester sends the request message, and neither the requester nor the message infrastructure attempts a retransmission in the case of a failure to deliver the message.
- *At least once.* The service requester continues to attempt to send the request until it receives acknowledgment from the service provider that the message was received. As a result, the service provider might receive more than one copy of the message. If the request is a simple query, this duplication isn't a major problem (although it will contribute to network overhead). However, in other cases, each message may need to carry a unique ID so that the service provider can recognize a duplicate message. Along with its acknowledgment, the service provider either sends the requested response or a "cannot process message" exception.
- *Exactly once.* The service requester makes its request, and the service provider guarantees in its reply that the request has been executed (or it sends an error message, if necessary). The "exactly once" mode of messaging requires an *endpoint manager* at either end of the message to relay messages and guarantee responses (which may simply be a timeout exception should the service provider fail to respond). Endpoint managers also frequently support the queuing of messages or more complex behaviors such as forwarding messages to other ervice providers. The exactly once mode is only applicable when both endpoints participate in the appropriate messaging infrastructure—for example, within an enterprise or between two companies who have configured their joint messaging infrastructure beforehand.

Note

A new protocol called the *Web Services Endpoint Language* (WSEL) is currently under development. WSEL will provide a format for handling endpoint management, including QoS, usage, and security characteristics, as well as contextual information such as legal and cost issues.

Although sophisticated messaging infrastructures are a possibility in such controlled situations, on the open Internet we must work within the constraints of HTTP. HTTP mandates a simple request/response mechanism with a set of standard error messages, but it lacks most of the features of reliable messaging. This is an area where more work must be done before business will be able to use Web Services over the Internet reliably.

Caution

Web Services QoS is also a bleeding-edge topic. Managed messaging infrastructures such as IBM's MQ can provide QoS capabilities, but work on global Web Services QoS is just getting underway.

Composition and Conversations

So far, we have been looking at Web Services as individual components: how to create, find, publish and implement single services. However, for Web Services to be truly useful in a global e-business environment, there must be a way to combine and coordinate collections of Web Services so they can be used to support complex, real-world business processes. The ability to use collections of Web Services falls into two general categories: *composition* of Web Services and *conversations* among Web Services.

Composition of Web Services

Composition essentially means combining multiple individual Web Services into larger components that are themselves Web Services. Composition of Web Services falls into two broad categories:

- Web Services can be combined within an enterprise in order to describe a business process. In this case, the composition of the Web Services follows a particular *usage* pattern.

- Web Services from multiple companies can be coordinated in order to describe partner interactions. In this case, the composition of the Web Services follows a particular *interaction* pattern.

In addition, Web Services can be composed *recursively*. A Web Service that is recursively composed of other Web Services can itself be used as a component in further compositions of Web Services.

Naturally, it makes sense to describe the composition of Web Services with an open, XML-based description language. This avenue of research is still very new, but the most progress has been made by IBM with its Web Services Flow Language (WSFL). The WSFL is an XML-based description language that describes both categories of Web Services in the preceding list.

Caution

Yes, the WSFL is a bleeding-edge topic as well. IBM makes it very clear that WSFL is its contribution to the discussion on Web Services composition and that it will participate in ongoing standards discussions. Whether WSFL will become an accepted standard, or how much it will change during the standards process, is anybody's guess.

In order to apply the WSFL, an enterprise would first identify a business process that it wishes to implement with Web Services. Then it would take that business process and identify the following:

- The *component business processes* (typically implemented in the form of existing Web Services) that make up the larger process.
- The *business rules* that determine the sequence of steps that form the business process.
- The *flow of information* that joins the individual process steps.

From these elements, the enterprise would create the WSFL flow model that defines the overall structure of the business process.

Note

More information on IBM's work on Web Services, including WSFL, can be found at `http://www-106.ibm.com/developerworks/webservices`. Although WSFL represents IBM's contribution to the area of XML-based business process and workflow definition grammars, it is my no means the only one. Others include the following:

- The ebXML Business Process Specification (see `http://www.ebxml.org`).
- The Business Process Modeling Language (`http://www.bpmi.org`).
- Microsoft's XLANG, which is the proprietary grammar at the heart of the BizTalk Server (at `http://www.gotdotnet.com/team/xml_wsspecs/xlang-c/default.htm`).

Conversations Among Web Services

A *conversation* between two collaborating Web Services is a sequence of requests and responses that is correlated into a particular group or unit of work. Conversations become important when there is a need for transactional properties to apply to the sequence of requests and responses.

The concept of a *transaction* is fundamental to the application of distributed computing. Although database transaction models and transaction-processing (TP) monitor programming models are typically sufficient in existing heterogeneous enterprise IT environments, the Web Services model requires a more flexible mechanism for handling transactional capabilities such as atomicity, phased commits, and rollbacks. (See Chapter 15 for an in-depth discussion of transactional capabilities.) Some differences between the two environments are as follows:

- Within enterprises, applications that support asynchronous messaging typically assume a chained, multiple-transaction model when crossing different messaging systems. Web Service collaborations, however, typically rely on asynchronous messages across enterprise boundaries and must support transactional capabilities in the absence of a single messaging system.
- The TP monitor infrastructure that manages transactions in heterogeneous enterprise environments typically provides a single span of control for executing transactions. Such systems must have sophisticated management and monitoring tools to avoid problems with failures. Web Service collaborations across different enterprises, however, have multiple spans of control.
- The ability of Web Service requests to combine multiple method calls into a single request, combined with the ability of Web Services to send and receive both synchronous and asynchronous messages, means that multiple-company Web Service collaborations will typically take much more time than the individual requests and responses in traditional transactional environments.

Because of these fundamental differences between traditional environments and the Web Services model, transactions must be handled differently. We require a more incremental approach to transactional capabilities, as follows:

- First, we need an *activity service* that specifies the operational context of a series of requests. Included in this operational context are the duration of the activity, the participants involved, and a description of the possible outcomes of the activity.
- Next, there is a need for a *conversation service* that provides request atomicity. Request atomicity guarantees that a particular set of Web Service operations either happen completely or not at all. The endpoint manager publishes the atomicity capability to the participants.
- The conversation service must also correlate sequences of requests into a single unit of work, by providing a structure for conversations that includes indications of the beginning and end of the conversations as well as success and failure outcomes. The conversation service must be able to accept a rollback command from either participant, and then it must provide the semantics of the rollback command to each participant.

Note

Hewlett-Packard has entered the Web Services fray by developing the Web Services Conversation Language (WSCL), which allows for the defining of business-level conversations or public processes supported by a Web Service. In addition, WSCL specifies the documents being exchanged as well as the sequence of the documents. However, WSCL does not (yet) describe how Web Services conversations will handle transactions. (Learn more about Hewlett-Packard's work with Web Services at `http://www.e-speak.hp.com`.)

Caution

The WSCL is on the bleeding edge, as well. In addition, Hewlett-Packard has not been as prominent a participant in the Web Services standards processes as IBM and Microsoft, so there is a somewhat greater possibility that WSCL will not become a standard compared to, say, WSFL.

Architecting Web Services

Software architects are at the vanguard of the software development lifecycle. If Web Services truly represent a paradigm shift in how distributed computing is performed, rather than merely an incremental improvement, it is up to the architects first to understand this shift and then to communicate it to their teams as well as their management.

Software architecture is a broad, somewhat-vague discipline that includes elements of design, abstraction, and aesthetics, as well as a more fundamental view of what really works and what doesn't. Architects touch upon the hardware, the network, the applications, and the interfaces as well as the users, the partners, and the marketplace. In order to architect complex, multifaceted systems, including those made up of Web Services, architects must exercise many ways of thinking and many ways of viewing the problems before them.

One established model for how architects visualize the systems before them is the *4+1 View Model of Software Architecture*, popularized by Philippe Kruchten of Rational Software. Whereas the four blind men each touch the elephant in a different place and therefore come to different understandings of it, the architect has clear vision, seeing the elephant from all four views. As a result, the architect has a comprehensive picture of the elephant.

This is the same with the 4+1 View Model. This model describes four distinct ways of looking at the architecture for a system, plus a fifth view that overlaps the others, as shown in Figure 14.4.

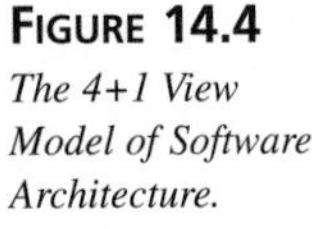

FIGURE 14.4
The 4+1 View Model of Software Architecture.

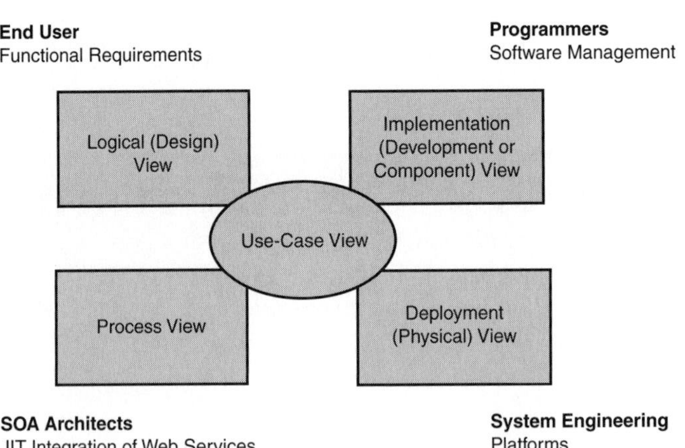

Each of the four main views takes the perspective of key stakeholders in the development process. The fifth view, the Use-Case View, overlaps the other views and plays a special role with regard to the architecture. This section approaches the Web Services model from each of the four views, demonstrating the different ways architects should envision Web Services. A discussion of the Use-Case View closes out the chapter.

Note

The 4+1 View Model of Software Architecture is introduced in *The Rational Unified Process* by Philippe Kruchten (Addison Wesley Longman, Inc., 1999) and covered more in depth in *Software Architecture for Product Families* by M. Jazayeri, et al. (Addison Wesley Longman, Inc., 2000). You can also find a good discussion of the model at `http://www.rational.com/products/whitepapers/350.jsp`.

The Implementation Architectural View: The Web Services Technology Stack

In general, the Implementation View (also called the *Development* or *Component View*) describes the organization of the software artifacts and also addresses issues of software management. The Implementation View of the SOA focuses on the Web Services technology stack, as shown in Figure 14.5.

Figure 14.5 shows a conceptual Web Services technology stack, where each layer on the left builds upon the capabilities of the layer beneath it. The vertical columns on the right represent capabilities that the architect must address at every level of the stack.

The base stack includes those technologies necessary to create and invoke Web Services. At the bottom is the network layer, which fundamentally allows Web Services to be available to service requesters. Although HTTP is the de facto standard network protocol, the architect may consider any of a number of other options, including SMTP (for e-mail), FTP, IIOP, or messaging technologies such as MQ. Some of these choices are request/response based, whereas others are message based; furthermore, some are synchronous, whereas others are asynchronous. The architect may find that in a large system, a combination of different network protocols is appropriate.

In the next two layers, SOAP is the XML-based messaging protocol that forms the basis for all interactions with Web Services. When running on top of HTTP, SOAP messages are simple POST operations with SOAP's XML envelope as the payload. SOAP messages support the publish, find, and bind operations that form the basis of the SOA, as shown previously in Figure 14.2. (SOAP is covered in depth in Chapter 15.)

FIGURE 14.5
The Web Services technology stack.

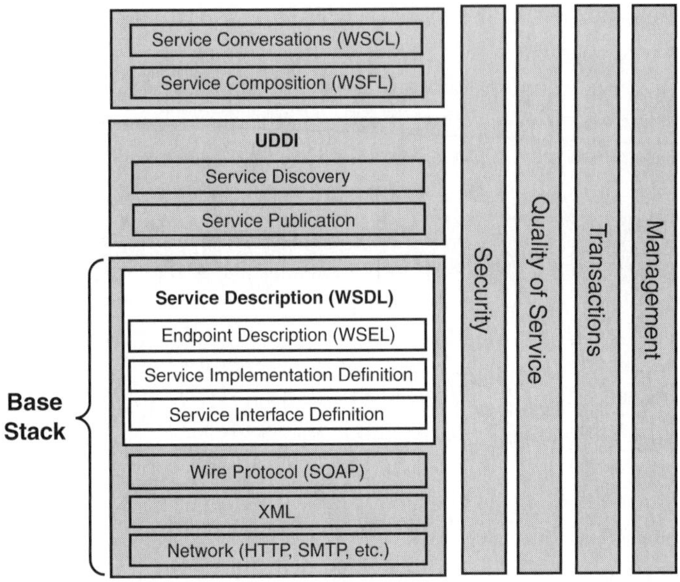

On top of the SOAP layer comes three layers that together form the service description. WSDL is the de facto standard for service descriptions, with the addition of the still-tentative WSEL for endpoint descriptions. The service interface definition contains the `binding`, `portType`, `message`, and `type` elements, which form the portion of the service description that is reusable from one implementation to another. (These elements are fully described in Chapter 16.)

The service implementation definition, however, contains those elements that are specific to each implementation: the `service` and `port` elements. A third party (say, a standards body) might specify the service interface definition for a particular type of Web Service, leaving the service implementation definition up to each implementation team.

Next comes the endpoint description, which introduces semantics to the service descriptions that apply to a particular implementation. Endpoint descriptions can contain security, QoS, and management attributes that help to define the policies for each of these vertical columns.

Once the architect has dealt with all the issues in the base stack, the Web Services are essentially fully constructed. Next, the development team uses UDDI to publish the services to a registry or another repository of information about available Web Services. Once Web Services are published, UDDI can then be used to discover them in the registries.

Only when the architect has dealt with the issues of service publication and discovery can he move on to the more complex issues regarding the interaction of multiple Web Services. The two protocols shown in Figure 14.5, WSFL and WSCL, are still in development, and it's not clear how these layers will be handled in the future.

One important lesson to be gained from the Web Services stack is that security, QoS, transactions, and service management each apply to every layer in the stack. The architect must therefore consider the intersection of each vertical column with each horizontal layer. For example, network security will likely be handled by HTTPS (SSL over HTTP), but the security of individual messages may still need to be handled by encrypted payloads and digital signatures, which are incorporated into the SOAP header. Securing the base stack is relatively straightforward, because it is internal to the enterprise; securing Web Services involved in publication and discovery across the Internet is another issue entirely.

QoS, as well, means different things at each layer. Network QoS involves network uptime, packet delivery, and valid HTTP messages. Reliable messaging, however, depends heavily on the capabilities of the endpoint manager, which uses WSEL or another endpoint description language. Transactions depend on endpoint descriptions, as well.

Transactions, in fact, must be handled on multiple levels of the service stack, because of the complexity of handling rollbacks in a multi-enterprise Web Services environment. To roll back a particular conversation, each operation within that conversation may need to be reversed. Alternatively, there may need to be a way to remember the earlier state of multiple systems in order to perform a rollback. In either case, there is no single span of control managing the transactional environment. Transactions may be some of the most intractable issues with Web Services today.

On top of all of these development and implementation concerns, the architect must also think about the management of Web Services. Management of Web Services will likely be handled by a management application, which may need to be built in-house. This management application must be able to do the following:

- Determine the availability and health of the Web Services infrastructure, including the network as well as the physical systems that support the execution of the Web Services.
- Determine the availability and health of the internal Web Services themselves. Web Services may need to be built with a management interface in order to support this level of management.

- Determine the availability and health of the service registries. Some of these registries may be internal to the enterprise, allowing for direct access to their inner workings, but other registries are external and may only expose a minimal interface for external management.
- Determine the availability and health of external Web Services, once they are discovered, attempt to invoke them. Again, these services are external and may not provide a management interface.
- Control and configure all internal systems, including the infrastructure as well as the Web Services themselves.

These management requirements emphasize the need for a standard way of building management interfaces for Web Services (as well as the infrastructure that supports them). In addition, there is clearly a need for a reporting and recovery process for publicly available Web Services (either on the open Internet or available to specific business partners). Partners should be able to access an interface that provides status reports on a company's services and infrastructure, without having to understand the details of how the company manages its internal infrastructure.

Caution

The work on standard management interfaces for Web Services is still very much on the drawing board, although there are some technologies, such as the Java Management Extensions (JMX), that can help to set a standard for the more general, language-neutral environment of Web Services. The JMX home page is at `http://java.sun.com/products/JavaManagement/`.

The Logical Architectural View: Composition of Web Services

The Logical (or Design) Architectural View starts with the end user's functional requirements and provides a top-down abstraction of the overall design of the system. In the case of B2B functionality (say, in the case of processing a purchase order), the user interface may be handled separately from the Web Services; therefore, the "end users" in this case are the businesses themselves. In other cases, Web Services may provide functionality to the user interface more directly.

In the B2B case, the functional requirements of a Web Services–based system will typically involve complex conversations among Web Services that participate in multi-step business processes. In addition, the individual Web Services involved are likely to be composed of component Web Services. As a result, an architect working from the Logical View will likely be concerned with workflows of Web Services.

For example, let's take the case of a buyer's Web Service contacting a seller's Web Service to make a purchase. Figure 14.6 shows a possible (simplified) workflow for this interaction.

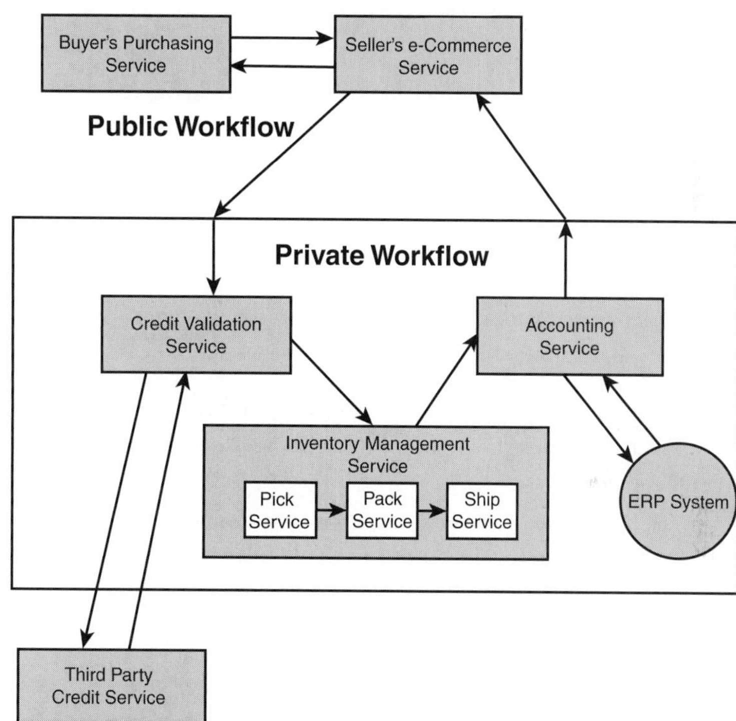

FIGURE 14.6
Simple e-commerce workflow.

This workflow consists of two separate workflows: a public workflow as well as one private to the seller. From the buyer's point of view, the seller is exposing a single public Web Service that is composed of separate Web Services in succession.

The interfaces to the two public services are both written in WSDL. The buyer has obtained the seller's service description beforehand—either by looking it up in a registry or through a prearranged relationship between the buyer and the seller. The buyer uses the service description to build the SOAP messages it exchanges with the seller.

Once the seller receives a request from the buyer, a sequence of business processes within the private workflow takes place. First, a credit-validation service sends a request to a third-party, credit-checking Web Service, which it may have established a preexisting relationship with. This third-party service is an example of an *enabling service*. Depending on the response from the third-party service, the seller continues with the e-commerce workflow or possibly sends a "credit rejected" response back to the buyer. (The architect must consider both the "rejected" special case as well as how to handle the situation where the third-party credit service is unavailable.) In a more general case, it will likely not be necessary to query this service if the seller has an established relationship with the buyer.

Once the buyer's credit is approved, the internal credit-validation service sends a request to the inventory-management service. This service is recursively constructed from individual component services (three of which are shown for illustration purposes, but in reality such services would be more complex). The architect must determine the interface for the inventory-management service as well as detail the workflow that takes place within the service.

The architect must work with several different elements in a complex workflow like this one, including the following:

- The *sequencing rules* that describe how the Web Services interact over time.
- The *information flows* between each of the services (including the necessary data mapping).
- The *service providers* responsible for executing each step. Is the inventory-management service responsible for executing any of its internal steps, or are they taken care of by the component services?
- The *associations* between activities in the workflow.
- The *operations* offered by each service provider.

The three component services within the inventory-management service may also represent applications that are not themselves Web Services. In such a case, the inventory-management service is responsible for communicating with each component via a preexisting framework, such as CORBA, DCOM, or J2EE.

Once the purchased item has been shipped (assuming there were no errors), the accounting service is responsible for interacting with the ERP system. This system is an example of a component that is not itself a Web Service. Typically, the architect will call for a wrapper that will present a Web Service interface to the rest of the system. In this case, the accounting service may itself be that wrapper, in which case the links between it and the ERP system would be implemented with the APIs provided by the ERP system.

This simple example appears to be a synchronous system—that is, there is a single, closed loop starting and ending at the buyer that every request follows to completion. In reality, however, some of the processes will be synchronous whereas others will be asynchronous. The inventory-management service will likely communicate with the buyer through the public e-commerce service to determine whether or not the product is in stock, and then the pick, pack, and ship process will take place asynchronously. As a result, the architect must also consider how the buyer (as well as the seller) will be able to monitor and control the asynchronous inventory service.

If this is a B2B example, then the buyer's purchasing service likely ties into the buyer's enterprise systems as part of its supply chain management system. However, in a Business to Consumer (B2C) situation, the buyer's purchasing service might be hosted on a B2C Web site. In this situation, the *user context* is a primary concern of the architect.

User context is a critical part of all consumer (and generally, individual user) focused Web Services, including Microsoft's .NET My Services initiative as well as Sun's SunONE framework.

Note

.NET My Services (formerly codenamed *Hailstorm*) is Microsoft's platform for building user-centric XML-based Web Services. Learn more about .NET My Services at `http://www.microsoft.com/myservices/`.

The Sun Open Net Environment (SunONE) is Sun's standards-based software vision, architecture, platform, and expertise for building and deploying Web Services on demand. Learn more about SunONE at `http://www.sun.com/sunone`.

The user context contains information about the user as well as information about the user's session, including the following:

- Demographic information, credit card information, and so on
- The user's physical location
- The user's locale (the user's language, currency, number format, and so on)
- The user's security level and permissions
- Personalization information that pertains to the Web site the user is visiting, including merchandise preferences, calendar information, buddy lists, and so on

Caution

User context issues are still under development, and there is not yet an established procedure for handling them. Microsoft is taking a centralized server approach to user context with its Passport Service, but there are prevalent concerns about storing information this sensitive in a central repository. It may make more sense to develop a distributed user context system that the users themselves manage, but work on this topic is ongoing.

The home page for Microsoft HailStorm is at `http://www.microsoft.com/net/hailstorm.asp`.

Information about SunONE, which includes work on user context, can be found at `http://www.sun.com/sunone/`.

The Deployment Architectural View: From Application Servers to Peer-to-Peer

The Deployment (or Physical) Architectural View maps the software to its underlying platforms, including the hardware, the network, and the supporting software platforms. Today, Web Services are hosted on application server platforms such as IBM's WebSphere, BEA's WebLogic, and Microsoft's Windows 2000. There are many benefits to building Web Services on top of platforms like these: They handle database access, load balancing, scalability, and interface support as well as provide a familiar environment for dealing with hardware and network issues.

Tip

Working with a particular vendor's platform typically requires the use of the vendor's tools. IBM provides the Web Services Toolkit for building Web Services, in addition to its WebSphere Studio Application Developer product, which is IBM's updated VisualAge for Java offering. Microsoft also provides a full suite of Web Service–creation tools as a part of its .NET offering. Many other vendors are introducing Web Services tools as well, in addition to several open-source contributions, including applications under the Apache banner. More information about these tools can be found in Chapters 15 and 16.

Because Web Services typically exchange messages over HTTP, a Web server is typically the desired host for supporting a Web Service. Both the Microsoft and the J2EE platforms share a similar developer model, as shown in Figure 14.7.

FIGURE 14.7
Web Services developer model.

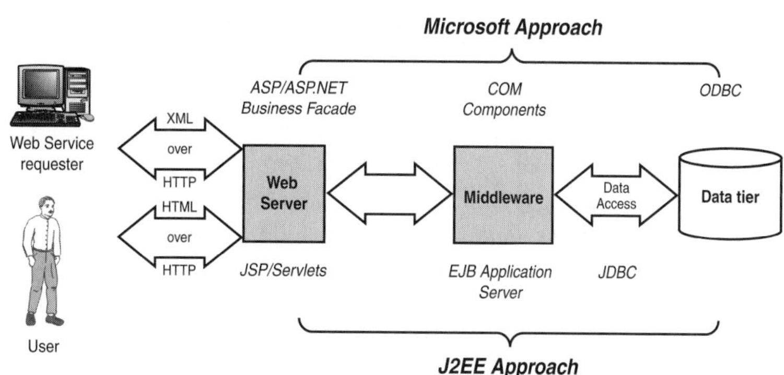

This model follows a traditional *n*-tier architecture, except that the Web server is also responsible for sending and receiving the XML messages that form the Web Services interface. The technology that supports Web Services is therefore already well understood; the fundamental difference between Web Services and Web pages is that pages are intended for humans to read, whereas Web Services expose an interface intended for machines.

Running Web Services off of Web servers is not the only way to support the services, however. It is also possible to build Web Services on a peer-to-peer (P2P) developer model. P2P, popularized by the Napster music service, is a distributed architecture that does not rely on central servers but rather distributes responsibility to systems (called *peers*) in the network. Unfortunately, P2P technologies are every bit as new and bleeding edge as Web Services, so only time will tell which P2P models will become established. The self-organizing promise of Web Services does lend itself to P2P, but a lot of work remains before we will see how this fascinating area will develop.

Note

One pioneer in the area of P2P-based Web Services is Cambridge, Massachusetts–based AVAKI (at `http://www.avaki.com`). AVAKI is building a scalable middleware platform that combines distributed and P2P computing capabilities. AVAKI's middleware platform is based on JXTA, which is Sun Microsystems' new set of P2P protocols. AVAKI's Peer Information Protocol is an XML-based interface protocol that supports interactions with Web Services. JXTA's home page can be found at `http://www.sun.com/jxta/`.

The Process Architectural View: Life in the Runtime

The Process Architectural View addresses all runtime issues, including processes, concurrency, and scalability. As the applications of Web Services move up the hierarchy of Web Service integration options to JIT integration (as shown previously in Figure 14.3), the Process Architectural View will take on increasing importance. In fact, the Process Architectural View will be where the bulk of the SOA architect's work will take place.

For example, let's take another look at the simple e-commerce workflow in Figure 14.6. If you just look at the figure, you might think that there's nothing much new here; this diagram could represent an e-commerce system based on a simple *n*-tier architecture.

The reason that the diagram doesn't immediately demonstrate the power of the Web Services model is that in the diagram, the buyer has already identified the seller, the seller has already identified its third-party credit service, and the seller's private workflow is already put in place. If all these statements are in fact true, then, yes, Web Services has little to offer over traditional *n*-tier architectures. On the other hand, let's take a JIT approach, as shown in Figure 14.8.

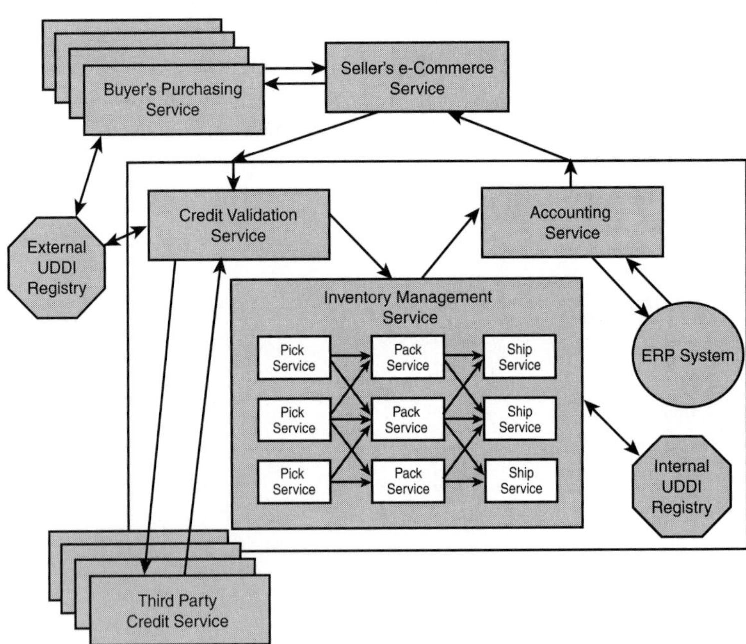

FIGURE 14.8
JIT e-commerce workflow.

Figure 14.8 shows an e-commerce workflow much like the one in Figure 14.6, except that multiple buyers have looked up the seller in a registry and have chosen to invoke the seller's e-commerce service. Likewise, the seller looks up third-party credit services in an external registry and looks up pick, pack, and ship services in an internal registry. (As before, these three services are used as examples rather than to indicate how inventory management would actually take place.) The inventory-management service then selects the internal components on-the-fly at runtime.

This example begs the following questions: What if the buyer sends an automatic query to a registry, identifies and qualifies an appropriate seller on-the-fly, and negotiates the purchase dynamically? What if the seller looks up a potentially different credit service every time, given a changing set of criteria such a service might need to meet? Even more significant, what if the seller's inventory-management service dynamically selects its pick, pack, and ship services at runtime, depending on supply chain issues such as availability, price, and logistics?

Herein lies the power of Web Services. The architect must be able to plan and structure processes where individual Web Services might be selected, queried, and invoked dynamically at runtime. Therefore, the Process View is the most important, and yet the least understood, of the architectural views of the SOA.

JIT integration also complicates scalability and redundancy issues. Many of these issues can be handled by the underlying software platform that supports the Web Services. However, with JIT integration, it is not necessarily possible to predict at design time which Web Services will be invoked or what service implementations they will expose. How do you plan for scalability and redundancy when you don't even know whether a particular component will be invoked at all?

Summary

It's difficult to write a chapter about something as bleeding edge as Web Services. You start the chapter with answers, and by the end, all you have are questions. Keep in mind, however, that there are two main audiences for this chapter: People who wish to architect Web Services, and people who wish to help define how Web Services should be architected. Of course, these two audiences overlap.

For those of you who wish to architect Web Services, you will need to tread lightly in those areas that are still in development. Open technologies are defined more by mobs than by committees: Everybody tries to get their particular way of doing something to be accepted by the community at large. Some succeed, but most fail; even those who succeed often see their brainchild changed before the work is done.

However, along with the risks of being an early adopter come the rewards. If you're building Web Services now, then chances are your company or institution is interested in exploring technologies before they are fully defined. That will put you ahead of the game as the technologies become better established.

And for those of you who read this chapter because you are interested in helping to define how Web Services should be architected, I hope you have found some of the material in this chapter to be controversial. There's no way to write a chapter like this and capture the prevailing wisdom, because there simply is no prevailing wisdom for many of these issues. In addition, you are reading this at least six months after it was written, and much will have changed in that interval. At the very least, I hope that I have gotten you to think about the Web Services model in new ways. If I have done that, then this chapter was successful.

Oh yes, you might be wondering why I haven't yet talked about the fifth architectural view: the Use-Case View. I saved this view for last for a reason. The Use-Case View is meant to drive the discovery and the design of the architecture as well as to validate each of the other views. The existence of use-cases, however, means that there already exists business users who know what they want a Web Services architecture to do, and that's not the case at this time. Business users don't even know what functionality is possible.

The functionality of Web Services today is understood in the context of existing solutions, because that's what people are familiar with. It is up to you as an early adopter to understand how the Web Services model and the SOA can enable a new paradigm of component technology. Only then will the capabilities of this new paradigm filter down to the world of global e-business.

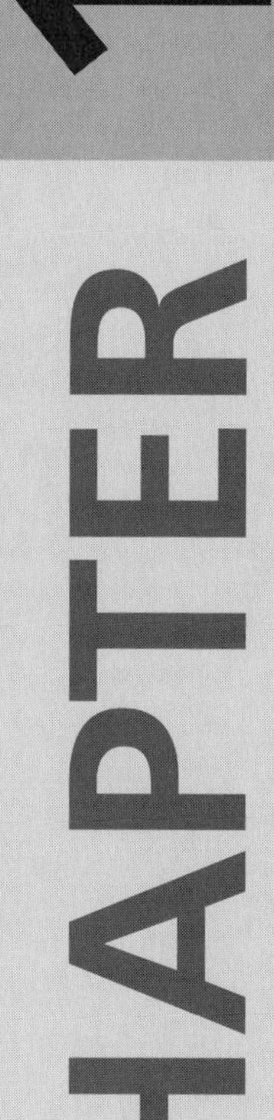

Web Services Building Blocks: SOAP

In This Chapter

The Simple Object Access Protocol (SOAP) is an XML-based messaging and remote procedure call (RPC) specification that enables the exchange of information among distributed systems. Initially proposed by Microsoft, SOAP has established itself as the de facto standard for an open, extensible, XML-based wire protocol.

SOAP has achieved its level of widespread acceptance for several reasons:

- It is an open specification, available for anyone to use.
- It is simple to write and is "human-readable."
- It is extensible, taking advantage of the power of XML to enable loose coupling between remote systems.
- It is a flexible protocol that is useful both in request/response and message passing/queuing architectures.

Even though SOAP has wide application in the distributed computing environment, probably its most significant role is as a building block for the Web Services model, introduced in Chapter 14, "Architecting Web Services."

In this chapter, you will learn

- The basics of SOAP syntax
- How to send and receive SOAP messages
- How to build SOAP implementations using industry-leading tools
- About advanced and bleeding-edge applications of SOAP

Introduction to SOAP

Basically, SOAP is a standard way of serializing the information needed to invoke services located on remote systems so that the information can be sent over a network (or "wire") to the remote system, in a format the remote system can understand, regardless of what platform the remote service runs on or what language it's written in. If you're familiar with RPC architectures such as CORBA and DCOM, this description of SOAP should sound familiar, because SOAP resembles the wire protocols underlying both architectures: the Internet Inter-ORB Protocol (IIOP) that underlies CORBA and Microsoft's Distributed Component Object Model (DCOM) protocol, respectively. In fact, SOAP can be thought of as a simplified XML-based replacement for these protocols.

Note

As of this writing, the SOAP specification is at version 1.1, and all the SOAP in this chapter refers to this version. A brief discussion of what's expected in version 1.2 comes at the end of the chapter. The official source for the SOAP specification is in a W3C note, which can be found at `http://www.w3.org/TR/SOAP/`.

Improved RPC

In order to understand SOAP's context, it helps to put it in perspective relative to RPC architectures in particular, and communications within distributed computing models in general.

The two dominant communications models throughout the history of distributed computing have been message passing/queuing and request/response. With message passing, a message sender can send a message at any time, and the messaging infrastructure is responsible for delivering the message whenever it can, thus typically offering *asynchronous* message delivery. With the request/response model, the message sender typically must wait until it receives a response from the recipient, in what is an example of *synchronous* message delivery. If the goal is to send data to a method hosted on a remote system and wait for its response, the request/response model is a natural fit. Message passing, however, is more appropriate when a response is not immediately required.

As a result, RPC architectures generally followed the synchronous request/response model, and when object-oriented architectures came into widespread use, Object RPC (ORPC) protocols such as CORBA's IIOP and DCOM became dominant in the distributed computing arena. However, both CORBA/IIOP and DCOM have several problems, including the following:

- Both CORBA and DCOM are single-vendor solutions. DCOM is expressly a Microsoft solution, and although CORBA is intended to be cross-platform, in reality it is typically only cost-effective when all the involved systems share a single Object Request Broker (ORB) platform.
- Both CORBA and DCOM have different, proprietary characteristics. For example, CORBA's payload parameter value format is the Common Data Representation (CDR), whereas DCOM's is the incompatible Network Data Representation (NDR). Likewise, CORBA uses Interoperable Object References (IORs) for endpoint naming, whereas DCOM uses OBJREFs.

- IIOP and DCOM are both binary protocols, which means they are not human-readable, and neither is firewall friendly. The firewall limitation in particular relegates both architectures to use primarily within individual enterprises.
- Both CORBA and DCOM are tightly coupled, which means that a change in the exposed methods of any distributed object requires programming changes in distributed objects that communicate with it. As a result, interfaces must be specified at design time, and any changes required during runtime involve expensive, time-consuming version upgrades.

Such is the environment that gave birth to SOAP. SOAP addresses each of these drawbacks to existing ORPC architectures:

- SOAP is built with open technologies and is an open specification. Because SOAP is built with XML and is itself managed by international standards bodies, SOAP is a *vendor-neutral* protocol.
- It follows, then, that SOAP's characteristics are also open. SOAP uses XML as its payload parameter value format and uses URIs (which are like URLs; more about URIs later) for endpoint naming. In addition, SOAP interfaces are described with the Web Services Description Language (WSDL), which is also an open technology. (More about WSDL in Chapter 16, "Web Services Building Blocks: WSDL and UDDI.")
- Because SOAP is based on XML, it is a text-based protocol. As a result, it is simpler than CORBA and DCOM. SOAP messages are human-readable and firewall friendly. SOAP messages are typically sent over HTTP, either over the standard port, 80, or the standard SSL port, 443. Human-readability is valuable for developing and maintaining the software.
- SOAP is a loosely coupled protocol. Because SOAP takes advantage of XML's self-describing capabilities, SOAP messages (in conjunction with WSDL) can indicate to their recipients their interface requirements. Therefore, it is possible to change SOAP message interfaces at runtime, as long as the underlying architecture supports just-in-time (JIT) integration. You can learn more about JIT integration in Chapter 14.

In addition, SOAP works quite well in messaging as well as RPC architectures. Although both CORBA and DCOM are inherently based on their request/response mechanisms, the SOAP protocol supports asynchronous messages as well as one-way messages that don't come in request/response pairs.

Improved Interoperability

If there is one phrase that strikes fear in the hearts of many a system integrator, it is "DCOM-CORBA bridge." Sure, DCOM and CORBA are technically interoperable via such bridges, but in reality, the custom integration needed to make such bridges work in real-world environments is extraordinarily expensive and time consuming. If such integration was just a matter of translating Network Data Representation (NDR) payloads to Common Data Representation (CDR) payloads, for example, then integration wouldn't be as great an issue. The problem is, however, that DCOM and CORBA handle location transparency in different ways.

> **Note**
>
> Location transparency is one of the main design goals of both ORPC architectures (as well as other architectures, such as Java RMI). *Location transparency* means being able to hide the communication tasks between remote objects by encapsulating them into classes so that a client object can access methods on a server object as though those methods were local to the client. In essence, for a client object to invoke a server object, it must request some executable code from the server to be marshaled and sent over the wire to the client, where it is unmarshaled.

Sending executable code over the network, naturally, opens a Pandora's box of issues, including security, flexibility, and the previously mentioned firewall unfriendliness. It is clearly problematic to unmarshal an object written in one language into an object supported on a different platform. SOAP's capabilities can help to resolve these issues with location transparency.

SOAP, in essence, is the XML-based replacement for the object serialization techniques used by the existing ORPC architectures. Using XML to structure the data serialization provides a "neutral third party" between CORBA and DCOM (as well as other proprietary RPC architectures). CORBA-SOAP and DCOM-SOAP bridges are much simpler to build and use than a CORBA-DCOM bridge, because they are simply XML interfaces to existing objects.

Key Building Block for Web Services

SOAP provides an additional advantage over traditional ORPC architectures: Because SOAP messages are self-describing, the method calls contained in a SOAP message can vary each time the message is sent. In addition, it is possible to marshal several method calls in a single SOAP message. With a traditional ORPC, each call to a remote method must be handled as a separate roundtrip. A SOAP message, however, can be constructed on-the-fly to send data to multiple methods. Used judiciously, this capability can more than compensate for the slowness of SOAP's text-based messages as compared to the binary messages of CORBA and DCOM.

The ability of SOAP messages to be constructed on-the-fly is the linchpin of the Web Services model. If you look at the Web Services stack in Figure 14.5, you'll see that SOAP is a key element in the foundation of Web Services. SOAP is ideally suited both for messages between Web Services and for messages that other systems exchange with Web Services. As explained in Chapter 14, the true power of Web Services lies in its JIT capabilities, and it is SOAP's extensibility—inherited from XML—that forms the basis for Web Services' new JIT paradigm.

Basic SOAP Syntax

Let's take a closer look at the inner workings of SOAP. SOAP provides three key capabilities:

- SOAP is a messaging framework, consisting of an outer `Envelope` element that contains an optional `Header` element and a mandatory `Body` element.
- SOAP is an encoding format that describes how objects are encoded, serialized, and then decoded when received.
- SOAP is an RPC mechanism that enables objects to call methods of remote objects.

It is possible to use SOAP only as a messaging framework or as a messaging framework and an encoding format. However, the most common use of SOAP as an encoding standard is to support its use as an RPC mechanism, as well.

SOAP Message Structure and Namespaces

Let's start with a simple example of a message we might want to send—a request to the server for a person's phone number. We might have an interface (here, written in Java) that would expose a method we might call to request the phone number:

```
public interface PhoneNumber
{
  public String getPhoneNumber(String name);
}
```

Let's say, then, that instead of using CORBA or RMI, our client sends an XML-formatted request to the server. This XML might look like the following:

```
<?xml version="1.0"?>
<PhoneNumber>
  <getPhoneNumber>
    <name>John Doe</name>
  </getPhoneNumber>
</PhoneNumber>
```

Notice that the root node corresponds to the Java interface, and the method as well as its parameter are nodes, too. We then use our client to create an HTTP request, and we put the preceding XML in the body of an HTTP `POST`. We might expect a response from the server that looks something like the following:

```
<?xml version="1.0"?>
<PhoneNumber>
  <getPhoneNumberResponse>
    <thenumber>
      <areacode>617</areacode>
      <numberbody>555-1234</numberbody>
    </thenumber>
  </getPhoneNumberResponse>
</PhoneNumber>
```

The root node retains the name of the interface, but the method name has the word "`Response`" appended to it, so the client can identify the correct response by appending "`Response`" to the calling method name.

In general, constructing request and response messages like the preceding ones is a simple but limited approach. The biggest limitation is that the vocabulary that the client and server use to exchange messages must be agreed upon beforehand. If there is a new method or a new parameter, both the client and the server must reprogram their interfaces. In addition, in a complex message, there could easily be confusion if two methods have parameters with the same name.

In order to resolve these limitations with such simple message formats, SOAP takes advantage of XML namespaces. Let's take a look at the same request message recast in SOAP:

```
<SOAP-ENV:Envelope
  xmlns:SOAP-ENV="http://schemas.xmlsoap.org/soap/envelope/"
  xmlns:xsi="http://www.w3.org/1999/XMLSchema-instance"
  xmlns:xsd="http://www.w3.org/1999/XMLSchema"
  SOAP-ENV:encodingStyle="http://schemas.xmlsoap.org/soap/encoding/">
```

```
<SOAP-ENV:Header>
</SOAP-ENV:Header>

  <SOAP-ENV:Body>
    <ns:getPhoneNumber xmlns:ns="PhoneNumber">
      <name xsi:type="xsd:string">John Doe</name>
    </ns:getPhoneNumber>
  </SOAP-ENV:Body>
</SOAP-ENV:Envelope>
```

Let's break down this request and take a closer look. First of all, its root node is `Envelope`, which has an optional `Header` section and a mandatory `Body` section. The SOAP `Envelope` is then enclosed in the outer transport envelope, which might be HTTP, SMTP, and so on. All SOAP messages are structured like this, as shown in Figure 15.1.

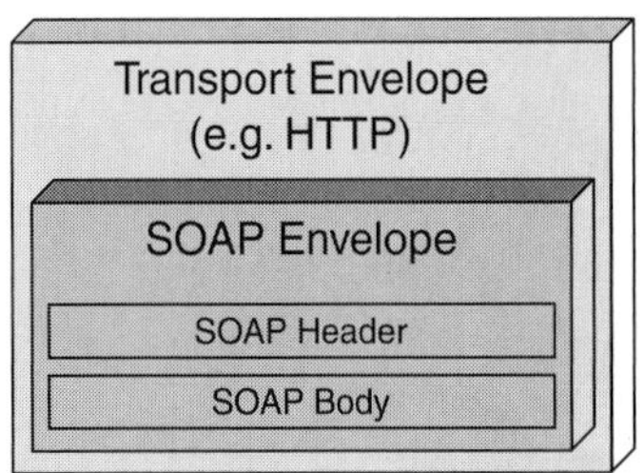

FIGURE 15.1
SOAP message structure.

Next, notice that the message takes full advantage of namespaces. Namespaces are a critically important part of SOAP (for more about namespaces, see Chapter 5, "The X-Files: XPath, XPointer, and XLink"). Namespaces differentiate elements and attributes with similar names, so they can both occupy the same document without confusion. In addition, namespaces are used for versioning so that the semantics of the XML tags can be updated or modified. Most important, however, namespaces allow the SOAP messages to be extensible: By referencing different namespaces, a SOAP message can extend its semantic scope (in other words, talk about different things), and the receiver can interpret the new message by referencing the same namespace.

You declare namespaces with the `xmlns` keyword. There are two forms of namespace declarations: default declarations and explicit declarations. In our sample request, all the declarations are explicit. Explicit declarations take the following form:

```
xmlns:SOAP-ENV=http://schemas.xmlsoap.org/soap/envelope/
```

The default declarations look like this:

```
xmlns="SomeURI"
```

Explicit declarations begin with the xmlns keyword, followed by a colon and a shorthand designation for the namespace. The SOAP-ENV namespace includes the <Envelope>, <Header>, and <Body> structural elements as well as the encodingStyle attribute, found at the URI http://schemas.xmlsoap.org/soap/envelope/, which is the standard URL for the SOAP-ENV namespace. An explicit declaration is used when taking advantage of a publicly available namespace, whereas default declarations are appropriate for custom namespaces.

Note

So, what are the differences among URLs, URIs, and URNs, anyway? A Uniform Resource Identifier (URI) is nothing more than a formatted string that uniquely identifies a resource. URIs come in two flavors: URLs and URNs. A Uniform Resource Locator (URL) includes an encoding of the underlying protocol that is used to locate the resource (the all-too-familiar "http://"), whereas a Uniform Resource Name (URN) is location independent and therefore provides no information about where to find the resource.

The syntax for HTTP URLs is as follows:

```
"http://" <host> [":" <port>] [<path> ["?" <query>]]
```

Here, <host> is the IP address or fully qualified domain name of the server; <port> is the TCP port number; <path> is the absolute path to the resource being requested, and the optional <query> is the query string suffix.

The syntax for URNs is quite different:

```
"urn:" <NID> ":" <NSS>
```

Here, <NID> is the namespace identifier, and <NSS> is a namespace-specific string. An example of a URN would be as follows:

```
urn:uuid:12345
```

In addition, the xsi namespace maps to http://www.w3.org/1999/XMLSchema-instance, and xsd maps to http://www.w3.org/1999/XMLSchema. Both are also standard namespaces. The xsd namespace includes the attribute string.

The Envelope element also contains the attribute:

```
SOAP-ENV:encodingStyle="http://schemas.xmlsoap.org/soap/encoding/"
```

The encodingStyle attribute informs the server receiving the message about the way that the message content is encoded, or *serialized*. The server needs this information to decode the Body element; as a result, the SOAP message is self-describing.

The `encodingStyle` attribute defined by `http://schemas.xmlsoap.org/soap/encoding/` is the only one defined by the SOAP specification, but it is not actually mandatory. An empty URI ("") can be used as the encoding style to disable any serialization claims from containing elements. In addition, you can select a more restrictive serialization rule by extending the path of the encoding style URI. In this case, the URIs indicating the serialization rules that you want to use must be written from most specific to least specific, as follows:

```
SOAP-ENV:encodingStyle="http://mysite.com/soap/encoding/restricted
➥http://mysite.com/soap/encoding/"
```

Next, let's take a look at the `Body` element of our SOAP request. The interface name `PhoneNumber` in the line

```
<ns:getPhoneNumber xmlns:ns="PhoneNumber">
```

is no longer a node name, as it was in our simplistic XML example. In our SOAP request, `PhoneNumber` refers to the namespace `ns`. The line

```
<name xsi:type="xsd:string">John Doe</name>
```

contains the `string` "John Doe" as the value for the element `name`, which the server will understand is the parameter for the `getPhoneNumber` method.

Now, let's take a look at the server's response message:

```
<SOAP-ENV:Envelope
    xmlns:SOAP-ENV="http://schemas.xmlsoap.org/soap/envelope/"
    xmlns:xsi="http://www.w3.org/1999/XMLSchema-instance"
    xmlns:xsd="http://www.w3.org/1999/XMLSchema"
    SOAP-ENV:encodingStyle="http://schemas.xmlsoap.org/soap/encoding/">
  <SOAP-ENV:Body>
    <getPhoneNumberResponse xmlns="SomeURI">
      <areacode>617</areacode>
      <numberbody>555-1234</numberbody>
    </getPhoneNumberResponse>
  </SOAP-ENV:Body>
</SOAP-ENV:Envelope>
```

The response message shows an example of a namespace with a default declaration in the following line:

```
<getPhoneNumberResponse xmlns="SomeURI">
```

In the case of a default declaration, the namespace found at `SomeURI` automatically scopes that element and all its children. As a result, the `<areacode>` and `<numberbody>` elements are defined in terms of the default namespace, instead of taking advantage of the `xsi` or `xsd` namespaces.

SOAP Envelope Element

The SOAP Envelope element is the mandatory top element of the XML document that represents the SOAP message being sent. It may contain namespace declarations as well as other attributes, which must be "namespace qualified." The Envelope element may also contain additional subelements, which must also be namespace qualified and follow the Body element.

SOAP does not define a traditional versioning model (for example, 1.0, 1.1, 2.0, and so on). Instead, SOAP handles the possibility of messages conforming to different versions of the SOAP specification by the way it handles the namespace associated with the Envelope element. This namespace, http://schemas.xmlsoap.org/soap/envelope/, is required by all SOAP messages. If a SOAP application receives a message with a different namespace, it must recognize this situation as a version error and discard the message. If the underlying protocol requires a response (as with HTTP), the SOAP application must respond with a VersionMismatch faultcode using the http://schemas.xmlsoap.org/soap/envelope/ namespace. (More about faultcodes later in the chapter.)

SOAP Header Element

The SOAP Header element is optional and is used for extending messages without any sort of prior agreement between the two communicating parties. You might use the Header element for authentication, transaction support, payment information, or other capabilities that the SOAP specification doesn't provide.

Let's take a look at a typical Header element:

```
<SOAP-ENV:Header>
  <t:Transaction xmlns:t="myURI"
      SOAP-ENV:mustUnderstand="1">
    3
  </t:Transaction>
</SOAP-ENV:Header>
```

The Header element is the first immediate child of the Envelope element, and child elements of the Header element are called *header entries*. In this example, the header entry is the Transaction element. Header entries must be identified by their fully qualified element names (in this case, xmlns:t="myURI", where the namespace URI is represented by myURI, and the local name is t).

The SOAP `Header` element may also optionally contain the following attributes:

- A SOAP `encodingStyle` attribute, which would indicate the serialization rules for the header entries.
- A SOAP `mustUnderstand` attribute (as in our example), which indicates whether it is optional or mandatory to process the header entry. This attribute is explained in this section.
- A SOAP `actor` attribute, which indicates who is supposed to process the header entry and how they are supposed to process it. The `actor` attribute is also explained in more detail in this section.

The value of the `mustUnderstand` attribute is either `1`, indicating that the recipient must process the header entry, or `0`, indicating that the header entry is optional. If this attribute doesn't appear, processing the header entry is assumed to be optional provide.

If the attribute is set to `1`, the recipient must either process the semantics of the header entry properly according to its URI or fail processing the message and return an error. Therefore, if there is a change in the semantics associated with a header entry, setting the `mustUnderstand` attribute to `1` guarantees that the recipient will process the new semantics.

In the preceding example, the `Transaction` element is mandatory, as indicated by the `mustUnderstand` attribute, and has a value of `3`, indicating which transaction the current message belongs to.

Caution

Because the `mustUnderstand` attribute is optional, you would think that you could avoid problems by not using it. However, the current Apache SOAP implementation doesn't support the `mustUnderstand` attribute, and as a result, Apache SOAP can't understand some SOAP messages sent by the Microsoft SOAP Toolkit, because that toolkit does send messages that use the `mustUnderstand` attribute. In other words, both tools follow the SOAP spec (in this instance, anyway), but they follow it in incompatible ways nevertheless.

The second optional header entry attribute is the `actor` attribute. The SOAP `actor` attribute indicates the recipient of the header entry. If there are only two parties involved in a message (namely, the sender and the recipient), the `actor` attribute is extraneous. However, in many cases, intermediaries will process a SOAP message on its way from the sender to the recipient. These intermediaries are typically interested in only part of the SOAP message. For example, a firewall may check the `Envelope` element for allowed URIs but may not be interested in the `Body` element.

If an intermediary receives a SOAP message and determines that part of the message is for itself, it must remove that part of the message before sending on the rest. Of course, the intermediary may also add to the message, as well. The `actor` attribute might be used to indicate that part of the message is intended for a particular intermediary or possibly for the final recipient. There is also a special URI:

```
http://schemas.xmlsoap.org/soap/actor/next
```

This URI can be used as the value for the `actor` attribute that indicates that the header entry is intended for the next application down the line to process the message provide.

SOAP Body Element

The mandatory `Body` element is an immediate child of the `Envelope` element and must immediately follow the `Header` element if a header is present. Each immediate child of the `Body` element is called a *body entry*. The `Body` element is used to carry the payload of the SOAP message, and there is a great deal of latitude in what you can place in the `Body` element. `Body` entries are identified by their fully qualified element names. Typically, the SOAP `encodingStyle` attribute is used to indicate the serialization rules for body entities, but this encoding style is not required.

The only `Body` entry explicitly defined in the SOAP specification is the `Fault` entry, used for reporting errors. The `Fault` entry is explained later in the chapter.

Data Types

The SOAP specification allows for the use of custom encodings, but typically you are likely to use the default encoding defined in `http://schemas.xmlsoap.org/soap/encoding/`. If you use this encoding, you get to take advantage of its data model, which is structured to be consistent with the data models of today's popular programming languages, including Java, Visual Basic, and C++.

First of all, the standard encoding provides for the terminology defined in Table 15.1.

TABLE 15.1 SOAP Terminology

Term	*Meaning*
Value	A string, the name of a measurement (including numbers, dates, and so on), or a combination of such values.
Simple value	A value that doesn't have named parts.

TABLE 15.1 continued

Term	*Meaning*
Compound value	An aggregate of values. For example, a complete street address (number, street, city, state, and zip code) would be a compound value. Arrays are also compound values.
Accessor	A role name or ordinal that distinguishes a value within a compound value. "Zip code" would be an accessor to the street address value.
Array	A compound value where the member values are distinguished solely by their ordinal position.
Struct	A compound value where the necessarily unique accessor name is the only distinction among member values.
Simple type	A class of simple values. For example, `string` is a simple type, whereas `"this string"` is a simple value that is an instance of the simple type.
Compound type	A class of compound values. Each instance of a particular compound type would have to share the same accessors.
Locally scoped	An accessor whose name is unique within a particular type but not across all types. Locally scoped accessors must be combined with the type name to be uniquely identified.
Universally scoped	An accessor whose name is based (directly or indirectly) on a URI and is therefore unique across all types.
Single-reference	A value that can be referenced by only a single instance of an accessor, as determined by the schema.
Multi-reference	A value that could potentially be referenced by more than one instance of an accessor, as determined by the schema.
Independent	An element that appears at the top level of a serialization.
Embedded	Any element that isn't independent.

Next, the standard encoding provides for SOAP's simple types, which are based on the "Primitive Datatypes" section of the XML Schema specification. SOAP's primitive data types are described in Table 15.2.

TABLE 15.2 SOAP Primitive Data Types

Data Type	*Meaning*
`SOAP-ENC:string`	Any string of Unicode characters that are allowed in a SOAP message.

TABLE 15.2 continued

Data Type	*Meaning*
`SOAP-ENC:boolean`	`true`, `false`, `1`, or `0`.
`SOAP-ENC:decimal`	A number such as 44.145629 or -0.32, with an arbitrary size and precision.
`SOAP-ENC:float`	The 4-byte IEEE-754 floating-point number that is closest to the specified decimal string.
`SOAP-ENC:double`	The 8-byte IEEE-754 floating-point number that is closest to the specified decimal string.
`SOAP-ENC:integer`	Any integer.
`SOAP-ENC:positiveInteger`	An integer that is strictly greater than zero.
`SOAP-ENC:nonPositiveInteger`	An integer that is less than or equal to zero.
`SOAP-ENC:negativeInteger`	An integer that is strictly less than zero.
`SOAP-ENC:nonNegativeInteger`	An integer that is greater than or equal to zero.
`SOAP-ENC:long`	An integer between -9,223,372,036,854,775,808 and +9,223,372,036,854,775,807.
`SOAP-ENC:int`	An integer between -2,147,483,648 and 2,147,483,647.
`SOAP-ENC:short`	An integer between -32,768 and 32,767.
`SOAP-ENC:byte`	An integer between -128 and 127.
`SOAP-ENC:unsignedLong`	An integer between 0 and 18,446,744,073,709,551,615.
`SOAP-ENC:unsignedInt`	An integer between 0 and 429,496,729.
`SOAP-ENC:unsignedShort`	An integer between 0 and 65,535.
`SOAP-ENC:unsignedByte`	An integer between 0 and 255.
`SOAP-ENC:duration`	A length of time given in the ISO 8601 extended format, represented by `PnYnMnDTnHnMnS (for example, 19951231T235959)`. The number of seconds can be a decimal or an integer. All the other values must be non-negative integers.
`SOAP-ENC:dateTime`	A particular moment of time on a particular day up to an arbitrary fraction of a second in the ISO 8601 format, which is `CCYY-MM-DDThh:mm:ss (for example, 1995-12-31T23:59:59)`. Put on a `Z` suffix to indicate coordinated universal time (UTC) or an offset from UTC.
`SOAP-ENC:time`	A time of day in the ISO 8601 format: `hh:mm:ss.sss`. A time zone specified as an offset from UTC may also be added.

TABLE 15.2 continued

Data Type	*Meaning*
`SOAP-ENC:date`	A particular date given in ISO 8601 format: `YYYYMMDD`
`SOAP-ENC:gYearMonth`	A particular month in a particular year in the form `YYYY-MM`.
`SOAP-ENC:gYear`	A year in the Gregorian calendar ranging from 0001 up or -0001 down. (There is no year zero.)
`SOAP-ENC:gMonthDay`	A particular day of a particular month in the form `MM-DD`.
`SOAP-ENC:gDay`	A particular day in the form `DD`.
`SOAP-ENC:gMonth`	A particular month in the form `MM`.
`SOAP-ENC:hexBinary`	Encoded hexadecimal binary data; each byte of the data is replaced by the two hexadecimal digits that represent its unsigned value.
`SOAP-ENC:base64Binary`	Base-64 encoded binary data.
`SOAP-ENC:anyURI`	An absolute or relative URI.
`SOAP-ENC:QName`	An XML name such as `SOAP-ENV:Body` or `Body`, which may have an optional prefix. However, nonprefixed names must be in the default namespace.
`SOAP-ENC:NOTATION`	The name of a notation declared in the current schema.
`SOAP-ENC:normalizedString`	A string that does not contain any carriage return (`\r`), linefeed (`\n`), or tab (`\t`) characters. Such strings are called *normalized*.
`SOAP-ENC:token`	A normalized string without any leading or trailing white-space and no runs of consecutive whitespace characters. Whitespace characters include the space itself, tabs, and so on (as well as the three characters disallowed in all normalized strings).
`SOAP-ENC:language`	An RFC 1766 language identifier (the RFC 1766 standard can be found at `http://www.ietf.org/rfc/rfc1766.txt`).
`SOAP-ENC:NMTOKEN`	An XML name token.
`SOAP-ENC:NMTOKENS`	A whitespace-separated list of XML name tokens.
`SOAP-ENC:Name`	An XML name.
`SOAP-ENC:NCName`	An XML name that does not contain any colons.
`SOAP-ENC:ID`	An `NCName` that is unique among other IDs in the same document.
`SOAP-ENC:IDREF`	An `NCName` used as an ID somewhere in the document.

TABLE 15.2 continued

Data Type	*Meaning*
`SOAP-ENC:IDREFS`	A whitespace-separated list of `IDREF` elements.
`SOAP-ENC:ENTITY`	An `NCName` that has been declared as an unparsed entity (not yet implemented consistently).
`SOAP-ENC:ENTITIES`	A whitespace-separated list of `ENTITY` names (also implemented inconsistently) .

These data types can be used directly in SOAP elements:

```
<SOAP-ENC:int>47</SOAP-ENC:int>
```

In addition, the data types support the `id` and `href` attributes, allowing multiple references to the same value:

```
<SOAP-ENC:string id="mystr">The string</SOAP-ENC:string>
<SOAP-ENC:string href="#mystr"/>
```

Furthermore, if the attributes are defined within a schema, you might have the following example:

```
<bodystring id="mystr">The string</bodystring>
<newstring href="#newstring"/>
```

In this case, the schema would include the following fragments:

```
<element name="bodystring" type="SOAP-ENC:string">
<element name="newstring" type="SOAP-ENC:string">
```

The only difference between this approach and declaring an element to be of type `"xsd:string"` is that `"SOAP-ENC:string"` allows for the `id` and `href` attributes.

Arrays

Arrays are examples of compound values, where the member values in an array are distinguished only by their ordinal value. Arrays can contain elements that are of any type, including nested arrays. Here is an example of an array containing integers:

```
<SOAP-ENC:Array SOAP-ENC:arrayType="xsd:int[2]">
  <SOAP-ENC:int>4</SOAP-ENC:int>
  <SOAP-ENC:int>33</SOAP-ENC:int>
</SOAP-ENC:Array>
```

Alternately, the same array can be represented with the use of the schema, as follows:

```
<myIntegers SOAP-ENC:arrayType="xsd:int[2]">
  <num>4</num>
```

```
  <num>33</num>
</myIntegers>
```

Here's the corresponding schema fragment:

```
<element name="myIntegers" type="SOAP-ENC:Array">
```

A third way of specifying types of member elements is with the `xsi:type` attribute in the instance, as shown here:

```
<SOAP-ENC:Array SOAP-ENC:arrayType="xsd:ur-type[3]">
  <item xsi:type="xsd:int">4</item>
  <item xsi:type="xsd:decimal">3.456</item>
  <item xsi:type="xsd:string">This is a string</item>
</SOAP-ENC:Array>
```

This example also shows how the types of the member elements of an array can vary.

It is also possible for arrays to be multidimensional. Here is an example of a two-dimensional array:

```
<myStrings SOAP-ENC:arrayType="xsd:string[2,3]">
  <str>Row 1 Column 1</str>
  <str>Row 1 Column 2</str>
  <str>Row 1 Column 3</str>
  <str>Row 2 Column 1</str>
  <str>Row 2 Column 2</str>
  <str>Row 2 Column 3</str>
</myStrings>
```

Arrays may also have other arrays or other compound values as member elements.

Finally, the SOAP specification defines two additional types of arrays: partially transmitted or varying arrays and sparse arrays. A partially transmitted array is an array that only has some of its elements specified. The `"SOAP-ENC:offset"` attribute indicates when the first specified element isn't the array's first element, as shown in the following example:

```
<SOAP-ENC:Array Type="xsd:string[5]" SOAP-ENC:offset="[2]">
  <str>The third element of the Array</str>
  <str>The fourth element of the Array</str>
</SOAP-ENC:Array>
```

Caution

Neither Apache SOAP 2.2 nor the Microsoft SOAP Toolkit 2.0 SP2 support partial or sparse arrays. The Apache implementation doesn't support multidimensional arrays, either.

SOAP handles sparse arrays by defining a SOAP-ENC:position attribute that indicates a member value's position within an array, as shown in the following example:

```
<SOAP-ENC:Array Type="xsd:string[5,5]">
  <str SOAP-ENC:position="[1,2]">Second row, third column</str>
  <str SOAP-ENC:position="[4,0]">Fifth row, first column</str>
</SOAP-ENC:Array>
```

Structs

In addition to arrays, structs are also examples of compound values, where the member values in a struct are identified by unique accessor names. A simple example of a struct is given here:

```
<elt:Purchase>
  <buyer>John Doe</buyer>
  <item>Widget</item>
  <count>2</count>
  <cost>14.47</cost>
</elt:Purchase>
```

The following schema fragment describes the struct:

```
<element name="Purchase">
  <complexType>
    <element name="buyer" type="xsd:string"/>
    <element name="item" type="xsd:string"/>
    <element name="count" type="xsd:int"/>
    <element name="cost" type="xsd:decimal"/>
  </complexType>
</element>
```

With structs, the name of the element is unique and identifies the element. The order of elements is irrelevant.

We can expand the preceding struct by giving the buyer element some child elements of its own:

```
<elt:Purchase>
  <buyer>
    <name>John Doe</name>
    <address>1 Web St.</address>
  </buyer>
  <item>Widget</item>
  <count>2</count>
  <cost>14.47</cost>
</elt:Purchase>
```

This is the best way of handling nested elements when they are single-reference. However, if the buyer element were multi-reference, which would be true in the case of a purchase (because John Doe would hopefully be expected to make additional purchases), then the following struct would be more appropriate:

```
<elt:Purchase>
  <buyer href="#Person-1"/>
  <item>Widget</item>
  <count>2</count>
  <cost>14.47</cost>
</elt:Purchase>
<elt:Person id="Person-1">
  <name>John Doe</name>
  <address>1 Web St.</address>
</elt:Person>
```

In this example, "John Doe" is an example of an independent element, which represents an instance of a type (in this case, Person) that is referred to by at least one multi-reference accessor (in this case, buyer). Such independent elements must be tagged with the id attribute and must be unique within the SOAP message.

Both of the two struct examples would be described by the following schema fragment:

```
<element name="Purchase" type="tns:Purchase">
  <complexType name="Purchase">
    <sequence minOccurs="0" maxOccurs="1">
      <element name="buyer" type="tns:Person"/>
      <element name="item" type="xsd:string"/>
      <element name="count" type="xsd:int"/>
      <element name="cost" type="xsd:decimal"/>
    </sequence>
    <attribute name="href" type="uriReference"/>
    <attribute name="id" type="ID"/>
    <anyAttribute namespace="##other"/>
  </complexType>
</element>
<element name="Person" base="tns:Person">
  <complexType name="Person">
    <element name="name" type="xsd:string"/>
    <element name="address" type="xsd:string"/>
  </complexType>
</element>
```

Note that the child elements of the sequence element might occur at most once, in which case the href attribute would not occur.

The preceding examples cover the breadth of what can be done with structs, but there are many different ways of building them. For example, it is also possible to nest multi-reference elements, for example, if a `Person` element might have more than one `address` element. In addition, elements can themselves be compound values.

Faults

The SOAP `Fault` element carries error messages (typically in response messages) or other status information. This element is optional, but if it is present, it must appear only once as a body entry.

Here is an example of a SOAP response message with a `Fault` element:

```
<SOAP-ENV:Envelope xmlns:SOAP-ENV="http://schemas.xmlsoap.org/soap/envelope/">
  <SOAP-ENV:Body>
    <SOAP-ENV:Fault>
      <faultcode>SOAP-ENV:Server</faultcode>
      <faultstring>Unable to process message</faultstring>
      <detail>
        <dtl:faultDetail xmlns:dtl="Some-URI">
          <message>Namespace mismatch</message>
          <errorcode>47</errorcode>
        </dtl:faultDetail>
      </detail>
    </SOAP-ENV:Fault>
  </SOAP-ENV:Body>
</SOAP-ENV:Envelope>
```

First, notice that the `Fault` element has three child elements. There are a total of four possible subelements to the `Fault` element:

- The `faultcode` element is mandatory and provides a mechanism for software applications to find the fault. SOAP defines four faultcodes (provided in the following list).
- The `faultstring` element is also mandatory and provides a human-readable explanation of the fault.
- The `faultactor` element is optional and is used when there are intermediaries in the message path. It parallels the SOAP `actor` attribute (described earlier), providing a URI that indicates the source of the fault.
- The `detail` element carries error information related specifically to the `Body` element and is mandatory if the message recipient could not process the `Body` element of the original message. (Error information about header entries must be carried within the `Header` element.) If the `detail` element is missing, the recipient of the fault message knows that the fault occurred before the `Body` element was processed.
- Other namespace-qualified `Fault` elements are also allowed.

As mentioned in the preceding list, SOAP provides for four faultcodes:

- A `VersionMismatch` faultcode indicates that the recipient found an invalid namespace for the SOAP `Envelope` element.
- The `MustUnderstand` faultcode indicates that a SOAP header entry with a `MustUnderstand` attribute set to `"1"` was not understood (or not obeyed).
- The `Client` faultcode indicates a problem with the request message itself. The problem might be malformed XML or missing information that is required by the recipient.
- The `Server` class of faultcodes indicates that the recipient was unable to process the message, but the problem was not directly caused by the request message. A typical `Server` faultcode would result from the server application failing to obtain required data from another system. The server may send a subsequent successful response if the problem is resolved.

Sending SOAP messages

The primary motivation for developing the SOAP specification has been to find a way to make RPC architectures simpler and less problematic. The problems with DCOM and CORBA—vendor dependence, firewall unfriendliness, and unnecessary complexity—led to the development of early XML-based RPC architectures, such as XML-RPC.

XML-RPC paved the way for SOAP. Although XML-RPC was a straightforward application of XML, it did not take advantage of XML namespaces and was therefore not fully extensible. For this reason, SOAP was originally thought of as a namespace-capable augmentation to XML-RPC.

Note

XML-RPC is a straightforward, simple set of implementations that enable disparate software systems to interact over the Internet. It was pioneered by Dave Winer of UserLand Software, who was also instrumental in the creation of SOAP. Although XML-RPC has a devoted following, it is gradually being superseded by SOAP. You can learn more about XML-RPC at `http://www.xml-rpc.com/`.

Even though SOAP is primarily intended to be used as part of an RPC architecture and its heritage is firmly in the RPC camp, it nevertheless does not require a synchronous request/response mechanism. In fact, SOAP supports four types of operations:

- A request-response operation, which is bidirectional. In this type of operation, the server receives a message from the client and replies with a response message.
- A solicit-response operation, which is also bidirectional, except that the server solicits a request from the client, who then responds, essentially putting the response before the request.
- A one-way message sent from the client to the server with no response message returned.
- A notification message sent from the server to the client.

In essence, the bidirectional messages are inverses of each other, as are the unidirectional ones. In addition to these four basic operations, SOAP also supports the forwarding by intermediaries, which can also be either unidirectional or bidirectional. Furthermore, SOAP faults are only supported by bidirectional messages.

Because of SOAP's flexibility regarding message type, in combination with the fact that it is a text-based protocol, SOAP messages can go over any number of different protocols: HTTP, SMTP, FTP, and so on. However, HTTP has become the predominant transfer protocol for SOAP because of its request-response mechanism, its ubiquity, and its familiarity. Nevertheless, it is still important to point out some asynchronous applications of SOAP as well.

SOAP and HTTP

HTTP supports two request methods: `GET` and `POST`. The `GET` method sends its parameters in the URL and is typically used to request Web pages from a Web server. The `POST` method sends data to the server in a payload that comes after the HTTP header. Because `POST` payloads can be of indefinite length, SOAP requests transmitted via HTTP are sent as HTTP `POST` requests.

Here's the format of a simple HTTP `POST` request that you might send when submitting a form on a Web page:

```
POST /mypath HTTP/1.1
Host: 123.45.67.89
Content-Type: text/plain; charset="utf-8"
Content-Length: 20

This is the payload.
```

The first line of the HTTP request contains the method, the URI of the recipient, and the HTTP version. The second line contains the IP address of the sender. The third line specifies the MIME type and the character encoding of the request, and the fourth line tells the server how many characters to expect in the payload. Following the fourth line is an extra carriage return/linefeed (required by the HTTP protocol) and then the payload itself, which is arbitrary text.

Now, let's take a look at an HTTP `POST` request that contains a simple SOAP message:

```
POST /mypath HTTP/1.1
Host: 123.45.67.89
Content-Type: text/xml
Content-Length: 300
SOAPMethodName: urn:mysite-com:PhoneNumber#getPhoneNumber

<SOAP-ENV:Envelope
  xmlns:SOAP-ENV="http://schemas.xmlsoap.org/soap/envelope/"
  SOAP-ENV:encodingStyle="http://schemas.xmlsoap.org/soap/encoding/">
  <SOAP-ENV:Body>
    <ns:getPhoneNumber xmlns:ns="PhoneNumber">
      <name>John Doe</name>
    </ns:getPhoneNumber>
  </SOAP-ENV:Body>
</SOAP-ENV:Envelope>
```

In this request, the URI `/mypath` indicates the SOAP endpoint: It is up to the server to translate this URI into the location of the application charged with accepting this request. The `Content-Type` for all SOAP messages must be `text/xml` (as opposed to `text/plain` for Web pages).

SOAP requests must also contain the additional `SOAPMethodName` HTTP header. This header indicates the method that is to be called (in this case, the `getPhoneNumber` method of the `PhoneNumber` class). This header is scoped by a URI using a `#` character as a delimiter. The payload for this request is simply the SOAP `Envelope` element.

Now, let's look at HTTP responses. In the case of a simple Web page, an HTTP response looks like this:

```
HTTP/1.0 200 OK
Content-Type: text/plain; charset="utf-8"
Content-Length: 38

<html><body>
617-555-6789
</body></html>
```

The first line of this response always contains the HTTP status code, which in this case is `200` (indicating success). Other failure codes include `400 Bad Request` and the all-too-familiar `404 Not Found`. The second and third lines are analogous to the request, as is the carriage return/linefeed. Finally, the server sends the payload, which in this case is the HTML for a Web page that displays John Doe's phone number.

A SOAP response looks pretty much the way you would expect:

```
HTTP/1.0 200 OK
Content-Type: text/xml
Content-Length: 374

<SOAP-ENV:Envelope
    xmlns:SOAP-ENV="http://schemas.xmlsoap.org/soap/envelope/"
    SOAP-ENV:encodingStyle="http://schemas.xmlsoap.org/soap/encoding/">
  <SOAP-ENV:Body>
    <m:getPhoneNumberResponse xmlns:m="urn:mysite-com:PhoneNumber">
      <areacode>617</areacode>
      <numberbody>555-1234</numberbody>
    </m:getPhoneNumberResponse>
  </SOAP-ENV:Body>
</SOAP-ENV:Envelope>
```

Note that the URN for the receiving class appears in the `getPhoneNumberResponse` element, but there is no `SOAPMethodName` HTTP header. Such headers are only required for HTTP requests and are not allowed in responses. In addition, if the server encounters an error and returns a SOAP fault, the first line of the HTTP header would be this:

```
500 Internal Server Error
```

Header Extensions

HTTP is a mature protocol that was developed to support the connectionless, stateless world of Web pages. However, HTTP's inability to guarantee message delivery threatened to constrain its usefulness in the world of Web Services. As a result, the HTTP extension framework was developed to allow for additional functionality within the confines of the HTTP specification.

> **Note**
>
> HTTP header extensions are part of an experimental RFC at the W3C. You can learn more about them at `http://www.w3.org/Protocols/HTTP/ietf-http-ext/`.

Here is an example of an HTTP `POST` request that takes advantage of the HTTP extension framework:

```
M-POST /mypath HTTP/1.1
Host: 123.45.67.89
Content-Type: text/xml; charset="utf-8"
Content-Length: 300
```

```
Man: "http://schemas.xmlsoap.org/soap/envelope/"; ns=01
01-SOAPAction: urn:mysite-com:PhoneNumber#getPhoneNumber

<SOAP-ENV:Envelope
...
```

The first line of the preceding request contains the `M-POST` method, where `M` indicates *mandatory*. A mandatory HTTP request must include at least one mandatory extension declaration, which uses either the `Man` or `C-Man` header field. (The `C-Man` header field is used for "hop-by-hop" requests that can traverse one or more intermediaries.)

Caution

Neither Apache SOAP 2.2 nor the Microsoft SOAP Toolkit 2.0 SP2 support the M-POST method, although SOAP::Lite does.

In this example, the `Man` header request indicates the default `Envelope` namespace and maps the header prefix `01` to the namespace. The next line then attaches this prefix to the `SOAPAction` field.

The server's response to this request (assuming there are no errors) appears as such:

```
HTTP/1.0 200 OK
Ext:
Content-Type: text/xml; charset="utf-8"
Content-Length: 374

<SOAP-ENV:Envelope
...
```

The `Ext:` header (or `C-Ext:` header, in the case of a hop-by-hop response) simply indicates that the mandatory extension declarations were fulfilled by the server.

SOAP and SMTP

The Simple Mail Transport Protocol (SMTP) is the established standard protocol for sending e-mail messages. Because SOAP envelopes are nothing more than text messages, e-mailing them is elementary on the surface. However, there are several issues that must be dealt with when using SMTP to send a message to an application.

A SOAP message sent via SMTP goes to a mailbox and waits for the server to act upon it. The mailbox will be typically provided by a Post Office Protocol (POP3) server. Therefore, in order for the server to access the SOAP message in a mailbox, the server will typically use a POP3-to-HTTP bridge to post the incoming message to the processing application, and then take the response and use an HTTP-to-SMTP bridge to send it back to the client. The client must then poll its own POP3 mailbox in order to accept the message.

Alternately, it is possible to custom-code a POP3-compliant application that can parse SOAP messages directly as well as create the responses. Furthermore, because SMTP is an asynchronous protocol, its best application may be for those SOAP messages that are unidirectional.

Caution

Apache SOAP 2.2 supports SMTP, but the Microsoft SOAP Toolkit 2.0 SP2 does not. Neither the Apache nor Microsoft Toolkits support POP3 or any other transport protocols for that matter (other than HTTP and HTTPS).

SOAP Implementations

As you have probably gathered by the cautions in this chapter, there are two leading SOAP implementations available today: Microsoft's SOAP Toolkit (currently at version 2.0 SP2) and Apache SOAP (now at version 2.2), which was originally created by IBM, who donated it to the Apache Foundation. The Microsoft Toolkit supports all COM-compliant languages—in particular, Visual Basic, and C#. The Apache implementation uses Java.

However, several other SOAP implementations are available, as well. Table 15.3 lists several of the most popular implementations.

TABLE 15.3 Some Popular SOAP Implementations

Vendor	*Languages*	*Platforms*	*Home Page*
Microsoft	Visual Basic, C#	Windows	`http://msdn.Microsoft.com/soap`
Apache	Java	UNIX, Windows	`http://xml.apache.org/soap`
SOAP::Lite	Perl	UNIX, Windows	`http://www.soaplite.com`

TABLE 15.3 continued

Vendor	*Languages*	*Platforms*	*Home Page*
Systinet WASP	C++, Java	UNIX, Windows	`http://www.systinet.com/` `➥wasp_overview.html`
GLUE	Java	UNIX, Windows	`http://www.themindelectric.com/` `➥products/glue/glue.html`

At this point in time, there are two main issues with the available SOAP implementations: First, how well do they support an overall Web Services implementation? Second, how interoperable they are? The discussion of how well each of the leading SOAP implementations supports Web Services appears in Chapter 16, in the discussion of WSDL and UDDI. The question of interoperability among SOAP implementations is also a critical issue for this nascent technology.

Microsoft SOAP Toolkit

The Microsoft SOAP Toolkit can be found at `http://msdn.Microsoft.com/soap`. You must have the Visual Basic runtime files and the Windows Installer installed on your system before you install the toolkit. The toolkit also requires Internet Explorer 5.0, or higher, and will install MSXML 3.0 SP1 (if it isn't already present). You will also need Visual Basic or another development tool that can compile DLL files, if you will be creating your own.

The SOAP Toolkit contains the following elements:

- A client-side component that enables an application to invoke Web Services operations that are described by a WSDL document.
- A server-side component that maps those operations to COM object method calls. These calls are described by the WSDL and Web Services Meta Language (WSML) files.
- Marshaling and unmarshaling components.
- A WSDL/WSML document-generator tool.

In order to exchange SOAP messages, you must set up the SOAP server and the SOAP client. The server requires a system running Internet Information Services (IIS). To set up the server, you can either choose an Internet Server API (ISAPI) server or an Active Server Pages (ASP) server as the listener. You then create an ActiveX DLL within Microsoft Visual Basic that contains the actual server code (sample code comes with the toolkit). Listing 15.1 shows a sample DLL that calculates a base rate or a replacement cost, which you will need to compile with Visual Basic.

LISTING 15.1 `CalcRateBase.vbs`—DLL File

```
Public Function CalcBaseRate(ByVal RawBaseRate As Double,
➥ByVal RelativeFactor As Double, ByVal TerritoryFactor As Double) As Double
    CalcBaseRate = RawBaseRate * RelativeFactor * TerritoryFactor
End Function

Public Function CalcReplacementCost(ByVal BaseRate As Double,
➥ByVal ReplacementCostFactor As Double) As Double
    CalcReplacementCost = BaseRate * ReplacementCostFactor
End Function

Public Function DisplayVersion() As String
    DisplayVersion = "Version 1.0"
End Function
```

Run the SOAP Toolkit Wizard and name your service with the toolkit. Then select the COM DLL file to analyze, as shown in Figure 15.2.

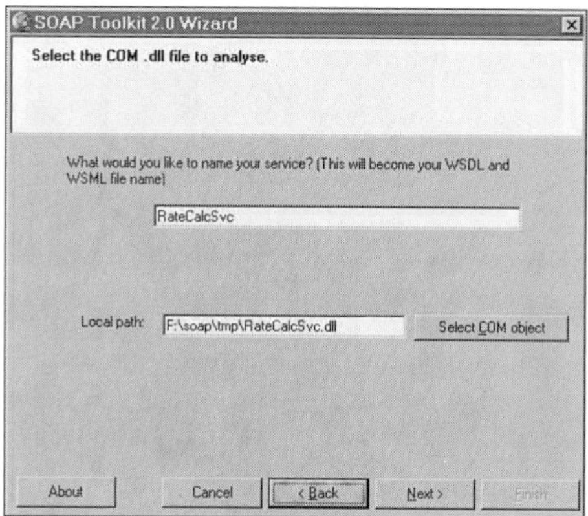

FIGURE 15.2
Selecting a COM DLL file.

Then select the services you would like to expose, as shown in Figure 15.3.

Next, create a virtual root using IIS and then create the WSDL file and the WSML files that describe the Web Service. (More about WSDL and WSML in Chapter 16.)

> **Note**
>
> The WSML file provides the information that maps the Web Service, as described in the WSDL file, to methods of the Server COM objects. WSML is a Microsoft-only specification.

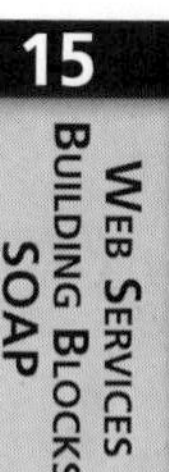

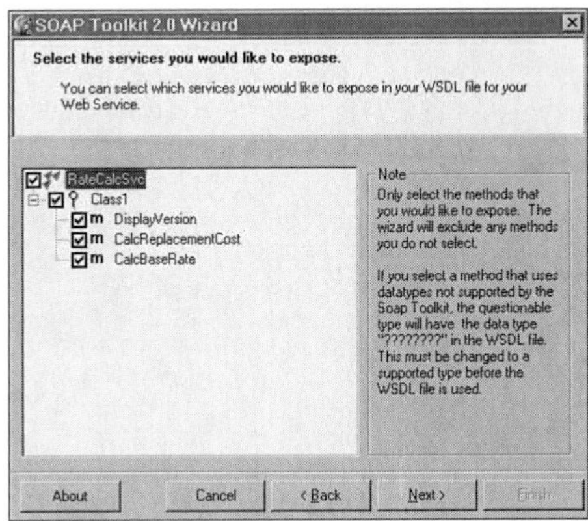

FIGURE 15.3
Exposing methods in a Web Service.

Listing 15.2 shows the WSDL file produced by the toolkit for our example.

LISTING 15.2 `RateCalcSvc.wsdl`—Generated WSDL File

```
<?xml version='1.0' encoding='UTF-16' ?>
<!— Generated 09/24/01 by Microsoft SOAP Toolkit
    WSDL File Generator, Version 1.02.813.0 —>
<definitions  name ='RateCalcSvc' targetNamespace = 'http://tempuri.org/wsdl/'
    xmlns:wsdlns='http://tempuri.org/wsdl/'
    xmlns:typens='http://tempuri.org/type'
    xmlns:soap='http://schemas.xmlsoap.org/wsdl/soap/'
    xmlns:xsd='http://www.w3.org/2001/XMLSchema'
    xmlns:stk='http://schemas.microsoft.com/soap-toolkit/wsdl-extension'
    xmlns='http://schemas.xmlsoap.org/wsdl/'>
  <types>
    <schema targetNamespace='http://tempuri.org/type'
      xmlns='http://www.w3.org/2001/XMLSchema'
      xmlns:SOAP-ENC='http://schemas.xmlsoap.org/soap/encoding/'
      xmlns:wsdl='http://schemas.xmlsoap.org/wsdl/'
      elementFormDefault='qualified'>
    </schema>
  </types>
  <message name='Class1.CalcBaseRate'>
    <part name='RawBaseRate' type='xsd:float'/>
    <part name='RelativeFactor' type='xsd:float'/>
    <part name='TerritoryFactor' type='xsd:float'/>
  </message>
  <message name='Class1.CalcBaseRateResponse'>
    <part name='Result' type='xsd:float'/>
  </message>
  <message name='Class1.CalcReplacementCost'>
    <part name='BaseRate' type='xsd:float'/>
    <part name='ReplacementCostFactor' type='xsd:float'/>
```

LISTING 15.2 continued

```
</message>
 <message name='Class1.CalcReplacementCostResponse'>
   <part name='Result' type='xsd:float'/>
 </message>
 <message name='Class1.DisplayVersion'>
 </message>
 <message name='Class1.DisplayVersionResponse'>
   <part name='Result' type='xsd:string'/>
 </message>
 <portType name='Class1SoapPort'>
   <operation name='CalcBaseRate'
        parameterOrder='RawBaseRate RelativeFactor TerritoryFactor'>
     <input message='wsdlns:Class1.CalcBaseRate' />
     <output message='wsdlns:Class1.CalcBaseRateResponse' />
   </operation>
   <operation name='CalcReplacementCost'
        parameterOrder='BaseRate ReplacementCostFactor'>
     <input message='wsdlns:Class1.CalcReplacementCost' />
     <output message='wsdlns:Class1.CalcReplacementCostResponse' />
   </operation>
   <operation name='DisplayVersion' parameterOrder=''>
     <input message='wsdlns:Class1.DisplayVersion' />
     <output message='wsdlns:Class1.DisplayVersionResponse' />
   </operation>
 </portType>
 <binding name='Class1SoapBinding' type='wsdlns:Class1SoapPort' >
   <stk:binding preferredEncoding='UTF-16'/>
   <soap:binding
       style='rpc' transport='http://schemas.xmlsoap.org/soap/http' />
   <operation name='CalcBaseRate' >
     <soap:operation
         soapAction='http://tempuri.org/action/Class1.CalcBaseRate' />
     <input>
       <soap:body use='encoded' namespace='http://tempuri.org/message/'
           encodingStyle='http://schemas.xmlsoap.org/soap/encoding/' />
     </input>
     <output>
       <soap:body use='encoded' namespace='http://tempuri.org/message/'
            encodingStyle='http://schemas.xmlsoap.org/soap/encoding/' />
     </output>
   </operation>
   <operation name='CalcReplacementCost' >
     <soap:operation
         soapAction='http://tempuri.org/action/Class1.CalcReplacementCost' />
     <input>
       <soap:body use='encoded' namespace='http://tempuri.org/message/'
            encodingStyle='http://schemas.xmlsoap.org/soap/encoding/' />
     </input>
     <output>
```

LISTING 15.2 continued

```
      <soap:body use='encoded' namespace='http://tempuri.org/message/'
            encodingStyle='http://schemas.xmlsoap.org/soap/encoding/' />
    </output>
  </operation>
  <operation name='DisplayVersion' >
    <soap:operation
          soapAction='http://tempuri.org/action/Class1.DisplayVersion' />
    <input>
      <soap:body use='encoded' namespace='http://tempuri.org/message/'
            encodingStyle='http://schemas.xmlsoap.org/soap/encoding/' />
    </input>
    <output>
      <soap:body use='encoded' namespace='http://tempuri.org/message/'
            encodingStyle='http://schemas.xmlsoap.org/soap/encoding/' />
    </output>
  </operation>
</binding>
<service name='RateCalcSvc' >
  <port name='Class1SoapPort' binding='wsdlns:Class1SoapBinding' >
    <soap: address location='http://10.68.1.7/rates/RateCalcSvc.WSDL' />
  </port>
</service>
</definitions>
```

And Listing 15.3 shows the corresponding WSML.

LISTING 15.3 RateCalcSvc.wsml—Generated WSML File

```
<?xml version='1.0' encoding='UTF-16' ?>
<!— Generated 09/24/01 by Microsoft SOAP Toolkit
    WSDL File Generator, Version 1.02.813.0 —>
<servicemapping name='RateCalcSvc'>
  <service name='RateCalcSvc'>
    <using PROGID='Project1.Class1' cachable='0' ID='Class1Object' />
    <port name='Class1SoapPort'>
      <operation name='CalcBaseRate'>
        <execute uses='Class1Object' method='CalcBaseRate'
             dispID='1610809344'>
          <parameter callIndex='1' name='RawBaseRate'
              elementName='RawBaseRate' />
          <parameter callIndex='2' name='RelativeFactor'
              elementName='RelativeFactor' />
          <parameter callIndex='3' name='TerritoryFactor'
              elementName='TerritoryFactor' />
          <parameter callIndex='-1' name='retval' elementName='Result' />
        </execute>
      </operation>
      <operation name='CalcReplacementCost'>
```

LISTING 15.3 continued

```
        <execute uses='Class1Object' method='CalcReplacementCost'
            dispID='1610809345'>
          <parameter callIndex='1' name='BaseRate' elementName='BaseRate' />
          <parameter callIndex='2' name='ReplacementCostFactor'
              elementName='ReplacementCostFactor' />
          <parameter callIndex='-1' name='retval' elementName='Result' />
        </execute>
      </operation>
      <operation name='DisplayVersion'>
        <execute uses='Class1Object'
            method='DisplayVersion' dispID='1610809346'>
          <parameter callIndex='-1' name='retval' elementName='Result' />
        </execute>
      </operation>
    </port>
  </service>
</servicemapping>
```

Finally, create an ASP application to handle incoming SOAP requests.

To set up the client, write a Visual Basic Scripting Edition (VBScript) application that calls the operations that your server provides. Listing 15.4 shows our sample client.

LISTING 15.4 `SoapClient.vbs`—Sample SOAP Client

```
Option Explicit

Dim soapClient,BaseRate, RelativityFactor, TerritoryFactor, AdjustedBase,
➥ReplaceCost, ReplaceCostFactor, TotalCost
set soapclient = CreateObject("MSSOAP.SoapClient")
On Error Resume Next

Call soapclient.mssoapinit("http://mysite.com/rates/RateCalcSvc.wsdl",
➥ "RateCalcSvc", "Class1SoapPort")

if err <> 0 then
  wscript.echo "Initialization Failed " + err.description
else
  wscript.echo "Initialization Successful "
end if
wscript.echo  ""
wscript.echo  ""

BaseRate = 303
RelativityFactor = .97
TerritoryFactor = 1.2
ReplaceCostFactor = .21
AdjustedBase = 0
```

LISTING 15.4 continued

```
wscript.echo  "Trying DisplayVersion()"
wscript.echo  soapclient.DisplayVersion() : wscript.echo  ""
if err <> 0 then
  wscript.echo   "ERRORS" :  wscript.echo  ""
  wscript.echo   "----------------------" : wscript.echo  ""
  wscript.echo   "General Error=" + err.description : wscript.echo  ""
  wscript.echo   "faultcode=" + soapclient.faultcode : wscript.echo  ""
  wscript.echo   "faultstring=" + soapclient.faultstring : wscript.echo  ""
  wscript.echo   "faultactor=" + soapclient.faultactor : wscript.echo  ""
  wscript.echo   "detail=" + soapclient.detail    : wscript.echo  ""
end if
wscript.echo  ""

wscript.echo  "Base Premium = " + BaseRate : wscript.echo  ""
wscript.echo  "Trying CalcBaseRate()"
AdjustedBase =
➥soapclient.CalcBaseRate(BaseRate,RelativityFactor,TerritoryFactor)
if err <> 0 then
  wscript.echo   "ERRORS" :  wscript.echo  ""
  wscript.echo   "----------------------" : wscript.echo  ""
  wscript.echo   "General Error=" + err.description : wscript.echo  ""
  wscript.echo   "faultcode=" + soapclient.faultcode : wscript.echo  ""
  wscript.echo   "faultstring=" + soapclient.faultstring : wscript.echo  ""
  wscript.echo   "faultactor=" + soapclient.faultactor : wscript.echo  ""
  wscript.echo   "detail=" + soapclient.detail   : wscript.echo  ""
end if
wscript.echo "Adjusted Base Premium = " + Cstr(AdjustedBase) : wscript.echo ""
wscript.echo  ""

wscript.echo  "Trying CalcReplacementCost()"
ReplaceCost = soapclient.CalcReplacementCost(AdjustedBase, ReplaceCostFactor)
if err <> 0 then
  wscript.echo   "ERRORS" :  wscript.echo  ""
  wscript.echo   "----------------------" : wscript.echo  ""
  wscript.echo   "General Error=" + err.description : wscript.echo  ""
  wscript.echo   "faultcode=" + soapclient.faultcode : wscript.echo  ""
  wscript.echo   "faultstring=" + soapclient.faultstring : wscript.echo  ""
  wscript.echo   "faultactor=" + soapclient.faultactor : wscript.echo  ""
  wscript.echo   "detail=" + soapclient.detail   : wscript.echo  ""
end if
wscript.echo  "Replacement Cost = " + ReplaceCost : wscript.echo  ""
wscript.echo  ""

TotalCost = ReplaceCost + AdjustedBase
wscript.echo  "Total Premium = " + TotalCost : wscript.echo  ""

set soapClient = nothing
```

The final step is simply to run the VBScript application.

Note

The SOAP Toolkit isn't the only Microsoft implementation of the SOAP protocol. SOAP is also an essential enabling technology for the BizTalk Framework, as of version 2.0. BizTalk Framework XML documents may be transmitted as SOAP messages and can even handle SOAP messages with attachments. Learn more about BizTalk in Chapter 18, "Using XML in the .NET Enterprise Servers."

Apache SOAP

You can find the open-source Apache SOAP 2.2 at `http://xml.apache.org/soap`. You will need to have the following tools installed on your system before you install Apache SOAP:

- Java 1.1 or higher.
- Apache Jakarta Tomcat 3.2.1 Web server and servlet engine, available at `http://jakarta.apache.org/`
- Apache Xerxes XML Parser 1.2.3, found at `http://xml.apache.org/xerces-j/`
- JavaMail (`mail.jar`), found at `http://java.sun.com/products/javamail/`, and the JavaBeans Activation Framework (`activation.jar`), found at `http://java.sun.com/products/beans/glasgow/jaf.html`

Once all the tools (including Apache SOAP) are installed and your `CLASSPATH` is correctly updated, you must configure Tomcat so that it can detect Apache SOAP. Edit the file `\jakarta-tomcat-3.2\conf\server.xml` and put the following entry near the end of the file:

```
<Context path="/soap" docBase="C:/soap-2_0/webapps/soap" reloadable="true">
</Context>
```

Next, launch Tomcat. You should see the output:

```
Starting tomcat. Check logs/tomcat.log for error messages
```

Now, point your browser to `http://localhost/soap` (including the port number, if you have chosen a port other than 80) to launch the Apache SOAP system.

Next, we need to write a Web Service in Java. Listing 15.5 shows a sample service that calculates a rate (in this case, returning the same value every time).

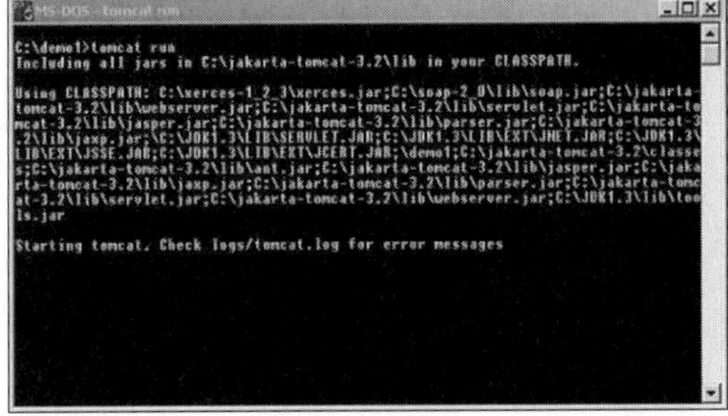

FIGURE 15.4
Starting the Tomcat server.

LISTING 15.5 `Exchange.java`—Sample Web Service

```
public class Exchange
  {
  public float getRate( String BaseRate, String ReplacementCostFactor )
    {
    System.out.println( "getRate( " + BaseRate +
        ", " + ReplacementCostFactor + " )" );
    return 1234.56F;
    }
  }
```

Put the directory that contains the `Exchange` class on your `CLASSPATH` and compile it. Restart Tomcat and run the admin client from your browser. From the admin client, click Deploy, and you'll see the screen shown in Figure 15.5.

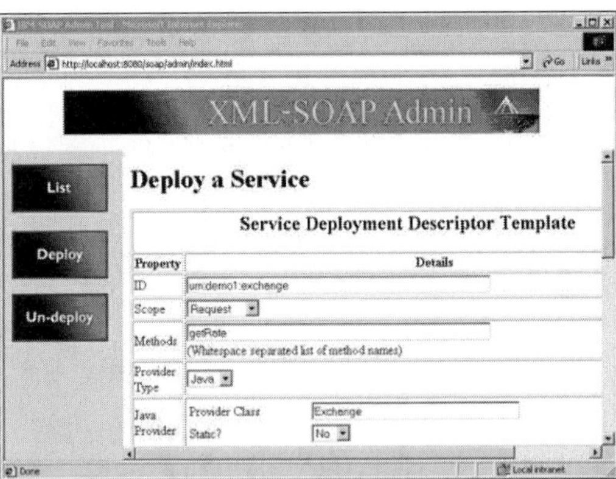

FIGURE 15.5
Deploying a Web Service.

Enter the necessary information, as shown in Figure 15.5, and click the Deploy button again. If you have successfully deployed your Web Service, you should see the screen shown in Figure 15.6.

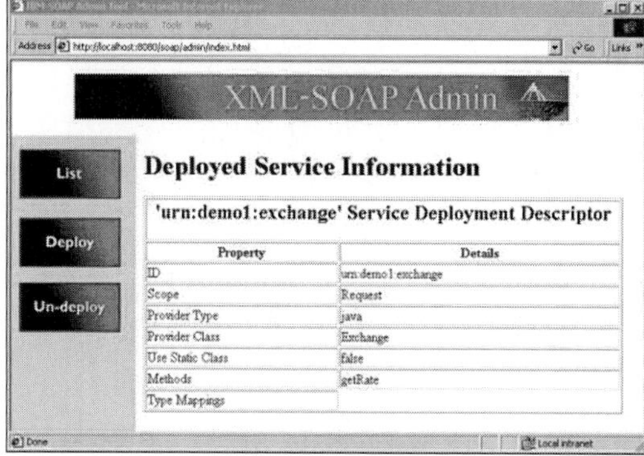

FIGURE 15.6
The URN of the Web Service.

Next, we must run our client application. Listing 15.6 shows a simple example of a Java client.

LISTING 15.6 `Client.java`—Sample SOAP Client

```
import java.net.*;
import java.util.*;
import org.apache.soap.*;
import org.apache.soap.rpc.*;
public class Client
   {
   public static void main( String[] args ) throws Exception
     {
     URL url = new URL( "http://localhost/soap/servlet/rpcrouter" );
     String urn = "urn:demo1:exchange";
     Call call = new Call(); // prepare to invoke the Service
     call.setTargetObjectURI( urn );
     call.setMethodName( "getRate" );
     call.setEncodingStyleURI( Constants.NS_URI_SOAP_ENC );  // the default
     Vector v = new Vector();
     v.addElement( new Parameter( "BaseRate", String.class, "12.34", null ) );
     v.addElement( new Parameter( "ReplacementCostFactor", String.class,
➥"56.78", null ) );
     call.setParams( v );
     try
       {
       System.out.println( "Service invoked:\n" + "  URL= " +
          url + "\n  URN= " + urn );
       Response response = call.invoke( url, "" ); // invoke the Service
       if( !response.generatedFault() )
         {
         Parameter r = response.getReturnValue(); // response was OK
         System.out.println( "Result= " + r.getValue() );
         }
```

LISTING 15.6 continued

```
      else
        {
        Fault f = response.getFault(); // error
        System.err.println( "Fault= " + f.getFaultCode() + ", " +
          f.getFaultString() );
        }
      }
    catch( SOAPException e ) // error sending call
      {
      System.err.println( "SOAPException= " + e.getFaultCode() + ", " +
        e.getMessage() );
      }
    }
  }
```

Compile and run the client, and you should see the following output:

```
Service invoked:
URL= http://localhost/soap/servlet/rpcrouter
URN= urn:demo1:exchange
Result= 1234.56
```

Finally, the output from the Tomcat server should include the following:

```
Processing SOAP request...
GetRate (12.34, 56.78 )
```

We have successfully invoked our Web Service!

Interoperability Issues

Interoperability among different SOAP implementations is especially important, because, well, interoperability is what Web Services are all about. What's the point of having loosely coupled services if they can only talk to systems that use the same implementation? The fact that interoperability is an issue at all is a symptom of the fact that Web Services are still on the bleeding edge. This issue is currently a topic of much discussion, and there is a good chance that the issue will be resolved in 2002.

The fundamental cause of most interoperability problems has to do with a single word: *may*. When the SOAP specification says that a particular feature *may* be implemented, it opens up the option that a particular vendor may choose not to implement the feature. Another implementation, however, may use the feature, causing the two implementations to be incompatible with each other.

Interoperability issues with SOAP implementations fall into three general categories:

- Transport problems, namely those involving the HTTP `SOAPAction` header.
- XML issues, typically involving the Byte Order Mark.
- SOAP problems, involving the `mustUnderstand` attribute or other unevenly implemented features of the specification.

Let's look at each of these issues in turn.

First, as discussed earlier, the `SOAPAction` header is mandatory in SOAP messages that go over HTTP. However, the SOAP specification allows for a null `SOAPAction`, which appears like this:

```
SOAPAction:
```

However, Apache SOAP does not have any way of interpreting a null header value, causing messages that have null values to be incompatible with those SOAP messages that have this header.

Second, there is the issue of the Byte Order Mark (BOM). A BOM is a nonprintable character that indicates the order of the bytes in a two-byte character encoding (like those for Japanese and Chinese). BOMs are required for two-byte encodings such as UTF-16, but they serve little purpose (even though they are not forbidden) for single-byte encodings such as UTF-8. Apache SOAP, for example, cannot interpret UTF-8-encoded SOAP messages that have a BOM, even though many text editors (such as Notepad) automatically place a BOM at the beginning of UTF-8-encoded text.

Finally, the third category of incompatibility issues has to do with inconsistent implementations of SOAP. Table 15.4 contains a reasonably comprehensive accounting of the current state of SOAP feature support in the three leading SOAP implementations.

TABLE 15.4 SOAP Compatibility Matrix

Feature	*Apache SOAP 2.2*	*SOAP::Lite 0.51*	*MS SOAP Toolkit 2.0 SP2*
	Data Types		
Custom encoding styles	Yes	No	Limited
	Arrays		
Single dimensional	Yes	Yes	Yes
Multidimensional	No	No	Yes
Partial	No	No	No
Sparse	No	No	No

TABLE 15.4 continued

Feature	*Apache SOAP 2.2*	*SOAP::Lite 0.51*	*MS SOAP Toolkit 2.0 SP2*
	Fault		
Actor	Limited	Limited	Limited
Complex detail	Yes	Yes	Yes
XML schema data types	Yes	Yes	Yes
	Attributes		
`mustUnderstand`	Yes	Limited	Limited
`actor`	Limited	Limited	Limited
`root`	Yes	Limited	No
`id/href`	Yes	Yes	Limited
	HTTP		
`M-POST`	No	Yes	No
Object serialization	Yes	Yes	Yes
UTF-8 support	Yes	Limited	Yes
	Transports		
SMTP	Yes	Yes	No
POP3	No	Yes	No
FTP	No	Limited	No
TCP	No	Yes	No
HTTP	Yes	Yes	Yes
	Attachments		
SOAP attachments support	Yes	Limited	No

Whenever a SOAP feature is not fully supported across different implementations, there is always the possibility of a failure to exchange SOAP messages correctly. The fact that relatively few rows in Table 15.4 contain only "Yes" is a clear indication of the immaturity of the SOAP protocol.

The Future of SOAP

It should be clear at this point that SOAP is a work in progress. On the one hand, current implementations are inconsistent in their support of the SOAP 1.1 specification. On the other hand, the current spec leaves much to be desired, as well. This section covers some of the most critical features either missing in the 1.1 spec or poorly supported by the current implementations.

SOAP with Attachments

At its core, SOAP consists of self-defining serialization rules that allow for the marshaling and unmarshaling of objects into a simple text stream. SOAP's focus on objects is quite understandable—after all, it is the Simple *Object* Access Protocol. However, for SOAP to be a truly useful wire protocol, it must be able to handle large binary objects that don't lend themselves to marshaling.

The SOAP Messages with Attachments specification (found at `http://www.w3.org/TR/SOAP-attachments`) uses the MIME Multipart/Related mechanism for handling attachments. This mechanism is the established protocol for handling e-mail attachments and is therefore well accepted in the technical community. When the technical community turned to the discussion of SOAP attachments using MIME, however, it had a problem: How to handle such attachments without burdening the SOAP specification with additional elements? The answer was to construct the SOAP message package as a Multipart/Related media type. In other words, a "SOAP message with attachments" package is actually a MIME Multipart/Related message, where the SOAP `Envelope` is one of the parts, instead of the MIME message being included in the SOAP `Envelope`.

Note

The SOAP with Attachments specification uses the Multipart/Related MIME media type, defined in RFC 2387, which can be found at `http://www.ietf.org/rfc/rfc2387.txt`. It also uses the URI schemes found in RFC 2111 and RFC 2557, found at `http://www.ietf.org/rfc/rfc2111.txt` and `http://www.ietf.org/rfc/rfc2557.txt`, respectively.

Here is how to construct the SOAP message package:

1. Put the SOAP message in the root body part of the Multipart/Related structure. The type parameter of the Multipart/Related media header will be the same as the `Content-Type` header of the SOAP message, (that is, `text/xml`).
2. To reference a MIME part, it must have either a `Content-ID` MIME header or a `Content-Location` MIME header.

3. To support HTTP, the `Content-Type: Multipart/Related` MIME header must appear as a HTTP header, and there should be no other MIME headers that appear as HTTP headers.

Let's take a look at an example of an HTTP `POST` request that contains a SOAP message package:

LISTING 15.7 `Post.txt`—Sample HTTP POST Request

```
POST /myPath.asp HTTP/1.1
Host: www.myServer.com
Content-Type: Multipart/Related; boundary=MIME_boundary; type=text/xml;
Âstart="<myFile.xml@myClient.com>"
Content-Length: 1234567
SOAPAction: http://schemas.myServer.com/myMethod
Content-Description: This is the optional message description.

—MIME_boundary
Content-Type: text/xml; charset=UTF-8
Content-Transfer-Encoding: 8bit
Content-ID: <myFile.xml@myClient.com>

<?xml version='1.0' ?>
<SOAP-ENV:Envelope
    xmlns:SOAP-ENV="http://schemas.xmlsoap.org/soap/envelope/">
  <SOAP-ENV:Body>
    <msg:myMsg id="myMsgId"
        xmlns:myMsg="http://schemas.myServer.com/myMethod">
    <myJPEG href="cid:myFile.jpeg@myClient.com"/>
    </msg:myMsg>
  </SOAP-ENV:Body>
</SOAP-ENV:Envelope>

—MIME_boundary
Content-Type: image/jpeg
Content-Transfer-Encoding: binary
Content-ID: <myFile.jpeg@myClient.com>

Raw JPEG image...
—MIME_boundary—
```

Note that there is a reference to the JPEG image file `myFile.jpeg` in the SOAP `Body` element.

SOAP Security

As discussed in Chapter 14, there are four basic requirements for secure message transmission: confidentiality, authorization, data integrity, and nonrepudiation. Sending SOAP messages over SSL-secured connections such as HTTPS provides for confidentiality and data integrity, but additional measures are required to ensure authorization and nonrepudiation, as well. The extension to SOAP that outlines a system for adding these security requirements is the Digital Signature (DS) specification, which is currently a W3C Note that can be found at `http://www.w3.org/TR/SOAP-dsig`.

The DS Note proposes a standard way to use the XML Digital Signature `[XML-Signature]` syntax to sign SOAP messages by defining the `<SOAP-SEC:Signature>` header entry. DS uses digital signatures to solve the problems of confidentiality, authorization, and so on. This header entry is provided in the following namespace:

```
http://schemas.xmlsoap.org/soap/security/2000-12
```

Next, the DS Note provides for the `SOAP-SEC:id` global attribute, which enables the `<ds:Reference>` element that is used to refer to the signed part of the SOAP `Envelope`. For example, Listing 15.8 below shows a SOAP message with a signature header entry:

LISTING 15.8 Ds.xml—SOAP Message with Signature Header Entry

```
<SOAP-ENV:Envelope
    xmlns:SOAP-ENV="http://schemas.xmlsoap.org/soap/envelope/">
  <SOAP-ENV:Header>
    <SOAP-SEC:Signature
        xmlns:SOAP-SEC="http://schemas.xmlsoap.org/soap/security/2000-12"
        SOAP-ENV:actor="some-URI"
        SOAP-ENV:mustUnderstand="1">
      <ds:Signature xmlns:ds="http://www.w3.org/2000/09/xmldsig#">
        <ds:SignedInfo>
          ...Encryption algorithm information goes here
          <ds:Reference URI="#Body">
             ...Encrypted digest goes here
          </ds:Reference>
        </ds:SignedInfo>
       <ds:SignatureValue>HiuKjIHKJH=...</ds:SignatureValue>
      </ds:Signature>
    </SOAP-SEC:Signature>
  </SOAP-ENV:Header>
  <SOAP-ENV:Body
    xmlns:SOAP-SEC="http://schemas.xmlsoap.org/soap/security/2000-12"
    SOAP-SEC:id="Body">
  ...Unencrypted SOAP message content goes here
  </SOAP-ENV:Body>
</SOAP-ENV:Envelope>
```

Note, first, that the `<ds:Signature>` element is part of the `<SOAP-SEC:Signature>` header entry, and the `URI` attribute of the `<ds:Reference>` element refers to the `<SOAP-ENV:Body>` element.

SOAP Transactions

For a set of messages to be considered a successful transaction, it must pass the ACID test. ACID is an acronym for the following:

- *Atomicity*. The set of messages in a transaction either all take place or none take place. If one fails, every system involved must be returned to the state it was in before the messages were sent (in other words, rolled back).
- *Consistency*. Transactions always operate on a consistent view of the data and always leave the data in a consistent state when a transaction is complete. Instances of data are considered to be consistent when they conform to the rules that apply to them (for example, if money is being transferred from a checking account to a savings account, the money can never be in both accounts at the same time).
- *Isolation*. Transactions are not able to interfere with each other. If a system supports multiple threads of execution, each transaction is unaware of others going on at the same time.
- *Durability*. Once a transaction is committed, its effects persist even if one or more of the involved systems fail subsequent to the transaction. If there is a system failure in the middle of a transaction, all involved systems roll back to their original state.

Database-management systems typically use a two-phase commit model to achieve the ACID requirements. However, the environment that SOAP messages move in lacks much of the infrastructure that databases rely on to execute transactions efficiently. SOAP messages may be asynchronous, potentially leaving a system in a locked or indeterminate state for an extended period of time. SOAP messages may also involve intermediaries, making two-phase commits impractical. In addition, SOAP messages are designed to move among different platforms with no tightly coupled framework supporting them.

Note

A two-phase commit contains two processes that typically occur in a fraction of a second: the *prepare phase*, where the initiating database, acting as the coordinator, requests that all the involved systems promise either to commit or roll back the transaction, and the *commit phase*, where the distributed systems respond that they are ready for the transaction, at which time the coordinator instructs them to commit the transaction. If anything goes wrong, the coordinator calls for all systems to roll back the transaction.

In order to address the limitations of the two-phase commit for SOAP messages, the SOAP Chained Transactions (SOAP-CTX) model has been proposed. (You can find SOAP-CTX at `http://www.newtelligence.com/news/soapchaindetrans01.asp`.) SOAP-CTX is based on a four-phase commit model that allows for intermediaries as well as for asynchronous messages. Here are the four phases in SOAP-CTX:

- *Enlistment.* The coordinator packages a batch of SOAP messages and marks them for processing by individual participants. Each participant extracts the messages intended for it and forwards the rest to the next participant.
- *Commit preparation.* Once the coordinator has received confirmation that each participant is able to commit the transaction, it informs the first participant to begin the commit process. The first participant then forwards the instruction up the chain of participants. Once a participant receives the instruction, it enters a "commit timeout" mode. If the execution command is not received before the mode times out, the transaction is rolled back.
- *Execution.* A "go" command is relayed through the chain of participants. Each participant that receives the "go" command enters a "rollback timeout" mode. If the "clean up" command isn't received before this timeout expires, the transaction is likewise rolled back.
- *Clean up.* When the coordinator receives word that each participant has received the "go" command, it issues the "clean up" command, which clears all the "rollback timeout" modes and completes the transaction.

Because the timeouts in the SOAP-CTX model can effectively be set to any value, this model handles asynchronous messages well. However, each participant must still be able to isolate transactions from one another. The SOAP-CTX model does not specify how each participant is supposed to implement the model.

SOAP 1.2

As of this writing, the 1.2 spec is a W3C working draft (found at `http://www.w3.org/TR/soap12`), but it may be accepted as the current version by the time you read this. Fortunately, there are no fundamental changes in the spec from version 1.1 to 1.2.

The 1.2 SOAP specification improves upon version 1.1 in the following areas:

- Ambiguities resulting from the order of header entries has been fixed. In version 1.1, an error in one header entry might prevent the rest of a message from being processed, thus leading to inconsistent behavior.

- More explicit error messages with strong recommendations on how to handle them.
- The inclusion of the final W3C XML Schema release.
- Improvements in the use of namespaces, which will better resolve ambiguities resulting from elements in different namespaces that share the same names.
- Improved envelope stability, which will improve interoperability among different implementations.

So, the good news is, SOAP is reasonably complete, and there won't be that much new in the next version. The bad news? There is a new protocol under development that may supersede SOAP altogether: the XML Protocol.

The XML Protocol

The new XML Protocol (XP) is a working draft that is still squarely on the drawing board (at both the W3C as well as the IETF; find it at `http://www.w3.org/2000/xp`). XP seeks to approach the same issues SOAP was designed to address, by starting with an "abstract model" that separates business workflow from SOAP's correlation of messages. Although it is generally understood that XP may supersede SOAP, it still remains to be seen whether there will be enough of a difference between the two to warrant such a move. There is also the possibility that the work going into XP will simply become a future version of SOAP.

The XP Working Group wants to include the following features in the specification:

- An envelope that allows for extensibility, evolvability, and a variety of different types of intermediaries (gateways, proxies, and so on)
- Operating system–neutral conventions for handling RPCs
- A serialization mechanism based on XML Schema data types
- An HTTP transport mechanism (which will remain optional, because XP messages can go over a variety of transport mechanisms)

If the preceding features look familiar, it's no surprise; after all, SOAP currently offers all these features, at least to some extent. That's one of the reasons why the technical community realizes that XP may not need to be distinct from SOAP at all. However, only time will tell.

Summary

There are books on the market today that say they're just about SOAP. Unfortunately, all of them are missing something: Either they really go into topics beyond SOAP, or they don't, but they should. It's no mistake that this chapter is in the middle of this book, because SOAP is nothing more than a building block.

SOAP by itself provides a way to exchange messages with Web Services, but it doesn't provide a way to find out what messages a Web Service might want to exchange. It also doesn't give you any way of finding Web Services or negotiating with them to establish a relationship that will allow you to exchange messages with them. The good news is that the technologies that provide these additional capabilities—WSDL and UDDI—are covered in Chapter 16.

CHAPTER 16

Web Services Building Blocks: WSDL and UDDI

In This Chapter

The *Web Services Description Language* (WSDL) and *Universal Description, Discovery, and Integration* (UDDI), along with SOAP, form the essential building blocks for Web Services. Each one, taken separately, serves its own particular purposes, but taken together, they provide the foundation for the just-in-time, Service-Oriented Architecture detailed in Chapter 14, "Architecting Web Services."

WSDL (often pronounced *wiz-dill*) is an XML-based format for describing Web Services. It describes which operations Web Services can execute and the format of the messages Web Services can send and receive. UDDI (pronounced, unfortunately, *U-D-D-I*) is a protocol that describes a standard way of setting up registries of Web Services, along with the methods of querying such registries for information about the Web Services they contain. Each UDDI registry's response to a query contains a WSDL message, which instructs the requester on how to interact with the desired Web Service. (Refer to Figure 14.2 in Chapter 14 for a picture of how these operations fit together.)

In this chapter, you will learn

- The basics of WSDL syntax
- How WSDL and SOAP work together
- How to use popular WSDL implementations
- The elements of UDDI and how they work together
- How to use the UDDI API
- How to use UDDI implementations to interact with existing UDDI registries
- The future of UDDI

Introduction to WSDL

You can think of WSDL as the *Empire Strikes Back* of Web Services. SOAP forms the foundation, UDDI gives you the payoff, but WSDL is essentially an intermediate technology that provides the missing link between the two. Nevertheless, it is a critical technology in its own right, even though it doesn't deserve its own chapter separate from UDDI.

Note

The WSDL standard is currently at version 1.1. The official source for the WSDL standard is in a W3C Note, which can be found at `http://www.w3.org/TR/wsdl`.

As explained in Chapter 15, "Web Services Building Blocks: SOAP," SOAP uses namespaces to create self-describing messages. Therefore, it should be possible for SOAP messages to provide the information needed to access the content of a message. However, there is no way to determine the name and type of each function parameter using SOAP, so you're stuck in a catch-22: There's no way to call a function with a SOAP message unless you already know about the function.

In the early days of SOAP, as well as its precursor XML-RPC (touched upon in Chapter 15), several languages sprang up that addressed this missing piece of the SOAP puzzle, including WebMethod's Web Interface Definition Language (WIDL), Microsoft's SOAP Contract Language (SCL) and Discovery of Web Services (DISCO), and IBM's Network Accessible Service Specification Language (NASSL). Then the UDDI Consortium of dozens of companies, headed up by IBM, Microsoft, and Ariba, began the process of hammering out the UDDI specification. It was readily apparent that there needed to be one language for describing Web Services—thus, WSDL was born, combining much of the benefits of its predecessors.

Basic WSDL Syntax

A WSDL document can be thought of as a contract between a client and a server. It describes what the Web Service can do, where it can be found, and how to invoke it. Essentially, WSDL defines an XML grammar that describes Web Services (and in general, any network service) as collections of communications endpoints (that is, the client and the server) that are able to exchange messages with each other.

WSDL documents use the following elements:

- `definitions`. Associates the Web Service with its namespaces.
- `types`. A container for data type definitions, typically using a XML Schema Definition (XSD) or possibly some other type system.
- `message`. An abstract, typed definition of the data contained in the message.
- `operation`. An abstract description of an action that the Web Service supports.
- `portType`. The set of operations supported by one or more endpoints.
- `binding`. A specification of the protocol and data format for a particular `portType`.
- `port`. An endpoint, defined in terms of a binding and its network address (typically a URL). This is not a TCP/IP port, which is represented by a number.
- `service`. A collection of related endpoints.

The structure of a typical WSDL document is shown in Figure 16.1.

FIGURE 16.1
WSDL document structure.

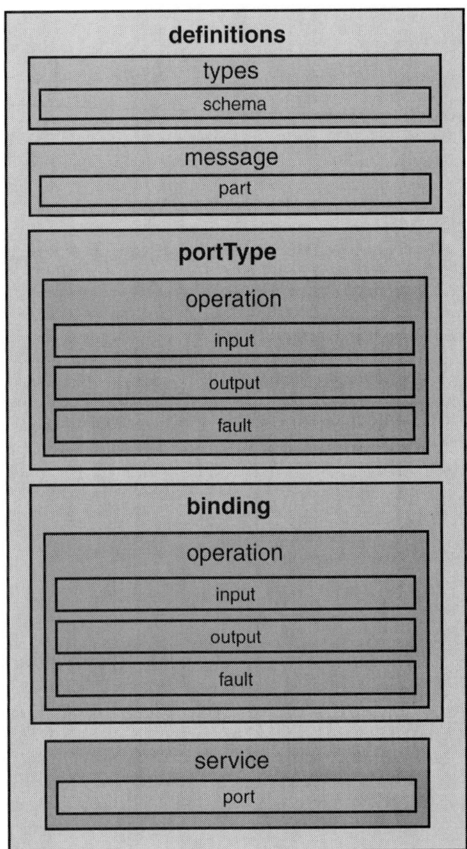

Let's take a look at a simple WSDL document example and break it down into its component elements:

```
<?xml version="1.0"?>

<definitions name="MyService"
    targetNamespace="http://mySite.com/myService.wsdl"
    xmlns:tns="http://mySite.com/myService.wsdl"
    xmlns:xsd1="http://mySite.com/myService.xsd"
    xmlns:soap="http://schemas.xmlsoap.org/wsdl/soap/"
    xmlns="http://schemas.xmlsoap.org/wsdl/">

<import namespace="http:/mySite.com/myService/schemas"
    location="http:// mySite.com/myService/myNameSpace.xsd"/>
```

```
  <types>
    <schema targetNamespace="http://mySite.com/myService.xsd"
        xmlns="http://www.w3.org/2000/10/XMLSchema">
      <element name="MyRequest">
        ...
      </element>
    </schema>
  </types>

  <message name="GetMyInput">
    <part name="body" element="xsd1:MyRequest"/>
  </message>

  <message name="GetMyOutput">
    <part name="body" element="xsd1:myParameter"/>
  </message>

  <portType name="MyServicePortType">
    <operation name="MyMethod">
      <input message="tns:GetMyInput"/>
      <output message="tns:GetMyOutput"/>
    </operation>
  </portType>

  <binding name="MyServiceSoapBinding" type="tns:MyServicePortType">
    <soap:binding style="document"
      transport="http://schemas.xmlsoap.org/soap/http"/>
    <operation name="MyMethod">
      <soap:operation
          soapAction="http://mySite.com/MyMethod"/>
        <input>
          <soap:body use="literal"/>
        </input>
        <output>
          <soap:body use="literal"/>
        </output>
    </operation>
  </binding>

  <service name="MyService">
    <documentation>My first service</documentation>
    <port name="MyServicePort" binding="tns:MyServiceBinding">
      <soap:address location="http://mySite.com/myService"/>
    </port>
  </service>

</definitions>
```

The `definitions` Element and Namespaces

First, we have the `definitions` element:

```
<definitions name="MyService"
    targetNamespace="http://mySite.com/myService.wsdl"
    xmlns:tns="http://mySite.com/myService.wsdl"
    xmlns:xsd1="http://mySite.com/myService.xsd"
    xmlns:soap="http://schemas.xmlsoap.org/wsdl/soap/"
    xmlns="http://schemas.xmlsoap.org/wsdl/">
```

Typically, this element defines a single Web Service, but it may define more than one. The `definitions` element typically contains the following attributes:

- `name`. An optional attribute that describes the overall service.
- `targetNamespace`. A typically unique namespace that defines the logical namespace that provides information about the service.
- `xmlns:tns`. An optional attribute that must be set to the same value as `targetNamespace`. By scoping references between sections of the WSDL document with the `tns:` prefix, one WSDL document can import another without running into the problem of element name clashes.
- `xmlns:xsd1`. An example of a custom namespace that is used here to define terms such as `MyRequest` and `MyParameter`.
- `xmlns:soap` *and* `xmlns:xsd`. Standard namespace definitions for SOAP-specific information and data types.
- `xmlns`. The default WSDL namespace, which contains `<definitions>`, `<message>`, `<service>`, and so on.

The `types` Element

The `types` element contains data type definitions that are required by the messages described in the WSDL document:

```
<types>
  <schema targetNamespace="http://mySite.com/myService.xsd"
      xmlns="http://www.w3.org/2000/10/XMLSchema">
    <element name="MyRequest">
      ...
    </element>
  </schema>
</types>
```

In this example, we are using an optional custom schema to define our complex types as well as a standard schema.

The message and portType Elements

Within the definitions element is one or more message elements:

```
<message name="GetMyInput">
  <part name="body" element="xsd1:MyRequest"/>
</message>

<message name="GetMyOutput">
  <part name="body" element="xsd1:myParameter"/>
</message>
```

A message element is simply one piece of information that moves between the client and server endpoints. Typical roundtrip remote method calls have two message elements—one for the request, and the second for the response. Each message can have any number of part child elements.

Note

Although most WSDL documents are used in RPC-style request/response pairs, WSDL also supports one-way messages. WSDL supports the same four types of operations that SOAP messages do (request-response, solicit-response, one-way, and notification), as explained in Chapter 15.

The definitions element also contains the portType element:

```
<portType name="MyServicePortType">
  <operation name="MyMethod">
    <input message="tns:GetMyInput"/>
    <output message="tns:GetMyOutput"/>
  </operation>
</portType>
```

The portType element contains one or more operation elements, each of which describes a specific message sequence. Each operation element corresponds to a message element. The portType element corresponds to a class (or an interface), and the operation element corresponds to one of its methods.

The binding Element

The binding element corresponds to a portType element implemented in a particular protocol, namely SOAP. The type attribute ties the binding element to the portType element. It is possible to use different protocols (such as CORBA or DCOM), or even more than one protocol, in which case you would have more than one `binding` element. Here's an example:

```
<binding name="MyServiceSoapBinding" type="tns:MyServicePortType">
  <soap:binding style="document"
    transport="http://schemas.xmlsoap.org/soap/http"/>
  <operation name="MyMethod">
    <soap:operation
        soapAction="http://mySite.com/MyMethod"/>
      <input>
        <soap:body use="literal"/>
      </input>
      <output>
        <soap:body use="literal"/>
      </output>
  </operation>
</binding>
```

The `service` Element

The `service` element represents a collection of `port` elements, where each port represents the availability of a binding at a particular endpoint:

```
<service name="MyService">
  <documentation>My first service</documentation>
  <port name="MyServicePort" binding="tns:MyServiceBinding">
    <soap:address location="http://mySite.com/myService"/>
  </port>
</service>
```

The `binding` attribute of the `port` element ties it to the corresponding `binding` element defined previously.

The `documentation` Element

You should also notice the `documentation` child element of the preceding `service` element. This element essentially allows you to provide a human-readable comment and is allowed in every other element as well.

The `import` Element

The `import` element is an optional element that allows you to break up a WSDL document into multiple documents. When present, it must immediately follow the `definitions` element. The following example imports a schema, but it is possible to import any WSDL elements, including the `definitions` element, essentially allowing you to import an entire WSDL document:

```
<import namespace="http:/mySite.com/myService/schemas"
   location="http:// mySite.com/myService/mySchema.xsd"/>
```

The `import` element is particularly useful for breaking up a WSDL document into interface and implementation documents.

Extensibility Elements

Finally, we come to extensibility elements, which allow elements in a WSDL document to represent specific technologies, including SOAP. They are typically used to specify binding information. Extensibility elements are optional and can occur in most WSDL document elements. Table 16.1 shows where extensibility elements can occur and why each one is used.

TABLE 16.1 WSDL Extensibility Elements

Location	*Purpose*
`definitions`	Introduces additional information to the entire WSDL document
`types`	Specifies a type system (other than XSD)
`operation`	Provides protocol-specific information for both the input and output message
`input`	Provides protocol-specific information for the input message
`output`	Provides protocol-specific information for the output message
`binding`	Provides protocol-specific information that applies to all operations in the bound `portType` element
`port`	Specifies an address for the port
`service`	Introduces additional information for the service
`fault`	Provides protocol-specific information for the fault message

The next section contains several examples of how to use extensibility elements to bind SOAP endpoints.

SOAP Binding

When using WSDL documents to describe Web Services that will exchange SOAP messages (that is, SOAP endpoints), you need to have a way to indicate within the WSDL document all the necessary information about the SOAP messages that will be exchanged. WSDL uses extensibility elements to provide this information. The SOAP binding that is provided with WSDL supplies the following information:

- An indication that the WSDL binding is bound to the SOAP protocol.
- How to specify the address for the SOAP endpoints.
- For the HTTP binding of SOAP, the URI for the `SOAPAction` HTTP header (explained in Chapter 15).
- A list of definitions for all `Header` elements in the SOAP `Envelope`.
- A way of specifying SOAP roots in XSD.

Let's take a look at some examples of the SOAP binding in WSDL.

`soap:binding`, `soap:operation`, `soap:header`, and `soap:body`

The following example shows a SOAP binding of a request/response operation over HTTP:

```
<binding name="MyServiceSoapBinding" type="tns:MyServicePortType">
  <soap:binding style="rpc"
      transport="http://schemas.xmlsoap.org/soap/http" />
  <operation name="MyMethod">
    <soap:operation SOAPAction="http://mySite.com/MyMethod" style="rpc" />
      <input>
        <soap:body use="encoded" namespace="http://mySite.com/myService"
            encodingStyle="http://schemas.xmlsoap.org/soap/encoding/" />
        <soap:header message="tns:MyMethod" part="MyHeader" use="literal"/>
      </input>
      <output>
        <soap:body use="encoded" namespace="http://mySite.com/myService"
            encodingStyle="http://schemas.xmlsoap.org/soap/encoding/" />
      </output>
  </operation>
</binding>
```

Note that the `style` attribute of the `soap:binding` element is set to `rpc`. In the case of a one-way operation over SMTP, for example, the style attribute would have a value of `document` (and `document` is the default if the attribute is omitted). The `transport` attribute (here, set to the URI of the HTTP binding in the SOAP specification) indicates to which transport of SOAP this binding corresponds.

The `soap:operation` element includes the `SOAPAction` attribute, which specifies the value of the `SOAPAction` header for this operation (required only for HTTP), as well as the `style` attribute, which indicates either RPC messages (containing parameters and return values) or documents.

The `soap:header` and `soap:body` elements define how message parts appear in the SOAP `Header` and `Body` elements, respectively. The `soap:header` and `soap:body` elements can each take up to four attributes:

- The optional `parts` attribute (not shown in our example) is used when parts of the message may appear outside the SOAP `Envelope`, as is the case when the message is in MIME `multipart/related` format. In that case, the value of the `parts` attribute indicates which parts appear within the SOAP `Envelope`.
- The required `use` attribute indicates whether the message parts are encoded. If the value of `use` is `encoded`, each message part references an abstract type using the `type` attribute. In this case, the encoding is specified by the `encodingStyle` attribute. The alternative to `encoded` is `literal`, which indicates that each part references a concrete schema using the `element` attribute (for simple parts) or the `type` attribute (for composite parts).
- The `encodingStyle` attribute's values are lists of URIs, which represent encodings used within the message, exactly like the corresponding attribute in the SOAP specification (see Chapter 15).
- The `namespace` attribute (not shown in our example) is an input to the encoding defined by the `encodingStyle` attribute.

soap:address, soap:fault, and soap:headerfault

There are a few additional elements in the SOAP binding worth mentioning. First, the `soap:address` element simply assigns a URI to a port:

```
<service name="MyService">
  <port name="MyServicePort" binding="tns:MyServiceBinding">
    <soap:address location="http://www.mySite.com/MyServiceURL/" />
  </port>
</service>
```

The `soap:fault` element specifies the contents of the SOAP `Fault` element:

```
<fault>
  <soap:fault name="MyFault" use="encoded"
      encodingStyle="http://schemas.xmlsoap.org/soap/encoding/"
<http://schemas.xmlsoap.org/soap/encoding/>/>
</fault>
```

Finally, the `soap:headerfault` element follows the syntax of the `soap:fault` element but refers to SOAP `Fault` in `Header` elements.

Other Bindings

In addition to the SOAP binding, the WSDL specification also provides for HTTP GET and POST bindings as well as a MIME binding. We're not going to cover how to use these bindings in depth. However, an outline of the various elements that each binding uses is provided in Table 16.2.

TABLE 16.2 Other WSDL Bindings

Element	*Example*	*Purpose*
	HTTP	
http:address	<http:address location="mySite.com/" />	Specifies the base URI for the port
http:binding	<http:binding verb="GET" />	Indicates the use of HTTP
http:operation	<http:operation location="myMethod" />	Specifies a relative URI for the operation
http:urlEncoded	<http:urlEncoded />	Indicates the message parts are encoded in the URL query
http:	<http:urlReplacement /> urlReplacement	Indicates the message parts are encoded in the URL using a replacement algorithm
	MIME	
mime:content	<mime:content part="img" type="image/gif" />	Conveys information about a MIME element
mime:	<mime:multipartRelated> multipartRelated	Aggregates an arbitrary set of MIME-formatted parts into one message
mime:mimeXml	<mime:mimeXml part="myXML" />	Specifies XML payloads that are not SOAP payloads

In addition, the MIME binding allows the soap:body element as a MIME element. This element will have a content type of text/xml.

WSDL Implementations

Because WSDL is a bridge technology in the sense that it bridges SOAP and UDDI, you're unlikely to find a WSDL toolkit that stands by itself. The two most popular WSDL implementations, therefore, are parts of other toolkits:

- *The Microsoft SOAP Toolkit.* This toolkit, covered in depth in Chapter 15, is primarily aimed at developers who want to work with SOAP in a Microsoft environment, although it does support Microsoft's UDDI implementation.
- *The IBM Web Services Toolkit* (WSTK). This toolkit provides WSDL support, several security enhancements, UDDI integration, and support for the IBM WebSphere application server. The WSTK also includes the open-source Web Services Description Language for Java Toolkit (WSDL4J).

WSDL the Microsoft Way

First, refer to the section "The Microsoft SOAP Toolkit," of Chapter 15 for a step-by-step illustration of how to generate WSDL files with the Microsoft SOAP Toolkit. The resulting WSDL file is shown in Listing 15.2. This file is standard WSDL, and it's generated automatically, so there is little to say about the file itself. However, the Microsoft implementation requires another file to map the invoked Web Service operations to COM object method calls. This additional file is expressed in the Web Services Markup Language (WSML), which is Microsoft's proprietary language for this particular purpose. The Microsoft SOAP Toolkit generates WSML files automatically; see Listing 15.3 for an example.

Note

You can learn more about WSML at `http://msdn.microsoft.com/library/default.asp?url=/library/en-us/soap/htm/soap_overview_72r0.asp`.

WSDL the IBM Way

The WSTK runs on Linux or Windows 2000/NT 4 and requires a recent installation of the Java Development Kit (JDK). Download the WSTK from `http://www.alphaworks.ibm.com/tech/webservicestoolkit`. The version used for this book is 2.4, but IBM warns developers to consider the toolkit to be alpha code.

The WSTK comes with several useful utilities, including the following:

- A limited version of IBM's WebSphere Application Server, suitable for running Web Services. It also supports the latest full version of WebSphere.
- Apache SOAP (which IBM originally produced and released as open source) and AXIS, which is an open-source SOAP implementation.
- WSDL4J, the WSDL Toolkit for Java.

- The XML4J XML Parser, which includes the Apache Xerces Java-based XML parser.
- LotusXSL-Java (based on Apache Xalan Java), which is an Extensible Style Language Transformations (XSLT) processor for transforming XML documents into HTML, text, or other XML document types.
- IBM UDDI4J, which is IBM's UDDI Toolkit for Java (more about this part of the WSTK later in the chapter), as well as a preview of IBM's UDDI Registry software.
- A demo implementation of Reliable HTTP (HTTPR).
- A prototype implementation of the XML Key Information Service Specification (X-KISS), which is part of the XML Key Management Specification (XKMS). X-KISS is a protocol for a trust service (that is, a third-party key registry) that resolves public key information contained in certain XML documents.
- A Web Services for Browser (WS4B) plug-in that provides programmatic access to any UDDI node from a standard browser.

Note

Reliable HTTP (HTTPR) is a transport-level protocol proposed by IBM that gives HTTP the reliability of proprietary messaging systems such as IBM's MQSeries. HTTPR defines how metadata and application messages that indicate how to add support for reliability at the transport level are encapsulated within the payload of HTTP requests and responses. Learn more about HTTPR at `http://www-106.ibm.com/developerworks/webservices/library/ws-phtt`.

The installation of the WSTK is straightforward, except that you must select a UDDI registry for the toolkit to access. You can use the local one provided with the toolkit or configure the toolkit to access a public registry. To use the WSTK, you must first have a Java client that accesses a Web Service. The toolkit comes with a Java class that is supposed to access a stock quote service provided by Nasdaq, but Nasdaq apparently no longer provides this service. For our example, therefore, we wrote a simple client that returns a placeholder instead of accessing a true Web Service, as shown in Listing 16.1.

LISTING 16.1 Demo Client Application `MyClass.java`

```
public class MyClass
  {
  public int MyMethod (String arg)
    {
    return 47;
```

LISTING 16.1 continued

```
    }

  public static void main ( String[] args )
    {
    System.out.println( "output" );
    }
  }
```

Note

Source code files for all numbered listings in this chapter can be found on the Sams Web site.

Next, we use the WSTK to generate the WSDL wrapper for our application. Launching the toolkit takes you to the dialog box shown in Figure 16.2.

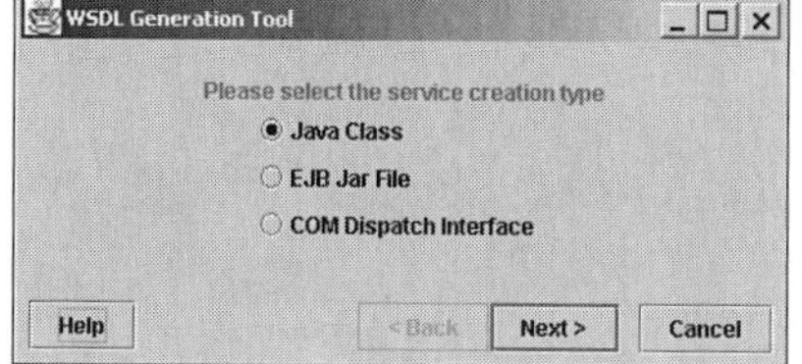

FIGURE 16.2
Selecting the service creation type.

From here, select Java Class and click Next to get to the Java Class WSDL Generator dialog box, as shown in Figure 16.3.

WSDL Generation Tool

Java Class WSDL Generator

Class Name: MyClass.class

Classpath: c:\myPath\

Output Filename: MyClass_Service.wsdl [Browse...]

Service Properties

Property Name	Value
Service Name	MyClass_Service
Service URN	urn:myclass-service
Target Namespace	http://www.myclassservice.com/MyClass
Binding URL	http://localhost:8080/soap/servlet/rpcrouter
WSDL URL prefix	http://localhost:8080/wsdl

Help | < Back | Next > | Cancel

FIGURE 16.3
The Java class WSDL generator.

Type in the necessary information about your client application and click Next to select your wrapper class methods, as shown in Figure 16.4.

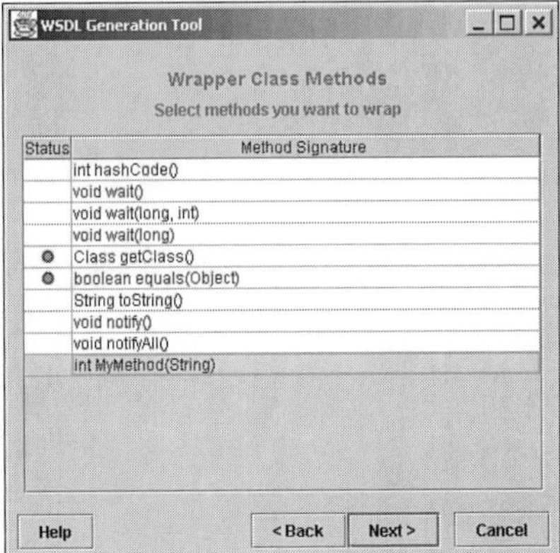

FIGURE 16.4
Selecting methods to wrap.

Select the methods in your application you wish to expose. Your methods shouldn't have red dots by them, or you will have to modify the WSDL manually to support complex data types that the WSTK cannot handle.

Finally, click Next to confirm your selection, as shown in Figure 16.5.

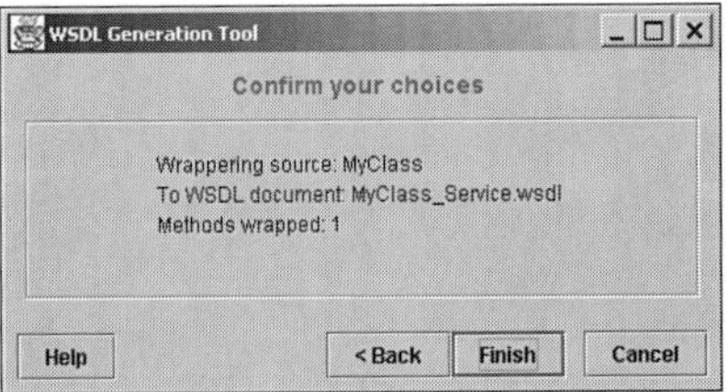

FIGURE 16.5
Confirming the creation of WSDL files.

You will get an error message at this point if the WSDL generation tool is unable to wrap the methods you have selected.

Clicking the Finish button will generate two WSDL files plus a deployment descriptor file. The first file the toolkit generates is the WSDL service implementation description, as shown in Listing 16.2.

LISTING 16.2 Generated File `MyClass_Service.wsdl`

```
<?xml version="1.0" encoding="UTF-8"?>

<definitions name="MyClass_Service"
```

LISTING 16.2 continued

```
    targetNamespace="http://www.myclassservice.com/MyClass"
    xmlns="http://schemas.xmlsoap.org/wsdl/"
    xmlns:interface="http://www.myclassservice.com/MyClass-interface"
    xmlns:soap="http://schemas.xmlsoap.org/wsdl/soap/"
    xmlns:types="http://www.myclassservice.com/MyClass"
    xmlns:xsd="http://www.w3.org/2001/XMLSchema">

  <import
      location="http://localhost:8080/wsdl/MyClass_Service-interface.wsdl"
      namespace="http://www.myclassservice.com/MyClass-interface">
</import>

  <service
      name="MyClass_Service">
    <documentation>IBM WSTK V2.4 generated
➥service definition file</documentation>
    <port
        binding="interface:MyClass_ServiceBinding"
        name="MyClass_ServicePort">
      <soap:address location="http://localhost:8080/soap/servlet/rpcrouter"/>
    </port>
  </service>

</definitions>
```

Note that Listing 16.2 contains an `import` element and a `service` element, but no `message`, `portType`, and `binding` elements. Instead, these elements are included in the service interface file, which is imported via the `import` statement. The service interface file is shown in Listing 16.3.

LISTING 16.3 Generated File `MyClass_Service-interface.wsdl`

```
<?xml version="1.0" encoding="UTF-8"?>

<definitions name="MyClass_Service"
    targetNamespace="http://www.myclassservice.com/MyClass-interface"
    xmlns="http://schemas.xmlsoap.org/wsdl/"
    xmlns:soap="http://schemas.xmlsoap.org/wsdl/soap/"
    xmlns:tns="http://www.myclassservice.com/MyClass-interface"
    xmlns:types="http://www.myclassservice.com/MyClass-interface/types/"
    xmlns:xsd="http://www.w3.org/2001/XMLSchema">

  <message name="InMyMethodRequest">
    <part name="meth1_inType1" type="xsd:string"/>
  </message>

  <message name="OutMyMethodResponse">
```

LISTING 16.3 continued

```
    <part name="meth1_outType" type="xsd:int"/>
  </message>

  <portType name="MyClass_Service">
    <operation name="MyMethod">
      <input message="tns:InMyMethodRequest"/>
      <output message="tns:OutMyMethodResponse"/>
    </operation>
  </portType>

  <binding name="MyClass_ServiceBinding" type="tns:MyClass_Service">
    <soap:binding style="rpc"
        transport="http://schemas.xmlsoap.org/soap/http"/>
    <operation name="MyMethod">
      <soap:operation soapAction="urn:myclass-service"/>
      <input>
        <soap:body
            encodingStyle="http://schemas.xmlsoap.org/soap/encoding/"
            namespace="urn:myclass-service"
            use="encoded"/>
      </input>
      <output>
        <soap:body
            encodingStyle="http://schemas.xmlsoap.org/soap/encoding/"
            namespace="urn:myclass-service" use="encoded"/>
      </output>
    </operation>
  </binding>

</definitions>
```

By separating the service implementation from the service interface, the WSTK allows the service to be changed without affecting the interface, thus providing for greater reuse and flexibility. This approach is an example of good design that is allowed, but not required, by the WSDL specification. The service interface document is created by a *service interface provider*, whereas the service implementation document is put together by the *service provider*. Although these two organizations may be the same entity, in practice they are typically different organizations.

In addition to the service and service interface files, the WSTK also produces a deployment descriptor file, as shown in Listing 16.4.

LISTING 16.4 Generated File `DeploymentDescriptor.xml`

```
<isd:service
    xmlns:isd="http://xml.apache.org/xml-soap/deployment"
```

LISTING 16.4 continued

```
    id="urn:myclass-service"
    checkMustUnderstands="false">
  <isd:provider type="java" scope="Application" methods="MyMethod">
    <isd:java class="MyClass" static="false"/>
  </isd:provider>
</isd:service>
```

The deployment descriptor file correlates each service with its URI. The WSTK's SOAP engine contains a hashtable of services deployed on the server, and the deployment descriptor provides the keys to the hashtable. The deployment descriptor serves a similar purpose for the WSML file in the Microsoft implementation, where the deployment descriptor provides a correlation to Java methods in each deployed service, whereas the Microsoft SOAP Toolkit uses WSML to correlate to COM object method calls.

Once these three files are written, you have successfully deployed your Web Service, and you should see the dialog box shown in Figure 16.6.

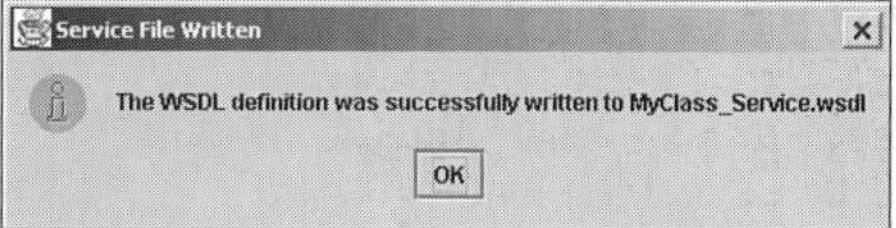

FIGURE 16.6
Service file written.

Introduction to UDDI

If WSDL is *The Empire Strikes Back*, then UDDI is *The Return of the Jedi*, concluding the chapters on Web Services. Universal Description, Discovery, and Integration (UDDI) is a platform-independent, open framework for describing services, discovering businesses, and integrating business services using the Internet as well as public registries of Web Services designed to store information about businesses and the services they offer. UDDI is also a specification for building such registries as well as an application programming interface (API) that exposes the functionality of the registries. Fundamentally, UDDI provides for the publication and discovery of Web Services, which are the key functional components of the Service-Oriented Architecture explained in Chapter 14, "Architecting Web Services."

The UDDI Consortium, established by hundreds of companies, emerged in response to a series of challenges posed by the new Web Services model. These challenges included the following:

- How do you discover Web Services?
- How should information about Web Services be categorized?

- How do you handle the global nature of Web Services? How do you provide for localization?
- How can interoperability be provided, both in the discovery and invocation mechanisms?
- How can you interact with the discovery and invocation mechanisms at runtime?

For UDDI to provide the foundation for Web Services registries, therefore, it had to serve two primary roles within the Web Services model: *Service publication* and *service discovery* (shown in Figure 14.2 in Chapter 14). The rest of this chapter addresses how UDDI's publication and discovery capabilities operate as well as how UDDI addresses the listed challenges.

Note

The home page for UDDI is at `http://www.uddi.org`. You can find specification documents, articles, whitepapers, and more at this URL. UDDI version 1.0 is currently in use, and version 2.0 documents are now available on the site, as well. This chapter covers functionality in UDDI 1.0, with a discussion on what is new in version 2.0 at the end of the chapter.

UDDI Basics

Public UDDI registries are hosted by *operator nodes*, which are companies such as Microsoft and IBM that have committed to running public UDDI nodes. The public registry system is loosely modeled after the Domain Name Service (DNS) system, in that there are multiple registries responsible for synchronizing their data with each other. Currently, each public UDDI node synchronizes with the others daily, but a more frequent schedule is in the works.

Likewise, as is the case with the DNS system, UDDI registries are not repositories of data; rather, in their roles as registries, they simply provide information on how to find and invoke Web Services. Just as the DNS system provides for unique domain names, UDDI relies on *globally unique identifiers* (GUIDs), which are URNs that uniquely identify the resources in each registry.

There are three levels of information available in each UDDI registry, which correspond roughly to the features of a phone book:

- *White pages*. These pages provide listings of companies that can be queried by name, text description, contact information, and known identifiers (like Dun and Bradstreet's DUNS numbers).

- *Yellow pages*. These pages allow for the looking up of companies by the kind of services they offer, organized into established business categories (industry codes, location, and products and services). These categories are organized into taxonomies.
- *Green pages*. These pages provide information about how to interact with companies' Web Services by exposing service descriptions and binding information.

Note

UDDI 1.0 supports three taxonomies:

- The North American Industry Classification System (NAICS), found at `http://www.naics.com`.
- The Universal Standard Products and Services Codes (UNSPSC), located at `http://www.unspsc.org`.
- The ISO 3166 Geographic Taxonomy, found at `http://www.iso.ch`.

UDDI 2.0 adds two more:

- The Standard Industrial Classifications (SIC), which has been superseded by NAICS.
- The GeoWeb Geographic Classification (no longer available online).

Starting with UDDI 3.0, any number of different taxonomies are potentially usable within UDDI registries.

By accessing the appropriate "pages," a service requester can obtain answers to the following questions:

- For a given industry, what Web Services interfaces have been published?
- Which of those interfaces are based on WSDL?
- Which companies have created implementations based on one of those interfaces?
- Which Web Services in a particular category are available?
- How does one contact a company about accessing the Web Services it publishes?
- What are the specifics of binding to and invoking a given Web Service?

The Structure of UDDI

The XML schema that provides the structure of UDDI defines four core types of information in a UDDI registry, as shown in Figure 16.7:

FIGURE 16.7
UDDI structure.

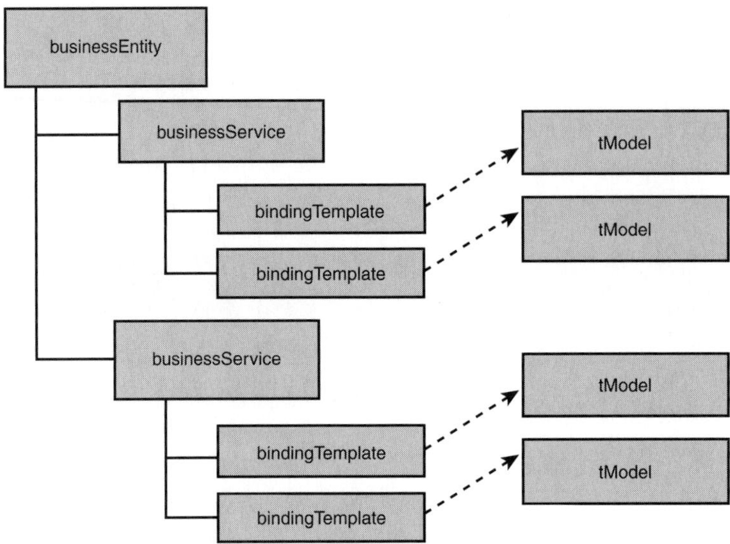

- *Business information.* Provided by the `businessEntity` element. The `businessEntity` element supports the "white pages" and "yellow pages" taxonomies, allowing for structured information about companies. This element is the top-level information manager for the information in the registry about a particular business.
- *Service information.* Provided by the `businessService` element. This element supports the "green pages" functionality. The `businessService` structure contains a group of Web Services related to a category of services or possibly a business process. Each `businessService` element contains one or more technical Web Services descriptions, which describe how to find and bind to each of the Web Services.
- *Binding information.* Provided by the `bindingTemplate` element, which is the element contained within the `businessService` element that provides the information needed to bind to and invoke a Web Service."
- *Specifications for services.* Enclosed within each `bindingTemplate` element are special elements that list references to information about specifications for services. These elements, called `tModel` elements (from "technical models"), are metadata about each specification, providing information on a specification's name, publishing organizations, and URLs to the specifications themselves. `tModel` elements have several uses within a UDDI registry, in particular, representing technical specifications for wire protocols (such as SOAP), interchange formats (WSDL), and sequencing rules. Each specification registered as a `tModel` in a UDDI registry receives a unique GUID.

It is important to point out that UDDI actually has no direct support for WSDL—or any other service description mechanism, for that matter. Instead, UDDI uses `tModel` elements to allow the specification of the service description mechanism to be flexible and independent of any single description language. At this time, however, WSDL is currently the preferred description language for UDDI registries.

tModel Structure

Understanding `tModel` elements is critical to understanding how UDDI works, because they form the basis of how UDDI deals with the meaning of the various specifications it deals with. The concept of a `tModel` is necessarily somewhat nebulous, because `tModel` elements consist of metadata (data about data). `tModel` elements provide a reference system for UDDI registries that is based on abstraction (in other words, a `tModel` can define just about anything).

The primary use for `tModel` elements within UDDI is to represent a technical specification—for example, wire protocols (such as SOAP), interchange formats, and the like. When two parties wish to communicate using a particular specification, they must share a mutually agreed on technical identity for the specification they share. This technical identity can be registered in a `tModel`. Once such a specification is uniquely defined in this way, other parties can refer to it by referring to its unique `tModel` identifier, which is called a `tModelKey`. `tModelKey` elements act as "technical fingerprints" that uniquely designate individual specifications.".

The other main use for `tModel` elements supports how UDDI handles its search capability. Searching, of course, is an essential part of UDDI's "find" capability. Searching is provided for in UDDI with the use of two structures: `identifierBag` and `categoryBag`. The `identifierBag` structure defines organizational identity. It consists of name/value pairs that record and define identification numbers—for example, "DUNS number 12345" or "SS# 987-65-4321." The `categoryBag` elements, on the other hand, are name/value pairs that correlate specific taxonomy information—for example, "Florists 45311" (from the NAICS taxonomy), "Massachusetts US-MA" (from the ISO 3166 Geographic Taxonomy), or "Boston 516499" (from the GeoWeb taxonomy). A particular florist in Boston, Massachusetts would possess all three of these `categoryBag` elements, as well as each identifier's supercategories. The `tModel`, then, is used to correlate different levels of these hierarchies—for example, to express the relationship that Boston is within Massachusetts, or that florists are retailers.

`tModel` elements have the structure shown in Figure 16.8.

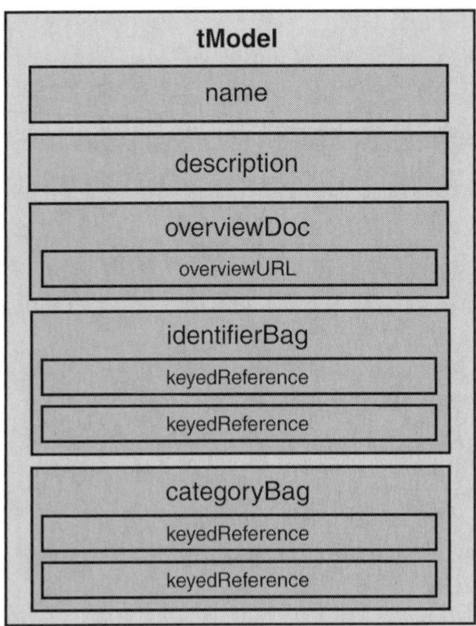

FIGURE 16.8
Structure of a `tModel`.

The `name` element is the only required element, and it's searchable, whereas the `description` is not. The `overviewDoc` element references remote descriptions or other instructions related to the `tModel`. Finally, the `identifierBag` and `categoryBag` elements contain searchable name/value pairs that reference identification numbers and taxonomy information, respectively. An example of a `tModel` is shown in the following section).

Publishing and Finding WSDL Descriptions in a UDDI Registry

In order to understand how UDDI uses WSDL as a description language, you must be clear on how WSDL documents are mapped to the UDDI structure. As discussed earlier, WSDL documents can be organized as service implementation and service interface documents. (Listing 16.2 shows a WSDL service implementation document, and Listing 16.3 shows the corresponding WSDL service interface.) The service implementation document maps to the UDDI `businessService` element, whereas the service interface document maps to the `tModel` elements, as shown in Figure 16.9.".

The first step in publishing a WSDL description in a UDDI registry is publishing the service interface as a `tModel` in the registry. Here are the steps to follow to create the appropriate `tModel`:

1. Set the `name` field of the `tModel` to the `targetNamespace` attribute of the `definitions` element in the interface document. This field is used to locate the appropriate `tModel`.

2. The `description` field of the `tModel` corresponds to the `documentation` element of the interface document. This field can have a maximum of 256 characters.
3. Set the `overviewURL` field of the `tModel` to the URL and binding specification in the interface document.
4. Set the `categoryBag` field of the `tModel` so that its keyed reference is `uddi-org:types` and its `keyValue` is `wsdlSpec`. This defines the UDDI entry as a WSDL service interface definition.

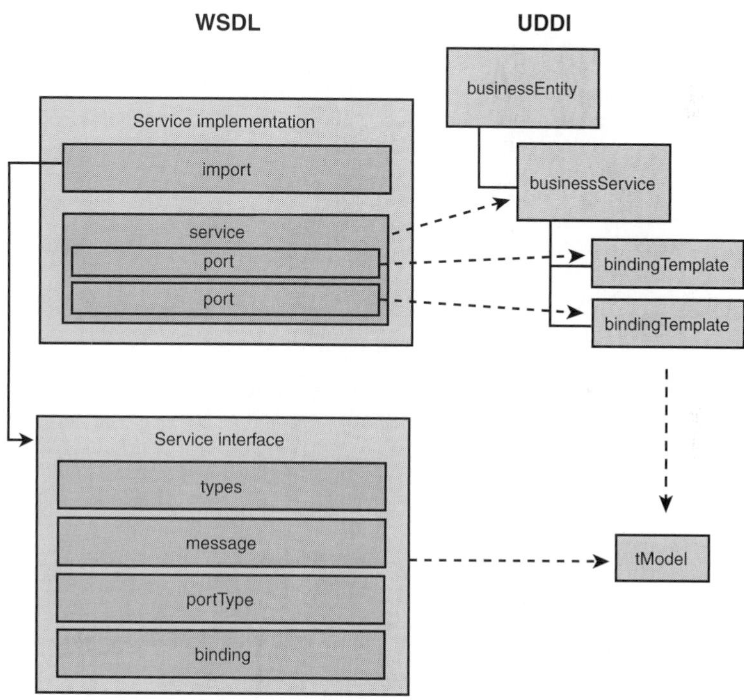

FIGURE 16.9
WSDL-to-UDDI mapping.

For example, if we take the interface document in Listing 16.3, we build the `tModel` in Listing 16.5.

LISTING 16.5 `tModel.xml`—A `tModel` Created from a WSDL Service Interface

```
<?xml version="1.0"?>
<tModel tModelKey="">
  <name>http://www.myclassservice.com/MyClass-interface</name>

  <description xml:lang="en">
    Service interface definition for our demo Service.
  </description>
```

LISTING 16.5 continued

```
  <overviewDoc>
    <description xml:lang="en">
      WSDL Service Interface Document
    </description>
    <overviewURL>
      http://www.myclassservice.com/MyClass-interface#MyClass_ServiceBinding
    </overviewURL>
  </overviewDoc>

  <categoryBag>
    <keyedReference tModelKey="UUID:C1ACF26D-9672-4404-9D70-889DFDA9D9F8"
        keyName="uddi-org:types" keyValue="wsdlSpec"/>
    <keyedReference tModelKey="UUID:DB77450D-9FA8-45D4-A7BC-9C8C7D998F8D"
        keyName="Sample Web Service"
        keyValue="12345678"/>
  </categoryBag>
</tModel>
```

Next, we must create the `businessService` and `bindingTemplate` elements that correspond to the WSDL service implementation document shown in Listing 16.2. The `businessService` has the following fields.":

- The `name` field of the `businessService` is set to the `name` attribute of the `service` element in the implementation document.
- The `description` field of the `businessService` comes from the `documentation` element in the implementation document.

The `bindingTemplate` has the following fields:

- The `description` field of the `bindingTemplate` comes from the first 256 characters of the `documentation` element of the `port` element, if it exists.
- The `accessPoint` field is set to the value of the `location` attribute of the `extension` element that is associated with the `port` element, in the case of a SOAP or HTTP binding.
- The `bindingTemplate` contains one `tModelInstanceInfo` field for each `tModel` it references.
- The `overviewURL` field directly references the service implementation document; however, it is only used to provide human readability.

Putting these instructions together, we can build the UDDI `businessService` that corresponds to the WSDL interface document in Listing 16.2. The `businessService` appears in Listing 16.6.

LISTING 16.6 `businessService.xml`—`businessService` and `bindingTemplate` Elements Created from a WSDL Service Implementation

```
<businessService businessKey="..." serviceKey="...">
  <name>MyClass_Service</name>

  <description xml:lang="en">
    IBM WSTK V2.4 generated service definition file
  </description>

  <bindingTemplates>
    <bindingTemplate bindingKey="..." serviceKey="...">
      <description></description>
      <accessPoint URLType="http">
        http://localhost:8080/soap/servlet/rpcrouter
      </accessPoint>
      <tModelInstanceDetails>
        <tModelInstanceInfo tModelKey="[tModel Key for Service Interface]">
          <instanceDetails>
            <overviewURL>
              http://localhost:8080/wsdl/MyClass_Service-interface.wsdl
            </overviewURL>
          </instanceDetails>
        </tModelInstanceInfo>
      </tModelInstanceDetails>
    </bindingTemplate>
  </bindingTemplates>

  <categoryBag>
    <keyedReference tModelKey="UUID:DB77450D-9FA8-45D4-A7BC-3663DA8D8CFB"
        keyName="Sample Web Service"
        keyValue="84121801"/>
  </categoryBag>
</businessService>
```

UDDI Invocation Model

Now that we can build a `businessService` and its various elements, let's step through the process for using a UDDI registry to find and invoke a Web Service.":

1. You use the UDDI business registry to locate the `businessEntity` information that was previously published by a company advertising a Web Service.
2. You either request more specific information about the `businessService` or request the entire `businessEntity` structure. This structure contains the relevant `bindingTemplate` information needed to connect to the service. You put this binding information into a cache.

3. You refer to the tModel key information in the bindingTemplate to obtain relevant information on the specifications needed to invoke the desired Web Service, and you use this information to write the program that will access the service.
4. The program invokes the Web Service using the bindingTemplate information that has been cached.
5. If the call to the Web Service fails, refresh the bindingTemplate information. If the new call succeeds, refresh the cache. Otherwise, keep trying.

By using cached binding information and taking a "retry on failure" approach, the UDDI registry infrastructure is not burdened by unnecessary calls but rather allows for seamless operation when binding information changes. This approach to scalability is quite similar to the way the DNS system works."

The UDDI API

The UDDI Programmer's API Specification, found at http://www.uddi.org/pubs/➥ProgrammersAPI-V1.01-Open-20010327_2.pdf, is complete and easy to use. It's also the authoritative source of information on the API. Therefore, it's of little value simply to repeat the content from that document here. Instead, this section will cover the API functions on a descriptive level in order to provide a broad introduction to the capabilities within the API. Be sure to refer to the API Specification for complete details.

Inquiry API

The publicly available inquiry functions provided by the UDDI API fall into two categories: the find_xx group, which enables programs to find information in a UDDI registry, and the get_xx group, which is used to retrieve information once it is found.

The inquiry queries are as follows:

- find_binding. Locates specific bindings within a registered businessService and returns a bindingDetail message that contains a bindingTemplate element's structure. If there are no matches, the returned bindingDetail will be empty. If an error occurs, a dispositionReport structure will be returned in a SOAP Fault element (SOAP Fault elements are covered in Chapter 15) .
- find_business. Locates information about one or more businesses and returns a businessList message. Searches can be performed on name elements (or partial name elements), identifierBag elements, categoryBag elements, tModelBag elements, or discoveryURL elements. tModelBag elements are collections of tModel

elements that allow searches for compatible bindings. If there are no matches, an empty businessList is returned. Errors are handled as they are with the find_binding query.

- find_service. Locates specific services within a registered businessEntity and returns a serviceList message. Searches can be performed on name elements (or partial name elements), identifierBag elements, categoryBags elements, or tModelBag elements. If there are no matches, an empty businessService structure is returned. Errors are handled as they are with the find_binding query.
- find_tModel. Locates one or more tModel information structures and returns a tModelList structure, which is a list of abbreviated information about tModel elements that match the search criteria. Search parameters, no match conditions, and error conditions are handled the same as the preceding queries.
- get_bindingDetail. Gets the full runtime bindingTemplate information that can be used to make one or more service requests by invoking the API of a registered business. This query returns a bindingDetail message. It's recommended that this query only be used when the bindingDetail that is stored in the cache is no longer valid.
- get_businessDetail. Gets the full businessEntity (identified by its businessKey) information for one or more businesses and returns a businessDetail message.
- get_businessDetailExt. Gets information about an extended businessEntity (also identified by its businessKey) for one or more businesses and returns a businessDetailExt message.
- get_serviceDetail. Gets full details for a given businessService structure (identified by its serviceKey) and returns a serviceDetail message.
- get_tModelDetail. Gets full details for a given tModel structure (identified by its tModelKey) and returns a tModelDetail message.

Publication API

The messages within the publication API fall generally into two categories: delete_xx, for deleting information from a registry, and save_xx, for inserting and updating information. In addition, there are three messages that involve the security of information within the registry.

Note

Other than requiring publication API calls to be authenticated and SSL-secured over HTTPS, the UDDI specification does not regulate the security of the information within a registry. Instead, it is up to each operator site to establish its own security protocols. UDDI handles authentication by requiring an authentication token (`authToken`) to be sent as a parameter in each of these calls, which the operator site must either validate or reject.

The publication queries are as follows:

- `delete_binding`. Removes an existing `bindingTemplate` from the `bindingTemplates` collection that is part of a specified `businessService` structure. The `bindingTemplate` is identified by its `bindingKey`. If successful, a `dispositionReport` with a single success indicator is returned (which is the case for each of the `delete_xx` messages).
- `delete_business`. Deletes a business by deleting registered `businessEntity` structures from the registry. The `businessEntity` is identified by its `businessKey`).
- `delete_service`. Deletes an existing `businessService` structure from the `businessServices` collection, which is part of a specified `businessEntity`. The `businessService` is identified by its `serviceKey`).
- `delete_tModel`. Used to delete registered information about one or more `tModel` structures. If there are any references to a `tModel` when this call is made, the `tModel` will be marked as deleted, or hidden, instead of being physically removed. Hidden `tModel` elements can still be accessed by their owner but are not returned in search results (resulting from the `find_tModel` query). However, the details in a hidden `tModel` are still accessible, so these should be nulled out with the `save_tModel` call (detailed later), if the owner wishes the details to be deleted).
- `discard_authToken`. Informs an operator site that a previously provided authentication token is no longer valid. This message is only relevant if the operator site caches the `authToken` elements).
- `get_authToken`. Requests an authentication token from an operator site (in other words, requests a login). This message is optional for operator sites that have an alternative means for handling authentication).
- `get_registeredInfo`. Requests a summary of the information currently managed by a given individual (returning both `businessEntity` and `tModel` keys), as identified by their authentication token).

- `save_binding`. Registers a new `bindingTemplate` structure or updates an existing `bindingTemplate` structure within one or more `bindingTemplate` structures. This call controls the information about the technical capabilities exposed by a registered business).
- `save_business`. Registers a new `businessEntity` structure or updates an existing `businessEntity` structure. This call has a broad scope in that it controls the overall information about the entire business. The new or changed `businessEntity` can be passed as a parameter, or one or more URLs to such structures can be passed instead, in an `uploadRegister` structure).
- `save_service`. Adds or updates one or more `businessService` structures exposed by a specified `businessEntity`. The `businessService` is passed as a parameter, allowing this call to move a `bindingTemplate` from one `businessService` to another, or a `businessService` from one `businessEntity` to another).
- `save_tModel`. Adds or updates one or more `tModel` structures. The parameters to this call include either the `tModel` to be added or one or more URLs in an `uploadRegister` that each point to a single `tModel` structure).

Vendor Implementations

The first two public UDDI registries to be made available (for both development and beta production) are IBM's (at `http://www-3.ibm.com/services/uddi/`) and Microsoft's (at `http://uddi.microsoft.com`). Both registries currently support UDDI 2.0, and both operator sites host production and test registries. As a result, it is possible to interact with both registries from either a Java or a Microsoft (Visual Basic or C#) platform.

Note

Most of the implementation work surrounding UDDI involves publishing, finding, and binding to existing public UDDI registries. However, it is also possible to build your own private UDDI registry. IBM is currently developing private UDDI registry software, which is available at `http://www.alphaworks.ibm.com/tech/UDDIreg`. You can also find open-source UDDI registry software based on Java, called jUDDI, at `http://www.juddi.org`. On the Microsoft side, the Microsoft UDDI SDK (discussed later) includes Microsoft UDDI Developer Edition, which is a lightweight UDDI registry implementation built on the .NET Framework.

In this section, we will focus on using the inquiry and publication APIs to interact with existing UDDI registries, starting with the Java platform.

UDDI4J (IBM)

UDDI4J is a Java-based implementation of the UDDI APIs written by IBM and released as open source. The home page for UDDI4J is `http://oss.software.ibm.com/developerworks/projects/uddi4j`, but the UDDI4J package is included in IBM's Web Services Toolkit (WSTK), which is available at `http://www.alphaworks.ibm.com/tech/webservicestoolkit`. This section assumes you have installed a recent version of Java as well as the WSTK.

The first example exercises the UDDI inquiry API. Our application, `FindMyBusiness`, searches the IBM test registry for all companies whose names begin with the letter *T*. The code for this example is provided in Listing 16.7.

LISTING 16.7 Inquiry API Application `FindMyBusiness.java`

```
import com.ibm.uddi.*;
import com.ibm.uddi.datatype.business.*;
import com.ibm.uddi.response.*;
import com.ibm.uddi.client.*;
import org.w3c.dom.Element;
import java.util.Vector;
import java.util.Properties;

public class FindMyBusiness
  {
  public static void main (String args[])
    {
    FindMyBusiness fmb = new FindMyBusiness ();
    fmb.run();
    System.exit(0);
    }

  public void run()
    {
    UDDIProxy proxy = new UDDIProxy();

    try
      {
      proxy.setInquiryURL
        ("http://www-3.ibm.com/services/uddi/testregistry/inquiryapi");
      }
    catch (Exception e)
      {
      e.printStackTrace();
```

LISTING 16.7 continued

```
        }
      try
        {
        BusinessList bl = proxy.find_business("T", null, 0);
        Vector businessInfoVector =
          bl.getBusinessInfos().getBusinessInfoVector();
        for (int i = 0; i < businessInfoVector.size(); i++)
          {
          BusinessInfo bi = (BusinessInfo)businessInfoVector.elementAt(i);
          System.out.println(bi.getNameString());
          }
        }
      catch (UDDIException e)
        {
        DispositionReport dr = e.getDispositionReport();
        if (dr!=null)
          {
          System.out.println ("UDDIException" +
            "\n faultCode:" + e.getFaultCode() +
            "\n operator:"    + dr.getOperator() +
            "\n generic:"     + dr.getGeneric() +
            "\n errno:"       + dr.getErrno() +
            "\n errCode:"     + dr.getErrCode() +
            "\n errInfoText:" + dr.getErrInfoText());
          }
        e.printStackTrace();
        }
      catch (Exception e)
        {
        e.printStackTrace();
        }
    }
}
```

First, we initialize the UDDI `Proxy` object in the following line:

```
UDDIProxy proxy = new UDDIProxy();
```

The UDDI `Proxy` object contains all the methods we'll need to access the UDDI registry. We then use the `setInquiryURL` method in the `Proxy` object to point to the proper registry. We could have pointed to IBM's production registry, either of Microsoft's registries, or another company's registry. In addition, we can point to our own test registry, if we have one running.

Next, we call the `find_business` method of the `Proxy` object in the following line:

```
BusinessList bl = proxy.find_business("T", null, 0);
```

This takes three arguments:

- The search parameter (here, the letter "T")
- A FindQualifiers object (here, set to null)
- The number of matches to return (0 indicating all matches)

We then place the results of this call into a Vector object. If an exception occurs, a UDDIException is thrown, which exposes a method that returns a DispositionReport object.

Next, let's utilize the publication API in the application SaveMyBusiness, which is shown in Listing 16.8.

LISTING 16.8 Publish API Application SaveMyBusiness.java

```
import com.ibm.uddi.*;
import com.ibm.uddi.datatype.business.*;
import com.ibm.uddi.response.*;
import com.ibm.uddi.client.*;
import org.w3c.dom.Element;
import java.util.Vector;
import java.util.Properties;

public class SaveMyBusiness {
  public static void main (String args[])
    {
    SaveMyBusiness smb = new SaveMyBusiness ();
    smb.run();
    System.exit(0);
    }

  public void run()
    {
    UDDIProxy proxy = new UDDIProxy();

    try
      {
      proxy.setInquiryURL
        ("http://www-3.ibm.com/services/uddi/testregistry/inquiryapi");
      proxy.setPublishURL
        ("https://www-3.ibm.com/services/uddi/
➥testregistry/protect/publishapi");
      }
    catch (Exception e)
      {
      e.printStackTrace();
      }
```

LISTING 16.8 continued

```
    try
      {
      System.out.println("\nGet authtoken");
      AuthToken token = proxy.get_authToken( "userid", "password" );
      System.out.println("Returned authToken:" + token.getAuthInfoString());
      System.out.println("\nSave 'My Business'");
      Vector entities = new Vector();
      BusinessEntity be = new BusinessEntity("", "My Business");
      entities.addElement(be);
      BusinessDetail bd =
        proxy.save_business(token.getAuthInfoString(), entities);
      }
    catch (UDDIException e)
      {
      DispositionReport dr = e.getDispositionReport();
      if (dr!=null)
        {
        System.out.println ("UDDIException" +
          "\n faultCode:" + e.getFaultCode() +
          "\n operator:"    + dr.getOperator() +
          "\n generic:"     + dr.getGeneric() +
          "\n errno:"       + dr.getErrno() +
          "\n errCode:"     + dr.getErrCode() +
          "\n errInfoText:" + dr.getErrInfoText());
        }
      e.printStackTrace();
      }
    catch (Exception e)
      {
      e.printStackTrace();
      }
  }
}
```

In this example, we initialize the `Proxy` object and the `InquiryURL` object as before, but now we also set the `PublishURL` object in the following line:

```
proxy.setPublishURL("https://www-3.ibm.com/services/uddi/testregistry/
protect/publishapi");
```

Recall that all publication API calls are conducted over HTTPS. Next, our application must log in to the registry by sending its username and password and obtaining an authorization token (`AuthToken`) in return:

```
AuthToken token = proxy.get_authToken( "userid", "password" );
```

Next, we must create a new `BusinessEntity` object and populate it with the desired properties. Here, we are only defining its name:

```
Vector entities = new Vector();
BusinessEntity be = new BusinessEntity("", "My Business");
entities.addElement(be);
```

Finally, we pass our new `BusinessEntity` to the registry, along with our `AuthToken`:

```
BusinessDetail bd = proxy.save_business(token.getAuthInfoString(), entities);
```

This saves our `BusinessEntity` in the UDDI registry.

The Microsoft UDDI SDK

The Microsoft UDDI SDK is available at `http://www.microsoft.com/downloads/release.asp?ReleaseID=30880`. The version used here is 1.5.2, which includes the UDDI SDK for Visual Studio 6, the UDDI Developer Edition 1.5 (Beta), and the UDDI .NET SDK (Beta) for Visual Studio .NET. To run the UDDI SDK, you will need the following Microsoft products:

- Windows 2000 Professional, Server, or Advanced Server
- Visual Studio .NET Beta 2
- SQL Server 2000 Desktop Engine (MSDE), Personal, Standard, or Enterprise Edition

First, let's go through a simple Visual Basic example that uses the inquiry API, again looking for companies that begin with the letter *T*, as shown in Listing 16.9.

LISTING 16.9 Inquiry API Visual Basic Application `FindMyBusiness.vb`

```
Imports Microsoft.Uddi
Imports Microsoft.Uddi.Business
Imports Microsoft.Uddi.Binding
Imports Microsoft.Uddi.Service
Imports Microsoft.Uddi.ServiceType

Module SaveMyBusiness

  Sub Main()
    Dim myReq As New UDDIEnv.RequestManager
    Dim reqEnv As New UDDIEnv.Envelope
    Dim respEnv As UDDIEnv.Envelope
    Dim inqMsg As New UDDI10.find_business
    Dim inqRsp As New UDDI10.businessList
    Dim res As UDDI10.businessInfo
```

LISTING 16.9 continued

```
    Set reqEnv.Plugin = inqMsg
    inqMsg.Name = "T"
    Set respEnv = myReq.UDDIRequest(reqEnv)
    Set respEnv.Plugin = inqRsp
    For Each res In inqRsp.businessInfos
      Debug.Print res.Name
    Next
  End Sub

End Module
```

First, we declare objects from the UDDI SDK, including the request manager, as well as envelopes and document objects for our request and response. Then we set up the request document with the request envelope:

```
Set reqEnv.Plugin = inqMsg
```

Next, we set our search criteria:

```
inqMsg.Name = "T"
```

Then we send our request to the registry, obtaining a response envelope in return:

```
Set respEnv = myReq.UDDIRequest(reqEnv)
```

Then we add the document object to the envelope to read the response and loop through the results:

```
Set respEnv.Plugin = inqRsp
For Each res In inqRsp.businessInfos
  Debug.Print res.Name
Next
```

Next, we cover an example that uses the publication API to register a business in a registry. The example in Listing 16.10 uses the publication API by first building a `tModel`.

LISTING 16.10 Publish API Visual Basic Application `SaveMyBusiness.vb`

```
Imports Microsoft.Uddi
Imports Microsoft.Uddi.Business
Imports Microsoft.Uddi.Binding
Imports Microsoft.Uddi.Service
Imports Microsoft.Uddi.ServiceType

Module SaveMyBusiness

  Sub Main()
    Publish.Url = "https://test.uddi.microsoft.com/publish"
```

LISTING 16.10 continued

```
    Publish.User = "username"
    Publish.Password = "password"

    Dim tm As New SaveTModel()
    tm.TModels.Add()
    tm.TModels(0).Name = "URN of tModel"
    tm.TModels(0).Descriptions.Add("en", "Description of tModel")
    tm.TModels(0).OverviewDoc.OverviewURL = "URL of WSDL"
    tm.TModels(0).CategoryBag.Add("uddi-org:types",
      "wsdlSpec", "uuid:c1acf26d-9672-4404-9d70-4863bc075ad9")
    Dim sTModelKey As String

    Try
      Dim td As New TModelDetail()
      td = stm.Send()
      sTModelKey = td.TModels(0).TModelKey
    Catch ue As UddiException
      Console.WriteLine(ue.Message)
      Return
    Catch e As Exception
      Console.WriteLine(e.Message)
      Return
    End Try

    Dim sb As New SaveBusiness()
    sb.BusinessEntities.Add()
    sb.BusinessEntities(0).Name = "My Business"
    sb.BusinessEntities(0).Descriptions.Add
      ("en", "Description of My Business")

    sb.BusinessEntities(0).BusinessServices.Add()
    sb.BusinessEntities(0).BusinessServices(0).Name = "My Business Service"
    sb.BusinessEntities(0).BusinessServices(0).Descriptions.Add
      ("en", "Description of My Business Service")

    sb.BusinessEntities(0).BusinessServices(0).BindingTemplates.Add()
    sb.BusinessEntities(0).BusinessServices(0).BindingTemplates(0).
➥Descriptions.Add("en", "Description of Binding")
    sb.BusinessEntities(0).BusinessServices(0).BindingTemplates(0).
➥AccessPoint.Text = "My Access Point"
    sb.BusinessEntities(0).BusinessServices(0).BindingTemplates(0).
➥AccessPoint.URLType = Microsoft.Uddi.Api.URLTypeEnum.Http

    sb.BusinessEntities(0).BusinessServices(0).BindingTemplates(0).
➥TModelInstanceDetail.TModelInstanceInfos.Add()
    sb.BusinessEntities(0).BusinessServices(0).BindingTemplates(0).
➥TModelInstanceDetail.TModelInstanceInfos(0).Descriptions.Add
      ("en", "Insert Description Here")
    sb.BusinessEntities(0).BusinessServices(0).BindingTemplates(0).
```

LISTING 16.10 continued

```
➥TModelInstanceDetail.TModelInstanceInfos(0).TModelKey = sTModelKey

    Try
      Dim bd As New BusinessDetail()
      bd = sb.Send()
      Console.WriteLine(bd)

    Catch ue As UddiException
      Console.WriteLine(ue.Message)
      Return
    Catch e As Exception
      Console.WriteLine(e.Message)
      Return
    End Try

  End Sub

End Module
```

First, we prepare to log in to the registry with the following lines:

```
Publish.Url = "https://test.uddi.microsoft.com/publish"
Publish.User = "username"
Publish.Password = "password"
```

Next, we must build a `tModel` in order to publish our WSDL files:

```
    Dim tm As New SaveTModel()
    tm.TModels.Add()
    tm.TModels(0).Name = "URN of tModel"
    tm.TModels(0).Descriptions.Add("en", "Description of tModel")
    tm.TModels(0).OverviewDoc.OverviewURL = "URL of WSDL"
    tm.TModels(0).CategoryBag.Add("uddi-org:types",
      "wsdlSpec", "uuid:c1acf26d-9672-4404-9d70-4863bc075ad9")
    Dim sTModelKey As String
```

The `CategoryBag.Add` call is necessary for the proper categorization of the `tModel`. Finally, we send the `tModel` to the registry:

```
Dim td As New TModelDetail()
td = stm.Send()
sTModelKey = td.TModels(0).TModelKey
```

If we are successful in saving our `tModel` to the registry, it will return a unique `tModelKey`, which we use later to bind our Web Service. In the next step, we create our business entry:

```
    Dim sb As New SaveBusiness()
    sb.BusinessEntities.Add()
```

```
    sb.BusinessEntities(0).Name = "My Business"
    sb.BusinessEntities(0).Descriptions.Add
      ("en", "Description of My Business")
```

Then we create the BusinessService:

```
    sb.BusinessEntities(0).BusinessServices.Add()
    sb.BusinessEntities(0).BusinessServices(0).Name = "My Business Service"
    sb.BusinessEntities(0).BusinessServices(0).Descriptions.Add
      ("en", "Description of My Business Service")
```

Next, we create the BindingTemplate:

```
    sb.BusinessEntities(0).BusinessServices(0).BindingTemplates.Add()
    sb.BusinessEntities(0).BusinessServices(0).BindingTemplates(0).
➥Descriptions.Add("en", "Description of Binding")
    sb.BusinessEntities(0).BusinessServices(0).BindingTemplates(0).
➥AccessPoint.Text = "My Access Point"
    sb.BusinessEntities(0).BusinessServices(0).BindingTemplates(0).
➥AccessPoint.URLType = Microsoft.Uddi.Api.URLTypeEnum.Http
```

Finally, we create the tModelInstanceInfo:

```
    sb.BusinessEntities(0).BusinessServices(0).BindingTemplates(0).
➥TModelInstanceDetail.TModelInstanceInfos.Add()
    sb.BusinessEntities(0).BusinessServices(0).BindingTemplates(0).
➥TModelInstanceDetail.TModelInstanceInfos(0).Descriptions.Add
      ("en", "Insert Description Here")
    sb.BusinessEntities(0).BusinessServices(0).BindingTemplates(0).
➥TModelInstanceDetail.TModelInstanceInfos(0).TModelKey = sTModelKey
```

Now we are ready to register our business with the UDDI registry:

```
Dim bd As New BusinessDetail()
bd = sb.Send()
```

The Future of UDDI

The companies that came together to establish UDDI realized that the specification would need to go through several versions for it to be truly useful. Therefore, they laid out a roadmap for at least the first three versions of UDDI:

- Version 1, released in September 2000, included three taxonomies and basic descriptions of services as well as provided registration services for business units.
- Version 2, rolled out as a public draft in June 2001, adds additional taxonomies, provides support for layered services, and is intended to provide registration services for corporations with multiple divisions.

- Version 3, now scheduled for a December 2001 release, adds support for custom taxonomies and workflows and will provide registration services for a wide range of associations.

  Once version 3 is released, the UDDI Consortium intends to turn the project over to a third-party standards body.

Because the version 2 specification is now available, it is possible to take a closer look. Version 2 will enable the following:

- *Descriptions of complex organizations.* Businesses will now be able to describe and publish their internal organizational structure, including their business units, departments, divisions, and subsidiaries.
- *Improved support for internationalization.* Businesses will now have more flexibility in describing their business and services in multiple languages and locales.
- *Additional categorization and identifier schemes.* Businesses will now be able to use additional industry-specific categories and identifiers to describe their businesses, providing additional vertical market support. It will be possible to validate these additional categories during registration through third parties such as industry associations.
- *Richer searching options.* Businesses will now be able to search registries using more expressive query parameters, using more fields, and using more complex combinations of fields.

Furthermore, there are some additional API calls in version 2 that support the new notion of `publisherAssertions`. A `publisherAssertion` describes the relationship between two specific registered businesses. New publication API messages include `add_publisherAssertions`, `set_publisherAssertions`, and `delete_➥publisherAssertions` for managing `publisherAssertions`. The inquiry API adds the `get_publisherAssertions` message as well as a `find_relatedBusinesses` and a `get_assertionStatusReport` call.

So, assuming the technologies included in UDDI mature and companies worldwide are able to publish their Web Services to the network of public UDDI registries, will UDDI enable one global e-marketplace? Possibly, but it is likely that UDDI will find its best use in other contexts. Here are some examples of how UDDI registries might participate in the world of global commerce:

- Corporate registries that provide a central repository of information about a single enterprise's Web Services. Essentially, this is an intranet model of a UDDI registry.
- UDDI registries that form an integral part of a vendor's enterprise offering. For example, a CRM or ERP vendor might re-architect its offering as a collection of loosely coupled Web Services, each registered in the package's own UDDI registry.

- An "extranet" application of a UDDI registry put up by one company for use by itself and its business partners.
- Private e-marketplaces are likely candidates for hosting their own UDDI registries. Each e-marketplace can qualify entries into the registry, providing a guarantee of quality and financial stability to its members.
- Industry consortia or Better Business Bureau–type organizations may host their own UDDI registries, offering either Web Services specific to particular vertical markets or Web Services from companies that have undergone a particular approval process.
- Finally, this list wouldn't be complete without including the global, universally available network of UDDI registries. Clearly, companies will be reluctant to invoke Web Services listed in such a registry without either a preexisting relationship with the Web Services provider or some kind of authentication or approval provided beforehand by a third party.

So, how will UDDI be used in the future? Only time will tell. There is no question, however, that the technology is positioned to provide value in many different business situations.

Summary

As we climb up the Web Services technology stack shown in Figure 14.5, we get into technologies that are less and less established. UDDI appears near the top of the stack, indicating that as of today, this part of the Web Services puzzle is still mostly on the drawing board. The public UDDI registries today are essentially toys for the technical people to play with, so that organizations on the bleeding edge can both learn about the new technologies and provide feedback to those people who are working on improving the technologies in future versions.

Therefore, it is important to keep in mind that UDDI shouldn't be avoided because it is incomplete and immature; on the contrary, these are perfectly good reasons to become involved. If you have read this chapter through to this point, you are likely one of the individuals who can help push this nascent technology to the next level. If you have learned anything from this chapter, it is hoped that you have learned that, above all else, UDDI has great promise.

Leveraging XML in Visual Studio .NET

In This Chapter

With the advent of the personal computer and the success of companies such as Microsoft, we saw a fundamental shift in computing from mainframes to smaller personal computers. Rather than having the software reside in one location, it was installed on each machine that needed to run it. Recently, however, with the new push toward distributed environments, we're seeing another shift. Applications are no longer constrained to being installed on every machine that needs to run them. In fact, with the Internet, the ultimate distributed environment, we're finding more and more applications taking advantage of distributed computing by having one global location from which to execute functionality.

Until now, Web development output has consisted of string concatenation to create strings that would then be returned to the user. For those of us who are used to working in object-oriented programming languages, this involved a huge shift in thinking. No longer could we visually development our forms, buttons, and controls. We had to construct a series of classes that created string output. The major drawback to this approach is that you have to remember two styles of programming: one for the distributed applications and one for nondistributed applications. Now, with the introduction of Visual Studio .NET, Microsoft promises to bridge that gap in such a way that one style will suffice for both. In this chapter, we'll cover

- Some basics on ADO.NET data providers
- Some basics on the `DataSet` class
- Some basics on the `DataTable` class
- Some basics on the `DataRelation` class
- Typed data sets
- Loading a data set from XML
- Writing XML from a data set

The .NET Strategy

For years, Microsoft has provided to developers a suite named Visual Studio that consists of a visual development environment for various programming languages that Microsoft produces. However, having the languages bundled together hasn't meant that developers can more easily use something written in another language. The only way in which to accomplish this has been to create a COM object or an ActiveX control. This means that although developers can use anything written in any language as a COM object, they are pretty limited in how that object's functionality can be extended.

Another major complaint by developers has been the nightmare involving different versions of various DLLs, often referred to as *DLL hell*. Basically, every new version of a DLL cannot break a previous version's functionality because one DLL might be referenced by many different applications, all of which could be expecting the DLL to provide different functionality. This has created a versioning nightmare for the providers of those DLLs.

After many years of this, Microsoft has finally introduced a new version of Visual Studio that promises to ease all these problems for developers. First and foremost is the concept of the Common Language Runtime (CLR). The CLR provides a single set of runtime files for use by every language within Visual Studio. In other words, if you write a Visual Basic .NET application, your application will use the same runtime libraries as if you had written the application in C#. This CLR allows for the inheritance of classes across languages. For instance, you can define a class in Visual Basic .NET and inherit from it in a C# application. Quite a nice feature—one that many of us have been requesting for years.

Visual Studio .NET also promises to ease the struggles created by DLL hell by having all DLLs referenced within the application directory. This means you no longer have one global repository for DLLs. Now, every DLL used by an application can be found within the application directory.

Although this may seem like a step back, at first, you have to understand some of the reasoning that went into this decision. Imagine a scenario in which you create an object that uses early binding to bind to various methods of, say, a COM object. What happens is that the early binding uses a pointer to an address for any methods and properties accessed. Once you're done coding your object, you package and ship it. Then, two years down the road, one or more of your users install an application that uses a newer version of the COM object you referenced for early binding in your object. If the authors of that object weren't careful, the pointer your object has to the addresses of the properties, events, and methods of the COM object may now be pointing to the wrong property, event, or method, which will cause a major application malfunction. If, instead, your object were to have a local copy of that same object, you wouldn't have to worry about that scenario unless someone specifically copied over the file.

Another interesting major feature of Visual Studio .NET is the framework included within it. Until now, VB developers really haven't been able to take advantage of classes in the Microsoft Foundation Classes (MFC) the way in which C++ developers have been able to. Although the Visual Studio .NET Framework is not the MFC, it does provide something that Visual Basic developers have never really had: a complete application framework. In fact, a concept that will be new to many Visual Basic developers is *inheritance*. The inheritance that existed in previous versions of Visual Basic was not really inheritance at all. Basically, VB developers were limited to defining a class and then creating instances of that class within their applications. Now, VB developers can take advantage of the full power of inheritance by defining a class and then defining another class based on that new class, and another subclass based on that class, and so on.

Another major complaint that developers have had in the past is that, until now, they could not create an Internet application using object-oriented programming because the Internet was still basically reduced to a series of string concatenations to generate output to the browser. Now, Microsoft has bridged that gap. The same programming you have done in the past for Windows applications can be used, with slight modifications, to develop Web-based applications. In fact, Microsoft has made the creation of Web Services even easier than before. By having the IDE really do all the extra work in registering the Web service, developers are now able to concentrate on providing the functionality rather than on how they expose that functionality as a Web Service. Microsoft has also invested a considerable amount of time and energy in making it simpler for you to take advantage of Web Services. With the new IDE, you can simply add a reference to a Web Service to your application and gain all the benefits of that service, just as if it were another class within your application—you no longer have to worry about the necessary SOAP calls to that Web service. Visual Studio .NET figures out those little details for you. All you have to do is make a call to the Web Service, just as if it were another resource residing on the local machine, pass in the necessary parameters, and store the results.

All in all, Visual Studio .NET promises to open up the door to a whole new level of application design and functionality.

ADO.NET

In the past, Microsoft introduced its "universal" data access engine, ActiveX Data Objects (ADO), which was based primarily on four objects: the `Connection`, the `RecordSet`, the `Command`, and the `Parameter` objects. Although this system provided a common method for data access using OLE DB data providers, it maintained a connection to the data store. In distributed applications, this became more and more of a limitation. As a result, Microsoft created ADO.NET.

ADO.NET utilizes XML as a data-interchange mechanism between the data store and the application. By taking advantage of XML for use as a data-transport mechanism, ADO.NET is able to function under a disconnected environment, thus making distributed applications easier to write. The core elements of the ADO.NET architecture are the data set and the data provider. This architecture has been designed to separate data access from data manipulation. How can it accomplish this? The answer is really quite ingenious: The primary component for data manipulation is the data set. However, the data set does not maintain a connection to the data store. As a result, the data set can be processed without the need for a connection to the data store; the connection is maintained by the data provider components.

An entire book could be devoted to the intricacies and nuances for the entire data-access strategy in Visual Studio .NET, but because this book is geared toward XML, this section will introduce the basic concepts necessary to understand how XML fits into ADO.NET. As a result, this section will not cover ADO.NET in its entirety. For more information, visit `http://msdn.microsoft.com/vstudio/nextgen/technology/adoplus.asp`.

The ADO.NET Data Provider

The ADO.NET data providers are comprised of components that facilitate connecting to a data store, executing commands against that data store, and retrieving the results, which can be processed by the data provider or can be placed into a data set. The ADO.NET data provider consists of the following four components:

- `Command`
- `Connection`
- `DataAdapter`
- `DataReader`

The base versions of these components can be found in the `System.Data` namespace. However, specialized versions can be found within the `System.Data.SqlClient` and `System.Data.OleDb` namespaces. The differences between the two are very slight. The `System.Data.SqlClient` namespace is optimized for access to a Microsoft SQL Server database, whereas the `System.Data.OleDb` namespace can be used to access any OLE DB–compliant database. Granted, the class names are different within the two namespaces, but the basic functionality remains the same.

Note

For either of the .NET data providers to work, you must have Microsoft Data Access Components (MDAC) 2.6 or later installed.

You should note that the `System.Data.SqlClient` namespace will only interact with Microsoft SQL Server versions 7.0 or later. What do you do if you have an earlier version of Microsoft SQL Server? You can still use the `System.Data.OleDb` namespace.

Also, you should note that the `System.Data.OleDb` namespace does not work with the OLE DB 2.5 interfaces (you must have MDAC 2.6 or later for this to work correctly) and the `System.Data.OleDb` namespace does not work with the OLE DB provider for ODBC (MSDASQL).

You can find more information about the Microsoft Data Access Components as well as the latest version of the MDAC at `http://www.microsoft.com/data/`.

The `System.Data.SqlClient` Namespace

The classes within the `System.Data.SqlClient` namespace are optimized for access to Microsoft SQL Server versions 7.0 or later. They consist of the following implementations of the key components of the .NET data providers:

- `SqlCommand`
- `SqlConnection`
- `SqlDataAdapter`
- `SqlDataReader`

In a normal programming scenario, a connection is made to the server using the `SqlConnection` class, and the `SqlDataAdapter` class is used in conjunction with the `SqlConnection` class to populate a `DataSet` class.

In its simplest form, the C# code would appear as follows:

```
string cConn = "Data Source=TRAVISNOTEBOOK\\SQL2000;Integrated
➥Security=SSPI;Initial Catalog=Northwind";
System.Data.SqlClient.SqlConnection oConn = new
➥System.Data.SqlClient.SqlConnection(cConn);

oConn.Open();

System.Data.SqlClient.SqlDataAdapter oDA = new
➥System.Data.SqlClient.SqlDataAdapter(
➥"Select * From Customers", oConn);
System.Data.DataSet oDS = new System.Data.DataSet();

oDA.Fill(oDS,"Customers");
oConn.Close();
```

Here's how the VB .NET code would appear (also in its simplest form):

```
Dim cConn As string = "Data Source=
➥TRAVISNOTEBOOK\SQL2000;Integrated
➥Security=SSPI;Initial Catalog=Northwind"
Dim oConn As System.Data.SqlClient.SqlConnection = new
➥System.Data.SqlClient.SqlConnection(cConn)

oConn.Open();

Dim oDA As System.Data.SqlClient.SqlDataAdapter = new
➥System.Data.SqlClient.SqlDataAdapter(
➥"Select * From Customers", oConn)
Dim oDS As System.Data.DataSet = new System.Data.DataSet()

oDA.Fill(oDS,"Customers")
oConn.Close()
```

These examples demonstrate how to create a connection to a Microsoft SQL Server 2000 database and how to use `SqlDataAdapter` to populate a `DataSet` object.

Note

One point deserves special attention here: The preceding code contains an explicit call to the `Close()` method of the `SqlConnection` object. Unless you explicitly call this method or the `Dispose()`method, the connection to the server will not be closed.

A `DataSet` object keeps the entire result set in memory, which for larger applications or larger result sets might not be the most optimal method of data retrieval. For this reason, Microsoft has included the `SqlDataReader` and `SqlCommand` classes. Using these classes in conjunction with each other allows an application to load one record at the time into memory. This means that at any given point in time, the application is using only enough resources to keep that one record in memory, whereas `DataSet` would use whatever resources it needed to keep all the records in memory. This may not be a big issue when you're dealing with a result set of 1,000 or so records, but when you're dealing with 10,000 or more, the memory problems quickly become apparent. For instance, let's say each record takes 100 bytes of memory. First of all, you're looking at somewhere around 100,000 bytes to keep the first `DataSet` object in memory. Second, you're looking at 1,000,000 bytes. That's a big difference—and that's just for one `DataSet` object; that's not counting the other objects that exist in the application to perform the actual processing and business logic needed. If you were to use the `SqlDataReader` class, no matter what, you'd only use 100 bytes at any given time, and 100 bytes versus 1,000,000 bytes is a big difference when you're talking about memory management and resource availability.

To populate a `SqlDataReader` class, you could write C# code as follows:

```
string cConn = "Data Source=TRAVISNOTEBOOK\\SQL2000;Integrated
➥Security=SSPI;Initial Catalog=Northwind";
System.Data.SqlClient.SqlConnection oConn = new
➥System.Data.SqlClient.SqlConnection(cConn);

oConn.Open();

System.Data.SqlClient.SqlCommand oCommand = new
➥System.Data.SqlClient.SqlCommand(
➥"Select * From Customers", oConn);
System.Data.SqlClient.SqlDataReader oDR =
➥oCommand.ExecuteReader();
```

```
.
.
.
oDR.Close();
oConn.Close();
```

For VB .NET, the code would appear as this:

```
Dim cConn As string = "Data Source=
➥TRAVISNOTEBOOK\SQL2000;Integrated
➥Security=SSPI;Initial Catalog=Northwind"
Dim oConn As System.Data.SqlClient.SqlConnection = new
➥System.Data.SqlClient.SqlConnection(cConn)

oConn.Open();

Dim oCommand As System.Data.SqlClient.SqlCommand = new
➥System.Data.SqlClient.SqlCommand(
➥"Select * From Customers", oConn)
Dim oDR As System.Data.SqlClient.SqlDataReader =
➥oCommand.ExecuteReader()
.
.
.
oDR.Close()
oConn.Close()
```

The drawback to using the `SqlDataReader` class is that it must maintain a constant connection to the data store. Once the data reader has been populated, you can move to the next record by calling the `Read()` method on the data reader. Also, once the data reader has been created, no other operations can be performed using the `Connection` object: It's too busy servicing the requests from the data reader to be of any use to any other objects. Therefore, until you call the `Close()` method on the data reader, the `Connection` object used for the data reader will be unable to process requests from other sources.

Note

You cannot directly instantiate a `SqlDataReader` object by using the `new` keyword. Instead, you must create it by calling the `ExecuteReader()` method on the `SqlCommand` object.

The `System.Data.OleDb` Namespace

The classes within the `System.Data.OleDb` namespace provide data-access mechanisms to an OLE DB–compliant database and consist of the following implementations of the key components of the .NET data providers:

- `OleDbCommand`
- `OleDbConnection`
- `OleDbDataAdapter`
- `OleDbDataReader`

Just as with the classes provided in the `System.Data.OleDb` namespace, in a normal programming scenario, a connection is made to the server using the `OleDbConnection` class, and the `OleDbDataAdapter` class is used in conjunction with the `OleDbConnection` class to populate a `DataSet` class.

In its simplest form, the C# code would appear as follows:

```
string cConn = "Provider=SQLOLEDB;Data Source=
➥TRAVISNOTEBOOK\\SQL2000;Initial Catalog=Northwind;
➥Integrated Security=SSPI;";
System.Data.OleDb.OleDbConnection oConn = new
➥System.Data.OleDb.OleDbConnection(cConn);

oConn.Open();

System.Data.OleDb.OleDbDataAdapter oDA = new
➥System.Data.OleDb.OleDbDataAdapter(
➥"Select * From Customers", oConn);
System.Data.DataSet oDS = new System.Data.DataSet();

oDA.Fill(oDS,"Customers");
oConn.Close();
```

For VB .NET, the code would appear as this:

```
Dim cConn As string = "Provider=SQLOLEDB;Data Source=
➥TRAVISNOTEBOOK\SQL2000;Initial Catalog=Northwind;
➥Integrated Security=SSPI;"
Dim oConn As System.Data.OleDb.OleDbConnection = new
➥System.Data.OleDb.OleDbConnection(cConn)

oConn.Open();

Dim oDA As System.Data.OleDb.OleDbDataAdapter = new
➥System.Data.OleDb.OleDbDataAdapter(
➥"Select * From Customers", oConn)
Dim oDS As System.Data.DataSet = new System.Data.DataSet()

oDA.Fill(oDS,"Customers")
oConn.Close()
```

These examples demonstrate how to create a connection to a Microsoft SQL Server 2000 database and how to use `OleDbDataAdapter` to populate a `DataSet` object.

Note

Notice the explicit call to the `Close()` method of the `OleDbConnection` object. Remember, just as with the `SqlConnection` class, unless you explicitly call this method or the `Dispose()` method, the connection to the server will not be closed.

As for implementing `OleDbDataReader`, the C# code would appear as follows:

```
string cConn = "Provider=SQLOLEDB;Data Source=
➥TRAVISNOTEBOOK\\SQL2000;Initial Catalog=Northwind;
➥Integrated Security=SSPI;";
System.Data.OleDb.OleDbConnection oConn = new
➥System.Data.OleDb.OleDbConnection(cConn);

oConn.Open();

System.Data.OleDb.OleDbCommand oCommand = new
➥System.Data.OleDb.OleDbCommand(
➥"Select * From Customers", oConn);
System.Data.OleDb.OleDbDataReader oDR = oCommand.ExecuteReader();
.
.
.
oDR.Close();
oConn.Close();
```

Here's the code for VB .NET:

```
Dim cConn As string = "Provider=SQLOLEDB;Data Source=
➥TRAVISNOTEBOOK\SQL2000;Initial Catalog=Northwind;
➥Integrated Security=SSPI;"
Dim oConn As System.Data.OleDb.OleDbConnection = new
➥System.Data.OleDb.OleDbConnection(cConn)

oConn.Open();

Dim oCommand As System.Data.OleDb.OleDbCommand = new
➥System.Data.OleDb.OleDbCommand(
➥"Select * From Customers", oConn)
Dim oDR As System.Data.OleDb.OleDbDataReader = oCommand.ExecuteReader()
.
.
.
oDR.Close()
oConn.Close()
```

Just as with `SqlDataReader`, the drawback to using `OleDbDataReader` is that it must maintain a constant connection to the data store. Once the `OleDbDataReader` object has been populated, you can move to the next record by calling the `Read()` method on `OleDbDataReader`. Also, once the `OleDbDataReader` object has been created, no other operations can be performed using the `OleDbConnection` object; it's too busy servicing the requests from the data reader to be of any use to any other objects. Therefore, until you call the `Close()` method on `OleDbDataReader`, the `OleDbConnection` object used for `OleDbDataReader` will be unable to process requests from other sources.

> **Note**
>
> You cannot directly instantiate an `OleDbDataReader` object by using the `new` keyword. Instead, you must create it by calling the `ExecuteReader()` method on the `OleDbCommand` object.

The ADO.NET `DataSet` Class

The `DataSet` class within the ADO.NET architecture is the core component for providing data access in a distributed and disconnected environment. One of the largest limitations in ADO is the lack of support for having multiple tables and such within a record set. You have to shape a single record set in ADO in order to build a hierarchical record set. However, ADO.NET is leaps and bounds ahead of Microsoft's first attempt at universal data access. Within ADO.NET, you have a sort of miniature database called a *data set.* No longer are you limited to having one table—you can have as many as desired. Plus, you can create relations between those tables and, furthermore, those tables can have constraints. All this is available through the `DataSet` class in the ADO.NET architecture.

A data set within .NET contains zero or more tables and zero or more constraints, which are accessed via `DataTableCollection` and `DataRelationCollection`, respectively. `DataTableCollection` contains zero or more `DataTable` objects, whereas `DataRelationCollection` contains zero or more `DataRelation` objects.

> **Note**
>
> Notice the use of the terminology "zero or more" for how many `DataTable` objects a data set may contain. Why is it "zero or more" and not just "one or more"? The answer is, until you use a data adapter, whether it's `SqlDataAdapter` or `OleDbAdapter`, to populate the data set, the data set will remain empty.

The `DataSet` class has a series of public instance properties that influence the way the `DataSet` instance behaves. Two of the biggest improvements in ADO.NET are the `Tables` and `Relations` collections. Table 17.1 lists some of the public instance properties available for the `DataSet` class.

TABLE 17.1 Some of the Public Instance Properties for the `DataSet` Class and Their Descriptions

Name	*Description*
`CaseSensitive`	Gets or sets a value indicating whether string comparisons within a `DataTable` object are case sensitive
`DataSetName`	Maintains the name of the `DataSet` object
`EnforceConstraints`	Indicates whether constraint rules are followed when attempting an update operation
`ExtendedProperties`	Retrieves the collection of custom user information
`HasErrors`	Indicates whether there are errors within one or more rows within the `DataSet` object
`Namespace`	Specifies the namespace for the `DataSet` object
`Prefix`	Specifies the prefix to use for the namespace for the `DataSet` object
`Relations`	A reference to a `DataRelationCollection` object
`Tables`	A reference to a `DataTableCollection` object

The `DataSet` class also includes a set of public instance methods to help the developer manipulate the data returned from the data store in a variety of ways. Table 17.2 lists some of the public instance methods available for the `DataSet` class.

TABLE 17.2 Some of the Public Instance Methods for the `DataSet` Class and Their Descriptions

Name	*Description*
`AcceptChanges`	Commits the changes made to the `DataSet` object since it was loaded or since the last time `AcceptChanges` was called
`BeginInit`	Initializes the `DataSet` object for use by a form or another component
`Clear`	Removes all rows from all tables within the `DataSet` object, effectively "clearing" it of all data

TABLE 17.2 continued

Name	*Description*
`Clone`	Creates a duplicate `DataSet` object containing the same structure, including all `DataTable` schemas, relations, and constraints, minus the data
`Copy`	Creates a duplicate `DataSet` object containing the structure and the data from the original `DataSet` object
`EndInit`	Ends the initialization of the `DataSet` object
`Equals`	Determines whether two object instances are equal
`GetChanges`	Gets a copy of the `DataSet` object containing the changes made since it was loaded or since the last time `AcceptChanges` was called
`GetXml`	Gets an XML document representing the data stored within the `DataSet` object
`GetXmlSchema`	Gets the XML schema for the structure in the `DataSet` object
`HasChanges`	Determines whether changes have been made to the data within the `DataSet` object
`InferXmlSchema`	Infers the XML schema from the specified `TextReader` object or file into the `DataSet` object
`Merge`	Merges the current `DataSet` object with another `DataSet` object
`ReadXml`	Reads the XML schema and associated data into the `DataSet` object
`ReadXmlSchema`	Reads the XML schema into the `DataSet` object
`RejectChanges`	Reverts all changes made to the data within the `DataSet` object since it was loaded or since the last time `AcceptChanges` was called
`Reset`	Resets the `DataSet` object to its original state
`ToString`	Creates a string representation of the `DataSet` object
`WriteXml`	Writes the data and the associated XML schema for the `DataSet` object
`WriteXmlSchema`	Writes the XML schema for the `DataSet` object

The DataTable Class

The DataTable class within ADO.NET represents a single, in-memory representation of a relational result set. The DataTable class can be found and referenced from the System.Data namespace. Data tables can be created by using a data adapter to "fill" a data set, or they can be created manually.

Here's the C# code for creating a data table manually:

```
System.Data.DataSet oDS = new DataSet();
System.Data.DataTable oTable = oDS.Tables.Add("Orders");

oTable.Columns.Add("OrderID", typeof(System.Int32));
oTable.Columns.Add("OrderQuantity", typeof(System.Int32));
oTable.Columns.Add("CustID", typeof(System.Int32));
```

Here's the code for VB .NET:

```
Dim oDS As System.Data.DataSet = new DataSet()
Dim oTable As System.Data.DataTable = oDS.Tables.Add("Orders")

oTable.Columns.Add("OrderID", typeof(System.Int32))
oTable.Columns.Add("OrderQuantity", typeof(System.Int32))
oTable.Columns.Add("CustID", typeof(System.Int32))
```

The preceding code examples create a new DataSet object and manually add a new table called Orders to the data set. Then, three columns are added to the Orders data table. All in all, this is a rather simple example of how to manually create a DataTable object and add it to a DataSet object.

A DataTable object consists of a collection of columns, constraints, and rows. The columns represent the fields within the result set, whereas the rows represent the individual rows of data within the result set. The constraints maintain a collection of the rules the result set must follow. Table 17.3 lists some the public instance properties for the DataTable class.

TABLE 17.3 Some of the Public Instance Properties for the DataTable Class

Name	*Description*
CaseSensitive	Specifies whether string comparisons within the table are case-sensitive
ChildRelations	A reference to a DataRelationCollection object for the child relations for the current DataTable object
Columns	A reference to a DataColumnCollection object for the columns for the current DataTable object

TABLE 17.3 continued

Name	Description
`DataSet`	A reference to the `DataSet` object to which this `DataTable` object belongs
`DefaultView`	A reference to a `DataView` object for this `DataTable` object
`DisplayExpression`	Specifies the expression that returns a value used to represent the `DataTable` object in the UI
`ExtendedProperties`	Maintains a collection of the user information
`HasErrors`	Indicates whether the `DataTable` object has an error within it
`MinimumCapacity`	Specifies the initial starting size for the current table
`Namespace`	Specifies the namespace used in the XML document that represents this table
`ParentRelations`	A reference to a `DataRelationCollection` object for all parent relations for the current `DataTable` object
`Prefix`	The prefix to use for the namespace specified
`PrimaryKey`	Specifies an array of columns to use as the primary key for the `DataTable` object
`Rows`	A reference to a `DataRowCollection` object containing all the rows for the result set used by the `DataTable` object
`TableName`	Specifies the name of the `DataTable` object

Just as the `DataSet` class contains a series of public instance methods to help with the overall manipulation of data, the `DataTable` class contains a series of methods designed to help with the manipulation of data within a single table. Table 17.4 lists some of the public instance methods for the `DataTable` class.

TABLE 17.4 Some of the Public Instance Methods for the `DataTable` Class

Name	Description
`AcceptChanges`	Commits the changes since the `DataTable` object was loaded or since the last time `AcceptChanges` was called
`BeginInit`	Initializes the `DataTable` object
`BeginLoadData`	Turns off notifications, indexes, and constraints when loading data
`Clear`	Clears all data from the `DataTable` object
`Clone`	Creates a copy of the structure of the `DataTable` object

TABLE 17.4 continued

Name	*Description*
`Compute`	Computes how many rows match the given filter criteria
`Copy`	Creates a copy of the `DataTable` object, complete with data
`EndInit`	Ends the initialization of the `DataTable` object
`EndLoadData`	Turns off notifications, indexes, and constraints when loading data
`GetChanges`	Gets a copy of the `DataTable` object containing the changes that have been made since it was loaded or since the last time `AcceptChanges` was called
`GetErrors`	Gets an array of `DataRow` objects that have errors in them
`ImportRow`	Copies a `DataRow` object into the `DataTable` object
`LoadDataRow`	Finds and updates a specific `DataRow` object
`NewRow`	Creates a new `DataRow` object for the `DataTable` object
`RejectChanges`	Reverts all changes made since the `DataTable` object was loaded or since the last time `AcceptChanges` was called
`Select`	Creates an array of `DataRow` objects matching a given criteria
`ToString`	Returns the `TableName` object and the `DisplayExpression` object as a string

The `DataRelation` Class

Most database engines use a series of relations to organize information contained in various tables. They allow the database to store the information that can be logically grouped together in one place, thus reducing the amount of duplicate information in the database. This ultimately speeds up data access and operations performed against the data. It also allows information stored in one table to be related to a series of other tables.

Since a `DataSet` object can be considered its own personal little database, it's important for the `DataSet` object to support a key concept of relational databases: table relationships. The `DataSet` class can support multiple `DataTable` objects, and in some cases, you may need to relate two or more of those `DataTable` objects together. This is where the `DataRelation` class comes in. This class manages a `DataTable` object's relationship with another `DataTable` object by creating that relationship between two `DataColumn` objects.

The following code shows a simple example of how to establish a relationship between two tables within a `DataSet` object using C#:

```
System.Data.DataColumn oParentColumn;
System.Data.DataColumn oChildColumn;
oParentColumn = oDS.Tables["Customers"].Columns["CustomerID"];
oChildColumn = oDS.Tables["Orders"].Columns["CustomerID"];

System.Data.DataRelation oRelation =
➥new System.Data.DataRelation("CustomerOrders",
➥oParentColumn, oChildColumn);
oDS.Relations.Add(oRelation);
```

Here's the code for VB .NET:

```
Dim oParentColumn As System.Data.DataColumn
Dim oChildColumn As System.Data.DataColumn
oParentColumn = oDS.Tables("Customers").Columns("CustomerID");
oChildColumn = oDS.Tables("Orders").Columns("CustomerID");

Dim oRelation As System.Data.DataRelation =
➥new System.Data.DataRelation("CustomerOrders",
➥oParentColumn, oChildColumn)
oDS.Relations.Add(oRelation)
```


The preceding code assumes the existence of a `DataSet` object that has two `DataTable` objects in it: one for the Customers table, which has a CustomerID field in it, and one for the Orders table, which also has a CustomerID field in it. The code then grabs a reference to the two `DataColumn` objects to be related, creates a new `DataRelation` object, and then adds the new `DataRelation` object to the `Relations` collection on the `DataSet` object.

Alternatively, these examples could be written in C# as follows:

```
System.Data.DataRelation oRelation = oDS.Relations.Add(
➥"CustomerOrders", oDS.Tables["Customers"].Columns[
➥"CustomerID"], oDS.Tables["Orders"].Columns["CustomerID"]);
```

Here's the code for VB .NET:

```
Dim oRelation As System.Data.DataRelation = oDS.Relations.Add(
➥"CustomerOrders", oDS.Tables("Customers").Columns(
➥"CustomerID"), oDS.Tables("Orders").Columns("CustomerID"));
```

In this case, we are using the `Add()` method of the `Relations` collection on the `DataSet` object to accomplish this task in a much shorter form.

Table 17.5 lists some public instance properties available in the `DataRelation` class.

Note

The DataColumn objects used to specify the relationship between two DataTable objects must be of the same type. In other words, if column A of the first table is an Integer type, then column A of the second table must also be an Integer type.

TABLE 17.5 Some of the Public Instance Properties Available for the DataRelation Class

Name	*Description*
ChildColumns	Holds a reference to the child DataColumn objects for the child table
ChildKeyConstraint	Holds a reference to the ForeignKeyConstraint object for the child table
ChildTable	Holds a reference to the child DataTable object
DataSet	Holds a reference to the DataSet object
ExtendedProperties	Gets the collection that stores customized properties
Nested	Specifies whether the DataRelation objects are nested
ParentColumns	Holds a reference to the parent DataColumn objects for the parent table
ParentKeyConstraint	Holds a reference to the UniqueConstraint object in the parent table
ParentTable	Holds a reference to the parent DataTable object
RelationName	Specifies the name of the DataRelation object

The only methods available on the DataRelation class are the ones available on every object within the .NET framework, although the ToString method has been overridden. Again, because every class in the .NET Framework inherits, ultimately, from Object, every class will have at a minimum the following four methods listed in Table 17.6. In the case of the DataRelation class, the ToString method returns the value of the RelationName property.

TABLE 17.6 Some of the Public Instance Methods Available for the `DataRelation` Class

Name	*Description*
`Equals`	Determines whether two objects instances are equal
`GetHashCode`	Serves as a hash function for a particular type
`GetType`	Gets the type of the current instance
`ToString`	Gets the string representation of the instance

The `DataView` Class

The `DataView` class is provided within the ADO.NET Framework to allow for the filtering and sorting of a data table by using a basic for SQL syntax. This provides an interface of Web Forms and Windows Forms for which controls may be bound. For instance, you could have a `DataTable` object that contains an entire set of data and a `DataView` object that provides a small subset of that data. This prevents having to make another roundtrip to the server to get that information.

The following C# code shows a simple method for creating a custom view of the data within the Customers data table for all customers within the city of Berlin.

```
System.Data.DataTable oTable = oDS.Tables["Customers"];
System.Data.DataView oView = new System.Data.DataView(oTable);

oView.RowFilter = "City='Berlin'";
```

Here's the code for VB .NET:

```
Dim oTable As System.Data.DataTable = oDS.Tables("Customers")
Dim oView As System.Data.DataView = new System.Data.DataView(oTable)

oView.RowFilter = "City='Berlin'"
```

Because the `DataView` class represents a subset of data contained within a `DataTable` class, the `DataView` has a set of properties, events, and methods specialized in dealing with subsets of data. Table 17.7 lists some of the public instance properties available on the `DataView` class.

TABLE 17.7 Some of the Public Instance Properties Available on the `DataView` Class

Name	*Description*
`AllowDelete`	Specifies whether delete operations are allowed
`AllowEdit`	Specifies whether edit operations are allowed

TABLE 17.7 continued

Name	*Description*
`AllowNew`	Specifies whether new rows may be created
`ApplyDefaultSort`	Specifies whether the default sort should be used
`Count`	Indicates the number of records in the `DataView` object that meet the filter criteria
`Item`	Returns a row of data from a specified table
`RowFilter`	Specifies the filter expression that rows must meet to be included in the `DataView` object
`RowStateFilter`	Specifies the row state that rows must meet to be included in the `DataView` object
`Sort`	Specifies one or more columns by which to sort the rows within the `DataView` object
`Table`	Specifies the `DataTable` object for the `DataView` object

In addition to the inherited methods mentioned in Table 17.6, the `DataView` class has some methods for performing actions against a particular filtered or sorted subset of data contained in a `DataTable` class instance. Table 17.8 lists some of the public instance methods available on the `DataView` class.

TABLE 17.8 Some of the Public Instance Methods Available on the `DataView` Class

Name	*Description*
`AddNew`	Adds a new row to the `DataView` object
`BeginInit`	Starts the initialization of the `DataView` object
`Delete`	Deletes a row at the specified index
`Dispose`	Disposes of the resources used by the `DataView` object
`EndInit`	Ends the initialization on the `DataView` object
`Find`	Finds the row in the `DataView` object that meets the specified primary key value
`GetEnumerator`	Indicates the enumerator used for the `DataView` object

XML Within ADO.NET

XML is at the core of the functionality provided by the ADO.NET architecture. It allows developers to more easily access data in a distributed/disconnected environment. The

XML support within the ADO.NET architecture is immense, and the majority of it can be found within the functionality provided and included with the `DataSet` class.

Data sets can be created directly from XML documents or streams, allowing a hierarchical set of data to be loaded and accessed in a relational manner. The data sets can then create XML documents representing the data in a hierarchical fashion and use XML as a transport mechanism to allow data sets to be easily transported via HTTP. In fact, if, for example, a Web service returns a `DataSet` object, for anything other than another .NET application, this will be returned as a DiffGram, which is explained later in this chapter. However, if a .NET application uses that same Web service, .NET is smart enough to "dehydrate" the `DataSet` object into XML for transport via HTTP and then "rehydrate" the DiffGram into a `DataSet` object on the other side, thereby simplifying data access and allowing the developer to concentrate on more important tasks, such as what to do with that data once it's returned.

The support for XML within ADO.NET doesn't stop there. In fact, it gets better. A developer can create "typed" data sets using XSD schemas to create a mapping between the data store and the data set. ADO.NET then uses these maps when accessing and updating information in the data store.

Typed Data Sets

Typed data sets within ADO.NET provide a sort of string-typing mechanism for data access. By creating this string typing, you can access the tables and columns within the data set by name rather than through collection-based methods. Another added benefit to using typed data sets is the ability of Intellisense to provide autocomplete features for tables and columns contained in the data set.

So, how do you create a typed data set? To illustrate this, we'll use the Northwind database included in SQL Server 2000 to create a sample typed data set for the Customers table. This example assumes you've either created a new project in VS .NET or have opened an existing one for which you'd like to create a typed data set. Once there, go to the Solution Explorer, right-click the main project solution item, and then select Add, Add New Item. This will bring up the Add New Item dialog box, as shown in Figure 17.1.

Select the Data Set item on the right side of the dialog box and enter a name for the XSD schema. For this example, we'll use the filename `CustomersDataSet.xsd`. Once you have entered the filename, click the Open button. This will take you back to the design area shown in Figure 17.2.

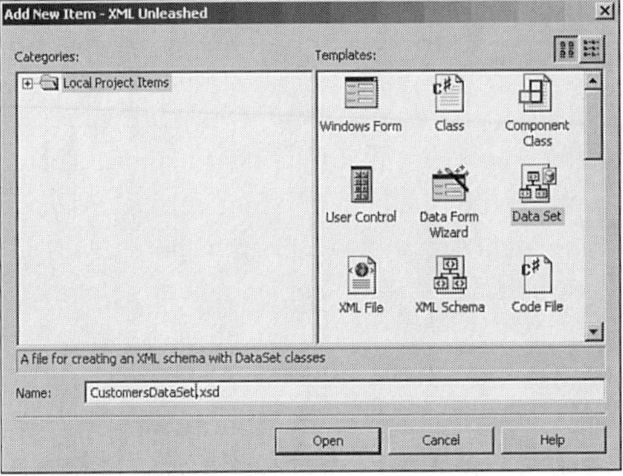

FIGURE 17.1
The Add New Item dialog box.

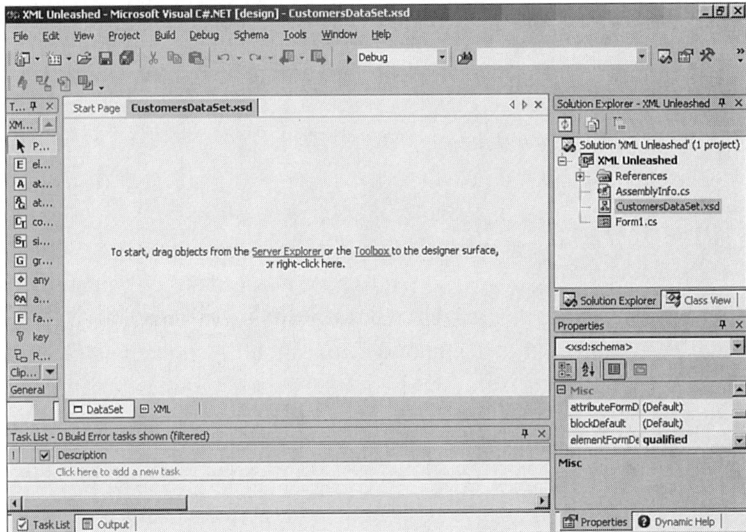

FIGURE 17.2
The Visual Studio .NET IDE after you've chosen to create a data set item.

Now, you need to open a connection to your data store. To accomplish this, from the main menu, select Tools, Connect To Database, which will bring up the Data Link Properties dialog box shown in Figure 17.3.

Using this dialog box, you will need to enter your connection information, such as the instance of SQL Server to connect to, how to log in to the data store, and what database to open. For our purposes, we'll use the Northwind database. Once, you've entered the information needed to open the connection, you can test the connection before committing the information by clicking the Test Connection button. Once you're confident of the connection information, you can open the connection by clicking the OK button.

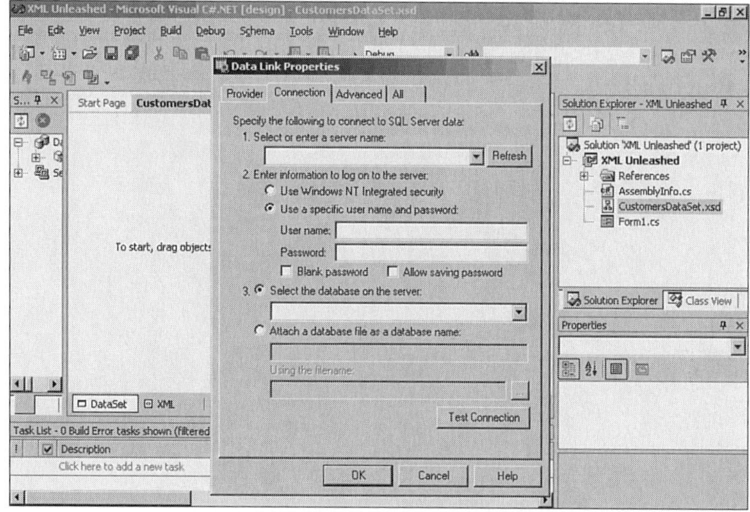

FIGURE 17.3
The Data Link Properties dialog box.

From here, you can navigate through Server Explorer to drag and drop items from your data store into the data set design area. For the purposes of our demonstration, select the Customers table and drag and drop it into the design area for the data set. Once you've completed this, your design area should look similar to Figure 17.4.

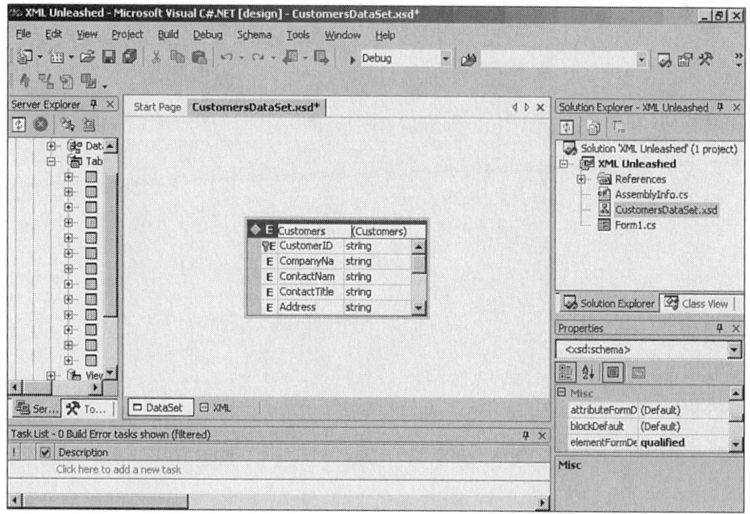

FIGURE 17.4
The data set design area after you've dragged and dropped the Customers table from the Northwind database in the Server Explorer.

You can now move this graphical item around on the design area, add or remove other tables, add or remove columns from the Customers table, and change the data types for each column. Once you have modified the data set definition, you can view the XML generated for it by clicking the XML button in the design area. Your screen should now appear similar to Figure 17.5.

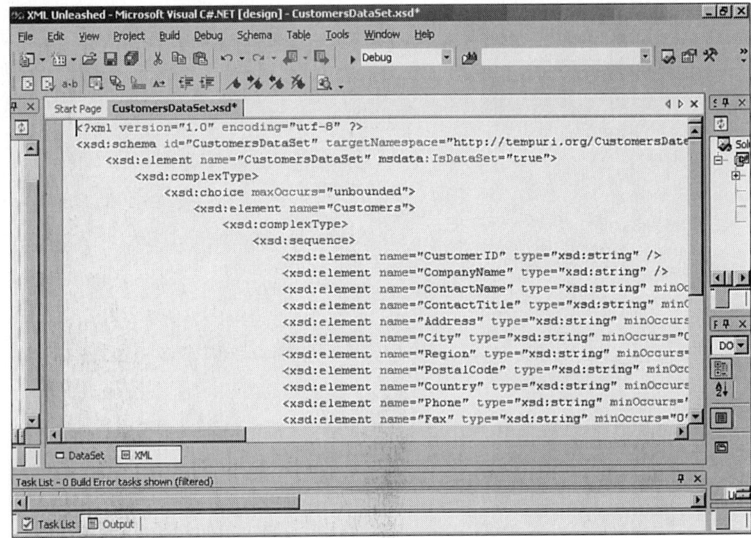

FIGURE 17.5
The XML view of the data set.

The actual XSD schema generated is shown in Listing 17.1.

LISTING 17.1 `CustomersDataSet.xsd` Contains the Information to Create a Typed Data Set for the Customers Table

```
<?xml version="1.0" encoding="utf-8" ?>
<xsd:schema id="CustomersDataSet" targetNamespace=
➥"http://tempuri.org/Customers.xsd"
➥elementFormDefault="qualified"
➥xmlns="http://tempuri.org/Customers.xsd"
➥xmlns:xsd="http://www.w3.org/2001/XMLSchema"
➥xmlns:msdata="urn:schemas-microsoft-com:xml-msdata">
  <xsd:element name="Customers" msdata:IsDataSet="true">
    <xsd:complexType>
      <xsd:choice maxOccurs="unbounded">
        <xsd:element name="Customers">
          <xsd:complexType>
            <xsd:sequence>
              <xsd:element name="CustomerID" type="xsd:string" />
              <xsd:element name="CompanyName" type="xsd:string"
➥minOccurs="0" />
              <xsd:element name="ContactName" type="xsd:string"
➥minOccurs="0" />
```

LISTING 17.1 continued

```
              <xsd:element name="ContactTitle" type="xsd:string"
➥minOccurs="0" />
              <xsd:element name="Address" type="xsd:string"
➥minOccurs="0" />
              <xsd:element name="City" type="xsd:string"
➥minOccurs="0" />
              <xsd:element name="Region" type="xsd:string"
➥minOccurs="0" />
              <xsd:element name="PostalCode" type="xsd:string"
➥minOccurs="0" />
              <xsd:element name="Country" type="xsd:string"
➥minOccurs="0" />
              <xsd:element name="Phone" type="xsd:string"
➥minOccurs="0" />
              <xsd:element name="Fax" type="xsd:string"
➥minOccurs="0" />
            </xsd:sequence>
          </xsd:complexType>
        </xsd:element>
      </xsd:choice>
    </xsd:complexType>
    <xsd:unique name="CustomersKey1" msdata:PrimaryKey="true">
      <xsd:selector xpath=".//Customers" />
      <xsd:field xpath="CustomerID" />
    </xsd:unique>
  </xsd:element>
</xsd:schema>
```

Now that we've modified and adjusted the data set's XSD schema, we can generate the typed data set by selecting (assuming you installed Visual Studio .NET in its default location) Start, Programs, Microsoft Visual Studio .NET 7.0, Visual Studio .NET Tools, Visual Studio .NET Command Prompt. This will bring up the Visual Studio .NET command prompt. By default, this will show up in the root directory. You will need to change this to your project's directory. In this example, we'll use `C:\Documents and Settings\Travis.TRAVISNOTEBOOK\My Documents\Visual Studio Projects\DevConADODemo\`. Once you're in your project directory, you can run a command-line program called `xsd.exe` to create your typed data set. The basic syntax for this program is shown here:

```
xsd /d /l:Language SchemaFileName [/n:NamespaceName]
```

The `/d` directive indicates that the program should create a typed data set. The `/l` directive specifies the language to use—for instance, `/l:CS` indicates that the data set should be generated in C#. Next, `SchemaFileName` is the name for your XSD schema file, and the `/n` directive allows you to specify a namespace to be generated for the typed data set, which will allow you to include that namespace within your applications. Figure 17.6 shows the command prompt for Visual Studio .NET with the full `xsd` command entered.

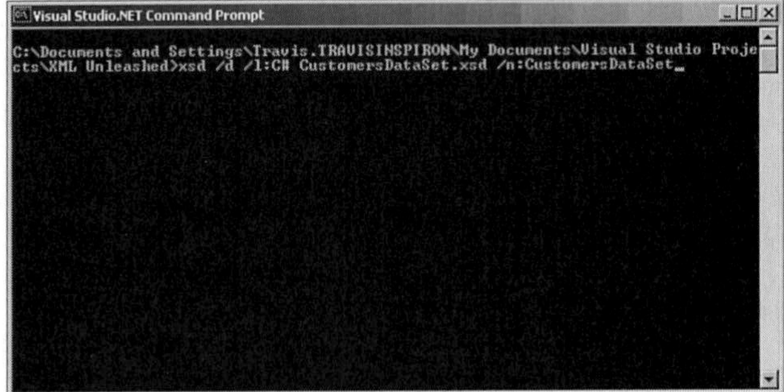

FIGURE 17.6
The full `xsd.exe` *command entered at the command line.*

Once this command has successfully executed, it will create a file with the same name, `CustomersDataSet`, with a `.cs` extension for C#. We can then go back into the Visual Studio .NET Solution Explorer, right-click the project, and then select Add, Add Existing Item. This will bring up the Add Existing Item dialog box. From here, you can select the file generated by the `xsd.exe` program and click the Open button to add it to the project, as shown in Figure 17.7.

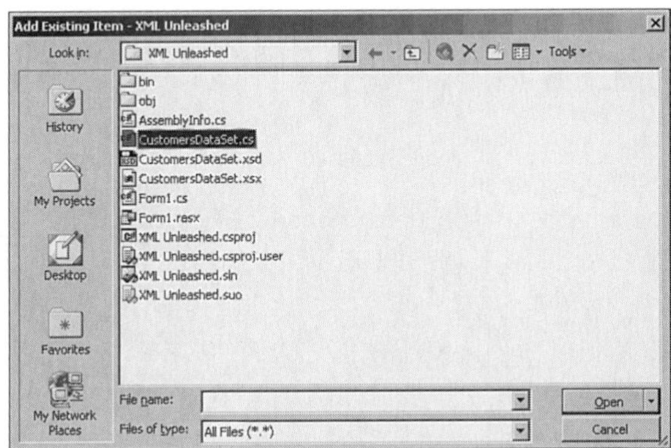

FIGURE 17.7
The Add Existing Item dialog box displays the new file generated by the `xsd.exe` *command-line program.*

This will add the file to your project, and you can then begin to use the newly created typed data set in your application. If you decide to generate a namespace, using the `/n` option, for your typed data set, as was done in the example, you can include it in your application by referencing that namespace as shown in the following code for C#:

```
using CustomersDataSet;
```

Here's the code for VB .NET:

```
Imports CustomersDataSet
```

> **Note**
>
> Remember that you do not have to include the newly created namespace in your application. You can still create all the objects contained within the namespace by specifying the namespace when you declare your variables.

Now you can create strongly typed variables based on your data set—in this example, `CustomersDataSet`. As mentioned before, one of the biggest benefits to using typed data sets is the use of Intellisense when accessing members from your typed data set, as shown in Figure 17.8.

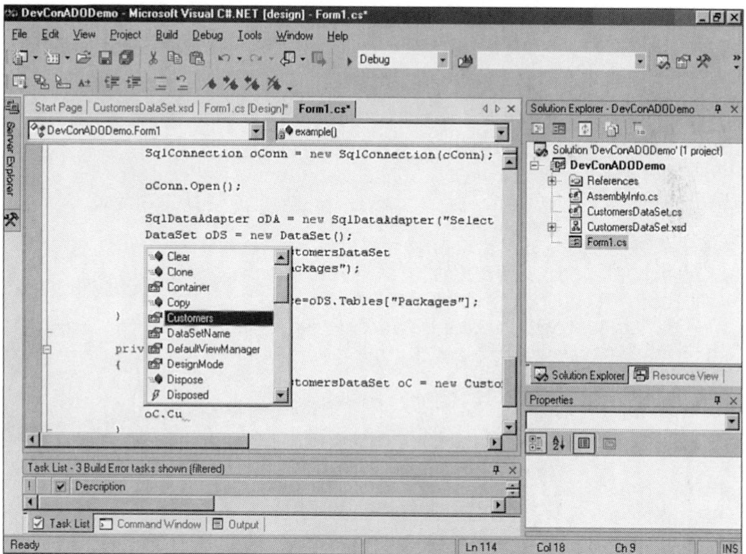

FIGURE 17.8
Using Intellisense for accessing members of a typed data set.

From Figure 17.8, you can see that we can directly access the Customers data table via a property on the `CustomersDataSet` object itself. In data sets that are not typed, you had to access the data table from the `Tables` collection on the `DataSet` object.

The following C# code demonstrates how to create the typed data set and sets the captions for the CustomerID and CompanyName columns:

```
string cConn = "Data Source=TRAVISNOTEBOOK\\SQL2000;Integrated
➥Security=SSPI;Initial Catalog=Northwind";
System.Data.SqlClient.SqlConnection oConn = new
➥System.Data.SqlClient.SqlConnection(cConn);

oConn.Open();

System.Data.SqlClient.SqlDataAdapter oDA = new
➥System.Data.SqlClient.SqlDataAdapter(
➥"Select * From Customers", oConn);
CustomersDataSet.CustomersDataSet oDS = new
➥CustomersDataSet.CustomersDataSet();

oDA.Fill(oDS,"Customers");
oConn.Close();

oDS.Customers.CustomerIDColumn.Caption = "Customer Id";
oDS.Customers.CompanyNameColumn.Caption = "Company Name";
```

Here's the code for VB .NET:

```
Dim cConn As string = "Data Source=
➥TRAVISNOTEBOOK\SQL2000;Integrated
➥Security=SSPI;Initial Catalog=Northwind"
Dim oConn As System.Data.SqlClient.SqlConnection = new
➥System.Data.SqlClient.SqlConnection(cConn)

oConn.Open();

Dim oDA As System.Data.SqlClient.SqlDataAdapter = new
➥System.Data.SqlClient.SqlDataAdapter(
➥"Select * From Customers", oConn)
Dim oDS As CustomersDataSet.CustomersDataSet = new
➥CustomersDataSet.CustomersDataSet()

oDA.Fill(oDS,"Customers")
oConn.Close()

oDS.Customers.CustomerIDColumn.Caption = "Customer Id"
oDS.Customers.CompanyNameColumn.Caption = "Company Name"
```

As you can see from the preceding code, we create the connection string to our SQL Server Northwind database, create the `SqlDataAdapter` object, create the `CustomersDataSet` object, use the `SqlDataAdapter` object to fill the typed `CustomersDataSet` object, close the connection to the database, and then set the column captions.

Loading an XML Document into a Data Set

XML is starting to play a bigger and bigger role in today's business world, and as a result, today's applications need to be able to perform extraordinary tasks based on XML documents or even XML fragments. Microsoft recognizes the importance of XML within today's industries and has attempted to integrate support for XML within its newest technologies, including Visual Studio .NET and the various .NET Enterprise server applications that will be discussed in Chapter 18, "Using XML in the .NET Enterprise Servers."

Because XML is the key technology that enables data sets to function, it's really a rather trivial task to load an XML document into a `DataSet` object. Why would you ever need to do this? Sometimes it may be easier to access an XML document in a relational manner rather than a hierarchical one. For these cases, Microsoft has included the ability to load XML documents directly into `DataSet` objects by calling the `ReadXml()` method. This method accepts two parameters. The first parameter is the XML source, and a second (optional) parameter indicates how the XML document should be loaded into the `DataSet` object.

The following C# code demonstrates a simple example of loading an XML file called `Customers1.xml` into a `DataSet` object:

```
System.Data.DataSet oDS = new System.Data.DataSet();
oDS.ReadXml("http://localhost/sql2000/template/customers1.xml");
```

Here's the code for VB .NET:

```
Dim oDS As System.Data.DataSet = new System.Data.DataSet();
oDS.ReadXml("http://localhost/sql2000/template/customers1.xml");
```

Notice that the second parameter isn't used in the preceding examples. By not explicitly passing an optional, second parameter, we leave it up to .NET to decide the best way to create the `DataSet` object from the given XML document. Also, the first parameter itself can be an XML stream, an XML document, or an `XmlReader` object because the `ReadXml()` method is overloaded. This gives you, the developer, added flexibility in application design by allowing you to load XML into a data set from multiple sources.

Note

It should be noted that if you load an XML document into a `DataSet` object that already has data, unless the source XML document is a DiffGram, Visual Studio .NET will not "merge" the XML document into the data set. To accomplish that, you'll have to load the XML document into a new `DataSet` object and call the `Merge()` method on the existing `DataSet` object to merge the two together.

Writing an XML Document from a DataSet Object

Just as you can load an XML document into a DataSet object to represent hierarchical data as relational data, you can create an XML document from a DataSet object, thereby allowing yourself to represent relational data in a hierarchical fashion. The XML can be retrieved from the data set as a string, an XML file, an XML stream, or an XMLWriter object, depending on whether you call the GetXml method or the WriteXml method. The GetXml method always returns an XML string, whereas the WriteXml method allows you to specify whether you want to create a file, write the XML to a stream, or write it to an XMLWriter object. It just depends on which output you desire. If you want the XML as a string, you can call the GetXml() method on the DataSet object, as shown in the following C# code:

```
string cConn = "Data Source=TRAVISNOTEBOOK\\SQL2000;Integrated
➥Security=SSPI;Initial Catalog=Northwind";
System.Data.SqlClient.SqlConnection oConn = new
➥System.Data.SqlClient.SqlConnection(cConn);

oConn.Open();

System.Data.SqlClient.SqlDataAdapter oDA = new
➥System.Data.SqlClient.SqlDataAdapter(
➥"Select * From Customers", oConn);
System.Data.DataSet oDS = new System.Data.DataSet();

oDA.Fill(oDS,"Customers");
oConn.Close();

string cXml;
cXml = oDS.GetXml();
```

Here's the code for VB .NET:

```
Dim cConn As string = "Data Source=
➥TRAVISNOTEBOOK\SQL2000;Integrated
➥Security=SSPI;Initial Catalog=Northwind"
Dim oConn As System.Data.SqlClient.SqlConnection = new
➥System.Data.SqlClient.SqlConnection(cConn)

oConn.Open();

Dim oDA As System.Data.SqlClient.SqlDataAdapter = new
➥System.Data.SqlClient.SqlDataAdapter(
➥"Select * From Customers", oConn)
Dim oDS As System.Data.DataSet = new System.Data.DataSet()

oDA.Fill(oDS,"Customers")
oConn.Close()
```

```
Dim cXml As string
cXml = oDS.GetXml()
```

From these examples, you can see that we create a connection string, open a connection to the database, create a `SqlDataAdapter` object, use the `SqlDataAdapter` object to fill the data set, close the connection to the database, and finally get the XML string for the data set. However, there is one limitation to this method: The `GetXml()` method only returns an XML string that represents the data within the data set, not the XML schema for it. To retrieve the XML schema, call the `GetXmlSchema()`method on the `DataSet` object, as shown in the following C# code:

```
string cConn = "Data Source=TRAVISNOTEBOOK\\SQL2000;Integrated
➥Security=SSPI;Initial Catalog=Northwind";
System.Data.SqlClient.SqlConnection oConn = new
➥System.Data.SqlClient.SqlConnection(cConn);

oConn.Open();

System.Data.SqlClient.SqlDataAdapter oDA = new
➥System.Data.SqlClient.SqlDataAdapter(
➥"Select * From Customers", oConn);
System.Data.DataSet oDS = new System.Data.DataSet();

oDA.Fill(oDS,"Customers");
oConn.Close();

string cXmlSchema;
cXmlSchema = oDS.GetXmlSchema();
```

Here's the code for VB .NET:

```
Dim cConn As string = "Data Source=
➥TRAVISNOTEBOOK\SQL2000;Integrated
➥Security=SSPI;Initial Catalog=Northwind"
Dim oConn As System.Data.SqlClient.SqlConnection = new
➥System.Data.SqlClient.SqlConnection(cConn)

oConn.Open();

Dim oDA As System.Data.SqlClient.SqlDataAdapter = new
➥System.Data.SqlClient.SqlDataAdapter(
➥"Select * From Customers", oConn)
Dim oDS As System.Data.DataSet = new System.Data.DataSet()

oDA.Fill(oDS,"Customers")
oConn.Close()

Dim cXmlSchema As string
cXmlSchema = oDS.GetXmlSchema()
```

These examples are the same as the ones for returning the XML string representation, except that instead of calling the `GetXml()` method to return the XML string for the data in the data set, we call the `GetXmlSchema()` method to return the XML schema for the data in the data set.

Persisting a `DataSet` as an XML File

Sometimes, however, you may wish to create an actual XML file with both the data and the schema information in it at the same time, or you may even wish to reduce the number of steps required to create an XML document file. In this case, you can call the `WriteXml()` method to immediately create an XML document file containing just the data, the data and the schema information, or a third type of XML document used extensively by ADO.NET—a DiffGram.

The following C# code demonstrates how to write an XML document with only the data based upon the data in the dataset:

```
string cConn = "Data Source=TRAVISNOTEBOOK\\SQL2000;Integrated
➥Security=SSPI;Initial Catalog=Northwind";
System.Data.SqlClient.SqlConnection oConn = new
➥System.Data.SqlClient.SqlConnection(cConn);

oConn.Open();

System.Data.SqlClient.SqlDataAdapter oDA = new
➥System.Data.SqlClient.SqlDataAdapter(
➥"Select * From Customers Where CustomerID Like
➥'A%'", oConn);
System.Data.DataSet oDS = new System.Data.DataSet();

oDA.Fill(oDS,"Customers");
oConn.Close();

oDS.WriteXml("c:\Customers.xml",
➥System.Data.XmlWriteMode.IgnoreSchema);
```

Here's the code for VB .NET:

```
Dim cConn As string = "Data Source=
➥TRAVISNOTEBOOK\SQL2000;Integrated
➥Security=SSPI;Initial Catalog=Northwind"
Dim oConn As System.Data.SqlClient.SqlConnection = new
➥System.Data.SqlClient.SqlConnection(cConn)

oConn.Open();
```

```
Dim oDA As System.Data.SqlClient.SqlDataAdapter = new
➥System.Data.SqlClient.SqlDataAdapter(
➥"Select * From Customers Where CustomerID Like
➥'A%'", oConn)
Dim oDS As System.Data.DataSet = new System.Data.DataSet()

oDA.Fill(oDS,"Customers")
oConn.Close()

oDS.WriteXml("c:\Customers.xml",
➥System.Data.XmlWriteMode.IgnoreSchema)
```

The preceding examples create an output file called `Customers.xml` in the root directory of C, as shown in Listing 17.2.

LISTING 17.2 `Customers.xml` Contains the XML Output from Calling `WriteXml` on the Data Set Without Including Schema Information

```
<?xml version="1.0" standalone="yes"?>
<NewDataSet>
  <Customers>
    <CustomerID>ALFKI</CustomerID>
    <CompanyName>Alfreds Futterkiste
➥</CompanyName>
    <ContactName>Maria Anders</ContactName>
    <ContactTitle>Sales Representative</ContactTitle>
    <Address>Obere Str. 57</Address>
    <City>Test</City>
    <PostalCode>12209</PostalCode>
    <Country>Germany</Country>
    <Phone>030-0074321</Phone>
    <Fax>030-0076545</Fax>
  </Customers>
  <Customers>
    <CustomerID>ANATR</CustomerID>
    <CompanyName>Ana Trujillo Emparedados y helados
➥</CompanyName>
    <ContactName>Ana Trujillo</ContactName>
    <ContactTitle>Owner</ContactTitle>
    <Address>Avda. de la Constitución 2222</Address>
    <City>México D.F.</City>
    <PostalCode>05021</PostalCode>
    <Country>Mexico</Country>
    <Phone>(5) 555-4729</Phone>
    <Fax>(5) 555-3745</Fax>
  </Customers>
  <Customers>
    <CustomerID>ANTON</CustomerID>
    <CompanyName>Antonio Moreno Taquería
➥</CompanyName>
```

LISTING 17.2 continued

```
    <ContactName>Antonio Moreno</ContactName>
    <ContactTitle>Owner</ContactTitle>
    <Address>Mataderos  2312</Address>
    <City>México D.F.</City>
    <PostalCode>05023</PostalCode>
    <Country>Mexico</Country>
    <Phone>(5) 555-3932</Phone>
  </Customers>
  <Customers>
    <CustomerID>AROUT</CustomerID>
    <CompanyName>Around the Horn</CompanyName>
    <ContactName>Thomas Hardy</ContactName>
    <ContactTitle>Sales Representative</ContactTitle>
    <Address>120 Hanover Sq.</Address>
    <City>London</City>
    <PostalCode>WA1 1DP</PostalCode>
    <Country>UK</Country>
    <Phone>(171) 555-7788</Phone>
    <Fax>(171) 555-6750</Fax>
  </Customers>
</NewDataSet>
```

The following C# code shows you how to create an XML file from a data set that includes the data and the schema information:

```
string cConn = "Data Source=TRAVISNOTEBOOK\\SQL2000;Integrated
➥Security=SSPI;Initial Catalog=Northwind";
System.Data.SqlClient.SqlConnection oConn = new
➥System.Data.SqlClient.SqlConnection(cConn);

oConn.Open();

System.Data.SqlClient.SqlDataAdapter oDA = new
➥System.Data.SqlClient.SqlDataAdapter(
➥"Select * From Customers Where CustomerID Like
➥'A%'", oConn);
System.Data.DataSet oDS = new System.Data.DataSet();

oDA.Fill(oDS,"Customers");
oConn.Close();

oDS.WriteXml("c:\CustomersWithSchema.xml",
➥System.Data.XmlWriteMode.WriteSchema);
```

Here's the code for VB .NET:

```
Dim cConn As string = "Data Source=
➥TRAVISNOTEBOOK\SQL2000;Integrated
➥Security=SSPI;Initial Catalog=Northwind"
```

```
Dim oConn As System.Data.SqlClient.SqlConnection = new
➥System.Data.SqlClient.SqlConnection(cConn)

oConn.Open();

Dim oDA As System.Data.SqlClient.SqlDataAdapter = new
➥System.Data.SqlClient.SqlDataAdapter(
➥"Select * From Customers Where CustomerID Like
➥'A%'", oConn)
Dim oDS As System.Data.DataSet = new System.Data.DataSet()

oDA.Fill(oDS,"Customers")
oConn.Close()

oDS.WriteXml("c:\CustomersWithSchema.xml",
➥System.Data.XmlWriteMode.WriteSchema)
```


The preceding examples create an XML file in the root directory of C called `CustomersWithSchema.xml` that includes the data and the schema information for it, as shown in Listing 17.3.

LISTING 17.3 `CustomersWithSchema.xml` Contains the Data and the Schema Information for the Data Set

```
<?xml version="1.0" standalone="yes"?>
<NewDataSet>
  <xsd:schema id="NewDataSet" targetNamespace="" xmlns=""
➥xmlns:xsd="http://www.w3.org/2001/XMLSchema"
➥xmlns:msdata="urn:schemas-microsoft-com:xml-msdata">
    <xsd:element name="NewDataSet" msdata:IsDataSet="true">
      <xsd:complexType>
        <xsd:choice maxOccurs="unbounded">
          <xsd:element name="Customers">
            <xsd:complexType>
              <xsd:sequence>
                <xsd:element name="CustomerID" type="xsd:string"
➥minOccurs="0" />
                <xsd:element name="CompanyName" type="xsd:string"
➥minOccurs="0" />
                <xsd:element name="ContactName" type="xsd:string"
➥minOccurs="0" />
                <xsd:element name="ContactTitle" type="xsd:string"
➥minOccurs="0" />
                <xsd:element name="Address" type="xsd:string"
➥minOccurs="0" />
                <xsd:element name="City" type="xsd:string"
➥minOccurs="0" />
                <xsd:element name="Region" type="xsd:string"
➥minOccurs="0" />
```

LISTING 17.3 continued

```
              <xsd:element name="PostalCode" type="xsd:string"
➥minOccurs="0" />
              <xsd:element name="Country" type="xsd:string"
➥minOccurs="0" />
              <xsd:element name="Phone" type="xsd:string"
➥minOccurs="0" />
              <xsd:element name="Fax" type="xsd:string"
➥minOccurs="0" />
             </xsd:sequence>
            </xsd:complexType>
           </xsd:element>
          </xsd:choice>
         </xsd:complexType>
        </xsd:element>
       </xsd:schema>
       <Customers>
         <CustomerID>AAAAA</CustomerID>
         <CompanyName>Test updategram</CompanyName>
         <ContactName>Test update</ContactName>
         <Address>Test</Address>
         <City>Test</City>
         <Phone>Test</Phone>
       </Customers>
       <Customers>
         <CustomerID>ALFKI</CustomerID>
         <CompanyName>Alfreds Futterkiste
➥</CompanyName>
         <ContactName>Maria Anders</ContactName>
         <ContactTitle>Sales Representative</ContactTitle>
         <Address>Obere Str. 57</Address>
         <City>Test</City>
         <PostalCode>12209</PostalCode>
         <Country>Germany</Country>
         <Phone>030-0074321</Phone>
         <Fax>030-0076545</Fax>
       </Customers>
       <Customers>
         <CustomerID>ANATR</CustomerID>
         <CompanyName>Ana Trujillo Emparedados y helados
➥</CompanyName>
         <ContactName>Ana Trujillo</ContactName>
         <ContactTitle>Owner</ContactTitle>
         <Address>Avda. de la Constitución 2222</Address>
         <City>México D.F.</City>
         <PostalCode>05021</PostalCode>
         <Country>Mexico</Country>
         <Phone>(5) 555-4729</Phone>
         <Fax>(5) 555-3745</Fax>
       </Customers>
```

LISTING 17.3 continued

```
  <Customers>
    <CustomerID>ANTON</CustomerID>
    <CompanyName>Antonio Moreno Taquería
➥</CompanyName>
    <ContactName>Antonio Moreno</ContactName>
    <ContactTitle>Owner</ContactTitle>
    <Address>Mataderos  2312</Address>
    <City>México D.F.</City>
    <PostalCode>05023</PostalCode>
    <Country>Mexico</Country>
    <Phone>(5) 555-3932</Phone>
  </Customers>
  <Customers>
    <CustomerID>AROUT</CustomerID>
    <CompanyName>Around the Horn</CompanyName>
    <ContactName>Thomas Hardy</ContactName>
    <ContactTitle>Sales Representative</ContactTitle>
    <Address>120 Hanover Sq.</Address>
    <City>London</City>
    <PostalCode>WA1 1DP</PostalCode>
    <Country>UK</Country>
    <Phone>(171) 555-7788</Phone>
    <Fax>(171) 555-6750</Fax>
  </Customers>
</NewDataSet>
```

Representing the `DataSet` as a DiffGram

In addition to creating a standard XML file with or without the schema information included, as mentioned earlier in this section, a third option is available to you: You can create a DiffGram. A DiffGram is a special form of XML file used by ADO.NET that includes original values, current values, and a unique identifier for every record.

The following C# code shows you how to create a DiffGram from a data set:

```
string cConn = "Data Source=TRAVISNOTEBOOK\\SQL2000;Integrated
➥Security=SSPI;Initial Catalog=Northwind";
System.Data.SqlClient.SqlConnection oConn = new
➥System.Data.SqlClient.SqlConnection(cConn);

oConn.Open();

System.Data.SqlClient.SqlDataAdapter oDA = new
➥System.Data.SqlClient.SqlDataAdapter(
➥"Select * From Customers Where CustomerID Like
➥'A%'", oConn);
System.Data.DataSet oDS = new System.Data.DataSet();
```

```
oDA.Fill(oDS,"Customers");
oConn.Close();

oDS.WriteXml("c:\CustomersDiffGram.xml",
➥System.Data.XmlWriteMode.DiffGram);
```

Here's the code for VB .NET:

```
Dim cConn As string = "Data Source=
➥TRAVISNOTEBOOK\SQL2000;Integrated
➥Security=SSPI;Initial Catalog=Northwind"
Dim oConn As System.Data.SqlClient.SqlConnection = new
➥System.Data.SqlClient.SqlConnection(cConn)

oConn.Open();

Dim oDA As System.Data.SqlClient.SqlDataAdapter = new
➥System.Data.SqlClient.SqlDataAdapter(
➥"Select * From Customers Where CustomerID Like
➥'A%'", oConn)
Dim oDS As System.Data.DataSet = new System.Data.DataSet()

oDA.Fill(oDS,"Customers")
oConn.Close()

oDS.WriteXml("c:\CustomersDiffGram.xml",
➥System.Data.XmlWriteMode.DiffGram)
```

The preceding examples create a DiffGram called `CustomersDiffGram.xml` in the root directory of C, as shown in Listing 17.4.

LISTING 17.4 `CustomersDiffGram.xml` Contains a DiffGram for the Data Set

```
<?xml version="1.0" standalone="yes"?>
<diffgr:diffgram xmlns:msdata=
➥"urn:schemas-microsoft-com:xml-msdata" xmlns:diffgr=
➥"urn:schemas-microsoft-com:xml-diffgram-v1">
  <NewDataSet>
    <Customers diffgr:id="Customers1" msdata:rowOrder="0">
      <CustomerID>AAAAA</CustomerID>
      <CompanyName>Test updategram</CompanyName>
      <ContactName>Test update</ContactName>
      <Address>Test</Address>
      <City>Test</City>
      <Phone>Test</Phone>
    </Customers>
    <Customers diffgr:id="Customers2" msdata:rowOrder="1">
      <CustomerID>ALFKI</CustomerID>
      <CompanyName>Alfreds Futterkiste
➥</CompanyName>
```

LISTING 17.4 continued

```
      <ContactName>Maria Anders</ContactName>
      <ContactTitle>Sales Representative</ContactTitle>
      <Address>Obere Str. 57</Address>
      <City>Test</City>
      <PostalCode>12209</PostalCode>
      <Country>Germany</Country>
      <Phone>030-0074321</Phone>
      <Fax>030-0076545</Fax>
    </Customers>
    <Customers diffgr:id="Customers3" msdata:rowOrder="2">
      <CustomerID>ANATR</CustomerID>
      <CompanyName>Ana Trujillo Emparedados y helados
➥</CompanyName>
      <ContactName>Ana Trujillo</ContactName>
      <ContactTitle>Owner</ContactTitle>
      <Address>Avda. de la Constitución 2222</Address>
      <City>México D.F.</City>
      <PostalCode>05021</PostalCode>
      <Country>Mexico</Country>
      <Phone>(5) 555-4729</Phone>
      <Fax>(5) 555-3745</Fax>
    </Customers>
    <Customers diffgr:id="Customers4" msdata:rowOrder="3">
      <CustomerID>ANTON</CustomerID>
      <CompanyName>Antonio Moreno Taquería
➥</CompanyName>
      <ContactName>Antonio Moreno</ContactName>
      <ContactTitle>Owner</ContactTitle>
      <Address>Mataderos  2312</Address>
      <City>México D.F.</City>
      <PostalCode>05023</PostalCode>
      <Country>Mexico</Country>
      <Phone>(5) 555-3932</Phone>
    </Customers>
    <Customers diffgr:id="Customers5" msdata:rowOrder="4">
      <CustomerID>AROUT</CustomerID>
      <CompanyName>Around the Horn</CompanyName>
      <ContactName>Thomas Hardy</ContactName>
      <ContactTitle>Sales Representative</ContactTitle>
      <Address>120 Hanover Sq.</Address>
      <City>London</City>
      <PostalCode>WA1 1DP</PostalCode>
      <Country>UK</Country>
      <Phone>(171) 555-7788</Phone>
      <Fax>(171) 555-6750</Fax>
    </Customers>
  </NewDataSet>
</diffgr:diffgram>
```

You can see from Listing 17.4 that a DiffGram is really just another XML grammar. The major item to notice is that each `<Customers>` element has a unique `diffgr:id` attribute. This allows the `DataSet` to resolve changes made to individual rows and fields in the various `DataTable` objects in the `DataSet`.

The `System.Xml` Namespace

XML within the .NET framework is a key component, and as such, Microsoft has provided a comprehensive set of classes to perform all sorts of tasks related to the operations dealing with XML. Everything from reading and writing XML, to parsing XML, to validating XML, to performing transformations on XML, and more can be found within the classes provided by the .NET framework.

The `System.Xml` namespace within the Visual Studio .NET Framework provides the set of classes necessary to perform everything from simple to complex operations on XML data. The following classes may be found within the `System.Xml` namespace:

- `XmlDocument`
- `XmlNode`
- `XmlNodeList`
- `XmlNamedNodeMap`
- `XmlDataDocument`
- `XmlWriter`
- `XmlTextWriter`
- `XmlReader`
- `XmlTextReader`

In addition to these classes, the `System.Xml` namespace contains a set of child namespaces that contain other classes to perform more specialized operations:

- `System.Xml.Schema`
- `System.Xml.Serialization`
- `System.Xml.XPath`
- `System.Xml.Xsl`

These namespaces, as you can probably guess by their names, provide classes to deal with specific operations or provide specific functionality related to schemas, serialization, XPath expressions, and XSLT transformations.

The `XmlDocument` Class

The `XmlDocument` class found in the `System.Xml` namespace is a .NET implementation of the core W3C Document Object Model (DOM), levels 1 and 2. Because this particular class is nothing more than another DOM for XML, we'll forego spending a lot of time going over how to use it, because Chapter 7, "Parsing XML Using Document Object Model," has already done a good job of teaching you how to use a DOM object. Instead, what we'll do here is list the various members of the `XmlDocument` class, such as the public instance properties of the `XmlDocument` class, as shown in Table 17.9.

TABLE 17.9 Some of the Public Instance Properties of the `XmlDocument` Class

Name	*Description*
`Attributes`	Holds a reference to an `XmlAttributeCollection` object
`BaseURI`	Indicates the base URI of the current node
`ChildNodes`	Holds a reference to an `XmlNodeList` object
`DocumentElement`	The root `XmlElement` for the document
`DocumentType`	Holds a reference to the `DOCTYPE` node within the document
`FirstChild`	Holds a reference to the first child node of the current node
`HasChildNodes`	Indicates whether the current node has any child nodes
`Implementation`	Holds a reference to the `XmlImplementation` object for the current document
`InnerText`	Specifies the concatenated values of the current node and all its children
`InnerXml`	Specifies the XML fragment of the children of the current node
`IsReadOnly`	Indicates whether the current node is read-only
`Item`	Returns the specified child element
`LastChild`	Holds a reference to the last child of the current node
`LocalName`	Indicates the local name of the current node
`Name`	Indicates the qualified name of the current node
`NamespaceURI`	Indicates the namespace URI for the current node
`NameTable`	Holds a reference to the `XmlNameTable` object associated with this implementation
`NextSibling`	Holds a reference to the next node following the current node
`NodeType`	Indicates the type of node

TABLE 17.9 continued

Name	*Description*
`OuterXml`	Returns the XML fragment of the current node and its child nodes
`OwnerDocument`	Holds a reference to the `XmlDocument` object for the current node
`ParentNode`	Holds a reference to the parent node of the current node
`Prefix`	Specifies the namespace prefix for the current node
`PreserveWhitespace`	Specifies whether whitespace should be preserved
`PreviousSibling`	Holds a reference to the node immediately preceding the current node
`Value`	Specifies the value of the current node
`XmlResolver`	Sets the `XmlResolver` object to use for resolving external resources

Chapter 7 covered the XML Document Object Model (DOM) in detail. Microsoft, ever striving to merge a defined "standard" and its vision of a "standard," hasn't forgotten how important the DOM is to developers. However, rather than simply use the current COM implementation of the DOM, Microsoft has decided to include a specialized class in the .NET Framework that is a DOM implementation that will run in the managed environment of the CLR. Table 17.10 lists the public instance methods available for the `XmlDocument` class.

TABLE 17.10 Some of the Public Instance Methods of the `XmlDocument` Class

Name	*Description*
`AppendChild`	Adds the specified node to the end of the child node of the current node
`Clone`	Creates a duplicate of the current node
`CloneNode`	Creates a duplicate of the current node
`CreateAttribute`	Creates an `XmlAttribute` object with the specified name
`CreateCDataSection`	Creates an `XmlCDataSection` object containing the specified data
`CreateComment`	Creates an `XmlComment` object containing the specified data
`CreateDocumentFragment`	Creates an `XmlDocumentFragment` object
`CreateDocumentType`	Creates an `XmlDocumentType` object

TABLE 17.10 continued

Name	*Description*
`CreateElement`	Creates an `XmlElement` object
`CreateEntityReference`	Creates an `XmlEntityReference` object with the specified name
`CreateNavigator`	Creates an `XPathNavigator` object for navigating this object
`CreateNode`	Creates an `XmlNode` object
`CreateProcessingInstruction`	Creates an `XmlProcessingInstruction` object with the specified name and data
`CreateSignificantWhitespace`	Creates an `XmlSignificantWhitespace` object
`CreateTextNode`	Creates an `XmlText` object with the specified text
`CreateWhitespace`	Creates an `XmlWhitespace` object
`CreateXmlDeclaration`	Creates an `XmlDeclaration` object with the specified values
`Equals`	Determines whether two object instances are equal
`GetElementById`	Gets the `XmlElement` object with the specified ID
`GetElementsByTagName`	Returns an `XmlNodeList` object containing a list of all descendant elements that match the specified name
`GetEnumerator`	Provides support for the `for-each` style iteration over the nodes in the specified node
`GetNamespaceOfPrefix`	Looks up the closest `xmlns` declaration for the given prefix that is in scope for the current node and returns the namespace URI in the declaration
`GetPrefixOfNamespace`	Looks up the closest `xmlns` declaration for the given namespace URI that is in scope for the current node and returns the prefix defined in that declaration
`GetType`	Gets the type of the current instance
`ImportNode`	Imports a node from another document into the current document
`InsertAfter`	Inserts a node immediately after the specified node
`InsertBefore`	Inserts a node immediately before the specified node
`Load`	Loads the specified XML data
`LoadXml`	Loads the XML document from the specified string

TABLE 17.10 continued

Name	*Description*
`Normalize`	Puts all `XmlText` nodes in the full depth of the subtree underneath the current node into a "normal" form, where only markup separates `XmlText` nodes (that is, there are no adjacent `XmlText` nodes)
`PrependChild`	Adds the specified node to the beginning of the child nodes for the current node
`ReadNode`	Creates an `XmlNode` object based on the information in an `XmlReader` object
`RemoveAll`	Removes all the children and/or attributes of the current node
`RemoveChild`	Removes the specified child node
`ReplaceChild`	Replaces the specified child node with another node
`Save`	Saves the XML document to the specified location
`SelectNodes`	Selects a list of nodes matching the XPath expression
`SelectSingleNode`	Selects the first node that matches the XPath expression
`Supports`	Tests whether the DOM implementation implements a specific feature
`ToString`	Returns a string that represents the current object
`WriteContentTo`	Saves all the children of the `XmlDocument` node to the specified `XmlWriter` object
`WriteTo`	Saves the `XmlDocument` node to the specified `XmlWriter` object

The `XmlDataDocument` Class

You've already seen how you can load hierarchical XML data into a data set so that you can access the information in a relational manner. You've also seen how you can create hierarchical XML data from a data set that can then be loaded into an `XmlDocument` object from which you can perform operations on that XML. However, the steps necessary to perform these tasks are less than ideal. Wouldn't it be great if you could simply load the information contained within a data set directly into a DOM object from which you could perform data manipulations? Believe it or not, within Visual Studio .NET, you can.

The Visual Studio .NET Framework provides a class that allows you to do just that. The XML framework and the ADO.NET Framework provide a unified programming model to access XML as well as relational data. The `XmlDataDocument` class within the XML framework provides the necessary bridge between ADO.NET and the XML framework. Table 17.11 lists some of the public instance properties of the `XmlDataDocument` class.

TABLE 17.11 Some of the Public Instance Properties Available on the `XmlDataDocument` Class

Name	*Description*
`Attributes`	Holds a reference to an `XmlAttributeCollection` object
`BaseURI`	Indicates the base URI of the current node
`ChildNodes`	Holds a reference to an `XmlNodeList` object
`DataSet`	Holds a reference to the data set that provides the relational data for the `XmlDataDocument` object
`DocumentElement`	The root `XmlElement` for the document
`DocumentType`	Holds a reference to the `DOCTYPE` node within the document
`FirstChild`	Holds a reference to the first child node of the current node
`HasChildNodes`	Indicates whether the current node has any child nodes
`Implementation`	Holds a reference to the `XmlImplementation` object for the current document
`InnerText`	Specifies the concatenated values of the current node and all its children
`InnerXml`	Specifies the XML fragment of the children of the current node
`IsReadOnly`	Indicates whether the current node is read-only
`Item`	Returns the specified child element
`LastChild`	Holds a reference to the last child of the current node
`LocalName`	Indicates the local name of the current node
`Name`	Indicates the qualified name of the current node
`NamespaceURI`	Indicates the namespace URI for the current node
`NameTable`	Holds a reference to the `XmlNameTable` object associated with this implementation
`NextSibling`	Holds a reference to the next node following the current node
`NodeType`	Indicates the type of node
`OuterXml`	Returns the XML fragment of the current node and its child nodes

TABLE 17.11 continued

Name	*Description*
`OwnerDocument`	Holds a reference to the `XmlDataDocument` object for the current node
`ParentNode`	Holds a reference to the parent node of the current node
`Prefix`	Specifies the namespace prefix for the current node
`PreserveWhitespace`	Specifies whether whitespace should be preserved
`PreviousSibling`	Holds a reference to the node immediately preceding the current node
`Value`	Specifies the value of the current node
`XmlResolver`	Sets the `XmlResolver` object to use for resolving external resources

Because `XmlDataDocument` is a subclass of the `XmlDocument` class, it inherits all the properties, events, and methods from the `XmlDocument` class. However, the `XmlDataDocument` class provides some additional methods that help manage relational data as hierarchical data. Table 17.12 lists some of the public instance methods available for the `XmlDataDocument` class.

TABLE 17.12 Some of the Public Instance Methods Available of the `XmlDataDocument` Class

Name	*Description*
`AppendChild`	Adds the specified node to the end of the child node of the current node.
`Clone`	Creates a duplicate of the current node.
`CloneNode`	Creates a duplicate of the current node.
`CreateAttribute`	Creates an `XmlAttribute` object with the specified name.
`CreateCDataSection`	Creates an `XmlCDataSection` object containing the specified data.
`CreateComment`	Creates an `XmlComment` object containing the specified data.
`CreateDocumentFragment`	Creates an `XmlDocumentFragment` object.
`CreateDocumentType`	Creates an `XmlDocumentType` object.
`CreateElement`	Creates an `XmlElement` object.
`CreateEntityReference`	This method is not supported by the `XmlDataDocument` class. If it's called, an exception will be thrown.

TABLE 17.12 continued

Name	*Description*
`CreateNavigator`	Creates an `XPathNavigator` object for navigating this object.
`CreateNode`	Creates an `XmlNode` object.
`CreateProcessingInstruction`	Creates an `XmlProcessingInstruction` object with the specified name and data.
`CreateSignificantWhitespace`	Creates an `XmlSignificantWhitespace` object.
`CreateTextNode`	Creates an `XmlText` object with the specified text.
`CreateWhitespace`	Creates an `XmlWhitespace` object.
`CreateXmlDeclaration`	Creates an `XmlDeclaration` object with the specified values.
`Equals`	Determines whether two object instances are equal.
`GetElementById`	This method is not supported by the `XmlDataDocument` class. If it's called, an exception will be thrown.
`GetElementFromRow`	Returns the `XmlElement` object associated with the specified `DataRow` object.
`GetElementsByTagName`	Returns an `XmlNodeList` object containing a list of all the descendant elements that match the specified name.
`GetEnumerator`	Provides support for the `for-each` style iteration over the nodes in the specified node.
`GetNamespaceOfPrefix`	Looks up the closest `xmlns` declaration for the given prefix that is in scope for the current node and returns the namespace URI in the declaration.
`GetPrefixOfNamespace`	Looks up the closest `xmlns` declaration for the given namespace URI that is in scope for the current node and returns the prefix defined in that declaration.
`GetRowFromElement`	Returns the `DataRow` object for the specified `XmlElement` object.
`GetType`	Gets the type of the current instance.
`ImportNode`	Imports a node from another document into the current document.
`InsertAfter`	Inserts a node immediately after the specified node.
`InsertBefore`	Inserts a node immediately before the specified node.
`Load`	Loads the specified XML data and synchronizes the `XmlDataDocument` object with the data set.

TABLE 17.12 continued

Name	*Description*
`LoadXml`	Loads the XML document from the specified string.
`Normalize`	Puts all `XmlText` nodes in the full depth of the subtree underneath the current node into a "normal" form, where only markup separates `XmlText` nodes (in other words, there are no adjacent `XmlText` nodes).
`PrependChild`	Adds the specified node to the beginning of the child nodes for the current node.
`ReadNode`	Creates an `XmlNode` object based on the information in an `XmlReader` object.
`RemoveAll`	Removes all the children and/or attributes of the current node.
`RemoveChild`	Removes the specified child node.
`ReplaceChild`	Replaces the specified child node with another node.
`Save`	Saves the XML document to the specified location.
`SelectNodes`	Selects a list of nodes matching the XPath expression.
`SelectSingleNode`	Selects the first node that matches the XPath expression.
`Supports`	Tests whether the DOM implementation implements a specific feature.
`ToString`	Returns a string that represents the current object.
`WriteContentTo`	Saves all the children of the `XmlDocument` node to the specified `XmlWriter` object.
`WriteTo`	Saves the `XmlDocument` node to the specified `XmlWriter` object.

You can see from Tables 17.11 and 17.12 that in addition to the properties and methods found in the `XmlDocument` class, the `XmlDataDocument` class has a few specialized properties and methods that integrate the `XmlDocument` class with the `DataSet` class.

The following C# code demonstrates how to create an `XmlDataDocument` object from a given data set:

```
string cConn = "Data Source=TRAVISNOTEBOOK\\SQL2000;Integrated
➥Security=SSPI;Initial Catalog=Northwind";
System.Data.SqlClient.SqlConnection oConn = new
➥System.Data.SqlClient.SqlConnection(cConn);

oConn.Open();
```

```
System.Data.SqlClient.SqlDataAdapter oDA = new
➥System.Data.SqlClient.SqlDataAdapter(
➥"Select * From Customers Where CustomerID Like
➥'A%'", oConn);
System.Data.DataSet oDS = new System.Data.DataSet();

oDA.Fill(oDS,"Customers");
oConn.Close();

System.Xml.XmlDataDoument oXML =
➥new System.Xml.XmlDataDocument(oDS);
```

Here's the code for VB .NET:

```
Dim cConn As string = "Data Source=
➥TRAVISNOTEBOOK\SQL2000;Integrated
➥Security=SSPI;Initial Catalog=Northwind"
Dim oConn As System.Data.SqlClient.SqlConnection = new
➥System.Data.SqlClient.SqlConnection(cConn)

oConn.Open();

Dim oDA As System.Data.SqlClient.SqlDataAdapter = new
➥System.Data.SqlClient.SqlDataAdapter(
➥"Select * From Customers Where CustomerID Like
➥'A%'", oConn)
Dim oDS As System.Data.DataSet = new System.Data.DataSet()

oDA.Fill(oDS,"Customers")
oConn.Close()

Dim oXML As System.Xml.XmlDataDocument =
➥new System.Xml.XmlDataDocument(oDS)
```

Basically, the preceding code loads the relational data into a `DataSet` object, and then we use that `DataSet` object as a parameter that is passed to the constructor of the `XmlDataDocument` object. At this point, Visual Studio .NET does something intriguing: You may modify and manipulate the data in either object—the `DataSet` object or the `XmlDataDocument` object—and the changes will be reflected in the other object. This means you still have one data source you may modify, but you have two different objects that allow you to do so, and each object picks up on the changes made in the other object.

Summary

The future of development using Microsoft products is beginning to change. The languages that we use to write our applications must be able to reduce the amount of work for us as the demands of our applications become increasingly more complex. Microsoft has answered this call with Visual Studio .NET by providing the Common Language Runtime, which every language within Visual Studio .NET can take advantage of, by providing increased support for Web services, and by revolutionizing Web development.

.NET promises to make developers more productive by allowing them to concentrate on the more important tasks of writing the actual business functionality needed within their applications, rather than worrying about how to get one portion of their applications to interface with something else. Microsoft has gone through great pains to incorporate XML into the .NET Framework as much as possible because it recognizes that XML is becoming an increasingly accepted standard for messaging, data representation, and more.

CHAPTER 18

Using XML in the .NET Enterprise Servers

In This Chapter

Microsoft has invested a considerable amount of time and energy into creating a complete series of components that will easily integrate together to solve many of the problems currently faced by businesses. In addition to Visual Studio .NET, Microsoft produces a set of "enterprise servers": BizTalk Server 2000 and SQL Server 2000, both of which are designed to "Web-enable" various enterprise aspects of companies. Everything from Business-to-Business communication and Business-to-Consumer communication to publishing real-time data on the Web. In addition, the .NET Enterprise Servers are designed to help build, deploy, and manage these Web-enabling solutions.

BizTalk Server is geared toward handling Business-to-Business (B2B) communication in an automated fashion, whereas SQL Server 2000 is Microsoft's answer to a database management system that handles scalability. In this chapter, you'll learn

- About the basic concepts of BizTalk Server 2000
- How to route documents in BizTalk Server 2000
- About the new `For XML` clause in SQL Server 2000
- How to query SQL Server 2000 using a URL query
- How to query SQL Server 2000 using a template query
- How to create annotated XSD schemas
- How to query SQL Server 2000 using an XPath query
- How to create XML updategrams
- How to submit XML updategrams to SQL Server 2000

BizTalk

Microsoft BizTalk Server 2000 is one of the .NET Enterprise Servers that makes Business-to-Business (B2B) communication happen. Many times, a single company can no longer provide everything to its customers. For instance, a bookstore may need to rely on a shipping partner to ship a book that a customer orders. In the past, these sorts of situations have been handled either by hand or by very complex automation routines that would provide this information to the partner in a "nightly dump" or similar manner. With the growing sophistication of today's applications, we need the ability to send these notifications in a more timely manner. This is what's known as *business-to-business communication*; it's the idea that one business relies on an outside partner to accomplish certain tasks and notifications of what's expected to be sent to the partner company. BizTalk Server is, in essence, a routing service that receives and routes B2B messages in a very efficient and flexible way. BizTalk Server 2000 allows you to set up business relationships with a large number of partnering organizations (which may all be using different standards), define the standards used by your business partners, and the map between the various standards with which you deal.

The BizTalk Management Desk can be considered the "BizTalk control center." This is where a typical BizTalk user would go to set up organizations, agreements, document formats, mapping and routing information, and so on. However, before we can discuss some of the more advanced management capabilities with BizTalk Server 2000, we first need to explore the basic items that make BizTalk Server 2000 tick.

Organizations

Organizations are the cornerstones of all BizTalk scenarios. Organizations simply are business partners. There's always a "home" organization (that's you) and at least one other organization with which the home organization does business.

Setting up organizations is easy. You can create a new organization through the File, New menu. An organization typically has little more than a name that identifies it. However, you can specify as many additional identifiers as you want. You can choose between standard identifiers, such as Dun & Bradstreet (DUNS) numbers, or you can set up custom identifiers.

Ports

A port can be considered the routing destination of a message, which can be an organization, as mentioned earlier, or an application, as you'll learn later in this chapter. Ports do not necessarily reference business partners, because there can be ports for routing messages or documents internally or for routing messages to the home organization. For instance, imagine a scenario in which Company B places an order with Company A (the home organization). That order is received and then routed to the home organization for processing.

You can create a new port from the File menu by choosing File, New, Port. When you're defining a port, one of the first settings that needs to be specified is the application name and the primary transport mechanism. The transport address specifies the mechanism and the destination to be used for the document. Here are the available mechanisms:

- HTTP and HTTPS
- SMTP
- File
- Message Queues
- Application Integrator Components
- Loopback

By specifying HTTP and HTTPS as the routing mechanism, you indicate that BizTalk needs to route the document to a Web server. A value of SMTP tells BizTalk to route the document as an e-mail, whereas a value of File signals to the BizTalk Server to route the document to a local file. Identifying a routing mechanism of Message Queues tells the BizTalk Server to invoke Microsoft Message Queuing Services when routing a document. The value Application Integrator Components lets you route documents to custom destinations, and the value Loopback let's you route the document/message back into the BizTalk Routing Services.

Frequently, you will encounter a scenario in which you must route a document or message to another organization. In this case, you'll need to specify the destination organization and the transport mechanism to use to route the document or message. Additionally, you can also set up security and encryption information as well as some other advanced settings. Okay, so now you know how to route a document once it's in the BizTalk system. However, you do not know how to get a document from an external source into the system in the first place. This is done through *channels*. Every port needs to have at least one channel in order to be useful. When you're creating a new port, BizTalk automatically asks you to create a new channel for the port (unless you deselect that option in the last step of the wizard) .

Channels

Channels route a message from an organization or application to the assigned port. During this process, the document may actually be converted or mapped from one standard into another standard. When setting up a port, you are automatically asked by the wizard to create a channel. Alternatively, you can right-click a port in the Management Desk and select New Channel, From an Organization, which also launches the Channel Properties Wizard.

To create a new channel, you'll need to specify a source organization, the type of "inbound" document to route, and the type of "outbound" document to create. This allows you to say, in essence, that you expect to receive a certain type of document and you need to route this document to a certain port in a particular format. If the inbound and outbound documents are different, the incoming document needs to be converted, or *mapped*. (We will discuss document maps later in this chapter.)

Document types have to be defined in BizTalk using schemas, which allows you to accept a business partner's document format as long as it is well defined and valid. However, just because you can accommodate a business partner's document format doesn't mean you have to use that format internally. In fact, you may have your own standard for the same document type.

Applications

In BizTalk, applications are not necessarily programs or components. They are simply sets of logically connected transactions. Applications are defined in the home organization's Organization definition. To create a new application, simply click the New button in the Applications page or the Organization Properties dialog box, specify a name, and you're finished.

Document Definitions

Document definitions comprise another important building block for BizTalk systems. All messages that are routed through BizTalk have to be defined, which is done using XML schemas. Document definitions can be very simple, specifying only a couple of fields in a document, or they can be very complex, defining field types and lengths and even BizTalk routing information.

Microsoft BizTalk Server 2000 provides a tool to create document definitions called the Document Editor. The BizTalk Document Editor is basically a schema editor with some special features for BizTalk. When you create a new document, the Document Editor allows you to base the new document on a template or to start with a blank document. You can then proceed to add new records and fields. By default, records are the equivalent of tags, and fields equate to attributes. However, you can change that and actually turn a field into a tag by changing the Type setting in the Declaration page. The major difference between records and fields is that records can have subrecords and fields as child items, whereas fields cannot. The editor basically gives you all the freedom XML schemas provide. You can set the data type, valid values, minimum and maximum content length, default values, whether a field or record is optional or required, the number of times a tag can occur, and much more.

In addition, the Document Editor can handle BizTalk-specific settings, such as routing information. BizTalk-specific information is specified in the Dictionary page. All this information is handled under the BizTalk namespace. You can add your own namespaces to provide information specific to your document format. Simply click the Namespace page to do so.

BizTalk document definitions can be stored as regular files on your hard drive or in a WebDAV repository.

Note

The BizTalk Document Editor can handle other formats besides XML. To switch to a different format, click the main document node, select the Reference page, and change the setting for Standard.

Document Maps

Document maps define how one document type is to be converted into another and are created using the BizTalk Mapper. To create a new map, select File, New from the menu bar and then select the source document definition and the destination document definition. This opens both document formats and displays them in the BizTalk Mapper. You can now start mapping documents, field by field, using simple drag-and-drop operations. The map is complete once all the fields in the destination receive a value from the source. This information is stored in a WebDAV repository or the local hard drive, where it can be referenced from BizTalk Server.

Note

Several fields from the source document type can be mapped to multiple fields in the destination document.

Also, not all the fields are necessarily straight maps. Some of them may need to use "functoids." These are the little boxes you see in the center of a map. The number of available functoids is large and ranges from simple string manipulation and mathematical functions to scientific calculations and even scripts.

WebDAV

Web-based Distributed Authoring and Versioning (WebDAV) is an extension to the HTTP protocol that allows users to collaboratively edit and manage files on remote Web servers and provides standard ways to handle issues such as locking and access control.

WebDAV is an open standard that is used by many companies, including Netscape, Novell, Xerox, Microsoft, and others. Microsoft Office 2000 represents one of the most popular implementations of the WebDAV standard for office collaboration.

Microsoft BizTalk Server 2000 uses WebDAV for authoring document definitions and maps (although you can also save these documents on your hard drive without using WebDAV).

For more information on WebDAV, refer back to Chapter 13, "XML and Content Management," or visit www.webdav.org.

Distribution Lists

Distribution lists allow you to route messages to several organizations at once, which is useful for distributing information such as price lists and catalogs. Regular ports always map to one and only one organization. A distribution list, though, is linked to an infinite number of ports that will receive the routed message. All these ports need to have a specified destination.

Note

A message routed to distribution lists cannot have routing information embedded within it. That just wouldn't make sense because the destination could be different for every port. Therefore, keep in mind that distribution lists cannot accept self-routing documents.

A distribution list is linked to a channel, just like ports are usually linked to channels, only this time, the distribution list spreads the information to a number of ports.

Submitting Documents

Now that you have a basic understanding of BizTalk Server and its most important components, features, and tools, it's time to submit your first document. To start, we'll do so using Visual Basic code.

Communication with BizTalk is handled through a COM-based interface, thus making document submission a simple process. Let's assume we want to route an XML document containing an order into BizTalk so we can process the order. We would take the XML document we wish to submit to BizTalk and, within a method in a Visual Basic object, write something like the following:

```
DIM loBT AS Object
DIM lvResult AS String

SET loBT = CREATEOBJECT("BizTalk.Interchange")
lvResult = loBT.Submit 1,SourceDocument, DocumentType,
➥"Organization Name", NameOfSourceOrganization,
➥"Organization Name","Home Organization"
```

As you can see, the code is rather simple and straightforward. We create an instance of the `BizTalk.Interchange` object and call the `Submit()` method, passing in the content of the source document (our XML document containing our orders). In this example, we are manually routing the document, which means we pass information about the document format as well as the source and destination organizations. Parameter 3 specifies the document type that has to be set up in the BizTalk Management Desk. Parameters 4 and 5 specify the source organization identifier and the actual name or the source organization. Parameters 6 and 7 do the same for the destination organization.

Assuming the XML document is valid according to the schema we set up, BizTalk Server will find a channel/port pair that matches the document type as well as the defined organizations.

In addition to explicitly specifying the source and destination organizations in the `Submit` method, the XML document itself can contain routing information. Such documents are known as *self-routing documents*. Self-routing documents contain information about the source organization, destination organization, document type, and organization identifiers. Basically, self-routing documents enable you to call the `Submit()` method and pass only the first two parameters. All this information has to be identified in the document definition to indicate to BizTalk Server where that information can be found. This is done using the Dictionary tab in the Document Editor.

Depending on the submitted message, the routing information can be contained in the actual message (this is typically the case in BizTalk Framework–compliant messages) or in an envelope.

When you're submitting a self-routing document, the basic steps are the same as with manually routed documents (discussed earlier), with the difference being that only the first two parameters are passed to the `Submit()` method.

SQL Server 2000

With the advent of XML and the increasing requirements for distributed applications in today's marketplace, a larger demand has been placed on the developer to provide messaging and data in an XML format. Providing data in XML format, until now, has consisted of querying data in the form of a cursor or ADO record set and using a conversion routine to convert the data into XML format. Now with the new features in SQL Server 2000, this task can be accomplished with minimal effort, which allows the developer to concentrate on the more important task of writing the business logic.

SQL Server 2000 allows the developer to query SQL Server data and receive that data in XML format through the use of a special clause: `FOR XML`. This clause provides three different options by which SQL Server can return data in XML format: `AUTO`, `RAW`, and `EXPLICIT`.

Issuing the SQL `SELECT` command with `FOR XML AUTO` will return the result set in XML format, with each record having a node whose tag name is the same as the table name on which the query was performed. Each node will have attributes equal to the field names specified in the query with values equal to the values of the fields within the table. Using the `FOR XML RAW` clause will return XML in which each record is represented by a node whose tag name is "row" and whose attributes are the fields from the query. The last option, `FOR XML EXPLICIT`, uses queries written in a specific format to return the XML in a specific format. However, these options are only available from within the SQL Server Query Analyzer or by accessing SQL server through a URL.

In this chapter, we will be using Web Release 2 for SQL Server 2000.

Configuring IIS

Before you can utilize the new XML support within SQL Server 2000, you must first configure it. Simply click Start, Programs, Microsoft SQL Server XML Tools, Configure IIS Support—Web Release 2. This will launch the configuration utility necessary to provide XML support within SQL Server 2000, as shown in Figure 18.1.

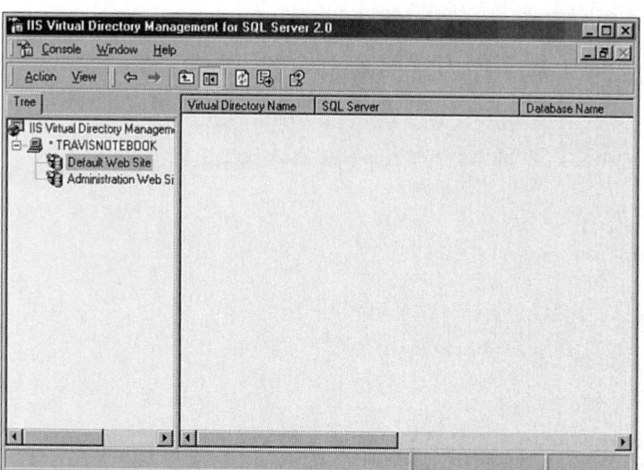

FIGURE 18.1
The IIS Virtual Directory Management Console is where you can administer the XML support for SQL Server.

Once you have the IIS Virtual Directory Management for SQL Server page open, drill down in the tree on the left side of the screen until you get to the Default Web Site node or the Web site from which you wish to access SQL Server 2000. On the right side of the screen, right-click and select New, Virtual Directory. This will bring up the New Virtual Directory Properties dialog box, where you enter information regarding how SQL Server 2000 should be configured to run when accessed from a URL, as shown in Figure 18.2.

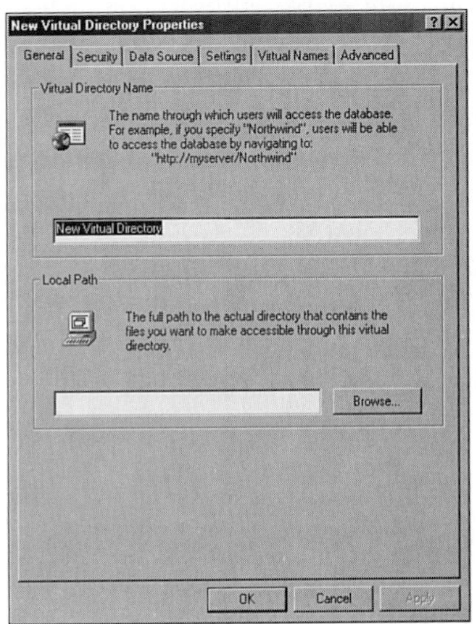

FIGURE 18.2
The General page of the Virtual Directory Properties dialog box.

On the "General" page, you will be required to give the new virtual directory a name and provide the physical path on the hard drive associated with this virtual directory. This first page determines how you may access SQL Server via HTTP. For instance, in the case of Default Web Site, if you enter a virtual directory name of SQL2000, you could access it via HTTP as `http://localhost/sql2000`.

The "Security" page, shown in Figure 18.3, is where you indicate how you wish to log in to SQL Server 2000.

The "Data Source" page, shown in Figure 18.4, allows you to specify the SQL Server installation to use and the database name to access.

The "Settings" page, shown in Figure 18.5, allows you to indicate the different types of queries that can be run: URL queries, template queries, and/or XPath queries, as well as whether HTTP POSTs are allowed.

FIGURE 18.3
The Security page of the Virtual Directory Properties dialog box.

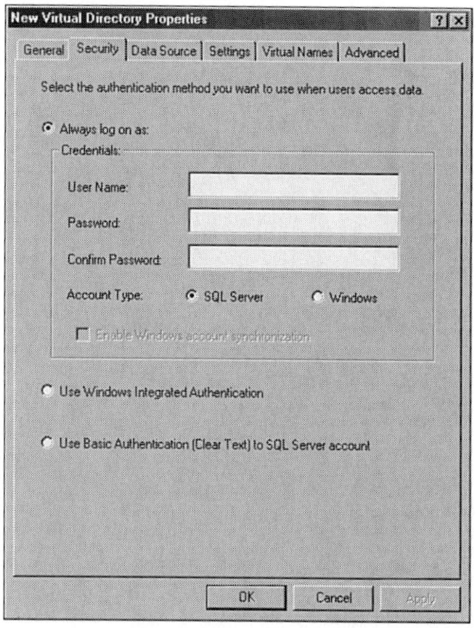

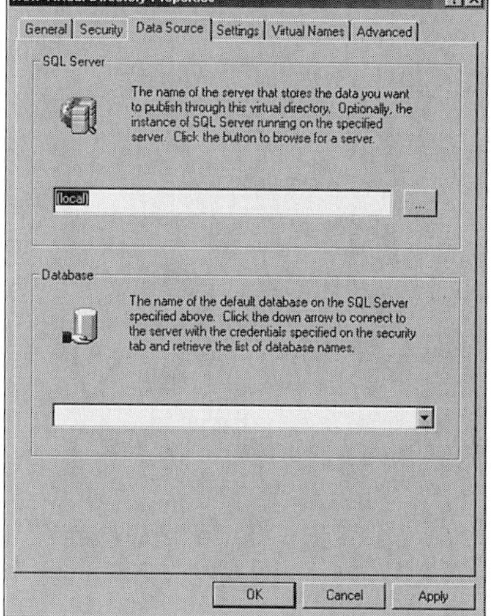

FIGURE 18.4
The Data Source page of the Virtual Directory Properties dialog box.

The "Virtual Names" page allows you to map various special virtual directories to your main SQL Server virtual directory. If you want to execute template queries, you'll need to at least create a template virtual directory here. If you want to use XPath queries, you'll need to create a schema virtual directory as well. Figure 18.6 shows you the "Virtual Names" page of the dialog box, whereas Figure 18.7 shows you the Virtual Name Configuration dialog box.

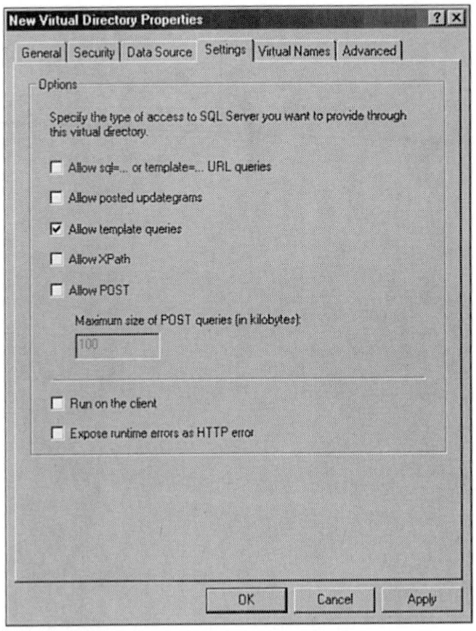

FIGURE 18.5
The Settings page of the Virtual Directory Properties dialog box.

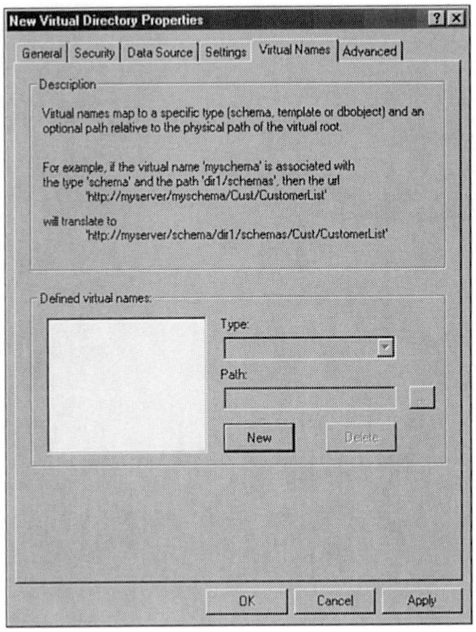

FIGURE 18.6
The Virtual Names page of the Virtual Directory Properties dialog box.

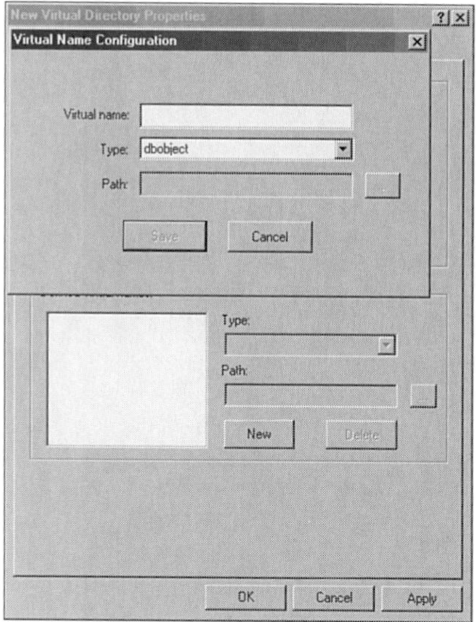

FIGURE 18.7
The Virtual Name Configuration dialog box.

There's one "Advanced" page on the dialog box for advanced configuration options. This page allows you to specify the SQL ISAPI DLL to use for the virtual directory as well as whether various items in memory, such as templates, schemas, and XSLT style sheets, should be cached. Figure 18.8 shows this final page.

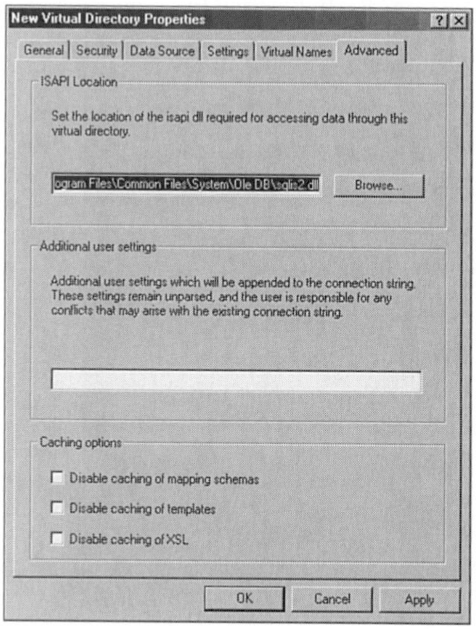

FIGURE 18.8
The Advanced page of the Virtual Directory Properties dialog box.

Once you've configured IIS to support XML for SQL Server 2000, you can begin accessing your new virtual directory via HTTP in the form of URL queries, template queries, and XPath queries.

URL Queries

The easiest way in which to test or become familiar with URL queries in SQL Server is to open Microsoft's Internet Explorer and enter queries into the address space available. It is important to keep in mind that the XML string returned by SQL Server 2000 is not well-formed XML; rather, it is an XML fragment. This is because there is no single root node from which all other nodes are children. However, a parameter can be passed along with the query itself to specify the root node, which will eliminate this problem by wrapping the returned XML string with the node specified.

For instance, the query

```
SELECT * FROM Customers
```

as a URL query looks like this:

```
http://localhost/sql2000?sql=Select+*+From+Customers+Where+
➥CustomerID+Like+'A%25'+For+XML+Auto&Root=Results
```

The preceding URL query returns all the records in the Customers table that have a CustomerID that begins with the letter *A*, wrapped with a root node called Results, as shown in Listing 18.1.

LISTING 18.1 The Output Returned from SQL Server 2000 for All Customers with a CustomerID beginning with *A*

```
<?xml version="1.0"?>

<Results>
  <Customers CustomerID="ALFKI" CompanyName="Alfreds
➥Futterkiste" ContactName="Maria Anders" ContactTitle=
➥"Sales Representative" Address="Obere Str. 57" City=
➥"Test" PostalCode="12209" Country="Germany" Phone=
➥"030-0074321" Fax="030-0076545"/>
  <Customers CustomerID="ANATR" CompanyName="Ana Trujillo
➥Emparedados y helados" ContactName="Ana Trujillo"
➥ContactTitle="Owner" Address="Avda. de la Constitución
➥2222" City="México D.F." PostalCode="05021" Country=
➥"Mexico" Phone="(5) 555-4729" Fax="(5) 555-3745"/>
  <Customers CustomerID="ANTON" CompanyName="Antonio Moreno
➥Taquería" ContactName="Antonio Moreno" ContactTitle=
➥"Owner" Address="Mataderos  2312" City="México D.F."
➥PostalCode="05023" Country="Mexico" Phone="(5) 555-3932"/>
```

LISTING 18.1 continued

```
  <Customers CustomerID="AROUT" CompanyName="Around the Horn"
➥ContactName="Thomas Hardy" ContactTitle="Sales
➥Representative" Address="120 Hanover Sq." City="London"
➥PostalCode="WA1 1DP" Country="UK" Phone="(171) 555-7788"
➥Fax="(171) 555-6750"/>
</Results>
```

In this example, each record is represented by a node called Customers whose attributes are the fields within the Customers table. The URL query used to return these results uses the `For XML Auto` clause. The `Auto` portion indicates to SQL ISAPI that it should produce an XML string with the specified table as the main element and that it should include the fields as attributes.

The `For XML Raw` clause will produce a slightly different XML grammar from the one created by `For XML Auto`.

For instance, the following URL query returns all records in the Customers table that have a CustomerID that begins with the letter *A*, wrapped in a root node called Results:

```
http://localhost/sql2000?sql=Select+*+From+Customers+Where+
➥CustomerID+Like+'A%25'+For+XML+Raw&Root=Results
```

The main difference here is that every record is represented by a tag named "row," as shown in Listing 18.2.

LISTING 18.2 Results Returned from SQL Server 2000 for All Customers with a CustomerID beginning with *A* Using the `For XML Raw` Clause

```
<?xml version="1.0"?>

<Results>
  <row CustomerID="ALFKI" CompanyName="Alfreds Futterkiste"
➥ContactName="Maria Anders" ContactTitle="Sales
➥Representative" Address="Obere Str. 57" City="Test"
➥PostalCode="12209" Country="Germany" Phone="030-0074321"
➥Fax="030-0076545"/>
  <row CustomerID="ANATR" CompanyName="Ana Trujillo Emparedados
➥y helados" ContactName="Ana Trujillo" ContactTitle=
➥"Owner" Address="Avda. de la Constitución 2222"
➥City="México D.F." PostalCode="05021" Country="Mexico"
➥Phone="(5) 555-4729" Fax="(5) 555-3745"/>
  <row CustomerID="ANTON" CompanyName="Antonio Moreno Taquería"
➥ContactName="Antonio Moreno" ContactTitle="Owner"
➥Address="Mataderos  2312" City="México D.F." PostalCode=
➥"05023" Country="Mexico" Phone="(5) 555-3932"/>
```

LISTING 18.2 continued

```
  <row CustomerID="AROUT" CompanyName="Around the Horn"
➥ContactName="Thomas Hardy" ContactTitle="Sales
➥Representative" Address="120 Hanover Sq." City="London"
➥PostalCode="WA1 1DP" Country="UK" Phone="(171) 555-7788"
➥Fax="(171) 555-6750"/>
</Results>
```

Both versions of the returned XML appear very similar to the way in which ADO stores and loads record sets in XML format. However, this may not always coincide with the grammar of XML that is expected within an application. For this reason, another parameter, `xsl`, can be included with the URL to specify an XSLT style sheet to use to transform the native XML grammar given by SQL Server 2000 into the expected grammar. Let's look at the following example of an XSLT style sheet called `Customers1.xsl`, which, in this case, resides in the root of the virtual directory SQL2000, as shown in Listing 18.3.

LISTING 18.3 `Customers1.xsl` Contains an XSLT Transformation for Use with Results Returned from SQL Server 2000

```
<?xml version="1.0"?>

<xsl:stylesheet xmlns:xsl="http://www.w3.org/1999/XSL/Transform"
➥version="1.0">
  <xsl:template match="/">

<CUSTOMERS>
  <xsl:for-each select="results/customers">

  <CUSTOMER>
    <CUSTOMERID><xsl:value-of select="@CustomerID"/></CUSTOMERID>
    <COMPANY><xsl:value-of select="@CompanyName"/></COMPANY>
    <CONTACT><xsl:value-of select="@ContactName"/></CONTACT>
    <ADDRESS><xsl:value-of select="@Address"/></ADDRESS>
    <CITY><xsl:value-of select="@City"/></CITY>
    <PHONE><xsl:value-of select="@Phone"/></PHONE>
  </CUSTOMER>

  </xsl:for-each>
</CUSTOMERS>

  </xsl:template>
</xsl:stylesheet>
```

As an example, the URL query

```
http://localhost/sql2000?sql=Select+*+From+Customers+Where+
➥+CustomerID+Like+'A%25'+For+XML+Auto&Root=Results&xsl=
➥Customers1.xsl
```

produces the results shown in Listing 18.4.

LISTING 18.4 Results Returned from SQL Server 2000 Using the `Customers1.xsl` Style Sheet to Transform the Native Results

```
<?xml version="1.0"?>

<CUSTOMERS>
  <CUSTOMER>
    <CUSTOMERID>ALFKI</CUSTOMERID>
    <COMPANY>Alfreds Futterkiste</COMPANY>
    <CONTACT>Maria Anders</CONTACT>
    <ADDRESS>Obere Str. 57</ADDRESS>
    <CITY>Test</CITY>
    <PHONE>030-0074321</PHONE>
  </CUSTOMER>
  <CUSTOMER>
    <CUSTOMERID>ANATR</CUSTOMERID>
    <COMPANY>Ana Trujillo Emparedados y helados</COMPANY>
    <CONTACT>Ana Trujillo</CONTACT>
    <ADDRESS>Avda. de la Constitución 2222</ADDRESS>
    <CITY>México D.F.</CITY>
    <PHONE>(5) 555-4729</PHONE>
  </CUSTOMER>
  <CUSTOMER>
    <CUSTOMERID>ANTON</CUSTOMERID>
    <COMPANY>Antonio Moreno Taquería</COMPANY>
    <CONTACT>Antonio Moreno</CONTACT>
    <ADDRESS>Mataderos  2312</ADDRESS>
    <CITY>México D.F.</CITY>
    <PHONE>(5) 555-3932</PHONE>
  </CUSTOMER>
  <CUSTOMER>
    <CUSTOMERID>AROUT</CUSTOMERID>
    <COMPANY>Around the Horn</COMPANY>
    <CONTACT>Thomas Hardy</CONTACT>
    <ADDRESS>120 Hanover Sq.</ADDRESS>
    <CITY>London</CITY>
    <PHONE>(171) 555-7788</PHONE>
  </CUSTOMER>
</CUSTOMERS>
```

In this case, our query is executed first, and then the XSLT style sheet is applied to perform the transformation.

Knowing that an XSLT style sheet can be applied to the result set, using another parameter (`contenttype`) will return the output in HTML format. Using the style sheet in Listing 18.5, coupled with the `contenttype` parameter, indicates that the resulting XML grammar should be interpreted as HTML.

LISTING 18.5 `Customers2.xsl` Contains an XSLT Transformation to Convert the Results into an HTML Table

```
<?xml version="1.0"?>

<xsl:stylesheet xmlns:xsl="http://www.w3.org/1999/XSL/Transform"
➥version="1.0">
  <xsl:template match="/">

<TABLE width="100%">
  <TR bgcolor="moccasin">
    <TD valign="top"><b>Customer Id</b></TD>
    <TD valign="top"><b>Company</b></TD>
    <TD valign="top"><b>Contact</b></TD>
    <TD valign="top"><b>Address</b></TD>
    <TD valign="top"><b>City</b></TD>
    <TD valign="top"><b>Phone</b></TD>
  </TR>

  <xsl:for-each select="Results/Customers">

    <TR bgcolor="white">
      <TD valign="top"><xsl:value-of select="@CustomerID"/></TD>
      <TD valign="top"><xsl:value-of select="@CompanyName"/></TD>
      <TD valign="top"><xsl:value-of select="@ContactName"/></TD>
      <TD valign="top"><xsl:value-of select="@Address"/></TD>
      <TD valign="top"><xsl:value-of select="@City"/></TD>
      <TD valign="top"><xsl:value-of select="@Phone"/></TD>
    </TR>

  </xsl:for-each>

</TABLE>

  </xsl:template>
</xsl:stylesheet>
```

Because we've specified that the content type should be text/HTML, a browser will be sure to interpret the resulting XML as HTML and display the results appropriately. In our case, by specifying the URL query

```
http://localhost/sql2000?sql=Select+*+From+Customers+Where+
➥+CustomerID+Like+'A%25'+For+XML+Auto&Root=Results&xsl=
➥Customers2.xsl&ContentType=text.html
```

we get the result set in Listing 18.6.

LISTING 18.6 The Results from Applying the `Customers2.xsl` Style Sheet to the Results Returned from SQL Server 2000

```
<?xml version="1.0"?>

<TABLE width="100%">
  <TR bgcolor="moccasin">
    <TD valign="top"><b>Customer Id</b></TD>
    <TD valign="top"><b>Company</b></TD>
    <TD valign="top"><b>Contact</b></TD>
    <TD valign="top"><b>Address</b></TD>
    <TD valign="top"><b>City</b></TD>
    <TD valign="top"><b>Phone</b></TD>
  </TR>
  <TR bgcolor="white">
    <TD valign="top">ALFKI</TD>
    <TD valign="top">Alfreds Futterkiste</TD>
    <TD valign="top">Maria Anders</TD>
    <TD valign="top">Obere Str. 57</TD>
    <TD valign="top">Test</TD>
    <TD valign="top">030-0074321</TD>
  </TR>
  <TR bgcolor="white">
    <TD valign="top">ANATR</TD>
    <TD valign="top">Ana Trujillo Emparedados y helados</TD>
    <TD valign="top">Ana Trujillo</TD>
    <TD valign="top">Avda. de la Constitución 2222</TD>
    <TD valign="top">México D.F.</TD>
    <TD valign="top">(5) 555-4729</TD>
  </TR>
  <TR bgcolor="white">
    <TD valign="top">ANTON</TD>
    <TD valign="top">Antonio Moreno Taquería</TD>
    <TD valign="top">Antonio Moreno</TD>
    <TD valign="top">Mataderos  2312</TD>
    <TD valign="top">México D.F.</TD>
    <TD valign="top">(5) 555-3932</TD>
  </TR>
  <TR bgcolor="white">
    <TD valign="top">AROUT</TD>
    <TD valign="top">Around the Horn</TD>
    <TD valign="top">Thomas Hardy</TD>
```

LISTING 18.6 continued

```
    <TD valign="top">120 Hanover Sq.</TD>
    <TD valign="top">London</TD>
    <TD valign="top">(171) 555-7788</TD>
  </TR>
</TABLE>
```

It is up to the individual browser to figure out how to display the resulting HTML. Also, some browsers, such as Internet Explorer version 6.0, will automatically interpret the resulting XML as HTML and display it appropriately even without the `contenttype` parameter being explicitly specified.

Template Queries

Another method of retrieving XML result sets from SQL Server 2000 is to template queries. These are XML files that tell SQL Server how to run queries, what the root node will be, what XSLT style sheet to apply, and so on. These files eliminate the need to specify a `SELECT` statement at the URL level.

In this case, our query (`Select * From Customers`), written as a template query, would appear as shown in Listing 18.7.

LISTING 18.7 `Customers1.xml` Contains a Template Query to Return All Customers from SQL Server 2000 Whose CustomerID Begins with *A*

```
<Results xmlns:sql="urn:schemas-microsoft-com:xml-sql">
  <sql:query>
    Select * From Customers Where CustomerID Like 'A%' For XML Auto
  </sql:query>
</Results>
```

Also, it returns the result set shown in Listing 18.8.

LISTING 18.8 The Results Returned from Navigating to the `Customers1.xml` Template Query

```
<?xml version="1.0"?>

<Results>
  <Customers CustomerID="ALFKI" CompanyName="Alfreds
➥Futterkiste" ContactName="Maria Anders" ContactTitle=
➥"Sales Representative" Address="Obere Str. 57" City=
➥"Test" PostalCode="12209" Country="Germany" Phone=
➥"030-0074321" Fax="030-0076545"/>
```

LISTING 18.8 continued

```
  <Customers CustomerID="ANATR" CompanyName="Ana Trujillo
➥Emparedados y helados" ContactName="Ana Trujillo"
➥ContactTitle="Owner" Address="Avda. de la Constitución
➥2222" City="México D.F." PostalCode="05021" Country=
➥"Mexico" Phone="(5) 555-4729" Fax="(5) 555-3745"/>
  <Customers CustomerID="ANTON" CompanyName="Antonio Moreno
➥Taquería" ContactName="Antonio Moreno" ContactTitle=
➥"Owner" Address="Mataderos  2312" City="México D.F."
➥PostalCode="05023" Country="Mexico" Phone="(5) 555-3932"/>
  <Customers CustomerID="AROUT" CompanyName="Around the Horn"
➥ContactName="Thomas Hardy" ContactTitle="Sales
➥Representative" Address="120 Hanover Sq." City="London"
➥PostalCode="WA1 1DP" Country="UK" Phone="(171) 555-7788"
➥Fax="(171) 555-6750"/>
</Results>
```

To run this query, save the template as `Customers1.xml` and store it in the template virtual directory beneath the main SQL Server 2000 virtual directory. Then, simply navigate to `http://localhost/sql2000/template/customers1.xml`, which returns the XML in the native SQL Server format.

Now let's replace the keyword `AUTO` with `RAW` in our template query, as shown in Listing 18.9.

LISTING 18.9 `Customers2.xml` Contains the Revised Query

```
<Results xmlns:sql="urn:schemas-microsoft-com:xml-sql">
  <sql:query>
    Select * From Customers Where CustomerID Like 'A%' For XML Raw
  </sql:query>
</Results>
```

Here's the result:

```
<?xml version="1.0"?>

<Results>
  <row CustomerID="ALFKI" CompanyName="Alfreds Futterkiste"
➥ContactName="Maria Anders" ContactTitle="Sales
➥Representative" Address="Obere Str. 57" City="Test"
➥PostalCode="12209" Country="Germany" Phone="030-0074321"
➥Fax="030-0076545"/>
  <row CustomerID="ANATR" CompanyName="Ana Trujillo Emparedados
➥y helados" ContactName="Ana Trujillo" ContactTitle=
➥"Owner" Address="Avda. de la Constitución 2222"
➥City="México D.F." PostalCode="05021" Country="Mexico"
➥Phone="(5) 555-4729" Fax="(5) 555-3745"/>
```

LISTING 18.9 continued

```
  <row CustomerID="ANTON" CompanyName="Antonio Moreno Taquería"
➥ContactName="Antonio Moreno" ContactTitle="Owner"
➥Address="Mataderos  2312" City="México D.F." PostalCode=
➥"05023" Country="Mexico" Phone="(5) 555-3932"/>
  <row CustomerID="AROUT" CompanyName="Around the Horn"
➥ContactName="Thomas Hardy" ContactTitle="Sales
➥Representative" Address="120 Hanover Sq." City="London"
➥PostalCode="WA1 1DP" Country="UK" Phone="(171) 555-7788"
➥Fax="(171) 555-6750"/>
</Results>
```

To apply a style sheet to the result set, the template query would appear as shown in Listing 18.10.

LISTING 18.10 `Customers3.xml` Contains the Query to Execute and the Location of Style Sheet to Use to Transform the Results

```
<Results xmlns:sql="urn:schemas-microsoft-com:xml-sql"
➥sql:xsl='../Customers1.xsl'>
  <sql:query>
    Select * From Customers Where CustomerID Like 'A%' For XML Auto
  </sql:query>
</Results>
```

This returns the results shown in Listing 18.11.

LISTING 18.11 The Results from Navigating to the `Customers3.xml` Template QUERY

```
<?xml version="1.0"?>

<CUSTOMERS>
  <CUSTOMER>
    <CUSTOMERID>ALFKI</CUSTOMERID>
    <COMPANY>Alfreds Futterkiste</COMPANY>
    <CONTACT>Maria Anders</CONTACT>
    <ADDRESS>Obere Str. 57</ADDRESS>
    <CITY>Test</CITY>
    <PHONE>030-0074321</PHONE>
  </CUSTOMER>
  <CUSTOMER>
    <CUSTOMERID>ANATR</CUSTOMERID>
    <COMPANY>Ana Trujillo Emparedados y helados</COMPANY>
    <CONTACT>Ana Trujillo</CONTACT>
    <ADDRESS>Avda. de la Constitución 2222</ADDRESS>
    <CITY>México D.F.</CITY>
    <PHONE>(5) 555-4729</PHONE>
```

LISTING 18.11 continued

```
  </CUSTOMER>
  <CUSTOMER>
    <CUSTOMERID>ANTON</CUSTOMERID>
    <COMPANY>Antonio Moreno Taquería</COMPANY>
    <CONTACT>Antonio Moreno</CONTACT>
    <ADDRESS>Mataderos  2312</ADDRESS>
    <CITY>México D.F.</CITY>
    <PHONE>(5) 555-3932</PHONE>
  </CUSTOMER>
  <CUSTOMER>
    <CUSTOMERID>AROUT</CUSTOMERID>
    <COMPANY>Around the Horn</COMPANY>
    <CONTACT>Thomas Hardy</CONTACT>
    <ADDRESS>120 Hanover Sq.</ADDRESS>
    <CITY>London</CITY>
    <PHONE>(171) 555-7788</PHONE>
  </CUSTOMER>
</CUSTOMERS>
```

As is the case with URL queries, you can format the final results to be displayed in HTML. In this case, simply change `Customers1.xsl` to `Customers2.xsl`. The result is the HTML table created earlier, as shown in Listing 18.12.

LISTING 18.12 The Results from Using the `Customers2.xsl` Style Sheet Instead in the `Customers3.xml` Template Query

```
<?xml version="1.0"?>

<TABLE width="100%">
  <TR bgcolor="moccasin">
    <TD valign="top"><b>Customer Id</b></TD>
    <TD valign="top"><b>Company</b></TD>
    <TD valign="top"><b>Contact</b></TD>
    <TD valign="top"><b>Address</b></TD>
    <TD valign="top"><b>City</b></TD>
    <TD valign="top"><b>Phone</b></TD>
  </TR>
  <TR bgcolor="white">
    <TD valign="top">ALFKI</TD>
    <TD valign="top">Alfreds Futterkiste</TD>
    <TD valign="top">Maria Anders</TD>
    <TD valign="top">Obere Str. 57</TD>
    <TD valign="top">Test</TD>
    <TD valign="top">030-0074321</TD>
  </TR>
  <TR bgcolor="white">
    <TD valign="top">ANATR</TD>
```

LISTING 18.12 continued

```
    <TD valign="top">Ana Trujillo Emparedados y helados</TD>
    <TD valign="top">Ana Trujillo</TD>
    <TD valign="top">Avda. de la Constitución 2222</TD>
    <TD valign="top">México D.F.</TD>
    <TD valign="top">(5) 555-4729</TD>
  </TR>
  <TR bgcolor="white">
    <TD valign="top">ANTON</TD>
    <TD valign="top">Antonio Moreno Taquería</TD>
    <TD valign="top">Antonio Moreno</TD>
    <TD valign="top">Mataderos  2312</TD>
    <TD valign="top">México D.F.</TD>
    <TD valign="top">(5) 555-3932</TD>
  </TR>
  <TR bgcolor="white">
    <TD valign="top">AROUT</TD>
    <TD valign="top">Around the Horn</TD>
    <TD valign="top">Thomas Hardy</TD>
    <TD valign="top">120 Hanover Sq.</TD>
    <TD valign="top">London</TD>
    <TD valign="top">(171) 555-7788</TD>
  </TR>
</TABLE>
```

Template queries can also accept parameters to help filter the result set. Specifying that we only want the customers whose CustomerID begins with the letter *A* is kind of short sighted. It would make a lot more sense to allow the value of the CustomerID to vary. Therefore, the template file could be rewritten as shown in Listing 18.13.

LISTING 18.13 `Customers4.xml` Contains a Parameterized Template QUERY

```
<Results xmlns:sql="urn:schemas-microsoft-com:xml-sql" >
  <sql:header>
    <sql:param name='CustomerId'>%</sql:param>
  </sql:header>
  <sql:query>
    Select * From Customers Where CustomerID Like @CustomerId For XML Auto
  </sql:query>
</Results>
```

In this example, we specify that the template query will accept one parameter, `CustomerId`, and that this parameter has a default value of `%`, which, in conjunction with the query, will return all records from the Customers table. To execute this query, we just provide the following URL:

```
http://localhost/sql2000/template/customers.xml?CustomerId=A%25
```

Now we can return any number of records from the Customers table. For instance, if we supply the URL

```
http://localhost/sql2000/template/customers.xml?CustomerId=B%25
```

we'd get the result set shown in Listing 18.14.

LISTING 18.14 The Results from Navigating to the `Customers4.xml` Template Query

```
<Results xmlns:sql="urn:schemas-microsoft-com:xml-sql">

  <Customers CustomerID="BERGS" CompanyName="Berglunds snabbköp"
➥ContactName="Christina Berglund" ContactTitle=
➥"Order Administrator" Address="Berguvsvägen  8" City=
➥"Luleå" PostalCode="S-958 22" Country="Sweden" Phone=
➥"0921-12 34 65" Fax="0921-12 34 67"/>
  <Customers CustomerID="BLAUS" CompanyName="Blauer See
➥Delikatessen" ContactName="Hanna Moos" ContactTitle=
➥"Sales Representative" Address="Forsterstr. 57" City=
➥"Mannheim" PostalCode="68306" Country="Germany" Phone=
➥"0621-08460" Fax="0621-08924"/>
  <Customers CustomerID="BLONP" CompanyName="Blondesddsl père
➥et fils" ContactName="Frédérique Citeaux" ContactTitle=
➥"Marketing Manager" Address="24, place Kléber" City=
➥"Strasbourg" PostalCode="67000" Country="France" Phone=
➥"88.60.15.31" Fax="88.60.15.32"/>
  <Customers CustomerID="BOLID" CompanyName="Bólido Comidas
➥preparadas" ContactName="Martín Sommer" ContactTitle=
➥"Owner" Address="C/ Araquil, 67" City="Madrid"
➥PostalCode="28023" Country="Spain" Phone=
➥"(91) 555 22 82" Fax="(91) 555 91 99"/>
<Customers CustomerID="BONAP" CompanyName="Bon app'" ContactName=
➥"Laurence Lebihan" ContactTitle="Owner" Address=
➥"12, rue des Bouchers" City="Marseille" PostalCode=
➥"13008" Country="France" Phone="91.24.45.40" Fax=
➥"91.24.45.41"/>
  <Customers CustomerID="BOTTM" CompanyName="Bottom-Dollar
➥Markets" ContactName="Elizabeth Lincoln" ContactTitle=
➥"Accounting Manager" Address="23 Tsawassen Blvd." City=
➥"Tsawassen" Region="BC" PostalCode="T2F 8M4" Country=
➥"Canada" Phone="(604) 555-4729" Fax="(604) 555-3745"/>
  <Customers CustomerID="BSBEV" CompanyName="B's Beverages"
➥ContactName="Victoria Ashworth" ContactTitle="Sales
➥Representative" Address="Fauntleroy Circus" City=
➥"London" PostalCode="EC2 5NT" Country="UK" Phone=
➥"(171) 555-1212"/>

</Results>
```

XPath Queries

Previously, when SQL Server 2000 initially shipped at the beginning of 2001, support had not been included for annotated XSD schemas. Therefore, everyone was forced to create annotated XDR schemas. However, with Web Release 2 for SQL Server 2000, support for creating annotated XSD schemas has been added. Although annotated XDR schemas are still supported for backward compatibility, the XDR schemas will most likely be phased out in favor of the XSD schemas.

Two basic attributes and one basic element are needed to author annotated XSD schemas. The attributes needed are `sql:field` and `sql:relation`. The element is `sql:relationship`. The `sql:relation` attribute is used to map an element to a table. This has the effect of creating one XML element for every record in the table. The `sql:field` attribute is used to map a particular attribute or node value to a field from the related table. The `sql:relationship` element is used to relate elements within the XML document to other elements. It defines the two tables and the join condition necessary to relate them together.

Using those attributes and elements, an annotated XSD schema can be authored to return data from SQL Server 2000 in a specific format. The only required attribute is `sql:relation`. This attribute refers to a table or view in the database and can be placed on an element in the XSD schema. The schema shown in Listing 18.15 is a simple example of using an `sql:relation` attribute in an annotated XSD schema for the Customers table in the Northwind database.

LISTING 18.15 `Customers1.xsd` Contains an Annotated XSD Schema for Customers Within the Northwind Database

```
<?xml version="1.0" encoding="UTF-8"?>
<xsd:schema xmlns:xsd="http://www.w3.org/2001/XMLSchema"
➥xmlns:sql="urn:schemas-microsoft-com:mapping-schema">
  <xsd:element name="CUSTOMER" sql:relation="Customers">
    <xsd:complexType>
      <xsd:attribute name="CustomerID" type="xsd:string"/>
      <xsd:attribute name="CompanyName" type="xsd:string"/>
      <xsd:attribute name="ContactName" type="xsd:string"/>
      <xsd:attribute name="Address" type="xsd:string"/>
      <xsd:attribute name="City" type="xsd:string"/>
      <xsd:attribute name="Phone" type="xsd:string"/>
    </xsd:complexType>
  </xsd:element>
</xsd:schema>
```

Because the sql:relation attribute is specified on an xsd:element element within our schema, the relation is inherited by all elements and attributes contained within the element declaration. This means we do not need to specify the sql:relation attribute on every <element> or <attribute> element within our schema. Because we defined our attribute names exactly how they exist in the Northwind database, we don't need to use the sql:field attribute. Keep in mind that XML is case sensitive. Therefore, the attribute names defined earlier must match exactly with the field names defined in the database for this XSD schema to work. This schema, when used for an XPath query for all customers within the City of London, returns an XML document whose structure matches that of the one defined in the schema, as shown here:

```
<?xml version="1.0"?>

<Results>
  <CUSTOMER City="London" CompanyName="Around the Horn"
➥CustomerID="AROUT" Address="120 Hanover Sq."
➥ContactName="Thomas Hardy" Phone="(171) 555-7788"/>
  <CUSTOMER City="London" CompanyName="B's Beverages"
➥CustomerID="BSBEV" Address="Fauntleroy Circus"
➥ContactName="Victoria Ashworth" Phone="(171) 555-1212"/>
  <CUSTOMER City="London" CompanyName="Consolidated Holdings"
➥CustomerID="CONSH" Address="Berkeley Gardens 12  Brewery"
➥ContactName="Elizabeth Brown" Phone="(171) 555-2282"/>
  <CUSTOMER City="London" CompanyName="Eastern Connection"
➥CustomerID="EASTC" Address="35 King George" ContactName=
➥"Ann Devon" Phone="(171) 555-0297"/>
  <CUSTOMER City="London" CompanyName="North/South" CustomerID=
➥"NORTS" Address="South House 300 Queensbridge"
➥ContactName="Simon Crowther" Phone="(171) 555-7733"/>
  <CUSTOMER City="London" CompanyName="Seven Seas Imports"
➥CustomerID="SEVES" Address="90 Wadhurst Rd."
➥ContactName="Hari Kumar" Phone="(171) 555-1717"/>
</Results>
```

The sql:field attribute may be used in conjunction with the sql:relation attribute to create elements or attributes that do not exactly match their definitions in the database, as demonstrated by the annotated XSD schema shown in Listing 18.16.

LISTING 18.16 Customers2.xsd Demonstrates How Fields from the Database Are Mapped to Attributes Within the Output XML Document

```
<?xml version="1.0" encoding="UTF-8"?>
<xsd:schema xmlns:sql="urn:schemas-microsoft-com:mapping-schema"
➥xmlns:xsd="http://www.w3.org/2001/XMLSchema">
  <xsd:element name="CUSTOMER" sql:relation="Customers">
    <xsd:complexType>
      <xsd:attribute name="Id" type="xsd:string" sql:field="CustomerID"/>
```

LISTING 18.16 continued

```
      <xsd:attribute name="Company" type="xsd:string" sql:field="CompanyName"/>
      <xsd:attribute name="Contact" type="xsd:string" sql:field="ContactName"/>
      <xsd:attribute name="Address" type="xsd:string"/>
      <xsd:attribute name="City" type="xsd:string"/>
      <xsd:attribute name="Phone" type="xsd:string"/>
    </xsd:complexType>
  </xsd:element>
</xsd:schema>
```

When the schema in Listing 18.16 is used in the same XPath query, it will return the following XML result set:

```
<?xml version="1.0"?>

<Results>
  <CUSTOMER City="London" Id="AROUT" Company="Around the Horn"
➥Address="120 Hanover Sq." Phone="(171) 555-7788"
➥Contact="Thomas Hardy"/>
  <CUSTOMER City="London" Id="BSBEV" Company="B's Beverages"
➥Address="Fauntleroy Circus" Phone="(171) 555-1212"
➥Contact="Victoria Ashworth"/>
  <CUSTOMER City="London" Id="CONSH" Company="Consolidated
➥Holdings" Address="Berkeley Gardens 12  Brewery"
➥Phone="(171) 555-2282" Contact="Elizabeth Brown"/>
  <CUSTOMER City="London" Id="EASTC" Company="Eastern Connection"
➥Address="35 King George" Phone="(171) 555-0297"
➥Contact="Ann Devon"/>
  <CUSTOMER City="London" Id="NORTS" Company="North/South"
➥Address="South House 300 Queensbridge" Phone=
➥"(171) 555-7733" Contact="Simon Crowther"/>
  <CUSTOMER City="London" Id="SEVES" Company="Seven Seas Imports"
➥Address="90 Wadhurst Rd." Phone="(171) 555-1717"
➥Contact="Hari Kumar"/>
</Results>
```

Now let's say we don't like having the fields mapped to attributes. Instead, we could use the schema in Listing 18.17 to produce an XML document with elements for the fields in the Customers table.

LISTING 18.17 `Customers3.xsd` Demonstrates How Fields from the Database Can Be Mapped to Elements Within the Output XML Document

```
<?xml version="1.0" encoding="UTF-8"?>
<xsd:schema xmlns:xsd="http://www.w3.org/2001/XMLSchema"
➥xmlns:sql="urn:schemas-microsoft-com:mapping-schema">
  <xsd:element name="CUSTOMER" sql:relation="Customers">
    <xsd:complexType>
```

LISTING 18.17 continued

```
      <xsd:all>
        <xsd:element name="CUSTOMERID" type="xsd:string"
➥sql:field="CustomerID"/>
        <xsd:element name="COMPANY" type="xsd:string"
➥sql:field="CompanyName"/>
        <xsd:element name="CONTACT" type="xsd:string"
➥sql:field="ContactName"/>
        <xsd:element name="ADDRESS" type="xsd:string"
➥sql:field="Address"/>
        <xsd:element name="CITY" type="xsd:string"
➥sql:field="City"/>
        <xsd:element name="PHONE" type="xsd:string"
➥sql:field="Phone"/>
      </xsd:all>
    </xsd:complexType>
  </xsd:element>
</xsd:schema>
```

If we use the preceding annotated XSD schema in the same XPath query as before, the XML shown in Listing 18.18 is returned by SQL Server 2000.

LISTING 18.18 The Resulting XML Document from Executing an XPath Query Against the `Customers3.xsd` Schema

```
<?xml version="1.0"?>

<Results>
  <CUSTOMER>
    <CUSTOMERID>AROUT</CUSTOMERID>
    <COMPANY>Around the Horn</COMPANY>
    <CONTACT>Thomas Hardy</CONTACT>
    <ADDRESS>120 Hanover Sq.</ADDRESS>
    <CITY>London</CITY>
    <PHONE>(171) 555-7788</PHONE>
  </CUSTOMER>
  <CUSTOMER>
    <CUSTOMERID>BSBEV</CUSTOMERID>
    <COMPANY>B's Beverages</COMPANY>
    <CONTACT>Victoria Ashworth</CONTACT>
    <ADDRESS>Fauntleroy Circus</ADDRESS>
    <CITY>London</CITY>
    <PHONE>(171) 555-1212</PHONE>
  </CUSTOMER>
  <CUSTOMER>
    <CUSTOMERID>CONSH</CUSTOMERID>
    <COMPANY>Consolidated Holdings</COMPANY>
    <CONTACT>Elizabeth Brown</CONTACT>
```

LISTING 18.18 continued

```
    <ADDRESS>Berkeley Gardens 12  Brewery</ADDRESS>
    <CITY>London</CITY>
    <PHONE>(171) 555-2282</PHONE>
  </CUSTOMER>
  <CUSTOMER>
    <CUSTOMERID>EASTC</CUSTOMERID>
    <COMPANY>Eastern Connection</COMPANY>
    <CONTACT>Ann Devon</CONTACT>
    <ADDRESS>35 King George</ADDRESS>
    <CITY>London</CITY>
    <PHONE>(171) 555-0297</PHONE>
  </CUSTOMER>
  <CUSTOMER>
    <CUSTOMERID>NORTS</CUSTOMERID>
    <COMPANY>North/South</COMPANY>
    <CONTACT>Simon Crowther</CONTACT>
    <ADDRESS>South House 300 Queensbridge</ADDRESS>
    <CITY>London</CITY>
    <PHONE>(171) 555-7733</PHONE>
  </CUSTOMER>
  <CUSTOMER>
    <CUSTOMERID>SEVES</CUSTOMERID>
    <COMPANY>Seven Seas Imports</COMPANY>
    <CONTACT>Hari Kumar</CONTACT>
    <ADDRESS>90 Wadhurst Rd.</ADDRESS>
    <CITY>London</CITY>
    <PHONE>(171) 555-1717</PHONE>
  </CUSTOMER>
</Results>
```

In addition to using the `sql:relation` and `sql:field` attributes, we can use the `sql:relationship` element, which must be used within the `<xsd:appinfo>` element, to produce nested XML documents in which elements may contain related child elements. Four attributes of the `sql:relationship` element must be specified: `parent`, `parent-key`, `child`, and `child-key`. The `parent` attribute specifies the parent table, and the `parent-key` attribute specifies the key on the parent table to use to relate it to a child table. The `child` attribute specifies the child table, and the `child-key` attribute specifies the key on the child table used to relate it to the parent table. When these four attributes are used in conjunction with the `sql:relationship` element, SQL Server 2000 is able to relate and nest XML elements using the values specified in the attributes of the `sql:relationship` element, as shown in the annotated XSD schema in Listing 18.19.

LISTING 18.19 `Customers4.xsd` Demonstrates How to Create a Relationship Between Two Tables

```
<?xml version="1.0" encoding="UTF-8"?>
<xsd:schema xmlns:sql="urn:schemas-microsoft-com:mapping-schema"
➥xmlns:xsd="http://www.w3.org/2001/XMLSchema">
  <xsd:element name="CUSTOMER" sql:relation="Customers">
    <xsd:complexType>
      <xsd:sequence>
        <xsd:element name="CUSTOMERID" type="xsd:string"
➥sql:field="CustomerID"/>
        <xsd:element name="COMPANY" type="xsd:string"
➥sql:field="CompanyName"/>
        <xsd:element name="CONTACT" type="xsd:string"
➥sql:field="ContactName"/>
        <xsd:element name="ADDRESS" type="xsd:string"
➥sql:field="Address"/>
        <xsd:element name="CITY" type="xsd:string"
➥sql:field="City"/>
        <xsd:element name="PHONE" type="xsd:string"
➥sql:field="Phone"/>

        <xsd:element name="ORDER" maxOccurs="unbounded"
➥sql:relation="Orders">
          <xsd:annotation>
            <xsd:appinfo>
              <sql:relationship parent="Customers" parent-key=
➥"CustomerID" child="Orders" child-key="CustomerID"/>
            </xsd:appinfo>
          </xsd:annotation>

          <xsd:complexType>
            <xsd:sequence>
              <xsd:element name="ORDERID" type="xsd:integer"
➥sql:field="OrderID"/>
              <xsd:element name="ORDERDATE" type="xsd:date"
➥sql:field="OrderDate"/>

              <xsd:element name="DETAILS" maxOccurs="unbounded"
➥sql:relation="[Order Details]">
                <xsd:annotation>
                  <xsd:appinfo>
                    <sql:relationship parent="Orders" parent-key=
➥"OrderID" child="[Order Details]" child-key="OrderID"/>
                  </xsd:appinfo>
                </xsd:annotation>
```

LISTING 18.19 continued

```
                <xsd:complexType>
                  <xsd:sequence>
                    <xsd:element name="ORDERID" type=
➥"xsd:integer" sql:field="OrderID"/>
                    <xsd:element name="PRODUCTID" type=
➥"xsd:integer" sql:field="ProductID"/>
                    <xsd:element name="UNITPRICE" sql:field=
➥"UnitPrice">
                      <xsd:simpleType>
                        <xsd:restriction base="xsd:decimal">
                          <xsd:fractionDigits value="2"/>
                        </xsd:restriction>
                      </xsd:simpleType>
                    </xsd:element>
                    <xsd:element name="QUANTITY" type=
➥"xsd:positiveInteger" sql:field="Quantity"/>
                  </xsd:sequence>
                </xsd:complexType>
              </xsd:element>
            </xsd:sequence>
          </xsd:complexType>
        </xsd:element>
      </xsd:sequence>
    </xsd:complexType>
  </xsd:element>
</xsd:schema>
```

Performing an XPath query for the customer with the CustomerID ALFKI against the preceding annotated XSD schema will produce the following result shown in Listing 18.20.

LISTING 18.20 The Results from an XPath Query Against `Customers4.xsd`

```
<?xml version="1.0"?>

<Results>
  <CUSTOMER>
    <CUSTOMERID>ALFKI</CUSTOMERID>
    <COMPANY>Alfreds Futterkiste</COMPANY>
    <CONTACT>Maria Anders</CONTACT>
    <ADDRESS>Obere Str. 57</ADDRESS>
    <CITY>Test</CITY>
    <PHONE>030-0074321</PHONE>
    <ORDER>
      <ORDERID>10643</ORDERID>
      <ORDERDATE>1997-08-25</ORDERDATE>
      <DETAILS>
```

LISTING 18.20 continued

```
        <ORDERID>10643</ORDERID>
        <PRODUCTID>28</PRODUCTID>
        <UNITPRICE>45.6</UNITPRICE>
        <QUANTITY>15</QUANTITY>
      </DETAILS>
      <DETAILS>
        <ORDERID>10643</ORDERID>
        <PRODUCTID>39</PRODUCTID>
        <UNITPRICE>18</UNITPRICE>
        <QUANTITY>21</QUANTITY>
      </DETAILS>
      <DETAILS>
        <ORDERID>10643</ORDERID>
        <PRODUCTID>46</PRODUCTID>
        <UNITPRICE>12</UNITPRICE>
        <QUANTITY>2</QUANTITY>
      </DETAILS>
    </ORDER>
    <ORDER>
      <ORDERID>10692</ORDERID>
      <ORDERDATE>1997-10-03</ORDERDATE>
      <DETAILS>
        <ORDERID>10692</ORDERID>
        <PRODUCTID>63</PRODUCTID>
        <UNITPRICE>43.9</UNITPRICE>
        <QUANTITY>20</QUANTITY>
      </DETAILS>
    </ORDER>
    <ORDER>
      <ORDERID>10702</ORDERID>
      <ORDERDATE>1997-10-13</ORDERDATE>
      <DETAILS>
        <ORDERID>10702</ORDERID>
        <PRODUCTID>3</PRODUCTID>
        <UNITPRICE>10</UNITPRICE>
        <QUANTITY>6</QUANTITY>
      </DETAILS>
      <DETAILS>
        <ORDERID>10702</ORDERID>
        <PRODUCTID>76</PRODUCTID>
        <UNITPRICE>18</UNITPRICE>
        <QUANTITY>15</QUANTITY>
      </DETAILS>
    </ORDER>
    <ORDER>
      <ORDERID>10835</ORDERID>
      <ORDERDATE>1998-01-15</ORDERDATE>
      <DETAILS>
        <ORDERID>10835</ORDERID>
```

LISTING 18.20 continued

```
        <PRODUCTID>59</PRODUCTID>
        <UNITPRICE>55</UNITPRICE>
        <QUANTITY>15</QUANTITY>
      </DETAILS>
      <DETAILS>
        <ORDERID>10835</ORDERID>
        <PRODUCTID>77</PRODUCTID>
        <UNITPRICE>13</UNITPRICE>
        <QUANTITY>2</QUANTITY>
      </DETAILS>
    </ORDER>
    <ORDER>
      <ORDERID>10952</ORDERID>
      <ORDERDATE>1998-03-16</ORDERDATE>
      <DETAILS>
        <ORDERID>10952</ORDERID>
        <PRODUCTID>6</PRODUCTID>
        <UNITPRICE>25</UNITPRICE>
        <QUANTITY>16</QUANTITY>
      </DETAILS>
      <DETAILS>
        <ORDERID>10952</ORDERID>
        <PRODUCTID>28</PRODUCTID>
        <UNITPRICE>45.6</UNITPRICE>
        <QUANTITY>2</QUANTITY>
      </DETAILS>
    </ORDER>
    <ORDER>
      <ORDERID>11011</ORDERID>
      <ORDERDATE>1998-04-09</ORDERDATE>
      <DETAILS>
        <ORDERID>11011</ORDERID>
        <PRODUCTID>58</PRODUCTID>
        <UNITPRICE>13.25</UNITPRICE>
        <QUANTITY>40</QUANTITY>
      </DETAILS>
      <DETAILS>
        <ORDERID>11011</ORDERID>
        <PRODUCTID>71</PRODUCTID>
        <UNITPRICE>21.5</UNITPRICE>
        <QUANTITY>20</QUANTITY>
      </DETAILS>
    </ORDER>
  </CUSTOMER>
</Results>
```

But wait, why is there so much interest in creating annotated XSD schemas? Unfortunately, these files have to exist to perform an XPath query. Basically, to perform an XPath query, the syntax is as follows:

```
http://servername/sqlvirtualdirectory/schemavirtualdirectory/
➥schemafilename/Xpathexpression?Root=RootNodeName
```

Because we've already covered the syntax for XPath expressions in Chapter 4, "Creating XML Schemas," we will not go over it again here. The main difference you need to keep in mind is the exclusion of the root element within the expression because it is not defined within the schema. For instance, the following XPath query would result in an error:

```
http://localhost/sql2000/schema/customers.xsd/Results/CUSTOMER?
➥Root=Results
```

Instead, you need to write this XPath query as follows:

```
http://localhost/sql2000/schema/customers.xsd/CUSTOMER?Root=Results
```

XML Updategrams

Rather than having to code multiple stored procedures to handle the inserting, updating, and deleting of records within a database, you can use XML updategrams instead. These XML documents are posted to SQL Server's virtual directory and are intercepted by the SQL ISAPI extension. By using various elements within an XML updategram, SQL Server can modify the data in the database accordingly.

The basic premise behind an XML updategram is that it behaves the same as a template and uses a snapshot of information, both before and after changes are made to the XML fragment, to determine how SQL Server must proceed. By using a combination of `<sync>` elements, which mark the beginning and end of a transaction, and `<before>` and `<after>` elements, SQL Server can determine whether a new record is being created or an existing record is being modified or deleted.

The `<before>` element identifies what the database's existing state is. The `<after>` element tells what the database's new state will be. The `<sync>` element indicates what a transaction encompasses. It contains one or more `<before>` and `<after>` elements, and all the pairs within a `<sync>` element will be executed as one transaction. Therefore, either everything within a `<sync>` element will be performed, or nothing will be performed.

Here's the basic structure of an XML updategram:

```
<ROOT xmlns:updg="urn:schemas-microsoft-com:xml-updategram">
  <updg:sync [mapping-schema= "XDRSchemaFile.xml"]>
    <updg:before>
       ...
    </updg:before>
    <updg:after>
       ...
    </updg:after>
  </updg:sync>
</ROOT>
```

Note the inclusion of the updategram namespace: `urn:schemas-microsoft-com:xml-updategram`. This namespace is required for XML updategrams. However, the actual namespace you decide to use within your updategrams is completely up to you. For instance, the following is also a perfectly valid XML updategram structure:

```
<ROOT xmlns:eps="urn:schemas-microsoft-com:xml-updategram">
  <eps:sync [mapping-schema="XDRSchemaFile.xml"]>
    <eps:before>
       ...
    </eps:before>
    <eps:after>
       ...
    </eps:after>
  </eps:sync>
</ROOT>
```

An XML updategram determines what function to perform based on the contents of the `<before>` and `<after>` elements, which is outlined as follows:

- If a record's XML definition appears only in the `<before>` element with no corresponding definition in the `<after>` element, the XML updategram performs a delete operation.
- If a record's XML appears only in the `<after>` element with no corresponding XML in the `<before>` element, an insert operation is performed.
- If the XML for a record appears in the `<before>` element and has a corresponding definition in the `<after>` element, an update operation is performed. In this case, the updategram updates the record instance to the values specified in the `<after>` element.

Mapping the XML to the Database

An XML updategram can map the XML back into the database either implicitly or explicitly. In other words, specifying the XDR schema in the updategram is optional as long as you follow a few simple rules. First and foremost, remember that you must use

FOR XML AUTO or FOR XML AUTO,ELEMENTS in order to use the default mapping that SQL ISAPI provides.

In simple insert, update, and delete scenarios, implicit mapping may be enough to perform the necessary operation on the given XML fragment. SQL ISAPI will attempt to map the elements and attributes back to the database in a fashion that's similar to how it maps the database to an XML fragment using FOR XML AUTO. The key for this approach to work, however, is that each element, which represents a table, must be named the same as the table name. Remember, XML is case sensitive. Also, each element or attribute that represents a field must be named likewise. For instance, the following XML updategram will insert a new customer into the Customers table of the Northwind database:

```
<ROOT xmlns:updg="urn:schemas-microsoft-com:xml-updategram">
   <updg:sync >
      <updg:before>
      </updg:before>
      <updg:after>
         <Customers CustomerID="TEST" CompanyName="Test insert comp."/>
      </updg:after>
   </updg:sync>
</ROOT>
```


By examining the preceding XML updategram, you can see how SQL Server identifies how it must behave. Given this XML updategram, SQL ISAPI sees that there is nothing in the <before> element that corresponds to anything in the <after> element, so it determines that an insert operation must be performed. SQL ISAPI also examines the contents of the <after> element and determines from the existence of the <Customers> element that a new record will be inserted into the Customers table. Furthermore, SQL ISAPI realizes that two fields will have values specified for them—CustomerID and CompanyName—based on the occurrence of attributes with those names.

For complex mappings, you can explicitly identify an annotated XSD schema to use in order to map the elements and attributes back to the appropriate tables and fields in the database. Each transaction unit, identified by a <sync> element, can have its own mapping schema to use to map elements and attributes back into the database.

Implicit Mapping in Updategrams

An element-centric updategram is comprised of elements that contain subelements. The elements map to a table in the database, and the subelements map to fields within that table. Therefore, to use element-centric mapping, we need an XML document that looks something like this:

```
<Customers>
   <CustomerID>TEST</CustomerID>
   <CompanyName>Test insert comp</CompanyName>
</Customers>
```

In this case, to perform an insert operation, we would construct the following updategram:

```
<ROOT xmlns:updg="urn:schemas-microsoft-com:xml-updategram">
   <updg:sync >
      <updg:after>
         <Customers>
                  <CustomerID>TEST</CustomerID>
                  <CompanyName>Test insert comp</CompanyName>
               </Customers>
      </updg:after>
   </updg:sync>
</ROOT>
```

Note

Although, this time, there is no `<before>` element, the updategram will still work. That's because for an insert operation, there is no corresponding information for the record; therefore, the `<before>` element is optional. The same holds true for a delete operation. Because there will not be any corresponding information after the deletion, the `<after>` element can be omitted.

For attribute-centric mappings, the `table` element contains attributes that map to fields within the table. Therefore, the previous example could be represented in an attribute-centric approach by using an XML document, like this:

```
<Customers CustomerID="TEST" CompanyName="Test insert comp"/>
```

An XML updategram like this one would also be used:

```
<ROOT xmlns:updg="urn:schemas-microsoft-com:xml-updategram">
   <updg:sync >
      <updg:after>
         <Customers CustomerID="TEST" CompanyName="Test insert comp"/>
      </updg:after>
   </updg:sync>
</ROOT>
```

Interestingly enough, a combination of element-centric and attribute-centric mappings can be used. As long as the elements and attributes map back into the database using the default mapping provided by `FOR XML AUTO`, the two approaches can be mixed. For instance, imagine the following XML document:

```
<Customers CustomerID="Test">
   <CompanyName>Test insert comp</CompanyName>
</Customers>
```

This record could be inserted into SQL Server by using an XML updategram like the following:

```
<ROOT xmlns:updg="urn:schemas-microsoft-com:xml-updategram">
   <updg:sync >
      <updg:after>
         <Customers CustomerID="TEST">
            <CompanyName>Test insert comp</CompanyName>
         </Customers>
      </updg:after>
   </updg:sync>
</ROOT>
```

Explicit Mapping in Updategrams

In the case of complex mappings, an annotated XSD schema can be specified for each transaction the XML updategram performs by specifying the name of the corresponding XDR schema in the `mapping-schema` attribute of the `<sync>` element. By doing this, explicit mapping is chosen, and every element and attribute of the XML document must map to the elements and attributes within the specified XSD schema. For example, in a simple case, an annotated XSD schema could contain the following:

```
<?xml version="1.0" encoding="UTF-8"?>
<xsd:schema xmlns:xsd="http://www.w3.org/2001/XMLSchema"
➥xmlns:sql="urn:schemas-microsoft-com:mapping-schema">
   <xsd:element name="CUSTOMER" sql:relation="Customers">
      <xsd:complexType>
         <xsd:attribute name="CustomerID" type="xsd:string"/>
         <xsd:attribute name="CompanyName" type="xsd:string"/>
         <xsd:attribute name="ContactName" type="xsd:string"/>
         <xsd:attribute name="Address" type="xsd:string"/>
         <xsd:attribute name="City" type="xsd:string"/>
         <xsd:attribute name="Phone" type="xsd:string"/>
      </xsd:complexType>
   </xsd:element>
</xsd:schema>
```

Using this schema, an XML document like the following could be placed into an XML updategram:

```
<CUSTOMER CustomerID="TEST" CompanyName="Test insert comp"
➥ContactName="Test contact" Address="Some address"
➥City="Unknown" Phone="9999999"/>
```

To insert this XML document into the Customers table of the Northwind database, we need to post an updategram like the following to the SQL Server virtual directory:

```
<ROOT xmlns:updg="urn:schemas-microsoft-com:xml-updategram">
   <updg:sync mapping-schema="SampleSchema1.xml">
      <updg:after>
         <CUSTOMER CustomerID="TEST" CompanyName=
➥"Test insert comp" ContactName="Test contact" Address=
➥"Some address" City="Unknown" Phone="9999999"/>
      </updg:after>
   </updg:sync>
</ROOT>
```

However, the XSD schemas and the corresponding XML documents that will be inserted can get quite complex. For instance, the XSD schema shown in Listing 18.19, maps fields and tables from the Northwind database into a hierarchical XML document.

Based on the schema in Listing 18.19, an XML document like the following could be placed into an XML updategram:

```
<CUSTOMER>
   <CUSTOMERID>TEST</CUSTOMERID>
   <COMPANY>Test insert comp</COMPANY>
   <CONTACT>Test contact</CONTACT>
   <ADDRESS>Test address</ADDRESS>
   <CITY>Test city</CITY>
   <PHONE>9999999</PHONE>
   <ORDER updg:at-identity="OrderId">
      <ORDERDATE>2001-07-23</ORDERDATE>
      <DETAILS>
         <ORDERID></ORDERID>
         <PRODUCTID>28</PRODUCTID>
         <UNITPRICE>45.6</UNITPRICE>
         <QUANTITY>15</QUANTITY>
      </DETAILS>
   </ORDER>
</CUSTOMER>
```

Given this XML document, the information could be inserted by creating the XML updategram shown in Listing 18.21.

LISTING 18.21 A Sample XML Updategram Using a Mapping Schema

```
<ROOT xmlns:updg="urn:schemas-microsoft-com:xml-updategram">
   <updg:sync mapping-schema="../Schema/Customers4.xsd">
      <updg:after>
         <CUSTOMER>
            <CUSTOMERID>TEST</CUSTOMERID>
            <COMPANY>Test insert comp</COMPANY>
            <CONTACT>Test contact</CONTACT>
            <ADDRESS>Test address</ADDRESS>
            <CITY>Test city</CITY>
            <PHONE>9999999</PHONE>
```

LISTING 18.21 continued

```
            <ORDER updg:at-identity="OrderId">
               <ORDERDATE>2001-07-23</ORDERDATE>
               <DETAILS>
                  <ORDERID>OrderId</ORDERID>
                  <PRODUCTID>28</PRODUCTID>
                  <UNITPRICE>45.6</UNITPRICE>
                  <QUANTITY>15</QUANTITY>
               </DETAILS>
            </ORDER>
         </CUSTOMER>
      </updg:after>
   </updg:sync>
</ROOT>
```

This example uses a new attribute for the updategram: `at-identity`. This attribute captures the identity value for the identity column of the referenced table and stores it in the specified variable for later use in the updategram, as shown in the `<ORDERID>` element contained in the `<DETAILS>` element.

NULL Handling in Updategrams

NULL fields in SQL Server are not returned in the XML document. However, it is sometimes useful to set a field to NULL. Using updategrams, this can be accomplished by using the `nullvalue` attribute on a `<sync>` element. When the `nullvalue` attribute is specified in an `<sync>` element, SQL ISAPI can determine that when it encounters the specified string, it should insert NULL into the field. For instance, to insert a NULL value into the CompanyName field of the Customers table in the Northwind database, we could use the following XML updategram:

```
<ROOT xmlns:updg="urn:schemas-microsoft-com:xml-updategram">
   <updg:sync updg:nullvalue=".NULL." >
      <updg:before>
         <Customers CustomerID="ALFKI"/>
      </updg:before>
      <updg:after>
        <Customers CustomerID="ALFKI" CompanyName=".NULL." />
     </updg:after>
   </updg:sync>
</ROOT>
```

When SQL ISAPI encounters the `.NULL.` value in the CompanyName attribute, it inserts NULL into the CompanyName field.

Executing Updategrams

Knowing how XML updategrams function is one thing, but how do we get SQL ISAPI to perform the necessary operations? Quite simply, we can post the updategram to the SQL Server virtual directory. This can be accomplished using an HTML page or the XMLHTTP COM object available in MSXML2. For instance, we could use the following code in Visual Basic to post an XML updategram to a SQL Server virtual directory called localhost/sql2000:

```
Dim loPost As New MSXML2.xmlHttp
Dim loXML As New MSXML2.DOMDocument

loXML.Async=.F.
loXML.loadXML MyUpdateGram
   ' Post the template.
loPost.Open "POST", "http://localhost/sql2000", False
loPost.setRequestHeader "Content-type", "text/xml"
loPost.send loXML
```

We can then query the ResponseText property of the XMLHTTP object to find out whether an error occurred and what the result was.

Summary

XML is quickly becoming the preferred method of passing information, not only for the Internet, but also across applications, and even within the same application. Until now, developers have been forced to create their own routines to automate messaging and to convert data contained within a database into XML.

Now, with BizTalk Server 2000 and SQL Server 2000, much of these tasks can be handled in a more efficient manner. That leaves the developer with more time to perform the important tasks of programming, by not having to worry about writing automated messaging systems or documenting routing systems and by not having to write conversion routines to convert relational data into XML. What else can be said, except that the future looks bright.

Applied XML

PART III

IN THIS PART

CHAPTER 19

Understanding XML Standards

IN THIS CHAPTER

So far, you have heard all about XML and the various components that make up the technology. Already you've been immersed in an alphabet soup of acronyms and abbreviations—XML, XSL, XPath, XLink, DOM, and SAX—and this is just the tip of the iceberg. There are literally hundreds of XML-based specifications and standards that leverage these "core" XML specifications. How can we identify these various initiatives and keep them separated in our minds from other initiatives and specifications?

In many different technology practices, a common metaphor has been used to identify the wide set of specifications and standards that impact that particular technology segment. This metaphor is called the *standards stack*, because it not only shows the various specifications and standards but also how they interrelate. This metaphor, which is more visual rather than logical, helps to separate and identify the key specifications worth tracking and those that are tangential to the problem being solved.

In this chapter, we will examine standards stacks and explore the stack that is most relevant to the XML universe. In particular, you will learn

- What exactly an XML standard is
- What organizations are involved in standards setting
- What the standards stack is
- What the horizontal "layers" in the XML standards stack are
- What the vertical "aspects" to the XML standards stack are
- What convergence is happening in the XML standards space

Standards and Vocabularies

At the XML '99 conference, Steve McVey of Sterling Commerce remarked, "XML is very flexible. Everyone can do their own thing, and, by golly, everyone is!" The increasing prevalence and use of XML as a key, important business tool has resulted in its use in every nook and cranny where data is consumed and produced. In the case of business and industry, its use has spurred the development of document structures and markup elements specific to industries, industry segments, and individual businesses. These specified document structures and markup elements are known as *vocabularies*. Just as in the English sense of the word, a *vocabulary* is a set of agreed-upon language constructs that mean the same things to all parties using them. In many ways, vocabularies that are defined within user communities and have a well-defined mechanisms for their maintenance are called *standards*. But this usage of the term *standard* is somewhat controversial. Many consider a standard to be one that has been in use by a large population for a given number of years, whereas others consider a standard to be a well-defined specification that addresses the needs of a wide user base. Despite the definition, the net result of the widespread use of XML has resulted in hundreds of industry vocabularies, specifications, and standards.

The Definition of "Standard" as Excerpted from the American Heritage Dictionary

Noun: **1.** A flag, banner, or ensign, especially: **a.** The ensign of a chief of state, nation, or city. **b.** A long, tapering flag bearing heraldic devices distinctive of a person or corporation. **c.** An emblem or flag of an army, raised on a pole to indicate the rallying point in battle. **d.** The colors of a mounted or motorized military unit.

2a. An acknowledged measure of comparison for quantitative or qualitative value; a criterion. **b.** An object that under specified conditions defines, represents, or records the magnitude of a unit.

3. The set proportion by weight of gold or silver to alloy metal prescribed for use in coinage.

4. The commodity or commodities used to back a monetary system.

5. *Something, such as a practice or a product, that is widely recognized or employed, especially because of its excellence.*

6a. A degree or level of requirement, excellence, or attainment. **b.** A requirement of moral conduct. Often used in the plural.

7. Chiefly British. A grade level in elementary schools.

8. A pedestal, stand, or base.

9. Botany. **a.** The large upper petal of the flower of a pea or related plant. **b.** One of the narrow upright petals of an iris. Also called banner, vexillum.

10. A shrub or small tree that through grafting or training has a single stem of limited height with a crown of leaves and flowers at its apex.

11. Music. A composition that is continually used in repertoires.

Adjective: **1.** Serving as or conforming to a standard of measurement or value.

2. *Widely recognized or employed as a model of authority or excellence: a standard reference work.*

3. *Acceptable but of less than top quality: a standard grade of beef.*

4. Normal, familiar, or usual: the standard excuse.

5. Commonly used or supplied: standard car equipment.

6. Linguistics. Conforming to established educated usage in speech or writing.

Etymology: Middle English, from *Old French estandard, rallying place*, probably from Frankish *standhard : *standan, to stand.

As you can tell from this dictionary excerpt, there are many, somewhat conflicting definitions of the word standard. Therefore, it is no surprise that technologists and business wonks cannot agree on what constitutes an XML "standard." However, the terms in italics represent some of the better definitions of what a standard is in the context of our discussion. To many, commonly accepted practices or products have earned "de facto" standard status. This includes the Windows platform, the metric system, and even the width of railroad tracks (see the sidebar later in this discussion). However, the use of the term *excellence* in the preceding definition has oft been questioned when used in combination with the word *standard*. Therefore, the more lenient definition of a commonly used or supplied technology has been applied. However, some XML specifications have yet to be adopted or even produced. How can the term *standard* apply to these specifications, then? Perhaps we can seek solace in the original definition of the word *standard* as derived from the Old French: rallying point. These efforts seek not to be known as pervasive and common but to serve as a rallying point for those in the industry to agree on terms, processes, and other conditions that may never have been possible in the past.

So, what exactly is an XML standard? This question is answered in two parts. The first concerns the nature of a standard itself. Some will take issue with the term *standard* when what may really be meant is *initiative*, *application*, or *recommendation*. Each of these terms has definite validity and good reasons why it should be used instead of the marshmallow-soft, inaccurate term *standard*. However, the lesser of all evils demands that some expression be chosen. Inaccurate as it is, various forces have compelled the use of the term *standard* when *agreement* is really what is meant. For the purposes of this chapter, a standard is considered to be an agreement among multiple parties about the definition, representation, or use of data and/or the technology used to exchange data. If the chosen term still offends you, the reader, we encourage a mental "search and replace" for *standard* with whatever term you find most appropriate.

Basically, standards are really about one thing: getting agreement. A standard represents a codified representation of an agreement on how to perform a process or implement a technology. For horizontal technologies, a standard represents an agreement on the representation or implementation of a technology. For example, in the United States, electrical outlets are 120 volts AC at 60 Hz using a particular outlet shape, whereas in the United Kingdom, electrical outlets are 220 volts AC at 50 Hz using a different outlet shape. On the other hand, vertical or business standards represent an agreement on a particular business process or methodology. For example, the United States legal system uses a specific language and process for the conduct of its operations and processes, whereas other legal systems use different languages and processes.

The second part of the answer to the preceding question is that the basis of all the standards mentioned in this document is that they define an XML tag set, document type definition (DTD), or a fragment thereof. Standards that do not comprise a definition of XML tags, DTDs, or their interchange are not covered in this chapter.

The types of entities that are creating standards are almost as wide and varying as the number of standards themselves, but they generally fall into one of the following categories:

- Governmental bodies
- International or nongovernmental formal standards bodies
- Vertical industry consortia
- Ad-hoc groups of companies
- Individual companies
- Academic institutions
- Individuals

Many equate standards with the individuals or organizations that create them. The reason for this is that the quality of a standard is dependent on the process that created it. Standards organizations differ on many areas that will determine how completely a specification is developed, and to what extent it will be used. These areas include the following:

- The level of enforcement
- The definition process
- The management process
- The number and nature of participants

Clearly, the level of enforcement of a standard depends on whether a governmental body or a group of companies has developed the specification in question. Many standards that are government created and regulated are enforced for practical, safety, or regulatory reasons and as a result have the force of law to back them up. However, governmental and many international standards have a more rigorous, rigid process by which they are defined and agreed to, whereas industry consortia and smaller company efforts are a more fluid and rapid process. In addition, as the standards efforts get smaller in scope, the nature of their management and the size of their participation becomes more "closed" and proprietary in scope.

What Is an Open Standard?

Many standards, whether created by industry, government, or individual companies, are touted as being "open" standards that can be adopted by the industry or market as a whole. Of course, this implies that *open* is a positive term, but what does it really mean? Some describe a technology or specification as "open" if they mean that it isn't proprietary. In that sense, the word is being used as an opposite to the word *proprietary*, which many consider to be pejorative. To many, *proprietary* means closed to outside development and viewing, closed minded, not customer centric, and slow to change. This is simply not the case with most proprietary standards, and so we must consider a different definition for *open*.

However, we are describing here not only specifications and standards that are "out in the open" and can be viewed in their entirety by all interested parties but also an "open process." An open process means that the forces and efforts that are employed in the creation of the specification itself are open. Meetings are publicized, held outside the confines of a single dominant company, and voting processes for modifications to the specification are well understood. Most importantly, any party that is interested in contributing and can bring resources to bear on a certain problem should be allowed to contribute in a truly "open" process. Although W3C and other organizations follow this open-process model, not all other XML specifications and "standards" do.

Another good definition of *openness* comes not in the definition of the specification but in the manner with which it is used. XML's "openness" means that it can be created by Corporation A's tools and processed by Corporation B, C, or D's tools or open-source applications and tools—or it can be created and processed in any combination of different tools and applications by different or competing tools vendors. For vendors of software applications who use "open" XML protocols and standards, this means that their software can be replaced. This is primarily an advantage to the consumer, who has increased choice in who and how they choose to have their problems addressed. However, this is also an advantage for the software vendor in that it can develop open interfaces that keep its software applications always current and open for modification. In addition, no company can do everything well. The adoption of open standards allows companies to "play well" with each other in the space and reinforce their own products' best features.

The Standards-Creation Process

The work that is done by standards committees falls into one of two camps: the least common denominator (LCD) or the greatest common denominator (GCD). As a result of the constant tug-of-war present in standards working groups, final specifications are a compromise of one of two sorts. In LCD specifications, the specification reflects all the elements that could be agreed upon by all parties. If this means that a specification with 60 elements was whittled down to only 10, then the result is the lowest common denominator with which all parties can agree. Another variation on this is that the specification contains all the suggestions of all the parties. This means that everyone at least has some of his or her suggestions embodied in the final result. This "greatest common denominator" approach results in a fat, bloated specification that is too large for everyone and not specific for anyone. LCD approaches result in specifications that are customized with add-ons that are often proprietary and company specific. GCD approaches result in specifications that are partially implemented on a selective basis with companies at odds over which parts of the specification they will choose to implement. Either solution is a poor choice for the implementing company.

One of the features of XML is that it is extremely easy to create a new document format. As a result, the proliferation of XML formats and standards is tremendous. Likewise, the potential for duplication of labor and competing standards is very high. These conflicting standards then require users to map between data formats as they cross industries or competing standards adoption. In the end, competing standards makes it a headache for everyone in the industry to adopt XML, and this is a potential barrier to long-term XML adoption.

With all this in mind, is technology even a consideration in developing standards, or is it just an excuse to get companies and industries together to agree on issues they may never have agreed on in the past? It is quite likely that XML is merely just a crutch for industries to lean on while they agree on a universal representation for a particular business process or technology representation.

Note

Here is an excerpt from an e-mail from Randolph J. Herber, originally from an unknown source, but widely circulated on the Internet, regarding the development and persistence of standards:

The U.S. standard railroad gauge (width between the two rails) is 4 feet, 8.5 inches. That's an exceedingly odd number.

Why was that gauge used? Because that's the way they built them in England, and the U.S. railroads were built by English expatriates.

Why did the English build them like that? Because the first rail lines were built by the same people who built the pre-railroad tramways, and that's the gauge they used.

Why did "they" use that gauge then? Because the people who built the tramways used the same jigs and tools that they used for building wagons which used that wheel spacing.

Why did the wagons have that particular odd wheel spacing? Well, if they tried to use any other spacing, the wagon wheels would break on some of the old, long distance roads in England, because that's the spacing of the wheel ruts.

So who built those old rutted roads? The first long distance roads in Europe (and England) were built by Imperial Rome for their legions. The roads have been used ever since.

And the ruts in the roads? Roman war chariots first formed the initial ruts, which everyone else had to match for fear of destroying their wagon wheels. Since the chariots were made for (or by) Imperial Rome, they were all alike in the matter of wheel spacing. The United States standard railroad gauge of 4 feet, 8.5 inches derives from the original specification for a Roman chariot. So the next time you are handed a specification and wonder what horse's ass came up with it, you may be exactly right, because the Imperial Roman war chariots were made just wide enough to accommodate the back ends of two war horses. Thus, we have the answer to the original question.

There's an interesting extension to the story about railroad gauges and horses' behinds. When we see a space shuttle sitting on its launch pad, there are two big booster rockets attached to the sides of the main fuel tank. These are solid rocket boosters, or SRBs. The SRBs are made by Thiokol at their factory in Utah. The engineers who designed the SRBs might have preferred to make them a bit fatter, but the SRBs had to be shipped by train from the factory to the launch site.

The railroad line from the factory had to run through a tunnel in the mountains. The SRBs had to fit through that tunnel. The tunnel is slightly wider than the railroad track, and the railroad track is about as wide as two horses' behinds. So, the major design feature of what is arguably the world's most advanced transportation system was determined over two thousand years ago by the width of a horse's behind!

Standards Organizations: Who Is Creating the Standards?

As mentioned earlier, it is almost as important to identify who is creating a given specification as detailing the specification itself. The organization that is producing the standard provides key signals about the quality, prospects of adoption, and longevity of the given specification. In fact, different organizations proposing the very same specification could meet drastically different challenges as they attempt to bring the specification to "market."

That's right, the word *market* can be applied in the context of discussing specifications and standards. After all, a specification is just words on a piece of paper or text in an electronic document. The specification needs to be adopted, used, and pulled in different directions by users of different needs before it can be considered to be a "standard." Therefore, a wide range of specifications-writing bodies have different amounts of influence and pull in the market. This section discusses the various institutions that are creating XML-based specifications and how they are influencing how XML specifications are being created today.

The World Wide Web Consortium (W3C)

In the XML world, the World Wide Web Consortium (W3C) is the preeminent standards-setting body. Hosted by the Laboratory for Computer Science at MIT, by INRIA and Keio University with support from DARPA, and by the European Commission, the W3C cut its teeth originally on the Hypertext Markup Language (HTML) and has maintained its position as the foremost standards-setting body for markup language ever since.

Founded by Tim Berners-Lee (the same individual who founded the Web itself) in October 1994, the W3C is focused on developing standards for the interoperability and technical evolution of the Web. To underscore this goal, the W3C has produced an impressive number of specifications, totaling over 35 in just five years that are in widespread use throughout the globe. The W3C has amassed support from a wide array of corporations, academic institutions, governmental and nongovernmental bodies, and private individuals. To say that its word is the gold currency of the industry is an understatement. In the words of the organization, W3C's technology specifications help make the Web a "robust, scalable, and adaptive infrastructure for a world of information."

To meet these needs, the W3C has a core set of goals that drive its specification development and direction. First and foremost is its commitment to universal access of Web functionality for all different cultures, educations, abilities, material resources, delivery platforms, and physical limitations. This goal is very much in sync with the design goals for HTML as well as XML. A second goal of the organization is to develop an environment called the "Semantic Web" that allows users to maximize their use of Web resources. Finally, the third part of its "three-legged stool" of goals is to develop a "Web of Trust" that helps to guide the development of the Web in consideration of the legal, commercial, and social issues raised by this technology.

The W3C promotes its mission to the millions of people using its specifications by soliciting feedback from its member organizations as well as the Web community at large. The W3C then utilizes this feedback to create Web technologies and specifications that can be published to the community as *recommendations*, which is the W3C non-politically charged word for *standard*. The technological framework is based on three central principles: interoperability, evolution, and decentralization. The interoperability principle requires that the various specifications must be able to work with each other and any two systems that comply to the specification should be able to communicate with each other. The evolution principle requires that specifications be able to change as the environment for the technology likewise changes. This latter principle addresses the fact that Internet technologies change at lightning speed, requiring specifications that can likewise stay up-to-date and relevant. The final principle centers on the fact that the Web is a decentralizing force, not having a central control authority or bottleneck. W3C standards must be able to scale to global proportions while simultaneously preventing bottlenecks, errors, or dependencies on central control mechanisms.

The W3C accomplishes its task through the use of working groups, interest groups, and coordination groups, which serve as the main specification generating documentation and communication activities of the organization. These groups are divided into five domains that facilitate these activities: the Architecture domain, which focuses on underlying "core" Web architectures, the Document Formats domain, which works on presentation-level specifications, the Interaction domain, which aims to improve user interaction and document creation on the Web, the Technology and Society domain, which seeks to synchronize technological developments with social, legal, and public policy concerns, and the Web Accessibility Initiative (WAI), which aims to improve the usability of the Web by individuals with disabilities. In addition, the Technical Architecture Group (TAG) was created in July of 2001 to provide a means for guiding, documenting, and synchronizing architectural issues as they appear in cross-technology environments. TAG will be important as the use of W3C technologies continues to proliferate.

Guided by these design principles, mission statements, and goals, the W3C organization has published dozens of recommendations and proposals at various states of development and approval. Table 19.1 shows some of these key specifications.

TABLE 19.1 W3C Recommendations as of October 2001

Recommendation	*Description*
Hypertext Markup Language (HTML)	HTML forms the core protocol for almost all Web functionality today. Currently at version 4.0, HTML will soon be superceded by its XML-based cousin, XHTML.

TABLE 19.1 W3C Recommendations as of October 2001

Recommendation	*Description*
Cascading Style Sheets (CSS)	CSS applies style and robust design capabilities to HTML, and early on, XML.
PNG and WebCGM	Two of W3C's specifications for graphics on the Web.
Document Object Model (DOM)	DOM provides an application programming interface (API) to structured languages such as XML and HTML.
Extensible Markup Language (XML)	XML, the reason why this book exists, is the powerful structured language that is making aves. The XML initiative ncludes the related pec-ifications XPath, Link, XPointer, XSL, and Forms.
MathML	MathML is a structured language for the communication of mathematical information.
Synchronized Multimedia (SMIL)	SMIL allows authors toIntegration Language create synchronized multimedia presentations on the Web.
Web Accessibility Guidelines	The Web Accessibility Initiative has published two recommendations to promote access to the Web for people with disabilities.
Platform for Internet Content Selection (PICS)	PICS describes a mechanism for content selection and filtering—in particular for filtering inappropriate material for minors.
Resource Description Framework (RDF)	RDF provides a metadata model and framework upon which a Semantic Web can be built.

Note

You can find out more about the W3C by visiting its Web site at `http://www.w3.org`.

The Internet Engineering Task Force (IETF)

Before the W3C even existed, the Internet Engineering Task Force (IETF) was the main source of technical specifications and policies for the Internet. First convening in 1986, the IETF has been creating the fundamental protocols and technologies that have been powering the Internet since it has been an ongoing concern.

Despite the wealth of specifications created by the IETF, it isn't a formal standards body per se. The IETF is a large, open, international community of network designers, operators, vendors, and researchers concerned with the evolution of the Internet architecture and the smooth operation of the Internet, but it doesn't have a formalized membership or organizational structure. It is formed as a loosely self-organized group of people who contribute their resources to solving various problems in the Internet space, but it doesn't operate as a corporation with directors, members, and dues. This simplistic structure has allowed the IETF to focus on one thing: the development and promotion of technical specifications for the Internet.

The group's core of the operations focuses on identifying and proposing solutions to important technical problems faced by the Internet community, specifying protocols to solve these problems, making recommendations for the adoption and standardization of those protocols, facilitating technology transfer for those protocols, and providing a forum for the exchange of information between the various participants in the adoption process.

Because the organization is a loose collection of voluntary contributors, the format for specifications generation is through IETF meetings and periodic gatherings. Anyone may register and attend these meetings because there are no formal membership processes. The IETF is nominally managed by the Internet Society (ISOC), but in a very much hands-off manner. The process of IETF standardization is managed by the Internet Engineering Steering Group (IESG). The IESG manages the output of the IETF working groups as well as helps to form and dissolve IETF working groups.

The IETF focuses on eight key areas of protocol development: application-level protocols, Internet protocols for routing packets and the Domain Name Service (DNS), operational and network-management protocols, routing protocols, security protocols, transport services, user services, and other general protocols.

IETF standards are published as "Request for Comments" (RFCs), although many of them carry much the same weight as general standards. There are, in fact, six kinds of RFCs: proposed standards, draft standards, Internet standards (or "full standards"), experimental protocols, informational documents, and historical standards. Every RFC first starts out as an Internet Draft (I-D). I-Ds can be written by any working group member; therefore, you can always tell a person who doesn't understand the IETF due to his bragging about publishing an Internet Draft (when it in fact takes no significant effort). Internet Drafts are tentative documents that are meant for readers to comment on, and they automatically expire after six months. Once an I-D is published, it is reviewed by other members of the various working groups and then is escorted through the standards process by various IETF and IESG members. Finally, once the draft has been approved by all parties, it becomes an RFC. Only the first three of the RFC classes (proposed, draft, and full) are considered to be actual standards within the IETF. Examples of IETF RFCs are shown in Table 19.2.

TABLE 19.2 Some IETF RFCs

RFC	*Description*
Hypertext Transfer Protocol (HTTP; RFC 1945)	Protocol for communicating between Web servers and browsers.
Simple Mail Transfer Protocol (SMTP; RFC 876)	Protocol for exchanging e-mail messages
File Transfer Protocol (FTP; RFC 959)	Mechanism for transferring binary and ASCII files over the Internet
Blocks Extensible Exchange Protocol (BEEP; RFC 3080)	An application protocol framework for connection-oriented, asynchronous request/ response interactions
WebDAV (RFC 2518)	Extensions to HTTP that enable remote collaborative authoring of Web resources

The registry system for the various IETF activities is managed by the Internet Assigned Numbers Authority (IANA). The IANA keeps track of the various protocol items as they are updated and managed. This includes such items as TCP port numbers and MIME types. Historically, IANA has also been the manager of the root of the Domain Name System (DNS), but this responsibility was passed to the Internet Corporation for Assigned Names and Numbers (ICANN) as the domain name market exploded with demand and swamped IANA's capability and authority.

Much of the IETF RFCs form the basis for XML and HTML standards, including the HTTP, SMTP, and FTP protocols as well as ongoing efforts based in XML to standardize various intermachine communication efforts.

Note

You can find out more about the IETF by visiting its Web site at `http://www.ietf.org`.

The Organization for the Advancement of Structured Information Standards (OASIS)

Another major standards-setting organization is the Organization for the Advancement of Structured Information Standards (OASIS), a nonprofit, international consortium of individuals, corporations, and organizations focused on building interoperable industry specifications based on public standards such as XML and SGML. Originally known as SGML Open, OASIS has its roots in the SGML language and was a consortium of small software vendors and large customers devoted to developing guidelines for interoperability among SGML products. As XML grew in popularity, it became obvious that OASIS's guidance and expertise in standards setting was needed in this new era of specification proliferation.

Today, OASIS has over 170 organizational members and is focused on simplifying interbusiness communications processes for all businesses. It does this by fostering communities of interest that are concerned with solving problems in a specific domain of expertise through open discussion and debate. OASIS as an organization doesn't set any standards or write specifications (its constituent Technical Committee members do); instead, it creates an open forum where its members can discuss market needs and directions as well as recommend guidelines for product interoperability. OASIS then consolidates, coordinates, and disseminates this information to its member organizations for approval and adoption.

Therefore, OASIS functions more like a community rather than an official standards body, such as the W3C or the collection of technicians that represent the IETF. OASIS has a simple membership and participation model: organizations and individuals who are members can participate in the standards definition and approval process. As a result, any group of at least three OASIS members can be authorized to create a community for development of a specific industry or community specification. These groups then form the core of the *Technical Committee* (TC), which can result in the production of specifications to be reviewed by the OASIS membership or the Internet community in general. Once a specification (known as a *committee specification*) is created by a TC group, at least three implementations of the specification must be created for approval of the OASIS membership. After a minimum of 10 percent of the membership has approved the specification, it becomes a formal specification under the OASIS umbrella, although users can make use of the specification before it becomes a formal OASIS standard.

In this manner, OASIS provides a central rallying point for the different types of technical specifications surrounding the structured languages of XML, SGML, and HTML. OASIS has only the following goals that TCs must meet as they develop specifications:

- They should be open to all OASIS members and casual observers.
- There should be a formal audit trail of work conducted in the TC.
- The specification development and voting process will be conducted in a democratic manner.
- The process should be flexible in the way that users can utilize the specification and the deliverables that are produced.
- The efforts should be scalable and language neutral to support the widest audience possible.

Because TCs are created by OASIS members, OASIS itself doesn't start any specification projects and doesn't have a technical agenda of its own. However, OASIS has the most interest in XML- and SGML-based projects that foster interoperability, vertical industry convergence, and cross-industry standards. A current list, as of October 2001, of OASIS projects is provided in Table 19.3.

TABLE 19.3 OASIS Technical Committees

Specification	*Description*
Access Control Markup Language	Defines a core schema and corresponding namespace for the expression of authorization policies in XML.
Business Transactions	Develops technology for business transactions on the Internet.
Conformance, XML Conformance, and XSLT Conformance	Various interoperability and conformance technical committees.
Customer Information Quality	Delivers XML standards for customer profile/information management to the industry.
Directory Services	The Directory Services Markup Language (DSML) bridges the world of directory services with the world of XML.
DocBook	DocBook is a DTD (both SGML and XML versions are available) that is particularly well suited to books and papers about computer hardware and software.
ebXML	A global XML-based set of technologies for business-to-business communication, integration, and commerce.

TABLE 19.3 continued

Specification	*Description*
Election and Voter Services	Develops a standard for the structured interchange of data among hardware, software, and service providers who engage in any aspect of providing election or voter services to public or private organizations.
HumanMarkup	A specification for the conveyance of human characteristics through XML.
RELAX NG	The purpose of this committee is to create a specification for a schema language for XML based on the TREX proposal.
Web Services Component Model (WSCM)	Creates an XML- and Web Services–centric component model for interactive Web applications.
Universal Business Language	Produces a synthesis of existing XML business libraries to develop a coordinated set of XML grammatical components that will allow trading partners to unambiguously identify the business documents to be exchanged in a particular business context.

Note

You can find out more about OASIS by visiting its Web site at `http://www.oasis-open.org`.

Governmental Bodies

Governments are also getting into the game of producing specifications for XML. This shouldn't seem all that amazing because governmental as well as nongovernmental organizations (NGOs) that are affiliated with official processes have long been in the practice of setting standards for acceptable communications. Many of these specifications are produced as a way of meeting various regulations for trade, safety, policy, or other reasons, rather than meeting a technological need. As a result, the specifications tend to be very rigorous and enforced.

In the XML space, two major governmental standards organizations stick out: the United Nations and the International Organization for Standardization (ISO). The United

Nations (UN) has long been in the process of building specifications for facilitating international commerce. The United Nations Centre for Trade Facilitation and Electronic Business, more commonly known as UN/CEFACT, is a UN-sponsored organization whose mission is to improve the ability of businesses and organizations to trade products and services in an effective and friction-free manner.

Founded in 1996, UN/CEFACT was created to respond to the rapidly changing technological environment and the need to officially recognize specific contributions to the global trade network. UN/CEFACT realized that progress needed to be made in reducing the amount of cumbersome and time-consuming paperwork, formalities, and procedures encountered by small and medium-sized businesses in their day-to-day trade. In the 1970s, the UN facilitated the development of a worldwide EDI message format and has since leveraged its experience, interest, and power in helping to craft the ebXML specification in conjunction with OASIS.

The International Organization for Standardization (ISO), whose name is derived from the Greek word *isos* and is not an acronym, isn't really a governmental body, but it forms the basis upon which many governmental regulations are based. ISO specifications are numbered and can cover anything from manufacturing and quality management processes, such as ISO 9001, to setting the size of metric screw threads. ISO is made up of an international federation of 140 national standards-setting bodies, and it operates in a very formal manner.

With over 12,000 standards comprising 300,000 pages of documentation, ISO develops its standards in a formal manner that aims at achieving widespread adoption and consensus. The standardization process is very structured, requiring specification candidates to first submit their proposals to their national standards bodies, which in turn propose these items for consideration of ISO as a whole. The process then follows a regimented series of steps for project definition, specification, and approval, requiring the consent of 75 percent of all voting members. As a result, it is no surprise that ISO standards can be several years in the making but have long-lasting effects. ISO has begun to specify XML-based standards that will surely be used for many years to come.

Note

You can find out more about UN/CEFACT by visiting its Web site at http://www.unece.org/cefact/index.htm.

You can find out more about ISO by visiting its Web site at `http://www.iso.ch`.

Of course, there are many other governmental and affiliated standards-setting organizations besides UN/CEFACT and ISO. Governments will always be the best place to establish a standard that can be enforced by law, regulation, and established guidelines of conduct.

Industry Consortia

Another source of standardization and technical specification is in formal groupings of vendors that share some aspect of their business in common. These consortia usually center around industry verticals, such as insurance, electronic components, and apparel, but can also be horizontal consortia, focusing on business requirements such as retail, manufacturing, and human resources. In any case, these groups are usually established to formalize the business processes and relevant standards for their industries. Technological automation and innovation forced many of these groups to come up with relevant electronic encodings for their products and services that can be shared within their industry.

A natural outgrowth of these organizations has been the development of industry-specific or horizontally applied XML-based vocabularies. Experience has shown that the vast majority of implementations of any technology will be in these vertical industries. After all, the implementation of technology in a specific industry is where the "rubber meets the road." Businesses of all shapes and sizes fall into a number of industry classifications and types, and there is no way that a particular specification can meet the different, and often diverging, needs of these various industries.

Examples of industry consortia include the Computing Technology Industry Association (CompTIA), focusing on the electronic component and information technology industries, ACORD, which solves problems for the insurance industry, and Health Level Seven (HL7), which focuses on similar problems for the healthcare industry.

Chapter 22, "Applied XML in Vertical Industry," covers information on these vertical industry standards and specifications in considerable detail, including more detail on the ACORD and HL7 efforts.

Birds-of-a-Feather Vendor Groupings

A less formal, but nonetheless effective, grouping of organizations can be thought of as the "birds-of-a-feather" vendor grouping. Such vendors come together when a specific problem needs to be solved. In these cases, the borders and differences between different industries may be blurred as the problem that needs to be solved becomes increasingly more critical to everyone's success. Alternatively, it just may be that a certain technological issue needs to be standardized before it can be put to use in any particular industry.

Whatever the root cause, the need to solve a given problem will motivate different organizations to come together to provide a technical specification to solve the problem.

Good examples of this loose organization of companies are the SyncML and Universal Description, Discovery, and Integration (UDDI) efforts. In the case of SyncML, vendors in the various mobile, wireless, computing, and portability industries got together to produce a single specification for synchronizing data between their various devices, systems, and platforms. UDDI's main objective was to produce a practical and quickly implemented central repository for Web Services components and descriptions. In both cases, the groups never existed prior to this point, and may not exist in the long term. Instead, the goal to produce a specification and solve a specific need drew them together.

The main issue in these problem-centric groupings of organizations is that their longevity and ability to enforce their respective specifications beyond the initial grouping of customers is in question. Because the firms get together for a specific reason, once the reason has been addressed, the group's need to exist comes into question. Another point of contention with these sorts of organizations is that they are often somewhat closed in their membership and solicitation of general feedback and scrutiny. For the firms that participate in these endeavors, their goal is to solve a problem, not serve as a standards body. Of course, in effect, these groups *are* standards bodies in what they are producing.

Individuals and Organizations

The final set of standards-setting and specification-creating bodies includes single companies and individuals. Vendors of all types of products and services are constantly being motivated to improve their products and services in a manner that is competitively advantageous. Many of them are looking to XML as a means for providing this capability. Some are also looking at XML as a way to provide extensibility and flexibility to their product while simultaneously providing an open API that users can interact with.

These needs are motivating the creation of *single-vendor standards*, which are really specifications created by large and small companies alike that have been published to the community at large for its usage. The most typical of these single-vendor standards are those published by the large software and technology companies Microsoft and Sun Microsystems. Each of these vendors has produced XML and other specifications that are being used by millions of users worldwide. Some would argue that the single-vendor standards are the ones more frequently in use, whereas some of the other consortia and standards body–driven specifications languish for years without any adoption. Of course, the major downside to this approach is that the specifications are rarely open for general review, comment, and improvement. Rather, users must rely on the vendors to continue to enhance, maintain, and document their specifications to the required level.

Also, motivated individuals have been creating XML specifications, such as ChessML, for general adoption by the general user community. These individuals are mainly motivated by simple needs or the desire to share their knowledge, and many of their resultant specifications are not widely adopted. Rather, they have been used to form a starting point or "straw man" proposal for the generation of specifications by larger and more well-funded standards organizations.

The Standards Stack

Given the number of specifications created by the diverse set of standards-setting and specification-creating bodies, as mentioned previously, it is important for us to be able to identify which standards solve which set of problems and which are in possible competition or conflict with each other. This categorization of standards is commonly done throughout many technology segments and usually takes the form of a visual representation model called a *stack*. As the visual metaphor suggests, a standards stack is much like a stack of pancakes: Each layer is a separately defined entity, but the various layers depend on each other for their technology and interoperability. The higher in the stack one goes, the more technology and specifications each layer is dependent on or references.

One of the most common standards stacks in use is the International Standard Organization's Open System Interconnect (ISO/OSI) network layer model. Shown in Figure 19.1, the OSI model shows how the various network protocols and technologies, such as Ethernet, TCP, and HTTP, relate to each other and compare to other specifications on the stack.

The OSI network model is in frequent use by many that use or create network protocol specifications. In a similar vein, as the use and proliferation of XML specifications grow, a similar stack needs to be created. However, there is one major difference between the OSI model and the need for modeling XML specifications. Network protocols have a fairly simplistic set of dependencies. Technology at one layer depends on the technology of the lower levels. Yet, this strict layering doesn't exist in the XML world. Rather, there are some aspects of XML specifications that exhibit layering behavior, whereas others can be applied to multiple layers in the stack. As a result, the network model has a two-part rendition that can be seen in Figure 19.2.

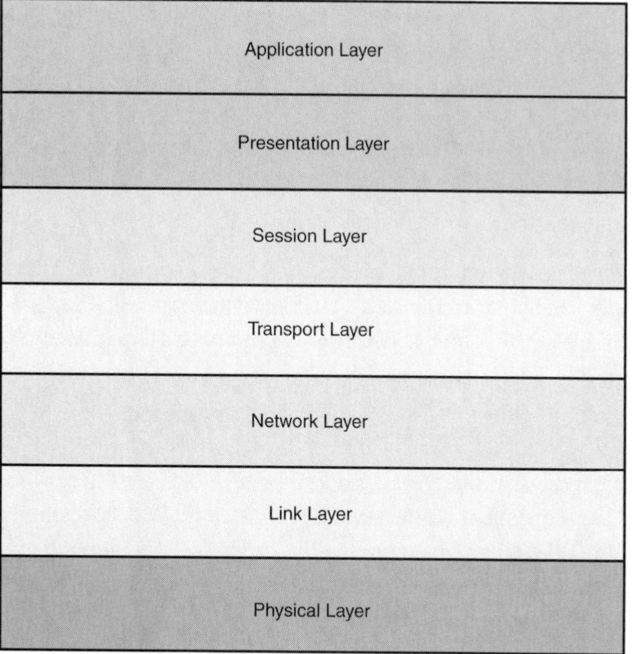

FIGURE 19.1
The OSI network model.

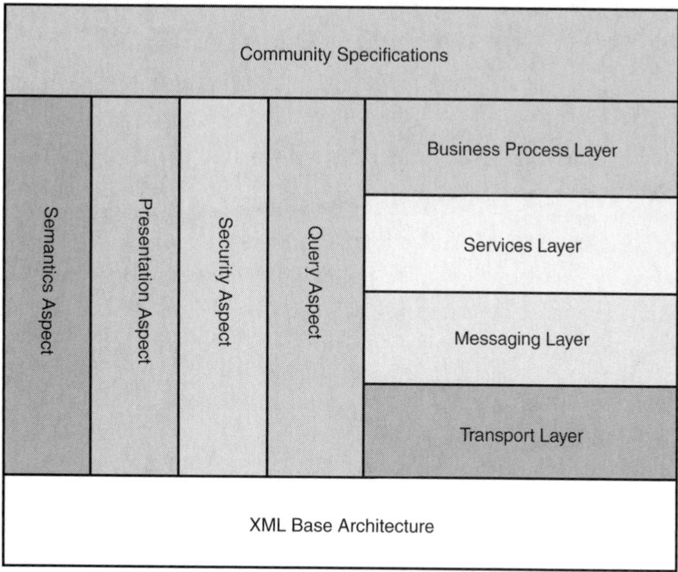

FIGURE 19.2
The XML standards stack.

As shown in this figure, the standards stack consists of many portions and can be divided into four main components:

- XML base architecture
- Technology layers
- Cross-layer aspects
- Community (vertical) specifications

As will be further detailed in the later sections, these various components aim to help users identify which part of the XML standards playing field they are standing on as well as provide a different set of specifications that solve different needs.

Standards Stack Layers

As detailed previously, the XML standards stack consists of a few horizontal layers, with each layer dependent on the layer below it, and a few horizontal aspects that can be applied to multiple layers. Even though the aspects can be applied to multiple XML standards stack layers, they too are dependent on at least one layer for their operation and technical completion.

Message-Oriented Protocols Versus Document-Oriented Specifications

When looking at the XML standards stack, you'll notice that one thing immediately stands out: Half of the diagram is "sideways." This can be interpreted in a number of ways, but most important of these is the very nature of how XML is being used.

As you have countless times been informed, XML is just a document format. There is nothing specific about XML that dictates in what context it can be used, how it is to be exchanged, or even how it is to be presented to the user. As a result, there are many uses for XML. In general, the uses for XML fall into two different camps: message-oriented protocols and document-oriented specifications. These two camps differ in their approach toward using XML and the requirements put upon the language.

Message-oriented protocols are focused at facilitating communication between two parties. They invariably involve a dialogue that has an initiating party and a responding party. Sometimes these conversations occur in a synchronous manner (parties open and maintain connections that are serviced until completion) or in an asynchronous manner (parties have an ongoing conversation with no real beginning or end). Typically, specifications targeted at meeting messaging needs are called *protocols*, because they specify a proper means of interaction between systems and users. Protocols also have a distinct set of layers in their architecture. One given protocol might depend on another layer for proper interaction with a system. As such, the message-oriented needs for XML are represented by the layer hierarchy shown at the right side of the diagram.

Document-oriented specifications are a different beast. They consider XML to be a way to represent information that may or may not be transmitted between users. The transmission aspect of XML is irrelevant to document-oriented specifications, just as the specifics of document representation are irrelevant to message-oriented protocols. Document-oriented specifications care specifically about how an XML document is represented or the information contained within the document is applied. As a result, document-oriented specifications can be applied to any XML document—and more specifically to any level of the message-oriented protocol stack. Due to the orthogonal nature of message-oriented protocols, it is represented by vertical bars that span the message-oriented protocol layers.

Because the XML base architecture forms a basis for all XML documents regardless of intent, and community specifications rely on both message- and document-oriented specifications for their operation, these two portions of the stack cut across both usage domains.

XML Base Architecture

All XML specifications share one thing in common: the use of XML. This seemingly circular reasoning is intended to establish the baseline for all specifications, namely the W3C XML Recommendation. This recommendation forms the base for all XML specifications; therefore, this layer in the XML standards stack is known as the *XML Base Architecture layer*.

Of course, a layer can't consist of just a single specification or protocol. First, we must acknowledge that the current release of the XML Recommendation, namely version 1.0, will most likely change and mutate over the course of its existence. As a result, the base won't consist of just one specification, but perhaps two or more that different specifications at higher levels in the stack may depend on. For example, when version 2.0 is released, perhaps some specifications will make use of it, whereas others will still depend on version 1.0. However, the greater reason for the existence of this layer in the stack is the fact that XML is surrounded by a host of other specifications that extend its reach into different technological areas. Many of these extend the "core" of what XML is and therefore represents additional specifications at this layer. For example, XML Schema, XLink, XPath, and DOM all represent additions to the base XML specification that enrich the language and provide support for the various upper levels of the hierarchy. As such, those are included in this layer.

So, what is the definition for the technologies that are included in this layer? We can define specifications and technologies in the XML Base Architecture layer as "those standards, specifications, protocols, and technologies that form a basis for the representation of XML documents for all parties and uses, regardless of industry, context, or usage." Therefore, it is clear that XML Schema falls into this layer, whereas XHTML, which is a presentational specification, does not.

XML Transport Layer

Because XML is just a data representation technology, it doesn't physically go anywhere. It needs to be transported from place to place in order for it to provide value to any set of parties in communication with each other—unless of course the XML documents are meant only to be stored and not exchanged. Traditionally and most typically, XML sits at a fairly high level in the OSI network model, usually at the Presentation and Application layers, so it can take advantage of many of the existing network protocols to get from point A to point B. Typically, XML documents are sent via the Hypertext Transfer Protocol (HTTP), Simple Mail Transfer Protocol(SMTP), or the File Transfer Protocol (FTP).

Despite this, there have been a number of efforts to utilize XML itself as a means for facilitating point-to-point communications, either by replacing some of the aforementioned protocols or by augmenting them for better transfer of XML documents. Because these use XML as their document format, it makes sense for the Transport layer to be above the XML Base Architecture layer, but more appropriately, all message-based protocols rely on a Transport layer for documents to be transmitted between communicating parties. One can simply use XML-based or non-XML-based protocols in the Transport layer, and it will be obvious that non-XML-based protocols don't depend on XML for their operation.

Some of these XML-based transport efforts include the Blocks Extensible Exchange Protocol (BEEP or BXXP) and Jabber. Both aim to use XML as a means for defining messaging transport protocols or as a framework for exchange of messages in a networked environment.

XML Messaging Layer

The Messaging layer of the XML standards stack is where much of the work happens in packaging XML documents for transmission between communicating parties. Although the Transport layer takes care of the actual message transmission, information is first needed to determine who is to receive the message, how it should be handled, and what to do in the eventuality of transmission failures. Many specification efforts call this layer the *Transport, Routing, and Packaging* (TRP) layer, although they aren't really specifying the transport mechanism per se but rather all the requirements needed by a transport protocol to handle the job effectively.

There are many components to the Messaging layer and issues that need to be taken into account when packaging and routing messages. Think of the Messaging layer as an envelope that surrounds the content to be transported. On a mail envelope, there are a few key features: a delivery address, a return address, postage, a postmark, and a physical envelope that keeps the contents away from prying eyes. These metaphors are quite relevant in the Messaging layer.

In the same manner that an envelope has a sending address and a return address, the Messaging layer specifies who is to receive the given content and who originated the content. This allows messages to be routed from place to place in a predictable fashion. However, the Messaging layer is more complex than the postal mail analogy in that many messaging specifications allow users to also specify intermediaries that can store and forward messages. Regardless of the technology used, this addressing or routing information is extremely important in the Messaging layer.

Postal mail also contains postage and a postmark. The direct analogy to this in the Messaging layer is the ability to specify transaction and nonrepudiation rules. Transaction rules dictate in what order the given message is to be processed, dependencies on other messages for processing, and timeouts for attempting to transmit to the receiving parties. This ensures that only the appropriate number of messages are processed in the correct order by the recipient. Nonrepudiation rules help ensure that a given message was in fact received by the other communicating party. Without a way of knowing whether the message was received and processed, it would be impossible to determine whether it just disappeared into the "ether." These features of transaction control and nonrepudiation help to ensure that message delivery is a reliable affair.

Finally, there is the issue of the envelope itself. The envelope serves two major purposes: to package the contents for delivery and to protect the contents from unauthorized access. Without the envelope, XML documents are just a loose assortment of metadata tags. The envelope provides a means for collecting and identifying these tags as a distinct data entity. In addition, the envelope can encrypt or otherwise restrict access to the contents contained within, in much the same way postal mail security envelopes protect their content from prying eyes.

Examples of XML messaging specifications include the Simple Object Access Protocol (SOAP), ebXML's Transport, Routing, and Packaging (TRP) layer, and the RosettaNet Implementation Framework (RNIF). The W3C is also working on a specification, called the XML Protocol, that will extend concepts provided in SOAP. Each of these Message layer protocols solve the aforementioned problems, but in their own way. This difference in implementation can cause problems in interoperability. For example, if we all wrote our addresses in different ways on an envelope, the Postal Service would be unable to deliver our mail. The same can be said for different Message layer specifications. It is important to consider the interoperability of these specifications as they come into more widespread use.

Services Layer

Once we have addressed the issues of transporting and packaging XML documents for shipment across a network, the next layer involves ascribing some functionality to these various intersystem communications. This is where the Services layer fits. The term *services*, in this context, describes a set of exposed application functionalities that can be accessed by machines in a distributed manner. Such functionality can take the form of actual application code or simply messages communicated between systems in the process of accomplishing some task. In either case, the Services layer addresses the specifications needed to accomplish these tasks.

The most common phrase heard nowadays with regard to services is *loosely coupled.* Systems that communicate using XML and Messaging layer protocols can exchange information without having to know too much about how the other system plans to process that information. Such systems are known as *loosely coupled systems.* The word *coupled* denotes that the two systems are connected to each other in some fashion, whereas the term *loosely* means that they are connected in the least restrictive of manners.

Services layer specifications accomplish this goal of providing loosely coupled systems by encapsulating system functionality in a manner that exposes required inputs and outputs while abstracting processing methodology. The best example of Services layer functionality is the Web Services Description Language (WSDL). WSDL forms a core component of the overall Web Services architecture that leverages SOAP as its routing and packaging layer. Because Services layer specifications expose application functionality while masking application processes, it is important for systems to understand the inputs and outputs required by the specific Services layer component. Protocols such as WSDL specify these things while also helping systems understand the data requirements of these inputs and outputs, error processing requirements, and general data handling.

Process Layer

Once application logic and functionality has been encapsulated and defined in the Services layer, turning that functionality into coordinated action is the responsibility of specifications in the Process layer. Process layer specifications concentrate on organizing individual functionality components into larger applications that aim to solve an overall business problem or meet a usage goal. In the same manner that software applications are a sum of their objects and program components, XML-based applications are the sum of their Service layer components.

Some of the key parts of turning functionality into action include the ability to wire service components together with workflow and logic. Process layer specifications aim to provide a mechanism to identify when certain pieces of functionality should be executed, the proper branching for evaluation of functionality results, and when various processes begin and end. The workflow behind an application helps to tie these disparate components into a cohesive system that embeds the logic of human-based systems into a machine-based exchange. Workflows also allow human interaction to occur at various points in the machine-to-machine dialogue.

Speaking of dialogue, the main goal of Process layer specifications is to organize these transactions into larger dialogues that represent an actual business function, rather than an application function. For example, a Process layer may embody a "Purchase Goods" process, which in turn actuality consists of many individual transaction-based functions such as "Request Product Availability," "Place Product Order," "Submit Purchase Order," and "Process Invoice."

Process layer specifications include RosettaNet Partner Interface Processes (PIPs), the Business Process Markup Language (BPML), and various workflow specifications.

Standards Stack Aspects

Whereas message-oriented protocols follow a very structured, regimented layer scheme, document-oriented specifications have no layering structure to them. Rather, these specifications can be applied to any level of the message-passing stack as well as the community vocabularies in the level above. As such, rather than having layers, the document-oriented specification's portion of the XML standards stack merely has "aspects" that are applied when they are needed.

In general, there are at least four major categories of document-oriented specification:

- *Presentation specifications.* These specifications detail how XML should be presented or modified in presentation for usability.
- *Security specifications.* These specifications provide a level of protection of XML information.

- *Query specifications*. These specifications assist in locating XML resources.
- *Semantics specifications*. These specifications help to apply meaning and context to XML documents.

Presentation Aspect

One of the major document-oriented specifications aspects involves those specifications that define how XML documents should be presented to the user. These presentation aspects help to transform any XML document on any layer of the XML standards stack into a form that can be visually understood and processed by humans. The goal of specifications in this stack is not to focus on machine processing of XML documents but rather on the human factor in using XML. Presentation specifications include the formatting of documents for display as well as the addition of graphical, multimedia, and timing elements.

Usability and information portability also are major factors addressed by presentation aspect specifications. Usability specifications focus on making information easier to use and access by users of all types. These specifications aim to meet the needs of those who are physically handicapped as well as to help to make information generally more accessible to all. Form technology and text-to-speech specifications are good examples of usability-focused presentation aspect specifications. Information portability specifications aim to make the information contained within more accessible to different devices, form factors, and systems. With the increased usage of cell phones, PDAs, and memory-constrained devices, various presentation aspect specifications have been created to enable the widest distribution of content as possible.

Major presentation aspect specifications include XHTML, XForms, and Scalable Vector Graphics (SVG), among others.

Security Aspect

With the increased distribution of content and sensitive data comes the need to protect that information. However, *security* is a catch-all word that actually embodies many different concepts around protecting information, all of which can be applied to XML documents.

The first level of security is the protection of information from prying eyes. Encryption specifications help to alleviate these concerns by masking XML data and preventing it from being used, viewed, or processed by parties that are not privy to the information. Encryption specifications make use of widely available techniques for protecting data, including advanced private-key protection mechanisms. Therefore, the strongest of protection technology can be used and applied to XML data.

Authentication provides another level of security to XML documents. Even though you may be able to decrypt an XML document, it is important for an application to verify that you are who you say you are. Numerous compromises in security occur when unauthorized users abscond data and make use of keys they should never have had access to. A variety of authentication specifications have been created to address this need.

A further level of security is provided by authorization and permission specifications that attempt to identify which resources a valid user has access to. These authorization specifications indicate the specific resources, information, or other digital assets a user can use and the restrictions on that use. These specifications include not only the assignment of user controls but also controls on the content to be exchanged to the user to prevent unauthorized duplication and use. Known as *Digital Rights Management* (DRM) specifications, these limits on the use of intellectual property are becoming increasingly popular in this era of the digital asset.

A final level of security is applied by privacy specifications that aim to make sure that those who are entitled to information don't intentionally or inadvertently spread the information to parties who aren't entitled to it. Increasingly, users are worried that their personal and private information will be shared with parties they have no intention of sharing their information with. Privacy specifications, and especially the Platform for Privacy Preferences (P3P), are aimed at giving users control of how their data will be used, shared, and stored. In this manner, all aspects of information security can be ensured.

Query Aspect

Another universal need for information, especially the richly structured information contained with XML, involves the ability to locate and make proper use of data. As is necessary in most database and data storage systems, the ability to query information is as important as the ability to store and represent that data. Query specifications are responsible for retrieving information and tagging it for proper identification and return.

A number of major XML specifications exist that help in the tagging of XML documents with metadata needed to assist in their proper retrieval. In addition, many proposals and specifications have been created to specify a language for the global query of these documents.

Semantics Aspect

Because XML allows users the ability to create any vocabulary and structure of their choosing, the main challenge is in synchronizing these vocabularies with other, incompatible representations. In addition, it has become important for machines to understand not only the literal encoding of documents but the intent and context of the human who created them. There is nothing that prevents different organizations from calling the same data element different things. Also, there is nothing that prevents these very same users from using the same name to mean entirely different things. For example, the meaning of the word *title* denotes different things to those in the publishing and insurance industries. Another major problem is the fact that different languages and cultures have different names for the same item. It is important for our representation of information to cross these conceptual, semantic, and language boundaries.

A major initiative called the Semantic Web is squarely focused on addressing these problems and producing specifications that add a contextual, or semantic, layer to the way we represent information in XML. The semantics aspect applies these specifications to all levels and layers of the XML standards stack. The immediate application of these specifications is to simplify and enable users to make better, more relevant searches for content. Many search engine responses to user inquiries result in large amounts of irrelevant information. To a machine, the information may seem relevant, but to a user the context of those responses is entirely inadequate. Besides, we should be able to search for a term in any language of our choice and have the results still be relevant to us even if it is presented in a different language.

A larger and more ambitious implementation of semantic aspect specifications is for machines and systems to make intelligent guesses as to our intent for the use of information and to retrieve data sources in an "educated" manner. In this vein, the Semantic Web approaches the goals of artificial intelligence as much as it solves needs for the XML user community. As semantic aspect specifications are developed, they will no doubt be applied to all levels of the XML standards stack.

Community Vocabularies Layer

As you've probably noticed, we've spoken about every part of the XML standards stack except for one: the Community Vocabularies layer. On top of all these various layers and aspects sits the Community Vocabularies layer. This is the layer where all the industry-specific implementations and problem-oriented specifications are created. In effect, this is where the "rubber meets the road." Community vocabularies, which can be vertical industry specifications and standards or cross-industry specifications, make use of all or some of the aforementioned technologies and specification layers to accomplish their goals.

Community vocabularies specify the actual metadata and information that represents how a given user community plans to make use of XML. These community vocabularies may represent a need in an industry, such as insurance or electronic component manufacturing, or a horizontal user community, such as online gaming or data warehousing. In any case, the vocabularies define the specifics of data interchange that can then be represented using Process layer specifications, utilizing Service layer components, packaged into Message layer messages, transmitted over Transport layer protocols, and utilizing any combination of security, presentation, query, and semantics aspects. Thus, the community vocabulary forms the top layer.

Although community vocabularies represent the absolute top of the XML standards stack, they often are some of the first specifications to be developed. The reason for this is quite simple: Some need motivated the desire to implement XML in the first place! In many cases, this was a desire to communicate between industry participants, such as in the financial services, manufacturing, or healthcare arenas. However, when it came time to implement these specifications, the various specification-writing bodies realized that some of their required pieces of functionality, as represented by the messaging-oriented protocol or document-oriented specification stack, didn't exist. The result was that industry-specific vocabularies had to define specifications that were of a more general nature. For example, the ACORD specification had many Message layer components defined in its early days. As layers of the XML stack become increasingly more developed, the breadth of individual community vocabulary specifications become increasingly more narrow.

However, while the scope of community vocabularies may be increasingly more focused as other layers of the stack become more developed, the number of community vocabularies are proliferating. There's a vast number of vertical industries and horizontal user communities that desire to define their own, specific XML vocabularies for interchange. In fact, the entire XML standards stack in actuality looks more like an upside-down pyramid when viewed from the perspective of how many different specifications there are in a given level. Whereas there are hundreds, if not thousands, of individual community vocabulary specifications at the top level, there are very few specifications at the XML Base Architecture layer, and the number increases as we move up the XML specification food chain. One may say that document-oriented specifications remain steady in number, but it can still be argued that the number of document-oriented specifications is greater than the number XML base architecture specifications and less than the number of community vocabulary implementations. Therefore, we have an inverse pyramid of usage, as shown in Figure 19.3, that helps to make our XML standards stack model even more accurate.

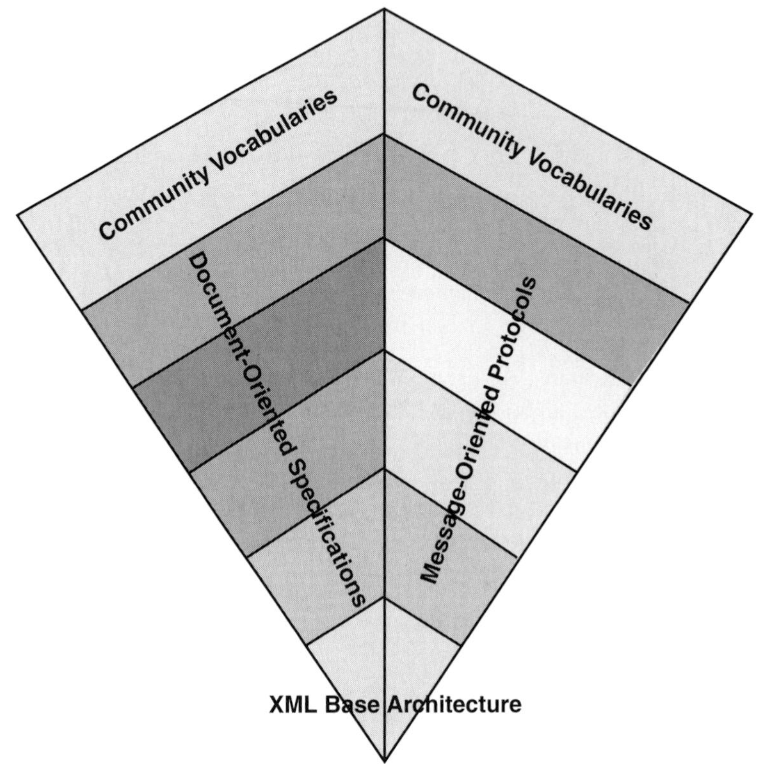

FIGURE 19.3
XML standards stack "pyramid."

Summary

As you have seen, the use of XML is pervading every nook and cranny where data and information are present. In the process of using XML, we have expressed a need to standardize and produce specifications to be shared with others. This need to standardize has resulted in an explosion of standards created by a wealth of different standards bodies and organizations. The resultant population of standards now needs to be categorized and segmented so we can better understand how the various specifications contribute to our needs and compete with each other.

The best metaphor for visually understanding how the various standards and specifications interact with each other is through the standards "stack." As illustrated in this chapter, the stack provides a means for understanding how different specifications relate to one another. The stack helps us understand which specifications may be dependent on or competitive with others. The standards stack also helps technology developers realize what technological areas have been implemented and which areas have yet to be addressed.

With the large number of standards and specifications, there is no doubt that a consolidation is due to occur in the next few months or years ahead. However, as history has taught us well, even as certain areas consolidate and present a more limited set of well-defined specifications, other areas of need will continue to expand and flourish. Wherever there are humans, there will be disagreement. And wherever there is disagreement, there will be a need to reach some sort of consensus. The XML specification and standards reflect this need to come to agreement and represent the agreement in a technical format that can be understood by machines as well as humans.

CHAPTER 20

Implementing XML in E-Business

In This Chapter

As you have seen from previous chapters in this book, XML can be applied in many ways to solve a variety of problems. However, some of the most important problems that XML is being applied to today are to solve critical business communication issues. Many attempts in the past, such as Electronic Data Interchange (EDI), have only had limited success in attempting to electronically connect the different parts of a business organization. XML plans to change this track record by introducing business-specific functionality aimed squarely at solving the business needs of all industries and all firms, large and small alike.

Yet there are many parts to the business equation. Enabling business collaboration and communication is a complex endeavor with many lessons to be learned from past experiences. As a result, successful implementations of e-business technologies and specifications require proper application of experience learned from past e-business endeavors in order to create stronger, more robust trading capabilities.

This chapter of the book explores these concepts and, in particular, helps you to learn

- What the "supply chain" is
- What exactly "e-Business" is
- What the various components of XML-based e-business standards and technologies are
- What has been attempted with EDI
- About the CommerceNet model for e-business communication
- About the XML/EDI hybrid approach
- About the ebXML approach
- About the RosettaNet approach

What Is the Supply Chain?

Before we can spend time talking about how XML facilitates commerce of all types, we first need to identify the ecosystem about which we are speaking. Commercial activity occurs within a well-defined system known as the *supply chain*, which consists of participants that are interrelated in much the same way that different species are related in a food chain. The supply chain, in effect, is comprised of the interactions between parties that are required to produce products or services and deliver them to customers. Figure 20.1 illustrates a supply chain that may be used for a manufacturing organization. For individual companies and industries, various portions of the supply chain may exist that may not exist for other companies and industries.

FIGURE 20.1
The supply chain.

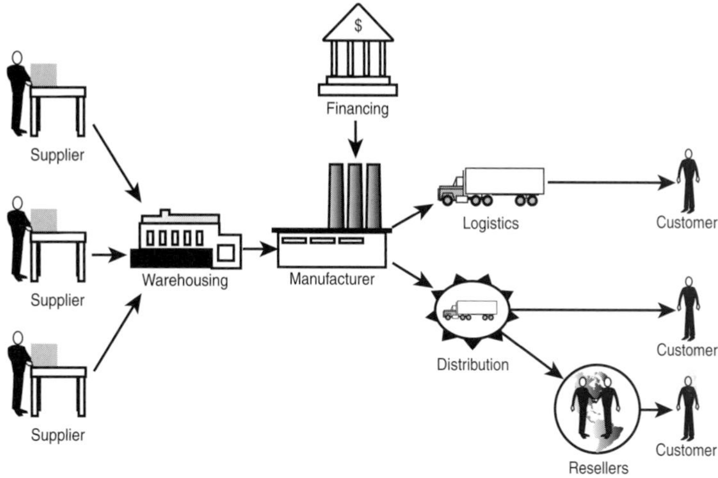

The supply chain has evolved to become a focal point for automation and electronically enabled processes. Because so many parties are involved in the process of getting a product from a company to its customers, optimizing the efficiency, lowering the cost, and increasing the return on investment (ROI) for each of the portions of the supply chain is a major goal of most supply chain management (SCM) techniques and technologies. SCM preceded the development of the Internet and XML by many years—and in some cases decades. As such, supply chain management concepts are not tied directly to Internet-centric modes of thought. In fact, the classical definition of SCM (as detailed on `http://www.stanford.edu/~jlmayer/Article-Webpage.htm`) is a "set of approaches utilized to efficiently integrate suppliers and clients (comprised of stores, retailers, wholesalers, warehouses, and manufacturers) so merchandise is produced and distributed at the right quantities, to the right locations, and at the right time, in order to minimize system-wide costs while satisfying service level requests."

The concept of the supply chain rapidly evolved shortly after the beginning of World War II. Prior to then, manufacturing and supply processes were mostly paper-based processes that linearly connected manufacturers, warehouses, wholesalers, retailers, and consumers. Some manufacturing processes were relatively straightforward, whereas others were hopelessly complex nightmares involving up to two dozen tiers of interaction. Each of these layers of interaction required people and paper trails. Compounding this problem, the linear nature of these processes made communication between arbitrary points on the network a time- and cost-intensive process. It was obvious that for the economy to be mobilized from a Depression-era inefficient system to a highly organized, efficient wartime manufacturing machine, vast changes needed to occur.

Old-style, multitier, linear supply chains had obvious inefficiencies that masked inventory, supply, and other production problems in independent layers of operation. An efficient supply chain would have to simplify and enable the flow of critical supply information between different points on the chain. World War II introduced a concept known as *operations research and management science* that helped to provide conceptual solutions to these problems. Originally, operations research was targeted at moving military goods and material to war fronts from supply factories at home. Obviously, efficiency was a primary concern.

Prior to the widespread use of computing and networking power to solve these problems, an interim solution known as *cross-docking* became a predominant method for optimizing efficiency. This method involved the manufacturing of products from multiple plants and shipping them to multiple distribution centers. These centers, in turn, distributed the products to multiple retail and outlet stores. This process reduced the dependency on warehousing and reduced the time in which manufactured goods reached their end destinations. Cross-docking results in the invention of a number of techniques and technologies still in use today, such as the *stock keeping unit* (SKU), which provides a numerical identifier for produced goods. The use of the SKU in combination with the newly developed barcode helped to enable electronic sorting and management of stock within a cross-docking facility.

This increasing automation of the portions of the supply chain allowed suppliers and consumers to gain increasing levels of awareness of the efficiencies in the supply chain process. Products could be tracked, via their SKU, from the time they're produced at numerous suppliers to the time they arrive at end-user locations. This increase in automation also allowed the chain to become less linear in nature. With a unifying means for identifying and sorting goods, multiple suppliers, distribution centers, and retail outlets could be used to reach the customer. The use of computers also reduced the need for paper to be the means for tracking these movements of goods and services.

Reducing supply costs has dramatic impact on the profitability of a business. In particular, supply chain efficiencies enable the following:

- Improved product margins (the profit per unit produced)
- Increased manufacturing throughput and productivity
- Better return on assets (net income after expenses)
- Shorter time to market for developed goods
- Better customer and supply chain relationships

The development of a supply chain is a fluid and constantly changing process. Supply chains are established upon the production of new products and services. Contracts are negotiated and put in place to arrange the supply of parts and materials. Management forecasts of demand and customer orders drive the creation of production plans. As parts are manufactured by various suppliers, inventory is managed. Agreements are signed with various sales and marketing channels, such as retail stores, to deliver these goods to the end customers. As sales are made, these channels deliver their forecasts and actual sales to help further streamline the product manufacturing and supply process.

These days, most products are complex in nature. Each finished product is assembled from parts and materials, which in turn are made of parts and materials, and so on, down to the most basic of parts and materials. Airplanes, automobiles, computers, and even tennis shoes are composed of dozens to millions of parts. Optimizing the supply chain to make sure that the right parts arrive in the right quantities at the right time is of extreme importance. The core unit of this aggregation of products into a final product is known as a *bill of materials* (BOM). The BOM identifies the constituent parts in a finished product. Any delays, production difficulties, or quality issues in constituent parts will delay production of the whole product.

Nowadays, the supply chain is more of a "web." Each manufacturer of finished goods has relationships with dozens or hundreds of suppliers, each of which have relationships with dozens or hundreds of manufacturing customers. These interrelationships have enabled the use of dynamic supply agreements that allow companies to constantly be on the lookout for better relationships and deals. The increasing globalization of business has resulted in suppliers existing anywhere in the world, covering many different countries, languages, and time zones. This globalization has added challenges and pressures in the effort to optimize supply chains.

The supply chain itself applies to two different ways of conducting business:

- Business to Consumer (B2C)
- Business to Business (B2B)

Business to Consumer (B2C)

All products have to get to customers at one point or another. In some cases, the consumers are actual individual consumers rather than business entities. Individual customers are a well-defined group of buyers that have long been the objects of marketing, advertising, and other targeted selling activities. Many of the early developments on the Internet were focused at helping businesses directly sell their goods to customers. This model of selling directly to individual end users of goods is known as *Business to Consumer* (B2C) sales processes.

The promise of B2C commerce is that it eliminates the "middlemen" and expenses of going through multiple distribution and sales channels before reaching the end customer. Of course, with the greater direct connection to the customer comes increased marketing, sales, and support costs that would otherwise be borne by various other elements in the channel. The most well-known B2C companies include Amazon.com, Buy.com, and other such direct-to-customer companies that provide services such as online banking, travel, online auctions, health information, and real estate.

Other than the increased complexity and potential cost in dealing with customers on a direct basis using B2C (or *dot-com*), a company implementing B2C techniques faces the danger of channel conflict, or *disintermediation*. This occurs when a manufacturer or service provider bypasses a reseller or salesperson and starts selling directly to the customer. This has been increasingly the case in such commodity industries as travel, banking, and electronic goods. However, disintermediation of the channel can seriously backfire, upsetting long-term relationships with dealers, distributors, and retailers.

Business to Business (B2B)

The other main source of customers for a business is other businesses. Transacting with other businesses as customers is a comparably much larger market than selling directly to end users. The Business to Business (B2B) market is estimated at over 10 times the size of comparable B2C markets. However, selling to businesses involves many differences and complexities that are not present in traditional B2C sales environments.

Of course, the major difference between B2C and B2B commerce is that the customers are different—B2B customers are other companies, whereas B2C customers are individuals. However, a more important difference between the two business goals is that B2B transactions are more complex and involved than the comparatively simpler B2C transactions. Selling to another business involves negotiating prices, sales terms, credit, delivery, and product specifications. Business buyers need to be approved in advance and their business needs to follow allowable parameters. Companies selling to other businesses also need to simplify and, in many causes, automate their purchasing interactions so that processes can be as smooth as possible. Whereas B2C transactions are made for the benefit of individuals, B2B transactions are for the most part important purchases for daily operations and the production of manufactured goods. Business-to-business activity is an online as well as offline phenomenon, although the term *B2B* has primarily been used to describe solely online transactions.

Electronic Data Interchange (EDI)

One of the first major attempts to electronically enable the supply chain was the development of the Electronic Data Interchange (EDI) specification. Although computers had been introduced into the supply chain since almost the first year they had been commercially available, processes and methods were far from standard. In addition, these systems needed an effective way of communicating between disparate points in the supply chain. Using telecommunications, companies could transmit data electronically over regular telephone lines or private networks and have the resultant data inputted directly into their trading partners' business applications.

However, this means of computer telecommunications only solved part of the problem in tying together the parts of the supply chain. These early electronic interchanges were based on proprietary formats agreed to in advance between trading partners. As the number of trading partners increased, it became increasingly more difficult to exchange data in a reliable manner. Estimates suggest that 70 percent of all computer input has previously been output from another computer. Each reentry of data is a potential source of error. It has also been estimated that the cost of processing an electronic requisition can be one tenth the cost of handling its paper equivalent. Therefore, a standard format for the exchange of data was needed. Work began in the 1960s as a cooperative effort between industry groups mainly in the transportation sector to produce such a standard format. In 1968 the United States Transportation Data Coordinating Committee (TDCC) was formed to coordinate the development of translation rules among four existing sets of industry-specific standards. It evolved to become the EDI specification in the 1970s, gaining first national and then international standard status in subsequent years. The stated goals of the EDI format were as follows:

- To reduce the labor-intensive tasks of exchanging data, including data reentry
- To be hardware independent and unambiguous in message content so that these messages could be used by trading partners of all types
- To provide a reliable means for the delivery of transactions and messages

One of the major features EDI has enabled is a concept called *vendor-managed inventory* (VMI). The concept around VMI is to shift the responsibility for analyzing sales and for deciding when the buyer will receive new product to the seller rather than the buyer. Using raw sales data sent by the buyer in EDI format, the seller is enabled to make judgments as to which products should be produced for sale. In this manner, risks and responsibilities are shifted from the buyer to the seller.

There are two primary syntaxes for EDI: The Accredited Standards Committee (ASC) X12, used mainly in North America, and the Electronic Data Interchange For Administration, Commerce, and Transport (EDIFACT), used in Europe and Asia.

EDI has historically used a standardized, secure, and reliable electronic transmission medium, originally known as the *value-added network* (VAN), to transmit individual EDI messages between participants in the supply chain process. The VAN provides a common connection point for participants by means of electronic mailboxes. The VAN functions in much the same way as a post office, providing not only a means to get messages from point to point, but also providing a means to guarantee that a message is received in a secure and robust manner. EDI participants dial in to a VAN, deposit all their outbound EDI messages, and simultaneously pick up any EDI messages destined for them.

VANs provide basic services, such as message tracking, that record whether and when messages arrive, are transferred, and are picked up. Faults and disputes can easily be resolved by referring to VAN audit trails. VANs also have the capability to deal with a wide variety of different computers and communication protocols. In effect, the VAN serves as an intermediary that helps to assist in the communication process by serving as a standard, neutral transportation layer—much the same role that the Internet plays today.

Although the VAN is considered by many to be an outdated mode for transportation of EDI messages, it nonetheless is in widespread use. There have been many efforts to move EDI transmission to the Internet, based on its capability for delivering messages at a relative low cost and with simplicity. However, many companies still rely on the VAN for reliable, robust, and secure transmission of their documents. Perhaps that may change in the future, but the VAN will have long-lasting influence as long as EDI remains in use.

EDI messages are text-based, positional, structured messages that are arranged into transaction sets. Each transaction set represents an exchange between supply chain partners in order to execute some business process. As a result, transaction sets are very focused in nature. The X12 Release 3030 contains 161 transaction sets. Many of them are quite specific; some are shown in Table 20.1.

TABLE 20.1 Sample EDI Transaction Sets

Transaction Set	*Description*
130	Student educational record (transcript)
810	Invoice
819	Operating expense statement
820	Payment-order/remit-advice

TABLE 20.1 continued

Transaction Set	*Description*
822	Customer account analysis
823	Lockbox
830	Planning schedule
832	Price/sales catalog
837	Healthcare claim
840	Request for quotation
843	Response to request for quote
844	Product transfer account adjust
845	Price authorization acknowledgment
846	Inventory inquiry
849	Response to product transfer
850	Purchase order
855	Purchase order acknowledgment
856	Ship notice/manifest
860	Purchase order change
861	Receiving advice
862	Shipping schedule
863	Report of test results
865	Purchase order change acknowledgment
867	Product transfer and resale report
869	Order status inquiry
870	Order status report
997	Functional acknowledgment

EDI transactions are processed by a well-choreographed set of software applications and systems. EDI software packages perform two fundamental tasks: encoding data into the EDI format and subsequently decoding response messages. Major components of this system include "translators" to go between EDI and non-EDI systems, "mappers" to associate differing versions of EDI transaction sets, connection software to facilitate and enable the use of VAN or Internet-based transfers, and internal software integration applications.

Despite the lofty goals of EDI, many of its core benefits have not come without costs and challenges. EDI systems aren't inexpensive to set up. Most EDI "hub" implementations average over $1 million to set up, whereas individual "spokes" require an investment averaging over $45,000—and these are just the primary implementation costs. Maintenance and ongoing services easily double this figure. In addition, systems take between several days to months before trading partners are up and running.

EDI systems also suffer from a shortage of skilled laborers who have the knowledge and education to support these systems, as well as the inability and unwillingness of trading partners to locate and hire these resources to manage their own implementations. In addition, EDI's long legacy has given it the sense of being an "old" technology whose time as come to be replaced by the "newer, better" thing. However, perhaps the largest challenge to EDI is its history of implementation. Traditional EDI implementations could only enlist 20 percent of a company's trading partners, which may account for a significant volume but still not enable a company to take full advantage of an electronically enabled supply chain. After all, these companies still have to support paper processes for these non-EDI-enabled partners.

E-Business and the Internet-Enabled Supply Chain

The advent of the Internet, XML, and online mechanisms have provided solutions to some of the problems of EDI. The low cost of Internet systems has spurred many companies to look at the technology as a means to lower the bar of entry into dynamic supply chain trading for small- and medium-sized companies. The net effect is to change the linear, somewhat-rigid supply chain into a flexible, Internet-based web of trading partners. In an e-business system, the center of operations is an informational hub that serves as a central point where multiple organizations can interact to pursue supply chain interactions. Transactional information is received, processed, and then forwarded to other nodes in the supply chain web.

Before we can talk about these solutions, we should first define what we mean by *e-business*. The basic definition of e-business is the marriage of traditional supply chain management techniques with Internet and Web technologies. E-business applications make extensive use of Internet technologies throughout all nodes in a supply chain operation. However, e-business is not a monolithic block of technology. In fact, it is comprised of three major components:

- E-commerce
- E-procurement
- E-collaboration

The Internet has changed all the rules, from servicing customers to licensing and installing applications.

E-Commerce

E-Commerce is not a concept that was invented with the Web. Rather, it has been around as long as there have been electronic means for exchanging commercial transactions. Electronic Data Interchange (EDI) has been around since the late 1960s and has been in use to exchange supply, shipping, and purchase information. However, in the context in which we are using the term here, *e-commerce* is just a piece of the overall e-business puzzle. It encapsulates the actual electronic transactions that take place within an organization without touching on relating processes that must occur around the transaction. Typically, e-commerce relates to individual transactions and not overall processes that are more general in nature.

The definition of e-commerce has been somewhat of a moving target, and at one point it encapsulated all forms of electronic business and commerce. However, as the term *e-business* emerged, *e-commerce* as a term was relegated to the point-of-sale and direct transactions that occur in an overall e-business environment. A typical e-commerce scenario is a customer placing an order for a product, which results in a series of transactions that occur to fill the product order and ship the product to the end-user destination. Therefore, e-commerce encapsulates the following concepts:

- Executing transaction requests and orders by customers
- Tying customer orders to business processes within an organization
- Order tracking
- Order error tracking and management
- Logging and auditing of commerce data

The *e* in e-commerce obviously stands for *electronic*, which necessarily means that commerce is transacted over networks and through computer and digital systems. The term *e-commerce* also applies to all intercompany and intracompany functions, including finance, sales, marketing, and manufacturing. E-Commerce can therefore cover transactions that occur via the Web, e-mail, EDI, file transfer, fax, teleconferencing, or interaction with a remote computer, and it can cover all forms of electronic business, including transferring electronic funds, using smart cards and digital cash, and doing business over digital networks.

The need for an organization to fill customer service and support requirements is also handled by e-commerce. Servicing customers by means of help desks, self-guiding support centers, knowledge databases, and interactive technical support with live agents is a key component of any e-commerce system. Companies that aim to directly serve their customers should also aim to satisfy their customer-support needs through these same systems.

E-Procurement

Whereas e-commerce usually refers to point transactions and purchases by individuals or organizations, *e-procurement* refers to processes by which a manufacturer obtains products from suppliers for its daily operations. By necessity, e-procurement transactions are enormous in quantity and value and therefore require a greater level of process control, workflow, and documentation. Typical procurement solutions cover all steps of the procurement process, ranging from supply order to acquisition and payment.

Due to its enormous volume and value, e-procurement is a sweet spot for many online B2B systems. E-Procurement has also been a target for aggregations of buyers and sellers—known as a *marketplace*—to achieve great economies of scale. These marketplaces allow industries to make large-scale purchasing and selling decisions across all participants in a given supply chain. Instead of working solely with local and large parts dealers, manufacturers and suppliers potentially can access a competitive, global market through electronically enabled marketplace e-procurement systems.

E-Collaboration

The final aspect of e-business systems is the ability to share information among supply chain participants in a process known as *e-collaboration*. E-Collaboration enables information sharing, collaborative planning, and collaborative product development. These systems store qualitative and quantitative information regarding supply chain processes and serve as a means to share critical supply and process information with other participants in a supply chain. These systems allow purchase orders, sales orders, invoices, checks, and other business documents to be shared within a well-defined community access area.

As mentioned earlier, a key area of e-collaboration is collaborative planning, which assists in group decision making in a cost-effective manner by considering different participants in the supply chain. Collaborative planning shares sales forecasts, production quotas, and replenishment plans that allow all parts of the extended organization to jointly reduce inventory costs and raise customer service levels. This collaborative decision-making process therefore leverages all available knowledge to make intelligent decisions on behalf of the whole chain.

E-collaboration also enables new product development by squeezing product delivery cycles and increasing development efficiency. By providing a common community for information exchange, these solutions enable real-time communication among engineers, product developers, and customer service representatives to provide feedback on the creation of new products. This process also allows users to make quick decisions on changes to suppliers and manufacturers.

Different Types of B2B Interaction

Not all models for business-to-business interaction are the same. As the technologies and mechanisms for e-business evolve, so too do the models for B2B business. In particular, B2B business models are migrating from long-term one-to-one relationships to rapidly changing and fluid many-to-many relationships. Rather than establishing fixed relationships with a set of identified supply chain partners, there has been an increasing trend towards fluid and in some cases spontaneous supply chain partnering. This section describes the various types of B2B relationships enabled by e-business systems.

First, it is important to identify the roles that parties play in B2B e-commerce. In general, they fall along four main types, with organizations playing multiple roles at different parts in the chain:

- *Buyers*. Customers such as individuals and businesses that purchase goods and services from suppliers. In the context of e-business, these buyers use electronic procurement systems.
- *Suppliers*. Businesses that market and sell goods or services to buyers directly or indirectly through sales and distribution channels. These suppliers use electronic procurements systems and marketplaces to sell their goods.
- *Marketplaces*. Third-party organizations that connect multiple buyers with multiple suppliers in an electronic market that allows for the arbitrary pairing of supplier product with buyer demand with a combination of services such as payment, credit, and logistics.
- *Service providers*. Third-party organizations that provide buyers, sellers, and marketplaces with services to facilitate commerce such as payment, credit, and logistics.

Direct Partnership

The simplest and most immediate form of supply chain relationship is the direct partnership. When suppliers and buyers are strategic to each other's needs, strong direct relationships are formed. Each business inherently and intimately knows the other's business needs, and thus electronic systems can be crafted around these requirements. Due to the intimate nature of the relationship, parties can take advantage of automated reordering through Electronic Data Interchange or the Internet, as well as vendor-managed inventory services. The supplier may even take on the burden of monitoring material levels at the buyer's sites. Although simple in nature and setup, direct partnerships require a large amount of trust and are very difficult to scale to any large number of partners. As such, direct partnerships are relegated to simple and direct relationships in industries that are critical and trust centric, such as munitions.

Multiparty Procurement

The predominant means for working with suppliers is through a multiple-party system using electronic procurement methods. As opposed to a direct partnership, multiple-party procurement is a more hands-off relationship with suppliers that allows a vendor to abstract elements of the working relationship without having to become intimately tied to its suppliers' businesses. However, these relationships are not completely fluid, because they involve long-term commitments and investments on behalf of both parties. Products in this channel arrangement are frequently supplied from multiple supplier locations to a single customer location. The primary challenge is in electronically enabling a significant enough population of suppliers so that costs may be reduced and efficiencies increased.

Agents and Distributors

Many products aren't directly transacted between buyer and seller but rather flow through intermediary channels that serve to add value. There are two primary categories of supplier channel: stocked and stockless. Stocked channels carry inventory and are responsible for making sure enough product is carried on-hand to meet buyer demand. Stockless channels provide value-add to the sales process without carrying inventory. This value-add includes sales, marketing, and service support to assist a company in "extending its enterprise" without having to carry the burden of inventory.

Stocked agents and distributors typically need to maintain a sufficient quantity of inventory for stocked items to meet delivery lead-time requirements. These channels then can actually rapidly assemble many small orders as they arrive from the buyer. These channels also make use of automated picking using sophisticated materials-handling systems. Due to the additional information and timing requirements, the addition of these parties in a supply chain greatly adds to the complexity of the overall solution.

Exchanges, Auctions, and Digital Transaction Hubs

A new and increasing form of B2B commerce involves the use of a "marketplace," which provides a single location where multiple buyers and sellers can accumulate their economic interests for the improvement of the overall sales process. Currently, marketplaces are a relatively new phenomenon, and transaction volumes are still very low among the majority of B2B marketplaces. However, as the Internet becomes more predominant in supply chains, there will no doubt be a turn of attention toward these efficiency-improving methods.

So-called "fulfillment e-marketplaces" help buyers locate sellers, and vice versa. They accomplish this by providing mechanisms such as dynamic partner discovery, exchanges, auctions, and reverse auctions that aim to set prices and establish relationships between trading parties. In general, marketplaces can be either public or private. Public marketplaces are open to any carrier or shipper that wishes to participate, whereas private marketplaces are restricted solely to member providers and users. Public marketplaces are "buying clubs," whereas private marketplaces are usually community sites aimed at attracting a focused group of commerce participants.

As opposed to arranging new partnerships between suppliers and buyers, which is the focus of the aforementioned "exchanges and auctions," digital transaction hubs are focused on reducing the cost of integration between buyers and sellers. In these transaction hubs, the relationships between suppliers and buyers are already established; they routinely buy and sell product from one another. These hubs let participants outsource noncore fulfillment activities and other services to achieve better efficiencies. This also allows service providers to interact with a single point of integration to work with multiple supply chain parties and therefore can offer value-added services, such as inventory, transportation, and supply chain management, at lower costs and greater economies of scale.

Components of E-Business XML Systems

E-business systems aren't monolithic structures. They are comprised of major segments of functionality that help to contribute to an overall solution for supply chain interactions. Because e-business in an Internet context, (especially using XML) is very new, not all components are necessarily implemented by all organizations. However, a complete e-business system needs to be comprised of the following elements:

- Enterprise and back-end integration
- Various network and foundational layers
- Messaging in a transport, routing, and packaging context
- Registries and/or repositories
- Data dictionaries
- Process and workflow
- Trading Partner Agreements
- Business vocabularies

Enterprise Integration

Because e-business systems are a core part of any business enterprise that interacts with suppliers and trading partners, they cannot exist outside of and be disconnected from enterprise back-end systems. As a result, e-business systems need to be tied to various back-end systems, including the following:

- Customer Relationship Management (CRM) systems
- Enterprise Resource Planning (ERP) systems
- Asset- and inventory-tracking systems
- Point-of-sale systems
- Warehousing, shipping, and logistics systems
- Financial and accounting systems
- Marketing, sales, and customer service systems

Enterprise integration provides connection hooks into these various systems by means of APIs, Enterprise Application Integration (EAI), file transfer, or other shared messaging techniques. Integration is a two-way street, meaning that e-business systems can extract data from these various knowledge repositories as well as enter data into them. In the process of this bidirectional interchange, these systems apply business logic processing and translation among different formats. Enterprise integration therefore provides a gateway to the back-end systems from which results are communicated to other processes in the chain.

Fundamental Network and Platform Layers

In order for much of these e-business processes to happen, various technology, network, and protocol layers need to exist. These various layers cover the following fundamentals for e-business exchange:

- Partner connection and document transport
- Security
- Development platform and tools

First, it is necessary for e-business messages to be transported between points and for business partners to physically get "connected" to a network. In the EDI model, the VAN handles these issues, plus many others covered by other segments of e-business technology. In this case, e-business messages are generally transported over well-known and popular Internet transport protocols, including the Hypertext Transfer Protocol (HTTP), Simple Mail Transfer Protocol (SMTP), and File Transfer Protocol (FTP). Each of these protocols provides different messages for asynchronous publishing of data, subscription to supply chains, message queuing, and synchronous request/response messaging models. Due to widespread adoption, a plethora of tools and techniques exist for proper and low-cost use of these transport mechanisms. Therefore, this component of e-business functionality provides a means for messages to "get on the wire."

Additional security layers are applied to these fundamental transport protocols to provide security of different levels, including these:

- Encryption
- Authentication
- Authorization and permissions
- Privacy

Encryption is commonly handled by the use of Secure Sockets Layer (SSL) over HTTP or SMTP, and authentication can be handled by means of digital certificates. Authorization and privacy layers are more proprietary in nature and are just not being solved in a standard, open manner. In general, e-business transactions need these security technologies and protocols in order for the relationships to be trusted.

This set of foundation components also provides some management capability of e-business systems to help discover the availability, existence, and condition of e-business systems. These components manage the quality of services for the overall system to ensure a consistent delivery of supply chain interactions.

Finally, the fundamental network components of e-business systems are the development tools and platforms for the construction of e-business systems, such as those powered by Web Services. Microsoft, Sun, HP, Oracle, and IBM all offer a number of e-business-enabling systems that can be built on to offer the rich functionality required. This portion of e-business functionality defines APIs that serve to connect e-business transaction systems with the back-end systems.

Messaging (Transport, Routing, and Packaging)

Just having a transport protocol is not enough to provide business-level, robust, and reliable communications between trading partners. EDI VANs have historically provided a number of other major features that have enabled partners to reliably conduct business with each other. As a result, the messaging layer, consisting of transport, routing, and packaging components, is the core to e-business systems.

Messaging systems provide a standardized message and envelope structure that serves to identify endpoints (and optionally intermediaries) in a given e-business transaction, specify how long messages are to be resent before timeout, and provide transaction controls and nonrepudiation (which helps to guarantee that messages are received by the end user). These components provide a certain level of session management and transaction coordination in a loosely coupled environment.

Messaging components also record sessions and other parameters that control reliable and secured messaging, among other features. As a result, messaging components serve as a basis for all e-business communications between parties.

Registry and Repository

E-Business services and capabilities are stored within repositories and registries—two terms whose meaning is often interchanged. Similar to the service offered by Universal Description, Discovery, and Integration (UDDI), registries and repositories serve as a central location where e-business services can be stored and later retrieved to dynamically discover business partners and their various capabilities, services, and business terms and conditions.

Data Dictionaries

Many portions of B2B information exchange require common knowledge of the vocabulary and acceptable items to be used within that vocabulary. These definitions of acceptable vocabulary usage can be found within a structure known as a *data dictionary*. These entities contain data structures, data types, constraints, and code lists of all the items necessary to compose valid business documents. In general, dictionaries specify the structure and semantics for particular business process documents.

Process and Workflow

Much of what differentiates e-business from simple e-commerce and individual transactional information is its ability to string multiple transactions into an overall business process to be executed. Many business process components, such as the "purchase order," are in fact composed of multiple individual transactions that must be executed in a particular order and with a given accepted workflow. In many e-business systems, these larger processes and workflows can be specified and exchanged in advance. Business processes can also be modeled with various technologies and those models shared to help craft the actual execution of e-business transactions.

Some business processes are applicable to a broad range of businesses, regardless of the vertical industry or locale, and despite specific characteristics of the business. These processes include many common business activities, such as invoicing, request for quote (RFQ), collaborative product development, purchasing, supply chain execution, and manufacturing. These general-purpose processes are defined so that they may be reused by other industries and businesses to achieve manageability and economies of scale. Other business processes are more specific to individual industries or organizations. These, too, may be defined as modifications to the generalized business processes or as new composites or sequences of established processes and workflow. Such examples include specific purchase order methodology, taxes, and production requirements.

Trading Partner Agreements

In the paper world, in order to execute any supply chain interaction, a contract must exist. This contract stipulates the terms and conditions of sale and the production of goods. In order to maintain a sense of legality and accountability, a similar process must exist in the electronic world. In e-business, this electronic form is known as a Trading Partner Agreement (TPA). The TPA includes a profile of a business partner's contractual agreement for transaction as well as its e-business system infrastructure and usage of protocols.

However, TPAs can be time consuming to negotiate and sign because they inevitably require businesses to use lawyers in the business process. They can sometimes raise thorny, intractable issues, and so some organizations may decide to forego TPAs because their costs appear to outweigh the benefits. Some TPAs and e-business systems, however, allow their users to prepare partial TPAs that, for example, send a declaratory letter to a trading partner asserting the company's position and policy on the issues that would otherwise be in the TPA.

Business Vocabulary

Much of the heavy lifting in an e-business system is actually accomplished in the actual document that describes a specific transaction. Of course, such transactions vary in distinct ways among different businesses, industries, geographies, and markets. As a result, business vocabularies have been defined by standards bodies of all sorts covering various business needs. These vocabularies are then used to construct the actual business content of a message. This message can contain product, finance, employee, or other business information. The actual terms to be used in the vocabulary are described by the data dictionary defined earlier in this section. Examples of business vocabularies include Health Level Seven (HL7) for the healthcare industry, ACORD for the insurance industry, the Open Travel Alliance (OTA) for the travel industry, and the Extensible Business Reporting Language (XBRL) for a variety of financial exchange needs.

Vocabularies are where the "rubber meets the road" in e-business transactions and include industry or supply chain–specific technical terms, properties, values, and taxonomic structures that are used to conduct commerce. In essence, it is the actual payload of a business transaction.

CommerceNet eCo Framework

Given the preceding definition of the various components of an e-business system, there are a variety of models to show how these various components interact to comprise a complete e-business system. One of the most accepted models for e-business interaction is the CommerceNet eCo Framework for e-business architectures.

The eCo Framework provides an architectural framework that enables businesses to dynamically discover each other on the Internet and interactively determine how they can do business with each other. The main goal of the eCo Framework, as defined in 1998, is to bring e-commerce and e-business processes from a systematic, technical level to a business level by providing a means for businesses to present accurate and stable interfaces to their partners in a loosely coupled manner, abstracting possible changes in an organization's internal processes, organization, or technology implementation. This allows potential trading partners in an e-business process to only describe what they do instead of agreeing on what they do or how they will do it.

The eCo Framework consists of an architecture and a set of semantic recommendations that serve to describe e-business systems in seven essential layers that answer the following critical business and systems issues:

- The location of other businesses and trading partners
- Determining whether partners want to do business with each other and how they can participate within a market
- The discovery of the services they offer
- The kinds of interactions to expect
- The protocols that will be accepted

- General issues that would prevent or allow systems to communicate
- Application interfaces
- Determining what modifications need to be implemented to ensure interoperability between systems
- Required information to exchange

The eCo Framework also provides guidelines and recommendations for creating e-business-focused semantic types and definitions to assist in automated processing. In addition, this semantic recommendation provides a means through which information on e-commerce systems can be communicated, a method for querying that information, and a definition of the structure that will be used to return that information.

Therefore, the eCo Framework is more of a business-level framework rather than a technical specification. The framework defined allows businesses to publicly define and expose their XML-encoded descriptions of their e-business systems in order to allow potential trading partners to get the information they need to enable interoperability. In order for this information exchange to occur between trading partners, a common understanding is needed of the basic components that make up an e-business environment and how those components relate as well as a common means for exposing information about these components.

Many subsequent efforts, such as Web Services, have borrowed from the eCo Framework in order to structure and guide their work. It is important to note that the eCo Framework is a theoretical guide and approach to e-business systems and not a specific implementation, per se. As such, it is up to efforts such as Web Services in the application-to-application realm and ebXML in the business-to-business realm to turn theoretical probability into practical reality.

The basic structure of the eCo Framework is outlined at `http://eco.commerce.net/how/index.cfm` and is shown in Figure 20.2.

The architecture is related as a layered "stack" that represents a typical e-business environment. Each layer is dependent on the layer beneath it. In the case of the eCo Framework, the layers are defined separately through "type registries" that define some aspect of information about the e-business environment and enable trading partners to obtain information at each layer of offered services for potential use.

As in other models, the Network layer describes the physical networks (in our case, Internet) that contain various marketplaces, or "markets," for supply chain interaction. Each market in the network is an independent aggregation of parties that are made up of one or more businesses described in the Businesses layer of the eCo Architecture. The

Market layer is responsible for business aggregation and identification, such as a business's location and other related information. A business can participate in multiple markets, and vice versa.

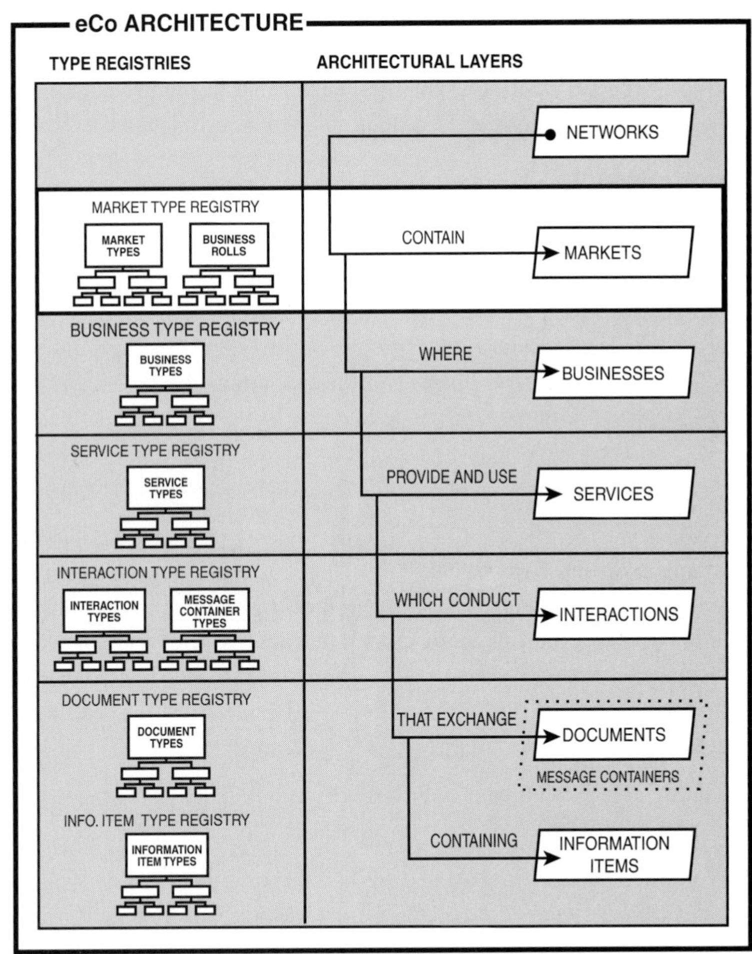

Figure 20.2
eCo Framework architecture structure (copyright CommerceNet).

The Services layer provides a means for businesses to describe the types of business services they offer, the required interfaces, and other information needed to actually make use of a particular business service, such as product ordering, payment, catalogs, or any other specific business process. These processes have their interfaces described in this Services layer. Some of these services may be defined in a standard manner within an industry or may be specific to an individual company. Services may be comprised of "subservices" that are also described in this layer. There also may be dependencies or invocations of other services in order for a given service to complete its execution.

The relationships and interactions between services are described in the Interactions layer, which describes the sequence, events, "choreography," and types of interactions allowed between service and process components. Each of these interactions contains a set of documents needed to actually perform the interaction or services request. Services are composed of a set of document exchanges that can be defined in the context of "interactions." Interactions are framed in a request/response mechanism that is event driven when a party requests a particular document from another. These documents are defined in the Documents layer of the eCo Architecture. The documents are the actual units of business dialog and interchange, which are composed of atomic elements described in the Information Items layer. Finally, we arrive at individual data elements and attributes that comprise each type of document used by an interaction. These data elements may be defined by industries and standards organizations, independently defined by businesses themselves, or a combination of both of these possibilities.

The eCo Architecture also defines a mechanism to query and access the actual information and properties described at each layer. This query mechanism allows trading partners to obtain information about a particular implementation of that layer and use that information to determine the extent to which it can interoperate with the other party. By examining all the layers implemented by a fully eCo-compliant system, prospective trading partners can make intelligent decisions about their interoperability with the system.

In addition to the architecture and mechanisms for querying that architecture, the eCo Framework defines "type registries" that are associated with each layer of the architecture and describe the various document and element type components in an e-business system. Type registries allow hierarchies of definitions to be asserted within a system, determine the equivalency of types in the same registry, and determine the relationships that exist between types. For example, a market for automotive parts might be further refined by breaking it down into markets for engines, tires, and so on. Registries also expose their interfaces in the same way that layers do so that their information can be accurately queried. As a difference with the previous definition of registries and repositories, these eCo registries are only used to store type information and not business documents, data dictionaries, or service descriptions. Each layer in the architecture is defined by referencing type definitions in one or more registries, with the notable exception of the Network layer. For example, businesses can type themselves by referencing a business registry, and documents can type themselves in a documents registry.

In this manner, a comprehensive architecture can be defined to enable the automatic interaction of business parties as required by e-business systems.

Note

For more information on the eCo Framework, visit the CommerceNet site at `http://www.commercenet.com/`.

XML/EDI

One of the first steps in attempting to get closer to an XML-based means for e-business interchange is the XML/EDI effort. This effort, in effect, is a combination of the best practices and technologies learned from EDI with the benefits that XML provides.

A lot of time and effort was put into making traditional EDI a success. Consequently, a lot of best practices and business process know-how was inserted into EDI specifications, software, and implementations. The desire to uproot these systems and replace them with completely redesigned ones makes some implementers hesitate, at best. However, the setbacks and challenges of EDI implementation have also thrown a wrench into many EDI rollouts. Therefore, a halfway solution must be found that can improve EDI with new technology while not throwing it completely out.

It is in this spirit that XML/EDI was created. The vision for XML/EDI is to allow organizations to deploy a system that allows each trading partner to exchange e-business information using XML and Internet technologies, leveraging not just the old structures of EDI data but also process control templates and business rules as well. XML/EDI consists of five major components:

- XML base specification
- EDI transaction sets
- Templates for process logic
- A global repository and reference dictionary
- Agents and implementation methods

These five components are combined to provide an e-business system that delivers e-business data as well as processes logic. By doing so, XML/EDI hopes to address the following list of requirements and solutions to the typical "ailments" of EDI:

- Reduce the cost of doing business
- Reduce the cost of entry into e-business
- Provide low-cost, easily implemented tools
- Improve data integration and accessibility

- Maintain appropriate security and control
- Utilize technology that can be extended and maintained with little adverse business impact
- Integrate with today's systems
- Utilize open standards
- Provide a successor to X12/EDIFACT and interoperability for XML syntaxes
- Be globally deployable and maintainable

It doesn't take much effort to simply encode EDI transaction sets into XML. Therefore, the real work and benefit is in encapsulating the various business processes, logic, and value-add that EDI provides beyond simple document encodings. XML/EDI has added the concepts of using process templates, the XML/EDI repository, and software agents as means to providing these benefits. Figure 20.3 illustrates the interaction of the five major components of XML/EDI. As you can see, XML and EDI are separate technologies, whereas the others are contained within the auspices of XML/EDI.

FIGURE 20.3
XML/EDI components.

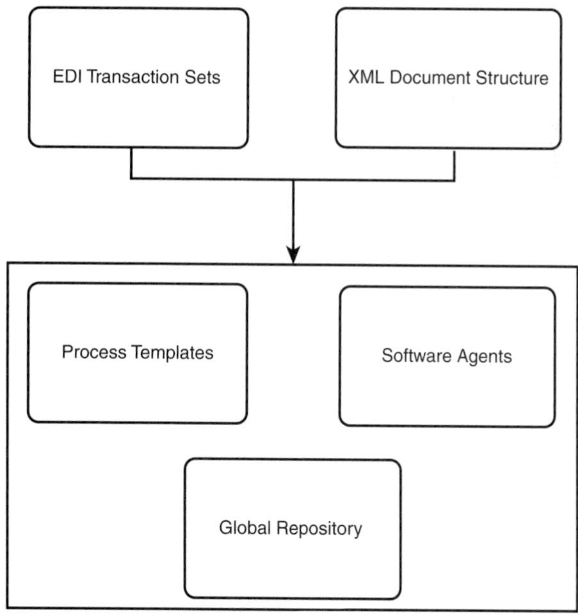

Process templates are built using XML and express work requirements throughout the system. They describe and control business context and process definitions that enable trading partners and users of the system to locate the correct components they need. As has been defined earlier, the XML/EDI repository provides a mechanism for users to define and look up meanings for the definitions of various e-business entities. As a result, described interfaces can be automatically searched and identified. The repository system provides a semantic foundation for e-business transactions while simultaneously enabling software agents to identify and reference business document entries.

In this regard, software agents serve several key functions and requirements. They are applied to process templates and interpret the results in order to determine work to be performed, and they interact with entries and definitions in the repository to apply and integrate the appropriate data per each business task. They accomplish this by searching the business repository and attaching the right template for processing.

The XML/EDI Initiative was started in 1997 mainly as a "grass-roots initiative" to promote the use of XML for e-business. Since then, the vision for XML-powered e-business has strongly gained ground, and the need to evangelize this vision has significantly decreased. As such, many of the concepts within XML/EDI have subsequently been used to form the foundation of the ebXML and UDDI work. Therefore, there isn't an overwhelming number of actual XML/EDI implementations, but rather the vision itself has helped craft the industry. For ongoing development efforts in XML-powered e-business, we need to look toward the work in ebXML, RosettaNet, and other such efforts.

Note

You can find more information about XML/EDI at the XML/EDI Group Web site at `http://www.xmlEDI-group.org/`.

ebXML

One of the major projects targeted at solving some of these e-business problems for small, medium, and large organizations is the e-business XML (ebXML) project, a joint project from UN/CEFACT and OASIS. EbXML is aimed squarely at making e-business transactions accessible to *all* businesses, including the smallest of business organizations.

EbXML was created in 1999 as a joint partnership by UN/CEFACT and OASIS in order to replace or augment existing EDI standards. The group saw the main challenge as being able to deliver the same value large organizations realized in the EDI specification to small- and medium-sized enterprises (SME). The ebXML group saw its main goal as producing an XML-based standard that would accelerate e-business deployment, reduce cost, be easy to support, and support worldwide business needs. It is for this reason that many say that ebXML "supports anyone, anywhere to do business with anyone else over the Internet." The specification intends for companies of all sizes to be able to dynamically locate each other via the Internet in order to conduct business through XML-based electronic messages.

The ebXML effort has been developed in an open environment, and as a result participation is free and open to anyone. The specification was also designed to be complimentary with existing standards and technical specifications such as UN/EDIFACT, ASC X12, and others. The goal was not to reinvent the wheel in e-business but rather to apply what was learned there to SMEs. The final result is a "plug-and-play" architecture that allows modular and incremental use of ebXML technologies by those interested. The end intent is that vendors will build applications that support these open standards that are affordable, easily developed, and available even for the smallest of organizations. The promise of ebXML is the ability to fulfill all business communication needs, but as we all know, ambition and end result sometimes do not meet.

The ebXML framework was developed as part of an intense, global effort that lasted only 18 months. As part of this process, UN/CEFACT was involved because it is one of only four international bodies that can enact legally binding standards. UN/CEFACT has previously lent its weight to the development and standardization of the global EDI format known as UN/EDIFACT. The final specification was delivered in May of 2001 in Vienna, Austria. At this event, a proof of concept demonstration was shown in which over two dozen companies and organizations demonstrated their implementations of ebXML.

The ebXML specification is comprised of three main infrastructure components and several other supporting technologies focused on such issues as document creation and business process definition. These architecture components are designed so they may be independently and modularly implemented. The ebXML infrastructure components include the following:

- Collaborative Protocol Profile (CPP)
- Core components
- Registry and repository
- Messaging
- Business process modeling

Needless to say, ebXML utilizes XML for the definition of all messages, process models, and supporting content. However, ebXML may transport any type of data, such as binary content or EDI transactions. It is notable that ebXML expresses trading partner agreements and business service interfaces in XML as well. The only major non-XML component of the architecture is the common business process models, which utilize established modeling standards such as the Unified Modeling Language (UML), the results of which are stored in a global registry.

It should be noted that there are not one but rather two ebXML architectures. One of these architectures describes the software components of the technical infrastructure and is known as a *product architecture*. The other architecture is focused on systems analysis and development and is known as a *process architecture*. The actualization of these different architecture models is realized in the Business Operational View (BOV) and Functional Service View (FSV), which are described later in this chapter.

Also, the ebXML architecture has been constructed in a way that its various components and sections, as described earlier, can be used independently and without dependency. This loosely related nature of the systems allows users to pick and choose those aspects of ebXML that are best suited to their operations without unnecessary baggage in supporting components they are not interested in.

Overview of ebXML Process

The process followed in the ebXML model can be simply described as two companies—Company A and Company B—that desire to conduct business in a trading partner relationship. First, the originating trading partner, Company A, looks up industry specifications and business processes and builds a local implementation. The company then creates a profile for its business, known as the Collaborative Protocol Profile (CPP), and registers it with the registry. Company A might wish to contribute new business processes to the registry or simply reference available ones. The CPP contains all the information necessary for potential trading partners to determine which business roles Company A is interested in, and which technologies and protocols it can engage in for these various roles.

After Company A registers itself in the registry, a prospective trading partner, Company B, can search the repository for Company A's CPP and check to make sure that its profile is compatible with Company B's requirements. The next step is that a Collaboration Protocol Agreement (CPA) is automatically negotiated between parties based on the conformance of the CPPs as well as associated protocols and other standards and recommendations. The final result is that the two organizations can now conduct business. The transactions are encoded in business messages that are encapsulated in ebXML message envelopes and conducted according to industry needs. The ebXML process is illustrated in Figure 20.4.

FIGURE 20.4
The ebXML process (courtesy ebXML).

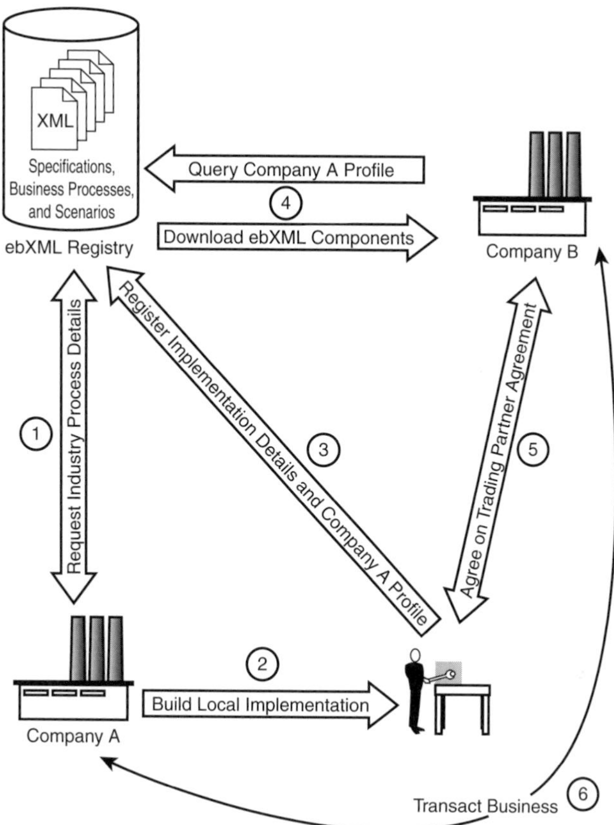

Collaborative Protocol Profile

The Collaboration Protocol Profile (CPP) describes a company's message-exchange capabilities, business processes, and business collaborations in a standardized and portable manner. The business processes that are described indicate how trading partners are to interact with the company. A business collaboration describes both "ends" of a B2B transaction, meaning that in a typical buyer-seller scenario, the CPP describes the selling process and semantics of the seller as well as the buying process and semantics of the buyer. The resulting CPP is stored with a registry to later be located and searched.

The Collaboration Protocol Agreement (CPA) is an addition to this model that describes the exact requirements and mechanisms for the transactions that two companies perform with each other. The CPA is formed by combining the CPPs of the two organizations and can be manually formed or automatically generated depending on the commerce transaction scenario. The CPA therefore becomes a binding contract that describes the terms and conditions for individual collaborations. The CPA is the actual implementation of a CPP by virtue of agreement on given terms. For example, if a CPP indicates that some property can be utilized in a transaction, the CPA will state that the given property *will* be used in a given commerce exchange.

The CPP specifies such properties as the contact information of an organization, supported network and file transport protocols, specific network addresses, security implementations, and business process specifications.

> **Note**
>
> The CPA and CPP specifications and examples can be found at the following sites:
>
> `http://www.ebXML.org/specs/cpa-example.xml`
>
> `http://www.ebXML.org/specs/cpp-example.xml`
>
> `http://www.ebXML.org/specs/ebCCP.pdf`

Core Components

An important part of the ebXML architecture is the specification of a set of ebXML schemas that contain formats for different types of shared business data such as dates, monetary amounts, tax formats, account owners, exchange contracts, and other specifications. These schemas are known as *core components* and are shared across all industries and user communities. The core components are meant to be the basic "atoms" of information used in business messages and are also known as *common business objects* in other e-business specifications. The schemas also provide a means to enable extensibility so that different types of information in different industries, geographies, or individual organizations can represent the same information in different ways.

In addition, ebXML describes a "core library" that defines a standard set of parts that will, in turn, be used by other ebXML elements. This library can contain such items as core processes that are referenced by more specific business processes.

Registry and Repository

The ebXML registry is a central storage facility that stores the data required for ebXML to interact with organizations and their profiles. The registry stores a variety of business-related information, including the core components, CPPs, business process and information meta models, and related documents or fragments, including Web Services documents, Java files, and even multimedia documents. The registry is the place where ebXML-participating businesses go before and during the conducting of electronic business transactions. Basically, when a business wants to start an ebXML relationship with another business, it queries a registry in order to locate a suitable partner and to find information about requirements for dealing with that partner.

The registry contains a set of query capabilities that allows users to search for relevant documents and potential business partners. Technologies such as the Java APIs for XML Registries (JAXR) can be used to query ebXML registries. In addition, the ebXML registry has a relationship with the more Web Services–centric Universal Description, Discovery and Integration (UDDI) registry.

UDDI was developed as a joint project co-sponsored by IBM, Microsoft, and Ariba and announced in September 2000. The main difference between the ebXML registry and UDDI's is that the ebXML registry is a local container for actual business information itself that can be of any type of content, including CPP, schemas, commonly used XML components, as well as Web Services, whereas the UDDI registry is mainly meant to be a global source of Web Services–related content. The UDDI registry system contains three types of information: white, yellow, and green pages. White pages store information about companies' organizational profiles, including their names and key services. Yellow pages categorize these organizations by industry standard codes or by physical geographical location. Green pages provide a mechanism for companies to store their actual services interfaces that allow them to interface with other organizations. It is quite feasible, however, for business partners to first search UDDI registries that could result in references to a CPP stored in an ebXML registry. Therefore, this becomes a two-step process, leveraging the benefits of both systems.

Originally, the ebXML registry was going to be a fully distributed, networked set of interacting registries that would provide transparent interaction to any ebXML-compliant registry through interfacing with a single source, but time constraints lead to the specification of just a single registry. Instead, the group now leverages its partnership with UDDI, as mentioned earlier.

In many cases, the terms *registry* and *repository* are used interchangeably, but in truth, the two perform different functions. The registry provides the interface and access mechanism, information model, and reference system implementation, whereas the repository provides the actual, physical information store.

Messaging

Messages specified by ebXML are sent between partners by means of the messaging architecture, which provides an "envelope" encapsulating a message with all necessary transmission semantics, including asynchronous or synchronous communications modes, transaction control, security, and reliability settings. The messaging service provides the means for the system to exchange a "payload," which may or may not be an actual ebXML business document. In addition to the enveloping and transmission capabilities, an ebXML message can specify routing instructions to ensure that a given party receives the document. EbXML messages utilize SOAP as the actual mechanism for message passing and extend the SOAP protocol via additional functionality to support attachments, security, and reliable delivery. The actual transport protocol, such as HTTP, SMTP, or FTP, is left to the user to implement.

Business Process and Information Modeling

As with all e-business systems, most of the intelligence in a system is stored not in the actual XML-encoded messages but in the business processes that surround the documents. Business process information includes transaction requirements, workflow and document processing, collaboration, and data encapsulation, among other related things. These business process documents describe how a business functions internally and how other organizations can appropriately interface with the company. As systems move from being human based to being machine automated, the appropriate electronic rendition of these processes is of utmost importance.

Business processes are formally described in ebXML by the Business Process Specification Schema (BPSS) and may also be modeled in UML. The BPSS describes all the activities that a business is interested in engaging in with its partners.

Using an XML DTD, BPSS provides a definition of an XML document that describes the way an organization does business. The CPA and CPP deal specifically with the technical and integration needs and aspects of a business but don't specifically deal with the business processes and workflow inherent in a company. Rather, the BPSS specifically handles modeling around the roles, specification of business document usage, general processes, workflow and document flow, security and legal aspects, transactions, acknowledgments, and overall status. The BPSS can then be used to create applications that automatically configure the system based on the specific business details of a trading partner.

In addition, users can use the UN/CEFACT Modeling Methodology (UMM), which utilizes UML, as a means to model ebXML business processes. UMM is an implementation of UML that specifically deals with methods for performing business and information modeling in the context of an e-business system. The model prescribes the specific items and their relationships that are to be produced from modeling analysis. The BPSS itself is just a subset of the UMM information model. To simplify the process, ebXML has produced simple "worksheets" that can enable nontechnical users to create information necessary for BPSS without performing full UMM modeling. These business process analysis worksheets and guidelines assist nontechnical analysts with the process of gathering the required data to describe a business process. In addition, ebXML has also produce a predefined catalog of common business processes that can be reused by more specific BPSS definitions. The group has produced a set of e-commerce patterns that are examples of common business patterns, a methodology for discovering core components in preexisting business documents or new processes, a set of standard naming conventions based on ISO 11179, and catalogs of core components and context drivers to assist in helping users to extend and build definitions of business messages.

The business process specification DTD declaration can be found in Listing 20.1.

LISTING 20.1 `ProcessSpecification` DTD Declaration (Courtesy of ebXML.org)

```
<!ELEMENT ProcessSpecification
          (Documentation*,
          (Include* | DocumentSpecification* |
            ProcessSpecification* | Package |
            BinaryCollaboration | BusinessTransaction |
            MultiPartyCollaboration)*)>
<!ATTLIST ProcessSpecification
          name    ID    #REQUIRED
          version CDATA #REQUIRED
          uuid    CDATA #REQUIRED >
```

As you can see, the ebXML process specification contains a root element called `ProcessSpecification`, which may contain references to other process or document specifications or other information. Each process specification has a globally unique identifier called "`uuid`" as well as a name and version that is specific to the model being represented. Within the process specification is a defined set of collaborations that are either `MultiPartyCollaboration` elements or `BinaryCollaboration` elements. These collaborations play roles for the transacting business parties. Listing 20.2 shows an excerpt of a sample package of collaborations.

LISTING 20.2 A Package of Collaborations (Courtesy of ebXML.org)

```
<Package name="Ordering">
  <!— First the overall MultiParty Collaboration —>
  <MultiPartyCollaboration name="DropShip">
    <BusinessPartnerRole name="Customer">
      <Performs authorizedRole="requestor"/>
      <Performs authorizedRole="buyer"/>
      <Transition fromBusinessState="Catalog Request"
```

Listing 20.2 continued

```
                  toBusinessState="Create Order"/>
    </BusinessPartnerRole>
    <BusinessPartnerRole name="Retailer">
      <Performs authorizedRole="provider"/>
      <Performs authorizedRole="seller"/>
      <Performs authorizedRole="Creditor"/>
      <Performs authorizedRole="buyer"/>
      <Performs authorizedRole="Payee"/>
...
  <BinaryCollaboration name="Request Catalog">
    <AuthorizedRole name="requestor"/>
    <AuthorizedRole name="provider"/>
    <BusinessTransactionActivity name="Catalog Request"
                                 businessTransaction="Catalog Request"
                                 fromAuthorizedRole="requestor"
                                 toAuthorizedRole="provider"/>
  </BinaryCollaboration>
```

Business Messages

The final element of ebXML architecture is the actual business messages themselves. These documents contain the business-level information that is sent as part of the e-business communication. The business message is wrapped in a number of layers as per the previous description. Business messages are wrapped within ebXML message envelopes, which in turn are wrapped in SOAP messages that are communicated via HTTP, SMTP, FTP, or some other protocol. The business message is simply considered to be a "payload" for the ebXML system.

Proof of Concept Demonstration

In order to verify that the concepts within the ebXML specification meet real-world requirements, a simultaneous effort to produce a "proof of concept" has been initiated by the group. The workgroup has demonstrated its progress at each quarterly ebXML meeting and has shown how the various components are integrated. Feedback is given to each ebXML working group on problems, challenges, and features discovered in the implementation. Resulting standards then reflect the results of the Proof of Concept team. The end result is to create a specification that is real-world tested (to some degree) and meets the needs of facilitating the implementation of cost effective e-business systems for SMEs. At the last meeting of the working group in May 2001, more than two dozen vendors participated in the Proof of Concept demonstration—and many of these participants are software vendors who no doubt will be releasing products based on ebXML.

More on ebXML Architecture

As mentioned earlier, there are really two different architectural views of ebXML. We have spent much time covering the technical architecture of ebXML but have not really spent much time with the conceptual thinking behind the initiative. It is important to realize that the teams responsible for the architecture approached the specification from a business workflow point of view. This resulted in the creation and selection of business components and objects that would be common to businesses across multiple industries, geographies, and markets. These objects, such as location, party, and address, would be designed not only to meet the specific needs of the various technical groups but also to be reused in multiple, unexpected ways in the future. In this manner, ebXML could be a constantly updated specification that unites cross-industry e-business needs with a standard technical definition.

The ebXML architectural model is a two-part conceptual model whose origin is in the OpenEDI group of UN/CEFACT. The first part of this model is the Business Operational View (BOV), which deals with the semantics of e-business data exchanges. This view of the model deals with the various operational requirements, agreements, and business obligations and requirements for an e-business exchange that applies to ebXML trading partners. Figure 20.5 illustrates the BOV.

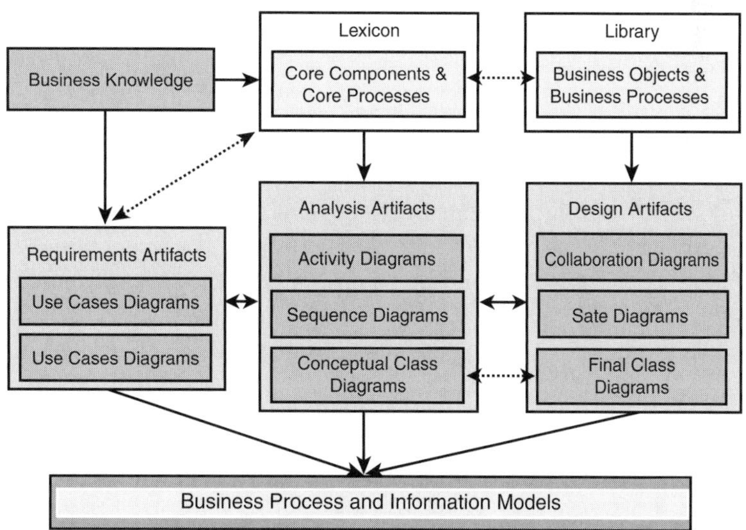

FIGURE 20.5
The Business Operational View (courtesy of ebXML.org).

The second part of the model is the Functional Service View (FSV), which deals more with the various deployment services and needs of ebXML. It deals with the stages in which ebXML systems are developed and deployed. The execution of the FSV consists of implementation, discovery and deployment, and runtime phases. The implementation phase is concerned with developing and creating ebXML-compliant systems and infrastructures. The discovery and deployment phase deals with the various aspects of discovering ebXML resources that can be manually or automatically configured for use in an ebXML system. Finally, the runtime phase deals with the actual execution and physical aspects of e-business exchange in a real-world ebXML scenario between trading partners.

In addition to these phases, it is important to note that the FSV has a specific focus on the information technology (IT) requirements for the implementation of a successful ebXML system. These various IT aspects include the following:

- Capabilities for implementation, discovery, deployment, and runtime scenarios
- Data-transfer infrastructure interfaces
- User application interfaces
- Protocols for interoperation of XML vocabulary deployments from different organizations

The registry serves as the means for actually delivering the BOV and FSV, because it provides a set of integral services for enabling the sharing of information, business processes, and related e-business data between ebXML trading partners. The FSV is shown below in Figure 20.6.

Future Development and Maintenance

As per the original stated objectives of the group, the ebXML effort was officially closed at the May 2001 meeting of ebXML in Vienna, Austria. The ongoing development and maintenance of the infrastructure of ebXML has officially been handed to the OASIS group, whereas the document definition, process discovery, and process definition components were moved to a group operating under the auspices of UN/CEFACT. In order to make sure that these two groups stay in sync, a formal coordinating committee was formed with frequent exchanges of progress.

Participation in ebXML is very high at the moment and consists of almost every large software vendor and XML-consuming organization currently in the market. Many associations, government standards bodies, and other groups are also members or otherwise affiliated with ebXML. Backers include a large number of high-tech, manufacturing, logistics, finance, and other companies of many different industries. Many standards groups are also working with ebXML, including the National Institute of Standards and Technology (NIST), W3C, and RosettaNet.

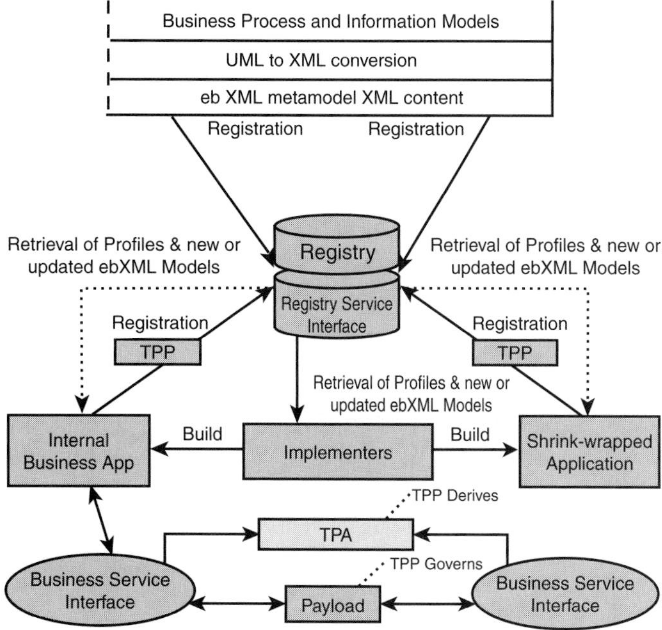

FIGURE 20.6
The Functional Service View (courtesy of ebXML.org).

RosettaNet

Named after the famed *Rosetta Stone* that helped in the understanding of ancient languages, RosettaNet not only seeks to standardize the grammar and language for Information Technology (IT) vendors to participate in e-business transactions but also to specify the business processes in which they take place. RosettaNet has gained much attention from the heavyweights and over 400 participants in the IT industry, many of which are also members of ebXML and other efforts. RosettaNet was formed in 1998 as an independent IT and electronic components–focused industry consortium formed by leading manufacturers, suppliers, distributors, and resellers. Its main goal is to produce an e-business specification for the industry that optimizes supply chain interactions. The result is a comprehensive set of standards and guidelines for an automated, Internet-based exchange of business information and transactions between trading partners. RosettaNet was an early proponent of defining B2B process standards in addition to simplifying business data formats, and perhaps their work has influenced the direction that other formats such as ebXML are headed. In essence, the group is focused on enabling businesses to conduct dynamic trade by means of providing flexible trading networks, improving operational efficiency, and presenting new business opportunities. An illustration of RosettaNet's role in e-business is shown in Figure 20.7, which references the eCo Framework as well.

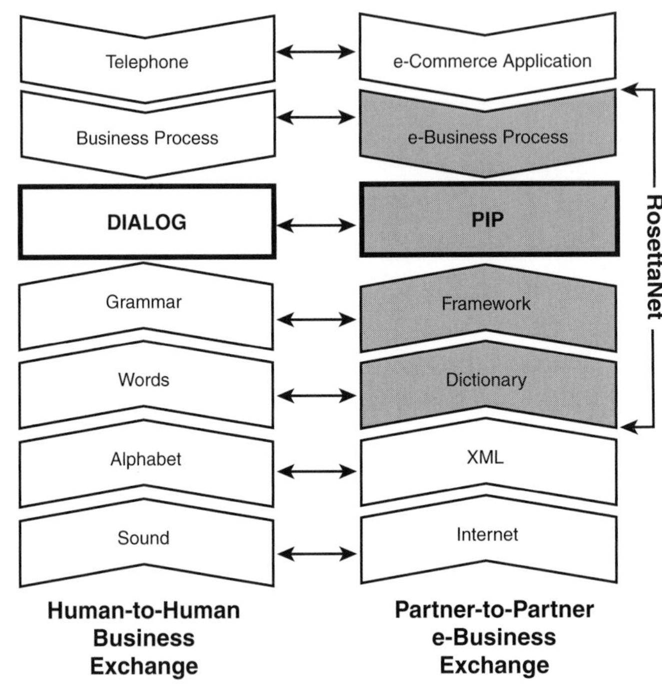

FIGURE 20.7
RosettaNet value proposition (courtesy of RosettaNet).

The main components of the RosettaNet e-business architecture consist of the following:

- Data dictionaries
- Partner Interface Processes (PIPs)
- The RosettaNet Implementation Framework (RNIF)
- Business process modeling and analysis

These components are described in the following subsections.

Data Dictionaries

The goal of RosettaNet dictionaries is to eliminate or reduce semantic confusion in supply chains due to differently defined terminology. There are actually two RosettaNet dictionaries: the Business Dictionary and Technical Dictionary. The RosettaNet Business Dictionary defines a common set of properties and data elements for describing business properties for specific industries. This includes definitions of catalog properties, partner properties, and business transaction properties.

The Technical Dictionary specifies common properties for IT products. The main goal is to simplify the process of locating and comparing the pricing and availability of similar products from multiple vendors. Dictionaries are applied on a per-industry basis, such as the Information Technologies Technical Dictionary or the Electronic Components Technical Dictionary.

Partner Interface Processes (PIP)

RosettaNet Partner Interface Processes (PIPs) control and coordinate the exchange of messages between internal IT systems and trading partners to support specific business-to-business processes. They are individual dialogs that contain the specific sequence of steps required to complete B2B processes such as catalog management, order management, inventory management, and customer service and support. Each PIP specification includes a business document that contains the required vocabulary, business process, and choreography of the message dialog. The PIPs also define the specific information exchange and transactions each step in the business process triggers. PIPs are grouped according to core processes known as *clusters*. These clusters include Administration, Partner, Product and Service Review, Product Introduction, Order Management, Inventory Management, Marketing Information Management, Service and Support, and Manufacturing. Table 20.2 provides a sample listing of PIPs dating from mid-2001.

TABLE 20.2 Examples of RosettaNet PIPs

PIP	*Description*
PIPIB1	Manage product information subscription
PIP2A1	Distribute new product information
PIP2A2	Query new product information
PIP2A5	Query technical information
PIP2A8	Distribute product SKU
PIP3A2	Query price and availability
PIP3A3	Transfer shopping cart
PIP3A4	Manage purchase order
PIP3A5	Query order status
PIP3A6	Distribute order status

The RosettaNet Implementation Framework

The RosettaNet Implementation Framework (RNIF) provides a structure for intersystem communication, messaging, transaction control, and response mechanisms as well as the implementation guidelines for creating components that facilitate the execution of PIPs. The RNIF core specification outlines the protocols used for the reliable, secure, quick and efficient exchange of PIPs and related business process information.

The RNIF is defined through the use of PIP implementation and message guidelines. These define the vocabulary, structure, and allowable data elements as well as values and value types for each message exchanged in a PIP. The message guidelines are composed of three major parts: the preamble header, service header, and service content. These are all packaged for transport as MIME messages that are packed, validated, and transmitted between RosettaNet participants through server-to-server transfers or transfers through an intermediate human-controlled browser.

Business Process Modeling and Analysis

Although the dictionaries, PIPs, and RNIF form the core of the RosettaNet specification, supporting business process modeling and analysis activities surround them in a layer of additional capabilities. The business process modeling involves a number of activities around identification and quantification of the various elements of a business process and the possible reengineering of those processes to simplify their implementation. It involves the creation of an "as-is" model of current business processes and generic "to-be" processes to be modeled in the RosettaNet architecture. A "blueprint" is created from the "to-be" model that identifies all the partner roles, interactions, and interfaces required to execute a business process. This includes specifications for PIP services, transactions, and messages. A PIP protocol is then created from the blueprint that results in a valid XML document based on the data dictionaries and RNIF.

Future of RosettaNet

A key element in this vision is a shift in strategy from being focused on providing a certain number of business process definition documents known as Partner Interface Processes (PIPs) to an e-business "ecosystem" that focuses more on proof-of-concept implementations, small subsets of existing PIPs, and implementation with a limited set of trading partners. Ten production milestones have been created that are meant to reflect real-world implementations and full-fledged tests of the capabilities of the RosettaNet specifications. Each of these milestones consists of a small ecosystem of companies committed to implementing a particular business process scenario, in a production or nontest capacity, by a certain date. Each milestone deals with different, specific problems within a supply chain. For example, in the Electronic Components industry, 15 companies are committed to implementing a closed-loop "Design Win Management" process by December 2001. Cisco's iHub project is committed to implementing 24 PIPs that provide greater supply and demand chain visibility by the third quarter of 2001. Each of these milestones is committed to tackling different business process scenarios and consists of three phases of implementation with a steadily increasing number of trading partners at each phase. Some of these processes will result in implementation of RosettaNet PIPs, whereas others will result in the creation of new processes to be defined by RosettaNet.

RosettaNet claims that each implementation of a "delivery-win" PIP saves each participant over $400,000 per trading partner. Rather than producing a laundry list of requirements, the organization is focused on an engagement model that stipulates that it can only focus on work that is supported by a significant number of board members. When these board members indicate that they want to attack a particular problem, RosettaNet then assigns resources and ramps up its work activities as quickly as possible. RosettaNet has announced another major milestone—the implementation of RosettaNet Basic, which is aimed at bringing the middle-tier of trading partners into the loop. This is done by greatly simplifying the process of implementing a RosettaNet solution, providing greater involvement of software developers and OEMs, and requiring large trading partners to perform RosettaNet-based exchanges with at first hundreds and then thousands of trading partners. RosettaNet Basic milestones are focused on defining use-cases and implementation guides, working with solution providers to specify a target price and implementation methodology, and encouraging solution providers to produce a series of product offerings based on the RosettaNet Basic requirements. RosettaNet and these solution providers will then market this offering to mid-tier trading companies.

RosettaNet is also flexing its international muscles by aiming to have a group of six Japanese companies and 60 of their trading partners communicating using RosettaNet specifications. Later, this same group will expand its scope to over a thousand trading partners. RosettaNet has also announced its support of the ebXML effort as well as support for the use of UDDI registries and repositories. In particular, RosettaNet is supporting the ebXML messaging service in its RosettaNet Implementation Framework (RNIF).

Note

For more information on RosettaNet, visit the RosettaNet Web site at `http://www.rosettanet.org`.

Summary

As you have seen, the world of e-business and supply chain management is quite involved. There are many steps to the various processes that enable companies to more efficiently communicate with their trading partners, suppliers, and customers of all types. As you have seen countless times before, XML provides a coherent, effective, and efficient solution to these various problems and has provided a number of improvements beyond technologies such as EDI that have attempted to solve these problems in the past.

Such XML standards and robust specifications, including ebXML and RosettaNet, have provided users with a framework by which they can reliably exchange e-business information and transact efficiently in a supply chain. The advent of these frameworks and their hopeful widespread use will no doubt herald an era when even the smallest business operation can effectively communicate online with its customers, suppliers, and partners.

Delivering Wireless and Voice Services with XML

In This Chapter

Of all the applications of XML discussed in this book, wireless and voice services are two of the most complex and problematic, and yet they are also the most promising. Both technologies play critical roles in many vendors' multiple touchpoint visions, from IBM's Pervasive Computing to AOL Time Warner's AOL Anywhere. Such vendors envision the Internet as a global enabler of communication among both business and consumer users anywhere, at any time. Such visions require that users are able to access Internet-based applications via multiple devices, including traditional telephones, mobile telephones, wireless PDAs, pagers, and whatever other devices are over the horizon.

The technology required to bring this vision of the ubiquitous Internet to life, however, has been unexpectedly challenging. Voice-recognition software, the key to voice services, is only just now maturing. The wireless world has also been struggling with its immaturity; wireless technology is characterized by competing communications protocols, inconsistent user interfaces, and confused, disillusioned users.

Unfortunately, the advantages of XML only apply to a relatively small portion of the issues surrounding wireless and voice services. XML can provide a simple way to format and translate data between the various interfaces and the back-office applications that talk to them. In addition, the XML-based technologies of XSL and XSLT are well suited to translating interface-neutral content for the wide variety of user interfaces. However, XML cannot improve voice recognition or solve the problem of incompatible wireless communication protocols. Therefore, it is important to read this chapter with a wary eye. Using the technologies described here is easier said than done.

In this chapter, you will learn

- What wireless and voice services are and how to incorporate them into a Web application architecture
- The application architecture for wireless services based on the Wireless Application Protocol (WAP) and how it fits into a multiclient Web application architecture
- How to develop applications using the Wireless Markup Language (WML), including an overview of the WML language and a development primer
- The application architecture for a VoiceXML service and how it fits into the multiclient Web application architecture, including an overview of the VoiceXML language.

The Vision of Ubiquitous Computing

Three essential elements make up the vision of ubiquitous computing:

- *Anywhere access.* Users are able to access desired services from any location, using whatever access device is convenient and appropriate for their current situation, including desktop computer, landline or mobile telephone, PDA, pager, public Internet terminal, and so on.
- *Parallel and complementary modes of access.* Parallel modes of access give users more options regarding when, where, and how they access a given service. An example of parallel modes of access would be a map and directions service that may be accessed via a standard PC Web browser or on a Web phone while the user is traveling. In this case, both modes of access have merits and are beneficial to the user under different circumstances. On the other hand, with complementary modes of access, a service is made accessible via a variety of modes that work together to deliver the service. For example, complementary modes of access would be found in a phonebook service where users can most efficiently create and manage their contact information using a desktop PC but access this information most efficiently via a Web phone.
- *Presentation-neutral application middleware.* As shown in Figure 21.1, different devices use different communication infrastructures, but they all access the same application on the back-office server. It is essential, therefore, for the applications running on that server to be "presentation neutral." Separate devices that are dedicated to supporting their corresponding interfaces best handle the formatting of data for presentation. XML and XSL provide excellent tools for implementing presentation-neutral middleware.

Figure 21.1 shows four separate access devices using different communication infrastructures to access a common application. A desktop user may use the standard Internet technologies of TCP/IP and HTTP to access the Internet directly. Alternately, a wireless PDA, two-way pager, or mobile phone user may use one of many wireless communication infrastructures to access the Internet via a WAP gateway. The mobile phone might also call into a VoiceXML gateway to interact with the common application via voice, which is also possible from a landline phone.

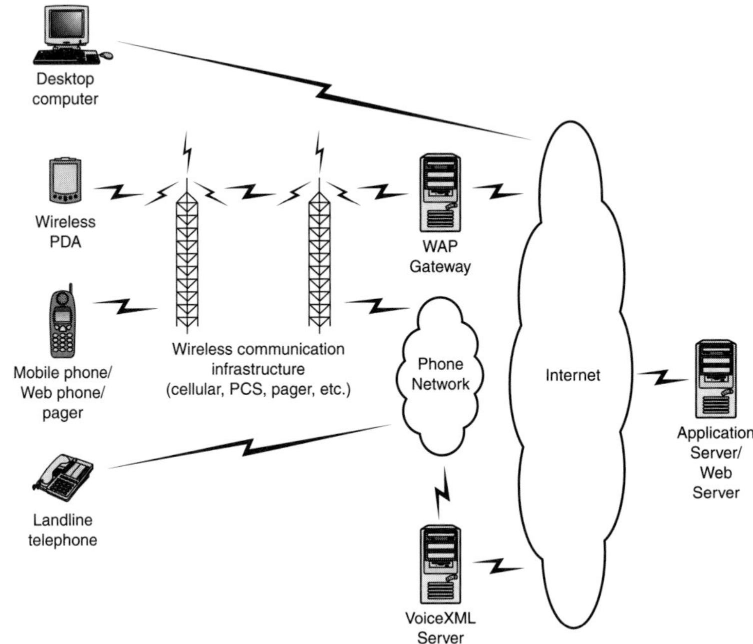

Figure 21.1
The ubiquitous computing multiclient Web application architecture.

Key Technologies

Ubiquitous computing is divided into two complementary modes of communication, simply because we have both eyes and ears. On the one hand, remote devices must display a graphical user interface that allows the user to communicate via the Internet. On the other hand, some devices must accept spoken commands and respond audibly—what might be called an *audible user interface*. In many ways, each mode of communication must be discussed separately. However, because of the requirement of presentation neutrality, there must be a core technology—based on XML—that's shared by the various communication modes.

Wireless Services: WAP and WML

The *Wireless Application Protocol* (WAP) is a specification for the delivery and presentation of information and telephony services via wireless networks on mobile phones, which are also called Web phones, as well as other wireless terminals. The current version of the WAP specification is 1.2.1, which is overseen by the WAP Forum, and is backed by major industry players, including Openwave, IBM, Sprint, Cingular, Ericsson, Motorola, and Nokia.

Note

The WAP Forum can be found at `http://www.wapforum.org`. The 1.2.1 specification can be found at `http://www.wapforum.org/what/technical_1_2_1.htm`.

WAP 1.2.1 uses the Wireless Markup Language (WML), an XML derivative modeled after HTML, for tagging content for presentation on mobile handsets. The version of WML that corresponds to WAP 1.2.1 is WML1, which, like HTML, suffers from a lack of extensibility. Although WAP has been endorsed by over 90 percent of the world's handset manufacturers, its adoption has been spotty, due to several problems—inadequate security, low-quality applications, ineffective business models, poor usability, and inconsistent implementations across different handset models. The upcoming WAP 2.0 specification, on the other hand, addresses most of the issues with WAP 1.2.1 and WML1.

Note

The W3C (at `http://www.w3.org`) is guiding the WML 2.0 specification, which can also be found at the WAP Forum (`http://www.wapforum.org/what/technical.htm`). For a more extensive treatment of WAP and WML, please see the book *WAP Development with WML and WMLScript* by Ben Forta (Sams Publishing, 2000).

The WAP 2.0 specification includes the following features:

- *Direct support for TCP and HTTP*. WAP 1.2.1 provided for the Wireless Session Protocol (WSP) and the Wireless Transaction Protocol (WTP), which had to be converted to TCP and HTTP at the WAP gateway. WAP 2.0 allows for HTTP and TCP at the handset and is also backward compatible with WAP 1.2.1.
- *The Wireless Application Environment (WAE)*. WAE provides for the interaction between WAP-based Web applications and wireless devices containing a WAP browser (called a *microbrowser*).
- *WAP 2.0 addresses the unique characteristics of wireless devices*. These include small screens, limited battery life and memory, as well as user interface considerations such as one-finger navigation.
- *The updated WML2 markup language converges with the Extensible Hypertext Markup Language Basic (XHTML Basic)*. The Compact Hypertext Markup Language (cHTML), the format used for the i-Mode service widely used in Japan, also converges with XHTML Basic. XHTML Basic is a core subset of the

Extensible Hypertext Markup Language (XHTML), which is appropriate for wireless devices.

- *WAP 2.0 supports two additional "mobile friendly" technologies.* These include the Composite Capabilities/Preference Profiles (CC/PP) framework for describing user preferences and device capabilities as well as the Cascading Style Sheets (CSS) Mobile Profile, which provides a subset of CSS version 2 targeted at mobile devices. (CC/PP can be found at `http://www.w3.org/Mobile/CCPP`, and the CSS Mobile Profile is located at `http://www.w3.org/TR/css-mobile`).
- *Support for WMLScript.* Also part of the WML specification is WMLScript, a subset of ECMAScript (the standards-based extension of JavaScript). WMLScript may be used to create and embed scripts in WML content (for client-side validation, for example). The WMLScript specification is part of the WML 2.0 specification.
- *Support for WAP Push.* This allows content to be sent to devices by server-based applications, allowing applications to send alerts to WAP devices without requiring them to poll the server.

Voice Services: VoiceXML

The other key technology behind ubiquitous computing is VoiceXML. Many of the popular Web services have interfaces that require minimal input and provide concise, high-value text-based output. Voice applications strive to deliver services such as stock quotes, weather, driving reports, and so on over any telephone. Such applications accept both voice and Dual-Tone Multiple Frequency (DTMF, commonly called *Touchtone*) key-presses for input and synthesized speech or prerecorded audio playback for output. VoiceXML is a XML-based markup language specification that allows Web sites to deliver voice-based services over telephones to users. To access such a service, a user calls a number with his telephone and connects to a voice portal running on a VoiceXML server (refer to Figure 21.1). The voice portal, driven by VoiceXML, in turn interacts over the Internet with the application that delivers the service to the user.

There are several reasons why a company may want to make a Web application accessible via voice:

- *Voice access is very low cost.* Users already have phones and phone service, so there is no initial cost to purchase a device or a special service for this mode of access.
- *Users are also familiar and comfortable with telephones, and telephones are globally available.* One of the most vexing problems facing wireless data services today is availability. By using the telephone as the client device to access voice services, companies can maximize coverage and availability with minimal additional infrastructure cost.

- *Voice access enables eyes and hands-free operation.* This makes voice access the only suitable choice in many situations, such as driving a car. Wireless PDAs, two-way pagers, and Web phones all require at least one hand and the user's eyes.
- *For companies that are already using Interactive Voice Response (IVR) systems, they have the incentive to move to voice portals driven by VoiceXML in order to consolidate all their services, thus reducing costs.* Traditional IVR systems are closed, proprietary systems, making it difficult for companies to build presentation-neutral applications.

Note

The VoiceXML specification can be found at `http://www.voicexml.org`. The specification has recently been released to the W3C, where it can be found at `http://www.w3.org/Voice`. For a more extensive treatment of VoiceXML, see the book *Voice Application Development with VoiceXML*, by Rick Beasley, Mike Farley, John O'Reilly, and Leon Squire (Sams Publishing, 2001).

VoiceXML is a relatively straightforward XML-based language. VoiceXML's features include the following:

- Interaction dialogs, including `<menu>` and `<form>`, which provide for user input
- Audio output, tagged with `<prompt>`, which provides either text-to-speech (TTS) or prerecorded audio streams
- Audio input, including speech recognition and Touchtone capabilities
- Presentation logic, including basic control flow commands as well as ECMAScript client-side scripting
- Event handling, including bad input, help, and error conditions
- Basic connection control, including call transfer, bridging, and disconnect

Building a VoiceXML application, however, is far more complex than the VoiceXML language itself. Creating a VoiceXML application involves the following steps:

- Designing the voice application and developing it with VoiceXML tools.
- Tuning the endpoint parameters to improve comprehension and speech quality.
- Tuning the grammars and parameters for the Automatic Speech Recognition (ASR) capability, essentially training the application to understand all relevant speech utterances.

- Setting up the VoiceXML generator, interpreter, and platform to provide the required availability, scalability, and redundancy to the application.
- Establishing a rigorous test suite and conducting thorough quality assurance.

As with wireless services, there's more to voice services than meets the eye. ASR is the weak link in any voice service, and even with a well-trained ASR system, there are still many steps to creating a functional XML-based interactive voice service. Furthermore, with wireless services, the current WAP specification is sorely lacking in usability and functionality, and even when the WAP 2.0 specification becomes established, developers are still faced with issues of backward compatibility, multiple communication protocols, and a seemingly never-ending variety of handset configurations. So, now that you've been suitably warned, let's proceed with the rest of the chapter.

The rest of the chapter addresses WML and VoiceXML by showing you how to use XSL style sheets to produce WML and VoiceXML from existing XML documents. The transformation examples will help you understand how to develop in WML and VoiceXML.

Wireless Applications with WAP and WML

This section discusses how to use a multiclient XML/XSL-based architecture to deliver Web applications to Web phones using WML. It presents the WML application architecture, which is used as a framework to introduce each of the components that collaborate to deliver WML Web applications. The phonebook business service is then presented as a sample business service to illustrate the delivery concepts and how to develop XML, XSL, and WML content to drive the multiclient architecture so that WML Web phones may access it.

A WML Application Architecture

The WML architecture consists of a number of major user and system components that together contribute to a system for human interaction with applications via telephony devices. Figure 21.2 shows the overall WML application architecture that is discussed in this section.

Here's a list of the components:

- *Mobile user*. The user of a WML-enabled Web phone.
- *Web phone*. A wireless phone equipped with a WML-compatible browser.
- *Base station*. A cellular base station in a wireless network that handles both voice and wireless data connections.

- *Telecommunications infrastructure*. The telecommunications provider's infrastructure for routing and managing telephone connections.
- *Phone*. A standard landline phone used by the phone user to receive a voice call in this example.

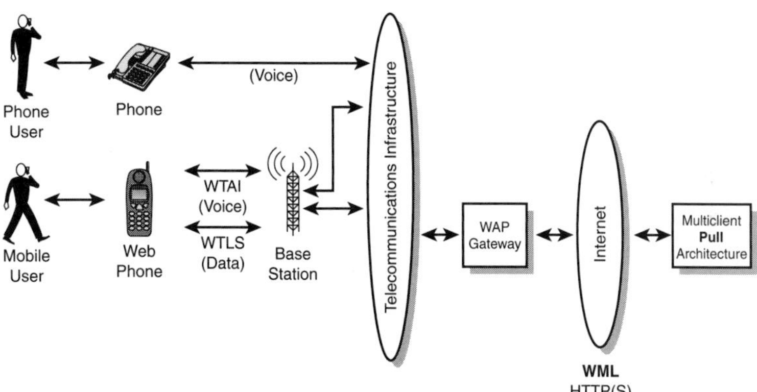

FIGURE 21.2
WML application architecture.

Note

Although a standard landline phone is being shown in this example, any type of telephone, including another wireless phone may receive such a voice call.

- *Phone user*. A user of a standard phone who is talking with the mobile user on a standard voice call initiated from a WML session.
- *WAP gateway*. A wireless system gateway that interfaces the WML browser to the Internet.
- *Multiclient pull architecture*. The architecture that delivers Web applications to a variety of different types of clients. The architecture is described as "pull" because when the mobile user issues a request, he waits while the request is being processed until the response is received.

WML Applications

Just because access to wireless and telephony-based services is enabled by technologies such as WAP and WML, it doesn't mean this is appropriate in all circumstances. It is important to realize what advantages and disadvantages these new technologies offer users and developers, and consequentially which business applications are most appropriate for use in this environment. As a result, it is important to review some of these benefits and challenges to adoption.

Advantages

Web phone access to wireless services has the following specific advantages:

- *Familiarity*. Phones are familiar and available to people, in contrast with other wireless devices, including wireless PDAs and two-way pagers.
- *Multifunction client devices*. Web phones can be used for wireless data as well as voice calls, although not concurrently.
- *Low cost*. Many users already have phones capable of accessing Web applications and simply need to activate this feature in their associated service plan.

Limitations

Mainly the technology's relative immaturity and the issues surrounding the combination of previously unrelated technologies evidence the limitations of this mode of access. In particular, the challenges include the following:

- Significant security holes in the WAP protocol
- Challenges to user experience due to different input paradigms
- Not eyes and hands free
- Small, monochrome user interface
- Inconsistent WML support

Security Holes in WAP

As a WAP gateway interfaces WML requests and responses, there is a point at which the request and supporting information is unencrypted, thus opening a potential security hole in the WAP architecture.

For most WML applications, this hole is not an issue because the providers that maintain the WAP gateway provide adequate security around the gateway so that this hole is not exposed for would-be attackers to access.

However, the next release of WAP, version 2.0, has been updated to overcome this security hole.

Challenges to User Experience Due to Different Input Paradigms

Web phones use methods of input that are unfamiliar to PC users:

- Alphanumeric input using the telephone keypad to enter individual characters
- Alpha entry using the "T9" system, which "guesses" at the user's intent as she presses keypad buttons
- Scrolling and "clicking" using unfamiliar handset-specific buttons

Not Eyes and Hands Free

Web phones require at least one hand as well as the attention of the user's eyes to operate them. This issue limits the usability of Web phones for wireless data access while driving, walking, or engaging in other activities that require the user's full attention.

Small Monochrome Screen

A typical Web phone screen is approximately 1×1 inch square and either is monochrome or has a few grayscale levels at most, thus effectively limiting the visual output of the phone to text or primitive icons only. This size of screen generally permits typically 4 lines of 15 characters per line and varies by Web phone model.

Inconsistent WML Support

Some inconsistency exists in the behavior across different models of Web phones. This is due in part to inconsistent or incomplete implementations of the WAP/WML specification or the introduction in some phones of proprietary features not supported by all phones.

The Profile of a Successful WML Application

Despite the aforementioned challenges, a number of forward-looking enterprises have embarked on the creation of WML-based applications, and some with a reasonable amount of success. As a result, a few characteristics of a successful WML application are outlined here to give the tentative WML application creator some insight into the types of business services that lend themselves well to this mode of access:

- Concise input. (Selecting options from a list is preferable to keying in text input.)
- Navigation requires a minimal number of steps (fewer than 10 is a starting rule of thumb).
- Concise text output.
- Sparing use of icon graphics.
- Retrieves volatile information that is important to the user.
- Information is required outside of business hours or away from the office.

Example: A Wireless Phonebook Service with WML

Regardless of the limitations of WML, there are many reasons to at least dive in and give the technology a try. The following example uses a phonebook service to illustrate WML access to business Web applications. The concepts discussed here are applicable to WML Web applications in general. This example is a common one—a user accesses a company phonebook, looks up a contact, and then calls the contact via the phone device.

Usage Scenario

This usage scenario outlines the chronological sequence of steps required to realize the goal:

- The user accesses the phonebook service to get a list of contact groups.
- The user selects a group to view a list of its contacts.
- The user selects a contact to view the details of that contact, including phone numbers.
- The user selects a phone number to call that contact.

Collaborations

The first three steps in the usage scenario each involve a separate type of request to the multiclient architecture, whereas the last step involves the Web phone using WTAI to initiate a voice call directly to a phone number retrieved from the phonebook service. To support the steps, the phonebook service retrieves data, selects the proper XSL style sheet, and transforms the data into WML for delivery to the gateway. For a diagram of the architecture that is applicable for these collaborations, refer to Figure 21.1 earlier in this chapter.

Developing the Content

This section discusses how to develop the content required to power the WML phonebook service. This content is presented in the order of the steps of the usage scenario outlined previously.

Accessing the Service to Get a List of Contact Groups

The user first enters the URL of the phonebook service into the Web phone using one of the two Web phone text-entry methods discussed previously. Here's an example:

```
https://www.MyDomain.com/servlet/Phonebook
```

Here, `www.MyDomain.com` is the domain of the business Web site providing the phonebook service.

The XML that is returned by the data component in response to this request appears in Listing 21.1.

LISTING 21.1 `Phonebook_Empty.xml`—Phonebook Service XML Empty Response

```
<?xml version="1.0" encoding="UTF-8"?>

<phonebook name="XYZ Inc" group="None"/>
```

This XML response conveys the name of the phonebook as `"XYZ Inc"` and the group as `"None"` to indicate that this phonebook XML document contains no contacts.

The XSL style sheet used by the phonebook view component to transform this XML response into WML is shown in Listing 21.2. The purpose of the style sheet is to transform the XML business data in the phonebook application so the data can be delivered as WML. If you need more information about using and developing with XSL, refer to Chapter 9, "Transforming XML with XSL."

LISTING 21.2 `GetListOfContactGroups_WML.xsl`—The XSL Used by the Phonebook View to Transform the XML into a WML List of Contact Groups

```
<?xml version="1.0" encoding="UTF-8"?>
<xsl:stylesheet version="1.0" xmlns:xsl="http://www.w3.org/1999/XSL/Transform">
  <xsl:param name="servlet" select="'undefined'"/>
  <xsl:template match="/">
    <xsl:text disable-output-escaping="yes">
      <![CDATA[<!DOCTYPE wml PUBLIC "-//WAPFORUM//DTD WML 1.1//EN"
➥"http://www.wapforum.org/DTD/wml_1.1.xml">]]>
    </xsl:text>
    <wml>
      <card id="SelectGroup">
        <do type="accept" label="OK">
          <go method="get">
            <xsl:attribute name="href"><xsl:value-of select="$servlet"/>
➥</xsl:attribute>
            <postfield name="mode" value="selectContact"/>
            <postfield name="group" value="$group"/>
          </go>
        </do>
        <p>
          <b><xsl:value-of select="phonebook/@name"/></b>
          <select name="group">
            <option>All</option>
            <option>[A-C]</option>
            <option>[D-F]</option>
            <option>[G-I]</option>
            <option>[J-L]</option>
```

LISTING 21.2 continued

```
            <option>[M-O]</option>
            <option>[P-S]</option>
            <option>[T-V]</option>
            <option>[W-Z]</option>
          </select>
        </p>
      </card>
    </wml>
  </xsl:template>
</xsl:stylesheet>
```

When the XML in Listing 21.1 is transformed using the XSL in Listing 21.2, it results in the WML response shown in Listing 21.3.

LISTING 21.3 `ListOfContactGroups.wml`—The WML Response for a List of Contact Groups

```
<?xml version="1.0" encoding="UTF-8"?>
<!DOCTYPE wml PUBLIC "-//WAPFORUM//DTD WML 1.1//EN"
➥"http://www.wapforum.org/DTD/wml_1.1.xml">
<wml>
  <card id="SelectGroup">
    <do label="OK" type="accept">
      <go method="get" href="/servlet/Phonebook">
        <postfield value="selectContact" name="mode"/>
        <postfield value="$group" name="group"/>
      </go>
    </do>
    <p>
      <b>XYZ Inc</b>
      <select name="group">
        <option>All</option>
        <option>[A-C]</option>
        <option>[D-F]</option>
        <option>[G-I]</option>
        <option>[J-L]</option>
        <option>[M-O]</option>
        <option>[P-S]</option>
        <option>[T-V]</option>
        <option>[W-Z]</option>
      </select>
    </p>
  </card>
</wml>
```

The output listing illustrates these characteristics of WML:

- The <wml> root element common to WML documents.
- The card-based paradigm. This WML document has a single card, as specified by the card element.
- The <do> element, to define and accept user input. This example specifies a soft menu at the base of the Web phone screen that will have the label OK and the type accept, meaning that when the user presses the key associated with the OK label, the Web phone will accept and submit the input.
- The <go> element, to define the submission method and arguments. The example uses HTTP GET. The first argument sets the parameter with the name mode to the value selectContact, informing the phonebook view that the request is intended to get the WML page required to select a particular contact of the phonebook. The second argument sets the parameter with the name group to the value of the local WML variable named group.
- The <p> element, which controls output display on the Web phone screen.
- The <b> element that indicates the enclosed text should be displayed in bold font to serve as a title for the phonebook being displayed.
- <select> element, which presents a list of options for the user. When the user selects an option, the form enclosed by the go element is submitted. In this case, the user is selecting the group containing the first letter of the last name of the contact she wishes to call.

When this WML is loaded into a Web phone, the screen appears as shown in Figure 21.3.

Selecting a Group to View a List of Its Contacts

Next, the user needs to select a group to view its contacts. In this example, we select the group [A-C] and submit the request by pressing OK. The ensuing collaborations generate the XML response in Listing 21.4.

LISTING 21.4 Phonebook_a2c.xml—The Phonebook Service XML Response for Contacts in a Selected Group

```
<?xml version="1.0" encoding="UTF-8"?>

<phonebook name="XYZ Inc" group="a2c">
  <contact id="e5678">
    <name>
      <firstname>Joe</firstname>
      <lastname>Ashworth</lastname>
    </name>
    <phone type="Work">
```

LISTING 21.4 continued

```
      <areacode>813</areacode>
      <number>9816084</number>
      <extension>4373</extension>
    </phone>
    <phone type="Home">
      <areacode>813</areacode>
      <number>3472341</number>
    </phone>
  </contact>
  <contact id="e9921">
    <name>
      <firstname>Bill</firstname>
      <lastname>Currie</lastname>
    </name>
    <phone type="Work">
      <areacode>813</areacode>
      <number>2367856</number>
      <extension>4373</extension>
    </phone>
    <phone type="Mobile">
      <areacode>813</areacode>
      <number>9835646</number>
    </phone>
  </contact>
</phonebook>
```

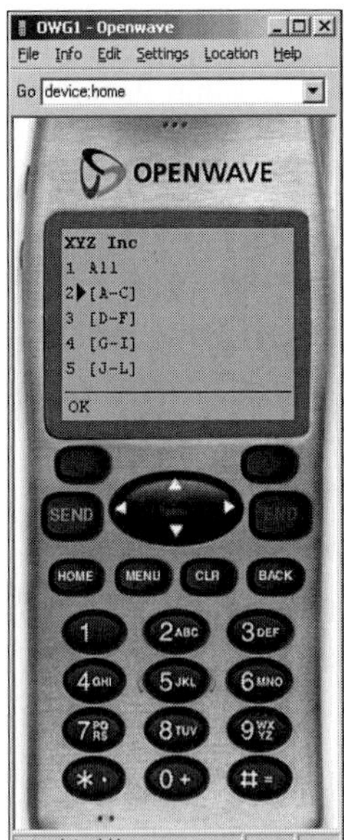

FIGURE 21.3
The Web phone emulator view of the WML response for a list of contact groups. Openwave UP.SDK 4.1 used for emulator. (Image of UP.SDK courtesy Openwave Systems Inc.)

The XSL used to transform Listing 21.4 is shown in Listing 21.5.

LISTING 21.5 `GetListOfContacts_WML.xsl`—The XSL Used by the Phonebook View to Transform the XML into a WML List of Contacts in a Group

```
<?xml version="1.0" encoding="UTF-8"?>
<xsl:stylesheet version="1.0" xmlns:xsl="http://www.w3.org/1999/XSL/Transform">
  <xsl:param name="servlet" select="'undefined'"/>
  <xsl:param name="group" select="'undefined'"/>
  <xsl:template match="/">
    <xsl:text disable-output-escaping="yes">
      <![CDATA[<!DOCTYPE wml PUBLIC "-//WAPFORUM//DTD WML 1.1//EN"
➥"http://www.wapforum.org/DTD/wml_1.1.xml">]]>
    </xsl:text>
    <wml>
      <card id="SelectContact">
        <do type="accept" label="OK">
          <go method="get">
            <xsl:attribute name="href"><xsl:value-of select="$servlet"/>
➥</xsl:attribute>
            <postfield name="mode" value="selectNumber"/>
            <postfield name="group" value="$group"/>
            <postfield name="contact" value="$contact"/>
          </go>
        </do>
        <p>
          <b><xsl:value-of select="phonebook/@name"/> -
➥<xsl:value-of select="$group"/></b>
          <select name="contact">
            <xsl:for-each select="phonebook/contact">
              <option>
                <xsl:attribute name="value"><xsl:value-of select="@id"/>
➥</xsl:attribute>
                <xsl:value-of select="name/firstname"/><xsl:text> </xsl:text>
➥<xsl:value-of select="name/lastname"/>
              </option>
            </xsl:for-each>
            <option><xsl:attribute name="onpick"><xsl:value-of
➥select="$servlet"/>?mode=selectGroup</xsl:attribute>[Back]</option>
          </select>
        </p>
      </card>
    </wml>
  </xsl:template>
</xsl:stylesheet>
```

The WML that is generated as a result of transforming the XML in Listing 21.4 with the XSL in Listing 21.5 is shown in Listing 21.6.

LISTING 21.6 `ListOfContacts.wml`—The WML Response for a List of Contacts in a Group

```
<?xml version="1.0" encoding="UTF-8"?>
<!DOCTYPE wml PUBLIC "-//WAPFORUM//DTD WML 1.1//EN"
➥"http://www.wapforum.org/DTD/wml_1.1.xml">
<wml>
  <card id="SelectContact">
    <do label="OK" type="accept">
      <go method="get" href="/servlet/Phonebook">
        <postfield value="selectNumber" name="mode"/>
        <postfield value="$group" name="group"/>
        <postfield value="$contact" name="contact"/>
      </go>
    </do>
    <p>
      <b>XYZ Inc - [A-C]</b>
      <select name="contact">
        <option value="e5678">Joe Ashworth</option>
        <option value="e9921">Bill Currie</option>
        <option onpick="/servlet/Phonebook?mode=selectGroup">[Back]</option>
      </select>
    </p>
  </card>
</wml>
```

As in the previous request, this output contains a single WML `card` element:

```
<card id="SelectContact">
```

This card contains two child elements: `do` and `p`. The function of these elements is the same as discussed for the previous request, except in this case the form submitted by the `go` child element of the `do` element includes `mode`, `group`, and `contact` parameters:

```
<go method="get" href="/servlet/Phonebook">
<postfield value="selectNumber" name="mode"/>
<postfield value="$group" name="group"/>
<postfield value="$contact" name="contact"/>
</go>
```

The `mode` parameter is set to the value `selectNumber`, indicating that the request is to get a WML view showing details of a contact, including phone numbers, that enables the user to select a number to call. The `group` parameter is set with the value `[A-C]` passed from the previous request. Lastly, the `contact` parameter is set to the employee ID of the contact selected in the selection list.

The display on the Web phone for this card includes a bold line at the top with the text `XYZ Inc - [A-C]`:

```
<b>XYZ Inc - [A-C]</b>
```

A selection list follows that assigns the value of the option selected to the variable named `contact`:

```
<select name="contact">
```

Two options for contacts in the list correspond to the two `contact` elements in the source XML:

```
<option value="e5678">Joe Ashworth</option>
<option value="e9921">Bill Currie</option>
```

The last option in the selection list appears on the Web phone screen as the text `[Back]`, informing the user that selecting this option causes the phonebook service to go back to the previous step:

```
<option onpick="/servlet/Phonebook?mode=selectGroup">[Back]</option>
```

This option enables users to drill down into a contact group to look at the contacts in that group and then navigate back to the list of contact groups to look at contacts in other contact groups.

When this WML is loaded into a Web phone, the screen appears as shown in Figure 21.4.

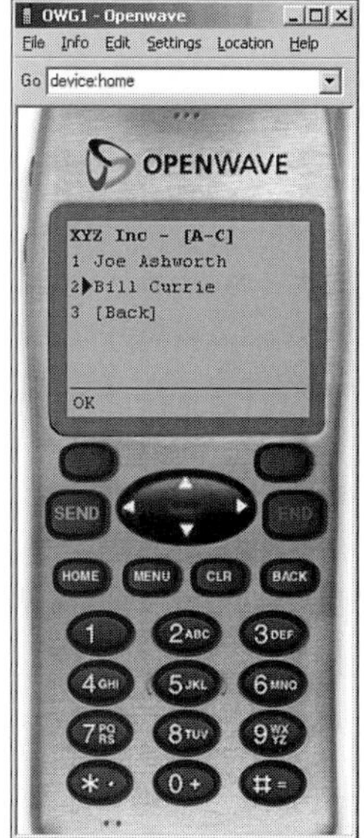

FIGURE 21.4
Web phone emulator view of WML response for list of contacts in group. Openwave UP.SDK 4.1 used for emulator. (Image of UP.SDK courtesy Openwave Systems Inc.)

Selecting a Contact to View Its Details

In this step, the user selects a contact from the list in order to see the details of that contact. In this example, the mobile user selects the contact with the name Bill Currie. The XML response to this request from the phonebook data servlet is shown in Listing 21.7.

LISTING 21.7 Phonebook_e9921.xml—The Phonebook Service XML Response for Contact Details

```
<?xml version="1.0" encoding="UTF-8"?>

<phonebook name="XYZ Inc" group="e9921">
  <contact id="e9921">
    <name>
      <firstname>Bill</firstname>
      <lastname>Currie</lastname>
    </name>
    <phone type="Work">
      <areacode>813</areacode>
      <number>2367856</number>
      <extension>4373</extension>
    </phone>
    <phone type="Mobile">
      <areacode>813</areacode>
      <number>9835646</number>
    </phone>
  </contact>
</phonebook>
```

Note in this XML that the group attribute of the phonebook element has the value e9921, indicating that this particular XML document contains the phonebook details for only one contact. The contact is Bill Currie, and two phone numbers are listed: a work phone number and mobile phone number. The XSL used to transform this XML is shown in Listing 21.8.

LISTING 21.8 GetContactDetails_WML.xsl—The XSL Used by the Phonebook View to Transform the XML into WML Contact Details

```
<?xml version="1.0" encoding="UTF-8"?>
<xsl:stylesheet version="1.0" xmlns:xsl="http://www.w3.org/1999/XSL/Transform">
  <xsl:param name="servlet" select="'undefined'"/>
  <xsl:param name="group" select="'undefined'"/>
  <xsl:template match="/">
    <xsl:text disable-output-escaping="yes">
      <![CDATA[<!DOCTYPE wml PUBLIC "-//WAPFORUM//DTD WML 1.1//EN"
➥"http://www.wapforum.org/DTD/wml_1.1.xml">]]>
    </xsl:text>
```

LISTING 21.8 continued

```
    <wml>
      <card id="SelectNumber">
        <do type="accept" label="Call">
          <go href="wtai://wp/mc;$(number)"/>
        </do>
        <p>
          <xsl:for-each select="phonebook/contact[1]">
            <b>XYZ Inc - <xsl:for-each select="name">
                <xsl:value-of select="firstname"/>
                <xsl:text> </xsl:text>
                <xsl:value-of select="lastname"/>
              </xsl:for-each>
            </b>
            <select name="number">
              <xsl:for-each select="phone">
                <option>
                  <xsl:attribute name="value"><xsl:value-of select="areacode"/>
➥<xsl:value-of select="number"/></xsl:attribute>
                  <xsl:value-of select="@type"/>
                  <xsl:text> - </xsl:text>
                  <xsl:value-of select="areacode"/>
                  <xsl:text> </xsl:text>
                  <xsl:value-of select="number"/>
                </option>
              </xsl:for-each>
              <option>
                <xsl:attribute name="onpick"><xsl:value-of select="$servlet"/>
➥?mode=selectContact&amp;group=<xsl:value-of select="$group"/>
➥</xsl:attribute>[Back]</option>
            </select>
          </xsl:for-each>
        </p>
      </card>
    </wml>
  </xsl:template>
</xsl:stylesheet>
```

The WML that is generated as a result of transforming the XML in Listing 21.7 with the XSL in Listing 21.8 is shown in Listing 21.9.

LISTING 21.9 `ContactDetails.wml`—The WML Response for Contact Details

```
<?xml version="1.0" encoding="UTF-8"?>
<!DOCTYPE wml PUBLIC "-//WAPFORUM//DTD WML 1.1//EN"
➥"http://www.wapforum.org/DTD/wml_1.1.xml">
<wml>
  <card id="SelectNumber">
    <do label="Call" type="accept">
      <go href="wtai://wp/mc;$(number)"/>
    </do>
    <p>
      <b>XYZ Inc - Bill Currie</b>
      <select name="number">
        <option value="8132367856">Work - 813 2367856</option>
        <option value="8139835646">Mobile - 813 9835646</option>
        <option onpick="/servlet/Phonebook?mode=selectContact&amp;group=[A-C]">
➥[Back]</option>
      </select>
    </p>
  </card>
</wml>
```

This WML is again similar to other previously presented WML documents, with a few differences highlighted here. The soft menu at the bottom of the Web phone screen is assigned the label "Call" to indicate that the user is not only making a phone number selection but is also initiating a call to that number:

```
<do label="Call" type="accept">
```

The URL to which the Web phone navigates once the phone number selection is made uses the WTAI interface in the Web phone to initiate a voice call, as indicated by the protocol of the URL, `"wtai"`. The `wp` part of this URL specifies that the WTAIPublic function library is to be used, and the `mc` part specifies that the `makeCall` function in the WTAIPublic library is to be invoked. Lastly, the `$(number)` part of the URL passes the phone number, including the area code, as an argument to the `makeCall` function. The value of this number variable is set just prior to navigating to this URL when the user selects a phone number in the selection list in the same WML card:

```
<go href="wtai://wp/mc;$(number)"/>
```

For more information on the WTAI syntax and other available functions, see the WTAI specification at the WAP Forum (`Wapforum.org`).

When this WML is loaded into a Web phone, the screen appears as shown in Figure 21.5.

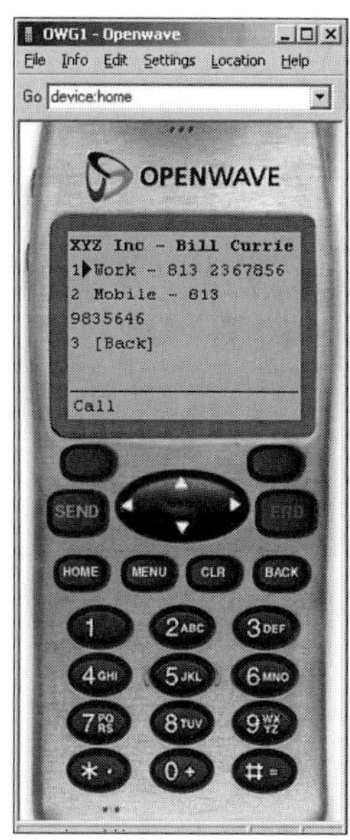

FIGURE 21.5
The Web phone emulator view of the WML response for contact details. Openwave UP.SDK 4.1 used for emulator. (Image of UP.SDK courtesy Openwave Systems Inc.)

Selecting a Phone Number to Call a Contact

When the user navigates to a phone number and presses the "Call" button, the WAP/WML wireless data connection from the Web phone is dropped and a voice connection through the public telephone network is established by the WTAI `makeCall` function.

WML Structure and Elements

This section briefly reviews the key elements of WML, including all the elements used in the preceding example. For a complete, detailed WML specification, see the WAP Forum (`www.wapforum.org`).

Figure 21.6 shows a high-level graphical view of the structure of a WML document. This view was derived from the WML 1.1 DTD (`www.wapforum.org/DTD/wml_1.1.xml`).

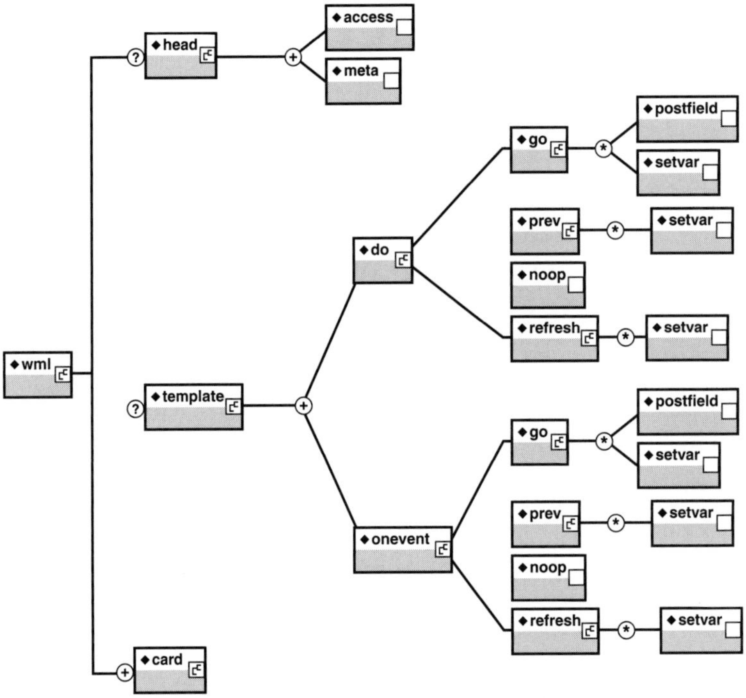

FIGURE 21.6
A high-level graphical view of the structure of a WML document.

FIGURE 21.6
continued

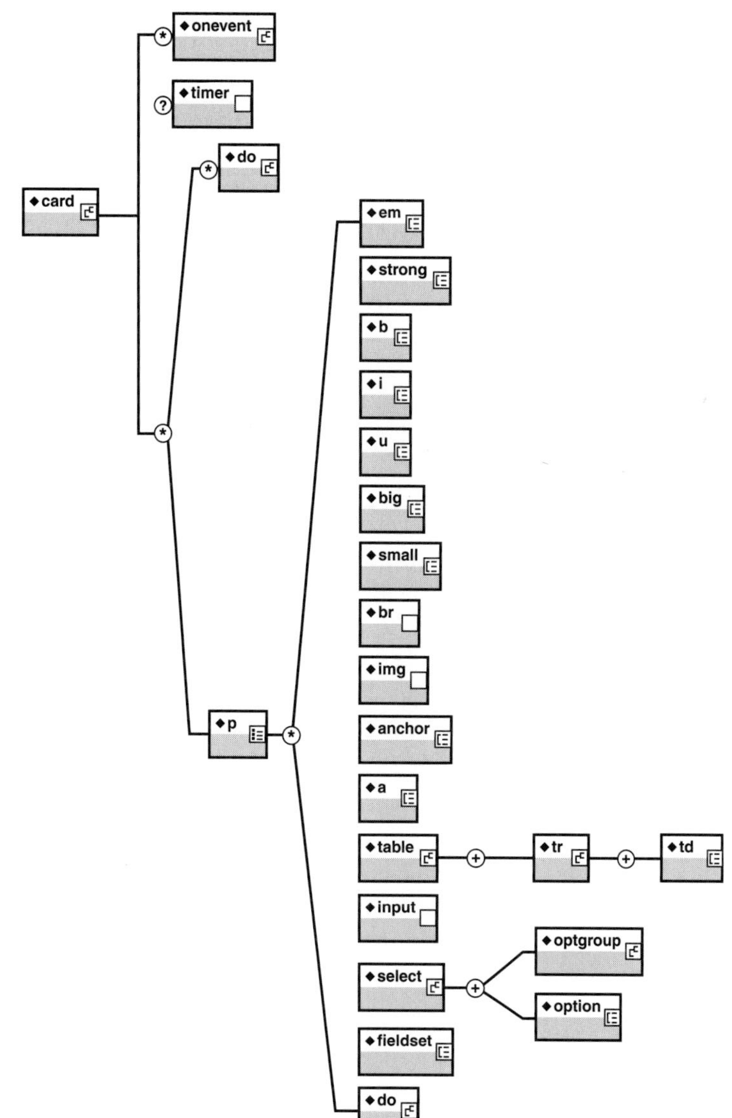

Table 21.1 provides descriptions of the various elements of WML.

TABLE 21.1 WML Elements with Descriptions

Element	*Description*
`a`	Short form of the anchor element.
`access`	Specifies access control information for the entire WML deck.
`anchor`	Specifies a hyperlink. This is the same as the shorter form element named `a`.
`b`	Renders child text with a bold font.
`big`	Renders child text with a large font.
`br`	Establishes the beginning of a new line.
`card`	A WML deck contains a collection of cards, the details of which are contained by these elements. There are a variety of card types, each specifying a different mode of user interaction—for example, some cards simply display information, whereas others get user input either using an option list or text input.
`do`	Provides a general mechanism for the user to act on the parent card when it is currently visible to the user. The representation of this element in the user interface is device dependent. For example, a `do` element may be visible as a soft menu on the bottom of the screen of the phone that may be activated by the user pressing the associated soft menu key. Alternatively, a `do` element could map to a voice-activated command sequence.
`em`	Renders child text with emphasis.
`fieldset`	Enables the grouping of related fields and text.
`go`	Declares a task to navigate to a URI. This URI may specify either another card in the current deck or some other static or dynamic WML deck on the Internet. When this task is executed, the target of the URI is loaded and displayed.
`head`	Contains information for the deck in general, including metadata and access-control information.
`i`	Renders child text with an italic font.
`img`	Specifies an image is to be included in the text flow.
`input`	Specifies a text-entry object to get user input.
`meta`	Contains generic meta-information relating to the WML deck. This meta-information is in the form of name/value property pairs.
`noop`	Specifies that nothing should be done (“no operation”).
`onevent`	Binds a task to a particular intrinsic event for the immediately enclosing element. For example, the `onenterforward` and `onenterbackward` intrinsic events may be specified at both the deck and card levels.
`optgroup`	Groups related options within a selection list into a hierarchy.

TABLE 21.1 continued

Element	*Description*
`option`	Specifies a single choice or option in a set of options associated with a user selection.
`p`	Contains presentation information for the card.
`postfield`	Specifies a property name/value pair for submission to a server during a URI request.
`prev`	Declares a "go back" task, indicating navigation to the previous URI on the history stack.
`refresh`	Declares a refresh task, indicating an update of the user agent context as specified by the `setvar` elements.
`select`	Lets the user provide input by picking from a number of enclosed options.
`setvar`	Specifies the variable to set in the current browser context as a result of executing a task.
`small`	Renders child text with a small font.
`strong`	Renders child text with strong emphasis.
`table`	Specifies a table in a card's presentation.
`template`	Declares a template for cards in the deck. Event bindings specified inside this element apply to all cards within the deck. However, a card element may override these bindings.
`timer`	Declares a card timer, providing a way to measure inactive or idle time.
`td`	Specifies a cell of a table.
`tr`	Specifies a row of a table.
`u`	Renders child text with an underline.
`wml`	Defines a deck and encloses all information and cards within the deck.

WMLScript

WMLScript is a script language used to provide programmatic control of mobile devices. WML is an extended subset of ECMAScript (formerly known as JavaScript), which has been modified to better support low-bandwidth communication and thin clients. For example, client-side scripting can be used to check the validity of user input, thus enabling errors or omissions to be detected prior to incurring the cost of a network request. This has benefits for both the client and server. The client experiences a faster response time and lower wireless network usage and associated cost. The server, on the other hand, experiences fewer bad or invalid requests, thus improving its signal-to-noise ratio and enabling it to scale to handle more clients. WMLScript can also enable the user to access facilities on the device—for example, in order to store a phone number in an address book on the device.

Note

WMLScript is not supported on some older Web phones. It is prudent to check the models of phones used by the intended end users and verify that they support WMLScript before using this feature in applications.

Development Primer

This section provides some general tips and outlines common pitfalls in WAP/WML service development. It also provides some references to complement those already made in the previous discussion to assist you with getting started in WML development.

Focusing WML Responses

WAP/WML services impose restrictions on the length of content returned in a single response. Some limits are as low as 512 bytes. Although some systems have a higher limit on the length of the content (rather than the length of content per card), the 512 figure serves a lowest-common denominator with which systems should conform. Consequently, it is necessary to focus information delivered to the client. For example, this can be achieved through a multistep hierarchical search, such as that used in the phonebook example presented previously. When responses exceed the limit, the mobile device typically returns an error rather than the subset of content that falls within the limit. Therefore, it is desirable to stay well within this limit because straying outside will cause a fatal application error.

Caching WML Responses

WAP gateways may cache WML responses. Sometimes, a user may expect a given request made previously to cause a hit on the business Web site, but this might not be the case due to the cached responses. This can be confusing and frustrating during development, testing, and demonstrations. Most Web phones provide a menu option to flush the cache and, in effect, force a request to hit the target business Web site.

Setting the WML MIME Content Type

In order for a Web server to serve a static WML page with the correct MIME content type, it must be configured to associate the `*.wml` extension with the MIME content type text/vnd.wap.wml. Failing to make this configuration will cause an error if a Web phone tries to access content via that Web server. Similarly, the *.wmls extension for WMLScript documents should be associated with the MIME content type text/vnd.wap.wmlscript. If BMP or WBMP images are used in WML content, the *.bmp and *.wbmp extensions should be associated with the image/bmp and image/vnd.wap.wbmp MIME content types, respectively.

Testing Usability

There is no substitute for extensive usability testing during the conceptual and prototyping phase of development to help identify subtle but potentially fatal usability issues. Where end users may not yet have Web phones or a service being tested is not yet live, it may be possible to conduct some preliminary usability testing with Web phone emulators, such as UP.SDK, as discussed previously in this section. However, there is no substitute for the real testing that should incorporate the real Web phones and live wireless network.

Getting Started

The Openwave Developer Program (developer.openwave.com) provides downloads of SDKs that may be used to start HDML and WML development and testing. This site also provides excellent training material and reference documentation as well as forums for the developer community.

For J2ME-enabled Web phones and other handheld devices, KBrowser from 4thpass (www.4thpass.com) is a microbrowser capable of accessing WML and WMLScript services.

Future WAP/WML Developments

Any system intended to live for more than a few years should be designed with sufficient flexibility to accommodate future changes. Although all changes cannot be anticipated, there are some that can. These expected future developments should be used to stress-test any design to ensure that it can adapt to meet future changes.

WML 2 and XHTML Basic

In WAP 2.0, WML converges with the core of XHTML, known as *XHTML Basic*, a standard overseen by the W3C. WML 2.0 is a markup language that extends the syntax and semantics of XHTML Basic and CSS Mobile Profile with the unique semantics of WML 1.0. HDML and cHTML (Compact HTML) are also both converging to XHTML Basic. XHTML is designed for Web clients such as mobile phones, PDAs, pagers, and set-top boxes that cannot handle the full XHTML markup language. One of the goals of XHTML Basic is to be a common markup language understood by a variety of Web clients. This promises to simplify the development of content for multiclient architectures. However, even in the event that XHTML Basic is wildly successful in becoming the de facto standard markup language for mobile devices in the long term, separate XSL transformations in a multiclient XML/XSL-based architecture will still be required for each client type (for example, to tailor content for different device capabilities).

3G Wireless Networks

Third-generation packet-based wireless networks promise to deliver higher rates, concurrent voice and wireless data services, and "always-on" wireless connectivity with data rates up to 2Mbps. These higher bandwidths and simultaneous voice and data channels promise to deliver more powerful multimedia services and a richer, more interactive user experience. When these more powerful networks are available and the number of clients capable of using them becomes significant, demand on multiclient architectures delivering Web applications to these clients will increase. Therefore, when you're designing multiclient architectures, it is wise to build into them the ability to scale to meet this future growth in demand.

Multimode

Currently, wireless services do not support voice and wireless data concurrently. However, as wireless networks, devices, and markup languages evolve and become available, wireless data and voice services will converge to enable future multimode services. For example, this will enable wireless data services, such as those currently driven by WML, to work in parallel with voice services, such as those currently driven by VoiceXML, in a hybrid multimode service. At the markup language level, the Synchronized Multimedia Integration Language (SMIL, pronounced *smile*) is a new standard overseen by the W3C that promises to provide a way to coordinate such hybrid or multimode services. SMIL is an XML-based markup language and may be easily generated from the multiclient XML/XSL-based architecture presented in this discussion, enabling it to easily adapt to deliver these new hybrid multimode services when client devices become able to handle them.

Wi-Fi (IEEE 802.1lb) and Bluetooth

Wi-Fi (`standards.ieee.org/wireless`) and Bluetooth (`www.bluetooth.com`) are both short-range wireless networks that promise to deliver Web applications to a variety of mobile devices, including PDAs and laptops in particular. Because these networks do not specify content types or markup languages to be used at the application level, they will not have a direct impact on multiclient XML/XSL-based architectures.

Voice Applications with VoiceXML

This section shows how to deliver VoiceXML Web applications from a multiclient XML/XSL-based architecture. The section includes information about the following:

- Voice portals and VoiceXML
- VoiceXML application architecture
- Advantages and limitations of voice access to Web applications
- An example of the phonebook business service used to illustrate service delivery with VoiceXML

Voice Portals and VoiceXML

Voice portals, specifically portals that support VoiceXML, contain the hardware and software required to interface the public telecommunications network to VoiceXML services on the Internet.

VoiceXML Application Input

Voice portals accept input from telephones in the form of voice and touchtones. In order to use voice input, voice portals need to be able to perform speech recognition. Application software can then act on the recognized input. Speech recognition is dependent on application grammars that tell the portal which sounds represent valid input. Because most VoiceXML applications need to be speaker independent, they are usually more accurate with smaller grammars.

Voice portals contain the software and hardware needed to recognize touchtone input. Touchtone input is useful for login and other input that must be very accurately recognized. It is also a more robust alternative to voice in noisy caller environments that can confuse speech recognition software.

VoiceXML Application Output

Voice portals deliver two kinds of output: synthesized speech and audio playback.

Speech synthesis, also known as *TTS* (text-to-speech), is the process of producing automated speech from words in text format. TTS is useful for services that output dynamic results. TTS is also useful while developing, testing, and refining a voice Web service because it may be changed rapidly at low cost.

Audio playback involves simply playing back a prerecorded audio file over the telephone. This mode of output has a lower computational cost and is therefore more suitable for static content and content that needs to be delivered in a more natural-sounding voice.

A VoiceXML Application Architecture

The various components of the voice application architecture are illustrated in Figure 21.7 and include the following:

- *Mobile user*. This is a user who wants to access voice Web applications.
- *Web phone*. This is a mobile phone being used to make telephone calls to voice Web applications.
- *Base station*. The cellular base station in the wireless network interacts with the Web phone via wireless network protocols.
- *Phone user*. This is a user with a standard landline phone accessing voice Web applications delivered via the voice portal.
- *Phone*. This is a standard landline phone connected to the telecommunications infrastructure.
- *Telecommunications infrastructure*. This is the global telephone network that enables any telephone to access voice Web applications via the voice portal.
- *Voice portal*. This is the hardware and software gateway through which users can access voice Web applications.
- *Multiclient pull architecture*. This is the XML/XSL-based architecture capable of delivering Web applications to multiple types of clients, including VoiceXML. This component is a pull architecture because clients make requests and then wait for a server response.

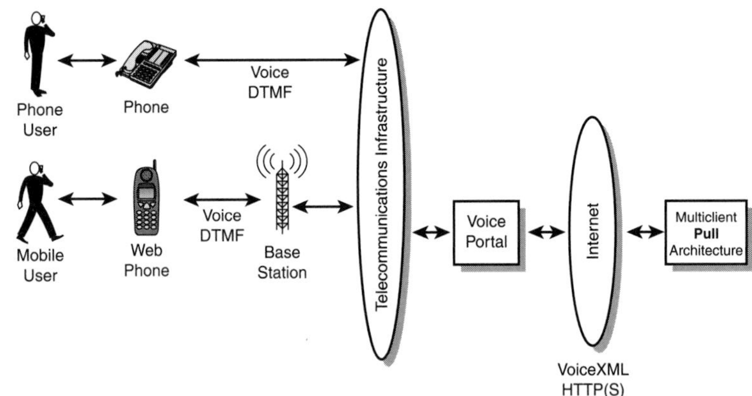

FIGURE 21.7
Voice application architecture.

Voice Portal Architecture

The components of the voice portal architecture are illustrated in Figure 21.8 and include the following:

- *Communications Interface Hardware*. Specialized boards that interface the voice portal with the telephone system and the Internet.
- *VoiceXML interpreter and controller*. The VoiceXML "browser" component that interfaces the telephone user and the VoiceXML application. It retrieves VoiceXML pages from the business Web site, interprets them, and executes them to control the voice Web service dialog.
- *Text-to-speech*. Converts text to speech and delivers it to the telephone user via the telephony hardware.
- *Audio playback*. Plays prerecorded audio for the telephone user via the telephony hardware.
- *DTMF (touchtone)*. Receives and interprets touchtone signals from the telephone user.
- *Speech recognition*. This is the input module responsible for interpreting speech input received from the telephone user.
- *Audio recording*. This is the input module that receives audio from the telephone user and records it.

FIGURE 21.8
Voice portal internal architecture.

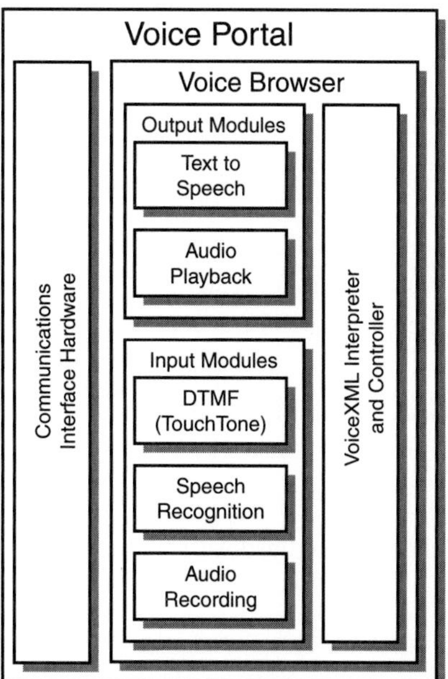

Advantages and Limitations of VoiceXML Applications

To understand what kinds of Web applications may be effectively delivered via voice over telephones, it is useful to review the advantages and limitations of this mode of access. In addition to the advantages outlined previously in this chapter for mobile access in general, here are some specific advantages of voice access:

- *Low cost.* Users already have telephones and service plans, so there is typically no extra initial or sustained cost associated with accessing voice Web applications.
- *High availability through pervasive coverage.* The global telephone network is the most pervasive network there is. Leveraging this network to deliver voice Web applications maximizes service access and availability.
- *Eyes- and hands-free operation.* Through appropriate hands-free headsets, telephones enable eyes- and hands-free operation, a requirement for many consumer and business situations.
- *Telephones are familiar tools.* Telephones are familiar to users, so there is less of an intimidation factor involved in using voice Web applications.

Here are some of the limitations of VoiceXML applications that you should consider when planning and designing voice Web applications:

- *Audio only.* Voice Web applications may deliver audio only. This makes voice Web applications unsuitable for services that require visual output.
- *New user interface paradigm.* Voice Web applications are a relatively new mode of access to the Internet. This makes the design and development as well as the use of these new services more challenging. As a result, usability testing and personalization are important to VoiceXML service development.
- *IVR stigma.* Many new users equate voice Web applications with rigid prompt/response Interactive Voice Response (IVR) systems. VoiceXML applications must overcome this perception before they will be accepted into mainstream use.

The Profile of a Successful VoiceXML Application

A few characteristics of a successful VoiceXML application are outlined in the following list to give you some insight into the types of business services that lend themselves well to this mode of access:

- Concise input (voice or touchtone only)
- Concise audio output

- High-value urgent information that is required as soon as it is available
- Information required outside of business hours or the office
- Services required at multiple locations
- Services required where users need to have eyes- and hands-free operation

Example: A Voice Phonebook Service with VoiceXML

In this example, a phonebook business service is used to illustrate VoiceXML access to Web applications.

The goal of this sample service is for the user to retrieve a telephone number for a contact and place a call to that contact.

Usage Scenario

This usage scenario outlines the chronological sequence of steps required to realize the goal:

- Access the phonebook service to get a list of contact groups.
- Select a group to view a list of its contacts.
- Select a contact to view the details of that contact.
- Select a phone number and call the contact.

Collaboration

Each of the first three steps in the usage scenario result in a request from the voice portal over the Internet using HTTP to the multiclient architecture running on the business Web site.

The last step, on the other hand, simply results in the voice portal transferring the user's call to the phone number of the contact he has selected to call.

The phonebook service retrieves data, selects an XSL style sheet, and transforms the XML to VoiceXML for delivery to the voice portal. The voice portal then interprets and executes the VoiceXML in order to conduct the voice phonebook Web service dialog with the end user over his telephone.

Developing the Content

This section reviews the content required to drive the multiclient XML/XSL-based architecture to deliver the voice phonebook Web service, as discussed in the previous usage scenario.

Accessing the Service to Get a List of Contact Groups

Users access VoiceXML applications by dialing a telephone number that connects them to the voice portal. For this example, we will assume a user has dialed the telephone number the voice portal associates with the phonebook service.

When a user calls the number, the voice portal loads the VoiceXML from the URL associated with the phone number:

```
https://www.MyDomain.com/Phonebook.vxml
```

> **Note**
>
> In order to shorten the voice application startup time, a voice portal can store the initial VoiceXML page. This enables the voice portal to execute the dialog without waiting for a response from the service URL.

In this case, `www.MyDomain.com` is the domain of the business Web site providing the phonebook service. The VoiceXML that is loaded from the initial URL is shown in Listing 21.10.

LISTING 21.10 `Phonebook.vxml`—The Initial VoiceXML for the Phonebook Service

```
<?xml version="1.0" encoding="UTF-8"?>
<!DOCTYPE vxml PUBLIC "-//Tellme Networks//Voice Markup Language 1.0//EN"
➥"http://resources.tellme.com/toolbox/vxml-tellme.dtd">
<vxml application="Phonebook.vxml">
  <form id="Introduction">
    <block>
      <audio>Welcome to the X Y Z corporation phone book.</audio>
      <goto next="/servlet/Phonebook?mode=selectGroup"/>
    </block>
  </form>
</vxml>
```

The first line of the document indicates that the VoiceXML is XML 1.0 compliant and has a UTF-8 character encoding:

```
<?xml version="1.0" encoding="UTF-8"?>
```

The next line indicates the document type (recall that in this example the VoiceXML is hosted by the Tellme Networks voice portal):

```
<!DOCTYPE vxml PUBLIC "-//Tellme Networks//Voice Markup Language 1.0//EN"
➥"http://resources.tellme.com/toolbox/vxml-tellme.dtd">
```

The root element of this document is the `vxml` element, which has an attribute named `application` that specifies that this VoiceXML document belongs to the `Phonebook.vxml` application:

```
<vxml application="Phonebook.vxml">
```

Different VoiceXML documents that belong to the same voice application specify the same value for this attribute. This is known as the *application scope* of the VoiceXML service and is the highest-level scope in a hierarchy of scopes possible in a VoiceXML service. VoiceXML documents within the same scope may share the same grammars. The `form` element has an `id` attribute with the value `Introduction`:

```
<form id="Introduction">
```

VoiceXML documents may contain multiple forms. The `id` attribute of any given form may be used to navigate to that form from either within the same VoiceXML document or from another VoiceXML document. This `form` element, in turn, contains a single child `block` element.

The `block` element contains an `audio` element that is converted to speech as an introduction to the phonebook service:

```
<block>
<audio>Welcome to the X Y Z corporation phone book.</audio>
<goto next="/servlet/Phonebook?mode=selectGroup"/>
</block>
```

After this introduction, the voice portal executes the other child `goto` element. This element instructs the voice portal to navigate to the next VoiceXML document in the service that may be loaded from the URL `/servlet/Phonebook?mode=selectGroup`.

The `goto` element causes the voice portal to send a request for a dynamically generated VoiceXML document from the multiclient architecture. The phonebook data responds to this request by generating the same XML response as in the case of the WML Web phone client, as shown in Listing 21.1 earlier in this chapter.

The phonebook view component identifies the client as a VoiceXML browser and loads the XSL style sheet shown in Listing 21.11.

LISTING 21.11 `GetListOfContactGroups_VXML.xsl`—The XSL Used by the Phonebook View to Transform XML into a VoiceXML List of Contact Groups

```
<?xml version="1.0" encoding="UTF-8"?>
<xsl:stylesheet version="1.0" xmlns:xsl="http://www.w3.org/1999/XSL/Transform">
  <xsl:param name="servlet" select="'undefined'"/>
  <xsl:template match="/">
```

Listing 21.11 continued

```
    <xsl:text disable-output-escaping="yes">
      <![CDATA[<!DOCTYPE vxml PUBLIC "-//Tellme Networks//Voice Markup Language
➥1.0//EN" "http://resources.tellme.com/toolbox/vxml-tellme.dtd">]]>
    </xsl:text>
    <vxml application="Phonebook.vxml">
      <menu id="SelectGroup">
        <prompt>Please select the key on your phone with the initial of the
➥last name of the person to call.</prompt>
        <choice dtmf="1"><xsl:attribute name="next"><xsl:value-of
➥select="$servlet"/>?mode=selectContact&amp;group=All</xsl:attribute>
➥all</choice>
        <choice dtmf="2"><xsl:attribute name="next"><xsl:value-of
➥select="$servlet"/>?mode=selectContact&amp;group=[A-C]</xsl:attribute>
➥(a to c)</choice>
        <choice dtmf="3"><xsl:attribute name="next"><xsl:value-of
➥select="$servlet"/>?mode=selectContact&amp;group=[D-F]</xsl:attribute>
➥(d to f)</choice>
        <choice dtmf="4"><xsl:attribute name="next"><xsl:value-of
➥select="$servlet"/>?mode=selectContact&amp;group=[G-I]</xsl:attribute>
➥(g to i)</choice>
        <choice dtmf="5"><xsl:attribute name="next"><xsl:value-of
➥select="$servlet"/>?mode=selectContact&amp;group=[J-L]</xsl:attribute>
➥(j to l)</choice>
        <choice dtmf="6"><xsl:attribute name="next"><xsl:value-of
➥select="$servlet"/>?mode=selectContact&amp;group=[M-O]</xsl:attribute>
➥(m to o)</choice>
        <choice dtmf="7"><xsl:attribute name="next"><xsl:value-of
➥select="$servlet"/>?mode=selectContact&amp;group=[P-S]</xsl:attribute>
➥(p to s)</choice>
        <choice dtmf="8"><xsl:attribute name="next"><xsl:value-of
➥select="$servlet"/>?mode=selectContact&amp;group=[T-V]</xsl:attribute>
➥(t to v)</choice>
        <choice dtmf="9"><xsl:attribute name="next"><xsl:value-of
➥select="$servlet"/>?mode=selectContact&amp;group=[W-Z]</xsl:attribute>
➥(w to z)</choice>
        <catch event="nomatch noinput help">
          <reprompt/>
        </catch>
      </menu>
    </vxml>
  </xsl:template>
</xsl:stylesheet>
```

The VoiceXML that is generated by transforming the XML in Listing 21.1 using the XSL in Listing 21.11 appears in Listing 21.12.

LISTING 21.12 `ListOfContactGroups.vxml`—The VoiceXML Response for a List of Contact Groups

```
<?xml version="1.0" encoding="UTF-8"?>
<!DOCTYPE vxml PUBLIC "-//Tellme Networks//Voice Markup Language 1.0//EN"
➥"http://resources.tellme.com/toolbox/vxml-tellme.dtd">
<vxml application="Phonebook.vxml">
  <menu id="SelectGroup">
    <prompt>Please select the key on your phone with the initial of the last
➥name of the person to call.</prompt>
    <choice dtmf="1" next="/servlet/Phonebook?mode=selectContact&amp;group=
➥All">all</choice>
    <choice dtmf="2" next="/servlet/Phonebook?mode=selectContact&amp;group=
➥[A-C]">(a to c)</choice>
    <choice dtmf="3" next="/servlet/Phonebook?mode=selectContact&amp;group=
➥[D-F]">(d to f)</choice>
    <choice dtmf="4" next="/servlet/Phonebook?mode=selectContact&amp;group=
➥[G-I]">(g to i)</choice>
    <choice dtmf="5" next="/servlet/Phonebook?mode=selectContact&amp;group=
➥[J-L]">(j to l)</choice>
    <choice dtmf="6" next="/servlet/Phonebook?mode=selectContact&amp;group=
➥[M-O]">(m to o)</choice>
    <choice dtmf="7" next="/servlet/Phonebook?mode=selectContact&amp;group=
➥[P-S]">(p to s)</choice>
    <choice dtmf="8" next="/servlet/Phonebook?mode=selectContact&amp;group=
➥[T-V]">(t to v)</choice>
    <choice dtmf="9" next="/servlet/Phonebook?mode=selectContact&amp;group=
➥[W-Z]">(w to z)</choice>
    <catch event="nomatch noinput help">
      <reprompt/>
    </catch>
  </menu>
</vxml>
```

This VoiceXML is similar to the VoiceXML discussed for the previous step, with some differences discussed here. The `vxml` root element contains one child `menu` element that prompts the user for some input and then interprets the response. The `id` attribute of the `menu` element has the value `SelectGroup`:

```
<menu id="SelectGroup">
```

VoiceXML documents may contain multiple `menu` elements. This `id` attribute may be used to navigate to menus either within the same VoiceXML document or in a different VoiceXML document.

The `prompt` child element contains text that is converted into speech by the text-to-speech output module of the voice portal; this indicates to the user what input is required to proceed to the next step in the dialog:

```
<prompt>Please select the key on your phone with the initial of the last name
➥of the person to call.</prompt>
```

After the prompt element is a range of choice elements, each one representing a valid option in the user's response to the previous prompt for input. In the following XSL snippet, the dtmf attribute of the choice element specifies that this option may be selected by pressing the touchtone key labeled "2" on the phone:

```
<choice dtmf="2" next="/servlet/Phonebook?mode=selectContact&amp;group=
➥[A-C]">(a to c)</choice>
```

Alternatively, the text child of the choice element—in this case, with the value (a to c)—indicates that the user may say "a to c" to select this option. The next attribute of this element indicates the URL that the voice portal should navigate to when the user selects this option. In this case, the URL is the phonebook servlet with the HTTP GET argument mode with the value selectContact, indicating that the response should enable the user to select a particular contact from the contact group named [A-C], as specified by the other HTTP GET argument, named group.

The catch child element of the menu element indicates to the voice portal that certain events should be caught and handled as specified in the content of this element. The event attribute specifies that the events for nomatch, noinput, or help should be caught when the user provides invalid input, no input, or asks for "help," respectively.

The reprompt child element of the catch element indicates to the voice portal that when any of these events are caught, the action taken should be to prompt the user for the input again, as described previously, and then wait for another input selection:

```
<catch event="nomatch noinput help">
<reprompt/>
</catch>
```

In a production application, these events would typically be handled separately and in a more user friendly manner.

Selecting a Group to View a List of Its Contacts

Next, the user selects option number 2, corresponding to contacts with last names having initials in the range [A-C]. The XML generated by the phonebook data component in response to this request is the same as for the WML Web phone client (refer back to Listing 21.4).

The phonebook view uses the style sheet shown in Listing 21.13 to transform the results.

LISTING 21.13 `GetListOfContacts_VXML.xsl`—The XSL Used by the Phonebook View to Transform the XML into a VoiceXML List of Contacts in a Group

```
<?xml version="1.0" encoding="UTF-8"?>
<xsl:stylesheet version="1.0" xmlns:xsl="http://www.w3.org/1999/XSL/Transform">
  <xsl:param name="servlet" select="'undefined'"/>
  <xsl:param name="group" select="'undefined'"/>
  <xsl:param name="lcletters" select="'abcdefghijklmnopqrstuvwxyz'"/>
  <xsl:param name="ucletters" select="'ABCDEFGHIJKLMNOPQRSTUVWXYZ'"/>
  <xsl:template match="/">
    <xsl:text disable-output-escaping="yes">
      <![CDATA[<!DOCTYPE vxml PUBLIC "-//Tellme Networks//Voice Markup Language
➥1.0//EN" "http://resources.tellme.com/toolbox/vxml-tellme.dtd">]]>
    </xsl:text>
    <vxml application="Phonebook.vxml">
      <menu id="SelectContact">
        <prompt>Got <xsl:value-of select="count(phonebook/contact)"/>
➥contacts. Please say the name of the contact you wish to call.</prompt>
        <xsl:for-each select="phonebook/contact">
          <choice><xsl:attribute name="next"><xsl:value-of select="$servlet"/>
➥?mode=selectNumber&amp;group=<xsl:value-of select="$group"/>&amp;
➥contact=<xsl:value-of select="@id"/></xsl:attribute>(
➥<xsl:value-of select="translate(name/firstname,$ucletters,
➥$lcletters)"/><xsl:text> </xsl:text><xsl:value-of select="translate(
➥name/lastname,$ucletters,$lcletters)"/>)</choice>
        </xsl:for-each>
        <catch event="nomatch noinput help">
          <reprompt/>
        </catch>
      </menu>
    </vxml>
  </xsl:template>
</xsl:stylesheet>
```

The VoiceXML that results from this transformation is shown in Listing 21.14.

LISTING 21.14 `ListOfContacts.vxml`—The VoiceXML Response for a List of Contacts in a Group

```
<?xml version="1.0" encoding="UTF-8"?>
<!DOCTYPE vxml PUBLIC "-//Tellme Networks//Voice Markup Language 1.0//EN"
➥"http://resources.tellme.com/toolbox/vxml-tellme.dtd">
<vxml application="Phonebook.vxml">
  <menu id="SelectContact">
    <prompt>Got 2 contacts. Please say the name of the contact you wish to
➥call.</prompt>
    <choice next="/servlet/Phonebook?mode=selectNumber&amp;group=[A-C]&amp;
➥contact=e5678">(joe ashworth)</choice>
    <choice next="/servlet/Phonebook?mode=selectNumber&amp;group=[A-C]&amp;
➥contact=e9921">(bill currie)</choice>
```

LISTING 21.14 continued

```
    <catch event="nomatch noinput help">
      <reprompt/>
    </catch>
  </menu>
</vxml>
```

In this case DTMF options for the `choice` elements are not available. The effect of this is that the user is required to say the name of the contact to select it. It is possible to enable DTMF selection if the service requires it.

Each `choice` element's `next` attribute points to the URL the voice portal should load and execute if the user selects it. The URL is composed of the location of the phonebook view component followed by `mode`, `group`, and `contact` arguments in HTTP `GET` syntax. The `contact` argument is assigned the value of the `id` attribute of the associated `contact` element in the source XML being transformed. This lowercase name that is the text child value of the `choice` element is effectively the grammar that indicates to the voice portal what the user will say to select this option.

The choice element illustrates a few characteristics of grammars:

- VoiceXML grammars are required to be in lowercase.
- The first and last names are separated by a space to indicate to the voice portal that the name is two words rather than one. This has bearing on the sounds the voice portal will expect when the user speaks this option.
- The phrase is enclosed in parentheses to indicate to the voice portal that the user needs to speak the first name followed by the last name for this option to be selected.

Selecting a Contact to View the Details of That Contact

We will assume that the user has selected Bill Currie in the previous step. In this step, the user gets Bill Currie's telephone numbers and selects one to call him. The XML generated by the phonebook data component in response to this request is the same as in the case of the WML Web phone, as shown previously in Listing 21.7. The XSL used to transform this XML into VoiceXML is shown in Listing 21.15.

LISTING 21.15 `GetContactDetails_VXML.xsl`—The XSL Used by the Phonebook View to Transform the XML into VoiceXML Contact Details

```
<?xml version="1.0" encoding="UTF-8"?>
<xsl:stylesheet version="1.0" xmlns:xsl="http://www.w3.org/1999/XSL/Transform">
  <xsl:param name="servlet" select="'undefined'"/>
```

LISTING 21.15 continued

```
  <xsl:param name="group" select="'undefined'"/>
  <xsl:param name="lcletters" select="'abcdefghijklmnopqrstuvwxyz'"/>
  <xsl:param name="ucletters" select="'ABCDEFGHIJKLMNOPQRSTUVWXYZ'"/>
  <xsl:template match="/">
    <xsl:text disable-output-escaping="yes">
      <![CDATA[<!DOCTYPE vxml PUBLIC "-//Tellme Networks//Voice Markup Language
➥1.0//EN" "http://resources.tellme.com/toolbox/vxml-tellme.dtd">]]>
    </xsl:text>
    <vxml application="Phonebook.vxml">
      <xsl:for-each select="phonebook/contact[1]">
        <menu id="SelectNumber">
          <prompt>There are <xsl:value-of select="count(phone)"/> phone numbers
➥for <xsl:value-of select="name/firstname"/><xsl:text> </xsl:text>
➥<xsl:value-of select="name/lastname"/>. Please select from the
➥following options:
            <xsl:for-each select="phone">
              <xsl:value-of select="translate(@type,$ucletters,$lcletters)"/>
➥<xsl:text> </xsl:text>
            </xsl:for-each>
            .
          </prompt>
          <xsl:for-each select="phone">
            <choice><xsl:attribute name="next">#Call<xsl:value-of
➥select="@type"/></xsl:attribute><xsl:value-of
➥select="translate(@type,$ucletters,$lcletters)"/></choice>
          </xsl:for-each>
          <catch event="nomatch noinput help">
            <reprompt/>
          </catch>
        </menu>
        <xsl:for-each select="phone">
          <form id="CallHome">
            <xsl:attribute name="id">Call<xsl:value-of select="@type"/>
➥</xsl:attribute>
            <block>
              <audio>Transferring call to Bill Currie at the <xsl:value-of
➥select="@type"/> phone number.</audio>
            </block>
            <transfer>
              <xsl:attribute name="dest"><xsl:value-of select="areacode"/>
➥<xsl:value-of select="number"/></xsl:attribute>
            </transfer>
          </form>
        </xsl:for-each>
      </xsl:for-each>
    </vxml>
  </xsl:template>
</xsl:stylesheet>
```

The VoiceXML that results from this transformation is shown in Listing 21.16.

LISTING 21.16 ContactDetails.vxml—The VoiceXML Response for Contact Details

```
<?xml version="1.0" encoding="UTF-8"?>
<!DOCTYPE vxml PUBLIC "-//Tellme Networks//Voice Markup Language 1.0//EN"
➥"http://resources.tellme.com/toolbox/vxml-tellme.dtd">
<vxml application="Phonebook.vxml">
  <menu id="SelectNumber">
    <prompt>There are 2 phone numbers for Bill Currie. Please select from the
➥following options: work mobile.</prompt>
    <choice next="#CallWork">work</choice>
    <choice next="#CallMobile">mobile</choice>
    <catch event="nomatch noinput help">
      <reprompt/>
    </catch>
  </menu>
  <form id="CallWork">
    <block>
      <audio>Transferring call to Bill Currie at the Work phone number.</audio>
    </block>
    <transfer dest="8132367856"/>
  </form>
  <form id="CallMobile">
    <block>
      <audio>Transferring call to Bill Currie at the Mobile phone
➥number.</audio>
    </block>
    <transfer dest="8139835646"/>
  </form>
</vxml>
```

This VoiceXML has one `menu` element, which enables the user to select the phone number to call, and two `form` elements—one for each phone number for the given contact. Each of the `form` elements serves to transfer the caller to the associated number. The values of the `next` attributes of the `choice` elements in the `menu` element are local URLs, each one pointing to a `form` element in the same VoiceXML document with an `id` attribute that has a value the same as the part of the URL after the # character. Key elements used in this form are the `transfer` elements that, when executed by the voice portal, cause it to transfer the caller to the given number. Here's the code:

```
<transfer dest="8132367856"/>
```

Selecting a Phone Number to Call That Contact

When the user hears the output of Listing 21.16, he says "work" in order to call Bill Currie at his work phone number. Control passes to the `form` in the same VoiceXML that has an `id` attribute with the value `CallWork`. The user is then notified that his call is being transferred. The call is then transferred to the number 813-236-7856. The user hears the call being transferred and then makes a connection with Bill Currie at his work number when he picks up the phone.

VoiceXML Structure and Elements

This section briefly reviews the key elements of VoiceXML, including all the elements used in the preceding example. For a complete detailed VoiceXML specification, see the VoiceXML Forum (`www.voicexml.org`).

Figure 21.9 shows a high-level graphical view of the main structure of a VoiceXML document. This view was derived from the VoiceXML 1.0 DTD (`www.voicexml.org/voicexml1-0.dtd`).

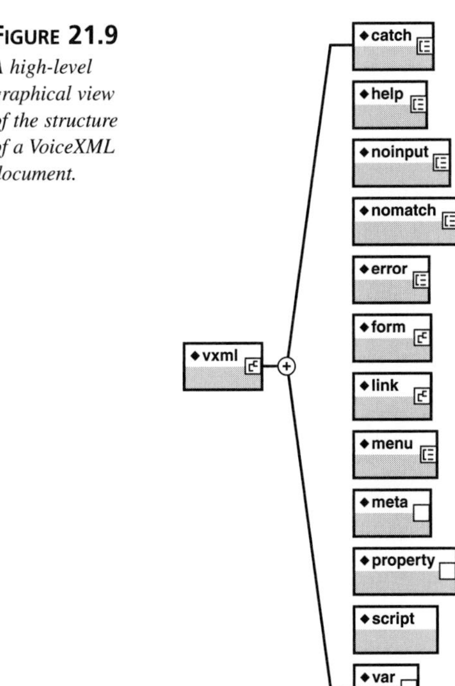

FIGURE 21.9
A high-level graphical view of the structure of a VoiceXML document.

FIGURE 21.9
continued

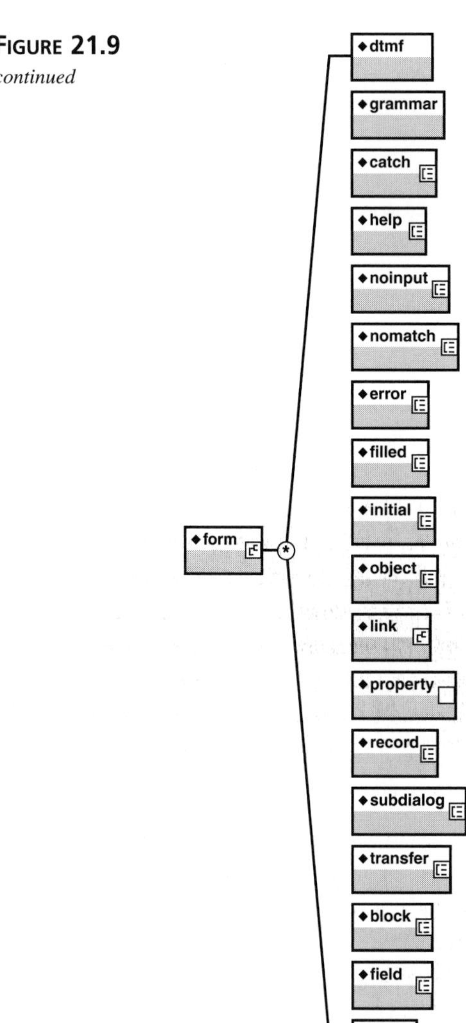

FIGURE 21.9
continued

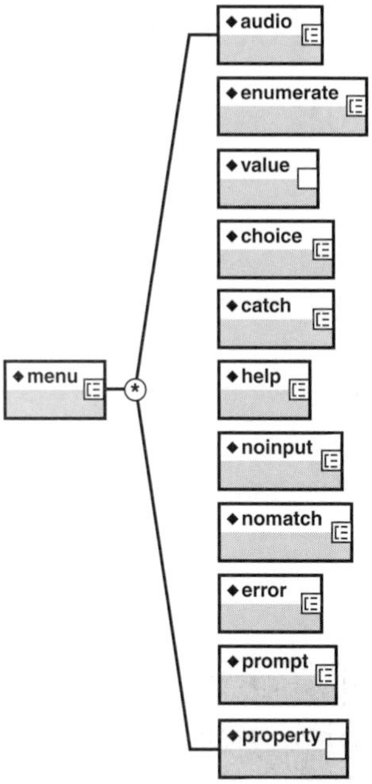

Table 21.2 provides descriptions of the elements shown in this figure.

TABLE 21.2 VoiceXML Elements with Descriptions

Element	*Description*
`assign`	Assigns a value to a variable that exists in the state maintained by the voice portal for the caller's session.
`audio`	Outputs some audio. The output can be either a prerecorded audio clip (for example, in the form of a WAV file) or in the form of synthesized speech generated from the text child of this element.
`block`	A container of procedural statements executed in sequence from first to last.
`break`	Inserts a pause in the speech output of a duration in milliseconds specified using an attribute.
`catch`	Catches an event either always or on some specified condition.
`choice`	Defines a menu item, including both the touchtone or speech input that may be used to select the choice and the URL to transfer control to upon selection of the choice.
`clear`	Resets one or more form item variables by setting their values to `undefined`.
`disconnect`	Disconnects a session, causing the voice portal to hang up the call from the user.

TABLE 21.2 continued

Element	*Description*
`div`	Specifies that the enclosed text is of a particular type (for example, a sentence or paragraph).
`dtmf`	Specifies a touchtone key grammar that serves as a set of valid phone key input options.
`else`	Used optionally in combination with `if` elements in conditional logic that may depend, for example, on the value of a variable.
`elseif`	Used optionally in combination with `if` elements in conditional logic that may depend, for example, on the value of a variable.
`emp`	Indicates that the enclosed text should be spoken with emphasis.
`enumerate`	Shorthand for automatically enumerating the choices available in a menu.
`error`	Catches an `error` event. Shorthand for a specific type of `catch` element that catches events of the `error` type.
`exit`	Exits a session by terminating all loaded VoiceXML documents and returning control to the interpreter.
`field`	Declares an input field in a form to get a user selection.
`filled`	An action executed when a user provides recognized input for a field.
`form`	A dialog for presenting information and collecting data from user input.
`goto`	Transfers execution to another form, dialog, or document.
`grammar`	Encloses a speech-recognition grammar that consists of a set of valid spoken inputs and the associated values that describe each option.
`help`	Catches a `help` event. Shorthand for a specific type of `catch` element that catches events of the `help` type.
`if`	Encloses conditional logic that may be executed, depending on the value of a variable, for example.
`initial`	Declares initial logic upon entry into a (mixed-initiative) form. In a mixed-initiative form, both the caller and the voice portal direct the conversation.
`link`	Specifies a transition common to all dialogs in the link's scope.
`menu`	A dialog for prompting the user and enabling her to select from a range of choices.
`meta`	Enables specification of data about the document.
`noinput`	Catches a `noinput` event (an event that occurs when no response is received from the user when expected).

TABLE 21.2 continued

Element	*Description*
`nomatch`	Catches a `nomatch` event (an event that occurs when a response is received from the user but is not recognized as valid).
`object`	Invokes a platform-specific object with parameters (for example, a speaker-verification object).
`option`	Specifies an option in a field, including the DTMF and/or speech required for the user to select the option as well as the value to assign to the `field` variable when the selection is made. Similar to the `choice` element for menus.
`param`	Used to specify name/value parameter pairs that are passed into `object` or `subdialog`.
`prompt`	Outputs synthesized speech or prerecorded audio to the user and then waits for a user response.
`property`	Sets the value of a property that controls the platform behavior (for example, timeouts).
`pros`	Specifies prosodic information about the enclosed text.
`record`	Records an audio sample and stores it in a field item variable.
`reprompt`	Plays a field prompt again (for example, when a field is revisited after a `nomatch` or `noinput` event).
`return`	Returns from a subdialog. This is similar in concept to a return from a function call in procedural logic.
`sayas`	Specifies how a word or phrase should be spoken. This enables finer control over the text-to-speech output.
`script`	Specifies a block of ECMAScript client-side scripting logic that will run on the voice portal.
`subdialog`	Invokes another dialog as a subdialog of the current one. This is similar in concept to a function call in procedural logic. It returns an ECMAScript object as the result of the subdialog.
`submit`	Submits values to the business Web site providing the voice Web applications.
`throw`	Throws an event that may be either a predefined event or an application-specific event.
`transfer`	Transfers the caller to another telephone number.
`value`	Inserts the value of an expression in a prompt (for example, a variable value).
`var`	Declares a variable and optionally assigns it a value.
`vxml`	The top-level root element in each VoiceXML document.

Development Primer

This primer provides important strategies for designing voice Web applications with VoiceXML.

> **Note**
>
> For more detailed information on developing VoiceXML applications, see *Voice Application Development with VoiceXML* (also from Sams publishing) on this subject.

Tips and Pitfalls for VoiceXML Development

The following subsections cover a few common tips and pitfalls concerning the development of VoiceXML services.

Usability Testing and Setting Expectations

Voice portals driven by VoiceXML represent a new paradigm in delivering Web applications to users. In order to win user acceptance and be successful in meeting business needs, voice Web applications must be thoroughly tested not only for functionally but also from a usability standpoint. Engaging end users early and often for usability testing also helps set their expectations for the final service, thus easing their acceptance of the deployed result.

Voice Service Robustness

Voice Web service interfaces are limited to audio interaction with the user. The user's ability to detect and correct problems with a voice Web service is therefore relatively limited when compared, for example, to a visual interface such as a Web browser. Consequently, in order to ensure that voice Web applications are robust enough to meet the needs of mission-critical enterprise systems, they must be able to gracefully handle a range of exceptions and error conditions. This includes, in particular, missing or invalid user input, help requests from users, and various system errors (for example, problems with the network connectivity between the voice portal and the business Web site delivering the voice Web applications).

Getting Started

A growing number of voice portals on the Web provide excellent services for developing, testing, and hosting deployed voice Web applications. These include but are not limited to the following:

- Tellme Networks (`www.tellme.com`)
- BeVocal (`www.bevocal.com`)
- VoiceGenie (`voicegenie.com`)
- Voxeo (`www.voxeo.com`)

Future VoiceXML Developments

Any system intended to live for more than a few years should be designed with sufficient flexibility to accommodate future changes. Although all changes cannot be anticipated, some can. These expected future developments should be used to stress-test any design to ensure that it can adapt to meet future changes.

Mainstream Use of Voice-Over-IP (VoIP)

In addition to telephones, Voice-over-IP (VoIP) can also be used to access voice Web applications via voice portals. In this case, the client side is a PC with speakers and a microphone, for example, and is connected to the voice portal over the Internet. As VoIP becomes a more popular method of communication, voice portals will seamlessly adapt to this new method of accessing voice Web applications. From the multiclient architecture standpoint, there will be no apparent difference between telephone clients or Voice-over-IP clients, except perhaps in the lack of a caller's phone number in the voice portal session.

Multimode Voice and Data Services

With new wireless networks that enable concurrent voice and data, new services will emerge that present hybrid voice and data interfaces×for example, interfaces that enable users to ask for directions and have the directions returned in a list that is cached on the client so that users can refer to it step by step. SMIL is a standard overseen by the W3C that's an XML markup language that promises to coordinate such multimedia interfaces. SMIL may be easily generated from the multiclient XML/XSL-based architecture, enabling it to seamlessly adapt to deliver these new hybrid multimode services when they appear.

Advanced Voice Processing on the Client Side

As telephone and other types of clients gain more computational power, there will be a shift as more of the voice-processing capability goes to the client side. With this trend, we can expect to see such clients start accepting content that drives their voice capabilities, just as VoiceXML drives voice portals today. This is good in that it reduces the load on the voice portal while improving the client response time. More voice handling on the client side also enables greater client privacy for certain applications because the audio does not have to propagate over a network to be interpreted. This trend can already be seen in the new advanced voice command functionality that is appearing in some higher-end mobile phones as well as in navigation systems appearing in cars.

Summary

To enable businesses to remain competitive, future Web service architectures need to be flexible, extensible, and facilitate the rapid addition of new client types and business Web applications. At the same time, these services need to be personalized to improve their usability. Furthermore, future architectures for Web applications cannot be dedicated to a single client type or mode of access. Rather, in order to maximize business investments in Web applications, maximize the potential user base, and empower the end user with more options, such Web applications architectures must have the flexibility to support multiple types of clients concurrently, including both voice and wireless clients in addition to Web browsers and external servers in a business extranet.

Such multiclient architectures modes of access will work either in parallel with each other when they present equivalent alternatives for the user, or they may be complementary choices when a service is delivered with multiple modes of access working together. XML and XSL are powerful technologies that enable the clean separation of content from presentation, and together with supporting tools and technologies they provide a solid foundation on which to build future multiclient architectures. WML provides a powerful markup language for the delivery of Web applications to Web-enabled phones and other mobile devices, whereas VoiceXML provides an equivalent markup language for the delivery of these services to telephones via voice portals. Web applications delivered using a multiclient XML/XSL-based architecture enable the same Web applications to be delivered concurrently to both Web phones with WML as well as telephones via voice portals driven by VoiceXML.

CHAPTER 22

Applied XML in Vertical Industry

In This Chapter

The majority of this book has dealt with what XML is, the various technologies that enrich the language, and how to implement XML in a variety of application scenarios. However, we have not yet talked about the myriad of ways that XML is actually being used and applied in different business scenarios. The actual, real-world implementation of XML is where the "rubber meets the road." Without widespread usage and adoption of XML, it is merely an abstract technology with lots of promise but little delivery. The "proof is in the pudding" when many businesses in different industries make use of XML in their day-to-day operations or in other business-critical capacities.

You may even be reading this book to gain a better understanding of how XML can benefit and improve the operations of your particular business or industry. As such, the vast majority of this book has addressed the technologies necessary for these implementations, but what remains are specific examples and advice for industry-specific implementations of XML technologies. This chapter will get you well on your way towards understanding how XML has benefited and impacted a variety of industries, ranging from manufacturing and health care to government and entertainment industries. In addition, for those readers who are now becoming familiar with XML from a technical viewpoint, this chapter provides real-world implementations of XML so that you can apply your technical skills to "nontechnical" industries and provide a quick return-on-investment (ROI) for your skills. In general, this chapter turns XML "promise" into XML "reality."

In this chapter, you will learn about

- The widespread use and adoption of XML by multiple industries
- How vertical industries approach the use of XML and create industry vocabularies
- The use of XML for document storage, manufacturing, process control, modeling, and messaging and communication
- Professional services' use of XML as applied to financial services, health care, insurance, legal, travel, and human resources industries
- Scientific and engineering use of XML and XML-based standards in the biotech, chemical, mathematical, and artificial intelligence industries
- The use of XML and relevant standards in the print, media, and entertainment industries
- The use of XML in manufacturing and supply chains in different industries
- Government, academic, and public-sector industry use of XML

The Vertical Industries

Before we can launch into a discussion of the different vertical industries, we must answer the question, What exactly is a vertical industry? The term *vertical* is used to define any user community that has a specific and focused set of needs that differ from other "parallel" industries. Horizontal technologies (or industries) are those that span all industries and don't apply to any particular industry specifically. In the context of our discussion, a vertical industry is a separately identifiable user community that bases its vocabularies on the horizontal technologies represented by XML. Figure 22.1 illustrates this concept.

FIGURE 22.1
Structure of standards.

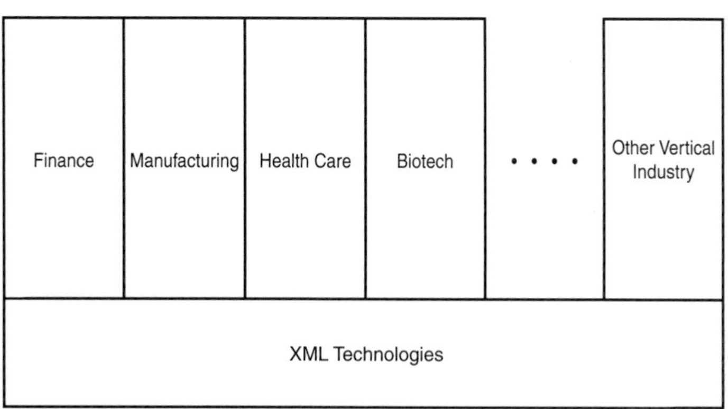

According to research conducted by ZapThink, an XML industry analyst firm, there are over 450 XML vocabularies publicly announced in various registries and reference sources as of October 2001. This number has grown from around 120 in February 2000 and 250 in August 2000. It seems as though the pace of new XML schema development is certainly not slowing. Approximately 70 percent of these vocabularies are vertical industry applications, with the remainder split between horizontal applications and general XML technologies and frameworks.

Note

You can view the vertical industry XML vocabulary listings mentioned earlier by visiting ZapThink's Web site at `http://www.zapthink.com/`.

Of course, the definition of vertical industries and horizontal technologies is a fuzzy art, at best, and many would argue that certain vertical industries are really horizontal industries, and vice versa. In fact, within our discussion of vertical industries, there are really two types of vertical industry markets:

- Purely vertical industries, such as electronic components
- "Horizontal" verticals, which are industries that in turn span multiple other industries. Good examples of this include shipping, human resources, and in many cases finance.

In addition, the vertical industry groups themselves clump into "birds of a feather" verticals that, while serving distinct user communities, share so many features in common that solutions for one user group will usually be applicable to the second user group. For example, the "manufacturing" industry is really a set of very distinct user communities, but solutions for any user group would generally result in applicable solutions for another. In that case, our discussion of the manufacturing vertical will usually be applicable to all birds of that feather.

In our discussions, we will group these two different types of vertical markets together and illustrate how they, in turn, make use of truly horizontal XML technologies.

Professional Services Standards

The use of XML is inextricably linked to the desire for people to communicate. Whereas some XML efforts focus on the communication between machines and devices, the focus of "professional services" standards is to enable the communication and processes of people. Professional services are those industries whose primary asset and product are people. There really is no "professional services" industry per se, but rather a collection of individual industries that together all share a number of things in common. Namely, they deal with people, provide services on a pay-per-service or on a pay-per-time basis, and require the management of time, people, and resources. In addition, professional services firms tend to call their customers and partners different things, including patients, clients, retainers, agents, brokers, and employees. Despite the differences in what they call things, they share many of their data models in common.

This section outlines what some of these professional services industries are doing with XML and some of the XML standards efforts that have been produced to meet the needs of these user groups.

Finance and Accounting

The finance industries of banking, accounting, securities trading, research and reporting, and economics have always needed timely, accurate, and critical access to information. As such, they have always been early implementers of electronic document exchanges. Automatic Teller Machines (ATMs) have implemented early forms of electronic commerce since the late 1970s. However, XML now allows for lower cost of delivery for this information; therefore, both existing and new standards are being created for the delivery of financial-related information. Of course, in this particular industry, security and time-sensitiveness are the key issues that XML standards must resolve.

The Extensible Business Reporting Language (XBRL)

One of the most important financial activities within a corporation is the reporting of financial or business data. Reporting of financial data happens throughout a business organization and even external to it. Business units, divisions, entire corporations, subsidiaries, partners, regulatory agencies, and the government all require financial reports of one sort or another. The strong need for this sort of business reporting is met with an equally strong challenge in the difficulty to share financial data across disparate systems. Typically, many systems in an organization store financial and related business information—accounting systems, supply-chain systems, Customer Relationship Management (CRM), sales and marketing, Enterprise Resource Planning (ERP), asset and inventory management, and human resources systems are just a few such repositories of financial and business data. Figure 22.2 illustrates the complex universe of financial reporting systems and interactions. The challenge is therefore great to have all these systems transmit their data in a common format that can then be aggregated for the purpose of creating consolidated balance sheets, reports of income, financial statements, financial information, nonfinancial information, regulatory filings, such as annual and quarterly financial statements, and other data necessary for the daily operation of the business and compliance with regulations.

The Extensible Business Reporting Language (XBRL) solves this problem by providing software vendors, programmers, and end users who adopt it a means to enhance the creation, exchange, and comparison of business reporting information. The primary users of the XBRL specification are those responsible for the preparation of financial information, intermediaries in those preparation and distribution processes, end users of business report information, as well as vendors who supply software and services to the previous user types. The overall intention is to balance the needs of these groups, creating a product that provides benefits to all groups. Although XBRL represents a new methodology for data information exchange, its goal is to facilitate current business reporting practice, not to change or set new accounting standards. The general goals of the format can be seen in Figure 22.3 and Figure 22.4.

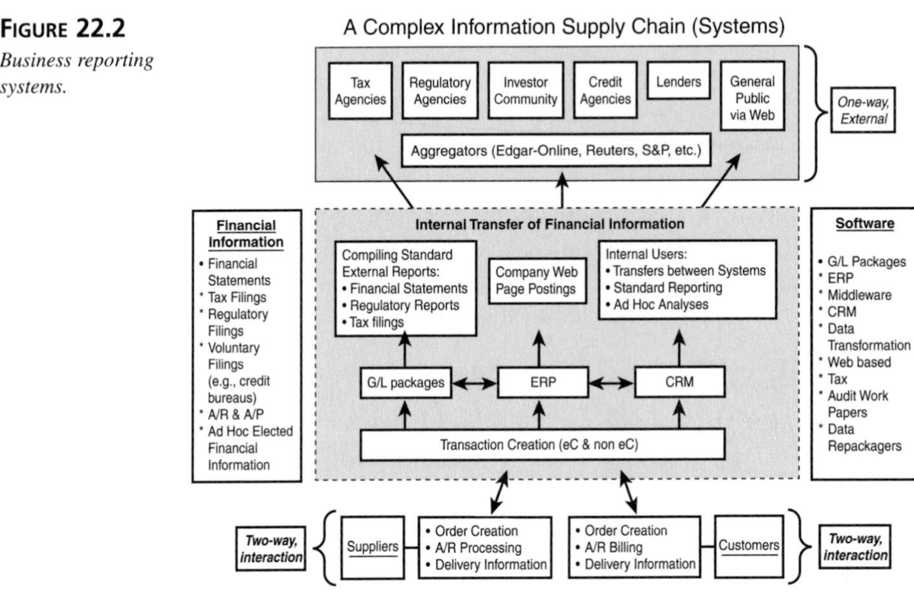

FIGURE 22.2
Business reporting systems.

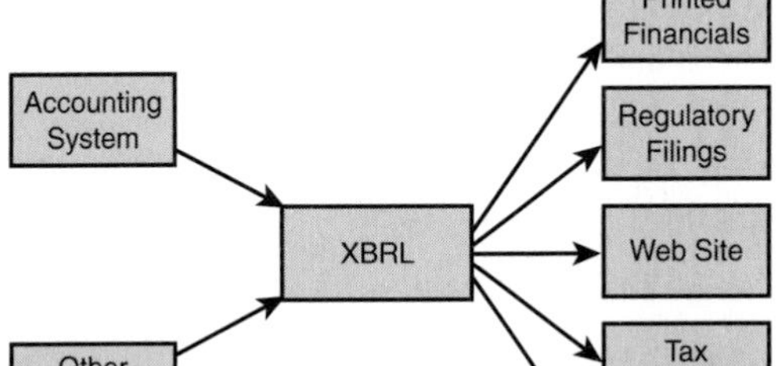

FIGURE 22.3
XBRL: Multiple outputs from a single specification.

XBRL provides users with a standard format in which to prepare, exchange, extract, and compare financial reports that can be subsequently presented in a variety of ways. The specification also facilitates the ability to "drill down" to detailed information, authoritative literature, audit information, and accounting working papers. XBRL instance documents transmit a set of financial facts. There is no constraint on how much or how little information these documents can contain. For example, an XBRL document can contain just a single item of financial information, such as what the cost of goods sold was for last quarter.

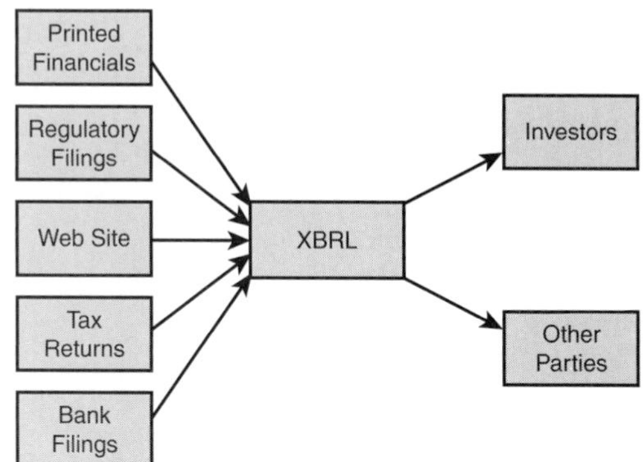

FIGURE 22.4
XBRL: Aggregating sources for common needs.

XBRL is not a single standard but rather a suite of many related standards. The specification is composed of a global specification that contains "taxonomies" or dependent standards that meet the requirements of specific user communities. The reason for this structure is quite necessary. In part, the reasons are geographic and political: The United States has a different kind of accounting system than the United Kingdom or Germany. These countries each have different policy standards and regulatory requirements. However, even within a country such as the United States, the way that health care companies report financial data is different from how banks report their data to the Federal Deposit Insurance Corporation (FDIC). Even the meaning of the term *cash* is different in various countries and industries. To further emphasize the need for local taxonomies, within industries and geographies, such as United States banking, there are different users who demand different kinds of reports. The tax administrator, controller, and investor relations officer all deal with different report requirements. Therefore, XBRL provides a mechanism not only to unify data exchange but also to bring together these various communities. In that manner, XBRL is actually two languages: one for financial "facts" that are standardized and one for financial "concepts" that are defined by communities.

Those that read the XBRL specification will find an interesting set of words used frequently, including *taxonomy*, *item*, and *tuple*. Many of these definitions are different from how other groups define these terms, so a careful reading of the definitions is necessary for a complete understanding of the specification. XBRL defines a *taxonomy* as an XML Schema instance that defines new *elements* that correspond to concepts referenced in XBRL documents. XBRL taxonomies can be regarded as extensions of the XML

Schema utilizing XML Link–based information. An important taxonomy utilized in many XBRL implementations is the set of elements that correspond to well-defined concepts within the U.S. Generally Accepted Accounting Principles (GAAP) applied to Commercial and Industrial (C&I) companies. That taxonomy includes concepts of "Accounts Receivable Trade, Gross," "Allowance for Doubtful Accounts," and "Accounts Receivable Trade, Net." An *item* corresponds to a fact that is usually, but not necessarily, a numeric fact being reported with respect to a given period of time about a given business entity. For example, company XYZQ's revenue of $7 million for the year 1998 is a numeric item, whereas a paragraph of text describing the principles of consolidation used to combine reports from the subsidiaries of XYZQ is a nonnumeric item. *Tuples* join these facts into logical groups so that they can be understood. The combination of the name, age, and compensation of a director of a company is an example of a tuple. On a similar note, an XBRL *group* is a less strictly combined set of related *items* that can appear in any order and can be interspersed among other text and elements in any XML document. Using the notion of the group, the specification avoids the direct creation of an XBRL document type. Rather, XBRL items can be embedded in any well-formed XML document, such as a press release or business document.

Within an XBRL document, there can be any number of XBRL items that refer to any number of taxonomies, although each individual item can itself only refer to only one taxonomy. Taxonomies can be composed together to extend other taxonomies. For example, the Financial Reporting for Commercial and Industrial Companies and U.S. GAAP taxonomies can be extended to include the term *physician salaries*, which extends the concept "expenses" that already exists there.

An XBRL taxonomy document is a valid instance of an XML Schema document. In fact, two XBRL schemas are imported by a taxonomy: the XBRL instance document schema, which defines abstract elements such as *item* and *tuple*, and the XBRL datatype schema, which defines XBRL standard data types, such as "monetary." See Listing 22.1 for a sample XBRL taxonomy definition and Listing 22.2 for a sample XBRL instance.

LISTING 22.1 XBRL Sample Taxonomy Element

```
<element name="statements.accountantsReport" type="string">
<annotation>
  <documentation>Report(s) issued by independent accountant or
     internal accountant.  If two reports are issued, two accountant
     report sections should appear</documentation>
  <appinfo>
     <xbrl:rollup to="statements" weight="0" order="3" />
     <xbrl:label xml:lang="en">Accountant's Report</xbrl:label>
     <xbrl:reference name="SAS" number="58" chapter="" paragraph=""
        subparagraph="" />
```

LISTING 22.1 continued

```
  </appinfo>
</annotation>
</element>
```

LISTING 22.2 XBRL Sample Instance (Truncated for Brevity)

```
<?xml version="1.0" encoding="utf-8"?>
<group
    xmlns="http://www.xbrl.org/core/xbrl-2000-07-31"
    xmlns:ci="http://www.xbrl.org/us/gaap/ci/2000-07-31"
    xmlns:gpsi="http://www.xbrl.org/us/gaap/ci/2000-07-31/sample"
    xmlns:csh="http://www.xbrlSolutions.com/labels"
    id="XXXXXXXXXX-AB"
    entity="NASDAQ:GPSI"
    period="1999-05-31"
    schemaLocation="http://www.xbrl.org/us/gaap/ci/2000-07-31
    http://www.xbrl.org/us/gaap/ci/2000-07-31/us-gaap-ci-2000-07-31.xsd
    http://www.xbrl.org/us/gaap/ci/2000-07-31/sample
   http://www.xbrl.org/us/gaap/ci/2000-07-31/sample/gpsi-custom-2000-07-31.xsd"
scaleFactor="3"
    precision="9"
    type="statements"
    unit="ISO4217:USD"
    decimalPattern="#.#"
    formatName="">

…
    <!--Revenues -->
    <group type="ci:grossProfit.salesRevenueNet">
        <group type="ci:salesRevenueGross.goods">
        <label href="xpointer(..)" xml:lang="en">License</label>
            <item id="IS-001" period="P1Y/1999-05-31">79685</item>
            <item id="IS-002" period="P1Y/1998-05-31">52949</item>
            <item id="IS-003" period="P1Y/1997-05-31">35919</item>
        </group>
        <group type="ci:salesRevenueGross.services">
        <label href="xpointer(..)" xml:lang="en">Service</label>
            <item id="IS-004" period="P1Y/1999-05-31">55222</item>
            <item id="IS-005" period="P1Y/1998-05-31">32710</item>
            <item id="IS-006" period="P1Y/1997-05-31">21201</item>
        </group>

        <label href="xpointer(..)" xml:lang="en">Total revenues</label>
        <item id="IS-007" period="P1Y/1999-05-31">134907</item>
```

LISTING 22.2 continued

```
        <item id="IS-008" period="P1Y/1998-05-31">85659</item>
        <item id="IS-009" period="P1Y/1997-05-31">57120</item>
    </group>
...
<!-- End of document group -->
</group>
```

> **Note**
>
> The complete sample code for XBRL can be found in the example with the filename `xbrlsample.xml`. The file can be downloaded from the Sams Web site.

The results of this document are shown in Figure 22.5.

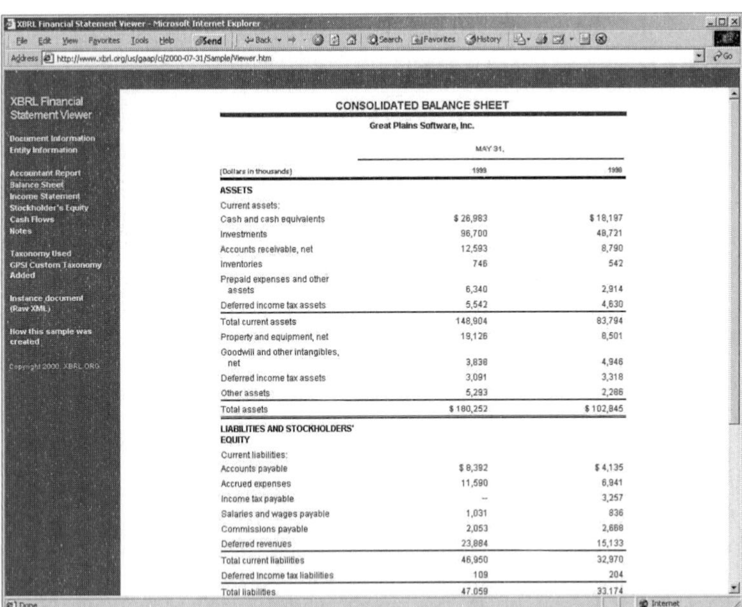

CONSOLIDATED BALANCE SHEET

Great Plains Software, Inc.

	MAY 31,	
(Dollars in thousands)	1999	1998
ASSETS		
Current assets:		
Cash and cash equivalents	$ 26,983	$ 18,197
Investments	96,700	48,721
Accounts receivable, net	12,593	8,790
Inventories	746	542
Prepaid expenses and other assets	6,340	2,914
Deferred income tax assets	5,542	4,630
Total current assets	148,904	83,794
Property and equipment, net	19,126	8,501
Goodwill and other intangibles, net	3,838	4,946
Deferred income tax assets	3,091	3,318
Other assets	5,293	2,286
Total assets	$ 180,252	$ 102,845
LIABILITIES AND STOCKHOLDERS' EQUITY		
Current liabilities:		
Accounts payable	$ 8,392	$ 4,135
Accrued expenses	11,590	6,941
Income tax payable	--	3,257
Salaries and wages payable	1,031	836
Commissions payable	2,053	2,668
Deferred revenues	23,884	15,133
Total current liabilities	46,950	32,970
Deferred income tax liabilities	109	204
Total liabilities	47,059	33,174

FIGURE 22.5
XBRL sample instance.

As you may have noticed, critical information is being contained and exchanged within XBRL. You would think that security would be a primary concern, but it's not even a consideration. The primary reason for this is that the group working with and managing the XBRL effort believes that other groups will solve this problem in a more complete and widely adopted manner. Therefore, XBRL will leverage those specifications when they become available.

XBRL is becoming increasingly widely supported. Its presence has spread the globe and has gotten support from such major establishments as the Securities Exchange Commission (SEC), the International Accounting Standards Board (IASB), and the International Federation of Accountants (IFACT). Every company and every industry in the world will soon use XBRL. As of October 2001, about 20 countries are getting involved with XBRL-based information exchange. In addition, the XBRL specification is increasingly working with other standards efforts to be the de facto standard for financial reporting within those other standards efforts. XBRL has formed connections with such notable standards as Health Level Seven (HL7), RosettaNet, Research Information Exchange Markup Language (RIXML), Investor Research Markup Language (IRML), and other efforts. Even though financial services users use XBRL, it is not exclusively about financial services. Users of the specification include government agencies, pharmaceutical companies, and manufacturing companies. Part of the reason for XBRL's widespread adoption is its rigorous requirements for working group members. Any group that wants to become an XBRL working group member must commit significant financial, technical, and public relations resources, as well as commit to incorporating XBRL in all of its financial reporting applications, both internal and external. These requirements ensure that the specification isn't merely given lip service.

Note

You can view the XBRL specification by visiting the XBRL Web site at `www.xbrl.org`.

Interactive Financial Exchange (IFX)

One of the most intensive uses of information in the financial sector is the exchange of transactional financial data. Transactional data is the day-to-day, minute-to-minute exchange of individual financial information such as funds transfers, stock purchases, credit inquiries, and other such information vital to a working economy. Given the vast quantity and importance of this data, it is no wonder that XML is increasingly being used to simplify and enhance the exchange of this information.

In particular, the Interactive Financial Exchange (IFX) specification provides a robust, scalable framework for the exchange of financial data and instructions. Even though the current implementation of IFX is in the XML format, the core specification is independent of a particular representational technology. Participating in the definition of this format are major financial players, service providers, and information technology vendors. IFX builds on previous industry experience, including the Open Financial Exchange (OFX) and GOLD specifications, which are currently implemented by financial institutions and service providers to enable electronic exchange of financial data between them and their customers. IFX didn't start out as an XML specification but rather as a generalized business messaging specification for financial transactions. It just was that XML was able to meet its needs before any other representational technology. Work on IFX has been going on for about four years. The IFX Forum is an open-membership, nonprofit corporation founded to maintain and facilitate the development of the IFX specifications. Current IFX Forum members include Microsoft, Checkfree, Bank of America, Wells Fargo, Citigroup, and Avalon.

Specifically, the IFX specification enables the exchange of online financial services information. The activities supported by IFX include bank, brokerage, mutual fund, and credit card statement downloads as well as electronic funds transfers, including recurring transfers, individual and recurring consumer and business payments, transaction history, current holdings, balances, and electronic bill presentment and payment. These transactions occur between a broad range of user types, known as *service providers*, including banks, brokerage houses, insurance companies, merchants, payment and bill processors, financial advisors, and government agencies.

The IFX specification also provides a certain amount of transaction and security robustness, as is necessary for the nature of the documents being exchanged. These features assure users that IFX messages are reliably executed, the information supplied is correct, and the results can be used for communicating and executing important financial transactions. IFX provides an suite of security options for further protecting the integrity of financial transactions. These security features include authentication of the parties involved, encryption of data, integrity of the information being exchanged, as well as robust protocols for error recovery.

The IFX specification is an XML messaging protocol that has two key parts: the infrastructure for sending financial messages and the specific content of those messages. The infrastructure concerns interparty communication within and outside company walls and provides common data elements and security. The specific content is focused on loans and credit, electronic bill presentment, and business and consumer banking needs.

IFX is a "message-oriented" standard in that the documents are used in a request/response mechanism. Clients send IFX message "requests" to servers that understand the format, which in turn return IFX message "responses" back to the client. As such, the IFX specification functions as a protocol that can be used in either batch or interactive communication styles. However, IFX is also transport neutral, supporting HTTP, SMTP, FTP, or any emergent protocol for exchange. IFX applies a single authentication context to multiple requests in order to reduce the overhead of user authentication. With an international focus, IFX supports multiple currencies, country-specific extensions, and different forms of encoding, such as Unicode.

IFX can be transmitted in an asynchronous or synchronous mode. This means that IFX messages can be sent without keeping the connection open for a response, or the connection session can wait for the transaction to be completed before terminating. This feature allows IFX servers the ability to complete a response at a later time. Sample IFX messages can be seen in Listings 22.3 and 22.4.

LISTING 22.3 Sample IFX Request Message

```
POST http://www.CSP.com/IFX.cgi HTTP/1.0
User-Agent:MyApp 5.0
Content-Type: text/xml
Content-Length: 1032

<?xml version="1.0" encoding="UTF-8" ?>
<?ifx version="1.0.1" oldfileuid="00000000-0000…" newfileuid="00000000-0000…" ?>

<!DOCTYPE IFX PUBLIC "-//IFX//DTD IFX1.0.1//EN"
"http://www.ifxforum.org/IFX1.0.1/xml/ifx.dtd"
[private markup]>
<IFX>" \>
   ... IFX requests ...
</IFX>
```

LISTING 22.4 Sample IFX Response Message

```
HTTP 1.0 200 OK
Content-Type: text/xml
Content-Length: 8732

<?xml version="1.0" encoding="UTF-8" ?>
<?ifx version="1.0.1" oldfileuid="00000000-0000…" newfileuid="00000000-0000…" ?>

<!DOCTYPE IFX PUBLIC "-//IFX//DTD IFX1.0.1//EN"
"http://www.ifxforum.org/IFX1.0.1/xml/ifx.dtd"
[private markup]>

<IFX>" \>
<Status>passed</Status>
<AcctId>1234567890</AcctId>
</IFX>
```

As you probably noticed, this message and the previous message are very similar. This is intentional. IFX request and response messages are relatively symmetric documents that can be exchanged by any party in a financial transaction.

IFX actually consists of a number of separate message types that address different needs. Table 22.1 lists some of those message types and the sorts of messages they describe.

TABLE 22.1 Sample IFX Message Types

Message Type	*Description*
Debit and credit messages	Authorize, commit, and reverse debits and credits for use in self-service, point-of-sale, and other applications that involve debiting or crediting an account.
Deposit account statement inquiry	Balance and transaction reporting as required in a corporate environment.
Single payment add	Business-to-business payment transactions.

The IFX framework is made up of implementation rules. Two communicating parties use the self-discovery features of IFX to exchange information about what they can and can't support for transactions. For example, a bill-presentment client needs to interact with a server that handles payments.

Subsequent development on the IFX specification has concentrated on adding substantial support for additional features, such as business-to-business and ATM transactions, including credit, debit, and management of "value media," such as stamps, dollar bills, and tickets. In general, the IFX specification is adding capabilities to support richer forms and types of payment that can be individually transmitted or conglomerated for payment in an aggregated fashion, such as payroll transactions.

IFX is also working in the loan credit application space and working with the insurance vertical industry standard, ACORD. In its next major v2.0 release, the IFX Forum is seriously considering how to better incorporate Web Services, and thinking about using SOAP as a transport mechanism.

Note

Find out more by visiting the IFX Web site at `http://www.ifxforum.org/`.

Insurance

Insurance is one of the most heavily paper document–dominated industries around. The need to document the entire insurance process, from customer acquisition to claims fulfillment (and everything in between), practically eclipses every other industry with the exception of perhaps health care. As such, the need to simplify the storage and exchange of this information has motivated groups to create industry standards, using XML as a possible base for these efforts. In this section, we focus on one of the major insurance industry XML efforts.

Association for Cooperative Operations Research and Development (ACORD)

The insurance business is driven by data, and the Property & Casualty (P&C) business is no exception. In the drive to utilize the Internet as a means for real-time exchange of insurance information between producers, carriers, rating bureaus, and service providers, the Association for Cooperative Operations Research and Development (ACORD) created an XML format for defining message-oriented P&C transactions. Leveraging the existing Interactive Financial Exchange (IFX) specification as a "base protocol," ACORD is defining an insurance industry format that contains transactions for Personal and Commercial Lines, Surety, Claims, and Accounting transactions. As a result, most of the business message structure, data types, and documentation conventions were borrowed from the IFX specification.

The organization was actually formed in 1970 for the development and promotion of standards for the insurance industry. ACORD's first XML standard to pass approval was its ACORD Property and Casualty and Surety (P&C and Surety) specification, developed in late 1998 and approved in 2000. ACORD's follow-up to this was the development of the ACORD Life insurance standard known as XMLife. A key aspect of the ACORD standards is its dependence on the IFX standard and its support of the e-business standardization effort ebXML. It also extends Automation Level 3, an EDI standard adopted in the insurance industry.

ACORD specifies all the aspects of the insurance lifecycle, from customer acquisition to claims fulfillment. These are divided along the lines of Property and Casualty, Life, and Surety insurance. ACORD specifies a very large and thick Document Type Definition (DTD) around the vocabulary and exchange mechanisms designed to meet these needs.

Due to its longevity and reputation,ACORD has the support of over 1,000 insurance carriers and groups, 25,000 agencies, the majority of software services and vendors, many nonprofit organizations, and the CPCU society. This, combined with its excellent work in the form of its XMLife and Property and Casualty standardization efforts, contribute to its excellent chances of success in surviving any battles with conflicting insurance industry standardization efforts.

For security, ACORD relies on channel-level encryption, such as SSL or SMIME, for privacy and data integrity. ACORD contains built-in mechanisms for authentication of user parties and transactions but does not provide any mechanism to protect privacy and guarantee data integrity between endpoints. As a result, the implementation relies on channel-level facilities for this functionality. Because ACORD follows the same architecture structure of IFX, it supports batch and interactive styles of communication and is application protocol independent, supporting HTTP, FTP, SMTP, or emerging protocols for transport.

The ACORD Global Standards Strategy Committee has also announced a project called "eMerge" that aims to integrate existing ACORD standards into a single common standard. The goal is to facilitate more effective and efficient movement of data between insurance trading partners. This project is an evolution of the XML standards that ACORD has supported since 1998. This new and evolving format will develop a single view of financial services by partnering with other standards bodies globally in an effort to facilitate straight-through processing (STP). Increasingly, the lines between insurance and the other financial services sectors are becoming blurred by virtue of increasingly shared data and implementations. Adoption of a common data-exchange structure will simplify and streamline data transfer both internal and external to an enterprise.

Major ACORD members involved in crafting the standards include such insurance and software industry vendors as Channelpoint, IBM, Manulife Financial, Marsh Inc., MetLife, Microsoft, Oracle, Principal Financial Group, SAFECO, Silverlake Software, The Hartford, Travelers, TowerStreet, and ZeBU.

Note

Find out more by visiting the ACORD Web site at `http://www.acord.org/`.

Health Care

Besides insurance, health care is the most heavily document-dominated industry. Every aspect of the care of patients must be documented, from patient acquisition and appointments, to specific treatment and payment. Therefore, many groups have emerged to solve the various documentation challenges associated with health care. In this section, we feature a few of those health care–related industry standards.

Much of the recent activity in XML-enabling health care can be attributed to one motivator: The Health Insurance Portability & Accountability Act (HIPAA) of 1996. This one law, also known as the Kennedy-Kassebaum Act, seeks to make major changes to the way medical information is stored and exchanged. It mandates that health care efficiency must be improved by standardizing electronic data interchange, and information must be maintained with the strictest confidentiality and security through the setting and enforcement of standards. In particular, HIPAA calls for the standardization of electronic patient health, administrative, and financial data, the establishment of unique health identifiers for individuals, employers, health plans, and health care providers, and the setting of security standards to protect the confidentiality and integrity of "individually identifiable health information," past, present, or future. And this all needs to be implemented by October 16, 2002 for the first part, and April 14, 2003 for the second. Otherwise, penalties up to $250,000 will apply!

XML is perfectly suited to providing all the requirements of HIPAA in a manner that also simplifies the requirements for integration with the tons of legacy systems that medical establishments have in place. Sounds like XML to the rescue. Of course, there are also lots of reasons besides HIPAA why XML should be implemented in the health care space, including platform neutrality, prevalence of tools, greatly reduced cost, a large set of skilled XML labor, and positive buzz—but none of these exerts as much pressure as HIPAA.

A few major standards hope to solve this problem, which is generally known as Electronic Patient Records (EPR). The front leader in this category is the Health Level Seven (HL7) standard. HL7 originally was a non-XML standard but is rapidly becoming a major influence in the XML space with its next standards release. HL7 specifies a health care industry–specific format that covers the needs for EPR, prescriptions, and medical insurance filings as well as medical imaging needs. Its next major release, v3.0, plans to support XML natively and has considerable backing.

For those who are interested in medical record XML standards but can't wait for the HL7 release, there are a number of other efforts by organizations aiming to "fill the gap" in meeting HIPAA requirements. These include the CISTERN specification, which builds upon HL7's prior releases. DocScope and Xchart are other private efforts to tackle the EPR problem.

In general, a growing body of work is being pursued in creating XML formats specifically for the health care industry, and especially the medical records industry. For more information, check out the "Healthcare" listing in the "XML in Industry" section of the `www.xml.org` Web site.

Health Level Seven (HL7)

Health Level Seven, whose name refers to the top level (the application level) of the International Standards Organization's (ISO) communications model for Open Systems Interconnection (OSI), is an American National Standards Institute (ANSI) approved Standards Developing Organization (SDO) focused on the health care arena. SDOs produce standards for a wide variety of domain areas in the health care space, ranging from pharmaceutical, medical devices, imaging, and insurance. The HL7 SDO focuses on standards for clinical and administrative data. More specifically, HL7 produces standards for the exchange, management, and integration of data that supports clinical patient care and the management, delivery, and evaluation of health care services. The goal of the Ann Arbor, Michigan–based nonprofit organization is to service its members, which include providers, vendors, payers, consultants, government groups, and others who have an interest in the development and advancement of clinical and administrative standards for health care. HL7 is also international in scope, with applications in Australia, Canada, China, Finland, Germany, India, Japan, Korea, The Netherlands, New Zealand, Southern Africa, Switzerland, and the United Kingdom.

The application level of the OSI model isn't concerned with the lower-level aspects of data communication (such as transport and routing) but rather addresses application data definition, exchange, error checking, security checks, participant identification, availability checks, and data structure.

Created in 1989, HL7 has been standardizing clinical and administrative data for health care, utilizing an EDI-like messaging specification. However, its latest release is a full-scale movement to XML. The most widely adopted of its specifications is patient and financial administration, which solves specific transactional issues such as admitting new patients to a hospital. HL7 solves the major problem of sharing this patient data with all the systems in a hospital that need to know about new patients. This standardization, widely used for patient administration, certain kinds of laboratory data, and to some extent for clinical observations, results in a high level of penetration by HL7 in the industry. Over 90 percent of U.S. hospitals use some portion of the HL7 standard, which is the highest adoption of any specification in health care. However, the scope and focus of the specification still leaves a lot of room for standardization. The specification was started so many years ago and was built up by accretion. The result was so broad based that it became difficult to add new functionality in the 1990s. As a result, the HL7 managing organization realized that it needed to go back and rethink the whole approach. It needed a more coherent model, and XML was the answer.

The HL7 created the Reference Implementation Model (RIM), which resulted in a grand simplification of the messages based on XML. The group working on the specification was looking at the fact that despite the best efforts of HL7, and despite intensive work to computerize patient records, the effort to move from paper-based to computer-based systems had stalled. About 85 percent of clinical information was still paper based. Therefore, even if hospitals used document management systems, the results were printed, and most still used paper, rather than the electronic form. The group realized that the attempt to computerize info relied on a highly regularized, normalized data model that did not fit clinical practice and the way doctors think of the clinical encounter. The various doctors looking at XML saw a means to create a new approach to standardizing clinical information that took advantage of the sparsely populated tree structure of XML. The result was a models-based approach using the RIM, a product of seven years of work in the industry. The final product was HL7 v3.0, a new version by number, but a completely new product in reality.

Because some countries have mandated the use of HL7 by law, there was good reason to maintain the old HL7 interfaces. Therefore, the organization took a scaled approach for gently moving the space from the EDI-like syntax of v2.4 to the XML-based v3.0. This resulted in three major products and versions of the HL7 specification:

- An informative specification called "v2.XML" that created an XML expression for the current generation of HL7 specs.
- The clinical document architecture (CDA), approved in November 2000, which took the new approach to standardizing clinical information using the ability of XML but didn't produce a formal version of the HL7 standard.
- The formal HL7 v3.0, which is a complete set of clinical messages that overlap the functionality of v2.0 but is derived from the RIM information model.

While contributing to v3.0, the CDA is not formally part of any specification. Instead, it helps users make the mental transition to the new way of doing things. The CDA is based on the RIM and uses HL7 methodology for deriving XML from a UML object model. The core component of information is what a physician is willing to sign. The model combines the concept of a persistent information unit, the concept of wholeness, and a signature to create an integrity-based system. As a result, the final specification is very elementary, almost like XHTML in its model, with a few other features related to the information model of clinical content. Listing 22.5 shows the CDA document hierarchy.

LISTING 22.5 CDA Document Hierarchy (from the HL7 Web Site)

```
CDA Level One
        CDA Level Two
              Level Two :: Progress Note
              Level Two :: Cardiology Progress Note
              Level Two :: Endocrinology Progress Note
```

LISTING 22.5 continued

```
            Level Two :: Diabetes Mellitus Progress Note
                CDA Level Three
                    Level Three :: Progress Note
                    Level Three :: Cardiology Progress Note
                    Level Three :: Endocrinology Progress Note
                    Level Three :: Diabetes Mellitus Progress Note
```

HL7 version 3.0 encapsulates all the functionality of previous versions but uses the new reference model and architecture for its representation. It also allows multiple representations of the expression, not limiting itself to XML. For example, one can express HL7 3.0 in IDL and ASN as well. The current functionality of HL7 is covered in Table 22.2.

TABLE 22.2 HL7 Functionality

Functionality	*Definition*
Control	Message definitions and interchange protocols
Patient administration	Admit, discharge, transfer, and demographics
Order entry	Orders for clinical services and observations, pharmacy, dietary, and supplies
Query	Rules applying to queries and to their responses
Financial management	Patient accounting and charges
Observation reporting	Observation report messages
Master files	Health care application master files
Medical records/ information management	Document management services and resources
Scheduling	Appointment scheduling and resources
Patient referral	Primary care referral messages
Patient care	Problem-oriented records
Laboratory automation	Equipment status, specimen status, equipment inventory, equipment comment, equipment response, equipment notification, equipment test code settings, and equipment logs/service
Application management	Application control–level requests and transmission of application management information
Personnel management	Professional affiliations, educational details, language detail, practitioner organization unit, practitioner detail, and staff identification

Listing 22.6 shows a sample HL7 CDA XML document excerpt.

LISTING 22.6 Sample HL7 CDA XML Document (Excerpt)

```
<?xml version="1.0"?>
      <!DOCTYPE levelone PUBLIC "-//HL7//DTD CDA Level One 1.0//EN" >
<levelone>
  <clinical_document_header>
    <id EX="a123" RT="2.16.840.1.113883.3.933"/>
    <set_id EX="B" RT="2.16.840.1.113883.3.933"/>
    <version_nbr V="2"/>
    <document_type_cd V="11488-4" S="2.16.840.1.113883.6.1"
      DN="Consultation note"/>
    <origination_dttm V="2000-04-07"/>
    <confidentiality_cd ID="CONF1" V="N" S="2.16.840.1.113883.5.1xxx"/>
    <confidentiality_cd ID="CONF2" V="R" S="2.16.840.1.113883.5.1xxx"/>
    <document_relationship>
      <document_relationship.type_cd V="RPLC"/>
      <related_document>
        <id EX="a234" RT="2.16.840.1.113883.3.933"/>
        <set_id EX="B" RT="2.16.840.1.113883.3.933"/>
        <version_nbr V="1"/>
      </related_document>
    </document_relationship>
    <fulfills_order>
      <fulfills_order.type_cd V="FLFS"/>
      <order><id EX="x23ABC" RT="2.16.840.1.113883.3.933"/></order>
      <order><id EX="x42CDE" RT="2.16.840.1.113883.3.933"/></order>
    </fulfills_order>
    <patient_encounter>
      <id EX="KPENC1332" RT="2.16.840.1.113883.3.933"/>
      <practice_setting_cd V="GIM"
        S="2.16.840.1.113883.5.1xxx" DN="General internal medicine clinic"/>
      <encounter_tmr V="2000-04-07"/>
      <service_location>
        <id EX="KXLPa123" RT="2.16.840.1.113883.3.933"/>
        <addr>
          <HNR V="970"/>
          <STR V="Post St"/>
          <DIR V="NE"/>
          <CTY V="Alameda"/>
          <STA V="CA"/>
          <ZIP V="94501"/>
        </addr>
      </service_location>
    </patient_encounter>
  </clinical_document_header>
  <body confidentiality="CONF1">
    <section>
      <caption>
```

LISTING 22.6 continued

```
        <caption_cd V="8684-3" S="2.16.840.1.113883.6.1"/>
        History of Present Illness
      </caption>
      <paragraph>
        <content>
          Henry Levin, the 7th is a 67 year old male referred for further
          asthma management. Onset of asthma in his teens. He was hospitalized
          twice last year, and already twice this year. He has not been able to
          be weaned off steroids for the past several months.
        </content>
      </paragraph>
    </section>
    <section>
      <caption>
        <caption_cd V="1234-X" S="2.16.840.1.113883.6.1"/>Plan
      </caption>
      <list>
        <item><content>Complete PFTs with lung volumes.</content></item>
        <item><content>Chem-7</content></item>
        <item>
          <content>
            Provide educational material on inhaler usage and
            peak flow self-monitoring.
          </content>
        </item>
        <item>
          <content>Decrease prednisone to 20qOD alternating with
18qOD.</content>
        </item>
        <item><content>Hydrocortisone cream to finger BID.</content></item>
        <item><content>RTC 1 week.</content></item>
      </list>
    </section>
  </body>
</levelone>
```

Note

A complete HL7 sample file, called `hl7cdasample.xml`, can be downloaded from the Sams Web site.

The complete version of this file is shown in a Web browser in Figure 22.6.

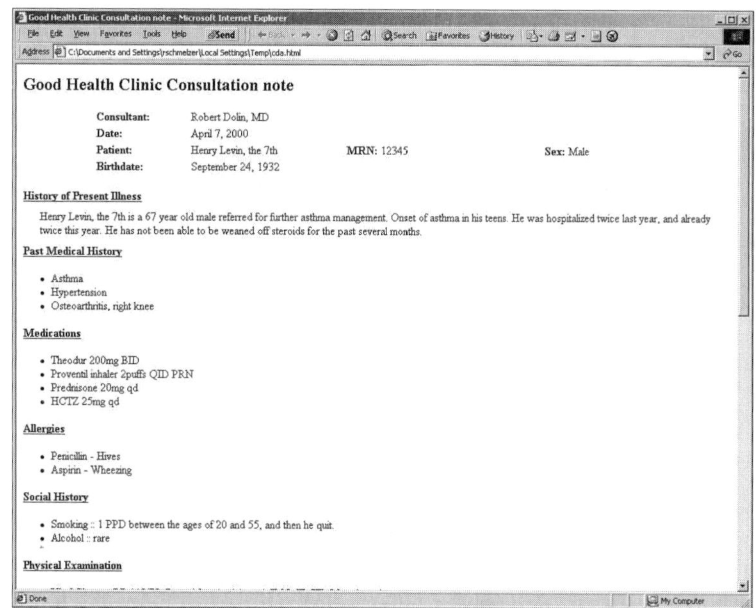

FIGURE 22.6
Visual representation of the HL7 CDA file.

Due to HIPAA's high visibility in the health care arena, HL7 has become significantly involved with HIPAA implementation as well as legislation. It has produced an addendum to the HIPAA specification to specifically enable certain aspects of the HIPAA-mandated electronic transmission of patient records. Future projects will include Home Health, Skilled Nursing Facility, Durable Medical Equipment (DME), End Stage Renal Disease (ESRD), and Preauthorization and Referrals.

> **Note**
>
> You can find out more by visiting the HL7 Web site at `http://www.hl7.org/`.

Legal Industry XML Standards

The judicial system has made good use of XML in the past few years. This section covers one of the more notable legal industry–focused standards that helps to simplify the process of exchanging information in the context of law interpretation and litigation.

Legal XML

Even lawyers need XML. The need to file court papers, exchange documents with other legal authorities and clients, and generally simplify life has resulted in the development of XML vocabularies focused on the legal profession. A number of these efforts combined to result in the Legal XML initiative, whose mission is to develop open, nonproprietary standards for legal documents and associated applications.

Legal XML began in November 1998 and rapidly grew to over 870 participants by 2001. It is made up of roughly 50 percent private legal companies, 25 percent government institutions, and 25 percent academic or nonprofit organizations, with a mostly United States–based population that is increasingly developing its presence in Australia, Canada, and Europe. Despite the novelty of applying XML to the legal profession, the "Legal XML" idea is actually quite dated. Soon after Charles F. Goldfarb, who himself was a lawyer, developed SGML, Alan Asay, a brilliant lawyer and technologist, created civil and criminal SGML Document Type Definitions (DTDs) for the Utah state courts. It only took the continued development of these original SGML documents, combined with the proliferation of the Internet and XML, to make Legal XML happen.

The issue of what is considered to be a "legal" document is an interesting one. Theoretically, almost every electronic document can be categorized as "legal," because the law is concerned with the exchange of day-to-day documents in the context of business as well as interpersonal interaction. However, this scope is too wide for any organization to build a credible standards base. Therefore, the Legal XML group has sought to address the legal documents that are of most importance and the need for standardization.

The domain of Legal XML documents is divided into various subdomains by virtue of their horizontal or vertical application. In this context, *vertical* describes specific legal document domains, such as public law (including legislation, bills, and statutes), private law (including contracts and wills), court filings, transcripts, judicial decisions, and publications (including legal books and law journals). *Horizontal* vocabulary describes general information of relevance to most legal documents, such as citations, general names and addresses, and general document structure, such as tables, outlines, paragraphs, and signatures. Legal XML standardizes these various horizontal and vertical vocabulary structures as well as coordinates their efforts within the larger legal community.

The Legal XML effort is divided into workgroups that focus on either horizontal or vertical domains, such as court filings and transcripts. These workgroups then develop specifications that define the actual technical XML standards. An additional two groups, called "Legal" and "Horizontal," then synchronize and harmonize the work of these various groups to make sure no redundant or contradictory work is done. As of this writing, Legal XML has not yet produced a final, "recommended" standard. However, the group has published its first proposed standard in the "Court Filing" area. The general approach that Legal XML takes to its work is the Greatest Common Denominator (GCD) approach, which solicits feedback from the community at large and then includes as many of those features as possible, making many of them optional. The discussion on the merits of this approach is discussed earlier in this chapter.

The Court Filing document describes the information required for electronic court filing and the structure of that information. It doesn't include any information that regards the actual content of the pleading, such as contracts, orders, or judgments. As such, the first proposed specification is somewhat basic, but it illustrates well the goals of the Legal XML group. The architecture makes use of a three-tier application model that uses three cooperating applications: the client (consisting of an application on the user's desk, called the Electronic Filing Provider [EFP]), the server (also known as the Electronic Filing Manager [EFM]), and the Case Management System.

The document specifies a `LegalEnvelope` element that is the root element of the Legal XML document. The `LegalEnvelope` element identifies the type of message and routing information as well as indicates the contents contained within. Within the `LegalEnvelope` element is a `Legal` entity that in the case of this proposal contains a `CourtFiling` element that specifies individual `Filing` elements. A sample of a Court Filing Subsequent Filing can be found in Listing 22.7.

LISTING 22.7 Legal XML Court Filing Example (`LegalEnvelope` omitted for brevity; it doesn't validate because it's an excerpt)

```
<?xml version="1.0" standalone="yes"?>
<!DOCTYPE LegalEnvelope SYSTEM "LegalEnvelope.dtd">
<!-- Creation date and time: 10-Mar-00 22:36Z -->
<LegalEnvelope Version="1.0">
    ...
<CourtFiling>
<Filing>
<Actors>
    <Actor ID="J01">
        <Title>Presiding Judge</Title>
        <Name ID="Ref01.n1">
            <Person>
            <FullName>Margret Marly Jefferson</FullName>
                <FirstName>Margret</FirstName>
            <MiddleName>Marly</MiddleName>
                <LastName>Jefferson</LastName>
            </Person>
        </Name>
        <Role>
            <RoleName>Presiding Judge</RoleName>
        </Role>
    </Actor>
</Actors>
```

LISTING 22.7 continued

```
<FilingInformation ID="Ref01.1">
    <SpecialHandling/>
    <CourtInformation>
        <Location ID="D1116"/>
    </CourtInformation>
    <CaseInformation>
        <FullCaseNumber>D1116-CR-99-218</FullCaseNumber>
        <CaseTitle>State v. Onereallybadman</CaseTitle>
        <CaseCategory>criminal</CaseCategory>
        <CaseYear>1999</CaseYear>
    </CaseInformation>
</FilingInformation>
<LeadDocument ID="Ref01.1.d1">
    <DocumentInformation>
An Actor is by reference to an Actor in the Filing Actors list.
        <Actors>
        <Actor ID="Ref01.n1.1" Reference="Ref01.n1"/>
        </Actors>
        <Submitted>
          <DateTime>
            <Date>20000202</Date>
            <Time>18:36Z</Time>
          </DateTime>
        </Submitted>
        <DocumentDescription>
            <DocumentTitle>
                Order for Pre-Trial Hearing has been scheduled
            </DocumentTitle>
            <DocumentType DocumentCode="8251">
                ORD: PRE-TRIAL/SCHEDULED
            </DocumentType>
        </DocumentDescription>
    </DocumentInformation>
    This document content shows a document residing on the web as the input .
        <DocumentContent ID="Ref01.1.d1.dc" MimeType="application/pdf"
href="ftp://nowhere.com/JudgeJefferson/cr/99/218/Orders/PretrialHearing.pdf"/>
        <Attachment ID="Ref01.1.d1.a1">
    An attachment to the lead document.
        <AttachmentDocumentInformation>
        <Submitted>
          <DateTime>
              <Date>20000202</Date>
              <Time>18:36Z</Time>
          </DateTime>
        </Submitted>
            <DocumentDescription>
                <DocumentTitle>Attached text</DocumentTitle>
                <DocumentType>Text</DocumentType>
            </DocumentDescription>
```

LISTING 22.7 continued

```
        </AttachmentDocumentInformation>
This shows text as the document content.
        <DocumentContent ID="Ref01.1.d1.a1.dc" MimeType="application/text">
        The attached image file provides new information in this case.
        </DocumentContent>
This is an attachment to an attachment.
        <Attachment ID="Ref01.1.d1.a1.a1">
            <AttachmentDocumentInformation>
            <Submitted>
              <DateTime>
                <Date>20000202</Date>
                <Time>18:36Z</Time>
              </DateTime>
            </Submitted>
            <DocumentDescription>
                <DocumentTitle>Attached image</DocumentTitle>
                <DocumentType>image</DocumentType>
            </DocumentDescription>
        </AttachmentDocumentInformation>
This shows a BLOB as the document content.
        <DocumentContent ID="Ref01.1.d1.a1.a1.dc" Size="8191"
        MimeType="image/jpeg" ContentEncoding="Base64">jk075pfb3205hafnbci ...
        asfawrq2357c=rqttpbc</DocumentContent>
        </Attachment>
        </Attachment>
    </LeadDocument>
</Filing>
</CourtFiling>
</Legal>
</LegalEnvelope>
```

Legal XML is a small but growing effort and is using its clout to promote its standards efforts. It also uses partnerships with existing organizations, such as the Joint Technology Committee of COSCA/NACM, the National Court Reporters Association, SEARCH, the California Administrative Office of the Courts, and LEXML, to help develop and promote its standards. Other XML efforts on the legal front include UELP, XCI, National Center for State Courts/Lexis, Washington State Bar XML Study Committee, Joint Technology Committee of COSCA and NACM, National Conference of State Legislatures, and Legal Electronic Data Exchange Standard (LEDES) for time and billing.

Note

You can find out more by visiting the Legal XML Web site at `http://www.legalxml.org/`.

Real Estate

With all the information required for the successful purchase or lease of real estate property, there's no doubt that XML standards will have a significant impact on this industry. The range of solutions required for the real estate industry ranges from the electronic exchange of property information to mortgage and financial transaction data. This section covers one of the more notable standards relating to mortgage and real estate finance.

Mortgage Industry Standards Maintenance Organization (MISMO)

Much of the paperwork and documentation in the real estate industry actually revolves around the mortgage, credit, and loan processes rather than in locating and describing real estate property listings. The process for purchasing a home through a credit agency is both rigorous and paper ridden. However, the Mortgage Industry Standards Maintenance Organization (MISMO), under the auspices of the Mortgage Bankers Association (MBA), is seeking to simplify this task by providing a single repository of XML DTDs for use in real estate finance transactions from origination through servicing.

The mechanism for these automated transactions is quite simple in comparison. For example, one company will send a standard MISMO Credit Request to another participating company that, in turn, responds with a standard MISMO Credit Response. These transactions include all data that each company requires to process the exchange. MISMO has defined three deliverables to accomplish these goals. The first deliverable is a mortgage data dictionary. This dictionary includes the data elements present in MISMO Standard transactions. The dictionary also contains corresponding definitions, XML tag names, data requirements, and sources for the definitions of the supplied terms. The second deliverable for MISMO is an XML architecture that leverages the Web as its transport. The final deliverable is a relational data model that is provided to explain the relationships between the defined data elements and the necessity of those elements in a particular transaction.

MISMO set out to standardize information regarding loan data that is sent between two organizations and is relevant to a specific point in time and can span multiple transactions between trading partners. However, the intention of the specification is not to provide a means for archival of loan data, although companies can archive the files as they are sent back and forth within the industry. Specifically, the data structures were not designed with archival in mind, but rather stateful data relevant to a particular instance in a transaction between organizations. Key elements of functionality in the specification include credit reporting, loan boarding, applications, service orders, underwriting, and supporting activities.

The overall MISMO information architecture consists of four levels that define the scope of various data elements and processes. The top level consists of common element types that define data entities, such as a person's name or the name of a city, and can be used in more than one part of the MISMO architecture. The mechanism for the definition of these common elements is through a global DTD. The second level consists of DTDs maintained by an editorial committee of domain experts that corresponds to the message type defined by that DTD. For example, the underwriting DTD is designed to serve the needs of underwriting activities, and it is under the editorial control of a committee of underwriting experts. Data types are inherited from the top level when there is a match or are defined when there isn't such a match. An editorial committee similarly controls the top-level, common meta-DTD to ensure consistency. The third level consists of a MISMO Union DTD that provides a means for MISMO messages to contain any number of any of the message types defined by committees in the second level. The MISMO Union, therefore, inherits all of the committee architectures of the other levels and gathers all the data for the industry in a single DTD for general release. The Union DTD can also be used as a source from which other DTDs may be derived, such as a Credit Reporting DTD or a Service Request DTD, or to create a DTD for the entire mortgage industry. The fourth and final level of the model consists of extensions to the MISMO Union that are contributed by other mortgage industry players, in order to serve their specific needs or the needs of their partners. MISMO calls this the *application translation layer* (ATL).

MISMO has published specifications that support mortgage insurance application, mortgage insurance loan boarding, bulk pricing, real estate services, credit reporting, and underwriting process areas. The specifications are freely available for industry implementation via the MISMO Web site.

Note

Find out more by visiting the MISMO Web site at `http://www.mismo.org/`.

Business Administration and Human Resources (HR)

As a relative latecomer to the XML game, the needs of business management and human resources (HR) should not be neglected in their needs to exchange information with regards to employees, business operations, and other needs in the discourse of business information. In this section, we will explore HR-XML, a standard covering administrative and HR-related needs that aims to improve efficiency and hence reduce the cost of managing an effective organization.

Human Resources XML (HR-XML)

Paperwork is the day-to-day rigor that comes part and parcel with being part of a human resources (HR) organization. Simplifying these daily chores using XML is an almost obvious "Ah Ha!" However, despite the fact that the industry has a single name, there is nothing common about the way human resources is done from company to company, especially crossing geographic and industry boundaries. Yet, a human resources XML known simply as HR-XML aims to eliminate these paper processes by eliminating the lengthy "discovery" periods typical of setting up internal and external company transactions today.

The HR-XML Consortium is an independent, nonprofit association dedicated to the development and promotion of XML-enabled human resources–related data exchanges. The stated mission of the HR-XML Consortium (which is located at `http://www.hr-xml.org/channels/about.htm`) is to "spare employers and vendors the risk and expense of having to negotiate and agree upon data interchange mechanisms on an ad-hoc basis." HR-XML actually consists of a number of related but separate working groups that address the different problem areas in HR. The Recruiting and Staffing Workgroup's mission is to define XML vocabularies that enable recruiting and staffing transactions among employers, staffing companies, application vendors, job boards, and job seekers. The first fruits of its labor was the development of the Staffing Exchange Protocol (SEP), which enables the posting of job or position opportunities to job boards and other recruiting and sourcing venues and the return of job seeker, or candidate, data related to those postings. SEP supports the updating and recalling of job postings, the supplying of contact information for a job candidate (where only partial information initially was supplied), and the supplying of employer feedback to job seeker suppliers on postings that have been filled. The Cross-Process Objects (CPO) Workgroup aims to develop a common vocabulary and data model for HR as well as developing schemas for common HR objects used across the consortium's domain-specific workgroups, such as `Person` and `Job` objects.

The Payroll Workgroup is developing schemas to support a comprehensive range of interfaces into and out of payroll, including one-way integration from HR and Benefits systems to Payroll systems. The workgroup also has a draft schema designed to support the export of defined benefits and 401(k) plan participant data from payroll systems to third-party administrators. The Benefit Enrollment Workgroup is developing a universal schema for communicating employee benefit enrollment information between employers and insurance carriers, managed care organizations, and third-party administrators. Some of the immediate problems that the organization plans to address are enrollment in health, dental, vision, life, 401(k), and other types of benefit programs and ensuring that benefits enrollment specifications can map to the EDI transaction sets mandated by the federal Health Insurance Portability Protection Act (HIPAA). The Technical Steering Committee has developed a "Provisional Envelope Specification" that aims to provide a temporary specification for how HR-XML messages are transmitted, but it is expected that as other messaging protocols such as ebXML are widely adopted, HR-XML will become compliant.

With over 100 member organizations, clear focus, and advanced development of its XML vocabulary, the HR-XML Consortium is well poised to make an impact on the HR industry and its use of XML. It does, however, face some challenges in getting the many different participants in the HR process using the standard, and the adoption issue is its primary challenge. However, in March 2001, over 24 major organizations involved in HR document exchange committed to using and adopting the HR-XML Consortium standards as part of their day-to-day document exchange.

Note

Find out more by visiting the HR-XML Web site at `http://www.hr-xml.org/`.

Travel and Hospitality

With the volume of information that is available nowadays for travel and leisure services, the need to enable the fairly arcane reservation and scheduling systems in place in the travel and hospitality industries has become more urgent. XML has been provided as a technology capable of meeting these next-generation needs.

Like the manufacturing, health care, and other industries using EDI, the travel industry has been previously dominated by older data formats and mechanisms that have attempted to solve similar problems in data exchange. In the case of the travel industry, the systems that have been widespread are Global Distribution Systems (GDSs). The goal of GDSs is to centralize, consolidate, and deliver travel supplier information for the online booking of reservations. The primary users of GDSs are travel agencies, but in the past few years a number of consumer-focused GDSs have been increasingly available over the Web. GDSs currently present information only on the companies that subscribe to their services and supply data to them, and the format is as arcane and inflexible as

EDI is for the manufacturing industry. Therefore, there is movement afoot to replace the GDS systems with an XML-based mechanism to extend the functionality of those systems.

Open Travel Alliance (OTA)

The hospitality and travel industries are undergoing rapid change in this wired era, and XML is helping along the way. While data formats and standards have long been a staple of the airline, hotel, and car-rental organizations, never before have these various components of the travel industry gotten together and agreed on any one common format. Evolving from the continuing work and effort of the Hospitality Industry Technology Integration Standards (HITIS), the Open Travel Alliance (OTA) aims to solve this critical problem.

The OTA was created in May 1999 as a means for generating a set of standards for the hospitality and travel industries. The OTA organization is a consortium of suppliers in many different sectors of the travel industry, including air, car rental, hotel, travel agencies, and tour operators, as well as related companies that provide distribution and technology support to the industry.

OTA's first deliverable is an XML-based specification that covers the various needs of airline, hotel, car, and entertainment facilities. The OTA effort is an outgrowth of work that has been going on for many years in HITIS. HITIS was mainly focused on the development of standard specifications for internal processes such as Point of Sale (POS), reservation, and Property Management Systems (PMS). However, HITIS was not really focused on standardizing systems to communicate externally with other properties, suppliers, partners, and customers. As such, HITIS focused "inside the property," and the OTA was created to solve the needs of standardizing "outside the property." The OTA effort, launched at first independently of HITIS, soon merged with the OTA effort as HITIS began to consider XML as a means for its internal specifications.

The first year of OTA specifications extended the HITIS standards and delivered a handful of transactions that had been partially defined as part of HITIS. However, in the past few months, OTA has been very active in the development of industry-specific vocabularies that can give industry players, as well as tools and software vendors, the opportunity to create solutions based on the OTA approach.

The OTA is comprised of five working groups focusing on each of the different sectors of the market: air, car, hotel, leisure supplier, and nonsupplier, as well as an interoperability committee to ensure consistency. Each industry group is defining transactions that are unique to its industry, and the infrastructure group is trying to define the elements that all these industries share in common. Although they're all operating under the auspices of OTA, in reality each industry group is working independently and progressing at its own rate. In the hotel industry group, most of the major hotels and chains are represented: Cendant, Bass, Marriott, Sheraton, Hilton, and many others. A few of these chains, such as Cendant and Bass, had people assigned to HITIS group prior to their involvement in OTA. Therefore, many of these firms had a vested interest in continued standards development. All the participants in the hotel group are very active, making substantial progress on the development of various hotel industry vocabularies and messages. The group meets face to face at least three or four times per year in addition to numerous conference calls between meetings.

The OTA specification is a message-oriented protocol that specifies requests and responses for various industry-specific actions. The major features in the hotel portion of the OTA specification include the ability to create, modify, and cancel reservations as well as create and pass rate information, detailed and complete rate structures, booking rules, price availability and applicability, room and property availability, and requests for generic availability within a certain geographic area across multiple properties. The latest OTA version, v4.0, is an integration of HITIS into OTA. The end result will be that continued development will be under the watch of OTA, rather than HITIS. Of the two organizations, OTA is most likely to exist in the long run.

There is continual discussion within the group about how OTA can interact with other standards efforts and identify how other standards groups and industries are defining similar vocabularies. However, it seems that getting the various industry groups within OTA to communicate and converge their standards efforts is not easy either. One of the big issues within OTA is getting internal agreement—never mind competing standards—on vocabulary and processes among the air, hotel, car, and related industries. To solve this issue, there are big efforts within OTA to normalize what each of the groups are producing and to ensure a level of cohesiveness throughout all the specifications. Currently, OTA has not integrated with other standards efforts, but as internal agreement occurs, there is no doubt that the organization will look to other standards groups to integrate, converge, and/or leverage its efforts.

On other fronts, however, OTA is working well with other standards groups. The organization is looking to tie itself more closely with the ebXML specification as a means for transporting industry messages in a standard manner. The infrastructure committee within the OTA is planning to use ebXML as a transport layer, wrapping its OTA messages within MIME wrappers as a means for transporting, routing, and packaging industry messages. In the hotel industry, the prevalent vocabularies have been defined by two organizations in particular: the Hotel Electronic Distribution Network Association (HEDNA) and the Hospitality Industry Technology Integration Standards (HITIS).

The HITIS standards leveraged previous efforts of the Windows Hospitality Interface Specifications (WHIS) for its base documents in the development of its standards. The OTA specifications, originally based in part on the WHIS and HEDNA development, have recently merged with HITIS efforts, thus combining many of the best efforts of previous generations.

The latest OTA specification, known as OTA 2001A, is actually divided into two parts: the OTA Infrastructure and the Profile Specification. The OTA Infrastructure section defines how OTA documents are exchanged in a secure and reliable manner between trading partners. The OTA 2001A Infrastructure specifies a request/response mechanism for transmitting messages and can support both synchronous and asynchronous messaging capability. The OTA Infrastructure makes use of the ebXML header and a modified version of the manifest part of that header document for transport, routing, and packaging. In addition, the OTA Infrastructure supports four basic message types: `Create`, `Read`, `Update`, and `Delete`. Each of these operations are applied to the profile that is described later in this section. Although `Create`, `Read`, and `Delete` operations apply to a document as a whole, the `Update` method utilizes XPath to enable partial record updating. In addition to these, the OTA 2001A Infrastructure has well-defined security features, including authentication, encryption, confidentiality, message integrity, and a separated control mechanism for altering these security features. The OTA Infrastructure specification only allows for a connection to one trading partner per message, but it supports multiple payloads that may include different operations or batch operations in one message.

The Profile Specification is the content that is transmitted in the OTA Infrastructure and specifies a common customer "profile" that individual travelers and organizations can fill out once and exchange among various travel services over the Internet. A *profile* is a standard vocabulary that communicates data about the identity of a person or company as well as the person's or company's contacts and various "affiliations," including loyalty programs, forms of payment, travel documents, and detailed travel preferences. Profiles allow users to define collections of travel preferences in terms of specific travel plans and experiences, which can also include preferences for various air, hotel, car, rail, and other travel services. Preferences can be simply defined or contain more complex condition-based choices and dependencies. The profile not only identifies an individual or company but also affiliated persons, such as family members, companions, or business colleagues, as well as affiliated agencies, such as travel agencies, travel clubs, or employers. Profiles are identified by a globally unique identifier, comprised of an identifying string in combination with a URL that specifies the location of the identifier.

Due to the sensitivity of travel information, the OTA 2001A specification contains strict privacy requirements that have also been detailed in previous versions of the specification. These privacy preferences allow customers and companies to indicate the data that can be shared with other parties. Various attributes specified with this privacy information indicate whether the data may be shared for the synchronization of system information, such as keeping all copies of the profile on remote sites identical with the original, shared for marketing purposes, or not shared at all.

Prior to any exchange of information, the parties engage in a conversation to determine the capabilities of each other's systems and their support for different transport protocols, security, and required fields. This is accomplished using nonversioned discovery messages. To deal with the situation of identifying trading partners, the OTA 2001A specification supports a simple trading partner model, or exclusive trading partner agreement, that involves linking one requestor to one supplier. Although OTA supports the dynamic discovery of trading partners and their capabilities, there is currently no capability to determine whether a proper contract exists or to verify the validity of the trading partner; therefore, the feature remains unsupported. The issue of dynamic partner discovery will no doubt be addressed in future specification releases or in conjunction with other standards efforts.

The Open Travel Alliance is one of the more successful and notable XML-based vertical industry standards currently in existence. Part of its positive publicity is due to the focus of the standard and its acceptance of existing efforts that have attempted to produce specifications relevant to the travel industries. In particular, it has gained the support of other travel and hospitality industry groups such as the Hotel Electronic Distribution Network Association (HEDNA) and the American Hotel & Motel Association (AH&MA), developers of the Hospitality Industry Technology Integration Standards (HITIS). This support has allowed OTA to excel in many capacities as far as standards development and adoption. OTA has recruited some of the most notable travel industry organizations, ranging from businesses such as United and Marriott, to industry associations such as AH&MA and HEDNA.

Their recent merger of efforts with HITIS (read the HITIS specification, available on the OTA Web site) continues to bolster its credibility within the industry and possibility for widespread adoption success. The true measure of success will come when the major Global Distribution Systems such as Sabre and Worldspan choose to use OTA as their primary means of communication instead of the more arcane ResTeletype (a 64-character code system) and UN/EDIFACT (an EDI-based protocol) systems. Some of the major GDS providers are part of the OTA effort, which seems to bode well for their future success. A sample OTA XML file excerpt can be found in Listing 22.8.

LISTING 22.8 Sample OTA XML File Excerpt

```
<Profile>
  <Customer>
    <PersonName NameType="Default">
      <NameTitle>Mr.</NameTitle>
      <GivenName>George</GivenName>
      <MiddleName>A.</MiddleName>
      <SurName>Smith</SurName>
   </PersonName>
   <TelephoneInfo PhoneTech="Voice" PhoneUse="Work">
     <Telephone>
       <AreaCityCode>253</AreaCityCode>
       <PhoneNumber>813-8698</PhoneNumber>
     </Telephone>
   </TelephoneInfo>
   <PaymentForm>
   ...
   </PaymentForm>
   <Address>
     <StreetNmbr POBox="4321-01">1200 Yakima St</StreetNmbr>
     <BldgRoom>Suite 800</BldgRoom>
     <CityName>Seattle</CityName>
     <StateProv PostalCode="98108">WA</StateProv>
     <CountryName>USA</CountryName>
   </Address>
   <RelatedTraveler Relation="Child">
     <PersonName>
       <GivenName>Devin</GivenName>
       <MiddleName>R.</MiddleName>
       <SurName>Smith</SurName>
     </PersonName>
   </RelatedTraveler>
     <RelatedTraveler Relation="Child">
       <PersonName>
         <GivenName>Amy</GivenName>
         <MiddleName>E.</MiddleName>
         <SurName>Smith</SurName>
       </PersonName>
     </RelatedTraveler>
     <RelatedTraveler Relation="Child">
       <PersonName>
         <GivenName>Alfred</GivenName>
         <MiddleName>E.</MiddleName>
         <SurName>Newman</SurName>
       </PersonName>
     </RelatedTraveler>
  </Customer>
</Profile>
```

Note

Find out more by visiting theOTA Web site at `http://www.opentravel.org/`.

Manufacturing

Businesses of all shapes and sizes have been impacted by the constant need to delivery more products or services at lower costs and greater margins. Businesses face pressures of time, competition, lack of resources, and, of course, greater revenue. Although these are the typical, everyday problems that businesses will deal with as long as there is a market, XML technologies and standards have attempted to solve some of these problems.

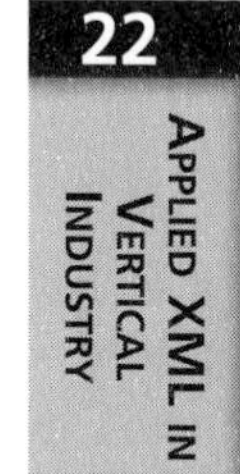

Once the general business issues are addressed, issues more specific to an industry or particular business remain. For example, how do utility companies communicate their billing needs to their customers? How do construction companies share planning and material requirements documents? There are also applications for XML in the manufacturing industries to provide functionality for data interchange between ordering systems and shop-floor scheduling systems, enabling machine and equipment communication, providing standardized bills of material as well as pack-and-ship systems, and simplifying software configuration.

Because Chapter 20, "Implementing XML in E-Business," deals with e-business standards, how does this section overlap with what we have dedicated an entire chapter to? The answer is simple: Manufacturing involves more than just supply-chain operations. E-Business specifications just cover the business part of manufacturing; we have to deal with the actual manufacturing process itself. Even before there was a formal supply chain to speak of, there were processes that resulted in the fabrication of products from raw materials. As the factory became an automated workplace, the need for paper and processes surely followed. It's these automation, assembly, factory, and associated processes that are moving from paper to electronic formats, and XML is empowering this revolution.

However, despite this focus on manufacturing, there aren't many shop floor and factory XML standards that have garnered widespread attention and adoption, so we'll focus on what it takes to get products from point A to point B (otherwise known as shipping and logistics).

Shipping and Logistics

As mentioned, many of the issues in producing product have to do with getting the manufactured product from one location to another. In many cases, we are talking about shipping, but more generally these activities are called *logistics*. Transporting goods in many ways is a horizontal industry, because it crosses so many industry boundaries. After all, products as diverse as running shoes, waterbeds, and automobiles all need to be transported. However, transportation and logistics are usually considered vertical industries because they have very domain-specific vocabularies and business processes.

The goal of shipping and logistics standards is to provide a common base for communicating shipping instructions, bills of lading, packaging, routing, and related logistic information. It would be unreasonable to assume that every industry that touches logistics should create identical vocabularies, so many logistics-focused vendors have come together to create standards that can be shared with other industry and standards organizations—and XML is the language of choice for enabling these possibilities.

TranXML

Originally formed as part of the transportation giant Union Pacific, Transentric branched off on its own in mid-2000 as an organization focused on solving the technological problems faced in the transportation, shipping, and logistics industries. Leveraging its 20 years of experience in developing semantic repositories for logistics and transportation needs, Transentric has developed an open, cross-vertical specification called TranXML for standardizing the way that transportation information is sent between customers and freight carriers.

In many ways, one can look at transportation as a "horizontal industry" that is applicable to multiple vertical industries. Industries as diverse as petroleum, automotive, computer manufacturing, textiles, and agriculture all rely on transportation as the means to get their products to market. Therefore, they have usually created vocabularies to express the various needs in describing transportation, shipping, and logistics information. Much of this information is the same, regardless of the industry being described. As such, transportation companies such as Transentric have sought to bring some order to the chaos by providing a single cross-industry definition of transportation needs. In standardizing this format, TranXML hopes to provide the benefit of cost savings and efficiency to the "small mom and pop" organizations. Also, TranXML serves an important role in enabling internal communication, interapplication integration, and communication with the systems of other trading partners.

Rather than creating a new semantic representation of this information, Transentric sought to leverage its years of experience in EDI and present a format that is easily exchanged with this format. EDI use is widespread in the transportation industry, and requiring a new format that uproots the existing technology would cause unnecessary difficulty in gaining acceptance and adoption. The TranXML specification therefore mirrors many of the existing X12 EDI specifications and uses an architecture that accepts EDI messages at one end, converts to an "XEDI" specification by means of an XML Solut-ions XML transformation tool, and results in a native XML format well suited to EDI integration. This EDI approach uses qualifiers as attributes, thus keeping compliance checking similar to X12. However, the EDI "conversion" only gets one halfway there, since it represents a simple transformation. The real added value of the TranXML group is that it uses its domain knowledge and expertise to transform these EDI-based elements into native XML code that differs based on interpretation of X12 standards. For example, equipment, name, and invoice structures are particular to individual industries and organizations.

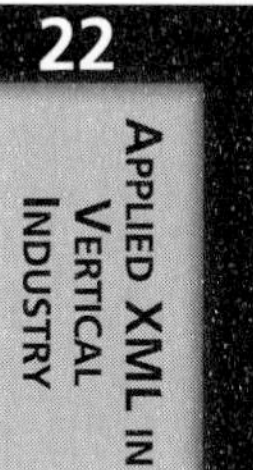

In April 2001, Transentric released eight TranXML schemas in support of its standards effort. These support applications such as load tendering, delivery, freight billing, reconciliation, scheduling/forecasting, and equipment ordering. Specifically, the schemas correspond to rail bills of lading, car location messaging, motor carrier bills of lading and load tender, shipment status and weight, terminal operations and intermodal ramp activity, and a dictionary for transportation terms and attributes. The next release of additional schemas will include rail waybills, car handling, shipper car orders, switch lists, advance shipping notices, and warehouse stock, shipping, and inventory.

One of the benefits of a single cross-industry transportation description such as TranXML is that it provides an easy and inexpensive way to implement new trading partner relationships, because it leverages EDI and provides a neutral format that enables both carrier and shipper legacy systems to exchange data. Because the format requires some of the capabilities of EDI, it has taken advantage of XML Schema, which provides more advanced grouping, data typing, attribute capabilities, and inheritance capabilities. Developed as an open standard, TranXML is designed to be vendor neutral, and licenses will be available free of charge.

Because the interest in transportation vocabularies, especially track and tracing functionality, is widespread among many industries, Transentric sought to form a neutral, independent organization for the promotion and continued development of the TranXML format. The mission of TranXML.org is to provide a neutral, cross-industry forum for the development of collaborative logistics supply-chain XML vocabularies and functions.

The collaborative effort will encourage participation by carriers, shippers, and third parties. TranXML.org also meets its goals by forming relationships with other standards organizations, such as the Chemical Industry Data Exchange (CIDX), RosettaNet, and the Joint Core Components group of ASC X12 and UN/EDIFACT. The important consideration is that a critical mass of carrier adoption (rail, ocean, motor, and air) is needed.

The group is working with other industries that share synergies due to shared transportation needs. For example, ChemXML is heavily drawn from X12 and EDIFACT directories and would also benefit from a TranXML relationship. TranXML has adopted the ebXML framework for transport, routing, packing, and security. It would like to work closely with the JCC but have some concerns about interest and overlap. Despite these concerns, TranXML is working to get involved with the JCC repository and ensure proper expertise in this domain area. RosettaNet also provides an opportunity to gain from a TranXML relationship, because its schemas provide only the basics for transportation and logistics need.

TranXML is a focused, detailed effort that is sure to gain adoption and attention by the industry as soon as the various vertical industry specification efforts realize that transportation, logistics, and shipping are not their core competencies. It is hoped that the TranXML.org group can promote its efforts and continue development to the extent that other specification efforts leverage its work. After all, it makes no sense to reinvent the wheel in transportation—that's where it was invented in the first place.

Note

For more information about TranXML, visit the Transentric Web site at `http://www.transentric.com/products/commerce/tranxml.asp`.

Architecture and Construction

The folks who are responsible for the creation of buildings, namely architects and the construction industry, are remarkably high tech for a seemingly low-tech industry. Building plans, layouts, and materials must be documented and stored. Daily operations, schedules, and dependencies must be tracked. The hundreds, if not thousands, of workers need to be coordinated and efficiently used. If anything, construction and architecture have just as much need for up-to-date information logistics as do traffic controllers and financial traders.

Architecture, Engineering, and Construction XML (aecXML)

Planning, engineering, and constructing buildings is a very labor- and paper-intensive process. The amount of paperwork needed to build anything, from a simple single-family residence to the most complicated of structures, is tremendous. Architecture, engineering, and construction (AEC) data sets are usually quite large and typically involve many types of unstructured, interrelated data that is created and used by many types of users and software applications. At any time in a project cycle, users such as the owner or operator of the subject facility, architects, designers, engineers, project managers, contractors, estimators, consultants, suppliers, product manufacturers, and government regulatory agencies may utilize the information for different reasons. Many of these participants are small to medium-sized companies and are only involved in small roles in the project for short periods of time, commonly working on multiple projects simultaneously. It is no surprise, then, that so many different systems of varying qualities are being used within the industry. It's important to solve this problem, because the industry generates hundreds of thousands of transactions worldwide and has annual expenditures in the trillions of dollars.

However, in every aspect of the building creation and operation process, the Internet and XML are making significant inroads. This means that proposals, design, estimating, scheduling, construction, ordering, and purchasing are being automated and simplified by way of XML-based standards, such as those enabled by International Alliance for Interoperability's (IAI) aecXML. The IAI-adopted aecXML provides a means for communicating information between participants involved in designing, constructing, and operating buildings, plants, infrastructures, and facilities. Applications, organizations, and individuals using the aecXML schema can coordinate and synchronize related project information among suppliers and purchasers of equipment, materials, supplies, parts, and services based on that technical information.

The initiative began in August 1999 as an independent effort by Bentley Systems and was soon moved to the administrative domain of the industry consortium International Alliance for Interoperability. As of October 2001, there are seven working groups, and over 600 interested participants are involved in the development of aecXML. The main principle behind the creation of the format is that project information can be entered once and reused where necessary, across organizational, geographical, and technological boundaries. In today's project-management processes, information is commonly reentered many times by many people, due to differences in the way that data is stored and represented, especially as projects pass from phase to phase and as new participants become involved in the project. As paper-based reports, specifications, and product catalogs are replaced by their electronic equivalents, searches for product information, specifications, and pricing and availability will be conducted, taking advantage of the Internet. This means that regulatory rules, requirements and guidelines, project submissions, and the review and approval processes will be automated similar to how other processes have been enabled using XML.

aecXML is an XML-based vocabulary used to represent and communicate information across the AEC industries. This information covers resources such as projects, documents, materials, parts, organizations, professionals, and activities such as proposals, design, estimating, scheduling, and construction. Some examples of this information include the following:

- Documents such as Request for Proposal (RFP), Request for Quotation (RFQ), Request for Information (RFI), drawings, specifications, addenda, bulletins, change orders, contracts, building codes, and purchase orders
- Building components such as catalog items, custom manufactured items, assemblies, and materials
- Projects such as design, construction, decommissioning, operations and maintenance, and facilities management
- Professional services and resources such as engineers, architects, contractors, suppliers, and specialties
- Organizations such as standards bodies and government agencies
- Software such as computer-aided design (CAD), estimating, project management, scheduling, and document management

However, aecXML is not intended to be a native file format because many of the applications used to support these needs have their own valuable file formats. Rather, aecXML will simply be a file-exchange mechanism using XML as its strength. The aecXML group envisions a utility within a software program that provides the option "Save as aecXML." This utility would export necessary information in the aecXML schema.

One of the key aspects of the format is the aecXML Framework, which includes a set of XML schemas to describe information specific to the information exchanges between participants involved in designing, constructing, and operating buildings, plants, infrastructures, and facilities. The aecXML Framework provides the AEC industry with common business interfaces and defines both the data to be exchanged among AEC participants and the processes ruling the exchange of that data. The Framework is composed of several components, including Common Object Schemas (COS), Domain Specific Schemas (DSS), Business Process Schemas (BPS), and the Implementation Framework (IF).

The COS serves as a component library that's composed of many reusable schema objects that are common to multiple AEC business domains. These objects, such as global elements, global attributes, complex types, and simple types are reused in different places of AEC business information exchange. There are two types of common objects:

non-AEC-specific and AEC-specific objects. AEC-specific objects are objects that have content specific to the AEC industry, whereas non-AEC-specific objects are objects can apply to any industry. Examples of AEC-specific objects are `Project`, `Contractor`, and `BuildingComponent`, whereas examples of non-AEC-specific objects are `Name`, `Email`, `Address`, and `Person`. The aecXML format defines some of these non-AEC-specific objects but plans to leverage objects from other formats, such as xCBL, as they become available. AEC-specific objects are derived from many sources, including IAI's Industry Foundation Classes (IFC), which are object models that allow for the exchange of dynamic information among platforms and applications serving the AEC community.

The aecXML Domain Specific Schemas (DSS) are sets of schemas built on the aecXML COS to describe static AEC information, whereas dynamic information such as business processes are defined in the BPS. These can be either an individual piece of business information or a natural grouping of AEC business components. Examples of DSS include objects such as `ChangeOrder`, which can be used to define the document flow of change order information within the BPS as `RequestForChangeOrder`, `ApprovedChangeOrder`, and `CompletedChangeOrder`. The DSS are operated through domains such as Project Management, Design, Schedule, and Plant. Each of these domains owns one or more schema namespaces that contain multiple schemas.

As stated in the aecXML specification, "the COS define the letters of the alphabet, the DSS define nouns, and the BPS define verbs." The BPS encapsulate the exchange of business data between AEC participants during the project life cycle. The aecXML BPS are sets of schemas that describe AEC industry-specific business processes, including the query of information, the business transaction, and the communication messages. The BPS describe detailed interactions and their respective activities between AEC participants, identify which data needs to be present to ensure requirements of both parties are being met, and choreograph AEC business documents with process interfaces. Examples of BPS include Send an Invoice, Submit a Purchase Order, Request for Information, and Request for Change Order.

The Implementation Framework provides a messaging framework for the exchange of aecXML messages. The IF supports the use of multiple different messaging framework standards such as ebXML, RosettaNet, and BizTalk. As a specification, aecXML is transport neutral and is not developing its own IF, rather relying on the preceding methods for transporting aecXML documents.

The aecXML initiative comprises constituents from industry, government, and research communities as well as end users. Since its inception, more than 600 organizations have expressed interest in this initiative on six continents. These organizations include architects, engineers, contractors, owner/operators, estimators, consultants, materials suppliers, and building product manufacturers.

Note

To find out more about aecXML, visit the aecXML Web site at `http://ww.aecxml.org`.

Scientific and Engineering

In the early 1990s, the Internet was being used, not by mainly commercial entities but by scientific and educational establishments. The foundation technologies for the Web—the Hypertext Transfer Protocol (HTTP) and the Hypertext Markup Language (HTML)—were created not for the sake of online e-commerce but to exchange research papers in the field of physics. Therefore, it makes complete sense that XML would be a hotbed of activity by those in various scientific, mathematic, and engineering fields. This section touches on two standards that have leveraged XML as their means of document exchange.

Biotech

The rapid increase in the use and exchange of data in the biological fields has demanded a better way for representing, storing, and exchanging this information. The use of information in biology has spawned its own field of study, bioinformatics, and the recent explosion in genetics research has likewise required an increasing amount of attention in standardizing information storage and exchange. To this end, XML has provided the technology to meet many of these needs.

Bioinformatic Sequence Markup Language (BSML)

Just as in every industry that has large data requirements, the bioinformatics industry has the challenge of integrating large quantities of heterogeneous information gathered from different sources and distributed locally and over the Internet. A bioinformatic sequence is the visual encoding of strings of nucleotides, the chemical makeup of our DNA. Individual nucleotides, such as adenosine, cytosine, guanine, taurine, and uracil, are encoded as “acgtu,” respectively. A sequence is an arbitrarily long string of these characters that corresponds to a particular encoding of genetic material. As researchers expand their knowledge of a particular organism’s genetic structure, the exchange of these strings of genetic encoding becomes increasingly more important. As is the case almost everywhere that data is present, XML can facilitate the discovery process by enabling the researchers to integrate and annotate these sequences. XML also enables the integration of this "genomic" information with related, or "extragenomic," information such as literature, images, and documents that support the particular genetic information being researched.

Developed by the National Human Genome Research Institute (NHGRI) and promoted by LabBook, Inc., the Bioinformatic Sequence Markup Language (BSML) is a proposed XML standard for the communication of bioinformatics data. The BSML standard is divided into two logical parts: Definitions and Display. The Definitions section encodes the bioinformatic data, including sequences, sets, sequence features, analytical outputs, relationships, and annotations. The optional Display section encodes information for graphic representation of the bioinformatic data. Multiple users can simultaneously access the same data and examine different links, files, and sequence views without having to make alterations to source documents. In addition, BSML allows users to include multiple annotations such as documents, tables, charts, and sequence features and graphs aligned to sequence maps. Although the specification of BSML doesn't require any specific browser or graphical interpretation technology, LabBook provides for a viewer that is tailored around the BSML application. In addition, LabBook develops and provides freely available tools that help create and manipulate BSML files.

The BSML specification's main goal is to represent genetic sequences and their graphic display properties. In particular, the specification describes the features of genetic sequences, represents relationships among sequences and their features, defines graphic objects that represent sequence features and relationships, provides representation of the relationships between sequences and source documents (such as sequence and genetic marker databases), and defines methods for storing and transmitting encoded sequence and graphic information. Listing 22.9 shows a sample BSML XML instance.

LISTING 22.9 Sample BSML Instance

```
<!DOCTYPE Bsml SYSTEM "bsml.dtd">
<Bsml>
 <Definitions>
  <Sequences>
   <Sequence id="SEQ1" title="ECRPOBC" seq-type="dna" units="bp"
             length="12337" shape="linear" strands="2">
   </Sequence>
  </Sequences>
 </Definitions>
 <Display>
  <Page>
   <View id="VEW1" seqref="SEQ1">
   </View>
  </Page>
 </Display>
</Bsml>
```

Even though LabBook has wrapped commercial products around the standard, BSML remains in the public domain and is supported by the LabBook efforts.

> **Note**
>
> To find out more about BSML, visit LabBook's BSML Web site at `http://www.labbook.com/products/xmlbsml.asp`.

Chemistry

In the same vein as biological information, chemistry and materials information also needs to be exchanged. This is especially vital in the various pharmaceutical, materials processing, plastics, petroleum, and other industries that rely on accurate chemical information to perform their tasks adequately. However, like any other industry, the processes have been formerly dominated by paper rather than electronic interchange. Various chemistry industry specifications, such as the Chemical Markup Language covered next, hope to change this by providing a deep level of specification for chemical properties as well as the required vocabularies for defining chemical industry interchange.

Chemical Markup Language

The foundations of the Chemical Markup Language (CML, or more officially known as XML-CML) can be traced all the way back to the original days of HTML, when the Internet was frequented mainly by academics rather than individuals and corporations. The original concept was to provide a platform-neutral means of exchanging information regarding chemical compositions. Originally formatted as an SGML DTD, CML began pursuing the XML direction soon after the language's development in 1996. Subsequently, CML became one of the first acknowledged domain-specific DTDs published for XML.

CML itself doesn't cover the entire spectrum of possibilities in the chemical industry. Rather, it focuses on representing molecules, which the CML Web site defines as "discrete entities representable by a formula and usually a connection table." CML further specifies a hierarchy for compound molecules, such as clathrates and macromolecules, reactions, and macromolecular structures/sequences. In addition, CML "has no specific support for physicochemical concepts but can support labeled numeric data types of several sorts, which can cover a wide range of requirements. It allows quantities and properties to be specifically attached to molecules, atoms, or bonds."

In many respects, CML forms a common basis for most chemical-domain XML vocabularies in much the same way that MathML forms the basis for many mathematical and scientific-domain XML vocabularies. CML also makes use of and leverages a number of other XML specifications, including Resource Description Framework (RDF), XHTML, SVG, PlotML, MathML, Dublin Core, and XML Schema, as its schema base.

CML supports spectra and other instrumental output, crystallography, organic and inorganic molecules, physicochemical quantities (including units), MO calculations, macromolecules (such as sequence protein and ligand), molecular hyperglossaries (including text and molecules), and hyperlinks. CML accomplishes this by specifying a core set of elements, such as `molecule` (to describe a connected set of atoms), `bond`, which describes a link between atoms within a molecule, `atomArray` and `bondArray`, which provide containers for atoms and bonds, and `electron`, which provides details of electrons in atoms, bonds, and molecules. Also specified are macromolecular, reaction, crystallography, and formula elements to describe the interaction of these various core elements. Macromolecular elements include `sequence`, to describe a macromolecular sequence, and `feature`, which describes features in a sequence. Reaction elements are specified by means of `reaction`, which describes a reaction that contains molecules and links between them. Crystallography and formulas are described by `crystal` and `formula`, which describe crystallographic unit cell and symmetry in fractional coordinates for atoms and provide a container for the representation of arbitrary chemical formulas using a text string with a convention attribute.

LISTING 22.10 Sample CML Document

```
<molecule convention="MDLMol" id="adrenalin" title="EPINEPHRINE">
  <date day="22" month="11" year="1995">
  </date>
  <atomArray>
    <atom id="a1">
      <string builtin="elementType">C</string>
      <float builtin="x2">-0.2969</float>
      <float builtin="y2">0.8979</float>
    </atom>
    <atom id="a2">
      <string builtin="elementType">C</string>
      <float builtin="x2">-0.2969</float>
      <float builtin="y2">-0.6121</float>
    </atom>
    <atom id="a14">
      <string builtin="elementType">H</string>
      <float builtin="x2">2.144</float>
      <float builtin="y2">2.8844</float>
    </atom>
  </atomArray>
  <bondArray>
    <bond id="b1">
```

LISTING 22.10 continued

```
      <string builtin="atomRef">a1</string>
      <string builtin="atomRef">a2</string>
      <string builtin="order">1</string>
    </bond>
    <bond id="b2">
      <string builtin="atomRef">a1</string>
      <string builtin="atomRef">a3</string>
      <string builtin="order">2</string>
    </bond>
    <bond id="b14">
      <string builtin="atomRef">a4</string
      <string builtin="atomRef">a14</string>
      <string builtin="order">1</string>
      <string builtin="stereo">H</string>
    </bond>
  </bondArray>
</molecule>
 <reaction title="Diels-Alder cycloaddition"
      id="simple_rxn_1" convention="stepwise">  <string title="description">
   Simple example of a A + B -> C reaction. See source for further information.
</string>
  <float title="yield" units="%">88</float>
  <string title="notes">taken from Vollhardt and Schore</string>
  <list title="reactionStep" id="simple_s_1">
   <string title="description">cycloaddition</string>
   <float title="yield" convention="%">88</float>
   <string title="notes">one step</string>
   <link title="reactant" href="simple_mol_reactant1" id="simple_lk_1"/>
   <link title="reactant" href="simple_mol_reactant2" id="simple_lk_2"/>
   <link title="reagent" id="simple_lk_3">
    <integer title="index">1</integer>
    <string title="solvent">Acetonitrile</string>
    <string title="temperature" convention="degC">100</string>
    <string title="duration" convention="hours">3</string>
    <string title="notes">reflux</string>
   </link>
   <link title="reagent" id="simple_lk_4">
    <integer title="index">2</integer>
    <string title="notes">workup</string>
   </link>
   <link title="product" href="simple_mol_product" id="simple_lk_5"/>
   <!-- also catalyst, intermediate, transition state as needed -->
  </list>
 </reaction>
```

Note

To find out more about CML, visit `http://www.xml-cml.org/`.

Print, Media, and Entertainment

The pervasiveness, applicability, and extensibility of XML has even impacted the fairly innocuous arena of general entertainment. Playing games, watching movies, and general entertainment is made even more enjoyable and intelligently enabled by XML technology.

NewsML

The news industry is dominated by one thing: content. In fact, there really is no separation of news from content, and as such the issues around content management are really the same as the issues around the creation and distribution of news. In the past, editorial environments would produce content to support various news products, which would require the content to be tailored to each format. Where there is data, especially document and structured data such what's present in the news industry, there is XML. In fact, there's a plethora of news- and content-related specifications that are squarely targeted at solving the needs of this space. In particular, the NewsML format, created initially by Reuters and supported by the International Press Telecommunications Council (IPTC), is a specification created for the definition, creation, exchange, and packaging of news articles and related content. NewsML further compliments and extends another IPTC standards effort, the News Industry Text Format (NITF), which specifies the content of news articles. Once you have the kind of rich format that NewsML provides, you can build news products for different user groups without creating lots of the reengineering needed for mixing different blends of news. Typical uses of NewsML include uses in and among editorial systems, between news agencies and their customers, between publishers and news aggregators, and between news service providers and end users.

The main functionality of NewsML falls along the following areas: providing neutrality of news format and media type, easier development of news items, collections of news items into larger news "stories," named relationships between news items, divisions of news stories into structures consisting of parts and named relationships between parts, alternative representations of those parts, explicit inclusion, inclusion by reference and exclusion of parts and alternatives, and attachment of metadata from standard and non-standard schemes. In addition, NewsML provides for strong versioning support, support for multiple display methods, and adaptation to delivery environments.

As such, NewsML can be considered to be a "container" for news items. As the NewsML Web site states, "NewsML makes no assumption about the media type, format, or encoding of news. NewsML provides a structure within which news objects, of whatever type, relate to each other. NewsML can equally represent text, video, audio, graphics, and photos. NewsML takes the view that any medium can be the main part of a news item and that objects of all other types can fulfill secondary, tertiary, and other roles in respect of the main part. Hence, NewsML allows for the representation of simple textual stories, textual stories with primary and secondary photos, the evening TV news—with embedded individual reports, and so on." An architecture diagram of the NewsML format is shown in Figure 22.7.

FIGURE 22.7
NewsML architecture.

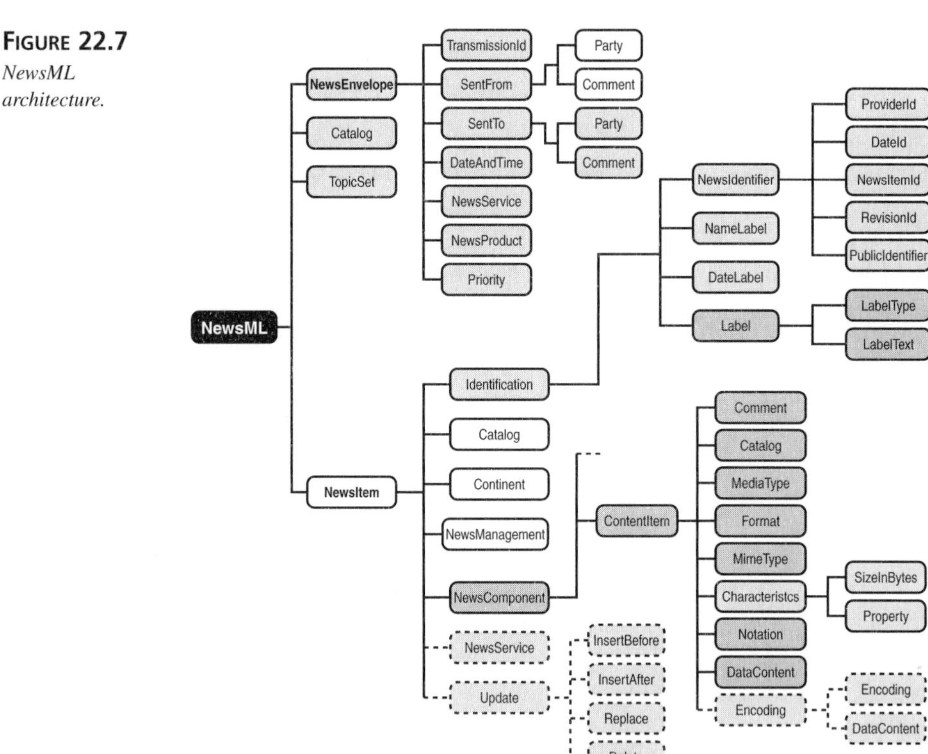

Because news stories develop over time, NewsML supports versioning and allows for the development of textual stories using takes. In addition, NewsML supports the attachment of components of news stories that can be available later to existing news story components. Another major feature of NewsML is the collection of news elements into a greater "story" that contains a variety of components that have the same "journalistic intent." To support this capability, NewsML allows the construction of relationships between news items and collections of news items, such as "see also," "related news," and "for more detail," so that these entities can exist in a web of such named relationships. The NewsML format also supports the authentication and signature of metadata and news item content because the value of news content, and its associated metadata, is highly dependent on its reliability.

The architecture of a NewsML document consists of components and named relationships between components. Most news items contain a "main" part and some number of secondary and tertiary parts that complement the main part in various ways. This could take the form of a textual main part and photos as secondary parts. In addition, news items themselves can be related to other news items so that a news item can be a component of another, and individual component can be represented in different ways so that users can select which version they wish to use or is most appropriate to their delivery environment. For example, part of a news item might be available in HTML, RTF, and PDF versions, with photos available at different resolutions and color depths utilizing the GIF or JPEG file format. This methodology also allows news items to be transmitted in print, on the Web, or over wireless delivery protocols because NewsML doesn't describe layout semantics. Each part of a news item and the news item as a whole can contain metadata that describes physical properties of the parts, information about the construction of the parts, such as author, publisher, and owner, and information about the content, such as the topic, category, and importance. Although NewsML provides the facility to describe news items, it doesn't specify any particular vocabulary for doing so and thus allows individual organizations to choose their metadata format.

NewsML can add as much information as needed for defining context that individuals can use to better locate and make use of news items. NewsML also gives users the opportunity to receive and aggregate news items from different vendors with similar metadata. Although the packaging features of NewsML are usable internally to produce what users might see on a Web page, it's the metadata that allows users to link stories with their real meanings.

NewsML is a document format and not a messaging protocol, so it can be delivered using other messaging or content-management messaging schemes such as SOAP, RSS, and ICE. An example of a NewsML file can be found in Listing 2.11.

LISTING 22.11 Sample NewsML File

```
<?xml version="1.0" encoding="UTF-8"?>
<!DOCTYPE NewsML PUBLIC "urn:newsml:iptc.org:20001006:NewsMLv1.0:1"
    "./DTD/NewsMLv1.0.dtd">
<?xml-stylesheet type="text/xsl" href="./stylesheets/IPTCNewsML.xsl"?>
```

Listing 22.11 continued

```
<NewsML>
 <Catalog Href="./catalog/mycatalog.xml"/>
 <NewsEnvelope>
  <DateAndTime>20001006</DateAndTime>
 </NewsEnvelope>
 <NewsItem>
  <Identification>
   <NewsIdentifier>
    <ProviderId>iptc.org</ProviderId>
    <DateId>20001006</DateId>
    <NewsItemId>SportsResultSample</NewsItemId>
    <RevisionId PreviousRevision="0" Update="N">1</RevisionId>
    <PublicIdentifier>
        urn:newsml:iptc.org:20001006:SportsResultSample:1
</PublicIdentifier>
   </NewsIdentifier>
  </Identification>
  <NewsManagement>
   <NewsItemType FormalName="News" Scheme="NewsItemType"/>
   <FirstCreated>20001006</FirstCreated>
   <ThisRevisionCreated>20001006</ThisRevisionCreated>
   <Status FormalName="Usable" Scheme="IptcStatus"/>
  </NewsManagement>
  <NewsComponent>
   <ContentItem>
    <DataContent><![CDATA[<FootballResult><Hteam>Arsenal</Hteam>
<Hscore>1</Hscore><Ateam>Chelsea</Ateam><Ascore>2</Ascore></FootballResult>]]>
</DataContent>
   </ContentItem>
  </NewsComponent>
 </NewsItem>
</NewsML>
```

Note

To find out more about NewsML, visit the Web site at `http://www.newsml.org/`.

A Final Note: XML Standards Adoption

Of course, with all these specifications, recommendations, standards, and initiatives being proposed, there is no guarantee that any of them—as well developed, well intentioned, and well positioned as they may be—will be adopted. The primary challenge in

XML is getting individuals and companies to actually use these formats. After all, these specifications are just text documents and XML files that represent a recommendation for the way things should be done in a particular industry or with a particular technology.

Many in various industries claim that these standards are repeating the errors of the past. In effect, the various groups are reengineering processes and vocabularies that were attempted with technologies and methodologies that had different or limited levels of success. Some say that members of the various working groups don't have enough experience to define the standards for their industries or the communities in general. However, there are others that say that standards and specifications have a life of their own—those that are worthwhile to adopt will be adopted, whereas others will simply fall by the wayside. The long-term adoption and success of these standards depends entirely on one thing: their usefulness.

Summary

As you have seen, XML has a very wide and broad application with every possible industry and market segment. Wherever there is the need for data representation and exchange, there will be XML. Will it be applicable in every scenario and every use case? Of course not, but it will definitely find a place to exist in every vertical industry and horizontal application that is relevant.

One of the things we can learn from such a widespread use and adoption of XML is that there is nothing specific about XML that restricts its use to a particular need of an industry or market segment. Whereas other data formats such as EDI and SGML may have been more appropriate for certain uses (EDI was never a good format for representing the structure of documents, and SGML was never good at representing e-business transactions), XML has no similar setbacks and misgivings. If anything, XML provides the "DNA" that allows it to be mutated into different solutions by different communities.

In this chapter, you have seen just a sample of what is currently available in the way of XML standards. In fact, over 450 such vocabularies exist as of October 2001, and these are only the ones that are publicly announced. For sure, there are thousands of private or proprietary implementations of XML that further expand the boundaries of what can be done with the language. It is up to you, the reader of this book, to make the most use of XML as one can within the confines of your industry. In the process, make use of the industry specifications, standards, and vocabularies that are within your grasp. By doing so, you not only meet your needs but help to further establish XML as a viable means for communicating business-relevant information.

The Semantic Web

Part IV

In This Part

CHAPTER 23

RDF for Information Owners

In This Chapter

The Resource Description Framework (RDF) gives information owners a way of expressing meaning on the Web that machines can understand (and humans will, ultimately, profit from). This chapter explains how RDF expresses machine-understandable meaning using its data model; the next chapter, on the Semantic Web, will show some of the good things that RDF makes happen. So, if you want the business case for RDF applications, skip ahead to Chapter 24, "The Semantic Web for Information Owners." If mastery of RDF syntax and semantics is what you're after, read on.

RDF is spelled out in a family of W3C specifications. Like many families, though, the RDF family members are not all quite at the same level of maturity, and not all of them agree with each other all the time. Therefore, to help you avoid the pitfall of spending a lot of time on parts of RDF that are either obsolete or immature, we'll first go through the specifications, giving extra attention to open issues and resources that will keep your expertise current.

RDF's data model gives RDF its power to express machine-understandable meaning, and that's what we'll look at next. Because the RDF data model is a graph, we'll study just enough graph theory to deal with that formalism and get through the model. Then, we'll go through the data model in detail, showing the RDF graph in both pictorial and XML syntax, all in ready-reference form. Then we'll do the same thing for RDF schema, and you'll see how RDF schema's class hierarchy allows the meaning of RDF instances to be constrained and validated.

Finally, we'll look at some angle bracket–type issues in handling RDF, such as how to embed RDF in Web pages, and so on.

Therefore, by the time you finish this chapter, your expertise will extend beyond the basics of RDF to

- The RDF family of specifications
- Issues with the specs and where to go to resolve them
- The RDF data model (and a little graph theory)
- What RDF schema validates and how it does so
- XML and pictorial RDF syntax

Basics of the Resource Description Framework

We often hear that XML tags add meaning to documents. And this is true, but it's meaning that only humans can intuit. For example, given the XML markup

```
<person name="Jane">
<sells product="books"/>
</person>
```

a human might use the intuitive tag names and attribute name/value pairs to infer that "Jane sells books" (among other things that people may do), but this is a leap of faith that a machine cannot make. True, the content models in a DTD or schema can enforce that `sells` nests within `person`, but it does not tell us anything about why the nesting takes place.

Note

RDF builds on XML terminology without changing it, so when you see *element*, *tag*, *attribute*, *DTD*, and other XML terms in this chapter, they have the same meanings as in the other chapters of this book.

Similarly, given the preceding markup, an XSLT style sheet could transform it into the following string:

```
"Jane sells books"
```

However, to the computer, this is just a string like many other strings. In the end, the computer has no power to do anything with the string other than display it. In particular, it can't make any logical connection between the string "Jane sells this book" and the string "My human wants to buy this book" and make the purchase. Such strings have meaning only to humans.

Tip

Uniform Resource Identifiers (URIs) tend to be quite long and cluttered with delimiters, slashes, and protocols like HTTP. To cut the clutter and also to make it easier for the code examples to serve as copy-and-paste templates, all URIs in this chapter will be represented as a string in square brackets, like this:

```
[uri]
```

You'll see this in Listing 23.1.

What we need is to go beyond the notion of a content model to a "meaning model," which is what the RDF data model provides. Listing 23.1 gives us the markup for the

RDF statement that has the meaning "Jane sells books," where "Jane" is in RDF's subject position, "sells" is in the predicate position, and "books" is in the object position. In this way, we use markup technology to tell the computer where the meaning is. Note that "[Jane]" and "[books]" are URIs, and sells is a name in the "[my]" namespace; you'll see why later.

LISTING 23.1 A Simple Statement in RDF

```
<rdf:Description about="[Jane]" xmlns:my="[my]">
 <my:sells rdf:resource="[books]"/>
```

The idea here is just as simple as when a teacher draws a subject/verb/object diagram on the chalkboard in grade school, as shown in Figure 23.1. If you want your sentence to mean anything, you have to put the words in the right order—and you and your listener have to know what the order is.

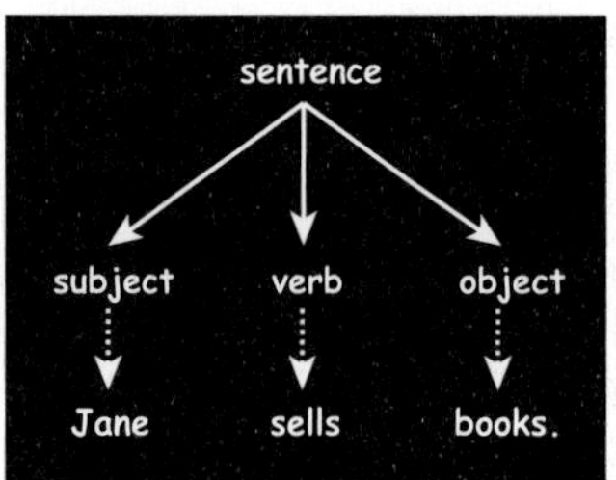

FIGURE 23.1
Grade school grammar for a subject/predicate/object statement.

What the teacher's syntax production does for students, in chalk, the RDF data model does for machines, in bits and bytes. Now let's look a bit more deeply into the three words that comprise RDF: resource, description, and framework.

Why resource? A *resource* is anything that has identity (Jane, for example). How do resources get identity? Through being identified by Uniform Resource Identifiers (URIs). Therefore, that which has identity is a resource, and that which is a resource has identity!

If you look back to Listing 23.1, you will see that both the subject and the object of the RDF statement are resources, because they are identified by URIs.

Not all resources (for example, Jane) are retrievable across a network. A URI can identify a Web page, of course, but also a printed book, a government agency, a human being, or an abstract concept.

Why description? A *description* is really just a container; it is a bucket for one or more statements. This idea, too, is pretty much straight from the grade school dictionary. If I ask Jane's friend (or maybe even her computer) for a description of Jane, I expect to get back a number of statements, one of which might be that "Jane sells books."

Note

We'll look at the notion of *statements* (also known as *triples*) in detail in this chapter when we discuss the RDF data model. For now, notice how many specifications must work together to weave statements into the Semantic Web: XML, of course, but also RDF, the "vocabularies" (the actual subjects and objects of sentences, to be defined by the RDF schema), and the URIs that link the Web pages together. In the next chapter, you will see that such sentences (or *statements*) can be generalized as the notion of a *conversation*. We will identify such conversations as the fundamental value proposition of the Semantic Web.

Why a framework? Natural languages such as English and Esperanto permit speakers to generate infinite numbers of sentences, to invent new words, and to give new meanings to old words, all based on a reasonably small set of rules. These rules comprise the framework of the language. In the same way, RDF sets rules that will enable humans and machines to make and understand infinite numbers of statements whose subjects and objects are resources.

The RDF Family of Specifications

Now that you understand the basic idea behind RDF, let's look at the family of RDF specifications in detail, noting their differing authority as well as where the interests of information owners are impacted. When we're done, you'll understand the maturity of the different parts of the RDF specification.

Core Specifications

RDF builds on two companion specifications. The model and syntax specification defines the triple in which RDF statements are made; the schema specification describes how to use RDF to build RDF vocabularies (collections of resources that can be used as predicates—the verbs in RDF statements).

Note

Here are the Web sites for the RDF core specifications:

- Resource Description Framework (RDF) Model and Syntax Specification (REC); `http://www.w3.org/TR/1999/REC-rdf-syntax-19990222` [RDFMS]
- Resource Description Framework (RDF) Schema Specification 1.0 (CR); `http://www.w3.org/TR/2000/CR-rdf-schema-20000327` [RDFS]

These core RDF specifications, in turn, build upon W3C's XML and Namespaces Recommendations, covered elsewhere in this book.

Recent Working Drafts and Notes

RDF is a very dynamic set of specifications, in part because of W3C's working draft/candidate recommendation/recommendation publication cycle, which encourages midcourse corrections based on implementation experience. Indeed, although institutionally W3C may be likened to a cathedral, in action (at least, in RDF) it may seem that the bazaar development model prevails, with all manner of goods on show or openly spilling amid a cacophony of raised voices: logicians, priests, and so on. In the sidebar, you will see the places to go to keep on top of RDF as it evolves.

Now, why are all these specifications of anything other than academic interest? In a word, *interoperability*.

RDF is not about my semantic site, my semantic department, or even my semantic enterprise. It is about the Semantic *Web*: It is a general solution for making statements that all machines (not just some machines) and all humans (not just some humans) can understand. Just as the strength of HTML is that it is simple and can be displayed anywhere, RDF's strength is that it can be (or should be) understood everywhere. It is (or should be) a *lingua franca*.

If RDF statements are not interoperable—that is, if they are not understood in the same way by all processors—then it's hard to see how the Semantic Web can come to be. Suppose that two processors have different understandings of a statement about a drug dosage? Or a statement in an aircraft repair manual? Or, if you are an information owner, your data? Mars Explorer crashed because one processor thought a measurement was in metric units, and a second processor thought the same measurement was in English units. On the Semantic Web, the impact of interoperability failure could come as lethal drug dosages, crashed airplanes, or corrupted data.

Note

Here are the recent notes and working drafts that seem most significant for interoperability issues at the time of this writing (October 2001):

- RDF Core Working Group, *RDF Issue Tracking*, `http://www.w3.org/2000/03/rdf-tracking/`.
- *URIs, URLs, and URNs: Clarifications and Recommendations 1.0, Report from the Joint W3C/IETF URI Planning Interest Group*, W3C Note, 21 September 2001, `http://www.w3.org/TR/2001/NOTE-uri-clarification-20010921/`.
- Dave Beckett, *Refactoring RDF/XML Syntax*, W3C Working Draft, 06 September 2001, `http://www.w3.org/TR/2001/WD-rdf-syntax-grammar-20010906/`.
- Patrick Hayes, *RDF Model Theory*, W3C Working Draft, 25 September 2001, `http://www.w3.org/TR/2001/WD-rdf-mt-20010925/`.
- Art Barstow, Dave Beckett, *RDF Test Cases*, W3C Working Draft 12 September 2001 `http://www.w3.org/TR/2001/WD-rdf-testcases-20010912/`.

These activities are coordinated by the RDF Core Working Group:

- `www.w3c.org/2001/sw/RDFCore`

First, let's take a look at *URIs, URLs, and URNs*. What is *not* addressed by *URIs, URLs, and URNs* is more critical than what *is*. The issue: Whether it is okay for URIs not to identify resources that can be retrieved over a network (for example, the person Jane). This issue is categorized as "unresolved."

Therefore, RDF's use of URIs, and the broader Web's use of URIs, may not be interoperable. Therefore, there is some uncertainty about whether the following application areas are in scope for RDF, because they would depend on URIs for resources that cannot be retrieved over a network:

- Government archives on physical media (for example, "reel/frame" numbers at the United States Patent and Trademark Office)
- Legal citations to volume, reporter, and page
- Warehouse applications
- Help lines (where the resource is a human's expertise)
- Disembodied concepts

Next, *Refactoring RDF/XML Syntax* raises further interoperability concerns. It summarizes the effects of reports from implementers. As it turns out, different RDF implementations, given the same markup, generate different graphs (instances of the RDF data model). Hence, the specification is ambiguous.

RDF Model Theory addresses interoperability concerns. It is an effort to enhance RDF's precision by respecifying the RDF data model using techniques for defining the semantics of statements that are more precise than the text of the existing specifications.

RDF Test Cases provide a way of testing and possibly allaying interoperability concerns. It is a draft set of machine-processable test cases corresponding to technical issues addressed by the [RDF] WG, again based on W3C's issues-tracking document, to which we now turn.

RDF Issue Tracking categorizes open issues in two ways:

- Under consideration
- Not yet under consideration

Here is a small selection of the issues that are under consideration as of this writing.

- *rdfs-xml-schema-datatypes*. The RDF schema spec should consider using XML Schema data types in examples and/or in some formal specification of the mapping of these data types into the RDF model.
- *rdfms-literal-is-xml-structure*. A literal containing XML markup should be treated as markup.

Here is a small selection of the issues that are on the list to be considered, but are not yet being considered:

- *rdfms-resource-semantics*. What is a resource? How do resources relate to other concepts such as URI and entity?
- *rdfms-identity-of-statements*. Does the RDF model allow more than one statement with the same triple of subject/predicate/object?
- *rdf-equivalent-representations*. RDFMS employs several syntactic representations when describing the RDF abstract model. Are they truly equivalent?

Most of these issues raise interoperability concerns for owners of RDF information. For example, *rdfms-formal-grammar*, by making the description of the data model and its XML representation more rigorous, should have the effect of making implementations more consistent. Similarly for *rdfs-xml-schema-datatype*: Why should RDF's integers or dates not be interoperable with XML schema's? *rdfms-resource-semantics* raises the lack of consistency between *URIs, URLs, and URNs* and *RFC2396*, noted earlier.

Finally, those philosophical bugbears—identity and equivalence—are wakened from hibernation by *rdfms-identity-of-statements* and *rdf-equivalent-representations*. For the first issue, the question is whether "Subject has an object" and "Subject has an object" are two statements, when processed by an RDF engine, or one. For the second, you will see shortly that there are several ways to represent the RDF data model in syntax. Are these representations truly equivalent? How could we be certain? Here again, these questions raise interoperability issues, because different RDF implementations could make different assumptions on these points.

Making the Case for RDF Investment

Finally, the $64,000 question: Assuming that avoiding reconversion of RDF data is a requirement, when should information owners and developers feel comfortable in making significant investments in RDF implementations?

This will depend on individual cases, of course. However, some general guidelines can be laid down. First, the interoperability issues of significance to the information owner and potential clients should be closed out at W3C. Monitor the *RDF Issue Tracking* site on this point. Second, there should be some W3C-recommended declarative specification for mechanically checking the validity of RDF instances—for example, a W3C XML schema or XML DTD. Third, there should be test cases for checking RDF processors. Monitor the *RDF Test Cases* site on this point. This site has test cases only for technical issues, not a test suite for RDF processing in general. If W3C does not create such a suite, perhaps some institution such as the National Institute for Standards (NIST) will.

The fundamental RDF value proposition (conversations) remains unaffected by any concern raised by these glances at the innards of the W3C issues-tracking process. You now have the background to assess the RDF data model in detail.

The RDF Data Model

The RDF data model is a graph: a mathematical construct that connects nodes and arcs in tinker toy–like fashion. Many find the fundamental simplicity of graphs very appealing. In this section, you will learn just enough graph theory to understand the basic mathematical characteristics of the RDF graph. As a developer, you will find this useful in selecting and tailoring graph algorithms for processing the RDF graph.

You will see that the RDF graph is a collection of statements (or *triples*). We will look at issues of representing RDF statements in syntax and go through the construction rules that allow an RDF graph to be created from XML syntax. We will conclude the chapter by summarizing how XML elements and attributes are assembled to create a representation of the graph for interchange.

Just Enough Graph Theory

The one-minute graph theorist would say that there are only two fundamental graph constructs:

- Nodes
- Arcs

Arcs may have labels and may be directed (such as a one-way street). Figure 23.2 shows the basic parts of graph, where "Jane" and "books" are nodes connected with a directed arc whose label is "sells."

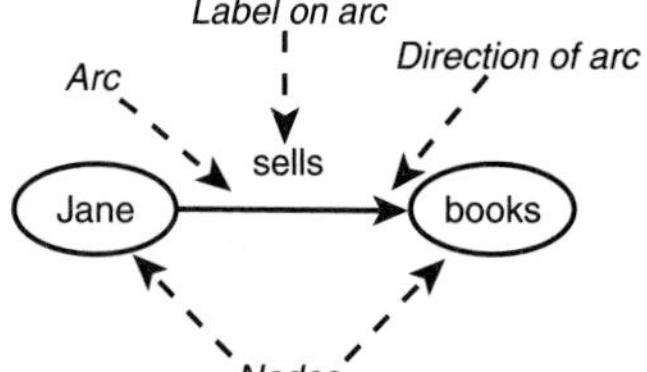

FIGURE 23.2
Basic parts of a graph.

A graph data model can be very powerful. Graph structures are used for many large-scale modeling tasks, including air traffic control, enterprise resource allocation, and so forth. Graphs can model both object-oriented and relational database systems, and they can be formalized mathematically. Therefore, it is possible (or at least should be possible) to assess the structures of RDF graphs mathematically and prove that some graphs are "better" than others, at least according to some formal criterion. These formal properties are useful for a data model to have, as we know from the power that relational algebra has given the relational model.

Graph literature is vast. Mainstream graph theory, accessible to the nonspecialist, seems to focus more on pleasing symmetries and visual elegance, but "real Web" graphs, such as the RDF graph, lack those characteristics. Figure 23.3 shows the sort of graph that seems of interest to academics.

The Web—a set of connections (arcs) between resources (nodes) that we must model in RDF to create the Semantic Web—lacks such symmetry. That said, we have already listed two formal characteristics of the RDF graph that a specialist would recognize:

- Directed
- Labeled

FIGURE 23.3
A graph that's not much like the Web.

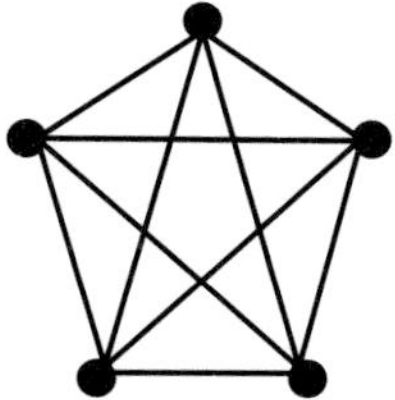

The one-minute graph theorist would add that RDF graphs are distinguished by the characteristics they lack as much as by the characteristics they possess. RDF graphs have the following characteristics:

- *Complete*. That is, all `<IT>Not complete</IT>` two nodes have an arc running between them. As you'll learn in the next section, RDF demands triples—two nodes connected by a labeled arc—and nothing less than triples. The elegant five-pointed star shown in Figure 23.3 is complete. A square, with its corners considered *nodes* and its sides *arcs*, is not complete, but a square with a corner-to-corner × would be.
- *Not connected*. It is *not* always possible to reach any node from any other node. (The sets of resources for two RDF triples might disjoint.)
- *Not symmetrical*. That is, an RDF graph is not like a triangle, a square, a star, or a buckyball; it is more like a model railroad track or the net.

In addition, the RDF graph is:

- *Cyclic*.

Figure 23.4 shows a cycle from node *C* to node *D* to node *E* and back to node *C*. In addition, the figure illustrates the other formal characteristics we have just discussed. The graph is complete. However, it is not connected: Nodes *F* and *G* can only be reached from each other, not from any of the other nodes in the graph. What's more, the graph isn't symmetrical around the vertical axis from *x* to *y*.

FIGURE 23.4
A graph that's much more like the Web.

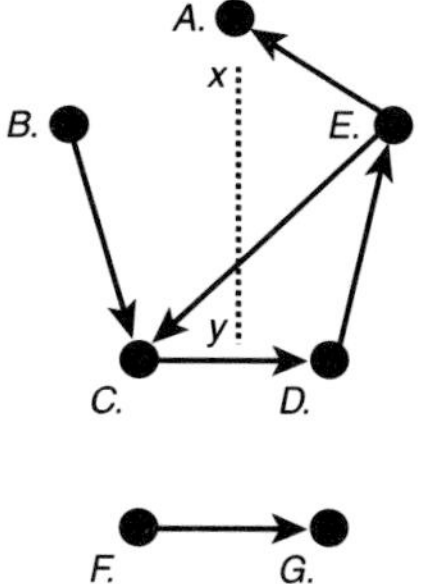

The RDF Graph

The RDF graph is the data model of RDF. It is a mathematical construct—a collection of triples—whose characteristics define the expectations of developers and information owners when RDF information is processed. Any RDF document should generate the same graph when processed by any RDF processor; that is the operational definition of interoperability.

The RDF Statement

An RDF statement is often called a *triple* because it has three parts, as you'll recall from the earlier blackboard discussion:

- Subject
- Predicate
- Object

We now ask, in RDF, what *are* subjects, predicates, and objects? The answer: They are all resources, uniquely identified on the Web by URIs. The exceptions to this answer are string literals and "anonymous nodes" (to be treated later in this chapter), which are resources but are not uniquely identified, except possibly by an RDF application for its own internal purposes.

Note

RDF has an alternative triplet of names for subject, predicate, and object. We could also say that the subject *resource* has a *property* (the predicate) whose *value* is the object.

In this and the next chapter, we are going to stick with the terms *subject*, *predicate*, and *object* because they suggest the natural connection between statements seen as sentences in a grammar and statements seen as propositions in some form of logic. This connection will provide the basis for conversations on the Semantic Web, as you'll see in the next chapter.

Finally, subject, predicate, and object are implicitly ordered: At least for speakers of the English language, subjects naturally come first, predicates in the middle, and objects at the end. Therefore, the directed nature of the RDF graph becomes intuitive. Jane, the subject, is always first, isn't she?

As you saw in our blackboard example, an RDF statement is like a simplified sentence in a natural language like English. Figure 23.5 shows the sentence "Jane sells books" in the form of an RDF graph. Jane (a nonretrievable resource represented by the URI `[Jane]`) is the subject node of the statement. Books (nonretrievable and represented by `[books]`) is the object node of the statement. Sells (`[sells]`) is the predicate, and it labels the arc between the subject and object. Because arcs in RDF are directed, running from subject to object, we always know which node is the subject and which node is the object.

FIGURE 23.5
A single statement in the RDF graph.

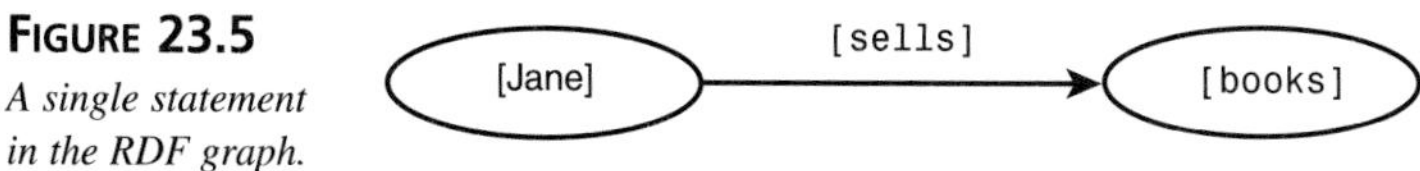

Now that you know that subjects, objects, and predicates are all resources on the Web and are uniquely identified, you can see that many statements (indeed, an infinite number of statements) can be made about any resource, and that any resource can be a subject or an object (or a predicate). Figure 23.6 shows the flexibility of the RDF graph, as it shows how to connect three statements: "Jane sells books," "books enrich publishers," and "publishers pay Jane." The figure shows that resources that are subjects in one statement can be objects in another, and vice versa.

FIGURE 23.6
Multiple connected statements in the RDF graph.

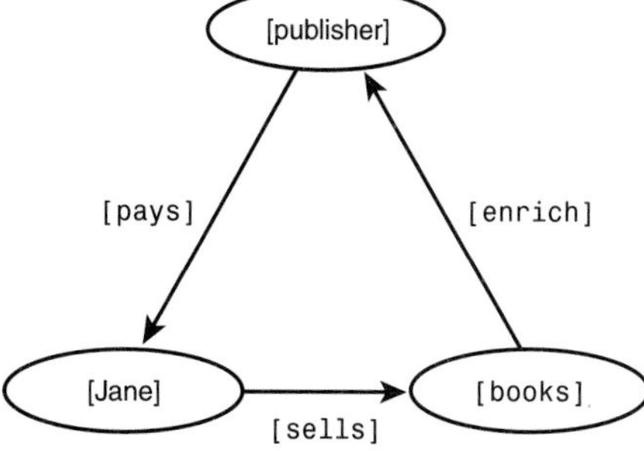

Figure 23.7 shows that we can even make statements about statements—in this case, "'Jane sells books' exemplifies a statement." This capability is called *reification*. Here are two examples of reification that show why it is useful:

- "John says that 'Jane sells books.'"
- "Morgoth the Vile says that 'Jane sells books.'"

Suppose I trust John: The reified statement "Jane sells books" is likely to be true, and I might go on to investigate the books she sells. Suppose I do not trust Morgoth: The reified statement is likely to be false, and I probably wouldn't invest the time to work out its implications. (This is a small example of the "web of trust," discussed in Chapter 24.)

Further, if RDF were not able to make statements about statements through reification, it would not be able to document or assert that its *own* statements are RDF statements, a strange limitation indeed. We'll look at reification in some detail later in this section.

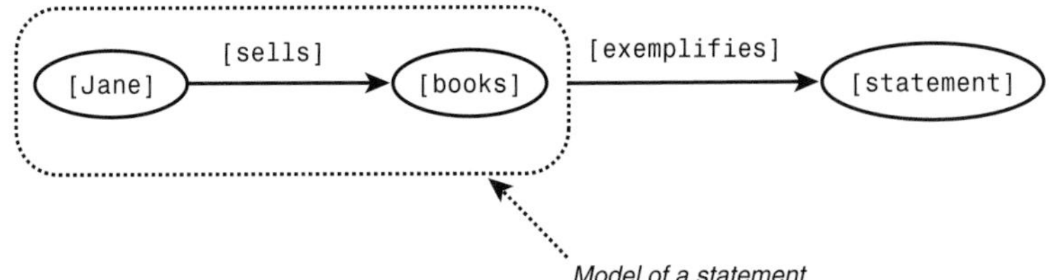

FIGURE 23.7
Statements about statements in the RDF graph.

To sum up: RDF triples (or statements) have subjects, predicates, and objects. Subjects, predicates, and objects are all resources, uniquely identified by URIs (except, again, for literals and anonymous nodes). Resources can participate in an infinite number of statements. Furthermore, we can make statements about (models of) statements. Before turning to the data model of RDF, which formalizes these relationships and provides the mathematical formalism to which all RDF notations must conform, we need to look at RDF syntax, because we will need to represent the model *in* syntax.

Caution

Strictly speaking, we do not make statements about statements in RDF but rather statements about *models* of statements, known as *higher-order statements*. That is what the dashed line around the issues in Figure 23.7 indicates. Reification will be examined in detail in "Constructing the RDF Graph from XML Syntax," where we will go through the complete inventory of RDF triples, showing how they are constructed in both pictorial and XML syntax.

Issues in RDF Syntax

RDF has a single data model, but the specification allows the model to be represented in several ways:

- Pictorially, in nodes and arcs diagrams
- Via XML serialization (which can be "abbreviated")
- Via curly brace serialization

Typically, graph-based modeling languages and data models have at least two syntactic representations. Conceptual graphs and the Unified Modeling Language (UML) both have a graphical and a serialized, linear notation, for example, as do most textbooks on graph theory. The compact, pictorial representation is used for communication between humans (authors, reviewers, and clients). The linear notation is used to interchange models between systems; the graphical notation is deconstructed into the linear notation by the sender and reconstituted into the pictorial notation by the receiver. The process of deconstruction and reconstitution works because the linear and graphical notations are formally equivalent. RDF is typical in this regard.

Caution

It is not completely clear that RDF's several linear and graphical notations are equivalent; see the discussion of the open issue *rdf-equivalent-representations* in "Recent Working Drafts and Notes," earlier. Because this means that different RDF processors could reconstitute different graphs from the same markup (or vice versa), an interoperability concern is raised.

However, RDF's XML syntax exhibits atypical features. First, there is no W3C XML schema (or even XML DTD) to which RDF instances must conform. Some implementers (that is, those outside the "RDF community" who are not necessarily true believers) believe that the lack of a clear syntax specification makes implementing the spec (at least interoperably) virtually impossible. (Later in this chapter, Table 23.2 attempts to sumarize RDF syntax.)

Second, RDF makes heavy use of a technique called *abbreviation*, where verbose and less-verbose versions of the XML are deemed to represent the RDF graph in the same way. (This is shown later in the chapter in Figure 23.15.)

Note

To some, RDF's profusion of syntaxes and use of abbreviation is a case of reinventing a square wheel. In SGML 10 years ago, any number of "variant concrete syntaxes" and forms of markup "minimization" were possible. Ultimately, the editors of XML 1.0, in a classic addition-by-subtraction design decision, removed such esoterica from SGML in the name of simplicity, implementation, and widespread adoption—goals achieved beyond the wildest dreams of the early proponents of "SGML on the Web." Maybe the RDF community could take a tip from this experience when thinking about syntax.

In this chapter, we will use the pictorial and XML syntax for examples. RDF is about statements, and the pictorial notation represents statements effectively. Even though the XML syntax is not particularly stable, it is likely to be understood by the many readers who will encounter it in other publications by the RDF community and when they're creating their own documents.

For completeness, here is the curly braces serialization of an RDF statement ("triple"):

```
{my:myPredicate,[mySubject],[myObject]}
```

In this notation, subjects, predicates, and objects are determined by order, not graphical images or angle brackets. Notice, too, that in curly braces notation, the predicate comes first, unlike the XML serialization and the pictorial notation.

Now that you understand how to represent RDF statements in both pictorial and XML syntax, we can now exhibit the formal data model of RDF.

The RDF Data Model

This section shows how the concepts of the RDF data model are classified, how these elements map to XML syntax, and how some "convenience" XML syntax enables the mapping of XML syntax to the RDF data model.

There are 10 concepts in the RDF formal model, as listed here:

- `RDF:Alt`
- `RDF:Bag`
- `RDF:Object`
- `RDF:Predicate`
- `RDF:Seq`
- `RDF:Statement`
- `RDF:Subject`
- `RDF:Type`
- `literal`
- `ord`

We'll discuss the meaning of each concept in turn. Most of them you are already familiar with. For example, `RDF:Subject`, `RDF:Predicate`, and `RDF:Object` are indeed the three parts of the RDF triple, and `RDF:Statement` is that triple (or statement).

The new concepts are `RDF:Alt`, `RDF:Bag`, and `RDF:Seq`. These concepts are called *containers*. Their names bear a suspicious resemblance to the old-time SGML Abstract Syntax content model connectors—`ALT`, `AND`, and `SEQ`—and indeed the semantics are similar. Each container concept represents a collection of subjects or objects, where the items in the collection have the following characteristics:

- *Mutually exclusive.* `RDF:Alt` (alternate). Like a content model with an `OR` (`|`) connector, one of the alternatives must be chosen.
- *Unordered.* `RDF:Bag` (collection). Like a content model with an `AND` (`&`) connector, the order in which the members of the bag are serialized is not significant. (A bag is a collection rather than a set, because detecting duplicate members of the collection is considered to be a validation function.)
- *Ordered.* `RDF:Seq` (sequence). Like a content model with a `SEQ` (`,`) connector, the order in which the members of the bag are serialized is significant.

The `ord` data model concept gives us, as you'll see later when we construct containers, a way to refer to a container's individual members.

Finally, the `literal` data model concept enables data (in XML, `#PCDATA`) to be incorporated into the RDF graph. The data is treated as primitive and is not interpreted in any way, even if it contains XML markup characters.

These 10 data model concepts are sorted into three buckets (object types):

- Properties
- Resources
- Literals

In this case, properties is a subset of resources.

You already know what resources and literals are. A property is just a predicate. In object-oriented (OO) design, resources correspond to objects and properties correspond to instance variables.

How do these object types map to the RDF triple? The RDF data model maps them as follows:

- *Subject.* `RDF:Alt`, `RDF:Bag`, `RDF:Seq`, and `RDF:Statement` (resource object type)
- *Predicate.* `RDF:Object`, `RDF:Predicate`, `RDF:Subject`, and `RDF:Type` (property object type)
- *Object.* `RDF:Alt`, `RDF:Bag`, `RDF:Seq`, `RDF:Statement`, `literal`, and `ord` (resource and literal object type)

How does the data model affect the nature of the statements we can make in RDF? First, objects of the type `Statement` can be the subjects and objects of sentences, but not the predicates of statements. For example, we cannot say "The man 'The man bit the dog' the dog," if indeed we would ever want to. Second, objects of the type `Object`, `Predicate`, `Subject`, or `Type` can be predicates in statements but cannot be subjects or objects. Finally, objects of type `literal` (data) can be the object of a statement but never the subject—that is, what the statement is "about." If you hear the idea expressed that RDF is about metadata (data about data), not data, this is the formal expression of that notion.

We now turn to mapping object types in the data model to XML elements. As it turns out, the following types all map directly to RDF XML elements: To create the RDF tag name, replace the string "RDF" in the concept name with the RDF namespace prefix, so `RDF:Alt` becomes `rdf:Alt`, for example.

The string "RDF" in the concept name is replaced in the tag name with the RDF namespace qualifier, except for `RDF:Type`, which maps to an attribute (this mapping is implicit in RDFMS but made explicit in RDFS):

- `RDF:Alt`
- `RDF:Bag`
- `RDF:Object`
- `RDF:Predicate`
- `RDF:Seq`
- `RDF:Statement`
- `RDF:Subject`
- `RDF:Type`

So far, we've been working top-down from the RDF data model to the RDF XML syntax. Working bottom-up from the formal grammar in the specification, we find the following XML convenience constructs:

- `rdf:about`
- `rdf:Description`
- `rdf:ID`
- `rdf:li`
- `rdf:resource`

These utility constructs comprise the scaffolding that is discarded when RDF XML syntax is processed into an RDF graph. The details of this process are given in the next section, "Constructing the RDF Graph from XML Syntax."

Tables 23.1, 23.2, and 23.3 summarize the relationships just described between data model object types, XML elements that map to these object types, and the utility XML constructs, respectively.

TABLE 23.1 Combining Data Model Elements into Statements

Subject Resources	*Predicate Properties **	*Object Resources/Literals*
RDF:Alt	RDF:Object	RDF:Alt
RDF:Bag	RDF:Subject	RDF:Bag
RDF:Seq	RDF:Predicate	RDF:Seq
RDF:Statement	RDF:Type	RDF:Statement
		ord
		literal

* *Properties are a subset of resources.*

TABLE 23.2 Mapping Data Model Elements to XML Syntax

Data Model Element	*XML String*	*XML Element*	*XML Attribute*
RDF:Alt	rdf:Alt	•	
RDF:Bag	rdf:Bag	•	
RDF:Object	rdf:object	•	
RDF:Predicate	rdf:predicate	•	
RDF:Seq	rdf:Seq	•	
RDF:Statement	rdf:statement	•	
RDF:Subject	rdf:subject	•	
RDF:Type	rdf:type		•
literal	#PCDATA		
ord	RDF:_*n* elements		

TABLE 23.3 Utility XML Constructs

XML String	*XML Element*	*XML Attribute*
rdf:about		•
rdf:Description	•	
rdf:ID		•
rdf:li	•	
rdf:resource		•

Constructing the RDF Graph from XML Syntax

This section provides pictorial and XML serialization representations for all the statement constructions specified in RDFMS.

Figure 23.8 summarizes the conventions we will use in the pictorial syntax for RDF. There are two kinds of nodes: circles (for nodes that represent resources) and rectangles (for nodes that represent literals). Nodes that do not represent resources (so-called *anonymous nodes*) are empty circles.

FIGURE 23.8
Pictorial syntax for RDF data model.

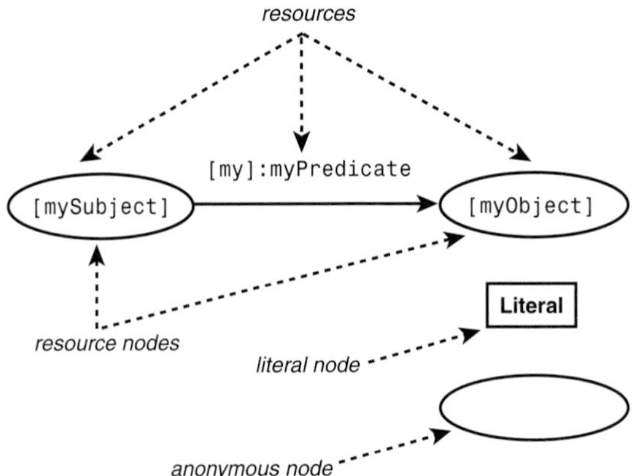

Listing 23.2 is the XML serialization of the pictorial statement in Figure 23.8. Notice the one-to-one equivalence between the pictorial and XML representations of the model. The `description` element with the value of its `about` attribute is equivalent to the subject node. The tag name `my:myPredicate` is equivalent to the predicate label on the arc that connects subject to object (when the namespace prefix is not expanded). The value of the `rdf:resource` attribute, `[myObject]`, is equivalent to the object node.

LISTING 23.2 Pictorial Syntax for RDF Data Model Serialized as XML

```
<rdf:Description about="[mySubject]" xmlns:my="[NS]">
 <my:myPredicate rdf:resource="[myObject]"/>
```

The XML serialization examples use three conventions, in addition to the conventions for showing URIs introduced earlier in this chapter. First, XML IDs and string literals are bold. Second, XML covered previously in the table and not repeated will be indicated with a bold ellipsis (...).

Finally, in the pictorial examples, namespace prefixes are replaced by the URIs to which they map when processed—in this instance, `my` to `[NS]`. This underscores the fact that namespaces are resources too.

Figure 23.9 shows the RDF statements that are reconstituted from the serialized children of `rdf:Description`. At the left, we see the RDF graph that is created by XML markup on the right.

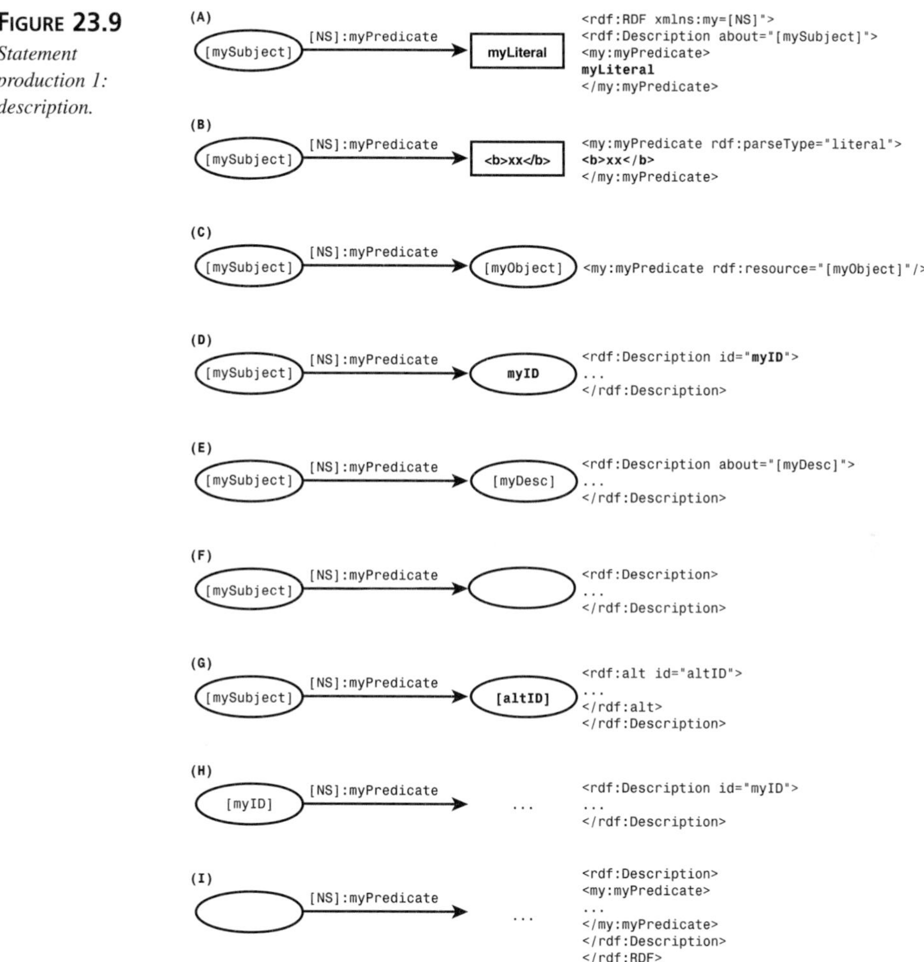

FIGURE 23.9
Statement production 1: description.

The subjects of the statements are created in three ways: as a node whose resource is identified by the URI in the value of the `rdf:Description` element's `about` attribute (statements *A* through *G*), as a node whose resource is identified by the value of the rdf:Description element's id attribute (statement *I*), and as an anonymous node, because the rdf:Description element has neither an about nor an id attribute.

The predicates of all the statements are created by expanding the namespace-qualified tag name (generic identifier) of the child element of rdf:Description, as in statements *A* through *C*. In the examples, the namespace prefix my in the markup is replaced by its namespace name [NS] in the graph, as given in the xmlns:my namespace declaration on the rdf:RDF element in production *A*. (The predicates for statements *D* through *J* are created as described earlier and are replaced in the markup by ellipses on the right side.)

When the child element of rdf:Description is not an RDF element, the objects for all the statements are created as nodes either from the #PCDATA contained in the predicate element (in the example, my:myPredicate), as in statement *A*; from XML markup contained in the predicate element when the predicate's rdf:parseType attribute has a value of literal, as in statement *B*; or from the resource identified by the URI in the value of the predicate element's rdf:resource attribute, as in statement *C*.

When the child element is an RDF element, it may be another rdf:Description element, as in statements *D* through *F*. As mentioned earlier, the resource of the object node may be identified with an ID (statement *D*), with the about attribute (statement *E*), or as anonymous (statement *F*).

The child element may also be an RDF container element; the object of the statement becomes the resource identified by the value of the id attribute of that container, as in statement *G*.

The objects and predicates in statements *H* and *I* are created as described earlier and are therefore replaced by ellipses on both the graph and markup sides.

Figure 23.10 shows how a single subject can be distributed over several objects in the graph using the aboutEach attribute.

There are two statements in Figure 23.10, although they both have the same subject ([mySubject]) and predicate ([myPredicate]), derived respectively from the rdf:Description and my:myPredicate elements, as shown previously in Figure 23.9.

The objects in the statements are created as nodes from the children of the RDF container element whose ID is the value of the aboutEach attribute on the containing rdf:Description element.

Figure 23.11 shows the RDF statements that are created in the graph when a serialized RDF container is reconstituted (rdf:Seq is used, but the same applies to rdf:Alt and rdf:Bag). The productions are parallel to Figure 23.9, with the container in place of rdf:Description and the list items in place of the predicate elements.

FIGURE 23.10
Statement production 2: distributed referents.

```
<rdf:RDF>
<rdf:Description about="mySubject"
 aboutEach="myBag">
<my:myMetaPredicate>
...
</my:myPredicate>
</rdf:Description>
<rdf:Bag ID="myBag">
<rdf:li resource="[this]"/>
<rdf:li resource="[that]"/>
</rdf:Bag>
</rdf:RDF>
```

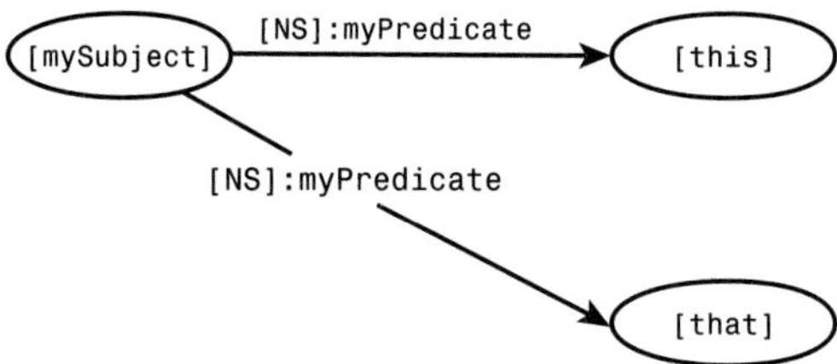

The subject of each statement is a node whose resource is the container element itself, identified by the value of its `id` attribute.

The predicates of each statement are nodes whose resources are the `rdf:li` elements, identified by their sequence within the XML markup, in the form `RDF:_1`, `RDF:_2`, up to `RDF:_n`, where *n* the number of list items, as generated by the RDF processor.

When the child element of the container element is not an RDF element, the objects for all the statements are created as nodes either from the `#PCDATA` contained in the predicate element (in the example, `rdf:li`), as in statement *A*; from XML markup contained in the predicate element when the predicate's `rdf:parseType` attribute has a value of `literal`, as in statement *B*; or from the resource identified by the URI in the value of the predicate element's `rdf:resource` attribute, as in statement *C*.

When the child element is an RDF element, it may be an `rdf:Description` element, as in statements *D* through *F*. As mentioned earlier, the resource of the object node may be identified with an ID (statement *D*), with the `about` attribute (statement *E*), or as anonymous (statement *F*).

The child element may also be an RDF container element; the object of the statement becomes the resource identified by the value of the `id` attribute of that container, as in statement *G*.

The objects and predicates in statements *H* and *I* are created as described earlier and are therefore replaced by ellipses on both the graph and markup sides.

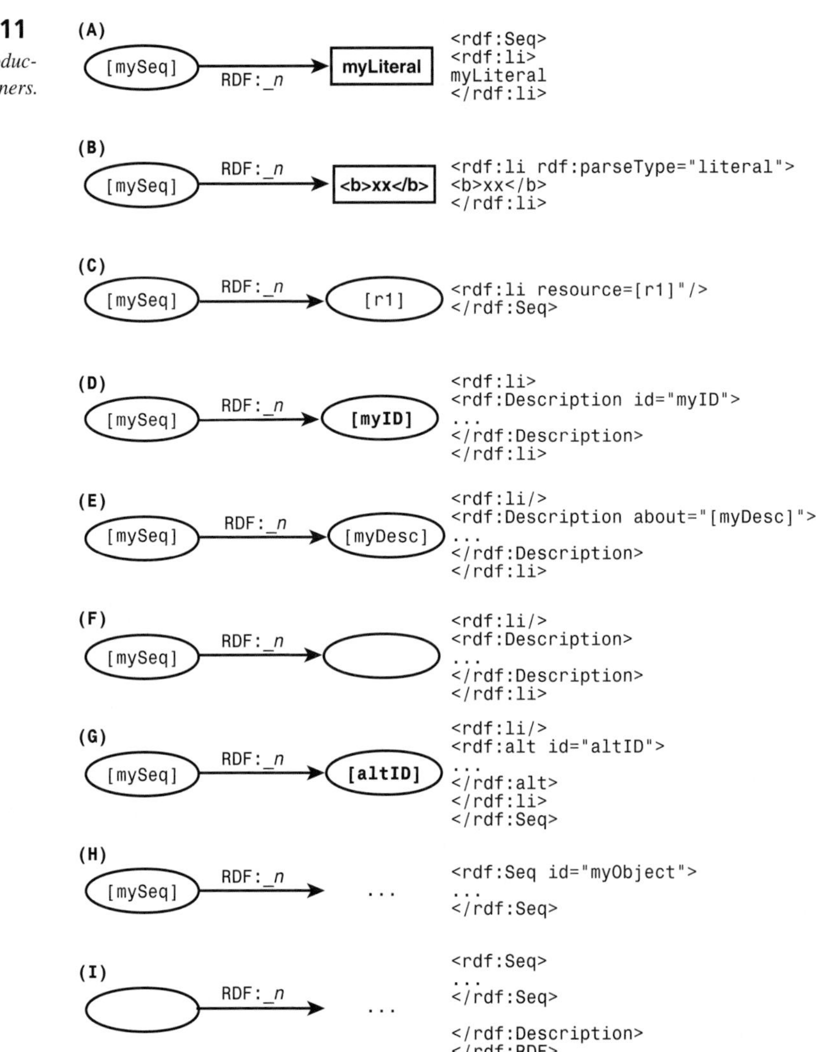

FIGURE 23.11
Statement production 3: containers.

Figure 23.12 shows the RDF statements that are created in the graph when the `aboutEachPrefix` feature is used on an `rdf:Description` element in the markup.

The subject of the statements is reconstituted from a serialized `rdf:Description` element, as shown previously in Figure 23.9. The predicate of the statements is reconstituted as for any serialized `rdf:Description` element, again as in Figure 23.9.

FIGURE 23.12
Statement production 4: containers defined by a URI pattern.

```
<rdf:RDF xmlns:my="[NS]">
<rdf:Description
 about="[mySubject]"
 aboutEachPrefix="[my]">
<my:myPredicate/>
</rdf:Description>

<rdf:Description about="[my]/foo.xml"/>
...
<rdf:Description about="[my]/bar.xml"/>
...
<rdf:Description about="[other]/foo.xml"/>
...
<rdf:Description about="[other]/bar.xml"/>
...
<rdf:Description about="[my]/baz.xml"/>
</rdf:RDF>
```

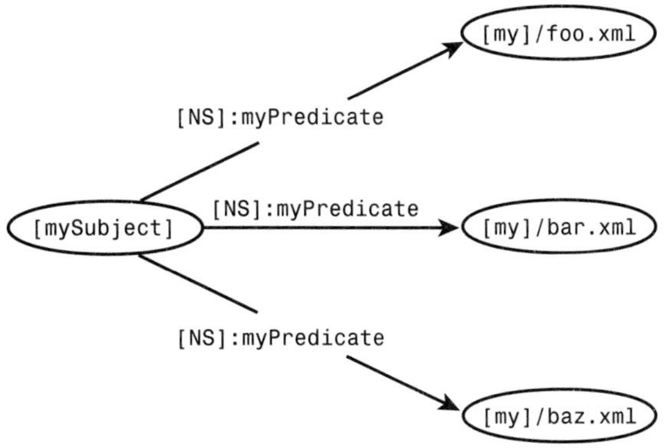

The objects of the statements are created as nodes from resources whose identifiers begin with the character string that is the value of the `aboutEachPrefix` prefix on the `rdf:Description` element. In Figure 23.12, the prefix is `[my]`. Therefore, the resources `[my]/foo.xml`, `[my]/bar.xml`, and `[my]/baz.xml` are objects of the statements, and the resources `[other]/foo.xml` and `[other]/bar.xml` are not objects.

Figure 23.13 shows how the same graph can be reconstituted from serialized `rdf:Description` elements that use attributes rather than element content for their subject and object resources.

Compare statement *A* with statement *C* in Figure 23.9. Whereas Figure 23.9 uses an element, `my:myPredicate`, for its predicate and the attribute value of its `rdf:resource` attribute for its object; statement *A* in Figure 23.13 uses the `my:myPredicate` attribute right in the `rdf:Description` element for the predicate and uses the value of that attribute for its object.

<rdf:RDF mlns:my="[NS]">
<rdf:Description
about="[mySubject]"
my:myPredicate="[myobject]"/>
(A)
[mySubject]
[NS]:myPredicate
[myObject]
<rdf:Description id="myDesc"
my:myPredicate="myLiteral"/>
(B)
[mySubject]
[NS]:myPredicate
myLiteral
<rdf:Description
about="mySubject"
aboutEach="[myBag]"
my:myPredicate="[foo]"/>
<rdf:Bag ID="myBag">
<rdf:li resource="[this]"/>
<rdf:li resource="[that]"/>
</rdf:Bag>
(C)
[mySubject]
[NS]:myPredicate
[this]
[NS]:myPredicate
[that]

FIGURE 23.13
Statement production 5: element and attribute equivalence in description.

Now compare statement *B* with statement *A* in Figure 23.9. Here again, the predicate serialized from a `my:myPredicate` element in Figure 23.9 is reconstituted from the serialized attribute of the same name in statement *B* in Figure 23.13. Also, the reconstituted object is not the value of an `rdf:resource` attribute but rather the value of the `my:myPredicate` attribute.

Finally, compare statement *C* with the distributed referent in Figure 23.10. Again, whereas Figure 23.10 uses an element (`my:myPredicate`) for the predicate, statement C in Figure 23.13 uses an attribute (`my:myPredicate`) on `rdf:Description`. Also, whereas Figure 23.10 uses the value of an `rdf:resource` attribute for the object, statement *C* uses the value of an attribute (`my:myPredicate`).

Figure 23.14 shows the graph that is constructed by embedding a namespace-qualified XML element inside an `rdf:Description` element. The subject is taken from the value of the `rdf:Description` element's `about` attribute. The predicate is `RDF:type`, and the object is the embedded XML element.

FIGURE 23.14
Statement production 6: typed node as descriptions.

[mySubject] —RDF:type→ [NS]:myType

```
<rdf:RDF xmlns:my="[NS]">
<rdf:Description about="[mySubject]">
<my:myType>
</my:myType>
</rdf:RDF>
```

Figure 23.15 shows the graph reconstituted from ordinary XML elements and attributes, where the tag and attribute names are "namespace qualified" within an RDF description element.

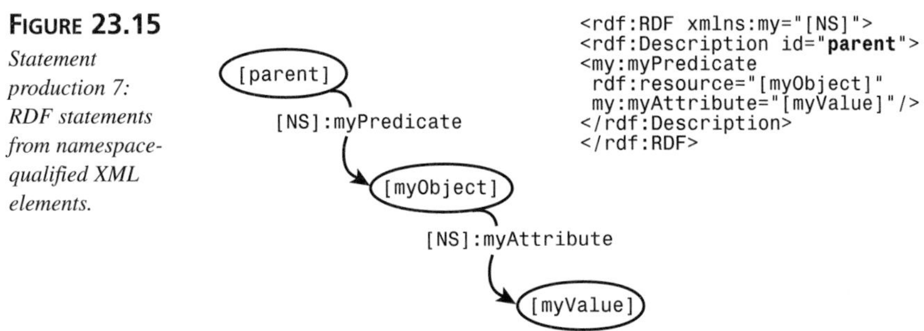


```
<rdf:RDF xmlns:my="[NS]">
<rdf:Description id="parent">
<my:myPredicate
 rdf:resource="[myObject]"
 my:myAttribute="[myValue]"/>
</rdf:Description>
</rdf:RDF>
```

FIGURE 23.15
Statement production 7: RDF statements from namespace-qualified XML elements.

The subject of statement *A* is the node reconstituted from the serialized parent `rdf:Description` element. The predicate of the statement is reconstituted from the namespace-qualified tag name of the child element. The object is reconstituted from the value of the `rdf:resource` attribute on that child element.

Statement *B* is a complete statement reconstituted from the child element itself. The subject of the statement is reconstituted from the value of the `rdf:resource` attribute. The predicate of the statement is reconstituted from another qualified attribute name on the child element (here, `my:myAttribute`). The object of the statement is reconstituted from the value of that attribute name (`my:myAttribute`).

In effect, then, any XML element can be caused to constitute RDF statements, as long as it uses namespace-qualified names in its element and attribute names.

Reification

Figure 23.16 shows the process of RDF reification: making a statement about a model of a statement.

Why would we make a statement about a model of a statement instead of a statement about a statement? First, we avoid problems of recursion. Second, we avoid problems with data integrity in any store of RDF statements we might have. Suppose that we have a store of RDF statements, all of which are true. We then wish to make this statement: "The statement 'blue is the same as green' is false." If we kept the statement "blue is the same as green" in our store of true statements, we lose our data integrity. We could, of course, make a separate store for statements that are false, but who would want to maintain such a system? The upshot is that we want to be able to make statements about *hypothetical* statements—statements that would act just like statements if only we made them. That way, our store of true statements remains uncorrupted.

The answer, as mentioned previously, is to make statements about models of statements (that is, hypothetical statements). Figure 23.16 shows how to do this. In Figure 23.16, Statement *A* is a statement about a model of statement *C*. Again, when we build a model of statement *C*, we say that we "reify" it. (Statement *C* has a dotted line around it to show that a reified statement may be purely hypothetical, such as "blue is the same as green.")

FIGURE 23.16
Statement production 8: reifications.

```
<rdf:RDF xmlns:rdf="[RDF]"xmlns:my="[NS]">
<rdf:Description about="[mySelf"]>
<my:myMetaPredicate rdf:resource="[myStatement]"/>
</rdf:Description>
<rdf:Statement>
<rdf:subject resource="[mySubject]"/>
<rdf:predicate resource="[myPredicate]"/>
<rdf:object>
<rdf:Description about="[myObject]"/>
</rdf:object>
<rdf:type resource="[rdf:statement]"/>
</rdf:Statement>
</rdf:RDF
```

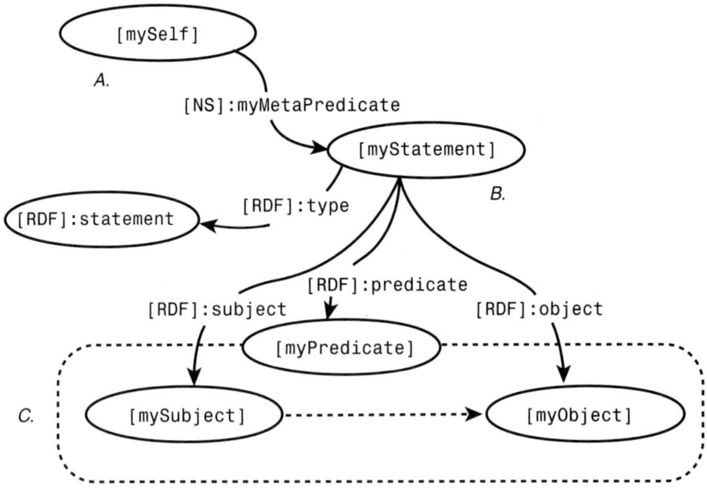

First, we construct a normal RDF statement using a description element, as detailed in Figure 23.9.

The subject of statement *A* is a node from the [myself] resource, which is the value of the about attribute of the rdf:Description element. ([mySelf] is the "reifier" of the hypothetical statement *B*.)

The predicate of statement *A* takes the expanded namespace-qualified tag name (here, my:myMetaPredicate).

The object of statement *A* (here, [myStatement]) is constituted by the value of the rdf:resource attribute on the predicate element.

The object of statement *A*—the resource [myStatement] (at *B*)—represents our statement model. Now, let's build that model. We know that statements have subjects, predicates, and objects. Therefore, we need to say that one predicate of [myStatement] is that it is a type of statement, a second predicate is that it has a subject, a third that it has an object, and a fourth that it has a predicate.

Therefore, one predicate of [myStatement] is that its [RDF]:type is [RDF]:Statement. A second predicate of [myStatement] is that it has an [RDF]:subject, the resource [mySubject].

A third predicate of [myStatement] is that it has an [RDF]:predicate, the resource [myPredicate], and a fourth predicate of [myStatement] is that it has an [RDF]:object, the resource [myObject].

Because statement *B* has all the predicates that a nonhypothetical statement has, RDF can treat it as a statement. (If it walks like a duck....)

RDF XML Syntax Summary

Tables 23.4 and 23.5 supply what is missing from the RDF specification—something approaching a DTD. Table 23.4 gives the attributes that RDF elements may have; Table 23.5 lists their content models.

In Table 23.4, the RDF elements label rows, and the RDF attributes label columns. An element that may have an attribute has a bullet (•) in its cell. For example, rdf:Description may have an id attribute or an rdf:about attribute.

TABLE 23.4 RDF XML Syntax: Elements and Attributes

XML Element	*XML Attributes[1]*										
	id	*about*	*about ➥EachPrefix*	*about ➥Each*	*type*	*bagID*	*type*	*qName attribute*	*resource*	*parse ➥Type[2]*	*_n*
<rdf:RDF>											
<rdf:Description>	•	•	•	•		•	•	•			
typed node (qName)	•	•	•			•	•	•			
<rdf:Seq>	•										•
<rdf:Alt>	•										•
<rdf.Bag>	•										•
<rdf:li>									•	•	•
<rdf:type>	•				•	•		•		•	
<rdf:predicate>	•				•	•		•		•	
<rdf:subject>	•				•	•		•		•	
<rdf:object>	•				•	•		•		•	
<rdf:statement>	•				•	•		•		•	

[1] All the attribute names except for ID and IDREF are qualified with the rdf: namespace prefix.

[2] Permitted values are "Literal" and "Resource"

[3] The <code>ID</code> and <code> about</code> attributes are mutually exclusive. Not all attributes can be used with element content: `bagID` *and* `resource`.

In Table 23.5, the RDF elements are on the left and their permitted content are on the right. For example, an `rdf:Seq` element can contain `rdf:li` elements.

TABLE 23.5 RDF XML Syntax: Permitted Content

XML Element	*Permitted Content*
`rdf:RDF`	`rdf:Description rdf:Alt rdf:Seq rdf:Bag rdf:type rdf:predicate rdf:subject rdf:object` typed node
`rdf:Description`	`rdf:type rdf:predicate rdf:subject rdf:object` "qname"
Typed node "qname"	`rdf:type rdf:predicate rdf:subject rdf:object`
`rdf:Seq`	`rdf:li`
`rdf:Alt`	`rdf:li`
`rdf:Bag`	`rdf:li`
`rdf:li`	string well-formed XML `rdf:Description rdf:Alt rdf:Seq rdf:Bag rdf:predicate rdf:subject rdf:object` typed node
`rdf:type`	string `rdf:Description rdf:Alt rdf:Seq rdf:Bag rdf:type rdf:predicate rdf:subject rdf:object`
`rdf:predicate`	string `rdf:Description rdf:Alt rdf:Seq rdf:Bag rdf:type rdf:predicate rdf:subject rdf:object`
`rdf:subject`	string `rdf:Description rdf:Alt rdf:Seq rdf:Bag rdf:type rdf:predicate rdf:subject rdf:object`
`rdf:object`	string `rdf:Description rdf:Alt rdf:Seq rdf:Bag rdf:type rdf:predicate rdf:subject rdf:object`
`rdf:statement`	`rdf:subject rdf:predicate rdf:object`

Note

Here are the XML namespace declarations for RDF:

- `rdf: http://www.w3.org/1999/02/22-rdf-syntax-ns#`
- `rdfs: http://www.w3.org/2000/01/rdf-schema#`

In this chapter, for readability, we show the first namespace as `[RDF]`, and the second as `[RDFS]` when expanding these URIs.

RDF Schema

Historically, RDF grew out of the need to specify a general-purpose mapping between specific bibliographic solutions using particular vocabularies. Here are some examples:

- The W3C Platform for Internet Content Selection (PICS)
- The Dublin Core (simple bibliographic data for Web pages)
- Site maps, subject taxonomies, thesauruses, and library classification systems
- The W3C Platform for Privacy Protection (P3P)

In this section, we look at how to use RDF schema to constrain, validate, document, and extend RDF vocabularies using the RDF typing system.

Validity in RDF Schema

RDF schema meets its requirement for generality by being a vocabulary for vocabularies (just as XML and SGML are languages for defining languages). We might imagine our teacher, still at the blackboard, being asked, "How do I know that this statement makes sense, even if all the words are in the right place?" She might answer, "Because some words can only be used with other words. Jane can sell books, but books can't sell Jane."

In RDF-speak, unlike general usage, a *vocabulary* is not just a list of words. Rather, an RDF vocabulary may be said to define:

- Subject validity (which predicates go with which subjects)
- Object validity (which predicates go with which objects)

For example, in the "Jane sells books" examples, we have a set of resources: `[Jane]`, `[sells]`, and `[books]`. If we define a schema against which to check this statement, `[Jane]` could be the subject in a statement where `[sells]` is the predicate. This is subject validity. Likewise `[books]` could be the object in a statement where `[sells]` is the predicate (and `[Jane]` could not). That is object validity.

RDF schema can define a vocabulary that accomplishes these validity constraints through what is called its *typing system*.

The RDFS Typing System

To "connect the dots" in the RDF typing system, we need to cover two concepts:

- `rdf:type`
- `rdfs:subclassOf`

`rdf:type` enables class/instance statements to be made. When a resource has a type, the resource is the object in a statement where the predicate is `[rdf:type]` and the subject is the type. Figure 23.17 shows an RDF statement that says that `[Rover]` is a type of `[dog]`. Rover can also be said to be an instance of the class dog, and every statement about the class of dogs can be made about Rover. However, instances are unique: There is only one Rover—*this* Rover.

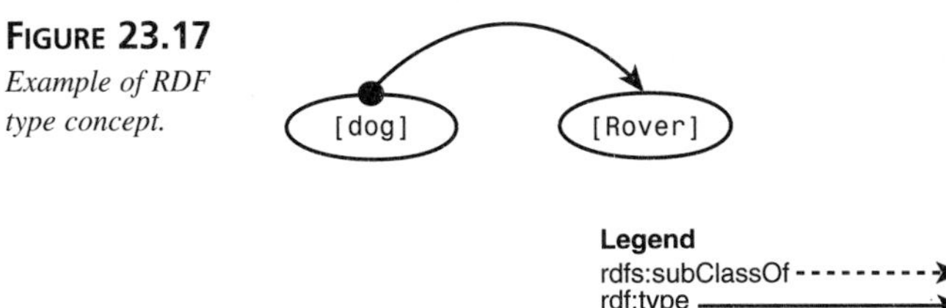

FIGURE 23.17
Example of RDF type concept.

`rdfs:subclassOf` enables subset/superset statements to be made. The class is the superset; the subclass is the subset. When a resource is a subclass, the resource is the object in a statement where the predicate is `rdfs:subClassOf` and the subject is an RDF class. Figure 23.18 shows that the class `[dog]` is a subclass of the class `[animal]` and that `[animal]` is a subclass of `[living being]`. You can also see that, in RDF, a class may be a subclass of more than one class; the class of dogs may also be a subset of the class of `[companion]`—a "companion animal" being (often) a pet.

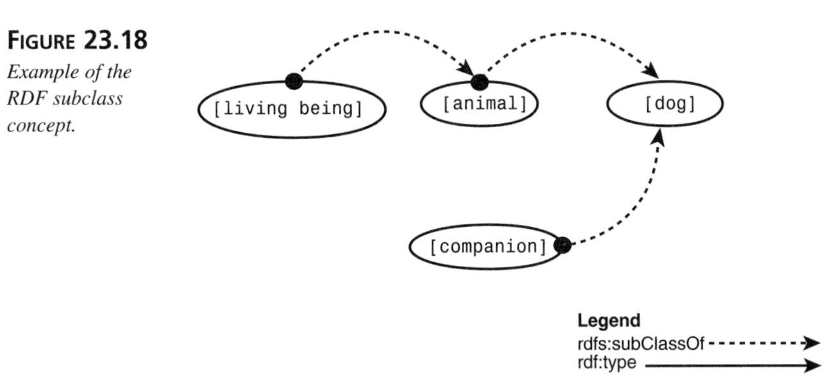

FIGURE 23.18
Example of the RDF subclass concept.

Class relations are said to be *transitive*. If class `[dog]` is a subclass of the broader class `[animal]`, and `[animal]` is a subclass of `[living being]`, then `[dog]` is also implicitly a subclass of `[living being]`. Figure 23.19 shows this relationship: There are not only arcs *A* and *B* between `[living being]` and `[animal]`, and between `[animal]` and `[dog]`, but also arc *C*, drawn explicitly between `[living being]` and `[dog]`. However, although such implicit arcs are present in the RDF graph, we generally simplify the pictorial representation of class relations to keep the graph less cluttered by leaving them out. A human can trace the class relations upward or downward, if necessary.

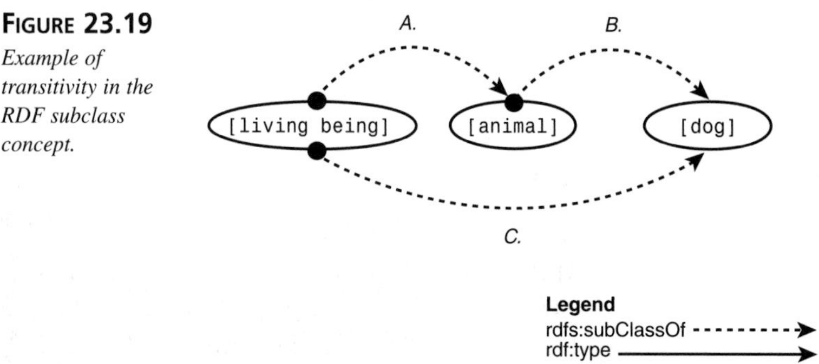

FIGURE 23.19
Example of transitivity in the RDF subclass concept.

We will look at more subtleties of classes, subclasses, and typing later when we look in more detail at the RDF hierarchy.

We now have what we need for an overview of the RDF class hierarchy. All the predicates in the RDFS typing system are either `rdfs:subClassOf` or `rdf:type`, as is shown in Figure 23.20. (The single exception to this rule is a use of `rdfs:subproperty`, discussed later.) The 16 RDF schema resources are divided into the following six categories:

- Validation
- Core
- Hierarchy
- Documentation
- Schema control
- Extensibility

Also, each schema resource is represented by a node.

We will discuss these categories and their resources, in order, in the remainder of this section (although validation concepts are divided into two parts).

Validation

We'll start with validation—even though it is nearer the bottom of the RDF class hierarchy than the top—because that's the operation many information owners will want to perform on their data, just as they want a database schema to control the quality of their

RDBMS and they want an XML DTD or XML schema to provide some level of quality assurance for their data. Recall that there are two forms of schema validation in RDF: object validity and subject validity. `rdfs:domain` handles subject validity; `rdfs:range` handles object validity.

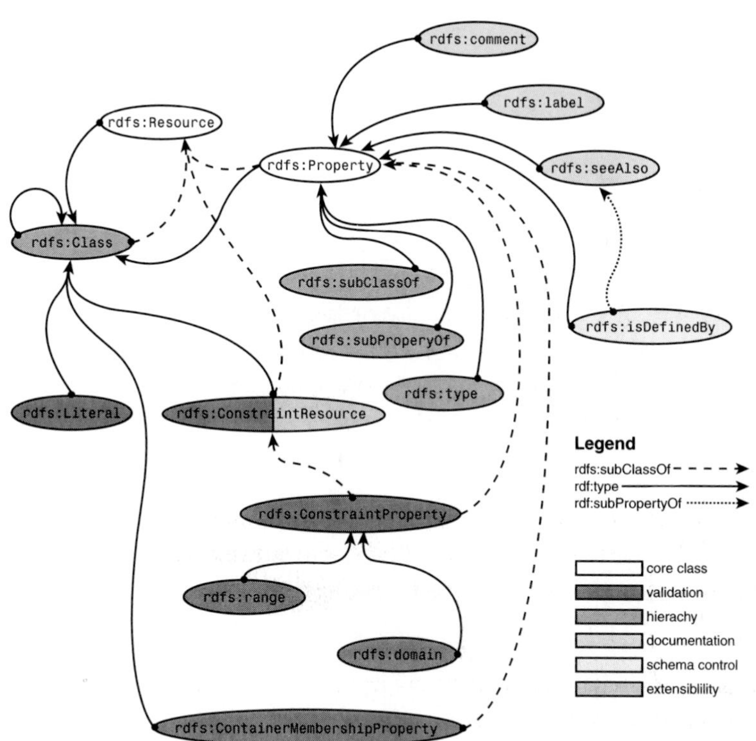

FIGURE 23.20
Class hierarchy for RDF schema showing types and subclasses.

`rdfs:domain`

`rdfs:domain` is a type of `rdfs:ConstraintProperty`. It constrains the classes of subjects (resources) for which the property is a valid predicate. If a property has no domain, it can be the predicate of any subject. A property may have more than one range. If a property has more than one `rdfs:domain` constraint, it may be the predicate of subjects that are subclasses of any one or all of the specified classes.

The range and domain of the `rdfs:domain` concept are specified only in a comment, so there is no pictorial representation of `rdfs:domain`.

rdfs:range

rdfs:range is a type of rdfs:ConstraintProperty. It constrains the classes of objects (resources) for which the property is a valid predicate. A property doesn't have to have a range. If so, the property can be used as an object in any statement. However, when imposed, the constrains of rdfs:range are stronger than those imposed by rdfs:domain. First, a property can have only one range. Second, the domain (subject) of an rdfs:range predicate must be an rdf:property, and its range (object) must be an rdfs:Class.

Core

Now that you understand the key concern of information owners—validation—let's move to the top of the RDF class hierarchy.

rdfs:Resource

rdfs:Resource is the root of the RDF class hierarchy (refer back to Figure 23.8). All things described by RDF expressions—all nodes and labels in the RDF graph—are instances of rdfs:Resource. rdfs:Resource is also a class. In fact, rdfs:Resource is a type of rdfs:Class, and rdfs:Class is a subclass of rdfs:Resource. (Remember, the RDF graph permits cycles!)

rdf:property

rdf:property represents the subset of RDF resources that are properties (see Table 23.1). rdf:property is a type of rdfs:Class and a subclass of rdfs:Resource. rdf:property has the "rdf" namespace prefix, rather than the "rdfs" prefix, because the RDF model has implicit properties, even if it lacks a schema.

rdf:type

As you have seen, rdf:type indicates that a resource is an instance of a specified class. That class must be an instance of rfds:Class or a subclass of rdfs:Class. This statement is true for the resource that is known as rdfs:Class, which is a type of itself. (The RDF graph, again, permits loops.)

Like rdf:property, rdf:type has the "rdf" namespace prefix, rather than the "rdfs" prefix, because the RDF model has implicit types, even if it lacks a schema.

Class Hierarchy

The class hierarchy in RDF is set up by with rdfs:class, rdfs:subClassOf, and rdfs:subPropertyOf (and rdf:type, which we've already looked at). Let's look at these three elements.

`rdfs:Class`

As you have seen, `rdfs:Class` is both a type of resource and a subclass of itself. However, RDF classes are both like and unlike classes as OO programmers may think of them. RDF classes are like OO classes in that, through transitivity, they can specify broad-to-specific categories such as "living being to animal to dog." RDF classes are unlike OO classes, first, because they have no methods—they don't *do* anything. (Markup never does.) Second, RDF classes could be called *extrinsic* rather *intrinsic*. Instead of defining a class in terms of features intrinsic to its instances, an RDF schema will define predicates in terms of the classes of subject or object to which they may be applied, extrinsically. (This allows testing for subject and object validity.)

Theoretically, URIs representing HTML documents, dogs, books, databases, and abstract concepts could all be members of the same class—the class of things that can be represented by RDF.

`rdfs:subClassOf`

`rdfs:subClassOf` is a type of `rdf:property`. It specifies a subset/superset relation between classes—a relation that is transitive, as you have seen. Only instances of the type `rdfs:Class` may have an `rdfs:type` property whose value is `rdfs:Class`. Importantly, a class can never be declared to be a subclass of itself or any of its own subclasses. (The RDF Schema specification cannot express this constraint formally, though it is expressed in prose.) Therefore, although the RDF graph may contain cycles, the class/subclass inheritance hierarchy that is a subgraph of the RDF graph remains a tree, whose nodes are only instances of `rdfs:Class`. Finally, RDF (unlike most object-oriented programming languages) permits multiple inheritance—that is, a class may be a subclass of several classes. (It could hardly be otherwise, because the Semantic Web must permit arbitrary combinations of RDF statements taken from multiple systems, each of which may have its own inheritance hierarchy.)

`rdfs:subPropertyOf`

`rdfs:subProperty` is a type of `rdf:property`. It enables properties to be specialized—a process similar to inheritance, except for properties instead of classes. Like the `subClassOf` predicate, `subPropertyOf` is transitive and forms a hierarchy that is a proper tree, like `rdfs:subClassOf`. Multiple specializations are also permitted.

Documentation

Documentation allows human-readable text to be attached to a resource, either as a label or a comment. Because the content of the documentation elements is only data, not statements, it does not affect the RDF graph in any way and therefore does not enable machine understanding of the resource.

rdfs:label

rdfs:label provides for a human-readable representation of a URI, perhaps for display. The domain (subject) of a label predicate must be an rdfs:resource. The range (object) must an rdf:literal.

rdfs:comment

rdfs:comment permits human-readable documentation to be associated with a resource. The domain (subject) of a comment predicate must be an rdfs:resource. The range (object) must an rdf:literal.

rdfs:seeAlso

rdfs:seeAlso is a cross-reference that gives more information about a resource. The nature of the information provided is not defined. The domain (subject) and range (object) of an rdfs:seeAlso predicate must both be rdfs:resource elements.

Schema Control

rdfs:isDefinedBy is a subproperty of rdfs:seeAlso. It's URI is meant to be the address of the RDF Schema for the subject resource. The domain (subject) and range (object) of an rdfs:isDefinedBy predicate must both be rdfs:resource elements.

General Constraints

We now turn to the issue of constraints in general (that is, beyond the constraints on domain and range, discussed earlier). At this point, there's one caveat: Because markup doesn't *do* anything, RDFS doesn't say what an application must do if a constraint is violated. That is up to the application.

rdfs:ConstraintProperty

rdfs:ConstraintProperty is a subclass of both rdfs:ConstraintResource and rdf:property. Both rdfs:domain and rdfs:range are instances of it.

Extensibility

rdfs:ConstraintResource is a type of rdfs:Class and a type of rdfs:Resource. It is present in the model so that other constraint properties besides domain and range may be subclassed from it.

Non-Model Validation

This type of validation is called "non-model" because expressing the notion that a literal should be checked for being a literal or that the auto-generated counter for container children should be derived from the actual number of children is something the RDF engine would have to do, not the data model.

rdfs:literal

`rdfs:literal` is a type of `rdfs:Class`. An `rdfs:literal` can contain atomic values such as textual strings. The XML `lang` attribute can be used to express the fact that a literal is in a human language, but this information does not become a statement in the graph.

rdfs:ContainerMembershipProperty

`rdfs:ContainerMemberShip` is a type of `rdfs:class` and subclass of `rdf:property`. Its members are the properties `_1`, `_2`, `_3`, and so on (the order in which the children of a container appear in the container, under the `ord` component of the data model).

Working with the Angle Brackets

This section provides a few techniques that the RDF community has found useful in RDF's brief history.

Here is a way to add RDF to HTML: Put it inside the `HEAD` element in the HTML page. Be sure to add the RDF namespace declarations so that an RDF processor can make use of the RDF markup, as shown in Listing 23.3.

LISTING 23.3 Embedding RDF into HTML

```
<HTML>
<HEAD>
<rdf:RDF xmlns:rdf="http://www.w3.org/1999/02/22-rdf-syntax-ns#"
xmlns:my="[mySchema]">
<rdf:Description rdf:about="[URI of the enclosing HTML document]">
<my:RDF1="data">
<my:RDF2="data">
</rdf:Description>
</rdf:RDF>
</HEAD>
...
</HTML>
```

Of course, you can substitute a more well-known URI for `[mySchema]` (for example, Dublin Core at `http://purl.org/dc/elements/1.0/Creator`).

If all fails, make the RDF a separate document and use an HTML `LINK` element with the URI of the document as the value for the `href` attribute and `meta` as the value of the `rel` attribute, as shown in Listing 23.4.

LISTING 23.4 Embedding RDF into HTML

```
<LINK rel="meta" href="[myRDFdocument]">
```

Summary

The Shakers sang, "'Tis a joy to be simple. 'Tis a joy to be free." How simple is RDF? And how free?

RDF is made from very few components. The RDF graph uses only three components: nodes, arcs, and labels on the arcs. An RDF statement has only three parts: subjects, predicates, and objects. What's more, if there were an RDF DTD or schema, it would declare only 11 elements.

Furthermore, RDF packs some punch despite its simplicity. It can be incorporated into any HTML document. Normal XML elements, when incorporated in RDF, become magically capable of making RDF statements.

Finally, there is the typing system that elegantly defines RDF in terms of RDF, itself, but is also a lightweight method of classifying all the resources on the Web.

And yet, there are times when it seems that RDF was designed by architects of the "more is more" school. There are times when, indeed, "less is more," and RDF is one of them. RDF's progress is hampered by the dense undergrowth of three (to date) different syntactical representations. Furthermore, RDF's notation for expressing element syntax in the form of attributes is tricky, but it flies in the face of SGML's bad experience with such tricks. The lack of a DTD or a schema makes validation harder than it needs to be for developers and information owners. Finally, RDF'ers seem to have a deep need to say the same thing in at least two different ways. In this chapter, we have tried to use the terminology of subject, predicate, and object consistently, but as briefly noted, there is an different, parallel set of terminology that speaks of named properties and values. Just as the syntactical representations may not be truly interoperable for machines, the terminologies might not be for humans. Many academics from many disciplines participate in the RDF community, and this makes conflation of conceptual vocabularies even more of a constant danger.

Therefore, the seeming simplicity of RDF presents a paradox. The simple graph, the simple data model, and the simple markup have enticed many developers to work with RDF. Yet, different interpretations of the syntaxes, as well as different readings of the vocabularies, have ensured that their work doesn't reconstitute the same RDF graph from the same markup. What's more, if interoperability is not achieved, RDF won't scale to the World Wide Web.

How free is RDF? It is, after all, the apple of the eye for the director of the W3C, and as everyone knows, the Semantic Web is the "next big thing." However, RDF is dependent on a number of other specifications, not all of them under W3C control. In particular, the clash of understanding between URIs as understood in RDF and as understood in the world of ordinary Web practice as governed by the IETF is worrisome, because if RDF and the installed base clash, it is not necessarily RDF that will win.

Nor is RDF now free from competition. The pragmatic William James once referred to truth as "the cash value of an idea." Well, giant software firms are investing in markup technologies that will enable anything to be bought and sold on the Web (including, I assume, ideas in the form of intellectual property). If these projects succeed—if indeed the only reason to make statements on the Web is to buy and sell resources—then what reason is there for RDF, simple though it may be?

Furthermore, RDF is no longer free of its own history. If fundamental questions need to be asked, will the community be able to ask them? For example, a reified triple is really a quad (refer back to Figure 23.16). Is this just happenstance, or is there a deep, pattern-language-type issue that needs to be addressed? Some semantics experts think so. Others complain that RDF is *too* simple; that it lacks the powers for inferencing that would enable developers to drive agents with it.

All of this serves to bring us back to the usual question: When and why does it make sense to invest in RDF technology? And that brings us to the usual answer: Look to your opportunity costs. If you are an information owner, investing in RDF now brings the certainty of rework later, because the specification is not particularly stable, and the RDF generated by different RDF software does not interoperate. If you are a developer, you may wish to begin work on RDF tools immediately so that when the specifications do mature and the RDF documents are interoperable, you can seize opportunities at once. If you are an RDF evangelist, you can take courage from the diligent and open efforts of W3C and the RDF community to address the interoperability issues with the spec and move forward rapidly to making RDF the foundation of the Semantic Web.

CHAPTER 24

The Semantic Web for Information Owners

In This Chapter

What is the Semantic Web? Recall the fable of the blind men and the elephant, where the blind man grappling the elephant's leg said, "An elephant is like a temple pillar! The blind man who lifted the elephant's trunk said, "An elephant is a snake," and the blind man who was brushed by the elephant's flapping ear said, "An elephant has fronds like a palm tree!" In speaking of something of the scale and scope of the Semantic Web, we are like those blind men, and the Web is like that elephant, except that the Semantic Web is an elephant under construction.

Therefore, we must understand the Semantic Web under conditions of uncertainty. First, we'll look at the ancestry of the Semantic Web, where you will see the two main lineages from which the Semantic Web inherits concepts: bibliography and knowledge representation. Some of these ancestors are still alive today and meeting requirements, giving us confidence that the fundamentals of the Semantic Web are sound.

Then, we'll look at the seven-layer architecture of the Semantic Web, as listed here:

- Unicode and URIs
- XML, XML Schema, and XML Namespaces
- RDF, RDF Schema, and Topic Maps
- Ontologies
- Logic
- Proof
- Trust

Note

Here is the W3C Web site for the Semantic Web activity:

`http://www.w3c.org/2001/sw/`

When the Semantic Web is constructed, its central value proposition will be conversations between people and machines. For example, take the following English sentence:

> Buy me a hardcover copy of Jane's book, in Chinese, if available for less than $39.95.

If this sentence is expressed using RDF statements and vocabularies (see Chapter 23, "RDF for Information Owners"), both machines and humans will be able to understand it. Furthermore, the machine (using the Ontology and Logic layers) will be able to draw inferences from the statement—and make further statements. For example, if the book is not available at the right price, the machine will be able to suggest an alternative book to the human as well as understand the human's answer. Also, if the human doesn't understand how the computer came to the conclusions it did, the computer's logic can be exposed by the Proof layer. Finally, if asking the computer for proof all the time is just too time-consuming, one can ask trusted and more tractable humans (or agents or machines) what they feel. We collect all these question and answer interactions under the heading of *conversation*—realizing that this could end up making machines seem more human than we expect them to seem today. In fact, conversation is what puts the semantics in the Semantic Web.

Precursors of the Semantic Web

Bibliography is the art of designing "finding aids" for collections of information. The standard bibliographic model enables a user to find anything, anywhere. Two of the most influential electronic implementations of the bibliographic model are Project Xanadu and the HyTime international standard (ISO 10744). These are the two main precursors of the Semantic Web, which is also an implementation of the bibliographic model.

Project Xanadu

Xanadu would have been the creation of the visionary Ted Nelson, coiner of the term *hypertext nonsequential writing*. Nonsequential writing is simple: It's what we do when we throw together chunks of bulleted content in PowerPoint and later put them in the correct order with the appopiate indents.. Of course, Nelson's vision was a little bit bigger than that. Imagine, first, that the relationships between bullet points are not expressed implicitly by sequence and indentation but explicitly in the form of an information overlay that links the bullet points. Second, imagine that each bullet point is on the Internet; and third, that each bullet point has a copyright owner who receives royalties in the form of an instantaneous micropayment every time his bulleted point (or even some characters inside it, according to a patented addressing scheme) is used in someone else's presentation. Finally, imagine that there's a worldwide franchise operation, a "Dunkin' Data" of sorts, that manages copyright issues and micropayments. Now imagine developing such a system before the Internet, before the word processor, before the personal computer, and when the `GOTO` statement was not yet universally considered harmful. That was Xanadu. "In Xanadu did Kubla Khan, A stately pleasure-dome decree…."

Xanadu was not, it should be noted, vaporware. A lot of labor went into its development; its release date simply slipped, slipped, and slipped into the indefinite future. Xanadu's legacy has both positive and negative aspects. On the bright side, Xanadu was the conceptual pioneer for software that implemented the standard bibliographic model. It set the bar, at least conceptually, for all subsequent hypertext systems, including the Semantic Web. Furthermore, if Xanadu didn't have all the answers, at least it posed many of the questions that still vex us today: How do we handle rights in an electronic publishing environment? How do we manage links, in particular when the endpoints of the link may change or vanish? How do we address into multiple data formats? None of these questions have definitive answers today. It may be a miracle that the Web works without solving any of these posers. However, it is likely that at least one of the questions—How do we handle rights in a global electronic publishing environment?—will have to be answered before the Semantic Web can reach its "full potential." (Semantics, after all, are a form of intellectual property.)

Xanadu also pointed out a major pitfall that other hypertext systems avoided. Xanadu was conceived as a complete business system; it was to be franchised. Subsequent attempts to implement the standard bibliographic model avoided this pitfall. Both HyTime (discussed later) and Web specifications generally are open and public documents that any business may take advantage of for free. Furthermore, many of the foundational technologies of the Web are open sourced. Therefore, Xanadu's franchise business model seems to be an evolutionary dead end.

Note

Here is the Xanadu web site:

`http://www.xanadu.com`

This is quite an irony, because the remaining cadre of Xanadu true believers regards the Web as irremediably broken.

Here's a Web site for a program that uses Xanadu-style links:

`http://www.gzigzag.org/`

HyTime

HyTime (ISO 10744) implemented the bibliographic model (find anything, anywhere) on the scale suitable for extremely large information owners (such as government agencies and manufacturing concerns). Because its addressing model enables the addressing of arbitrary chunks of information and their presentation in arbitrary order, it is also a hypertext system.

HyTime is the oft-unacknowledged intellectual precursor of at least three of the foundational technologies of the Semantic Web shown in this chapter and in Chapter 23. It built the foundation for links as information overlays, used graphs as a data model, and enabled semantic links.

First, HyTime was the first markup technology to treat links as an information overlay and to advocate that they be separately stored, rather than embedded within their source or target documents (as in HTML a elements). We see this architectural decision carried through in the W3C XLink, XPointer, and XPath specifications (covered elsewhere in this book). This architecture is also used both by RDF and the XTM effort (XML Topic Maps, covered later in this chapter), both of which specify lightweight information overlays above sets of resources, rather than being embedded within the resources.

Second, HyTime was the first markup technology to use graphs as a data model. (The graph data model of RDF, and graphs generally, are discussed in Chapter 23.) This was the famous Grove Paradigm, where Grove stands for *Graph Representation of Property Values*. HyTime faced the problem of addressing into representations of data structures in many formats, not just XML, and without being dependent on any particular programming paradigm (such as object orientation). As it turned out, the formal properties of graphs were fit for the purpose of representing most data structures. SGML and HyTime itself were described using Groves, and techniques were developed to describe other data formats. Both RDF and XTM topic maps faced the problem of representing a data model for their interchange syntax (or, in the case of RDF, *syntaxes*) and adopted a graph formalism for the same reason.

Third, HyTime was the first markup technology to implement semantic links—links where the semantics of the link endpoints could be more sophisticated and explicit than the simple and implicit "source" and "target" semantics of vanilla HTML. Here again there is a clean line of inheritance to W3C specifications through XLink, but the RDF statement can be perceived as nothing but a semantic link with three endpoints: the subject, the object, and the predicate.

HyTime is sometimes reviled for being too big and too complicated. It is certainly not in the mainstream of Web development. However, where the problems are big and complex, HyTime still finds a ready welcome, particularly in truly humongous technical documentation projects for aircraft and/or weapons systems, where its stability, power, and robustness really shine. For example, both the European and U.S. standards for Interactive Electronic Technical Manuals (IETMs) are specified in HyTime.

Note

Here is the Web site for the HyTime specification:

`http://www.ornl.gov/sgml/wg8/docs/n1920/html/n1920.html`

Here is a reader's guide to the standard:

`http://www.hytime.org/papers/htguide.html`

Here is the Web site for AECMA 100D, an IETM that uses HyTime constructs:

`http://www.aecma.org/Publications/Spec1000d/1000d.htm`

Architecture of the Semantic Web

W3C has described a seven-layer architecture for the Semantic Web, from the bottom to the top:

- Unicode and URIs
- XML, XML Schema, and XML Namespaces
- RDF, RDF Schema, and Topic Maps
- Ontologies
- Logic
- Proof
- Trust

As you can see, these layers move from the very concrete to the abstract, even ethereal. Most people have seen a URI (layer 1), but few (maybe none) have thought through what trust might mean, let alone how it might be specified so that it can be processed by machines. The bottom three layers are well specified enough that some issues can be raised with them—particularly at the interfaces of the layers. The top four layers are (like our elephant) very much under construction. This section describes the seven layers. Needless to say, there is a lot more detail in the concrete layers than in the blue-sky thinking at the top.

Note

Here is a Web site that illustrates the seven layers of the Semantic Web:

`http://www.w3.org/2000/Talks/1206-xml2k-tbl/slide10-0.html`

Unicode and URIs

At the lowest layer of the Semantic Web are specifications for the characters used by documents on the Semantic Web (Unicode) and for identifying documents (URIs). Because URIs are made from characters, we'll look at characters first.

Unicode

In the beginning, there was ASCII, and that was good. When the World Wide Web was starting out, that is. The original HTML specifications used the SGML Reference Concrete Syntax, which boiled down to using ASCII (the American Standard Code for Information Interchange), and the browser manufacturers followed along. They used the SGML entity facility to map characters that were not included in the ASCII character set, such as curly quotes, bullets, and so forth, using (whether or not they knew it) the famous ISO entity sets with which so many consultants were able to pad their deliverables.

ASCII was good because it was a very successful standard (or vice versa). It was totally transparent and portable—as long as you used the Western European alphabet nd didn't need any accented characters. If you needed accents (in French, for example) or Cyrillic, Greek, or Hebrew characters, then the SGML entity system became more than a little verbose. (Imagine using `β` whenever you wanted to write β throughout an entire document!) However, if you used a nonalphabetic writing system, ASCII was totally unhelpful.

Enter Asian character sets, which are often nonalphabetic and run to many thousands of characters. After all, WWW doesn't stand for *Western-European Wide* Web—it stands for *World* Wide Web. What to do?

The answer was to build a bigger code space. ASCII, at maximum, provides for 256 characters—barely enough for English, and far too few for even one Asian character set, and absurdly small when Chinese, Japanese, Hangul, Thai, their many historical variations, as well as all the other Asian characters sets (including Khmer and Vietnamese) are taken into account.

Unicode built the bigger code space. (One reason for XML's worldwide success is that it uses Unicode in the form of UTF-8.) Unicode is, essentially, a giant code table. It maps characters, which are abstract entities (such as "LATIN CHARACTER CAPITAL A," a Japanese Hiragana syllable, or a Chinese ideogram), to code points, which are unique numeric values ("U+0041" for Latin "A"), to byte serializations or *encodings*. Rendering engines, in turn, map byte serializations to visual representations of characters (such as capital "A" in the font Garamond), called *glyphs*. Unicode does not standardize glyphs.

There are three Unicode encodings: UTF-32, with one 32-bit code unit per one code point; UTF-16, with one or two 16-bit code units per code point; and UTF-8, with one to four 8-bit code units per code point. UTF-8 is the subset of Unicode in which XML documents are encoded. It aims to preserve the characteristics of ASCII so that file systems, parsers, and other software that rely on ASCII remain backward compatible with Unicode.

As already mentioned, Unicode is required by XML. Other languages and specifications that require Unicode are Java, ECMAScript (JavaScript), LDAP, and CORBA 3.0. Companies that have adopted Unicode include Apple, HP, IBM, Microsoft, Oracle, SAP, Sun, Sybase, Unisys, and other industry leaders. It is supported in all modern browsers, numerous products, and most operating systems. Therefore, if you're a developer writing on a platform that doesn't handle Unicode or an information owner making the assumption that all characters are ASCII, take a hard look at your assumptions. Importantly, Unicode "guarantees" that no characters will be removed or reinterpreted in ways that are incompatible with the existing standard.

Up until now, we've been using the word *Unicode* for the standard that solves our code space problem. In fact, there are two standards:

- Unicode
- ISO 10646

Unicode is a semicommercial effort; ISO 10646 is an international standard. Fortunately, in 1991 both efforts decided that the world didn't need two competing solutions for the code space problem and agreed to keep their code tables in sync with each other and coordinate future extensions. They have kept their agreement. All characters are at the same positions in the code tables and have the same names in Unicode and ISO 10646.

Are there differences between Unicode and ISO 10646? Yes. ISO 10646 is focused mainly on its code tables. Unicode also gives information relevant to implementers, particularly for implementers of high-end composition systems. It provides rendering algorithms for scripts (such as Arabic), mixing bidirectional text (such as Latin left-to-right text and Hebrew right-to-left text), sorting and string comparisons, and so forth. However, ISO 10646 has more complete coverage of Chinese, Japanese, and Korean sample glyphs.

Are there differences between Unicode and ISO 10646 that affect the Semantic Web directly? Again, yes, and again the answer turns on code space.

First, there are some differences between the XML view of the world at W3C and the Unicode view of the world. For example, W3C does not consider some Unicode characters suitable for XML. W3C feels it is better to use the HTML `<BR>` tag or some other markup equivalent than to use Unicode line and paragraph separators. Other issues arise when Unicode characters are specified to handle functions that are handled, or better handled, by markup. Examples here include list item marker characters (better handled with a style sheet), bidirectional text (specified in HTML 4.0), object replacement (better handled with an HTML `src` attribute or equivalent), and others.

Note

Here's the W3C site for XML and Unicode issues:

`http://www.w3.org/TR/unicode-xml/`

Potential users of Unicode also have issues with it, especially Chinese/Japanese/Korean/Vietnamese (CKJV) users. Character set issues in general, and East Asian character sets in particular, are extremely intricate and culturally bound. (There is one, possibly apocryphal, story of country representatives feuding over whom would be "first" in the code table.)

Some CKJV issues are process issues. Due to the large number of Asian character sets, and the huge numbers of ideographs within each set, some sets and Unicode does not cover many characters. Unicode 3.0 has almost 28,000 ideographic characters. However, by some estimates, there are 160,000 ideographs yet to be standardized. Even if this estimate is high, given that the Unicode process, like any standards process, is by nature slow, some CKJV users are bound to remain skeptical of Unicode for some time.

Some of these skeptics will, of course, be classical scholars who study works that use characters or character sets that are no longer widely used. However, here we should consider that these works may have great cultural significance. How would English writers and speakers feel if the Unicode process had not yet standardized on the characters used to represent the works of Shakespeare or the New Testament in Greek?

Note

Here are the Web sites for Unicode, ISO 10646-1, and the Internet Engineering Task Force (IETF), respectively:

http://www.unicode.org/

http://www.iso.ch

http://www.ietf.org/rfc/rfc2279.txt

The normative editions of Unicode and ISO 10646 (http://www.iso.org) are available in book form:

- The Unicode Consortium (Editor). *The Unicode Standard*, Version 3.0. Addison-Wesley, 2000.
- ISO/IEC 10646-1:2000, Information Technology—*Universal Multiple-Octet Coded Character Set (UCS)*—Part 1: Architecture and Basic Multilingual Plane.
- ISO/IEC 10646-2:2001, Information Technology—*Universal Multiple-Octet Coded Character Set (UCS)*—Part 2: Supplementary Planes. (Available in English only.)

Here is where to find information on UTF-8:

- The Unicode Standard, Chapter 8
- ISO 10646, Annex D
- http://www.ietf.org/rfc/rfc2279.txt

Hobbits, elves, dwarves, and wizards may be interested in the following tongue-in-cheek proposal to put J.R.R. Tolkien's Tengwar character set into Unicode:

http://anubis.dkuug.dk/jtc1/sc2/wg2/docs/n1641/n1641.htm

URIs

Unicode is the first part of level 1 of the Semantic Web; the URI is the second part. Now, URIs are made out of characters, so the issues of internationalizing character sets, as we just discussed, potentially impact URI interoperability. Furthermore, URIs pose interesting technical and philosophical issues in their own right (known as the *identification problem*). So, let's look at URIs and their impact on the Semantic Web in detail.

On the second day, Tim Berners-Lee created the Uniform Resource Locator (URL). It, too, was good. Having in mind the overarching goal of creating a system whereby scientists could communicate their results, he sought to create an addressing system that could be scribbled on a cocktail napkin in a bar; in this he succeeded. URLs are definitely human readable, as opposed to the multiline incantations and arcane sequences of digits that preceded the URL.

Let's process a URL, just to get the terminology clear. Here is a sample (fake) URL:

```
http://jane.books.com/hardbacks/chinese
```

If you typed this into your browser (and the URL weren't fake) here is what would happen: The browser would divide the URL into scheme, domain name, and path name, and then resolve the result.

First, the browser would split the URL on the scheme (before the `://` part). That scheme tells the browser how and to whom to delegate locating a resource. (This "how and to whom" is called a *transfer protocol*; `HTTP` is an example.) Next, the browser looks for a "top-level domain" in the URL (here, `.com`) and, reading backwards, passes the domain name `jane.books.com` to a Domain Name System (DNS) router, which interprets the string and connects the browser to the `jane.books.com` server. Finally, Jane's server resolves the remaining path name into a Web page, and returns that document to the browser, which displays it.

So far, so good. The URL certainly works. But today, we have transitioned from the notion of a UR*L* that locates to a UR*I* that identifies, and in that transition some problems have arisen:

- The internationalization problem (a scalability problem)
- The privatization problem (a scalability problem)
- The terminology problem (a semantic problem)
- The identity problem (a semantic problem)

Let's turn to the internationalization problem first. Again, character set issues raise their ugly heads. On the one hand, URIs are to be 7-bit ASCII (as specified in RFC 2396). On the other hand, we have URIs embedded in XML documents that not only are UTF-8 Unicode but may contain XML general entities such as `&`. What to do? The answer: Perform a mini data conversion effort on-the-fly in the browser, in which the general entities in the URL sequence are converted to Unicode characters, and the resulting sequence is converted to UTF-8. In that sequence, each UTF-8 character is used if it corresponds to a 7-bit ASCII character. Otherwise, it is escaped into hex, and written like `%hh`, where `h` is one of the two 7-bit ASCII characters making the hexadecimal number in the Unicode code table for the desired character in UTF-8.

In this process, the original use-case behind URLs—human readability—has been left far behind. A netizen in the world's largest emerging market and oldest continuous commercial civilization (that is, a Chinese person) who wished to scribble a URI on a cocktail napkin would see nothing but a morass of percent signs (even assuming that all his characters were in UTF-8)! Furthermore, if he wanted to use his URI for marketing and print it on a billboard (like Western firms do), which version of his URL would he use? The one in the characters his customers could read, or the one that they saw in the browser's address box after conversion to UTF-8? Our Chinese netizen can't use his own character set for his own URI! This is the internationalization problem for URLs in a nutshell.

Enter the second problem: the privatization problem. Because there is a market for internationalized domain names, at least one registry service (a service that ensures the uniqueness and hence the value of domain names as assets) has opened an internationalized domain service intended to "catalyze" the work of the Internet Engineering Task Force (IETF) in writing the specifications for internationalized domain names. Well and good, but what will happen if the catalysis fails? Will the registries decide to deny their customers services, or will they fragment the World Wide Web by introducing domain names that are not universally resolvable?

These problems would seem simple enough to resolve, at least in theory (just like Unicode—make a bigger name space). Enter problem three: Not all the people who are charged with resolving these problems use the same terminology. One key nonstandardized piece of terminology, at least in the world of URIs, is the term *URI reference*.

Recall from earlier the sample URI

```
http://jane.books.com/hardbacks/chinese
```

which addresses an entire document. What if we only want to address a fragment of that document? We would use a URI reference, which would look like this:

```
http://jane.books.com/hardbacks/chinese#id42
```

Here, `id42`, in an XML document, would be the ID of an XML element, or *fragment identifier*. However, although the W3C world uses the term *URI reference* in RDF for the combination of a URI and a fragment identifier, this term is not recognized in the IETF world where URIs are defined. The impact? Think back to internationalization for a moment—URIs, being in the scope of IETF efforts, are 7-bit ASCII, but fragment identifiers, being outside IETF, are not! Our Chinese entrepreneur, still trying to write a legal URI reference on his dampening cocktail napkin, would end up with percent signs everywhere up to the hash mark, and then nice, readable (to him) characters after the hash mark.

Caution

As of this writing, neither W3C nor IETF has decided how one recognizes ID attributes in a well-formed XML document that lacks a DTD or W3C schema to define the attributes that have values of type `ID`.

Finally, we have the identity problem. Between the original definition of URLs in RFC 1630 and their standardization in RDF 2396, URLs became a subset of URIs; what was location became a subset of identification. But what is it, exactly, that URIs identify?

Now, the change to URIs was motivated by the perfectly reasonable desire to solve the huge infrastructure problem that locations on the Web, like it or not, change. If the path name portion of the URL represents a real path to a real document on a real machine, the URL will break if the document is renamed or moved, if the machine gets a new domain name, or if the machine is down. The concept of a URI introduced a level of indirection, in that the identifier may remain stable, even if the path name of the document (its location) changes. Of course, it turns out that most of this indirection can be managed at the file-system level by the server, and so URI, which was supposed to turn into an umbrella concept for other UR*s, such as URC (Uniform Resource Citation) and URN (Uniform Resource Name), really turned into a fancier name for a URL.

However, there is a crucial semantic difference between a URL and a URI. Because the conceptual association between the URI and a physical file has been severed, the URI became free to identify anything, including resources that are not available on the Net, such as physical books, the person Jane, and abstract ideas. RDF uses URI references in just this way (see Chapter 23).

However, let's put ourselves in the place of a browser and server once more. When we-the-browser are given a URI reference, how do we know, from the URI alone (which is all we do know about) whether the URI is a document to display or an identification of a nonretrievable resource such as the person Jane or the concept of love? Using the HTTP protocol, how do we-the-server distinguish between a URI that identifies the person Jane and an Error 404? In Zen terms, how do we distinguish the pointing finger from the moon?

The answer is that now we can't. As of this writing, there is no standard way to distinguish between URIs that have failed to retrieve resources and URIs that are not meant to retrieve resources at all. Today, the Semantic Web suffers from one of the most basic confusions possible: between the identity of a thing and the thing itself. There are at least two alternative solutions: URIs could change to include such a semantic, and the semantic could be handled at a higher layer above URIs.

Note

Here are the Web sites for the URI specifications:

`http://www.ietf.org/rfc/rfc1630.txt`

`http://www.ietf.org/rfc/rfc2396.txt`

Here is a Web site that provides design guidelines for URIs:

`http://www.w3.org/Provider/Style/URI.html`

Here is a Web site on issues of identity on the Semantic Web:

`http://www.w3.org/2001/03/identification-problem/`

XML Specifications

XML, XML namespaces, and XML Schema are covered elsewhere in this book. In this section, we will focus on one XML specification, *XML Topic Maps* (XTM), that addresses the issues that bubble up to the middle layers of the Semantic Web architecture from the Unicode and URI layers. As you'll recall, two of those issues are internationalization and identity.

First, we'll briefly describe XTM topic maps. Then we'll compare and contrast the topic approach to the problem with the RDF approach.

Note

Here are the Web sites for the topic map specifications:

`http://www.topicmaps.org (for the XTM specification)`

`http://www.topicmaps.net (for the data model)`

The ISO standard from which the XTM specification was derived can be found here:

`http://www.ornl.gov/sgml/sc34/document/0058.htm`

Note that further work on the data model is proceeding under the aegis of ISO.

Topic maps are a bibliographic solution. They were originally designed to provide an interchange syntax for finding aids such as indexes, thesauruses, glossaries, and taxonomies. Like most solutions that involve bibliographic issues (see the discussions of DDC and AECMA 1000D), topic maps evolved into a solution for modeling relations between information resources. Topic maps were evolved rapidly by the members of a small team working closely together.

Topic maps create associations among topics, which are electronic proxies for subjects (*subjects* being subject matter—stuff people talk about). Subjects can be addressable (a Web page) or nonaddressable (the person Jane or the concept of love). Users are encouraged to develop and use Published Subject Indicators (PSIs) for their nonaddressable subjects. Unlike RDF, the topic map data model has a number of "pre-reified" constructs optimized for modeling; these constructs include the topic basename associations, where a topic can be given a label within a scope.

Topic maps address the internationalization problem in a way that RDF labels and comments do not. In topic maps, basenames that can be scoped by human languages are built in to the data model. Therefore, a topic map information overlay can be adjusted to give topics names that are appropriate to the user, whether the user's preference is for English, French, or Chinese. Because RDF labels and comments use the XML `lang` attribute, which is not part of the RDF data model, RDF solutions must use ad-hoc solutions for a function that topic maps build in.

Topic maps address the identity problem that bubbles up from URIs. RDF has no built-in way to distinguish between resources that fail to be retrieved (such as a document on a downed server) and resources that can never be retrieved (such as the concept love). Topic maps, by explicitly distinguishing in their XML markup between addressable (that is, retrievable) and nonaddressable subjects, solves the identity problem.

Ontology

Ontology (like semantics) is another one of those words that, having been appropriated by the software community, has gained new meanings. In philosophy, ontology is the study of being; a formal account of what exists. For the Web, ontology combines taxonomy with inference rules. A taxonomy is a system that classifies things that exist, often in the form of a tree. For example, the taxonomy of the animal kingdom descends from order through kingdom, phylum, class, order, family, genus, and species. Because animals are classified on the basis of their physical characteristics, we make inferences: If all members of the genus fish have gills, and a trout is a fish, then trout have gills.

Ontologists also have a notion of an ontological commitment—that being the ontology we choose to make the basis of our inferences. For example, assume we must choose between a universe that is Euclidean, where the geometry of space is flat, and a universe that is Riemannian, where it is curved. This ontological commitment will affect our inferencing rules: If the universe is flat, parallel lines will never meet. If it is curved, parallel lines will meet.

Pragmatically, ontologies exist just so communities of interest can use them to share commitments. A large part of the library community, for example, has made an ontological commitment to the Dewey Decimal Classification (DDC).

However, the boundaries of the twin notions "taxonomy" and "inferencing rules" are just a bit fuzzy. After all, a DTD could be seen as a classification system for element types in markup languages, and a DTD enables inferencing rules for instances of those types in its content models. Even a URI can be viewed as a taxonomy of URLs, URCs, URNs, and so forth.

Fortunately, the W3C has formed an ontology working group, so we may hope for a more precise approach. This will be necessary for the Semantic Web, because without ontologies to allow communities of interest to agree formally on the meaning of XML namespaces, there is no possibility of creating meaning that machines can understand, because the predicates of RDF statements are implemented with namespaces.

Note

Here's the home page of the newly charted W3C ontology working group:

`http://www.w3.org/2001/sw/WebOnt/`

There are many existing ontologies the Semantic Web could leverage. Two of the most important are DDC and MeSH (Medical Subject Headings). There are also many meta-ontologies: ontology languages to create ontologies. Three of the most important are Cyc, Conceptual Graphs, and OIL. Let's look at these ontologies in detail. Next, we'll look at the meta-ontologies.

DDC

DDC is the numerical classification scheme that one sees on the spines of paper books in libraries. Of course, because DDC classifies the content of books, it could just as well be used online—for example, as an ontology in the Semantic Web.

Devised by Melvil Dewey in 1873, DDC uses a taxonomy of Arabic numerals separated by dots to create classifications based on subject matter. For example, 500 represents natural sciences and mathematics in general, 530 represents physics, and 531 classical mechanics. (The addressing system of the HyTime-compliant specification AECMA 1000D uses the same numbering principles, but for a taxonomy of part-whole relationships for aircraft assemblies and subassemblies.)

An interesting artifact of the numbering systems are that short numbers are higher in the taxonomic hierarchy than long ones, because the more specific the subject matter, the more digits are required to describe it. DDC therefore implies inferencing rules, as well as a taxonomy, and is therefore a first-class ontology.

Note

Here is the Web site for DDC:

`http://www.oclc.org/oclc/fp/index.htm`

MeSH

MeSH is an ontology, too, but organized quite differently from DDC. It is a controlled vocabulary thesaurus, where (as in the writer's tool *Roget's*) terms are associated with links such as synonym, antonym, homonym, and so forth. (Chapter 23 shows how such associations could be represented in RDF with the terms as nodes connected with labeled arcs: *True* and *false* would be two words connected by an arc labeled "antonym," for example.)

MeSH terms can be organized both alphabetically and in a conceptual hierarchy. In the former, *ankle* would follow *anatomy*; in the latter, *ankle* would be a narrower subject under the broader subject *anatomy*. Therefore, there are multiple points of entry into the MeSH ontology; this is a general characteristic of information overlays such as RDF and topic maps. Like DDC, MeSH's hierarchy implies inferencing rules, and MeSH is therefore a first-class ontology.

Conceptual Graphs

Conceptual Graphs (CG) is a language in which ontologies can be created. It uses graph structures to express meaning in a way that humans can read and machines can process. CGs are similar to RDF when considered as syntax, in that they can be represented both graphically and textually. Here is an example of CG syntax in text form:

```
[Go]-
 (Agnt)->[Person: Joe]
 (Dest)->[City: Manhattan]
 (Inst)->[Train].
```

The words in square brackets (`[Go]`)are concepts; the words in parentheses (`(Dest)`) are relations. Arcs that connect relations to concepts are shown as arrows (`->`). The preceding CG statement translates to "Joe is going to Manhattan by train." The essential concept—the verb—is `[Go]`; the individual `[person: Joe]` is an `(Agent)` that can perform actions such as `[Go]`ing to the individual `[City:Manhattan]` in an `(Inst)`rumental relation with a `[Train]`.

CG enables the definition of taxonomies in the form of relations between concepts. CG also supports inferencing rules in the form of First Order Logic (FOL), which we will briefly cover when we examine the next layer of the Semantic Web.

Note

Here is the Web site for CG:

`http://users.bestweb.net/~sowa/cg/index.htm`

Cyc

Cyc (pronounced *psych*), like CG, is an ontology and an ontology definition language, but its approach is completely different. Cyc intends to realize the artificial intelligence (AI) dream of enabling machines to use common-sense reasoning. However, instead of working from the top down (the classical AI approach), with the hierarchy's root and the axioms for inferencing rules, Cyc works from the bottom up. The Cyc project collects and formalizes common-sense rules (over one million so far) and allows common-sense conclusions to emerge from the interactions between the rules.

For example, a common sense rule is, "If it rains, take an umbrella." Or so it would seem. In fact, this rule can be heavily qualified by contextual rules, which also need to be entered. (For example, the rule presumes that the agent who may or may not take the umbrella is sane, not dead, not quadriplegic, not on the planet Venus, and so on.)

Fortunately, after 17 years of development, enough rules have been collected to allow Cyc to be productized and a significant portion of the rules base made public. It may be that Semantic Web developers will consider that this particular wheel need not be reinvented; if so, they will find Murray Altheim's XML version of Cyc a useful tool.

Note

Here's the Web site for Cyc:

`http://www.cyc.com`

Murray Altheim has translated the Upper Cyc ontology into XML syntax using XTM topic maps. Here is the site:

`http://www.doctypes.org/cyc/cyc-xtm-20010227.html`

OIL

Ontology Inferencing Layer (OIL) is our last ontology definition language. Rather than create an FOL-enabled syntax from the top down (like CG) or a vast inferencing system from the bottom up (like Cyc), OIL is a layer on top of the W3C RDF specification (see Chapter 23).

OIL (not yet a W3C effort, although cited there inherits concepts from three communities. First, the AI community supplies OIL with the notion of "*frames* with *slots*," or, in object-oriented (OO) terms, with classes that have attributes. Second, the knowledge representation community brings the notions of *concepts* and *roles* in description logic, which OIL maps to the notions of *classes* and *attributes*, respectively. Description logic (unlike the OO notation) has well-understood mathematical properties that enable inferencing rules. Finally, the markup technology community brings XML syntax and the RDF modeling primitives (`instanceOf` and `subClassOf`). OIL extends RDF to create a full-fledged modeling language.

Here is an example of OIL syntax:

```
class-def Book
slot-def Price
domain Product
class-def Janes Book
subclass-of Book
 slot-constraint PublishedBy
has-value "Janes Publisher"
```

This is a typical OO class hierarchy. Because Jane's book is a subclass of book, it inherits the properties of book (such as price). Whether the OO hierarchy is necessary or sufficient to create an ontology seems an open question: neither CG nor Cyc are considered OO technologies.

Note

Here is the Web site for OIL:

```
http://www.ontoknowledge.org/oil/
```

Logic

If RDF provides for a statement using a simple subject/object/predicate model, we can think of First Order Logic (FOL) in the Logic layer as enhancing RDF statements with richer syntax and more semantic power, within a world or universe of discourse specified by the ontological commitments made in the Ontological layer. (If our ontological commitment is to the DDC, we will reason from different premises than we would if our commitment was to MeSH, Cyc, or DAML.)

FOL statements are richer syntactically than RDF statements because they can use constructs that are like natural language conjunctions (Boolean operators, such as "and") and demonstratives (variables, such as "this"). FOL statements are more powerful because they can explicitly assert what is true—part or all of a world (the quantifiers, such as "there exists"). Other forms of logic may coexist with FOL on the Logic layer of the Semantic Web, but FOL provides a baseline functionality.

FOL typically uses a formal notation of its own (called *Peano notation*), but in this section, for accessibility, we'll just use English-like phrases in italic. For the existential quantifier ∃, for example, we will write the words *there exists*.

Briefly, here are the informal synthesis of the key concepts in FOL. We will elaborate the statement "Roses are red" in our examples.

The following concepts are defined by the user:

- *Constants.* Individuals in the world (resources, such as "rose").
- *Functions.* Mapping resource to resource (properties, such as "color-of(rose) = red").
- *Relations.* Mapping resources to truth values (true and false).

These concepts are supplied by FOL itself:

- *Variable symbols. x* and *y*.
- *Boolean values. True* and *false*.
- *Conjunction.* Rose is red, *and* violet is blue.

- *Disjunction*. Rose is red, *or* rose is yellow.
- *Negation*. Rose *is not* blue.
- *Inference*. *If* rose is red, *then* violet is blue.
- *Equivalence.* Rose is red *if and only if* sugar is sweet.

There are two kinds of quantifiers:

- *Universal. For all* x.
- *Existential. There is* an x.

FOL also has assembly rules building up sentences from terms and atoms:

1. A *term* (denoting a resource) is a constant symbol, a variable symbol, or a function of *n* terms.
2. An *atom* (which has a truth value) is either a relation of *n* terms or two atoms connected with *and* or *or.*
3. A *sentence* is an atom, or, if *S* is a sentence and *x* is a variable, then a sentence is preceded by an existential quantifier: *There exists* an *x* such that *x* is *S*. (Note that the existential quantifier implicitly apples only within our world.)

A well-formed formula (WFF) is a sentence with all variables "bound" by universal or existential quantifiers. For example, "*There is* a rose *such that* roses are red" has "rose" as a universally quantified variable, but not "red."

Notice that rules 1 through 3 are recursive: Terms are defined in terms of, well, terms, atoms in terms of atoms, and sentences in terms of sentences. We'll use this characteristic to break the following example into its components.

Now, why on earth would these rules matter to the Semantic Web? Let's take the sentence with which we began this chapter:

> Buy me a hard-cover copy of Jane's book, in Chinese, if available for less than $39.95.

This is a pretty complicated sentence, and a machine might well wish to break it down into its component parts. Those parts turn out to be easily expressible in FOL.

First, let's replace "Jane's book" with the variable *book* and make that variable explicit where the rules of English (unlike the rules of logic) allow it to be implicit:

> Buy me a hard-cover copy of *book*, in Chinese, if *book* is available for less than $39.95.

Now, because the definition of "sentence" is recursive, let's break this sentence down into sentences. The English is deceptive—it looks like we are saying "There is a hard-cover copy of book", but, in fact, because we can't buy the book if it doesn't exist, we'll translate the phrase to a relation, because a relation has a truth value. We'll also assign each sentence to a constant:

A := *book* (hard-cover)

B := *book* (Chinese)

X := *book* (available)

Y := *book* (price, < $39.95)

Now, because sentences are atoms, and atoms can be connected with Booleans, we can construct the following inference:

If ((A and B) and (X and Y)) then…

This means that we will purchase Jane's book only if it is available, in Chinese, in a hard-cover version, and at the right price. Notice that all the sentences can be easily represented by RDF statements (as shown in Chapter 23), but the FOL variables abstract away from the RDF syntax, which shows the layered design of the Semantic Web in action to a good effect.

But how to express the imperative "Buy me the book"? First, we need to make a little more explicit what is implicit. How would we represent the purchase? With the following sentence:

P := *book* (purchased)

Our sentence now reads like so:

If ((A and B) and (X and Y)) then P.

As it turns out, we have now represented a transaction in FOL. But as you know, an entire transaction has a truth value, because it takes place in the time between the "if" and "then": The last copy of Jane's book might be sold, in which case we would want to roll back the credit card purchase statement in P. Can we represent this in FOL? For convenience, we would put our transaction sentence into a variable:

T := if ((A and B) and (X and Y)) then P.

However, all we really need to do is assert:

T

Why? A sentence is an atom, and atoms have truth values. Therefore, if T is true, our Semantic Web–aware system should commit the transaction. Otherwise, it should not.

Note

An excellent resource for understanding the mathematical background of the technologies that enable the Semantic Web can be found at John Sowa's site:

http://users.bestweb.net/~sowa/misc/mathw.htm

Proof

The Logic layer provides a language for describing the truth or falsity of statements we might make in a universe of discourse. But suppose we want to question the conclusions of the Logic layer? We would get the Proof layer to expose the steps in the reasoning that led the Logic layer to make the inference it did. For example, the truth of the FOL relation

Book (Chinese)

might be proved by exhibiting the value "Mandarin" in the book title's XML `lang` attribute.

The vision is that once an XML-based interchange syntax for proofs is developed, Semantic Web users (whether machine or human) will begin to exchange proofs as well as to mix and match them—and in a process akin to evolutionary programming, good proofs will drive out bad ones.

If the Logic layer of the Semantic Web enters uncharted territory, the Proof layer enters the whitespace on the map. There are no W3C specifications in process for it. The closest implementation experiences to the Proof layer seem to fall into two disciplines:

- Formal methods for proving programs correct
- Automated theorem proving

Neither technology has gained broad acceptance, although both have been used with success on extremely large-scale projects. Automated theorem proving is used in hardware verification by chip manufacturers, for example.

Note

Here's a useful Web site on formal methods in software development:

http://www.afm.sbu.ac.uk/

Z (pronounced *zed*) is a well-known language for formal program specification based on set theory and FOL. Here's the Web site for Z:

http://www.afm.sbu.ac.uk/z/

Trust

If the Proof layer enters the whitespace of the Semantic Web's conceptual map, the Trust layer is deep within it. Remember, again, that the Logic layer provides a language for describing the truth or falsity about statements we might make in a universe of discourse. Suppose, again, that we don't trust the conclusions of the Logic layer, but we don't have the time or the inclination to run a proof. What to do? In the physical world, we might ask a friend whose judgment we trust whether she trusts the Logic layer to come to the right conclusion on the facts given to it. On the Semantic Web, we ask a network of friends the same question. This is the notion of a "web of trust."

Note

A site that shows the "web of trust" built by PGP (Pretty Good Privacy) users who have exchanged digital signatures can be found here:

`http://bcn.boulder.co.us/~neal/pgpstat/`

The Annotea project enables any resource to be annotated with comments, notes, reviews, warnings, cautions, notes, and so on in the form of an information overlay. The Annotea project will innovate web-of-trust Semantic Web applications by combining these annotations with XML digital signatures.

Here is the Web site for Annotea:

`http://www.w3.org/2001/Annotea/`

Digital Signatures

In the architecture of the Semantic Web, digital signatures are involved in the RDF and RDF Schema, Ontology, Logic, and Proof layers. Digital signatures are worthy of a book in their own right, so we will only briefly summarize them here. Thinking back to the example of purchasing Jane's book in Chinese, you would probably want the following assurances:

- That the publisher to whom you sent the price of the book was the real publisher and not some fly-by-night operation
- That the inferencing engine that told you the book was in pinyin was not a hacker
- That the shipping arrangements were made with a reputable shipper

The problem is the same in each case: the publisher, inferencing engine, and shipper need to be authenticated in some way. This is what digital signatures do. They are encrypted chunks of data with which Semantic Web users can verify that information comes from a trusted source. I, for example, can sign all my RDF statements with my signature so that people know these are my RDF statements and only mine.

There are some beginnings of digital signatures today, in the form of Always Trust Content check boxes from this or that manufacturer. in the web of trust, levels of trust will be gradated, so we can give 100 percent of our trust to a few friends in a web of trust, 1 percent of our trust to the statements of a denizen of a chat room, and other levels in between.

Here is the W3C site for digital signatures:

```
http://www.w3.org/Signature/
```

This site lists current and past versions of proposals and software that conforms to the specs.

Also, a wonderful science fiction novel on encryption issues, including digital signatures, is Neal Stephenson's *Cryptonomicon* (HarperCollins, 2000).

How Do Semantics Get into the Semantic Web?

No one would ever say that the Semantic Web is the world's largest artificial intelligence project—that would be political and marketing suicide. Nor would anyone ever point out that when the AI bubble burst, a lot of its practitioners moved into the field of bibliography, since bibliography involves building models of worlds, a project familiar to them, because a world view is one thing an AI would need in its "mind" to be or at least seem, well, "intelligent." Nor that both RDF and topic maps have their roots in building bibliographic worlds. Not even that many technologies in widespread use today (such as full-text search and semantic networks) started out as pieces in the great AI puzzle. So I will refrain from saying any of those things.

Nevertheless, I will say that the Semantic Web certainly partakes of the AI nature. Let's start with the notion that the fundamental value proposition of the Semantic Web is a conversation. Why? Because that is what a collection of statements (the RDF subject/predicate/object structure, or the topic map association) can be. Let's take our book order example once more:

> Buy me a hard-cover copy of Jane's book, in Chinese, if available for less than $39.95.

Remember that we translated this sentence into FOL, and you saw how a machine that understands FOL (as represented in RDF, for example) could act upon that logic to purchase Jane's book. (Because accurate machine translation of idiomatic English is a long way off, we'll assume that the human user communicated to the machine through an interface of some kind; for example, a GUI that assembles the FOL sentences, or an Englishized version of FOL syntax that users can just type in.)

Now suppose one of the FOL relations, such as

> *Book* (Chinese)

is not true. Now, the whole sentence is not true. What should the publisher do? One option, of course, would be to roll back the transaction and tell the customer to come back another day. A better option is for the publisher to have a smart Semantic Web–based system with additional relations in it. For example,

> script (Chinese, Traditional Characters)
> script (Chinese, Simplified Characters)

where traditional characters are Chinese ideographs, and the simplified characters are Chinese written using Latin characters, are both true. Therefore, when the original FOL constant, Chinese, is replaced by the constant Traditional Characters or Simplified Characters, the FOL statement representing the preconditions for the transaction becomes true and the transaction can proceed—or rather, it could, if the user authorizes it. The Semantic Web–based system tells the user the following information:

> Your book is not available in Chinese.
> Your book is available in Chinese traditional characters.
> Your book is available in Chinese simplified characters.

The system displays the books, and the user can add the books to her shopping cart in the usual way—or engage in further conversation with the system. (Topic maps have the potential for exactly the same sort of human/machine interaction; because humans are the ultimate arbiters of subject identity, any topic map system worth its salt must engage in conversation with the user whenever issues of subject identity come into question.)

The key concept is *conversation*. The user has stated something to the machine, the machine has responded to the user with more statements, and the cycle may persist indefinitely (like many conversations do). Naturally, I won't remind you here of a classic AI project, Eliza, where the machine imitated a not-very-insightful psychiatrist by parsing the user's input, transforming it, and writing it back out to the user.

User: I feel curiously oppressed, Doctor.

Eliza: Can you tell me what you mean by "oppressed"?

User: You're the doctor, why don't you tell me?

Eliza: Can you tell me what you mean by "why"?

And so on and so forth. Interestingly, some patients reported gaining relief from these "conversations." Most Eliza sites would be "sticky"—although a Freudian Eliza site, where the analyst is expected to be entirely silent, probably would not be.

Note

Topic maps have a community of interest devoted to ideas of conversation as applied to computer-assisted learning. Here's a good Web site for ideas on this subject:

`http://www.thinkalong.com`

And here's a good Web site to see practice in this area:

`http://www.CollegeUnits.com/courses.html`

The latter site represents knowledge in the form of a graph structure, reminiscent both of the RDF and topic map data models, and of John Sowa's conceptual graphs.

Now let's put the notion of conversation on hold for just a moment and ask the seemingly unrelated question, "What do we mean by semantic?" Some place semantics under the curse of the S-words, where words such as *syntax*, *semiotics*, *signify*, *sign* (as well as *standard* and specification) generate endless religious controversies about their true meaning. I prefer to use the markup community's definition of semantics:

Semantics is that upon which people do not agree.

Alternatively, one could use the programming community's definition:

Semantics is that which enables my program.

Then again, one could use the layperson's definition:

Semantics has to do with the meaning of words.

Markup/people; programs/machines. The cultural (if not, necessarily) technical dichotomies persist. The markup community's definition can at least be operational. But are there any factors that all the definitions have in common? Yes. It takes two to make semantics. This is equivalent to Wittgenstein's apothegm that there are no private languages. A word that I make up in my head, and use only in my head, can't be said to have meaning. It is also equivalent to saying that meaning, whatever it may be, can be found in conversations. (If the patient's conversations with Eliza had been without meaning, doubtless no placebo effect would have occurred.)

This concept locates both meaning and semantics in the conversations occurring on the Semantic Web; conversations over a network are what make the Web "semantic." Now, no one would ever say that this means that the Semantic Web, if successful, would be a large-scale implementation of AI. That's science fiction stuff, probably wrong, and certainly suicidal from a professional standpoint. So, I won't say that the famous Turing Test boils down to having a conversation, and if we can have conversations with Semantic Web–enabled machines, then they (and we, for that matter) have passed the Turing Test.

Granted, Turing's imitation game is still pretty easy for a human to win; one simply poses a question whose answer would be "obvious" to a human but not to a machine: The conversation breaks down because the bounds of the machine's microworld overflow, and the machine fails to imitate a human successfully. The way to avoid any therapeutic benefit from a conversation with Eliza is to feed Eliza gibberish. Garbage in, garbage out applies to machines, although not necessarily to humans. And humans have all kinds of garbage readily available for conversation, including lies, jokes, irony, paradox, rhetoric, and everything represented by the S-words.

Nevertheless, to say that the machines of the Semantic Web won't be able to have every kind of conversation with humans is not to say that their conversations with us (and with each other) will not be meaningful, or that the Semantic Web fails the Turing Test definitively. (In fact, I never said it took the test, because that would have involved mentioning AI.) After all, there are people who cannot—cannot because their brain structure does not permit them to do so—appreciate jokes, irony, paradox, or rhetoric. They might fail the Turing Test. Are their conversations therefore not meaningful? Are they then not fully human?

Note

Alan Turing's original article on the Turing Test (or the *Imitation Game*) can be found at the following Web site:

`http://cogprints.soton.ac.uk/abs/comp/199807017`

For an interesting discussion of a highly intelligent human who might not play the Imitation Game successfully, see Temple Grandin's *Thinking in Pictures and Other Reports from My Life with Autism* (Doubleday, 1995.)

Searle's "Chinese Room Argument" is a refutation of the Turing Test:

`http://www.cogsci.soton.ac.uk/bbs/Archive/bbs.searle2.html`

Summary

So, you've seen the historical precursors of the Semantic Web, each of which implemented the standard bibliographic model: the doomed but valiant Project Xanadu as well as the vilified but influential ISO standard HyTime.

We've looked at the seven layers in the Semantic Web. It's more-fragile-than-we-think foundations in URIs and Unicode, and the problems those foundational technologies cause for higher layers, in terms of internationalization and identity. We've looked at ontologies, where users select the vocabularies in which they will make ontological commitments and converse with the Semantic Web. We've looked at how logic will determine the truth value of statements made using those vocabularies. We've seen how the Proof layer will empower users to check the results of the Logic layer.

Finally, we've seen how humans (and machines) can build a web of trust so that the laborious processes of logic and proof can be replaced with a little help from our friends—machine or human. This is the conversation that humans and machines can have: the Semantic Web.

Appendix

PART V

IN THIS PART

Extensible Markup Language (XML) 1.0 (Second Edition) Specification

In This Appendix

This appendix is taken from the W3C Recommendation 6 October 2000 that is available at `http://www.w3.org/TR/REC-xml`.

Previous versions:

`http://www.w3.org/TR/2000/WD-xml-2e-20000814`

`http://www.w3.org/TR/1998/REC-xml-19980210`

Editors:

Tim Bray, Textuality and Netscape <tbray@textuality.com>

Jean Paoli, Microsoft <jeanpa@microsoft.com>

C. M. Sperberg-McQueen, University of Illinois at Chicago and Text Encoding Initiative <cmsmcq@uic.edu>

Eve Maler, Sun Microsystems, Inc. <eve.maler@east.sun.com> - Second Edition

Copyright Notice

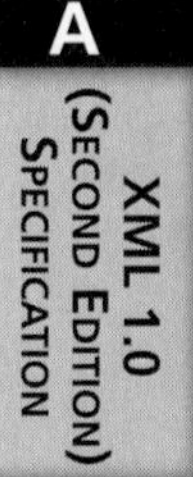

Abstract

The Extensible Markup Language (XML) is a subset of SGML that is completely described in this document. Its goal is to enable generic SGML to be served, received, and processed on the Web in the way that is now possible with HTML. XML has been designed for ease of implementation and for interoperability with both SGML and HTML.

Status of This Document

This document has been reviewed by W3C Members and other interested parties and has been endorsed by the Director as a W3C Recommendation. It is a stable document and may be used as reference material or cited as a normative reference from another document. W3C's role in making the Recommendation is to draw attention to the specification and to promote its widespread deployment. This enhances the functionality and interoperability of the Web.

This document specifies a syntax created by subsetting an existing, widely used international text processing standard (Standard Generalized Markup Language, ISO 8879:1986 as amended and corrected) for use on the World Wide Web. It is a product of the W3C XML Activity, details of which can be found at `http://www.w3.org/XML`. The English version of this specification is the only normative version. However, for translations of this document, see `http://www.w3.org/XML/#trans`. A list of current W3C Recommendations and other technical documents can be found at `http://www.w3.org/TR`.

This second edition is not a new version of XML (first published 10 February 1998); it merely incorporates the changes dictated by the first-edition errata (available at `http://www.w3.org/XML/xml-19980210-errata`) as a convenience to readers. The errata list for this second edition is available at `http://www.w3.org/XML/xml-V10-2e-errata`.

Please report errors in this document to `xml-editor@w3.org`; archives are available.

Note

C. M. Sperberg-McQueen's affiliation has changed since the publication of the first edition. He is now at the World Wide Web Consortium, and can be contacted at `cmsmcq@w3.org`.

Table of Contents

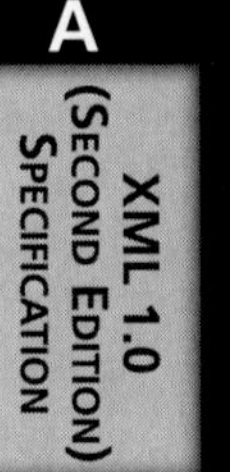
A
XML 1.0
(SECOND EDITION)
SPECIFICATION

Appendices

1 Introduction

Extensible Markup Language, abbreviated XML, describes a class of data objects called XML documents and partially describes the behavior of computer programs which process them. XML is an application profile or restricted form of SGML, the Standard Generalized Markup Language [ISO 8879]. By construction, XML documents are conforming SGML documents.

XML documents are made up of storage units called entities, which contain either parsed or unparsed data. Parsed data is made up of characters, some of which form character data, and some of which form markup. Markup encodes a description of the document's storage layout and logical structure. XML provides a mechanism to impose constraints on the storage layout and logical structure.

[Definition: A software module called an XML processor is used to read XML documents and provide access to their content and structure.] [Definition: It is assumed that an XML processor is doing its work on behalf of another module, called the application.] This specification describes the required behavior of an XML processor in terms of how it must read XML data and the information it must provide to the application.

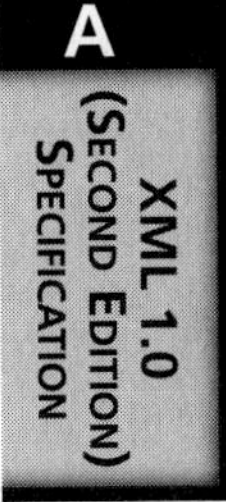

1.1 Origin and Goals

XML was developed by an XML Working Group (originally known as the SGML Editorial Review Board) formed under the auspices of the World Wide Web Consortium (W3C) in 1996. It was chaired by Jon Bosak of Sun Microsystems with the active participation of an XML Special Interest Group (previously known as the SGML Working Group) also organized by the W3C. The membership of the XML Working Group is given in an appendix. Dan Connolly served as the WG's contact with the W3C.

The design goals for XML are:

- XML shall be straightforwardly usable over the Internet.
- XML shall support a wide variety of applications.
- XML shall be compatible with SGML.
- It shall be easy to write programs which process XML documents.
- The number of optional features in XML is to be kept to the absolute minimum, ideally zero.
- XML documents should be human-legible and reasonably clear.
- The XML design should be prepared quickly.
- The design of XML shall be formal and concise.
- XML documents shall be easy to create.
- Terseness in XML markup is of minimal importance.

This specification, together with associated standards (Unicode and ISO/IEC 10646 for characters, Internet RFC 1766 for language identification tags, ISO 639 for language name codes, and ISO 3166 for country name codes), provides all the information necessary to understand XML Version 1.0 and construct computer programs to process it.

This version of the XML specification may be distributed freely, as long as all text and legal notices remain intact.

1.2 Terminology

The terminology used to describe XML documents is defined in the body of this specification. The terms defined in the following list are used in building those definitions and in describing the actions of an XML processor:

may

[Definition: Conforming documents and XML processors are permitted to but need not behave as described.]

must

[Definition: Conforming documents and XML processors are required to behave as described; otherwise they are in error.]

error

[Definition: A violation of the rules of this specification; results are undefined. Conforming software may detect and report an error and may recover from it.]

fatal error

[Definition: An error which a conforming XML processor must detect and report to the application. After encountering a fatal error, the processor may continue processing the data to search for further errors and may report such errors to the application. In order to support correction of errors, the processor may make unprocessed data from the document (with intermingled character data and markup) available to the application. Once a fatal error is detected, however, the processor must not continue normal processing (i.e., it must not continue to pass character data and information about the document's logical structure to the application in the normal way).]

at user option

[Definition: Conforming software may or must (depending on the modal verb in the sentence) behave as described; if it does, it must provide users a means to enable or disable the behavior described.]

validity constraint

[Definition: A rule which applies to all valid XML documents. Violations of validity constraints are errors; they must, at user option, be reported by validating XML processors.]

well-formedness constraint

[Definition: A rule which applies to all well-formed XML documents. Violations of well-formedness constraints are fatal errors.]

match

[Definition: (Of strings or names:) Two strings or names being compared must be identical. Characters with multiple possible representations in ISO/IEC 10646 (e.g. characters with both precomposed and base+diacritic forms) match only if they have the same representation in both strings. No case folding is performed. (Of strings and rules in the grammar:) A string matches a grammatical production if it belongs to the language generated by that production. (Of content and content models:) An element matches its declaration when it conforms in the fashion described in the constraint [VC: Element Valid].]

for compatibility

[Definition: Marks a sentence describing a feature of XML included solely to ensure that XML remains compatible with SGML.]

for interoperability

[Definition: Marks a sentence describing a non-binding recommendation included to increase the chances that XML documents can be processed by the existing installed base of SGML processors which predate the WebSGML Adaptations Annex to ISO 8879.]

2 Documents

[Definition: A data object is an XML document if it is well-formed, as defined in this specification. A well-formed XML document may in addition be valid if it meets certain further constraints.]

Each XML document has both a logical and a physical structure. Physically, the document is composed of units called entities. An entity may refer to other entities to cause their inclusion in the document. A document begins in a "root" or document entity. Logically, the document is composed of declarations, elements, comments, character references, and processing instructions, all of which are indicated in the document by explicit markup. The logical and physical structures must nest properly, as described in 4.3.2 Well-Formed Parsed Entities.

2.1 Well-Formed XML Documents

[Definition: A textual object is a well-formed XML document if:]

- Taken as a whole, it matches the production labeled document.
- It meets all the well-formedness constraints given in this specification.
- Each of the parsed entities which is referenced directly or indirectly within the document is well-formed.

Document

```
[1]    document    ::=    prolog element Misc*
```

Matching the document production implies that:

- It contains one or more elements.
- [Definition: There is exactly one element, called the root, or document element, no part of which appears in the content of any other element.] For all other elements, if the start-tag is in the content of another element, the end-tag is in the content of the same element. More simply stated, the elements, delimited by start- and end-tags, nest properly within each other.
- [Definition: As a consequence of this, for each non-root element C in the document, there is one other element P in the document such that C is in the content of P, but is not in the content of any other element that is in the content of P. P is referred to as the parent of C, and C as a child of P.]

2.2 Characters

[Definition: A parsed entity contains text, a sequence of characters, which may represent markup or character data.] [Definition: A character is an atomic unit of text as specified by ISO/IEC 10646 [ISO/IEC 10646] (see also [ISO/IEC 10646-2000]). Legal characters are tab, carriage return, line feed, and the legal characters of Unicode and ISO/IEC 10646. The versions of these standards cited in A.1 Normative References were current at the time this document was prepared. New characters may be added to these standards by amendments or new editions. Consequently, XML processors must accept any character in the range specified for Char. The use of "compatibility characters", as defined in section 6.8 of [Unicode] (see also D21 in section 3.6 of [Unicode3]), is discouraged.]

Character Range

```
[2]     Char    ::=     #x9 | #xA | #xD | [#x20-#xD7FF] | [#xE000-#xFFFD] |
➥[#x10000-#x10FFFF] /* any Unicode character, excluding the surrogate blocks,
FFFE, and FFFF. */
```

The mechanism for encoding character code points into bit patterns may vary from entity to entity. All XML processors must accept the UTF-8 and UTF-16 encodings of 10646; the mechanisms for signaling which of the two is in use, or for bringing other encodings into play, are discussed later, in 4.3.3 Character Encoding in Entities.

2.3 Common Syntactic Constructs

This section defines some symbols used widely in the grammar.

S (white space) consists of one or more space (#x20) characters, carriage returns, line feeds, or tabs.

White Space

```
[3]    S    ::=    (#x20 | #x9 | #xD | #xA)+
```

Characters are classified for convenience as letters, digits, or other characters. A letter consists of an alphabetic or syllabic base character or an ideographic character. Full definitions of the specific characters in each class are given in B Character Classes.

[Definition: A Name is a token beginning with a letter or one of a few punctuation characters, and continuing with letters, digits, hyphens, underscores, colons, or full stops, together known as name characters.] Names beginning with the string "xml", or any string which would match (('X'|'x') ('M'|'m') ('L'|'l')), are reserved for standardization in this or future versions of this specification.

Note

The Namespaces in XML Recommendation [XML Names] assigns a meaning to names containing colon characters. Therefore, authors should not use the colon in XML names except for namespace purposes, but XML processors must accept the colon as a name character.

An Nmtoken (name token) is any mixture of name characters.

Names and Tokens

```
[4]    NameChar    ::=    Letter | Digit | '.' | '-' | '_' | ':' | CombiningChar
➥| Extender
[5]    Name    ::=    (Letter | '_' | ':') (NameChar)*
[6]    Names    ::=    Name (S Name)*
[7]    Nmtoken    ::=    (NameChar)+
[8]    Nmtokens    ::=    Nmtoken (S Nmtoken)*
```

Literal data is any quoted string not containing the quotation mark used as a delimiter for that string. Literals are used for specifying the content of internal entities (EntityValue), the values of attributes (AttValue), and external identifiers (SystemLiteral). Note that a SystemLiteral can be parsed without scanning for markup.

Literals

```
[9]    EntityValue    ::=    '"' ([^%&"] | PEReference | Reference)* '"'
➥|  "'" ([^%&'] | PEReference | Reference)* "'"
[10]    AttValue    ::=    '"' ([^<&"] | Reference)* '"'
|  "'" ([^<&'] | Reference)* "'"
```

```
[11]    SystemLiteral    ::=    ('"' [^"]* '"') | ("'" [^']* "'")
[12]    PubidLiteral    ::=    '"' PubidChar* '"' | "'" (PubidChar - "'")* "'"
[13]    PubidChar    ::=    #x20 | #xD | #xA | [a-zA-Z0-9] | [-
➥'()+,./:=?;!*#@$_%]
```

Note

Although the EntityValue production allows the definition of an entity consisting of a single explicit < in the literal (e.g., <!ENTITY mylt "<">), it is strongly advised to avoid this practice since any reference to that entity will cause a well-formedness error.

2.4 Character Data and Markup

Text consists of intermingled character data and markup. [Definition: Markup takes the form of start-tags, end-tags, empty-element tags, entity references, character references, comments, CDATA section delimiters, document type declarations, processing instructions, XML declarations, text declarations, and any white space that is at the top level of the document entity (that is, outside the document element and not inside any other markup).]

[Definition: All text that is not markup constitutes the character data of the document.]

The ampersand character (&) and the left angle bracket (<) may appear in their literal form only when used as markup delimiters, or within a comment, a processing instruction, or a CDATA section. If they are needed elsewhere, they must be escaped using either numeric character references or the strings "&" and "<" respectively. The right angle bracket (>) may be represented using the string ">", and must, for compatibility, be escaped using ">" or a character reference when it appears in the string "]]>" in content, when that string is not marking the end of a CDATA section.

In the content of elements, character data is any string of characters which does not contain the start-delimiter of any markup. In a CDATA section, character data is any string of characters not including the CDATA-section-close delimiter, "]]>".

To allow attribute values to contain both single and double quotes, the apostrophe or single-quote character (') may be represented as "'", and the double-quote character (") as """.

Character Data

```
[14]    CharData    ::=    [^<&]* - ([^<&]* ']]>' [^<&]*)
```

2.5 Comments

[Definition: Comments may appear anywhere in a document outside other markup; in addition, they may appear within the document type declaration at places allowed by the grammar. They are not part of the document's character data; an XML processor may, but need not, make it possible for an application to retrieve the text of comments. For compatibility, the string "—" (double-hyphen) must not occur within comments.] Parameter entity references are not recognized within comments.

Comments

```
[15]    Comment    ::=    '<!--' ((Char - '-') | ('-' (Char - '-')))* '-->'
```

An example of a comment:

```
<!-- declarations for <head> & <body> -->
```

Note

Note that the grammar does not allow a comment ending in —>. The following example is not well-formed.

```
<!-- B+, B, or B--->
```

2.6 Processing Instructions

[Definition: Processing instructions (PIs) allow documents to contain instructions for applications.]

Processing Instructions

```
[16]    PI    ::=    '<?' PITarget (S (Char* - (Char* '?>' Char*)))? '?>'
[17]    PITarget    ::=    Name - (('X' | 'x') ('M' | 'm') ('L' | 'l'))
```

PIs are not part of the document's character data, but must be passed through to the application. The PI begins with a target (PITarget) used to identify the application to which the instruction is directed. The target names "XML", "xml", and so on are reserved for standardization in this or future versions of this specification. The XML

Notation mechanism may be used for formal declaration of PI targets. Parameter entity references are not recognized within processing instructions.

2.7 CDATA Sections

[Definition: CDATA sections may occur anywhere character data may occur; they are used to escape blocks of text containing characters which would otherwise be recognized as markup. CDATA sections begin with the string "<![CDATA[" and end with the string "]]>":]

CDATA Sections

```
[18]    CDSect    ::=    CDStart CData CDEnd
[19]    CDStart    ::=    '<![CDATA['
[20]    CData    ::=    (Char* - (Char* ']]>' Char*))
[21]    CDEnd    ::=    ']]>'
```

Within a CDATA section, only the CDEnd string is recognized as markup, so that left angle brackets and ampersands may occur in their literal form; they need not (and cannot) be escaped using "<" and "&". CDATA sections cannot nest.

An example of a CDATA section, in which "<greeting>" and "</greeting>" are recognized as character data, not markup:

```
<![CDATA[<greeting>Hello, world!</greeting>]]>
```

2.8 Prolog and Document Type Declaration

[Definition: XML documents should begin with an XML declaration which specifies the version of XML being used.] For example, the following is a complete XML document, well-formed but not valid:

```
<?xml version="1.0"?> <greeting>Hello, world!</greeting>
```

and so is this:

```
<greeting>Hello, world!</greeting>
```

The version number "1.0" should be used to indicate conformance to this version of this specification; it is an error for a document to use the value "1.0" if it does not conform to this version of this specification. It is the intent of the XML working group to give later versions of this specification numbers other than "1.0", but this intent does not indicate a commitment to produce any future versions of XML, nor if any are produced, to use any particular numbering scheme. Since future versions are not ruled out, this construct is provided as a means to allow the possibility of automatic version recognition, should it become necessary. Processors may signal an error if they receive documents labeled with versions they do not support.

The function of the markup in an XML document is to describe its storage and logical structure and to associate attribute-value pairs with its logical structures. XML provides a mechanism, the document type declaration, to define constraints on the logical structure and to support the use of predefined storage units. [Definition: An XML document is valid if it has an associated document type declaration and if the document complies with the constraints expressed in it.]

The document type declaration must appear before the first element in the document.

Prolog

```
[22]    prolog    ::=    XMLDecl? Misc* (doctypedecl Misc*)?
[23]    XMLDecl    ::=    '<?xml' VersionInfo EncodingDecl? SDDecl? S? '?>'
[24]    VersionInfo    ::=    S 'version' Eq ("'" VersionNum "'" | '"'
➥VersionNum '"')/* */
[25]    Eq    ::=    S? '=' S?
[26]    VersionNum    ::=    ([a-zA-Z0-9_.:] | '-')+
[27]    Misc    ::=    Comment | PI | S
```

[Definition: The XML document type declaration contains or points to markup declarations that provide a grammar for a class of documents. This grammar is known as a document type definition, or DTD. The document type declaration can point to an external subset (a special kind of external entity) containing markup declarations, or can contain the markup declarations directly in an internal subset, or can do both. The DTD for a document consists of both subsets taken together.]

[Definition: A markup declaration is an element type declaration, an attribute-list declaration, an entity declaration, or a notation declaration.] These declarations may be contained in whole or in part within parameter entities, as described in the well-formedness and validity constraints below. For further information, see 4 Physical Structures.

Document Type Definition

```
[28]    doctypedecl    ::=    '<!DOCTYPE' S Name (S ExternalID)? S?
('[' (markupdecl | DeclSep)* ']' S?)? '>' [VC: Root Element Type]
                                    [WFC: External Subset]
                                    /* */
[28a]    DeclSep    ::=    PEReference | S [WFC: PE Between Declarations]
                                    /* */
[29]    markupdecl    ::=    elementdecl | AttlistDecl | EntityDecl |
NotationDecl | PI | Comment  [VC: Proper Declaration/PE Nesting]
                                [WFC: PEs in Internal Subset]
```

Note that it is possible to construct a well-formed document containing a doctypedecl that neither points to an external subset nor contains an internal subset.

The markup declarations may be made up in whole or in part of the replacement text of parameter entities. The productions later in this specification for individual nonterminals (elementdecl, AttlistDecl, and so on) describe the declarations after all the parameter entities have been included.

Parameter entity references are recognized anywhere in the DTD (internal and external subsets and external parameter entities), except in literals, processing instructions, comments, and the contents of ignored conditional sections (see 3.4 Conditional Sections). They are also recognized in entity value literals. The use of parameter entities in the internal subset is restricted as described below.

Validity constraint: Root Element Type

The Name in the document type declaration must match the element type of the root element.

Validity constraint: Proper Declaration/PE Nesting

Parameter-entity replacement text must be properly nested with markup declarations. That is to say, if either the first character or the last character of a markup declaration (markupdecl above) is contained in the replacement text for a parameter-entity reference, both must be contained in the same replacement text.

Well-formedness constraint: PEs in Internal Subset

In the internal DTD subset, parameter-entity references can occur only where markup declarations can occur, not within markup declarations. (This does not apply to references that occur in external parameter entities or to the external subset.)

Well-formedness constraint: External Subset

The external subset, if any, must match the production for extSubset.

Well-formedness constraint: PE Between Declarations

The replacement text of a parameter entity reference in a DeclSep must match the production extSubsetDecl.

Like the internal subset, the external subset and any external parameter entities referenced in a DeclSep must consist of a series of complete markup declarations of the types allowed by the non-terminal symbol markupdecl, interspersed with white space or parameter-entity references. However, portions of the contents of the external subset or of these external parameter entities may conditionally be ignored by using the conditional section construct; this is not allowed in the internal subset.

External Subset

```
[30]    extSubset     ::=    TextDecl? extSubsetDecl
[31]    extSubsetDecl    ::=    ( markupdecl | conditionalSect | DeclSep)* /* */
```

The external subset and external parameter entities also differ from the internal subset in that in them, parameter-entity references are permitted within markup declarations, not only between markup declarations.

An example of an XML document with a document type declaration:

```
<?xml version="1.0"?> <!DOCTYPE greeting SYSTEM "hello.dtd"> <greeting>Hello,
world!</greeting>
```

The system identifier "hello.dtd" gives the address (a URI reference) of a DTD for the document.

The declarations can also be given locally, as in this example:

```
<?xml version="1.0" encoding="UTF-8" ?>
<!DOCTYPE greeting [
  <!ELEMENT greeting (#PCDATA)>
]>
<greeting>Hello, world!</greeting>
```

If both the external and internal subsets are used, the internal subset is considered to occur before the external subset. This has the effect that entity and attribute-list declarations in the internal subset take precedence over those in the external subset.

2.9 Standalone Document Declaration

Markup declarations can affect the content of the document, as passed from an XML processor to an application; examples are attribute defaults and entity declarations. The standalone document declaration, which may appear as a component of the XML declaration, signals whether or not there are such declarations which appear external to the document entity or in parameter entities. [Definition: An external markup declaration is defined as a markup declaration occurring in the external subset or in a parameter entity (external or internal, the latter being included because non-validating processors are not required to read them).]

Standalone Document Declaration

```
[32]    SDDecl    ::=    S 'standalone' Eq (("'" ('yes' | 'no') "'") | ('"'
('yes' | 'no')
➥'"'))  [VC:Standalone Document Declaration]
```

In a standalone document declaration, the value "yes" indicates that there are no external markup declarations which affect the information passed from the XML processor to the application. The value "no" indicates that there are or may be such external markup declarations. Note that the standalone document declaration only denotes the presence of external declarations; the presence, in a document, of references to external entities, when those entities are internally declared, does not change its standalone status.

If there are no external markup declarations, the standalone document declaration has no meaning. If there are external markup declarations but there is no standalone document declaration, the value "no" is assumed.

Any XML document for which standalone="no" holds can be converted algorithmically to a standalone document, which may be desirable for some network delivery applications.

Validity constraint: Standalone Document Declaration

The standalone document declaration must have the value "no" if any external markup declarations contain declarations of:

- attributes with default values, if elements to which these attributes apply appear in the document without specifications of values for these attributes, or
- entities (other than amp, lt, gt, apos, quot), if references to those entities appear in the document, or
- attributes with values subject to normalization, where the attribute appears in the document with a value which will change as a result of normalization, or
- element types with element content, if white space occurs directly within any instance of those types.

An example XML declaration with a standalone document declaration:

```
<?xml version="1.0" standalone='yes'?>
```

2.10 White Space Handling

In editing XML documents, it is often convenient to use "white space" (spaces, tabs, and blank lines) to set apart the markup for greater readability. Such white space is typically not intended for inclusion in the delivered version of the document. On the other hand, "significant" white space that should be preserved in the delivered version is common, for example in poetry and source code.

An XML processor must always pass all characters in a document that are not markup through to the application. A validating XML processor must also inform the application which of these characters constitute white space appearing in element content.

A special attribute named xml:space may be attached to an element to signal an intention that in that element, white space should be preserved by applications. In valid documents, this attribute, like any other, must be declared if it is used. When declared, it must be given as an enumerated type whose values are one or both of "default" and "preserve". For example:

```
<!ATTLIST poem  xml:space (default|preserve) 'preserve'>

<!-- -->
<!ATTLIST pre xml:space (preserve) #FIXED 'preserve'>
```

The value "default" signals that applications' default white-space processing modes are acceptable for this element; the value "preserve" indicates the intent that applications preserve all the white space. This declared intent is considered to apply to all elements within the content of the element where it is specified, unless overriden with another instance of the xml:space attribute.

The root element of any document is considered to have signaled no intentions as regards application space handling, unless it provides a value for this attribute or the attribute is declared with a default value.

2.11 End-of-Line Handling

XML parsed entities are often stored in computer files which, for editing convenience, are organized into lines. These lines are typically separated by some combination of the characters carriage-return (#xD) and line-feed (#xA).

To simplify the tasks of applications, the characters passed to an application by the XML processor must be as if the XML processor normalized all line breaks in external parsed entities (including the document entity) on input, before parsing, by translating both the two-character sequence #xD #xA and any #xD that is not followed by #xA to a single #xA character.

2.12 Language Identification

In document processing, it is often useful to identify the natural or formal language in which the content is written. A special attribute named xml:lang may be inserted in documents to specify the language used in the contents and attribute values of any element in an XML document. In valid documents, this attribute, like any other, must be declared if it is used. The values of the attribute are language identifiers as defined by [IETF RFC 1766], Tags for the Identification of Languages, or its successor on the IETF Standards Track.

Note

[IETF RFC 1766] tags are constructed from two-letter language codes as defined by [ISO 639], from two-letter country codes as defined by [ISO 3166], or from language identifiers registered with the Internet Assigned Numbers Authority [IANA-LANGCODES]. It is expected that the successor to [IETF RFC 1766] will introduce three-letter language codes for languages not presently covered by [ISO 639].

Warning

(Productions 33 through 38 have been removed.)

For example:

```
<p xml:lang="en">The quick brown fox jumps over the lazy dog.</p>
<p xml:lang="en-GB">What colour is it?</p>
<p xml:lang="en-US">What color is it?</p>
<sp who="Faust" desc='leise' xml:lang="de">
  <l>Habe nun, ach! Philosophie,</l>
  <l>Juristerei, und Medizin</l>
  <l>und leider auch Theologie</l>
  <l>durchaus studiert mit heißem Bemüh'n.</l>
</sp>
```

The intent declared with xml:lang is considered to apply to all attributes and content of the element where it is specified, unless overridden with an instance of xml:lang on another element within that content.

A simple declaration for xml:lang might take the form

```
xml:lang NMTOKEN #IMPLIED
```

but specific default values may also be given, if appropriate. In a collection of French poems for English students, with glosses and notes in English, the xml:lang attribute might be declared this way:

```
<!ATTLIST poem   xml:lang NMTOKEN 'fr'>
<!ATTLIST gloss  xml:lang NMTOKEN 'en'>
<!ATTLIST note   xml:lang NMTOKEN 'en'>
```

3 Logical Structures

[Definition: Each XML document contains one or more elements, the boundaries of which are either delimited by start-tags and end-tags, or, for empty elements, by an empty-element tag. Each element has a type, identified by name, sometimes called its "generic identifier" (GI), and may have a set of attribute specifications.] Each attribute specification has a name and a value.

Element

```
[39]    element    ::=    EmptyElemTag
   | STag content ETag [WFC: Element Type Match]
    [VC: Element Valid]
```

This specification does not constrain the semantics, use, or (beyond syntax) names of the element types and attributes, except that names beginning with a match to `(('X'|'x')('M'|'m')('L'|'l'))` are reserved for standardization in this or future versions of this specification.

Well-formedness constraint: Element Type Match

The Name in an element's end-tag must match the element type in the start-tag.

Validity constraint: Element Valid

An element is valid if there is a declaration matching elementdecl where the Name matches the element type, and one of the following holds:

- The declaration matches EMPTY and the element has no content.
- The declaration matches children and the sequence of child elements belongs to the language generated by the regular expression in the content model, with optional white space (characters matching the nonterminal S) between the start-tag and the first child element, between child elements, or between the last child element and the end-tag. Note that a CDATA section containing only white space does not match the nonterminal S, and hence cannot appear in these positions.
- The declaration matches Mixed and the content consists of character data and child elements whose types match names in the content model.
- The declaration matches ANY, and the types of any child elements have been declared.

3.1 Start-Tags, End-Tags, and Empty-Element Tags

[Definition: The beginning of every non-empty XML element is marked by a start-tag.]

Start-tag

```
[40]    STag    ::=    '<' Name (S Attribute)* S? '>' [WFC: Unique Att Spec]
[41]    Attribute    ::=    Name Eq AttValue [VC: Attribute Value Type]
    [WFC: No External Entity References]
    [WFC: No < in Attribute Values]
```

The Name in the start- and end-tags gives the element's type. [Definition: The Name-AttValue pairs are referred to as the attribute specifications of the element], [Definition: with the Name in each pair referred to as the attribute name] and [Definition: the content of the AttValue (the text between the ' or " delimiters) as the attribute value.]Note that the order of attribute specifications in a start-tag or empty-element tag is not significant.

Well-formedness constraint: Unique Att Spec

No attribute name may appear more than once in the same start-tag or empty-element tag.

Validity constraint: Attribute Value Type

The attribute must have been declared; the value must be of the type declared for it. (For attribute types, see 3.3 Attribute-List Declarations.)

Well-formedness constraint: No External Entity References

Attribute values cannot contain direct or indirect entity references to external entities.

Well-formedness constraint: No < in Attribute Values

The replacement text of any entity referred to directly or indirectly in an attribute value must not contain a <.

An example of a start-tag:

```
<termdef id="dt-dog" term="dog">
```

[Definition: The end of every element that begins with a start-tag must be marked by an end-tag containing a name that echoes the element's type as given in the start-tag:]

End-tag

```
[42]    ETag    ::=    '</' Name S? '>'
```

An example of an end-tag:

```
</termdef>
```

[Definition: The text between the start-tag and end-tag is called the element's content:]

Content of Elements

```
[43]    content    ::=    CharData? ((element | Reference | CDSect | PI |
➥Comment) CharData?)* /* */
```

[Definition: An element with no content is said to be empty.] The representation of an empty element is either a start-tag immediately followed by an end-tag, or an empty-element tag. [Definition: An empty-element tag takes a special form:]

Tags for Empty Elements

```
[44]    EmptyElemTag    ::=    '<' Name (S Attribute)* S? '/>' [WFC: Unique Att
➥Spec]
```

Empty-element tags may be used for any element which has no content, whether or not it is declared using the keyword EMPTY. For interoperability, the empty-element tag should be used, and should only be used, for elements which are declared EMPTY.

Examples of empty elements:

```
<IMG align="left"
 src="http://www.w3.org/Icons/WWW/w3c_home" />
<br></br>
<br/>
```

3.2 Element Type Declarations

The element structure of an XML document may, for validation purposes, be constrained using element type and attribute-list declarations. An element type declaration constrains the element's content.

Element type declarations often constrain which element types can appear as children of the element. At user option, an XML processor may issue a warning when a declaration mentions an element type for which no declaration is provided, but this is not an error.

[Definition: An element type declaration takes the form:]

Element Type Declaration

```
[45]    elementdecl    ::=    '<!ELEMENT' S Name S contentspec S? '>' [VC:
Unique Element Type Declaration]
[46]    contentspec    ::=    'EMPTY' | 'ANY' | Mixed | children
```

where the Name gives the element type being declared.

Validity constraint: Unique Element Type Declaration

No element type may be declared more than once.

Examples of element type declarations:

```
<!ELEMENT br EMPTY>
<!ELEMENT p (#PCDATA|emph)* >
<!ELEMENT %name.para; %content.para; >
<!ELEMENT container ANY>
```

3.2.1 Element Content

[Definition: An element type has element content when elements of that type must contain only child elements (no character data), optionally separated by white space (characters matching the nonterminal S).][Definition: In this case, the constraint includes a content model, a simple grammar governing the allowed types of the child elements and the order in which they are allowed to appear.] The grammar is built on content particles (cps), which consist of names, choice lists of content particles, or sequence lists of content particles:

Element-content Models

```
[47]    children    ::=    (choice | seq) ('?' | '*' | '+')?
[48]    cp    ::=    (Name | choice | seq) ('?' | '*' | '+')?
[49]    choice    ::=    '(' S? cp ( S? '|' S? cp )+ S? ')' /* */
    /* */
    [VC: Proper Group/PE Nesting]
[50]    seq    ::=    '(' S? cp ( S? ',' S? cp )* S? ')' /* */
    [VC: Proper Group/PE Nesting]
```

where each Name is the type of an element which may appear as a child. Any content particle in a choice list may appear in the element content at the location where the choice list appears in the grammar; content particles occurring in a sequence list must each appear in the element content in the order given in the list. The optional character following a name or list governs whether the element or the content particles in the list may occur one or more (+), zero or more (*), or zero or one times (?). The absence of such an operator means that the element or content particle must appear exactly once. This syntax and meaning are identical to those used in the productions in this specification.

The content of an element matches a content model if and only if it is possible to trace out a path through the content model, obeying the sequence, choice, and repetition operators and matching each element in the content against an element type in the content model. For compatibility, it is an error if an element in the document can match more than one occurrence of an element type in the content model. For more information, see E Deterministic Content Models.

Validity constraint: Proper Group/PE Nesting

Parameter-entity replacement text must be properly nested with parenthesized groups. That is to say, if either of the opening or closing parentheses in a choice, seq, or Mixed construct is contained in the replacement text for a parameter entity, both must be contained in the same replacement text.

For interoperability, if a parameter-entity reference appears in a choice, seq, or Mixed construct, its replacement text should contain at least one non-blank character, and neither the first nor last non-blank character of the replacement text should be a connector (| or ,).

Examples of element-content models:

```
<!ELEMENT spec (front, body, back?)>
<!ELEMENT div1 (head, (p | list | note)*, div2*)>
<!ELEMENT dictionary-body (%div.mix; | %dict.mix;)*>
```

3.2.2 Mixed Content

[Definition: An element type has mixed content when elements of that type may contain character data, optionally interspersed with child elements.] In this case, the types of the child elements may be constrained, but not their order or their number of occurrences:

Mixed-content Declaration

```
[51]    Mixed    ::=    '(' S? '#PCDATA' (S? '|' S? Name)* S? ')*'
   | '(' S? '#PCDATA' S? ')'  [VC: Proper Group/PE Nesting]
    [VC: No Duplicate Types]
```

where the Names give the types of elements that may appear as children. The keyword #PCDATA derives historically from the term "parsed character data."

Validity constraint: No Duplicate Types

The same name must not appear more than once in a single mixed-content declaration.

Examples of mixed content declarations:

```
<!ELEMENT p (#PCDATA|a|ul|b|i|em)*>
<!ELEMENT p (#PCDATA | %font; | %phrase; | %special; | %form;)* >
<!ELEMENT b (#PCDATA)>
```

3.3 Attribute-List Declarations

Attributes are used to associate name-value pairs with elements. Attribute specifications may appear only within start-tags and empty-element tags; thus, the productions used to recognize them appear in 3.1 Start-Tags, End-Tags, and Empty-Element Tags. Attribute-list declarations may be used:

- To define the set of attributes pertaining to a given element type.
- To establish type constraints for these attributes.
- To provide default values for attributes.

[Definition: Attribute-list declarations specify the name, data type, and default value (if any) of each attribute associated with a given element type:]

Attribute-list Declaration

```
[52]    AttlistDecl    ::=    '<!ATTLIST' S Name AttDef* S? '>'
[53]    AttDef    ::=    S Name S AttType S DefaultDecl
```

The Name in the `AttlistDecl` rule is the type of an element. At user option, an XML processor may issue a warning if attributes are declared for an element type not itself declared, but this is not an error. The Name in the `AttDef` rule is the name of the attribute.

When more than one `AttlistDecl` is provided for a given element type, the contents of all those provided are merged. When more than one definition is provided for the same attribute of a given element type, the first declaration is binding and later declarations are ignored. For interoperability, writers of DTDs may choose to provide at most one attribute-list declaration for a given element type, at most one attribute definition for a given attribute name in an attribute-list declaration, and at least one attribute definition in each attribute-list declaration. For interoperability, an XML processor may at user option issue a warning when more than one attribute-list declaration is provided for a given element type, or more than one attribute definition is provided for a given attribute, but this is not an error.

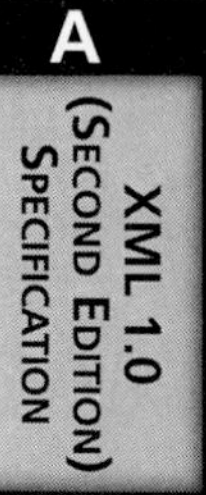

3.3.1 Attribute Types

XML attribute types are of three kinds: a string type, a set of tokenized types, and enumerated types. The string type may take any literal string as a value; the tokenized types have varying lexical and semantic constraints. The validity constraints noted in the grammar are applied after the attribute value has been normalized as described in 3.3 Attribute-List Declarations.

Attribute Types

```
[54]    AttType    ::=    StringType | TokenizedType | EnumeratedType
[55]    StringType    ::=    'CDATA'
[56]    TokenizedType    ::=    'ID' [VC: ID]
    [VC: One ID per Element Type]
    [VC: ID Attribute Default]
   | 'IDREF' [VC: IDREF]
   | 'IDREFS' [VC: IDREF]
   | 'ENTITY' [VC: Entity Name]
   | 'ENTITIES' [VC: Entity Name]
   | 'NMTOKEN' [VC: Name Token]
   | 'NMTOKENS' [VC: Name Token]
```

Validity constraint: ID

Values of type ID must match the Name production. A name must not appear more than once in an XML document as a value of this type; i.e., ID values must uniquely identify the elements which bear them.

Validity constraint: One ID per Element Type

No element type may have more than one ID attribute specified.

Validity constraint: ID Attribute Default

An ID attribute must have a declared default of #IMPLIED or #REQUIRED.

Validity constraint: IDREF

Values of type `IDREF` must match the Name production, and values of type `IDREFS` must match Names; each Name must match the value of an `ID` attribute on some element in the XML document; i.e. `IDREF` values must match the value of some ID attribute.

Validity constraint: Entity Name

Values of type `ENTITY` must match the Name production, values of type `ENTITIES` must match Names; each Name must match the name of an unparsed entity declared in the DTD.

Validity constraint: Name Token

Values of type `NMTOKEN` must match the `Nmtoken` production; values of type `NMTOKENS` must match `Nmtokens`.

[Definition: Enumerated attributes can take one of a list of values provided in the declaration]. There are two kinds of enumerated types:

Enumerated Attribute Types

```
[57]    EnumeratedType    ::=    NotationType | Enumeration
[58]    NotationType    ::=    'NOTATION' S '(' S? Name (S? '|' S? Name)* S? ')'
[VC: Notation Attributes]
    [VC: One Notation Per Element Type]
    [VC: No Notation on Empty Element]
[59]    Enumeration    ::=    '(' S? Nmtoken (S? '|' S? Nmtoken)* S? ')'
[VC: Enumeration]
```

A `NOTATION` attribute identifies a notation, declared in the DTD with associated system and/or public identifiers, to be used in interpreting the element to which the attribute is attached.

Validity constraint: Notation Attributes

Values of this type must match one of the notation names included in the declaration; all notation names in the declaration must be declared.

Validity constraint: One Notation Per Element Type

No element type may have more than one NOTATION attribute specified.

Validity constraint: No Notation on Empty Element

For compatibility, an attribute of type NOTATION must not be declared on an element declared EMPTY.

Validity constraint: Enumeration

Values of this type must match one of the Nmtoken tokens in the declaration.

For interoperability, the same Nmtoken should not occur more than once in the enumerated attribute types of a single element type.

3.3.2 Attribute Defaults

An attribute declaration provides information on whether the attribute's presence is required, and if not, how an XML processor should react if a declared attribute is absent in a document.

Attribute Defaults

```
[60]    DefaultDecl    ::=    '#REQUIRED' | '#IMPLIED'
   | (('#FIXED' S)? AttValue) [VC: Required Attribute]
    [VC: Attribute Default Legal]
    [WFC: No < in Attribute Values]
    [VC: Fixed Attribute Default]
```

In an attribute declaration, #REQUIRED means that the attribute must always be provided, #IMPLIED that no default value is provided. [Definition: If the declaration is neither #REQUIRED nor #IMPLIED, then the AttValue value contains the declared default value; the #FIXED keyword states that the attribute must always have the default value. If a default value is declared, when an XML processor encounters an omitted attribute, it is to behave as though the attribute were present with the declared default value.]

Validity constraint: Required Attribute

If the default declaration is the keyword #REQUIRED, then the attribute must be specified for all elements of the type in the attribute-list declaration.

Validity constraint: Attribute Default Legal

The declared default value must meet the lexical constraints of the declared attribute type.

Validity constraint: Fixed Attribute Default

If an attribute has a default value declared with the #FIXED keyword, instances of that attribute must match the default value.

Examples of attribute-list declarations:

```
<!ATTLIST termdef
          id      ID      #REQUIRED
          name    CDATA   #IMPLIED>
<!ATTLIST list
          type    (bullets|ordered|glossary)  "ordered">
<!ATTLIST form
          method  CDATA   #FIXED "POST">
```

3.3.3 Attribute-Value Normalization

Before the value of an attribute is passed to the application or checked for validity, the XML processor must normalize the attribute value by applying the algorithm below, or by using some other method such that the value passed to the application is the same as that produced by the algorithm.

- All line breaks must have been normalized on input to #xA as described in 2.11 End-of-Line Handling, so the rest of this algorithm operates on text normalized in this way.
- Begin with a normalized value consisting of the empty string.
- For each character, entity reference, or character reference in the unnormalized attribute value, beginning with the first and continuing to the last, do the following:
- For a character reference, append the referenced character to the normalized value.
- For an entity reference, recursively apply step 3 of this algorithm to the replacement text of the entity.
- For a white space character (#x20, #xD, #xA, #x9), append a space character (#x20) to the normalized value.
- For another character, append the character to the normalized value.

If the attribute type is not CDATA, then the XML processor must further process the normalized attribute value by discarding any leading and trailing space (#x20) characters, and by replacing sequences of space (#x20) characters by a single space (#x20) character.

Note that if the unnormalized attribute value contains a character reference to a white space character other than space (#x20), the normalized value contains the referenced character itself (#xD, #xA or #x9). This contrasts with the case where the unnormalized value contains a white space character (not a reference), which is replaced with a space character (#x20) in the normalized value and also contrasts with the case where the unnormalized value contains an entity reference whose replacement text contains a white space character; being recursively processed, the white space character is replaced with a space character (#x20) in the normalized value.

All attributes for which no declaration has been read should be treated by a non-validating processor as if declared CDATA.

Following are examples of attribute normalization. Given the following declarations:

```
<!ENTITY d "&#xD;">
<!ENTITY a "&#xA;">
<!ENTITY da "&#xD;&#xA;">
```

the attribute specifications in the left column below would be normalized to the character sequences of the middle column if the attribute a is declared NMTOKENS and to those of the right columns if a is declared CDATA.

Attribute specification	*a is NMTOKENS*	*a is CDATA*
a=" xyz"	x y z	#x20 #x20 x y z
a="&d;&d;A&a;&a;B&da;"	A #x20 B	#x20 #x20 A #x20 #x20 B #x20 #x20
a="

A

 B
" | #xD #xD A #xA #xA B #xD#xA | #xD #xD A #xA #xA B #xD #xD |

Note that the last example is invalid (but well-formed) if a is declared to be of type NMTOKENS.

3.4 Conditional Sections

[Definition: Conditional sections are portions of the document type declaration external subset which are included in, or excluded from, the logical structure of the DTD based on the keyword which governs them.]

Conditional Section

```
[61]    conditionalSect    ::=    includeSect | ignoreSect
[62]    includeSect    ::=    '<![' S? 'INCLUDE' S?
'[' extSubsetDecl ']]>'  /* */
    [VC: Proper Conditional Section/PE Nesting]
[63]    ignoreSect    ::=    '<![' S? 'IGNORE' S?
'[' ignoreSectContents* ']]>' /* */
    [VC: Proper Conditional Section/PE Nesting]
[64]    ignoreSectContents    ::=
Ignore ('<![' ignoreSectContents ']]>' Ignore)*
[65]    Ignore    ::=    Char* - (Char* ('<![' | ']]>') Char*)
```

Validity constraint: Proper Conditional Section/PE Nesting

If any of the "<![", "[", or "]]>" of a conditional section is contained in the replacement text for a parameter-entity reference, all of them must be contained in the same replacement text.

Like the internal and external DTD subsets, a conditional section may contain one or more complete declarations, comments, processing instructions, or nested conditional sections, intermingled with white space.

If the keyword of the conditional section is INCLUDE, then the contents of the conditional section are part of the DTD. If the keyword of the conditional section is IGNORE, then the contents of the conditional section are not logically part of the DTD. If a conditional section with a keyword of INCLUDE occurs within a larger conditional section with a keyword of IGNORE, both the outer and the inner conditional sections are ignored. The contents of an ignored conditional section are parsed by ignoring all characters after the "[" following the keyword, except conditional section starts "<![" and ends "]]>", until the matching conditional section end is found. Parameter entity references are not recognized in this process.

If the keyword of the conditional section is a parameter-entity reference, the parameter entity must be replaced by its content before the processor decides whether to include or ignore the conditional section.

An example:

```
<!ENTITY % draft 'INCLUDE' >
<!ENTITY % final 'IGNORE' >

<![%draft;[
<!ELEMENT book (comments*, title, body, supplements?)>
]]>
<![%final;[
<!ELEMENT book (title, body, supplements?)>
]]>
```

4 Physical Structures

[Definition: An XML document may consist of one or many storage units. These are called entities; they all have content and are all (except for the document entity and the external DTD subset) identified by entity name.] Each XML document has one entity called the document entity, which serves as the starting point for the XML processor and may contain the whole document.

Entities may be either parsed or unparsed. [Definition: A parsed entity's contents are referred to as its replacement text; this text is considered an integral part of the document.]

[Definition: An unparsed entity is a resource whose contents may or may not be text, and if text, may be other than XML. Each unparsed entity has an associated notation, identified by name. Beyond a requirement that an XML processor make the identifiers for the entity and notation available to the application, XML places no constraints on the contents of unparsed entities.]

Parsed entities are invoked by name using entity references; unparsed entities by name, given in the value of ENTITY or ENTITIES attributes.

[Definition: General entities are entities for use within the document content. In this specification, general entities are sometimes referred to with the unqualified term entity when this leads to no ambiguity.] [Definition: Parameter entities are parsed entities for use within the DTD.] These two types of entities use different forms of reference and are recognized in different contexts. Furthermore, they occupy different namespaces; a parameter entity and a general entity with the same name are two distinct entities.

4.1 Character and Entity References

[Definition: A character reference refers to a specific character in the ISO/IEC 10646 character set, for example one not directly accessible from available input devices.]

Character Reference

```
[66]    CharRef    ::=    '&#' [0-9]+ ';'
   | '&#x' [0-9a-fA-F]+ ';' [WFC: Legal Character]
```

Well-formedness constraint: Legal Character

Characters referred to using character references must match the production for Char.

If the character reference begins with "&#x", the digits and letters up to the terminating ; provide a hexadecimal representation of the character's code point in ISO/IEC 10646. If it begins just with "&#", the digits up to the terminating ; provide a decimal representation of the character's code point.

[Definition: An entity reference refers to the content of a named entity.] [Definition: References to parsed general entities use ampersand (&) and semicolon (;) as delimiters.] [Definition: Parameter-entity references use percent-sign (%) and semicolon (;) as delimiters.]

Entity Reference

```
[67]    Reference    ::=    EntityRef | CharRef
[68]    EntityRef    ::=    '&' Name ';' [WFC: Entity Declared]
    [VC: Entity Declared]
    [WFC: Parsed Entity]
    [WFC: No Recursion]
[69]    PEReference    ::=    '%' Name ';' [VC: Entity Declared]
    [WFC: No Recursion]
    [WFC: In DTD]
```

Well-formedness constraint: Entity Declared

In a document without any DTD, a document with only an internal DTD subset which contains no parameter entity references, or a document with "standalone='yes'", for an entity reference that does not occur within the external subset or a parameter entity, the Name given in the entity reference must match that in an entity declaration that does not occur within the external subset or a parameter entity, except that well-formed documents need not declare any of the following entities: amp, lt, gt, apos, quot. The declaration of a general entity must precede any reference to it which appears in a default value in an attribute-list declaration.

Note that if entities are declared in the external subset or in external parameter entities, a non-validating processor is not obligated to read and process their declarations; for such documents, the rule that an entity must be declared is a well-formedness constraint only if standalone='yes'.

Validity constraint: Entity Declared

In a document with an external subset or external parameter entities with "standalone='no'", the Name given in the entity reference must match that in an entity declaration. For interoperability, valid documents should declare the entities amp, lt, gt, apos, quot, in the form specified in 4.6 Predefined Entities. The declaration of a parameter entity must precede any reference to it. Similarly, the declaration of a general entity must precede any attribute-list declaration containing a default value with a direct or indirect reference to that general entity.

Well-formedness constraint: Parsed Entity

An entity reference must not contain the name of an unparsed entity. Unparsed entities may be referred to only in attribute values declared to be of type ENTITY or ENTITIES.

Well-formedness constraint: No Recursion

A parsed entity must not contain a recursive reference to itself, either directly or indirectly.

Well-formedness constraint: In DTD

Parameter-entity references may only appear in the DTD.

Examples of character and entity references:

```
Type <key>less-than</key> (&#x3C;) to save options.
This document was prepared on &docdate; and
is classified &security-level;.
```

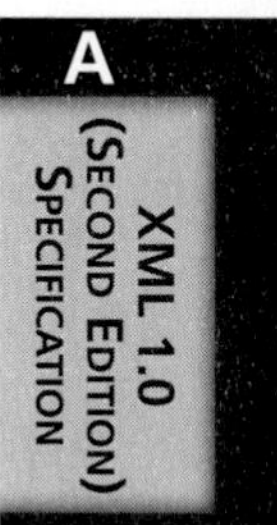

Example of a parameter-entity reference:

```
<!-- declare the parameter entity "ISOLat2"... -->
<!ENTITY % ISOLat2
         SYSTEM "http://www.xml.com/iso/isolat2-xml.entities" >
<!-- ... now reference it. -->
%ISOLat2;
```

4.2 Entity Declarations

[Definition: Entities are declared thus:]

Entity Declaration

```
[70]    EntityDecl    ::=    GEDecl | PEDecl
[71]    GEDecl    ::=    '<!ENTITY' S Name S EntityDef S? '>'
[72]    PEDecl    ::=    '<!ENTITY' S '%' S Name S PEDef S? '>'
[73]    EntityDef    ::=    EntityValue | (ExternalID NDataDecl?)
[74]    PEDef    ::=    EntityValue | ExternalID
```

The Name identifies the entity in an entity reference or, in the case of an unparsed entity, in the value of an ENTITY or ENTITIES attribute. If the same entity is declared more than once, the first declaration encountered is binding; at user option, an XML processor may issue a warning if entities are declared multiple times.

4.2.1 Internal Entities

[Definition: If the entity definition is an EntityValue, the defined entity is called an internal entity. There is no separate physical storage object, and the content of the entity is given in the declaration.] Note that some processing of entity and character references in the literal entity value may be required to produce the correct replacement text: see 4.5 Construction of Internal Entity Replacement Text.

An internal entity is a parsed entity.

Example of an internal entity declaration:

```
<!ENTITY Pub-Status "This is a pre-release of the
 specification.">
```

4.2.2 External Entities

[Definition: If the entity is not internal, it is an external entity, declared as follows:]

External Entity Declaration

```
[75]    ExternalID    ::=    'SYSTEM' S SystemLiteral
   | 'PUBLIC' S PubidLiteral S SystemLiteral
[76]    NDataDecl    ::=    S 'NDATA' S Name [VC: Notation Declared]
```

If the NDataDecl is present, this is a general unparsed entity; otherwise it is a parsed entity.

Validity constraint: Notation Declared

The Name must match the declared name of a notation.

[Definition: The SystemLiteral is called the entity's system identifier. It is a URI reference (as defined in [IETF RFC 2396], updated by [IETF RFC 2732]), meant to be dereferenced to obtain input for the XML processor to construct the entity's replacement text.] It is an error for a fragment identifier (beginning with a # character) to be part of a system identifier. Unless otherwise provided by information outside the scope of this specification (e.g. a special XML element type defined by a particular DTD, or a processing instruction defined by a particular application specification), relative URIs are relative to the location of the resource within which the entity declaration occurs. A URI might thus be relative to the document entity, to the entity containing the external DTD subset, or to some other external parameter entity.

URI references require encoding and escaping of certain characters. The disallowed characters include all non-ASCII characters, plus the excluded characters listed in Section 2.4 of [IETF RFC 2396], except for the number sign (#) and percent sign (%) characters and the square bracket characters re-allowed in [IETF RFC 2732]. Disallowed characters must be escaped as follows:

Each disallowed character is converted to UTF-8 [IETF RFC 2279] as one or more bytes.

Any octets corresponding to a disallowed character are escaped with the URI escaping mechanism (that is, converted to %HH, where HH is the hexadecimal notation of the byte value).

The original character is replaced by the resulting character sequence.

[Definition: In addition to a system identifier, an external identifier may include a public identifier.] An XML processor attempting to retrieve the entity's content may use the public identifier to try to generate an alternative URI reference. If the processor is unable to do so, it must use the URI reference specified in the system literal. Before a match is attempted, all strings of white space in the public identifier must be normalized to single space characters (#x20), and leading and trailing white space must be removed.

Examples of external entity declarations:

```
<!ENTITY open-hatch
         SYSTEM "http://www.textuality.com/boilerplate/OpenHatch.xml">
<!ENTITY open-hatch
         PUBLIC "-//Textuality//TEXT Standard open-hatch boilerplate//EN"
```

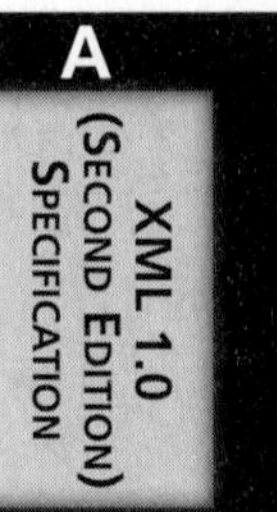


```
        "http://www.textuality.com/boilerplate/OpenHatch.xml">
<!ENTITY hatch-pic
        SYSTEM "../grafix/OpenHatch.gif"
        NDATA gif >
```

4.3 Parsed Entities

4.3.1 The Text Declaration

External parsed entities should each begin with a text declaration.

Text Declaration

[77]	TextDecl	::=	'<?xml' VersionInfo? EncodingDecl S? '?>'

The text declaration must be provided literally, not by reference to a parsed entity. No text declaration may appear at any position other than the beginning of an external parsed entity. The text declaration in an external parsed entity is not considered part of its replacement text.

4.3.2 Well-Formed Parsed Entities

The document entity is well-formed if it matches the production labeled document. An external general parsed entity is well-formed if it matches the production labeled extParsedEnt. All external parameter entities are well-formed by definition.

Well-Formed External Parsed Entity

[78]	extParsedEnt	::=	TextDecl? content

An internal general parsed entity is well-formed if its replacement text matches the production labeled content. All internal parameter entities are well-formed by definition.

A consequence of well-formedness in entities is that the logical and physical structures in an XML document are properly nested; no start-tag, end-tag, empty-element tag, element, comment, processing instruction, character reference, or entity reference can begin in one entity and end in another.

4.3.3 Character Encoding in Entities

Each external parsed entity in an XML document may use a different encoding for its characters. All XML processors must be able to read entities in both the UTF-8 and UTF-16 encodings. The terms "UTF-8" and "UTF-16" in this specification do not apply to character encodings with any other labels, even if the encodings or labels are very similar to UTF-8 or UTF-16.

Entities encoded in UTF-16 must begin with the Byte Order Mark described by Annex F of [ISO/IEC 10646], Annex H of [ISO/IEC 10646-2000], section 2.4 of [Unicode], and section 2.7 of [Unicode3] (the ZERO WIDTH NO-BREAK SPACE character, #xFEFF). This is an encoding signature, not part of either the markup or the character data of the XML document. XML processors must be able to use this character to differentiate between UTF-8 and UTF-16 encoded documents.

Although an XML processor is required to read only entities in the UTF-8 and UTF-16 encodings, it is recognized that other encodings are used around the world, and it may be desired for XML processors to read entities that use them. In the absence of external character encoding information (such as MIME headers), parsed entities which are stored in an encoding other than UTF-8 or UTF-16 must begin with a text declaration (see 4.3.1 The Text Declaration) containing an encoding declaration:

Encoding Declaration

```
[80]    EncodingDecl    ::=
S 'encoding' Eq ('"' EncName '"' | "'" EncName "'" )
[81]    EncName    ::=    [A-Za-z] ([A-Za-z0-9._] | '-')*
/* Encoding name contains only Latin characters */
```

In the document entity, the encoding declaration is part of the XML declaration. The EncName is the name of the encoding used.

In an encoding declaration, the values "UTF-8", "UTF-16", "ISO-10646-UCS-2", and "ISO-10646-UCS-4" should be used for the various encodings and transformations of Unicode / ISO/IEC 10646, the values "ISO-8859-1", "ISO-8859-2", ... "ISO-8859-n" (where n is the part number) should be used for the parts of ISO 8859, and the values "ISO-2022-JP", "Shift_JIS", and "EUC-JP" should be used for the various encoded forms of JIS X-0208-1997. It is recommended that character encodings registered (as charsets) with the Internet Assigned Numbers Authority [IANA-CHARSETS], other than those just listed, be referred to using their registered names; other encodings should use names starting with an "x-" prefix. XML processors should match character encoding names in a case-insensitive way and should either interpret an IANA-registered name as the encoding registered at IANA for that name or treat it as unknown (processors are, of course, not required to support all IANA-registered encodings).

In the absence of information provided by an external transport protocol (e.g. HTTP or MIME), it is an error for an entity including an encoding declaration to be presented to the XML processor in an encoding other than that named in the declaration, or for an entity which begins with neither a Byte Order Mark nor an encoding declaration to use

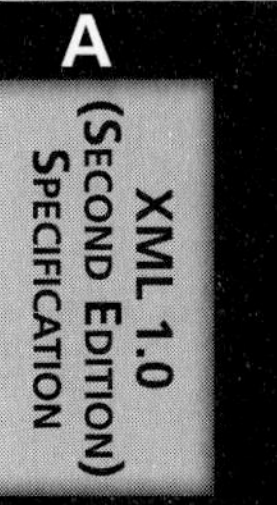

an encoding other than UTF-8. Note that since ASCII is a subset of UTF-8, ordinary ASCII entities do not strictly need an encoding declaration.

It is a fatal error for a TextDecl to occur other than at the beginning of an external entity.

It is a fatal error when an XML processor encounters an entity with an encoding that it is unable to process. It is a fatal error if an XML entity is determined (via default, encoding declaration, or higher-level protocol) to be in a certain encoding but contains octet sequences that are not legal in that encoding. It is also a fatal error if an XML entity contains no encoding declaration and its content is not legal UTF-8 or UTF-16.

Examples of text declarations containing encoding declarations:

```
<?xml encoding='UTF-8'?>
<?xml encoding='EUC-JP'?>
```

4.4 XML Processor Treatment of Entities and References

The table below summarizes the contexts in which character references, entity references, and invocations of unparsed entities might appear and the required behavior of an XML processor in each case. The labels in the leftmost column describe the recognition context:

Reference in Content

as a reference anywhere after the start-tag and before the end-tag of an element; corresponds to the nonterminal content.

Reference in Attribute Value

as a reference within either the value of an attribute in a start-tag, or a default value in an attribute declaration; corresponds to the nonterminal AttValue.

Occurs as Attribute Value

as a Name, not a reference, appearing either as the value of an attribute which has been declared as type ENTITY, or as one of the space-separated tokens in the value of an attribute which has been dclared as type ENTITIES.

Reference in Entity Value

as a reference within a parameter or internal entity's literal entity value in the entity's declaration; corresponds to the nonterminal EntityValue.

Reference in DTD

as a reference within either the internal or external subsets of the DTD, but outside of an EntityValue, AttValue, PI, Comment, SystemLiteral, PubidLiteral, or the contents of an ignored conditional section (see 3.4 Conditional Sections).

Entity Type

	Parameter	*Internal General*	*External Parsed General*	*Unparsed*	*Character*
Reference in Content	Not Recognized	Included	Included if valdiating	Forbidden	Included
Reference in Attribute	Value Not recognized	Included in literal	Forbidden	Forbidden	Included
Occurs as Attribute	Value Not recognized	Forbidden	Forbidden	Notify	Not recognized
Reference in Entity Value	Included in literal	Bypassed	Bypassed	Forbidden	Included
Reference in DTD	Included as PE	Forbidden	Forbidden	Forbidden	Forbidden

4.4.1 Not Recognized

Outside the DTD, the % character has no special significance; thus, what would be parameter entity references in the DTD are not recognized as markup in content. Similarly, the names of unparsed entities are not recognized except when they appear in the value of an appropriately declared attribute.

4.4.2 Included

[Definition: An entity is included when its replacement text is retrieved and processed, in place of the reference itself, as though it were part of the document at the location the

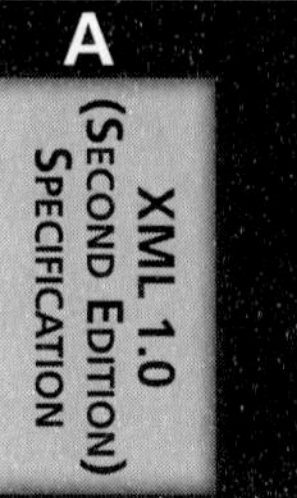

reference was recognized.] The replacement text may contain both character data and (except for parameter entities) markup, which must be recognized in the usual way. (The string "AT&T;" expands to "AT&T;" and the remaining ampersand is not recognized as an entity-reference delimiter.) A character reference is included when the indicated character is processed in place of the reference itself.

4.4.3 Included If Validating

When an XML processor recognizes a reference to a parsed entity, in order to validate the document, the processor must include its replacement text. If the entity is external, and the processor is not attempting to validate the XML document, the processor may, but need not, include the entity's replacement text. If a non-validating processor does not include the replacement text, it must inform the application that it recognized, but did not read, the entity.

This rule is based on the recognition that the automatic inclusion provided by the SGML and XML entity mechanism, primarily designed to support modularity in authoring, is not necessarily appropriate for other applications, in particular document browsing. Browsers, for example, when encountering an external parsed entity reference, might choose to provide a visual indication of the entity's presence and retrieve it for display only on demand.

4.4.4 Forbidden

The following are forbidden, and constitute fatal errors:

- the appearance of a reference to an unparsed entity.
- the appearance of any character or general-entity reference in the DTD except within an EntityValue or AttValue.
- a reference to an external entity in an attribute value.

4.4.5 Included in Literal

When an entity reference appears in an attribute value, or a parameter entity reference appears in a literal entity value, its replacement text is processed in place of the reference itself as though it were part of the document at the location the reference was recognized, except that a single or double quote character in the replacement text is always treated as a normal data character and will not terminate the literal. For example, this is well-formed:

```
<!-- -->
<!ENTITY % YN '"Yes"' >
<!ENTITY WhatHeSaid "He said %YN;" >
```

while this is not:

```
<!ENTITY EndAttr "27'" >
<element attribute='a-&EndAttr;>
```

4.4.6 Notify

When the name of an unparsed entity appears as a token in the value of an attribute of declared type ENTITY or ENTITIES, a validating processor must inform the application of the system and public (if any) identifiers for both the entity and its associated notation.

4.4.7 Bypassed

When a general entity reference appears in the EntityValue in an entity declaration, it is bypassed and left as is.

4.4.8 Included as PE

Just as with external parsed entities, parameter entities need only be included if validating. When a parameter-entity reference is recognized in the DTD and included, its replacement text is enlarged by the attachment of one leading and one following space (#x20) character; the intent is to constrain the replacement text of parameter entities to contain an integral number of grammatical tokens in the DTD. This behavior does not apply to parameter entity references within entity values; these are described in 4.4.5 Included in Literal.

4.5 Construction of Internal Entity Replacement Text

In discussing the treatment of internal entities, it is useful to distinguish two forms of the entity's value. [Definition: The literal entity value is the quoted string actually present in the entity declaration, corresponding to the non-terminal EntityValue.] [Definition: The replacement text is the content of the entity, after replacement of character references and parameter-entity references.]

The literal entity value as given in an internal entity declaration (EntityValue) may contain character, parameter-entity, and general-entity references. Such references must be contained entirely within the literal entity value. The actual replacement text that is included as described above must contain the replacement text of any parameter entities referred to, and must contain the character referred to, in place of any character references in the literal entity value; however, general-entity references must be left as-is, unexpanded. For example, given the following declarations:

```
<!ENTITY % pub    "&#xc9;ditions Gallimard" >
<!ENTITY   rights "All rights reserved" >
<!ENTITY   book   "La Peste: Albert Camus,
&#xA9; 1947 %pub;. &rights;" >
```

then the replacement text for the entity "book" is:

```
La Peste: Albert Camus,
© 1947 Éditions Gallimard. &rights;
```

The general-entity reference "&rights;" would be expanded should the reference "&book;" appear in the document's content or an attribute value.

These simple rules may have complex interactions; for a detailed discussion of a difficult example, see D Expansion of Entity and Character References.

4.6 Predefined Entities

[Definition: Entity and character references can both be used to escape the left angle bracket, ampersand, and other delimiters. A set of general entities (amp, lt, gt, apos, quot) is specified for this purpose. Numeric character references may also be used; they are expanded immediately when recognized and must be treated as character data, so the numeric character references "<" and "&" may be used to escape < and & when they occur in character data.]

All XML processors must recognize these entities whether they are declared or not. For interoperability, valid XML documents should declare these entities, like any others, before using them. If the entities lt or amp are declared, they must be declared as internal entities whose replacement text is a character reference to the respective character (less-than sign or ampersand) being escaped; the double escaping is required for these entities so that references to them produce a well-formed result. If the entities gt, apos, or quot are declared, they must be declared as internal entities whose replacement text is the single character being escaped (or a character reference to that character; the double escaping here is unnecessary but harmless). For example:

```
<!ENTITY lt     "&#38;#60;">
<!ENTITY gt     "&#62;">
```

```
<!ENTITY amp    "&#38;#38;">
<!ENTITY apos   "&#39;">
<!ENTITY quot   "&#34;">
```

4.7 Notation Declarations

[Definition: Notations identify by name the format of unparsed entities, the format of elements which bear a notation attribute, or the application to which a processing instruction is addressed.]

[Definition: Notation declarations provide a name for the notation, for use in entity and attribute-list declarations and in attribute specifications, and an external identifier for the notation which may allow an XML processor or its client application to locate a helper application capable of processing data in the given notation.]

Notation Declarations

```
[82]    NotationDecl    ::=    '<!NOTATION' S Name S (ExternalID | PublicID) S?
➥'>'
[VC: Unique Notation Name]
[83]    PublicID    ::=    'PUBLIC' S PubidLiteral
```

Validity constraint: Unique Notation Name

Only one notation declaration can declare a given Name.

XML processors must provide applications with the name and external identifier(s) of any notation declared and referred to in an attribute value, attribute definition, or entity declaration. They may additionally resolve the external identifier into the system identifier, file name, or other information needed to allow the application to call a processor for data in the notation described. (It is not an error, however, for XML documents to declare and refer to notations for which notation-specific applications are not available on the system where the XML processor or application is running.)

4.8 Document Entity

[Definition: The document entity serves as the root of the entity tree and a starting-point for an XML processor.] This specification does not specify how the document entity is to be located by an XML processor; unlike other entities, the document entity has no name and might well appear on a processor input stream without any identification at all.

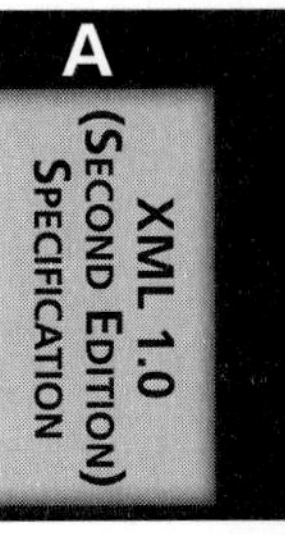

5 Conformance

5.1 Validating and Non-Validating Processors

Conforming XML processors fall into two classes: validating and non-validating.

Validating and non-validating processors alike must report violations of this specification's well-formedness constraints in the content of the document entity and any other parsed entities that they read.

[Definition: Validating processors must, at user option, report violations of the constraints expressed by the declarations in the DTD, and failures to fulfill the validity constraints given in this specification.] To accomplish this, validating XML processors must read and process the entire DTD and all external parsed entities referenced in the document.

Non-validating processors are required to check only the document entity, including the entire internal DTD subset, for well-formedness. [Definition: While they are not required to check the document for validity, they are required to process all the declarations they read in the internal DTD subset and in any parameter entity that they read, up to the first reference to a parameter entity that they do not read; that is to say, they must use the information in those declarations to normalize attribute values, include the replacement text of internal entities, and supply default attribute values.] Except when standalone="yes", they must not process entity declarations or attribute-list declarations encountered after a reference to a parameter entity that is not read, since the entity may have contained overriding declarations.

5.2 Using XML Processors

The behavior of a validating XML processor is highly predictable; it must read every piece of a document and report all well-formedness and validity violations. Less is required of a non-validating processor; it need not read any part of the document other than the document entity. This has two effects that may be important to users of XML processors:

Certain well-formedness errors, specifically those that require reading external entities, may not be detected by a non-validating processor. Examples include the constraints entitled Entity Declared, Parsed Entity, and No Recursion, as well as some of the cases described as forbidden in 4.4 XML Processor Treatment of Entities and References.

The information passed from the processor to the application may vary, depending on whether the processor reads parameter and external entities. For example, a non-alidating processor may not normalize attribute values, include the replacement text of internal entities, or supply default attribute values, where doing so depends on having read declarations in external or parameter entities.

For maximum reliability in interoperating between different XML processors, applications which use non-validating processors should not rely on any behaviors not required of such processors. Applications which require facilities such as the use of default attributes or internal entities which are declared in external entities should use validating XML processors.

6 Notation

The formal grammar of XML is given in this specification using a simple Extended Backus-Naur Form (EBNF) notation. Each rule in the grammar defines one symbol, in the form

```
symbol ::= expression
```

Symbols are written with an initial capital letter if they are the start symbol of a regular language, otherwise with an initial lower case letter. Literal strings are quoted.

Within the expression on the right-hand side of a rule, the following expressions are used to match strings of one or more characters:

```
#xN
```

where N is a hexadecimal integer, the expression matches the character in ISO/IEC 10646 whose canonical (UCS-4) code value, when interpreted as an unsigned binary number, has the value indicated. The number of leading zeros in the #xN form is insignificant; the number of leading zeros in the corresponding code value is governed by the character encoding in use and is not significant for XML.

```
[a-zA-Z], [#xN-#xN]
```

matches any Char with a value in the range(s) indicated (inclusive).

```
[abc], [#xN#xN#xN]
```

matches any Char with a value among the characters enumerated. Enumerations and ranges can be mixed in one set of brackets.

```
[^a-z], [^#xN-#xN]
```

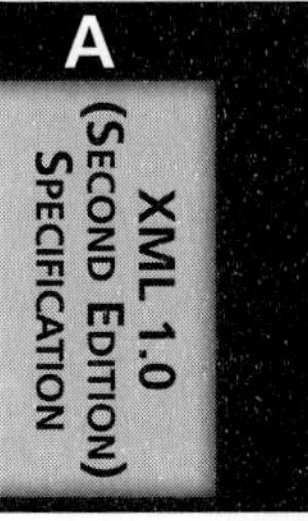

matches any Char with a value outside the range indicated.

`[^abc], [^#xN#xN#xN]`

matches any Char with a value not among the characters given. Enumerations and ranges of forbidden values can be mixed in one set of brackets.

`"string"`

matches a literal string matching that given inside the double quotes.

`'string'`

matches a literal string matching that given inside the single quotes.

These symbols may be combined to match more complex patterns as follows, where A and B represent simple expressions:

`(expression)`

expression is treated as a unit and may be combined as described in this list.

`A?`

matches A or nothing; optional A.

`A B`

matches A followed by B. This operator has higher precedence than alternation; thus A B | C D is identical to (A B) | (C D).

`A | B`

matches A or B but not both.

`A - B`

matches any string that matches A but does not match B.

`A+`

matches one or more occurrences of A.Concatenation has higher precedence than alternation; thus A+ | B+ is identical to (A+) | (B+).

`A*`

matches zero or more occurrences of A. Concatenation has higher precedence than alternation; thus A* | B* is identical to (A*) | (B*).

Other notations used in the productions are:

/* ... */

comment.

[wfc: ...]

well-formedness constraint; this identifies by name a constraint on well-formed documents associated with a production.

[vc: ...]

validity constraint; this identifies by name a constraint on valid documents associated with a production.

A References

A.1 Normative References

IANA-CHARSETS

(Internet Assigned Numbers Authority) *Official Names for Character Sets*, ed. Keld Simonsen et al. See `ftp://ftp.isi.edu/in-notes/iana/assignments/character-sets`. IETF RFC 1766

IETF (Internet Engineering Task Force). *RFC 1766: Tags for the Identification of Languages*, ed. H. Alvestrand. 1995. (See `http://www.ietf.org/rfc/rfc1766.txt`.) ISO/IEC 10646

ISO (International Organization for Standardization). *ISO/IEC 10646-1993 . Information technology — Universal Multiple-Octet Coded Character Set (UCS) — Part 1: Architecture and Basic Multilingual Plane.* [Geneva]: International Organization for Standardization, 1993 (plus amendments AM 1 through AM 7). ISO/IEC 10646-2000

ISO (International Organization for Standardization). *ISO/IEC 10646-1:2000. Information technology — Universal Multiple-Octet Coded Character Set (UCS) — Part 1: Architecture and Basic Multilingual Plane.* [Geneva]: International Organization for Standardization, 2000. Unicode

The Unicode Consortium. *The Unicode Standard, Version 2.0.* Reading, Mass.: Addison-Wesley Developers Press, 1996. Unicode3

The Unicode Consortium. *The Unicode Standard, Version 3.0.* Reading, Mass.: Addison-Wesley Developers Press, 2000. ISBN 0-201-61633-5.

A.2 Other References

Aho/Ullman

Aho, Alfred V., Ravi Sethi, and Jeffrey D. Ullman. *Compilers: Principles, Techniques, and Tools*. Reading: Addison-Wesley, 1986, rpt. corr. 1988. Berners-Lee et al.

Berners-Lee, T., R. Fielding, and L. Masinter. *Uniform Resource Identifiers (URI): Generic Syntax and Semantics*. 1997. (Work in progress; see updates to RFC1738.) Brüggemann-Klein

Brüggemann-Klein, Anne. Formal Models in Document Processing. Habilitationsschrift. Faculty of Mathematics at the University of Freiburg, 1993. (See `ftp://ftp.informatik.uni-freiburg.de/documents/papers/brueggem/habil.ps`.) Brüggemann-Klein and Wood

Brüggemann-Klein, Anne, and Derick Wood. *Deterministic Regular Languages*. Universität Freiburg, Institut für Informatik, Bericht 38, Oktober 1991. Extended abstract in A. Finkel, M. Jantzen, Hrsg., STACS 1992, S. 173-184. Springer-Verlag, Berlin 1992. Lecture Notes in Computer Science 577. Full version titled *One-Unambiguous Regular Languages* in Information and Computation 140 (2): 229-253, February 1998. Clark

James Clark. Comparison of SGML and XML. See `http://www.w3.org/TR/NOTE-sgml-xml-971215`. IANA-LANGCODES

(Internet Assigned Numbers Authority) *Registry of Language Tags*, ed. Keld Simonsen et al. (See `http://www.isi.edu/in-notes/iana/assignments/languages/`.) IETF RFC2141

IETF (Internet Engineering Task Force). *RFC 2141: URN Syntax*, ed. R. Moats. 1997. (See `http://www.ietf.org/rfc/rfc2141.txt`.) IETF RFC 2279

IETF (Internet Engineering Task Force). *RFC 2279: UTF-8, a transformation format of ISO 10646*, ed. F. Yergeau, 1998. (See `http://www.ietf.org/rfc/rfc2279.txt`.) IETF RFC 2376

IETF (Internet Engineering Task Force). *RFC 2376: XML Media Types*. ed. E. Whitehead, M. Murata. 1998. (See `http://www.ietf.org/rfc/rfc2376.txt`.) IETF RFC 2396

IETF (Internet Engineering Task Force). *RFC 2396: Uniform Resource Identifiers (URI): Generic Syntax*. T. Berners-Lee, R. Fielding, L. Masinter. 1998. (See `http://www.ietf.org/rfc/rfc2396.txt`.) IETF RFC 2732

IETF (Internet Engineering Task Force). *RFC 2732: Format for Literal IPv6 Addresses in URL's*. R. Hinden, B. Carpenter, L. Masinter. 1999. (See `http://www.ietf.org/rfc/rfc2732.txt`.) IETF RFC 2781

IETF (Internet Engineering Task Force). *RFC 2781: UTF-16, an encoding of ISO 10646*, ed. P. Hoffman, F. Yergeau. 2000. (See `http://www.ietf.org/rfc/rfc2781.txt`.) ISO 639

(International Organization for Standardization). *ISO 639:1988 . Code for the representation of names of languages.* [Geneva]: International Organization for Standardization, 1988. ISO 3166

(International Organization for Standardization). *ISO 3166-1:1997 . Codes for the representation of names of countries and their subdivisions — Part 1: Country codes* [Geneva]: International Organization for Standardization, 1997. ISO 8879

ISO (International Organization for Standardization). *ISO 8879:1986. Information processing — Text and Office Systems — Standard Generalized Markup Language (SGML).* First edition — 1986-10-15. [Geneva]: International Organization for Standardization, 1986. ISO/IEC 10744

ISO (International Organization for Standardization). *ISO/IEC 10744-1992 . Information technology — Hypermedia/Time-based Structuring Language (HyTime).* [Geneva]: International Organization for Standardization, 1992. *Extended Facilities Annexe.* [Geneva]: International Organization for Standardization, 1996. WEBSGML

ISO (International Organization for Standardization). *ISO 8879:1986 TC2. Information technology — Document Description and Processing Languages.* [Geneva]: International Organization for Standardization, 1998. (See `http://www.sgmlsource.com/8879rev/n0029.htm`.) XML Names

Tim Bray, Dave Hollander, and Andrew Layman, editors. *Namespaces in XML.* Textuality, Hewlett-Packard, and Microsoft. World Wide Web Consortium, 1999. (See `http://www.w3.org/TR/REC-xml-names/`.)

B Character Classes

Following the characteristics defined in the Unicode standard, characters are classed as base characters (among others, these contain the alphabetic characters of the Latin alphabet), ideographic characters, and combining characters (among others, this class contains most diacritics) Digits and extenders are also distinguished.

Characters

[84]	Letter	::=	BaseChar| Ideographic
[85]	BaseChar	::=	[#x0041-#x005A] | [#x0061-#x007A] | [#x00C0 #x00D6] | [#x00D8-#x00F6] | [#x00F8-#x00FF] |

[#x0100-#x0131] | [#x0134-#x013E] | [#x0141-#x0148] | [#x014A-#x017E] | [#x0180-#x01C3] | [#x01CD-#x01F0] | [#x01F4-#x01F5] | [#x01FA-#x0217] | [#x0250-#x02A8] | [#x02BB-#x02C1] | #x0386 | [#x0388-#x038A] | #x038C | [#x038E-#x03A1] | [#x03A3-#x03CE] | [#x03D0-#x03D6] | #x03DA | #x03DC | #x03DE | #x03E0 | [#x03E2-#x03F3] | [#x0401-#x040C] | [#x040E-#x044F] | [#x0451-#x045C] | [#x045E-#x0481] | [#x0490-#x04C4] | [#x04C7-#x04C8] | [#x04CB-#x04CC] | [#x04D0-#x04EB] | [#x04EE-#x04F5] | [#x04F8-#x04F9] | [#x0531-#x0556] | #x0559 | [#x0561-#x0586] | [#x05D0-#x05EA] | [#x05F0-#x05F2] | [#x0621-#x063A] | [#x0641-#x064A] | [#x0671-#x06B7] | [#x06BA-#x06BE] | [#x06C0-#x06CE] | [#x06D0-#x06D3] | #x06D5 | [#x06E5-#x06E6] | [#x0905-#x0939] | #x093D | [#x0958-#x0961] | [#x0985-#x098C] | [#x098F-#x0990] | [#x0993-#x09A8] | [#x09AA-#x09B0] | #x09B2 | [#x09B6-#x09B9] | [#x09DC-#x09DD] | [#x09DF-#x09E1] | [#x09F0-#x09F1] | [#x0A05-#x0A0A] | [#x0A0F-#x0A10] | [#x0A13-#x0A28] | [#x0A2A-#x0A30] | [#x0A32-#x0A33] | [#x0A35-#x0A36] | [#x0A38-#x0A39] | [#x0A59-#x0A5C] | #x0A5E | [#x0A72-#x0A74] | [#x0A85-#x0A8B] | #x0A8D | [#x0A8F-#x0A91] | [#x0A93-#x0AA8] | [#x0AAA-#x0AB0] | [#x0AB2-#x0AB3] | [#x0AB5-#x0AB9] | #x0ABD | #x0AE0 | [#x0B05-#x0B0C] | [#x0B0F-#x0B10] | [#x0B13-#x0B28] | [#x0B2A-#x0B30] | [#x0B32-#x0B33] | [#x0B36-#x0B39] | #x0B3D | [#x0B5C-

#x0B5D] | [#x0B5F-#x0B61] | [#x0B85-#x0B8A] | [#x0B8E-#x0B90] | [#x0B92-#x0B95] | [#x0B99 #x0B9A] | #x0B9C | [#x0B9E-#x0B9F] | [#x0BA3-#x0BA4] | [#x0BA8-#x0BAA] | [#x0BAE-#x0BB5] | [#x0BB7-#x0BB9] | [#x0C05-#x0C0C] | [#x0C0E-#x0C10] | [#x0C12-#x0C28] | [#x0C2A-#x0C33] | [#x0C35-#x0C39] | [#x0C60-#x0C61] | [#x0C85-#x0C8C] | [#x0C8E-#x0C90] | [#x0C92-#x0CA8] | [#x0CAA-#x0CB3] | [#x0CB5-#x0CB9] | #x0CDE | [#x0CE0-#x0CE1] | [#x0D05-#x0D0C] | [#x0D0E-#x0D10] | [#x0D12-#x0D28] | [#x0D2A-#x0D39] | [#x0D60-#x0D61] | [#x0E01-#x0E2E] | #x0E30 | [#x0E32-#x0E33] | [#x0E40-#x0E45] | [#x0E81-#x0E82] | #x0E84 | [#x0E87-#x0E88] | #x0E8A | #x0E8D | [#x0E94-#x0E97] | [#x0E99-#x0E9F] | [#x0EA1-#x0EA3] | #x0EA5 | #x0EA7 | [#x0EAA-#x0EAB] | [#x0EAD-#x0EAE] | #x0EB0 | [#x0EB2-#x0EB3] | #x0EBD | [#x0EC0-#x0EC4] | [#x0F40-#x0F47] | [#x0F49-#x0F69] | [#x10A0-#x10C5] | [#x10D0-#x10F6] | #x1100 | [#x1102-#x1103] | [#x1105-#x1107] | #x1109 | [#x110B-#x110C] | [#x110E-#x1112] | #x113C | #x113E | #x1140 | #x114C | #x114E | #x1150 | [#x1154-#x1155] | #x1159 | [#x115F-#x1161] | #x1163 | #x1165 | #x1167 | #x1169 | [#x116D-#x116E] | [#x1172-#x1173] | #x1175 | #x119E | #x11A8 | #x11AB | [#x11AE-#x11AF] | [#x11B7-#x11B8] | #x11BA | [#x11BC-#x11C2] | #x11EB | #x11F0 | #x11F9 |

[#x1E00-#x1E9B] | [#x1EA0-#x1EF9] | [#x1F00-#x1F15] | [#x1F18-#x1F1D] | [#x1F20-#x1F45] | [#x1F48-#x1F4D] | [#x1F50-#x1F57] | #x1F59 | #x1F5B | #x1F5D | [#x1F5F-#x1F7D] | [#x1F80-#x1FB4] | [#x1FB6-#x1FBC] | #x1FBE | [#x1FC2-#x1FC4] | [#x1FC6-#x1FCC] | [#x1FD0-#x1FD3] | [#x1FD6-#x1FDB] | [#x1FE0-#x1FEC] | [#x1FF2-#x1FF4] | [#x1FF6-#x1FFC] | #x2126 | [#x212A-#x212B] | #x212E | [#x2180-#x2182] | [#x3041-#x3094] | [#x30A1-#x30FA] | [#x3105-#x312C] | [#xAC00-#xD7A3]

[86] Ideographic ::= [#x4E00-#x9FA5] | #x3007 | [#x3021-#x3029]

[87] CombiningChar (::= [#x0300-#x0345] | [#x0360-#x036) 1] | [#x0483-#x0486] | [#x0591-#x05A1] | [#x05A3-#x05B9] | [#x05BB-#x05BD] | #x05BF | [#x05C1-#x05C2] | #x05C4 | [#x064B-#x0652] | #x0670 | [#x06D6-#x06DC] | [#x06DD-#x06DF] | [#x06E0-#x06E4] | [#x06E7-#x06E8] | [#x06EA-#x06ED] | [#x0901-#x0903] | #x093C | [#x093E-#x094C] | #x094D | [#x0951-#x0954] | [#x0962-#x0963] | [#x0981-#x0983] | #x09BC | #x09BE | #x09BF | [#x09C0-#x09C4] | [#x09C7-#x09C8] | [#x09CB-#x09CD] | #x09D7 | [#x09E2-#x09E3] | #x0A02 | #x0A3C | #x0A3E | #x0A3F | [#x0A40-#x0A42] | [#x0A47-#x0A48] | [#x0A4B-#x0A4D] | [#x0A70-#x0A71] | [#x0A81-#x0A83] | #x0ABC | [#x0ABE-#x0AC5] | [#x0AC7-#x0AC9] | [#x0ACB-#x0ACD] |

			[#x0B01-#x0B03] | #x0B3C | [#x0B3E-#x0B43] | [#x0B47-#x0B48] | [#x0B4B-#x0B4D] | [#x0B56-#x0B57] | [#x0B82-#x0B83] | [#x0BBE-#x0BC2] | [#x0BC6-#x0BC8] | [#x0BCA-#x0BCD] | #x0BD7 | [#x0C01-#x0C03] | [#x0C3E-#x0C44] | [#x0C46-#x0C48] | [#x0C4A-#x0C4D] | [#x0C55-#x0C56] | [#x0C82-#x0C83] | [#x0CBE-#x0CC4] | [#x0CC6-#x0CC8] | [#x0CCA-#x0CCD] | [#x0CD5-#x0CD6] | [#x0D02-#x0D03] | [#x0D3E-#x0D43] | [#x0D46-#x0D48] | [#x0D4A-#x0D4D] | #x0D57 | #x0E31 | [#x0E34-#x0E3A] | [#x0E47-#x0E4E] | #x0EB1 | [#x0EB4-#x0EB9] | [#x0EBB-#x0EBC] | [#x0EC8-#x0ECD] | [#x0F18-#x0F19] | #x0F35 | #x0F37 | #x0F39 | #x0F3E | #x0F3F | [#x0F71-#x0F84] | [#x0F86-#x0F8B] | [#x0F90-#x0F95] | #x0F97 | [#x0F99-#x0FAD] | [#x0FB1-#x0FB7] | #x0FB9 | [#x20D0-#x20DC] | #x20E1 | [#x302A-#x302F] | #x3099 | #x309A
[88]	Digit	::=	[#x0030-#x0039] | [#x0660-#x0669] | [#x06F0-#x06F9] | [#x0966-#x096F] | [#x09E6-#x09EF] | [#x0A66-#x0A6F] | [#x0AE6-#x0AEF] | [#x0B66-#x0B6F] | [#x0BE7-#x0BEF] | [#x0C66-#x0C6F] | [#x0CE6-#x0CEF] | [#x0D66-#x0D6F] | [#x0E50-#x0E59] | [#x0ED0-#x0ED9] | [#x0F20-#x0F29]
[89]	Extender	::=	#x00B7 | #x02D0 | #x02D1 | #x0387 | #x0640 | #x0E46 | #x0EC6 | #x3005 | [#x3031-#x3035] | [#x309D-#x309E] | [#x30FC-#x30FE]

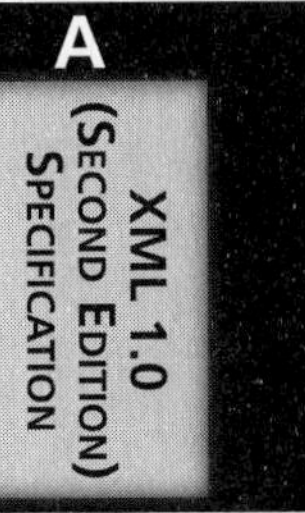

The character classes defined here can be derived from the Unicode 2.0 character database as follows:

Name start characters must have one of the categories Ll, Lu, Lo, Lt, Nl.

Name characters other than Name-start characters must have one of the categories Mc, Me, Mn, Lm, or Nd.

Characters in the compatibility area (i.e. with character code greater than #xF900 and less than #xFFFE) are not allowed in XML names.

Characters which have a font or compatibility decomposition (i.e. those with a "compatibility formatting tag" in field 5 of the database — marked by field 5 beginning with a "<") are not allowed.

The following characters are treated as name-start characters rather than name characters, because the property file classifies them as Alphabetic: [#x02BB-#x02C1], #x0559, #x06E5, #x06E6.

Characters #x20DD-#x20E0 are excluded (in accordance with Unicode 2.0, section 5.14).

Character #x00B7 is classified as an extender, because the property list so identifies it.

Character #x0387 is added as a name character, because #x00B7 is its canonical equivalent.

Characters ':' and '_' are allowed as name-start characters.

Characters '-' and '.' are allowed as name characters.

C XML and SGML (Non-Normative)

XML is designed to be a subset of SGML, in that every XML document should also be a conforming SGML document. For a detailed comparison of the additional restrictions that XML places on documents beyond those of SGML, see [Clark].

D Expansion of Entity and Character References (Non-Normative)

This appendix contains some examples illustrating the sequence of entity- and character-reference recognition and expansion, as specified in 4.4 XML Processor Treatment of Entities and References.

If the DTD contains the declaration

```
<!ENTITY example "<p>An ampersand (&#38;#38;) may be escaped
numerically (&#38;#38;#38;) or with a general entity
(&amp;amp;).</p>" >
```

then the XML processor will recognize the character references when it parses the entity declaration, and resolve them before storing the following string as the value of the entity "*example*":

```
<p>An ampersand (&#38;) may be escaped
numerically (&#38;#38;) or with a general entity
(&amp;amp;).</p>
```

A reference in the document to "*&example;*" will cause the text to be reparsed, at which time the start- and end-tags of the *p* element will be recognized and the three references will be recognized and expanded, resulting in a *p* element with the following content (all data, no delimiters or markup):

```
An ampersand (&) may be escaped
numerically (&#38;) or with a general entity
(&amp;).
```

A more complex example will illustrate the rules and their effects fully. In the following example, the line numbers are solely for reference.

```
<?xml version='1.0'?>
<!DOCTYPE test [
<!ELEMENT test (#PCDATA) >
<!ENTITY % xx '&#37;zz;'>
<!ENTITY % zz '&#60;!ENTITY tricky "error-prone" >' >
%xx;
]>
<test>This sample shows a &tricky; method.</test>
```

This produces the following:

- in line 4, the reference to character 37 is expanded immediately, and the parameter entity "*xx*" is stored in the symbol table with the value "*%zz;*". Since the replacement text is not rescanned, the reference to parameter entity "*zz*" is not recognized. (And it would be an error if it were, since "*zz*" is not yet declared.)
- in line 5, the character reference "*<*" is expanded immediately and the parameter entity "*zz*" is stored with the replacement text "*<!ENTITY tricky "error-prone" >*", which is a well-formed entity declaration.
- in line 6, the reference to "*xx*" is recognized, and the replacement text of "*xx*" (namely "*%zz;*") is parsed. The reference to "*zz*" is recognized in its turn, and its replacement text ("*<!ENTITY tricky "error-prone" >*") is parsed. The general entity "*tricky*" has now been declared, with the replacement text "*error-prone*".
- in line 8, the reference to the general entity "*tricky*" is recognized, and it is expanded, so the full content of the *test* element is the self-describing (and ungrammatical) string *This sample shows a error-prone method.*

E Deterministic Content Models (Non-Normative)

As noted in 3.2.1 Element Content, it is required that content models in element type declarations be deterministic. This requirement is for compatibility with SGML (which calls deterministic content models "unambiguous"); XML processors built using SGML systems may flag non-deterministic content models as errors.

For example, the content model *((b, c) | (b, d))* is non-deterministic, because given an initial *b* the XML processor cannot know which *b* in the model is being matched without looking ahead to see which element follows the *b*. In this case, the two references to *b* can be collapsed into a single reference, making the model read *(b, (c | d))*. An initial *b* now clearly matches only a single name in the content model. The processor doesn't need to look ahead to see what follows; either *c* or *d* would be accepted.

More formally: a finite state automaton may be constructed from the content model using the standard algorithms, e.g. algorithm 3.5 in section 3.9 of Aho, Sethi, and Ullman [Aho/Ullman]. In many such algorithms, a follow set is constructed for each position in the regular expression (i.e., each leaf node in the syntax tree for the regular expression); if any position has a follow set in which more than one following position is labeled with the same element type name, then the content model is in error and may be reported as an error.

Algorithms exist which allow many but not all non-deterministic content models to be reduced automatically to equivalent deterministic models; see Brüggemann-Klein 1991 [Brüggemann-Klein].

F Autodetection of Character Encodings (Non-Normative)

The XML encoding declaration functions as an internal label on each entity, indicating which character encoding is in use. Before an XML processor can read the internal label, however, it apparently has to know what character encoding is in use—which is what the internal label is trying to indicate. In the general case, this is a hopeless situation. It is not entirely hopeless in XML, however, because XML limits the general case in two ways: each implementation is assumed to support only a finite set of character encodings, and the XML encoding declaration is restricted in position and content in order to make it feasible to autodetect the character encoding in use in each entity in normal cases. Also, in many cases other sources of information are available in addition to the XML data stream itself. Two cases may be distinguished, depending on whether the XML entity is presented to the processor without, or with, any accompanying (external) information. We consider the first case first.

F.1 Detection Without External Encoding Information

Because each XML entity not accompanied by external encoding information and not in UTF-8 or UTF-16 encoding *must* begin with an XML encoding declaration, in which the first characters must be '*<?xml*', any conforming processor can detect, after two to four octets of input, which of the following cases apply. In reading this list, it may help to know that in UCS-4, '<' is "*#x0000003C*" and '?' is "*#x0000003F*", and the Byte Order Mark required of UTF-16 data streams is "*#xFEFF*". The notation ## is used to denote any byte value except that two consecutive ##s cannot be both 00.

With a Byte Order Mark:

00 00 FE FF	UCS-4, big-endian machine (1234 order)
FF FE 00 00	UCS-4, little-endian machine (4321 order)
00 00 FF FE	UCS-4, unusual octet order (2143)
FE FF 00 00	UCS-4, unusual octet order (3412)

FE FF ## ##	UTF-16, big-endian
FF FE ## ##	UTF-16, little-endian
EF BB BF	UTF-8

Without a Byte Order Mark:

00 00 00 3C *3C 00 00 00* *00 00 3C 00* *00 3C 00 00*	UCS-4 or other encoding with a 32-bit code unit and ASCII characters encoded as ASCII values, in respectively big-endian (1234), little-endian (4321) and two unusual byte orders(2143 and 3412). The encoding declaration must be read to determine which of UCS-4 or other supported 32-bit encodings applies.
00 3C 00 3F	UTF-16BE or big-endian ISO-10646-UCS-2 or other encoding with a 16-bit code unit in big-endian order and ASCII characters encoded as ASCII values (the encoding declaration must be read to determine which)
3C 00 3F 00	UTF-16LE or little-endian ISO-10646-UCS-2 or other encoding with a 16-bit code unit in little-endian order and ASCII characters encoded as ASCII values (the encoding declaration must be read to determine which)
3C 3F 78 6D	UTF-8, ISO 646, ASCII, some part of ISO 8859, Shift-JIS, EUC, or any other 7-bit, 8-bit, or mixed-width encoding which ensures that the characters of ASCII have their normal positions, width, and values; the actual encoding declaration must be read to detect which of these applies, but since all of these encodings use the same bit patterns for the relevant ASCII characters, the encoding declaration itself may be read reliably
4C 6F A7 94	EBCDIC (in some flavor; the full encoding declaration must be read to tell which code page is in use)
Other	UTF-8 without an encoding declaration, or else the data stream is mislabeled (lacking a required encoding declaration), corrupt, fragmentary, or enclosed in a wrapper of some kind

Note:

In cases above which do not require reading the encoding declaration to determine the encoding, section 4.3.3 still requires that the encoding declaration, if present, be read and that the encoding name be checked to match the actual encoding of the entity. Also, it is possible that new character encodings will be invented that will make it necessary to use the encoding declaration to determine the encoding, in cases where this is not required at present.

This level of autodetection is enough to read the XML encoding declaration and parse the character-encoding identifier, which is still necessary to distinguish the individual members of each family of encodings (e.g. to tell UTF-8 from 8859, and the parts of 8859 from each other, or to distinguish the specific EBCDIC code page in use, and so on).

Because the contents of the encoding declaration are restricted to characters from the ASCII repertoire (however encoded), a processor can reliably read the entire encoding declaration as soon as it has detected which family of encodings is in use. Since in practice, all widely used character encodings fall into one of the categories above, the XML encoding declaration allows reasonably reliable in-band labeling of character encodings, even when external sources of information at the operating-system or transport-protocol level are unreliable. Character encodings such as UTF-7 that make overloaded usage of ASCII-valued bytes may fail to be reliably detected.

Once the processor has detected the character encoding in use, it can act appropriately, whether by invoking a separate input routine for each case, or by calling the proper conversion function on each character of input.

Like any self-labeling system, the XML encoding declaration will not work if any software changes the entity's character set or encoding without updating the encoding declaration. Implementors of character-encoding routines should be careful to ensure the accuracy of the internal and external information used to label the entity.

F.2 Priorities in the Presence of External Encoding Information

The second possible case occurs when the XML entity is accompanied by encoding information, as in some file systems and some network protocols. When multiple sources of information are available, their relative priority and the preferred method of handling conflict should be specified as part of the higher-level protocol used to deliver XML. In particular, please refer to [IETF RFC 2376] or its successor, which defines the *text/xml* and *application/xml* MIME types and provides some useful guidance. In the interests of interoperability, however, the following rule is recommended.

- If an XML entity is in a file, the Byte-Order Mark and encoding declaration are used (if present) to determine the character encoding.

G W3C XML Working Group (Non-Normative)

This specification was prepared and approved for publication by the W3C XML Working Group (WG). WG approval of this specification does not necessarily imply that all WG members voted for its approval. The current and former members of the XML WG are:

- Jon Bosak, Sun (*Chair*)
- James Clark (*Technical Lead*)
- Tim Bray, Textuality and Netscape (*XML Co-editor*)
- Jean Paoli, Microsoft (*XML Co-editor*)
- C. M. Sperberg-McQueen, U. of Ill. (*XML Co-editor*)
- Dan Connolly, W3C (*W3C Liaison*)
- Paula Angerstein, Texcel
- Steve DeRose, INSO
- Dave Hollander, HP
- Eliot Kimber, ISOGEN
- Eve Maler, ArborText
- Tom Magliery, NCSA
- Murray Maloney, SoftQuad, Grif SA, Muzmo and Veo Systems
- MURATA Makoto (FAMILY Given), Fuji Xerox Information Systems
- Joel Nava, Adobe
- Conleth O'Connell, Vignette
- Peter Sharpe, SoftQuad
- John Tigue, DataChannel

H W3C XML Core Group (Non-Normative)

The second edition of this specification was prepared by the W3C XML Core Working Group (WG). The members of the WG at the time of publication of this edition were:

- Paula Angerstein, Vignette
- Daniel Austin, Ask Jeeves

- Tim Boland
- Allen Brown, Microsoft
- Dan Connolly, W3C (*Staff Contact*)
- John Cowan, Reuters Limited
- John Evdemon, XMLSolutions Corporation
- Paul Grosso, Arbortext (*Co-Chair*)
- Arnaud Le Hors, IBM (*Co-Chair*)
- Eve Maler, Sun Microsystems (*Second Edition Editor*)
- Jonathan Marsh, Microsoft
- MURATA Makoto (FAMILY Given), IBM
- Mark Needleman, Data Research Associates
- David Orchard, Jamcracker
- Lew Shannon, NCR
- Richard Tobin, University of Edinburgh
- Daniel Veillard, W3C
- Dan Vint, Lexica
- Norman Walsh, Sun Microsystems
- François Yergeau, Alis Technologies (*Errata List Editor*)
- Kongyi Zhou, Oracle

I Production Notes (Non-Normative)

This Second Edition was encoded in the XMLspec DTD (which has documentation available). The HTML versions were produced with a combination of the `xmlspec.xsl`, `diffspec.xsl`, and `REC-xml-2e.xsl` XSLT stylesheets. The PDF version was produced with the html2ps facility and a distiller program.

INDEX

Symbols

A

B

D

E

G

J

K

L

M

N

O

P

S

T

U

V

X-Z

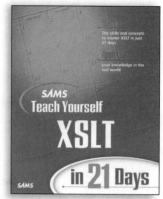

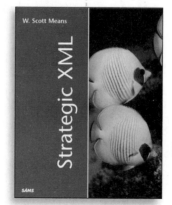